D1092806

THE OXFORD
COMPANION TO
CLASSICAL
LITERATURE

THE OXFORD COMPANION TO CLASSICAL LITERATURE

SECOND EDITION

EDITED BY

M. C. HOWATSON

OXFORD

UNIVERSITY PRESS

OXFORD

UNIVERSITY PRESS

Great Clarendon Street, Oxford OX2 6DP

Oxford University Press is a department of the University of Oxford.
It furthers the University's objective of excellence in research, scholarship,
and education by publishing worldwide in

Oxford New York

Auckland Cape Town Dar es Salaam Hong Kong Karachi Kuala Lumpur
Madrid Melbourne Mexico City Nairobi New Delhi Shanghai Taipei Toronto

With offices in

Argentina Austria Brazil Chile Czech Republic France Greece
Guatemala Hungary Italy Japan South Korea Poland Portugal
Singapore Switzerland Thailand Turkey Ukraine Vietnam

Oxford is a registered trade mark of Oxford University Press
in the UK and in certain other countries

Published in the United States
by Oxford University Press Inc., New York

© Oxford University Press 1989

Database right Oxford University Press (maker)

First Edition 1937
Second Edition 1989
First issued in paperback 1997
Reissued in hardback 2005

All rights reserved. No part of this publication may be reproduced,
stored in a retrieval system, or transmitted, in any form or by any means,
without the prior permission in writing of Oxford University Press,
or as expressly permitted by law, or under terms agreed with the appropriate
reprographics rights organization. Enquiries concerning reproduction
outside the scope of the above should be sent to the Rights Department,
Oxford University Press, at the address above

You must not circulate this book in any other binding or cover
and you must impose this same condition on any acquirer

British Library Cataloguing in Publication Data
Data available

Library of Congress Cataloging in Publication Data
Data available

ISBN 0–19–861418–7   978–0–19–861418–0
ISBN 0–19–860081–X(Pbk)   978–0–19–860081–7(Pbk)

6

Printed in Great Britain
on acid-free paper by
Clays Ltd, St Ives plc

PREFACE

SIR PAUL HARVEY wished the original *Oxford Companion to Classical Literature* to be a handbook of information for readers of the literatures of Greece and Rome, and of modern works which touched upon the classical world. Harvey by no means limited himself to books and authors. He included entries outlining the history of Greece and Rome, the most important myths, science, geography, religion and thought, as well as many features of ancient life and society. But since his day new discoveries and reappraisals have been made. The decipherment of Linear B and archaeological excavations have greatly increased our knowledge of the earliest civilization that can be called Greek, while advances in scholarship have brought better understanding of, for example, the period we call Hellenistic and, we like to think, the subject we define as myth. However, not only has our knowledge increased but, more significantly, the perspective has changed. Harvey wrote for readers who had acquired some knowledge of the classical world in their schooldays, along with Greek and Latin. Nowadays those who seek information about that world approach it from a wide variety of backgrounds and assumptions. Readers of today are in some respects more ignorant than those of fifty years ago, but in others more sophisticated and demanding. Though fewer people know the ancient languages, many more have visited the countries in which they were once spoken, and have read the guide-books, toured the museums, or watched television programmes. Moreover we nowadays perceive our classical heritage differently. We are more aware than we used to be that literature must be set against its society and institutions, and that it cannot be separated from the history and thought of its times.

This new *Companion* takes account of these changed circumstances in a revised and enlarged edition. The indispensable book summaries are still Harvey's, and the pattern and proportions of the whole work are closely based on his: anyone who attempts to revise one of his *Companions* can feel nothing but admiration for the original conception and execution. But in detail, assumptions, and emphasis it is very different—more attention is paid to (for example) the philosophy and political institutions of the ancient world—and the extent is very much greater. A few entries on technical subjects such as metre are naturally written with classical specialists in mind, but in general the book requires no knowledge of Greek or Latin: it is for any reader who is curious to find out about the classical world.

Given the nature of the book I have tried to present the generally accepted view (or indicate the range of possibilities) in every case rather than be over-lavish in the use of 'possibly' and 'perhaps'. I may therefore on occasions sound more dogmatic than I feel, or achieve more consistency and coherence, especially in the matter of dates, than the evidence would warrant. To keep within reasonable bounds some topics have been drastically simplified, such as the histories of Athens and Rome, but even superficial information as guidance seemed better than no information at all. This *Companion* maintains the policy of the original in not being a dictionary of classical mythology. To make it so would have increased its bulk threefold and changed its focus. Only those names and stories which occur most often in literature are included.

The period covered begins with the entry of the Greeks into Greece in about 2200 BC. Its stopping-point is not so easily identifiable. Readers will find that from the third century AD there are entries for Christian writers who were important from a classical viewpoint. From this time to the closing of the philosophy schools at Athens in AD 529 only the most significant people and events are selected for inclusion, but the fate of classical literature is traced in outline through the Dark Age to the Renaissance.

A discretionary policy of cross-referencing has been adopted. An asterisk before a word draws the reader's attention to its existence as a separate entry only where more information may be found of direct relevance to the subject. The reader can assume an entry for main topics such as the history of Greece and Rome, large wars, and major authors and important works of literature.

Some guidance is given in the headwords to their pronunciation in English. Classicists should note that in many cases the English stress accent or syllabic length does not coincide with the Greek or Latin original. All Greek is transliterated (v = y, χ = ch). Proper nouns are spelt by and large in the Latinized form in which they have become familiar in English, but where these are headwords their transliterated Greek form is also given. Roman names generally appear under the *nomen* (second name, or middle name of three), e.g. Gaius *Marius*, Quintus *Fabius* Maximus; but in many cases where the subject is best known by his *cognomen* or third name the entry is under that headword, e.g. Marcus Tullius *Cicero*, Tiberius Sempronius *Gracchus*. Where there are several individuals with the same name, the entries appear in chronological order.

A chronological table and set of maps are included at the end of the book. The chronological table records the major literary and historical events from 2200 BC to AD 529. The maps aim to show only those places mentioned in the text, irrespective of size and importance; omitted are places east of Iran, which are here relevant only to the journeys of Alexander the Great. Geographical names are given in classical form (except for those which are very commonly used in English even in a classical context, e.g. Athens, Adriatic Sea). Modern equivalents, where they are judged to be helpful or interesting, are shown in italics.

I owe a considerable debt of gratitude to many people: to the Principal and Fellows of St Anne's College for leave of absence, and in particular to

Margaret Hubbard, Gwynneth Matthews, Barbara Mitchell, Emily Kearns, and Mary Whitby for generously undertaking duties which were properly mine; to Catriona, Gabrielle, James, and Robert Howatson for their contribution of an entry apiece, and for warm encouragement; to Robert for pertinent if searing comment; to Mark Bostridge for constructive help; to Rachel Woodrow and Janet Randell for flawless typing; to the editors of the Press for their great patience and unobtrusive advice. The painting on the jacket was the inspired suggestion of Mr David Ekserdjian, to whom I give warm thanks.

I am very deeply obliged to Alastair Howatson, my most dedicated reader and critic. I have striven to satisfy his exacting standards as well as his admiration for Cicero. My inadequacies and errors will, I know, be pointed out in customary trenchant fashion by the classical undergraduates past and present of St Anne's College.

M. C. H.

St Anne's College, Oxford
October 1988

CONTENTS

A

Abas, in Greek myth, son of *Lynceus (2) and Hypermnestra, father of *Acrisius and *Proetus.

Abdē'ra, Greek city on the coast of *Thrace, founded in the seventh century BC and re-founded in the sixth by Ionians from Teos in Asia Minor, among them the Greek lyric poet *Anacreon. It was the birthplace of the sophist *Protagoras and the philosopher *Democritus, but was nevertheless proverbial for the stupidity of its inhabitants.

Absy'rtus, see APSYRTUS.

Abȳ'dus, Milesian colony on the Asiatic side of the Hellespont, at its narrowest point. Here Xerxes crossed to Europe in 480 BC. See PERSIAN WARS and also LEANDER.

Acadē'mica (*Academics*), dialogue by *Cicero ((1)5) discussing the philosophical views of the Greek New *Academy, particularly the Sceptic view of *Carneades on the impossibility of attaining certain knowledge. The work was originally in two books, entitled *Catulus* and *Lucullus* respectively after the chief interlocutors, Q. Lutatius Catulus (consul in 78 BC) and L. Licinius *Lucullus. Cicero, Lucullus, and Catulus had all attended the lectures of the (moderate) Sceptic *Philo of Larisa and his successor as head of the Academy, Antiochus of Ascalon. While Cicero's 'publisher' *Atticus was having copies made of this work, Cicero remodelled it into four books. Both 'editions' went into circulation; of the first edition we possess the second book, *Lucullus*; of the second edition we possess part of the first book, known as *Academica posteriora*. The scene of the conversations is laid at various villas on the shores of the gulf of Naples; their date was supposed in the first edition to be before 60 BC, in the second to be near the time of composition (45 BC). In the *Academica posteriora* the scholar *Varro (1) expounds the evolution of the doctrines of the Academy, from early dogmatism to the Scepticism of Arcesilaus and Carneades. In *Lucullus* that interlocutor attacks the position of the Sceptics. Cicero defends the Sceptic view and approves Carneades' doctrine of accepting what seems most probably true.

Acadē'mus, see ACADEMY.

Academy (Akadēmia or Akadēmeia; the earlier Greek name was Hekademeia), originally a shrine in olive groves sacred to the hero Akademos (or Hekademos) on the western side of Athens near the hill of Colonus. In classical times it was also the site of a gymnasium, surrounded by gardens and groves. Here, perhaps as early as the 380s BC, Plato established his school, consequently known as the Academy; it survived continuously until AD 529, when the Christian emperor Justinian closed the philosophy schools in Athens. Plato was buried nearby. Sulla cut down the trees during his siege of Athens in 87–86 BC, but they must have grown again, for Horace, who studied at Athens, refers to the 'woods of Academus' (*Epistles* II. 2. 45). Finds on the site in the twentieth century include schoolboys' slates, some with writing on them.

Although the Academy gave its name to a school of philosophy which, broadly speaking, continued to teach philosophy and science in accordance with Plato's own teaching (see PLATO 3), its doctrines naturally changed direction several times before it was closed. For this reason, and for convenience, ancient writers several centuries after Plato divided the history of the Academy into periods designated by numbers or, more usually, by the terms Old, Middle, and New; they did not always agree (nor do authorities today) on where the divisions occurred.

The *Old Academy* describes the period when the school was headed by Plato and his conservative successors Speusippus, Xenocrates, Polemon, Crantor, and Crates, down to 265 BC.

The *Middle Academy* is the term often used for the period initiated by Arcesilaus (or Arcesilas) of Pitane (*c*.315–242 BC) who gave the school the *Sceptical approach which it kept with minor variations until the leadership of Antiochus of Ascalon in the first century BC. Arcesilaus followed that aspect of Plato which was derived from Socrates' negative style of argument, in which no positive conclusion is reached (see ELENCHUS). He was perhaps influenced by the Scepticism of Pyrrhon; like the Sceptics he and his successors attacked the *Stoic doctrine of knowledge, that 'clear and certain perceptions' lead to direct apprehension of reality.

The *New Academy*, sometimes taken to include Arcesilaus, is more usually agreed to have started in the mid-second century BC under *Carneades (d. 129), who developed Scepticism further (and for whose views there is more evidence). Using the Stoic terms he argued, like them, that reality can be grasped only by 'perceptions', and therefore our conduct must be guided by perceptions that are 'persuasive', i.e. seem true or probable. By this admission of 'probability' as a guide to conduct, the New Academy differs from Scepticism proper, though it still maintains that, since there is no criterion by which a true perception can be shown to be true, we must always reserve our judgement.

The destruction of the Academy with its library during the sack of Athens by the Roman general Sulla in 86 BC broke the direct link with Plato. Antiochus of Ascalon, head of the (Fifth) Academy from 86 to 68 BC, abandoned the Scepticism of his predecessor Philo of Larisa and aimed to return to what he thought was genuine Platonism by maintaining that there was essential agreement between the doctrines of the Old Academy, the Aristotelians (*Peripatetics), and the Stoics. Although not original he exerted great influence; his lecture audience included Cicero, to whom his eclecticism appealed and who later proclaimed himself an Academic (see *ACADEMICA*). For the development of Platonism after Antiochus see MIDDLE PLATONISM.

Little is known of the Academy in the following centuries until it appears in the fifth century AD as a centre of Neoplatonism, particularly under the leadership of *Proclus, who powerfully influenced the form in which the Greek philosophical inheritance was passed on to Renaissance Europe.

Aca'rnan, son of *Alcmaeon.

Aca'stus, son of *Pelias and Anaxibia, and brother of Alcestis. He sailed with the *Argonauts against his father's wishes; see also PELEUS.

acatalectic, metrical term; see METRE, GREEK 6.

Acca Lare'ntia or **Larentina,** an obscure Roman goddess who was worshipped at the Larentalia on 23 December. According to one of several conflicting legends she was the wife of the herdsman *Faustulus, mother of the original Fratres Arvales (see ARVAL PRIESTS) and the nurse of Romulus and Remus.

accents, Greek. The invention of accent marks as a guide to the pronunciation of classical Greek, denoting not stress but the pitch of the voice, has been attributed to the Alexandrian scholar.*Aristophanes of Byzantium c.200 BC. It may have been prompted by the need to guide Greek speakers in the pronunciation of by then unfamiliar words (e.g. in Homeric epic) and to teach the language to foreigners. Papyri of this period show that accents were used sporadically at first and usually to distinguish between otherwise ambiguous words. They were not used regularly in manuscripts until the beginning of the tenth century. The system now used

in our Greek texts is an early Byzantine refinement on previous systems. The low tones are left unaccented, except in a few cases where the grave accent is used, and the high and compound tones are indicated by the acute and circumflex accents. Although the classical Greek accent was tonal it is unlikely that Greek words had no variations of stress, and by the fourth century AD and on into modern Greek the tonal accent has been replaced by a stress on the same syllable. Under a mistaken impression that the accents had nothing to do with the original pronunciation, many Greek texts were printed without them in England in the eighteenth century, the University Press at Oxford adopting this practice as its official policy. It was largely the influence of the English scholar Richard Porson (1759–1808) that caused it to be reversed.

accidence, that aspect of grammar which concerns the inflexions, or various endings, of words.

A'ccius or **Attius Lucius** (170–c.86 BC), Latin poet and dramatist of Pisaurum in Umbria. He was a younger contemporary of *Pacuvius and the last great Roman tragedian. Cicero records that he heard him lecturing early in the 80s. Fragments of some 46 named tragedies are extant, most of those which are recognizable being free translations of Greek tragedies. He also wrote two fabulae *praetextae on Decius Mus and Brutus the Liberator. Accius created for his tragedy a vigorous and dignified style much admired by later rhetoricians. He was an influential figure in his day, and of great importance for the development of Latin literature. Cicero quoted him often and Virgil imitated him. His Atreus contained the tyrant's phrase *oderint dum metuant* ('let them hate, so long as they fear'), said by Suetonius to have been frequently quoted by the emperor Caligula.

His other works show him as a scholar with a particular interest in spelling reform (e.g. using u and s, not y and z), and a collector and critic of the works of his predecessors. His books include the *Annales*, books of hexameter poetry on months and festivals, and the *Didascalica*, on the history of the Greek and Roman theatre and other literary matters, from Homer to Accius himself. The few surviving fragments suggest that it may have been written in a mixture of prose and verse, thus anticipating the Menippean satires of *Varro (1).

Ace'stes (Aigestēs, Aigestos), in Virgil's *Aeneid*, son of the river-god Crimisus and a Trojan woman, Egesta or Segesta; he entertains Aeneas and his comrades in Sicily. The city of Egesta (Segesta) was originally named Acesta after him by its founders, the Trojan followers of Aeneas who remained in Sicily.

Achae'a, Achae'ans (Achaioi). In historical times these denoted two regions and peoples, one in south-east Thessaly (Phthiotan Achaea), the other a narrow strip in the north of the Peloponnese between Elis and Sicyon, a territory comprising twelve small towns forming a loose confederacy. In Homer the names are used both in a restricted and in a general sense. They may denote the region and people in south Thessaly where Achilles lived, and also the people in the north-east Peloponnese (Argolis), the followers of Agamemnon who ruled Mycenae and the surrounding area. But they may also denote, by extension, Greece and the Greeks in general. Modern scholars sometimes use the name 'Achaeans' to refer to the Greeks of the *Mycenaean period. One of the peoples mentioned in the Hittite tablets of the thirteenth century is the Akhkhijava, whom some scholars identify with Achaeans, seeing in the Hittite descriptions confirmation of Homer's picture of a powerful Greek confederacy in the late Bronze Age.

In the eighth century BC Peloponnesian Achaea founded an important group of colonies at the southern extremity of Italy (including Sybaris and Croton; see COLONIZATION, GREEK 2) which formed the greater part of what was known as Magna Graecia. Otherwise it plays little part in Greek history until the third and second centuries BC when the *Achaean Confederacy became the chief power in Greece.

From 146 BC this area was attached to the Roman province of Macedonia, but in 27 BC the name Achaea was given to the senatorial province which included a large part of Greece.

Achaean Confederacy or **League.** Founded in 280 BC and apparently considered part of an older confederacy, this consisted firstly of Achaean cities in the Peloponnese which had detached themselves from the rule of Macedon; secondly and most importantly it admitted non-Achaeans on terms of equality, a successful step forward in the growth of federal states that had scarcely been attempted hitherto. Since the Achaean Confederacy was in practice a federal state, it functioned more nearly like a representative government than a normal city-state, though the Achaeans kept their primary assembly until c.200 BC. It was headed first by two generals, then after 255 BC by one. Immediate re-election was forbidden. Ten *demiourgoi*, 'officers', administered and presided over the council and assembly.

The power and influence of the Confederacy increased under the leadership of Aratus of Sicyon, who was normally its general in each alternate year from 245 until his death in 213. By sound statesmanship and diplomacy he made the Confederacy the leading power in the Peloponnese, with Corinth as its chief stronghold. When the Spartans seemed likely to destroy the Confederacy, Aratus took the Achaeans into alliance with Macedon in 224. This alignment lasted until the Confederacy went over to Rome in 198. During most of the period from 208 to 182 the general was *Philopoemen who reorganized the army and was particularly successful in military campaigns against Sparta, which he overcame in 188. But the Confederacy frequently came into conflict with Rome, and after defeating the Macedonians at Pydna in 167 Rome deported to Italy a thousand eminent Achaeans, including the historian *Polybius, for political investigation; they were released in 150. In 148 there was again trouble with Sparta. Rome intervened and imposed harsh terms on the Confederacy, which rebelled and declared war; but after a short struggle it was completely defeated by Mummius in 146 and dissolved. See ROME 5.

Achaeme'nidae, the first royal house of Persia, so named from the legendary hero Achaemenes (Persian, Hakhāmanish), founder of the family. To this family belonged Cyrus, Cambysēs, and Darius (see PERSIAN WARS). The line perished in 330 BC at the hands of Alexander the Great.

Acha'rnians (Acharnēs), Greek comedy by *Aristophanes, produced at the Lenaea in 425 BC by Callistratus, perhaps because the author was too young to produce it himself. It is his first surviving play, and won first prize in the dramatic competition.

The Athenians had for six years been suffering the horrors of the *Peloponnesian War, the devastation of their territory, plague in the overcrowded city, and shortage of food, but their spirit was unbroken. The Acharnians (inhabitants of an Attic deme lying north-west of Athens near the foot of Mount Parnes), of whom the chorus of the play is composed, had been among the chief sufferers, their territory having been repeatedly ravaged.

The play opens with Dikaiopolis, an Athenian farmer, sitting and waiting for the meeting of the assembly, sighing for the good times of peace. Amphitheos ('demigod') appears, sent by the gods to arrange peace with Sparta, but unfortunately lacking the necessary travelling-money. This Dikaiopolis provides, but the treaty with Sparta is to be a private one for himself alone. Amphitheos presently brings the treaty, narrowly escaping from the chorus of bellicose and infuriated Acharnians. Dikaiopolis celebrates with a procession consisting of his daughter and servants, and this leads to a dispute between Dikaiopolis and the chorus on the question of peace or war, in which *Lamachus, portrayed as a typical general, takes part. Dikaiopolis is allowed to make a speech before being executed as a traitor; and to render this more pathetic borrows from the tragedian Euripides some of the stage properties that make his tragedies so moving. As a result the chorus

are won over to the pro-peace view of
Dikaiopolis. After the *parabasis* (see COMEDY,
GREEK 3), in which the poet defends his position,
there is a succession of amusing scenes illustrating the benefits of peace. A Megarian comes to
Dikaiopolis to buy food (Athens had been
trying to starve out Megara by a blockade),
offering in exchange his little daughters disguised as pigs in sacks. A Boeotian brings eels
and other good things, and wants in return local
produce of Attica; he is given an informer tied
up in a sack. A farmer wants peace-salve for his
eyes, which he has cried out over the loss of his
oxen; and so on. Finally Lamachus has to march
off through the snow against the Boeotians, and
returns wounded by a vine-stake on which he
has impaled himself, while Dikaiopolis celebrates the *Anthesteria with the priest of
Dionysus.

This play has been interpreted as a serious plea
for peace on the part of the poet.

Achā'tēs, in Virgil's *Aeneid*, the faithful friend
and lieutenant of Aeneas, frequently referred to
as *fidus Achates*, 'faithful Achates'. He is in the
epic tradition of faithful friends, comparable
with Patroclus, friend to Achilles, and Pirithous,
to Theseus.

A'cheron, in Greek myth, one of the rivers of
the Underworld (see HADES). The name was also
that of an actual river in southern Epirus, which,
issuing from a deep and gloomy gorge, passed
through the lake Acherusia and after receiving
the waters of the tributary Cocytus fell into
the Thesprotian Gulf. In Hellenistic and Latin
poetry the name denoted the Underworld itself.

Achillē'id (*Achillēis*), epic poem in hexameters
by the Roman poet *Statius on the story of
*Achilles, of which only the first book and part
of the second exist, the work having been cut
short by the poet's death. The poem describes
how Thetis, anxious that her son Achilles shall
not take part in the Trojan War (from which
she knows he will not return), removes him
from the care of the Centaur *Chiron to the
island of Scyros. It relates his adventures there in
the disguise of a girl, his discovery by Ulysses,
and departure for Troy.

Achi'llēs (Akhilleus), in Greek myth, only son
of the mortal *Peleus, king of Phthia in
Thessaly, and Thetis, a sea-nymph, daughter of
Nereus (see also PARIS, JUDGEMENT OF). In the
Trojan War Achilles was the chief hero on the
Greek side; Homer draws his portrait once and
for all in the *Iliad*, the plot of which turns on
Achilles' ungovernable anger. He came to Troy
with a contingent of fifty ships and many
followers usually referred to as Myrmidons (for
which name see AEACUS). When he sulked in his
tent and refused to fight after his quarrel with
Agamemnon, as related in the *Iliad*, the Greeks
were driven back to their ships and almost

overwhelmed. Then followed the intervention
and death of his friend Patroclus in the battle at
the hands of the Trojan hero Hector, and
Achilles' terrible grief. After reconciliation with
Agamemnon, he slew Hector, taking further
vengeance for Patroclus' death by dragging the
body behind his chariot. The *Iliad* ends with
Achilles, purged of anger and grief, allowing
Priam, Hector's father, to ransom the body.

The *Aethiopis* tells how Achilles killed
Penthesilea, queen of the Amazons, who was
fighting on the Trojan side. Mourning her for
her beauty, he was mocked by *Thersites and
killed him in a rage; subsequently he killed
*Memnon. Soon afterwards he was himself
killed, shot in the heel by Paris (or by Apollo);
see below. Odysseus saw him in the
Underworld (*Odyssey* 11), but it was said later
that he lived immortal on an island in the Black
Sea. After the fall of Troy his ghost claimed
Polyxena, daughter of Priam, as his prize, and
she was sacrificed on his tomb.

In these accounts Achilles has a passionate
nature and seems more savage than the other
Greeks. His treatment of Hector's body and his
sacrifice of Trojan prisoners at Patroclus' funeral
are both stigmatized as evil deeds. When roused
to anger he spares no one and has no respect for
a visible god, but he shows great devotion to his
friend Patroclus. He is aware that his life is fated
to be short, his death at Troy having been
foretold.

The poets of the *Epic Cycle and later
authors add to the story of Achilles. It was said
that in infancy he was dipped in the river Styx
by his mother Thetis (or anointed with *ambrosia by day and held in the fire at night) to make
him invulnerable. She was interrupted by
Peleus, and in anger abandoned her husband and
the child, who remained vulnerable in the heel
by which she had held him; it was in his heel
that Achilles according to epic tradition received
his death wound from an arrow shot by Paris.
He had his education from the Centaur *Chiron.
When the Greek contingents were gathering for
Troy, Peleus or Thetis, seeking to save him from
his fated death, hid him on the island of Scyros at
the court of King Lycomedes dressed as a girl and
called, according to one source, Pyrrha. (Suetonius says that the emperor Tiberius liked to
puzzle the scholars at his court with questions
such as, 'What was the name of Achilles when he
hid himself among the girls?') The king's
daughter Deidameia bore him a son *Neoptolemus (sometimes called Pyrrhus). When the seer
Calchas told the Greeks that Troy could not be
captured without Achilles, Odysseus sought him
out, after which he went willingly to Troy, by
way of Mysia, where he wounded *Telephus,
Aulis, where the incident concerning *Iphigeneia took place, and Tenedos, where he slew
Tenes, king of the island and son of Apollo.
There are also various stories of his exploits at

Troy not related in the *Iliad*, notably the killing of *Cycnus (2) and *Troilus.

Achi'llēs Ta'tius, see NOVEL, GREEK.

Ācis, see GALATEA.

Aco'ntius, youth from the Greek island of Ceos who being in love with an Athenian girl Cydippē threw her an apple on which he had written, 'I swear to Artemis to marry none but Acontius'. This she read aloud, as was usual in the ancient world, and being thus bound by oath she fell ill whenever her parents tried to marry her elsewhere. In this way Acontius won her.

A'cragas (Lat. Agrigentum, modern Agrigento—until 1927 Girgenti), one of the richest and most famous of the Greek cities in Sicily, founded *c.*580 BC on the south-west coast by a colony from nearby Gela, itself a joint Cretan and Rhodian foundation. It first came to power under the tyrant *Phalaris and continued to prosper under the tyrant *Theron who, together with *Gelon tyrant of Gela, inflicted a notable defeat on the Carthaginians at Himera in 480 BC. After Theron's death his son Thrasydaeus was overthrown and a democracy established in which the philosopher *Empedocles took part. The democracy continued until Acragas was sacked by the Carthaginians in 406. It revived to some extent in the time of Timoleon (d. *c.*334 BC; see SYRACUSE 3) but suffered badly in the Punic Wars. In the time of the Roman governor Verres it was again wealthy, and with the rest of Sicily received full Roman citizenship after Julius Caesar's death in 44 BC.

Acri'sius, in Greek myth, son of Abas, king of Argos, and father of *Danae. His brother was Proetus.

Acro'polis ('upper town'), the citadel, standing on high ground, of a Greek town. The Acropolis of Athens is a rocky plateau about 50 m. (165 ft.) high, the flat summit measuring about 300 m. east to west and 150 m. north to south, and inaccessible except by a steep slope on the west. It was the fortress and sanctuary of Athens. Already by the thirteenth century BC it had been enclosed by a massive wall (see ATHENS I). There are few remains of the *Geometric period actually on the Acropolis, although there are graves and pottery from this time in the *Ceramicus. Scanty remains of the *Archaic period show that there were important buildings on the Acropolis by the end of the seventh century, by which time the Mycenaean wall had declined in importance; after the expulsion of the *Peisistratids in 510 BC the Acropolis was no longer a fortress. All previous fortifications, buildings, and statues were destroyed in the Persian occupation of 480–479 BC (see PERSIAN WARS). The walls were rebuilt by

*Themistocles and *Cimon and in celebration of the final defeat of the Persians a statue of Athena Promachos by *Pheidias was erected in the 450s. It stood 10 m. (33 ft.) high, and the helmet and spear-tip were visible to sailors at Sunium. Pheidias was directed by *Pericles to superintend the latter's general scheme for the rebuilding of the Acropolis. First came the *Parthenon, then the *Propylaea, Temple of *Athena Nikē, and *Erectheum, as well as many lesser sanctuaries such as that of *Artemis Brauronia. There was also a large number of marble slabs and columns, with inscriptions of decrees, memorials, casualty-lists, treaties and alliances, public accounts, inventories, etc. Many of these inscriptions, more or less mutilated, have survived. Later ages added few buildings, and pagan worship persisted until the fifth century AD. See ATHENS 2.

acta, under the Roman empire, an emperor's enactments which magistrates and succeeding emperors swore to observe, unless they had been explicitly rescinded immediately after an emperor's death.

acta senatūs ('enactments of the senate'), under the empire, the official record of proceedings in the senate.

acta diurna ('daily events'), a gazette of social and political news published daily from 59 BC and read both in Rome and in the provinces.

Actae'on, in Greek myth, son of *Aristaeus and Autonoē, daughter of *Cadmus. For some offence, either because he boasted that he was a better hunter than Artemis or because he came upon her bathing, the goddess changed him into a stag, and he was torn to pieces by his own hounds.

A'ctium, promontory in the south of Epirus, off the west coast of Greece, where Octavian defeated the fleets of Antony and Cleopatra on 2 September 31 BC (see ROME 7). This battle marked the end of the Roman republic and introduced the empire. Early in 31 Octavian had landed an army in Epirus in the hope of surprising Antony's fleet in the Ambracian Gulf. In this he had been disappointed, for Antony had succeeded in bringing up his army for the defence of the fleet and establishing it at Actium. For several months the armies and fleets of the two generals confronted each other. Late in August, Antony decided to fight a battle at sea; but what precisely were his plans is uncertain. The fight began at dawn. At first the heavier ships of Antony appeared to be prevailing; but presently the sixty Egyptian ships of Cleopatra's contingent were seen to set sail and make off southwards, Antony himself following in a swift quinquereme. Most of his fleet seems to have surrendered, and his army shortly afterwards went over to Octavian.

Ade'lphoe or **Adelphi** ('brothers'), Roman

comedy by *Terence adapted from Menander and Diphilus (see COMEDY, GREEK 6), produced in 160 BC.

Aeschinus and Ctesipho are the two sons of Demea. Ctesipho is brought up by his father in the country, but Aeschinus is entrusted to his uncle Micio and brought up in the town. The theme of the comedy is the contest between two methods of education. Demea makes himself hated and distrusted by his harshness and frugality; Micio makes himself loved and trusted by his indulgence and open-handedness. Aeschinus has seduced an Athenian girl Pamphila, living in modest circumstances, whom he loves and wishes to marry. Ctesipho, whom his father believes a model of virtue, has fallen in love with a music-girl. Aeschinus, to help his brother, carries off this girl from the slave-dealer to whom she belongs and brings her to Micio's house. He is therefore suspected of carrying on an affair with her just when his own girl-friend needs his support. The truth becomes known; Aeschinus is forgiven by Micio and his marriage arranged. Demea is mortified at the revelation of Ctesipho's behaviour. Finding that his boasted method of education has earned him only hatred, he suddenly changes his attitude and makes a display of geniality, forcing his old bachelor brother into a reluctant marriage with the bride's mother, endowing one of her relatives with a farm at his brother's expense, and obliging him to free his slave and give him a good start in life—showing that even geniality can be overdone.

The *Adelphoe* was played at the funeral games of Aemilius *Paullus.

ad Here'nnium, Rheto'rica, see RHETORICA.

Admē'tus, in Greek myth, son of Pheres and king of Pherae in Thessaly. When Zeus killed *Asclepius for restoring Hippolytus to life, Apollo, the father of Asclepius, furious at this treatment of his son, took vengeance on the *Cyclopes who had forged Zeus' thunderbolt, and slew them. To expiate this crime Zeus made him for a year the servant of Admetus, who treated him kindly. Apollo in gratitude helped him to win *Alcestis as his bride. At the bridal feast it was revealed that Admetus was fated to die imminently, but Apollo again intervened and by making the Fates drunk persuaded them to grant Admetus longer life, provided that at the appointed hour of his death he could persuade someone else to die for him. Admetus' father and mother having refused, his wife Alcestis consented, and accordingly died. Just after this, Heracles, on his way to one of his Labours, visited the palace of Admetus who, in obedience to the laws of hospitality, concealed his wife's death and welcomed the hero. Heracles presently discovered the truth, went out to intercept Death, set upon him, and took from him Alcestis, whom he then restored to her husband.

For Euripides' treatment of the story see *ALCESTIS.*

administration, public, see ATHENS 3, ROME 12.

Adoniazū'sae, the title of Idyll 15 of *Theocritus.

adonean, see METRE, GREEK 8 (i).

Adō'nis, in Greek myth, a beautiful youth, son of *Cinyras, king of Cyprus, by his daughter Zmyrna or Myrrha. Their union was brought about by Aphroditē in revenge for Zmyrna's refusal to honour the goddess. When her father discovered the truth and was about to kill her the gods turned her into a myrrh tree. Adonis was born from this tree. He was very beautiful from birth, and Aphrodite fell in love with him. One story says that she placed him in a chest and gave him to Persephone to take care of, and Zeus decreed that for part of the year he should stay with her and for the remaining part with Aphrodite. Another story relates that Adonis, having been brought up by nymphs, was out hunting when Aphrodite met him and fell in love with him. He was killed by a wild boar, and from his blood sprang the rose, or from Aphrodite's tears the anemone.

The story of Adonis has been explained as a vegetation myth, in which the god dies every year and is restored to life with the growth of new crops. The name could be oriental in origin, from the Semitic *Adon,* 'Lord'. Other explanations of this strange myth have been suggested. The cult of Adonis reached Athens probably from Cyprus in the fifth century BC; his festival was marked by women mourning and lamenting his death, and by the setting on the house-tops of the 'Gardens of Adonis', seedlings in shallow soil which withered as soon as they sprang up.

adoption. In Athenian society the original purpose of adoption was to ensure the survival of the family and the continuance of its religious rites by allowing a citizen who had no son to choose an heir, usually from among his relatives. The principle that adoption imitates nature was not accepted, and the adoption of a daughter's husband as son was regular practice. Despite the religious aspect there is no doubt that in Greece as in Rome financial considerations were important in cases of adoption.

In Roman society, for all legal purposes, the adopted person was in the same position as if he or she had been the natural child of the adopter, succeeding to name and rank, and subject to the same restrictions on marriage within the family as a natural child.

Adra'stus, mythical king of Argos at the time of the conflict of Polyneices and Eteocles for the kingdom of Thebes (see OEDIPUS). He was the son of Talaus and Lysimachē. After a quarrel with another branch of the royal family he fled to Sicyon, where the king made him his heir. He became king of Sicyon, but then made his peace at Argos and returned there, giving his sister Eriphylē in marriage to Amphiaraus. To his court came the exiles *Tydeus and Polyneices. The latter married his daughter Argeia, the former her sister Dēipylē. Adrastus undertook to restore them to their kingdoms and began by leading an army, the *'Seven against Thebes', to set Polyneices on the throne of Thebes. When the expedition was defeated, Adrastus escaped, thanks to the swiftness of his horse Arīon, the offspring of Poseidon and Demeter. In his old age he successfully led the sons of the Seven, the *Epigonoi, against Thebes, but died on his way home from grief at the loss of his son, Aegialeus, who alone had fallen in the attack. His grandson Diomedes became king.

Adriatic Sea (Gk. Adrias, Lat. Mare (H)Adriaticum or (H)Adria), the gulf between Italy and the Balkan peninsula; in the south it meets the Ionian Sea (east of Sicily). Its name is derived from the Etruscan town of Atria (or Hatria; modern Adria), not very far from the mouth of the Po. The Adriatic is notoriously stormy.

adultery. In Greece and Rome there was no adultery unless a married woman was concerned. In Greece a man who caught another in the act of criminal intercourse with his wife might kill him and, if he could prove the adultery had occurred, go unpunished; or he might inflict other punishment, or enter a legal prosecution against him, in which case the penalty was very severe. He might also take a sum of money off the adulterer by way of compensation. The husband of a proved adulteress lost his privileges of citizenship if he continued to cohabit with her. The adulteress was excluded from all temples and religious gatherings.

In Roman law the offended husband was not allowed quite so much freedom of self-redress, especially after the *lex Julia* (Julian law) of 18 BC. Only in certain circumstances might he kill the adulterer. A special court tried cases of adultery and the usual punishment was banishment for wife and adulterer, to different islands. The Christian emperors introduced severer penalties, Constantine making the adulterer's offence capital.

advocate, SEE LAW, AT ATHENS 3; AT ROME I (ii).

Ae'a, in the story of the *Argonauts, the realm of *Aeētēs, later identified with Colchis.

Ae'acus, in Greek myth, son of Zeus and the nymph Aegina. He married Endeis and became the father of *Telamon (father of the Greater Ajax) and of *Peleus (father of Achilles). He was a man of great piety. His prayers once ended a drought in Greece; on another occasion when the inhabitants of his island, Aegina, were destroyed by a plague, Zeus, to reward him, re-peopled it by creating human beings out of ants (*myrmēkes*); they were therefore called Myrmidons, the name by which the subjects of Peleus and Achilles are known in Homer. After his death he became, with *Minos and *Rhadamanthys, a judge of the dead in the Underworld, imposing punishments for misdeeds in life.

Aeae'a (Aiaiē), in Homer's *Odyssey*, the island of *Circē, situated in the stream of Ocean (see OCEANUS).

aediles, at Rome, originally two plebeian magistrates, named from the *aedes* or temple of *Ceres, where they superintended the cult, one which was particularly important to the *plebs*. Their administration was soon extended to public buildings in general and especially to the archives (decrees of the senate and resolutions of the *plebs*). In 367 BC their number was increased to four by the addition of two *curule aediles elected from the patricians. The office of aedile was elective and annual, not an essential part of the *cursus honorum* but the lowliest office to permit its holder to enter the senate. The aediles had charge of temples, buildings, markets, and, until the time of Augustus, the Games (see LUDI), which many aediles saw as a means of gaining popularity and votes. They also had charge of the corn supply until Julius Caesar entrusted this burden to special officers (see ANNONA).

Ăē'don, in Greek myth, daughter of Pandareōs and wife of Zēthus. Envying Amphion's wife *Niobē for her many children, she plotted to kill them. By mistake she slew her own child, Itylus (or Itys), and mourned for him so bitterly that the gods changed her into a nightingale, *aedon*. (Compare the story of Procne: see PHILOMELA.)

Ae'dui or **Haedui,** Gallic tribe which in Roman times occupied a region corresponding with modern Burgundy. Their chief town was Bibractē (Mont-Beuvray, near Autun). They became allies of Rome c.121 BC, and gave support to Julius Caesar during most of the Gallic Wars, joining Vercingetorix (of the Arverni) somewhat reluctantly in his revolt of 52 BC; see *COMMENTARIES* I (book 7). Under the empire they were the first Gallic tribe to have members in the senate at Rome.

Aeē'tēs, in Greek myth, king of Colchis; he was the son of *Helios, brother of *Circē, and father of *Medea. See ATHAMAS and ARGONAUTS.

Aega'tēs I'nsulae, islands off Lilybaeum in Sicily, near which was fought in 241 BC the naval battle in which C. Lutatius Catulus, the Roman admiral, defeated the Carthaginian fleet, so terminating the First *Punic War.

Aegean Sea (Aigaios pontos), the part of the Mediterranean between Greece and Asia Minor. The origin of the name is uncertain but was connected by some with Greek *aigis*, 'storm' and by others with Aegeus, father of *Theseus.

Aegeus, see THESEUS.

Aegi'aleus, son of Adrastus and the only one of the *Epigonoi to be killed in the expedition against Thebes.

Aegi'mius, the king of Doris in Greece who asked Heracles for help to expel the *Lapiths from his land. Heracles asked as his reward the right of his descendants to claim asylum in Doris. Later the *Heracleidae (from whom the Dorian kings claimed descent) were believed to have settled there, and thus were 'Dorians'. Aegimius' sons Dymas and Pamphylus together with Heracles' son Hyllus gave their names to the three Dorian tribes. See DORUS.

Aegī'na. 1. Nymph, daughter of the river-god Asopus, who was carried to the island (see below) by Zeus, to whom she bore *Aeacus.
2. Island of some 90 sq. km. (35 sq. miles) in the Saronic Gulf, about 20 km. (13 miles) south-west of Athens, famous in Greek myth, as the realm of *Aeacus, and in history. Around 1100 BC it was conquered by the Dorians who introduced the Dorian dialect and customs (see DORIAN INVASION). In the seventh century it became subject to the Argive tyrant *Pheidon. It soon developed great commercial importance and gradually built up a navy which by 500 BC had no rival in Greece. It was ruled by an aristocracy, its citizens were enriched by commerce, and the arts flourished. In 506 began the long feud with neighbouring Athens, whose navy was developed partly to combat the Aeginetan threat. Aegina did not support the Greek cause in the first Persian invasion of 490 (see PERSIAN WARS) but fought on the Greek side in the battles of 480 with outstanding bravery. In 457/6 she was decisively defeated by Athens and compelled to join the *Delian League (see ATHENS 2 (ii)). In 431, at the outbreak of the *Peloponnesian War, which the Aeginetans helped to foment, the Athenians expelled the whole population from the island and resettled it with Athenian *cleruchs. The exiles were restored by Lysander in 405, after which Aegina played a minor role in history.

The name 'Aeginetan' was given to one of the principal scales of weights and measures current throughout Greece (see MONEY).

aegis, attribute of the Greek gods Zeus and Athena, usually represented as a goat-skin or skin-covered shield, later having a fringe of snakes and a *Gorgon's head, used to frighten enemies and protect friends.

Aegi'sthus, see PELOPS.

Aegospo'tami (Aigospotamoi, 'goat's rivers'), small river in the Thracian Chersonese, with at one time a town of the same name on it. Off the mouth of the river Athens suffered her final naval defeat of the *Peloponnesian War in 405 BC. For the famous fall of a meteorite there see ANAXAGORAS.

Aegy'ptus. 1. See DANAUS. 2. See EGYPT.

Ae'lian (Claudius Aeliānus) (AD *c*.170–235), a Greek rhetorician, a *Stoic, who taught at Rome. His writings were much drawn upon by later moralists. His extant works are: *On the Characteristics of Animals*, a collection of excerpts and anecdotes of a moralizing nature in seventeen books; and *Historical Miscellanies* (usually known as *Varia Historia*), a similar collection dealing with human life and history in fourteen books.

Ae'lius Aristei'des, see ARISTEIDES.

Ae'lius Lampri'dius, see HISTORIA AUGUSTA.

Ae'lius Spartia'nus, see HISTORIA AUGUSTA.

Aemi'lius Paullus, Lucius, see PAULLUS.

Aenē'as, in Greek and Roman myth, one of the Trojan leaders in the Trojan War, son of *Anchises and the goddess Aphroditē (at Rome, Venus), and the subject of Virgil's Latin epic, the *Aeneid*. In the account of the Trojan War given in Homer's *Iliad* he is not depicted as an outstanding hero, being descended from the younger branch of the Trojan royal house (Priam, king of Troy, was of the older branch), but the Greek god Poseidon prophesies of him that he and his descendants will rule over the Trojans. Hence there developed, after Homer, the legend of his flight from ruined Troy with his father, son *Ascanius, and the *penates (indicative of his pious and dutiful nature), and of his subsequent wanderings. (See TABULA ILIACA.) Hellanicus the Greek *logographer writing in the fifth century BC makes the first certain literary allusion to Aeneas crossing the Hellespont and coming to the West; he may even allude to his being in Italy. There is no evidence that the Romans at that time thought of him as their founder, although artistic evidence shows that Aeneas was known in Etruria by the late sixth century BC. The Greek historian *Timaeus a century or so after Hellanicus speaks of Lavinium as Aeneas' first foundation in Italy. These were Greek views of Italy, attributing to Greek heroes (or in this case a Trojan hero) the settlement of the known West. Perhaps at the same period *Alba Longa began to claim that Aeneas was the ancestor of her kings. Rome soon took over, however, and developed the legend of Aeneas as founder of the Romans, national pride leading her to connect her own history with that of the Greek world. When *Pyrrhus launched his attack against Rome in 281 BC he saw himself as the descendant of Achilles making war on a colony of Troy. The story of Rome's Trojan origin took full shape in the third century BC when it was synthesized with the chronologically difficult legend of the foundation of Rome by *Romulus (a descendant of Aeneas through his mother). Probably both the Roman historian *Fabius Pictor and the Roman poet *Ennius filled the gap between the supposed dates of the fall of Troy (1184) and Romulus' foundation of Rome (753) with a sojourn by Aeneas' descendants at Alba Longa. Certainly by the third century BC the story later known to Virgil was well-established and familiar. From the second century BC the Julian *gens* ('clan'), Julius Caesar above all, exploited their descent from Aeneas and Venus for political aggrandizement. Virgil, while celebrating in the *Aeneid* the Trojan ancestry of Octavian, adopted son of Julius Caesar, also re-created Aeneas as a national hero.

Aeneas is portrayed by Virgil as *pius*, 'dutiful', conscious of his heavy destiny as founder of Rome, obedient to the will of the gods, a responsible leader to his followers, and a devoted father and son.

Aene'as Ta'cticus ('the tactician'), probably Aeneas of Stymphalus, an Arcadian general of the fourth century BC, named 'Tacticus' for his military treatises, one of which has survived, 'On the defence of fortified positions'. It is interesting for revealing social and political conditions in early fourth-century Greece, as well as for being a work outside the Attic literary tradition of its time.

Ae'nĕid (*Aenēis*), Latin epic poem in twelve books of hexameters by *Virgil, composed during the last ten years of his life, 29–19 BC, after the battle of Actium (31 BC) had finally established the rule of Octavian (later the emperor Augustus). The poem is designed to celebrate the origin and growth of the Roman empire, the achievements both of Rome and of Augustus. The groundwork is the legend of Aeneas, the Trojan hero, who survived the fall of Troy and after long wanderings founded a Trojan settlement (Lavinium) in Latium in Italy, named after his Italian bride Lavinia, and became through his (Trojan) son Iulus the ancestor of the *gens* *Julia and founder of *Alba Longa (and ultimately of Rome). Virgil was still working on the poem when he died, and indications of its incompleteness are some sixty half lines scattered throughout the poem which the poet would have expected to complete. It is unlikely that he intended to go beyond the present ending. There seems to have been pressure put on the poets of the day, perhaps by *Maecenas, to produce an epic on Augustus. Horace and Propertius both declined to do so, but from the introduction to the third book of the *Georgics* it seems clear that Virgil was

promising such a work. In the event he produced an epic not simply on Augustus but on the origins of Rome. Even so Augustus eagerly awaited its completion, and in 23 BC had the poet read to the imperial family books 2, 4, and 6.

The poem is immensely complex. Its framework is Homeric epic, which entailed the presence of the gods and their interference in human action, as well as exploits of a heroic nature; individual episodes are indebted to Attic tragedy and to the *Argonautica* of *Apollonius Rhodius, as well as to the ancient Roman poets *Naevius and *Ennius, but it is permeated by Roman themes, Roman values, and Roman history. At a simple level the Roman people and their chief families are glorified by the representation of their ancestors in the heroic age; at the same time the triumphs of Roman history are shown prospectively, as leading up to the reign of Augustus. Not only Rome, but also Italy, is shown as part of the scheme of things. One striking feature of the poem is the conception of Italy as a single nation, and of Roman history as a continuous whole from the founding of the city to the promise of the empire. The religious beliefs underlying the poem are far more profound than the epic machinery of gods and goddesses of myth. Ancient beliefs and practices, treated with reverence, coexist with philosophical ideas taken from the Greeks and modified by Roman attitudes. The theology of book 6, and the moral issues of books 4 and 12, raise questions which defy a final answer. The love affair between Dido and Aeneas in book 4 in particular has been the subject of much debate, and the poet has been censured for giving such a shabby portrayal of Aeneas while so powerfully enlisting our sympathies for the Carthaginian Dido. But it is his great achievement, here and throughout the poem, to reveal not only Rome's divinely ordained destiny to rule, to pacify, and to civilize, but also the terrible suffering entailed, for conquerors and conquered alike, for the noble and the less noble, and for those caught up in the fates of others: Creusa, Turnus, Lausus, Pallas, and Mezentius. The two passages cited by Samuel Johnson (1709–84) for their supreme quality are the descriptions of the tomb of Polydorus in book 3 and of the Trojan ships turned into sea-nymphs in book 9, neither appealing particularly to modern sensibility.

The *Aeneid* was edited after Virgil's death by his friends *Varius Rufus and Plotius Tucca. The events are as follows.

Book 1. Aeneas, who in the seven years since the fall of Troy has been making his way to Latium in Italy with the Trojan fleet, has just left Sicily. The goddess Juno, enemy of Troy and guardian of Carthage (which she knows is fated to be destroyed by a race of Trojan descent), has the wind-god Aeolus let loose a storm on the fleet. Some of the ships are wrecked, but the sea-god Neptune calms the storm; Aeneas and the remaining ships reach the Libyan coast. The Trojans are well received by Dido, queen of the newly founded Carthage; she has fled from Tyre, where her husband Sychaeus has been killed by his brother Pygmalion, the king. The goddess Venus, mother of Aeneas, fearful of both Juno and the Tyrians, arranges that Dido should fall in love with Aeneas.

Book 2. At Dido's request, Aeneas relates the fall of Troy and the subsequent events: the building of the Trojan Horse and the cunning of Sinon, the death of *Laocoon, the firing of the city, the desperate but unavailing resistance by the Trojans, Priam's death and Aeneas' own flight at the bidding of Venus; he tells how he carried his father Anchises on his shoulders and took his son Iulus (Ascanius) by the hand, how his wife Creusa, who followed, was lost, and his destiny revealed to him by her ghost.

Book 3. Aeneas continues his story. He and his companions build a fleet and set out. They land at Thrace, but leave after Aeneas finds there the grave of his murdered kinsman Polydorus, and hears his voice; they sail on to Delos. The Delian oracle tells them to seek the land that first bore the Trojan race. This they wrongly think means Crete, from which they are driven by a pestilence. Aeneas now learns that it means Italy. On their way there the Trojans land on the island of the *Harpies and attack them. The Harpy Celaeno prophesies that they shall found no city until hunger makes them 'eat their tables' (see book 7). At Buthrotum in Chaonia they find Helenus the seer (son of Priam) and Andromache. The seer tells Aeneas the route he must follow, visiting the Cumaean Sibyl and founding his city where by a secluded stream he shall find a white sow with a litter of thirty young. Going on his way, Aeneas visits the country of the *Cyclopes in Sicily; his father dies at Drepanum. From there he reaches Libya.

Book 4. Dido, though bound by a vow to her dead husband, confesses to her sister Anna her love for Aeneas. Juno and Venus arrange that the union of Dido and Aeneas should be sealed when a hunting expedition is interrupted by a storm and they take shelter in the same cave. The rumour of their love reaches Iarbas, a neighbouring king, who has been rejected by Dido and now in his anger appeals to Jupiter. The god commands that Aeneas should leave Carthage. When Dido realizes that the fleet is preparing to sail, she confronts Aeneas and pleads with him. He replies that he has no choice, and must go to Italy even against his will. Dido's fury does not stop the Trojan preparations, and even a last entreaty from her fails to weaken Aeneas' resolve. She prepares for death, and, having seen the Trojan fleet depart, takes her own life while cursing Aeneas and his descendants.

Book 5. The Trojans return to Sicily and are received there by their compatriot *Acestes. It is a year since Anchises died in the same place, and the anniversary is celebrated with sacrifices and games. The first event of the latter is a race between four ships. Gyas, captain of *Chimaera*, angrily pushes his helmsman overboard when he loses the lead to Cloanthus in *Scylla*; Sergestus in *Centaur* runs aground; Mnestheus in *Pristis* overtakes Gyas but just fails to catch Cloanthus. There follows a foot-race in which the leader, Nisus, having slipped and fallen, deliberately trips Salius so as to let his friend Euryalus win. In a boxing match between the Trojan Darēs and Entellus of Sicily, Aeneas stops the fight when Darēs is savagely attacked by the Sicilian. Next comes a competition with bows and arrows, and finally a display by thirty-six young horsemen led by Ascanius, an event which was later to become a tradition at Rome (see LUDUS TROIAE). Meanwhile the Trojan women, weary of their long wanderings, are incited by Juno to fire the ships; but only four are destroyed before a rain-storm quenches the flames in answer to Aeneas' prayer. Later the Trojans set sail again, some staying behind to found a new city under Acestes. The helmsman Palinurus falls asleep and is lost overboard.

Book 6. Aeneas visits the Cumaean *Sibyl and she foretells the trials he will face in Latium. At her bidding he plucks the *Golden Bough and descends with her through the cave of Avernus to the Underworld. Arriving at the river Styx they see the ghosts of the unburied dead unable to cross; among them is the helmsman Palinurus, who recounts his fate and begs for burial. On seeing the Golden Bough, Charon allows Aeneas and the priestess to cross the Styx; they send *Cerberus to sleep with a drugged cake. Beyond his cave they find various groups of the dead: infants, those unjustly condemned, those who have died of love (among them Dido, unmollified by the excuses Aeneas offers), and those killed in battle. They arrive at the entrance to Tartarus, where the worst sinners suffer torments, but go on until they reach Elysium, where the souls of the virtuous live in bliss. Here Aeneas greets his father Anchises, but tries in vain to embrace him. Aeneas sees ghosts drinking at the river *Lethē, and Anchises explains how they are the ones who will be reincarnated: over a long period they have been purged of all evil and now drink the waters so as to lose all memory. (This doctrine of rebirth may have been taken by Virgil from Plato or from Orphic–Pythagorean traditions: see MYSTERIES.) Anchises points out the souls of men who are destined to be illustrious in Roman history: Romulus, the early kings, the great generals, Augustus himself, and his nephew *Marcellus (to whose brief life Virgil makes touching allusion). After this Aeneas and the Sibyl leave the Underworld through the Ivory

Gate, by which false visions are sent to mortals (the significance of this has been much debated). This book contains these lines (851–3) on the destiny of Rome which are central to the poem:

> tu regere imperio populos, Romane, memento;
> hae tibi erunt artes: pacisque imponere morem,
> parcere subiectis, et debellare superbos.

> (Roman, let your concern be to command the nations; your skills shall be these: to impose the rule of peace, to spare the submissive, and to crush the proud.)

Book 7. Aeneas and the Trojans reach the mouth of the Tiber and land in Latium. They fulfil the prophecy of the Harpy Celaeno (see book 3 above) by eating the bread cakes which they have used as platters during a meal. Lavinia, the daughter of Latinus, king of Latium, has many suitors of whom the most favoured is Turnus, king of the Rutulians; but Latinus has been told by his father's oracle that she must marry not a Latin but a stranger who will arrive. Ambassadors from the Trojans are welcomed by Latinus, who offers Aeneas alliance and his daughter in marriage. Juno sees the Trojans preparing to settle and summons the Fury Allecto, who stirs up mad hostility to the Trojans in queen Amata, Lavinia's mother, and in Turnus. When Ascanius is hunting, Allecto causes him to wound a stag which is kept as a royal pet, and a fight ensues. Latinus is powerless to stop the preparations for war, and the Italian tribes gather under their leaders; among these, apart from Turnus, are Mezentius, scorner of gods and a hated tyrant, Messapus, Virbius (son of *Hippolytus), and the Volscian warrior-maiden *Camilla.

Book 8. The god of the river Tiber encourages the anxious Aeneas, telling him to seek alliance with the Arcadians under Evander, who have founded a city on the Palatine hill (which will in the future be part of Rome). Rowing up the river, Aeneas sees on the bank a white sow with her litter, as had been prophesied. Evander promises his support. Vulcan, at the request of Venus, makes armour for Aeneas. Evander, who has shown Aeneas a number of places in his city which will eventually be famous sites in Rome, urges alliance with the Etruscans. Venus brings Aeneas his armour; it includes a shield on which are depicted various events in the future of Rome, down to the battle of Actium.

Book 9. Aeneas has told the Trojans to keep to their camp in his absence, and they refuse to join battle even when Turnus and his forces surround them. When Turnus tries to set fire to the Trojan ships, Neptune changes them into sea-nymphs. At night Nisus and Euryalus leave the camp in order to summon Aeneas. They kill a number of the enemy in their drunken sleep, but are seen by a mounted column and surrounded; both are killed, after Nisus has bravely tried to save his friend. The Rutulians attack the Trojan

camp, and Ascanius, in his first feat of battle, kills one who has been shouting taunts. Turnus is cut off inside the camp, and kills many Trojans before plunging into the river to escape.

Book 10. On Olympus the gods debate the conflict. Aeneas secures the alliance of Tarchon, king of the Etruscans, and sets out with him and with Pallas, Evander's son, to return to the Trojans. Turnus attacks them as their ships reach the shore. In the battle which follows Turnus kills Pallas. Juno contrives a phantom of Aeneas; Turnus pursues it on board a ship which bears him away. Aeneas wounds Mezentius and reluctantly kills the latter's son Lausus as he tries to protect his father; Mezentius mounts his faithful horse Rhaebus for a last attack on Aeneas before horse and rider are both killed.

Book 11. Aeneas celebrates the Trojan victory and laments the death of Pallas. The Latins send ambassadors and a truce is arranged. King Latinus and the Italian chiefs debate; Drances proposes that Turnus, being mainly responsible for the war, should settle it by meeting Aeneas in single combat. Turnus, scornful of Drances, accepts the challenge. The Latins now hear that the Trojans and Etruscans are advancing against them; Camilla and her Volscian cavalry confront the attackers. In the battle which follows Tarchon drags Venulus from his horse; Arruns seeks out and kills Camilla, who is avenged by Opis, messenger of the goddess Diana. The Volscians are defeated.

Book 12. The Latins are discouraged, and Turnus decides to fight Aeneas alone despite the efforts of Latinus and Amata to dissuade him. Preparations for the duel are made, but the Rutulians, already anxious about the outcome, are stirred up to intervene by Turnus' sister Juturna; the two armies join battle again. Aeneas is wounded by an arrow, but Venus heals him and he pursues Turnus; then Aeneas sees that the city of the Latins is unguarded and turns the Trojan army to attack it with fire. Amata, distraught, takes her own life. Turnus seeks out Aeneas and the armies draw back while the two leaders fight. Aeneas wounds Turnus with his spear and finally, enraged by the sight of his enemy wearing the spoils taken from Pallas, kills him with his sword.

Aeo'lic. 1. For the dialect see DIALECTS, GREEK. 2. For the metre see METRE, GREEK 8 (i).

Ae'olis, the name given in classical times to the territory in the northern part of the west coast of Asia Minor, from the Troad to the river Hermus, which had been occupied by Aeolian Greeks (for the name see AEOLUS (2)). These Greeks, around the end of the second millenium BC, migrated from Boeotia and Thessaly and founded their first settlements in Lesbos; from there they spread northwards and along the coast; see MIGRATIONS and DIALECTS.

Ae'olus. **1.** Described in Homer's *Odyssey* as the son of Hippotēs, a mortal and a friend of the gods, to whom Zeus gave control of the winds. He was later thought of as the god of the winds. He lived on the floating island of Aeolia. He received Odysseus hospitably and gave him a leather bag in which he had secured those winds adverse to the latter's voyage. Virgil depicts him as keeping the winds imprisoned in a cave (*Aeneid* 1. 50–9). He is sometimes confused with (2).

2. Son of *Hellen and the legendary ancestor of the Aeolians; he was the father of *Sisyphus, *Athamas, *Salmoneus, *Alcyone, Calycē (mother of *Endymion), *Canacē, and other children.

Ae'pytus, see MEROPE.

aera'rium, the treasury of the Roman state, situated in the Temple of Saturn below the Capitol, and containing also some state documents. It was controlled by the quaestors under the general supervision of the senate. The *aerarium sanctius* was a 'special reserve fund' drawn upon only in emergencies. The treasury was maintained into the empire but many revenues were increasingly diverted to the imperial treasury, the *fiscus.

The *aerarium militare* was founded by the emperor Augustus in AD 6 to provide pensions for discharged soldiers.

Ǎě'ropē, wife of Atreus, seduced by Thyestes (see PELOPS).

aes, see MONEY, 2.

Ae'schinēs, Athenian orator and great rival of *Demosthenes (2), born in Athens *c.*390 BC or earlier. Only three of his speeches survive. Of obscure family, he was (at least according to Demosthenes) first an assistant in his father's school, then a tragic actor, then a soldier, taking part in the battle of Mantinea in 362, then a clerk under *Eubulus, who controlled Athenian finances. By 348 he had embarked on a public career. In this year (or perhaps in 346), when it was known that under Philip II Macedonian influence was spreading as far as the Peloponnese, Eubulus proposed a scheme for concerted Greek action against aggressors so that no state would need to seek Macedonian help, and sent Aeschines to Megalopolis to dissuade the Arcadians from dealings with Philip. The scheme failed, Athens realized the necessity of making peace with Philip, and an embassy under the leadership of *Philocrates, including Aeschines and Demosthenes, was hastily sent to negotiate terms. Peace and alliance between Philip and Athens (and the Second Athenian League) were finally agreed in 346 but not until Philip had made further advances, thus bringing the Peace into disrepute (see PHILIP (1) 2). Demosthenes was now anxious to dissociate himself from the

Peace, and became implacably hostile to Aeschines, who supported it, choosing to believe that he had been won over by Macedonian bribes. In 346/5 Demosthenes began a prosecution against him for his part in the peace negotiations, with the support of Timarchus. The latter was a man long active against Philip but notorious for his private life. Aeschines replied with a speech of counter-accusation, *Against Timarchus* (still extant), in which he invoked a law forbidding those of known misconduct from addressing the assembly. He was successful, but the mood of Athens was becoming more hostile to Macedon.

In 343 Demosthenes attacked again in a speech *On the False Embassy*, as if Aeschines had been solely responsible for the discredited Peace, and had supported it because he was bribed. Aeschines replied in a speech of the same title (which also survives) and was narrowly acquitted. He continued to be influential in the Assembly and in 340 was sent as one of Athens' representatives to the *Amphictyonic Council, where he failed notably in statesmanship. He provoked a *Sacred War at the very time when unity was essential to avoid furnishing Philip with an opportunity to intervene in Greek affairs. Philip's subsequent invasion ended with the defeat of Athens and Thebes at *Chaeronea in 338. Aeschines was a member of the embassy sent to negotiate with Philip after the battle. In 336 Ctesiphon proposed that Demosthenes should be crowned in the theatre at the *Dionysia for his services to the city. Aeschines indicted Ctesiphon for the alleged illegality of the proposal but did not proceed with the indictment until 330 when Athens was in almost complete isolation, with no prospect of liberation from Macedon. In his speech *Against Ctesiphon* he attacked the whole career of Demosthenes as injurious to Athens. Demosthenes replied in his speech *On the Crown* with such devastating effect that Aeschines failed to obtain the necessary fifth of the jury's votes to save him from a fine. He retired from Athens to Rhodes where he died in about 322. At Rhodes he gave declamations, and once delivered his speech *Against Ctesiphon*. When the islanders expressed amazement that it did not win he replied, 'You would not wonder if you had heard Demosthenes'.

Aeschines was not a professional rhetorician. A story tells that when the Rhodians asked him to teach rhetoric he replied that he was ignorant of it himself. He seems not to have written speeches for others, and it is probable that he received no rhetorical training, but he was thoroughly familiar with all the conventions. He was famous for his dignified presence and splendid voice. His speeches, of which only the three named above were known to ancient critics, are characterized by a fondness for the legalities of the case, an astute use of diversionary tactics, and vivid descriptions. In ancient as well as modern times he has suffered from comparison with Demosthenes. The general aim of his activities was to find a compromise between Athens and Macedon which would leave Athens independent and at peace, and inevitably he had to trust Macedon to some extent. This policy was not a noble one, nor was it possible to give it rhetorical expression. In consequence he avoided the deeper issues of policy, and in contrast with Demosthenes, who was for ever generalizing and broadening the issues, he seems lacking in a wider vision.

Ae'schylus (525–456 BC), the earliest Greek tragic poet whose work survives. Born at Eleusis, near Athens, of a noble family, he witnessed in his youth the end of tyranny at Athens, and in his maturity the growth of democracy. He took part in the Persian Wars, at the battle of Marathon in 490 (where his brother was killed) and probably at Salamis in 480 (which he describes in the *Persians*). At some time in his life he was prosecuted, it was said, on the charge of divulging the Eleusinian *mysteries, but exculpated himself. He visited Syracuse at the invitation of the tyrant Hieron I more than once (see SYRACUSE 1) and died at Gela in Sicily; an anecdote relates that an eagle dropped a tortoise on his bald head and killed him. Soon after his death it was decreed as a unique honour that anyone who wished to produce his plays should be 'granted a chorus' (see TRAGEDY 1). He had a son, Euphorion, like himself a tragic poet.

Aeschylus wrote some eighty to ninety plays (including satyric dramas) and won his first victory in the dramatic competitions of 484. He won at least thirteen victories in his lifetime. In his early days he was the rival of Pratinas, Phrynichus, and Choerilus of Athens, and in later life of Sophocles, who defeated him in 468. Seven plays only have come down to us, six of which we know to have come from prize-winning tetralogies: the *Persians*, produced in 472, the *Seven Against Thebes* in 467, the *Oresteia* trilogy, comprising the *Agamemnon*, the *Choephoroe*, and the *Eumenides*, in 458, and the *Suppliants*; this last used commonly to be regarded as the earliest play because of certain archaic features, but a papyrus fragment published in 1952 containing a note on its production shows that it cannot have been produced before 468, and 463 is a likely date. The other surviving play, *Prometheus Bound*, has several features not found elsewhere in the plays. Its date is uncertain, but it seems not to be an early work.

Aeschylus is generally regarded as the real founder of Greek tragedy: by increasing the number of actors to two and diminishing the part taken by the chorus he made true dialogue and dramatic action possible. Either he or

Sophocles added a third actor, and three are used in his later plays. He also had a liking for spectacular effects and for mechanical devices. He displays a similar taste in his long and magnificent descriptions, e.g. of the battle of Salamis in the *Persians* and the fall of Troy in the *Agamemnon*. His language has a matching grandeur which to the succeeding generation seemed occasionally to border on the bathetic, to judge from the criticism in Aristophanes' comedy the *Frogs. He coins long compound words and is lavish with epithets and bold metaphors, creating striking and memorable images which often gain in significance from repetition throughout a play or trilogy. His principal characters are drawn without complexity or elaboration; they are not so much individual as 'typical', governed by a single dominating idea. The choruses also show 'typical' characterization; they have a role to play and are intimately involved in the action. Their songs are relevant, often explaining the significance of events that preceded the action.

It has always been for many people the religious and moral ideas of Aeschylus that give his drama a lasting significance. The action of an Aeschylean tragedy, which is of the kind that Aristotle in the *Poetics calls 'simple', flows inexorably on towards its end without any intervening surprise or complication, because the events that precipitated it have occured long before. One effect of this form of plot is to suggest the slow but certain workings of divine justice. It is by suffering that men eventually learn that whatever happens is the will of a just Zeus. By his design the rival claims of men and of deities are eventually reconciled and made to work together to produce universal order. This is one moral that can be drawn from the *Oresteia* and also, as far as we can see, from the trilogies that contained the *Suppliants* and the *Prometheus Bound*. But this is not to say that Aeschylus relieves men of their ordinary human responsibility: 'the doer shall suffer'. Aeschylus accepts the moral presuppositions of his time: guilt is inherited; the guilty man, 'the doer', shall suffer but it may be in the person of his son. Guilt may even produce fresh guilt, as in the case of Orestes. Another presupposition is that great prosperity deludes men into committing acts of insolence that lead to destruction, and once set upon that path there is no turning back. To Aeschylus these were the lessons not only of history but of the events of his own time.

Aescula'pius, the Latin form of the name of the Greek god of healing, *Asclepius. His cult was brought to Rome from the famous temple at Epidaurus in Argos in 293 BC, after the Romans had consulted the Sibylline books (see SIBYL) because of a severe pestilence. The temple, with a sanatorium, stood on the island of the river Tiber.

Aeson, see ARGONAUTS.

Aesop (Aisōpos), the traditional composer of Greek *fables. The story of his life, which was already known to Herodotus in the fifth century BC, has been overlaid by many fictions, but it seems likely that he came from Thrace and lived as a slave on the island of Samos in the early sixth century. See also RHODOPE.

Aesō'pus, Claudius, celebrated Roman tragic actor in the first century BC. Horace rates him as the equal of his contemporary *Roscius, the great comic actor. He was a friend of Cicero, and during the latter's exile helped to move popular feeling in his favour by allusions to him on the stage. Cicero says that he had great power of facial expression and gesture.

aether (aither), the rarefied and pure atmosphere in which the Greeks imagined the gods to live, commonly called the 'upper air'; often by extension the sky generally. In Greek myth, Aither (Sky) is an elemental deity, father of *Tartarus.

Aethio'pia, see ETHIOPIA.

Aethio'pica, novel by Heliodorus; see NOVEL, GREEK.

Ae'thiopis, lost poem of the *Epic Cycle, ascribed to Arctinus of Miletus, a sequel to the *Iliad.*

Aethra, in Greek myth, daughter of Pittheus, king of Troezen, and mother of *Theseus.

Aetna. 1. Europe's highest active volcano, in Sicily. Eruptions were attributed in literature to the mythical monster *Typhon or the Giant Enceladus (see GIANTS) imprisoned by Zeus beneath the mountain; occasionally it was described as the workshop of *Vulcan. Various notable eruptions are recorded in antiquity (see PINDAR (Pythian 1)). **2.** The name given to the city of Catana (Gk. Katanē, modern Catania) at the foot of Mount Aetna by Hieron I, tyrant of Syracuse, when he refounded the city in 475 BC, removing the former inhabitants and re-peopling it with Dorian mercenaries. In 461 these were expelled and the old name restored. The name Aetna was then transferred with the mercenaries to the nearby city of Inessa.

Aetna, Latin didactic poem in 645 hexameters of unknown authorship. It is attributed by its manuscripts and doubtfully by *Donatus (1) to Virgil, but is almost certainly not by him. The authorship and date have been the subject of much speculation with no agreement reached, but the style seems to point to the first century AD. The author rejects mythological explanations and attributes eruptions to the action of wind at high pressure in cavities of the earth on subterranean fires (substantially the same explanation as that of Lucretius, 6. 680). The poem is enlivened by digressions and closes with a story to illustrate justice in natural events: on the occasion of a sudden eruption the inhabitants of Catana hastily fled, each carrying the property he thought most precious; they were overwhelmed, but a certain Amphinomus and his brother, who carried away nothing but their aged father and mother and their household gods, were spared.

Aeto'lia, Aetolian Confederacy or **League.** Aetolia was a country of central Greece, bounded on the west by Acarnania and on the south by the Corinthian Gulf. Its most famous town, near the coast, was Calydon. Since its only coast was marshy and lacked a harbour, Aetolia's history was that of a land-power. In the fifth century BC she was undeveloped and organized not in cities but in tribes (Thucydides reports that one tribe was said to speak an almost unintelligible dialect and to eat raw meat). She grew in power after 370 BC when the Aetolian League was formed, which developed further after the death of Alexander the Great in 323. The League was governed at first by an assembly of all free Aetolian citizens (including the citizens of federated cities in adjoining territory); at the head of it was a general elected annually. The council (*boulē* or *synedrion*), composed of delegations from the confederate cities in proportion to their military contingents, contained some thousand members. Hence much of the leadership fell to a small committee of the council, the *apoklētoi*. The assembly, however, retained the decision of peace and war. From about 290 the League occupied Delphi, and gradually extended its territory until by 220 it controlled the whole of central Greece outside Attica, and became Macedonia's chief rival in the peninsula and Rome's first ally in Greece. Later, the League's hostility to Rome and co-operation with Antiochus III in his war with Rome (see SELEUCIDS) brought about its downfall, and after Antiochus' defeat in 189 the Aetolians were forced to become Roman subject-allies.

Afrā'nius, Lucius (active *c.*160–120 BC), writer of Roman comedies (*fabulae *togatae), of which only scanty fragments and forty-two titles survive. He may also have been an advocate in the law-courts. His plays depicted Italian life and characters; Horace says (*Epistles* II. 1. 57) that admirers compared him with the Greek writer of comedy *Menander. Afranius acknowledges his indebtedness to Menander, but the extent of it is unknown. The popularity of his plays continued under the empire; the emperor Nero staged a realistic and costly performance of 'The Fire', allowing the actors to keep what furniture they could save from a house which was actually set on fire.

Africa. The Greeks called the African continent, or the part of it they knew, Libya. The name Africa was given by the Carthaginians to the territory around Carthage, and was applied subsequently to all of the known continent; it was retained by the Romans when they made the Carthaginian territory a Roman province after the Third Punic War (146 BC). The province was gradually expanded with the planting of new Roman colonies until under the empire it stretched along the north coast from Cyrenaica (which remained Greek-speaking; see CYRENE) to the Atlantic. The area was heavily urbanized; during the second century AD African senators at Rome (who included the orator Fronto) comprised the largest group from the western provinces. The wealth of Roman Africa was proverbial, and was derived chiefly from the export of vast quantities of corn. In the third century Christianity spread rapidly in the province; Cyprian, Tertullian, and Augustine were all African by birth. For the later history see CARTHAGE. See also EGYPT.

afterlife. In Greece and Rome there was no generally accepted religious dogma on an afterlife. An unequivocal acceptance of human mortality, a consciousness that in this respect we are totally apart from the gods, pervades Greek literature. Yet a belief in some sort of survival after death was general and many often contradictory ideas existed side by side. The most primitive and long-lasting belief was that the dead lived on in their tombs, where offerings were regularly made to them by their families (see ANTHESTERIA). From earliest times Greek religious beliefs were a strong influence in Italy, and from the later years of the republic the Graeco-Roman world was essentially one in its religious and philosophic views of the afterlife. For specifically Italian beliefs see MANES and LEMURES.

The most general belief of antiquity, given its essential form by Homer, was that all the dead dwell below the earth in the realm of *Hadēs and *Persephonē, good and bad alike, leading a shadowy and cheerless existence. But Homer also speaks of *Elysium or the Isles of the Blest, situated at the ends of the earth, whither certain favoured heroes may pass, exempted by the gods from death; he also shows traces of a belief that Hades and Persephone may punish serious offenders after death, and that the gods can be propitiated by prayers and sacrifice. From the sixth century BC onwards ideas of happiness after death for those who have deserved well in this life are expressed, together with ideas of punishment in the Underworld or *Tartarus for the wicked, and of reincarnation and even transmigration of souls. These ideas are particularly associated with the names of *Orpheus and *Pythagoras, and with the Eleusinian mysteries (see MYSTERIES), where both righteousness and

initiation in this life are the prerequisites for happiness in the next.

To these religious beliefs in some sort of life after death Plato gave a philosophic foundation, using his theory of Ideas or Forms to argue that the soul is immortal, though he never describes precisely what he means by immortality. His passionate conviction that the good man can suffer no harm, and that man's soul is akin to what is divine and eternal, profoundly influenced later thought.

Many philosophers after Plato suspended judgement about the immortality of the soul (see ACADEMY and SCEPTICS). Aristotle allowed immortality of a non-personal kind to part of a man's soul. The Epicureans (see EPICURUS) believed that the soul was made of atoms as the body is, and so dies with the body. To the Stoics death was no evil, but they made no dogmatic pronouncements on an afterlife, allowing simply that the soul might survive for some time in an unspecified form. It was partly these philosophic speculations on the soul that lent strength to the teachings of the mystery religions. These religions, which grew up in the Hellenistic age and flourished still more in Roman times, offered as their highest promise a happy afterlife, however it was thought of, and thus helped to foster the feeling, which was a feature of the religious beliefs of late antiquity, that the soul survived death.

Agamē'dēs, see TROPHONIUS.

Agame'mnon, in Greek myth, son of *Atreus, brother of *Menelaus, husband of *Clytemnestra, king of Mycenae, or Argos, and leader of the Greek forces in the Trojan War. He is represented in Homer's *Iliad* as a valiant fighter, a proud and passionate man, but vacillating in purpose and easily discouraged. His quarrel with *Achilles is the mainspring of the poem's action. The *Odyssey* tells how, on his return from Troy, he was feasted in the palace of his wife's lover, and there murdered by them both, together with his captive *Cassandra. This story is retold by later authors, with minor variants (see especially ORESTEIA). All accounts include a son *Orestes among his children, who avenged his father's murder, usually with the help of his sister *Electra. The *Cypria* is the earliest witness to the story that Agamemnon was required to sacrifice his daughter Iphigeneia to atone for an offence against Artemis, who in anger was keeping the Greek fleet wind-bound at Aulis.

Agamemnon. 1. Greek tragedy by *Aeschylus; for the plot see ORESTEIA.

2. Roman tragedy by Seneca the Younger (see SENECA (2) 4). The play shows variation in details from the *Agamemnon* of Aeschylus. The ghost of Thyestes is introduced urging Aegisthus to the crime, and Aegisthus strengthens a

weaker Clytemnestra's resolve. Cassandra is not murdered with Agamemnon but later. Electra appears and contrives the escape of her brother Orestes.

Agani'ppē, spring sacred to the Muses on Mount *Helicon in Boeotia; compare HIPPO-CRENE.

Agapē'nor, in Greek myth, leader of the Arcadian contingent against Troy in the Trojan War. On the way back he arrived at Cyprus where he founded the city of Paphos.

Aga'thias (AD c.531–c.580), Greek poet and lawyer who lived most of his life in Constantinople. He made a collection of epigrams written by his contemporaries, generally known as the *Cycle*, which partially survives in the Greek *Anthology. The Anthology also contains about a hundred of Agathias' own poems, some highly artificial and mannered, others, particularly the love poems, warm and charming. Later he started a *History* which was to bring the narrative of *Procopius' *Wars* up to his own day, but he died when he had completed only five books, covering the years 553–9.

Aga'thoclēs, see SYRACUSE 3.

A'gathon (b. c.445 BC), Athenian tragic poet, perhaps the most important apart from the three great tragedians (see TRAGEDY 4) and celebrated for his good looks. Less than forty lines of his work survive. His first victory in the dramatic competitions was gained at the Lenaea in 416 BC when he was probably under 30. It is the banquet held at his house to celebrate this victory that forms the setting of Plato's *Symposium. Agathon was an innovator: he was the first to construct a tragedy on an imaginary subject with imaginary characters rather than taking it from Greek myth; he made the songs of the chorus mere interludes (*embolima*, 'interpolations') without reference to the subject of the play, thus preparing the way for the division of the tragedy into acts; and he also introduced some changes in the character of the music. Aristophanes in the *Thesmophoriazusae* parodies Agathon's lyrics, hinting that they are voluptuous and effeminate and at one point describing them as like the walking of ants, and also makes fun of his effeminate appearance. When, towards the end of the Peloponnesian War, Agathon, like Euripides, withdrew to the court of Archelaus of Macedon, Aristophanes in the *Frogs* (84) regrets his abandonment of Athens. He died in Macedon c.400.

Aga'vē (Agauē), in Greek myth, the mother of Pentheus (see BACCHAE). For the pantomime with this title see STATIUS.

Agdi'stis, the Phrygian name of *Cybelē; see also ATTIS.

Agē'nōr, in Greek myth, king of Tyre, twin-brother of *Belus, and father of *Cadmus and *Europa.

age'ntes in rebus, see POLICE.

ager pu'blicus, 'state land' or 'public land', land confiscated during the Roman conquest of Italy (see ROME 4), from communities that put up a strong resistance or subsequently rebelled. (Some land in the provinces could also be so described.) Some of the land was assigned to individuals and much was allocated to colonies, but from earliest times most of it became the subject of dispute between the *plebs* who wished it to be distributed among themselves and the patricians who preferred to maintain public ownership so that they could be *possessores*. The *possessores* were supposed to pay dues to the state in return for occupying the land, and the amount of land that could be held was limited by the Licinian laws (see LICINIAN–SEXTIAN LAWS), but in practice both dues and laws were evaded. After the extensive confiscations of the Second Punic War some *ager publicus* was leased by the censors and brought in a good rent to the state, but vast tracts especially in the south were held by *possessores* and mostly used for ranching. The aim of the *Gracchi was to reimpose the Licinian laws and to distribute the excess land in smallholdings which were to remain state property and whose holders paid a tax. An end was put to many disputes by a law of 111 BC which said that all state land was to become the private property of its occupants. (There were of course several categories of land that remained state-owned, e.g. roads.) The question of *ager publicus* became an issue on several occasions afterwards as victorious generals like Sulla, Julius Caesar, and Octavian wanted land for their veterans. It was not until the time of the emperor Augustus that a pension scheme, as a means of support other than grants of land, was devised for discharged soldiers (see AERARIUM). Under the empire all state land gradually passed into the administration of the emperor.

ager Roma'nus, 'territory of Rome', see ROME 4.

Agesilā'us (c.444–360 BC), king of Sparta from 399. He was chosen king in place of his nephew, who was the direct heir, through the influence of the Spartan general *Lysander. He was lame, and his opponents drew attention to the warning of an ancient oracle against a 'lame reign' at Sparta. But he was a man of great efficiency and Spartan virtues. His successful campaigns against the Persians in 396–395 and his victory over the Boeotians and Athenians at Coronea in 394 are related by his friend the Athenian historian *Xenophon in his Hellenica. Spartan intervention in the affairs of autonomous states, which Agesilaus condoned, resulted in an alliance between Thebes and Athens which his invasions of Boeotia in 378 and 377 did not succeed in disrupting. His refusal in 371 to admit *Epaminondas' claim to represent all Boeotia at the peace congress in Sparta precipitated the battle of Leuctra at which Sparta lost the leadership of Greece. In the years of humiliation which followed he organized the defence of the city. Sparta needed money, and in order to earn a subsidy Agesilaus conducted an expedition in aid of an Egyptian prince against Persia in 361. In this he met his death. His Life was written by *Nepos and by Xenophon (see below).

Agesilā'us, one of the minor works of Xenophon, a biographical essay on his friend the Spartan king (see above). Xenophon relates in some detail the campaign of Agesilaus against the Persian satrap Tissaphernes in 395 BC and the march back to Greece through Macedonia and Thessaly, and gives a full description of the battle of Coronea at which, according to Plutarch, Xenophon fought for his friend against his fellow-countrymen. The remaining events of Agesilaus' reign are touched on more briefly. Xenophon then passes from his deeds to his virtues, and ends with an encomium on his piety, justice, wisdom, and patriotism.

A'giads (Agiadai), the name of the senior royal house at *Sparta, derived from the name of a legendary Dorian king Agis, son of Eurysthenes (see HERACLEIDAE), who made the original inhabitants of Sparta subject to the Dorian invaders (see DORIAN INVASION). The junior branch was the Eurypontid.

agōn ('contest'). **1.** In Greece and later at Rome, a public festival at which competitors contended for a prize, usually in chariot- and horse-races and athletics but occasionally in musical or dramatic competitions. See ATHLETICS; FESTIVALS; GAMES, PUBLIC; and LUDI.

2. The 'debate' in Attic Old Comedy; see COMEDY, GREEK 3 (iii).

a'gora, in Greek literally 'assembly', especially of the people; then 'place of assembly', market place (Lat. *forum*), or city centre of a Greek city. For the agora of Athens see ATHENS I; for *agora*, 'assembly', see ECCLESIA.

Agri'cola, Gnaeus Julius (AD 40–93), from the Roman colony of Forum Julii (Fréjus)—as was the poet Gallus—Roman general and governor of *Britain (see 4), on whose career his son-in-law the historian *Tacitus wrote *Agricola*, a laudatory monograph (see below). Agricola did his early military service in Britain as *tribunus militum* to the governor Suetonius Paulinus, in the troubled times which culminated in Boudicca's rebellion. He proceeded to be quaestor, tribune of the people, praetor, and then in AD 71–3 commander of the Twentieth Legion in Britain. After that he became governor of Aquitania and then consul for part of 77, and finally returned to Britain late in 77 or in 78 as

governor. In Britain his sympathy and justice towards the provincials enabled him to pacify the country while his military skills, particularly his good eye for terrain, helped him to extend Roman occupation northward into Scotland. This advance was made by stages during 80 and 81, with gains consolidated by fortifications including some on a line between the rivers Forth and Clyde. In 84 Agricola finally succeeded in bringing about a pitched battle with the highlanders at Mons Graupius (a much-sought battlefield, but the discovery of a large Roman camp near Inverurie in Aberdeenshire suggests that it may be the mountain now called Bennachie). Phrases from the speech attributed by Tacitus to the Caledonian leader Calgacus, exhorting his troops before the battle, have become famous: *omne ignotum pro magnifico est* ('what men know nothing about they see as wonderful'), and *ubi solitudinem faciunt, pacem appellant* ('when they create a desolation they call it peace'). Agricola's victory in this battle was final for its generation. After it, in 85, he was recalled and given no further command. He lived long enough to see Rome abandon the system of forts with which he had blockaded the highlands and secured the northern frontier. The excavations at Inchtuthil in Perthshire are a notable revelation of an outpost systematically demolished before it had been properly occupied. Agricola was remembered by later Roman historians for his circumnavigation of Britain after his campaign in Scotland. His civil policy encouraged urbanization and he founded many small quasi-independent 'states' in southern Britain to fill the administrative gap caused by moving the legions north.

Agri'cola, monograph by Tacitus in praise of the Roman general Agricola; see above. It includes an account of Britain and its tribes, the continual rain and cloud, and the long days and short nights of summer, but it is somewhat vague about the geography.

agriculture
1. To own and work a small agricultural estate was always a source of the highest social prestige, in Greece and Rome. In Mycenaean Greece it would appear that most villagers were the serfs of their king, but from at least the eighth century BC onwards the agricultural land was divided into small estates farmed by the owners and their slaves (how this came about is not known). In Greece, the first requirements for good crops were the irrigation and fertilization of the poor soil. Up to the fifth century BC and beyond it was common to leave the land fallow for a year after a crop of wheat or barley, and the importance of good manuring was realized. Where manure was not plentiful the farmers resorted to ploughing into the land a nearly mature bean crop, or at least growing a leguminous crop after a grain harvest. The

frequency of ploughing also depended on the richness of the soil; ploughing three times a year was usual. Wheat and barley figure prominently in the agricultural inventories of *Linear B tablets of the late second millennium BC. By the fifth century simple crop rotation was common and the potentialities of the various types of land were realized. Larger estates worked by slaves grew up, but small peasant holdings were still the general rule. For the pattern of the agricultural year see GREECE.

2. At Rome during this time agriculture was still domestic, carried on by the family of the landowner, on a small scale and by primitive methods, and devoted mainly to the production of grain. The family was self-sufficient, and it was this simple state of self-sufficiency that later reformers continually and unsuccessfully tried to restore. Sheep and cattle rearing became more profitable in the fourth century when the Volscian and Sabine hills were taken into the Roman territory. The third and second centuries brought Rome into contact with the more scientific agriculture first of Carthage and then of Greece and the Hellenistic East. The works of the fifty or so Greek writers on agriculture known to Cicero have all perished (only a Byzantine compilation, the *Geoponica*, survives); however, much of their teaching is known to us through the Latin hand-books of Cato, Columella, Varro, and Palladius. It was in Italy during the late republic and early empire that a peak of efficient agricultural production was reached, stimulated partly by the great variety of soils encountered in the various regions. The richest land yielded uninterrupted crops by a three-fold rotation; a vastly increased technical knowledge brought about the invention of new implements and the improvement of the land; there was specialization and organized division of labour. These developments began in the second century BC on the large agricultural estates known as *latifundia*, which grew up when landlords who had amassed wealth from the wars, or from provincial governorships, bought up the properties of smaller farmers and leased large tracts of *ager publicus*. Originally these estates were worked by gangs of slaves, now cheaply available through the recent wars, under the supervision of bailiffs, *vilici*; when slave labour ceased to be so plentiful in the first century BC the *vilici* continued to cultivate the home farms but leased the other farms to *coloni*, tenant farmers, and collected their rent. On many *latifundia*, however, especially in the south of Italy, stock-rearing or the cultivation of the vine and the olive were seen to be more profitable than arable farming. Thus the small cultivator totally disappeared from the scene in much of Italy and with him many of the imagined virtues of a simple rustic life.

3. Sheep and cattle formed an important part of the agricultural economy of Greece and Rome

from earliest times. Dry meadows and water meadows, often artificially produced by irrigation, were considered the most profitable kind of land, being free from risk of disaster and producing a double return in hay and pasturage. Sheep, pigs, goats, and (in small numbers) oxen all appear on the Linear B tablets. Oxen were bred to do all the heavy work of the farm and cows for the milk that was used to make cheese (butter and milk as such being scarcely ever consumed). Sheep and goats were valued for being cheese producers, but their chief value, as in the case of cattle, lay in their clip and hides rather than in their meat. (For the ancients' low consumption of meat see FOOD.) *Horses served no agricultural purpose; breeding them, for racing or for war, was a rich man's pursuit. Mules were bred to be beasts of burden, for light ploughing and for drawing travelling carriages. Pigs were raised for food, and poultry and game as well as the smaller wild birds were fattened for the table, by the Romans especially in ways unpleasantly suggestive of modern battery farming. The Romans also cultivated snails and dormice as items of luxury. Beekeeping was as important to the ancients as sugar production to us, and by the time of the empire had become highly technical. See HONEY.

The cultivation of the vine, the olive, and the fig was practised in eastern Mediterranean countries from the earliest times; figs, olives, olive-oil, and wine are all mentioned on the Linear B tablets. In many parts of Greece they were a more important crop than grain: the destruction of the vines and olives in Attica by the invading Spartans at the start of the Peloponnesian War was a considerable blow to the Attic farmers. Italy came more slowly to their cultivation, but by the first century BC such large plantations of them flourished on many *latifundia* that Italian wines had largely replaced the earlier Greek imports, and Italian olive oil was being sold in Greece.

By the end of the second century AD Mediterranean agriculture had become the unity that we see today. The agricultural advances that had come piecemeal from various parts of that world were spread throughout the empire, and put into practice by the *coloni* and by discharged soldiers who farmed their own small properties after the gradual disappearance of slave labour. After the fall of the empire in the fifth century AD, agriculture in the west did not break down; the late Roman pattern survived as the basis of agriculture in modern Europe.

4. *Agricultural implements.* Manual implements, basically the spade, the hoe, the bill-hook, and the sickle, remained much the same in Greece throughout antiquity. In Italy, however, the great variety of soils produced much variety in design, as did the growth of more scientific and

specialized farming. But hoe cultivation was never superseded by the plough since persistent tillage of the fallow was necessary between grain crops and it was usually recommended that the growing corn as well as other crops should be hoed regularly. Machines were somewhat rare. The laborious business of threshing, i.e. separating the grain from the chaff, was originally effected by spreading out the corn on specially prepared floors and beating it with flails or, more commonly, having animals tread it. An advance on this was the Greek invention of yoking the animals to a treading machine, *tribulum*, a heavily weighted board with flints embedded in its underside; an improved version in which the flints were replaced by toothed rollers, the so-called 'Punic wagon', was a legacy from Carthage. The most significant mechanical invention was the *vallus*, a reaping machine equipped with a toothed frame, which was driven through the standing corn and tore off the heads of grain, depositing them in a container. The machine was much used in the open fields of Gaul.

5. In references to the plough by classical authors it is not always easy to understand exactly what sort is meant, since their terminology varies, as does the English. The only surviving description of a Roman plough, that given by Virgil (*Georgics* I. 169), adds to the confusion. However, we know that the design of all classical ploughs is symmetrical, to raise the earth evenly on each side of the furrow. Basically the plough had three parts, which might all be made from the one piece of timber, especially if a young tree had been encouraged to grow in a shape to suit the purpose. There was the pole, beam, or tongue of the plough (Lat. *temo*, Gk. *rhymos* or *histoboios*), to one end of which the oxen are yoked, and which could be the trunk of the tree. At the other end of this pole, curving downwards into the ground, should be the sole or share-beam (Lat. *dentāle*, Gk. *elyma*). This might be sharpened and used as it stood as the plough-share (Lat. *vomis*, Gk. *hynnis*), but usually it was sheathed with bronze or iron. If the share-beam was not integral with the pole, it was mortised into a piece of strong timber known as the plough-beam or plough-tree (Lat. *buris*, Gk. *gyes*) which was connected to the pole. As he guided the plough, the ploughman forced the share into the soil to a sufficient depth by means of a handle, usually mortised into the share-beam; but here some confusion arises because the ancients seem to have used to describe this handle not only the proper name *stiva*, in Latin, or *echetlē* in Greek (stilt or plough-tail), but also the term for the plough-beam, no doubt because it often appeared to be a protraction of the latter. Pliny mentions ploughs with a wheeled fore-carriage to ease the labour of working heavy soil.

Agrige'ntum, see ACRAGAS.

Agri'ppa. 1. Marcus Vipsā'nius Agrippa (64–12 BC), the life-long friend and supporter of the emperor Augustus and the holder of important military and naval commands. He defeated Sextus *Pompeius in 36, and commanded the left wing at Actium in 31 BC to bring about the defeat of Mark *Antony. After this he helped to manage the affairs of Rome and in 23 BC Augustus, when he was seriously ill, probably intended that Agrippa should succeed him. He continued until his death to be Augustus' right-hand man in the government of the empire.

Agrippa was an honest and able administrator, whose personal tastes were simple. He devoted his life and his immense wealth (probably due to his first marriage; see below) to Rome and the empire, and left most of his property to Augustus at his death. Among his many public works were the building of the *Pantheon and the first great public *baths at Rome, and the renewal of the water-supply and sewage systems (see AQUEDUCTS and CLOACA MAXIMA). He built the harbour, Portus Julius, on the Lucrine Lake, and also carried out many works in the provinces; the system of main roads radiating from Lugdunum (Lyons) is his. He wrote an autobiography and a geographical commentary (see MAPS), both now lost. He married first the daughter, known as Attica, of Cicero's friend Titus Pomponius *Atticus; she bore him a daughter Agrippina who was to marry the emperor Tiberius. Secondly, he married Augustus' niece Marcella; thirdly, Augustus' daughter Julia, who bore him five children including Gaius and Lucius Caesar who were adopted by Augustus but died young (AD 2 and 4 respectively), and Agrippina, who married Germanicus.

2. Marcus Vipsanius Agrippa Po'stumus (12 BC–AD 14), son of Agrippa (1) and Julia, daughter of the emperor Augustus; he was born after his father's death, as his *cognomen* indicates. Along with Tiberius he was adopted by Augustus in AD 4, but was passed over by the emperor for the throne because of his boorish ways, and soon after Augustus died in 14 was put to death, possibly by order of Tiberius.

3. Marcus Julius Agrippa, see HEROD (2).

Agrippī'na. 1. Vipsānia Agrippina (d. AD 20), daughter of *Agrippa (1) and Attica, and first wife of the emperor Tiberius.

2. Agrippina the Elder (*c.*14 BC–AD 33), daughter of *Agrippa (1) and Julia, and wife of *Germanicus to whom she bore nine children. She was present at his death-bed in Syria and brought back his ashes to Rome. The hostility that she showed to Tiberius, whom she suspected (without evidence) of causing her husband's death, led to her arrest in 29 and banishment by the senate to the island of Pandataria (Ventotene). She starved herself to death in 33. She was the mother of the emperor Caligula (see GAIUS CAESAR).

3. Agrippina the Younger (AD 15–59), daughter of (2) above, married to Cn. Domitius *Ahenobarbus, to whom she bore one son, later the emperor Nero. She was exiled on suspicion of plotting against her brother the emperor Caligula in 39, and was recalled in 49 by Claudius, her uncle, who married her when she was widowed. She persuaded Claudius to adopt Nero, and when Claudius died in 54 she was generally believed to have poisoned him to make way for Nero. In the early years of the latter's reign she was almost co-regent with him, but eventually lost her influence through her imperious ways. In 59 Nero had her murdered at Baiae after he had failed to drown her by scuttling her ship.

Ahenoba'rbus later **Aenobarbus**, 'bronze-beard', the *cognomen* (see NAMES) of a distinguished branch of the Roman *gens*, the Domitii. Legend relates that the *Dioscuri had announced to an early member of the family the victory of Lake Regillus (496 BC), and to prove their supernatural powers had stroked his black beard, which immediately turned bronze-coloured. One Cn. Domitius Ahenobarbus, after fighting against Julius Caesar in 49 BC and being subsequently pardoned by him, was one of the republican leaders after Caesar's death, and commanded a fleet against the triumvirs. He was later reconciled to Mark *Antony, accompanied him in his expedition against the Parthians in 36, and was with him in Egypt. Abandoning Antony he joined the cause of Octavian before the battle of Actium in 31, and died soon afterwards. He figures in Shakespeare's *Antony and Cleopatra*.

Another Cn. Domitius Ahenobarbus, consul in AD 32, married *Agrippina (3), daughter of Germanicus, and was father of the emperor Nero. Suetonius described him as 'wholly despicable'. The timely death of the emperor Tiberius saved him from being charged with treason, adultery, and incest. According to Suetonius, the family possessed a streak of vicious cruelty. Of one member the orator Licinius *Crassus remarked, 'Should his bronze beard really surprise us? After all, he has a face of iron and a heart of lead.'

Aïdēs, Aïdō'neus, variant forms of *Hades.

Ai'gialeus, see AEGIALEUS.

Aisa, see FATE.

aither, see AETHER.

Ajax (Aias). 1. In Greek myth, son of *Telamon, king of Salamis, and Eriboea or Periboea (called Telamonian Ajax or 'the Greater Ajax', to distinguish him from (2) below), leader of the Salaminians who were with the Greeks at the siege of Troy. He is represented by Homer in the *Iliad* as being of great size and of dogged courage, the 'bulwark' of the Achaeans, who repeatedly leads the Greek attack or covers the retreat. His characteristic attribute is the all-enveloping Mycenaean body-shield. In the *Odyssey* his death is mentioned in a version that has become famous through Sophocles' tragedy *Ajax* (see below) and was narrated in the *Little *Iliad*. After Achilles' death there was a dispute between Ajax and Odysseus over who should receive his armour as a mark of personal prowess, and by the votes of the Greek leaders the armour was adjudged to Odysseus; Ajax went mad with resentment and killed himself. In fact various stories of his death were told in antiquity.

2. In Greek myth, son of Oileus (or Ileus), 'the Lesser Ajax', the captain of the Locrian contingent on the Greek side at the siege of Troy and the fastest runner, brave but arrogant and hated by the gods, particularly Athena. He was killed by the sea-god Poseidon on the way home from Troy for boasting that he had escaped from ship-wreck without divine aid. At the fall of Troy he dragged king Priam's daughter Cassandra by her hair from the altar of Athena, together with the statue (*Palladium) which she was embracing (a story told in the *Iliupersis*). For this impiety the Locrians continued to make atonement (until the second century BC), by sending every year two maidens of noble birth to serve in the temple of Athena at Troy. The girls had to reach the temple unseen or be killed by the townspeople.

Ajax, Greek tragedy by *Sophocles, of uncertain date, perhaps his earliest surviving play and written before 441 BC.

Ajax son of Telamon (see (1) above), bitterly resentful that Achilles' arms had been awarded to Odysseus, planned a night attack on the Greek leaders but, having been driven mad by the goddess Athena, killed cattle and sheep instead. When the play opens he is still mad and gloating over his supposed captives, but he recovers and is stricken with shame, while his concubine Tecmessa and the chorus of Salaminian sailors try to soothe him. He calls for his son Eurysaces, gives him his shield, and in his grief resolves upon suicide. After an interval Ajax speaks more calmly before going away to purify himself and to bury his sword. The chorus and Tecmessa are reassured, only to learn from his half-brother Teucer that the seer Calchas has declared calamity can be averted only if Ajax, who has angered the gods by his arrogance, is kept within his tent for that day. But it is too late; Ajax is found having fallen upon his sword. Menelaus forbids his burial, as an enemy to the Greeks; Agamemnon confirms the edict but is persuaded by Odysseus to relent, and Ajax is carried to his grave.

alae, 'wings', in the Roman army before the Social War (90–88 BC), two contingents of allied troops posted one on each flank of the Roman legion; later it had the restricted sense of 'cavalry'. After the army reforms of the emperor Augustus the name was applied to the cavalry contingents among the *auxilia*, auxiliary troops raised from outside Italy, under the command of the *praefectus equitum.

A'laric, the Visigothic leader who after several defeats finally succeeded in entering Rome in August AD 410 and plundered it for three days. It was the first time the city had been occupied by a foreign enemy since the Gallic invasion of 390 BC, and the civilized world was profoundly shocked. The sack is memorably described by Gibbon in his *Decline and Fall of the Roman Empire*, ch. 31. Alaric died soon after. (See VISIGOTHS.)

Ala'stor. 1. In Greek myth, son of Neleus who, like all the sons of Neleus except Nestor, was killed by Heracles.

2. 'Avenger', a supernatural agent who exacts vengeance for a crime.

Alba Longa, very ancient Latin city (see LATIUM) built on the northern slope of the Alban Mount near modern Castel Gandolfo some 20 km. (13 miles) south-east of Rome; it was traditionally founded *c*.1152 BC by Aeneas' son Ascanius, who moved his seat of government there from Lavinium. It appears once to have headed a league of Latin cities, but lost its primacy in Latium in about the seventh century BC, being destroyed allegedly by Rome in the reign of Tullus Hostilius. It was never rebuilt. (See ROME 2.)

Albinova'nus Pedo, Roman poet of the early first century AD, friend of Ovid, admired by Martial. He wrote elegies and epigrams and an epic poem on Theseus, all now lost. He was also the author, in the time of Tiberius (emperor AD 14–37), of a poem on the North Sea expedition of *Germanicus, of which some twenty hexameters survive in a quotation by the Elder Seneca.

Albion, the ancient (Celtic or pre-Celtic) name for Britain, soon ousted by the Celtic 'Britannia' (see BRITAIN 1). The Romans connected it with *albus*, 'white', and referred it to the cliffs of Dover.

Albu'nea, the *Sibyl who lived at Tibur (Tivoli) in central Italy and had a cult there. Her oracular verses were deposited in the Capitol at Rome, with the Sibylline books.

Alcae'us. 1. Greek lyric poet (b. before 620 BC) from Mytilene, chief city of Lesbos. Until recent years his poetry survived only in quotations made by later authors, but since the decipherment in the twentieth century of certain Egyptian papyri (see PAPYROLOGY) much more of his poetry has come to light, though the tattered fragments have yielded very few complete poems. Many of the poems concern the politics of the time, in which Alcaeus was closely involved. After the overthrow of the ruling family, the Penthilidae, Mytilene was governed by a series of tyrants, Melanchrus (612–609), Myrsilus, and *Pittacus (590–580), all of whom were generally opposed by Alcaeus' family or party. There was a closing of ranks when the Lesbians, Alcaeus among them, fought under Pittacus against the Athenians, *c*.606 BC, for the possession of Sigeum, a key stronghold on the Hellespont. Athens held Sigeum and Alcaeus describes himself as abandoning his shield in the retreat, as the poet Archilochus did before him. At some stage when Pittacus was ruling, Alcaeus went away to Egypt and his brother Antimenidas became a mercenary of Nebuchadnezzar, king of Babylon. He was eventually reconciled with Pittacus before the latter laid down the tyranny in 580, and returned home. The date of his death is unknown.

His poetry consists of lyrical songs, mostly monodies (see LYRIC POETRY) in two- or four-lined stanzas, in a great variety of metres. Many of these were later adapted to Latin poetry by Horace (see METRE, LATIN 3 (iii)), who imitated and wrote variations upon Alcaic themes throughout the Odes. As well as writing of politics and personalities with passion and gusto, Alcaeus composed love-songs (not always in his own person), now almost totally lost, drinking-songs (see SYMPOSIUM), and hymns to the gods, all with simple directness, economy, and little imagery. (In some of his political poems he writes allegorically, using the image of the ship of state tossed by storm to describe political strife.) His language was the Aeolic vernacular spoken in Lesbos at that time, with a few Homeric forms (see DIALECTS, GREEK 2).

2. Greek comic poet, writer of Old Comedy, known to be active at the beginning of the fourth century BC.

3. An epigrammatist of the third to second century BC who has some fifteen epigrams in the Greek *Anthology.

4. In Greek myth, a son of *Perseus and father of *Amphitryon; see also ALCIDES.

alca'ic, see METRE, GREEK 8 (i) and LATIN 3 (iii).

Alce'stis, in Greek myth, daughter of Pelias and Anaxibia, wife of *Admetus. Her father would let her marry only a suitor who could yoke a lion and a boar to a chariot and drive it, a condition fulfilled by Admetus with the help of the god Apollo. See also below.

Alce'stis, Greek drama by *Euripides produced in 438 BC in place of a satyr play (see SATYRIC DRAMA). The tetralogy of which it was the final play (and which included the famous *Telephus*) won second prize in the dramatic competition. It contains a certain burlesque element provided by the character of the genial, drunken Heracles, and a happy ending.

In the story, Heracles rescues Alcestis from Death and restores her to her husband *Admetus. The latter is represented at first as an ingenuous egoist, fond of his wife, deeply grieved to lose her, and indignant with his father for refusing to make the required sacrifice in her place. But he returns from his wife's burial sorrowfully, and with self-knowledge. Alcestis is a virtuous wife, accepting as natural the duty of dying for him, and concerned in a practical way for the future of her children. Heracles is an attractive character, relaxing between the Labours that form the main business of his life, to enjoy himself and do a good turn for a friend.

Alcibi'adēs, Athenian politician of noble family, born in or shortly before 450 BC, the elder son of Cleinias and Deinomachē, daughter of the Alcmaeonid Megacles, and a man of remarkable looks and talent. After his father was killed at Coronea in 446 he was educated by his guardian Pericles, and became a follower and friend of Socrates. His first military service was at the siege of Potidaea (432–430), where Socrates also served, and he was present at the battle of Delium in 424, when the Athenians were routed by Thebes. His experience led to his election as *strategos* in 420, probably at the earliest legal age, and at a time when he had already become a leader of the extreme democrats. His ambitious imperialism contributed most to the breakdown of the Peace of Nicias (made in 421) and to the launching in 415 of the Sicilian Expedition, of which he was appointed one of the three leaders. The mutilation of the *Hermae just before its departure was believed to be the work of Alcibiades and his associates, and he was also accused of profaning the Eleusinian mysteries (see MYSTERIES); nevertheless it was decided that he should embark and be tried later. When summoned back to Athens from Sicily for this purpose, he was allowed to make the journey in his own ship, but escaped at Thurii.

In his absence Alcibiades was condemned to death and his property confiscated. He made his way to Sparta, where he gave the Spartans the valuable advice that their general Gylippus should be sent to aid the Syracusans, and that Decelea in Attica should be occupied as a permanent threat to Athens. In 412 he went to Ionia and with a Spartan squadron fomented revolt against Athens first in Chios and then more widely, but he soon became distrusted by the Spartans (perhaps an intrigue with the wife of the Spartan king Agis had soured relations). He entered into negotiations with Tissaphernes, the Persian satrap, who tantalizingly seemed to support neither the Athenian nor the Spartan cause. He was now anxious to return to Athens. After months of delicate diplomacy the Athenian fleet at Samos made him general in the summer of 411, and from then until 406 he directed their war operations with brilliant success. In 407 the restored democracy at Athens recalled him, hoping to find in him a capable commander and a means of alliance with the Persians, but defeat in the sea-battle at Notium (fought against his orders) in 406 lost him his prestige, and he was not elected *strategos* for 406/5. He retired to the Thracian Chersonese, where the good advice he gave to the Athenian commanders before the battle of Aegospotami in 405 was disregarded and the Athenians suffered total defeat. He was finally assassinated in Phrygia in 404, perhaps through the influence of the Thirty Tyrants and Lysander.

The chief authority for the career of Alcibiades is Thucydides. Alcibiades figures in Plato's *Symposium* and the spurious Platonic dialogue that bears his name, and there are Lives of him by Nepos and Plutarch. He was an outstandingly able politician and military leader, with great personal magnetism, but his unscrupulous personal ambition, his vanity, and his dissolute life aroused the distrust of the Athenians at times when his leadership might well have been a decisive factor in the *Peloponnesian War. In Aristophanes' *Frogs* (produced in 405), when the tragic poets are required to give a sample of their political advice, it is their opinion of Alcibiades that is sought: Aeschylus thinks it 'wiser not to rear a lion's whelp, but if you do, you must accept its ways'. One of his most spectacular acts was to enter seven chariots for the Olympian games (perhaps those of 424 BC), in which he won first, second, and fourth places. He married Hipparetē, daughter of Hipponicus (son of *Callias) who was reputed to be the richest man in Greece. Alcibiades' career is referred to in two speeches of Lysias directed against his son, the younger Alcibiades, b. *c.*416, for whom Isocrates wrote one in support.

Alcibi'adēs, spurious dialogue attributed to *Plato.

Alci'damas (early fourth century BC), Greek *sophist and rhetorician from Elaea in Aeolis, pupil and follower of Gorgias, and opposed to the teaching of Isocrates. One genuine work of his survives, 'On the Sophists', in which the author argues in favour of extempore rather than prepared speeches.

Alcī'das, Spartan admiral in the early part of the Peloponnesian War.

Alcī'dēs (Alkeidēs), in Greek myth, a name meaning 'descendant of Alcaeus' used to designate Heracles, whose mortal father *Amphitryon was son of Alcaeus.

Alci'nŏus, in Homer's *Odyssey*, king of the Phaeacians in Scheria, father of *Nausicaa, who received Odysseus on his wanderings and sent him home to Ithaca on a magic ship.

A'lciphron (*c.* AD 200), Greek writer, author of fictitious letters (of which we have about a hundred) purporting to be by Athenians of various classes of society, depicting Athenian life in the fourth century BC.

Alcmae'on or **Alcmeon,** in Greek myth, son of *Amphiaraus. In accordance with his father's command he became leader of the expedition of the *Epigonoi which took Thebes. On his return, in further execution of his father's commands, he avenged him by slaying his own mother Eriphylē (or, in some sources, the matricide came before the expedition). For this murder he was (like Orestes) pursued from place to place by the Furies. At Psophis in Arcadia he received partial purification from Phegeus, whose daughter Arsinoē, or Alphesiboea, he married. To her he gave the necklace of Harmonia (see CADMUS (I)). But the crops of the country began to fail, and Alcmaeon set out again to discover a land on which the sun had not shone when he murdered his mother. This he found in an island newly thrown up at the mouth of the river Achelõus, between Acarnania and Aetolia in Greece. Here he married Callirrhoē, a daughter of Achelous. She in turn begged for the necklace of Harmonia, and Alcmaeon obtained it from Phegeus on a false pretence. But the brothers of Arsinoe waylaid and killed him, afterwards shutting their sister up in a chest because she protested, and selling her as a slave. Acarnan and Amphoteros, the sons of Alcmaeon and Callirrhoe, avenged their father by killing Phegeus and his sons; the fatal necklace was dedicated to Apollo at Delphi. A later story tells that it was stolen by a Phocian when Phocis was at war with Philip of Macedon, and brought ill luck to the thief.

Alcmaeo'nidae (Alkmeōnidai), a noble (Eupatrid) Athenian *genos prominent in politics. Its origins are obscure, but its name seems to derive from that Alcmaeon who commanded the Athenian forces in the First *Sacred War from *c.*595 BC onwards, and who in 592 won his family's and Athens' first victory at the Olympian games. The first notable member of this family was Alcmaeon's father *Megacles (I) who as archon in perhaps 632 incurred a hereditary pollution (see CYLON) which put all his descendants under sentence of banishment, a sentence that was periodically enforced upon them for political reasons. Banished at some time after 632 they were back in Athens under Solon. Alcmaeon's son Megacles (2) married the daughter of Cleisthenes, tyrant of Sicyon. Banished again during the tyranny of *Peisistratus (who was briefly and unsuccessfully married

to a daughter of Megacles (2)) they returned once more to Athens before the archonship in 525 of Cleisthenes, son of Megacles (2), but the tyrant *Hippias expelled them yet again. They finally succeeded in overthrowing Hippias and returned in 510. In the fifth century the pollution was invoked at intervals by political enemies. *Pericles, like *Alcibiades an Alcmaeonid on his mother's side, was able to ignore the Spartan appeal to the pollution in 432; it does not appear to have been invoked against Alcibiades.

Alcman, Greek *lyric poet who lived in Sparta in the second half, perhaps the last quarter, of the seventh century BC. In antiquity it was a matter of dispute whether he was a Laconian or whether he came from Sardis in Lydia. His works contain no direct reference to contemporary history but seem to belong to a period of peace, and are mainly choral lyrics for the festivals. His poems were collected in six books, now all lost except for a few quotations and papyrus fragments. His *partheneia ('maidensongs') were especially celebrated but we hear also of hymns and wedding songs. Most of the surviving fragments defy classification, but one or two are obviously from love-songs, of which he was said to be the inventor. The longest fragment of his poetry and the earliest piece of choral lyric we possess is from a *partheneion. It was found on an Egyptian papyrus and shows the unaffected charm and freshness of his writing. His dialect is for the most part the Laconian vernacular with some Homerisms. His simple metres are markedly dactylic, with some iambo-trochaic and aeolic elements (see METRE, GREEK 8 (i) and (ii)). It is not certain whether his lyric was *triadic in structure or composed in stanzas.

Alcme'na (Alkmēnē), see AMPHITRYON.

A'lcmeon, see ALCMAEON.

Alcy'onē. 1. In Greek myth, a daughter of *Aeolus (2) and wife of Cēyx, son of Eosphorus ('morning star'). They were changed into birds, she into the halcyon (kingfisher), he into the bird of his name (perhaps a tern or gannèt), either because he was drowned at sea and her despair was so great that the gods reunited them, or because of their impiety (they called themselves Zeus and Hera). 'Halcyon days' were fourteen days of calm weather around the winter solstice, supposed to be sent by Aeolus when the halcyon bird was brooding. **2.** One of the *Pleiades.

Aldus Manutius (Aldo Manuzio, 1449–1515), the great Venetian editor and printer of classical and humanistic texts whose name has been given to his own works (Aldine press, Aldine edition, etc.), and borrowed by later publishing enterprises. His books were distinguished by the accuracy as well as by the beauty of the typography. To him, or his engraver, we owe the sloping type known as italic, said to be a copy of contemporary handwriting. He also pioneered the introduction of the small octavo edition to replace the cumbersome folio. Both innovations appeared in the 1501 edition of Virgil. His press-mark is the anchor entwined by a dolphin. His work helped to popularize the classics, and Greek in particular. In twenty-one years the press produced twenty-seven first editions of Greek authors. See TEXTS, TRANSMISSION OF ANCIENT 8.

Ale'cto, see FURIES.

Aleu'adae, one of the leading aristocratic families of Thessaly (the other was the Scopadae; see SIMONIDES). They sided with Persia and conspired with Xerxes during the Persian Wars, and vigorously opposed the tyrants of Pherae (see JASON and ALEXANDER (I)).

Alexander (Alexandros). 1. **Alexander of Pherae** (in Thessaly), nephew and successor of *Jason, tyrant of Pherae 369–358 BC. He was opposed by most of the cities of Thessaly and allied himself with Athens to counteract Theban expansion. When the Theban general *Pelopidas visited him on one of his expeditions, he detained the general as a hostage until the latter was eventually rescued by a second Theban expedition in 367. As the result of a fresh appeal from Thessaly in 364, Pelopidas marched against him and defeated him at Cynoscephalae, but was himself killed. Later, a larger Theban army defeated Alexander and forced him to become the ally of the Thebans. In 362 he felt free to make piratical raids against Athens and raided the Piraeus. He was assassinated in 358 by his wife's brothers.

2. Alexander the Great, Alexander III of Macedon (356–323 BC), son of Philip II and Olympias of Epirus.

1. In his youth, Alexander was tutored by Aristotle. He early showed his intelligence and power of command; when only 18 he led the Macedonian cavalry with distinction at the battle of Chaeronea (338) which saw the defeat of Thebes and Athens by Macedon. When his father was murdered in 336 he succeeded without opposition as the only capable male heir to the kingdom of Macedon and the leadership—virtual dictatorship—of the Greek citystates (see ATHENS 2 (v)). He immediately put to death Philip's baby son, by his latest wife Eurydice (also known as Cleopatra), whose birth threatened his expectations, and some months later ordered the assassination of Eurydice's uncle, Attalus, at the time the commander in Asia of the Macedonian and Greek forces. Before his death Philip had been about to lead an army against Persia in punishment for the wrongs inflicted on Greece in the Persian Wars

150 years earlier. Alexander aimed to continue this war, but first he secured his position in Greece and stabilized the northern frontiers by defeating the Danubian tribes of that area. It was while he was at Corinth that he is reputed to have met the *Cynic philosopher Diogenes.

A false rumour of Alexander's death caused several Greek states to revolt (335), but only Thebes openly rebelled. Alexander arrived in Greece from the north with startling rapidity (his most impressive military quality) and stormed the city. The other Greek states were asked to decide Thebes' fate, and voted for its destruction. Only the house of the poet Pindar was spared.

2. With his Greek territory secured and left in the control of his general Antipater, Alexander crossed the Hellespont into Asia in 334 to join the remnants of his father's advance army. He had a force of about 43,000 men and a fleet of the Greek allies with about fifty warships. Like the mythical Greek hero *Protesilaus on his way to Troy, Alexander, who modelled his behaviour on the Homeric heroes, was the first ashore; he visited Troy and paid sacrifice at the tombs of various heroes. He soon achieved his desire for a pitched battle with the Persians, and at the river Granicus defeated Darius III and a slightly smaller Persian army. As a result of the battle, from which Darius escaped unscathed, Alexander's way into Asia Minor had been opened up. He moved fast and took the cities of Sardis and Ephesus. A series of Greek cities on the coast opened their gates to him. The Persians, and such Greek supporters as they had, resisted only at certain strongholds; most of Caria yielded but Miletus had to be fought for; after Miletus Alexander felt confident enough to disband the fleet. Halicarnassus fell only after a stubborn siege. Democracies were re-established in these cities which, though he came as the leader of a league of Greek states, became virtually a part of Alexander's own empire.

Having completed the conquest of western and southern Asia Minor Alexander reached Gordium, the ancient capital of king *Midas' Phrygian empire. Here he is said to have sliced through with his sword the knot which bound the shepherd Gordius' chariot to its yoke and which no man had ever been able to undo (see GORDIAN KNOT), thus proving, according to local legend, his destiny to rule 'Asia', that is the whole Persian empire. Perhaps the idea of an Alexander of mythical prowess was already being propagated. At Gordium in the spring of 333 Alexander heard that the Persian commander Memnon had been successful in winning back some Greek cities, but it was Alexander's good fortune that the able Memnon fell ill and died; after his death the Persian efforts lacked decisiveness.

Still in pursuit of Darius, Alexander marched east to the border of Phrygia, then south through Cappadocia and through the narrow pass into Cilicia. His conquest of Asia Minor could now be regarded as complete. At Tarsus he fell ill through bathing in the ill-reputed river Cydnus but was saved by his physician Philip. Meanwhile Darius had gathered together a large army from his eastern empire and was preparing to fight a decisive battle. The armies met late in 333 at Issus, on the coast, in the north-east corner of the Mediterranean Sea. Alexander's cavalry charge began the Persian defeat, which turned into a rout when Darius was seen to leave the battle at a crucial juncture. He escaped capture but left behind his wife, mother, and children. Alexander's chivalrous behaviour to them was notable. Included in the booty was a precious casket in which Alexander decided to store his copy of Homer's *Iliad*. He took as his mistress and kept for five years Barsiṇē, a Persian noblewoman. Darius offered generous terms for peace, and Alexander's refusal is the first sign that he aimed at the conquest of the whole Persian empire rather than at the limited objectives of Philip and the Greeks. An anecdote relates that when his general Parmenio said he would accept the terms if he were Alexander, the latter replied, 'So would I if I were Parmenio.'

3. Darius began to muster a huge army for what was to be his last battle, while Alexander spent the year after Issus in occupying Phoenicia, Palestine, and Egypt. His most striking success was in taking Tyre in 332 after a protracted siege in which he built a causeway over 1 km. (½ mile) of sea to support his siege machines. This feat was closely rivalled during the subsequent siege of Gaza, when he constructed an artificial mound higher even than the tell on which Gaza was perched, in order to be able to use his *catapults to good effect. Egypt, rich in men and grain, which had been under Persian rule since its conquest by *Cambyses in 525 BC, welcomed Alexander enthusiastically, perhaps crowning him Pharaoh of Upper and Lower Egypt. Early in 331 he sailed from Memphis northwards down the Nile to the Delta, and was struck by the commercial and military possibilities of its western side as a site for a city. Thus began *Alexandria, 'like a navel at the middle of the civilized world', based, like all the cities founded by Alexander, on an earlier military fort. From Egypt he made a gratuitous journey to the desert oracle of Zeus *Ammon at the oasis of Siwa. He kept secret the questions he asked and the answers he received, but the priest had already hailed him as 'Son of Ammon', a title that added another dimension to the myth, and gave evidence for his belief in his own descent from Zeus.

4. When Alexander left Egypt in the spring of 331, making for Persis, the original home province of the Persians, Darius had had over a year in which to mobilize his forces. These awaited Alexander east of the river Tigris at Gaugamela (near Arbela); once more the Persians were routed and Darius fled. After the battle Alexander turned south to Babylonia, a land of exceptional fertility which had fallen to the Persians 200 years previously and whose city now welcomed him as a deliverer; thence he proceeded to the province and Persian palace of Susa at the end of the Royal Road, which stretched for some 2,500 km. (1,500 miles) across the Persian empire from Sardis. Early in 330 Persepolis, the ritual centre of that empire and symbol of all that was most hateful to the Greeks, fell to Alexander and was sacked by his soldiers. It was subsequently burnt to ashes by his hand, perhaps not altogether intentionally: the story is that the Greek courtesan Thais incited him to this act, which he later regretted. The enormous treasure which he found at Persepolis was transported to a central treasury at Hamadan under his trusted general Parmenio. He released from service all the allied troops and Thessalian cavalry; thus the war in future was no longer an act of Greek vengeance but a private campaign fought by Alexander to his own interest. When Darius was found soon after this murdered by Bessus the satrap of Bactria, thus ending the line of the Achaemenidae, Alexander held himself to be the legitimate ruler of the Persian empire, bound to punish the regicide Bessus and to treat further resistance as rebellion. He assumed, significantly, parts of the Persian royal dress, the striped tunic, girdle, and diadem. His friend Hephaestion approved; others did not. It was now clear that his aim was the conquest of the whole empire.

5. The pursuit of Bessus took Alexander into Outer Iran and lasted from 330 to 327, during which time he subdued the vast tracts of Hyrcania, Areia, Drangiana, Bactria, and Sogdiana. While in Drangiana Alexander discovered a plot against his life implicating his officer Philotas, Parmenio's son. He had Philotas put to death, and acting swiftly sent a message to Hamadan ordering the assassination of Parmenio himself merely on suspicion: he could not afford to risk the disloyalty of a general who commanded the cross-roads of the empire, the treasury, and an army.

Advancing from Drangiana Alexander performed his most brilliant feat in taking his army across the snows of the Hindu Kush, mountains which his men believed must be in the Caucasus because they thought they saw the marks of the chains which had confined *Prometheus, and from the summit of which, according to Aristotle, one might espy the eastern rim of the world. Alexander descended into Sogdiana, and eventually captured and killed Bessus. He founded another Alexandria on what is now Kandahar. In 328 he reached the furthest north-east boundary of the Persian empire, the river

Jaxartes (Syr Darya), and here he founded Alexandria Eschatē, 'the furthest' (now known as Leninabad). Later that year, while the army rested in Samarkand, a violent quarrel arose at a banquet between Alexander and Cleitus, an elderly officer and life-long friend. Alexander seized a weapon and killed Cleitus with one blow, a rash act of which he bitterly repented, retiring to his tent in the manner of Achilles in Homer's *Iliad.*

By early 327 Alexander had overcome the last resistance in the north-east borders by the spectacular capture of two apparently impregnable mountain fortresses. Among the captives was Roxane, the daughter of a Sogdian baron, whom Alexander loved at sight and immediately married. In the same year another plot was discovered against his life; it implicated Callisthenes, a kinsman of Aristotle and the expedition's historian, who was imprisoned and eventually killed. (Callisthenes was reputed to have refused Alexander the obeisance, *proskynēsis*, traditionally given to the Persian kings. Although *proskynesis* might involve no more than kissing the tips of one's fingers towards a person or god, to the Greeks it meant prostration, which they regarded as impious when offered to men.)

6. In summer 327 Alexander descended to the plains of India. His motives for doing so will never be certain, but perhaps India appealed as much to his curiosity as to a longing for further conquest. For the Macedonians it was a mythical world full of wonders, the home of the god Dionysus whose cult was strong in Macedonia. None of these wonders made more impact on the West than the Gymnosophists ('naked philosophers'), whose meetings with Alexander became part of his legend and whose asceticism became an ideal to many. Alexander's advance was opposed by the local Indian chieftains, and he had to storm several mountain fortresses, most notably that of Aornos (Pir-Sar) which, legend has it, even Heracles had been unable to capture. In 326 he crossed the Indus and reached the river Hydaspes (Jhelum). Here he fought his last great pitched battle to defeat the local king Porus and his formidable elephants. This was the last battle too for *Bucephalas, Alexander's horse since childhood, which was wounded and died soon after the battle. Alexander advanced quite easily through the rest of the Punjab to the river Hyphasis (Sutlej) and contemplated proceeding across India to the Ganges, of which he now heard stories for the first time, but his army, exhausted by the monsoon as much as by the campaigning, refused to go further. Alexander gave way and turned back to the Hydaspes. Here an enormous fleet was constructed to transport the army—perhaps as many as 120,000 men—and its baggage downstream. It was put under the command of Nearchus, while Onesicratus, who wrote an account of the expedition, had charge of

Alexander's ship. Army detachments accompanied the boats along each shore. There was still fighting to be done, however, and it was while storming Multan that Alexander was so gravely wounded that his army at first believed him dead. He reached the Indus delta in summer 325, and started on a land march homewards leaving Nearchus to explore the sea-route up the Persian Gulf. Alexander chose a route through the waterless waste of Gedrosia (Baluchistan) at the cost of enormous loss of life. The fleet suffered too but arrived safely.

When Alexander reached Susa he found misgovernment and disloyalty among his subordinates, whom he ruthlessly purged. His friend and treasurer Harpalus fled to Greece with a large sum of money (see DEMOSTHENES (2) 1). There was unrest in Greece, especially about Alexander's proclamation that exiles should be allowed to return to their cities. At mid-summer he arranged marriages between his officers and men and Persian women, and encouraged those soldiers who had Asian mistresses to keep them as official wives. He himself married Stateira, daughter of Darius. Undoubtedly anger and jealousy were felt by some at the equality of status the Orientals now seemed to enjoy, particularly when large numbers of Persians were enrolled into the army, and these feelings found expression in a mutiny at Opis in 324 when Alexander tried to send some veterans home to Macedonia. He executed the ringleaders and retired in anger to his tent, thus frightening his troops into a change of heart. In the autumn his intimate friend Hephaestion died, and Alexander gave himself up to passionate expressions of grief, as, in Homer's *Iliad*, Achilles did for Patroclus. Afterwards he returned to Babylon where he was engaged on schemes for the opening of a sea-route from the mouth of the Euphrates to Egypt. Here in 323 he fell suddenly ill at a drinking party, perhaps through fever, perhaps through poison, and after ten days died. His body was finally brought to rest in Alexandria, where three centuries later his coffin was seen by the young emperor Augustus. It was probably destroyed in the riots of the late third century AD.

7. Alexander is the greatest general of antiquity. This position he owes partly to the splendidly organized Macedonian army and its technically improved siege weapons, partly to his own versatile and intelligent strategy, but much more to qualities that were uniquely his: an unprecedented speed of movement, resolution in tackling the seemingly impossible, personal involvement in the dangers of battle and the rigours of campaigning, and a heroic sense of style in all that he did. To these qualities as well as to his generosity Alexander owed his ascendancy over the army. His most unusual characteristic was his double sympathy with the life styles of the Persians as well as the Greeks,

manifest in his desire to see Macedonians and Persians alike ruling his empire. This policy was not popular and may have been partly the cause of the plots against his life and the quarrel with Cleitus.

Alexander clearly felt an intense concern for religion and showed scrupulous respect for local gods wherever he encountered them. In his lifetime he was widely acclaimed as divine, the son of Zeus, and he seems to have believed in his own divinity and to have been encouraged in this belief by his mother. Certainly he strove to emulate those other sons of gods, the Homeric heroes. His most lasting achievement was to extend the Greek language and institutions over the eastern world in such a way that he brought about an absolute break with the past. No region once conquered and settled by Alexander resumed its old ways uninfluenced by the conquest. The Greek city-states too never regained the independence that they lost with Philip. The centre of the (*Hellenistic) Greek world shifted to Alexandria, and with that shift arose a new kind of Greek culture.

8. *The literature concerning Alexander.* The principal extant authority for the history of Alexander's campaigns is the *Anabasis* of *Arrian, who used as sources the writings, now lost, of Alexander's officers Ptolemy (later King Ptolemy I Soter of Egypt), Aristobulus of Cassandreia, and the sea-captain Nearchus, all of whom were sympathetic to Alexander. He may also have used Alexander's lost journal (*Ephemerides*), but some scholars doubt the existence of an authentic journal. There is also a tradition, which may be seen in the fragmentary history of Quintus *Curtius, of writers hostile to Alexander, who represented him as a tyrant corrupted by power; most of them are of the *Peripatetic (Aristotelian) School, whose hostility was natural enough after Callisthenes' death. Plutarch's Life is compiled from every kind of source, good and bad. The most influential tradition, however, stems from the narrative of Cleitarchus, written in the third century BC and known to us through the writings of *Diodorus Siculus; Cleitarchus introduced the fabulous, an element that was further developed in the various Eastern versions of Alexander's life. From Latin versions supposedly translated from Callisthenes the legends passed into French poetry of the eleventh and twelfth centuries, thus giving the twelve-syllabled alexandrine line its name. There are two Old English works of the eleventh century based on the Latin legend, but it is from the French poems that the Alexander legends passed into the Middle English metrical romances such as 'King Alisaunder'.

3. **Alexander of Aphrodisias** (flourished *c.* AD 200), the most important of the early commentators on Aristotle. Of his commentaries (in Greek) a few survive, and his works are widely quoted by later writers.

4. Alternative name for *Paris (1).

Alexandra, see LYCOPHRON (2).

Alexa'ndria, city on the north coast of Egypt, near the Canopic or western mouth of the Nile, founded by Alexander the Great in 331 BC on a virtually virgin site, occupied only by a village and fort called Rhacotis; it was the first of his many foundations. On a barren coast this area alone had possibilities for a harbour to accommodate a large fleet and for further development. There was a long bay west of the silt-producing mouths of the Nile, protected by the island of Pharos (now joined to the mainland by a bridge of silted-up land), with a ridge of rising ground parallel to the coast between the sea and Lake Mareotis (Maryût) inland; the climate was equable. According to the historian Arrian, Alexander himself established where the main points of the city, the agora and the temples, should be, and drew the line of the city walls with the meal which his soldiers were carrying, a good omen for the city's future prosperity. After Alexander's general Ptolemy had established his authority in Egypt, the seat of government was transferred from the ancient city of Memphis to Alexandria. The new city grew rapidly and soon became the first city of the Hellenistic world, a centre of learning as well as of commerce and industry. In the Roman period it counted as the second city of the empire, after Rome itself. It did not decline until the Arab conquest in the seventh century caused Egypt to look towards Asia rather than towards Europe. The plan of ancient Alexandria is difficult to reconstruct, partly because of subsidence, which has resulted in much of the ancient city being covered by the coastal waters, and partly because of modern building and reconstruction of the coast. It was laid out on the sandy ridge running east and west between Lake Mareotis and the sea. A broad street ran east and west through the centre of it and was crossed by another running north and south. On the island of Pharos, which Alexander connected with the mainland by a mole over a kilometre long so as to provide a double harbour, a lighthouse, also known as the *Pharos, was built, probably in the reign of Ptolemy II Philadelphus. It seems to have been the first of its kind. Near the eastern sea-harbour lay the area known originally as 'the Palaces' and as Brucheion in the Roman period, in which stood royal palaces and buildings, shrines, pleasure-gardens, and a zoo built by Ptolemy II. It occupied much of the northern and central area of the city, perhaps a square mile in total, and was clearly the most pleasant part to live in. Here also was the Museum, and perhaps the Library, about whose location the literary sources are silent, and the *Sēma* (or *Sōma*), the tomb of Alexander, whose body was brought to the city by Ptolemy I Soter and encased in a magnificent gold coffin. (This was later removed by Ptolemy X when short of funds, and replaced by alabaster.) To the south-west of this, in the ancient Egyptian quarter (Rhacotis; see above), stood the Serapeum (temple of Serapis), built on a largely artificial hill by Ptolemy III Euergetes and greatly extended in Roman times. It is the only temple in Alexandria that has been excavated. Here still stands today the column known as 'Pompey's Pillar', dedicated to the emperor Diocletian. In the Ptolemaic period the city was divided into five 'quarters'. The Jews' quarter, the best-known, occupied the north-east angle of the city, and the Jews, who were here from the reign of Ptolemy VI Philometor (b. 186 BC) onwards, had their own ethnarch and council. The royal residence itself seems to have been on a promontory in the harbour which has now disappeared. Above the harbour a large theatre was built. Also in that area were the *emporion* (the general trading centre), warehouses, and the Caesareum, the temple of the emperor Augustus, finally destroyed in AD 912. Of the two obelisks which stood before it, one was given to Britain in 1877 and stands, known as Cleopatra's Needle, by the Thames in London, the other in 1879 to New York where it was erected in Central Park. Both had been brought to Alexandria from a temple in the ancient Egyptian city of Heliopolis.

By 200 BC Alexandria was the largest city in the world (later to be surpassed by Rome). Intermarriage between Greeks and Egyptians began in the second century BC, and the mixed population (with the exception of the Jews and some of the Greeks) gradually blended into a more or less homogeneous whole. Under the Ptolemies the city was nominally a democracy. Under the Romans it was assigned to the emperor, and Augustus refused it any self-government. In AD 200 it was given a senate by the Roman emperor Severus. See ALEXANDRIAN LIBRARY, MUSEUM, HELLENISTIC AGE, PTOLEMIES.

Alexandrianism, Latin, term used of the influence of the Alexandrian school of Greek poets of the third and second centuries BC (see HELLENISTIC AGE) on Roman poets of the first century BC, of whom Catullus is the only surviving representative. The chief features of the school were a development of new, miniature genres, especially epyllion, elegy, and epigram; a regard for form, which left a lasting impression on Latin literature; the cult of erudition; and the emergence of a subjective and personal way of writing. See NEOTERICS.

Alexandrian Library. This famous library may have been founded by Ptolemy I Soter (see PTOLEMIES) but was greatly augmented by his son Ptolemy II Philadelphus. Such evidence as there is suggests that it was in the 'palace quarter' of *Alexandria, perhaps adjacent to the Museum, and was supplemented by a subsidiary

building near the Serapeum. At its head was placed a series of distinguished scholars, Zenodotus, Apollonius Rhodius, Eratosthenes, Aristophanes of Byzantium, Apollonius the Eidograph, Aristarchus; the poet Callimachus also worked there. It is variously said to have contained 100,000 to 700,000 volumes. It is also said that Ptolemy II purchased the library that Aristotle had formed; and that Ptolemy III appropriated the official copies of the texts of Aeschylus, Sophocles, and Euripides (see LYCURGUS 3), forfeiting the large deposit he had paid when borrowing them from Athens. The library became the great centre of literature in the Hellenistic world and the practice of its copyists was probably decisive in the forms of book production. Callimachus made catalogues (*pinakĕs*) of its contents. There was keen rivalry between the kings of Alexandria and *Pergamum in the enlargement of their respective libraries. According to Plutarch, in 47 BC when Julius Caesar was in Alexandria the main library was burnt, but more probably it was a storehouse of books accidentally destroyed. Later legend magnified this destruction.

Alexandrian literature, see HELLENISTIC AGE 3 and 4.

Alexandrian scholars, see HELLENISTIC AGE 6.

Alexandrian War, see *BELLUM ALEXANDRINUM.*

Alexipha'rmaca, see NICANDER.

Ale'xis (*c.*375–275 BC), Greek comic poet of Middle and New Comedy, who lived most of his life at Athens. He was a prolific writer. It is difficult to assess from his few remaining fragments the part he played in the transition from the older to the newer forms of comedy, but he seems to have used the kind of plot especially associated with New Comedy, concerning love affairs of an intricate kind, and to have had a pleasant wit. His fame continued to Roman times when his plays were adapted by Roman comedians. See also COMEDY, GREEK 5.

a libe'llīs, a ratiō'nibus, ab epi'stulīs, see ROME 12.

Alle'cto, see FURIES.

allegory. Allegory in literature is the presentation of a subject under the guise of another suggestively similar. It was rarely written deliberately by the Greeks (but see ALCAEUS (1)). As a device of literary interpretation its most flourishing period was in the late fifth century BC when certain sophists found in the poets, particularly Homer and Hesiod, 'hidden meanings' of a cosmological or ethical nature. This kind of allegorizing was closely connected with etymology, at that time a pseudo-science which dealt in the 'true' meaning of words and names as revealed by assonances. Plato and the Alexandrian scholars rejected allegorical interpretation of literature. Its main proponents were the Stoic philosophers (third century BC onwards), who used it for the illustration and corroboration of their doctrines, and from them derive the surviving collections of allegorical interpretations of Homer.

The Romans, following the Greeks, found certain moral meanings implicit in Homer, and Horace took over Alcaeus' allegory of the 'ship of state', but they did not compose large-scale allegories. Instead they used numerous poetic conceits and personifications (such as calling the sea Neptune) often in a way that suggests rather the influence of symbolic painting. A Roman innovation was the allegorical representation of contemporary persons and events, as in Virgil's *Eclogues*, but perhaps this too had been done before by Theocritus (in Idyll 7), and scholars of both poets still dispute the degree of correspondence with real people. The profundity and ambiguity of much of the *Aeneid* led interpreters from the fourth century onward to find in it an allegory of ideas rather than of facts. Allegory entered Christian literature from Stoic sources. See also BUCOLIC.

A'llia, a small stream flowing into the Tiber about 18 km. (11 miles) north of Rome, near which the Romans suffered a notable defeat by the Gauls in 390 BC (see ROME 4). The disaster occurred on the anniversary (18 July) of the ambush of the Fabii (see FABIA, GENS) by the Veientes in 479 BC.

alliteration, the literary device in which two or more words in close connection begin with the same letter (see ASSONANCE). It was not a common device of Greek poetry, but is a feature in Latin saturnian verse (see METRE, LATIN I), and was adopted thence by later Roman poets including Ennius and Virgil; as when Ennius writes:

fraxinu' frangitur atque abies consternitur alta.
pinus proceras pervortunt.

('The ash tree is shattered and the lofty fir laid low. They overturn the tall pines.')

It is carried to grotesque excess by the same poet in the line:

o Tite tute Tati tibi tanta tyranne tulisti.

('O Titus Tatius, such great things you brought upon yourself, arrogant ruler.')

A'lmagest, see PTOLEMY.

Alō'adae, Alōī'dae, see OTUS.

alphabet

1. *Greek*. The earliest examples of Greek writing to survive are all inscribed on Greek pottery from the second half of the eighth century BC, and examples are found almost simultaneously in all parts of the Greek world, from Ischia off the coast of south Italy in the West to Rhodes in

the East. In these examples the writing runs from right to left in odd-numbered lines and from left to right in even-numbered lines, a form known as **boustrophēdon*, 'as the ox turns'.

The standard Greek alphabet, still in use today, is as follows:

Small letters	Capital letters	Greek names	English equivalents
α	A	alpha	a
β	B	bēta	b
γ	Γ	gamma	g
δ	Δ	delta	d
ε	E	epsīlon	ĕ
ζ	Z	zēta	z (pronounced sd)
η	H	ēta	ē
θ	Θ	thēta	th
ι	I	iōta	i
κ	K	kappa	hard c or k
λ	Λ	lam(b)da	l
μ	M	mū	m
ν	N	nū	n
ξ	Ξ	xī	x (pronounced ks)
o	O	omīcron	ŏ
π	Π	pī	p
ρ	P	rhō	r (or rh)
σ, s†; or c	Σ, C	sigma	s
τ	T	tau	t
υ	Y	upsī'lon	u (usually transliterated y)
φ	Φ	phī	ph
χ	X	chī	kh (sometimes transliterated ch)
ψ	Ψ	psī	ps
ω	Ω	ōmega	ō

†*s* is the form used at the end of a word; c is an alternative to either form.

A distinction between 'capital' and 'small' letters was not clearly made until the ninth century AD; see BOOKS AND WRITING 6. Small letters are used conventionally in what follows.

The alphabet from alpha to tau was taken over from a north Semitic alphabet (probably a Phoenician script used in Syria); its introduction to Greece is perhaps reflected in the myth which tells how *Cadmus, son of Agenor king of Tyre, brought letters to *Thebes, the city he had founded. The shapes of the letters, their names and their order are virtually the same in both alphabets but they do not necessarily represent the same sounds. The Semitic alphabet has no characters for vowels, and the Greek therefore used for its vowels Semitic characters for consonants not in use in Greece. Thus Semitic consonant characters were used for α, ε, o, and ι. The character for upsilon was taken over from a *cursive Phoenician script and added to the alphabet after tau. In Greece local variations lasted for centuries. Some dialects had an extra letter, F, between epsilon and zeta, pronounced like English w and called first 'wau' by the Greeks and later *digamma. It disappeared in pre-classical times from the Attic–Ionic dialects and does not appear in the standard alphabet given above. Other letters were added after upsilon to represent the sounds ph and kh. The alphabet thus obtained, comprising the first 22 letters of the 24 listed above, was used by the Athenians down to the end of the fifth century BC. The sounds represented have not changed, except that the letter eta (η) up to that time stood for the aspirate (h). Epsilon (ϵ) was written to represent all forms of the e sound and omicron (o) for all forms of the o sound. In 403 BC, in the archonship of Eucleides, Athens adopted the more developed East Ionic (Milesian) alphabet which distinguished between short and long o sounds by using o and ω respectively, and between short and long e by using η for the latter, as well as admitting diphthongs in its spelling to express variations of these sounds. The letter ψ was also introduced for the sound ps. All Ionic dialects, however, lacked the aspirate, and when the East Ionic alphabet was adopted the aspirate (for which η was no longer available) was ignored in writing. In some scripts this deficiency was remedied by the sign ⊢ (the left half of capital eta). The Alexandrian scholar *Aristophanes of Byzantium subsequently introduced both ⊢ and ⊣ written above initial vowels to mark the presence or absence of the aspirate (known as 'rough breathing' and 'smooth breathing'). These are written in modern texts as ' and ' respectively.

2. *Latin*. The Latin alphabet seems to have come from an early form of Etruscan script which was itself derived from the (Euboean) Greek alphabet as used at Cumae (in Campania), a colony of Chalcis in Euboea. The early Latin alphabet was the same as its modern English derivative except that it lacked the letters G, J (for which I did duty), U, W (for which V also served), Y, and Z. The character X represented the sound ks (unlike the Greek X, which represented the sound kh). H represented the aspirate (for its varying significance in Greek see 1 above). Greek gamma was represented by the character C which was at first used for the G sound as well as for the K sound (compare the names Gaius and Gnaeus which when abbreviated were written in archaic fashion C. and Cn.); the character G was introduced in the third century BC. Originally the character K was written instead of C where the following letter was A, but it was later replaced by C and K became redundant (a relic of this old spelling is *Kalendae*, 'the Calends'). The letter Q (from Greek ϙ, koppa, found in some Greek alphabets after pi), originally written instead of C before O and U, was later used only before U (English q). Z was introduced to express the original ds sound in

words borrowed from Greek, and was added at the end of the alphabet, its seventh place in the Greek alphabet (after digamma) having been occupied by G. The Latin f sound was most closely represented by the Greek digamma. V (a form of capital upsilon) represented both the vowel and the semi-vowel U. Y (the usual form of capital upsilon) was added in the late republic to transliterate Greek words containing upsilon.

See also BOOKS AND WRITING and EPIGRAPHY.

Alphesiboe'a, see ALCMAEON.

Alphē'us (Alpheios), one of the largest rivers in Greece, rising in Arcadia in the Peloponnese and, after receiving many tributaries (including the Erymanthus and the Ladon), flowing through Elis to the Ionian Sea. The plain of *Olympia is situated by the side of it. Its waters were fabled to pass unmixed through the sea and to be mingled with the fountain of *Arethusa in the island of Ortygia near Syracuse; perhaps the subterranean passage of the river in the upper part of its course gave rise to this myth.

Alps. There is no evidence that the early Greeks knew of the existence of these mountains; the Roman conquest of Cisalpine Gaul and Hannibal's invasion of Italy in the third century BC brought detailed information. The campaigns of Julius Caesar in Gaul opened up the Alps until by the second century AD a dozen passes were known and at least five paved roads built across them.

altar. As almost every religious act in the ancient world was accompanied by sacrifice, altars as sacrificial tables were an indispensable part of the cult of a god or hero (but not of an Underworld deity, to whom offerings were made in pits). Thus altars as a focus for worship existed long before *temples, and after temples were built the altar generally stood outside, opposite the main door. Altars were commonly block-like in form, or sometimes they had a flight of steps up to a platform, but there were also small altars at which only incense was burnt and bloodless sacrifices offered. Private houses often had their own small altars, or the hearth, as a sacred place, served as such. Altars were places of refuge for suppliants, who then came under the protection of the deity concerned.

Althae'a, in Greek myth, mother of *Meleager.

Amalthē'a (Amaltheia), in Greek myth, the goat that suckled the infant *Zeus in Crete; or a nymph (according to one version the daughter of Melissus, king of Crete) who fed Zeus with the milk of a goat. Zeus gave her the horn of the goat; it had the power of producing whatever its possessor wished, and was known (in Latin) as the *cornu copiae*, 'horn of plenty'.

Amā'ta, in Virgil's *Aeneid*, the wife of *Latinus and mother of *Lavinia.

Amazons (Amāzonĕs), legendary nation of female warriors supposed by the Greeks to have lived in the time of the heroes. Their home is always situated on the bounds of the known world, usually in remote north-east Asia. They figure in the exploits of various Greek heroes down to Alexander the Great, who according to legend met their queen on the borders of India, and are very popular in art from at least the seventh century BC. Their name, supposedly meaning 'breastless', was said to derive from their custom of cutting off the right breast to facilitate the use of arms in battle. Their occupations are hunting and fighting, always from horseback. They propagate their kind by associating for a time with men from a neighbouring tribe and rearing only their daughters. They are mentioned in Homer's *Iliad* and appear as allies of the Trojans in the poems of the Epic Cycle; their queen Penthesilēa was killed by Achilles. They also play a part in the careers of Heracles (see HERACLES, LABOURS OF 9) and *Theseus.

Ambarvā'lia, 'the procession round the fields', at Rome, a solemn annual purification of the fields of the *ager Romanus* ('Roman territory'), at which sacrificial animals, pig, sheep, and ox (*suovetaurīlia*), were led around the old boundaries of Rome. Sacrifice was offered at particular points. This ceremony may be identical with the sacrifice to the Dea Dia performed by the *arval priests. See also TIBULUS.

A'mbiorix, leader of the Gallic tribe of the Eburōnēs in their revolt against the Romans in 54–53 BC. He successfully evaded capture. See *COMMENTARIES* I (books 5 and 6).

Ambrose, Saint (Aurēlius Ambrŏsius) (*c.* AD 340–97), bishop of Milan, born of a Christian family at Trier, his father being prefect of Narbonese Gaul. He was educated at Rome and entered on an official career, and at an early age was made governor of the region of Milan with the title of consul. On the death in 374 of Auxentius, the *Arian bishop of Milan, Ambrose was chosen to replace him by popular acclamation, although he was a Christian only by belief, and unbaptized. He received baptism and the priesthood after his appointment. He was famous as an upholder of orthodoxy, and as a preacher. He exercised mounting influence over the Roman emperors, his aim being the establishment of an empire which excluded all errors of belief—paganism, Judaism, and Arianism. Hence he persuaded the emperor Valentinian II to withstand the plea of *Symmachus and the Roman aristocracy to restore the Altar of Victory (384), and he would not countenance the building of an Arian church in Milan or a synagogue in Callinicum on the Euphrates. He excommunicated the pious emperor Theodosius I for the vengeance-killings of 7,000 at Thessalon-

ika in 390, and that emperor's decision in 391 to put an end to all pagan worship was no doubt owing to Ambrose's influence. Ambrose used his knowledge of Greek to study philosophy and theology, and a knowledge of these sources is apparent in his commentaries and sermons (which were a great influence on *Augustine's conversion). His treatise on the duties of priests, *De officiis ministrorum*, is modelled on Cicero's *De officiis*. His letters, panegyrics, and sermons are a primary source for the history of his period. Of the hymns attributed to him, a few are certainly authentic, but he was not the author of the *Te Deum*, as tradition relates. The Ambrosian Library at Milan (founded in 1609) is named after him.

ambrosia and **nectar,** the mythical food and drink of the gods, associated with divine immortality. A mortal who took them became immortal; shed on a corpse they kept it from decay. Various things connected with the gods are described as ambrosial, sometimes with the connotation of 'sweet-smelling'.

Ammiā'nus Marcellī'nus (*c.* AD 330–95), the last great Roman historian who wrote in Latin, although in fact he was a Greek born at Antioch. His history in 31 books was a continuation of the histories of Tacitus, covering the years AD 96–378, from the death of Domitian to the disastrous defeat of the Romans by the Goths at Adrianople in 378. Books 1–13 have been lost. The remaining books 14–31 deal in extreme detail with the years 353–78 which cover events in his own lifetime, many of which he witnessed himself and, it is believed, reported accurately. As a young man he joined the army and served on the eastern frontier, and in Gaul under *Julian (later emperor) whom he admired profoundly but not uncritically. He took part in Julian's fatal campaign in Persia and later visited Egypt and Greece. In 378 he settled in Rome, where he wrote his history; his friends included *Symmachus, the leading literary figure at the time. Ammianus' narrative is interesting and enlivened by digressions—on the Egyptian obelisks and their hieroglyphics, earthquakes, lions in Mesopotamia, the artillery of his time, and includes a famous description of the *Huns (31.2). He writes largely without prejudice on the various nations dealt with, on the Christians, and on the emperors themselves. His style, which he was never fully in command of, was ornate and rhetorical, and partly based on Tacitus; it was much admired by later writers.

Ammon or **Amo(u)n,** Egyptian god represented sometimes as a ram, whose oracle at the oasis of Siwa in the Libyan desert became known to the Greeks probably through the north African Greek colony of Cyrene. Its fame rivalled that of Delphi and Dodona, and it was consulted on a notable occasion by *Alexander the Great. The poet Pindar wrote a hymn to the god, and his cult had arrived at Athens by the fourth century BC. Ammon was usually portrayed in the Greek world with the head of Zeus bearing a ram's curling horns. See also ANDROMEDA.

amoebe'an verse, literary form found mainly in bucolic poetry, for example in Theocritus and Virgil, consisting of couplets or 'stanzas' assigned alternately to two characters, usually in singing matches where the verses of one character are capped by the other.

Amō'res, fifty love-poems by the Roman poet *Ovid, written in the elegiac metre, some of them among his earliest works. There were two editions, the first in five books published perhaps in 20 BC, possibly under the title *Corinna.* This is lost; what we possess is the second edition in three books, published a little before 1 BC.

Most of the poems are studies or sketches of love in different moods, nearly always of sophisticated love, acted out in the city of Rome in the context of a pleasure-seeking, leisured society. They are polished, contrived, and amusing, the product of wit rather than of passion. 'Corinna' figures prominently in them, but it is doubtful whether she had any real existence. There are interesting illustrations of contemporary life—a scene at the circus, or a festival of Juno, for example. Poem III. 9 is a touching lament for the death of the poet *Tibullus.

Amphiarā'us, in Greek myth, an Argive hero and seer, son of Oikles, who played an important part in the stories of the Greek *Epic Cycle which relate to a generation earlier than the heroes of the Trojan War. He married Eriphylē, whom Polyneices bribed, with the necklace of Harmonia (see CADMUS), to persuade Amphiaraus to take part in the expedition of the Seven against Thebes (see OEDIPUS), although the seer knew that none of the Seven except Adrastus would return from it alive. He set out reluctantly, but before starting commanded his children to avenge his death by killing their mother, and by making a second expedition against Thebes (see ALCMAEON). He attacked Thebes but was driven off, and as he fled was swallowed up in a cleft in the ground made by Zeus' thunderbolt. Thus originated the famous oracular shrine of Amphiaraus at Oropus, where oracles were given by the interpretation of dreams.

amphi'ctyony (amphiktyoneia), religious association or league of Greek communities who lived in the neighbourhood of, and had some responsibility for, the shrine of a god (from *amphictuones,* 'dwellers around'). The most important amphictyonic league was that of Delphi, whose sanctuaries were the temples of Apollo at Delphi and of Demeter at Thermopylae. Many of the principal peoples of Greece, including Thessalians, Dorians, and Ionians, belonged to it. The assemblies of this League met twice a year, alternately at Delphi and Thermopylae. It administered the temple of Apollo and conducted the Pythian games; it also had political importance, since the votes of its members could be manipulated by powerful states to their own advantage (see PHILIP (1)). *Sacred wars were occasionally proclaimed against violators of amphictyonic laws. The foundation of the amphictyony was attributed in antiquity to an eponymous Amphictyon, son of Deucalion and brother of Hellen (the ancestor of the Greeks).

Amphī'on and Zethus, see ANTIOPE.

Amphi'polis, city founded by a colony of Athenians in 437 BC, of great strategic and commercial importance, particularly in the Peloponnesian War. Situated near the coast on the east bank of the river Strymon, the boundary between Macedonia and Thrace, it commanded the only crossing-place on the southern reaches of that river and thus the route into Greece from the Hellespont, and was the depot for the gold and silver mines of Mount Pangaeus, controlled by Athens, as well as for the timber needed by the Athenian navy. In 424 BC during the Peloponnesian War Amphipolis surrendered to the Spartans; the historian Thucydides was held responsible for the loss and exiled. In an unsuccessful attempt to recapture it in 422 the Athenian and Spartan commanders Cleon and Brasidas were both killed. Amphipolis was to have been restored to Athens by the Peace of Nicias in 421 but it remained practically independent, despite Athenian pressure, until it was annexed by Philip II of Macedon in 357 BC (see PHILIP (1) 1).

amphitheatre, Roman theatre constructed in a circular or elliptical shape so as to contain the combats of *gladiators, wild animals, and even ships and to make them visible to a large number of spectators. Amphitheatres were said to have been introduced into Rome by Julius Caesar's supporter Curio, though they were apparently in existence earlier in the provinces; the one at Pompeii was built nearly twenty years earlier, in about 70 BC. Rome's first permanent stone amphitheatre was erected in 29 BC at a time when many others were being constructed throughout the empire. Imperial architects rapidly evolved very large buildings with ingenious systems for access and circulation. The most famous is the *Colosseum in Rome (AD 80). See ARCHITECTURE 2.

Amphitrī'tē, Nereid (see NEREUS), wife of the god *Poseidon.

Amphi'truo, Roman comedy by *Plautus (c.195 BC), perhaps an adaptation of a Greek comedy by Philemon, on the mythical subject of the cuckolding of Amphitryon (see below) by the Greek god Zeus (in Plautus' play, the Roman god Jupiter). Jupiter takes on the appearance of Amphitruo after the latter's departure for war, and seduces his virtuous wife Alcmena. Plautus calls the play a *tragico-comoedia* because of the unusual blend of contrasting elements, the morally virtuous but unwittingly unchaste wife, and the burlesque situation of the outraged husband. Foils are provided by the god Mercury and Sosia, the long-suffering but cheerful slave. The theme proved popular with later comic dramatists, Molière, John Dryden (with music by Henry Purcell), and in more recent times, Jean Giraudoux.

Amphi'tryon, in Greek myth, son of Alcaeus king of Tiryns, and Astydameia; grandson of *Perseus. His sister Anaxo married her uncle Electryon (brother of Alcaeus), king of Mycenae, and their daughter Alcmena was betrothed to Amphitryon. After the death of his sons in a feud Electryon handed over his kingdom to Amphitryon, but the latter, while helping to recover stolen cattle, unfortunately killed Electryon and so had to take refuge with Creon, king of Thebes. Alcmena wished Amphitryon to avenge her brothers before she would marry him, and this he did; but during his absence Zeus fell in love with her and just before Amphitryon's return visited her in the guise of her husband. Alcmena gave birth to twin sons, Iphiclēs the child of Amphitryon and Heracles the child of Zeus.

Amū'lius, see ROME 2.

A'mycus, in Greek myth, a son of the god Poseidon and king of the Bebrycēs (a people of Bithynia), and a mighty boxer. When the *Argonauts came to his country, Polydeuces accepted his challenge and knocked him out. The Bebryces broke into the ring to avenge their king, but were routed by the Argonauts.

Amȳmō'nē, in Greek myth, one of the fifty daughters of *Danaus, rescued from a satyr and seduced by the god Poseidon, who created the spring Amymone in commemoration.

Ana'băsis (*Kyrou anabasis*, 'Cyrus' expedition inland'), prose narrative in seven books by *Xenophon, describing the expedition of the younger Cyrus, son of king Darius II of Persia, against his elder brother Artaxerxes II, the then king. Xenophon published the first part under the pseudonym of Themistogenes of Syracuse, but in the second part he abandoned the pretence and magnified his own role in the expedition.

Cyrus, who was satrap of Lydia, was disappointed that he had not been chosen to succeed his father, as the favourite son. His resentment against his brother was increased, according

to Xenophon, when he was arrested by Artaxerxes, soon after his accession, on a false charge of conspiracy. Cyrus prepared to attack Artaxerxes, and recruited an auxiliary force of 10,000 Greeks. Xenophon describes the long march of Cyrus' expedition, the 'Ten Thousand', which he accompanied at the invitation of his friend Proxenus, one of the Greek generals, from Sardis to the neighbourhood of Babylon in 401 BC. It was interrupted by the reluctance of some of the troops to proceed when they discovered the true object of the expedition, which had been concealed from them. The majority were persuaded to go on, and fought in the battle of Cunaxa, near Babylon; Cyrus himself was killed, and his Asiatic troops took flight.

This disaster dismayed the Greeks, but they resisted the attempts of Artaxerxes to induce them to surrender. Their dismay increased when the satrap *Tissaphernes, who had been conducting the negotiations on the Persian side, lured the Greek generals into his quarters to have them seized and beheaded. At this point Xenophon induced the remaining officers to reorganize the force and arrange a safe retreat. Cheirisophus commanded the van while Xenophon took the more dangerous command at the rear. His advice on the route and his courage and resourcefulness enabled the Greek army, after great hardships and severe fighting in the mountains of Armenia, to reach the Black Sea. Xenophon's account includes a famous description (IV. 7. 20–6) of the scene when the Greeks, climbing Mount Theches, at last saw the sea and cried '*thalatta, thalatta!*'. They now reached comparative safety at Trapezus, a Greek colony on the Black Sea coast; but difficulties had still to be overcome, and there was dissension among the troops before they reached Byzantium. After spending a winter in the service of the treacherous Seuthes, a Thracian, Xenophon handed over the remnant of the Ten Thousand to the Spartan Thimbron, for the war against Persia. In his narrative Xenophon's piety is noticeable: he takes no important decision without sacrificing to the gods and being guided by the omens.

Anacha'rsis, according to Herodotus, a Scythian prince of the sixth century BC who travelled widely and acquired a high reputation for wisdom. On his return to Scythia he was put to death for trying to introduce the cult of Magna Mater (see CYBELE). Later writers made him the guest of Solon at Athens and include him among the Seven Sages. He was traditionally supposed to have despised all Greeks except the Spartans, and thus arose the picture of him as a 'noble savage' uttering *Cynic diatribes against a corrupt civilization. The sayings and letters attributed to him furnished a model for Montesquieu and Oliver Goldsmith, writing in the early part of the eighteenth century.

Ana'creon (b. *c.*570 BC), Greek lyric poet, born in the Ionian city of Teos on the coast of Asia Minor, whence he migrated when the Persians threatened and joined other Teians in the foundation of Abdera in Thrace. Some time later he moved to the court of Polycrates, tyrant of Samos *c.*533–522, to whom he wrote many poems, though in the extant fragments Polycrates' name is nowhere found. After the fall of Polycrates, Hipparchus, brother of the Athenian tyrant Hippias, brought him to Athens; it is probable that after Hipparchus' murder he went to Thessaly. The place of his death, at an advanced age, is unknown. He wrote in the Ionic Greek dialect perhaps five books of lyric, iambic, and elegiac poetry from which only a few complete poems survive, more often in the quotations of later grammarians and metricians than in fragments of papyrus (see PAPYROLOGY). Most of his surviving fragments are from poems composed in simple metres (especially anacreontics and glyconics; see METRE, GREEK 8 (i)), which speak most memorably of love and the convivial pleasures (see SYMPOSIUM). His love poems are tender and delicately sensuous, often characterized by a self-deprecating humour and verbal wit that give a nice touch of ambiguousness to the tone of some of them. They are far removed from the mere 'prettiness' of later imitators (see below).

Anacreontēa, body of short poems mostly on amorous or convivial themes composed at various times in late antiquity. They were modelled not very accurately on the style and subject matter of Anacreon and often ascribed to him, so much so that his fame in Europe after the Renaissance depended very largely on these imitations. With their literary conceits and prettiness the best of them have a charm that disguises their slightness.

anacrū'sis, 'upbeat' in metric, an alternative term for *arsis.

anagnō'risis, 'recognition', see POETICS.

Analy'tica prio'ra and *posterio'ra,* treatises on logic by *Aristotle (4 (i)).

a'napaest, see METRE, GREEK I (iii).

Anatolia, 'the East', the late Greek name for that part of Asia which is roughly equivalent to modern Turkey. It is now used to denote that part of the world in ancient times.

Anaxa'goras (*c.*500–*c.*428 BC), of Clazomenae in Ionia, the first philosopher to reside in Athens, probably between 480 and 430 (the chronology of his life is disputed). He became the friend and mentor of Pericles. Later he was prosecuted for impiety (and perhaps for having Persian sympathies) by Cleon and so withdrew to Lampsacus, where he founded a school and was held in high esteem. He appears to have written only one book, *On Nature*, a prose work

of which several extensive fragments are preserved by quotation. He belongs to the Ionian tradition of philosophy (see PHILOSOPHY I and PROSE I), and his interests were in cosmology and physics, but conflicting testimonies make it difficult to reconstruct his thought. His universe is composed of 'seeds' of every distinct substance, which take their quality from their prevailing component but contain at the same time infinitesimal particles of every other substance ('everything has a share of everything'). Changes in things therefore occur as a consequence of the regrouping of the constituent substances. The animating principle of plants and animals and the initiator of cosmic motion is Mind, *Nous*, which is 'the finest of all things and the purest', and is itself separate and unmixed, omnipresent and eternal. In this cosmology Mind starts a rotary motion which gradually spreads and separates the seeds, the dense, moist, cold, and dark going to the centre and their opposites to the circumference. To Anaxagoras the heavenly bodies were huge stones ('the sun is larger than the Peloponnese') torn from the earth and rendered incandescent by their motion. This view may have been influenced by the famous fall of a meteorite in the region of Aegospotami in 467. Anaxagoras believed that the earth was flat and floated on air, but he understood that the heavenly bodies rotated and that the moon received its light from the sun, and he therefore grasped the principle of eclipses. Doctrines such as his, destructive of the traditional and official pantheon, exerted great influence on late fifth-century thought.

Anaxima'nder (Anaximandros) (*c.*610–545 BC), Ionian philosopher of Miletus, the first Greek known to have written (*c.*546) a book in prose, a treatise on nature, now lost except for one quotation. It was said that he introduced into Greece the gnomon (the vertical rod whose shadow indicates the sun's direction; see CLOCKS), and to have constructed the first map of the earth and the first celestial globe (this last is improbable).

Anaximander is the first philosopher we know of who tried to explain rationally the origins of the world and of mankind. He declared that the origin of all things was the Unbounded (*to apeiron*), which is 'the divine' (*to theion*), being immortal and indestructible. This 'enfolded' and 'controlled' the *cosmos*, or indeed many *cosmoi* (whether successive or co-existent is not clear). The most important forces at work in the cosmos and the agents of physical change were pairs of opposites, chiefly the hot and the cold, the wet and the dry. Anaximander thought that the earth was shaped like a drum of a column, its people living on its upper surface. Of his many interesting ideas about details of our cosmos two are notable. Alone of the Presocratics he explained why the earth remains in the same place without postulating some material support, declaring that there was no reason why what was symmetrically placed in the middle, equidistant from the extremities, should move downwards rather than in any other direction. The second is his conjecture about the origins of animal and human life. He supposed that the first living creatures were produced by spontaneous generation from mud by the action of the sun, and this became a standard account. Further, he inferred from the helpless condition of men in infancy that they could not have survived in primitive conditions without protection, and so conjectured that in the beginning they were reared in fish-like creatures from which they burst out when they were able to nourish themselves.

Anaxi'menēs, of Miletus (flourished *c.*546 BC), Ionian philosopher and younger contemporary of Anaximander. His writings are lost and our knowledge of them depends on the statements of later writers. For Anaximenes the originative principle (*archē*) of the cosmos was air; when air was rarified as fire or condensed as water or earth these elements compounded together could make up the wide diversity of the natural world. Furthermore air was the actual breath of the cosmos and so its ever-living and therefore divine source. Anaximenes thought that the earth was flat and shallow—'table-like'—and supported by air. His theory of condensation and rarefaction as observable means of change from the basic form of matter to the diversity of natural substances was his important contribution to the thought of his time.

anceps ('ambivalent'), in *metre (see 1), a syllable that can be scanned either long or short.

Anchi'sēs, in Greek myth, a Trojan prince, great-grandson of Tros (see TROY) and a member of the younger branch of the Trojan royal house. The goddess Aphroditē fell in love with him, and the child of their union was *Aeneas. Anchises when drunk boasted of the goddess's favour and was struck blind, or paralysed, by the thunderbolt of Zeus. We are told in the *Aeneid* that he was carried from burning Troy on his son's shoulders, and accompanied him in his wanderings. Tradition gives many accounts of his death; Virgil places it at Drepanum in Sicily (see *Aeneid*, 3, 5, and 6).

anci'lia. At Rome a shield (*ancīle*) was said to have fallen from heaven during the reign of *Numa (715–673 BC), and an oracle declared that the seat of empire would lie wherever that shield should be. Thereupon Numa caused eleven other shields to be made like it, so that, if a traitor should wish to remove it, the genuine shield could not be distinguished. These shields were of the ancient 'figure of eight' shape, known from Mycenaean art, and were preserved in the Temple of Mars (part of the old royal palace in the Forum) in the custody of the

*Salii and carried round the city yearly in solemn procession in the month of March, the shield being supposed to have fallen on the first day of that month. On a declaration of war, the Roman general moved the shields, with the words 'Awake, Mars!'

Ancus Ma'rcius, one of the legendary kings of Rome; see ROME 2.

Ancȳrā'num Monumentum, see MONUMENTUM ANCYRANUM.

Ando'cidēs (*c.*440–*c.*390 BC), one of the earlier Attic orators and member of an ancient aristocratic Athenian family which traced its descent from the god Hermes. He was accused of having shared in the mutilation of the Hermae in 415 (see PELOPONNESIAN WAR 5) and of having profaned the Eleusinian mysteries (compare ALCIBIADES), and in order to secure his own immunity and, he claimed, to save his father, who had been implicated, confessed to taking part in these affairs. He subsequently repudiated the confession, but at the time his account was accepted by the Athenians. He retired from Athens and began to trade as a merchant when a decree was passed limiting his rights as a citizen. We possess three of his speeches, the first, 'On his Return', delivered in the *ecclesia*, probably in 410, when he unsuccessfully pleaded for the removal of the limitation on his rights; the second, 'On the Mysteries', was made in 399 when, having been restored to full public rights under the amnesty of 403, he successfully defended himself against a charge of still being subject to the former limitation (the sixth speech in the works of Lysias is apparently part of the prosecution); it is interesting as an eye-witness account of an intriguing event in Athenian history. His third speech, 'On the Peace', is a political discourse urging peace with Sparta in 390, the fourth year of the Corinthian War. The Athenians rejected the peace, and Andocides retired into exile and oblivion. He was not, like the other orators, a trained or professional rhetorician, but a man of ability and shrewdness, who excelled in a natural and persuasive eloquence.

A'ndria ('woman of Andros'), the first comedy of *Terence, produced in 166 BC. An anecdote, perhaps apocryphal, relates that Terence appeared before *Caecilius by order of the *aediles to read his first play to him when Caecilius was at dinner. The latter was so impressed that Terence was invited to share the meal.

Pamphilus, a young Athenian, has seduced Glycerium, supposed to be the sister of a courtesan from Andros, and is devoted to her. His father, Simo, has arranged a match for him with the daughter of his friend Chremēs. But Chremes has heard of the relations between Pamphilus and Glycerium and withdraws his consent to the match. Simo conceals this and pretends to go on with preparations for an immediate marriage, hoping by this means to put an end to the affair. Pamphilus, learning from his cunning slave Davus that the intended marriage is a pretence, temporizes and offers no objection. Simo now persuades Chremes to withdraw his objection, so reducing Pamphilus to despair. At this stage Glycerium bears a son to Pamphilus, and Davus arranges to have this made known to Chremes, who now finally breaks off the match. At this point an acquaintance newly arrived from Andros reveals to Chremes that Glycerium as a child was shipwrecked there in circumstances which show that she is in fact his daughter. Chremes and Simo consent to the marriage of Pamphilus and Glycerium, and all ends happily.

The play contains the often-quoted phrases *hinc illae lacrimae*, 'hence those tears', and *amantium irae amoris integratiost*, 'the quarrels of lovers are the renewal of love'.

Androclus and the Lion, see GELLIUS, AULUS.

Andro'mache, in Greek myth, daughter of Ēëtiōn king of Thēbē in Cilicia, and wife of *Hector. Her father and brothers were killed by Achilles, her mother taken prisoner and ransomed. Her son Astyanax was put to death by the Greeks after the fall of Troy (see TROJAN WOMEN) and she herself fell to the lot of Neoptolemus to whom she bore three sons, Molossus (eponym of the Molossians), Pielus, and Pergamus (named after the citadel of Troy). The conflict between her and Hermione, the jealous, childless wife of Neoptolemus, is the theme of Euripides' play *Andromache*. After Neoptolemus' death she married the Trojan seer Helenus, a son of Priam, and lived in Epirus. When Helenus died she was taken by her son Pergamus to Asia Minor, where he founded the city of Pergamum.

Andro'mache, Greek tragedy by *Euripides, probably produced c.426 BC, in the early part of the Peloponnesian War.

The play deals with that period in the life of *Andromache when she was living as the concubine of Neoptolemus in Thessaly. She had borne him a son, Molossus. After ten years Neoptolemus had married Hermione, daughter of Menelaus; she remained childless and suspected that this was the doing of her hated rival Andromache. Helped by Menelaus, Hermione takes advantage of the absence of Neoptolemus on a journey to Delphi to draw Andromache, by the threat to kill Molossus, from the shrine of Thetis where she had taken refuge, in order to kill both mother and son. They are saved by the intervention of the aged Peleus, the grandfather of Neoptolemus. *Orestes, who has contrived the murder of Neoptolemus at Delphi and who arrives unexpectedly, carries off Hermione, to whom he had been betrothed before Neoptolemus had claimed her. The death of Neoptole-

mus is announced. Thetis appears and arranges matters. The odious character which the poet attributes to (the Spartan) Menelaus has been seen as according with the feeling against Sparta which prevailed at this time at Athens.

Andro'meda (Andromedē), in Greek myth, daughter of Cepheus king of the Ethiopians and his wife Cassiopeia. The latter had offended the Nereids (sea-nymphs) by boasting that her daughter was more beautiful than they. Thereupon they complained to the sea-god Poseidon, who sent a sea-monster to ravage the country. The oracle of *Ammon said it could be appeased only by the sacrifice of Andromeda, who was accordingly fastened to a rock on the sea-shore. Perseus changed the monster to stone by showing it the Gorgon's head, and married Andromeda, after first fighting and turning to stone her uncle Phineus, who had been betrothed to her and who now attacked him. Their children included Alcaeus and Electryon.

Androni'cus, Lucius Livius, see LIVIUS ANDRONICUS.

Andro'tion, Against, speech in a public prosecution by Demosthenes. See DEMOSTHENES (2) 4.

Ane'cdota, see PROCOPIUS.

anima'lium, Historia, treatise by *Aristotle (4 (iii)).

Anna, sister of *Dido. According to the poet Ovid, Anna came to Italy after *Aeneas had established himself there, and was entrusted by him to his wife Lavinia. But Lavinia was jealous of her, and Anna fled to the river Numicius and was taken by the river-god into his care. The story is not in Virgil's *Aeneid*.

Anna Pere'nna, ancient Roman goddess whose festival was celebrated on the Ides (15th) of March. This was a feast at what used to be the first full moon of the year, since by the old reckoning (see CALENDARS) March was the first month. She is usually explained as being a year-goddess but her name and attributes are not clear, though obviously connected with the year (*annus*). She had no mythology. Ovid (*Fasti* 3) gives several explanations of her, perhaps of his own invention. He also paints a vivid picture of the Roman crowd celebrating the festival by picnicking on the banks of the Tiber, returning home drunkenly at night.

Annā'lēs. 1. Of Ennius, see ENNIUS. **2.** Of Tacitus, see below.

Annals (*Annales* or *Ab excessu divi Augusti*, 'from the death of the late emperor Augustus'), a history of the reigns of the Julio-Claudian emperors Tiberius, Caligula, Claudius, and Nero, by Tacitus, written after his *Histories*. There is evidence that Tacitus was still writing it in AD 116. The surviving portions are books

1–4, a small piece of 5, 6, part of 11, 12–15, and part of 16. The work is notable for its style, concise to the point of obscurity, its sustained dignity and vividness, and its epigrammatic sayings, memorable for their irony or melancholy. The record is in the main gloomy and depressing, and although Tacitus bears occasional witness to the efficient civil administration of the empire, the emphasis seems to be rather on the crimes, the sycophancy, the informing, and the oppression that marked this period at Rome. Tacitus claims to write without partiality and prejudice, to aim at saving worthy actions from oblivion while recording evil deeds for posterity (3.65), but he has in fact a republican bias. It is generally recognized that the impression he gives of Tiberius is unduly dark, and the life of debauchery imputed to him in his last years at Capri inherently improbable. The most important matters covered in the surviving books are as follows.

Book 1 (AD 14–15). After a rapid review of the reign of Augustus, the author passes to that of Tiberius, relating the suppression by Germanicus of the mutiny of the legions in Pannonia and Germany in 14, and his first two campaigns (14–15) against the Germans. There is a notable description of the visit of the Roman army to the scene of the disaster of Varus.

Book 2 (AD 16–19). The third campaign of Germanicus (16), in which he defeats Arminius. His expedition to the East with Cn. Piso (17), and his death, suspected to have been due to Piso.

Book 3 (AD 20–2). The return of Agrippina, the widow of Germanicus, to Italy, and the trial (20) and suicide of Piso. The growth of luxury and sycophancy at Rome.

Book 4 (AD 23–8). The character and career of Sejanus, who, in league with Livia, the wife of Drusus (son of Tiberius), has Drusus poisoned (23) and plots against the children of Germanicus. The proposal of his marriage to Livia is set aside by Tiberius. In 26 Tiberius withdraws to Capri. The increase in the activity of informers and in judicial murders, such as that of Cremutius Brutus, accused of having in a history praised Brutus and Cassius.

Book 5 (AD 29). The death of Julia Augusta or Livia (29), mother of Tiberius. The story of the conspiracy and fall of Sejanus in 31, which formed part of this book, is lost.

Book 6 (AD 31–7). Tiberius at Capri; his vicious life, anguish, and ferocity. The death of Drusus (son of Germanicus) by starvation in prison, and of Agrippina his mother (33). The ceaseless bloodshed at Rome, by executions and suicides. The death of Tiberius in 37, and a summary of his life.

Book 11 (AD 47–9). The seventh year of the reign of Claudius (47). The excesses of Messalina, her marriage with Silius, the dismay of the emperor, and the execution in 48 of Silius and

Messalina at the urging of the freedman Narcissus.

Book 12 (AD 49–54). Claudius marries in 49 his niece Agrippina, daughter of Germanicus. Through her influence her son, the future emperor Nero, is adopted by Claudius, preferred to his own son Britannicus, and married to his daughter Octavia. Silanus, to whom Octavia had been betrothed, is brought to ruin and death in 49 by Agrippina. Seneca is recalled from exile to be Nero's tutor. The insurrection in Britain and the defeat (50) of Caratacus, king of the Silures, who is brought to Rome and pardoned. Claudius is poisoned by Agrippina, and Nero becomes emperor (54).

Book 13 (AD 55–8). The promising beginning to the reign of Nero, who is restrained by Seneca and Burrus, the prefect of the praetorians. Cn. Domitius Corbulo is sent to the East to resist Parthian aggression. Agrippina, whose influence is weakened, takes up the cause of Britannicus; Nero has him poisoned (55) and Agrippina removed from the palace. Nero in love with Poppaea Sabina.

Book 14 (AD 59–62). The attempt to remove Agrippina by scuttling her ship, followed by her brutal murder (61). The great rising of 61 in Britain under Boudicca, and its suppression (London is mentioned as much frequented by merchants and trading vessels). Armenia is recovered from the Parthians by the Romans under Corbulo. The death of Burrus in 62 and the retirement of Seneca. Nero marries Poppaea; his virtuous former wife Octavia is banished to Pandataria (Ventotene) and there murdered.

Book 15 (AD 62–5). The ignominious defeat of Caesennius Paetus in Armenia, followed by the reduction of the country by a Roman army under Corbulo to a dependency of the empire (63). The great fire of Rome, which devastates ten out of the city's fourteen districts, and its rebuilding on an improved plan. The persecution of the Christians, to whom Nero attributes the fire. The conspiracy of C. Calpurnius Piso and the putting to death of Seneca and Lucan in 65.

Book 16 (AD 65–6). The extravagances of Nero, who appears in public as a singer; the death of Poppaea (65). The suicide of the Stoic Thrasea and the banishment of his son-in-law Helvidius in 66. In chapter 16 of this book, one of the last surviving, Tacitus laments the melancholy and monotonous record of bloodshed. The part relating to the last two years of Nero's reign is lost.

annals, annalists. From the beginning of Roman history (see ROME 1 and 2) to 400 BC scarcely any records were kept, but from c.300 BC regular records of magistrates and 'the most important records', the so-called *annales maximi*, were inscribed by the **pontifex maximus* on the *tabulae pontificum*, 'tables of the priests', displayed outside his official residence. These tables constituted the first annals, from which Ennius took the title of his historical epic, but for a long time the information they contained was minimal and mainly sacral (names of the magistrates for the year, and records of wars and eclipses, for instance). The first historians of Rome, the so-called senatorial historians, Fabius Pictor, Cincius Alimentus, Postumius Albinus, and C. Acilius, writing in Greek in the first half of the second century BC, owed very little to the annals and were really continuing the tradition of Hellenistic Greek historical writing (see HISTORIOGRAPHY, GREEK). Cato the Censor, writing his history of Rome, the *Origines*, at this time, was also continuing the Greek tradition but writing in Latin. Under his influence the first systematic reconstruction of Roman history based on Roman evidence was made by the 'old' annalists Cassius Hemina and Calpurnius Piso, writing in the second half of the second century BC. Then P. Mucius Scaevola (d. *c*.115 BC), *pontifex maximus* in 130, ended the annual display of the annals and authorized their publication, in eighty books, from the earliest times up to his own day, involving for the regal period legendary speculation and for the early republic a reconstruction of events in the light of tradition. The arrangement of this historical work determined the form adopted by all later Roman historians, including those who, like Valerius Antias and Claudius Quadrigarius, expanded the records in rhetorical style. A few historians, like Licinius Macer and Aelius Tubero, appear to have checked their material, but most annalistic historians like Livy accepted both the narrative form and the content of their sources. See HISTORIOGRAPHY, ROMAN.

annō'na, the Roman corn supply. During the republic the supply was under the general supervision of the senate who arranged for the distribution of subsidized corn during famines and prevented speculation, although the market was normally free. From 299 BC this duty fell to the *aediles who were also in charge of imported grain, mostly from Sicily and Sardinia. Nevertheless shortages were frequent and fresh legislation often followed a famine. C. *Gracchus was the first to enact a corn law (*lex frumentaria*) for the benefit of impoverished citizens, which provided that the state should sell a certain quantity of grain each month at a fixed (probably subsidized) price. Subsequent political leaders of the people (e.g. Saturninus) lowered the price, until Clodius in 58 BC made distributions free. Julius Caesar appointed two new aediles (*aediles ceriales*) to manage the distributions, and limited the numbers receiving free corn to 150,000. Augustus took over responsibility for the corn supply, which subsequently remained under imperial control, and

raised the number of recipients to 200,000. He appointed an equestrian officer, the *praefectus annonae*, to organize supplies, and this became an important office. Under later emperors its importance and complexity increased enormously. Most of the grain was now imported from Egypt and Africa. The cities of Italy and the provinces looked after their own supplies, but the government in Rome gave help in time of famine. During the empire a special tax was imposed on Italy and the provinces, the *annona militaris*, to provide food for the army, which the soldiers then received free. Henceforward the word 'annona' chiefly denotes this tax.

Antae'us, in Greek myth, a giant, son of the god Poseidon and Gaia (Earth), who lived in Libya. Heracles wrestled with him while on his way to fetch the golden apples of the Hesperides (see HERACLES, LABOURS OF 11). Whenever he was thrown, he arose stronger than before from contact with his mother Earth. Heracles, perceiving this, lifted him in the air and crushed him to death.

Antei'a, see BELLEROPHON.

Antē'nor, one of the elders of Troy during the siege. He was in favour of restoring Helen to the Greeks, since she had been taken by treachery. It was said that the Greeks, recognizing his fairness, spared him and his family when the city was captured. Later legend made him out a traitor to the Trojans, telling the Greeks to steal the *Palladium and build the Wooden Horse. Several stories were told of what happened to him after the Trojan War. One legend known to Livy, which may be as old as Sophocles' lost tragedy *Antenoridae* ('sons of Antenor'), relates that Antenor led the Eneti, who had lost their king at Troy, from Paphlagonia to the head of the Adriatic Sea, where they settled in Venetia and founded the city of Patavium (Padua).

Anthestē'ria, at Athens, an important festival, lasting three days, of the god *Dionysus, which gave its name to the month Anthesterion (February–March), signifying the time of year when the flowers (*anthē*) begin to appear. It was the custom to garland with flowers children who were 3 years old, and children participated in the festival, perhaps because Dionysus was in some aspects the god of life and growth. As he was also god of wine, wine was much in evidence; the first day was the *pithoigia*, 'jar-opening', when the new wine was tasted and offered at the shrine of Dionysus in the Marshes, *en limnais* (the marshes which were the home of the Frogs in Aristophanes' comedy of that name). The second day was called *khŏĕs*, 'wine-jugs', the *khous* being a type of pot with a wide curving belly, short neck, and trefoil mouth, numbers of which survive in miniature form, having evidently been given to children as presents. Much drinking took place, and there was a procession in which Dionysus (perhaps personified by a masked actor) was borne along on a ship mounted on wheels, and was supposed to 'marry' the wife of the archon basileus (see ARCHONS (i)). At the end of Aristophanes' Acharnians the hero Dikaiopolis prepares to celebrate the feast of the wine-jugs while the general Lamachus has to go off to war. The third day was called khytroi, 'pots', in which a mixture of all kinds of vegetables was boiled and offered to the god Hermes Chthonios, 'of the Underworld', on behalf of the dead, to placate their hostility. It was a day of ill-omen, when the spirits of the dead (keres) were thought to roam the city. At the end of the day they were banished with the cry, 'Be gone, keres, the Anthesteria are over!'

A'nthimus, Greek doctor who wrote soon after AD 511, in the form of a letter to Theodoric the Great (see GOTHS), a short Latin treatise 'on dietetics', De observatione ciborum, half medical text-book, half cookery book. The book is of great interest for the picture it gives of the eating and drinking habits of a Germanic people, and for the unclassical nature of the author's language which he had learnt entirely from the speech of the people (see LATIN 4).

anthology
1. Greek. The word anthologia, literally 'flower-gathering', has come to denote a collection of extracts from literary works, and particularly a collection of poems. Many collections of poems were made in Greece from the fourth century BC onwards. These have been lost as separate entities, but a vast collection of short poems, mostly in the elegiac metre, ranging in time from the seventh century BC to the tenth century AD, survives in what we know as the Greek Anthology. The basis of this collection went back many centuries. The earliest source of which we know is the Garland compiled by *Meleager in the early years of the first century BC; it contains poems attributed to some fifty poets from *Archilochus to Meleager himself. Few were more than eight lines long. Another anthology of epigrams written after Meleager's time was compiled around AD 40 by Philip of Thessalonika. The next most notable collection was the Syllogē or Cycle made c. AD 560 by the Byzantine poet and scholar *Agathias from epigrams written by his contemporaries and himself. These three anthologies became the principal sources for an important and comprehensive anthology compiled c. AD 900 by the learned Constantine Cephalas, an official of the Imperial Palace at Byzantium, but perhaps never completed or published in the normal way. All these various collections have perished as such; the surviving Greek Anthology, a collection of sixteen books of epigrams, is derived from two Byzantine compilations which were based on Cephalas' work but with many additions.

The first and larger is the Palatine Anthology, so-called because the unique tenth-century manuscript that contains it was found in the Count Palatine's Library at Heidelberg. The second is a collection made by the scholarly monk Planudes in about 1300, and the only one known until the Palatine manuscript was discovered by the young French scholar Salmasius in 1606. Those epigrams of Planudes which are not found in the Palatine manuscript are now published as book 16 of the Palatine Anthology.

The Greek Anthology contains a wide variety of poems, many of great charm. There are epitaphs (including the famous epitaphs attributed to Simonides), dedications, reflections on life and death and fate, poems on love, on family life, on great poets and artists and their works, and on the beauties of nature. A certain proportion are humorous or satirical, making fun of doctors, rhetoricians, athletes, etc., or of personal peculiarities, such as Nicon's long nose.

The dedicatory poems form perhaps the group that throws most light on ancient Greek life. There are dedications not only of arms, but of many kinds of implements and articles of daily use: a girl about to marry offers up her dolls and toys, a traveller his old hat, 'a small gift, but given in piety'.

2. Latin. The Anthologia Latina is the title given to a collection of some 380 short Latin poems made in Africa during the early sixth century AD and preserved in the famous Codex Salmasianus (named after its former owner Salmasius: see above) of the seventh or eighth century. The collection contains poems written by African poets during the Vandal occupation (fifth to early sixth century) and a few miscellaneous earlier pieces, including the *Pervigilium Veneris and three epigrams of the philosopher Seneca. It played an influential part in the development of medieval Latin poetry.

Anticle'a (Antikleia), in Greek myth, the wife of Laertēs and mother of *Odysseus.

anti'dosis, 'exchange'. Wealthy Athenians were required to undertake certain public services (see LITURGY) as a form of taxation. A citizen who felt that his assessment was unfair might challenge some other, whose means he thought greater than his own, either to undertake the service or to make an exchange, antidosis, of properties. This might lead to a law-suit, if the other citizen refused.

Antidosis, On the, see ISOCRATES.

Anti'gonē. In the version of the myth of *Oedipus most familiar to us from Greek literature, Antigone is one of the four children (two daughters and two sons) of Oedipus by his union with his mother Jocasta. Antigone's part in the myth seems to have originated largely in fifth-century Attica. She accompanied the blind Oedipus after his banishment from Thebes, and they eventually arrived at Colonus, near Athens. When Oedipus' sons Polyneices and Eteocles died by each other's hand as they fought for the kingdom of Thebes, Jocasta's brother Creon, now king of Thebes, forbade the burial of Polyneices as being the aggressor. Antigone refused to accept this decree, gave the body a token burial, was discovered, and by Creon's order walled up alive in a tomb although she was betrothed to his son Haemon. She hanged herself and Haemon stabbed himself beside her body. This is the version of Sophocles' *Antigone* (see below). Euripides in his (lost) play *Antigone* told a modified version.

Anti'gonē, Greek tragedy by *Sophocles, probably written in 441 BC.

Creon, king of Thebes, has forbidden the burial of the body of Polyneices (see above). Antigone resolves to defy his decree, performs funeral rites for her brother, and is caught and brought before the king. She pleads that her act is in accordance with the overriding laws of the gods. Creon is unrelenting and condemns her to be immured alive in a cave. Her sister Ismenē, who has refused to share in Antigone's actions, now claims a share in her guilt and punishment, but the king regards her as demented. Creon's son Haemon, who is betrothed to Antigone, pleads with his father in vain; he leaves with a warning that he will die with her. The seer Teiresias threatens the king with the terrible consequences of his defying the divine laws, and Creon, at last moved, goes to the cave. He finds Haemon clasping the dead body of Antigone, who has hanged herself. Haemon lunges at Creon with his sword, but misses and then kills himself. Creon returns to his palace, to find that his wife Eurydicē, in despair, has taken her own life.

Anti'gonus and **Anti'gonids.** The first bearer of the name Antigonus of whom we know was one of the generals of Alexander the Great, the son of a noble Macedonian family, who was satrap of Phrygia at the time of Alexander's death in 323 BC and eventually aspired to rule all the empire; see MACEDONIA 2. He was defeated and killed at the battle of Ipsus in 301. His grandson Antigonus II Gonatas, son of Demetrius Poliorcetes, established in Macedonia the Antigonid dynasty, which maintained a partial control over Greece. After Gonatas the most prominent of the Antigonids was his grandson *Philip V (238–179 BC) who by provoking Rome into the Macedonian Wars (see MACEDONIA 3 and ROME 5) was largely responsible for bringing Greece under Roman domination. After the Macedonian army was practically annihilated by the Romans at the battle of Pydna in 168 BC the Antigonids were dethroned and the Macedonian realm broken up into four federal republics. In 146 BC it became a Roman province.

Anti'lochus, in Greek myth, son of Nestor, in Homer's *Iliad* a brave fighter for the Greeks in the Trojan War. The *Aethiopis* described how he was killed defending his father against Memnon.

Anti'machus, of Colophon (flourished *c.*400 BC), the first Greek 'scholar-poet' and as such a forerunner of the Hellenistic poets, anticipating them in their learned obscurities. He wrote an epic on Thebes, and in his long elegiac poem *Lydē* was the originator of narrative *elegy, a genre in which he had many imitators. Only scanty fragments of his works survive. The *Lyde* was much admired by some Hellenistic poets, but objected to by *Callimachus (see his *Answer to the Telchinēs*) on the grounds of excessive length and obscurity.

Anti'nŏus. 1. In Homer's *Odyssey*, the most arrogant of the suitors of Odysseus' wife Penelope, and the first of them to be killed by Odysseus.
2. Bithynian youth of great beauty and a favourite of the emperor *Hadrian. He was drowned in the Nile in AD 130 and gossip surrounded his death with romantic legends. Hadrian founded the city of Antinŏopolis on the Nile and erected temples in his memory. Antinous was frequently represented in sculpture, and some of these representations survive.

A'ntioch (Antiocheia), on the river Orontēs, the capital of ancient Syria, founded by Seleucus I (see SELEUCIDS) about 300 BC, and named after his father. Antiochus I, the Great, king of Syria 223–187 BC, adorned it with works of art, a theatre, and a library. It became a centre of trade and a city of pleasure; the Greek poet Aratus of Soli lived for a time at the court of Antiochus I (281–261 BC) and the Greek poet Euphorion was appointed librarian of the public library. Antiochus IV Epiphanes (175–163 BC), an ardent lover of classical Greek culture, considerably beautified the city. Antioch was prominent in Christian life: it was here that Christians were first so called (Acts 11: 26), and the city ranked after Rome and Jerusalem as the third Patriarchal see. After the inauguration of Constantinople in AD 330 Antioch gradually ceased to be a principal city of the East. It was destroyed in the Persian invasion of AD 538 and never fully recovered. Many other cities founded by the Seleucids, besides the capital, bore the name Antioch.

Anti'ochus. 1. The name of several of the Seleucid kings of Asia; see above, and SELEUCIDS.
2. Of Ascalon, see ACADEMY.

Anti'opē. 1. In Greek myth, daughter of Nycteus, king of Boeotia. Her story has come down to us chiefly through Euripides' tragedy *Antiope*, now lost. Antiope was seduced by Zeus and became the mother of the twin brothers

Amphion and Zethus. To avoid her father's anger she fled to Sicyon. Nycteus in despair killed himself, but first charged his brother, Lycus, who was king of Thebes during the minority of *Laius, to punish Antiope. Lycus captured Sicyon and imprisoned Antiope; her treatment was made more cruel by the jealousy of Dircē, the wife of Lycus. At last Antiope escaped and joined her sons, now grown to maturity. These revenged her by tying Dirce to the horns of a bull, so that she was dragged to death; and they killed or deposed Lycus. Amphion and Zethus now became rulers of Thebes and built its walls. (In Homer's *Odyssey* they are represented as the city's first founders.) Amphion was a harper of such skill that the stones were drawn into their places by his music. He married *Niobē, and Zethus married the nymph Thebē, whence the name of Thebes.

2. Another name for Hippolytē, queen of the Amazons.

Anti'pater (Antipatros). 1. (397–319 BC), one of the most able generals of Philip II of Macedon and subsequently of his son Alexander (the Great). During Alexander's absence in the East he was the governor of Macedonia and the Greek states. After the death of Alexander he suffered an uprising from a league of Greek states but was eventually victorious; he drove the Athenian orator Demosthenes to suicide by demanding his surrender. He remained loyal to the Macedonian dynasty, and it was his death in 319 that precipitated the break-up of Alexander's empire. His son was *Cassander. See MACEDONIA 2.

2. Of Sidon (flourished c.120 BC), Greek writer of short elegiac poems, some of which are preserved in the Greek *Anthology.

Anti'phanes, Greek poet of Middle Comedy; see COMEDY, GREEK 5.

A'ntiphon (c.480–411 BC), Attic orator whose surviving speeches are the earliest we have. He gained a great reputation by writing speeches for others to deliver on their own behalf (litigants at Athens were required to plead in person), but he himself remained in the background until he revealed his ability by guiding the oligarchic revolution and establishing the rule of the *Four Hundred in Athens in 411. After their overthrow he was put to death by the restored democracy. The speech he delivered in his own defence was widely admired; a few fragments of it have been found on papyrus. His name is a common one in Attica and this fact together with his many-sided activity make it difficult to separate him from the sophist Antiphon, with whom he is often confused or identified; it does not, however, seem likely that the extreme right-wing views of Antiphon the orator and the sophist's proclamation of the equality of all men could co-exist in the same person. We possess three of the orator's speeches for murder trials, and also three so-called *'Tetralogies', rhetorical exercises in which the author composes two speeches for the accuser and two for the defendant in imaginary murder trials. These lucid and well-constructed speeches show the sophistic trait of arguing not so much on the evidence of witnesses as on the inherent probabilities of the case.

Antiquita'tes rerum huma'narum et divina'rum, see VARRO (1).

Anti'sthenes, see CYNIC PHILOSOPHERS.

Anti'stius La'beo, Marcus, see LABEO.

Antonines, Age of the, strictly, the period of the Roman Empire from AD 138 to 192. It is part of that peaceful age famously described by Edward Gibbon in the third chapter of his *Decline and Fall of the Roman Empire*: 'If a man were called to fix the period in the history of the world, during which the condition of the human race was most happy and prosperous, he would, without hesitation, name that which elapsed from the death of Domitian to the accession of Commodus.' During this time the throne passed from Nerva to Trajan, Hadrian, Antoninus Pius, Marcus Aurelius, and Commodus. Only the last three were Antonines.

Antonine Wall, see BRITAIN 5 and ANTONINUS PIUS.

Antoni'nus Pius, Roman emperor AD 138–61, born in 86 at Lanuvium (Città Lavinia) and named Titus Aurelius Fulvus Boionius Antoninus. His family had originated in Gaul but settled at Rome; both his father and grandfather had been consuls. He won fame for his integrity as proconsul of Asia and joined the emperor Hadrian's circle of advisers. He earned the respect of the emperor, who adopted him as successor not long before his death. Antoninus maintained good relations with the senate and his reign was peaceful and orderly, without striking incident. His policies were benificent and mildly progressive, lacking extravagance; his reign is marked by a general sense of well-being, aptly expressed in Aristeides' oration 'To Rome'. He married *Faustina (1). It was in his reign, in 142, that the wall of turf known as the Antonine Wall was built in Britain between the Forth and Clyde estuaries by his lieutenant Lollius Urbicus (see BRITAIN 5).

Anto'nius, Marcus. 1. (143–87 BC), one of the greatest orators of his day, consul in 99, a member of the party of Sulla, and put to death by the supporters of Marius. He was grandfather of the famous Mark Antony (see next entry). He is one of the chief interlocutors in Cicero's *De Oratore*.

2. **Mark Antony,** see ANTONY, MARK below.

Antony, Mark (Marcus Antonius) (*c*.82–30 BC), grandson of Marcus Antonius (above). After serving under Aulus Gabinius in the East and under Julius *Caesar in Gaul, he was one of the tribunes in 49, when he supported Caesar against the senatorial (republican) side, joined him before the crossing of the Rubicon, and held a command in the ensuing campaigns in Italy and Epirus. After Caesar's victory at the battle of Pharsalus (48), Antony remained in Italy as second-in-command during the lawless period of Caesar's absence. He was Caesar's colleague in the consulship when the latter was assassinated in 44; his eloquence won over the people, so that he was in a favourable position to take over the leadership of the Caesarians, while remaining conciliatory towards the senate. However, his leadership was threatened by Caesar's heir *Octavian, who sided with the senate in opposition to Antony. Civil war broke out between Caesarians and republicans. It was at this time that *Cicero ((1) 5) delivered his speeches against Antony known as the *Philippics*, and powerfully contributed to raising the republican opposition to him. Antony was defeated by the republican Decimus Brutus at the battle of Mutina in 43. At this time Octavian had joined forces with the senate, but after Mutina the differences between him and Antony were settled, and Octavian, Antony, and Lepidus were appointed as a triumvirate to rule for five years. *Proscriptions followed, in which Cicero and his brother were sacrificed to Antony's desire for vengeance. In 42 Antony, sharing the command with Octavian, defeated the republicans Marcus Brutus and Cassius at Philippi.

Afterwards a division of the Roman world was made, in which the East was assigned to Antony, the West to Octavian. But hostilities soon broke out between the two leaders, temporarily settled by the treaty of Brundisium in 40, and by the marriage of Antony to Octavian's sister Octavia (Antony's wife *Fulvia having died in 40). This marriage interrupted his liaison with *Cleopatra, queen of Egypt, which had begun when he met her at Tarsus in Cilicia in 41. Their association was resumed in 37. Both stood to profit by it: Antony would have at his disposal the resources of Egypt to further his scheme of obtaining complete power over the East; Cleopatra would be confirmed in her rule over Egypt, which was none too secure. In 37 the triumvirate was prolonged for another five years. But the campaign which Antony undertook against the Parthians in 36 was unsuccessful, and the elimination of Lepidus from the triumvirate sharpened the rivalry between Antony and Octavian. After subduing Armenia in 34 Antony returned to Alexandria, the Egyptian capital, where he lived like an oriental ruler. He made donations of large parts of the eastern provinces to form kingdoms for Cleopatra,

*Caesarion, and his three children by Cleopatra. On the last day of 33 the agreement between Antony and Octavian came to an end, and in the following year he divorced Octavia. Having alienated the sympathy of Rome he gave Octavian the opportunity to declare a national war against Cleopatra. The result was decided by Octavian's victory in the sea-battle at Actium in 31, when Cleopatra's sixty ships sailed away, followed by Antony himself. In 30 Octavian invaded Egypt; Alexandria capitulated, and Antony took his own life. Shakespeare's play *Antony and Cleopatra*, being based on Plutarch's Life of Antony, may give a romantic and distorted view of events.

Anū'bis, in Egyptian religion, the jackal-headed god who conducted the souls of the dead to the region of immortal life, identified by the Greeks with *Hermes.

A'nytē, Arcadian poetess of Tegea who lived in the early third century BC. Some eighteen of her epigrams survive in the Greek *Anthology. They have great charm and are among the first pastoral descriptions of wild nature in Greek literature, and also include the first epitaphs for animals.

A'nytus, one of the three accusers who brought Socrates to trial, a wealthy Athenian, a moderate in politics, represented by Plato in the *Meno* as an enemy of the *sophists. He may have thought that by attacking Socrates he was acting in the best interests of Athens.

Ao'nia. The Aonians were, according to legend, ancient inhabitants of Boeotia. Aonia is the name sometimes used by learned poets to denote Boeotia; the Muses who frequented Mount Helicon in Boeotia are sometimes called Aonidēs.

Apatu'ria (Apatouria), see PHRATRIAI.

ape'lla, the assembly of the people at Sparta (see SPARTA 2).

Ape'llēs, the greatest painter of antiquity, born at Colophon in Ionia in the first half of the fourth century BC. He studied under the Ephesian painter Ephorus and the Sicyonian Pamphilus, and later worked at Corinth and Athens, and at the Macedonian court. The distinctive quality of his work was grace and charm, coupled with ease of execution. (It was said that the tone of his pictures was due to a secret varnish.) He painted mainly portraits, but a famous picture was that of Aphroditē Anadyomenē, 'Aphrodite rising from the sea', wringing the sea-water from her hair. This picture the emperor Augustus acquired for 100 talents. Apelles was the favourite painter of Alexander the Great, and painted several portraits of him, generally in some allegorical situation. See PAINTING.

Aphai'a, see BRITOMARTIS.

A'phobus, Against, speeches by Demosthenes against his fraudulent guardian; see DEMOSTHENES (2) 2.

Aphrodī'tē, the Greek goddess of love, beauty, and fertility, identified by the Romans with *Venus. She has two alternative genealogies: according to Hesiod she sprang from the foam (*aphros*) of the sea that gathered about the severed parts of the god Uranus when he was castrated by his son *Cronus. To Homer she is the child of Zeus and Dionē; Homer also calls her 'the Cyprian', and it was probably from Cyprus, in the Mycenaean age, that she first entered Greece. Many of her attributes indicate her partially oriental origin and her kinship with the Asian goddess Astarte. This is borne out by the legend that she first landed either at Paphos in Cyprus or at Cythera (an island off the Laconian coast), whence her title 'Cytherean'. Homer makes her the wife of Hephaestus. When her amorous intrigue with *Ares was discovered, the pair were caught in a net by Hephaestus and exposed to the ridicule of the assembled gods. Aeneas is her son by the Trojan *Anchises, and she always supported the Trojan cause against the Greeks (see TROJAN WAR). In later literature she is the mother of *Eros. For other legends about her see ADONIS and PARIS, JUDGEMENT OF. Although she was primarily a goddess of love, she was also a protector of sailors and a goddess of war. Two common titles of Aphrodite are Urania ('heavenly') and Pandemos ('popular'), cult names which Plato interpreted as symbolizing intellectual and sensual love. She had a famous sanctuary on Mount Eryx on the north-west coast of Sicily. This the Romans especially honoured, because Aphrodite, as the mother of Aeneas, passed for their ancestress. The title of Venus Erycina, who had a temple at Rome on the Capitol, outside the Colline Gate, was derived from the sanctuary on Mount Eryx.

Api'cius, Marcus Gavius, gourmet of the reign of Tiberius (AD 14–37). His recipes were written down; but the work on cookery which bears the name of Caelius Apicius is thought to be a compilation of a later period, perhaps the fourth century. It is sometimes entitled *De opsoniis et condimentis sive de re culinaria libri decem*, 'Ten books on catering and seasoning, or on cookery'.

Apis, see OSIRIS.

Apocolocynto'sis, title of a Menippean satire (see MENIPPUS) by *Seneca (2), formed from the words *apotheosis*, 'deification', and *colocynta*, 'pumpkin'. Manuscripts give the further title *Ludus de morte Claudii*, 'a joke about the death of Claudius'. It was written early in the reign of the emperor Nero in mockery of the deification of his predecessor Claudius; the pumpkin perhaps alludes to the latter's stupidity. It describes Claudius' arrival in heaven, the difficulty of finding out who he is because of his stammer, and the proposal of the deified emperor Augustus that he should be deported to the Underworld because of the murders he has committed. Here he meets his victims and is brought for trial before *Aeacus. Following Claudius' own system Aeacus hears the case against him and pronounces sentence without listening to the defence. Claudius is finally made clerk to one of his own freedmen.

Apollina'ris Sido'nius, see SIDONIUS.

Apo'llō (Apollon)

1. *In Greek myth.* The god Apollo was the son of *Zeus and *Leto, and twin brother of Artemis. The most characteristically Greek of all the gods, he embodied youthful but mature male beauty and moral excellence, and was associated especially with the beneficent aspects of civilization, giving to Greek culture its ideal of the beautiful, athletic, virtuous, and cultivated young man. Apollo was the god of plague but also of healing, of music (especially the lyre), archery (but not war, nor hunting), and prophecy; the god also of light (whence his epithet Phoebus, 'the bright'), sometimes identified with the sun. He was also associated with the care of flocks and herds, whence the epithet Nomios, 'of the pastures'. There is no certain occurrence of his name in the *Linear B tablets.

Apollo's first feat was to seize *Delphi for his abode; in doing so he destroyed the dragon Python, its guardian deity who personified the dark forces of the Underworld, an act he had to expiate by exile and purification. His 'fusion' with this earlier deity explains his title Apollo Pythios, 'Pythian Apollo'. Of his many loves, the most famous was that for Coronis, mother of *Asclepius. Others loved by Apollo include Cassandra, the Cumaean Sibyl, Cyrenē, Daphne, Hyacinthus, and Marpessa (see individual entries).

Apollo was not worshipped at Delphi before the eighth century BC. His origins are uncertain, but it is believed that he came either from somewhere north of Greece or from Asia. One of his most common epithets is Lykeios, and Homer's *Iliad* connects him with Lycia. Moreover, in that epic he is an enemy of the Greeks. There are also many oracles of Apollo in Asia Minor. But his Asian origin remains unproved. How and why he became a prophetic god in Greece is not known, but he is so from our earliest records. Delphi was the most important of his oracular shrines but those in Ionia at Branchidae and Claros were notable, and he had a famous shrine on the holy island of Delos. All Greece worshipped him and respected him. Apart from favouring Troy in the *Iliad*, Apollo was usually impartial in politics.

Notable departures from impartiality occurred when the Delphic Oracle began by supporting the Persians in the Persian Wars, and when it supported Sparta in the Peloponnesian War. The *Homeric Hymns to the Delian and the Pythian Apollo relate the story of his birth and of the founding of his Pythian temple. The *paean was traditionally sung to him.

2. *In Roman religion.* Apollo was introduced early into Italy, partly through Etruria and partly through the Greek settlements in Magna Graecia, but he was never properly identified with a Roman god. He was first introduced as a god of healing, but soon became prominent as a god of oracles and prophecy. In Virgil he figures in both these characters, but especially as the giver of oracles; the Cumaean Sibyl was his priestess. In Virgil's *Eclogues* Apollo appears also as the patron of poetry and music. The oldest temple to him in Rome was erected in 432 BC. For the games instituted in his honour see LUDI I (iv). His cult was further developed by the emperor Augustus, who took him as his special patron and erected to him a great temple on the Palatine.

Apollodō'rus, of Athens (flourished *c*.140 BC), the author of a long treatise in Greek prose 'On the gods', and of a 'Chronicle' (*Chronike syntaxis*), a chronological work of some importance, written in iambic trimeters, covering the period from the fall of Troy to 144 BC. Only fragments of these survive. He also wrote a *Bibliothekē*, a study of Greek heroic mythology, but the uncritical work that survives under this name was probably compiled in the first or second century AD.

Apollo'nius. I. **Apollonius Rhō'dius** (*c*.295–215 BC), Hellenistic Greek poet from Alexandria who spent the later part of his life in Rhodes. He was tutor to Ptolemy III Euergetēs and at some point head of the Alexandrian Library. Apollonius' main work, which survives, is the *Argonautica*, an epic on the story of Jason and the *Argonauts, narrating in four books the voyage of the *Argo* to Colchis by way of the Propontis and the Black Sea (books 1–2), the winning with Medea's aid of the Golden Fleece (book 3), and the return (to Iolcus in Thessaly) by the Danube, Po, Rhone, Mediterranean, and North Africa (book 4). This was the only epic before Virgil's *Aeneid* that could be compared with Homer in subject and extent, and the first epic to give a prominent place to love—Medea's for Jason. For the effect this had in subsequent writing the *Argonautica* holds a significant place in the history of European literature. Apollonius in true Hellenistic literary style combines poetry with scholarship and erudition, but he also excels in delicate psychological portrayal, and in this lies the perennial charm of book 3. The structure of the work as a whole has frequently been criticized, perhaps

undeservedly, but there are many individual scenes which are brilliantly contrived. A late and probably unreliable tradition tells of a quarrel between the poets Apollonius and *Callimachus which it represents as the consequence of a bitter controversy between writers of long traditional epics and writers of short and highly polished poems. Callimachus was said to have been victorious and Apollonius to have retired to Rhodes in consequence, but it was the long epic that continued in popularity. Apollonius was much admired in late antiquity and is one of the few Hellenistic poets whose work survived in medieval manuscripts.

2. **Apollonius of Pergē** in Pamphylia (active second half of the third century BC), mathematician, who founded the branch of geometry known as 'conics', the study of cones, and whose terminology and methods were accepted by all students of the subject. His work on conics largely survives (four books in Greek, three in Arabic, and one lost), though much on other topics has disappeared. *Hypatia wrote a (lost) commentary on the 'Conics'. In theoretical astronomy too Apollonius did work of fundamental importance, and among mathematicians in antiquity he ranks second only to Archimedes.

3. **Apollonius of Tya'na,** in Cappadocia (b. *c*.4 BC), a wandering Pythagorean philosopher and mystic who attained so great a fame by his wonder-working powers that divine honours were paid to him. He wrote a life of Pythagoras and other works, of which hardly anything has survived. His own life was written by *Philostratus.

4. **Apollonius Dy'scolus** ('bad-tempered') (second century AD), the author of several treatises which first placed Greek grammar on a scientific basis. He lived in poverty at Alexandria and wrote numerous works, only four of which survive, on the pronoun, conjunction, adverb, and syntax. His writings were much used by *Priscian. He was father of Aelius *Herodianus, who wrote on Greek accents.

5. **Apollonius of Tyre,** see NOVEL 2.

Apology of Socrates (*Apologia Sokratous*, 'speech in defence of Socrates').

I. The speech, as related by *Plato, made by *Socrates in the Athenian law-courts in answer to the charge of impiety that was brought against him. How far it represents the words actually used by Socrates is unknown.

Socrates distinguishes between previous vague accusations (that he speculated about physical questions, and made the worse cause appear the better) and the specific charge of impiety now brought by Meletus. On the former, he explains that he is neither a *sophist nor a natural philosopher; his only wisdom consists in knowing that he knows nothing. Instigated by an oracle, he has sought constantly to find a wiser man than himself, but has found none. He has gone to those who had a reputation for wisdom, and finding they had none has tried to convince them of his; this has provoked their enmity and given rise to these accusations. Socrates turns next to Meletus and cross-examines him on his particular charge. He then addresses the judges and declares himself unrepentant: he will persist in the practices complained of, for he must continue, in obedience to the divine voice, to preach the necessity of virtue. If they kill him, they will be injuring themselves, for he is the gadfly sent by the gods to stir Athens to life.

Socrates is convicted and the death penalty is proposed. The speech assumes a loftier tone. Why should he propose an alternative punishment? As a benefactor of Athens he ought to be rewarded. Imprisonment, exile, a fine, would certainly be evils, but as for death he does not know whether it is an evil or a good. Nevertheless he suggests a fine of thirty minas, which his friends will guarantee since he himself has no money. He is sentenced to death, and in his final words prophesies that many will arise after his death to condemn his judges. He comforts his friends with regard to his own fate, for death is either a dreamless sleep or a journey to a place of true justice, where he will be able to converse with Hesiod and Homer and the heroes. Nothing evil can happen to a good man; if he is to die, it must be better for him. He forgives his accusers and judges.

2. An account by *Xenophon of Socrates' defence in the same trial. At the time *Xenophon was taking part in the expedition of Cyrus (see ANABASIS), and he relies on the authority of Hermogenēs, a friend of Socrates who is mentioned in Plato's *Phaedo as present at the execution. This account is intended to bring out especially that Socrates was willing to die, not for the spiritual reasons given by Plato, in (1) above, but in order to escape the disabilities of old age. His pleas are here stated with less elaboration than by Plato.

apo'phradēs, unlucky days in the Greek calendar.

apparito'rēs, public servants, scribes and lictors, who attended Roman magistrates. They were generally freedmen or sons of freedmen and received a salary from the state.

appeal (in Roman law, *appellatio, provocatio*). The right of appeal against a capital sentence at Rome dates from a *lex Valeria* (Valerian law) of 300 BC. During the second century BC the right was extended to citizens outside Rome. There was no appeal against the judgement of a private judge in civil cases until the end of the republic. Thereafter appeal was allowed, to the magistrate who appointed the trial judge and eventually to the emperor.

Appendix Virgilia'na, collection of short Latin poems mostly dating from *Virgil's lifetime or soon after, ascribed to Virgil in late antiquity but of very doubtful authenticity. The collection comprises the following:

Catalepton, ('on a small scale'), fourteen epigrams, perhaps identical with the *Epigrammata* attributed to Virgil by Donatus and Servius; a few are possibly authentic. The title had been used earlier by *Aratus for a collection of short poems.

Ciris, an *epyllion of Alexandrian inspiration relating the story of Scylla, daughter of Nisus. Ciris is the mythical bird into which Scylla was changed. The poem contains Virgilian verses and phrases often inappropriately adapted to a new context. Not by Virgil.

Cōpa ('dancing girl'), a short elegiac poem containing phrases from Virgil and Propertius, describing with a lively vigour and charm a tavern girl who dances to castanets to entertain her customers. Not by Virgil.

Culex ('gnat'), a poem in hexameters telling the story of a shepherd who kills a gnat that has saved his life. The ghost of the gnat later appears to the shepherd, reproaches him, and describes the Underworld. Though this poem was widely believed in antiquity to be by Virgil it is a later pastiche of Virgilian phrases.

Dirae, transmitted as one hexameter poem in the manuscripts but usually edited as two: *Dirae,* 'furies', in which a farmer curses the soldiers who have dispossessed him of his farm, and *Lydia,* in which the poet laments in pastoral style his separation from his mistress. Neither is by Virgil.

Elegies on Maecenas, two elegies on *Maecenas' death, handed down in the manuscripts as one continuous poem.

Moretum, 'the salad', a realistic and only mildly mock-heroic poem in hexameters about a farmer's preparation of a meal, much in the spirit of the *Georgics.* It vividly describes the farmer rising early on a winter morning, lighting his fire, grinding his corn in a hand-mill, collecting from the garden the ingredients for his salad and preparing his meal; then starting for his day's work at the plough. Not by Virgil.

Priapea, three small poems ascribed to Virgil among a collection of eighty addressed to the god *Priapus, not by Virgil but made in the reign of Augustus.

Aetna, see the entry AETNA.

A'ppian (Appianos), of Alexandria (flourished *c.* AD 160). He practised as a lawyer in Rome and compiled narratives in Greek of the various Roman conquests from the earliest times to the accession of Vespasian, in twenty-four books. Of these, nine books survive complete and there are portions of others. The most valuable are books 13–17 which describe the civil wars between 146 and 70 BC.

Appian Way, see ROADS 2.

A'ppius Claudius, consul in 451 BC; see CLAU-
DIUS (1).

A'ppius Claudius Caecus, famous Roman
*censor (312–308 BC); see CLAUDIUS (2).

Apple of Discord, see ERIS.

Apsy'rtus, in Greek myth, brother of *Medea.

Apule'ius, Lucius (flourished *c.* AD 155), author
of the only Latin novel that survives entire. He
was born at Madaura in Africa, on the borders
of Numidia and Gaetulia. On a journey to
Alexandria, when a young man, he fell ill,
was nursed by a rich widow named Aemilia
Pudentilla, and married her. Her relatives
brought an action against him on the charge of
having won her by the use of magic. His
Apologia or speech for the defence survives.
From this we learn that he had inherited a
considerable fortune but had wasted it, that he
was deeply interested in natural science, and that
the accusation of magic was founded on trivial
grounds. That Apuleius was in fact much
interested in magic appears from many passages
of his novel, the *Metamorphoses* (see below). He
was acquitted and subsequently settled at Carthage, from where he travelled among the
African towns, lecturing in Latin on philosophy.
We possess a collection, perhaps made by a later
admirer, of excerpts from these lectures, under
the name *Florida* ('anthology'). Two populariza-
tions of Platonic philosophy are attributed to
him, *De dogmate Platonis* ('On the beliefs of
Plato') and *De deo Socratis* ('On the god of
Socrates'), as well as a free translation (*De
mundo*, 'On the world') of the *Peri kosmou*
attributed falsely to Aristotle.

The work for which he is famous is his
Metamorphoses or *Golden Ass*, a Latin romance in
eleven books. A version of the same story also
exists in Greek, *Loukios e onos*, 'Lucius or the
Ass', doubtfully attributed to *Lucian; both
works probably derive from the *Metamorphoses*
of an unknown Lucius. This original was
remodelled by Apuleius and enlarged by many
incidental tales.

The romance takes the form of a narrative
recounted in the first person by a young man
named Lucius, a Greek, whose adventures begin
with a visit to Thessaly, the reputed home of
sorceries and enchantments. There, while being
too curious about the black art, he is accidentally
turned into an ass, falls into the hands of
robbers, and becomes an unwilling and much-
beaten partaker in their exploits. Some of the
robber stories are excellent, but the most
beautiful and famous of the stories embedded
in the novel is the exquisite tale of Cupid and
*Psyche. After many vicissitudes, in the course
of which he serves one of the strange bands of
wandering priests of *Cybele, and becomes a

famous performing ass, Lucius is transformed
back into human shape by the favour of the
goddess *Isis, and appears to become Apuleius
the author himself. The last portion of the work
refers to his initiation into the mysteries of Isis
and Osiris and bears witness to the interest
shown in his day to oriental religions. The many
realistic details that he gives vividly illuminate
the popular life of his time. The style of the
novel resembles the exuberantly Asianic style
of oratory (see ORATORY 1), with vocabulary
drawn from a variety of registers, archaic,
poetic, Greek, and colloquial. The baroque
effect is fascinating and moving.

Apu'lia, region of south-east Italy, modern
Puglia. Its dry but fertile soil was excellent for
sheep-rearing and Apulian wool was famous.
The region was extensively Hellenized. In the
late fourth century BC it became subject to
Rome and remained loyal against *Pyrrhus. In
the *Punic and *Social Wars however many
Apulians revolted and Apulia was much devastated in consequence. Wolves were common in
the wilder parts.

Aquae Sulis, modern Bath, the tribal capital of
the Belgae in Britain. The hot springs were
developed from the end of the first century AD
and a temple to Sulis Minerva was built, of
which fragments remain. Many inscriptions
record the presence of visitors from Britain and
abroad at this health resort. In Saxon times the
site was deserted, the ruins being described in an
eighth-century poem.

aqueducts (Lat. *aquae*, 'waters'), one of Rome's
greatest contributions to architecture and public
amenity, the structures built to supply Rome
and other cities of the Roman empire with
water. Whereas Greek cities were usually
supplied with water from their numerous
natural springs, often elaborated into artificial
fountains, early Rome had only the river Tiber
and wells sunk in the city, and it was the
unwholesomeness and inadequacy of these supplies that led to the development of aqueducts to
bring large quantities of pure water from the
distant hills. The water was carried as far as
possible underground, in stone-built channels
lined with a special cement. There were
frequent inspection points, and the conduits had
to be kept clear of deposits. Open channels on
substructures of solid masonry or arches were
for the most part used only on the approach to
the city. The channels were built with a more or
less uniform gentle gradient. Pipes were also
used occasionally for parts of the route, allowing
water to be carried across intervening low
ground, as well as for the distribution system in
the city; according to their situation and size
they might be made of terracotta, lead, wood,
or leather.

Our detailed knowledge of the aqueducts of

Rome is derived from the book *De aquis urbis Romae* by *Frontinus, who was in charge of the Roman aqueducts in the late first century AD. He expressed a natural pride in these practical contributions made by Rome to architecture: 'With so many indispensable structures for so many aqueducts, compare, if you will, the idle pyramids or the useless, though famous, works of the Greeks' (*De aquis* 1. 6). In his day there were nine; when Rome fell to Alaric in AD 410 there were eleven. Rome's first two aqueducts were both tunnelled underground: they were the *Aqua Appia*, 18 km. (11 miles) long, built in 312 BC by the censor Appius *Claudius Caecus who also built Rome's first great road, and the *Anio Vetus* (named after the river Anio, now Aniene, its source), about 70 km. (44 miles) long, built 272–269 BC and paid for with booty captured from Pyrrhus. The third aqueduct, the *Aqua Marcia* built by command of the senate 144–140 BC, was the first to carry water on long arched sections. This was one of Rome's most important aqueducts, almost 100 km. (62 miles) long with 11 km. (7 miles) above ground. Its excellent cold water made good the deficiencies of the almost undrinkable *Anio Vetus*. The *Aqua Tepula* was built in 125 BC, the *Aqua Julia* in 33 BC by M. *Agrippa. In 19 BC he constructed the *Aqua Virgo* to supply his baths in the Campus Martius. The emperor Augustus built the *Aqua Alsietina* in 2 BC, its water so bad that it can only have been intended for gardens and for the mock sea-battles he staged in the amphitheatre. The two most magnificent aqueducts were the *Aqua Claudia*, AD 47, and the *Anio Novus*, AD 52, built by the emperor Claudius. The *Anio Novus* was 95 km. (59 miles) long and the highest of the aqueducts, some of its arches being over 30 m. (98 ft.) high. Near Rome these two aqueducts were united to form two channels on the same arches, the *Claudia* below and the *Anio Novus* above. Further aqueducts built at Rome were the *Aqua Traiana* (by the emperor Trajan) in 109 and the *Aqua Alexandrina* (by the emperor Alexander Severus) in 226. There were also important aqueducts in the provinces, the most striking being the Pont du Gard near Nemausus (Nîmes) in southern France.

The aqueducts were vastly expensive to build and maintain, and the works were usually a liability to the community. Under the republic the *aediles were mainly responsible for the water supply; during the empire a large staff was employed to see to the efficient maintenance of the system. The whole water-course through the aqueducts was public property; when the water arrived it was stored in reservoir buildings, *castella*, and piped thence to public fountains, baths, and private consumers, who paid a rent for the privilege. In early times all water was applied to public purposes, and citizens were allowed for private use only the water that leaked from flaws in the pipes. Later, citizens were allowed to rent a water supply by inserting a branch pipe into the main. Under the empire private reservoirs were allowed which supplied the cisterns in the houses renting a supply, and a complicated administration came into existence to prevent householders from defrauding the state.

A'quilo (Gk. Boreas), the north wind; see WINDS.

Aquī'nas, Thomas, see TEXTS, TRANSMISSION OF ANCIENT 7.

Arabia. The name Arabia was first applied to the desert region on the northern coast of the Arabian peninsula that lies east of the Nile delta and merges with Syria. Later it was extended to the whole peninsula. The Greeks and Romans were familiar with this area and with the eastern shore of the Arabian Gulf, and their knowledge was increased after the exploratory voyages of Alexander's admirals in the later part of the fourth century BC. The interior however always remained unknown. Arabia was regarded by the ancients as the land of spices and proverbially rich. It had vast stretches of desert grass fragrant with aromatic herbs, which also provided pasturage for its famous horses, and the fruitful terraced districts near the west coast grew balsam, aloe, myrrh, and frankincense. But Arabia stood on many trade routes and many of her exports—spices and precious stones—came from India or lands further east. When Egypt came under Roman rule in the first century AD the Romans traded directly with southern Arabia and India, and the old 'incense route' to the north diminished in importance. In the seventh century AD occurred the sudden movement that became the Arab conquest of the Near East, Egypt, North Africa, and Spain, begun by Mahomet in 622, checked by the Arab defeat at Constantinople in 717 but not ceasing to be a political force until the tenth century. The flowering of Arab culture that accompanied the movement left a legacy in Europe, particularly in Spain, while the Arabs themselves absorbed much from Greek philosophy and played a part in its survival (see ARISTOTLE 5 and TEXTS, TRANSMISSION OF ANCIENT 3 and 7).

Ara'chnē ('spider'), in Greek myth, a woman of Lydia who challenged the goddess Athena to a contest in weaving. She depicted in her web the amours of the gods, and Athena, angered at her presumption and choice of subject, tore the web to pieces and beat the weaver. Arachne in despair hanged herself, but Athena turned her into a spider.

Ara Ma'xima ('greatest altar'), the altar of *Hercules at Rome, which stood in the *Forum Boarium. It was here that, as related by Virgil in the *Aeneid* (book 8), Aeneas found *Evander sacrificing. The spot was connected with the legend of Hercules and *Cacus. Tithes of booty and commercial profits, etc., were offered at the altar.

Ara Pācis ('altar of peace'), in the Campus Martius at Rome, constructed during the years 13–9 BC by order of the senate to commemorate the safe return of the emperor Augustus from Gaul in the former year. The walls of the small court surrounding the altar were covered with beautiful sculptures, most notably including a representation of the procession on the day it was consecrated (4 July 13 BC), with portraits of Augustus' family and other leading citizens. The whole monument has now been reconstructed (under cover) with most of its surviving sculptures incorporated.

Ara'tus. 1. A Greek perhaps from Soli in Cilicia (c.315–c.240 BC), who came to Athens and subsequently spent part of his life at the court of *Antigonus Gonatas, king of Macedon; there he wrote hymns for the king's marriage. His best known work, and the only one still extant, is a didactic poem, the *Phaenomena* ('astronomy'), in 1,154 hexameters, describing with elegant clarity and little mythological allusion the relative positions of the chief stars and constellations, and their risings and settings; it is based on a prose treatise of the same name by the mathematician and astronomer *Eudoxus of Cnidus. The last 400 lines of the poem, dealing with meteorology, were sometimes given the separate title *Diosemeia*, 'weather signs'. This part was derived from a similar work, perhaps by Theophrastus. The *Phaenomena* achieved immediate fame, which it enjoyed until the end of antiquity, and found many commentators. Its language is Homeric Greek but the thought is consistently Stoic. It was translated into Latin by Cicero in his youth, and the latter part of it also by *Germanicus and *Avienus. Cicero's translation is thought to have had considerable influence on the style of Lucretius. Other poems were ascribed to Aratus but have not survived. The apostle Paul, who also came from Cilicia, quotes from the *Phaenomena* when preaching to the Athenians (Acts 17: 28).

2. Of Sicyon, general of the *Achaean Confederacy.

Arbē'la, town in Assyria; near it was fought in 331 BC the battle of Gaugamela (sometimes called the battle of Arbela) in which Alexander the Great finally overthrew Darius. See ALEXANDER (2) 4.

arbitration (Gk. *diaita*, Lat. *arbitrium*). The submission of a dispute, public or private, to the judgement of a neutral party was practised by the Greeks from very early times. Our knowledge of its details, which is fullest in respect of Athens, comes mainly from inscriptions. Its influence was greatest in inter-state relations,

and some notable cases are almost legendary, as the arbitration of Sparta in the dispute between Athens and Megara for possession of Salamis in the time of Solon, c.600 BC. By the mid-fifth century BC peace treaties normally had a clause requiring both parties to submit to arbitration in the event of a dispute, and arbitration became a recognized and frequent means of averting wars. For arbitration in private law-suits see LAW, AT ATHENS 3.

When Rome became a power in the Hellenistic world the senate took over the role of the kings who had often acted as arbitrators in disputes between Greek cities and leagues. At first Rome did not enforce acceptance of her awards. However, with the expansion of the Roman empire the international character of arbitration disappeared: the subject peoples could turn nowhere but to Rome; arbitration entered the sphere of provincial administration and became the duty of special commissioners.

arboriculture. After the Persian Wars, and particularly in the Hellenistic age, Greece (and later Rome) cultivated many trees for their fruit: apple, pear, cherry, and plum; fig and date; pistachio, carob, walnut, and almond. Under the Roman empire these fruits spread over the known world, as far as climate permitted. The cultivation of fig and date were of economic importance to the African and eastern parts of the Mediterranean world, including Greece, from Minoan times. The shortage of timber around much of the Mediterranean was partially remedied by plantations in Attica and elsewhere. Under the Roman empire state plantations were established and private plantations encouraged.

Arca'dia, region of Greece in the centre of the Peloponnese, very mountainous, especially in the north. The most prosperous parts were the eastern plains of Orchomenus, Mantinea, and Tegea. Among its rivers were *Alpheus, *Stymphalus, and *Styx. It was a land of villages and so was of little direct importance in Greek politics, although *Mantinea and *Tegea were involved in Spartan expansion, particularly in the fifth century BC. Its chief strength lay in its man-power. Under *Epaminondas an Arcadian confederacy was formed in the fourth century BC against Sparta (see MEGALOPOLIS) and it later joined the *Achaean Confederacy. Arcadia's isolated geographical position is the reason for several of its distinctive features. The inhabitants regarded themselves as the most ancient people of Greece. Their dialect, which is not seen in extant literature and is known only from inscriptions, closely resembles that of Cyprus, an area similarly cut off from later Greek influences, and is consequently known as Arcado-Cypriot (see DIALECTS, GREEK). It seems to be closest to Mycenaean Greek, a fact which suggests that Arcadia, with its mountainous and

inaccessible countryside, remained largely un-
penetrated by invading Dorians (see DORIAN
INVASION). Arcadia also preserves remarkable
myths and cults; the gods Hermes and Pan are
particularly connected with the country. According to one tradition Zeus was born on
Mount Lycaeus (see LYCAON). Through *Evander, said to have been an Arcadian, Arcadia is
connected with the origins of Rome. A famous
temple of Apollo was built at Bassae. The
idealized picture of the pastoral life of Arcadia,
the home of Pan, is due to the Roman poet
Virgil, who made it the setting of *bucolic
poetry (see ECLOGUES). The Latin tag familiar
from seventeenth-century pastoral paintings, et in
Arcadia ego, often translated as 'I too ⟨have lived⟩
in Arcadia', may more correctly mean 'I ⟨am
found⟩ in Arcadia as well', and refer to death.

Arcesila'us or **Arce'silas.** 1. The name of
many of the ruling dynasty of *Cyrene in
North Africa, which ruled from the foundation
of the colony (c.630 BC) for some 200 years.
     2. Of Pitanē in Aeolis, see ACADEMY.

Archaic age, name given to one of the five
periods of the Greek era (defined on the basis of
pottery styles). It begins c.620 BC and ends in
480. Compare PROTO-GEOMETRIC, GEOMETRIC,
ORIENTALIZING, and CLASSICAL. The term Archaic age is sometimes used more widely to
describe the period from c.750 to 480 BC.

Archelā'us, king of Macedon c.413–399 BC; see
MACEDONIA 1.

archers. In Homer the heroes did not usually
use the bow in war, but the ordinary soldiers
did. By historical times the bow and arrow were
no longer used as weapons of war in Greece,
except in Crete, though Persian archers were
greatly feared. Cretan archers were often used as
mercenaries and Scythian archers were employed in fifth-century Athens as a police force,
with additional recruits from the poorer citizens. More use was made of archers in the armies of the Hellenistic age. The Roman army too
used detachments of archers, but they were usually recruited from Crete or the allies. See ARMY.

archetype, see TEXTUAL CRITICISM.

Archidā'mus, see ISOCRATES.

Archi'lochus, Greek poet from the island of
Paros, who lived probably around the mid-
seventh century BC and wrote short poems in a
variety of metres, elegiac, iambic, and trochaic.
Little is known of his life; he took part in the
colonization of Thasos and fought there, and
was reputedly killed in a battle between Paros
and Naxos. His poetry survives only in the
quotations of later writers and some papyrus
fragments. Ancient tradition says that he fell in
love with Neobulē, daughter of Lycambes, but
her father forbade the marriage, and Archi-

lochus avenged himself with such biting satires
that father and daughter hanged themselves.
Some lines of his verse seem to confirm the
existence of Neobulē; one poem recovered from
a papyrus vividly recounts the poet's seduction
of her younger sister. Other fragments confirm
his ancient reputation for being an innovator in
metre, language, and subject matter. His *iambic poems in particular show a great variety of
tone—mockery, enthusiasm, melancholy, and a
mordant wit. The poems are remarkable for
their strongly personal note. His self-consciously
anti-heroic epigram on the shield he left behind
in battle had a considerable literary following
(see ALCAEUS (1) and HORACE; a fragment
suggests that even Anacreon had a similar
experience). See also SYMPOSIUM.

Archimē'dēs (c.287–212 BC), born at Syracuse,
son of an astronomer Pheidias, the greatest
mathematician of antiquity, an astronomer,
physicist, and inventor. He probably studied at
Alexandria and subsequently lived at the court
of Hieron II, tyrant of Syracuse, where he was
killed at the capture of the city by the Romans
under Marcellus. Popular history (see Plutarch's
Life of Marcellus) knew him as the inventor of
marvellous machines which helped to postpone
the fall of Syracuse, and other devices such as the
screw for raising water and the compound
pulley. It attributed to him the boast, 'Give me a
place to stand, and I will move the earth', and
the exclamation 'eureka' ('I have found it') when
he discovered how to test (by specific gravity)
whether base metal had been introduced into
Hieron's gold crown, after observing in his bath
the displacement of water by his body.
     Cicero, who was quaestor in Sicily in 75 BC,
discovered the tomb of Archimedes near one of
the gates of Syracuse, overgrown with brambles
and forgotten. By Archimedes' own wish it was
marked by a column depicting a cylinder
circumscribing a sphere, which recalled his
discovery that their volumes were in the ratio 3 : 2.
     In his breadth and freedom of vision Archi-
medes ranks as one of the greatest mathematicians of all time. In his work called the Sand-reckoner he
describes a system for expressing very large
numbers verbally in Greek when the language
stops at a myriad, 10,000 (10,000 × 10,000 becomes 'a second myriad' and so on). He showed
that he understood the nature of a numerical
system as no one else did in antiquity. A number of
his treatises survive on various topics including the
circle, the sphere, and the cylinder, and notably on
hydrostatics, a science which Archimedes invented. Two more of his works survive only in
Arabic.

architecture
1. Greek. The earliest forms known to us are
found in the remains of the *Mycenaean age
dating from the sixteenth to the twelfth
centuries BC, where the most characteristic

feature is the construction of palaces surrounded by so-called Cyclopean fortification walls built of huge polygonal blocks of stone fitted together. The nucleus of the palace complex is the megaron, 'hall', a structure whose history goes back to Neolithic times. In the Mycenaean palaces it consists of a portico, a vestibule, and a main room with a circular low hearth in the centre surrounded by four columns supporting the roof. All other subsidiary rooms and corridors lead off from the megaron. The columns were made of wood and tapered. The post-and-lintel method of spanning openings was mainly used, though the beehive-shaped tombs were constructed with horizontal courses of stone which gradually came together to form a vault, and passages were roofed with the inverted-V arch. With the decline of the Mycenaean civilization, architecture in Greece was reduced to very simple materials and forms. Its subsequent re-emergence was based on the temple rather than the great house or palace. The earliest Greek *temples, of brick and timber construction, appear to date from the latter part of the ninth century BC. Religious architecture developed during the next three centuries, not only in Greece proper (especially at Delphi and Olympia) but also in Asia Minor (notably in the temples of Artemis at *Ephesus and of *Hera at Samos) and in Magna Graecia and Sicily (especially Selinus and Acragas). In the temples of the sixth century BC monumental architecture reached a high level. It culminated in the fifth century in such temples as those of Aphaia in Aegina, of Bassae in the Peloponnese, and particularly in the group of temples erected on the *Acropolis of Athens in the second half of the fifth century, the *Parthenon, the *Erechtheum, and the temple of *Athena Nikē. The great architects of this period were Callicratēs and Ictinus, architects of the Parthenon, and Mnesiclēs, of the *Propylaea.

Temples were built on platforms approached by steps. The width was generally about half the length, but there was great variety in the proportions, the arrangement of columns, and the details of design. Temples can be distinguished by the number of columns at the end façades (front and back), for example 'hexastyle' having six columns, 'decastyle' ten; a temple completely surrounded by a peristyle, i.e. a covered colonnade with a single row of columns, is known as 'peripteral'. It was in the treatment of these outer colonnades that the famous orders of architecture were evolved. There were three orders in Greek architecture, defining styles which were based essentially on the form of the column.

(i) The Doric style was the oldest, evolved during the seventh century BC and appearing first at Corinth, and it was the normal style of mainland Greece, Sicily, and Magna Graecia. The column of the Doric order had no base but rose directly from the floor, tapering slightly from about a quarter of the way up and having a ratio of height to maximum diameter in the region of five or six. It had wide, shallow flutings (usually twenty in number), and was surmounted by a capital consisting of a basin-shaped circular moulding and a plain, square slab. On the capitals rested the entablature, of which the lowest member was the architrave, a rectangular beam of stone stretching from column to column. Above this was the frieze, divided into triglyphs, surfaces cut by vertical grooves into three parts, and *metopes, square panels set back from the triglyphs and decorated with sculpture. Above the frieze was a projecting cornice; at the ends of a ridge roof there were also two raking cornices, the three enclosing a triangular panel (the tympanum) to form the pediment.

(ii) The Ionic style developed in Ionia and the Aegean islands in the late sixth century BC. In the Ionic order the column was more slender, with a ratio of height to maximum diameter of about eight or nine, and deeper flutes (normally twenty-four). It stood on a base, and the capital was decorated with volutes (spiral scrolls). In place of the Doric triglyph frieze was a row of small projecting blocks, the dentils, but sometimes also a continuous decorated frieze.

(iii) The Corinthian order was essentially a development of the Ionic. Introduced in the later part of the fifth century, the column and entablature remained as in Ionic but the capital was of an inverted bell shape decorated with acanthus leaves. Imported to Rome, the Corinthian became the great imperial order.

In the finest temples certain refinements to please the eye were introduced: horizontal lines were given a slight upward curve; the columns had a slight inward inclination and entasis, or convex outline, and those at the corners had small variations in diameter and spacing. Many other forms of Greek building, however, remained rudimentary until comparatively late. The unroofed *theatre and the open *stadium and *gymnasium were still simple in form in the fifth century BC, and houses were unpretentious in plan and construction. The building material most commonly used was unbaked brick on a stone foundation, even for city walls. Some city walls and important temples were of solid stone, and in the fifth century fine marbles were increasingly used where available, with closely fitted joints and polished surfaces. An important feature of later Greek public architecture was the *stoa.

2. *Roman*. The Romans took over from the Greeks the traditional building forms of the temple and the stoa (which led to the *basilica), as well as some decorative features. These they transformed into buildings of impressive grandeur through their own particular architectural innovations: the arch, and concrete. Concrete

appeared late in the third century BC and, being lighter and cheaper, began to replace ashlar. Its properties allowed an architecture in which much larger areas could be roofed than by any form of stone construction, and which also took advantage of its fireproof and damp-resistant qualities (as in monumental baths, for example). It allowed the Romans to build *amphitheatres which did not rely for support on the natural contours of the site, or on an earth-filled solid foundation, but rested on a substructure consisting of a network of passages. It also enabled them to use the principle of the arch to develop, by the time of the emperor Augustus, the vaulted roof and the dome; of the latter there is an early surviving example at Baiae, but the most spectacular is that of the *Pantheon. Bricks were used as a facing for concrete; so also were marble, wall-mosaics, and moulded stucco, with the result that the decorative appearance of a structure increasingly concealed its function: this was true of interiors in particular. Exteriors, on the other hand, were sometimes comparatively plain. The new features in the architecture of the early empire are embodied in such buildings as Nero's *Golden House, Domitian's palace on the Palatine, and Hadrian's villa at Tivoli, characterized by their inner light and sense of space. Typical of the period also was the triumphal arch, erected in isolation as a monument, which became a symbol of Roman conquest. The first commemorative arches at Rome were erected by L. Stertinius in 196 BC, but it was not until the empire that these monuments became a conspicuous feature.

To the three orders of Greek architecture (see 1 above) the Romans added in the early empire a fourth, the 'composite', a combination of Ionic and Corinthian.

architheō'ria, see LITURGY.

archons (*archontĕs*), name given in most Greek states including Athens to the holders of the highest office, who had wide judicial as well as executive duties. When Athens ceased to be ruled by kings (supposedly in the eleventh century BC; see CODRUS), the government devolved by gradual degrees upon three archons elected from the aristocracy, at first for ten years but from 683 BC for only one year; after 487 BC the one-year appointments were made by lot.

The archons were: (i) the *archon basileus*, 'king archon', who took over the religious duties of the former kings; he was responsible for the ancient religious ceremonies, in particular the *mysteries, the *Lenaea, and the *Anthesteria, and presided over the council of the *Areopagus; (ii) the polemarch (*polemarchos*), whose original function was to command the army but who lost this power to the *strategoi* after 487 but when the archonship was decided by lot; he took over certain religious duties and legal functions concerning persons who were not Athenian citizens; (iii) the eponymous archon (*archon eponymos*), so called because his year of office was known and identified by his name. The eponymous archon was the chief magistrate until 487 BC, and always remained the nominal head of state. His legal duties were the widest and included the protection of all property and of the family; he also directed the festivals of the *Panathenaia and the *Dionysia. The political struggles of the seventh and sixth centuries centred upon elections to this office, but after 487 it was no longer coveted by the politically ambitious.

At some time in the seventh century six *thesmothetai*, 'legislators', were added as additional archons whose duties were mainly legal, and who presided as magistrates over many types of lawsuit. *Solon at the beginning of the sixth century BC made the office of archon open to the two highest census-classes in the state, thus making the qualification one of property rather than birth. After 457 the office was opened to the third census-class, and no one of lower property qualification was in practice excluded. Ex-archons entered the Areopagus as life-members, a fact which added importance to their office in early times but ceased to be significant when they were appointed by lot, because then the Areopagus too lost its political importance.

Archȳ'tas, of Tarentum (flourished *c*.400 BC), Pythagorean philosopher and mathematician, interested in music and mechanics, and a friend of Plato. He was also a military commander and repeatedly led the forces of his city in successful campaigns. Among his inventions were the screw, the pulley, and the rattle, and he is said to have solved (by geometry) the problem of the proportion between the sides of two cubes having the volume ratio two. Some fragments of his mathematical works survive. He figures in an ode of Horace (I. 28), where he is addressed as a 'sand-reckoner' (compare ARCHIMEDES).

Arcti'nus, see AETHIOPIS, EPIC CYCLE, and ILIUPERSIS.

Arctu'rus, see BOOTES.

Areopagī'ticus, see ISOCRATES.

Areo'pagus (Areios pagos), the 'hill of Arēs' at Athens, west of the Acropolis and separated from it by a depression; also the name of the ancient council that met on it. According to legend, it was so called because there Ares was tried by the gods and acquitted of the murder of Halirrhothios, Poseidon's son, who had raped Ares' daughter at that place. Again according to legend, as found in the *Eumenides* of Aeschylus (see ORESTEIA), it was there that Orestes was tried for the murder of his mother Clytemnestra, the goddess Athena having referred the case to a tribunal of Athenian citizens.

Originally the council known as the Areopagus must have existed to advise the king, and was composed exclusively of *Eupatridae, aristocrats. Its influence increased as the monarchy declined until in the seventh century it was virtually the government. After the reforms of *Solon its membership was recruited from all ex-*archons, who remained members for life, and who now represented the wealthy as opposed to the merely aristocratic elements, so that it became a less exclusive body. Its constitutional powers were redefined and to some extent limited by *Cleisthenes, but it remained powerful down to the Persian Wars. With the rapid advance of democratic institutions its great powers seemed out of place. It may have declined in prestige as it declined in political power after 487 BC, when the archons were appointed by lot and it was no longer men of the greatest ability who were recruited. In 462 *Ephialtes deprived it of its 'guardianship of the laws' and circumscribed its jurisdiction. It remained the court for murder trials but lost all political importance. It was still in existence in the fourth century AD.

The term *boulē, 'council', usually refers to a second body which was distinct from the Areopagus and dated from the time of Cleisthenes, although it has also been thought that Solon created a second council at the time when he reformed the Areopagus.

Ārēs, in Greek myth, the only son of *Zeus and his wife *Hera, the god of war or, rather, of warlike frenzy. He is of no great importance in mythology, although he is one of the twelve Olympian gods, and plays no very glorious part in the stories in which he appears. He is a stirrer of strife, unchivalrous, and does not always have the advantage in encounters with mortals (see for example OTUS AND EPHIALTES); nor does he ever develop into a god with a moral function, like Zeus or Apollo. He is frequently associated with the goddess *Aphroditē, wife of Hephaestus, and she bore him *Harmonia. Their amorous intrigue was the subject of a tale told at the Phaeacian court by the bard Demodocus in Homer's *Odyssey*. The Romans identified him with *Mars, a god of greater dignity and importance. See also AREOPAGUS.

Arē'tē, in Homer's *Odyssey*, the wife of Alcinous, king of the Phaeacians.

A'rethas, see BYZANTINE AGE and TEXTS, TRANSMISSION OF ANCIENT 3.

Arethū'sa (Arethousa). **1.** One of the *Hesperides.

2. A spring on the island of Ortygia, in the harbour of Syracuse. According to legend the river-god *Alpheus fell in love with the nymph Arethusa when she bathed in his stream in Arcadia. She fled from him to Ortygia and was changed into a fountain (by Artemis, in one version); but Alpheus flowed under the sea to Ortygia to be united with the fountain. It was believed in antiquity that there was a real connection between the two and that a cup thrown into the river would be recovered from the spring.

arge'i, bundles of rushes, made to resemble men bound hand and foot, which according to Ovid were carried from 'shrines of the *argei*' to the Tiber on 14 May in each year by a procession of *pontifices, *Vestal Virgins, the priestess of Jupiter, and the magistrates, and thrown into the river from the *Pons Sublicius by the Vestal Virgins. There were twenty-seven of the shrines throughout the city; perhaps that number was thought particularly lucky, being the cube of three. The meaning of the rite is disputed. The *argei* may have been offerings to the river-god to pacify him and induce him to tolerate the bridge across his stream, or a substitute for human sacrifice in times of acute famine; such a sacrifice is said to have been performed in 440 BC. There seems to have been a saying at Rome which refers to this practice: *sexagenarios de ponte*, 'off the bridge with the 60-year-olds'.

Argēs, one of the *Cyclopes.

Argīlē'tum, at Rome, district north-east of the Forum, between the Esquiline and the Quirinal hills. It was occupied by artisans and shopkeepers, including booksellers and shoemakers.

Arginu'sae (Arginousai), small islands south of Lesbos, off which in 406 BC the Athenian fleet heavily defeated that of Sparta, capturing or destroying seventy Spartan ships. The Athenians lost twenty-five ships whose crews were not rescued owing to bad weather. It was thought at Athens that insufficient efforts had been made to take up the dead and save the wounded and drowning, and the blame was laid on the eight generals who had been present. Two of them fled; the remaining six were condemned to death by the assembly in a wave of popular anger, sentence being pronounced on all the accused together instead of each being judged, as was constitutional, separately. These were executed, including Pericles, son of the great statesman, and Thrasyllus (see also THERAMENES and THRASYBULUS (2)). Socrates, one of the presidents of the assembly (*prytaneis*) at the time, bravely opposed the illegality of the proceedings.

Argonau'tica, see APOLLONIUS (I), VALERIUS FLACCUS, and VARRO ATACINUS.

A'rgonauts (Argonautai), in Greek myth, the heroes who sailed on the ship *Argo* with Jason to recover the Golden Fleece, and the subject of many stories. Jason was the son of Aeson (son of Cretheus and Tyro), who was the rightful king of Iolcus in Thessaly, but the throne had been usurped by Aeson's half-brother Pelias (son of the god Poseidon and of Tyro). Jason had been sent for safety and education to the centaur Chiron. Pelias had been warned that he would be killed by a descendant of Aeolus (see AEOLUS (2)) who would come to him wearing only one sandal. This prophecy was fulfilled when Jason, grown up, returned to Iolcus to claim his inheritance, having lost a sandal while carrying an old woman (the goddess Hera in disguise) across a river. Pelias promised to restore the throne to him if he would first recover the Golden Fleece. This was the fleece of the ram that had carried away Phrixus and Hellē (see ATHAMAS), and had been hung in the grove of Ares at Colchis, at the eastern end of the Black Sea, guarded by a dragon that never slept. Jason undertook the task, and embarked in the *Argo* at Pagasae with some fifty of the chief heroes of Greece. These must originally have come from Thessaly, the home of the *Minyans (as the Argonauts are often called), but later story-tellers added heroes from different times and traditions, such as Heracles. Heroes most generally said to have been on the expedition include Orpheus, Peleus, Telamon, the Dioscuri, Zetēs and Calais, Idas and Lynceus, Tiphys the helmsman, Argus, who built the ship, Admetus, Augeas, and Neleus' son Periclymenus. Acastus joined at the last moment. Many of the stories concern dangers which are overcome by the particular virtue of one hero or another (e.g. Polydeucēs by his boxing defeated *Amycus). For other adventures see HYLAS, HYPSIPYLE, PHINEUS, and SYMPLEGADES.

The expedition eventually reached Colchis, where the king Aeētēs expressed willingness to surrender the fleece if Jason would perform certain apparently impossible tasks. These included yoking to a plough a pair of fire-breathing bulls with bronze hooves, and ploughing a field and sowing it with teeth from *Cadmus' dragon; from these armed men would arise whose fury would be turned against Jason. With the help of the magic arts of *Medea, the king's daughter, who fell in love with Jason, the tasks were successfully accomplished, and Jason and Medea and the other Argonauts returned to Iolcus with the fleece. The account of the expedition now divides into several main variants describing adventures in many parts of the Mediterranean and Black Sea areas. Some stories have the Argonauts returning to Greece by sailing west along the stream of *Ocean, either to the north or the south, and entering the Mediterranean by the Pillars of Hercules. For the rest of Jason's story, see MEDEA. Jason was said to have died at Corinth, killed, according to one version, as he sat under the old *Argo* by a falling piece of her woodwork. For the subsequent adventures of Medea, see THESEUS.

The story of the Argonauts is one of the oldest Greek sagas, containing many elements from folk-tale including two of the most popular themes, that of sending a hero on a dangerous voyage to get rid of him, and that of confronting him with a series of difficult tasks, in which he is helped to success by an unexpected ally.

Argos, Greek city in the north-east Peloponnese 5 km. (3 miles) from the sea, on a site occupied since prehistoric and Mycenaean times. The name often signifies also the territory belonging to the city, sometimes called Argolis ('the Argolid'). In Homer the name is used to describe (i) the city, of which Diomedes was king, (ii) the kingdom of Agamemnon, who was Diomedes' overlord, and (iii) by extension the whole of the Peloponnese, as opposed to Hellas, i.e. Greece north of the Isthmus of Corinth. Hence the name 'Argives' in Homer frequently means 'Greeks'. In the stories of the *Dorian Invasion, Argos became the stronghold of Temenus, the eldest of the *Heracleidae. It probably retained leadership of the Peloponnese until challenged by Sparta in the seventh century BC. Argos defeated Sparta at the battle of Hysiae in 669, perhaps under the leadership of its king *Pheidon, a legendary figure to whom no certain date can be ascribed. However, the wide power which Argos won under Pheidon did not survive his death, and thereafter, largely influenced by jealousy of Sparta, Argos played a secondary and not always very glorious role in the history of Greece (see also CLEISTHENES (2)). At the time of the *Persian Wars its unfaithfulness to the Greek cause was concealed under a mask of neutrality. A democratic government was introduced and Argos allied itself with Athens against Sparta in 461 BC. In the first part of the *Peloponnesian War it remained neutral. In 420, after the Peace of Nicias and as a result of the efforts of Alcibiades, it joined Athens and shared the latter's defeat at Mantinea in 418. Argos sided with Philip II of Macedon and was one of the last cities to join the *Achaean Confederacy after a period of rule by tyrants.

The great Argive goddess was Hera, worshipped at the *Heraeum some 10 km. (6 miles) north of Argos. Argive sculptors were outstanding in the early classical period, notably *Polycleitus. For Argive myth see ADRASTUS.

Argus. 1. In Greek myth, the herdsman that Hera set to watch *Io, given the epithet Panoptēs because he had eyes all over his body; when Hermes killed him, Hera placed his eyes in the peacock's tail.

2. The craftsman who built the ship *Argo* (see ARGONAUTS).

3. In Homer's *Odyssey* (7. 292) the dog which recognizes its master Odysseus on his return and then dies.

Aria'dnē, in Greek myth, daughter of *Minos and Pasiphae. When *Theseus came to Crete she fell in love with him and gave him the thread by which he found his way out of the labyrinth after killing the Minotaur. He then fled, taking her with him, but abandoned her on the island of Dia (Naxos). There the god Dionysus found her, married her, and made her immortal.

Arian heresy, Arianism, heresy of the Christian church in the fourth century AD, named after its originator Arius, which denied the divinity of Christ. A compromise with orthodoxy was reached at a Council of 359, which led St *Jerome to describe that year as one in which 'the whole world groaned and marvelled to find itself Arian'. After that, support for the heresy declined sharply (though remaining strong among the Goths) and orthodoxy was re-established at the Council of Constantinople in 391. See also CONSTANTINE.

Ari'cia, town in a hollow of the Alban hills about 25 km. (16 miles) south-east of Rome. In a grove near the town was the famous seat of worship of the goddess *Diana.

Arimaspians, legendary people of the far north who were one-eyed, and fought with griffins who guarded a hoard of gold. They were supposedly written about by the poet *Aristeas of Proconnesus.

Arī'on. 1. Greek lyric poet, perhaps of the seventh century BC, said to have been born at Methymna in Lesbos, but largely a figure of legend. He is said to have been a pupil of the lyric poet *Alcman and to have spent the greater part of his life at the court of *Periander, tyrant of Corinth. He visited Italy where he amassed much wealth. On his return he was thrown overboard by the sailors, who wanted his treasure, but a dolphin, charmed by the song he had been allowed to sing before his death, carried him to land. To Arion was attributed the creation of the *dithyramb as a literary composition. He was also connected with the birth of tragedy, which perhaps means that his type of dithyramb helped eventually to produce tragedy. Nothing survives of his work.
2. Name of a legendary horse, the offspring of *Poseidon and Demeter. It belonged to the Argive hero *Adrastus and its speed enabled him to escape after the failure of his expedition against Thebes.

Ariovi'stus, chief of the Germanic Suebi, called into Gaul c.71 BC to assist a Gallic tribe in local warfare and then impossible to dislodge. The Roman senate acquiesced in his conquests but he was eventually routed by Julius Caesar in 58 BC and died soon after.

Aristae'us, in Greek myth, son of the god Apollo and the Thessalian nymph Cyrenē, whom Apollo carried off to the region in North Africa which bears her name. Aristaeus was a god of various kinds of husbandry, including bee-keeping, and of hunting. He fell in love with *Eurydicē who, trying to escape from him, trod on a serpent and died from its bite. The dryads avenged her by killing all his bees. According to Virgil (*Georgics* 4. 315), after this calamity Aristaeus, on his mother's advice, consulted the god Proteus, appeased the dryads and obtained new swarms from the carcasses of bulls. Aristaeus married Autonoē, daughter of Cadmus, and became the father of *Actaeon.

Arista'goras, tyrant of Miletus, the instigator of the Ionian revolt against Persia in 499 BC. See PERSIAN WARS.

Arista'rchus. 1. Of Samos (b. c.320 BC), an astronomer who is famous for hypothesizing that the earth revolves about the sun, and that it rotates about its own axis. His only extant treatise, however, presupposes a geocentric universe.
2. Of Samothrace (c.215–c.143 BC), head of the *Alexandrian Library from c.180 to c.145 BC and the originator of professional scholarship. He produced commentaries on Greek classical authors and treatises on particular topics, especially Greek grammar, scraps of which still survive in the ancient notes on classical authors which are found in some manuscripts (see SCHOLIUM). His most notable contribution to scholarship was his critical edition of Homer, followed by his editions of, or commentaries on, Hesiod, Archilochus, Alcaeus, Pindar, the tragedians, and Aristophanes, and among prose writers, Herodotus. His editions were accompanied by a full apparatus of critical signs (see TEXTS, TRANSMISSION OF ANCIENT I and HELLENISTIC AGE 6).

Ari'steas, of Proconnesus (an island in the Propontis), an early Greek traveller of, probably, the seventh century BC, and supposedly the possessor of magical powers which enabled him to leave the body and return to it at will. He was a devoted follower of Apollo and introduced the cult of the god at Metapontum in south Italy. Inspired by Apollo he visited the peoples of the far north beyond the Black Sea, reaching the Issedonēs, beyond whom lay the Arimaspians. He wrote about his travels in an epic poem of three books, the *Arimaspeia*, which was subsequently regarded as a source of geographical and historical information. Scanty fragments survive which are purported to come from this poem.

Aristei'dēs. 1. (d. c.468 BC), Athenian statesman known as 'the Just', a cousin of *Callias, famous for his rectitude, patriotism, and moderation. He was one of the *strategoi at the battle of Marathon in 490 (see PERSIAN WARS), and *archon in 489/8. He came into conflict with *Themistocles when the latter rose to power, and as a consequence was ostracized in 482.

According to a story told by Plutarch, who wrote his Life, an illiterate citizen requested Aristeides to vote in favour of his ostracism; on being asked what harm Aristeides had ever done him, he replied, none, he did not even know the man, but he was sick of hearing him always called 'the Just'. Aristeides returned from exile in 480, in the general amnesty issued under the Persian threat; he held a command at Salamis, and led the Athenian contingent at Plataea (for an anecdote see NYMPHS). His greatest achievement was in the apportionment of tribute by the *Delian League, when he fixed each member's contribution, a task entrusted to him on account of his justice and discretion. He served Athens faithfully, and died in about 467. We have a Life of him by Nepos as well as that by Plutarch.

2. Of Miletus, see MILESIAN TALES.

3. Aelius Aristeides (AD 117–89), Greek rhetorician of the Second *Sophistic. Born in Mysia, he was educated at Pergamum and Athens, and spent much of his life giving demonstrations of his oratory in the chief cities of the Greek world. Fifty-five of his compositions are extant. The best known is his eloquent encomium of Rome, but these works are now read chiefly for the light they throw on the social history of Asia Minor in his day. When on a visit to Rome at the age of 26, he was struck down by an illness, perhaps psychological in origin, from which he suffered for the rest of his life. He sought a cure in the temple of *Asclepius at Pergamum, and left an account of the dreams he experienced there in a book called 'Sacred Teachings' (*hieroi logoi*), which is interesting as a record of the personal religious experiences of a pagan, and valuable as evidence for the practice of *incubation. He was known to the physician *Galen, who cited him as an example of one whose power of oratory had 'caused his whole body to waste away'.

Aristi'ppus, of Cyrene, a pupil of *Socrates. It was probably not he but his grandson who founded the Cyrenaic school of philosophy, and was the first to teach its characteristic doctrine, that immediate pleasure is the only end of action; knowledge is based on sensation, and the present moment is the only reality. His works are entirely lost.

aristocracy. The Greek word means 'rule of the best', and originally denoted government by the hereditary nobility. At Athens, before the rise of *democracy ('rule of the people') the land-owning nobles were the ruling class of the city-state, prominent by birth, wealth, and personal prowess (see EUPATRIDAE and ATHENS 2 (i)). They governed the state through a council (see AREOPAGUS) whose authority was unchallenged. After the eighth century BC society changed throughout Greece, and wealth, not birth, became the criterion for power. New sources of wealth—*mines, trade, and (small scale) industry—brought into prominence a class who were not necessarily of noble birth, but who were rich and also important because of the part they played in the army, as heavy-armed foot-soldiers, *hoplites. As a consequence the councils which governed city-states were gradually reconstituted to admit these people (for Athens, see SOLON and BOULE), and non-aristocrats rose to the same political levels as the nobles. Aristocracy in Greece often developed into *oligarchy, but for a long time aristocratic families dominated political life. Sparta and Thessaly remained strongly aristocratic throughout the classical period. The poems of *Theognis (of Megara) show the views of an aristocrat alarmed by the effect of wealth in disturbing the old social and political order, while the odes of the Theban poet *Pindar reflect some of the ideals of the aristocratic life. For aristocracy at Rome see REPUBLIC.

Aristo'crates, Against, speech in a public prosecution by *Demosthenes (2).

Aristodē'mus. 1. One of the *Heracleidae, father of Eurysthenēs and Proclēs.

2. The only one of *Leonidas' three hundred Spartans to return home after the battle of Thermopylae (480 BC), having missed the fighting through sickness. He was disfranchised, and according to Herodotus (7. 230), 'no man would give him a light for his fire or speak to him; he was called Aristodemus the coward.' At the battle of Plataea in the following year he redeemed himself by fighting recklessly to the death.

3. Legendary Messenian hero of the First Messenian War against Sparta (see SPARTA 1). He killed his daughter in consequence of an oracle which said that the sacrifice of a maiden would ensure the preservation of Messenia. He became king and was at first victorious over the Lacedaemonians, but later, despairing of ultimate success, committed suicide over his daughter's grave.

Aristogei'ton, see HARMODIUS.

Aristo'menēs, legendary Messenian hero of the Second Messenian War against Sparta (see SPARTA 1), who was eventually defeated.

Aristo'phanēs. 1. (*c*.445, or earlier, –*c*.385 BC), Athenian comic poet, writer of Old Attic Comedy (see COMEDY, GREEK 3), son of Philippos of the deme Kydathenaion in Athens. Virtually nothing is known of his life. He may have lived or owned property on Aegina. Eleven of his plays survive; we also have some 32 titles and many fragments. His plays may be dated as follows:

427 *Daitaleis* ('banqueters', people of an imaginary deme of that name), now lost. Fragments of two speeches survive. The play won second prize in the dramatic competitions.

426 *Babylonians*, produced at the Dionysia, now lost. Afterwards Aristophanes was apparently prosecuted by Cleon for his 'attacks on the magistrates' in the presence of the allies (who were bringing their tribute to Athens as members of the *Delian League). No penalty seems to have been imposed. The play may have won first prize.

425 **Acharnians*, produced at the Lenaea, the first of his surviving comedies; it won first prize.

(These three plays were not produced by Aristophanes, but by a certain Callistratus; the reason is not known for certain, but it may have been that Aristophanes was under the customary age.)

424 **Knights* (Lenaea, first prize).

423 **Clouds* (Dionysia), on the subject of Socrates and the new learning. It was perhaps too subtle for popular taste; it won third prize (i.e. came last). It was rewritten by Aristophanes in the form we now have; we know that he substituted two scenes showing hostility to the new school. This second edition was not produced at either of the great festivals.

422 **Wasps* (Lenaea, second prize).

421 **Peace* (Dionysia, second prize).

414 **Birds* (Dionysia, second prize).

411 **Lysistrata* (produced by Callistratus) and **Thesmophoriazusae* (probably at the Lenaea and Dionysia respectively).

405 **Frogs* (Lenaea, first prize).

392 (probably) **Ecclesiazusae*.

382 **Plutus*, the second play of this name.

After these, Aristophanes wrote two comedies which he gave to his son Araros to produce, but which are now lost. One of them, the *Kokalos*, we are told, started the type of New Comedy (see COMEDY, GREEK 6), introducing romantic features which are characteristic of the plays of Menander. Aristophanes' plays down to 421 show him as the chief representative of Old Comedy, but from the *Birds* onwards he introduced significant changes in the structure.

Aristophanes' language is colourful and imaginative, his lyric poetry subtle and varied in tone. His humour lies largely in exaggeration, parody, and satire, directed against new movements in thought or culture, and prominent men who are suitable for this treatment. No group or class is exempt, and as a result it is notoriously difficult to decide what moral or political lesson, if any, we are meant to derive from a play. The sympathetic characters are in the main people who wish to be left alone to enjoy their private lives in a traditional way, untroubled by wars and politicians and intellectuals, but they themselves are often narrowly self-seeking, and no final decision is made as to who, or which cause, is 'right'. Plato in his **Symposium* represents Aristophanes as an agreeable and convivial companion who gives an amusing turn to a serious discussion, and this is perhaps the light in which to regard much of his work. It does not appear in fact to have affected the course of events.

Aristophanes had a direct influence on English literature, notably on the comedies of Ben Jonson (1572/3–1637), Thomas Middleton (1580–1627), and Henry Fielding (1707–54).

2. Aristophanes of Byzantium, head of the *Alexandrian Library *c.*200 BC. He was a scholar of wide learning, the teacher of *Aristarchus, who continued along the lines laid down by his master. Aristophanes made the first critical editions of several Greek poets, including Homer, Hesiod, Anacreon, Pindar, and Aristophanes (1). He is said to have invented or regularized Greek *accents; and he devised a set of critical signs to indicate passages in manuscripts suspected of being interpolations or otherwise noteworthy; see TEXTS, TRANSMISSION OF ANCIENT 1.

A'ristotle (Aristotelēs) (384–322 BC), Greek philosopher.

1. *Life.* Aristotle was born at Stageira in Chalcidice, the son of Nicomachus, physician to Amyntas II (father of Philip II), king of Macedon. In 367 he came to Athens, and for the next twenty years was a pupil of Plato, until the latter's death in 347. In that year he left Athens. It may be the case that when Plato was succeeded as head of the *Academy by Speusippus, Aristotle found the latter's mathematical kind of philosophy repugnant. Perhaps more probable is the theory that Aristotle left Athens for political reasons, because Demosthenes and his anti-Macedon party were in the ascendancy. However that may be, in the same year his home town of Stageira was destroyed by the then king of Macedon, Philip II, and Aristotle settled at Assos in the Troad, where there was a small colony of philosophers from the Academy. These were supported by Hermias, the enlightened tyrant of the neighbouring city of Atarneus, to whom Aristotle later wrote a poem of praise and whose niece, Pythias, he married. He remained there for three years, probably lecturing and writing, until the philosophers were driven out after the murder of Hermias. Aristotle retreated to Mytilene in Lesbos (where he met *Theophrastus), teaching there until 343/2. It was during his stay at Assos and Mytilene that he conducted many of his zoological researches. At the end of that time he was invited by Philip to be tutor to his 13-year-old son *Alexander (the Great). His teaching of Alexander was probably mainly in Homer and the dramatists (he was said to have prepared for his pupil an edition of the *Iliad*), but the need for some political education may have stimulated Aristotle's own interest in politics (a lost work is entitled 'Alexander, or On Colonization').

In 335, when Alexander had succeeded to the throne and started on his expedition to Asia, Aristotle returned to Athens and taught there in a *gymnasium built in a grove sacred to Apollo Lykeios and known in consequence as the Lyceum. Here he was said to have lectured to his pupils in the morning and the general public in the evening. The kind of philosophy he taught came to be known as the Peripatetic, owing its name to the covered court (*peripatos*) where the students walked up and down. Scholarly research of all kinds was carried on, literary, scientific, and philosophical. Aristotle collected manuscripts and maps, and formed the first considerable library of antiquity as well as a museum of natural objects, in the assembling of which he is said to have been helped by Alexander. At some time during this period Pythias died, and Aristotle lived afterwards with Herpyllis, by whom he had a son Nicomachus. He enjoyed the friendship and protection of Antipater, whom Alexander had made governor of Macedon and Greece. After the death of Alexander in 323 the anti-Macedonian party at Athens became dominant, and Aristotle, having obvious Macedonian connections, was charged with impiety on the grounds that his poem to Hermias befitted a god, not a man, an accusation probably political in origin. Rather than let the Athenians 'sin twice against philosophy' (the first time being the execution of Socrates) Aristotle left his school to Theophrastus and departed from Athens. He died the following year at Chalcis in Euboea, where in the last months of his life he lamented his isolation. His will, reproduced by *Diogenes Laertius, shows him to have been of a kindly and affectionate disposition.

2. *The general character of his work.* Aristotle left a vast number of works—some 400 were attributed to him—on a great variety of subjects, but only about a fifth has survived. The works we now possess belong mostly to the later period of his life and were never published in his lifetime. Those that were read in classical antiquity, by Cicero and his friends for example, were the published works of his early life and are now lost. Sometimes referred to as the 'exoteric works' (i.e. works for the 'outside' public), they were written in a fluent and polished style for the general reader, and were undoubtedly Platonic in their general assumptions (though the extent to which Aristotle in his early life adhered to the tenets of the Platonic Academy is still a matter of debate). At his death Aristotle bequeathed to Theophrastus, his successor as head of the Lyceum, not only his books but also his manuscripts. The manuscripts comprised his full lecture-notes, which had not been prepared for publication, sometimes called the 'acroastic works' (Gk. *akroasthai*, 'to attend a lecture'); it has come about by chance that the works of Aristotle which we now possess are in

origin lecture-notes, reworked over a number of years and never intended to be read by the public. They may have been set in order after Aristotle's death by his colleague Eudemos of Rhodes and his son Nicomachus. There is a tradition that Theophrastus left the manuscripts to a certain Neleus of Scepsis, whose heirs put them in a cellar to preserve them from the book-collecting kings of Pergamum (for an example of the collecting mania of the Hellenistic period see ALEXANDRIAN LIBRARY). What use was made of them in the third and second centuries BC is not clear, but they cannot have been entirely unknown: there were lists of the titles in circulation, made by or for the librarians of the Alexandrian Library, and some Stoic philosophers seem to have had some knowledge of Aristotle's logic. Eventually, in a crumbling condition, the manuscripts were sold and went to Athens, whence Sulla shipped them to Rome as part of his war-booty after the Mithridatic War (89–85 BC). There they were edited by the head of the Lyceum at Athens, Andronicus of Rhodes, and this edition is the basis of all our surviving manuscripts of Aristotle both in Greek and in other languages. It was circulated and closely studied and commented upon as being more profound and original than the published books; as a consequence the latter ceased to be read and were eventually lost.

3. The works of Aristotle may be divided into three classes:

(i) The early popular works of philosophy, mostly in dialogue form, published by Aristotle himself and now lost except for fragments preserved by quotation in later writers. These include the *Protrepticus* ('exhortation to philosophy') which served as a model for Cicero's *Hortensius* (itself a crucial influence on the young *Augustine, but now lost). They were Platonic in tone.

(ii) Large collections of historical and scientific facts, made by Aristotle sometimes in cooperation with others and now mostly lost. They included lists of the victors at the Olympian and Pythian games and the *didascaliae (records of the dramatic performances at Athens), traces of which remain in our scholia to the extant Greek plays. The only work from this class to have survived almost entire is the *Athenaiōn politeia*, 'constitution of the Athenians', the first in a collection of 158 such accounts of the constitutions of the Greek states, recovered from an Egyptian papyrus in 1890.

(iii) Philosophical and scientific works, many of which are still extant.

There are very few indications by which one may date Aristotle's works or arrange them in order of composition (and by their nature most reached their present form after being reworked over a number of years: see 2 above). On the whole they seem to reflect a progressive withdrawal from Plato's influence, although some of the works that show opposition to Plato could date from Aristotle's early years at the Academy. He did not believe in the separate existence of unchanging Ideas (or Forms) nor did he accept them as sufficient explanation of the facts of change and motion—an explanation he was still seeking in his latest work. He did not feel, as Plato felt, that physical science was founded on mathematics; hence in his physical works he was sometimes led to argue from plausible but mistaken assumptions, in the absence of actual measurement. In astronomy, for example, he made many errors, and his influence on later thought was a retarding one. In biology, however, a science which he brought into existence, exact measurement is less crucial in its early development, and his combination of close observation and acute reasoning made an outstanding contribution to knowledge. Politics he viewed in similar fashion, as a study which depends on observation and whose function it is to discover general laws governing the rise and fall of political systems, always with a practical end in view. His thought is distinguished partly by an inspired common sense which makes him avoid extremist views. This does not mean that he accepts half-hearted compromise, rather that he always recognizes equally the parts played by the senses and the intellect, the claims of mind and body; in this spirit he advocates the rule of the middle class as being the steadiest element in a state. His other striking characteristic is his love of order and system, and to this aspect of his mind we are greatly indebted for the classification of the sciences to which we still adhere, and for much of our philosophical terminology. Many of the terms that he first introduced—universal and particular, premiss and conclusion, subject and attribute, form and matter, potentiality and actuality—have become commonly used both in philosophy and outside it.

4. *Extant works.* The surviving treatises may be classified as follows.

(i) *On logic*, a group which much later came to be called the *Organon* ('tool' or 'instrument'), consisting of six treatises known as: **Categoriae* ('predicates'), *De interpretatione* ('on interpretation'), *Analytica priora* and *posteriora* ('prior' and 'posterior analytics'), *Topica* ('topics'), and *De sophisticis elenchis* ('refutations in the manner of the sophists'). In these Aristotle was the first to explore the science of reasoning, both formal (in the *Prior Analytics*) and scientific (in the *Posterior Analytics*), on the basis of the syllogism, which he discovered. His analysis, as far as it went, was admirable and still remains valid. The Schoolmen of the Middle Ages summarized his teaching on this subject in the famous mnemonic lines beginning '*barbara, celarent, darii, ferioque prioris...*', in which the vowels indicate the nature of the major and minor premisses and

conclusion of the various moods of the syllogism, A representing a universal affirmative ('all S is P'), E a universal negative ('no S is P'), I a particular affirmative ('some S is P'), O a particular negative ('some S is not P'). Aristotle himself used letters to stand for the terms of propositions.

(ii) *On metaphysics*, a mixture of treatises or lecture notes from different periods, put together by Andronicus of Rhodes (see 2 above) and called by him *Metaphysica* because in his edition they came 'after the physics' (*meta ta physika*). From this the branch of philosophy now known as metaphysics takes its name, but Aristotle's name for the subject is *prōtē philosophia*, 'primary philosophy'. The fourteen books, known by letters of the Greek alphabet, cover a range of topics concerned with basic realities, including the 'being' of things (*to on*, compare English 'ontology'), matter, form, substance, and essence. The Aristotelian 'form', the intelligible nature of a thing, differs from the Platonic 'idea', at least as Aristotle conceived it, in being immanent in the thing and not existing apart from it. Aristotle concludes that the universe must have a single, unchanging, final cause (see (iii) *a* below), an 'unmoved mover' engaged in the eternal activity of pure thought or contemplation (*theōria*), giving supreme happiness. This 'unmoved mover', who may be called God, has no interest in the universe but the latter ultimately depends on him, since the eternal circular motion of the stars which brings about the change of seasons and the rhythm of birth, reproduction, and death, is in imitation of God's activity. People, through their possession of mind (*nous*), can imitate God by themselves engaging in pure thought (although only briefly and intermittently), and this is their highest activity.

(iii) *On natural science* (physics, biology, psychology). The treatises in this group are: (*a*) *Physica* ('physics'), an examination of the constituent elements of things that exist by 'nature' ('nature' being an 'innate compulsion to movement'), and a discussion of such notions as matter and form, time, space, and movement, with an exposition of the four causes, the material cause (that out of which a thing comes to be), the formal cause (the intelligible nature of a thing, that in virtue of which it is what it is), the motive (or efficient) cause (the immediate origin of a change) and the final cause (the end or aim of the change); (*b*) *De caelo* ('on the heavens'), on the movement of celestial and terrestrial bodies (Aristotle knew that the earth was spherical, but thought it was situated at the centre of the universe); (*c*) *De generatione et corruptione* ('on coming into being and passing away'); (*d*) *Meteorologica*, principally on weather phenomena; (*e*) a group of works on biology: the nine books of the *Historia animalium*, ('inquiry into animals'), a collection of facts on animal life, showing acute observation (Aristotle knew, for instance, that whales were mammals), and a series of treatises in which he deals with the classification of animals, their reproduction, and the adaptation and evolution of their organs (he lays stress on final causes in the problems of organic life); (*f*) *De anima* ('on the soul'), a treatise in three books on the proposition that soul and body are two aspects of a single living thing, in the relation of form to matter. Thus the soul, which is the life force, does not survive the death of the body, though Aristotle seems also to say that the soul of man possesses a portion of 'active reason' which is immortal and eternal, and is perhaps akin to God; (*g*) several monographs known collectively as *Parva naturalia* ('short works on nature'), on the general physiological conditions of life.

(iv) *On ethics and politics*. Aristotle wrote two ethical treatises to which he gave the title *Ēthika*, 'matters to do with character', known as the *Nicomachean* and the *Eudemian Ethics*. These cover much the same ground, though with certain important differences of view. The relation between the two works is still a matter of debate; the former is the better known. It is in the main a study of the end to which conduct should be directed. Aristotle accepts 'happiness', *eudaimonia*, doing well, making a success of life, as the end of human action, and wants to instruct men how to achieve it. For a person to be happy he must do well those things which are distinctively human. Humans are distinguished from other animals by possessing intellect, 'the god within us'. The happiness that is distinctively human is therefore achieved by intellectual activity. Not all human virtue is intellectual; there is also moral virtue. Aristotle defines the latter as a disposition to choose a certain mean, as determined by 'a man of practical wisdom' (*phronimos*), between two opposite extremes of conduct; a mean, for instance, between asceticism and yielding to uncontrolled impulses. Aristotle lays stress on the notion of moral intention, but virtue of character is also important.

Virtue cannot be practised by the solitary individual: 'a human being is by nature a political animal' (i.e. it is our nature to live in a city, *polis*). In the eight books of the *Politica* ('politics'), Aristotle discusses the science of politics from the point of view of the city-state, which he assumes to be that most conducive to the fullest life of the citizen. He thinks the state was developed naturally by the grouping of families in villages, and of villages in a state, for the purpose of securing for the citizens a good and self-sufficing life. Since this moral end, and not material purpose, is the essential characteristic of the state, it is necessary that the power should rest, not with the wealthy or with the whole body of free citizens, but with the good.

He discusses citizenship, the classification of actual constitutions, and the various types of these, their diseases and the remedies; he recognizes the advantages of democracy, but finds the highest type in the monarchy of the perfect ruler if such is available, and failing this in an aristocracy of men of virtue and enlightenment. But this, too, is difficult, and on the whole he regards a limited democracy as the constitution best suited to the practical conditions of Greece in his day. He regards slavery as a natural institution, so far as it is based on the inferiority of the nature of the slave rather than on right of conquest. But the master must not abuse his authority, and slaves must have the hope of emancipation.

As the work has come down to us it is neither uniform nor complete; the various parts may well have been composed at different times. Books 7 and 8, containing the discussion of the ideal state, seem to belong to an early text in which the purely constructive method of Plato is followed. Books 4–6, dealing with actual historical states and containing an allusion to the death of Philip II of Macedon (in 336), must have been written later, when Aristotle had at his disposal the collection of the 158 constitutions of which the *Athenaion politeia* is the only survivor (see 3 (ii) above). That traces the development of the Athenian constitution from the earliest times (the first chapters are missing) down to the fall of the Thirty Tyrants (404), and then describes the mature democracy of Aristotle's own day.

(v) *On rhetoric and poetry*. Aristotle's *Rhetoric* deals with methods of persuasion, divided into those by which the speaker produces on his audience a favourable view of his own character, those by which he produces emotion, and thirdly argument, whether by means of example or of enthymeme (Gk. *enthymema*, the rhetorical form of the syllogism, based on probability). It then discusses style (of which the leading characteristics should be clearness and appropriateness) and arrangement. The object of this treatise is practical, how to compose a good speech (see RHETORIC).

See also POETICS for Aristotle's treatise of that name.

5. *The influence of Aristotle*. The influence that Aristotle exerted on later generations of philosophers and scientists was immense, by the stimulus he gave, by the instruments of investigation which he invented, and by his actual contributions to knowledge. In western Europe in the early Middle Ages, down to about AD 1200, it was mainly his writings on logic, and not all of these, that were known and studied and became such a rigorous influence upon the disputations of medieval Schoolmen. Aristotelian logic more than any other single influence formed the European mind. His writings on science and philosophy, however, followed a

different path. From about AD 800 onwards they were translated and expounded by the Arabs, first in the East and then, as a result of the Arab conquest, in Spain. The Arab versions were then retranslated into Latin and these Latin texts made their way from Spain into the rest of Europe, where they had previously been unknown, at the beginning of the thirteenth century. At first the study of these new writings was prohibited, but in the hands of Albertus Magnus (1206–80) and Thomas Aquinas (c.1225–74) they soon became the basis of a Christian philosophy which was a fusion of theology and Aristotelianism.

When at the end of the thirteenth century the Latin translations from Arabic were superseded by more accurate translations made directly from the Greek, Aristotle's authority in virtually all aspects of learning was absolute. It was particularly unfortunate that astronomy, which with alchemy made up the entire scientific interest of the Middle Ages, was the one subject in which Aristotle went furthest astray in believing the earth to be a stationary sphere and the universe geocentric. Dante and Chaucer, for example, who both had a considerable knowledge of astronomy, exhibit the Aristotelian view; when Galileo (1564–1642) disputed the truth of it, it was against a very Aristotelian Christianity that he was offending. Galileo's English contemporary Francis Bacon (1561–1626), though contemptuous of the ancient philosophers in general, adopts Aristotle's division of the four causes, and entitles part of his own work the *Novum Organum*. In the sphere of literature, Aristotle's *Poetics* was regarded as an authority from Elizabethan days onward, and in English literature we find references to it in the writings of Sir Philip Sidney (1554–86), Ben Jonson (1572/3–1637), and John Milton (1608–74).

Aristo'xenus (b. between 375 and 360 BC), philosopher and musical theorist, pupil of Aristotle, passed over by him for headship of the *Lyceum in favour of Theophrastus. He was famous in antiquity for his works on rhythm and on harmonics, parts of which have survived. His exposition of the theory of harmonics in particular was a strong influence for many centuries. He also had a deep interest in the ethical and educational value of music.

Arminius, see VARUS (2).

army. 1. Greek

1. In Homer the warrior, armed with spear and sword and protected by a helmet and figure-of-eight-shaped shield made of an ox-hide strengthened with bronze, rode out to battle in a chariot. From this he dismounted to encounter some opposing champion. They both began by throwing spears at each other, and then proceeded to close combat with swords. This method of fighting, fitting for heroic dignity, was not used in historic times. However, there are also passages which show the hero armed with the breastplate and greaves of later times.

From the early seventh century BC the Greeks changed their style of fighting and began to use *hoplites (heavy-armed infantry) in massed formation, a method which characterized Greek warfare for many centuries. Whereas in earlier times expert fighters had attacked each other individually, supported by a mass of lightly armed troops, in the new system success depended upon several ranks of hoplites keeping in formation and using their weight to charge and break down the enemy's lines. Changes in armour followed: hoplites were armed with bronze breastplate, helmet with nose- and cheek-pieces, and greaves, and used a round or elliptical shield secured to the left arm by a central arm-band, with a handgrip near the rim. Every man's shield projected to his left and covered his neighbour's unprotected right side. Hence came the Greek conception of courage, realized in the good man who stands his ground, so described by Tyrtaeus and Plato. The heavy hoplite shield was useless in flight since it could not be slung round to protect the wearer's back; in retreat it was better thrown down, as the poet *Archilochus discovered. The spear, some two or more metres long, was no longer a missile but was used for thrusting, especially at the neck of the enemy above the top of the breastplate. When the spear was lost the hoplite took to his short, straight, iron sword. The social and political effect of the introduction of the hoplite system was considerable. The middle class, the class that could afford the hoplite armour and provided the substantial numbers of trained fighters on which the cities depended, now claimed its share of power in the state, breaking the monopoly held by the aristocrats (see ARISTOCRACY). Thus the formation of hoplite armies was a significant factor in the shifting of political power in seventh- and sixth-century Greece.

2. At Athens in the fifth and fourth centuries BC military service was obligatory on all male citizens, and from the age of 18 to 20 they underwent military training as recruits (see also EPHEBOI). They were categorized according to the system of property-classes instituted by *Solon: thus the cavalry, service in which entailed heavy expense, was formed mainly from the *hippeis, the knights (always scarce in Greece, apart from Thessaly and Macedon); the hoplites were drawn from the *zeugitai* (as well as from the richer *metics), those who could equip themselves with full personal armour but were not rich enough to maintain horses. The *thetēs* served as light infantry or in the fleet; they had no fixed equipment and very little military efficiency. Between the ages of 20 and 49 a male Athenian formed part of the active army. From

50 to 60 he was retained, with the recruits and the remaining metics, for garrison duty only. There was no standing army in fifth-century Greece; the citizen body was conscripted as required. Athens might expect to put in the field an army having roughly 10,000 hoplites. The cavalry (1,000 in number after 446) were organized in ten squadrons, the hoplites in ten regiments (*taxeis*) based on the ten tribes. Each regiment was divided into battalions (*lochoi*) and was commanded by a taxiarch. The hoplite received, on service, pay at two obols a day, and subsistence allowance at the same rate (in the cavalry the allowance was one drachma). Military officers, *strategoi*, taxiarchs, etc., were elected (not chosen by lot) annually, but unlike most of the civil officials might be re-elected indefinitely (see also POLEMARCH).

3. At Sparta, where the whole life of the male citizens was organized with a view to the military efficiency of the state, liability to foreign military service extended from 20 to 60 years of age, and a high degree of mobility and dexterity in the use of weapons was maintained by constant exercises. It seems to have been from Sparta that the hoplite system spread through Greece. At Sparta more completely than elsewhere the citizens were the hoplites; having a vote in the *apella* (assembly) depended on being or having been a hoplite. The Spartans deliberately kept secret the strength of their army. At the battle of Mantinea in 418 BC it consisted, according to Thucydides, of seven companies (*lochoi*) of 512 spearmen, subdivided into 16 platoons (*enomotiai*) of 32, each with its commanding officer, thus securing rapidity of movement and flexibility. It seems probable that before the end of the Peloponnesian War the organization was modified, and a formation called a *mora* introduced, numbering about 600 men subdivided into platoons as before. Four such *morai* fought under Cleombrotus at the battle of Leuctra in 371 BC, but the number of full Spartan citizens included in them was only about 700. With the dwindling number of citizens, the ranks were increasingly filled with *perioikoi* (see SPARTA 2), supplemented in great emergencies by helots. Cavalry appears to have played a subordinate part in the Spartan army. This army was unique not only in its tactical organization (which amazed Xenophon) but in having a uniform and military flute-players. As in all Greek armies the men had to supply their own arms and fend for themselves in provisions.

4. In the early part of the fourth century BC the increasing use of mercenary troops, drawn especially from the wilder parts of Greece, became important. These professional troops, known as peltasts from the small, light, leather shield (*pelte*) which they carried, were armed with a javelin and were more mobile than the hoplites. In the Corinthian War (see CORINTH) of this period, a force of peltasts, with improved weapons, was organized by the Athenian Iphicrates, and was used with great success against the Spartans. Mercenary service grew in importance during the fourth and later centuries, and Greek mercenaries were largely employed by the Persian kings and their satraps (Xenophon and the Ten Thousand are a conspicuous example: see ANABASIS). *Epaminondas introduced the *phalanx and the tactical approach based on it; it was further developed by *Philip II of Macedon. The military successes of his son Alexander the Great were principally due to his skilful use of cavalry, who were more numerous in his than in earlier Greek armies. His cavalry delivered flank attacks, while the phalanx attacked the enemy front. In the narrative of Alexander's battles we constantly find him commanding in person the best of the cavalry and delivering the decisive blow. The successors of Alexander (see DIADOCHI) relied largely on great masses of untrained oriental troops, doubling the depth of the phalanx and thus further diminishing its mobility. Pyrrhus appears to have tried to remedy this defect in his wars with Rome by breaking up the phalanx into a number of columns with bodies of Italian troops placed between them; but he failed to overcome the Roman resistance. The later eastern adversaries of Rome, such as Philip V, Perseus, and Antiochus III, were even less successful.

5. *Greek siege-craft*. Siege warfare made no great progress before the fifth century BC. In earlier days Greek citadels on rocky hills, or walled towns such as Thebes, were impregnable and, treachery apart, had to be reduced by blockade. In the fifth century we first hear of siege engines (chiefly rams, scaling ladders, and screens for protection). The defence still had the advantage, as may be seen from the account given by Thucydides (2. 75) of the successful resistance offered by the Plataeans in 429 to the engines of the Spartan besiegers. Potidaea resisted Athenian siege for three years (432–430). Such blockades were very expensive. A great advance in siege-craft was made when, at the beginning of the fourth century, Dionysius I of Syracuse introduced the use of *catapult. Essentially a large cross-bow of increased range and power, it was developed into an engine capable of discharging heavy missiles against fortifications. During this century sieges began to be conducted more scientifically, with covered approaches, mines, movable towers and various types of catapult. These were largely developed by the engineers of Philip II, and successfully employed by Alexander. The methods of defence were likewise improved. Countermines were sunk to upset towers, catapults were extensively used against the besieging engines, and fire-arrows and similar devices used to set them on fire. A well-equipped city could still resist a siege, but few could afford the expense. Hence, after

Alexander, besiegers generally had the whip-hand. Among the most notable sieges of the fourth century were that of Tyre by *Alexander and the unsuccessful siege of Rhodes by Demetrius Poliorcetes (see MACEDONIA 2 and RHODES).

2. Roman

1. Probably from the earliest times it was the duty of Roman citizens to give military service, but because of the expense this duty would in practice have devolved upon the rich. By a reform traditionally ascribed to Servius Tullius citizens were grouped for service according to their means, so that most could serve in some capacity, although some minimum property qualification remained, except in times of crisis, until the reforms of *Marius at the end of the second century BC. As the need for longer campaigns grew, pay was introduced (tradition-ally during the siege of Veii in 406 BC) and the state began to assume responsibility for the maintenance of its armies.

2. The largest unit in the army was the legion, which had nominally consisted of 6,000 foot soldiers in 60 centuries (*centuriae) of 100 men, was reduced to half this size in the early republic, and was restored to a nominal 6,000 by Marius. In practice it was always liable to fall below its nominal strength. From about the fourth or third century BC the tactical formation of the legion was in three lines of heavy-armed infantry, each comprising ten maniples of two centuries each. The front line were known as hastati (hasta, 'spear'), the second principes ('men in the prime of life'), and the third triarii ('third-liners'). In the early republic the equipment of the infantry was still based on that of the Greek hoplites. Probably well before the mid-second century BC the pilum, a spear mainly for throwing, had replaced the hasta for the first two lines; the triarii, who were veterans held in reserve, retained the hasta for some time longer. Standard equipment now included the gladius, a short sword worn on the right side, and the scutum, a long shield which replaced the older round sort. Leather or bronze helmets and bronze breastplates or mail corselets were worn; greaves were no longer used once the scutum became common. In addition to the heavy infantry there were attached to the legion light-armed soldiers, velitēs, in numbers comparable to each of the heavy ranks, and a number of cavalry. The Roman cavalry, like the Greek, were originally drawn from the richest class, the equitēs (see EQUESTRIAN ORDER), but by the end of the second century BC the cavalry were no longer recruited from Rome, nor even from Italy. (Rome's Italian allies, even before they obtained citizenship, were required as a matter of course to provide contingents for the army.) During the last 200 years of the republic, and especially during the civil wars, troops from many countries outside Italy, known as auxilia,

'auxiliaries', were used to make up numbers. By the reforms of Marius both the cavalry and the velites were provided entirely by auxilia (see also ALAE). In these reforms also the formation of the legion changed: the cohort of three maniples became the tactical unit, ten of these making up the legion; the eagle, adopted as the standard of each legion, was carried by the first maniple of the first cohort. Marius abolished conscription, as well as the property qualification which then stood at 4,000 asses, having been reduced from an original figure in excess of 10,000. This, with the enfranchisement of Italians, meant that the Roman army was now a professional body of volunteers, consisting of the legions from Italy and the foreign auxilia. There were also contingents for special purposes, such as archers and slingers. The pay of a legionary was 120 denarii a year, from which the cost of rations was deducted, and enlist-ment was for sixteen years. The legions were commanded by tribunes (see TRIBUNI MILITUM). Julius Caesar increased the pay to 225 denarii and put legates in command, over the tribunes (see LEGATI).

3. In the first century BC the Roman army had become virtually a standing army, based largely in the provinces and expanded when need arose. The soldiers came to owe their allegiance more to their generals than to Rome, and looked to them for rewards which could include not only booty but also land on retirement. The generals in turn could look to their legions for political as well as military support, and were able to challenge the state itself: it was this conflict of interests which helped to bring about the civil wars of the first century BC and the fall of the republic (see ROME 6 and 7). The first true standing army, including the auxilia, was established by the emperor *Augustus. The legionaries enlisted for sixteen years plus a further four in a corps of veterans (sub vexillo, 'under the flag', as opposed to sub aquila, 'under the eagle'); these were later extended to twenty and five years respectively. The pay of a legionary remained at 225 denarii under Augustus (it was increased to 300 by Domitian and there were further increases under later emperors); he received a substantial gratuity on discharge. Local recruitment became common. Legionaries were not allowed officially to marry during their service. The number of legions varied somewhat, but under Augustus was around 25. They had numbers and sometimes names also, and were attached to fixed head-quarters. (The numbers of those legions lost in the *Varus disaster, 17, 18, and 19, were never used again.) Cohorts of auxiliaries were attached to the legions or used for garrisons, the auxiliary cavalry (alae) attached to each legion numbering typically 120. The basic pay of an auxiliary, although variable, was much less than a legion-ary's, and he enlisted for twenty-five years.

After that time, he was granted citizenship, civic rights for his descendants, and perhaps other privileges; these were engraved on his *diploma* (pl. *diplomata*), a pair of small bronze tablets constituting a certificate of discharge.

4. During the empire the army included the highly paid *praetorian guard at Rome, where there were also other special corps: a city police (*cohortes urbanae*) and a fire brigade (*vigiles*), both recruited from freedmen. But the greatest part of the army was stationed on the empire's frontiers. These were defended by forts (*castella*) and by various other means. Under Domitian a series of small earth forts was used, backed by larger stone forts at wider intervals; from Trajan onwards the defence was a ditch backed by a wall of stone or earth including forts at regular intervals (for Hadrian's Wall and the Antonine Wall see BRITAIN 5). See also CAMP and ELEPHANTS.

5. *Roman siege-craft*. Siege warfare developed in the Roman army in much the same way as in the Greek armies. Blockade was increasingly replaced by assault as the devices of the Greeks came to the knowledge of the Romans and were developed by them. The *testudo* ('tortoise') was a Roman device by which interlocked shields formed a screen under which a scaling party could approach the walls; another protective device was the *musculus*, a long gallery on wheels with a sloping roof, used by Caesar at Massilia (see *COMMENTARIES* 2 (books 1 and 2)). The lines of the besieging forces were protected from the besieged by trenches and pits, and from a relieving force likewise (as at Alesia in Gaul in 52 BC; see *COMMENTARIES* 1 (book 7)) by a rampart and palisade. A large movable tower could be brought along a causeway (*agger*) built up to the walls, and from it the attackers could cross by drawbridges. The chief engine of destruction was the ram (*aries*), a heavy beam tipped with iron, sometimes swung on ropes but in more developed versions mounted on a wheeled frame. The catapult and the *ballista used twisted ropes for propelling arrows and heavier missiles, and the *onager* was a large sling; these were used especially by the defenders.

Arpī'num, town in Latium, the birthplace of Marius and Cicero.

arre'phoroi, see PANATHENAIA.

A'rria. 1. Wife of Caecina Paetus, who, when her husband was ordered to death under the emperor Claudius, 'taught her husband how to die', stabbing herself and handing him the dagger with the words *Paete, non dolet* ('It doesn't hurt, Paetus').

2. The daughter of the above and wife of *Thrasea, a Stoic philosopher put to death by Nero.

A'rrian (Flavius Arrianus), b. AD 85–90, a Greek of Nicomedia in Bithynia, a successful officer in the Roman army, who became *consul suffectus* (129 or 130) and legate (131–7) in Cappadocia. He retired to Athens, where he was archon in 145/6. He was author of various extant works in Greek: a valuable *Anabasis* ('expedition up-country') *of Alexander* (the Great), in seven books, narrating his campaigns, with an eighth book, *Indikē*, describing India and Indian customs and relating the voyage of Nearchus in the Persian Gulf; an *Encheiridion* or manual of the philosophy of his master *Epictetus, and *Diatribai*, a record of the same philosopher's lectures which he attended in Greece, four books of which survive from an original eight; *Periplous* ('circumnavigation') of the Black Sea; *Cynegeticus* ('on hunting') purporting to supplement the treatise attributed to Xenophon; and other minor works. See also ALEXANDER THE GREAT 8.

Arsacids, the royal dynasty of Parthia from *c.*250 BC–*c.* AD 230.

Ars amatō'ria, poem in three books of elegiacs by *Ovid, written not before 1 BC. Its title means 'treatise on love'; it is in fact a mock-didactic poem on the art of seduction, written for a cultivated and pleasure-loving society where love is a game to be played with style and good humour. The first two books consist of instructions to men, the third of instructions to women on how to entice men. There are intriguing glimpses of Roman life and manners—the circus, the theatre, the banquet. The work was very popular, and quotations from it have been found on the walls of Pompeii. With its frivolous attitude to sexual morality it seems to have been one reason why the emperor Augustus banished the poet.

Arsi'nŏē. 1. In Greek myth, daughter of Phegeus and first wife of *Alcmaeon.

2. The name of several princesses among the ruling *Ptolemies of Egypt (who were of Macedonian descent). The most important was Arsinoe II (*c.*316–270 BC), daughter of Ptolemy I and Berenice, who married first Lysimachus, one of the generals and successors of Alexander the Great, secondly her step-brother Ptolemy Ceraunus, and thirdly her brother Ptolemy II Philadelphus, thus becoming queen of Egypt. Her influence contributed to the brilliance of court life and the great expansion of Ptolemaic power overseas, and she and her husband were both deified in their lifetime. Her death was lamented in an elegy by Callimachus.

3. Greek settlement founded by Ptolemy II in the Faiyum (an oasis some 80 km. (50 miles) south of Cairo in Egypt), of which extensive ruins survive. It was the first source in modern times of papyri of Greek texts (see PAPYROLOGY).

arsis, in metric, the up (or weak) beat. The metrical foot (see METRE, GREEK I) was divided between *arsis* (sometimes known as *anacrusis*) and *thesis*, the down (strong) beat. The terms are often confused and used in the opposite of these (original) senses.

Ars poe'tica, title by which *Horace's poetic *Epistle to the Pisos* soon became known (see EPISTLES). The poem takes the form of a letter of advice on the pursuit of literature, addressed to a father and two sons whose identity is as uncertain as the date of composition, which is perhaps about 19 BC. It is in the same tradition as Aristotle's *Poetics* and perhaps owes something to earlier Latin didactic poems, but the purpose of the *Ars poetica* in the form Horace gave it has always puzzled critics. First, as a treatise it is far from systematic. Where Aristotle is analytical and descriptive Horace is impressionistic, personal, and allusive. Transitions from one subject to another are abrupt and the arrangement seems haphazard. Secondly, its concentration on epic and drama seems irrelevant to the contemporary Roman literary scene. An ancient commentator said that Horace selected his material from the similar treatise of Neoptolemus of Parium, a Hellenistic Greek writer of the third century BC, but the structure of the *Ars poetica* and Horace's practice elsewhere suggest rather that he used no one Greek source but selected from among several sources those precepts which agreed with his own views on poetic style and were suitable for imaginative poetic treatment.

The appeal of the *Ars poetica* is summed up by Alexander Pope (1688–1744) in his *Essay on Criticism*:

> Horace still charms with graceful negligence,
> And without method talks us into sense.

Its lively autobiographical approach and its expression of personal standards in literature make it unique as a work of criticism in the ancient world. Many of its apt phrases, the *ridiculus mus* ('ridiculous mouse') of bathos, *in medias res* ('in the middle of things'), of an abrupt beginning, the 'purple patch' (*purpureus pannus*) and the reference to 'Homer nodding' (*dormitat Homerus*), have passed into common literary parlance. It exercised a great influence in later ages on European literature, notably in French drama through Boileau's *Art poétique* written in imitation, and was translated into English (1640) by Ben Jonson.

art, Greek and Roman. See ARCHITECTURE, GEMS, MOSAIC, PAINTING, PORTRAITURE, SCULPTURE, and TOREUTIC ART. It is remarkable that under these headings the names of many Greek artists appear, but of no Roman. Even the greatest achievements of Roman art—Ara Pacis, Trajan's Column, the Pantheon—are all anonymous. The Romans seem to have attributed art not to its creators but to its patrons, hence the Baths of Caracalla or Diocletian, the Arches of Titus or Constantine.

Artaphe'rnēs. 1. Half-brother of Darius I, king of Persia. He took a leading part in suppressing the Ionian Revolt against Persia in 499 BC (see PERSIAN WARS).

2. Son of (1), who with Datis commanded the Persian expedition which was defeated at the battle of Marathon in 490 BC.

Artaxe'rxēs, name of several Persian kings.

Artemidō'rus, of Daldis in Lydia (late second century AD), author of an extant Greek treatise *Oneirocritica* ('interpretation of dreams'); see DIVINATION.

A'rtemis, in Greek myth, the daughter of Zeus and *Leto, and twin sister of Apollo; a goddess universally worshipped in Greece. The etymology of her name is still unclear, nor is there agreement on whether or not it occurs on *Linear B tablets, but she is closely connected with Asia Minor. For the myth of her birth see APOLLO. She is by origin a goddess of wildlife, but her worship is found in cities through her association with women. She brings fertility to mankind and to the beasts; she is the goddess who helps women in child-birth, but she is also the virgin huntress to whose arrows is ascribed their sudden death. She has a fairly slight mythology. Her principal adventure was the slaying of *Orion, and she is associated with *Hippolytus and the death of *Callisto. She plays an undignified part in the *Iliad* where she is beaten by Hera with her own bow and sent away weeping. *Brauron in Attica was the site of a famous cult of the goddess; and a festival, the Brauronia, at which little girls 'acted the bear' in her honour, was held there.

Artemis was often in ancient times confused with *Hecatē, whose functions were similar, and *Selenē, another goddess of women. She was also identified with foreign goddesses having similar functions, such as the Cretan goddess *Britomartis. The most notable identification was with the great goddess of *Ephesus ('Diana of the Ephesians'). From there the worship of this 'Artemis' spread to Massilia (Marseilles) and thence to Rome, where the temple of Diana on the Aventine had a statue modelled on the Ephesian type.

Artemi'sia. 1. (early fifth century BC) daughter of Lygdamis, ruler of a Carian kingdom which included Halicarnassus, and after his death regent of his kingdom. With five ships she accompanied Xerxes on his invasion of Greece in 480 (see PERSIAN WARS), and is said by Herodotus (himself from Halicarnassus) to have shown bravery and resource at the battle of Salamis.

2. Sister and wife of *Mausolus of Caria in whose memory she built the Mausoleum at Halicarnassus *c*.353 BC. She instituted a literary competition in which the most famous rhetoricians of the age took part, including Isocrates and Theopompus, who won the prize.

Artemi'sium, promontory on the north-west coast of Euboea, where the Greek fleet was stationed during Xerxes' expedition against Greece in 480 BC, and whence they were forced to withdraw (see PERSIAN WARS).

Arundel Marbles, see MARMOR PARIUM.

arval priests or **brothers** (*fratres arvales*), the most ancient college of priests in Rome, already in existence under the early republic and restored by the emperor Augustus. They were so called from offering public sacrifices for the fertility of the fields (*arvum*, a ploughed field). For their mythical origin see ACCA LARENTIA. Many of their records survive in inscriptions. The college had twelve members chosen for life from the most distinguished senatorial families; from imperial times they seem to have included the reigning emperor. Their most important ceremony took place in May in honour of the agricultural goddess *Dea Dia, in a grove on the Via Campania 8 km. (5 miles) from Rome. The famous song of the priests, the *carmen arvale*, has been preserved on an inscription of AD 218; it dates originally from the sixth or fifth century BC and is the oldest surviving specimen of Latin poetry. Other surviving inscriptions recording vows and offerings they were required to make are important for the history of Latin script in Rome and also for the chronology of the empire, since many events in the house of the reigning emperor were commemorated by the priests. Compare SALII.

Arverni, Gallic tribe which for a long time fought the Aedui for the supremacy of Gaul. In 52 BC Vercingetorix, the son of a former Arvernian king, led the Gallic revolt against Julius Caesar (see *COMMENTARIES* I (book 7)).

arx ('citadel'), at Rome, the north-east summit of the Capitoline hill, the citadel proper. The temple of *Juno Moneta was here.

Asca'laphus, in Greek myth, the son of Acheron who revealed that Persephonē while in the Underworld had eaten some pomegranate seeds, obliging her to remain there for part of each year. According to Ovid, Persephone turned him into an owl for his betrayal.

Asca'nius or **Iūlus,** in Roman legend, son of Aeneas and, according to Virgil in the *Aeneid*, the Trojan princess Creusa; he accompanied his father to Italy after the fall of Troy. The historian Livy mentions an alternative version in which his mother was the Italian princess *Lavinia. The gens *Julia at Rome claimed descent from him.

asclē'piad, see METRE, GREEK 8 (i).

Asclēpi'adēs, of Samos (b. *c*.320 BC), also called Sicelidas, one of the earliest writers of the Greek literary *epigram, and in particular of the love epigram, in the Hellenistic age, a contemporary of Philetas and Theocritus. Many of his poems survive in the Greek *Anthology. He gave his name to the 'asclepiad' metres, used earlier by Sappho and Alcaeus, because he revived them.

Asclē'pius (Lat. Aesculapius), the Greek god of healing. Strictly speaking he was a hero, the son of the god Apollo (himself a healing god) and a mortal, Coronis, daughter of Phlegyas. Apollo killed Coronis for being unfaithful to him. (Regretting it afterwards, he turned the crow which had told him of her infidelity from a white bird into a black.) He saved his unborn child Asclepius, and entrusted him to the care of the centaur *Chiron. From him Asclepius learned the art of medicine. Answering the prayer of the goddess Artemis he restored to life her favourite Hippolytus, son of Theseus. Zeus, angered at his interference, slew Asclepius with a thunderbolt; Apollo in his turn was angry at the death of his son, and in revenge killed the *Cyclopes who had made the thunderbolt. To expiate this murder Apollo became for a year the slave of *Admetus. Homer in the *Iliad* represents Asclepius as the father of Machaon and Podaleirius, the doctors of the Greek army at the siege of Troy.

There is still controversy as to whether Asclepius was originally a god or, more probably, a nearly-divine type of hero, but certainly by classical times he had overshadowed other healing gods and heroes and was worshipped as a god and the founder of medicine. The most famous seat of his cult was at Epidaurus. From there lesser shrines were founded in other places, notably at Athens in 420 and at Rome in 293 BC (see AESCULAPIUS). There is a tradition that the poet Sophocles played a prominent part in establishing the Athenian cult. Epidaurus was much frequented by patients from all parts of the Greek world for the cure of their disease by the ritual of *incubation, the nature of the cure being indicated by means of a dream experienced in sleep (see also DIVINATION). Many inscriptions found at Epidaurus and at Athens describe successful cures, achieved perhaps sometimes through faith but also through normal medical treatment. In historical times the Asclepiadae were a clan (*genos*) which practised medicine as a hereditary skill, tracing their descent from Asclepius and perhaps deriving their science partly from the priestly cult. They seem to have admitted to membership doctors from other families (compare HOMERIDAE). Asclepius was closely associated with the snake, and in instituting new shrines a sacred snake was always taken from the temple at Epidaurus. In art he is often shown bearing a staff, sometimes entwined with a snake; he is sometimes accompanied by a dog. See also ARISTEIDES (3).

Ascō'nius Pediā'nus, Quintus (9 BC–AD 76), the writer of a historical commentary on Cicero's speeches, of which a fragment survives, discovered in 1416 in a ninth-century manuscript at St Gall by the Italian humanist Poggio Bracciolini.

Asia

1. *The continent.* The early Greek geographers until *c.*500 BC divided the land mass of the world into two roughly equal parts, Europe in the north and north-west, and Asia including Africa (Libya) to the south and south-east. By the time of Herodotus in the fifth century BC they had separated Africa from Asia and set the boundaries of the latter at the Indian Ocean in the south and the river Tanais (Don) in the north. Herodotus saw Asia Minor as a peninsula jutting into the Mediterranean Sea. Asia extended east as far as India, beyond which the earth was desert and unknown, with the river Oxus apparently marking its northern boundary. Not until the expedition of Alexander the Great towards the end of the fourth century BC did the Greeks have any detailed knowledge of the eastern regions of the continent. The conquest by the Romans of Asia Minor and Syria and their wars with Mithridates and the Parthians in the first century BC greatly increased their knowledge not only of western Asia but more especially of the Caucasian north, a region of which the Greeks were almost totally ignorant. The Romans' taste for luxuries such as silk and spices led to their exploration of the ancient trade routes and even to contact with Chinese merchants.

2. *The Roman province.* When Attalus III of Pergamum died in 133 BC he bequeathed his kingdom to the Romans. It included all of Greek Asia Minor; its eastern boundary was a line from Bithynia in the north to Lycia in the south and it later included Phrygia. It was rich in natural resources and had flourishing agriculture, industry, and trade. As a consequence of the exactions of Roman governors and profiteers, it was ready to join Mithridates VI, king of Pontus, who, seeking to extend his territory, occupied most of Asia Minor in 88 BC. He was forced by the Roman general Sulla to make peace in 84 and to give up all his conquered territory. Sulla reorganized the province and its system of taxation, but it continued to suffer from periodic exactions. During the partition of the provinces between Augustus and the senate after 27 BC, Asia became a senatorial province to be governed by a proconsul. It was essentially made up of many city states, some of which remained nominally free under Roman rule. Their rivalries prevented any real sense of provincial unity but individual city-states were often enriched by the pride of their citizens. During the first two centuries of the empire Asia enjoyed great prosperity. The coastal cities retained a sophisticated Greek society but those

of the interior became Hellenized only gradually, and always retained something of their non-Greek background. In the fourth century when Constantinople became the capital of the eastern Roman empire, Asian traffic was inclined to stop there, no longer passing on to Greece and Italy as it had for centuries. Thus Asia was deprived of the western influences which over the centuries had helped to mould its complex character.

Asia Minor, the peninsula in the extreme west of Asia bounded by the Black Sea and Propontis, the Aegean and the Mediterranean, and, on the east, by the mountains to the west of the upper course of the Euphrates. It is a largely fertile country which was inhabited from earliest times by a variety of tribes from Asia and Europe. Greek tradition said that as a consequence of the *Dorian Invasion into mainland Greece many of the dispossessed emigrated to the coast of Asia Minor and there planted the Greek language and customs. The north was colonized by Aeolians said traditionally to have come from Thessaly and Boeotia (see AEOLIS). To the south of them were the Ionians, who were to be more prominent in history, said to have come from Attica; their part of the coast was called *Ionia. Further south again were Dorian colonies from the Peloponnese and Crete. The actuality was of course much more complicated than this fairly simple picture: the settlers were of more mixed origin and the colonization may have taken two centuries, from the tenth to the eighth BC. However, settlements quickly prospered. City life developed, first under kings and then under oligarchies, and trade in the Aegean, around the Black Sea and in the interior of Asia Minor itself, created further prosperity. Folk memories of heroic life in Mycenaean Greece flowered into epic poetry (see HOMER), and scientific thinkers speculated about the nature of the physical universe on the supposition that some underlying principle could be discovered (see PHILOSOPHY 1). Perhaps these developments were in part due to the influence of the Asiatic peoples: over the centuries the Greeks adopted the Asiatic modes of music, introduced eastern myths into their religion (see e.g. CYBELE), and were strongly influenced by their art, science, and technology.

In the seventh and sixth centuries BC great political changes came about in Asia Minor. By the end of the seventh century the Assyrian empire had been overthrown by the *Medes, a people from the mountainous country southwest of the Caspian Sea. They advanced into eastern Asia Minor and clashed with *Lydia, a rich and powerful kingdom created by Gyges (*c.*685–657 BC). After a battle in 585 a frontier was established between the two kingdoms at the river Halys. Gyges had brought the Greek cities in Asia Minor under Lydian control and by the time of Croesus (*c*.560–546 BC), the last king, most of them paid tribute to Lydia; but they still retained considerable freedom and their trade prospered, no doubt helped by their adoption of the Lydian invention of coinage (see MONEY 1). Both Lydia and Media, however, were to fall to a new empire, that of the Persians, who lived in the hilly area north-east of the Persian gulf. In the mid-sixth century, under the leadership of Cyrus they conquered in succession the Medes, the Lydians, and the Babylonians, and under Cyrus' son Cambyses they conquered Egypt. Asia Minor was absorbed into the Persian empire; the Greek cities had to pay tribute, supply troops, and appoint tyrants acceptable to Persia. When Darius became king of the Persian empire in 521 BC the Greeks in Ionia became increasingly discontented for political and economic reasons and decided in 499 to revolt. This revolt was finally crushed by the Persians in 494 but the Ionians were not entirely without success, for the Persians now set up democracies in the Greek cities. From this point the history of Greek Asia Minor becomes bound up with that of Greece proper. See PERSIAN WARS, EPHESUS, and MILETUS.

Asianism, name given to the artificially mannered style of Greek oratory which developed in the period after Demosthenes (d. 322 BC); see ORATORY 1.

Asina'ria ('she-ass'), farcical Roman comedy by *Plautus, adapted from the Greek comedy of the same name, *Onāgros* (or *Onagos*) of Demophilus.

Demaenetus, an indulgent father, wishes to help his son Argyrippus to save the prostitute Philaenium from an old procuress, but he is tyrannized by his wife Artemona, who keeps tight control of the purse-strings. By a trick of one of his slaves he gets possession of twenty minae which were to be paid to Artemona's steward for some asses which have been sold (whence the name of the play), and father and son spend the evening banqueting with Philaenium. But a rival for the girl's favours, furious at finding himself anticipated, warns Artemona; she descends on the party, and with dire threats removes her husband.

The saying *homo homini lupus* ('man is a wolf to man') is taken from the play (l. 495).

Asi'nius Po'llio, see POLLIO.

Aspā'sia, of Miletus, the mistress of the Athenian statesman *Pericles; she was perhaps of free birth. She lived with Pericles from some time in the 440s until his death in 429 BC, the association beginning five years or more after Pericles divorced his wife. She had the reputation of being a woman of intellect who conversed with Socrates. Naturally enough she was often attacked for supposedly influencing Pericles' political actions, and was a target for writers of comedy. She bore Pericles a son, also called Pericles, who was legitimated by decree after the death in the plague of 430 of his father's two sons by his lawful wife. After Pericles' death she was said to have married the democratic politician Lysicles and to have borne him a son.

Asphodel, Plain of, in Homer's *Odyssey*, the place in the Underworld (see HADES) where all the dead dwell, leading a shadowy continuance of their former life in the world. The asphodel (whence 'daffodil') is a flowering plant of the lily family; in Hesiod it is given as an example of the cheapest and plainest food.

Aspis ('shield'), Greek comedy by *Menander, a substantial part of which has been recovered on a papyrus.

One of three brothers has died, leaving a son and daughter. The son Cleostratus goes off to the wars, leaving his sister under the protection of their uncle Chaerestratus. Cleostratus is reported dead, leaving his property to his sister. By Greek law the closest male relative of an heiress (within the permitted degree) was entitled to marry her. Chaerestratus was already planning to marry the girl to his stepson, but now his brother Smicrines tries to marry her for her money. A plot is laid to trick Smicrines into offering marriage to Chaerestratus' daughter instead, but Cleostratus, alive after all, returns. The play probably ended with the marriages of the cousins and the discomfiture of Smicrines.

The play is enlivened by the character of the resourceful slave Daos who engineers the deception and must be typical of many such slaves in other of Menander's plays, but now known chiefly from Roman comedy.

Assa'racus, great-grandfather of Aeneas (for genealogy see TROY).

assembly, see ECCLESIA, APELLA, and COMITIA.

assonance, the noticeable recurrence of a sound in successive words; compare ALLITERATION.

1. *Greek*. The Greeks occasionally employed assonance for the sake of its aesthetic effect but took no pains to avoid it when no effect was intended, even when the repetition of sound seems to us displeasing. To judge from a comic fragment, fault was found with Euripides for excessive use of the letter sigma, but his extant plays are not noticeably more sigmatic than the rest of Greek literature. Punning assonance sometimes occurs, but not always for humorous effect; many Greek thinkers believed that there was a significant connection between similar-sounding words. Hence phrases like *pathei mathos* ('through suffering comes knowledge') and *soma sema* ('the body is a tomb') acquired deeper meaning. There is little evidence for deliberate rhyming in epic or drama, though it

seems occasionally to happen in the final lines of a scene, or in a proverbial phrase. Prose writers avoided rhyme, except for conscious and mannered stylists like Isocrates.

2. *Latin.* The kind of assonance known as alliteration, often obtrusively and artlessly employed, is a common feature of early Latin poetry. By the time of Virgil, however, it had come to be employed with great subtlety and with emotional effect. A similar development is seen in prose, Cicero using the device with more point and less obtrusiveness than his predecessors. Tacitus uses alliterative pairs of words with great effect. The Roman ear seems to have enjoyed the judicious repetition of similar terminations in the more impassioned parts of oratory, an aspect of assonance employed more subtly by the poets. This usage easily turns into a species of rhyme found occasionally in poetry of all periods, but used deliberately in the accentual hymns from the fifth century AD onwards and with great beauty in the secular medieval lyrics.

Aste'ria, in Greek myth, sister of *Leto and mother, by the Titan Persēs, of Hecatē. Being pursued by Zeus she turned into a quail, leapt into the sea and became Ortygia ('quail island'), afterwards known as Delos.

Aste'ropē, one of the *Pleiades.

Astrae'a, 'starry maiden' (later applied as an epithet to Queen Elizabeth I of England), the constellation Virgo, identified with Justice (Gk. *Dikē*), the last god to leave the earth, by *Aratus. She was supposed to have lived among men in the *Golden Age, retired to the mountains in the Silver Age, and finally, during the wickedness of the Bronze Age, fled to heaven.

astra'galoi, 'knucklebones', used in various simple games especially by women and children. They were also used as *dice, since the four faces were of different shapes, one flat, one irregular, one concave, and one convex; these were given the respective values 1, 6, 3, and 4.

astrology. The study of the heavenly bodies as predicting or influencing the fate of individuals was ultimately due to the Babylonians, deriving from their cult of planetary gods and their observations and calculations concerning the movements of the heavenly bodies. The belief underpinning astrology, common to educated people generally and to most philosophical schools (the Epicureans were the exception), was that the cosmos was a unity, and that whatever happened in the heavens was bound to affect or be reflected in events on earth. As it was possible to predict the recurrence of celestial phenomena by prolonged observation and calculation (astronomy), so it might also be possible to predict terrestrial events by observation of the heavenly bodies (astrology). Astrology could therefore

appeal for various scientific, religious, and philosophical reasons to the educated as well as the uneducated, and it came to be generally believed that the fortunes of an individual depended upon the aspect of the sky at the moment of his birth, and that astrologers could give guidance accordingly.

Astrology does not seem to have exerted any influence on Greek life until after the third century BC, in the wake of Alexander the Great, though the cosmological speculations of the Greek philosophers paved the way for it. Berossus of Babylon is said to have set up a school of astrology in the island of Cos *c*.280 BC, and it has been thought that his writings, now lost, transmitted Babylonian astrology to the Greek world; by the next century it had spread to Rome, and a vogue for it began when a number of manuals began to circulate widely. Cato and Ennius expressed hostility, but in the next century believers included Sulla, Posidonius, and Varro (but not Cicero). Vitruvius, Propertius, and Ovid all professed to believe, and Augustus published his horoscope. From the first century AD onwards virtually everyone, Christians, pagans, and Jews alike, accepted the predictability of fate and the maleficent powers of the planets (see MANILIUS). A few of the best minds held out against this tyranny, usually with the argument (Plotinus and Origen) that while stars, by reason of the universal 'sympathy' pervading the cosmos, may indicate the future, they cannot *determine* it. Rome particularly was sensitive to the potential political dangers, and periodically at times of national crisis banished all professional astrologers (e.g. 139 and 33 BC). However, no permanent ban was intended, and the emperors themselves frequently had recourse to horoscopes. Thrasyllus, the astrologer of Tiberius, acquired great influence. It was not until the fourth century, with Augustine's emphatic denial of its validity, and with the advent of the Christian emperors, that the practice of astrology was officially banned. Nevertheless for the ordinary man it retained an axiomatic validity until the seventeenth century and beyond. See also PTOLEMY.

Astrono'mica, didactic poem on astrology by *Manilius.

astronomy. The science of astronomy (to which Rome contributed nothing) developed comparatively late in Greece and, being for the Greeks essentially a system for predicting the positions of the heavenly bodies, it covered only a part of what we understand by the term. In the classical period interest was confined to observations of the solstice and equinox and of the rising and setting of the most obvious stars and constellations, for the practical ends of navigation and establishing a *calendar. The fifth-century Athenian astronomer *Meton tried to correlate the lunar year with the solar year in a

19-year cycle (c.435 BC), but it seems that his system was not incorporated into the Athenian calendar, and he won immortality rather as the comic 'town-planner' in Aristophanes' *Birds*. It is very doubtful whether the Presocratic philosophers actually made the astronomical discoveries attributed to them (see THALES); their theories were purely speculative although individuals reached some of the truths necessary for a science of astronomy, such as that the earth is a sphere (believed by the Pythagoreans) and that the moon receives its light from the sun (found in Parmenides, Empedocles, and *Anaxagoras). Anaxagoras also understood the principles of eclipses. Not till the fourth century can we be sure that the Greeks identified the five planets known to the ancient world, Venus, Mercury, Mars, Jupiter, and Saturn (see EUDOXUS). In that century became crystallized the picture of the cosmos which was accepted by Aristotle (see 4 (iii)) and given final shape in the second century AD by *Ptolemy, who was able to calculate the position of all the known heavenly bodies at a given moment, predict eclipses, and foretell the appearance and disappearances of the planets and fixed stars. At the centre of the cosmos was the earth, a globe suspended in space and composed of the cold, heavy impurities of the universe, whose weight had taken it to the centre. The earth was surrounded by a system of concentric spherical shells, rotating at various speeds and about various axes; on these were carried the moon, sun, planets, and fixed stars. The terrestrial atmosphere reached as far as the moon. The outermost sphere, that of the fixed stars, was composed of the rarest of all elements, the aether, and revolved daily about the earth. Ptolemy in his *Almagest* gave canonical form to this view of the cosmos, and his work remained uncorrected except in small details throughout all antiquity until Copernicus (1473–1543) and Galileo (1564–1642). For a heliocentric view of the universe see ARISTARCHUS (1). See further the names cited under MATHEMATICS.

Asty'anax, known also as Skamandrios, the son of Hector and *Andromachē, born during the siege of Troy and thrown from its battlements by *Neoptolemus or killed by Odysseus after the capture of the city.

asty'nomoi, petty officials in Athens chosen annually by lot with the principal duty of keeping the streets clean and free of obstruction.

Atala'nta (Atalantē), in Greek myth, daughter either of Iasos, an Arcadian, or of Schoeneus, a Boeotian; in either case her mother was *Clymenē. She was a huntress, averse to marriage, and loved by *Meleager with whom she took part in the Calydonian boar-hunt. She refused to marry any man who could not defeat her in a race, and any suitor whom she defeated was put to death. Hippomenēs (or Milanion) took up the

challenge, and on the advice of Aphroditē carried with him three golden apples which she gave him. He dropped these at intervals and, as Atalanta could not resist the temptation to stop and pick them up, won the race. Their son was *Parthenopaeus in most accounts.

Ata'rgatis, often known simply as 'the Syrian goddess', worshipped as a fertility goddess at Hierapolis (Bambycē) where her temple was the greatest and holiest in Syria. Her consort was Hadad. In the second century BC her worship spread to a number of Hellenic cities, but appeared only sporadically in the West. *Lucian describes the cult, and *Apuleius the life of her Galli, wandering priests.

Ātē, in Greek myth, the personification of blind folly in the grip of which the victim cannot distinguish between right and wrong, advantageous and disadvantageous courses of action.

Ateius Ca'pito, Gaius, see CAPITO.

Ate'llan farces (*fābulae Atellānae*), named after the town of Atella in Campania, ancient dramatic performances apparently in the form of coarse comedies of low life. There were certain stock characters, Maccus the fool, Dossennus the hunchback, Mandūcus the glutton, Pappus the greybeard, etc., who were probably introduced in ridiculous situations. Some of the later titles suggest burlesques of mythology. Atellan plays became popular at Rome, probably in the third century BC, and were acted by amateurs. They were revived in more literary form, with the same stock characters but with a written plot in verse, by Pomponius of Bononia and Novius, who probably flourished early in the first century BC. These revivals were acted by professional comedians, were staged after the end of performances of tragedy, and seem often to have been tragic parodies. They continued intermittently until the end of the first century AD. Only fragments survive. See OSCAN.

A'thamas, in Greek myth, son of *Aeolus (2) and king of Thebes. The myth of his family is variously told, but in essentials is as follows. By his first wife Nephelē, a cloud-goddess, he had two children, Phrixus and Hellē. His second wife Ino, daughter of Cadmus, conceived a bitter hatred of her step-children, who escaped death on a winged and golden-fleeced ram which carried them away across the sea. Helle became giddy and fell into that part which is in consequence called the Hellespont. Phrixus arrived safely in Colchis, where Aeētēs the king received him hospitably. The ram was sacrificed to Zeus and its golden fleece hung up in Colchis and guarded by a dragon. For the rest of this myth see ARGONAUTS, and for the fate of Athamas, Ino, and her two sons see DIONYSUS.

atheism. In the ancient world charges of 'atheism' were levelled both against those who denied the existence of any kind of divinity and against those who rejected a traditional polytheism. Unbelief of either kind did not usually incur any penalty except when it was so publicly proclaimed as to exacerbate other feelings, as in fifth-century Athens when the *sophists had created a gulf between old and new beliefs, or in Rome under the empire when the 'atheistic' Christians refused to burn incense on the emperor's birthday. At times of crisis Athens and Rome were both liable to take alarm at signs of atheism that might offend the gods or be of evil omen. Tertullian (*Apologeticum* 40) observed that at every natural disaster the cry goes up, 'Christians to the lions!' The charge of atheism was sometimes made as an expression of general abuse, or with political undertones. Thus Socrates, who seemed to criticize some traditional views of the gods but was scrupulous in his religious observances and had a strong religious sense, was charged with being an atheist.

Athē'na or **Athē'nē,** the patron goddess of Athens. In Homer she is generally called Athene, in tragedy Athenaia. The (abbreviated) form Athena became common in the fourth century BC. She was worshipped in the *Parthenon, her great temple on the Acropolis, and throughout Greece, the islands, and the colonies. Whether Athens is named after the goddess or the goddess after Athens is an ancient argument, but the latter is generally considered more probable. Her name is perhaps to be found on a *Linear B tablet from Cnossus, and she is probably a prehellenic deity. She is sometimes known as Pallas Athene for reasons which remain obscure; Pallas was sometimes understood to mean 'maiden', sometimes 'brandisher' (of weapons). Equally obscure is the meaning of her name Tritogeneia, 'Trito-born', for which a number of explanations was given in antiquity. In classical times she was pre-eminently the city goddess of Greece, and had temples not only on the Acropolis at Athens but also on the citadels of Argos, Sparta, and Larisa (in Thessaly). In Homer, despite the fact that she is the enemy of Troy, she is still the goddess of the Trojan citadel; see PALLADIUM. She was *par excellence* a war-goddess, and is most frequently represented in art as armed, but in addition she was the patroness of all urban arts and crafts, especially spinning and weaving, and so ultimately the personification of wisdom. She is also the inventor of the musical instrument the *aulos* (a flute; see MUSIC I). The principal myth concerning her relates to her birth. She was the daughter of Zeus and *Mētis. Zeus swallowed Metis for fear she should give birth to a son stronger than himself. In due time the god Hephaestus (or Prometheus, it was sometimes said) opened Zeus' head with an axe and Athena emerged, fully armed and uttering her war-cry. She is

regularly regarded as virgin; Zeus gave Hephaestus leave to marry her, and from his unsuccessful attempt sprang the Athenian king *Erichthonius. She also strove with *Poseidon for possession of Attica, a contest in which she emerged victorious by producing the olive tree. (For another myth see ARACHNE.) She is generally represented as a goddess of severe beauty, in armour, with helmet, *aegis, spear, and shield (sometimes bearing the Gorgon's head); she often has an owl sitting on her shoulder, especially in fifth-century Athens, in reference to her stock epithet *glaukōpis* which appears to mean 'owl-faced' but could also be interpreted as 'bright-eyed'. See also ATHENA NIKE, TEMPLE OF, and compare MINERVA.

Athenae'um, at Rome, the emperor Hadrian's famous institute for lectures and recitations by rhetors and other literary figures.

Athenae'us (flourished *c.* AD 200), of Naucratis, Greek author of the *Deipnosophistai* ('men learned in the arts of the banquet') in fifteen books. Twenty-three learned men (some having the names of real persons, such as Galen and Ulpian) are represented dining together at Rome on several occasions, and conversing on all aspects of food and on a wide range of other subjects. In reality Athenaeus was an industrious collector of excerpts and anecdotes, which he reproduces as conversation. The work is a fruitful source of information on the literature and usages of ancient Greece; it survives except for the first two books and part of the third, which we have only in a later epitome.

Athēnaiōn politeia. **1.** A treatise by *Aristotle (see 3 (ii)). **2.** A political pamphlet attributed to Xenophon (see CONSTITUTION OF THE ATHENIANS (2)).

Athēna Nīkē, Temple of. A shrine to the goddess Athena Nike ('of victory') existed by the mid-sixth century on the *Acropolis at Athens, to the right of the (later) *Propylaea. Pausanias called it the Temple of Wingless Victory. An inscription indicates that it was decided in 448 BC to erect a new altar and temple of marble, but construction did not begin until 427, and was presumably completed by 424 when the statue was dedicated. It was built in the Ionic order (see ARCHITECTURE I (ii)), entirely of white marble, and richly decorated with sculptured reliefs. Around 410 the wall surrounding the temple, the Nike parapet, was erected. The temple visible today in a good state of preservation has been reconstructed after being pulled down in the seventeenth century and the marble used to build defences.

Athens (Athenai, Lat. Athenae), the chief city of *Attica, in Greece.

I. *Topography.* The city in classical times stood about 5 km. (3 miles) from the sea at its nearest point, in the central plain of Attica, surrounded by mountains on all sides except the south. It is enclosed on the north-west by Mount Parnes, on the north-east by Mount *Pentelicus, on the south-east by Mount *Hymettus, and (less important) on the west by Mount Aegaleus. The citadel of Athens, the *Acropolis, sometimes called simply *polis*, from being the original 'city', is a squareish rock rising steeply out of the plain. Immediately west of it is a second hill, the *Areopagus, and to the south-west a third, the *Pnyx. To the north-east and outside the city wall of Themistocles (built soon after the expulsion of the Persians in 479 BC) stands the peaked mountain of Lycabettus. To the east and west of the city flow the Ili(s)sus (joined by the Eridanus) and the Cephi(s)sus. The Themistoclean wall of the city was breached by a dozen gates, the most used of which was the *Dipylon in the north-west. Some 75 m. (80 yds.) to the south was the Sacred Gate from which the Sacred Way led to Eleusis. (Near this gate the army of the Roman general Sulla broke through the wall in 86 BC, slaughtering so many Athenians in the narrow streets that their blood streamed through the gate into the suburbs.) Communication between Athens and her harbours Piraeus and Phalerum was protected by the *Long Walls.

The commercial, social, and political centre of the city was the *agora*, 'market-place'. The old agora, the first at Athens, was supposedly built by Theseus and probably situated on the lower part of the north slope of the Acropolis. It contained the *Eleusinion and the *Prytaneum. By the seventh century BC the expanding city needed an enlarged agora, which was established north of the Acropolis and the Areopagus and formed part of the *Ceramīcus (potters' quarter) in a region where the oldest cemeteries are found, dating from Mycenaean to Geometric times. Archaeological excavations have shown that the area began to be developed in the time of Solon, at the beginning of the sixth century. The agora here became that of classical Athens; it was finally destroyed in the invasions of the Heruli (a Germanic tribe from the Black Sea area) in AD 267. In classical times some of the buildings dated from the time of the Peisistratids (second half of the sixth century BC), notably: the Enneakrounos or fountain-house, which has been probably identified in the south-east of the agora; the temple of Apollo Patrōos ('guardian'); the Altar of the Twelve Gods (see PEISISTRATUS); the *Olympieum; the old Bouleutērion, built at the beginning of the sixth century for the newly created *boule*; and the shrine of Theseus. (See also METROON.) It is possible that the original *orchestra*, 'dancing floor', stood here, where the collapse of stands for spectators seems to have resulted in the construction of both the Theatre of Dionysus (see DIONYSUS, THEATRE OF) and the *Odeum, in

Pericles' time. By the end of the fifth century the agora included among other buildings the new Bouleuterion, recently built to the west of the old, the Tholos, the Temple of Hephaestus (usually called the Thēsēum because it was identified as the shrine where the bones of Theseus were buried by Cimon), the Stoa of Zeus Eleutherios, and the Stoa Basileios.

2. *Historical outline.*

(i) The Acropolis was continuously inhabited from Neolithic times (*c*. 5000 BC). In the *Mycenaean period a palace was built on it, and it was fortified by a wall in the second half of the thirteenth century BC. (This was during the imagined lifetime of Athens' national hero *Theseus; for other myths relating to this early period see ERECHTHEUS, ERICHTHONIUS, and CECROPS.) Some scholars see in the fortification an indication of the *synoikismos*, synoecism (i.e. amalgamation), of the various communities in *Attica into one state, with Athens as the capital city (see Thucydides 2. 15). This event, traditionally ascribed to Theseus, is certainly historical, and was celebrated annually at Athens, but it was probably a gradual process, and when it was completed we do not know. At any rate by the twelfth century Athens was strong enough to resist the *Dorian Invasion, and to be the springboard of the eleventh-century *migrations from the mainland to Ionia. The Athenians of the classical period flattered themselves that they were autochthonous, 'sprung from the soil', i.e. that they were an indigenous people, unlike the Dorians, who were invaders. The archaeological evidence supports their idea of continuity with the Mycenaean world: it indicates that the city was occupied continuously during the *Dark Age, and after 900 BC was perhaps the most prosperous community in Greece, originating the Geometric style in pottery (see POTTERY I (iv)). Scanty remains of the Archaic period which followed show that there were important buildings there by the end of the seventh century. During this time the Mycenaean wall ceased to be important (disastrously so by 480 BC: see PERSIAN WARS). The *Peisistratids used the Acropolis as a place of refuge, but after the expulsion of the tyrants in 510 BC it ceased to be a fort.

In early times Athens, like other Greek states, was ruled by kings. Traditionally the last king was *Codrus, who was succeeded by elected *archons, and Athens became an *aristocracy. Although the archonship was an elected office, the aristocrats, being rich and powerful, monopolized it. The attempt by *Cylon to overthrow them and become tyrant (*c*.632) failed. Despite the legislation of *Draco (621) their position was not weakened until the reforms of *Solon in 594 BC. These however could not prevent tyranny at Athens, and the popular leader Peisistratus seized power in the mid-sixth century. The period of the Peisistratid tyrants, lasting until 510 BC, saw a considerable increase in the city's material prosperity and cultural standing. After the expulsion of *Hippias, the reforms of *Cleisthenes established a true *democracy (see also ECCLESIA, BOULE, and AREOPAGUS).

(ii) At the beginning of the fifth century BC Athens was a powerful state. But her intervention in the Ionian Revolt was unsuccessful and exposed her to the menace of Persia, where the exiled tyrant Hippias was trying to enlist help to get himself restored to power at Athens. The first Persian invasion was defeated at Marathon (490). When the second invasion came ten years later, Athens, under the influence of *Themistocles, had built a strong navy, and she emerged from the struggle with the city in ruins and her territory ravaged but with her fleet intact, her prestige increased, and her position as leader of all the Ionian Greeks acknowledged. The war with Persia was effectively ended with *Cimon's victory at the river Eurymedon c.466. Athens alone possessed a fleet capable of protecting Greece and the Aegean islands against Persian attack. The Ionian Greek cities which had rebelled against Persia accepted the leadership of Athens, and this was the origin of the *Delian League (477). As head of this league and by means of her colonies on the shores of the Aegean and the Black Sea (see COLONIZATION, GREEK 3) Athens became, under the guidance of Cimon and *Pericles, an imperial power. Through the constitutional reforms of *Ephialtes and Pericles in 462 democracy reached its fullest development: the citizens were entirely self-governing, political offices were open to all, and the citizens were paid for undertaking their political duties, so that even the poorest could afford to exercise their rights.

The rebuff of Cimon by the Spartans c.462 was ultimately a contributory factor to developing hostility between Athens and Sparta. War broke out between Athens and the Peloponnesians, led by Sparta, in 460 (sometimes known as the First Peloponnesian War) and lasted until 446. Aegina fell to Athens after a long blockade (457–456), and the Athenian general Tolmides sailed in triumph around the Peloponnese. The Delian League was being turned into an empire, by land as well as by sea; this was the period in which the first *cleruchies were established. A somewhat indecisive victory by the Spartans over the Athenians at Tanagra in Boeotia in 457 was decisively reversed at Oenophyta two months later. This gave the Athenians control of Boeotia, which they kept until 446 when they were defeated at Coronea by a Boeotian rising. In the interval Athens suffered a setback when her expeditionary force to *Egypt was defeated in 454. The Peace of *Callias c.450 finally brought the war with Persia to a formal conclusion, and the Thirty Years' Peace was made with Sparta in 446; although this ended Athens' possible hopes for a land-empire it acknowledged her right to keep her sea-empire. See also PENTEKONTAETIA.

(iii) The peace with Sparta lasted only fifteen years. By 431 Sparta was not alone in being alarmed by Athenian expansion, and when in that year Sparta entered upon war much of Greece looked to her as liberator. For the events of this war, lasting until 404, see PELOPONNESIAN WAR. The failure of the *Sicilian Expedition (413) was the signal for the revolt of many of Athens' subject-allies, which she made vigorous and partially successful efforts to suppress. The latter part of the war was marked also by the co-operation against her of Sparta and Persia, who were helped by the plotting of the Athenian aristocrat *Alcibiades, now in exile. In the city itself the democracy was temporarily overthrown by oligarchic revolution. A council of *Four Hundred was established in 411, nominally supplemented by an assembly of five thousand. The revolt of Euboea at this time caused deep alarm at Athens, but the *oligarchy was deposed within the year, and in 410, after Athens won a notable sea-battle at Cyzicus, the Spartans sued for peace. The demagogue *Cleophon was influential in the newly restored democracy, which lasted until the surrender of the Athenians in 404. Athens emerged a dependant of Sparta, impoverished, her population severely depleted, the Long Walls destroyed, all her overseas possessions lost, including the cleruchies, and the fleet reduced to twelve ships. Sparta imposed an oligarchy on the city, and for eight months in 404–403 Athens was ruled by the *Thirty Tyrants. However, she soon regained her democracy and her freedom; Sparta, deeply involved in Persia (see SPARTA 3), recognized Athenian independence and allowed her to rebuild her fleet and restore the Long Walls. In 395 Athens had joined Thebes, Argos, and Corinth in their attempt to overthrow the Spartan supremacy (see THEBES and SPARTA 4), an attempt that failed in its object and was ended when friendly relations between Sparta and Persia were restored and the king of Persia imposed the pro-Spartan Peace of Antalcidas or King's Peace (387/6). The king regained possession of the Ionian cities of Asia Minor and remained master of the Aegean Sea.

The fifth century was the great age of Attic culture: its most famous writers at this time, some of whose works still survive, include Aeschylus, Sophocles, Euripides, Herodotus, Thucydides, Aristophanes, and Antiphon.

(iv) Political interest in the early fourth century is focused on the rivalry between Sparta and Thebes, in which Athens played only a secondary role. In 377 Athens started to make alliances in order to protect herself against Sparta, and thus the Second Athenian League (or Confederacy) was formed (the first is known as the Delian League: see above), composed of various islands and cities of the Aegean, Corcyra, and other states. Athens retained her commercial supremacy, and in 376 Chabrias (a professional soldier) won back her supremacy at sea by a decisive naval victory over Sparta near Naxos. The most prominent Athenian statesman of this period was *Callistratus, whose general policy was based on harmony with Sparta and a balance of power between that city and Thebes. The latter, led by *Epaminondas, was now aspiring to the leadership of Greece, and Athens, having supported the Thebans until their victory over the Spartans at Leuctra in 371, was more influenced by jealousy of neighbouring Thebes than by the old rivalry with Sparta. In the ensuing struggle between these two, Athens was in alliance with Sparta in 369, and an Athenian contingent fought on the Spartan side at Mantinea in 362. Athens was reviving the alliances of the old Delian League in the Aegean (see TIMOTHEUS (2)) and causing discontent and suspicion among her allies. A revolt of these broke out in the Social War (357–355), at the end of which the independence of the principal members of the League was recognized. Athens was still strong enough in sea-power to safeguard the passage of her essential food supplies from the Hellespont, but by this time *Macedon was rising in importance and threatening the Athenian position in the north Aegean.

(v) For the growth of Macedonian power see MACEDONIA I and PHILIP (1). Faced with the threat of Macedon, Athens had to choose between two policies: to attempt to recover the leadership of Greece, or to come to terms with Philip, with some loss of independence. The 'peace' party included the statesman *Eubulus, the orator *Aeschinēs, the general *Phocion, and the statesman Philocratēs (see also ISO-CRATES); the 'war' party was led by the orators *Demosthenes, *Lycurgus, and *Hypereides. The eloquence of Demosthenes prevailed, and a final battle between Athens and Thebes on the one side and Philip on the other was fought at Chaeronea in 338. Athens was defeated, and was obliged to accept Philip's moderate terms (the loss of the Hellespont) and join the Hellenic confederacy which he organized. It cannot be known to what extent Philip would have allowed Athens to remain independent had the peace party been successful; Demosthenes' policy may have been the only one that left her a chance of freedom. After the risings that followed the accession of Philip's son in 336 (see ALEXANDER (2)) Athens enjoyed a period of tranquillity. The death of Alexander in 323 appeared to give the Greeks an opportunity to recover their freedom, but in the so-called *Lamian War (323–322) Athens with the other Greek states was defeated at Crannon by *Antipater. Demosthenes took poison to avoid capture. The democrats were reinstated at

Athens under the brief rule of Polyperchon (the immediate successor of Antipater as regent of Macedonia), but *Cassander, Antipater's son, restored in the main his father's constitution and appointed as his governor at Athens in 317 the distinguished Athenian citizen *Demetrius of Phalerum, a friend of the philosopher Aristotle. His ten years' governorship was a period of peace and prosperity for the city. Yet when *Demetrius Poliorcētēs, son of Antigonus (see MACEDONIA 2), captured the city from Cassander in 307 he was looked upon by the Athenians as a liberator, and was granted divine honours.

The fourth century shows the last phase of the intellectual and cultural pre-eminence of Athens. The character of her intellectual activity had become less creative and more analytical and critical. It was the age of Plato and Aristotle, the great orators, and New Comedy. Art became more realistic, less infused with the old religious ideas, no longer centred on the interests of the city state. See MYTH and HELLENISTIC AGE.

(vi) The third century BC saw the end of the political importance of Athens. The Chremonidean War (266–262) is notable as the last occasion when Athens took the lead against Macedon. Supported by Sparta and king Ptolemy II Philadelphus of Egypt, she revolted against Antigonus Gonatas (see MACEDONIA 3), was besieged, and finally surrendered through famine. The war took its name from the Athenian statesman (and pupil of the Stoic philosopher Zeno) who initiated the alliance. In 229, on the death of Demetrius II, son of Gonatas, Athens recovered her freedom and except for one attack by Philip V, grandson of Gonatas, had a peaceful existence until 88 BC. After the defeat of the *Achaean League by the Roman consul Mummius in 146 BC Greece became a Roman protectorate (not a province until the time of Augustus), but Athens and Sparta did not have to pay taxes to Rome. There was a revival of material prosperity, and the great quadrennial festival of Athens at Delos was restored. This prosperous period came to an end with the Mithridatic War of 89–85, when Athens, which had sided with *Mithridates, was sacked and in part destroyed by the Roman general *Sulla (see 1 above). Greece suffered severely, both from Sulla and from the barbarian allies of Mithridates, who sacked Delphi. Even greater ruin followed from the Roman civil wars of the first century BC, and endured until the emperor Augustus made Greece a Roman province in 27 BC.

In spite of her political decline Athens retained much of her intellectual prestige and remained pre-eminent for the study of philosophy (see HELLENISTIC AGE 2). She was patronized in the second century BC by the *Attalids of Pergamum, who adorned the city with colonnades (see STOA) and sculptures. It became fashionable for Romans to go to the philosophical schools of Athens as to a university. *Atticus lived there for many years; Cicero and his son and Horace were among those who studied in the city. Horace, and in a later age Lucian, appreciated the peaceful charm of Athens compared with the turmoil of Rome. Athens enjoyed some revival of her former glories in the second century AD under the emperor Hadrian and the Antonines, and in the fourth century Julian the Apostate was a lover of the city. The end of her period of intellectual eminence came in AD 529, when the Christian emperor Justinian ordered the closing of her schools of philosophy.

3. *Administration in the fifth and fourth centuries BC*. For the workings of the democratic government see DEMOCRACY. The chief administrative officials were the *archons (whose functions were largely ceremonial and judicial) and the *strategoi*. Next in order of importance were the financial officers, of whom the chief were the ten *tamiai* (treasurers) of the goddess Athena. There were also ten *pōlētai*, who sold confiscated property and franchises, and made contracts for public works, ten *praktores*, who collected judicial fines, and ten *logistai*, who audited the accounts of outgoing *magistrates. The policing and care of the city were in the charge of ten *astynomoi* (five for Athens and five for Piraeus), while street repairs were looked after by five *hodopoioi*. There were also market inspectors (*agoranomoi*) and inspectors of weights and measures. All these were chosen by lot. The *hellenotamiai*, the treasurers of the Delian League, who had responsibility for a great deal of money, were probably elected, as also were such technical officials as the surveyor of the water-supply and commissioners of public works. The policing of the city was carried out by a body of 300 Scythian archers, who were slaves belonging to the state; and there was a board known as the Eleven, under which were the executioners, the gaolers, and the officials who arrested criminals, all these subordinates also being public slaves. Such slaves were also employed in many clerical duties, some of them important, such as care of the archives.

4. *Economic conditions*. For a reflection of life in Greece before the eighth century BC (seen through epic poetry and therefore distorted) see HOMERIC AGE. The end of that period saw the decline of the self-sufficient household (*oikos*) and the rise of the city (*polis*), an increasing complexity of social and political life, and greater prosperity. Land was converted from animal to arable farming; the population increased steeply, and the soil became insufficient to support it. These changes were no doubt all connected. One problem was caused by the practice of dividing estates among heirs, to the disadvantage of small landowners whose heirs found themselves inheriting property too small to support them. A great part of the land was in any case held by the wealthy and powerful and worked by tenant farmers. From the ninth century onwards the development of trading for metals and luxury goods brought profit to artisans and merchants. See also AGRICULTURE and COLONIZATION, GREEK 1 and 2; and for economic discontent at the end of the seventh century see SOLON.

Our knowledge of the size of the population at Athens during the fifth and fourth centuries BC is very imperfect (see POPULATION); nevertheless, it is clear that in this period the soil of Attica was never able to feed its people, and Athens imported large quantities of wheat, dried fish, salt meat, and cattle, as well as raw materials such as copper, wood, ivory, wool, flax, papyrus, and some manufactured articles such as furniture. She exported wine and oil, silver, marble, pottery, arms, and books. Her ships sailed to all parts of the Mediterranean and, especially, to the Black Sea, the principal source of the Athenian corn supply. Traffic by land was, in contrast, difficult and extremely expensive.

Some idea of the cost of living may be formed from the following data. At the end of the fifth century a building worker or a rower on a trireme would receive one drachma a day, but would be unlikely to earn more than 300 drachmas in a year; a juror would receive half a drachma (three obols; see MONEY 1). A day's ration of corn for a man (his staple food) amounted to one *choenix*, one forty-eighth of a *medimnus* (see WEIGHTS AND MEASURES). The price of a *medimnus* of corn fluctuated during the fifth century, but seems not to have exceeded four drachmas. If to the cost of corn is added as much again for *opsonion*, 'relish', i.e. meat, fish, vegetables, or fruit, then it can be estimated that a single man could feed himself for a little over a drachma a week. In the fourth century the daily wages of skilled labour rose to two or two-and-a-half drachmas, those of unskilled labour remaining at one drachma or rising a little above that. The *Theoric fund provided subsidies to the poor to pay for their entertainments, such as the entrance charge for the theatre. To provide land for the poor, thousands were established as *cleruchs in territories overseas.

Private houses, in contrast with public buildings at Athens, were conspicuously mean, constructed either of a framework of wood or of sun-dried bricks. Their cost could be correspondingly low: figures mentioned by the orators range from 3 to 120 minas (300 to 12,000 drachmas), and 50 minas (5000 drachmas) seems to have been regarded as a large sum to pay for a house. (For comparison, to build a trireme might cost one talent, or 60 minas.) The annual rent of a house was usually set at 8 per cent of its capital value. *Banking was highly organized by the end of the fifth century; banks lent money on mortgage, on cargoes, or on personal security, and issued letters of credit to correspondents abroad. The bank founded by Antisthenes and Archestratus at the end of the fifth century BC, and carried on in the fourth century by the famous *Pasion, had large foreign transactions, especially with Byzantium; when Pasion retired it had a capital of 50 talents.

Urban industries were conducted on a comparatively small scale. The largest factory we know of was that of the *metic Cephalus, father of the orator Lysias, which employed 120 slaves on the manufacture of shields. The two factories belonging to the father of the orator Demosthenes employed respectively 33 on the manufacture of arms and 20 on the manufacture of beds. The shoemaker who figures in a mime of Herodas had 13 assistants. Even ship-building appears to have been carried on in a large number of small yards. Many industries were purely family affairs in the hands of an artisan and his wife. There is occasional mention of large fortunes at Athens, but they do not appear to have been numerous. *Callias was reputedly the richest man in Greece, and is said to have had 200 talents; *Nicias had 100. Both these fortunes were derived from mining enterprises.

See also FINANCE, GREEK.

Athens, Constitution of, see CONSTITUTION OF THE ATHENIANS.

athletics. Athletics were in origin games played in preparation for war. In Greece from Homeric times athletic contests were an essential part of the Greek way of life and the most important element in many religious festivals, arousing passionate interest. The important contests in classical times were for men only, but there were separate competitions for women, especially at Sparta. From the first century AD onward women's events were included in general athletics meetings; they were chiefly running races, but women's wrestling also featured. Greek male athletes were distinguished in one respect from other nationalities including Romans in that by the fifth century BC at the latest they practised and competed at all times entirely naked. Women customarily wore a short tunic. The pattern of athletics competitions was strongly influenced by the Olympian games, whose supremacy from 776 onwards resulted in their own rules and restricted programme becoming the norm; see GAMES, PUBLIC. The usual athletic events are listed below.

(i) *Running.* The ancient race course was essentially a rectangle about 200 m. (220 yds.) long with a starting line at each end and a turning post in the middle of each of these lines (see STADIUM). In the 'single' foot-race (*stadion*), the competitors ran the length of the track; in the 'double' foot-race (*diaulos*), they had to make an abrupt turn around the post and run back again (oddly enough there are no references in Greek literature to the possibility of foul play or falls during this manœuvre). The long-distance race comprised 12 laps of the stadium (about 4,800 m.). By the middle of the fifth century BC races were started by a mechanical starting gate. The race in (hoplite) armour, in time reduced to a symbolic helmet and shield, was introduced at the Olympian games of 520 BC and became less esteemed as time went on. Relay races never occurred in the stadium in regular programmes of athletics but took place at separate festivals when the runners ran through the streets and handed on a lighted torch.

(ii) *Wrestling.* Classification in Greek wrestling was by age rather than weight, so fortune favoured big men, and in the important Games professionalism crept in. At a lower level, however, wrestling remained the most popular Greek sport. The *palaestra* or wrestling school was for centuries a feature of every Greek city. All Greek athletes oiled themselves before exercise; wrestlers in addition dusted themselves with powder to ensure a good grip. A wrestling match was for the best of three falls; a fall was judged to be when a man's shoulders, or perhaps his knees, touched the ground.

(iii) *Boxing.* A boxing match was not divided into rounds but continued uninterrupted until a contestant was knocked out or raised a hand in acknowledgement of defeat. Boxing gloves took the form of soft leather wound round the wrists and knuckles both as protection and to prevent cutting the opponent's face. The magnificent Hellenistic bronze of a resting boxer in the Terme Museum at Rome shows the details clearly. We do not know for certain what blows were permitted and what forbidden, but the rules were enforced by referees with forked sticks for beating offenders. Men in training used earguards and softly padded gloves, and practised with a punch-ball as well as by shadow-boxing. (Boxing played a large part in the gladiatorial shows in Rome but then the gloves were loaded with lead and even spiked to draw blood. The emperor Augustus was said to have been particularly keen on boxing, but perhaps in its less violent Greek form.)

(iv) *The pancration.* This was a specialized form of all-in wrestling in which the aim was to get an opponent to admit defeat when he was in danger of strangulation or a broken limb. The only tactics we know to have been forbidden were biting and gouging out an opponent's eye. After the fourth century BC the event became increasingly professional and increasingly popular as it became more violent. Success in this event was highly esteemed.

(v) *The pentathlon.* Competitors in this contest had to enter five events, namely long jump, foot race, throwing the discus, throwing the javelin, and wrestling. We do not know the origin of the pentathlon, nor how the victor was chosen. It is unlikely that the Greeks used any system of reckoning points since they were interested only in victory and not in second and third places. It seems that by a process of elimination only the two best competitors were selected for the final event, the wrestling. By the Christian era the pentathlon had declined in popularity compared with the other contests.

(vi) *Javelin.* Distance was the aim in athletic javelin-throwing, but the javelin had to land on its point. The Greeks always threw with the help of a thong wound tightly round the shaft leaving a loop hitched over the fingers of the throwing hand, to increase the leverage of the throwing arm and so add to the speed of projection, and to impart spin so as to keep the javelin steady in flight and carry it much further. The competitor was allowed five throws, only the best one counting.

(vii) *Discus.* The discus was a circular plate of stone or metal, slightly convex, of roughly the same size as the modern athletic discus. Specimens are known up to 7 kg. (15 lb.) in weight. Throwing the discus was an event entered by heavy men. The method of throwing is illustrated by vase-paintings and statues, notably the Discobulus of Myron. The discus was held in the right hand with the arm straight, then swung back and released with an underarm pull. The aim was to throw it from a fixed space to the greatest distance. As with the javelin, only the best of five throws counted.

(viii) *Long jump.* All we know about the Greek long jump is that the athlete always used jumping weights, from which it has been inferred that the contest was for a standing rather than a running jump (where weights reduce the distance covered). It is not known how many jumps each competitor was allowed.

The Greeks and Romans did not usually keep records of the distances they threw or jumped, and so we cannot know what they achieved in athletics. The Etruscans practised most of the events in the Greek athletic programme, as their tomb-paintings show, although they did not follow Greek practice in competing naked. The Romans often experimented with Greek athletic events, but they never wholly accepted them as part of their way of life. The earliest Greek-style Games in Rome took place in 186 BC at a time when enthusiasm at Rome for Greek culture was at its height. We hear of other Greek Games being promoted during the first century BC, but in general their appeal was only to the leisured and literary classes. During the Augustan period we hear of wealthy young Romans taking up Greek athletics for amusement, but on the whole, despite the favourable attitude of some Roman emperors, notably Nero, the general Roman contempt at this time for most things Greek prevailed in this sphere also. The *gymnasia were seen by many as hotbeds of vice threatening the traditional Roman methods of training for war.

Athos, headland on the most easterly of the promontories of Chalcidice, with a mountain some 2,000 m. (6,600 ft.) high rising sheer from the sea, sacred to Zeus. To avoid the sea passage around Mount Athos when he was invading Greece, the Persian king Xerxes cut a canal through the isthmus (483–481 BC). Athos is now the site of several monasteries.

Ath. Pol., i.e. *Athēnaiōn politeia,* see CONSTITUTION OF THE ATHENIANS.

atī'mia, the loss of all or some civic rights by a citizen of a Greek city in punishment for certain offences concerning the state. The loss of rights might be temporary or permanent.

Atla'ntis, huge mythical island thought of as situated off the Straits of Gibraltar, first mentioned in literature in Plato's dialogues *Timaeus* and *Critias.* The name is derived from Atlas (see below). Its empire supposedly came into contact with the Athenians in prehistoric times and was defeated, the island being afterwards swallowed up in great earthquakes and floods. There has been frequent speculation as to whether the myth embodied folk memories of, for example, the Minoan civilization of Crete or the eruption at Thera (Santorini).

Atlas, in Greek myth, a Titan, son of *Iapetus and Clymenē; he married the *Oceanid Pleionē. His name probably means 'he who carries' or 'he who endures'. In Homer he is the father of Calypso but usually his daughters are the *Pleiades, and sometimes the *Hyades and the *Hesperides too. He is the guardian of the pillars of heaven (which hold up the sky), and later as punishment for his part in the revolt of the Titans he had to hold the sky up himself. He became identified with the western part of the Atlas mountains in north-west Africa, and sometimes with the southern Pillar of Hercules. A later tale said that *Perseus had turned him into stone with the Gorgon's head. When Heracles was seeking the apples of the Hesperides (see HERACLES, LABOURS OF 11) Atlas offered to fetch them if Heracles would hold up the sky; he then refused to take back his burden until tricked into doing so by the hero.

atomists, see DEMOCRITUS.

Ato'ssa, wife of *Darius I, king of Persia, and mother of Xerxes.

A'treus, in Greek myth, one of the sons of *Pelops; he was king of Mycenae, husband of Aerope, and father of Agamemnon and Menelaus. After Pelops was cursed by the dying Myrtilus, each generation of the family came to disaster. Pelops' brother Thyestes seduced Aerope and aimed at the kingship of Mycenae. Atreus banished him, but later pretended to be reconciled and invited him to a banquet at which he served up to Thyestes the flesh of his own children. Thyestes fled, then later married his own daughter Pelopia and became the father of Aegisthus, who was to be a further agent of the curse. The details of this story are variously told.

A'trium Libertā'tis ('hall of liberty'), at Rome, a building containing the offices of the *censors, their records, and some laws engraved on bronze tablets. In Cicero's time the judicial examination of slaves by torture was carried out here, as well as their *manumission.

A'trium Vestae ('hall of Vesta'), residence of the *Vestal Virgins, east of the Forum at Rome. The visible remains are of imperial times, but republican foundations have been discovered.

A'tropos, 'irresistible', one of the three *Fates. Her function, according to the poets, was to cut off the thread of life.

Atta, Titus Quintus (d. 77 BC), Latin poet, composer of comedies of the kind called *fabulae* *togatae, of which very few fragments survive. He is said to have excelled in female character portrayal.

A'ttalids, the ruling dynasty of *Pergamum in the third and second centuries BC. When after the death of Alexander the Great his generals succeeded to his empire (see DIADOCHOI) and divided it among themselves, Philetaerus was put in command of Pergamum, under the suzerainty of the general Seleucus (later Seleucus I; see SELEUCIDS) and he became the founder of the Attalid dynasty. He was succeeded by his nephew Eumenes I (d. 241 BC) who secured the city's independence from the Seleucid empire. He in turn was succeeded by his second cousin Attalus I who, by driving back and confining the *Galatians to an area of *Phrygia, obtained power and prestige and took the title of king. For a time Attalus was able to bring under his control nearly the whole of Seleucid Asia Minor. In 201 the Pergamenes and the Rhodians became embroiled with *Philip V of Macedon, and took the decisive step of asking Rome for help. This gave Rome the pretext for the Second Macedonian War and for intervention in Greek affairs. As the ally of Rome against Antiochus III at the great victory of Magnesia (189 BC), Pergamum established its position as the leading state in Asia Minor, receiving the bulk of the dominions ceded by Antiochus. In 172 Eumenes II of Pergamum, son of Attalus I, again incited Rome against Macedonia and provided the pretext on which war was declared against *Perseus in 171. Eumenes' brother Attalus II succeeded him, and continued the Attalid policy of caretaking for Rome in the East. He was succeeded in 138 by Attalus III, son of Eumenes II. The dynasty ended with the latter's death in 133, and his bequeathing of his dominions to Rome; they became the Roman province of Asia Minor.

The Attalids ruled over what was constitutionally a Greek city-state, but they had wide powers of interference and ruled directly over the native population of the surrounding country. This country possessed natural resources including silver mines but its wealth, for which the Attalids were proverbial, lay in its agricultural produce and the dependent industries of wool and parchment (a word derived from Pergamum). The Attalids were devoted patrons of art and literature, and under their influence Pergamum became one of the most beautiful of all Greek cities, famous for its library and school of architecture.

Atthis (i.e. *Atthis historia*, 'history of Attica'), name given to a type of chronicle dealing with the history of Athens and Attica, popular from c.350 to 250 BC out of nostalgia for the past glories of Athens. The pattern seems to have been set by *Hellanicus' history published soon after 404 BC. The contents of *Atthides* were traditional and concentrated on mythology, origins of cults, and descriptions of political institutions. The writers are referred to as 'atthidographers'. Only fragments of their work survive.

Attic (adj.), see ATTICA below.

A'ttica, the country around *Athens (its chief city), a mountainous and largely arid area forming the south-east promontory of central Greece, about 2,500 sq. km. (1,000 sq. miles) in extent. Attica is dominated by its four mountain systems, Aegaleus, Hymettus, Pentelicus, and Laurium, which divide the land into three plains, to the west the Thriasian plain with its chief town Eleusis, in the centre the Attic plain, and to the east the Mesogeia. The main rivers of Attica, which are full only in winter or after heavy rains, are the Cephi(s)sus and the Ili(s)sus. For the most part the soil is very sparsely watered, better adapted for olives and figs than for corn. In ancient times grapes were cultivated but did not produce a famous wine. The honey, however, was particularly fine, especially that of Hymettus. The country is too hilly and dry for horse-breeding, but sheep and goats flourished. Fish was plentiful in the coastal waters. Of natural resources, Attica was famous for its dazzling white Pentelic marble, and the grey, blue, and black marble from Hymettus. Its potters' clay was excellent, and there were silver and lead at Laurium (see MINES). Attica originally consisted of many separate communities, traditionally twelve in the time of the king *Cecrops, which were later fused into a single Athenian state, an achievement attributed to *Theseus but in fact a gradual process probably lasting into the seventh century BC. Athens became the capital city, although local loyalties remained and even during the sixth century aristocratic families still lived independent lives in the countryside. It was the tyranny of *Peisistratus and even more the reforms of *Cleisthenes which finally broke local ties and brought the whole of Attica under a centralized government at Athens.

A'ttica, Pompō'nia, see AGRIPPA (1).

Attic dialect, see DIALECTS.

Attic drama, see DRAMA, COMEDY, TRAGEDY.

A'tticism, see SOPHISTIC, SECOND.

Attic Nights, see GELLIUS.

A'tticus, Titus Pompō'nius (110–32 BC), intimate friend of *Cicero ((1) 1), born at Rome of an equestrian family. In 85 he left the turbulence and bloodshed of Rome for Athens, where he lived for many years (whence his *cognomen* Atticus, i.e. 'of Attica'). He adopted the *Epicurean philosophy and took no active part in the politics of the ensuing troubled period, but maintained an attitude of neutrality and friendship with all parties. He helped Marians and Pompeians; he protected Cicero's wife Terentia when Cicero went into exile, and Antony's wife Fulvia and his lieutenant Volumnius at the time of *Mutina (43 BC). In consequence he was spared by Antony in the proscriptions. He became the friend of the emperor Augustus, and his daughter Attica married *Agrippa. (Their daughter Vipsania married Tiberius and was mother of the younger Drusus.) His sister Pomponia married Cicero's brother Quintus. The series of Cicero's letters to Atticus begins in 68, and their friendship, which started when they were students together, continued until Cicero's death. In both public and private life Cicero constantly turned to him for sympathy and advice. Atticus had inherited a considerable fortune, with which he bought land in Epirus, and which he gradually increased by judicious investment until he became very wealthy. He had strong literary tastes; he kept a large staff of slaves trained in copying and binding manuscripts, and he helped in the circulation of Cicero's writings. His own works, which have not survived, included a *Liber annālis* ('annals'), an epitome of Roman history in one book dealing with laws, wars, and political events from the earliest times down to his own day; and a genealogical treatise on certain Roman families and the magistracies they had held. He also helped to establish 753 BC as the date of the founding of Rome (see CALENDARS). He committed suicide in 32 BC when suffering from an incurable illness. We have a Life of him by *Nepos.

A'ttila, king of the Huns AD 434–53 (known as Etzel in medieval German saga); he ruled an empire stretching from the Alps to the Caspian Sea. In 452 he invaded Italy and sacked several cities, but was persuaded to withdraw without entering Rome. While preparing to invade the eastern empire again, having ravaged it in the 440s, he died suddenly on his wedding night. His exploits and death are the subjects of chapters 34 and 35 of Edward Gibbon's *Decline and Fall of the Roman Empire.* See FALL OF ROME.

Attis, in mythology, the youthful consort of the Phrygian goddess *Cybelē (also known as Agdistis in Phrygia). The Phrygian version of his myth relates that he was the son of Nana, daughter of the river god Sangarius (a river in Asia Minor). She conceived him after gathering the blossom of an almond-tree sprung from the severed male organs of Agdistis/Cybele who, born both male and female, had been castrated by the gods. When Attis wished to marry, Cybele, who loved him and was jealous, drove him mad so that he castrated himself and died. There are many variants of this myth, which, among other things, purports to explain why Cybele's priests, *Galli, are eunuchs. Attis appears only rarely in Greece, but with Cybele became an accepted deity at Rome under the emperor Claudius. For a poem on the subject of Attis see CATULLUS.

A'ttius, Lucius, see ACCIUS.

Au'fidus, river in Apulia (south Italy), on which stood Venusia, the birthplace of Horace, who refers in his poems to its swift and roaring current. It was on the banks of this river that Hannibal defeated the Romans at the battle of Cannae in 216 BC.

Augē, in Greek myth, the mother by Heracles of *Telephus.

Auge'as (Augeiās), king of Elis whose stables Heracles was required to clean as one of his Labours (see HERACLES, LABOURS OF 6). *Trophonius and Agamedes, the legendary architects, are said to have built his treasury.

augury and **auspices,** divination by observing the habits of birds. The terms 'auguries' and 'auspices' were used interchangeably. Augury was as common for the Greeks as for the Romans, but it was the latter who made it a complete system governed by fixed rules and practised by a *college of augurs (elected for life) who alone were authorized to 'take the auspices', that is, read the signs. The function of augury was not to reveal the future but to tell whether or not a proposed course of action had the approval of the gods. Signs might be offered unsolicited, but often were deliberately sought; of the latter the best-known example is the observation by the Romans of sacred chickens, carried by armies in the field. Food was given to these birds and if they ate it greedily so as to drop some from their mouths it was a good sign. When, before the sea-battle of Drepanum between Rome and Carthage in 249 BC, they refused to eat, the Roman admiral threw them overboard, saying, 'Then let them drink'; the Romans were, of course, defeated. If wild birds were to be observed, the augur indicated with a wand the part of the sky to be observed (the *templum*, the word also used for an area of ground consecrated for the augur's use), dividing it into left and right, front and back regions. He would stand facing south or east; the significance of a bird's flight or cry varied according to the direction from which it came (see also OMENS). The auspices were taken before any important military or public event (and in early times before many private events too), but the officer responsible had the power to reject the advice of the augurs if he so pleased: see above. Another notable occasion was the morning of the battle of Lake Trasimene in 217 BC, during the Second Punic War, when the consul C. Flaminius ignored the auguries with disastrous results. Cicero, although an augur himself, wrote *De divinatione* ('on divination') to disprove the possibility of divination. The emperor Augustus seems to have believed in the auspices. See also DIVINATION and HARUSPICES.

Augusta, see AUGUSTUS, THE.

Augustā'lēs, at Rome under the empire, the name of several priesthoods or offices of an honorific nature. On the death of the emperor Augustus, his successor Tiberius instituted the college of *sŏdālēs Augustales* ('companions of Augustus') to attend to the worship of the (deified) Augustus and his family. The members were chosen from the most important people in the state. Similar priests were appointed for the worship of other emperors after their decease. In many Italian and some provincial towns a board of six men, the *sēviri*, was set up to oversee the cult of 'Rome and Augustus'. These were drawn largely from the class of freedmen who were no longer admitted automatically to full Roman citizenship, but whose loyalty could in this way be encouraged.

Augustā'lia, see LUDI 2 (ii).

Augustan age of Latin literature, a term applied to the period following the *Ciceronian age, of which the empire of Augustus was the formative influence. It spans roughly the time from the assassination of Julius Caesar in 44 BC to the death of Ovid in AD 17 (Augustus died in AD 14); its great authors were Virgil, Horace, Tibullus, Propertius, Ovid, and Livy. It started with the turmoil, destructions, and slaughter of the civil war, saw the death of republican government after the battle of Actium in 31 BC (see ROME 7), and ended after the restoration of tranquillity and order following nearly a century of revolution. Political activity as it existed under the republic came to an end with the institution of the empire (see AUGUSTUS); Augustus' ambition was to restore something of

the spirit of the republic in its heyday, and to imbue the Italian people with the old Roman traditions and virtues. To some extent freedom of political and historical inquiry and expression were limited; hence perhaps the eclipse of oratory and prose literature in general. The support given to Augustus' policy by the poets and historians of the time gives to their literature its unique flavour. This support was deliberately enlisted by the emperor himself and by other patrons in high official positions, men such as *Maecenas and *Messalla. Their writings are serious and mature; their themes, often drawn from the moralizing tradition, come alive because the authors are themselves inspired by love of Italy and the traditional Roman values. Even Ovid and Propertius, who appear often to ignore contemporary politics, show the pleasure they feel in the Italian scene. The poetry in particular is characterized by an increasing technical refinement and, what is less obvious, by a subtle and enriching blend of Greek and Roman themes, which requires from its readers a more intellectual appreciation. See also ROME 9.

Augu'stine (Aurēlius Augustīnus, AD 354–430), St Augustine of Hippo, born in Roman Africa at Thagastē (Souk Ahras, in Algeria). He was the son of a pagan father and a Catholic mother, Monica, who brought up her son as a Christian and was a dominant influence on his early life. Both parents were determined to give Augustine a good classical education, but though he revelled in the Latin poets he failed to learn Greek, the only Latin-speaking philosopher in antiquity to be virtually ignorant of that language. At 19 he read Cicero's *Hortensius* (now lost), an exhortation to the study of philosophy, and was fired with a passionate desire to acquire wisdom. This he sought in the heretical Christian sect of the Manichaeans who expounded a *Gnostic form of Christianity based on a supposed conflict between light and darkness, where Christ was represented as the principle of wisdom and goodness in eternal opposition to a principle of evil. Attracted by their claim to offer reason where the church appealed only to authority, Augustine remained a Manichaean for nine years, during which time he taught rhetoric at Carthage, Thagaste, and Rome, and was finally chosen by *Symmachus to be professor of rhetoric at Milan. His mother arranged for him an advantageous marriage (which never came about) with an heiress, and he had to send back to Africa, with a pang, his concubine with whom he had lived for fifteen years and who had borne him a son. However, under the influence of *Ambrose, whose intellect he respected, and the Neoplatonic writings of *Plotinus and *Porphyry, read in a Latin translation, Augustine was converted to Neoplatonism and Catholicism almost at the same time, and did not discard Platonism for many years. In 387 after a long inward struggle he was baptized and renounced the secular life; in the same year his mother died while they were both on the return journey to Africa. He arrived in Africa in 388 and never left it again. During a visit to the sea port of Hippo in 391 he was seized by the people and ordained priest somewhat against his will, and in 395 he was consecrated coadjutor bishop of Hippo. The rest of his life was spent in his see, where he died on 28 August 430 while the Vandals were besieging the town.

Augustine's Christianity was based on his central preoccupation as a bishop, biblical exegesis. During his episcopate he had to combat the heresies of Manichaeism, *Donatism, and Pelagianism; through these struggles his own theology was formulated. His teaching about the Fall of Adam and original sin, from which mankind can be saved only by the grace of God, showed that Augustine believed in predestination, and this side of his teaching exercised a great influence on subsequent Western theologians, especially John Calvin. His early works, written before and immediately after his baptism, were criticisms of ancient philosophies from the Christian standpoint, but after his appointment to the bishopric his writings became more polemical and doctrinal. The *De doctrina Christiana* ('on Christian learning', begun 396–7), on a scheme of Christian education, outlines a literary culture that was to be subordinated to the Bible. *De Trinitate* ('on the Trinity', 399–419) gives a philosophical account of the doctrine of the Trinity. His autobiography, the *Confessions* (c.397–400), is a highly selective account of his life to the time of his conversion, in which he analyses the heart's restless search to return to its Maker. The title is to be taken in its biblical sense of 'praising'; it is Augustine's thanksgiving for his conversion. The composition of *De civitate Dei* ('the city of God') in 413–26 arose out of the *Fall of Rome to *Alaric in 410, an event which had dismayed the civilized world.

Augustine wrote some ninety-three books as well as letters and sermons; his ancient biographer felt that no man could ever read them all. These works moulded the thought of Western theology down to the thirteenth century, when, with the rediscovery of *Aristotle (see 5), Christian philosophers such as Thomas Aquinas built up their systems on an Aristotelian basis, and there was a reaction against Augustinianism.

Augustodu'num (Autun), see BIBRACTE.

Augustus (63 BC–AD 14), the first of the Roman emperors. He was born Gaius Octavius on 23 September, son of the niece of Julius *Caesar. For the family history see OCTAVIAN. After his adoption by Caesar he was named

C. Julius Caesar Octaviānus (Octavian; see NAMES 2), and after 27 BC was known by his title Augustus. When Caesar was murdered in 44 and his will revealed that he had adopted Octavian and named him as his heir, Octavian left Greece where he had been finishing his education and returned to Italy at the age of 19 to avenge Caesar (see ROME 7). With political acumen he won the support both of Caesar's veterans and of moderate republicans who had been opposed to Caesar, including *Cicero ((1) 6), and reached a compromise with Mark *Antony, the leader of the Caesarian party, and M. *Lepidus, a provincial governor and rather vacillating Caesarian. Together they set up a *triumvirate in 43 and ruled Rome and the empire, Octavian obtaining Africa, Sicily, and Sardinia as his provinces. When (the dead) Julius Caesar was deified in 42 (see RELIGION, ROMAN 3) Octavian became *divi filius*, 'son of a god', and hence acquired a divine aura. Differences between the triumvirs were reconciled by the treaty of Brundisium in 40, and Antony married Octavian's sister Octavia, an event which some people think occasioned Virgil's fourth *Eclogue. Octavian married *Livia to whom he remained devoted throughout his life although she did not bear him children. Meanwhile Octavian's influence had grown considerably, and when in 36 he compelled Lepidus to retire from the triumvirate he was in sole control of Rome's western empire. Antony's liaison with the Egyptian queen *Cleopatra, which alienated him from Rome, strengthened Octavian's position still further. In 31 war was declared against Cleopatra; taking her side, Antony was defeated at the sea-battle of Actium and committed suicide. In this year Octavian had regularized his authority by being elected consul, and now his ostensible duty was to restore the republic; yet this duty had to be reconciled with the fact that he had no intention of resigning the absolute power he now wielded.

In 27 Octavian laid down his *de facto* dictatorship and handed back the government of the state to the senate, thereby formally restoring the republic. However, he retained the consulship, and Spain, Gaul, Syria, and Egypt as his provinces, together with command over the greater part of the army, and possibly other powers as well. He received in addition, at the proposal of L. Munatius Plancus, the title of Augustus (Gk. *sebastos*, 'reverend') which set him above the entire state. By this title Octavian was thereafter known, and together with the designation *Imperator* ('general', the origin of the English 'emperor'), it subsequently became part of the formal title of the Roman emperors (see following entry). He also came to be designated, informally at first, *princeps*, i.e. 'first citizen', a term often used under the republic, especially in the plural, to describe influential statesmen, former consuls and the like. This was the title he preferred. In 2 BC the senate, on the proposal of *Messalla, conferred on him the ancient republican honorific title *pater patriae*, 'father of his country'. His actual authority was overwhelming. In 23 he resigned the consulship but instead received for life the tribunician authority, which in effect gave him complete control. During subsequent years he organized the provinces and made religious and moral reforms aimed at restoring the old Roman virtues of simplicity, hard work, and faithful and prolific marriages. In this aim he was widely supported by the influential literary figures of the age (see AUGUSTAN AGE). The premature deaths of promising young men in his family thwarted plans for his successor and he was compelled to accept *Tiberius, son of Livia by a previous marriage. (For Augustus' plans for the succession see MARCELLUS (2), AGRIPPA (1) and (2), and DRUSUS (3).) When he died in AD 14 it was decreed that he should be deified and accepted among the gods of the state (see RELIGION, ROMAN 4). His life had been for the most part an exemplification of the virtues he preached. Republican government had been over before he came to power, but he tried to establish internal peace based on Roman traditions without offending sectional interests. In this his achievement was immense. However, he leaves behind an impression of a man in whom ideals were always subordinated to a ruthlessly practical end.

Augustus, the (Gk. *sebastos*, 'reverend'), title held exclusively by all the Roman emperors except Vitellius. When the emperor *Diocletian established a tetrarchy by dividing the empire among four rulers in AD 293, he established two nominally joint emperors who shared the title of Augustus to rule the eastern and western halves of the empire, each with a subordinate ruler, designated a Caesar, who might expect to succeed to the higher rank. By personal authority the senior Augustus could hope to remain in effect sole emperor. Although the system failed as a means of establishing the succession, the titles and their general application survived. The title 'Augusta' was bequeathed by the emperor Augustus to his wife Livia, and after Domitian was held by the wife of the reigning emperor.

Aulis, town of Boeotia in central Greece, celebrated as the place where the Greek fleet assembled for the expedition against Troy and where Agamemnon sacrificed his daughter *Iphigeneia to Artemis to allay the contrary winds.

aulos, flute; see MUSIC 1.

Aululā'ria ('pot of gold'), Roman comedy by *Plautus, probably adapted from a Greek comedy by *Menander. The prologue is spoken by the *lar familiaris* (see LARES).

Euclio, an old miser, has found a pot full of treasure buried in his house. He hides it and continues to pretend poverty, for fear that the treasure will be taken from him. His daughter Phaedria has been seduced, at a feast of Ceres, by Lyconides, a young man who is now repentant and wishes to marry her. But meanwhile his uncle Megadorus approaches Euclio with a view to marrying her himself. Euclio, thinking that Megadorus has designs on the treasure, takes it away from his house and hides it in one place after another. He is seen by a slave of Lyconides, who removes it. Euclio is in despair at its loss. (The end of the play is lost, but it may be supposed that Lyconides restores the treasure to Euclio, who in gratitude agrees to his marriage to Phaedria.)

The play is especially noteworthy for the character of the old miser, on whom Molière's character Harpagon in *L'Avare* (1669) is closely modelled. It includes the famous incident in which Euclio kills a cock which is scraping the earth near his treasure, because it is evidently bent on theft.

Aulus Ge'llius, see GELLIUS.

Aure'lian (Lucius Domitius Aurelianus) (*c.* AD 215–75), Roman emperor 270–5, a brilliant soldier who was successful against Gothic invasions, and a man of humble origin made emperor by the army. His most famous campaign was against *Zenobia, queen of Palmyra.

Aurē'lius, Marcus (AD 121–80), Roman emperor from 161 to his death. He was born M. Annius Verus, of consular family; his father and grandfather had the same name. He received a careful education from the best tutors, including *Fronto (in Latin) and *Herodes Atticus (in Greek). While still young he won the favour of the emperor Hadrian (who punningly and aptly called him *Verissimus*, 'most true'). When Hadrian adopted *Antoninus Pius as his successor in 138, the latter adopted Marcus. In 145 he married Faustina, Antoninus' daughter (and his own cousin). He became emperor in 161, and shared the throne with Lucius Verus (who had also been adopted by Antoninus) until Lucius' death in 169. His reign was dominated by warfare against invaders on all the important frontiers. His twelve books of 'Meditations' (*ta eis heauton*) were written, in Greek, during the last ten years of his reign while he was on campaign. They were not published until after his death; by whose agency is not known. As a young man he had adopted *Stoicism through the influence of one of his tutors, Apollonius of Chalcedon, and was the last great proponent of that philosophy. Except for the first book, in which he pays his debts of gratitude, the 'Meditations' are arranged in no systematic order but appear just as he wrote them, as a series of entries in personal diaries, and record his thoughts about the meaning of world-order and the relationship of man to it. Hence they have an immediacy and intensity that impart a strongly personal feeling to traditional Stoic moralizing. They show him to be disillusioned and despondent, seeking fortitude against the fear of death, the cares of this world, and the misdeeds and injustices of others. Thus he is better known than any other Roman statesman or emperor since Cicero. Part of the correspondence between him and his tutor Fronto has survived. He was succeeded as emperor by his son Commodus.

Aurō'ra, see EOS.

Ausō'nia, Ausō'nes, poetic names for Italy and Italians, in Latin and Greek; Ausonia was derived from *Ausones*, an ancient, perhaps Greek, name for the inhabitants of middle and south Italy, who have been variously identified. The word was possibly connected with the same root as Oscus or Opicus.

Ausō'nius, Decimus Magnus (*c.* AD 310–*c.*393), Latin poet, the son of a physician of Burdigala (Bordeaux), educated there and at Tolosa (Toulouse). After teaching rhetoric at Burdigala for thirty years he was appointed tutor to Gratian, son of the emperor Valentinian I. With his pupil he accompanied Valentinian's expedition against the Germans in 368–9. When Gratian succeeded his father Ausonius received rapid official advancement, becoming prefect of the Gallic provinces, and later of others, and finally consul in 379. After the murder of Gratian he returned to his family estate at Burdigala, where he appears to have spent most of the remainder of his life. He was nominally at least a Christian, but without any depth of religious feeling: he tried to dissuade his pupil Paulinus (later St Paulinus of Nola) from abandoning the world for a life of religion.

Ausonius wrote a great deal of verse in a variety of metres, showing great technical ability. There are over a hundred epigrams, some of which are in Greek. He seems to have written on any theme that presented itself, such as the names of the days and months, or the properties of the number three. He particularly delighted in verse catalogues: the professors of Burdigala, the famous cities of the world, the Twelve Caesars, the Seven Sages. He delighted also in such feats of skill as the composition of a prayer in forty-two *rhopalic hexameters beginning *spes deus aeternae stationis conciliator* ('God, | our hope | of haven | safe for ever, | uniter of all'). His more important and interesting poems are the *Ephēmeris* ('a day's events'), a description of a normal day in his life (when and where are not clear), his awakening, talking with his various servants, and so on; and the *Mosella,* a long hexameter poem describing in considerable detail the beauties of the river Moselle and the life that goes on around it. His prose writing includes a long *Grātiarum actio,* or thanksgiving for his consulship, addressed to Gratian.

auspices, see AUGURY.

auster, the south wind (Gk. *notos*). See WINDS.

Auto'lycus, in Greek myth, a son of the god *Hermes and a master of trickery and thieving. He received from his father the gift of making himself and his stolen goods invisible, or of changing the appearance of the latter so as to escape detection, but he was outwitted by *Sisyphus. He was the father of Anticlea, mother of Odysseus.

Auto'medon, in Homer's *Iliad,* the charioteer of Achilles.

Auto'noë, in Greek myth, daughter of Cadmus, mother of *Actaeon.

auxi'lia, 'auxiliaries', in the Roman army, troops enlisted from outside Italy. The emperor Augustus set up a permanent auxiliary army. See ARMY, ROMAN 2.

A'ventine, the most southerly of the seven hills of Rome. It remained outside the *pomerium* or city boundary for religious reasons until AD 49. It was the scene of the story of Hercules and *Cacus, whose cave Evander showed to Aeneas (Virgil, *Aeneid* 8. 184). It was a quarter occupied by the plebeians; a temple of Diana stood on the summit.

Ave'rnus, lake near Cumae and Naples. Close to it was the cave by which Aeneas descended to the Underworld (Virgil, *Aeneid* 6). The name was sometimes used for the Underworld itself. It was supposed to be derived from the Greek *aŏrnos,* 'without birds', and the lake was in consequence thought to have no bird life.

Avēs, see BIRDS.

Aviā'nus (flourished *c.* AD 400), Roman poet, author of forty-two *fables (based on those of *Babrius) written in elegiac couplets, which were popular in medieval schools. Nothing is known of his life.

Avie'nus, Rufius Festus (more correctly, Avienius; fourth century AD), by his own account a native of Volsinii (Bolsena) and twice proconsul. He was the author of an extant translation of *Aratus into Latin hexameters, as well as of a 'description of the world' (a translation of *Dionysius Periegetes) and a 'maritime shore', a wildly confused account of the coastal regions of the Mediterranean and elsewhere. He was a descendant of Musonius Rufus, the Stoic philosopher.

axō'nĕs, in the *Prytaneum at Athens, tablets of wood revolving about a vertical axis on which were written the laws of Draco and of Solon.

B

Ba'brius, Greek writer of fables who lived probably in the second century AD but about whom nothing is known. The fables exist today in two books, of which the second is incomplete. They are written in verse in the choliambic metre (see METRE, GREEK 5 (iii)) in the ordinary language of the period and are based on the fables of *Aesop with some apparently original additions. They remained very popular in later centuries and were frequently paraphrased in Greek prose and verse.

Bacchae ('women of Bacchus', i.e. female celebrants of the rites of Bacchus or Dionysus), Greek tragedy by *Euripides probably written during the poet's stay in Macedonia and found after his death in 406 BC. It was subsequently produced at Athens (probably in 405) by the poet's son (or nephew) also named Euripides, together with *Iphigeneia in Aulis* and *Alcmaeon in Corinth* (the latter now lost).

*Dionysus, divine son of Zeus and the Theban Semelē, travelling through the world to make himself known to men as a god, comes to Thebes, where his divinity has been denied even by Semele's sister Agavē, mother of Pentheus, king of Thebes. Dionysus has driven the women of Thebes mad and compelled them to celebrate his rites on Mount Cithaeron. Pentheus is implacably hostile to the new religion in spite of the remonstrances of his grandfather Cadmus and of the seer Teiresias, and imprisons Dionysus (who claims to be not the god himself but a votary). Dionysus proves his power over material things by causing Pentheus to bind a bull in his stead and by making an earthquake destroy the palace. A messenger arrives and describes the behaviour of the Theban women on the mountains. Dionysus induces Pentheus to disguise himself as a woman in order to see for himself, and then engineers Pentheus' discovery by the women, who tear him to pieces. Agave, in her frenzy, bears his head triumphantly to Thebes. It is only when she recovers that she finds she has killed her son. The family of Cadmus is doomed to banishment from Thebes and the play ends with their departure.

The *Bacchae* is about a supposed historical event, the introduction into Greece of a new religion which by Euripides' time had long been accepted as part of Greek life. Worship of Dionysus offered a different religious experience from that expressed in the cult of the traditional Olympian gods, and this play shows the power of Dionysus, a power beyond good and evil, and the fate of those who resist him.

Bacchanā'lia, Latin name for the fundamentally Greek religious rites (*orgia*) of the god *Dionysus, derived from his alternative name of Bacchus. They are chiefly known from the description by Livy in his history of Rome of the wild excesses and criminal acts committed by the devotees under the cloak of religion, after the rites had been introduced to Rome from Etruria and south Italy. As a consequence the senate in a celebrated decree of 186 BC banned the Bacchanalia from Rome and Italy. See also MYSTERIES.

Bacchants (Bacchantēs, Bacchanals, Maenads), women inspired to ecstasy by the Greek god *Dionysus (sometimes called Bacchus), as described by Euripides in the *Bacchae. They are depicted wearing the skins of fawns or panthers and wreaths of ivy, oak, or fir and carrying a thyrsus (a wand wreathed in ivy and vine leaves, topped with a pine cone). Freed from the conventions of normal behaviour they roamed the mountains with music and dancing and inspired by the god performed supernatural feats of strength, uprooting trees, catching and tearing apart wild animals, and sometimes eating the flesh raw.

bacchī'ac, in Greek metre the sequence ᴗ − −. (See METRE, GREEK 1 (ix).)

Bacchī'adae, royal clan in *Corinth who claimed descent ultimately from Heracles (see HERACLEIDAE) but more immediately from Bacchis, king of Corinth perhaps c.900 BC. The monarchy was overthrown in 747 (the traditional date) and thereafter the city was governed by a Bacchiad oligarchy until 657 BC when they too were destroyed by *Cypselus who made himself tyrant. The Bacchiadae supposedly laid the foundation for Corinth's greatness in colonization, maritime affairs, trade, and in particular pottery.

Ba'cchidēs ('girls called Bacchis'), Roman comedy by *Plautus, adapted from the Greek comedy of *Menander *Dis exapaton* ('the double deceiver').

The opening of the play is missing, but the situation is clear. A young man Pistoclerus is searching in Athens on behalf of an absent friend Mnesilochus for a courtesan Bacchis of Samos.

He finds that she has visited her sister, also called Bacchis, and succumbs himself to the sister's charms. When Mnesilochus arrives he is horrified to learn that his friend is making love to 'Bacchis'. The confusion about the supposed disloyalty is soon cleared up. Chrysalus the slave of Mnesilochus is the pivot of the play. In contrast with Lydus, the paedagogus of Pistoclerus, who rushes off to inform the boy's father of his misbehaviour, Chrysalus aids his young master in his love affair, lying unblushingly and resourcefully. Having been foiled in his first attempt to extract from the young man's father the money for the affair, he succeeds with a second ingenious trick and likens himself to a conqueror of Troy. Finally, the sisters beguile the fathers of the two young men into forgiveness and all ends happily.

Bacchus, alternative name (probably Lydian in origin) for the Greek god *Dionysus, and his usual name in Latin.

Bacchy'lides, Greek lyric poet and nephew of the poet *Simonides, born at the end of the sixth century BC in the island of Ceos, and dying probably in the middle of the fifth century. His poetry survived only in quotations until, at the end of the nineteenth century, the British Museum acquired the remains of two papyrus rolls containing fifteen epinician odes (see EPINIKION) and six *dithyrambs. A few small fragments have turned up since. Bacchylides seems to have been employed by the same patrons who employed his uncle Simonides and also *Pindar, whose great rival ancient scholars believed him to be. Pindar and Bacchylides both composed odes for at least two victories won in the great Games by Hieron tyrant of Syracuse: thus Bacchylides' Ode 5 and Pindar's O. 1 both commemorate the horse-race at the Olympian games of 476 BC, and Ode 4 and P. 1 the chariot-race at Delphi in 470. The epinician odes of Bacchylides contain the same elements as Pindar's odes contain—central mythical narrative, passages praising the victor, his country, and the gods, passages of moralizing—but he lacks Pindar's profundity and brilliant imaginative gifts. His strength lies in his moving and dramatic narratives, as is also apparent in the dithyrambs. Ode 18, a dithyramb, is unique in surviving choral lyric in being wholly a dialogue, between the leader of the chorus representing Aegeus, king of Athens, and, presumably, the remainder of the chorus who represent his followers. Aegeus has heard the news of the imminent arrival of a young hero and in reply to questions elaborates on the deeds of the young man whom he does not yet know to be his son Theseus. Perhaps the form of the poem was influenced by contemporary drama, but it is tempting to see in this dithyramb's unparalleled dramatic style a survival of an older

form of dithyramb which Aristotle believed to be the precursor of *tragedy (see 1). Bacchylides also wrote *hymns, *paeans, maiden-songs (see PARTHENEION), *hyporchemata, and *encomia, very little of which survives.

Bacis, the proper name commonly given in Greece to a male prophet, as Sibyl to a prophetess.

Baiae, small place near Cumae on the Bay of Naples, perhaps originally its port, first famous for its warm springs containing a variety of minerals and then, from before the time of Cicero, a fashionable Roman resort. Lucullus, Pompey, and Caesar all had villas here, as did the later Roman emperors, and it soon became notorious for its dissipations.

Balbus, common *cognomen* (see NAMES 2) in several Roman *gentes. It originally denoted one who had an impediment in his speech.

    Lucius Cornelius Balbus, a native of Gades (Cadiz), who had Roman citizenship conferred upon him in 72 BC through Pompey's influence, for his services to Rome in the war against Sertorius in Spain, and took a Roman name. He moved to Rome where, with Pompey's favour, he soon became a man of considerable importance. Prudently he cultivated Caesar's favour also, and partly brought about the coalition between Caesar, Pompey, and Crassus in 60 BC. His influence made him many enemies who engineered his prosecution in 56 for illegally assuming Roman citizenship, but he was successfully defended by Cicero in an extant speech. In the civil war he was outwardly neutral while privately favouring Caesar, and subsequently Octavian. In 40 he became Rome's first foreign-born consul. His published diary has not come down to us, but a few of his letters to Cicero survive. (His namesake and nephew is also mentioned in Cicero's correspondence.)

Balius, see XANTHUS.

balli'sta, military machine invented in Hellenistic Greece but used most effectively by the Romans. It projected stones weighing up to a talent or more for a distance of nearly half a kilometre against enemy fortifications, but at a comparatively slow rate of discharge. It was capable of breaching walls of brick and wood, but was ineffective against dressed stone. The machine worked on the principle of the crossbow, the twisted cords being made from animal hair (or even women's hair) and sinews, and the tension built up by some kind of winch or lever. The details are not clear.

Bandu'sia, Italian fountain made famous by Horace in *Odes* III. 13; it was probably located near Horace's Sabine farm, although there is also evidence suggesting that it was a spring near his birthplace Venusia.

banks. In early Greece temples lent money to the local population and served as repositories for safe-keeping. Bankers were originally money-changers who set up tables at festivals and, for commission, changed the money of travelling merchants into the local coin. (Promissory notes were unknown, hence trade with foreign cities could only be carried on through individuals who paid and received ready cash.) In Athens bankers were commonly *metics. Since they possessed secure means of storing money they naturally took into safe-keeping articles of value and especially money belonging to travellers from which they could make payments to a third person on behalf of the depositor. In order to effect payment a depositor called in person on his banker. A written order to a banker requesting payment to a third person first occurs in the Hellenistic age, and the endorsement of a cheque to be given as payment to a third person may have been unknown before then. The Ptolemaic empire (see PTOLE-MIES) created a public banking system of considerable complexity to collect the king's revenues and pay out his charges, and may have used this form of payment as well as primitive bills of exchange. Since most rich Athenians kept their money locked up in their own houses it is likely that those who deposited money with a banker did so in order to profit by it, and that the banker paid them interest if the money was deposited for a sufficient length of time for him to make loans from it to others. In Greece interest was usually reckoned by the month and not by the year. It seems that a banker lent money without any assurance that his depositors would not want their money back at very little notice. Banks were small firms, and though bankers such as *Pasion became immensely rich, banking was a risky business; at moments of crisis (e.g. in 371 BC when the Theban victory over the Spartans at Leuctra caused panic withdrawals at Athens) many banks failed.

Roman bankers were in the main drawn from the *equites. Their firms were comparatively small and were similar in function to their Greek counterparts, although in some areas more sophisticated. They evolved a method of clearing between banks in and outside Rome, so that sums of money banked in Rome could then be paid (e.g. to residents in the provinces by a banker in that place) without the transfer of actual money. Most of this banking procedure was preserved by Europeans and Arabs throughout the Middle Ages.

barbarian, onomatopoeic word originally used adjectivally by Homer to describe the speech of the Carians of south-west Asia Minor, though he nowhere speaks of barbarians. The name came later to be applied to all non-Greek-speaking peoples, and was subsequently applied to the Persians in particular when their rise to power threatened Greek freedom in the early fifth century BC. The word thus came to have a cultural rather than a merely linguistic significance, and described people outside the orbit of the Greek city-states, whether or not they spoke Greek (see MACEDONIA 1); barbarians were therefore thought to be uncivilized, cowardly, cruel, treacherous, and lacking in self-control. The world was sometimes thought of as divided between Greeks with their virtues and barbarians with their vices. Intellectuals from Democritus and Euripides onwards occasionally emphasized instead the natural unity of all mankind. *Eratosthenes (2) in his second book of the *Geographica*, denying the usefulness of dividing the land-mass into three continents, digresses into a plea that people should be divided not into Greeks and barbarians but into good and bad: 'for many Greeks are bad, and many barbarians civilized, notably the Indians and Arians, and again the Romans and Carthaginians, who enjoy such admirable forms of government.'

Alexander the Great may have tried to give these ideas some political reality by founding cities where Greeks and barbarians could coexist on a basis of complete equality, but the old division prevailed. The Romans adopted the word 'barbarian' and its general significance, but expanded its reference to include anyone not Greek or Roman. The Roman comic poet, Plautus, whose plays were adaptations from the Greek, uses the word from the Greek point of view for comic effect to describe a Roman or Italian.

For the barbarian invasions across the Roman frontiers in the fourth and fifth centuries AD which led to the collapse of the empire see FALL OF ROME and BRITAIN 8.

basi'lica, from the Greek adjective meaning 'royal (house)', the name applied by the Romans to a large public hall, usually divided into aisles by rows of columns, with a semicircular apse at one end. It was used for commercial, religious, or judicial purposes, and was essentially a Roman development of the Greek *stoa. The earliest known was built in Rome by Marcus Porcius Cato in 184 BC. A form of basilica with aisles flanking a nave and terminating in an apse exercised an important influence on Christian church-architecture of the fourth century.

Bassae, in Greece, in south-west Arcadia, the site of one of the best-preserved temples of the fifth century BC, dedicated to Apollo and built by Ictinus, who designed the Parthenon. The sculptured frieze is now in the British Museum.

Ba'ssarids (Bassarides), in Greek, Thracian *Bacchants; also the title of a lost play by Aeschylus. The name appears to mean 'those who wear fox-skins'.

Bath (city of), see AQUAE SULIS.

baths. From ancient times in order to bath Greeks and Romans sat in tubs and had water poured over them.

In Greece, bathing was not the social institution it became in Roman times. Public baths existed, but frequent use of warm water was sometimes regarded as excessively luxurious, especially by the Spartans, except to relax the muscles after exercise. A kind of soap was used as well as the strigil (a curved instrument made of metal or bone) to remove oil and dirt from the skin. After bathing both men and women anointed themselves with oil. At Athens the water in which a bride was bathed was taken from the fountain of Callirrhoe. Steam baths were known from the fifth century BC.

The Roman baths are one of the most characteristic of their institutions, found universally in the Roman world and enjoyed by all classes of society. During their earlier history the Romans bathed only for the sake of cleanliness; Scipio Africanus (236–184 BC) is known to have had a heated bath in his villa. The earliest known public baths are found at Pompeii and date from the early first century BC. The process of bathing changed radically with the invention of the system for carrying hot air from a furnace through passages under floors (*hypocausts), and through ducts embedded in room walls. With this providing warm water and hot air, by the middle of the first century BC the use of public and private baths had become general, and though public baths were intended at first for the poor they were soon made use of by all classes. Baths were communal, each being roughly the size of a small, shallow swimming-pool. The price of a bath was a *quadrans*, the smallest piece of coined money, virtually worthless. The essential rooms for public baths were the changing-room (*apodyterium*), the cold-bath room (*frigidarium*), to which some bathers confined themselves, and a warm-bath room (*caldarium*). Larger establishments might include a warm room (*tepidarium*), a hot vapour bath (*laconicum*), a sweating-room (*sudatorium*), suites of recreational rooms, exercise grounds (it was usual to take exercise before bathing), colonnades, and gardens. Rhetoricians and authors sometimes recited their works there. These buildings were the natural medium for the development of concrete vaulted *architecture, and the surviving baths in Italy and especially Rome strongly influenced the style of Renaissance architecture. Though mixed bathing was not unknown women more usually had separate (and inferior) baths adjoining those of the men.

Bathy'llus, see PANTOMIME.

Batrachomyoma'chia ('battle of the frogs and mice'), a short Greek mock-epic poem in the style of Homeric epic, sometimes attributed to Homer in antiquity and difficult to date but perhaps of the fifth century BC. The story derives from a fable of Aesop; a mouse Psīcharpax ('crumb-stealer') is invited by a frog Physignathos ('puff-cheek') son of Peleus to ride on his back to visit his watery kingdom. Unfortunately, at the sight of a water-snake the frog dives and the mouse is drowned. But the incident has been seen by another mouse, and a one-day Homeric war ensues between the mice and the frogs, in which the mice seem to be winning. At the request of Athena, Zeus intervenes, and having failed with thunderbolts sends crabs to quell the strife.

Battus, the leader of a body of Dorian Greeks who left the island of Thera in about 630 BC at the bidding of the Delphic Oracle, to colonize *Cyrene in Libya (North Africa). Battus, like other founders, achieved semi-mythical status, and the stories told about him have a strong element of folk-tale. He was said to be a descendant of the ancient race of heroes known as the *Minyae and of the *Argonaut Euphemus. His strange name has been variously interpreted, as the Libyan word for king or as meaning 'stammerer' from his supposed speech impediment. His descendants ruled Cyrene for more than two hundred years. The father of the poet Callimachus was a Cyrenaean of royal descent called Battus; hence the poet is often called 'Battiades' ('son of Battus').

Baucis, see PHILEMON.

Ba'vius and M(a)e'vius, two Latin poets sarcastically alluded to by Virgil in his third Eclogue, otherwise unknown: it is perhaps the same Mevius who is attacked in Horace's tenth Epode. Ancient commentators thought they were bad poets jealously critical of their talented contemporaries, and they have since become proverbial in that role.

Bē'driacum, midway between Cremona and Verona in Cisalpine Gaul, the site of two decisive battles in AD 69 when the forces of the Roman emperor Otho were defeated by the supporters of Vitellius, who succeeded to the empire, and whose own forces were defeated some months later by Vespasian's.

Belgae, population group occupying part of Gaul in Roman times. Their area was bounded in the south by the rivers Seine and Marne, in the west by the sea, and in the east and north by the Rhine. They claimed to be of German descent. Some tribes passed into Britain from about 100 BC onwards and settled in the south and south-west. The Belgae of Gaul were subdued by Julius Caesar in 57 BC but continued to give trouble for the subsequent thirty years.

Belisā'rius, outstanding general of the Roman emperor Justinian (reigned AD 527–65). His greatest victories were the recovery of Africa from the Vandals in 533, and in 540 of Italy from the Ostrogoths, whose king and nobles (as well as much treasure) he took back with him when he was recalled through court intrigues to Constantinople, the capital of the Roman empire at that time. He returned to Italy in 546 but was again recalled; the Ostrogoths were not finally crushed until 553, and then by another general, Narses. Belisarius' last victory was against the Bulgarians in 559. In 563 he was accused of a conspiracy against Justinian, and died in 565. There was a tradition that his eyes were put out and that he ended his life as a beggar in the streets of Constantinople. His extraordinary career, his unusual loyalty to the person of the emperor, and his devotion to his influential wife Antonina, a former actress, are all graphically recorded in exhaustive detail by the historian *Procopius.

Belle'rophon (or Bellerophontēs), in Greek myth, son of Glaucus (the son of Sisyphus) and Eurymedē; in some accounts his father was said to be the god Poseidon. His grandson was the Glaucus in the *Iliad*. He was an ancient Corinthian hero, and his adventures sound similar to those of Heracles and Theseus. He spent some time at the palace of Proetus, king of Argos, whose wife Anteia (sometimes called Stheneboea) fell in love with him. When he rejected her Anteia accused him to her husband of trying to seduce her. Proetus, unwilling to violate the laws of hospitality by killing Bellerophon in his house, sent him to Iobates, Proetus' father-in-law and king of Lycia, with a sealed letter requesting the king to execute Bellerophon. The king accordingly set him a number of tasks likely to prove fatal, killing the *Chimaera, defeating the Solymi and the *Amazons, but Bellerophon with the aid of the winged horse *Pegasus was always victorious. He became reconciled to the king and married his daughter. Afterwards he incurred the wrath of the gods by trying to ride Pegasus to heaven, but the horse threw him. He ended his life a lonely outcast.

Bellō'na (in the old form of the name, Duellona), the Roman goddess of war, sometimes thought of as the wife or sister of Mars. She had no *flamen and no festival, and virtually no mythology. Her first known temple was that vowed by Appius Claudius Caecus while fighting the Etruscans in 296 BC and built in the Campus Martius near the Circus Flaminius. Since the temple lay outside the *pomerium* or city boundary of Rome, it was used by the senate to give audience to foreign ambassadors and returning generals (see TRI-UMPH) whom it was not considered prudent to admit into the city. Here also stood the pillar symbolizing the enemy's frontier over which the *fetialis* threw a spear when a declaration of war was made. The Greek equivalent of Bellona was recognized to be *Enyo.

Bellum Africum ('the African war'), short record of Julius *Caesar's four months' war in Africa (47–46 BC) against the supporters of Pompey. The author is not known for sure, though some have thought it was *Hirtius; the contents suggest that he was a soldier who took part in the campaign but was not in Caesar's confidence.

Bellum Alexandrī'num ('the Alexandrian war'), a continuation of Julius *Caesar's history of the civil war (see COMMENTARIES 2), probably written by *Hirtius. It describes the war of 48–47 BC in Egypt, where Caesar, following his pursuit of Pompey, remained to settle the Egyptian succession by restoring *Cleopatra as ruler. It ends with Caesar's victory at Zela in August 47 (see CAESAR 3).

Bellum cīvī'le ('the civil war'). 1. History in three books by Julius *Caesar of the first two years of the civil war between him and Pompey begun in 49 BC; see COMMENTARIES 2.
   2. Title of an epic poem by the Latin poet *Lucan on the civil war between Julius Caesar and Pompey, often miscalled *Pharsalia*.

Bellum Gallicum, see COMMENTARIES 1.

Bellum Hispanie'nse ('the Spanish war'), account of Julius *Caesar's final campaign of the civil war fought in Spain in 45 BC against Pompey's sons and Labienus, ending in Caesar's victory at Munda. The author is unknown but was probably a soldier in Caesar's army. The text, written in uneducated Latin, has not been accurately preserved.

Bellum Jugurthī'num, see SALLUST.

Bellum Pū'nicum, see NAEVIUS.

Belus, in Greek myth, king of Egypt, son of Poseidon and of Libya or Eurynomē, twin-brother of *Agenor, father of Aegyptus and *Danaus. Through his sons he became the ancestor of several royal houses in Greece and Africa. Belus was also the name of Dido's father.

Bendis, in Greek myth, a goddess originally worshipped in Thrace and identified with Artemis. Her cult was accepted officially at *Piraeus in 430–429 BC for the benefit of resident Thracians. Her festival, which included a torch-race on horseback, is the occasion of Plato's dialogue the *Republic*.

Beneve'ntum (Benevento), one of the most important cities of Samnium in southern Italy, made a Roman colony with Latin rights in 268 BC. It was of strategic importance to the Romans in the Second *Punic War because of its proximity to Campania. A new colony was established there by Augustus.

Berenī'cē. 1. Born c.340 BC, half-sister and third wife of *Ptolemy I Soter, king of Egypt (hence known as Berenice I). Their children were Ptolemy II Philadelphus and Arsinoë II, who married her brother as his second wife (his first wife being Arsinoe I).

2. Daughter of Ptolemy II and Arsinoe I and sister of Ptolemy III, born *c.*280 BC and married to Antiochus II, king of Syria. After his death she and her son were murdered by Antiochus' first wife.

3. Daughter of the king of Cyrene, born *c.*273 BC and married to Ptolemy III Euergetes in 247. In 246 Ptolemy set out for Syria to support, too late, the claims of his sister's son to the throne of Syria (see (2) above). On his departure, his wife Berenice dedicated to the gods a lock of her hair as an offering for his safe return. This lock mysteriously disappeared. Conon, the court astronomer, claimed flatteringly to have discovered it in a hitherto unnamed constellation, seven faint stars near the tail of Leo, thereafter known as *Coma Berenices* (*Berenikēs plokamos*), 'the lock of Berenice'. This event was celebrated in an ingenious and entertaining poem by *Callimachus, in which the lock of hair addresses the reader; the poem has become better known to us in recent years through the discovery of several papyrus fragments containing it. *Catullus' poem 66 is virtually a translation of it into Latin. Alexander Pope (1688–1744) based upon it his *Rape of the Lock*, in which Belinda's curl which had been snipped off is wafted to heaven as a new star.

4. Born AD 28, daughter of *Herod of Acts 12 (who is usually known as Agrippa I) and great-granddaughter of *Herod the Great, king of Judaea. After the death of her second husband she lived with her brother Agrippa II, and to allay suspicion of incest married the king of Cilicia (AD 54). She soon left him, however, and returned to her brother, with whom she was living when the apostle Paul spoke his defence before them both (Acts 25, where she is called Bernice). She and her brother tried in vain to dissuade the Jews from rebelling against Rome in AD 66, and when war broke out they both sided with the Romans. When Titus, the son of the Roman emperor Vespasian, was fighting in Judaea in 67–70, he fell in love with her, and after she visited Rome in *c.*75 they lived openly together for three or four years. This liaison was unpopular and Titus was compelled to send her away when he succeeded to the throne in 79. *Juvenal mentions her contemptuously in his Satire 6. She is the Berenice who was the heroine of tragedies by Corneille (1606–84) and Racine (1639–99).

Bērō'ssus, priest at Babylon in the third century BC who wrote a history of Babylon in three books in Greek, of which only quotations survive. Also ascribed to him were works on astronomy and *astrology, which are known only from references in later writers.

Bī'as, brother of the Greek seer *Melampus.

Bibra'cte (Mont-Beuvray), in central Gaul, the chief town and hill-fort of the Aedui. In 12 BC its inhabitants were transferred to a new town near by, Augustodunum (Autun).

Bi'bulus, Marcus Calpu'rnius, Julius *Caesar's colleague in the aedileship and praetorship and finally in the consulship of 59 BC. After being ineffectual in trying to block Caesar's agrarian laws he shut himself up in his house for the rest of the year, ostensibly to watch for omens and so make Caesar's legislation technically invalid. This gave rise to the joke that it was the consulship not of Caesar and Bibulus but of 'Julius and Caesar'. Upon his proposal Pompey was elected sole consul in 52 BC. He was proconsul of Spain in 51 and commander of Pompey's fleet against Caesar in 49. He died in 48. His wife was Porcia, daughter of Marcus Porcius Cato of Utica, who subsequently married Marcus Brutus, one of Caesar's murderers.

biography

1. *Greek*. Greek biography proper was a late development, though rudimentary forms of it can be seen in the dirge and the funeral oration and in the character sketches of the historians, e.g. of Pausanias and Themistocles in Thucydides. In the fourth century BC appear the *Cyropaedia*, *Memorabilia*, and *Agesilaus* (see under separate titles) of Xenophon, as well as the *Evagoras* of *Isocrates, which all approach true biography. It was Aristotle's pupils in the fourth and third centuries BC who developed an interest in biography and gave a more systematic form to its composition. The tradition persisted among the Alexandrian scholars who valued biographical information about classical authors as a means of explaining their writings, and among those historians who aimed to entertain their readers by giving prominence to outstanding personalities. (Polybius, the only Hellenistic historian we still possess, is not representative of this school.) None of this work survives except in fragments. Over two hundred years later *Plutarch (second century AD) owed the form of his *Lives* largely to his Hellenistic predecessors, but he clearly distinguished between biography and history, and the scope of his work was original. His biographies were markedly moral in tone, since his aim was to exemplify the virtue displayed by the careers of great men; hence his concentration upon the characters of his heroes. In the early third century AD *Diogenes Laertius wrote a compendium of the lives and doctrines of the Greek philosophers, but it is merely a synthesis of earlier compositions.

2. *Roman*. Roman biography developed from a native tradition of funeral orations and sepulchral inscriptions which listed the achievements of the dead man in considerable detail. Many generals and politicians wrote accounts of their

careers in order to justify their actions; Sulla, for example, wrote his memoirs in twenty-two books. Under the empire memoirs were written by the emperor or members of his family, by Augustus and Tiberius, for example. All these works are lost. The most important surviving biographies are those of famous men by Cornelius *Nepos (first century BC), of Agricola by his son-in-law *Tacitus (end of the first century AD), of the Twelve Caesars by *Suetonius (Tacitus' younger contemporary), and of the later emperors by the writers of the *Historia Augusta.

The only autobiography that reveals the writer's own inner life and thoughts is the Confessions of St *Augustine (written c. AD 397–400), though the Meditations of Marcus *Aurelius (AD 121–80) may be compared with it.

Bīon 1. Bion the Borysthenite, Greek popular philosopher who was born c.325 BC in the Greek colony of Olbia in Scythia, near the estuary of the river Borysthenes (Dnieper). His family was enslaved to a rhetorician but Bion received a good education and was eventually freed. He studied in the various philosophical schools in Athens but became an adherent of no one school. He seemed closest to the *Cynics whose caustic wit and anti-establishment attitudes he shared. Most of his life he spent wandering from city to city, lecturing and teaching for money. He popularized the Greek diatribē ('spoken address') as a written sermon, so that it could reach a wider audience; and the connotation of abusiveness which the word has acquired in modern times derives from Bion's humorous but sharp attacks on human faults and weaknesses. His influence on the Latin satires of Lucilius and Horace was notable. He died c.246 BC. Fairly extensive fragments of his writing survive.

2. Of Smyrna, the last Greek pastoral poet known to us by name; he lived at the end of the second century BC, and is generally linked with the pastoral poet *Moschus. Virtually nothing is known of his life; according to the anonymous Lament for Bion (attributed to Moschus), he lived in Sicily and died by poisoning. He wrote in hexameters in the (literary) Doric *dialect, and seventeen fragments of his poems (some may even be complete) survive. Since the Renaissance he has been credited with the Lament for Adonis, perhaps intended for recitation at a festival. The pastoral element in his work is slight, most of the poems being playfully erotic.

Birds (Ornithes, Lat. Aves), Greek comedy by *Aristophanes which won second prize at the City Dionysia in 414 BC. In 415 the Athenian fleet had set out on the Sicilian Expedition (see PELOPONNESIAN WAR) and its success was still in the balance. The Birds is an escapist fantasy in which two Athenians, Peisetairos ('the per-suader') and Euelpides ('the optimist'), dissatisfied with life in Athens and its endless lawsuits, go to look for the mythical Tereus (see PHILOMELA) who has been turned into a bird and might know of a more suitable place to live. Tereus suggests various countries, but there are objections to them all. Peisetairos now has a brilliant idea: let the birds all unite and build a great walled city in the air, and they will defy both men and gods; they will intercept the smoke from the sacrifices on which the gods are nourished. The chorus of birds, at first hostile, is won over, and the birds quickly set about building the city, to be called Nephelokokkygia ('cloudcuckooland', from nephelē, 'cloud', and kokkyx, 'cuckoo'), under the direction of Peisetairos and Euelpides, who grow wings to suit their new condition. Then various unwelcome visitors arrive: a priest, a needy poet with a hymn in honour of the new city, an oracle-monger, *Meton the famous astronomer (to lay out the streets), a superintendent, and a statute-seller. They are all appropriately dealt with. The new city is now finished, when a guard comes in with the news that a god has escaped the birds' blockade. The god, who turns out to be Iris, sent to enquire why sacrifices have stopped on earth, is seized and told that birds are now the gods, and finally goes off in tears to complain to her father. Meanwhile people have become bird-mad and want wings. Further visitors arrive: a father-beater, because young cocks fight their fathers (he is reminded that young storks must feed their fathers); Cinesias the lyric poet, because he wants to soar on airy pinions; an informer, who would find wings useful for serving writs; and the god Prometheus, who hides from Zeus under a parasol while he tells of the food shortage among the gods and advises Peisetairos to make hard terms with them and insist on having Basileia ('sovereignty'), daughter of Zeus, to wife. Then come ambassadors from the gods, Poseidon, Heracles, and a god from the barbarous Triballians (democracy being in full swing among the Olympian gods also). Thanks to the greediness of Heracles, gods and birds are reconciled, Peisetairos gets the sceptre of Zeus as well as Basileia; he is hailed as the highest of the gods, and preparations are made for his wedding.

Bitōn, see CLEOBIS.

Boadicē'a (the usual, but textually incorrect, English form of Boudicca), the wife of the British king of the Iceni, a tribe living in East Anglia. At the king's death in AD 61 Roman insolence towards her family caused her to lead a British revolt against Roman rule while the Roman governor Suetonius Paulinus was campaigning in Anglesey. During the revolt the British sacked Camulodunum (Colchester), Londinium (London), and Verulamium (St Albans). At his return the governor routed her forces and she is said to have taken poison (Tacitus, *Annals* 14). See BRITAIN 4.

Bocchus, see JUGURTHA.

Boeō'tia, country of central Greece, bordering Attica on the north-west. Its two main cities were (Boeotian) Orchomenus and Thebes, both standing in rich plains, good for breeding horses and growing wheat. It possessed the two famous mountains of *Cithaeron and *Helicon. In classical times much of the northern plain where Orchomenus stood was covered by the shallow Lake Copāis (now drained), famous for its eels, into which the waters of the Boeotian Cephisus and its tributaries flowed. The land was occupied from Neolithic times onward and was clearly important in the Bronze Age. Mycenaean remains at Orchomenus and myths about the wealth of the Minyae who migrated there from Thessaly suggest that this city was older than Thebes, but the rise of the latter and the flooding of Lake Copais contributed to its decline.

Most Boeotian myth centres on the city of Thebes (see CADMUS, HERACLES, OEDIPUS), whose power at any one time determined the importance of Boeotia's role in the history of the period. Thebes was never strong enough, however, to enforce its authority over all the cities of Boeotia and combine them into one state. The cities of Thespiae and Plataea often figured in Boeotian politics. The affairs of Boeotia were managed by a confederacy of cities, but some cities were unwilling members and Plataea in particular made ties with Athens to protect her independence. Boeotia played an equivocal part, if she was not actively disloyal to Greece, in the Persian Wars. When Athens was seeking to extend her power in the mid-fifth century BC she invaded and defeated the Boeotians at the battle of Oenophyta in 457, and thus compelled all the cities except Thebes to acknowledge her supremacy, but the independence of Boeotia was restored ten years later when Athens was defeated at Coronea. A further defeat at Delium in 424 put an end to Athenian hopes of reconquering Boeotia. The fourth century saw the extension of Theban supremacy over the rest of Boeotia, particularly under the leadership of Epaminondas, and the Thebans' defeat of Sparta at Leuctra in 371 and again at Mantinea in 362. Like the rest of Greece, Boeotia could not resist the rise of Macedon under Philip, and after the defeat of Theban and Athenian forces at Chaeronea in 338 and the destruction of Thebes in 335 by Philip's son (Alexander the Great) Boeotia rapidly declined. In Roman times nothing remained of most Boeotian cities except their ruins and their names.

To the Athenians particularly the Boeotians seemed dull and thick-witted, a condition which Cicero and Horace ascribed to the dampness of the atmosphere. It seems true that Boeotia was backward artistically, but its contribution to music and literature was considerable: Hesiod, Corinna, Pindar, and Plutarch were all Boeotians. The *dialect in the classical period was Aeolic, as spoken in Lesbos and Thessaly, but had some features in common with west Greek and a vowel-system peculiar to itself.

Bōē'thius (Anicius Manlius Sevērīnus Boethius) (*c.* AD 476–524), Latin philosopher and (Christian) theological writer, son of the consul for 487 and belonging to a family which had held many high offices of state in the fourth and fifth centuries. Boethius was himself consul in 510 and won the favour of the Ostrogothic 'king' of Italy, Theodoric (see GOTHS), who retained the Roman civil administration in Italy and made Boethius his *magister officiorum* (head of the civil service). However, in 523 Boethius was suspected of treachery through defending a senator accused of conspiring with the emperor in the East (Byzantium), was imprisoned, and put to death in 524. He was buried at Pavia and was regarded as a Catholic martyr (because Theodoric was an Arian, i.e. a heretic) and canonized as 'St Severinus'. His importance derives from his being the last Latin-speaking scholar of the ancient world to have a genuine mastery of Greek. After him no one in the West had first-hand acquaintance with Greek philosophy until the rediscovery of Aristotle in the twelfth century (see TEXTS, TRANSMISSION OF ANCIENT 7).

In his early life Boethius' declared aim was to translate and write commentaries upon all the writings of Aristotle and Plato in order to construct a harmony out of the two philosophies. This huge task was never completed, but his translations of and commentaries on Aristotle's logical works and *Porphyry's Introduction (*Isagōgē*) to Aristotle as well as some logical works of his own played a highly influential role in medieval education and ensured that knowledge of Aristotle was never totally extinguished in the western world. His handbooks of arithmetic, music, geometry, and astronomy (the *quadrivium*) were also much used in the medieval schools (the two former books survive). There also survive several Christian treatises, on the doctrine of the Trinity and on the Incarnation. His literary fame depends on the book he wrote in prison, the *Consolation of Philosophy*, a dialogue between himself and a personified Lady Philosophy. This work influenced the thought of the Middle Ages as much as any other. It consists of five books in prose interspersed with thirty-nine short poems in thirteen different (and metrically accurate) metres in the style of Menippean satire (see MENIPPUS). Philosophy, who ousts the Muses, comes to console the prisoner; she reminds him of the sufferings of other thinkers such as Socrates, and invites him to lay bare his troubles. Boethius describes the ingratitude with which his integrity has been met, and laments the triumph of injustice. Philosophy reminds him of the mutability of fortune and the vanity of those things which the world esteems good. The only real good is God. Boethius asks how, under a beneficent God, evil can exist or pass unpunished (book 4), and is answered by a justification of divine government followed by a discussion on free will. It is a moving work, written from the heart, and it provided comfort to innumerable readers of the Middle Ages, as is shown by the hundreds of manuscripts of it which exist today, and the fact that it was translated into more European languages than any other book except the Bible. Its translators include Alfred the Great, Chaucer, and Queen Elizabeth I. Its tone, though theistic, is largely pagan and classical and it ignores the specifically Christian consolations, owing more perhaps to Stoicism and Platonism. Gibbon called it 'a golden volume'. Compare CASSIODORUS.

Bona De'a, Roman fertility goddess worshipped exclusively by women, sometimes identified with Fauna. Rites in her honour were celebrated annually at the house of the chief magistrate, under the leadership of his wife assisted by the *Vestal Virgins, and these were attended only by women. It was these rites that *Clodius violated in 62 BC by entering in female disguise.

books and writing
1. Writing had developed in the Near East and Egypt long before the skill reached Greece. In late Bronze Age Greece a script known as *Linear B was used on clay tablets but as far as we can tell only for making official inventories and not for literary purposes, and it did not survive the collapse of this civilization in about 1150 BC. Homer makes an obscure reference to writing (*Iliad* 6. 166ff.) but seems to have thought of the Homeric world as illiterate and bookless. The classical Greeks believed, certainly correctly, that their system of writing derived from Phoenicia (see CADMUS). Archaeological and literary evidence suggests that writing became widespread in Greece between 750 and 650 BC. See also ALPHABET.

2. Throughout the ancient world the commonest writing material was papyrus. The oldest papyrus roll known to us is Egyptian and is dated to about 3000 BC. We have no firm evidence on when papyrus came into general use in Greece, but it is hard to think that it could be later than the time of the poet Archilochus (*c*.680–640 BC) when it seems that poetry in general came to be written down. The chief rival to papyrus as writing material was animal skins; Herodotus says that the Ionians used the skins of sheep and goats when papyrus was unavailable. Papyrus was perhaps originally imported into Greece from the Phoenician town of Byblos from which the Greeks took their name for papyrus and

thence for book (*biblos*—hence 'bible'). It was made from the pith of a water plant which in antiquity grew mainly in the Nile. The pith was peeled off into thin strips; one layer of strips was laid down with the fibres running from top to bottom and another layer was superimposed with the fibres running from side to side, the two layers being hammered together without the use of glue. The sheet was then dried and the surface polished. The writing was normally on the side on which the fibres ran from side to side (recto). Frequently the back (verso) was used subsequently for a non-literary text. In rare cases the text on the recto is continued on the verso and the roll is then called an opisthograph. The sheets thus produced, with a maximum width of about 40 cm. (16 in.) and a normal height of about 23 cm. (9 in.), were pasted together side by side so as to form a continuous roll, the joins being virtually invisible in rolls of good quality. The pasted sheets were called in Greek *kollēmata*. In later times the Greek term for the 'first sheet' of a legal document on which was written the authentication for what followed was *prōtokollon*, hence English 'protocol'. The Library at Alexandria (see ALEXANDRIAN LIBRARY) was probably responsible for introducing standardization in book production. Papyrus was bought in rolls, not sheets, usually about 10 m. (33 ft.) long. With writing of average size such a roll could contain a book of Thucydides, or two of the shorter books of Homer. The work was written in vertical columns of 5–10 cm. (2–4 in.) wide throughout the length of the roll, with a margin between the columns and a broader margin at top and bottom. Scribes seem not to have been concerned to keep a regular number of lines to a column or of letters to a line. The minimum of help is given to the reader: *punctuation and even spacing between words are non-existent or at best erratic, and enlarged initial letters are not used. A short stroke under the line (*paragraphos*) often indicated where there was a pause in the sense or a change of speaker in dramatic texts (but the name of the speaker was hardly ever given). *Accents appear, if at all, only in poetic texts; *punctuation where it exists takes the form of a single point level with the top of the letter. Scribes wrote in black ink made from a dense carbon black. (The Athenian orator Demosthenes mocks Aeschines for having to get up early to 'grind the ink' for his father's school.) A hard reed pen was used for writing. Titles were written at the end of a roll (the part least liable to damage); a roll was usually identified by a label (Gk. *sillybos*, Lat. *titulus*) which hung from it as it lay on a shelf or in a pigeon-hole or box. A roller (Gk. *omphalos*, Lat. *umbilīcus*) might be attached to the end of the papyrus, ornamented with projecting knobs. The rolls comprising a long work or the complete works of an author might be kept together in a cupboard (Lat.

armārium) or bucket (Lat. *capsa*). A reader would undo the roll with his right hand, and roll it up, as he proceeded, with his left.

The alternative material to papyrus was vellum (Lat. *vellus*, 'skin', 'hide') made from the skins of cattle, sheep, and goats. The skins were scraped, rubbed with pumice, and dressed with alum. This material was later known as parchment, a name derived from the city of *Pergamum which was famous for its manufacture. (In modern usage, parchment is made from the skin of sheep and goats, vellum from that of calves, lambs, and kids.)

3. Books to the classical Greeks were essentially a substitute for recitation. It is not till the fifth century BC at Athens that we find the beginnings of a book trade, fostered by the large number of prose books written by the *sophists for educational purposes. Plato has Socrates say that a book by the philosopher Anaxagoras could be bought in the *orchestra* (in the agora at Athens) for a drachma or less. In the fourth century BC books became relatively common and the practice of reading seems to have become firmly established; *Isocrates certainly wrote for private reading (though in antiquity reading always meant reading aloud). Aristotle and his school formed a large collection of books. In the third and subsequent centuries the output of books greatly increased when educated slaves were employed as copyists and the production of papyrus and later of parchment was organized by the Hellenistic kings. (The story was told that in the second century BC a king of Egypt, jealous of the library at Pergamum, placed an embargo on the supply of papyrus to that city, where parchment was promptly invented.)

4. The Latin word for book, *liber*, 'bark', originated at an early time when books in Rome were written on bark, but the introduction of Greek literature into Rome in the third and second centuries BC propagated the papyrus roll. Very few papyrus fragments of Latin books have survived compared with Greek because the conditions which allow survival are found in Egypt, a Greek-speaking area. On the other hand, Latin literature is much richer than Greek in information about books and the book trade. From the first century BC we hear of booksellers with their staffs of copyists. Cicero had his writings published by *Atticus, and Horace mentions the Sosii as booksellers. The demand for books increased and it became the fashion for rich Romans to have a library. The price of books seems to have been moderate; Martial says that a copy of his first book of epigrams might be had for five denarii. There was no law of copyright and authors did not profit directly from the sale of their books.

5. A papyrus roll (Lat. *volumen*, English 'volume') was not very convenient to use. It had to be manipulated by both hands and rewound after use. Athenian vase-paintings show readers getting into difficulties with twisted rolls, and they were easily torn. From Homer onwards sets of wooden tablets hinged on a ring or leather thong had been used for notes or letters. The tablets were either whitened and written on in ink or, more usually, coated with wax and the writing scratched on with a stylus (the wax could be smoothed again with the blunt end); thus the Latin verb 'to write', *exarare*, meant originally 'to plough up', because the stylus furrows the wax like a plough-share. From these tablets there slowly developed from the first century AD the book in modern form, known as a codex, made from folded sheets of papyrus or parchment, put together quire by quire (eight leaves, sixteen pages), stitched at the spine and bound with wooden boards. The codex had several advantages over the papyrus roll: it was very easy to consult, since the pages could be turned forwards or backwards at will; both sides of the pages could be written on; it could hold four or five times as much text as a roll; and it was longer-lasting. It is noticeable that the Christians adopted the codex form quite early, perhaps because the sayings of Jesus were originally recorded in a parchment notebook of the kind used by lawyers and businessmen, perhaps also because the codex gave ease of reference. By the fourth century it had superseded the papyrus roll, and parchment was preferred to papyrus. From this and the following century come the earliest surviving manuscripts of classical authors. The roll form was retained for public documents through the Middle Ages to modern times. Paper was introduced from China by the Arabs in the ninth century, but its use did not become common until the twelfth century.

6. *Writing.* Greek books were written with remarkably little change from the time of the early papyri down to the manuscripts of the mid-ninth century AD in a majuscule ('large letters') script known as *uncial. The letters, resembling capitals, were large, rounded, and individually formed. A well-written manuscript in this hand possessed a dignified beauty, but the script was slow to write and took up a lot of room. In the mid-ninth century a new bookhand, minuscule ('small letters'), was introduced which could be written more quickly and economically; see TEXTS, TRANSMISSION OF ANCIENT 3. The earliest dated minuscule manuscript we possess is of the Gospels (the 'Uspensky Gospels'), dated to 835.

The writing of Latin manuscripts followed a similar pattern. During the classical period Latin books were written in majuscule, either in square capitals (for luxury books) or (more usually) in rustic capitals; the latter was a more fluid or careless-looking variety of the former, and it continued in use until the early sixth century AD. Meanwhile, in the fourth century, the uncial form of majuscule emerged as a bookhand, along with a less formal version known as half-uncial, which included some letter forms employed in the everyday business hand. Uncial and half-uncial writing continued until well into the ninth century AD and beyond. Meanwhile in the late seventh and eighth centuries experiments had been taking place in many parts of Europe to find a fast, neat, economical script. In continental Europe a minuscule script developed out of the old Roman *cursive handwriting used for business and official correspondence, whereas in Ireland such a script developed rather out of half-uncial. However, it was in France that a particularly fine and lucid minuscule hand evolved in the eighth century which became the bookhand of Europe. The letters were regular, rounded, and separate. This hand slowly came to predominate, reaching England in the tenth century, and was in use everywhere by the end of the twelfth. For italic see ALDUS MANUTIUS. See also EPIGRAPHY, LIBRARIES, and TEXTS, TRANSMISSION OF ANCIENT 5.

Boō'tēs ('ox-driver' or 'waggoner'), a smaller constellation near the larger one known as the Wain. When the Wain is known as the Great Bear, Bootes is called Arctophylax, 'guard of the Bear'; it is also sometimes called Arcturus, wrongly, since that name properly denotes only one star of the constellation. See also CALLISTO.

Bo'reas, in Greek, the north wind (Lat. *aquilo*); in Greek myth, son of the Titan Astraios ('starry one') and Eōs ('dawn'). His native land was said to be Thrace. He carried off as wife the nymph Oreithyia, daughter of Erechtheus, an early king of Athens, and was thus thought by the Athenians to be specially connected with them. They instituted a state cult for him after he destroyed the Persian fleet at Cape Sepias in 480 BC (see WINDS). He was the father of Zētēs and Calăis, mentioned among the *Argonauts.

Bory'sthenēs, river of Scythia (south Russia), the modern Dnieper.

Bo'sporus ('ox-ford'), sometimes 'Bosphorus'. 1. The Thracian Bosporus, the strait connecting the Sea of Marmora (Propontis) with the Black Sea, and separating Europe from Asia. According to Greek myth it was here that the heifer *Io crossed from one continent to the other (perhaps from Asia to Europe). The strong current and the winding channel made it dangerous to shipping. 2. The Cimmerian Bosporus, the straits connecting the Black Sea with the Sea of Asov. It also is said to derive its name from a crossing made by Io.

Bou'dicca, the textually correct form of *Boadicea.

boulē. In those Greek states where the government was carried out by an assembly of citizens and a council, the general Greek name for the latter was *boule*. This was a specially appointed body of citizens, which implemented the decisions of the sovereign assembly and administered the day-to-day running of the state. In classical Athens the boule consisted of five hundred (male) citizens over 30 years old, fifty from each of the ten *tribes, appointed annually by lot by the *demes (acting as voting districts) of Athens and Attica, from those who were willing to stand and had survived a preliminary scrutiny. No one could serve on the boule more than twice in a lifetime. Hence a large proportion of the male population served at some time in their lives, though there is some evidence that on occasions the well-to-do were over-represented (it must therefore have been possible to interfere with the drawing of lots). Although it was not on the whole an independent body anxious to enforce its own views, evidence suggests that it occasionally acted on its own initiative without the knowledge of the assembly.

*Solon at the beginning of the sixth century BC was credited with the creation of the original boule at Athens, but the origin of the boule as it functioned in classical times lies in the reforms of *Cleisthenes at the end of the sixth century. The boule had two main functions: it supervised the activity of the magistrates and did administrative work itself, either by meeting in full session or through committees; and it prepared the agenda for meetings of the *ecclesia ('assembly'). Under the first heading, it saw to the maintenance of the fleet and the docks, organized all the state finances, and had the care of public buildings and certain state cults and sacrifices. Under the second heading, it considered every motion to be placed on the agenda of the ecclesia. This does not mean that the boule directed policy; no doubt it drafted decrees on uncontentious issues, but on highly controversial matters it merely put the question on the agenda of the ecclesia. Any citizen could then propose an amendment, an alternative version, or outright rejection. The boule also had a judicial capacity, in which it scrutinized citizens' eligibility for various offices and tried some criminal cases.

The boule sat every day except for festivals. Each tribe's representatives served as presidents (*prytaneis) for one-tenth of the year (this period being known therefore as a prytany). The prytaneis were on duty every day and it was they who summoned the boule and the ecclesia. Every day they dined in the public hall (*tholos). One of their number was chosen by lot to be foreman and chairman of any meeting of the boule or ecclesia held on his day: for that day and never again he was custodian of the state seal, the treasuries, and the archives. Socrates was one of the prytaneis when the eight Athenian generals were being tried by the assembly after the battle of *Arginusae in 406 BC and objected to putting the motion that was to pronounce sentence on all the accused together.

During the oligarchic revolutions of 411 and 404 BC, the boule was replaced by oligarchic councils (see ATHENS 2), but it was restored when democracy returned and continued to function throughout the Hellenistic and Roman periods. (For the council at Sparta see GEROUSIA.)

bouleutē'rion, at Athens, 'council-chamber'; see METROON.

boustrophē'don (lit. 'as the ox turns'), in Greek *epigraphy, a term used to describe the script on early Greek inscriptions in which the lines of writing run alternately from right to left and from left to right, as the ox pulls the plough in successive furrows. The letters also are turned round to face the appropriate direction. See also ALPHABET.

boxing, see ATHLETICS (iii).

Bra'sidas (d. 422 BC), the most distinguished Spartan general in the early years of the *Peloponnesian War. In the first year of the war, 431, he saved the town of Methonē on the south-west coast of the Peloponnese which was being besieged by the Athenians. In consequence he was appointed the senior magistrate (ephor) at Sparta. He took part in the Spartan attempt to dislodge the Athenians from Pylos in 425, but held relatively subordinate commands until 424 when he was sent north to damage Athenian interests in Thrace; there he gained possession of several important cities in alliance with Athens, including Amphipolis and Tor-onē. The Athenians blamed the historian Thucydides, who was with his fleet at Thasos, for allowing Amphipolis to be surrendered without resistance, and exiled him. Brasidas continued operations in Thrace until 422, when he had to face without reinforcements a fresh Athenian army under Cleon sent to recoup the losses. The Athenians took back Torone but failed to recover Amphipolis, and in the battle both Cleon and Brasidas were killed. Brasidas was accorded the singular honour of burial within the walls of Amphipolis, and his tomb received yearly sacrifices as if he were a hero. Thucydides records three speeches in his name and clearly admired his resourcefulness. He permanently damaged the Athenian cause in a vital part of their empire.

Brauron (modern Vraona), in east Attica, one of the twelve ancient Attic townships tradition-ally united by Theseus into a single Athenian state. It was well known from ancient times for the worship of Artemis, who had an important temple there and in whose honour a festival, Braurōnia, was held annually. This was cele-brated with particular splendour every fourth year. The cult was in some way associated with

*Iphigeneia; local legend said that her sacrifice took place there rather than at Aulis, but that a bear was substituted for her. It was chiefly for women; its notable feature was that young girls between the ages of 5 and 10 wearing saffron dresses 'acted the she-bear', supposedly in atonement for the killing of a bear belonging to Artemis. Originally no girl might be married until she had performed this ritual bear-dance; by classical times the ritual was part of the Athenian state religion and was performed only by the daughters of noble families.

Brennus. 1. Leader of the Gauls (mostly Senones, a Celtic people) who invaded Italy in 390 BC (or 387), defeated the Romans at the river Allia, 19 km. (12 miles) from Rome, and then captured Rome apart from the Capitol. Legend relates that the Gauls massacred the priests and old patricians as they sat silently in their chairs of state in the porticoes of their houses. For the part supposedly played by the Capitoline geese in saving the Capitol, see MANLIUS. Legend also relates that, after six months' siege, when the gold which the Gauls accepted as the ransom of Rome was being weighed and a Roman tribune complained of false weights, Brennus threw his sword into the scale with the words, '*vae victis*', 'woe to the conquered'. Roman pride handed down the story that Brennus and his army were annihi-lated before they could leave Italy (see CAMIL-LUS). It has been suggested that the name Brennus was attributed to him in later times from the Gallic chieftain who invaded Greece in 280–279 BC (see below).

2. The leader of a Celtic people from Gaul who in 280–279 BC overran Macedonia and thence Greece. He was checked by a force of Athenians and others at Thermopylae, but finally turned their position as the Persians had done in 480 BC. He was defeated and wounded at Delphi and committed suicide in 278. The Gauls retreated with great loss.

brevis bre'vians ('the shortening short'), phon-etic tendency in popular Latin speech trans-ferred to less formal kinds of Latin verse (e.g. comedy) whereby a short syllable shortens a following long syllable if the latter is preceded or followed by an accented syllable (e.g. *bŏ'nīs* might be scanned ∪∪). See METRE, LATIN 2.

Bria'reōs (Lat. Briareus), one of the three hundred-armed giants (see HECATONCHEIRES), the sons of Uranus (Heaven) and Gaia (Earth), to be distinguished (as e.g. Virgil and Callima-chus did not) from the other *Giants who were also the offspring of these parents. Briareos was also called Aegaeon. He and his two brothers fought with Zeus against the *Titans and were rewarded by being set to guard the Titans imprisoned in Tartarus. When the other Olympian gods were about to put Zeus in chains, Briareos, summoned by Thetis, saved him.

Briga'ntēs, numerically the largest tribe in Britain, whose territory in the north of England stretched from coast to coast and from Hadrian's Wall (and, in the west, beyond it) to as far south as a curved line between the Mersey and the Humber, taking in the Peak District but excluding east Yorkshire. Under Queen Cartimandua (see BRITAIN 3) relations with Rome were friendly, but the territory was annexed by Rome in the seventies AD.

Brīsē'is, in the *Iliad*, Achilles' captive slave-concubine taken from him by Agamemnon, when the latter at the wish of Apollo had to return his own concubine Chryseis to her father. Hence the anger of Achilles, which is the theme of the *Iliad*.

Britain

1. *Britain before the Roman conquest.* Britain probably became known to the Mediterranean world in the fifth century BC through the Phoenicians of Carthage, the great traders and voyagers of the ancient world, because south-west Britain was one of the few western sources of tin, a necessary component of bronze very scantily diffused in the Mediterranean area. Greeks of the fifth century heard only vague stories about the 'Tin Islands' (*Cassiterides), but in the late fourth century a Greek navigator from Massilia (Marseilles), *Pytheas, visited Cornwall and the tin-depot at St Michael's Mount on his circumnavigation of Britain. (It may have been Pytheas who recorded the name of this country as the 'Pretannic Isles', a name of uncertain origin; it may be related to the Latin name *Picti*, Picts, i.e. 'painted' or 'tattooed'. The word *pretan* meaning 'tin' is apparently first found in an Egyptian demotic papyrus.) By the second century BC regular trade routes between Britain and the Mediterranean were established, Gallic merchants and especially the tribe of the Veneti from south Brittany acting as intermediaries until Julius Caesar disrupted trade in 56 BC.

It is not possible to discern Caesar's purpose in invading Britain in 55 BC after he had conquered and pacified Gaul. There were certainly connections other than trade between Britain and Gaul: Britons fought in the Gallic armies and rebellious Gauls sought refuge in Britain. Britain was the source of that Druidism which Caesar saw as the most powerful political force among the Gauls. He may have felt that his conquest of Gaul was hardly secure without at least a show of Roman strength in Britain; total conquest may not have been his intention.

It now seems likely that Caesar found in Britain an Iron Age culture not radically different from that of Gaul. Iron appears to have been first used in Britain in the late seventh century BC, brought, some think, by invaders, of whom it has been postulated that several waves came in successive centuries. The evidence for hostile invasion is not clear; it is at least possible that the change to iron was an innovation adopted peacefully by a long-established population under the influence of Iron Age cultures on the Continent. There is stronger evidence for a considerable influx of Belgic peoples in the late second century BC, whether peaceful or not we cannot be sure. Caesar in his *Gallic Wars* says that the 'seaward' part of Britain was populated by these more recent arrivals. The Belgae, living in northern France and the Low Countries, were probably constrained to move into Britain under pressure from the expanding German tribes (Cimbri and Teutones) who even threatened Italy in the late second century BC (see MARIUS).

The pattern of life that the Romans found in Britain was by no means homogeneous, but naturally varied with the physical features and climate. Land in the lowlands of the south and east was suitable for settlement and agriculture; communication inland and to the Continent was relatively easy, and the area was receptive both to new settlers and to new ideas. In the highlands of the west and north there was probably little cultivation; the people lived a pastoral and perhaps semi-nomadic life. Caesar, who never penetrated far enough to see for himself, was nevertheless well-informed when he wrote that they 'do not sow corn but live on milk and meat, and dress in skins'. The Britons lived in separate, self-governing tribes who found co-operation difficult, and were far from envisaging any form of centralized government. Tribal hill-forts, a feature of British life certainly since the Bronze Age and perhaps going back to Neolithic times, seem to have served variously as refuges in war and settlements in peacetime. In the first century BC among the southern and eastern peoples, perhaps in the main the recent Belgic invaders, a new and more advanced pattern seems to have evolved, evidenced by denser agricultural occupation of the fertile valleys, with enclosed meadows and fixed boundaries, all of which suggest a more settled form of land-ownership. Occupations were more specialized and organized; slave-labour may even have been used. In hill-forts, where a rudimentary street system sometimes existed, and in the larger valley settlements, the beginnings of something approaching urbanization may be detected. The art of this period, seen in the metalwork of weapons, mirrors, and personal ornaments, is of great beauty and high technical achievement, but the quantity found is small, suggesting that it was confined to an aristocratic class.

There is scarcely any trace, in place-names or elsewhere, of a language earlier than Celtic; all the places mentioned by Caesar have Celtic names. This fact suggests that at the time of the

Roman conquest the use of the Celtic language was universal, even in the far north of Scotland and in Ireland, and it is difficult to find evidence to account for this ubiquity.

2. *The Roman invasions of 55 and 54 BC.* The first invasion was in the nature of a reconnaissance and the Romans had several setbacks. The soldiers disembarked on the beaches around Deal in Kent, showing great reluctance in the face of the enemy until the standard-bearer of the 10th legion leaped into the sea first. The troubles culminated in severe damage to the anchored fleet through storm and high tide. Caesar withdrew his forces at the end of the summer, having gained useful experience but no lasting advantage. The invasion of the following year was a more serious affair. A fleet of over 800 vessels conveyed five legions and 2,000 cavalry to a landing in roughly the same area as before. In the operations that followed Caesar crossed the river Thames (Tamesis or Tamesa) to attack the British commander Cassivellaunus, king of the Catuvellauni, the most powerful of the southern tribes. The fact that the Britons appointed a common leader shows the extent of their alarm. Caesar crossed the Thames at its only fordable point, a place as yet unknown. Tribes favourable to Rome betrayed the whereabouts of Cassivellaunus' stronghold, perhaps at Wheathampstead in Hertfordshire; Caesar attacked and captured it, forcing Cassivellaunus to make moderate terms: to give hostages and to pay tribute. Caesar then withdrew to Gaul, where he feared an uprising.

3. *The conquest and occupation of Britain.* Britain was now a recognized part of the Roman world, though Rome was not to invade again for another century. In the thirties and twenties BC the Latin poets Virgil and Horace sometimes speak as if the emperor Augustus was on the verge of annexing Britain, but nothing came of it: in his reign and that of his successor Tiberius Rome's military attention was diverted elsewhere. Our knowledge of Britain for the century between 54 BC and AD 43 is considerably greater than for the previous century, through the evidence of inscriptions and coins as well as literature and archaeology in general, so that it is possible to draw a reasonably complete map of the tribes and know something of the policies of their rulers. It was a time of complicated political strife in the south-east. The Catuvellauni *c.*15 BC came to be ruled by a certain Tasciovanus, one of whose family, Cunobelinus (the Cymbeline of medieval legend and Shakespeare), minted coins at Colchester (Camulodunum), formerly the stronghold of the Trinovantes tribe. These latter and the Catuvellauni were now probably united under one king. Trade between this area and Rome, attested by the many Roman artefacts found here, suggests that no open hostility was felt for Rome; it has been argued that in west Britain

there was more enmity. In AD 39/40 Cunobelinus banished his son Adminius, who fled to the Continent and surrendered to the Romans. The emperor Gaius (Caligula) hailed this event as a great victory and perhaps then conceived the idea of an invasion. He had his troops drawn up on the Channel coast before the venture was abandoned, for unknown reasons. Cunobelinus died between AD 40 and 43, and was succeeded by his sons Togodumnus and Caratacus (Welsh 'Caradoc'); Claudius succeeded Gaius as emperor in AD 41. Soon after, rivalry between British tribal leaders turned to open war, with the possibility that much of Britain might be united under Cunobelinus' sons, contrary to Rome's interests. Claudius was himself eager to acquire a military triumph to strengthen his position. In 43 he therefore assembled on the Channel coast a formidable army under Aulus Plautius and some experienced legionary commanders (one was the future emperor Vespasian), consisting of four legions, the 2nd, 9th, 14th, and 20th, and auxiliaries, a total force of perhaps 40,000 men. At first the men refused to embark, feeling they were being sent beyond the known world, and had to be persuaded by the emperor's freedman Narcissus, sent especially from Rome. One group of the army landed at Richborough (Rutupiae), where the great camp can still be seen, and another probably near Chichester (Noviomagus Regensium, sometimes referred to as Regnum). Plautius' aim was to subdue the kingdom of Cunobelinus' sons. He won a decisive victory on the Medway, and shortly afterwards Togodumnus was killed. The setback stiffened British resistance to such an extent that Plautius was alarmed and, it is related, sent for Claudius, as ordered to do if he met with difficulties. This has seemed incredible to some historians, but Claudius subsequently arrived with reinforcements, captured Colchester—whether he played an active part himself in the fighting is disputed—and received the submission of many tribes. Caratacus escaped, eventually joining the Silures of south Wales to encourage resistance to Rome. The land of Cunobelinus was made a Roman province, with Colchester the capital, garrisoned by the 20th legion. A fort was built at St Albans (Verulamium).

Claudius pursued the policy of having client kingdoms around the province: such were the Iceni of Norfolk and the Brigantes in the north, though the latter felt themselves to be largely independent. An important client king was *Cogidubnus, whose land centred on the Chichester area of west Sussex (the palace excavated at Fishbourne is almost certainly his). Plautius was made governor of the province with orders to secure the rest of the country. His commander Vespasian campaigned successfully in the south and west, penetrating perhaps to Devon and Cornwall and winning a reputation that was to prove valuable later when the succession to the imperial throne was in question. By 47 when Plautius' term as governor ended, the 9th legion had pushed the frontier up to the Humber or beyond, and the lowlands of the south and east were under Roman control. The road known as the Foss(e) Way, from the mouth of the river Axe, east of Exeter (Isca Dumnoniorum) to Lincoln (Lindum), may indicate the general limit of Roman authority. Ostorius Scapula, the new governor, had to put down attacks from tribes outside the province as soon as he took office. In 49 he planted a colony of army veterans at Colchester (at about this time the governor's administration moved to London (Londinium)) and in 51 defeated Caratacus, who had become the leader of British opposition to Rome, and who fled after the battle to Cartimandua, queen of the Brigantes. But Cartimandua had submitted to Rome and surrendered him to the Romans, who kept him in honourable captivity. The Silures, however, were not reduced and continued to give serious trouble to the Romans.

4. *AD 58–96 (death of the emperor Domitian).* In 58 C. Suetonius Paulinus, a distinguished military commander, became governor of Britain and had two successful military campaigns, probably in north Wales because in 60 he made an assault on Anglesey, a rebel sanctuary, and was confronted by a horde of fierce soldiers, frantic women, and Druids. These he defeated, but was recalled from Anglesey to the province by news of a rebellion. Prasutagus, king of the Iceni, had died leaving the emperor (Nero) co-heir with his own two daughters. The governor's officers and especially the financial secretary (*procurator*) of the province behaved as if the whole territory had fallen into the possession of Rome, plundering and evicting and treating the natives as slaves, and finally flogging the queen Boudicca and raping her daughters. The revolt (probably starting in 60) rapidly spread from the Iceni to the Trinovantes, who had lost their land to the colonists at Colchester, and to neighbouring tribes. Colchester was overrun and destroyed almost immediately, and the British turned towards the flourishing commercial centre of London. On the way they met Q. Petilius Cerialis at the head of part of the 9th legion. He and his cavalry escaped but the infantry were annihilated. Suetonius hastened with his cavalry towards London but not having sufficient troops he did not try to defend it: London and St Albans were sacked and burnt. The inhabitants killed in the three towns numbered 70,000. Suetonius rejoined his infantry somewhere in the Midlands, and with 10,000 men met the far more numerous force of Boudicca and utterly destroyed it. The queen died soon after, perhaps by taking poison. There followed the ruthless destruction of the lands of all the tribes involved, but the new procurator Julius

Classicianus arranged the replacement of Suetonius by a more moderate governor, Petronius Turpilianus. With his appointment began a long period of stability in the south. The massive tombstone of Classicianus was found in London and is now in the British Museum.

In 71 Cerialis, the military commander mentioned above, was made governor of Britain. Since surviving the defeat of the 9th legion he had distinguished himself by quelling the rebellion of Civilis, chief of the Batavians, on the Rhine. He now conquered the greater part of the Brigantian territory, where revolt had broken out and Cartimandua had lost her throne, and established the 9th legion at York (Eburacum) which became the chief Roman military centre in the north of England. His successor in 74, Sextus Julius *Frontinus, subdued the Silures and built a new fortress at Caerleon-on-Usk (Isca Silurum). Easy communication was now established with Wales. Cn. Julius *Agricola, the father-in-law of Tacitus, who succeeded Frontinus in (probably) 78 completed his work in Wales, nearly annihilating the Ordovices and annexing Anglesey (Mona). In 79 Agricola pacified north-west England, and after the campaigning season began the task of making Roman civilization and all its trappings seem desirable to the natives. The following year he overran the lowlands of Scotland and reached the line of the Forth and the Clyde in 81. In 83 he moved further north to forestall a possible rising by northern tribes, and in 84 inflicted a famous defeat on the Caledonians at Mons Graupius, the site of which has long been debated. The fleet was sent around the north of Britain, and thus confirmed that it was an island. Garrisons were to be established in eastern Scotland north of the Forth, but it was now the end of the campaigning season. Agricola was recalled to Rome after being governor for more than six years. A legion was withdrawn, and by the end of the century, or soon after, Scotland beyond the line of the Forth and the Clyde was abandoned. The opportunity never came again to embrace the whole island in one province.

5. *AD 96–286.* For about forty years after the recall of Agricola there is no literary source for the history of Britain and we have to rely on archaeology. In the early years of the second century the unlucky 9th legion ceased to exist in York, and it used to be thought that its men were cashiered after a shameful defeat. It now appears that it was withdrawn from Britain before it finally disappeared from history. Under the emperor Trajan (98–117) there seems to have been a withdrawal from the south of Scotland and a new boundary created along the line between the Solway and the Tyne, confirmed by the subsequent emperor Hadrian (117–138) with the most elaborate frontier in the Roman world, which was begun after the

emperor's visit in 122. 'Hadrian's Wall' much of which can still be seen, ran from Wallsend-on-Tyne in the east to Bowness-on-Solway in the west, 118 km. (74 miles) in all. It was built of stone 2.5 or 3 m. (8 or 10 ft.) thick and about 6 m. (20 ft.) high including the parapet; a section at the western end, where limestone is scarce, was built in turf and converted to stone some decades later. It was fronted to the north by a ditch of varying width and depth, and fortified by garrison forts, mile-castles, and turrets. Behind it, to the south, was another ditch (the *vallum*) and, later, a military road. The construction of this great fortification was complicated and took most of the decade to complete. It acted as a base for patrols, it cut off raiders from the north, and produced settled conditions in the south in which the economy and the arts of peace could flourish. Under Hadrian the Romanization of the province proceeded rapidly; the cities were adorned with great public buildings as well as larger town houses, and the increasing complexity of local administration involved many more of the population in the Roman way of life.

Soon after Antoninus Pius became emperor in 138 he initiated a sudden change of policy. The governor of Britain, Q. Lollius Urbicus, advanced once more into southern Scotland, reconquered the lowlands, and built a new frontier wall of turf faced by a ditch across the line of the Forth and the Clyde, 60 km. (37 miles) long, less elaborate than Hadrian's Wall but of the same basic plan, with forts interspersed with smaller stations. There is little direct evidence as to why the frontier was moved, but the most probable reason was that the province would seem more secure if southern Scotland was under control and there was a shorter frontier to afford a greater concentration of forces. If the Romans hoped for peace in which to achieve the Romanization of this area they were disappointed; they seem to have suffered severely in a revolt in the 150s, even if they were finally victorious. The history of this period is confused, but the Antonine Wall seems to have been abandoned in *c.*163. Not long after 180 what is described as the greatest war of the emperor Commodus' reign occurred in Britain. Tribes from the north swept over Hadrian's Wall, ravaged widely, and destroyed a Roman force. A punitive campaign was successfully waged in 184, followed by withdrawal to the Wall. Roman influence was accepted in the lowlands but the tribes remained autonomous.

After the assassination of the emperor Commodus in 192, Clodius Albinus, governor of Britain, became a rival to the new emperor, Septimius Severus, and eventually claimed the throne. In 196 he crossed with an army to Gaul, where he was defeated by Severus in 197 and committed suicide. His withdrawal of troops from Britain gave the opportunity to those who hated Rome, especially those beyond the Wall, to vandalize and loot, but the widespread repairs on forts and particularly on the Wall that took place in the early years of Severus' reign seem, in the light of recent evidence, to be the rebuilding needed after years of neglect rather than the legacy of large-scale rebellion and invasion, as was hitherto believed. In 208 Severus himself arrived in Britain (accompanied by his sons and formidable wife Julia Domna) to direct a punitive expedition into Scotland. This was carried out without a decisive victory, and Severus was planning a further campaign when he died in 211. None the less the British frontier remained unbreached until 296. At some time in the early third century Britain was divided into two provinces, the northern having its centre at York and the southern at London. For the rest of the century it remained relatively undisturbed and moderately prosperous, untypically so if it is compared with the convulsions elsewhere in the empire in this period.

6. *AD 286–336*. Early in the reign of Diocletian (284–305), Saxon and Frankish raiders became troublesome on the northern coasts of Gaul. Carausius, a native of the Low Countries, was put in charge of the fleet. He dealt successfully with the raiders but kept the booty for himself. His arrest and execution were ordered, whereupon he declared himself emperor and seized the provinces of Britain in 286 or 287, making the island independent of the central government in Rome. Carausius was left in peace for some years, and his government of Britain was efficient and successful. (See DIOCLETIAN for the division of the empire into four commands.) But in 293 the Caesar Constantius inflicted notable defeats on his continental bases, and soon afterwards Carausius was assassinated by one of his chief associates, Allectus, who himself seized the provinces of Britain. Carausius has often been credited with building the 'Saxon shore' forts constructed late in the third century for the defence of the south-east coasts of Britain, but they were probably built by the emperor Probus (276–82). In 296 Constantius launched an invasion against Allectus, and the latter was killed in battle. Constantius thereby regained the provinces, which needed considerable reconstruction. An expedition was undertaken against the tribes beyond the Wall. In 306, when Constantius had become senior Augustus (emperor), he was joined by his son *Constantine for another invasion of Scotland, and won a great victory. Shortly after, he died at York and his son succeeded as Caesar. Constantine had soon to leave for Gaul, but during the first half of the fourth century Britain enjoyed peace and prosperity. Constantine became an enthusiastic Christian, attributing his victory at the Milvian Bridge in 312 to the intervention of the Christian God; in 313 the

Edict of Milan gave the Christian Church freedom of worship (see CHRISTIANITY). In 314 three British bishops attended the Council of Arles (see 9 below).

7. *AD 337–370*. Constantine died in 337 and out of the ensuing chaos his son Constantine II emerged as senior Augustus with command over Britain, Gaul, and Spain. He invaded Italy, the domain of his brother Constans, in 340, and was killed in battle. Some unknown crisis brought Constans unexpectedly to Britain in 343, perhaps attacks by Picts and Scots beyond the Wall and by Saxon and Frankish marauders in the south. By 368 the threat to British security was alarming, and in that year a concerted attack was made by the tribes in the north, the west coast, and the south-east; the country was overrun and London threatened. It was two years before a military commander Theodosius (the Elder), a Spaniard, sent by the emperor Valentinian, could restore order. He drove out the invaders and again repaired the Wall. Once more Britain had a firm government and secure defences, but it was to be only forty years before it ceased to be part of the Roman empire.

8. *The end of Roman Britain*. In 370 Britain seemed prosperous and secure, but the growing power of barbarians outside the empire threatened all Europe. From 383 to 407 not only were there repeated withdrawals of troops from Britain, but the army there set up claimants to the throne who took large forces across the Channel to fight for their claim. In 383 when the emperor Gratian lost favour in Britain, the army supported their commander Magnus Maximus, who was long remembered as a hero in Celtic folk-memory. He took an army to Gaul, no doubt depleting the defences to do so. Gratian was killed and Maximus became in effect the ruler of the western empire. In 388 he was defeated and put to death by the emperor Theodosius I (son of Theodosius the Elder: see 7 above). After his death sea-borne raids on Britain by the Picts, the Irish, and the Saxons continued until in 396–8 naval expeditions were sent against them under the command of *Stilicho, regent of the young emperor Honorius, and some sort of security was regained in 399. But troops, including many drawn from the native population, were still being withdrawn for the defence of Italy, and in 401 for the war against Alaric, leader of the invading *Visigoths. In 406 came a barbarian invasion of Gaul, and the year ended with large numbers crossing the frozen Rhine. Some British commanders realized that it would be impossible to defend Britain if Gaul fell, and a new claimant to the throne, Constantine III, crossed to Gaul with an army in 407, winning control there and in Spain the following year. Disorder soon broke out again with rebellion in Spain and in Gaul. A letter from the emperor Honorius in 410, the year in which Alaric and his Visigoths sacked Rome, is often interpreted as advice to the Britons, who had suffered serious Saxon incursions since 408, to see to their own defence. Roman rule in Britain lapsed and was never to be permanently reimposed. By *c.*450 the barbarians were in Britain to stay. (See also FALL OF ROME.)

It is unlikely that there was much political change for at least as long as expectation remained of the Romans resuming command. Soon after 400 effective occupation of Hadrian's Wall had ceased. Many of the villas continued to be occupied for some years further; some met a violent end, others fell into decay; very few became Saxon manors. Industry declined sharply and coinage became scarcer. Towns too declined, but some would receive Germanic settlers and continue to be occupied. Christianity became a significant force only at the end of the fourth century, but thereafter it was the leading religion and gained influence through monasteries which were centres of learning as well as of devotion (see TEXTS, TRANSMISSION OF ANCIENT 4, 5).

9. *Britain under the Romans*. Romanization affected every aspect of British life. Perhaps its chief tool was the Latin language, the essential *lingua franca* in a country that was to contain so many nationalities, particularly in the army. Since Celtic was almost exclusively a spoken language, anyone who wished to write had to do so in Latin. For many people Latin was no more than a second language, but Agricola saw to it that the sons of the leading Britons received a traditional Roman education and thus absorbed Latin culture.

One of the most prominent features of Roman occupation was the development of properly planned cities in a country that had hitherto had nothing more than villages (see the mention of hill-forts in 1 above). The process was rapid, and by the end of the first century there were numerous cities, tribal capitals (*civitates*) such as Winchester (Venta Belgarum), Chichester, Cirencester (Corinium), and Dorchester (Durnovaria), and settlements of veteran soldiers (*coloniae*) at Colchester, Gloucester (Glevum), and Lincoln; York, though a first-century foundation, became a *colonia* later. St Albans, founded at this time, was perhaps the only British city to be chartered as a *municipium* with the privileged status that attended this title. Even small towns were very often built on a grid-system. Almost every town had an engineered water-supply leading to public baths (a Roman necessity) and fountains, and sometimes to individual houses, with drains and sewers as well. In the town centre were the forum and basilica (town hall); many towns had their own theatre, and outside the walls (with which all towns were eventually surrounded) some arena suitable for the presentation of games. The city of Bath (Aquae Sulis) was the centre of an important healing-cult and also a pleasure resort for prosperous Romans and Britons. London was an important commercial and military centre from half-way through the first century AD, and was soon the administrative capital for the whole province, though no date can be given for its formal title as such.

The Romans may not have introduced any technical advance in agriculture, but it is clear that in Roman Britain agriculture became much more intensive. At least three-quarters of the population must have engaged in farming, but they had to support as well as themselves a much larger non-agricultural population than in the Iron Age. The army on the Wall and in the fortresses in highland areas was probably supplied with grain from pockets of arable farming in those parts, and the large herds of cattle that grazed there provided the huge quantities of leather needed. By the fourth century at the latest, Britain was self-sufficient in grain. A much larger population is nowadays postulated for Iron-Age and Roman Britain than hitherto, four to six million being suggested for the fourth century, with a sharp decline setting in in the fifth. More intensive cultivation was made possible by the new network of communications and the pacification of the country, which made land more accessible and workable. Large farms or agricultural estates, centred on a villa, with part perhaps leased to tenants, were organized so as to bring in a profit for the owner, and for that reason contributed to agricultural efficiency. The widespread distribution of goods, showing that the people were heavy consumers of manufactured products, was made possible by the provision of roads and perhaps even canals, and the better organization of travel by sea. Roads were built primarily for military and political purposes, but they must also have helped to promote the large volume of trade. They were well-maintained even into the fifth century. (See ROADS 2.)

The value of British mineral deposits, gold, silver, lead, iron, copper, and tin, is attested from earliest times and was exploited by the Romans as soon as they had won some measure of control. Timber was another valuable commodity, for building, for bridges, wharves, and the construction of large machines such as cranes, and also for minor trades. It was the main source of fuel, but coal too was used, from open-cast mines, both for metal-working and (probably) for domestic purposes. Certainly in the south-west it was burnt in the central-heating furnaces. The geographer Solinus writing in about AD 200 was amazed at the strange glowing coals on an altar in Bath. Pottery, particularly the finer wares, was imported, but some was made locally and by the second half of the second century Britain was producing large quantities of her own. Textiles were in demand,

and the British duffle coat (*byrrus Britannicus*) seems to have been special. There was considerable demand for decorative pieces of Whitby jet, and many small businesses flourished in individual shops in the towns.

The Belgae had introduced coinage to Britain in the late Iron Age, and after their settlement coins began to be struck in the island. It is doubtful whether they were used as currency to any degree; with occasional Roman coins, they seem to have been used rather as gifts or symbolic offerings. Coinage really came with the Romans, as necessary payment to the army and to facilitate trade. London eventually had its own mint, until *c*.326. Early in the fifth century coinage seems to have become no longer the normal means of exchange, a failure due perhaps to lack of confidence in money and associated with the collapse of large-scale industry and the withdrawal of the army.

The Celtic art of Britain in pre-Roman times (with its fondness for intricate, curvilinear patterns and non-representational forms) was very different indeed from classical art. After AD 43, with the import from the classical world of pottery and metal goods, British artists were quick to imitate the classical art forms and adopt the new craft of stone sculpture, as well as to try their hand at a new kind of architecture, and this art pervaded all levels of society through objects of everyday use. The best of Romano-British art retains something of the Celtic spirit, so that it has an original character of its own. In Wales and the north of England the old art forms lingered on, and in Ireland and the north of Scotland much remained unchanged. The end of the fourth century saw the beginning of a revival of Celtic art originating in the west, under Irish influence.

The Romans were tolerant of foreign deities and usually tried to equate them with their own gods. The Celtic Britons seem to have believed in one supreme god and a host of lesser deities, some widely worshipped, others purely local. The Romans sometimes had difficulty in identifying specific Celtic gods since they were not as clearly defined nor as anthropomorphic as Roman gods and tended to be powers of nature, often associated with water. The Celtic priesthood of the Druids was suppressed, partly perhaps because it provided a focus for resistance to Rome, more probably because its practice of human sacrifice was intolerable. But many primitive cults and customs survived during the Roman occupation, probably including the Celtic cult of severing the heads of their enemies (the head was considered the seat of personality), and sacred groves continued to be important as shrines. At the same time the Romans introduced the worship of their own gods, especially of the triad of Jupiter, Juno, and Minerva, to be joined from the mid-first century onwards by the cult of the deified Roman emperors of the past and of the spirit (*genius* or *numen*) of the living emperor linked with that of the goddess Roma (Rome). This cult inspired loyalty to Rome and imparted some sense of unity to the Romanized Britons, but it was largely impersonal. More personal needs were perhaps satisfied by a variety of classical and oriental deities, Mithras and Isis for example, brought in by individuals, which offered something in the nature of mystical and spiritual experience and laid down codes of conduct for adherents. The most important of the religions to arrive was Christianity. This faith reached Britain by the beginning of the third century at the latest: the most probable date for the martyrdom of St Alban, the first British martyr, is 208/9. By 314, when three British bishops, a priest, and a deacon attended the Council of Arles, the episcopate was obviously established. Christianity may have had little hold on Britain until the Edict of Milan published by the emperor Constantine in 313 gave certain regulations in favour of Christians, and indeed pagan cults continued to flourish through the middle of the fourth century. But by the end of that century Christianity had made considerable progress, and by the fifth century was advancing as a popular movement, firmly enough entrenched to survive the invasion of the pagan Saxons.

Brita'nnicus (Tiberius Claudius Britannicus) (AD 41–55), son of the Roman emperor *Claudius and his wife *Messal(l)ina. He was displaced as heir by the young *Nero, after whose accession he soon died, perhaps by poison.

Britoma'rtis, Cretan goddess of hunters and fishermen, frequently identified with the Greek goddess *Artemis after the introduction of the latter into Crete. Her name is said to mean 'sweet maiden'. *Minos king of Crete pursued her for nine months, and finally to avoid him she leaped over a cliff into the sea but was caught and saved by fishermen's nets—hence she is also called *Dictynna (from the Greek word meaning 'net'). She escaped to Aegina, where she was worshipped under the name of Aphaia, in a temple whose ruins still survive.

Bro'mius, name of the Greek god *Dionysus meaning 'noisy', 'boisterous', from the Greek verb meaning 'to roar'.

Brontēs, see CYCLOPES.

bronze, compound of copper and tin (usually in the proportion 9 : 1) that came into general use in the ancient world in the third millennium BC and remained so until replaced (though not entirely) by iron in the eleventh century BC. See BRONZE AGE below.

Bronze Age, in mainland Greece, the period from *c*.2800 to *c*.1050 BC (see GREECE); in Crete and the Aegean islands it began a little earlier, *c*.3000 BC. It was followed by the Iron Age,

c.1050–850 BC (which mostly coincides with the Greek *Dark Age). The various periods into which the Greek Bronze Age is subdivided for more precise reference are called Helladic I, II, etc. (see MYCENAE). Similar subdivisions of the Cretan Bronze Age are known as *Minoan I, II, etc. In Italy the Bronze Age was the period from *c*.1800 to *c*.1000 BC. See ITALY.

Brundi'sium (modern Brindisi), the best harbour on the east coast of Italy, situated on the heel, and the nearest Italian town to the eastern Adriatic coast. It was made a Latin colony in 246 BC. Connected to Rome by the Via Appia, it was the regular port of embarkation for Greece and Epirus. It was from Brundisium that Cicero and Ovid set out on their respective exiles, and it is a journey to Brundisium in company with, among others, Virgil, that Horace describes in *Satires* I. 5. Here Virgil subsequently died, in 19 BC, on his way home from Greece. Lucan in the *Pharsalia* relates Pompey's departure from the same port, and Tacitus (*Annals* 3. 1) the arrival there of Agrippina bringing home the ashes of Germanicus. The Treaty of Brundisium was made in 40 BC between Mark Antony and Octavian, at the insistence of soldiers in both armies when war between the two seemed imminent. To strengthen the alliance Antony married Octavian's sister Octavia.

Bru'ttii, see ITALY.

Brutus, name of a Roman plebeian family of the *gens Junia, the Junian clan, which traced its descent from L. Junius Brutus (see 1 below) and included the Brutus (see 2 below) who murdered Julius Caesar.

1. Lucius Junius Brutus. According to Roman tradition he became consul in 509 BC after overthrowing the rule of the Etruscan kings at Rome. He pretended to be an idiot (*brutus*) in order to escape the fate of his brother who had been murdered by their uncle, Tarquinius Superbus, the (last) Roman king. When *Lucretia was raped by Tarquinis' son, Brutus summoned the people, obtained the banishment of the Tarquin family, and was elected consul with L. Tarquinius Collatinus (Lucretia's husband). He was famous for his strict justice and put to death his own two sons who were attempting to restore the Tarquins. He was killed fighting an Etruscan army which was engaged in the same attempt.

2. Marcus Junius Brutus, *c*.85–42 BC, the prime assassin of Julius *Caesar. In 49 BC he joined in the civil war on Pompey's side against Julius Caesar, but after the former's defeat at Pharsalus he sought Caesar's pardon, which was granted. In *c*.45 he married Porcia, the daughter of M. Porcius *Cato whom he greatly admired and by whose republican sympathies he was influenced. In 44 Caesar appointed him as praetor, and he appeared to bear Caesar's dictatorship with equanimity, but *Cassius, a fellow-praetor, prevailed upon him to lead a conspiracy to murder Caesar, playing upon his patriotic desire to follow his famous ancestor and restore the republic. It is related by Suetonius that Caesar gave up the struggle against his murderers when he saw Brutus among them, exclaiming in Greek, *kai su, teknon* ('even you, my child!'). (The Latin version, 'Et tu, Brute!' ('even you, Brutus!') was made famous by Shakespeare.) Soon after the assassination Brutus was forced to leave Italy through public hostility and went to Greece, and with Cassius he prepared to resist the army of the *triumvirs Antony, Lepidus, and Octavian. In the autumn of 42 Antony and Octavian defeated Brutus and Cassius at *Philippi in eastern Macedonia, and Brutus committed suicide.

In his youth Brutus acquired a love of learning which never left him. He was one of Cicero's favourite literary adversaries, and Cicero seems to have felt affection for him, while failing to win him over to his own way of thinking in oratory, philosophy, or politics. In his treatise *Brutus* (see below) Cicero made him one of the speakers, and he dedicated to Brutus his *Orator*, *De finibus*, and *Tusculan disputations*. In Cicero's correspondence some letters of Brutus survive from which we learn of his financial dealings with the people of Salamis (in Cyprus); these throw a different light on his character: he lent money to the town at 48 per cent interest, and was prepared to go to any length to recover the debt.

3. Decimus Junius Brutus, one of the assassins of Julius Caesar (not to be confused with Marcus Junius, 2 above, to whom he was only distantly related). As a young man he served under Caesar in Gaul and fought for him in the civil war against Pompey. Caesar trusted Brutus so completely that he promised him the governorship of Cisalpine Gaul and allowed him to be his escort to the senate house on the day of his assassination. After Caesar's murder Brutus retired to Cisalpine Gaul and refused to surrender it to Mark Antony. The latter proceeded to besiege him and his republican forces in Mutina (43 BC), but with the aid of a senatorial army Brutus succeeded in repulsing him. Later, however, finding himself under attack by both Octavian and Antony, he tried to cross over to M. Brutus (2 above) in Macedonia, but was betrayed and killed. See ROME 7.

Brutus (or *De claris oratoribus*), treatise by *Cicero ((1) 5) on eminent Roman orators. Written in 46 BC with the purpose of defending Cicero's own oratorical practice, it gives interesting details of his early life and training as an orator and his gradual rise to the highest position. It purports to record a recent conversa-tion between Cicero, M. Junius Brutus (see previous entry), and *Atticus, in which Cicero ends an introductory section on Greek orators by referring to the Attic, Asianic, and Rhodian schools of *oratory, commending some of the qualities of the Asianists as well as of the Atticists. He reviews the long series of Roman orators from Brutus the Liberator (supposedly consul in 509 BC), but more particularly from Cethēgus, consul in 204 BC, 'the marrow of persuasion' according to Ennius, to his own times, giving a brief description of each. A few of the most eminent orators, especially Crassus, Antonius, and Q. Scaevola, are discussed at greater length. *Calvus is criticized for the plain style of his severe Atticism, and Cicero embarks on a polemic against the self-styled Atticists of his acquaintance. *Hortensius, on the other hand, is praised for his particular style of Asianism. Cicero defends himself against the charge of Asianism by showing that he is in the natural line of development of Roman oratory.

Būce'phalas ('ox-head'), the black horse of Alexander the Great, his favourite for twenty years, which died probably of wounds at the battle fought against the Indian Porus at the river Hydaspes (Jhelum) in 326 BC. In his memory Alexander founded the town of Bucephala (probably Jhelum on the west bank of the river in west Pakistan) near the site of Bucephalas' last river crossing. The popular story was that the horse was given to Alexander by his father Philip who had received it from a Greek friend Demaratus. It proved unmanage-able until the 12-year-old Alexander, observing that it shied at its own shadow, turned its head to the sun, soothed, and then mounted it.

bucolic poetry, pastoral poetry. The name 'bucolic' is derived from the Greek word for herdsmen, *boukoloi*, and was first used to describe the poems (known as *idylls) of the Greek poet *Theocritus, who invented the genre of pastoral poetry. These were imitated by the Greek poets *Bion and *Moschus, and later most notably by the Roman poet Virgil (in the *Eclogues); it was Virgil who gave the genre its location (Arcadia in Greece), its typical form, and many of the motifs subse-quently used by later European pastoral poets. In the typical pastoral poem the herdsmen-poets sing of themselves, their loves, and their music in a stylized Greek landscape with Pan and the nymphs. At its best the artful simplicity of pastoral poetry conceals a subtlety of composi-tion that most appeals to a sophisticated taste able to appreciate its studied remoteness from the realities of a shepherd's life. Many of its features are found in Milton's poem *Lycidas* (1637). Because of its limited subject-matter and easily recognized conventions pastoral poetry came to be used as a vehicle for *allegory or veiled social comment as early as Virgil. See also GENRE and ELEGY.

bulla, locket made of metal or leather containing an amulet, worn by free-born Roman children round the neck, by boys until they assumed the *toga virilis* (see DRESS) and by girls probably until their marriage. The custom seems to be derived from the Etruscans, and was no doubt apotropaic.

burial and cremation. The Greeks and Romans either placed their dead in coffins and buried them in the earth or burned them on pyres and later collected the ashes and bones into vessels which they then buried. The practice varied from time to time and sometimes both methods existed side by side; as far as we can tell it was not determined by ideas about the fate of the soul after death. The Greeks of the Mycenaean age (*c.*1600–1100 BC) mostly buried their dead. After this time the custom of cremation gradually spread from the Near East, and the Homeric poems reflect the practice of the Geometric age in which cremation was commoner but inhumation was known. In fifth-century Greece inhumation was commoner than cremation, perhaps because the scarcity of wood made the latter expensive. In Rome cremation gradually became more prevalent. Young children were usually buried, not cremated, often near houses; presumably they were not thought liable to cause pollution. Most burials in Greece and Rome took place outside the city to avoid pollution, often beside roads, for the sake of convenience, with an engraved slab (*stelē*) or column to identify the dead (see DIPYLON). In Greece the bodies of executed criminals were thrown into the sea or open pits, but at Rome they were allowed burial. In classical Rome, those who died without heir were buried at night; they included those who died young, and slaves (who by their status could have no heirs). There being no family to care, ritual offerings were not made to the corpse. Greek funeral offerings seem rarely to have been made with any serious intent to deposit with the dead his personal possessions or to equip him for an afterlife, and the tradition of providing a coin as fee to Charon for his service as ferryman, or a lamp and shoes for the journey, was not universally observed. It was essential to cover a body, burned or not, with earth—three handfuls sufficed for a symbolic burial—to prevent it from polluting the gods and their altars and to allow the spirit of the dead to pass into the Underworld. Hence burying the dead, by whatever means, was a universal act of piety. All people engaged in a funeral were considered to be polluted and could not mingle with other people until they had been purified. In Rome a polluted house would be marked by branches of cypress or pitch pine hung outside the door. Large

households in Rome or burial clubs (**collegia*) often placed vessels containing the ashes of their dead in a joint tomb called a *columbarium*, 'dovecot', each urn in its own *nidus* 'pigeonhole' (see CATACOMBS). Both Jews and Christians objected to cremation, and by the fifth century the practice had died out in the Roman empire.

Burrus, see SENECA (2) 1.

Būsī'ris (Bousīris), in Greek myth, a king of Egypt, son of Poseidon, who, in order to end a drought, on the advice of a seer, sacrificed to Zeus all strangers who arrived in his kingdom. The seer himself, being from Cyprus, was the first victim. Soon afterwards ***Heracles arrived and killed Busiris and his son and all his attendants.

Byzantine age, term describing Greek history and culture of the period from (at its widest) AD 330 until 1453, derived from the name of the capital of the eastern Roman empire, the Greek city ***Byzantium. The period begins in the later Roman empire (see PRINCIPATE) when the emperor ***Constantine the Great transferred his residence from Rome to Byzantium and renamed the city Constantinople. In AD 395, at the death of the emperor Theodosius the Great, the empire was divided between his two sons, Arcadius ruling from Byzantium/Constantinople in the East and Honorius from Rome in the West. Thereafter there was complete separation of administration and even of succession. When the western empire collapsed in the fifth century (see FALL OF ROME) relations between east and west declined. The last eastern emperor to use Latin as the official language of imperial government at Byzantium was Justinian, with whose reign (527–65) the Byzantine age (or Byzantine empire) is sometimes said to begin. Greek literature, no longer pagan, was now centred on Byzantium, and had lost its classical stamp under Roman, Eastern, and Christian influences. The Greek pronunciation had changed, syllables in Byzantine Greek having different quantities from classical Greek (see METRE, GREEK 1), with the result that after the second century AD it was no longer possible, except for a few deliberately archaizing poets, to write verse in the old classical metres. New literary genres appeared, such as Christian hymns and saints' lives. The kind of Greek used by authors varied widely, from the most ornate imitations of classical literary Greek to the very different near-vernacular. Poetry was rarely written; an exception is the lively epic poem *Digenes Akritas* written in literary Greek but in lines 15 syllables long with an accentual rather than a quantitative rhythm. It was an age of prose, of theology and history particularly; notable historians include ***Procopius, Anna Comnena (1083–after 1148), and Michael Psellus (*c*.1019–*c*.1078) (the last two outside the scope of this work). Many writers were occupied with lexicons, abridgements of classical works, and commentaries on them, and played an important part in the preservation and transmission of the ancient authors. Such men include Photius (patriarch *c*.820–*c*.893), Arethas, Archbishop of Caesarea (*c*.850–*c*.944), many of whose beautiful manuscripts still survive, and Eustathius, Archbishop of Thessalonika (d. *c*.1195). The period ended in 1453 with the fall of what was still officially the eastern Roman empire and the capture of Byzantium/Constantinople by the Ottoman Turks. See also SOPHISTIC, SECOND and TEXTS, TRANSMISSION OF ANCIENT 2 and 3.

Byzantium, Greek city by the Propontis (the Sea of Marmora), at the southern end of the Bosporus on the European side, later renamed Constantinople (see below) and now Istanbul. It was magnificently situated, commanding the two opposite shores of Europe and Asia with the advantages of security and great facility for trade. It was originally founded by Megarians in the seventh century BC, opposite Chalcedon (the 'city of the blind', so called by the Delphic oracle because its earlier Megarian founders had failed to choose the superior site of Byzantium). Ruled by Persia from 512 to 478 BC, then alternately under Athenian and Spartan dominion in the fifth and fourth centuries, Byzantium was a formal ally of Athens from *c*.378 to 357 BC, and then again when successfully resisting Philip of Macedon in the famous siege of 340–339. The help supposedly given by the goddess Hecatē on this occasion was commemorated on Byzantine coins by her symbol of crescent and star (adopted by the Turks as their device after they captured the city in AD 1453). The city suffered severely from the Celtic (Gallic) invasions of the third century BC (see GALATIANS) and the Byzantines paid the invaders huge sums in blackmail, recompensing themselves by exacting tolls from traffic in the Bosporus and thus getting involved in a war with Rhodes. Byzantium subsequently passed into the Roman empire, while remaining Greek in culture, and was chosen by the emperor *Constantine for his new capital (AD 330), to be known thereafter in the West as Constantinople. When the Roman empire in the West finally collapsed in the fifth century under barbarian invasions (see FALL OF ROME) the eastern empire and its capital, firmly in the Greek world, flourished. The city's position as the capital of the eastern empire was interrupted in 1204 when it was captured by the French and Venetians (collectively known as Latins) during the Fourth Crusade, and became the seat of the Latin empire until restored to Greek possession in 1261. The last emperor, Constantine XIII, was killed when the city and empire fell to the Turks in 1453. See also BYZANTINE AGE.

C

Cabei'ri (Kabeiroi), in Greek religion, gods apparently non-Greek in origin (their name has been thought to have Semitic connections) who, together with a mother goddess, were the object of a *mystery cult since early times. Their genealogy was variously given; sometimes they were described as the sons of *Hephaestus. Aeschylus gave the name *Kabeiroi* to one of his plays, now lost, in which they appeared as the chorus, receiving the Argonauts on Lemnos, and describing themselves as great wine-drinkers. Their mysteries were celebrated from early times on the north Aegean islands of Lemnos and Samothrace in particular, and from before the sixth century at Thebes. By the fifth century they were known in Athens; the historian Herodotus was an initiate. After the time of Alexander the Great (late fourth century BC) their cult spread rapidly over the Greek world, but little is known about it.

Cācus, in Roman myth, a fire-breathing monster, son of Vulcan, who was supposed to have lived on a hill at Rome (Aventine according to Virgil) and who terrorized the country. As *Hercules was driving home to Greece the cattle he had stolen from the monster Geryon, he rested at the site of the future Rome, where he was entertained by *Evander. Cacus stole some of the cattle and dragged them into his cave tail first so that it was impossible to follow their traces. When the remaining cattle passed the cave those within began to bellow and were thus discovered; Hercules then killed Cacus. Virgil may have invented this story. Cacus seems to have originated in Etruscan myth, where he was a seer on the Palatine.

Cadmē'a (Kadmeia), the citadel of Thebes, named after the city's founder *Cadmus.

Cadmus. 1. In Greek myth Cadmus was the legendary founder of the city of Thebes (in Boeotia), son of Agenor king of Tyre (in Phoenicia), who was sent to look for his sister Europa after she had been carried off by Zeus in the shape of a bull. By the advice of the Delphic Oracle he abandoned the search; he was told that he would meet a cow which he should follow until it lay down; there he should found a city. The cow led him to the site of Thebes; when he sent his companions to fetch water for sacrifice from a nearby spring they were all killed by the dragon guarding it. Cadmus slew the dragon and at the instruction of the goddess

Athena sowed half the dragon's teeth (Athena kept the other half for Aeētēs, king of Colchis, to give to Jason). A crop of armed men sprang up whom he set fighting by throwing a stone among them, and they fought each other until only five survived. These five, the Spartoi ('sown men'), helped to build the *Cadmea and in historical times were held to be the ancestors of the Theban nobility. Zeus gave Cadmus as bride Harmonia, the daughter of Ares and Aphrodite, and all the gods attended the wedding. Cadmus gave his bride as a present a necklace made by Hephaestus which subsequently was to play a fatal part in the Theban story (see AMPHIARAUS and ALCMAEON). Their daughters, all of whom met disaster, were Ino, Semelē (mother of *Dionysus), Autonoē, and Agavē (mother of Pentheus). Cadmus eventually abdicated in favour of Pentheus, but returned after the latter's death (see BACCHAE). He and his wife finally withdrew to Illyria, where they were changed into snakes and carried off by Zeus to Elysium. Cadmus was said to have civilized the Boeotians and taught them the art of writing with Phoenician letters (from which in fact the Greek *alphabet is derived). A large number of objects from the Near East has been found in the Kadmeion or royal palace of Thebes, suggesting possible Phoenician influence. Because in Theban mythical history victory so often entailed disaster for the victors, a 'Cadmean victory' was proverbial in Greek (compare 'Pyrrhic victory'; see PYRRHUS).

2. Of Miletus, see LOGOGRAPHERS.

Caeci'lius Stā'tius, Gaul from northern Italy, probably Mediolanum (Milan), taken prisoner of war in 223 or 222 BC, brought to Rome as a slave and manumitted, and subsequently the chief Roman comic dramatist of his day. He was the friend of the poet Ennius and came in point of time between the dramatists Plautus and Terence. He was still alive in 166 to pass judgement on the latter's *Andria. No complete play of his survives, but some forty-two titles are known, of which sixteen derive from Menander, the Greek writer of New Comedy. Some fragments survive in quotations. See COMEDY, ROMAN.

Cae'lius Rufus, Marcus (82–48 BC), young Roman with political ambitions, friend and pupil of Cicero from 66 to 63, when he broke away and associated with Catiline for a while. After a successful prosecution in 59 of Antonius,

Cicero's colleague in the consulship in 63, Caelius became popular in fashionable circles and rented a house in the desirable Palatine quarter near *Clodia, perhaps supplanting the poet Catullus in her affections, if he is the Rufus whom Catullus mentions. Their affair was over by 56, the year in which he was prosecuted by L. Sempronius Atratinus after he had himself successfully prosecuted the latter's father earlier in the year. It would appear that Clodia was the driving force behind the case. Cicero defended him in a notable speech which still survives (see CICERO (1) 4), and Caelius was acquitted. Clodia thereafter disappears from view, a coincidence which may indicate the social importance of Caelius' victory. He was tribune in 52, a supporter of Milo and enemy of Pompey. In 51 Cicero went to Cilicia as governor, and during his year's absence Caelius kept him informed of home affairs in seventeen witty and politically acute letters which survive in Cicero's correspondence. In 49, as civil war became imminent, he declared for Caesar, but soon grew discontented; he joined Milo in raising a rebellion in south Italy, but it was easily suppressed by Caesar, and Caelius and Milo were both killed.

Caesar, the name of a Roman patrician family of the *gens *Julia*, one of the most ancient clans in Rome, which traced its origin back to Iulus, son of Aeneas. The name 'Caesar' (see 6 below) survived into modern times in the Russian 'Tzar' and German 'Kaiser'. Julius Caesar's adopted son *Octavian (later the emperor Augustus) added it to his own name, as did his adopted son, the emperor Tiberius, and his successors. Although the Caesarian branch of the Julian clan became extinct with the death of Nero, succeeding emperors tended to assume the name as a title, until '*Augustus' became the title of the reigning emperor, 'Caesar' that of the emperor's designated heir or second-in-command.

Gaius Julius Caesar, Roman general, statesman, and dictator, b. 12 July 100 BC, assassinated 15 March (the Ides) 44 BC. (For Ides, see CALENDARS 5.)

1. *100–62 BC.* He was the son of Gaius Caesar, who died before attaining the consulship, and Aurelia. His father's sister married Marius and in 83 he himself married Cornelia the daughter of Cinna (the opponent of Sulla), so that from the beginning he was associated in politics with the popular party (see POPULARES). He served his first military campaign in Asia in 81, but he came to public attention by two (unsuccessful) prosecutions in Rome. He then retired to Rhodes to study under a Greek rhetorician (M. Antonius Gnipho, who also taught Cicero), but on the way was captured for ransom by pirates whom, soon after his release, he caught and crucified, as he had promised he would during his captivity. He returned to Rome in 73 and

became a senator before 70, supporting *Pompey when the latter as consul repealed some of Sulla's revisions of the constitution. During these years he spent money lavishly, much of it borrowed from *Crassus, to court popularity. In 68 he went as quaestor to Hispania Ulterior (Further Spain). His wife Cornelia died, and on his return in 67 he married one of the Pompeian family, no doubt in order to cement an alliance. In 65 he was elected to the aedileship, an office whose holder was expected to spend lavishly on buildings and public entertainments. He spent with unparalleled generosity and won especial favour with his restoration of the statues and trophies of Marius. In 63 he was prominent in the successful prosecution of Rabirius in order to further the cause of the popular party (see CICERO (1) 2), and opposed Cicero's execution of *Catiline's supporters. In the same year he was elected *pontifex maximus*, to the shame of his aristocratic rivals, and to the praetorship for 62. The end of his praetorship was marked by the scandal arising from *Clodius' profanation of the Bona Dea mysteries in Caesar's house by appearing disguised as a woman. As a consequence Caesar divorced his wife Pompeia because, according to Plutarch, 'his wife must be above suspicion'.

2. *61–50 BC.* Caesar's successful governorship of Further Spain in 61 established his reputation as a general, although he had hitherto had very little military experience, and enabled him to clear his debts. On his return he made an informal alliance with Pompey and Crassus (often called by modern scholars 'the first triumvirate'), and was elected consul for 59 together with *Bibulus whose vetoes he notoriously disregarded. His legislation satisfied the personal ambitions of Pompey and Crassus, and as proconsul in 58 he took for himself the governorship of Illyricum (Dalmatia), Cisalpine Gaul (northern Italy), and Transalpine Gaul (southern France).

The next nine years were occupied in the conquest of the rest of *Gaul (the Gallic War), brilliantly described in his *Commentaries. In the early years there is no evidence of discord with Pompey, who in 59 married Julia, the daughter of Caesar by his first wife Cornelia. Caesar himself married as his third wife *Calpurnia, the daughter of L. Calpurnius Piso who was consul in 59. By 56 Caesar regarded the conquest of Gaul as complete, and spent 55 and 54 in sending expeditions to *Germany and *Britain. The compact with Pompey and Crassus had been renewed at Luca (Lucca) in 56; these two became consuls for 55 and renewed Caesar's command for a further five years. However, in 53 Crassus was killed fighting the Parthians, and Pompey and Caesar were left alone at the head of the state. Pompey's wife Julia, who had formed a bond between them, had died in childbirth the previous year. Sporadic revolts in

Gaul in 53 culminated in a general rising in 52 under Vercingetorix, which Caesar put down after the most difficult fighting of his career. The pacification of Gaul was completed by 50. Meanwhile the civil disturbances at Rome (see ROME 7) led to the appointment of Pompey as sole consul for 52, and his measures included a law that allowed Caesar to stand for the consulship in his absence. Caesar's governorship expired in 49 and he therefore needed the consulship for 48 if he was not to become a private citizen, liable to prosecution by his political enemies in Rome. The senate wished to recall him before there could be any risk of his becoming consul while still at the head of his army, and the consul C. Marcellus proposed that he should lay down his command by 13 November. Pompey hesitated whether to give his support, but finally threw in his lot with Caesar's enemies.

3. *49–44 BC.* On 7 January 49 the senate ordered Caesar, now at the river *Rubicon, the boundary between Cisalpine Gaul and Italy, to disband his army. On 10 January Caesar nevertheless crossed the Rubicon with his army, and the civil war was launched. Pompey was entrusted by the senate with the whole management of the war on behalf of the republic, but he was outmanœuvred and fled to Greece, and within three months Caesar was master of Italy with a large measure of popular support. He was prudently merciful to the defeated, in strong contrast with earlier Roman leaders and their proscriptions. Rather than pursue Pompey to Greece he went to Spain, where in a brief and brilliant campaign he forced the surrender of the Pompeian army at Ilerda (Lerida). In 48 he followed Pompey to Epirus in Greece and suffered a reverse at Dyrrhachium from the latter's powerful army; however, he defeated Pompey at *Pharsalus and pursued him to Egypt, but on his arrival found him already murdered. After Ilerda, Caesar had been appointed dictator in order to hold the consular elections (in which he was elected consul) and pass some necessary legislation, but, that done, he had laid down the dictatorship. When news of his victory at Pharsalus reached Rome he was again nominated dictator, this time for a year. Throughout the winter of 48 he was occupied with a difficult war (the Alexandrian War; see *BELLUM ALEXANDRINUM*) to establish *Cleopatra VII, now his mistress, on the throne of Egypt; and he thereby gave the Pompeian forces time to regroup. Soon afterwards Cleopatra had a son (*Caesarion), claiming him to be by Caesar. Before returning to Rome, Caesar marched through Syria and Pontus to defeat Pharnaces, king of Pontus and son of the famous Mithridates. This he did in 47 at Zela, a victory which he announced with his famous boast, *veni, vidi, vici,* 'I came, I saw, I conquered'. In Rome he was elected to his third dictatorship, but before

the year ended he set out for Africa where he defeated the Pompeians (i.e. republicans) at Thapsus in 46 (the consequent suicide of *Cato at Utica became an inspiration for later republicans). On his return to Rome he was given the dictatorship for another ten years and in four magnificent triumphs celebrated his victories over foreign enemies (not those over other Romans).

He now turned to legislation to bring about many much-needed reforms, none of such long-lasting benefit as the reform of the calendar with the assistance of Sosigenes, the Alexandrian mathematician (see CALENDARS 4). This (Julian) calendar remained in operation until it was further reformed in the sixteenth century. In the midst of these activities Caesar was called to Spain where a republican revolt had broken out, led by Pompey's two sons and Caesar's own former officer Labienus. They were finally defeated in the hard-fought battle of Munda (45). Among the army and the people Caesar's popularity was enormous, and the senate granted him virtually monarchical power as well as extraordinary emblems of monarchy; but, although he attempted to conciliate powerful senators by merciful treatment of his enemies, his evident intention of putting an end to republican government forever and keeping the supreme power within his own family led to a conspiracy against his life, led by *Cassius and *Brutus, and he was stabbed to death in the senate house in 44 BC. (Dante in the *Inferno* put these two with Judas Iscariot in the lowest circle of Hell.)

4. Caesar's amazing ability and energy were in the main used for the benefit of Rome; he had re-established order and had begun to restore the economic situation, he was lavish in granting citizenship to provincials and had abolished tax-farming in Asia and perhaps in other provinces (see PUBLICANI); he enlarged the senate to 900, even recruiting its members from outside Italy. He had many other projects in mind, such as that of codifying the law, and was planning an expedition to Parthia at the time of his death.

5. His *Commentaries* (i.e. 'notes') on the Gallic war, and the (unfinished) three books on the civil war are his only writings that survive entire. The title of the former was chosen deliberately to suggest that it was not history that was being written but rather a bald record of events written in the third person, and therefore an objectively truthful account. Caesar wished, in fact, to create the impression that he was a simple soldier fighting necessary wars for the good of Rome, so as to refute the charges of his political enemies that he was fighting for personal aggrandizement. Nevertheless, despite its political purpose, the *Gallic War* is unique as a contemporary account of a foreign war written by a Roman general, in lucid,

unrhetorical Latin. Each book seems to have been composed at the end of the year with which it deals and perhaps sent individually to Rome. The work was published as a whole probably in 51 BC. The *Civil War* is rather more obviously a political pamphlet, with the theme that his enemies had forced war upon him, but the narrative is occasionally relieved by a human touch or a flash of sardonic humour. The *Bellum Africum*, *Bellum Alexandrinum*, and *Bellum Hispaniense* were written by members of Caesar's staff.

6. Caesar also wrote a number of other books which have not survived: a collection of jokes and sayings, later suppressed by Augustus as too frivolous; a grammatical work on declensions and conjugations, composed while he was crossing the Alps and dedicated to Cicero; an irritated reply, *Anticato*, to Cicero's panegyric of Cato (see 3 above), and a number of poems, of which a verse epigram to Terence survives. He was an outstanding orator, described by Cicero as the most eloquent of Romans. We have Lives of Caesar by Plutarch and Suetonius. Several portrait busts considered authentic show a clean-shaven, austere face, with hair combed forward in later life to conceal baldness, as Suetonius described him. He was tall, pale, with keen black eyes, and took pains over his appearance. It was related that he was born by being cut from his mother's womb, the so-called Caesarian section, but this story is also told of the first member of the Julian *gens* to take the name Caesar, in order to explain the name by deriving it from *caesus*, 'cut'.

For 'Caesar' as a title under the Roman empire see AUGUSTUS.

Caesa'rion, the nickname given by the Alexandrians, and generally accepted, to Ptolemy XV (Ptolemaeus Caesar), the son of Cleopatra VII, born in 47 BC and said by her to have been fathered by Julius Caesar. Octavian, Caesar's adopted son and heir, had him executed in 30 BC, perhaps seeing him as a rival.

caesū'ra ('cut'), place in a metrical line where a break between words regularly occurs, dividing the line into two unequal parts; see METRE, GREEK 2.

Calabria, in ancient times the heel of Italy, not, as now, the toe. It was very fertile despite its dryness, and its great heat in summer. It was famous for olives, fruit, wine, and horses. Brundisium was its chief city.

Ca'laïs and Zētēs, in Greek myth, sons of Boreas, the north wind. They were of human shape but had wings on their shoulders. They took part in the expedition of the *Argonauts to recover the Golden Fleece, in the course of which they saved *Phineus from the Harpies. On their way home they were killed in revenge by Heracles on the island of Tenos, because on the voyage to Colchis they had persuaded the other Argonauts to leave him behind on the coast of Bithynia (on the Propontis) when he was frantically searching for the lost *Hylas. Heracles erected two pillars over their grave, one of which moved whenever the north wind blew.

ca'lcĕus, the leather shoe worn by Romans in the city; see DRESS 2.

Calchas, the seer of the Greek army in the Trojan War. At the opening of Homer's *Iliad* he reveals the reason for the plague in the Greek camp. After Homer he is introduced into several narratives relating to the capture of Troy, such as Agamemnon's sacrifice of his daughter Iphigeneia and the construction of the Trojan Horse. See also MOPSUS.

Caledō'nia, the name used by Tacitus and other Romans to describe Britain north of the Firth of Forth.

calendars

1. Virtually all peoples have used the period between one new moon and the next, the lunar month, as a measure of time, although, since this period comprises $29\frac{1}{2}$ days, the months inaugurated by each new moon cannot contain a constant number of whole days. The succession of seasons is determined by the yearly cycle of the earth around the sun in roughly $365\frac{1}{4}$ days, that is, the solar year, which is about eleven days longer than twelve lunar months. Hence, when the solar year is divided into twelve months, the beginning of each month cannot in general correspond exactly with the appearance of the new moon.

The Greek calendar

2. All Greek states had a civil year of twelve months with 29 and 30 days alternately, each month beginning with the new moon. Since the year thus contained only 354 days, adjustment to fit the solar year had to be made, and the magistrates did this by adding ('intercalating') extra months or fractions of months as need arose. It seems that they did this empirically, without consulting astronomers, although they may have taken into account the eight-year cycle (ninety-nine lunar months approximate closely to eight solar years, the error being one and a half days) and a still better nineteen-year cycle discovered by *Meton in 432 BC. Festivals of the gods were celebrated according to the civil calendar rather than according to the phases of the moon. Every Greek state had its own names for the months, usually derived from festivals celebrated at that time, and its own views on intercalation, so that what was in principle the same month relating to the same new moon varied by a few days from state to state. The names of the months in the Athenian

calendar (which we know best), and the modern months to which they roughly correspond, are:

Hekatombaion (in which *hecatombs were offered), July; the civil year normally began with the first new moon after the summer solstice, but was probably affected by intercalary months.

Metageitnion, August.

Boedromion, September.

Pyanopsion, October, named after an Athenian festival to Apollo.

Maimakterion, November, named after the festival of Zeus Maimaktes, 'the boisterous'.

Poseideon, December. The normal intercalary month at Athens was a second Poseideon.

Gamelion, January, so named because it was the popular month for a wedding (*gamos*).

Anthesterion, February, named after the Anthesteria ('feast of flowers'), the three-day festival of Dionysus at Athens.

Elaphebolion, March, named after the festival of Artemis the 'deer-shooter'. The Spartans called this month Artemisios.

Munychion, April, named after a festival of Artemis who had a shrine at Munychia.

Thargelion, May, named after a festival to Apollo and Artemis.

Skirophorion, June, named after a festival to Demeter or Athena.

We do not know when names were first given to the months, but the festivals celebrated are very ancient. Some scholars have thought that a few names may appear in the *Linear B texts; Homer mentions none; Hesiod mentions one, but his calendar (see *WORKS AND DAYS*) is not the civil but the natural one used by sailors and farmers, based on the change of seasons marked by the rising and the setting of stars, the appearance of flowers and the behaviour of animals. Thucydides (5. 20) found this the best method for dating the Peloponnesian War so as to be universally understood.

3. The civil year, beginning roughly in July (see *Hekatombaion* above), was named at Athens after the chief archon and at Sparta after the first ephor whose terms of office coincided with it. A second civil calendar was in operation at Athens, the *prytany or the bouleutic calendar, by which assemblies were convened and affairs of state dated. In this the year was divided into 'prytanies', each prytany comprising the fraction of a year (one tenth in the fifth and fourth centuries BC when there were ten tribes) for which the members of one particular tribe performed the executive function of the council (*boule*). Official dating was done at Athens by naming the *archon of the year and the presiding tribe. The days within the Greek month or the prytany were sometimes divided into three periods of (mostly) ten days (decades) and the days within each decade denoted by number, but there were many variations.

The Roman calendar

4. The original Roman calendar, attributed to Romulus, was purely agricultural, consisting of ten very irregular months totalling 304 days running from March to December ('month ten', *decem*), with an uncounted gap in the winter when no agricultural work was possible. The change to a twelve-month lunar calendar (perhaps with an intercalary month of 22 or 23 days) was attributed to Numa, and another tradition suggests that in *c*.450 BC the decemvirs tried to amend (or even invent) the intercalary system. However, no system of regular intercalation successfully adjusted this lunar calendar to the solar year, and from 218 BC to Caesar's reform of 45 BC the *pontiffs adjusted the calendar as seemed best to them. In 153 BC January was made the first month. By Caesar's day the Roman year consisted of 355 days divided into these twelve months: *Januarius*, 29 days; *Februarius*, 28; *Martius*, the original first month, 31; *Aprilis*, 29; *Maius*, 31; *Iunius*, 29; *Quintilis* 'fifth month' (later *Iulius*), 31; *Sextilis*, 'sixth month' (later *Augustus*), 29; *September*, 'seventh month', 29; *October*, 'eighth month', 31; *November*, 'ninth month', 29; *December*, 'tenth month', 29.

This Roman calendar corresponded with neither the sun nor the moon, and by 46 BC the civic and solar years were discrepant by about three months. On the advice of the mathematician Sosigenes, Caesar gave the year 46 BC 445 days to remove the discrepancy, and from 1 January 45 made the year consist of 365 days, with the individual months having essentially the same length as in the modern calendar. He also introduced the leap year, at first used every three years in error; from 8 BC it occurred every four years, as now. The extra day (now 29 February) was added by repeating 24 February, the so-called 'bissextile' day (lit. 'the sixth day twice', i.e. five days before the Kalends of March: see 5 below). In this Julian calendar the year is about eleven minutes longer than the solar year. Between the Council of Nicaea (see CONSTANTINE THE GREAT) in AD 325 and the late sixteenth century the accumulated difference amounted to ten days; accordingly Pope Gregory XIII omitted ten days from 1582 and suggested that three intercalary days be omitted every four hundred years. England eventually adopted this Gregorian calendar in 1752, but the modern calendar is essentially the Julian, which is still used for dates before 1582.

5. The days in the Roman month were reckoned in relation to three named days: the first of the month, the Kalends (*Kalendae*); the fifth (or seventh in a month of 31 days), the Nones (*Nonae*); and the thirteenth (or fifteenth in a month of 31 days), the Ides (*Idus*). The number of the day was calculated by counting backwards from the next named day, the named day and the day to be numbered both being

included in the count. Thus 28 May was *a(nte) d(iem) V Kal(endas) Jun(ias)* ('the fifth day before 1 June'). Days were marked in the calendar *F*, *C*, or *N* according as they were *fasti*, days on which the court of the *praetor urbanus* was open for business; *comitiales*, days on which *comitia* might be held; or *nefasti*, days on which no public business was transacted. (See also DIES FASTI.) For the Roman 'week' see NUNDINAE.

6. The Romans dated their year by the names of the consuls. In both Greece and Rome the calendar year became concurrent with the civil year, i.e. the magistrate's year of office, whatever the month in which it began. At Athens the civil year began with the month *Hekatombaion*, usually after the summer solstice (see 2 above); at Rome after 153 BC it began on 1 January. It was probably Caesar's intention when he reformed the Roman calendar in 46 BC to begin the year with the shortest day, 24 December, but in the event the start was delayed for seven days in order to make the first reformed year begin on the day of the new moon.

The method of dating by magistrates is only effective if the series of names continues uninterrupted. (From Diodorus we have a list of Athenian archons from 480 to 302 BC; for Roman history we have a complete list of consuls from the foundation of the republic in 509 BC to AD 541, although in at least the first two centuries the names may be largely fictitious.) Dating by eras, where the years are numbered consecutively from an agreed starting-point, e.g. the foundation of Rome, has obvious advantages. In the fifth century BC some Greeks had used to establish an era the periodic Panhellenic games, especially the Olympian games, whose first recorded victor won in 776 BC and which recurred every four years. The first list of Olympian victors was said to have been published by the sophist Hippias in the second half of the fifth century BC, and afterwards kept up to date, and Thucydides uses the names of notable victors to date historical events. The numbering of Olympiads (the four-year periods between games) and the counting of years within an Olympiad probably goes back to the Greek scholar *Timaeus (fourth to third century BC), and from his time on most Greek dates were synchronized with the Olympiads. This system lasted until the Byzantine age. The Romans did not widely use the era *ab urbe condita* ('from the foundation of Rome', abbreviated to AUC), perhaps because the date we now accept as traditional, 753 BC, was disputed. Under the empire, years were dated by the names of consuls and also by the regnal years of emperors; many local eras were also used. The method of reckoning by *indictions was introduced by the emperor Diocletian and from AD 312 dates were reckoned in fifteen-year periods. This practice originated in the system of taxation; it was regularly used for dating financial years and sometimes for dating other documents even up to the Middle Ages and beyond. A number was used for the position of a year within an indiction, but quite often a writer did not bother to number the indictions themselves systematically.

The method of dating by the years of the Christian era was introduced in the mid-sixth century by Dionysius Exiguus, a Scythian monk who lived at Rome. He took as year 1 the year of Jesus' birth, which he believed to be 753 AUC. In fact Jesus was born a few years earlier. It has to be remembered, in calculating dates, that the year AD 1 was preceded by the year 1 BC (i.e. there is no year 0), and that therefore the interval between e.g. 5 BC and AD 5 is 9 and not 10 years.

See also CLOCKS.

ca'liga, the heavy hob-nailed open boot worn by Roman soldiers, from which was derived the nickname of the emperor Gaius, 'Caligula'. See DRESS 2.

Cali'gula ('little boot': see above), the popular name of the Roman emperor *Gaius Caesar.

Ca'llias, rich and distinguished fifth-century Athenian politician who was said to have negotiated the 'Peace of Callias' *c*.450 BC which finally ended the wars between Athens and Persia. Thucydides' failure to mention this treaty in his history has led some scholars to deny its existence, but hostilities between Athens and Persia ceased at this period until 413 BC. Callias was remembered for having married *Cimon's sister (or half-sister) Elpinicē for love and without a dowry.

Calli'cratēs, Greek architect of the fifth century BC, associated with Ictinus and Pheidias in the building of the *Parthenon.

Calli'machus, Greek poet and scholar of the Hellenistic age, who was born *c*.310–305 BC in Cyrene (North Africa) and died *c*.240. He is occasionally referred to as Battiades (i.e. 'son of *Battus'). During the reign of Ptolemy II Philadelphus, king of Egypt 285–246 BC, he arrived at Alexandria and was commissioned by the king to prepare the great catalogue (*pinakĕs*) of all the books in the *Alexandrian Library. This enormous undertaking (the catalogue ran to 120 volumes) not only benefited the library but actually influenced the poet's style: like other Hellenistic poets who combined poetry with scholarship he found in his researches material to be polished and incorporated in his verse. During this time Callimachus produced several prose works of scholarship which have not survived. Of his many poetical works the only ones to survive intact are the six Hymns and perhaps sixty-one short epigrams. The Hymns were modelled on the (so-called)

*Homeric Hymns but were not, like the latter, intended for recitation at festivals. Rather they were complex literary compositions, designed to be recited to, or read by, a cultivated audience appreciative of an intriguing narrative and a learned and sometimes ironic imitation of an earlier form. Hymn 1 is to Zeus, 2 to Apollo, 3 to Artemis, and 4 to Delos; Hymn 5, 'The Baths of Pallas', is written in elegiac couplets, unlike the others which are in hexameters; Hymn 6, to Demeter, tells the gruesome story of the insatiable hunger of Erysichthon. In the *epigrams Callimachus plays subtly with the conventions of this (relatively new) literary form. The epigrams which appeal most to us seem to reflect the poet's own experiences and emotions.

The rest of Callimachus' surviving poetry exists only in fragments, most of it on papyri discovered in the twentieth century; it includes the *Aitia*, the *Hecălē*, the *Iambi*, a lyric poem called *Apotheosis of Queen Arsinoe*, and an elegiac poem, *Victory of Sosibius*. The *Aitia* ('causes') was an elegiac poem in four books, comprising about 7,000 lines. The first two books have an elaborate framework: the poet is transported in a dream to Mount Helicon where (like the poet Hesiod) he is instructed by the Muses, in his case in the origins of all kinds of mythical lore connected with Greek history, customs, and religious rites. None of the stories except for one is known from earlier literature, and the sources appear to have been local histories. The style is learned and allusive but it is enlivened by dry humour and is not without true poetic touches. The third and fourth books, which were probably composed much later, do not have this framework, and are a collection of separate 'causes'. The first and last poems are in praise of the queen Berenice, the last being the famous *Plokamos* (Lat. *Coma*) or *Lock of *Berenice*. This was later translated into Latin by Catullus in poem 66, which in its turn became the model for Alexander Pope's *Rape of the Lock* (1712). The *Aitia* was also imitated by Ovid in his *Fasti*. By way of introduction to the whole work Callimachus composed the *Answer to the *Telchines*, apparently his critics, who belittle his achievement because he has not written one long continuous poem on an epic theme. His reply is that the small-scale poem is more attractive; moreover Apollo himself has commanded the poet to 'cultivate a slender Muse' and 'tread an unworn path'. As he reputedly said elsewhere, 'a big book is a big evil'; poetry should aim at small-scale perfection. A late tradition relates that chief among his opponents was the epic poet *Apollonius Rhodius, who was thought to be the object of Callimachus' (lost) verse invective, *Ibis*, later translated and adapted to his own purposes by Ovid. (See also ANTIMACHUS.)

Hecale is an example of the kind of epic Callimachus approved, an *epyllion perhaps about a thousand lines long (now known only in fragments) in which the poet tells how Theseus was on his way from Athens to Marathon to fight the Marathonian bull when a storm arose and the hero took shelter in the hut of an old woman, Hecale, who prepares a simple meal for him (the source perhaps of a similar meal in the hut of Philemon and Baucis in Ovid's *Metamorphoses*). When Theseus returns from killing the bull he finds that Hecale has died and men are digging her grave.

The fragmentary *Iambi* consist of thirteen short poems, in iambic and choliambic metres, which look back to the sixth-century vituperative poet *Hipponax; they are satirical in tone and often criticize contemporary literary attitudes.

Callimachus was a writer of astonishing output (reputedly 800 volumes) and remarkable originality and versatility, who aimed to be both a poet and a man of taste and erudition. His contribution to the development of a new literary taste in a new cosmopolitan society was very considerable (see HELLENISTIC AGE). His blend of sensitivity and detachment, elegance, wit, and learning, had a profound influence on later Roman poets, especially Catullus, Ovid, and Propertius (the last thought of himself as the Roman Callimachus), and through them on the whole European literary tradition.

Callī'nus (first half of the seventh century BC), the first Greek poet known to have written in elegiac couplets (see METRE, GREEK 4). He lived in the Greek city of Ephesus in Ionia on the coast of Asia Minor, and the few fragments of his poetry which survive refer to the barbarian invasions of '*Cimmerians and Trerians' from south Russia. In the only fragment of any length he exhorts his fellow-countrymen to take up arms and defend their country.

Callī'opē ('fair-voice'), in Greek (and Roman) myth one of the *Muses. When, in later Greek literature and art, each Muse is made the patron of a particular branch, Calliope is represented as the Muse of epic poetry, with writing tablet and stylus. Orpheus was sometimes said to be her son.

Calli'rhŏē ('fair-flowing'). **1.** Daughter of Oceanus and mother of Geryon.

2. Daughter of the river-god Achelous, wife of *Alcmaeon, and mother of Acarnan and Amphoterus. See also CHAEREAS AND CALLIRHOE.

3. The famous spring at *Athens (see 1, and PEISISTRATUS).

Calli'sthenēs, Greek historian, born *c.*370 BC, a relation of Aristotle under whom he studied at Stageira. All his works, including his history of Alexander the Great, are lost. He collaborated with Aristotle in the preparation of a complete list of the victors at the Pythian games from the earliest time. He accompanied Alexander on his expedition east as the historian of the campaigns; his biography of the king, which was widely read, extolled him as the champion of panhellenism, claiming him to be the son of Zeus. However, he quarrelled with Alexander, was suspected of being involved in Hermolaus' conspiracy against him, and was put to death in 327. This murder earned for Alexander the strong hostility of the school of Aristotle. Because of his adulatory and rhetorical style of history, Callisthenes' name became attached to an early version of the popular *Alexander Romance* (see ALEXANDER (2) 8).

Calli'sto, in Greek myth, nymph attendant upon the goddess Artemis; she was loved by Zeus and became mother of Arcas, the mythical ancestor of the Arcadians. She was changed into a bear, either by Zeus, to save her from the anger of his consort Hera, or by Hera or Artemis out of vengeance. In this form she wandered about until her son, now grown up, met her when out hunting and would have killed her with his spear. But Zeus turned both into constellations, the Great Bear and the Little Bear (Arctophylax, also known as *Boötes).

Calli'stratus, distinguished Athenian orator and statesman of the fourth century BC. He was elected *strategos* in 378 when the Second Athenian League was founded and influenced Athenian policy from 371 to 361 (see ATHENS 2 (iv)). He realized that Thebes was becoming more of a threat to Athens than was Sparta, but he and others nevertheless allowed the Thebans to gain possession of Oropus in 366. He was subsequently prosecuted, but successfully defended himself in a speech which is said to have inspired *Demosthenes to study oratory. In 361 he was again prosecuted and went into exile before the death sentence was pronounced. He eventually returned to Athens, miscalculating the popular mood, and was then put to death.

Calpu'rnia. 1. The daughter of *Piso Caesonius (the object of Cicero's speech *In Pisonem*), and the third wife of Julius Caesar, whom she married in 59 BC. Calpurnia's affection for Caesar survived his proposal, made in 54 after the death of his daughter Julia, Pompey's wife, that he should divorce her and marry Pompey's daughter to keep up the family connection, and she tried to keep him from the senate on the day of his murder.

2. Third wife of *Pliny the Younger, whom she accompanied to Bithynia.

Calpu'rnius Si'culus, Titus, the otherwise unknown Latin author of seven pastoral poems (an additional four appended and attributed to him in the manuscripts are by Nemesianus), usually thought to be writing between AD 50 and 60. Three of these poems, Eclogues 1, 4, and 7, are courtly poems aimed to flatter the

emperor (Claudius or Nero), while the remainder are more strictly pastoral. Eclogue 1, on the dawn of a new Golden Age signified by an omen in the sky (taken to be the comet of AD 54, the year of Nero's accession), resembles the fourth Eclogue of Virgil; Eclogue 2 is an *amoebean contest between a shepherd and a gardener; in Eclogue 3 Lycidas sings a love-song in remorse for having beaten his faithless mistress; in Eclogue 4 Corydon and his brother Amyntas sing the praises of the emperor, and their patron Meliboeus is asked to lay their poetry before him; in Eclogue 5 an old shepherd advises a younger on the care of goats and sheep; Eclogue 6 is a singing-match between two shepherds, broken off by a quarrel; in Eclogue 7 Corydon has been to Rome and describes a display of wild beasts given by the emperor in the amphitheatre. Calpurnius' poems are full of reminiscences of Augustan poetry and especially of Virgil's *Eclogues*.

Calvus, Gaius Lici'nius, 82–*c.*47 BC, son of the Roman annalist Licinius Macer (see ANNALS), a celebrated love poet in his day and a successful lawyer, who employed the austere Attic style of *oratory; his speeches against Vatinius were still used as models of oratory a century later. He was also a friend of Catullus, the *salaputium disertum* ('eloquent dwarf') of the latter's poem 53 (and the recipient of poems 14, 50, and 96). The very scanty fragments of his verse that survive—from epithalamia, a narrative poem, and satiric epigrams (attacking Pompey and Caesar)—at least show that his range was similar to that of Catullus.

Ca'lydon, Greek town in Aetolia, in Greek myth ruled over by Meleager, and famous for being once ravaged by a boar sent by Artemis. For the Calydonian boar-hunt see MELEAGER.

Caly'pso, in Greek myth, a goddess or nymph, the daughter of Atlas, who lived on the island of Ogygia where *Odysseus was washed up after being shipwrecked. She kept him there for seven years and promised to make him immortal if he would be her husband, but Zeus sent Hermes to order her to release him, and she gave him materials to make his own boat. Some stories make her the mother by Odysseus of Auson, the eponymous ancestor of the Ausonians of Italy.

Cambȳ'sēs, king of Persia 530–522 BC, son of Cyrus the Great. His main achievement was the conquest of Egypt in 525 BC, which established Persian rule there for two centuries. Greek writers, perhaps following a hostile Egyptian tradition, represent him as impious and tyrannical.

Camē'nae, Italian goddesses perhaps originally associated with water, and identified with the Greek Muses since *Livius Andronicus invoked the Camenae at the beginning of his Latin translation of Homer's *Odyssey*. They had a grove and a spring outside the Porta Capena at Rome from which the Vestals drew water daily for their rites.

Cami'lla, known only from Virgil's *Aeneid* and perhaps a Virgilian invention, a maiden-warrior of the Volsci, and ally of Turnus. When she was a baby her father Metabus, king of the Volscians, was driven out for his cruelty, and arrived with his baby daughter at the flooded river Amasenus. He tied her to a spear, dedicated her to the goddess Diana (Lat. *camilla*, 'religious attendant'), and threw her across the river to safety. He then swam across himself. In the *Aeneid* she is killed by the Etruscan Arruns.

Cami'llus, Marcus Fū'rius, according to Livy 'the saviour of his country and second founder of Rome' after its occupation by the Gauls *c.*390 BC. He was a Roman statesman and general of the early fourth century BC whose exploits were greatly embellished in later times. His first historical victory was the important capture of the Etruscan town of Veii in 396 BC, after which he dedicated a golden basin to Apollo at Delphi in fulfilment of a vow. Roman matrons contributed jewellery for it, and in return for their generosity received the privilege of riding in covered carriages (see CARMENTIS). Soon afterwards Camillus reduced Falerii. To this campaign belongs the famous story of the local schoolmaster who brought his pupils to Camillus' camp with the suggestion that they should be used as hostages to secure the town. Camillus, refusing to profit by treachery, returned the children safely, and sent the schoolmaster back in chains. The citizens were so struck by this example of Roman justice that they surrendered.

According to tradition Camillus was accused of appropriating booty and went into exile, but was recalled as dictator when the Gauls captured Rome *c.*390 (see BRENNUS). He is supposed to have annihilated the Gauls and recovered the gold with which the Romans were on the point of buying them off, but it is possible that Roman patriotism invented the story. Later, Camillus reputedly conquered the Volsci and the Aequi and steered Rome through the civil crisis following the Gallic invasion. He reasserted the power of the patricians and put down a revolution of the people led by *Manlius Capitolinus, but he was a moderating influence during the civil strife between patricians and plebeians that ended in 367 (see LICINIAN–SEXTIAN LAWS), and marked the return to peace by founding a temple to Concord built at the foot of the Capitoline hill. He was five times dictator, and a reform of Roman military organization is attributed to him.

camp, Roman. The camp in its stereotyped form was a part of Roman military organization from earliest times, so well known in fact that no Roman historian bothers to describe it, and for a written description we rely on the account of the Greek historian Polybius (second century BC). He describes a typical camp for an army led by one consul and consisting of two legions (in his account, about 9,000 Roman troops; but see ARMY, ROMAN I) and an equal number of Italian allies. It is square, with each side measuring about 2,000 Roman feet (about 600 m. or 650 yds.). The *praetorium* ('general's tent') lay off centre, towards one side. For a full Roman army of two consuls and four legions there would be two *praetoria*, one for each consul, back to back in the middle of a double camp which formed two squares. When only a single consular army was encamped the *praetorium* lay in a protected position between the legions. Across the front of the *praetorium* ran a roadway (*via principalis*, 'main road') ending in gates on two sides of the camp. The legions and most of the allies were encamped by *centuries (two to a maniple or six to a cohort) beyond the *via principalis* in streets running at right angles to it, and were divided in half (at the fifth cohort) by another road parallel to the *via principalis*, the *via quintana* ('fifth road'). In front of the *praetorium* stood the tents of the tribunes (six to each legion) on the *via principalis*, and beside it were the open space that served as *forum* and the *quaestorium* (for the quaestor and his department). At the rear of these areas ran a third road, parallel to the other two, behind which were the quarters for selected auxiliaries (*extraordinarii*) and foreign levies (*auxilia). The whole camp was surrounded by a ditch (*fossa*) and fortified by a palisade (*vallum*) made from stakes, of which each Roman soldier carried two. Between the palisade and the tents was a space, *intervallum*, 200 (Roman) feet wide. A street led from the front and rear of the *praetorium* across the camp, to gates on the remaining two sides, so that there were in all four gates to the camp.

In the permanent camps (*castra stativa*) and even the forts, furnished with wooden and eventually stone buildings, the detailed arrangements were different but the characteristic features remained the same. The tradition of the soldiers digging themselves in at night continued, and their experience at this made it possible for armies on campaign to construct siege works and build roads and bridges with remarkable speed.

The remains of republican camps at Numantia in Spain offer a fairly clear picture of their structure. A camp of the imperial period is described in a treatise attributed to *Hyginus; examples are well-preserved in Scotland and in Northumberland.

Campā'nia, territory in Italy south of Latium, lying between the Apennines and the Tyrrhenian Sea, and extending south to the Surrentine promontory (Sorrento). A volcanic plain, it is exceptionally fertile, and many wealthy Romans had villas there. It included the port of Puteoli and the towns of Cumae, Capua, Baiae, Neapolis (Naples), Pompeii, and Herculaneum. The Sabelli conquered Campania in the fifth century BC and brought with them their language, *Oscan, which was still spoken at Pompeii in the first century AD. The Campanians surrendered their territory to Roman authority in 343 BC. The emperor Augustus joined Campania to Latium, which thereby acquired the former name, the Campagna of today.

Campus Martius ('field of Mars'), at Rome, originally pasture-land belonging at first to the Tarquins, but after their expulsion to the Roman state. It was the park and recreation ground of the Romans; see GAMES, PRIVATE 2. Situated outside and to the north-west of the city boundary, in early times it was the exercise ground of Roman armies and the meeting-place of the *comitia centuriata*. It took its name from an altar to Mars erected there. Public buildings were gradually erected on it, and in 221 BC the censor C. Flaminius constructed there the circus that bore his name. Later, in 52 BC, Pompey built close to this the first permanent theatre in Rome. In the late republic and during the empire imposing buildings and colonnades were erected there. For the *horologium* of Augustus see CLOCKS.

Camulodū'num (modern Colchester, in Essex), capital of the British king Cunobelinus (Shakespeare's Cymbeline), captured by the emperor Claudius in AD 43, made a colony in 49, sacked by Boudicca in 60, and subsequently rebuilt.

Canacē, in Greek myth, daughter of Aeolus and Enaretē. She fell incestuously in love with her brother Macareus, and for this reason was put to death by her father, or, according to some accounts, committed suicide.

Candau'lēs, king of Lydia, killed by *Gyges c.685 BC.

candidā'tus ('whitened'), in Rome, a candidate for a magistracy, so called because he wore a white toga specially brightened with chalk when greeting electors in the forum.

canē'phori, 'basket-bearers', in Greece, maidens who bore baskets on their heads in religious processions; in particular, those from noble families who did so in the procession to the temple of Athena Polias at the *Panathenaea at Athens, and who were required to be chaste. To be rejected as unsuitable, as *Harmodius' sister was by Hipparchus, was a grave insult. The baskets contained all that was needed in the sacrificial ceremony.

Canī'nius Re'bilus, Roman senator who achieved fame when Julius Caesar appointed him consul at noon on the last day of the year 45 BC for the remainder of the day (the consul of that year having died on his last day of office). This was the consulship in which, according to Cicero's joke, no one breakfasted and the consul never slept.

Cannae, village in Apulia in Italy, the scene of a great defeat inflicted on the Romans by Hannibal in 216 BC. The consul Aemilius Paulus and (it was said) 50,000 Romans were killed in the battle. See PUNIC WARS 2.

canons, selective lists of Greek authors, dating from ancient times. By the mid-fourth century BC it was recognized at Athens that there were only three outstanding tragic dramatists, Aeschylus, Sophocles, and Euripides, who comprised the tragic canon, but the first authoritative lists, at least of the poets, seem to have been drawn up by the Hellenistic scholars, *Aristophanes of Byzantium and *Aristarchus, in the third and second centuries BC. These lists can only be reconstructed from later references and there is no unanimous agreement on their contents, but it seems clear that they named as the best *iambographers Archilochus, Hipponax, and Semonides; as the best epic poets Homer and Hesiod; as the best writers of Old Comedy Eupolis, Cratinus, and Aristophanes; and of lyric poetry Pindar, Bacchylides, Sappho, Anacreon, Stesichorus, Simonides, Ibycus, Alcman, and Alcaeus. Lists of orators, historians, and philosophers were subsequently compiled, although only that of the Attic orators rivalled in fame the lists of the poets. The ten best Attic orators were deemed to be Antiphon, Lysias, Andocides, Isocrates, Isaeus, Demosthenes, Aeschines, Lycurgus, Hypereides, and Deinarchus. The authors themselves were called in Greek, *hoi enkrithentes*, 'those selected', and in Latin, *classici*, i.e. 'of the first class' (see also CLASSIC), but there was no term for 'selective list' until the scholar Ruhnken in 1768 originated the use of 'canon' in this sense (Gk. *kanonēs*—originally 'rods', then carpenters' 'rules', hence metaphorically 'standards of excellence').

ca'ntica, in Roman comedy and particularly in Plautus, the parts that were sung or recited to a musical accompaniment. They were an invention of Roman dramatists. See COMEDY, ROMAN 2 (at the end).

cantō'res Euphoriō'nis, see EUPHORION 2.

Căpănē'us, in Greek myth, one of the *Seven against Thebes. He climbed the walls of Thebes boasting that not even Zeus would stop him, and was destroyed by Zeus' thunderbolt. His wife Evadne committed suicide by throwing herself on to his funeral pyre.

Cape'lla, Martiā'nus, see MARTIANUS CAPELLA.

Ca'pito, Gaius Ateius, eminent Roman legal writer of the early empire. He was a supporter of imperial (as opposed to republican) government, but in legal matters a conservative, in both respects contrasting with his ultimately more successful rival *Labeo.

Capitō'lium or **mons Capitōlī'nus,** the Capitoline hill, one of the hills of Rome; it had two peaks, the south-west summit known as the Capitol and the northern one known as the *arx ('citadel'). However, these two last terms are used indiscriminately by ancient as well as modern writers to signify the whole hill as well as one or other of the summits. From earliest times the hill was used not so much for habitation as for a citadel and a religious centre. The Capitol was the site of the temple to Iuppiter Optimus Maximus, 'Jupiter best and greatest', and his companions, the goddesses Juno and Minerva; it was therefore the most sacred part of Rome. According to tradition it was begun by the king Tarquin and dedicated in the first year of the republic, 509 BC. Here sacrifice was offered by magistrates on taking office, and by victorious generals in a *triumph. It was burnt in 83 BC but subsequently rebuilt. On the Capitol also stood the ancient temple of *Jupiter Feretrius, associated with an oak-tree, and reputedly founded by Romulus. The *Tarpeian Rock lay close to the Capitol. For the legend of the saving of the Capitol from the Gauls by the sacred geese see MANLIUS CAPITOLINUS.

Captī'vī ('prisoners of war'), Roman comedy by *Plautus, the Greek original of which has not survived. There are no women in the play, and the characters are more high-minded than is usual in Plautus.

One of the two sons of Hegio has been taken prisoner by the Eleans; the other was kidnapped when a child by a slave and has not been heard of since. Some Eleans have now been taken prisoner in a war and Hegio has bought two of them, Philocrates and his slave Tyndarus, in the hope of effecting an exchange for his captured son. The slave is to be sent to Elis to negotiate, but he secretly changes identity with his master in order to release him. The trick is revealed unintentionally by an Elean fellow-prisoner and Hegio, thinking that he will not now recover his son, sends Tyndarus loaded with fetters to work in the quarries. Presently Philocrates returns bringing with him Hegio's captive son and the slave who stole his second son. The slave reveals that the boy had been sold to the father of Philocrates and is in fact Tyndarus. The dramatic ironies and the dignified behaviour of the two prisoners make this one of Plautus' most interesting plays.

Ca'pua, in western Italy, the chief city of *Campania, to which it gave its name, and

famous for its luxury. In 216 BC after the Roman defeat at Cannae (see PUNIC WARS 2) it went over to the Carthaginian side, but was recaptured by Rome in 211 and severely punished: its leading citizens were beheaded, the others exiled, and its territory became the property of the Roman state. It had no municipal privileges until after 90 BC.

Caraca'lla, nickname of Aurelius Antoninus, Roman emperor AD 211–17; it was derived from the long, hooded Celtic cloak which he introduced. The son of Lucius Septimius Severus and *Julia Domna, he was mentally unstable, and murdered his younger brother Geta. His most significant act was to grant citizenship to all free inhabitants of the Roman empire in 212.

Carā'tacus (the spelling Caractacus is incorrect), in Welsh, 'Caradoc', British king AD 42–51, the son of Cunobelinus (Shakespeare's Cymbeline; see BRITAIN 3). After the death of his father and brother and the capture by the Romans of his capital Camulodunum (Colchester) in AD 43, Caratacus escaped to Wales and organized resistance to Rome. After being again defeated in 51 he fled to Cartimandua, queen of the Brigantes in Yorkshire, but she handed him over to the Romans. Thereafter he lived in honourable captivity in Rome.

Carau'sius (Marcus Aurēlius Mausaeus Carausius), general from the Low Countries who c. AD 287 seized the provinces of Britain. See BRITAIN 6.

Ca'ria, region in south-west Asia Minor south of the river Maeander, inhabited largely by a people who claimed to be indigenous, but including the Dorian Greek cities of Cnidus and Halicarnassus. Under the rule of *Mausolus in the fourth century BC the country became thoroughly Hellenized. Carian *hoplite soldiers of the seventh century BC are said to have been the first to fight as mercenaries (see EGYPT).

Cari'stia, Roman family feast. See PARENTALIA.

Carmen Saeculā're, choral hymn in the sapphic metre written by *Horace in 17 BC at the command of the emperor Augustus, to be performed at the *ludi saeculares ('secular games') by a choir of twenty-seven boys and twenty-seven girls. A marble inscription recording the ceremony and the part played by Horace still survives. The ode is in the form of a prayer addressed to Apollo and Diana, and the achievements of Augustus are commemorated.

Carme'ntis or **Carme'nta,** in Roman myth, a prophetic goddess, mother of *Evander the first settler at Rome. She may have been a water-goddess, and she was certainly a goddess of protection in childbirth, worshipped by matrons. A minor *flamen was assigned to her, and her festival, the Carmentalia, was on 11 and

15 January. It was said to have been inaugurated by the senate in the third century BC to mark the successful protest of Roman women who refused to have children until the senate restored their right, recently taken away from them, to ride in carriages (see CAMILLUS). One of the gates of Rome near the foot of the Capitoline hill was named after her, the Porta Carmentalis.

Carnē'a (Karneia), festival held at Sparta and in other Doric states at harvest time, from which the Doric name of the month Karneios (August–September) is derived. It was held in honour of Apollo, who had probably ousted some earlier god Karnos or Karneios. It in part symbolized the military life of Sparta, but it also had a rural character, and included a race between boys carrying bunches of grapes. A musical contest was added, which attracted poets and musicians from all parts of Greece.

Carne'adēs, *c.*213–129 BC, of Cyrene (North Africa), an important Greek philosopher, a *Sceptic whose headship of the *Academy at Athens marks a new turn in the development of Scepticism (which had been originated by *Pyrrho in the fourth century BC and taken up by Arcesilaus in the third). He was already head of the Academy in 155 BC, when he was sent as one of three philosophers on an embassy to Rome; there he won fame for giving, on two consecutive days, first a lecture in praise of justice and then another in which it was proved not to be a virtue but a civil compact to maintain society. He followed the fashion of his Sceptic predecessors and published nothing, but his arguments were recorded by his pupils, notably by Clitomachus, through whom they have survived in the philosophical writings of *Cicero ((1) 5). His influence was considerable. He argued at length against the Stoic belief that knowledge about the world was attainable if it was based upon sense impressions which recorded the facts (or objects) correctly, and that the percipient could be sure that the sense impressions were correct through their complete conformity with the facts perceived. Carneades did not believe that the percipient could be sure; sense impressions have no particular characteristics by which one may distinguish those that are correct from those that are not. Therefore he thought, like Arcesilaus, that knowledge was unattainable, but he allowed that some sense impressions are 'persuasive', i.e. seem probable, while others are not. For the purposes of life we have to assume the truth, or the falsity, of many sense impressions, but we should not assert it, because the truth about facts or objects may actually be quite different from our perception of them. Carneades attacked many Stoic and Epicurean dogmas, exposing their improbabilities and the often shaky arguments on which they were based. The Stoics modified some of their

theories in the light of his criticism. After Carneades the tradition of (moderate) Scepticism in the Academy was continued by Philo of Larisa (head of the Academy 109 BC). Cicero declared himself an adherent of the 'New' Academy of Arcesilaus, Carneades, and Philo.

Carrhae, city in northern Mesopotamia, scene of the defeat of the Roman general M. Licinius *Crassus by the Parthians in 53 BC.

Carthage, city occupying a strong strategic position on the Tunisian coast of North Africa, founded by colonists from Phoenician Tyre, traditionally in 814 BC though the earliest archaeological evidence dates from a century later. For its foundation legend see DIDO. It gradually outstripped other Phoenician cities in North Africa (Utica was the chief rival) because of its good trading position and excellent harbour, founded numerous colonies of its own in Africa, exercised direct rule over the native population of the surrounding territory, which the Carthaginians eventually turned into rich agricultural land, and controlled the African Nomads (Numidae). In general the native population was harshly ruled by Carthage and eager to revolt. The government was oligarchic; the two chief magistrates, called by the Romans *suffetēs*, were elected annually from among the rich and aristocratic. The generals were elected separately. Membership of the powerful senate was for life, and the citizens had only limited powers. Aristotle admired the equilibrium of aristocratic and democratic elements in the constitution which made for stability. Carthage was pre-eminently a commercial state, carrying on trade all along the coasts of the Mediterranean and maintaining control of sea-routes to the west, especially the important tin-routes. Voyages of exploration were undertaken along the Atlantic coasts of North Africa and Spain.

By *c.*600 BC it was clear that Carthaginian interests would conflict with those of the Greeks. In *c.*535 the Etruscan and Carthaginian fleets drove colonists from *Phocaea out of Corsica (Phocaea, an Ionian Greek city in Asia Minor, was an important colonizer in the western Mediterranean). In the same period Carthage established control of southern Sardinia and west Sicily, as well as consolidating her hold on southern Spain. By the time of the First *Punic War (264 BC) all the islands of the western Mediterranean belonged to Carthage. With the Roman republic she made commercial treaties to prevent Rome from interfering with Carthaginian trade; the earliest reputedly dated from 508 BC, the first year of the republic. For three centuries Carthaginians and Greeks fought over Sicily. In 480 BC a large Carthaginian expedition was defeated by the Sicilian (Greek) tyrants Gelon and Theron at Himera, reputedly on the same day as the Persians were defeated at Salamis. The Punic Wars between Carthage and

Rome were precipitated when Carthage occupied Messana (Messina) in north-east Sicily, and when they ended in 146 BC Carthage was utterly destroyed. Rome decreed that no house should be built nor crop planted, but the site was colonized by Julius Caesar and Augustus and the colony became the capital of the enlarged province of *Africa. By the second century AD Carthage had become the largest city in the west after Rome.

Carthaginian religion was oriental in origin, and even after the Roman destruction of 146 BC the Carthaginians continued to worship their grim gods Melkart, Baal-Hammon, and Eshmoun, and to practise human sacrifice. Carthage never developed an artistic style of her own but adapted Greek and Egyptian art forms. Her agricultural skill made the wealth of her cornlands proverbial, and after her recovery, under the Roman emperors, she exported half a million tons of corn annually. The agricultural treatise of the Carthaginian Mago, in thirty-two books, was translated into Latin. Under the empire Carthage became first a famous educational centre, especially for law and rhetoric, and then a focus for Christianity in the west, especially in the time of Tertullian and Cyprian (second and third centuries AD). Carthage fell to the Vandals in 439 and became the capital of their king Gaiseric, but after the victory of Belisarius in 533 it remained loyal to the Roman empire in the east until the Arab conquest at the end of the seventh century.

Cartima'ndua, British queen of the *Brigantes who made a treaty with the Roman emperor Claudius. In AD 51 she handed over the fugitive *Caratacus to Rome. She divorced her husband Venutius and married one of his officers, but in 68 Venutius defeated Cartimandua and regained the kingdom. In order to rescue the queen the Romans advanced further north into Britain; see BRITAIN 3.

Carya'tids (Karyātidĕs), the Greek name for columns supporting a roof that are carved in the form of women in long drapery. The most famous are the six which supported the roof of the small porch on the west end of the *Erechtheum, one of which is now in the British Museum; others are found in the porch of the Siphnian treasury at Delphi. The derivation of the name is unknown; one suggestion is that it means 'maidens of Caryae', a place in Laconia, and it is perhaps connected with the girl dancers who performed there in honour of Artemis.

Casca. Two brothers so named joined the conspiracy against Julius Caesar in 44 BC. One of them, Publius Longus, was the first to strike Caesar at his assassination. Both killed themselves after the defeat of the republicans at Philippi in 42 BC.

Ca'sina, Roman comedy by *Plautus, adapted from a play by the Greek writer of New Comedy, Diphilus (see COMEDY, GREEK 6).

An elderly Athenian and his son have both fallen in love with Casina, a slave-girl who has been rescued from exposure as a baby and brought up in their household. The father wants to have her married to his bailiff, the son to his own attendant Chalinus, each for his own purpose, while the father's wife, aware of her husband's scheme, plots on her son's behalf. Lots are drawn to settle the matter and the father wins, but at the wedding the bailiff is fobbed off with Chalinus dressed as a bride, who beats both bailiff and father. Casina is found to be a freeborn Athenian and marries the son.

Cassa'nder (Kassandros), c.358–297 BC, Macedonian, son of the general *Antipater who helped Alexander the Great to succeed to the throne of Macedon after the death of his father Philip II. Cassander was sent to Alexander at Babylon in the last months of the latter's life; he seems to have personally disliked Alexander. After the latter's death he was involved in the power-struggles among the generals and eventually procured the deaths of Alexander's mother, wife, and son. He managed to establish himself as his father's successor and ruled over Macedon and most of Greece, but spent the rest of his life trying to keep his territory. He founded the city of Thessalonika (Salonika) and rebuilt Thebes. See MACEDONIA 2.

Cassa'ndra (also called Alexandra), in Greek myth, the prophetic daughter of *Priam, king of Troy, and Hecuba his wife. For Homer, who knows nothing of her prophetic gifts, she is the most beautiful of Priam's daughters. It was according to a later tradition that she was loved by Apollo and given the gift of prophecy, but when she refused his love he condemned her to the fate of always prophesying truthfully but never being believed. She appears in Greek tragedy in this role, vainly foretelling the fall of Troy. When Troy was captured, Ajax the Locrian, son of Oileus, found her in the temple of Athena clinging to the sacred statue of the goddess (the *Palladium), dragged her away, and raped her. To expiate this sacrilege the Locrians were obliged to send two maidens to Troy every year for a thousand years to serve as slaves in Athena's temple; if they were caught by the inhabitants before reaching the temple they were executed. This obligation continued into the second century BC. After the sack of Troy Cassandra was awarded to the Greek commander *Agamemnon as his concubine, but on their return to Mycenae she was murdered by his wife Clytemnestra.

Cassiodō'rus (Flāvius Magnus Aurēlius Cassiodōrus), c. AD 490–583, Christian Roman statesman and writer. Born in south Italy the son of a praetorian prefect of Theodoric, king of the *Goths, he too served Theodoric, was consul in 514, and pursued a public career until the 540s. He then retired to his estates to devote himself to scholarship and the Christian life, as a monk in the monastery he founded at Vivarium in Bruttium (Calabria). He published twelve books of his *Variae epistulae* ('various letters'), the most important letters and edicts he had written for the Gothic kings to the notable personages of the day, and a valuable source to us for sixth-century history. Among his other writings were a *History of the Goths*, of which a summary survives, a brief history of the world down to AD 519, very popular in medieval times, and some grammatical works. The chief literary work of his later life was the *Institutiones* ('institutions'), a guide to the religious and secular education of his monks, the secular part being based on the *seven liberal arts. It also gives instruction about the copying of manuscripts, in which Vivarium was very active, but not, as far as can be seen, in the area of classical Latin texts. Nevertheless Cassiodorus played a part in the transmission of a literate culture to the western medieval world. Compare BOETHIUS.

Cassiope'ia or **Cassiepeia**, in Greek myth, wife of Cepheus king of the Ethiopians; she boasted that her daughter *Andromeda (or possibly she herself) was more beautiful than the Nereids; in consequence Poseidon sent a sea-serpent to ravage the land, to which Andromeda was to be sacrificed until *Perseus saved her life. After their deaths Cassiopeia and her family became constellations.

Cassite'rides ('tin islands'), name given by the Greeks to all the unknown lands in the northwest of Europe producing tin, but probably with special reference to the west of England and the Scillies. Herodotus in the fifth century BC knew that tin came to Greece reputedly from these islands, but did not know by what route nor where the islands were to be found. *Pytheas, the late fourth-century Greek explorer from Massilia (Marseilles), said he visited Cornwall and the tin depot at St Michael's Mount, but was not universally believed. The Phoenicians, from their colony at Gades (Cadiz) in Spain, or from Carthage, were probably the first to discover a sea-route to Cornwall in the eighth or seventh centuries BC, but they kept their sea-routes secret, hence Herodotus' ignorance. A Roman, P. Crassus, while governor in Spain *c.*95 BC, is credited with making the sea-route between Cornwall and Spain generally known.

Ca'ssius, Gaius Longi'nus, one of the murderers of Julius Caesar in 44 BC; he was *quaestor to M. *Crassus at the battle of Carrhae in 53 BC where he succeeded in extricating a division of

the Roman army from the disaster. He supported Pompey in the civil war and was given a naval command, but on hearing of Pompey's defeat at Pharsalus in 48 BC abandoned the war and later obtained Caesar's pardon. He was *praetor peregrinus* in 44 when he played a leading part in the conspiracy against Caesar. After the assassination he had to withdraw from Rome and in the senate's distribution of provinces was allocated Syria, where he defeated Caesar's supporter Dolabella. After Caesar's murderers were outlawed in the autumn of 43, he joined Brutus in Thrace to meet the triumvirs. In the first battle of Philippi in 42 his camp was captured and he ordered his slave to kill him.

Ca'ssius Dīo, Coccēiā'nus, also known as Dio Cassius, *c.* AD 150–235, Roman historian from Nicaea in Bithynia. He was twice consul at Rome and governor of Africa and Dalmatia. He wrote a small book on dreams and portents, and a history of the civil wars of 193–7 (both lost), but his major work was the history of Rome (written in Greek) in eighty books, from the landing of Aeneas in Italy down to AD 229. Books 36–54, covering the years 68–10 BC, survive complete, books 55–60 (9 BC–AD 46) in an abbreviated form, and books 79–80 (AD 217–20) in part. The rest of the history has to be pieced together from the summary descriptions of Byzantine historians of the eleventh and twelfth centuries. He is an important witness for contemporary events and a valuable commentator on the political aspects of history through his own experience, but he is unreliable about republican institutions and the style is coloured by his rhetorical training.

Cassivellau'nus, king of the British tribe of Catuvellauni, the most powerful of the southern tribes, and commander of the British forces that resisted Julius Caesar's second invasion of Britain in 54 BC. When Caesar discovered and captured his stronghold, perhaps at Wheathampstead in Hertfordshire, Cassivellaunus was forced to make terms. See BRITAIN 2.

Castā'lia, in Greek myth, the nymph who, when pursued by Apollo, threw herself into the spring on Mount Parnassus near Delphi. The spring was held sacred to Apollo and the Muses. All who wished to consult the Delphic Oracle were required to purify themselves in its waters. It may still be seen a little to the north-east of *Delphi. To the Romans, 'drinking the waters of Castalia' signified poetic inspiration, since Apollo was the god of poetry.

Castor and Pollux (Gk. Polydeukēs), twin sons of Leda, brothers to Helen of Troy. For their story see DIOSCURI.

castra, see CAMP.

catacombs, term used to describe the Christian

cemetery associated with the church of St Sebastian on the Via Appia, 5 km. (3 miles) south of Rome. It seems to have been derived originally from the name of the locality, but since the cemetery was peculiar in that it was constructed in the form of narrow underground galleries and chambers cut in the rock, it came to be applied to all cemeteries tunnelled underground. Recesses in the walls held one to four coffins (inhumation was the rule) and were sealed with a stone slab or tiles. The practice resembles that of the Roman tomb known as a *columbarium* (see BURIAL) which held the urns of the cremated dead, but was probably derived from the similar Jewish form of burial. The walls and ceilings were often painted, giving us the earliest examples of Christian art. The catacombs at Rome are the most extensive known, stretching for hundreds of kilometres along the main roads outside the city. About a century after Christianity became the official religion of the Roman empire in AD 325, the catacombs ceased to be used and became instead an object of pilgrimage. During the Middle Ages the existence of catacombs was entirely forgotten, until a chance discovery in 1578 brought them to public attention again.

catalectic, see CATALEXIS.

Catale'pton, see *APPENDIX VIRGILIANA.*

catale'xis (adjective, 'catalectic'), see METRE, GREEK 6. When the same metrical sequence or metron is repeated several times before a pause is reached, the final metron is often an abbreviated form of the preceding metra; catalexis is then said to occur and the abbreviated metron is described as catalectic.

Catalogue of Women (Gk. Ē(h)ōiai, Lat. Ē(h)-ōeae), Greek hexameter poem ascribed to *Hesiod in antiquity but probably not earlier than the sixth century BC. It was a continuation of his *Theogony* in five books, containing accounts of the women who had been loved by the gods and become the mothers of heroes. Some parts of the work survive in quotation and in papyrus fragments. The title was derived from the Greek words introducing each new group of heroines, ē hoiai ('or such as . . .').

catapult, artillery weapon used mainly by the Romans, but said to have been first employed in the Greek world by Dionysius, tyrant of *Syracuse (see 2) in the late fifth century BC. Like the *ballista* it relied on torsion, but discharged an iron-headed arrow about 3 kg. (6 lb.) in weight. It was also used to project incendiary materials and, later, the mysterious 'Greek fire', which was a key weapon in the Byzantine empire from the seventh century AD.

Categories (*Katēgoriai,* Lat. *Categoriae,* 'predicates'), one of the six logical works which comprise Aristotle's *Organon* (see ARISTOTLE 4 (i)), a treatise on the ten different types of predicate, or classes, into which the attributes of things (e.g. their substance or their size) may be divided.

catharsis, see POETICS.

Ca'tiline (Lucius Sergius Catilīna), d. 62 BC, a Roman patrician of disreputable character from a relatively obscure family, legate of Sulla, who rose to political prominence in the 60s of the first century BC. He was praetor in 68, governor of Africa for the following two years, and on his return was prosecuted for extortion and so prevented from standing for the consulship until he was finally acquitted. He was defeated for the consulship of 63 by Cicero, who captured the vote of the *optimates*; they might otherwise have supported Catiline but were alarmed by what his intentions might be. He was exploiting the widespread unrest in Italy at that time among many classes of society and proposing the cancelling of debts, and was said to have had the support of Julius Caesar. Defeated for the consulship of 62 also, he laid plans for revolution, against which Cicero could not take action until he had manoeuvred Catiline into leaving Rome, and had obtained written evidence to convince the senate of Catiline's intentions. The *senatus consultum ultimum* was passed late in 63 and the leaders of the conspiracy still in Rome were arrested and executed. Catiline was now in open rebellion against the state; the consul Antonius marched out with an army, and defeated and killed him early in 62. Catiline's severest critics, Cicero and Sallust, credit him with bravery and qualities of leadership, but his actions were prompted by a desperate ambition. See also CICERO (1) 2.

Cāto, Marcus Po'rcius 1. 'The Elder' or 'the Censor', 234–149 BC. He was born of peasant stock at Tusculum, fought in the Second *Punic War as military tribune, and embarked on a political career under the patronage of L. Valerius Flaccus who was impressed by Cato's stern morality. He was quaestor in Sicily, and returning to Rome via Sardinia he is said to have found the poet Ennius there and brought him to Rome. He was praetor in 198 and consul with Flaccus in 195, when he unsuccessfully opposed the repeal of the Oppian law limiting women's finery. He was governor in Spain where he won a *triumph for his military operations. During the 180s Cato was prominent in attacking the *Scipios, and hostile to their attempts to introduce Greek culture to Rome (although this did not prevent him from learning Greek himself in his later years). He was elected to the censorship in 184, an office he held with a severity which became proverbial. He applied himself to reforming the lax morals of the Roman nobility and checking the extravagance of the wealthy. His ideal was a return to the primitive simplicity of a mainly agricultural state. Late in life he went as a commissioner to Carthage and was so impressed by the danger to Rome _from her reviving prosperity that, henceforth, when asked for his opinion in the senate, whatever the subject under debate, he always declared 'Carthage must be destroyed' (*Carthago delenda est*). He had the satisfaction of seeing the Third Punic War under way before his death.

Cato wrote treatises for his son on varied topics. *Origines* ('beginnings') in seven books dealt with the foundation legends of Rome and the Italian cities (whence the title), and the history of recent wars. This discursive work (now lost) was the first of its kind in the Latin language (earlier Roman annalists wrote in Greek; see HISTORIOGRAPHY, ROMAN), and as well as stimulating the study of history it laid the foundation of Latin prose style. He wrote with greater sophistication than is suggested by his precept, *rem tene: verba sequentur* ('stick to the meaning: the words will follow'). His *De agri cultura* ('on agriculture'), sometimes known as *De re rustica*, which in large part survives, deals with the cultivation of vines, olives, and fruit, and cattle-grazing for profit, the precepts and recipes based on his experience, with prayers and spells included as well. His advice to sell off a slave when he is too old to be profitable is notorious. Cato was also a successful orator; one hundred and fifty of his speeches were known to Cicero. The surviving fragments show shrewdness and wit, honesty and simplicity. When prosecuted in old age on a capital charge he spoke his defence with undiminished vigour but was conscious of the difficulty of convincing the jury: 'How hard it is for one whose life has been passed in a preceding generation to plead his cause before men of the present.' Cicero makes him the principal interlocutor in his dialogue *De senectute*. For an anecdote concerning his views on divination see *De divinatione*.

Dicta Catōnis, 'the sayings of (Marcus) Cato', a collection of Latin moral maxims in prose and (mostly) verse, was an immensely popular school-book in the Middle Ages, translated into several European languages. From the sixteenth to the nineteenth century, editions of the work have called the author, erroneously, 'Dionysius Cato'.

2. 'Of Utica' (Lat. Uticensis), 95–46 BC, great-grandson of Cato (1), a man of unbending Stoic principles and absolute integrity, who was impelled by his devotion to the Roman tradition and his desire to emulate the virtue of his great-grandfather to support senatorial government and the republican cause. He was influential in persuading the senate to execute Catiline's fellow-conspirators in 63 BC (see CICERO (1) 2), accusing Julius Caesar of being an accomplice, and was the chief antagonist of the so-called 'first triumvirate' of Caesar, Pompey, and Crassus. He was so much of an annoyance to them that they arranged for Clodius to propose a law which sent him away to annex Cyprus. After his return Cato continued to oppose the triumvirs, and when Pompey became sole consul in 52 Cato felt that Pompey had abandoned republican principles. He withdrew from public life and, after the civil war began in 49, despaired of Rome. Nevertheless he held Sicily for the senate. When Caesar's supporter Curio landed, he withdrew to join Pompey, but was not present at the battle of Pharsalus. He proceeded to Africa, where his march around the Great Syrtis (gulf of Sirte) became famous as a feat of endurance. There he heard of Pompey's death and, subsequently, of Caesar's victory over the senatorial party at Thapsus. All Africa, except Utica, surrendered to Caesar, and Cato, after seeing to the safety of his friends, committed suicide, having spent the previous night reading Plato's *Phaedo*. One letter of his survives in Cicero's correspondence, civilly refusing to use his influence in procuring Cicero a triumph. His death conferred its own nobility on the losing republican side, to inspire Romans with a republican ideal long after republicanism was dead. Virgil in the *Aeneid* (book 8) makes him a judge in Elysium.

cats, see PETS.

Catu'llus, Gaius Vale'rius, *c.*84–*c.*54 BC, Roman poet, born in Verona, son of a wealthy man whose acquaintances included Julius Caesar. As a young man he went to Rome and joined the fashionable literary circle (see NEOTER-ICS), addressing poems to Cicero, Cornelius Nepos, and Hortensius among others, and freely insulting Caesar and Mamurra. Very little is known of his life except what can be gleaned from his poems: that he spent a year (57 to 56) with his friend *Cinna in Bithynia on the staff of the governor, Gaius *Memmius; that he saw his brother's grave in the Troad; that he returned from abroad to a villa at Sirmio on Lake Garda. At Rome he fell in love with a married woman of some social standing whom he calls Lesbia, but whose real name was probably *Clodia, the sister of P. Clodius Pulcher and the wife of Q. Metellus Celer. Some poems suggest that she deserted Catullus for Cicero's young protégé *Caelius. Catullus addressed twenty-five poems to Lesbia which chronicle his love affair from an idyllic beginning to final disillusionment.

His poems fall into three groups. 1–60 are short pieces, in hendecasyllables or other lyric metres (iambics, scazons, and in one case glyconics; see METRE). They are varied in subject and manner, embracing incidents of daily life, expressions of friendship, satires political lampoons, love poems, even a hymn to Diana; poem 51 is a translation of an extant poem by the Greek poet Sappho. This collection was for the most part made by the author and shows traces of a careful arrangement. The second group, 61–64, are longer poems: 61 is an epithalamium for a friend, 62 another wedding song, 63 an extraordinary metrical feat, a poem in galliambics (see METRE, LATIN 3 (iii) d) on the legend of Attis, a young man who, in religious frenzy for the goddess Cybelē, emasculates himself and lives to regret it; 64 is an *epyllion on the marriage of Peleus and Thetis, consisting mostly of a digression on the story of Ariadne. The first four poems of the third group, 65–68, are longer elegiac poems, 66 being a translation of *Callimachus' poem, *The Lock of *Berenice*; 69–116 form a sequence of epigrams in elegiacs on a wide range of subjects. The second and third groups of poems were perhaps collected and arranged by an editor. The first and third groups both contain love poems, expressing happiness and disillusionment, and witty and malicious occasional poems, but the poems of the third group are not perhaps so adventurous or experimental; they express the poet's feelings in more traditional Roman terms. Groups one and two were more obviously written under the influence of Hellenistic Greek poetry in racy, often erudite language (the blend of the fashionable colloquial and the obscure is peculiarly Catullus' own), sometimes ingeniously fitted to metres hitherto purely Greek. Catullus was the leading figure among the new poets of the day who were looking for inspiration not to past Romans but to the Greeks, both to the learned, polished poets of the Hellenistic age and to the more direct lyric poets of earlier centuries, such as Sappho. Part of his appeal lies in his versatility, but it is as a love poet that he is chiefly remembered. He was the first ancient poet to describe the progress of one deeply felt love affair, and in this he exerted a wide influence on his successors, on Tibullus, Propertius, and Ovid and others whose works are lost. We are fortunate to have his poems, for they nearly perished. The three manuscripts in which they are preserved are descended from the only text of the poems known to have survived into the fourteenth century. See TEXTS, TRANSMISSION OF ANCIENT 6.

Ca'tulus, Quintus Lutā'tius, Roman consul in 102 BC with *Marius and joint victor over the Cimbri in 101 BC, also with Marius. Catulus, resentful of his colleague's greater reputation, became one of his chief opponents. When Marius and Cinna captured Rome in 87 BC they not surprisingly proscribed him (see PROSCRIPTION), and he committed suicide. He was a cultured man, a competent orator—Cicero introduced him into his *De oratore*—and a writer of epigrams, two of which survive. His son of the same name is an interlocutor in Cicero's *Academica*.

Catuvellau'ni, the most powerful tribe in south-east Britain at the time of Julius Caesar's invasions, ruled by *Cassivellaunus. See BRITAIN 2.

Caudine Forks (Furculae Caudīnae), the defile of Caudium in Samnium where the Roman army in 321 BC was obliged to surrender to the Samnites (see ROME 4). The site has never been certainly identified.

cavalry, see HORSES and *CAVALRY COMMANDER* below.

Cavalry Commander, The (*Hipparchikos*), a treatise by the Athenian *Xenophon on the duties of a cavalry commander, perhaps written *c.*357 BC. As a young aristocrat Xenophon had been a member of the cavalry and was particularly interested in horses (see also his treatise, *HORSEMANSHIP*). The Athenian cavalry contained one thousand horsemen, one hundred from each of the ten tribes, under two commanders. Xenophon addresses himself to someone about to hold one of these commands. He gives advice on the selection and training of the recruits, the care of the horses, the choice of subordinate officers, the qualities required of a commander, and his duties both in the ceremonial functions of the cavalry and on active service (including tactics, ruses, etc.).

Cēbēs, of Thebes, a Pythagorean philosopher and associate of Socrates who plays an important part in the discussions in Plato's *Phaedo. In the *Crito he is one of those who are prepared to help Socrates escape from prison. An allegorical composition on the life of man, known as the *Pinax* ('picture') of Cebes, has been wrongly ascribed to him.

Cecrops, the mythical first king of Athens, sprung from the earth (i.e. aboriginal) and represented as serpent-shaped below the waist. The state of Attica was sometimes called Cecropia after him. By Aglaurus he had three daughters (for their story see ERICHTHONIUS). The contest between Athena and *Poseidon for possession of Attica took place in his reign, and in some accounts he was the judge, awarding the land to Athena.

Celae'no. 1. One of the *Pleiades. 2. One of the *Harpies.

Ce'lĕus, see DEMETER.

Celsus. 1. **Aulus** or **Aurelius Cornelius Celsus,** Roman encyclopaedist of whom very little is known. He lived in the reign of the emperor Tiberius (AD 14–37). Of his encyclopaedia, *Artes* ('arts'), eight books, on medicine, survive. After giving a brief history of medicine, which is important for reconstructing Hellenistic doctrines, he surveys the whole field of medical science as it was known at Rome in his day, but without adhering to any one school.

Consideration of diet and of the general principles of treatment are followed by a survey of diseases, classified as internal or external, and their treatment, and a discussion of pharmaceutical preparations; the final two books deal with diseases that are to be remedied by surgery, perhaps the most interesting and advanced part of the work. Much of the practice described was not superseded until the nineteenth century. Celsus' book was largely unknown until it was rediscovered and printed in the fifteenth century, from which time it became immensely popular, in part because of the simple and elegant style of the Latin in which it was written.

2. Greek-speaking Platonist philosopher of the second century AD who wrote the first comprehensive attack on Christianity; large parts of it survive in *Origen's reply, *Contra Celsum* ('against Celsus').

Celts, term used by ancient and modern writers to describe a population group occupying in prehistoric and historic times lands mainly north of the Mediterannean, from the Spanish peninsula and the British Isles in the west to Galatia in central Asia Minor (see GALATIANS). Their unity can be recognized from the fact that they had a common speech, evinced in place-names, and from a common artistic style. It is generally thought that the Celts spread from the region of the Upper Danube during the Bronze Age. Celtic tribes invading from across the Rhine and settling in Gaul came to be known themselves as Gauls. Hence the invaders of Italy who sacked Rome in *c.*370 BC and who entered the Balkans and raided Delphi in 279 BC and crossed the Hellespont in 278 are referred to either as Celts or as Gauls. The latter gave their name to the territory of Galatia, where Celtic was still spoken in the fifth century AD. The Celts in Europe were overrun by invading Germans crossing the Rhine from the third century BC onwards and by the migrations of the Cimbri and Teutones soon after 120 BC, and so they withdrew from Bohemia and south Germany. They were also conquered by Rome in the Gallic wars and some, e.g. the Belgae, became assimilated to their invaders.

censors, magistrates at Rome, two in number, who were elected every five years but held office for eighteen months only, in order to take the census, i.e. make up the official list of citizens and carry out the solemn purification, *lustrum*, which concluded it and which gave its name to the interval of five years between each purification. The registration of citizens took place in a special building on the Campus Martius. The censors exercised a general supervision over the conduct of citizens, but their power and prestige derived from their duty of revising the roll of senators, removing those who had acted against law and morality and replacing them by others.

They also had the duty of making contracts for public works and for the farming of taxes, and of leasing state lands. Throughout the middle and late republic the censorship stood at the head of the *cursus honorum*, but its authority was reduced by the legislation of *Sulla. The emperors tended to take censorial powers upon themselves to revise the composition of the senate (see CENSUS below).

census, register of citizens prepared at Rome since the time of the kings for the purposes of taxation and military service. The citizens were registered in tribes and distributed in five classes according to their wealth; each class was divided into *seniores*, those over the age of forty-five and usually beyond military service, and *iuniores*. A census was normally held every few years, but in the later republic the practice lapsed. It was revived by the emperor Augustus, who extended it to the provinces, the inhabitants supplying information about their property essential for the equitable levying of taxes.

centaurs, in Greek myth, a race of creatures with the body and legs of a horse but the chest, head, and arms of a man, said to be the offspring of *Ixion and Nephelē ('cloud'). They lived on Mount Pelion in Thessaly, and symbolized for the Greeks the appetites of animal nature and perhaps barbarism. When their neighbours the Lapiths were holding a feast for the wedding of their king Pirithous with Hippodamia, and invited the centaurs, the latter tried to carry off Hippodamia and other women; this event is depicted in the Parthenon metopes and on the temple of Zeus at Olympia. The centaurs were routed and driven from Thessaly to the Peloponnese. Individual centaurs have myths of their own; see NESSUS, PHOLUS, and CHIRON.

centu'mviri, 'the hundred men', at Rome, a special civil court numbering in fact 105 men during the republic, three from each of the thirty-five tribes, and increased under the empire to 180; these sat as jury for certain trials, mostly relating, it seems, to property and inheritance. Under the empire they were divided into four courts which usually sat separately but might sit as a single body in important suits.

centu'ria, 'century', the smallest unit of the Roman legion containing nominally one hundred men; each legion comprised sixty centuries divided into thirty maniples or, later, ten cohorts. According to tradition, Servius Tullius founded a new political assembly based on the centuries (see COMITIA).

centurion, the highest-ranking professional officer in the Roman army (compare LEGATI and TRIBUNI MILITUM), who commanded a 'century' (see CENTURIA). Every cohort had six centurions, each with his own title.

Ce'phalas, see ANTHOLOGY I.

Ce'phalus. 1. In Greek myth, the husband of Procris, daughter of Erechtheus. Eos ('dawn') fell in love with him, causing dissension between husband and wife. Artemis (or Minos) gave Procris a hound which always caught its quarry and a spear which never missed its mark; these Procris gave to Cephalus and a reconciliation followed. But Eos made Procris jealous of the time Cephalus spent hunting. Procris hid in a bush to watch him and he, thinking that he heard an animal stir in the bush, hurled his spear and killed her. These two are 'Shafalus' and 'Procrus' in the Pyramus and Thisbe scene of Shakespeare's *A Midsummer Night's Dream*.

2. The old man in Book I of Plato's *Republic*, the father of the Attic orator *Lysias.

Cēphī'sus or **Cephissus.** 1. The main river of the plain of Athens, rising in Mount Parnes, flowing past Athens about 3 km. (2 miles) to the west and into the bay of Phalerum. Its clay bed provided the material for Athenian pottery.

2. The main river of Phocis and Boeotia, emptying into the lake Copaïs.

Ceramī'cus (Kerameikos), the potters' quarter at Athens, an area north-west of the Acropolis. When the Themistoclean city wall was built this quarter was divided into the Inner and Outer Ceramicus. The part outside the walls was used as a burial ground; the agora was included in the inner part.

Ce'rberus, in Greek myth, monstrous dog guarding the entrance to the Underworld, the offspring of *Typhon and *Echidna. He had three (or fifty) heads and a mane or tail of snakes. As one of the labours imposed on him by Eurystheus, Heracles dragged Cerberus out of the Underworld, showed him to Eurystheus, and then returned him. Aeneas on his descent was told to drug him with a specially prepared cake: hence the expression 'a sop to Cerberus'.

Ce'rcidas, *c.*290–*c.*220 BC, Greek poet and statesman from Megalopolis in Arcadia of whose poems only seven fragments survive. They come from the *Meliambi*, a title Cercidas invented to describe satirical poems in lyric metre. He seems to have been hostile to the tyranny at Megalopolis in his own day, and achieved fame as a lawgiver. He was strongly influenced by the *Cynic school of philosophy.

Cercō'pes, in Greek myth, a pair of monkey-like dwarves whose mother Theia told them to beware of a certain Melampyges ('black-buttocks'). *Heracles caught them trying to steal his armour and slung them upside down from a pole borne across his shoulders. They found themselves staring straight at his buttocks, covered with black hair, and thus understood the warning. Their jokes at his hairiness so amused Heracles that he let them go.

Cērēs, an Italian divinity representing the generative power of nature, in later times identified with the Greek *Demeter. In cult she was associated with *Tellus, the earth-goddess. Her worship at Rome was very ancient, as is clear from the existence of a *flamen cerialis and the occurrence of the festival of the Cerialia (held on 19 April) in the calendars, but very little is known of it. Her most famous cult was that on the Aventine hill at Rome. In 496 BC under the stress of famine the Sibylline books were consulted and recommended the introduction of the worship of the Greek gods Demeter, Korē, and Iacchus, to be identified with the Roman Ceres, Liber, and Libera. The temple was completed in 493 and became a centre of plebeian activities. Games were instituted which became a prominent feature of the Cerialia. Little is known about the ritual of the festival, except the peculiar custom of tying lighted brands to the tails of a number of foxes which were then let loose in the Circus Maximus. As a deity of the earth Ceres also received sacrifice after a funeral, as a means of purifying the house of the deceased.

Cēto, in Greek myth, daughter of Pontus (Sea) and Gaia (Earth) and mother of the *Graiae and the *Gorgons.

Cē'yx, in Greek myth, husband of *Alcyonē.

Chae'reas and Calli'rrhŏē, title of a Greek *novel by Chariton.

Chaeronē'a (Khairōneia), in Boeotia, the scene of the defeat of the Thebans and Athenians by *Philip II of Macedon in 338 BC, commemorated by the erection of a large stone lion; by whom or when is not known. The lion was smashed in the Greek War of Independence (1821–2) and restored in the late nineteenth century. Under it were found the bones of some two hundred and fifty-four men, perhaps of the *Sacred Band. Chaeronea was also the scene of the defeat of Mithridates by Sulla in 86 BC, and the birthplace of Plutarch.

Chalcē'don, Megarian colony on the Asiatic side of the Bosporus opposite Byzantium, called by the Delphic Oracle 'the city of the blind' because its colonizers missed the then unoccupied and superior site of Byzantium across the channel. See COLONIZATION, GREEK 3.

Chalci'dicē, promontory in Macedonia between the Thermaic and Strymonic Gulfs terminating in three smaller peninsulas. It was first colonized by Chalcis in the eighth century BC.

Chalci'dic League. The cities of *Chalcidicē, revolting from the *Delian League and Athenian imperialism in 432 BC, formed a Chalcidic League with a common capital at *Olynthus. The member cities shared common citizenship and laws, and circulated their own coins. In the 380s the League expanded to embrace part of Macedonia including the capital Pella, and its ambitions grew to include its less willing neighbours, by force if necessary. Sparta, asked to intervene by some of the threatened cities, forced the League to capitulate in 379 and become subordinate allies. If the Chalcidic League had survived it might have been a check on the growth of Macedonian power. The Chalcidians soon joined a league with Athens, but Athenian activity in the 360s, aimed ultimately at regaining possession of Amphipolis (an independent city in that area, formerly an Athenian colony but lost after the Peloponnesian War), alienated Olynthus and the other Chalcidian cities. Philip II of Macedon reduced these cities in the 350s, and Olynthus, the last to hold out, was completely destroyed in 348 BC despite some Athenian help. See also DEMOSTHENES (2) 4.

Chalcis, chief city in Euboea, on its west coast, and separated from the mainland of Greece only by the narrow strait of the Euripus. It was an important link with trading routes from Greece to the east in the eighth century BC. During this century (probably) it fought with neighbouring Eretria for possession of the Lelantine Plain. Chalcis planted colonies in Italy, Sicily, and the north Aegean and became a great manufacturing and trading city, but was subject to Athens during the greater part of the fifth and fourth centuries BC.

Chāos ('gaping void'), in Greek mythical cosmogony the first created being. It was scarcely personified at all but was that out of which came the primeval deities Gaia (Earth), Tartarus, Erebus (Darkness), and Nyx (Night).

Charactē'rĕs, see THEOPHRASTUS.

Chara'xus, brother of *Sappho.

Chārēs, c.400–c.325 BC, famous Athenian general and commander of naval operations, notably against Philip II of Macedon. His troops were mercenaries whose pay he had to find himself. He fought at *Chaeronea and continued to hold commands until his death.

Chariclē'a and Theā'genēs, alternative title of the novel *Aethiopica* by Heliodorus. See NOVEL 1.

chariot-races. There were chariot-races in the panhellenic *festivals in Greece from early times. The chariot was two-wheeled and resembled those described by Homer which were used to carry the warrior and his charioteer to the battle line, low and rounded in the front, open at the back, on low wheels. The *Linear B tablets from Cnossus (in Crete) indicate that chariots were a regular part of military equipment at that time.

They are described as decorated and painted, inlaid with ivory and fitted with bronze or even silver, the wheels made of elm or willow. A military chariot was usually drawn by two horses, one on each side of the pole, by means of a yoke. The traditional date on which racing chariots with four horses first competed at Olympia is 680 BC. The extra horses were commonly harnessed one to each side of the yoked horses by means of traces. Pausanias describes an elaborate arrangement for starting the chariot-race at Olympia, where it was the opening event, inaugurating the games in a blaze of splendour. The chariots were placed in an arrowhead formation; to compensate those at the outer edges with further to travel, a staggered start was arranged by releasing ropes in sequence, beginning with those at the outer edge. The start was signalled by trumpet calls and a device which raised a bronze eagle and lowered a bronze dolphin. The largest number of chariots known to have entered for a Greek chariot-race is forty-one: only one finished. The course of the hippodrome at Olympia, which was typical, was flat and marked by a starting line at least 250 m. (275 yds.) wide and two turning posts, one at each end, but had no barrier between the up and the down lanes; the two turning posts were about 400 m. (440 yds.) apart. The race was twelve laps long, almost 10 km. (6 miles). The fame of winning a chariot-race in Greece belonged not to the charioteer but to the owner. It was thus possible for a woman to win the event; the first to do so at Olympia was Cynisca, sister of king *Agesilaus of Sparta, in 396 and 392 BC.

The Roman chariot-races, which the Romans instituted in imitation of the Greek, came to be one of the great entertainments of the Roman world. The Roman racing chariot was similar to the Greek, except that the board forming the front was higher. Chariot-races began at Rome in republican times and were held in the Circus Maximus, where the lanes were divided by a low wall known as the *spina*. They competed in heats of seven laps, usually six chariots at a time. (For the method of starting the races at Rome see CIRCUS.) In republican times the chariots belonged to wealthy individuals (as they did in Greece). Under the Roman empire they belonged to associations of contractors who were distinguished by colours, red and white at first, later blue and green as well. The emperor Domitian added purple and gold, but these colours seem not to have lasted beyond his reign. There was keen partisanship among the public and betting on the colours. Successful charioteers earned huge sums of money. Pliny tells how Caecina of Volaterrae, a chariot owner, had homing swallows, daubed with paint, to announce his victories. In the later empire the people frequently expressed their disapproval of the government by supporting and cheering the colours which were not favoured by the emperor or his officials (see JUSTINIAN).

Cha'rites (sing. Charis), see GRACES.

Cha'riton, author of a Greek novel, *Chaereas and Callirhoe*; see NOVEL I.

Cha'rmidēs, title of a dialogue by *Plato in which Charmides plays a large part. He was from an aristocratic Athenian family, cousin of Critias, uncle of Plato, and friend of Socrates. He took part in the oligarchic revolution of 404 BC and died with Critias fighting against Thrasybulus in 403.

Chāron. 1. In Greek myth, the ferryman who conveyed the dead in his boat across the river Styx to their final abode in the Underworld, provided they had received the proper rites of burial and paid the fare (an obol, placed in the mouth of the corpse). He is unknown to Homer, but is mentioned by Aeschylus, and plays memorable parts in the *Frogs* of Aristophanes and book 6 of Virgil's *Aeneid*.
   2. Of Lampsacus, see LOGOGRAPHERS (1).

Chary'bdis, in Greek legend, a whirlpool in a narrow channel of water, traditionally sited in the Straits of Messina. Homer (*Odyssey* 12) pictured it as a female monster, daughter of Poseidon and Gaia, who sucked in seawater and spewed it out three times a day. The equally dangerous *Scylla was on the opposite shore, so that Odysseus had to decide which to avoid as he sailed between them. The two have become proverbial to describe equally unpleasant alternatives.

Cheiron, see CHIRON.

Che'rsonese (chersonēsos, 'peninsula'). 1. Thracian Chersonese (Gallipoli), projecting into the north-east of the Aegean Sea, separated from Asia Minor by the Hellespont. It was important as a wheat-growing district and more especially because it lay on a main route between Europe and Asia and so controlled the corn-supply from the Crimea. It was acquired by the elder *Miltiades *c.*560 BC and remained a family possession until the younger Miltiades abandoned it to the Persians in 493 BC. After the Persian Wars the Athenians planted *cleruchies there. It was threatened by *Philip II of Macedon, and this threat was one of the chief grounds of hostility between Athens and Macedon. It was finally ceded to Philip in 338 BC.
   2. Tauric Chersonese, in the Black Sea, the modern Crimea.

Chersonese, On the, political speech by Demosthenes. See DEMOSTHENES (2) 4.

chīa'smus (from the form of the Greek letter chi, X), figure of speech in which the terms in the second of two parallel phrases are in reverse order to the corresponding terms in the first;

e.g. odit *populus Romanus* privatam *luxuriam*, publicam *magnificentiam* diligit (Cicero, *Pro Murena* 32): 'The Roman people *hate* private luxury but *public* display they *love*.'

Chīlon, *ephor at Sparta in 536 BC, famous for his wisdom. His exact contribution to the political life of sixth-century Sparta is uncertain but he may have helped to extend Spartan influence through the *Peloponnesian League. He was included among the *Seven Sages of Greece.

Chīmaera, in Greek myth, a fire-breathing monster with the head of a lion, body of a she-goat, and tail of a snake, the offspring of *Typhon and *Echidna. It was killed by *Bellerophon, mounted on the winged horse Pegasus.

Chīos, large island in the Aegean Sea off the coast of Asia Minor, settled by Greeks from Ionia. It became part of the Persian empire under Cyrus in the sixth century BC and its citizens fought bravely in the unsuccessful Ionian revolt against Persia in the 490s. As a member of the *Delian League it remained loyal to Athens until 413 BC. At its defection, Athens laid waste the island but failed to take the city. It was allied to Athens again in the first half of the fourth century BC, but again revolted and regained its independence in 354. The island was famed in antiquity for its wine and figs, and had a distinguished literary tradition, claiming to be the birthplace of Homer; see HOMERIDAE.

Chīron (Kheirōn), in Greek myth, a *centaur, but, unlike the others, the son of Philyra and Cronus; he owed his shape, half man and half horse, to the fact that Cronus assumed the shape of a horse when he approached Philyra so as to escape the jealous notice of his wife Rhea. In consequence Chiron's nature was different from that of the other centaurs; he was wise and kind, and instructed by Apollo and Artemis he was skilled in medicine, music, hunting, and the art of prophecy. He became the tutor of some of the most famous of the Greek heroes, Asclepius, Jason, and Achilles. He was the grandfather (through his daughter Endeis) of Peleus, saving him by restoring his sword when he was abandoned weaponless by Acastus on Mount Pelion, the Thessalian home of the centaurs. Chiron also helped him to win his bride Thetis. Like the other centaurs he was driven out of Thessaly into the Peloponnese by the Lapiths. When Heracles came in pursuit of the Erymanthian boar and was involved in a fight with the centaurs, one of his poisoned arrows scratched Chiron. Although immortal Chiron suffered great pain and, wishing to live no longer, transferred his immortality to the Titan Prometheus. Zeus set him in the sky as the constellation Centaurus.

chitōn, tunic worn next to the skin by the Greeks. See DRESS 1.

chlamys, short cloak worn by Greek horsemen, soldiers, etc. See DRESS 1.

Chloris, see FLORA.

Chŏē'phoroe or *Chŏē'phori* (Khŏēphoroi), 'Libation Bearers', the second tragedy in the *Oresteia* trilogy by Aeschylus.

Choe'rilus. 1. Of Athens, a tragic poet who wrote plays from *c*.523 BC onwards and competed against Aeschylus in the drama festivals. Virtually nothing else is known of him. See TRAGEDY 1.
2. Of Samos, an epic poet contemporary with Alexander the Great. See EPIC 1.

choĕs, see ANTHESTERIA.

chōlia'mbic (or scazon), in metre, the so-called 'limping iambic' line in which the penultimate syllable, short in an iambic line, is long (see METRE, GREEK 5 (iii)).

choral lyric, see LYRIC POETRY 1.

chorē'gia, at Athens, a form of *liturgy or public service in which individual wealthy citizens were expected to bear the expense of providing a chorus for one or other of the various lyric and dramatic contests (at the *Panathenaea, *Thargelia, *Dionysia, and *Lenaea), and hence were known as *choregoi.* The expense was considerable: in 405 BC, when Athens was seriously impoverished by the Peloponnesian War, *choregia* at the Great Dionysia was shared between two *choregoi. Choregoi* chose the members of their chorus and paid for their costumes, training, and rehearsal room. It was a misfortune for a *choregos* to be assigned to a bad poet, and equally for a poet to have a mean *choregos*; a generous one might procure a victory by putting on an impressive spectacle. The assigning was probably done by drawing lots. The prize for the winning *choregos* in the *dithyrambic contest was a tripod which was then dedicated to the god; in Athens the 'street of the tripods' (*hoi tripodĕs*) was named from these dedications which lined the street.

chŏ'riamb, in *metre, the metron $-\cup\cup-$.

chorodida'skalos, in Athens, the trainer of a chorus performing in one of the various lyric and dramatic contests, usually the poet himself. See CHOREGIA.

chŏrus (*chŏros,* 'dance'). In Greece the dance was an important part of public religious ceremonies, performed by a troupe to whom the name 'chorus' was also given. By archaic times the chorus sang as well as danced in performances of choral *lyric poetry, usually under a leader. As well as this the chorus had a role in tragedy and comedy. It is generally believed that Attic tragedy had its origin in the kind of choral lyric known as the dithyramb, sung and danced in honour of the god Dionysus (see TRAGEDY 1), and that comedy likewise developed out of the cheerfully insulting songs sung by bands of revellers as they accompanied the *phallus in Dionysiac processions (see COMEDY, GREEK 2). If this is the case, the fact that the chorus continued to play an important role in all fifth-century drama is entirely natural. The chorus sings the lyric passages (which are themselves referred to as 'the choruses') to flute accompaniment. Like the actors the chorus was masked (as in Dionysiac ritual). In tragedy it always performed in character as a group of people involved in the action; the chorus-leader, known as the *coryphaeus* or *hēgemon,* is sometimes made to converse briefly with the characters. Sophocles was said to have raised the number of the tragic chorus from twelve to fifteen, as it remained thereafter. It entered the *orchestra* (see DIONYSUS, THEATRE OF) on the audience's right in quadrangular form, three or five abreast. The chorus-leader stood in the middle of the row nearest to the audience; sometimes this role was taken by the *choregos* (see CHOREGIA). The chorus in Old Comedy comprised twenty-four members and was of central importance, the characters represented often giving the play its name, e.g. *Frogs* and *Wasps,* and their entry being a high point in the play. They threw off their assumed character in part at least of the *parabasis* (see COMEDY, GREEK 3 (iv)) and addressed the audience on behalf of the poet. After the fifth century the role of the chorus in tragedy and especially in comedy became much reduced: in Middle and New Comedy its role became entirely non-dramatic, and a song from a chorus (not included in the text of the play) became merely a device for dividing one act from the next. The Roman adaptations of Greek tragedy and the comedies of Plautus and Terence did not include a chorus.

Chremōnidē'an War. The Athenian nationalist statesman Chremonidēs carried a decree, probably in 266 BC, by which Athens joined the Peloponnesian anti-Macedonian coalition and led a revolt against Macedon and its ruler Antigonus Gonatas. Athens was besieged and surrendered in 262 BC. See ATHENS 2 (vi).

Chrēstoma'thia, see PROCLUS.

Christianity in the Roman world. Christians first became known to the Romans as a troublesome Jewish sect. Suetonius writing in the early years of the second century AD about the reign of the emperor Claudius (AD 41–54) describes them causing continuous disturbances in Rome. Tacitus' earlier reference to the originator of their sect, Christus, being executed by Pontius Pilate in Tiberius' reign (AD 14–37) is the only mention in pagan Latin literature of Pilate's role.

The Jews had been allies of Rome since they had fought the *Seleucids together in the second century BC. Moreover the Jews were an ancient people, and for both reasons they were legally entitled to follow their national religion. Tolerance of their religion persisted, and was safeguarded by legislation even when relations between Rome and the increasingly nationalistic Jews deteriorated towards the end of the first century BC, and became still worse after AD 6 when Judaea was made a Roman province. The Christians, regarded by the Romans no differently from the Jews, benefited from this official tolerance, as is shown in the Acts of the Apostles. But the Jews in general were implacably hostile to the Christians and anxious to embroil them with the authorities. After the burning of Rome in AD 64, Nero found the Christians convenient scapegoats for the fire. Although the official Roman attitude towards Jews and Christians underwent no change for another century, the mutual hostility between the two increased as well as that of the general pagan public to both, which resulted in intermittent persecution in various parts of Asia (reflected in the book of Revelation). It was from Bithynia in Asia in AD 112 that the Roman governor, the Younger Pliny, wrote his famous letter to the emperor Trajan asking how he was to deal with the Christians. It is clear that at this time Christians had to behave provocatively before official notice was taken of them, and also that many of them were not unwilling to be martyred. By the end of this century, however, thoughtful pagans saw Christianity not merely as a nuisance to the state but as a threat to its safety and stability. Christians seemed bound together by mysterious ties into secret societies to which they owed more loyalty than to the state. Since traditional Roman religion was in the nature of a contract between men and gods, by which the gods protected Rome as long as they received their due worship, some token participation in pagan religious ceremonies was one of the demands made of the Christians by the Roman government. By refusing to take part the Christians evinced not only that irritating 'obstinacy' for which they were notorious but disloyalty to Rome.

During the latter part of the second century a coherent Christian creed was beginning to emerge, and a case for Christianity could be stated to pagan intellectuals. In the third century it seems that some pagans attempted to absorb the Christian God into their pantheon: the emperor Alexander Severus (AD 222–35) is said to have kept in his private chapel, and paid equal reverence to, statues of Orpheus, Abraham, Christ, and *Apollonius of Tyana. The end of his reign marked the end of a long period of official toleration of Christians. The emperor

Decius (249–51) initiated the first systematic attempt to exterminate them, at a time when a united effort was needed to repel the barbarians pressing on the frontiers, and the now numerous Christians were feared as a dissident force. On the death of Decius in 251 this persecution collapsed but subsequent emperors, Valerian and Gallienus, revived the attacks, the worst in the western empire being that of 258–9. The last serious attempt by the government to suppress Christianity was that of Diocletian in 303 (see EUSEBIUS), but he forbade the killing of Christians; they were in any case now too numerous in the countryside as well as in the towns for any measure he took to be successful. Persecution of Christians ended in the West with his abdication in 305, though it dragged on in the East until 311 when Galerius granted them religious toleration. In 313 *Constantine issued certain regulations in favour of Christians, known as the Edict of Milan, and in 325 at the Council of Nicaea Christianity became in effect the religion of the Roman empire. The attempt by the emperor *Julian (360–3) to restore paganism was short-lived, and the pious *Theodosius I (emperor 378–95) gave the final endorsement to Constantine's espousal of Christianity. He listened with favour to petitions for the conversion of pagan temples to churches and turned a blind eye to attacks on them. The pagan rhetor *Libanius complained bitterly about the destruction of rural shrines around Antioch by bands of marauding monks. In 391 Theodosius laid a total ban on all pagan cult (though not on pagan belief). Although for nearly a century after some still hoped that a pagan emperor might arise to restore the old religion, this ban was never lifted.

For the spread of Christianity in Britain see BRITAIN 9.

Chro'nica, see NEPOS, EUSEBIUS, and JEROME.

chroniclers. For Greek, see LOGOGRAPHERS; for Roman see ANNALS.

chronology, see CALENDARS.

Chrȳsā'or ('golden sword'), in Greek myth, the (perhaps monstrous) son of Poseidon and the *Gorgon Medusa, and brother of the winged horse Pegasus; the brothers sprang from the blood spilt when Perseus decapitated Medusa. Chrysaor married Callirhoē and became the father of Geryon and Echidna.

Chrȳsē'is, in Homer's Iliad, the daughter of Chrȳsēs, priest of Apollo on the island of Chrȳsē near Troy. When the Greeks sacked the island they gave her to Agamemnon as his gift of honour. He took her as his concubine, declaring that he preferred her to his wife Clytemnestra, and refused the rich ransom offered by Chryses. Chryses prayed to Apollo, and after the Greeks suffered in consequence nine days of pestilence

Agamemnon agreed to return Chryseis on condition that he should receive in compensation the girl Briseis who had been given as a prize of war to Achilles. Hence arose the anger of Achilles, one of the main themes of the *Iliad*.

chryselepha'ntine ('of gold and ivory'), term used to describe certain Greek statues made of wood overlaid with gold and ivory, such as *Pheidias' statue of Athena in the Parthenon.

Chrȳsi'ppus, *c*.280–207 BC, Greek *Stoic philosopher. He became head of the Stoa in succession to *Cleanthes by whom he was converted to Stoicism after being educated at the Academy under the *Sceptic Arcesilaus. His voluminous writings (now lost) gave Stoicism coherence and logic, and became recognized as Stoic orthodoxy.

Chrȳsŏ'themis, see ELECTRA (1).

Ci'cero. 1. Marcus Tu'llius Cicero, 106–43 BC, Roman orator and statesman.

1. *Early life, 106–64 BC.* Cicero was born on 3 January 106 at Arpinum (Arpino) in the Volscian mountains some 110 km. (70 miles) south-east of Rome, the elder of two sons of a wealthy *eques*, the family being distantly related to the general Gaius *Marius. His early promise suggested a career as advocate and politician, and he was sent to Rome to study law under the two great lawyer-politicians of the day, the *Scaevolas (3 and 4), as well as philosophy under Philo, the former head of the Academy at Athens, and Diodotus the Stoic. At the age of 17 Cicero saw military service in the *Social War, serving under Pompeius Strabo, the father of *Pompey the Great, who was Cicero's exact contemporary and whose acquaintance Cicero probably made at this time. Throughout his life Cicero was to remain a supporter of Pompey, seeing him as the one man who could save Rome from external enemies and internal lawlessness while preserving the republican constitution. Also serving under Strabo was the young *Catiline (see 2 below). During the turbulent eighties Cicero completed his forensic education. His earliest surviving speech is *Pro Quinctio* of 81, a complicated partnership case of which the result is unknown, but we know that the opposing advocate was Hortensius, the greatest orator of the day. Cicero's reputation was established in the following year (80) by his successful defence of Roscius of Ameria (*Pro Roscio Amerino*) on a charge of parricide. Both speeches had a political aspect; in the latter Cicero courageously attacked Sulla's powerful freedman Chrysogonus. At this point (79) Cicero left Rome to spend two years abroad to improve his health and pursue his studies under the Greek masters of rhetoric and philosophy. At Athens he studied with another young Roman, Titus Pomponius *Atticus, who was to become his lifelong friend and, since Atticus spent most of his life away

from Rome, his most valued correspondent (see 7 below). In Rhodes Cicero visited *Posidonius, the great scholar and Stoic philosopher.

At about this time, either before he left for Greece or soon after his return in 77, he married his wife Terentia. Perhaps to this period after his return belongs his defence of his friend the comic actor Roscius (*Pro Roscio comoedo*). In 76 he was elected quaestor at the minimum age (of 30), as with every subsequent office he held, and so qualified for membership of the senate, remaining a member until his death. He served his quaestorship (75) at Lilybaeum (Marsala) in west Sicily; after his return to Rome in 74 he never willingly left Italy again (but see 4), refusing provincial governorships both after his praetorship and after his consulship. In the next few years he was occupied with legal work in the courts, particularly on behalf of the *equites*, through which he gained wealth and eventually political support. The (fragmentary) speech *Pro Tullio* may have been delivered in 72; in it Cicero defends a man with the same family name as his own in a boundary dispute with a veteran of Sulla's army. His reputation was unshakeably established in 70 with his brilliant prosecution of C. *Verres, the corrupt governor of Sicily from 73 to 71, at the request of the Sicilians. First Cicero had to defend his right to act as prosecutor (which he did successfully) against the claim of Q. Caecilius, who would have colluded with Verres (Cicero's speech on this occasion is the *Divinatio in Q. Caecilium*). Verres was defended by the famous Hortensius, but the latter was never called upon to speak: after Cicero's first speech for the prosecution (*actio prima*) Verres threw up the case and retired into exile in Massilia (Marseilles). Cicero's immense labours in gathering evidence for this case were not to be wasted; he published as well as his first speech the five long sections that were to comprise the *actio secunda* ('second stage' of the trial), and they made his reputation as Rome's leading advocate and fearless opponent of corruption. This was the year (70) in which the consuls Pompey and *Crassus broke down the Sullan constitution, by restoring to the tribunes their full political powers and taking away from the senate the right to control legislation and the law courts. In his speeches Cicero made it clear that he supported Pompey and the cause of reform.

In 69 Cicero became aedile, and to this year belong two speeches; they are the (incompletely preserved) *Pro Fonteio*, in which Cicero defended M. Fonteius on a charge of extortion as governor of Gaul, and *Pro A. Caecina*, in a case involving subtle legal points connected with inheritance of land. In 66 Cicero became praetor at the minimum age of 40. In this year he delivered in public assembly his first purely political speech, *Pro lege Manilia*, in which he supported, against strong *optimate opposition, the proposal of the tribune Manilius that Pompey should be appointed to the command of the war in the East against Mithridates. In this Cicero was to some extent motivated by self-interest: it would be invaluable to his political ambitions to have the backing of the powerful Pompey. His other important speech of this year was *Pro Cluentio*, a forensic masterpiece in which he successfully defended the rich *eques* Cluentius on a charge of poisoning his step-father.

During the years from 66 to 63 Cicero gradually moved away from his earlier reform-ist position and moved closer to the position of the conservative *optimates*, while men like Publius Crassus, Julius *Caesar, Gaius Antonius, and Catiline (the last two Cicero's rivals for the consulship in 63) propagated schemes for radical social reform.

2. *63–62 BC: Cicero's consulship.* In the elec-tions of 64 Cicero, a *novus homo*, a 'new man' with no advantages of birth, stood for the consul-ship of 63 and came top of the poll, *consul prior*, at the earliest permissible age, 42, *suo anno*, 'in his own year'. His candidature was successful partly because the *optimates* were alarmed by the revolutionary inclinations of Catiline, who might otherwise have been their candidate. His colleague in the consulship was Gaius Antonius, an ally of Catiline. As consul in 63 Cicero delivered the speeches *De lege agraria* (or *Contra Rullum*), arguing successfully that the legislation proposed by the tribune P. Servilius Rullus to bring about the distribution of land was fraudulent. The speech *Pro Rabirio* of the same year was in defence of an elderly *eques* charged by the popular party (at the instigation of Caesar; see also LABIENUS) with having killed, thirty-seven years before, the tribune Saturninus after the *senatus consultum ultimum* had been passed by the senate. The prosecution was in fact questioning the validity of such a resolution and drawing popular attention to the possibility of its abuse. The trial was abandoned, but Cicero was clearly seen to be a moderate conservative, in opposition to Caesar and the popular party who had brought about the prosecution. At the elections held in 63 for the consulship in 62, Catiline was again a candidate, and the natural leader of those desperate for much-needed economic reform. Again he was defeated. He seems to have hoped for some sort of aid from Cicero's colleague Antonius, but Cicero won over the latter by offering him the governorship of the more profitable province of Macedonia instead of Cisalpine Gaul. Catiline saw that his only chance of success lay in the violent seizure of power. Cicero discovered his plans and, having convinced the senate of the imminence of an uprising followed by a massacre at Rome, persuaded them to pass the *senatus consultum ultimum*. He still had no firm evidence against Catiline, however, and when he addressed the

senate on 8 November 63 in the most famous of all his speeches, his first *In Catilinam*, Catiline was present. Immediately afterwards Catiline left Rome. His departure was followed by Cicero's exposition of events to the people on 9 November (his second speech *In Catilinam*), and the arrest of five prominent citizens, who were leading conspirators in treasonable correspond-ence with envoys of the Allobroges (a Gallic tribe), on 2–3 December. In a third speech Cicero explained the new developments to the people. The fourth was delivered in the senate (5 December) on the question of the punishment of the prisoners, a speech of studied impartiality. The consul designate Silanus proposed the death penalty; Caesar proposed life imprisonment, a novel penalty in Roman law. Marcus *Cato spoke warmly in favour of the death penalty and carried the senate with him. Cicero had the sentence carried out at once. The army of Catiline now began to disperse; those remaining with their leader were cut to pieces in battle a month later. Although it was the senate's decision to execute the five, the act was a violation of an arrested citizen's right to a trial and was justified only by the passing of the *senatus consultum ultimum*. Cicero never doubted that he had saved the state from grave danger, and he wrote of his action in prose and verse, both in Latin and in Greek (see 8 below). During this crisis Cicero found himself called upon to defend (and did so successfully) the second consul designate, L. Murena, on an ill-timed charge, brought by Marcus Cato, of bribery in the elections (see PRO MURENA).

3. *From 62 to Cicero's banishment in 58.* Cicero never forgot, nor allowed anyone else to forget, the glory of 63, and Marcus Cato saluted him as 'father of his country' (*pater patriae*). But the legality of the execution of the arrested conspir-ators was soon questioned by the popular party. Cicero thought that he could bring about a union of all sound and respectable men of property from both the senatorial and eques-trian classes, his *concordia ordinum*, 'harmony between the *orders', but by the end of 61 it became clear that this was a delusion. In 62 he had delivered two speeches, *Pro Sulla* and *Pro Archia*. At the end of that year Publius *Clodius, who later emerged as a powerful popular leader, was detected while in disguise as a woman at the (female) mysteries of the Bona Dea, and prosecuted. Although he obtained an acquittal by bribery, his attempt to set up an alibi was defeated by the evidence of Cicero, who thereby incurred Clodius' hatred. Also at the end of the year Pompey returned from the East to Italy. The jealousy and hostility of the senate frustrated his political ambitions, but when Caesar returned from his governorship of Spain in 60 and was about to enter on his consulship in 59, he and Pompey formed a political alliance with Crassus, called in modern times 'the first

triumvirate'. It appears that Caesar made advances to Cicero with a view to including him in the alliance, but Cicero could not reconcile himself to Caesar's unconstitutional attitude and bravely but unwisely adopted a course of opposition. In 59 he spoke on behalf of Gaius Antonius, his colleague in the consulship of 63 and now accused of misconduct in his province (see 2 above), and made some complaint of the evil state of the times. On the same day Clodius was adopted into a plebeian family in order to become eligible to be tribune of the plebs, a process which required the consent of the *pontifex maximus*, namely Caesar. Cicero's only surviving speech of this year (59) was *Pro Flacco*, a defence on a charge of extortion in his province of one of the praetors of 63 who had effected the arrest of the Catilinarians. In it he took the opportunity to appeal to popular sentiment in his own favour. When Caesar renewed his overtures and Cicero again refused, Caesar seems to have allowed Clodius to get his revenge. As tribune for 58 Clodius brought in a bill aimed at Cicero, proposing to outlaw anyone who had put Roman citizens to death without trial. Cicero found himself without any obvious support; he therefore yielded to Clodius' threats and left Rome for exile in March 58.

Clodius now carried a decree exiling Cicero by name and confiscating his property. Cicero's magnificent house on the Palatine was destroyed (and part consecrated to *Libertas*, 'liberty', an ironic touch by Clodius), and his villa at Tusculum badly damaged. He spent his exile in Macedonia, at Thessalonika in 58 with the quaestor Gnaeus Plancius, moving at the end of the year to Dyrrhachium. He was utterly crushed by his misfortune and consumed by self-pity. But Pompey lost little time in starting to bring about Cicero's recall, with the support of the tribune *Milo, who employed violence as freely as Clodius.

4. *57–45*. Cicero was recalled by a law of the people on 4 August 57 and reached Rome a month later, to an enthusiastic welcome. In the two speeches *Post reditum* he thanked the senate and people for his recall. His speeches during the ensuing period arise out of his struggles to secure public compensation for the damage to his property (*De domo sua* and *De haruspicum responso*) and out of his support for those responsible for his recall. Thus in 56 he defended P. Sestius (*Pro Sestio*), a tribune who had exerted himself on his behalf, against a charge of rioting brought by Clodius. This speech, largely occupied with Cicero's own services and an attempt to rally aristocratic feeling against the triumvirs, contains some of the orator's finest passages. The speech *In Vatinium* was an attack on Vatinius, one of the witnesses, a supporter of Caesar's who had tried to get Sestius convicted. The speech *Pro Caelio* succeeded in obtaining the acquittal of a fashionable young friend, M. *Caelius Rufus, on charges that included conspiracy to murder an Egyptian envoy and the attempted poisoning of Caelius' former mistress Clodia, the sister of Clodius (and almost certainly the 'Lesbia' of *Catullus). The attack on Clodia herself is Cicero's most brilliant *tour de force*.

Cicero hoped that the political manœuvrings of 57 and 56, which took place against a background of increasing civil violence, would end in the break-up of the triumvirate, but in April 56 Caesar, Pompey, and Crassus renewed their political union and Cicero was forced to accept the situation and make his peace with Caesar, who always behaved with generosity towards him. Cicero's capitulation was evident in the speeches of 56, *De provinciis consularibus* ('on provinces governed by consuls') in favour of the prolongation of Caesar's command in Gaul, and *Pro Balbo*, a defence of the citizenship procured by Pompey for a rich Spaniard, Balbus, who was also a friend of Caesar's. In letters to his close friends Cicero reveals the blow that his pride has suffered. He had some satisfaction in speaking against his old enemy L. Calpurnius *Piso (*In Pisonem*) when the latter had been recalled from the governorship of Macedonia largely as a result of Cicero's attacks on him in *De provinciis consularibus* (see above). In 54 he defended his friend Plancius, who had received him during his exile in Macedonia (see 3 above), on a charge of electoral corruption (*Pro Plancio*), and Rabirius, a partisan of Caesar, on a charge of extortion (*Pro Rabirio Postumo*) as well as M. Aemilius Scaurus, ex-governor of Sardinia, on a similar charge (of this speech we have only fragments). The worst humiliations came in 54 when, at the behest of the triumvirs, he was forced to defend his enemies, Vatinius for bribery (successfully), and (unsuccessfully) on a charge of extortion the hated Gabinius, who as consul in 58 had made no attempt to prevent Cicero's exile. He was mortified by his failure in 52 to defend Milo successfully when the latter was charged and condemned for the murder of Clodius, and had to content himself with sending to the exiled Milo the speech *Pro Milone*, perhaps the finest of all his speeches. It is an elaboration of the one he tried to deliver when he lost his nerve, presented as he was with a court room packed with Clodian supporters and the hostile soldiers of Pompey. Milo is said to have congratulated himself that it was not delivered, otherwise he would have been acquitted and never have known the excellent seafood for which Massilia (Marseilles) was already famous. In 53 Cicero was somewhat comforted by being elected augur.

During the 50s, as he withdrew from the collapsing world of republican politics, he found consolation in writing on philosophy and rhetoric, and arguing against his literary antagonists, who were principally Julius Caesar, *Calvus, Marcus *Brutus, and Asinius *Pollio. By the end of 55 he had finished *De oratore, a treatise in three books on rhetoric, designed to replace his early work on the same subject, De inventione ('on invention'), written before he was 25; it was followed, perhaps in the late 50s, by a briefer essay on rhetoric, Partitiones oratoriae ('divisions of oratory'), in which Cicero answers his young son's questions on the orator's craft. From this period also comes the *De republica (of which we have only parts, including the *Somnium Scipionis), and *De legibus ('on laws'), which seems to have been begun in 52, though it was not completed until 45 and was probably published after Cicero's death. There was to be a further outpouring of philosophical works between 46 and 44. Meanwhile Cicero was reluctantly obliged to govern the province of Cilicia from summer 51 to summer 50 under the new regulations of Pompey's law for the government of the provinces (see also PROV-INCES, ROMAN). He disliked leaving Rome but he carried out his duties honestly and efficiently, winning a victory over the brigands and returning to Rome with the *fasces of his lictors wreathed in fading laurels. He found Rome on the brink of civil war, and when war did break out he left the city, with many of the senatorial party. Pompey had accepted the command of the republic's forces in Italy, but after he withdrew with them to Epirus in Greece Cicero was in the deepest trouble and perplexity. He decided to remain in Italy, and followed Pompey only at a later stage. After the defeat of the Pompeians at Pharsalus in the summer of 48 (at which battle he was not present because of illness), he returned to Italy. A period of anxious suspense was ended in 47 when Caesar came to Italy and the two were completely reconciled. At last Cicero could return to Rome.

At first he remained detached from public life, attending meetings in the senate but not speaking, regarded with suspicion by both sides. But he began to entertain the faint hope that when the civil war was finally over Caesar might perhaps set about restoring constitutional government. In 46 he delivered his first import-ant speech for five years, Pro Marcello, a speech of thanks to Caesar for pardoning M. Marcellus who as consul in 51 had launched the attack on him which ultimately precipitated the civil war (see CAESAR 2); it contains a famous sentence, satis diu vel naturae vixi vel gloriae ('I have lived long enough for the demands of nature or fame'). In 45 he spoke Pro Ligario, a defence of Q. Ligarius, tried as an enemy of Caesar, a speech whose eloquence is said to have moved Caesar to acquit the accused; and in the same year he delivered the speech Pro rege Deiotaro, defending the tetrarch of Galatia on a charge of attempting to murder Caesar. Shortly after Cato's death at Utica (Utique) in 46, Cicero, at

Brutus' suggestion, wrote a panegyric on him, now lost. It displeased Caesar, who replied to it in a work, also lost, called Anticato.

In 46 Cicero divorced his wife of some thirty years, Terentia, and shortly after married Publilia, who had been his ward. In 45 his beloved daughter *Tullia died, and Cicero was overwhelmed with grief. A famous letter of consolation (Epistulae ad familiares IV. 5) was written to him by the jurist *Sulpicius. Publilia offended Cicero by her lack of sympathy, and this second marriage also ended in divorce. These personal blows were made harder to bear by Cicero's growing realization that Caesar was never going to attempt to restore the republican constitution, and he took what consolation he could in literary composition.

5. Philosophical and literary writings. Between 46 and 44 Cicero wrote *Brutus, a history of Roman oratory, *Orator, a picture of the accomplished speaker, and other works on rhetoric: the Topica ('matters relating to com-monplaces'), dealing with kinds of arguments, supposedly derived from Aristotle's work of the same name; De optimo genere oratorum ('on the best kind of orators', perhaps written in 52), of which only a part survives; a preface to his (lost) translations of the two Greek orations *De corona of Demosthenes and Against Ctesiphon of Aeschines (this work may not be by Cicero). In 45 he wrote the Consolatio ('consolation') on the deaths of great men, a work (of which fragments survive) occasioned by the death of Tullia; Hortensius (now lost), a plea for the study of philosophy which greatly moved St *Augustine; *Academica, on the views of the Athenian 'New' Academy, and in particular of *Carneades; and *De finibus bonorum et malorum, on the different conceptions held by philo-sophers of the 'chief good'. After these works he wrote during 45 and 44 Tusculanae disputationes ('*Tusculan Disputations') on the conditions of happiness, the most intensely felt and expressed of all his philosophical works; *De natura deorum, the views of different philosophical schools on the nature of the gods; *De fato ('on fate', of which only fragments survive), a discussion of free will; the two charming essays *De senectute and *De amicitia; *De divinatione, the examination of Stoic belief concerning fate and the possibility of prediction, published soon after Caesar's murder; and his last work on moral philosophy, *De officiis, finished in November 44 and written for the edification of his son. It was altogether a wonderful output for two or three years.

As a philosopher Cicero claimed to be a follower of the 'New' Academy of Carneades which held that certain knowledge was impossi-ble, and that practical conviction based on probability was the most that could be attained. But while his general attitude was that of the New Academy, he was an eclectic, that is to say he did not adhere to any one school, but picked from among the doctrines of the various Greek schools those which commended themselves to his reason; and in questions of morality he was inclined (e.g. in *De finibus*, the *Tusculan Disputations*, and *De officiis*) to accept the positive Stoic teaching. He believed in the existence of a divine being, and maintained that it is prudent to keep up traditional rites and ceremonies. Finally, in *De fato* he shows his belief in the freedom of the will against Stoic fatalism. He did not claim that his philosophical works were original but he popularized Greek thought and created a Latin philosophical vocabulary. The works *De senectute*, *De amicitia*, *De officiis*, the *Tusculan Disputations*, and the *Somnium Scipionis* (detached from the *De republica* which was ultimately lost) had considerable influence on the Fathers of the early Church, St *Jerome (despite his misgivings), St *Ambrose (whose manual *De officiis ministrorum*, 'on the duties of a Christian', was modelled on the Ciceronian original), and St Augustine. The heretical Pelagians also drew largely on Cicero. In the Middle Ages, when Cicero's political and oratorical works had yet to be rediscovered (see TEXTS, TRANSMISSION OF ANCIENT 8), these books were studied extensively, and handed on to the European world a knowledge of Greek philosophy which was not otherwise attainable.

6. *The Philippics and Cicero's death, 44–43.* When a heterogeneous collection of men, united only in their desire to put an end to despotic rule, murdered Caesar in 44, Cicero was not invited to join them, although he greeted the news with delight. For several months he remained aloof from politics, but he still ardently desired to see the restoration of the republic. Everything hinged on Mark *Antony, Caesar's ally and consular colleague, and he, striving not only to restore public order but to maintain his leading position in the state, was prepared to fight Brutus and Cassius for the leadership. The arrival on the political scene of Caesar's nephew *Octavian, who drew to his side Antony's Caesarian supporters, posed a further threat to Antony. When, after several months of confusion and perplexity, the political alignments were becoming clear, and Antony had left Rome for Cisalpine Gaul to lay siege to the republicans under Decimus *Brutus at Mutina, Cicero put himself at the head of what was left of the senatorial party. He gave full expression to his hatred of the Caesarian tyranny in fourteen orations against Antony which he entitled *Philippics*, after the patriotic speeches delivered by the Athenian orator Demosthenes against Philip II of Macedon. In fact Cicero delivered his *First Philippic* to the senate on 2 September, before Antony left for Cisalpine Gaul, and it is relatively conciliatory in tone although it attacks Antony's recent behaviour. But Antony's reply stimulated Cicero to compose the *Second Philippic* and publish it in December, after Antony's departure; it was a masterpiece of political invective against the man who had tried to make Caesar king.

The *Third Philippic* (20 December) is an exposition to the senate of his policy—support for Decimus Brutus and Octavian against Antony. Cicero had accepted the overtures which Octavian made to him, ignoring the fact that Octavian could never be reconciled to Caesar's murderers, the republicans Marcus Brutus and Cassius, who were winning victories in the East. In the *Fifth Philippic*, delivered on 1 January 43, in which he describes 20 December as the day on which he began to rebuild the republic, he proposed the grant of the powers of propraetor to Octavian. The *Fourth* and *Sixth* (19 December 44 and 4 January 43) were addressed to the people. Cicero thus took the position of leader of the state, stimulating the consuls Hirtius and Pansa to send an army to Mutina to destroy Antony and restore constitutional government. The series of these speeches continues until the *Fourteenth*, the last of all Cicero's surviving speeches, celebrating the defeat of Antony at Mutina. But the rejoicing was premature: both the consuls leading the army were killed; Antony re-formed his army and was strengthened by the defection to him of *Lepidus and Pollio with their legions. Cicero was still deceived into believing that Octavian intended to destroy Antony, but instead Octavian marched on Rome with his legions to demand the consulship, and obtained it on 19 August 43. He then proceeded to make his peace with Antony, rescinding sentences outlawing the latter and Lepidus, and at the end of October all three met to agree on a three-fold division of power, the (second) triumvirate. They were to prosecute the war jointly against Brutus and Cassius in the East, money and land were to be obtained to satisfy their troops, and old scores settled by widespread *proscriptions. On the first list sent to Rome Antony wrote Cicero's name. On 7 December 43 his soldiers caught Cicero in a not very resolute attempt to escape by sea, and he bravely submitted to execution. His head and hands were displayed on the *Rostra in Rome. His old enemy Verres (see 1 above), still in exile at Massilia, heard of his death before he too was proscribed by Antony, reputedly for the sake of his art treasures. Cicero's son Marcus (see (3) below) survived him.

7. *Letters.* Perhaps, ironically, to his detriment, Cicero is known to us more intimately than anyone else in the ancient world through his voluminous correspondence covering the period 68 to 43. Over 800 of his letters survive in which, with complete candour and mostly with little thought of publication, he recorded his moods and actions. The first we hear of publication is in July 44 when he writes about making a small collection of his letters to *Tiro

and Atticus (see also 1 above). Because he was closely involved in the politics of a momentous period in history, and wrote to correspondents of the most diverse political views as well as to members of his household, the letters are an invaluable historical source. They have come down to us in four collections, which include some letters from his correspondents, and comprise: those written to Atticus (*Epistulae ad Atticum*) between 68 and 43; those written to more than ninety other friends and relations (*Epistulae ad familiares*) published by Tiro; those to his brother Quintus (*Epistulae ad Quintum fratrem*; see (2) below) written when the brothers were separated, chiefly between 59 and 54; and twenty-five letters written to Marcus Brutus (*Epistulae ad Brutum*) all written in 43. There are no letters for the years of Cicero's consulship (63) or the preceding year.

8. *Poems.* Cicero's very early poetry has perished but there survive a large part of the *Aratea* (469 consecutive hexameter lines and some fragments) and his translation of the *Phaenomena* of *Aratus, a Greek didactic poem; his philosophical works also contain snippets from Homer and the Greek tragedians in his own Latin version, and a few lines survive of an epic *Marius*. His famous poems were the autobiographical ones of self-glorification, the three books *De consulatu suo* ('on my consulship') written in 60, and, some five years later, three further books *De temporibus suis* ('on my times'). Little has survived of them except a passage of seventy-two lines on his consulship and the two notorious lines which aroused the derision of his contemporaries for their jingling sound and boastful expression, *cedant arma togae, concedat laurea laudi* (or *linguae*) ('Let arms submit to civil power, let military laurels yield to praise' or 'speech'), and *o fortunatam natam me consule Romam* ('O happy Rome, born in my consulship'). Despite his poetic failings he furthered the development of the Latin hexameter and had some influence on *Lucretius and perhaps Catullus.

9. *Cicero's influence on literature and thought.* Cicero was a man of great versatility of intellect. Lasting political success eluded him because of his support for what turned out to be a lost cause. His consulship in 63 was famous; he was a political force of whom serious account had subsequently to be taken by whoever aimed at controlling the political scene; his devotion to his country was selfless and never in doubt. But his immense success as consul left him with an exaggerated idea of what it was possible for him to achieve politically, and his enthusiasm for the restoration of the old form of the republic was sadly unrealistic; he was not able—nor was anyone—to deal with the serious economic and social issues which lay behind the politics of the day, and it is often said that he lacked judgement and constancy of purpose. His lasting greatness lies in his exceptional mastery of the Latin language. He was the greatest orator that Rome produced. In his prose treatises as well as in his oratory, he wrote in lucid and unaffected Latin and in a complex periodic style that was logical and coherent, rhythmical and sonorous. His prose became a model for later writers in Latin and helped to mould the style of many authors writing in the languages of modern Europe.

In his forensic speeches, mostly written for the defence, he was adept at selecting those aspects of a case on which he might speak to his client's advantage, at relating an engrossing narrative that furthered his cause, at rising to heights of emotion where appropriate, and at employing his considerable powers of wit, irony, and ridicule. He was unusual in being able to expound the theory of his art in a series of valuable treatises on rhetoric. He exemplified his own precept that an orator needed to have a wide knowledge by constant reading and study, especially of the Greek philosophers. Hitherto the Latin language was not adapted to expressing general philosophic ideas and lacked a suitable vocabulary. Cicero succeeded in expounding the Greek philosophical systems partly by introducing into Latin a range of new words to express the ideas. These ideas were not arid theories but, adapted to the Roman environment and Roman attitudes, underpinned Cicero's life as a practical man of action. Though ultimately suspending belief in the existence of gods he was, nevertheless, convinced of the essential rightness of the Stoic doctrine that all humans possessed a spark of the divine, which bound man to man and demanded that we treat each other with a common respect.

Cicero's reputation was somewhat eclipsed in the two centuries after his death; his views on rhetorical education had little influence, and Latin prose style tended to avoid Ciceronian fullness and balance in favour of what was striking and epigrammatic. His letters were probably published in the course of the first century AD but aroused no particular interest, nor was his philosophy much read. Some Christians saw him as a symbol of the pagan culture which should be rejected, but his good sense and his style ensured that he was studied by Christian apologists needing an acceptable language to express their beliefs to a pagan audience, and sometimes needing the arguments too. Thus *Minucius Felix in the third century based his own dialogue on Cicero's *De natura deorum*, and *Lactantius was famed for his 'Ciceronian eloquence' (see also the end of 5 above). Those books that seemed to prefigure or echo Christian wisdom were especially favoured in Christian reading and education: *Somnium Scipionis*, *De officiis*, *De amicitia*, *De senectute*. From the early Middle Ages until the nineteenth century Cicero's influence on literature and ideas was profound. The poet Petrarch

(1304–74), seeing in Cicero the exemplar of the good life, searched eagerly for Ciceronian manuscripts and rediscovered some of the speeches and the *Epistulae ad Atticum* (see 7 above). The speech *Pro Archia*, discovered at Liège in 1333, gave him great pleasure for its praise of poetry, but the *Epistulae ad Atticum*, found at Verona in 1345, shocked him at first with their revelation of Cicero's personality, and caused him to compose his famous letters of reproach to Cicero's shade. Fifty years later Cicero's *Epistulae ad familiares* were found. In the new light shed on Cicero many came to review their own attitudes towards political action, and indeed towards the education of a statesman. The Renaissance scholars admired and imitated his language and style, but, more importantly, saw him as the ideal of civilized man, brilliant, humane, practical in the discharge of civic duties, and enjoying a refined leisure. Those who imitated only the letter without imbibing the spirit of the man earned the ridicule of Erasmus. Interest in his Latin style became less intense towards the end of the sixteenth century when taste turned to Seneca and Tacitus, and in any case the various vernaculars established themselves as respectable vehicles of composition, themselves much influenced by Ciceronian style. In England in the seventeenth century the language of John Milton and of the Authorized Version of the Bible show their indebtedness. The eighteenth century with its cool rationalism felt a special affinity to Cicero, and David Hume, in his ethics as well as in his literary style, owed much to him. English statesmen knew him well. Edward Gibbon ardently admired him, and in France (and America) his freedom from dogma and his open-minded speculations struck a chord among aspiring revolutionaries. Throughout all these centuries every educated person had read something of Cicero's philosophical writings. In the nineteenth century his reputation as a statesman collapsed, largely under the attacks of the historian Theodor Mommsen, unsympathetic to republicanism; his philosophical writings too ceased to exert their previous influence and seemed unoriginal and excessively moralistic, and interest turned towards their Greek sources. Nevertheless, Ciceronian 'humanity' is still the ideal that lies at the base of much of modern civilization.

2. **Quintus Tu'llius Cicero,** 102–43 BC, younger brother of the orator ((1), above), an able soldier and administrator. He was praetor in 62, and governor of Asia 61–59, where he received from his brother two long letters of advice (*Epistulae ad Quintum fratrem* I. 1 and 2). He served as legate with Caesar in Gaul during 54–51, taking part in the invasion of Britain, and then joined his brother in Cilicia. He followed Pompey in the civil war, was pardoned after Pharsalus, and took no further part in public life. He and his son died in the proscriptions of 43. He had wide literary interests but his works do not survive, except for four letters to his brother. He married Pomponia, sister of his brother's friend Atticus.

3. **Marcus Tu'llius Cicero,** born 65 BC, only son of the orator ((1) above) and his wife Terentia. He was taken out to Cilicia with his father in 51. He fought with a squadron of cavalry in Pompey's army in 49/8, was pardoned after the battle of Pharsalus, joined Sextus Pompeius after Philippi, but took advantage of the amnesty after 39 to return to Rome. He was consul with Octavian for a brief period in 30; subsequently he governed Syria and after that we hear no more of him. An apologetic letter survives (*Ad familiares* XVI. 21) written by him to *Tiro in response to letters from his father and Atticus which expressed displeasure at his idle life while a student in Athens. In it he gives a careful account of his reformed mode of life.

Ciceronian age, of Roman literature, a term sometimes used to signify the period in Latin literature that roughly coincided with the manhood of Cicero and the last years of the republic, about 70 to 30 BC (see ROME 8). The writers of the period apart from Cicero include Lucretius, Catullus, Sallust, and Varro. Virgil is generally associated with the Augustan age although he had written the *Eclogues* and *Georgics* by 30 BC.

Cili'cia, country on the eastern half of the south coast of Asia Minor. In Homer's *Iliad* the Cilices, after whom the country is named, inhabited the southern Troad, but after the Trojan War some Greeks, under the leadership of *Mopsus the seer, applied the name to this new region in which they settled. The western area was rough and mountainous, but the east consisted of a large and very fertile plain. In the second century BC it became a pirate stronghold and the Romans constituted it as a province in 102 BC to deal with the menace. The pirates were not suppressed until Pompey's campaign of 67 BC. Cicero was governor of Cilicia in 51–50 (see CICERO (1) 4). Its most important city, autonomous until annexed by Pompey in 66 BC, was Tarsus, the seat of a famous school of philosophy and birthplace of the apostle Paul.

Cimme'rians (Kimmerioi), a people who belong partly to legend and partly to history. In Homer's *Odyssey* (book 11) they are a fabulous people living on the edge of the world by the shore of *Oceanus, shrouded in mist and in perpetual darkness. Here Odysseus gained access to the spirits of the dead. In Herodotus they are a historical people driven from their home (the biblical Gomer) north of the Black Sea in the eighth and seventh centuries BC by nomadic Scythian tribes. In the early seventh century they overturned Midas' kingdom of Phrygia (at which Midas took poison), attacked Lydia, killing the king Gyges, and in c.644 BC, during the reign of his son Ardys, took the capital Sardis, except for the citadel. The Greek poets Callinus and Archilochus bear witness to the terror they inspired in Ionia. Then plague struck them and they retreated east. Some who remained were finally expelled about 600 BC by Alyattes, king of Lydia.

Cīmon, Athenian statesman and soldier, son of *Miltiades and the Thracian Hegesipylē, born c.510 BC. It seems to have been thought that he owed some of his features—his great height, shaggy hair, and slowness of wit—to his Thracian ancestry. He entered politics shortly after 480 and was already prominent enough to be one of the official Athenian envoys sent to Sparta in 479. He was *strategos* in 478 and thereafter held that office frequently. He helped *Aristeides win the allegiance of the Greeks in Asia Minor and the islands for Athens rather than Sparta, and from 476 to 463 was commander in nearly all the operations of the *Delian League. In 475 he conquered the island of Scyros, drove out the pirates, and brought back in triumph to Athens what were supposed to be the bones of the Athenian hero Theseus who was said to be buried there. Cimon's greatest military achievement was the defeat of the Persian fleet at the mouth of the Eurymedon, perhaps in 466. Subsequently he reduced Thasos in 463 after a two-year siege when that island revolted from the Delian League.

During the seventies Athens was under the control of a limited number of aristocratic families whose authority was maintained by the political skills of Aristeides and the wealth and military successes of Cimon. These families kept on good terms with Sparta, but there was a democratic faction in Athens which saw Sparta as the natural political enemy and was in favour of radical political reform. When Cimon returned to Athens in 463 he was prosecuted by *Pericles and other democrats for failing to take further aggressive action, but was acquitted. He then (462) persuaded the Athenians to let him lead an army to help Sparta against a rebellion of *helots following the serious earthquake of 464, but the Spartans, not trusting Athenian motives, dismissed him. This ignominy discredited those sympathetic to Sparta and brought about Cimon's fall. In 461 he was ostracized; tradition states that he was recalled before the full ten years of exile had elapsed in order to conduct the delicate Athenian peace negotiations in the war with Sparta and the Peloponnesians (see ATHENS 2 (ii)). In c.451 Athens and Sparta concluded a five years' truce. Cimon led a last campaign against Persia to recapture Cyprus and died there c.450.

Cincinnā'tus, Lucius Quinctius, a legendary Roman hero who, according to tradition, was called from the plough to be dictator in 458 BC,

when the Roman army under the consul Mincius was blockaded by the Italian tribe of the Aequi on Mount Algidus. He defeated the enemy, resigned his dictatorship after sixteen days, and returned to his farm. He is often referred to as being typical of old-fashioned Roman simplicity and frugality.

Cinē'sias, Athenian *lyric (especially dithyrambic) poet who lived in the second half of the fifth century BC. Of his work nothing of interest survives. He was much mocked by his contemporaries, especially Aristophanes, for his free style of music, as well as for his personal appearance and for impiety, and contributed to the disappearance of the chorus from Attic comedy (see COMEDY, GREEK 3). Plato, in *Gorgias*, condemned him as a poet who aimed at producing pleasure rather than good.

Cinna. 1. **Lucius Cornelius Cinna,** brother of Julius Caesar's wife Cornelia, praetor in 44 BC. He had republican sympathies and expressed approval of Caesar's murder. He may have died in the later proscriptions. See also (2) below.

2. **Gaius Helvius Cinna,** Roman poet and friend of *Catullus, whom he accompanied to Bithynia in 57 BC; his *epyllion *Zmyrna* was greatly admired by his contemporaries for its vast erudition in the Alexandrian manner. He also wrote erotic poetry in various metres, of which only very small fragments survive. The ancient sources identify him with the tribune of 44 BC who, after the murder of Caesar, was lynched by the angry mob in mistake for Cornelius Cinna (see above) who had spoken publicly against the dictator on the previous day (or 'for his bad verses' according to Shakespeare).

Ci'nyras, mythical king of Cyprus and founder of the cult of Aphroditē in that island. He was the father of *Adonis through an unwitting union with his daughter Zmyrna (or Myrrha). He was regarded as a seer and musician, and sometimes said for that reason to be the son of Apollo. (See also PYGMALION.)

Circē, in Homer's *Odyssey* (book 10), a goddess living on the fabulous island of Aeaea (later identified by the Romans with the promontory of Circeii in Latium), powerful in magic, who turned Odysseus' men into swine. Odysseus resisted her magic by means of the mythical herb moly. Circe was the daughter of *Helios and Persē, and the sister of Aeētēs; by Odysseus she was the mother of two or three sons, one of whom was *Telegonos. Milton in *Comus* makes the magician Comus the son of Circe and Bacchus.

circe'nsēs, at Rome, contests and other displays in the *circus, including *chariot-races. *Panem et circenses* ('bread and circuses') were, according to the poet Juvenal (10. 81), the only things that the degenerate Roman people cared about.

circus, in Roman times, originally a circular or oval space in which public displays, games, and especially *chariot-races were held. In its developed form it was a rectangular enclosure with one end semi-circular in shape and the other enclosed by the stables for (usually) twelve teams of horses. The stables were built in a curve in such a way that all teams had an equal distance to travel before they started on the course proper. A low wall ran down the centre of the course with turning-posts at each end, dividing the area into two runs. Seats for spectators were built in storied groups around the perimeter on three sides.

The most famous circus was the Circus Maximus ('the biggest circus', so-called because it excelled the others in size and splendour). Situated on the plain between the Palatine and Aventine hills, in republican times and under the early empire it was the chief place of amusement for the Roman people. It was reputed to have originated in the time of Tarquinius Priscus, king of Rome in the sixth century BC, was added to during the republic and rebuilt by Julius Caesar, and reached its greatest size and splendour in the reconstruction of the emperor Trajan. A lap was approximately 1500 m. (1,650 yds.) long. Other circuses in Rome were the *Circus Flaminius* of 221 BC in the Campus Martius, the *Circus Gai et Neronis* or *Vaticanus, c. AD* 40, the site of Christian martyrdoms, near where St Peter's basilica was to be built, and (the best preserved) the *Circus of Maxentius* on the Via Appia, dedicated in AD 309. Compare STADIUM.

Ciris, see APPENDIX VIRGILIANA.

Cirrha, see CRISA.

Cisal'pine Gaul, see GAUL.

Cistellā'ria ('casket'), Roman comedy by *Plautus, adapted from a comedy by the Greek comic poet *Menander, *Synaristōsai* ('breakfasters'). The plot turns on the discovery by means of a casket of the true parentage of a foundling girl, Selēnium, who has passed into the care of a courtesan and has become the mistress of a young man Alcesimarchus. She is found to be the daughter of a citizen, Dēmipho, and is thereupon married to her lover.

Cithae'ron, the westerly part of the mountain range which separates the north of Attica from Boeotia. The summit was sacred to Zeus, but the mountain was also sacred to Dionysus, and on one of the crests was a famous cave of the *nymphs. It was the scene of several myths and legends including the metamorphosis of *Actaeon, the death of Pentheus (see *BACCHAE*), and the exposure of *Oedipus.

cǐ'thara, stringed musical instrument, an elaborate form of the lyre, the most important stringed instrument for the Greeks. See MUSIC 1.

citizenship.
1. *Greek.* Citizenship meant full membership of a city (see POLIS); the qualifications for membership depended on the constitution of each city (see ARISTOCRACY, DEMOCRACY, OLIGARCHY). In all constitutions citizenship was an exclusive right for a limited number; in Athens the qualifications changed with time as the constitution became more democratic (see SOLON and CLEISTHENES (2)), but there was always a section of the population who were not citizens (see METICS). Descent from full citizen parents, legitimately married, was the usual qualification, and in Athens from 451 to 338 BC was generally necessary (see PERICLES). (An exception was the admission to citizenship of those metics who manned the ships at the battle of Arginusae in 406 BC.) At other periods the requirement was less stringent. Adult male citizens were members of the *ecclesia and so shared in lawmaking and electing magistrates, and acted in the law-courts and the *dokimasia. Women's share in the privileges of citizenship was limited by their having no political rights and being ineligible to own property (see WOMEN, POSITION OF). Only citizens were entitled to own land. In order to take up his citizen rights the Athenian male youth at the end of his eighteenth year was registered by his father or guardian as a member of the family *deme, after his qualifications had been scrutinized. The duties of a citizen were to obey the laws, worship the city's gods, and (for men) perform military service and make financial contributions as required. Citizenship was lost by *atimia or *exile. From the fourth century BC onwards grants of citizenship to foreign individuals became increasingly common.

2. *Roman.* Full Roman citizenship, originally limited to the inhabitants of Rome, was in early times extended to the citizens of colonies set up in Roman territory and to the citizens of some Italian communities which, having surrendered their independence to Rome, had been fully incorporated into the Roman state. The normal qualification for citizenship was to be the child of two legitimately married Roman citizens or, in certain cases, of one citizen and one foreign parent; a grant of citizenship could be conferred by a decree of the people (or, later, the emperor). No Roman citizen could also be a citizen of another independent state. In the early (aristocratic) republic, citizens were divided into *patricians and *plebeians, of whom the former enjoyed more rights in the matter of voting, and a monopoly of office (see MAGISTRACIES), while the latter had to struggle for political equality (see ROME 3). Entire Italian communities (see MUNICIPIUM) also became citizens of Rome,

with the rights and duties of citizenship but without the vote. After the Social War (90–88 BC: see ROME 6), Roman citizenship was extended to all the Italian allies (see SOCII), so that Rome ceased to be a city-state and became more like a capital city. By that time all male citizens had voting rights in the various assemblies at Rome (see COMITIA and REPUBLIC, ROMAN), the right to stand for office, and rights of trade and of intermarriage (*commercium* and *conubium*; see LATIN RIGHTS). Women had no political rights and were unable to own property.

Citizenship entailed certain duties for males, according to varying liability, notably in military service, the payment of direct taxes (see FINANCE, ROMAN), and civil obligations such as the maintenance of roads and waterworks. For the poorest class whose only contribution to the state was their children see PROLETARII. Under the empire the political rights of citizens became insignificant, but the rights of *commercium* and *conubium* remained valuable, as did the citizen's right of appeal to a higher magistrate, ending with appeal to the emperor, against a judgement in a law-court. Citizenship was granted to all free inhabitants of the empire in AD 212, by the emperor Antoninus Caracalla. See also SLAVERY.

city, city-state (in Greece), see POLIS.

City of God, see DE CIVITATE DEI.

civil war, at Rome. This term denotes any one of three periods of civil war at Rome, first between Marius and Sulla from 88 to 82 BC, secondly between Pompey and Julius Caesar from 49 to 45 BC, and thirdly between Antony and Octavian from 44 to 30 BC (see ROME 6 and 7).

Civil War, commentaries by Julius Caesar; see COMMENTARIES 2.

clan, see GENOS and GENS.

classic (classics, classical). The English terms are derived from the Latin adjective *classicus* meaning 'of the highest class' (of the five classes of Roman citizens divided by Servius Tullius on a property basis). Aulus Gellius in the second century AD seems to have been the first to use the adjective figuratively to describe a writer, but Cicero had already taken the noun *classis* ('class') from its political and military sphere and used it to describe a 'class' of philosophers (see also CANONS). Renaissance scholars writing in Latin adopted the adjective to describe Greek and Latin authors in general, and from this the modern usage is derived. The terms are sometimes used with a narrower, temporal meaning to describe what is thought to be the best period, in a cultural sense, of the Greek and Roman civilizations. Thus, the classical period of ancient Greece was most of the fifth and fourth centuries BC, roughly from the defeat of

the Persians in 480 to the death of Alexander the Great in 323 BC, and that of Rome the first century BC and the following century up to the death of Augustus in AD 14, sometimes referred to as the Golden Age. (Compare ARCHAIC, ORIENTALIZING, GEOMETRIC, PROTO-GEOMETRIC, and HELLENISTIC AGE.)

Classiciā'nus, Julius, see BRITAIN 4.

Claudian (Claudius Claudiānus), the last great Latin poet in the classical tradition. He was born at Alexandria in the late fourth century AD and came to Italy before 395. Although a native Greek speaker, he turned to composing in Latin and became immediately successful as a court poet under Honorius, the young emperor in the West, writing in hexameters a number of eulogies of him and his ministers and, in particular, a three-book panegyric of the general and regent *Stilicho. (The date of his death is inferred from his silence about Stilicho's achievements after 404.) He also wrote poems savagely abusing Honorius' political enemies, mostly in the eastern empire (ruled by Honorius' young brother Arcadius), attacking in particular Rufinus, the guardian of Arcadius, and the eunuch Eutropius, Rufinus' successor. He wrote an (incomplete) *epyllion of 526 lines on the defeat of Gildo who led an uprising in Africa, and another on Stilicho's defeat of the Visigothic king Alaric at Pollentia (Pollenza). In these poems Claudian shows sincere enthusiasm for the Roman empire, great technical and rhetorical skill, and a vigour at times reaching high eloquence, although both his panegyric and his invective are extravagant. He makes abundant use of allegory and mythological episode and allusion. In addition to the political poems he wrote an epithalamium and four shorter poems for Honorius' marriage to Stilicho's daughter Maria. His finest work, as it seems today, is *The Rape of Proserpine*, divided into four books, of which 1,100 lines survive; he tells with great charm the familiar story of Proserpine's abduction by Pluto in the field of Enna. He also wrote a number of short pieces, idylls and epigrams, mostly in elegiacs (see METRE, GREEK 4), on a great variety of subjects—the Nile, the phoenix, a porcupine, a lobster, a statue, a landscape, etc. The best-known is the idyll on the 'Old man of Verona', imitated from Virgil's description of the old gardener of Tarentum (*Georgics* 4. 125), subsequently translated by the seventeenth-century English poet Abraham Cowley. Although Honorius' court was Christian, Claudian's poetry shows a predilection for the old pagan religion and it is probable that he remained unconverted. He was honoured for his work by a bronze statue erected in the Forum of Trajan, the inscription from which has survived and is in Naples.

Claudia Quinta, see CYBELE.

Claudius. 1. Appius Claudius, Roman patrician leader of the decemvirs (*decemviri, commission of ten men) appointed in 451 BC to draw up a written code of laws, the *Twelve Tables, in response to the agitation of the *plebs*. The traditions concerning these events are inextricably confused. The decemvirs, when reappointed for a second year, appear to have become oppressive, and Appius' conduct towards *Virginia provoked their overthrow in 449. Appius was arrested but committed suicide before he was brought to trial (Livy 3. 33). To later Romans he came to symbolize aristocratic arrogance. See FLAVIUS, ROME 3.

2. Appius Claudius Caecus ('blind'), the famous Roman censor (in 312 BC), reputedly a proud and obstinate man with original and broad views. He used his censorship to extend membership of the senate to rich citizens of the lower classes, and even to the sons of freedmen. Their support as well as heavier taxation enabled him to build Rome's first aqueduct, Aqua Appia, and the Via Appia (Appian Way) from Rome to Brundisium (Brindisi) on which he founded the market town and staging-post Forum Appii. In his old age, when blind, he successfully attacked the proposals of *Pyrrhus for peace (279/8 BC), in a famous speech still circulated in Cicero's day. He is the first Roman prose-writer whose name is known to us. Cicero says that he was a notable orator, and that some of his funeral orations were still read. He composed aphorisms in Saturnian verse (see METRE, LATIN I) of which a few have survived; they include 'a man is the creator of his own fortune', *faber est suae quisque fortunae*.

3. Tiberius Claudius Nero Germa'nicus (10 BC–AD 54), son of the elder *Drusus and Antonia, daughter of Mark Antony, the Roman emperor Claudius from 41 until his death. Hampered by some physical disability and the general belief that he was mentally deficient in some way, he led a retired life and devoted himself to scholarship, producing a history of the reign of Octavian and another from the death of Julius Caesar, as well as histories of Etruria and Carthage, and an autobiography. None of these works has survived. When the emperor *Gaius (Caligula) was murdered, Claudius was the only surviving adult male of the Julio-Claudian line, and was proclaimed emperor by the praetorian guard almost, it seemed, by accident, after being discovered in hiding, and against the wishes of the senate who wanted to restore the republic. Claudius took part in the invasion of Britain in AD 43 and was present at the capture of Camulodunum (Colchester). In 48 he divorced his wife *Messallina, by whom he had a daughter Octavia and a son Britannicus, for her infidelity, and married his niece *Agrippina, whose son *Nero he adopted.

It was generally believed that his death four years later was caused by a dish of mushrooms poisoned by Agrippina. His subsequent deification was the subject of a satire by *Seneca (2), entitled *Apocolocyntōsis*.

clau'sula ('sentence-ending'). In Greek and Latin rhetoric, the closing words of a sentence (or of a clause ending in a strong stop) are rhythmically very important and often follow a regular metrical sequence based on syllable length (for explanation of the symbols and terms in what follows see METRE, GREEK I). Greek rhetorical theory gives few precise details, but Aristotle recommends the sequence $\cup\cup\cup-$. In Latin, most of the clausulae of Cicero's speeches conform to a definite type in which a cretic $(-\cup-)$ is followed by one or two trochaic feet $(-\cup)$ or by a second cretic, the last syllable, according to Cicero, being anceps. Thus: *non haberemus* $-\cup--\times$, *(in)commodo civitatis* $-\cup-\vdots-\cup-\times$, or *cessit audaciae* $-\cup--\cup\times$. Cicero also commonly 'resolves' the cretic, e.g. $\widehat{\cup\cup}\cup--\times$, $-\cup\widehat{\cup\cup}-\times$, etc. Strongly avoided is the hexameter ending $-\cup\cup-\times$. Quintilian (x. 2. 18) says that an orator likes to end a sentence with *esse videatur*, $-\cup\widehat{\cup\cup}-\times$, thinking this to be an excellent imitation of Cicero.

Clea'nthēs (c.331–c.232 BC), of Assos in the Troad, successor of Zeno, the founder of *Stoicism, as head of that school of philosophy from c.261 to his death. He was said to have defined Zeno's instruction to 'live consistently' as meaning 'to live consistently with nature'. In his ethical teaching he stressed disinterestedness, saying that to do good to others with a view to one's own benefit was no different from feeding cattle in order to eat them. His Stoicism was pervaded by a religious fervour expressed in the thirty-eight surviving hexameter lines of a hymn to Zeus, in which Zeus is envisaged as the spirit that permeates and rules the universe, and human beings as the only living things that have a semblance to him. Parts of the poem express the Stoic view that all events are the will of a perfect God, and that men's acceptance of this fact will bring them peace of mind. Other small fragments of Cleanthes' works survive.

Clei'sthenes. 1. Tyrant of Sicyon c.600–570 BC, of the family of Orthagoras, the original founder of the tyranny c.665 BC. His policy was consistently anti-Dorian and anti-Argive (Sicyon had originally been occupied by Dorians from Argos but retained a large pre-Dorian element in its population). In this he was carrying on the policy of earlier Orthagorids. He would not allow rhapsodes to recite the Homeric poems because of their frequent references to Argives, and expelled the Argive hero *Adrastus from his tomb in Sicyon. This, together with his substitution of insulting names for the old Dorian tribe-names (see PHYLAI) in Sicyon, seems to have led to war with Argos. Earlier, Cleisthenes had taken a leading part in the *Sacred War of c.590 in support of Delphi against Crisa. His daughter Agaristē married the *Alcmaeonid Megacles and was mother of the Athenian Cleisthenes: see (2) below. For her marriage see HIPPOCLEIDES.

2. *Archon in (perhaps) 525, d. after 507 BC, the founder of Athenian democracy, son of Megacles the Alcmaeonid who married Agaristē the daughter of Cleisthenes, tyrant of Sicyon (see 1 above). It was said that by promising that his family would in part pay for the rebuilding of the temple at Delphi he persuaded the priestess to tell all Spartans who consulted the Delphic Oracle that they must first overthrow the tyranny of the *Peisistratids at Athens. When the Spartan king *Cleomenes I was successful in expelling the tyrant *Hippias (son of Peisistratus) in 510 and those exiled had returned, there was a movement in favour of oligarchy by the aristocracy in Athens, led by Isagoras and supported by Cleomenes. At this point Cleisthenes put himself forward as the champion of democracy and overthrew the aristocrats. He then proceeded to pass far-reaching political reforms of a democratic nature. He broke up what remained of the old political organization based on family groups, and in particular on the four Ionian *tribes (phylai), and substituted a new system based on topography. He divided the territory of Attica, including the city of Athens, into *demes (dēmoi), local communities or parishes, possibly on the basis of existing demes. All citizens were enrolled in one or other of the demes, and many *metics and freedmen were admitted to the *citizenship. Cleisthenes then grouped all the demes into ten new tribes so as to ensure that no tribe had a continuous territory or represented a local interest; on the contrary, each contained groups of demes (*trittyes) from the city region, from the coast, and from the interior. By these means groups of people in various parts of Attica were brought together and required to act in common, and the old parties acting out of purely local interest were abolished. The organization of the army depended on the tribes, each of which contributed a regiment of hoplites and a squadron of cavalry. The original *phratriai, 'clans' (subdivisions of a tribe), survived in the constitution as a kind of religious community for carrying out certain cults, and Cleisthenes probably compelled them to admit those whom he had enfranchised so that no citizen was excluded. Each tribe furnished annually fifty members to the *boulē ('council'), taken by lot from the demes of the tribe in proportion to their populations. These groups of fifty acted in turn as the executive committee of the boule (see PRYTANY), each group holding office for one tenth of the year. Cleisthenes subordinated the boule and the *Areopagus to the supreme authority of the *ecclesia, 'assembly' of all the citizens, which met regularly and might deal with any important state matter. In one respect Cleisthenes was conservative: he seems to have retained Solon's restrictions on eligibility for the higher offices of state. The archons could be chosen only from the two wealthiest classes of the population, and the *Eupatridae retained the monopoly of priestly offices. It is possible that *ostracism was introduced by Cleisthenes to protect his constitution, which was accepted and remained the basis of the later democracy. At his death Cleisthenes received a public burial in the *Ceramicus.

Cleitus, brother of the foster-mother of Alexander the Great and one of his cavalry commanders. He saved Alexander's life at the battle of the Granicus (334 BC), but was subsequently murdered by him in a drunken brawl in 327.

Clement of Alexandria, born at Athens c. AD 150, one of the early Greek Fathers of the Church. Clement was converted to Christianity and sought instruction from Pantaenus, head of the Catechetical School of Alexandria. He succeeded the latter as head in 190, but in 202 persecution forced him to flee. He was conspicuous for his wide knowledge of Greek literature, especially of Greek philosophy. His writings abound in quotations from the Platonic and Stoic philosophers, and from Homer, Hesiod, and the dramatists. He died between 211 and 216. Many of his writings are lost; the most important of those surviving are the Protrepticus, 'exhortation' to the Greeks, designed to demonstrate the superiority of Christianity to the pagan religions and philosophies, and showing familiarity with the Greek Orphic and Eleusinian mysteries (see MYSTERIES); the Paedagōgus ('tutor'), a course of instruction on Christian life and manners; and Strōmateis ('miscellanies'), dealing mainly with the relationship (and inferiority) of Greek philosophy to Christian philosophy, but regarding it as also a divine gift to the world. His conception of Christianity has been criticized for being tinged with Hellenism and therefore not wholly orthodox.

Cle'obis and Bitōn, sons of the Argive priestess of Hera, who were described by Solon to Croesus, according to a story in Herodotus (1. 31), as having been among the happiest of men. When on one occasion the oxen for the priestess's chariot were not brought in time, her sons drew it for some distance to the temple. She prayed to Hera to grant them the greatest blessing possible for mortals, and the goddess caused them to fall asleep in the temple and die in their sleep. Their statues, erected by the Argives at Delphi in the early sixth century BC, have been found there.

Cleo'menēs. 1. **Cleomenes I**, from *c*.520–*c*.490 BC king of Sparta of the *Agiad line. He expelled the tyrant *Hippias from Athens in 510. In 508 he supported the aristocratic faction in the city, led by Isagoras, against *Cleisthenes, and by invoking the hereditary curse of the *Alcmaeonidae, to which family Cleisthenes belonged, compelled him and his supporters to retire. When Cleomenes arrived in Athens and attempted to set up Isagoras and his friends in a narrow oligarchy, there was a popular uprising; after being besieged in the Acropolis both were obliged to withdraw, and Cleisthenes was able to return. Later Cleomenes failed in attempts to restore first Isagoras and then the tyrant Hippias, obstructed in both cases by his fellow king Demaratus. The latter also prevented him from punishing Aegina in 491, when that island was suspected of favouring Persia before the outbreak of the Persian War.

2. **Cleomenes III**, b. *c*.260 BC, king of Sparta from 235 to 219. Following the social ideals of his predecessor Agis IV, whose widow he married, he attempted to restore Spartan power by a series of reforms designed to rehabilitate the constitution of *Lycurgus; they entailed abolishing the ephorate, cancelling debts, making a new distribution of land, and restocking the citizen body from *perioikoi and *metics. This was in 226–225, when Cleomenes had already built up a strong position in the state by his successful wars against the *Achaean League. The reforms were in part carried out, but in 222 Cleomenes was defeated at Sellasia by the Achaeans under Aratus of Sicyon and fled to his patron Ptolemy III Euergetes in Egypt; there he committed suicide in 219. He was a nationalist and an idealist whose ideals lived on after him, but in practical terms he made no lasting gains.

Clēon (d. 422 BC), Athenian politician prominent during the first part of the Peloponnesian War, the son of a rich tanner. His first known political acts were attacks on *Pericles in 431 and 430. After Pericles' death in 429 he succeeded him as the most influential politician of his day. In 427 he proposed the decree (carried but rescinded the following day) to execute all the men of Mitylene after the suppression of its revolt. He favoured the ruthless pursuit of victory in the war, by any means so long as it brought power, glory, and wealth to the Athenian people. After the Athenian victory at Pylos in 425 (see PELOPONNESIAN WAR 3) he thwarted the Spartan peace proposals. He attacked for incompetence the generals who were unsuccessfully besieging the Spartans on the island of Sphacteria, and when Nicias proposed to hand over the command to him he was forced to accept. With the help of the general Demosthenes, Cleon was able to make good his promise to take Sphacteria and

bring home the prisoners within twenty days. He gained popularity with the people at this time by raising the pay of the dicasts (see LAW, AT ATHENS) from two to three obols, and would certainly have supported, if he did not originate, the measure greatly increasing the tribute paid by the allies (see DELIAN LEAGUE). In 423 he secured a decree for the destruction of Scione and the execution of its citizens (carried out in 421). After Athenian setbacks in Thrace he was elected *strategos and commanded the expedition to that area, but after some successes he was defeated and killed at Amphipolis by the Spartan general Brasidas, who was himself mortally wounded (422). His death and that of Brasidas removed the principal obstacles to the Peace of Nicias, which was concluded in 421.

A vivid but hostile picture of Cleon as a coarse and unscrupulous *demagogue is presented by Thucydides and by Aristophanes, and we have no independent witnesses who might give a less prejudiced view. His influence lay in his forceful and bullying style of oratory, antiintellectual and anti-aristocratic in tone, and his appeal to the emotions and prejudices of the people. He seems to have aimed at short-term goals, but Athens' poor stood to benefit by his policies, at the expense of her allies.

Cleopa'tra VII (69–30 BC), daughter of Ptolemy XII Auletēs, king of Egypt (d. 51 BC), appointed by him as his successor with her younger brother, Ptolemy XIII, to whom she was nominally married. (By Ptolemaic custom she could not rule alone.) She was expelled in 48 by her brother's party but reinstated by Julius *Caesar (see 3), who was in Egypt in pursuit of Pompey. When in the consequent war, the Bellum Alexandrinum, Ptolemy XIII lost his life Cleopatra married another younger brother, Ptolemy XIV, but was effectively sole ruler. By now she was Caesar's mistress: according to a well-known story she had gained entry to his apartment in a bale of cloth. In 47 she gave birth to a son, *Caesarion, declaring that Caesar was the father. In 46 she followed Caesar to Rome, returning to Egypt after his murder. When Ptolemy XIV died soon after, perhaps poisoned by her, she made her son co-ruler. In the Roman civil war following Caesar's murder she naturally sided with the triumvirate against the murderers. In 41 she met Mark *Antony at Tarsus in Cilicia; he spent the winter of 41–40 in Alexandria, and she bore him twins, a son and a daughter. After 37 she and Antony were in permanent association, and by 32, when Rome declared war on Cleopatra (alone), the association was seen as a threat to the Roman empire and to Octavian. The Romans believed she had boasted that she would dispense justice from the Capitol. After their defeat in the sea-battle at *Actium (31), in which her fleet caused a sensation by fleeing, Cleopatra and Antony sought peace terms from Octavian, but without success. Alexandria was surrendered in 30 and Antony committed suicide. Cleopatra was ordered to leave for Rome, and apparently committed suicide to avoid the shame of participating in Octavian's triumph. The story that she died by the bite of an asp (said to be painless) was accepted enthusiastically by the Romans as appropriate for a barbarian queen, and reported with some reservations by the historians.

Cleopatra was Greek by descent (the name is found in Homer), from Alexander's general Ptolemy Soter, and with her ended the Macedonian dynasty of the *Ptolemies in Egypt. We do not know her true character behind the romantic tales; she clearly had personal courage, and she wielded sufficient power to be feared by the Romans. Her beauty, charm, and melodious voice were outstanding; on her famous nose the French philosopher Pascal observed that had it been shorter the whole history of the world would have been different.

Clě'ophon, Athenian politician prominent in the latter part of the Peloponnesian War, and a leader of the people (*demagogue) after the restoration of democratic rule in 410 BC. He introduced a dole of two obols a day for poor citizens. His manner was as aggressive as *Cleon's, and he prevented the Athenians from accepting Sparta's peace offers in 410 and 405. He was prosecuted and condemned to death by the *oligarchs in 404.

cle'psydra, the water-clock, consisting essentially of a vessel with a small opening at the bottom through which water was allowed to trickle. It was originally used to measure the time for which people were allowed to speak in the lawcourts at Athens and appears to have been in common use from at least the second half of the fifth century BC (see LAW, AT ATHENS 3). As used in the courts the clepsydra did not measure time absolutely, but vessels of similar construction were used in ordinary life for dividing the time from sunrise to sunset into twelve equal parts, so far as that could be achieved. The vessel itself might be graduated, or there could be a graduated container to catch the outflow. The difficulty of maintaining an even flow of water was one cause of inaccuracy, but refinements were introduced to overcome this, and to compensate for seasonal variation in the period of daylight. The clepsydra was introduced into Roman lawcourts by Pompey during his third consulship (52 BC). See CLOCKS and EMPEDOCLES.

clěruch (klērouchos), Athenian citizen who held an allotment (klēros) of land in a foreign country. A cleruchy (klērouchia) or group of such cleruchs differed from a colony in that the former retained their Athenian citizenship, did not create a new, independent community, and did not even necessarily reside on their allotted land. This kind of settlement on conquered territory (Greek and foreign) was introduced in the last years of the sixth century BC and was much developed in the fifth, when it became an important feature in the Athenian imperial system. It ensured a sort of permanent garrison in foreign territory and in that of the allies (see DELIAN LEAGUE), in addition to providing land for the poor. The leader of a cleruchy was known as the oecist (oikistes). Important cleruchies were in Chalcis (506, and again c.446), Naxos, the Thracian Chersonese, Lemnos, Euboea (446), and Aegina (431). See also COLONIZATION, GREEK.

client, at Rome, in early republican times, a free man who entrusted himself to a powerful *patron to whom he rendered services and from whom he received protection; a freedman became automatically the client of his former owner. The *Twelve Tables recognized the tie of clientship as legally binding. The client would show his patron respect, particularly by greeting him in the morning, attend him in the streets, and give him political support. In return the client would receive daily a dole of food or money (sportula). Under the empire the client became almost indistinguishable from the *parasite, the subservient hanger-on, familiar from the satires of Juvenal and Martial. Certain conquered foreign states are sometimes spoken of as 'clients' of Rome, and some individuals and families in Rome built up a large following of foreign 'clients'.

Clĭo (Kleiō), see MUSES.

Cloā'ca Ma'xima, the great sewer of Rome, originally an open watercourse, later vaulted and paved. Starting from Argiletum it carried the waters from the Esquiline, Viminal, and Quirinal hills to the river Tiber by way of the *Forum Romanum, which was then sufficiently drained to allow large-scale building. Its construction was attributed to the Tarquins, and more particularly to Tarquinius Superbus in the late sixth century BC. It was first enclosed in the third century BC, and much of the existing sewer is the work of M. Vipsanius *Agrippa in c.33 BC. It still forms part of the drainage system of the modern city. (See CRATES 4.)

Cloa'nthus, in Virgil's Aeneid, a companion of Aeneas. He figures in the boat-race (book 5).

clocks (horologia; sing. Gk. hōrologion, Lat. hōrologium). In ordinary life the Greeks and Romans referred to the time of day in descriptive terms, 'first light', 'midday', etc. The hour, when used, was not a twenty-fourth part of the astronomical day but one-twelfth of the time from sunrise to sunset (or sunset to sunrise), and its length therefore varied with latitude and season. The clocks which were used to measure these hours in the ancient world were all variants of two basic kinds, the shadow-clock or sundial and the water-clock (*clepsydra). The earliest preserved examples have been found in Egypt. According to Herodotus, the Greeks learned the use of the shadow-clock from the Babylonians. (A later tradition ascribed the invention to *Anaximander or Anaximenes.) In its simplest form it consisted of a vertical staff, the *gnōmōn*, set up in a place exposed to the sun so that its shadow might be measured. Another version was the *pŏlŏs*, a concave basin in the centre of which a *gnomon* was erected. The shadow-clock had disadvantages other than its dependence on sunshine: it required different scales according to latitude, and for dividing the period of daylight into equal parts it required, like the water-clock, seasonal correction. The first clocks brought to Rome in the third century BC were shadow-clocks in the form of sundials, *sōlāria*, erected in public view. The most famous was one captured in Sicily in 263 BC and set up on a column behind the Rostra, but it was unfortunately not adapted to the latitude of Rome. P. Scipio Nasica, during his censorship of 159 BC, erected a public clepsydra which told the hours of day and of night. A magnificent shadow-clock was erected by Augustus in the Campus Martius, its *gnomon* an Egyptian obelisk (see HOROLOGIUM OF AUGUSTUS). Clocks were also kept by private individuals (see HEROPHILUS); Cicero sent one to Tiro. The Alexandrian inventor Ctesibius was said to have designed a water-clock in which dripping water turned wheels which gradually elevated a small statue whose pointing stick indicated the passing hours. Clepsydrae were used by the Romans in their military camps to measure the four watches into which the night was divided. See also HOROLOGION OF ANDRONICUS.

Clō'dia, in Rome, b. *c*.95 BC, second of the three sisters of P. *Clodius and wife of Q. Metellus Celer (consul in 60), notorious for her profligacy. Among her lovers was the poet *Catullus, who celebrated her as 'Lesbia' (the identification is virtually certain). Cicero paints a vivid picture of her in his letters and especially in his speech of 56, *Pro Caelio* (see CICERO (1) 4). She may have been still alive in 45 BC.

Clō'dius. 1. Publius Clodius Pulcher, b. *c*.92 BC, Roman patrician of the famous Claudian *gens*, who, like his sister Clodia (see above) and some other members of the *gens*, used the plebeian form of the name. He was notorious for his violence and profligacy, and as the enemy of Cicero. For his profanation of the mysteries of the Bona Dea in 62 BC, his hatred of Cicero, resulting in the latter's exile in 58, his

feud with Milo, and his violent death in 52 see CICERO (1) 3 and 4.

2. Decimus Clodius Albīnus, governor of Britain at the end of the second century AD. See BRITAIN 5.

Cloe'lia, according to Roman legend, one of the Roman hostages given to the Etruscan king Lars *Porsen(n)a in the course of his war with the newly founded Roman republic (510 BC). She escaped by swimming across the Tiber to Rome, but had to be handed back to Porsenna; he freed her, however, together with some of her companions, in admiration of her bravery, thus initiating a reconciliation between the two sides. The Romans erected an equestrian statue to her on the Via Sacra.

clothes, see DRESS.

Clōtho, 'spinner', one of the three Greek *Fates.

Cloudcuckooland, see BIRDS.

Clouds (*Nephelai*, Lat. *Nūbēs*), Greek comedy by *Aristophanes, ridiculing Socrates as a typical *sophist and corrupt propagator of ridiculous new ideas among the young. The play was originally produced at the City *Dionysia of 423 BC but won only third (and last) prize, and Aristophanes, who seems to have thought it his best play to date, set about rewriting it. We have only the (incompletely) revised version dating from the period 418–416, which was never performed.

Strepsīadēs ('twister'), an elderly dishonest farmer, has been financially ruined by his fashionable wife and horse-loving son Pheidippidēs. He has heard of Socrates, a man who can make the worse cause appear the better, and hopes that he will teach his son how to defraud his creditors. As his son refuses to enter Socrates' school (the *phrontistērion*, 'think-shop'), Strepsiades decides to go himself. He is told he must resign himself to hard work and simple living, and is introduced to the Clouds who (and not Zeus, as generally believed) are the deities who produce thunder and rain. But Strepsiades is too stupid and too much concerned with his debts to learn very much, and Pheidippides has to take his place as pupil. Socrates hands Pheidippides over to be instructed by Right and Wrong in person. A contest between these two (one of the substituted scenes) follows, in which Wrong is victorious. Strepsiades, by the aid of what little he has learnt, is able to confute his creditors. But the tables are turned on him when, as a result of the same learning, Pheidippides starts to beat his father (and threatens to beat his mother too), and proves that he is justified in doing so. Strepsiades, disgusted with the new education and repenting of his dishonesty, sets fire to Socrates' school and drives the inmates away.

clubs, in Greece and Rome, associations of

people who shared the same function (e.g. priests, magistrates: see COLLEGIUM), the same profession, or the same worship. In Greece, clubs existed as early as the beginning of the sixth century BC, and political clubs (*hetaireiai*) were common in fifth-century Athens as were those devoted to the cult of a hero or a god not yet admitted into state worship, e.g. Asclepius. They proliferated in the Hellenistic period and throughout the Greco-Roman world, playing a valuable part in uniting diverse elements of the population, men and women, free men and slaves, Greeks and foreigners, and pleasurably fulfilling social needs. At Rome, most clubs were either military, industrial, or purely funeral. The primary object of all three was to provide honourable burial for their deceased members, but in doing so they fostered the social life and the general well-being of their members. The military clubs were mainly associations of ex-servicemen. Young men formed sporting clubs. Clubs or guilds of craftsmen were formed at Rome from very early times; according to tradition they were first founded by Numa. They do not seem to have exercised any functions comparable with those of a modern trade union, and their funds were expended on the burial of members, common worship, and various festivities, rather than for the benefit of the sick and needy. Complete freedom of association was allowed, although some clubs which became involved in political action in the Ciceronian age were suppressed. Under Augustus every club had to be sanctioned by the senate or the emperor, and in general the sanction was freely given. The administration of clubs gave satisfaction to many humble people excluded from the higher rungs of municipal life.

Cly'menē, name of several women in Greek myth of whom the following are the most important.

   1. Daughter of Oceanus and Tethys and wife of the Titan Iapetus, by whom she became the mother of Atlas, Prometheus, and Epimetheus (see individual entries).

   2. Daughter of *Minyas and wife of *Cephalus; as a result of her union with *Helios she became the mother of Phaethon. She was also the mother of *Atalanta.

Clytemne'stra (Klytaim(n)ēstrā), in Greek myth, daughter of Tyndareus king of Sparta, and Leda; sister of Helen (of Troy), Castor, and Polydeuces (Lat. Pollux). She married Agamemnon king of Mycenae and became the mother of Iphigeneia (or Iphianassa), Chrysothemis, Electra (or Laodicē), and Orestes. During Agamemnon's absence in the Trojan War she took Aegisthus as lover, and upon Agamemnon's return with Cassandra, his Trojan concubine, she killed them both, Agamemnon in the bath. When Orestes reached manhood he killed his mother and

Aegisthus. The chief interest of her story for the authors who related it is the variety of motives it admits for the murder of Agamemnon, and the different characterizations it therefore makes possible.

Cnidus, Greek city on the coast of Caria in south-western Asia Minor, a Lacedaemonian colony, and one of the six Dorian colonies in Asia Minor known collectively as the Dorian Hexapolis, namely Cnidus, Cos, Halicarnassus (before its expulsion), and the three cities of Rhodes: Lindus, Ialysus, and Camirus. Owing to its favourable situation it acquired great wealth from trade. Famous citizens include *Ctēsias and *Eudoxus. Aphroditē was worshipped there, and the Cnidians, who seem to have been fond of art, possessed the statue by *Praxiteles of the goddess naked; they refused the king of Bithynia's offer to pay their public debt in exchange for it. (See also DELPHI.) In the fifth century BC Cnidus developed a flourishing medical school; with Cos it became the main centre for teaching medicine, with its own particular doctrines and practices (see MEDICINE).

Cnossus (Knōsos or Knōssos), the most famous city of *Crete in ancient times, situated near the middle of the north coast of the island about 6 km. (4 miles) inland. Its foundation was attributed to the legendary king *Minos who also built there the *labyrinth to contain the Minotaur. Sir Arthur Evans, who first excavated the palace and surrounding city at Cnossus from 1900 onwards, gave the name Minoan to the civilization of the third and second millennia BC which was revealed by his work. The palace was built on top of a 'tell' of debris, 6 m. (20 ft.) deep, from a neolithic settlement. Several similar palace-cities have been excavated in Crete, built first soon after 2000 BC and rebuilt and extended in the course of the following millennium; but that of Cnossus is so far the largest, the main building alone covering 1.2 hectares (3 acres), and the city around it perhaps 1 sq. km. (0.4 sq. mile). The striking features of the palace are the large central court and the many storage rooms which witness to its importance as an economic centre. The large number of clay tablets discovered in the palace, written in *Linear B, are all concerned with the administration. The palace was finally destroyed in about 1350 BC, having been occupied earlier by (Mycenaean) Greeks from the mainland. See also RELIGION, GREEK 1.

Cock, The, see LUCIAN.

Coclēs, Publius Horā'tius, the legendary Roman hero Horatius, the subject of the best known of the *Lays of Ancient Rome* by the nineteenth-century English writer Thomas Macaulay. With two companions, Sp. Larcius and T. Herminius, Horatius held at bay the whole Etruscan army under Lars *Porsen(n)a while the wooden Sublician bridge over the Tiber into Rome was being cut down behind them. At the moment of its collapse he sent back his two companions and held the position single-handed, finally jumping into the river and swimming back to the city.

Cocy'tus, in Greek myth, one of the rivers of *Hades. It was also the name of a tributary of the Acheron in Epirus.

cōdex, see BOOKS AND WRITING and JUSTINIAN.

codex Sinaïticus, one of the most celebrated manuscripts of the Greek Bible, probably dating from the late fourth century (see SEPTUAGINT and JEROME). It was found in the monastery of St Catherine on Mount Sinai in the mid-nineteenth century, acquired by the Tzar of Russia, and bought by the British Museum (for £100,000) in 1933.

Codrus, in Athenian legend, son of Melanthus, descendant of *Neleus, and a member of the Messenian royal family. When the Dorians captured Messenia, Codrus came to Athens; there he became king at the time when the Dorians conquered the Peloponnese. When they invaded Attica (roughly in the eleventh century BC; see DORIAN INVASION) they were told by an oracle that they would be victorious if they spared the king. Codrus, hearing this, entered the Dorian camp in disguise, provoked a quarrel, and was killed; the Dorians then withdrew. One tradition said that because no one was thought worthy to succeed such a king, the kingly office was thereafter abolished, and *archons appointed instead. The first archonship was held by Codrus' son Medon, from whom *Solon and *Peisistratus claimed descent. Another tradition made a later descendant the first archon.

Cogidu'bnus, client king of the British Atre-bates from *c.* AD 43 to 75. The villa at Fish-bourne, near Chichester in Hampshire, may have been built for him. (See BRITAIN 3.)

cognō'men, see NAMES 2.

cohort, in the Roman army, the tenth part of a legion, nominally 600 men. A legion varied in size at different periods, and therefore a cohort actually comprised between 300 and 600 men. The first cohort seems always to have been regarded as superior to the rest. Occasionally the word is used in the general sense of 'battalion' to denote a body of troops distinct from the legion. The general's personal bodyguard was known as the *cohors praetoria,* which under the empire turned into the *praetorian guard.

coinage, see MONEY AND COINS.

Cōlax ('flatterer'), Greek comedy by *Men-ander, made use of by Terence for his own *Eunuchus. Some fragments of *Colax* have been

recovered from papyri but it is difficult to reconstruct the plot. It concerned an arrogant Greek professional soldier.

Colchis, country at the eastern end of the Black Sea, bounded on the north by the Caucasus, famous in Greek legend as the destination of the *Argonauts and the home of *Medea. It was also known as Aea. Its river, Phasis, was sometimes regarded as forming the boundary between Europe and Asia, its navigable waters taking sailors from the Black Sea as far east as they could go.

Colise'um, see COLOSSEUM.

collē'gium ('college'), at Rome, an association of people who shared the same function, e.g. *magistrates and priests.
1. *Magisterial.* In the Roman republic every magistracy was filled by at least two officials so as to prevent political power falling into the hands of one man. Magistrates holding the same office (e.g. the two consuls) were *collegae,* 'colleagues'. This principle of equal *imperium* was a feature which greatly impressed foreigners.
2. *Priestly.* Each of the several priesthoods at Rome, including the *fetiales, *pontifices, and *augures* (see AUGURY), had its own *collegium.* (See also CLUBS.) The *collegium pontificum* ('college of pontiffs') included as well as the pontiffs the *flamens, *Vestal Virgins, and *rex sacrorum.* The priestly colleges, which had some of the characteristics of a modern club, were famous for their good dinners.

Colline Gate, at Rome, on the north-east side of the city, the scene of a battle in 82 BC in which *Sulla, after his return from the first Mithridatic War in the East, finally overcame the Marian forces and made himself master of Italy.

cōlon, see METRE, GREEK 8 (i).

colō'ni. 1. Tenant farmers in Italy who tilled public land or the land of private landlords. See AGRICULTURE 2 and LATIFUNDIA.
2. Members of a Roman colony (see COLON-IZATION, ROMAN 1).

colonization. 1. Greek
1. *General.* The first great age of Greek colon-ization, during which Greek cities were founded around the coasts of the Mediterranean and the Black Sea, was from the mid-eighth to the mid-sixth century BC. It may be regarded as a continuation of the movement which took Greek settlers across the Aegean to found the Greek cities in Asia Minor, very roughly from the eleventh to the early eighth century BC (see MIGRATIONS, GREEK). The city-states undertook colonization independently, so that the settlers in each colony came from only one or two cities. The main impetus in the eighth century

seems to have been land shortage in Greece and consequent poverty and famine; the amount of land that could be cultivated was very limited, and the traditional Greek pattern of inheritance was equal division between all the sons. There were also political reasons. In some states the aristocratic form of government, being exclusive and oppressive, bred discontent, so that men were encouraged to seek better conditions for themselves elsewhere. Occasionally the prospect of profitable trade may have been an inducement. Information from traders determined the situation of some colonies, which therefore tended to be founded on trade routes; for example, Massilia (Marseilles; see below) controlled the route up the Rhone valley. In a climate of opinion generally favourable to colonization, special factors were sometimes influential: Cyrene in North Africa was founded as a consequence of a prolonged drought in the island of Thera; the Greek cities of southern Asia Minor were unable to expand inland because the countries of the hinterland were far too strong for them; hence Rhodes and Miletus sent colonies overseas. The founding emigrants took with them fire from the sacred hearth of their city (see RELIGION, GREEK 2), and the state appointed an official oecist (*oikistes*, 'founder') as head of the venture. A Greek colony was normally an independent sovereign state, not politically dependent on its mother city, though ties between the two were often close. The *Delphic Oracle had the opportunity to play an important political role during the early period of colonization, being regularly consulted on choice of site and of patron deity.

2. *Greek colonization in the West.* The Greek colonists first sought fertile areas which were easily defended and possessed good harbours. Thus Sicily and south Italy (where the Greek cities came to be known collectively as Magna Graecia, 'Great Greece') were settled first, the pioneer in this direction being (Ionian) Euboea. Euboeans may well have been the first settlers in Corcyra (Corfu) also, an island in the north-west of Greece off the coast of Epirus, before they were dispossessed by Corinthians (see below). The Euboean cities Chalcis and Eretria founded *Cumae north of the Bay of Naples, traditionally the first Greek colony in the West and for some time the most distant. The original settlement had been on the island of Pithecusae (Ischia) *c.*750 BC, but a little later there was a move to the mainland.

From there the Cumaean Greeks exercised strong influence on the neighbouring Italian peoples, perhaps introducing the Greek alphabet and a knowledge of Greek religion. Cumae became an important centre of trade both with the inhabitants of the Italian peninsula and with the people beyond the Alps. The Euboeans also, together with Ionians from the Aegean island of Naxos, founded the first Greek colony in Sicily,

also called Naxos, in 734 BC, on a tongue of lava jutting into the sea north-west of Mount Etna. Within six years the Naxians themselves sent two colonies further south and colonized Leontini and Catana. For centuries these three colonies possessed the richest land in Sicily. In addition to these colonies the Euboeans founded during the same period (*c.*730) Zanclē on the north-east coast of Sicily, later named Messana by Messenian immigrants and itself the founder of Himera (648), and Rhegium (Rhēgion) on the toe of Italy opposite. The (Dorian) Corinthians too were active colonists. They left a colony at *Corcyra (having first, it appears, ousted the Euboeans) on that same expedition which had as its aim the foundation of *Syracuse (733). See also CYPSELUS.

Syracuse eventually became the most brilliant and populous city of Sicily, and in her turn founded Camarina (598). Other important colonies in Sicily were Dorian also. Megara founded Megara Hyblaea (728) north of Syracuse, from where a century later colonists, joined by others from the mother-city, founded Selīnus. Crete and Rhodes founded Gela in 688, and Gela subsequently (580) founded Acragas (Lat. Agrigentum). Acragas and Selinus were the most westerly points in Sicily reached by Greek colonization; beyond these the island was in Phoenician hands. Meanwhile Achaeans from the Peloponnese settled most of the colonies in south Italy. *Sybaris (720) and its rival *Croton (709), their principal foundations, became extremely wealthy owing to their fertile territories. However, Taras, better known by its Latin name Tarentum, in the 'instep' of south Italy, was a Dorian colony, founded by the so-called Partheniai, political undesirables despatched safely away from *Sparta after the First Messenian War; it was the only Laconian colony. One important venture in the extreme west remains to be mentioned: Phocaea, the most northerly Ionian Greek city in Asia Minor, opened up *Spain and *Tartessus between 640 and 550, and founded the colony of Massalia (Lat. Massilia, now Marseilles) in about 600 BC, apparently to control the trading route up the Rhône; the Massalians in turn established settlements in many directions, inland at the future Arles, along the Riviera (Agathe, Agde; Antipolis, Antibes; Nīcaea, Nice), westward at Pyrēnē (whence 'Pyrenees'), and at the future Malaga on the coast of Spain. For another Phocaean colony see ELEA.

3. *Greek colonization around the north Aegean, Black Sea, and Propontis.* For colonization in this area only approximate dates can be given. The chief founders of colonies in the north Aegean were Euboeans from the cities of Chalcis and Eretria, Megarians, Corinthians, and inhabitants of the islands and cities of Asia Minor, notably Miletus. In the late eighth and early seventh centuries BC the Chalcidians of Euboea founded

so many cities on the three-pronged promontory south of Macedonia that the whole area acquired the name Chalcidicē. Some of the chief cities, however, were founded by other states, notably *Potidaea by the Corinthians, on the neck of the western prong. Along the coast of Macedonia and Thrace, from the Euboean towns of Pydna and Methonē eastwards, colonies were planted up to the Hellespont, where the Lesbians founded Sestus and the Milesians Abȳdus early in the seventh century BC. At about that time the Megarians gained control of the Bosporus by founding first *Chalcedon (c.680) on the eastern side, and then, chided by the Delphic Oracle for their blindness, *Byzantium (c.660) on the western side. The Milesians established Cyzicus on the Propontis and took the lead in planting colonies around the Black Sea, perhaps as early as the mid-seventh century onwards. They founded Sinōpē and its daughter city Trapezus (Trebizond) on the southern shore, and among other settlements on the western shore the important town of Olbia in the north-west corner. In the sixth century Greek colonists went further east, reaching the Tauric Chersonese (the Crimea) and occupying Panticapaeum on its easternmost tip, opposite the mouth of the Tanais (Don), which became the commercial centre of the region, and the Megarians from Byzantium founded Heraclēa on the same peninsula. The Athenians had in Attica a large territory into which to expand, and therefore colonized relatively late: their first colony, c.610 BC, was situated at Sigēum, on the route from the corn-growing areas around the Black Sea, their aim being to protect their corn-route. In the mid-sixth century BC the Thracian Chersonese, also on the corn route, passed into the control of the elder *Miltiades, who went there with settlers. Athenian settlers were on Lemnos and Imbros c.499, Byzantium was captured in 478, and Scyros was captured and colonized in 476. In 436, after earlier attempts had been unsuccessful, Athens colonized Amphipolis, a city on the east bank of the Strymon, strategically and commercially important. The Greek colonies on the Black Sea had great economic importance as centres of trade, for as well as exporting large quantities of corn grown on the fertile Scythian plains, they also supplied slaves, gold, dried or salted fish, cattle, and horses; they in turn imported wine and oil (see also CORN SUPPLY).

4. *Greek colonization in the South and East.* In general Greek settlers were excluded from developed parts of the Mediterranean world such as Egypt and the Syrian coast, although occasionally trading settlements were established by the invitation of a ruler. Posideion (Al Mina), founded in the eighth century BC at the mouth of the Orontes in Syria, may have been such a settlement. The best known settlement of this type is *Naucratis in Egypt, on the Canopic

(west) branch of the Nile, founded according to Strabo by Milesians in the seventh century. In 550 BC in the reign of the Pharoah Amasis it became the sole emporium for Greek traders and thus the main centre for cultural relations between Greeks and Egyptians. The important and prosperous colony of *Cyrene in North Africa was founded in 630 from the Dorian island of Thera in the south Aegean, under the leadership of Battus, and augmented two generations later with new settlers from Crete and the Peloponnese. It is the only known colony where the founder successfully established a ruling dynasty.

5. As a result of these enterprises, the sixth century BC saw Greek colonies scattered along most of the shores of the Mediterranean and Black Sea 'like frogs round a pond', as Plato said, not united under any central control, but at liberty to work out their own destinies, with important consequences for the history of western civilization. They were the basis for the diffusion of Greek culture, and being themselves subject to the influence of their surroundings they transmuted and developed that culture in original ways, giving it new life and variety.

The second great period of Greek colonization was under *Alexander the Great, when Alexander himself founded a large number of colonies spread over the many territories he had conquered, in Persia, Mesopotamia, Egypt, India, and Afghanistan. These colonies were designed to keep his conquests peaceful and stable, to spread Greek civilization, and to foster trade, and Alexander's successors followed the same policy: hence the numerous cities in the East bearing such names as Alexandria, Antioch, and Seleucia. They were mostly situated in Asia Minor, Syria, and Egypt, but some were in more distant regions, Persia and India.

See also CLERUCH.

2. Roman

1. *Early Roman colonies.* The earliest colonies of Roman citizens were sent out by the state and not founded by private initiative as in Greece. They were designed for military defence, to guard the coastline, and were limited to Italy only. Ostia was by tradition Rome's first colony (soon after 350 BC), followed by Antium (338) and Tarracina (329). Others were added as Roman territory expanded. In 218 BC there were twelve such seaboard colonies, all fortified towns endowed with a certain area of public land acquired by conquest. Being within Roman territory, the inhabitants of these colonies retained their Roman citizenship though they might be too far from Rome to exercise their rights.

The *Latin colonies*, so-called, had a different constitution. (The title refers not to the people forming the colony but to their political rights (see LATIN RIGHTS); after the final defeat of the

Latin League in 338 BC Latin colonies were largely composed of Romans.) They were independent states, subject to Rome's control only in foreign policy and in their obligation to supply contingents to the Roman army. Those members who had Roman citizenship surrendered it, but had rights of trade under the protection of the Roman courts, and of intermarriage with Roman citizens. By the end of the second century BC, colonies were established throughout Italy, guarding a large number of strategic points. All colonists were known as *coloni*.

2. *Roman colonies in later republican and imperial times*. From the second century BC the character of Roman colonization underwent a change; colonies began to be founded more frequently and for economic reasons, some of them overseas. The first (abortive) foundation outside Italy was the colony Junonia, set up by Gaius *Gracchus on the territory of Carthage in 122, and in 118 Narbo Martius (Narbonne) was successfully founded in Provence. Those colonies of Gracchus and of Julius *Caesar which were more successful, notably that at Corinth, were mostly designed to provide land for the poor and to redevelop derelict areas. Other colonies (e.g. *Sulla's and those of the first triumviral period) were founded to supply land for veterans. Among the notable colonies of later republican times were Corduba (Cordoba) in Spain, and Aquae Sextiae (Aix) and Arelātē (Arles) in Gaul. Africa too became an important area of Roman colonization: *Marius settled many of his veterans there, and numbers of Italians went to Cirta and other African cities for commercial reasons.

The process of colonization in outlying parts of the empire was continued under the Roman emperors, largely for the purpose of providing land for veterans, and many cities were founded or enlarged. The imposing ruins of some of these still remain. In other cases colonies were the outcome of the military system of stationing legions in permanent fortresses on the frontiers. Semi-civilian settlements grew up near these fortresses and were the origins of modern cities such as Colōnia Agrippīna (Cologne), Lindum (Lincoln), and Eburācum (York).

colonnade, row of columns joined by an entablature (see ARCHITECTURE 1 (i); see also STOA).

colo'nus, see COLONI.

Colō'nus, deme or district of Attica, about 1.5 km. (1 mile) north-west of the *Dipylon at Athens, the legendary scene of the death of *Oedipus, and the birthplace of Sophocles.

Colosse'um, at Rome, the name by which the Flavian *amphitheatre has been known at least since the eighth century AD (it is first found in a work attributed to Bede (673–735)). Its name is derived from a large statue (see COLOSSUS) of the emperor Nero which stood nearby. It was situated at the foot of the Esquiline hill, east of the Forum, and was begun by the emperor Vespasian, completed under his sons Titus and Domitian, and dedicated by Titus in AD 80. Displays of wild beasts and gladiatorial shows were held there and the arena could be flooded for mimic sea-fights (see NAUMACHIAE). It continued to be used for such purposes until the sixth century. The truth of the tradition that it was the scene of many Christian martyrdoms in the early Church has been questioned. Gibbon's assertion in his celebrated description of the Colosseum (*Decline and Fall,* ch. 12) that it held 80,000 people may be an exaggeration, but it was capable of holding at least 50,000.

Colo'ssus of Rhodes (Gk. *kolossos,* 'a more than lifesize statue'), a bronze statue of the Greek sungod Helios, one of the *Seven Wonders of the ancient world. It was cast by Charēs of Lindus to stand at the entrance of the harbour (the tradition that it stood astride the entrance is unlikely to be true), and was 70 cubits high (30–5 m., 100–15 ft.). It was overthrown by an earthquake in 224 BC, sixty-six years after its erection.

columba'rium, see BURIAL.

Colume'lla, Lucius Junius Moderā'tus, Spaniard from Gades (Cadiz) in Spain who served as a tribune of the Roman army in Syria. In about AD 60–5 he composed a treatise on farming, *De re rustica,* in twelve books. It deals with the various aspects of a farmer's life and work, the choice of a farm, its cultivation, livestock, fishponds, bees, and gardens, while the last two books expound the duties of the bailiff and his wife. All the books are written in prose except for book 10, which in rather uninspired hexameters deals with gardens, a topic which Virgil, in the last book of the *Georgics,* had said he was leaving to others. Columella writes as a practical farmer who is distressed by the decline of Italian agriculture, remedy for which he sees in knowledge, hard work, and interest on the part of the landowner. He is a warm admirer of the *Georgics.* His prose is simple and dignified, without affectation. He also wrote a shorter manual on agriculture, of which one book on trees, *De arboribus,* is extant.

comedy. 1. Greek. The only Greek comedy we possess is Athenian. For that reason it is also known as Attic comedy (from the state of Attica, of which Athens was the chief city).

1. *Background.* Comedies at Athens, like tragedies, were produced under the auspices of the state and were a matter for competition (compare TRAGEDY 1). They obtained state recognition later than tragedies, having previously

been produced by performers at their own expense. They were first produced at the annual festival of the City *Dionysia in 486 BC (when a certain Chionides won the competition) and at the *Lenaea (another Dionysiac festival) c.440 BC. Before and after the Peloponnesian War (431–404 BC), five comedies were performed annually at each festival; during the war the number is said to have been reduced to three for reasons of economy. Comic dramatists (often called comic poets because the plays were written in verse) who wished to have their plays performed 'applied for a *chorus' to the magistrate in charge of the festival, who chose the successful applicants. At the City Dionysia the magistrate was the eponymous archon, at the Lenaea the archon basileus. The duty of providing a chorus fell upon rich citizens (see CHOREGIA). The dramatists, who received payment, usually presented only one play each, and were in competition for first prize, which may have been no more than a garland of ivy. At the Lenaea a prize seems also to have been given for the best comic actor, but not at the City Dionysia until the late fourth century. Ten judges were appointed by lot from among the citizens, according to an elaborate method designed to avoid corruption. It seems to be the case that no Greek wrote both tragedies and comedies; when, at the end of Plato's Symposium, Socrates forces Agathon, who wrote tragedies, and *Aristophanes, who wrote comedies, to admit that the same man could write both, the admission was intended to be paradoxical (but see ION OF CHIOS).

2. The origin of Greek comedy. The earliest comedy we possess, the Acharnians of Aristophanes, was produced in 425 BC; we do not know how it differed from the earliest comedies performed in Athens, nor how comedy started in the first place. Aristotle in the Poetics saw Athenian comedy developing from two influences. The first was 'the leaders of the phallic songs', i.e. the leaders of the bands of revellers who accompanied the phalloi in procession during the Dionysiac festival in Athens, exchanging banter with the members of the procession and with the onlookers. This theory is supported by the Greek word for comedy, kōmōidia, which means 'kōmos-singing' and is derived from the Greek kōmos, a procession of revellers singing and dancing (not from kōmē, 'village', as Aristotle thought); also Old Comedy (see below) in Athens gave an important role to the chorus, retained a phallic element, and was associated with the worship of Dionysus. The second influence Aristotle detected was that of Sicilian drama (having in mind the comedies of *Epicharmus, who was slightly older than the first Athenian comic dramatists), which he thought accounted for the element of 'plot' in Athenian comedy (as distinct from lampoons). Aristotle also thought comedy might have originated with the Megarians, both those in mainland Megara and those who had migrated to Sicily, who had comic performances of their own. Whether in fact Epicharmus or the Megarians influenced the development of Athenian comedy, it is impossible to say.

3. Old Comedy (Aristophanic Comedy). The term 'Old Comedy' denotes the comedies produced in Athens in the fifth century BC. Of all these works the only complete plays surviving are eleven by Aristophanes, and of these the last two (Ecclesiazusae and Plutus) were written in the fourth century BC and are different in character from the rest, notably in the much reduced role of the chorus. Our knowledge of Old Comedy therefore depends upon Aristophanes' other nine plays, all produced in the last quarter of the fifth century. However, there are sufficient resemblances between these plays, late in the tradition though they are, and the fragments of the other playwrights (see 4 below), to allow cautious generalizations about the nature of Old Comedy.

An Aristophanic comedy is elaborate in structure and may be divided into the following parts (found with some variations in the first nine plays).

(i) prologos, 'prologue', an expository opening scene before the entrance of the chorus.

(ii) parodos, 'the entry of the chorus', a scene in which the chorus enters and is characterized and introduced to the audience; it is usual for it then to oppose either the hero or the hero's enemies with great vigour. The parodos ends with a short scene that effects a transition to the next section.

(iii) agon, 'debate', between two adversaries with arguments for and against the crucial issue of the play. It regularly takes the form of a pair of speeches in tetrameter metre (the so-called 'epirrhematic syzygy') and the first speaker is always the loser. Some plays have no agon in the formal sense but instead have a scene with a similar function. The agon is concluded by a scene or two punctuated by choral songs.

(iv) parabasis, 'coming forward'. After the agon all the characters leave the stage, the chorus 'comes forward' and the chorus-leader addresses the audience directly in anapaestic tetrameters, the subject matter having little to do with the plot. The anapaests end in a long sentence to be spoken in one breath (pnīgos, 'the choke'). There usually follows a choral song (odē), some trochaic lines (epirrhema), another song (antodē), and an antepirrhema, but the term parabasis is often used to refer to the anapaests only.

It is possible that in the parodos, agon, and parabasis we have a reminiscence of a kind of komos in which a contest arose, and which ended in an address to the onlookers.

(v) Following the parabasis comes a number

of episodes (*epeisodia*), separated by brief choral songs, sometimes carrying on the main plot, but usually only illustrating the conclusion arrived at in the *agon*.

(vi) *exodos*, final scene, in which the predominant note is rejoicing, generally leading up to a feast or wedding. The play may conclude with a *cordax* or riotous dance.

A comedy required for its performance three or four actors, occasionally with the support of supernumeraries, and a chorus of twenty-four members (all men). The chorus was of primary importance. Many plays took their titles from the chorus (e.g. *Acharnians*, *Wasps*, *Birds*), whose costume and dances provided spectacle. The actors' costumes were an exaggeration of reality, with grotesque masks (which included hair) and body padding and, probably, a large phallus for male characters. The costume was consonant with the robust nature of Old Comedy, in which the jokes were much concerned with sex and excretion and expressed in uninhibited language. The comedy took as its starting point a fantastic scheme on the part of the hero, the achievement of which, wholly impossible in real life, constituted the plot. A few prominent citizens were mercilessly ridiculed; in some comedies they figure in major roles, either in their own names, e.g. Socrates in *Clouds*, Euripides in *Thesmophoriazusae*, or in thin disguise, e.g. Cleon as the Paphlagonian in *Knights*. Topical comment on personalities, events, and institutions of the day (e.g. the lawcourts in *Wasps*) was pervasive. The more extreme aspects of contemporary democratic politics, the more ridiculous developments in education, music, and literature, even the indignities of war, were seized upon and exaggerated for comic effect. The gods, or certain gods, were similarly treated with irreverence, but never in such a way as to deny their reality. It is difficult to see how far serious social comment lay behind the jokes. Altogether, Old Comedy was a humane blend of religious ceremony, satire and criticism (political, social, and literary), wit and buffoonery.

4. *Authors of Old Comedy*. Of the authors of Old Comedy other than Aristophanes we know little. *Magnēs* was the leading dramatist of the second quarter of the fifth century, and won first prize an unequalled eleven times at the City Dionysia. We have the titles of twenty-seven comedies by *Cratīnus* (*c*.520–*c*.423 BC), who won first prize six times at the City Dionysia and three times at the Lenaea. Aristophanes mocked him in *Knights* (424 BC), declaring that drink had brought about his decline. The following year Cratinus had his revenge, his play *Pȳtinē* ('bottle') beating Aristophanes' *Clouds*. *Cratēs* won three victories in the City Dionysia, the first in 450 BC. We have the titles of six of his plays. Aristotle in the *Poetics* says that he was the first Athenian comic dramatist to

create plots rather than write lampoons of individuals. *Pherecratēs* imitated the style of Crates, and won victories between 440 and 430 BC. We have some nineteen titles of plays by him. *Eupolis* produced his first play in 429 BC; he won first prize three times at the Lenaea and at least once at the City Dionysia. He died some time after 415 BC. We have nineteen titles and many fragments, including some fairly substantial papyrus fragments. Though he was highly regarded by the Greeks, the fragments so far discovered do not rival Aristophanes. There was also a comic playwright called *Plato*, writing from *c*.425 to 390 BC. Of these the two greatest after Aristophanes, as the Greeks thought, were Cratinus and Eupolis.

5. *Middle Comedy*. This term is used to describe Athenian comedy of the period *c*.400–*c*.323 BC (between Old and New Comedy), almost all of which is lost. It was a period of experimentation and no single type of play can be said to represent it exclusively. The defeat of Athens at the end of the Peloponnesian War (404 BC) was reflected in comedy by the evolution of a type that was cosmopolitan and less Athenian in character. Aristophanes' *Ecclesiazusae* (probably 391) and *Plutus* (388) are thought of as typical early examples. The *parabasis* disappeared, the role of the chorus declined sharply, the padded costume and the phallus were given up. Plots based on mythology continued to be popular in the first half of the period, but political themes and comment gradually disappeared, to be replaced by satire of familiar types in society, the professional soldier and the courtesan, for example. Emphasis came to be put on the realities of ordinary life. We know the names of about fifty dramatists of this period, of whom the most famous (after Aristophanes) were Antiphanēs, Eubulus, and *Alexis; but Aristophanes apart, no complete play survives, although we have a large number of fragments.

6. *New Comedy*. New Comedy is the name given to Athenian comedy of the period *c*.323–*c*.263 BC, that is, from the death of Alexander the Great to the death of Philemon, the last great dramatist of New Comedy. (The latter's death is memorably described in the *Florida* of Apuleius.) The plays of New Comedy adhere to a recognizable pattern which is a final development from Old Comedy. They were divided into five acts, separated by irrelevant choral interludes performed by a chorus which took no other part in the play and whose songs have not survived. Padded costume had been abandoned but masks were retained; in other respects the actors wore ordinary Athenian dress. The dramatists set their plays in Athens and were themselves based in Athens, but many of them were drawn there from other cities. They made few references to prominent Athenian citizens or politicians, and in general political

comment was rare. Their plots were concerned
with some stereotyped but relatively realistic
episodes in the private life of the well-to-do
family, cosmopolitan rather than narrowly
Athenian. Their success lay in the delineation
of character, especially as expressed by mood
and feeling. These characteristics gave New
Comedy a wide and long-lasting appeal, and
the plays enjoyed great popularity for many centuries in the Graeco-Roman world. It is ironic
therefore that the Attic Greek in which they
were written, foreshadowing the international
koinē (see DIALECTS (1) 3), was considered in the
Byzantine age to be inferior to Attic speech of
the fifth century BC, and thus unsuitable for the
Byzantine schoolroom. As a result manuscripts
of the plays were not circulated or copied and
none has survived to the present day. However,
a number of papyrus finds (see PAPYROLOGY) has
restored to us large parts of several plays of
*Menander, and we have fragments of some
other dramatists. Apart from Menander, the
most famous was Philemon (c.361–263 BC). He
was probably born in Syracuse, but became an
Athenian citizen. Sixty titles are known and
over two hundred fragments. His technique can
be gathered from Plautus' adaptation of his
plays. Diphilus from the Milesian colony of
Sinopē on the Black Sea was another dramatist
of the second half of the fourth century BC.
Again, about sixty titles are known, and a few
of his plays were adapted by Plautus.

2. Roman

1. *Background.* Drama at Rome had its origin in
the third century BC, but two centuries later
there was disagreement as to how, when
exactly, and where it arose. Livy's version of its
origin (see below) is only one of several. He
states (7. 2) that it began with the dances,
accompanied by the flute, of players brought
from Etruria in 363 BC to propitiate the gods
because of an outbreak of plague. Young men of
Rome imitated these dances, adding a dialogue
in verse, roughly improvised and, according to
Livy, similar to the *Fescennine verses (whatever these may have been) which Horace saw as
the origin of comedy. These entertainments
were thought of as giving place to a somewhat
more developed but still plotless dramatic
performance, the *satura* or medley (see SATIRE),
with appropriate musical accompaniment.
*Livius Andronicus (c.284–204 BC), a Greek
from Tarentum, was the first, according to
Livy, to abandon the *satura* and compose a play
with a plot. With him a more serious and artistic
form of drama became established. Probably
several elements went to the development of
Roman comedy: Etruscan mimetic dances (*per-
sona*, 'mask', and *scaena*, 'stage', are Etruscan
forms of the Greek words *prosōpon* and *skēnē*)
and perhaps Fescennine dialogue; *satura*; and
*Atellan farce, familiar in Rome by the end of
the third century BC, but perhaps imported

much earlier. The *mime too was known in
Rome well before the end of the third century.
With audiences prepared by these primitive
dramatic forms, Greek (New) Comedy was first
introduced by Livius Andronicus in translation
in 240 BC and gained a temporary hold. Greek
comedy found its first important native Italian
exponent in *Naevius, more than thirty of
whose comedies have titles known to us,
mostly, it would seem, translations of Greek
New Comedy, but possibly including original
comedies set in Italy. He was followed by
*Plautus, *Caecilius Statius, and *Terence, all
imitators and adaptors of New Comedy; their
plays were known in consequence as *fabulae
palliatae, 'plays in Greek cloaks'. But some
attempts were made, by the middle of the
second century BC, to write comedies in which
characters and scenes were Italian although the
structure was Greek. These were called *fabulae
togatae, 'plays in togas'. Unfortunately none of
these plays survives, except for a few brief
quotations. Lucius Afranius (b. c.150 BC) was the
most famous of their authors. Roman comedy
practically ceased to be written in the first
century BC, supplanted by the more popular
mime, which had no claim to literary merit.
The last recorded revival at Rome of a comedy
by Plautus, *Pseudolus*, was staged in Cicero's
day.

2. *Performance of Roman comedy.* There had
always been an audience at Rome for dramatic
performances of one sort or another. From the
third century BC days were set aside for stage
performances at the public games (see LUDI), and
besides regular festivals there were occasional
performances at such events as the funeral games
of distinguished men. Audiences were drawn
from all social classes, but, in general, Roman
audiences were less knowledgeable and appreciative than their counterparts in Athens, and had
less respect for actors and for the occasion.
Horace alleged that an audience will demand a
bear or boxers in the middle of a play. Plautus in
the prologue to *Poenulus* enumerates an amazing
list of activities he would prefer the audience to
desist from, of which letting the baby cry is the
least. Roman actors, always men except in
mimes, were generally slaves (see THEATRE), and
if free men, were thought too disreputable to
vote or to serve in the army (but see ROSCIUS).
There was no strict limitation upon the number
of actors, as there was in Greece, and many plays
require at least five speaking actors. Oddly
enough, it is not known for sure if masks were
worn in Roman adaptations of Greek drama,
but they were worn in the native Atellan drama.
Though the texts of the plays of Plautus have
been divided into five acts since the Renaissance,
and those of Terence since ancient times, they
were written to run continuously, and they did
not employ a chorus, although they included
parts that were declaimed or sung. The scenes of

spoken dialogue were written in iambic senarii and are called *dīverbia*. All other parts are called *cantica*, and include (*a*) trochaic and iambic septenarii, forming melodramatic recitals, declaimed by the actor to a musical accompaniment, and (*b*) the lyric parts sung by the actor (or a concealed substitute) with a flute accompaniment. For the metre of Roman comedy see METRE, LATIN 2. (See also PANTOMIME and SOCCUS.)

co'mites, see COMPANIONS.

comi'tia (plural noun), name given to a (political) assembly of the Roman people to vote on business presented to them by magistrates. As the people were divided into *curiae, *centuriae, and tribus (see TRIBES 2), so the three types of comitia were curiata, centuriata, and tributa (the last known also as *concilium plebis.) The resolutions of the comitia had to be ratified by the senate. The meetings had to be held on the proper day, after the auspices had been taken, on an inaugurated site (see COMITIUM). (When the people were summoned as a whole and not by particular groups, the assembly was called a *contio*; when only a part of the people was summoned, the assembly was properly called a *concilium*.) The *comitia* continued to exist at least formally until the third century AD. See REPUBLIC, ROMAN.

1. *comitia centuriata*. According to Roman tradition, the political assembly instituted by Servius Tullius (king of Rome, traditionally from 578 to 535 BC) based on the *centuries of the Roman legions. Its real date of origin is a matter of doubt; some authorities put it after 450. It was organized so as to give the preponderance of power to the wealthy classes (see REPUBLIC, ROMAN). It elected all the chief magistrates in the republic, acquired the sole right to declare war, had the power of legislation (upon the proposals submitted by consuls or other magistrates with 'power to command' *imperium), and acted as court of appeal against the death penalty. As a legislative body its power was limited by the veto of the senate. This restriction was practically removed by the Publilian law (339 BC) which required the senate to ratify in advance proposals that were to be presented to it. Ratification later became a mere formality. This assembly, being in origin an army and therefore not allowed to assemble within the city, met in the *Campus Martius. The citizens could appear at it wearing armour; on the Janiculum hill nearby a red flag flew which could be lowered in the event of an Etruscan raid (see PRO RABIRIO).

2. *comitia curiata*. From regal times the Roman people were divided for the exercise of their political rights and duties into thirty groups called *curiae, 'wards' or local communities (like the Attic demes), the meeting of which constituted the popular assembly, *comitia curiata*. It had

no legislative powers, but it met to hear matters of interest to the community, and it formally sanctioned important matters such as the succession of a new king or the declaration of war. During the *republic it ratified, by the formal *lex curiata de imperio*, the conferment of power on the newly appointed chief magistrates. It also dealt with cases of adoption, transference of a patrician to a plebeian family, election to certain priesthoods, and other religious matters. In late republican times meetings of the *comitia curiata* were purely formal: an assembly of thirty lictors was a sufficient quorum.

3. *comitia tributa*. The assembly more properly called *concilium plebis.

Comi'tium, the chief place of political assembly in republican Rome, a paved area about 75 sq. m. (90 sq. yds.) on the north-west side of the Roman Forum. It was a *templum*, or inaugurated area (see TEMPLES 2), and here in early republican times took place most of the assemblies of the Roman people for purposes other than elections (see CAMPUS MARTIUS). On the north side of it stood the *Curia, and on the south the *Rostra.

Commentaries, on the Gallic War and on the Civil War (*Commentarii de bello Gallico* and *Commentarii de bello cīvīli*), memoirs by Julius *Caesar concerned with, respectively, his campaigns in *Gaul from 58 to 52 BC and the civil war against *Pompey which culminated in the battle of Pharsalus (48 BC).

1. *The Gallic War.*

Book 1. After a brief geographical description of Gaul, Caesar starts with an account of the migration of the *Helvetii into Gaul, of how the Romans pursued them and drove them back, and finally resettled them in their old homes. He then relates the increasing invasion of Gaul by Germans, his decision to put an end to it, the fruitless negotiations with their king Ariovistus, and the great battle north-east of Vesontio (Besançon) in which the Germans were routed (58).

Book 2. The Belgic tribes (see BELGAE), threatened by the Roman advance and stirred up by discontented Gauls, combine for war against Rome. The prompt movement of Caesar against them upsets their plans; a series of fights ends in a critical battle against the Nervii (a Belgic tribe) on the river Sabis (Sambre) and they are virtually exterminated. An expeditionary force under P. Crassus meanwhile subdues the tribes on the Atlantic seaboard, and the whole of Gaul is temporarily reduced to quiet (57).

Book 3. Some predatory African tribes are subdued by Servius Galba. Certain Armorican tribes (in Brittany) led by the Veneti (from south Brittany) revolt, and although the Romans have little experience of their kind of naval warfare the rebels are defeated by the makeshift Roman fleet and its unexpected tactics. Their allies are dealt with in smaller campaigns.

Book 4. The German tribes of the Usipetēs and Tencteri invade Gaul and are crushed by Caesar near the river Mosa (Meuse). Caesar follows up this success by crossing the river Rhenus (Rhine) to demonstrate Roman power. He makes his first expedition to Britain, which had supported Gaul against the Romans. A small force lands in Kent in face of fierce opposition. Caesar's fleet at anchor is badly damaged by storm, and the British manner of chariot-fighting throws his troops into confusion. He withdraws his force from Britain in September (55).

Book 5. The second invasion of Britain with a larger force. After its landing, a storm again destroys many of the transports. Caesar reaches and fords the Thames, captures the stronghold of the chief Cassivelaunus, and obtains his surrender (see BRITAIN 2). Caesar takes hostages, fixes the tribute payable by Britain, and withdraws to the Continent (at this point the book includes a geographical description of Britain). During the winter the Gauls revolt, taking advantage of the dispersal of the legions in widely separated winter quarters. The Eburones under Ambiorix annihilate the Roman garrison at Aduatuca and then, gathering their allies, lay siege to the camp of Q. *Cicero in the territory of the Nervii. Cicero is rescued from a dangerous situation only by the rapid advance of Caesar with two legions from Samarobriva (Amiens). Further signs of revolt appear during the winter. Idutiomārus, leader of the rebellious Treveri, is killed in a surprise attack by the Romans (54).

Book 6. Various punitive expeditions are made by the Romans in the north-east of Gaul, the chief of them directed against Ambiorix (the leader of the Eburones in the capture of Aduatuca; see book 5). His kingdom is ravaged but he himself escapes. A company of German horsemen cross the Rhine to plunder what they can in the territory of Ambiorix, but at the suggestion of one of their Gallic prisoners they attack instead Aduatuca, where the baggage of the Roman army is stored. They nearly capture this fort by their surprise attack, but the Romans drive them off (53). The book contains an account of the customs of the Gauls and Druids, and of the Germans.

Book 7. The disturbed state of Italy (*Clodius having been murdered early in 52 BC; see CICERO (1) 3 and 4) encourages the Gauls to a general revolt, begun by the Carnūtes, who massacre the Roman residents in Cēnabum (Orleans). A coalition of the principal tribes is formed under Vercingetorix, leader of the Arverni (who gave their name to Auvergne), and threatens the frontier of the Roman province of Transalpine Gaul. Caesar hastens back from Italy, makes the province secure, and crosses the Cevennes in midwinter, drawing Vercingetorix south to defend Auvergne. Leaving behind D. *Brutus to divert Vercingetorix' attention Caesar himself rapidly travels to the country of the Lingones (Langres) and gathers his troops together. He recaptures Cenabum and besieges Avaricum (Bourges), capital of the Bitūriges. In spite of the attempts of Vercingetorix to relieve the town, and hardships suffered from the cold and from scarcity of supplies, the Romans occupy it and in revenge for past sufferings butcher all the inhabitants. Caesar moves to attack Gergōvia, capital of the Arverni. During the siege of this very difficult position, the rashness of some of the Roman troops in the course of a carefully planned attack, leading to an over-hasty assault on the town gates, results in heavy loss. This and news that the Aedui, hitherto faithful allies of Rome, were planning to revolt, leads Caesar to withdraw from Gergovia and make for the territory of the Aedui. Without hindrance from Vercingetorix he rejoins *Labienus in the north. Labienus has been sent out against the Senonēs (who gave their name to Sens) and the Parisii, but an uprising of the Bellovaci, as a consequence of their hearing that Caesar has retreated from Gergovia, has put him in danger. He extricates his troops by a skilful manoeuvre and joins Caesar at Sens. The united army moves against Vercingetorix, who is again threatening the province of Transalpine Gaul, follows him to his stronghold Alĕsia (Mont Auxois), lays siege to it, and in spite of the efforts of a great army of Gauls to relieve it, captures the stronghold as well as Vercingetorix after fierce fighting (52).

Book 8, a continuation of the others, was written by A. *Hirtius. Books 1–7 were published in 51 BC.

2. *The Civil War.*

Book 1 narrates the opening of the war, after the senate had voted that Caesar should lay down his military command and he, in defiance, had crossed the *Rubicon with his army. Caesar rapidly overruns Italy, and Pompey, under pressure, retires first to the south Italian port of Brundisium (Brindisi) and then across to Epirus in north-west Greece, before Caesar can close the harbour. Caesar therefore turns west to Massilia (Marseilles), starting to lay siege to it, and then to Spain, where his strategy in the neighbourhood of Ilerda (Lerida) secures the surrender of Pompey's lieutenants Afrānius and Petrēius.

Book 2 relates the continuation of the siege of Massilia and its surrender, the conquest of western Spain, and the disastrous North African campaign of Caesar's lieutenant, C. Curio, whose rashness brings about the annihilation of his force by king Juba. All the events of the first two books take place in 49 BC.

Book 3 relates the operations of Caesar in 48

against Pompey in Epirus, the unsuccessful attempt to blockade Pompey at Dyrrhachium, Caesar's withdrawal to Thessaly where he is reinforced by fresh troops, the battle of Pharsālus where Caesar's veterans defeat Pompey's numerically superior forces, and Pompey's flight to Egypt, where he is murdered through the agency of the Egyptian king's advisers. The work ends with an account of the political situation in Egypt, Caesar's activities there, and the grave danger to which he and his forces are exposed.

commerce, see ATHENS 4 and ROME 13.

commercium and conubium, rights of, see LATIN RIGHTS.

Co'mmodus, Lucius Ae'lius Aurē'lius (AD 161–92), Roman emperor from 180 to his death, elder son of Marcus *Aurelius. Late in his reign he became insane, renamed Rome Colonia Commodiana ('colony of Commodus'), and believed himself to be the reincarnation of Hercules. When he determined to appear in public as consul and gladiator, his ministers engineered his assassination.

commū'nes loci, 'commonplaces'; in *rhetoric, 'arguments that can be transferred to many places', which were published in handbooks of rhetoric and practised in schools. They seem to have originated with the Greek *sophists Gorgias and Protagoras.

companions. In early Greece, retainers attached to a king by personal ties of service. The institution is also found in the Macedonian monarchy, and the 'companions' of Philip II and Alexander the Great followed them in their campaigns. In Philip's day the companions comprised an élite body of cavalrymen chosen on the grounds of ability to accompany him in battle. From these he selected his counsellors. Under the Roman emperors, those who accompanied the emperor abroad were semi-officially called his 'companions', *comites.*

Compitā'lia, at Rome, the festival of the *lares of the crossroads (*compita*). The festival was a movable one, held on a day announced by the city praetor early in January (see FERIAE) to mark the end of the agricultural year. It was said to have been instituted by the king Servius Tullius, the son of a slave-woman by the *lar familiaris.* Slaves had a share in the festival and were allowed a great deal of licence. It fell into disuse during the civil wars but was restored by Augustus.

cōmus, see COMEDY, GREEK 2.

conceptī'vae, fē'riae, see FERIAE.

conci'lium plē'bis (also known as the *comitia tributa*), at Rome, the meeting of the *plebeians by *tribes, under the presidency of their *tribunes, instituted around the mid-fifth century BC. Patricians were excluded from the meetings. Its resolutions, *plēbi scita*, were recognized as binding on patricians and plebeians alike after 287 BC (see ROME 3). It elected the tribunes and (plebeian) *aediles. See also COMITIA.

Concord, Temple of. According to tradition the first Temple of Concord at Rome was dedicated by M. Furius Camillus in 367 BC to celebrate the end of civil strife over the Licinian rogations (see LICINIAN–SEXTIAN LAWS). It was restored by L. Opimius in 121 BC after the death of C. Gracchus and again by the emperor Tiberius in AD 10 from the spoils of his German campaigns. It stood in an elevated position at the west end of the Forum. The senate often met there and it was the setting for some of Cicero's great political speeches. It was there too that Sejanus was condemned to death.

conco'rdia o'rdinum, see CICERO (1) 3.

confarreā'tio, at Rome, the oldest and most solemn form of *marriage, in classical times only necessary for and perhaps confined to certain priesthoods. Bride and bridegroom sat with veiled heads on joined seats covered with the skin of a sacrificed sheep. A cake made of *far* (coarse wheat) was of some significance in the ceremony; it may have been offered to Jupiter Farreus, in whose honour this marriage ritual was performed. The *flamen dialis* and *pontifex maximus* were present. The marriage was indissoluble except by an elaborate ceremony.

Cōnon. 1. One of the Athenian commanders at the battle of Aegospotami between Athens and Sparta at the end of the *Peloponnesian War (405 BC). He escaped from the Athenian disaster with eight ships, and made his way to *Evagoras in Cyprus where he helped revive Persian sea-power. He was subsequently appointed with Pharnabāzus to command the Persian fleet against Sparta, and in 394 defeated the Spartans at Cnidus, destroying their naval power and avenging Aegospotami. He returned to Athens and with the help of the Persian fleet completed the rebuilding of the *Long Walls.

2. Of Samos (third century BC), mathematician and astronomer, who settled in Alexandria. He is best known for his discovery (*c.*245) of the new constellation, the Lock of *Berenice (see also CALLIMACHUS), and he worked on solar eclipses; nothing of his writings survives. He was a close friend of Archimedes, who writes of him with admiration.

Consōlā'tio ad Lī'viam ('consolation to Livia'), a Latin elegiac poem, incorrectly attributed to Ovid, ostensibly written on the death of the empress Livia's son Drusus while campaigning in Germany in 9 BC.

Consōlā'tio ad Ma'rciam, ad He'lviam, ad Poly'bium, see SENECA (2).

Constantine I, the Great (Flāvius Valerius Constantīnus Augustus), *c.* AD 285–337, emperor of Rome, son of Constantius, the *Augustus in the West (see BRITAIN 6). He was with his father in Britain at the latter's death (AD 306) at York, and was there proclaimed Augustus by the army; Galerius, the Augustus in the East, granted him only the rank of Caesar, and Severus became Augustus in the West. A complicated power struggle between rival claimants occupied the following years, brought to a head by the death of Galerius in 311. Early in 312 Constantine invaded Italy and marched on Rome. In a battle near the Milvian bridge across the Tiber he defeated Maxentius who had declared himself Augustus in the West; Maxentius was drowned in the Tiber while making his escape. Welcomed as deliverer by the senate, Constantine thus became the senior Augustus. *Eusebius says that years later Constantine told him that in the course of his march on Rome he had seen a vision of the cross of Christ against the sun, and beneath it the words 'In this conquer'. Before the walls of Rome Constantine saw a further vision telling him to have the soldiers mark their shields with the Christian monogram, the Greek letters chi and rho (the first two letters of the Greek word *Christos,* Christ) intersecting. Constantine regarded his victory as showing the favour of the Christian God. In 313 Constantine and Licinius, an imperial claimant, met at Milan and agreed to grant Christians complete religious freedom. It is sometimes thought that a formal proclamation of this policy was made, and it is referred to as the Edict of Milan. Later that year Licinius became Augustus in the East. In 316 (probably) and again in 323 war broke out between Constantine and Licinius, and the latter began to persecute the eastern Christians. In 324 Constantine, after several battles, forced the surrender of Licinius, whom he soon executed for fresh intrigues. Constantine was now sole Augustus and emperor. One of his early decisions was to establish a new imperial residence at *Byzantium for strategic reasons, the site proving commercially advantageous also. In 330 the new residence was formally dedicated and the city renamed Constantinople. It was predominantly a Christian city, although the dedication ceremony had contained both pagan and Christian elements. It still contained pagan temples but many churches were soon erected. In the course of the fourth century the city acquired many of the institutions and public buildings of the old Rome, a senate and a palace, and even traditional Roman festivals and free grain distributions to the people.

While ruler in the West only, where paganism strongly predominated, Constantine had supported the Christian cause, but after he had settled in the East his favour was more apparent. His personal attitude to Christianity is difficult to ascertain from his seemingly inconsistent acts, but he became convinced of the superiority of the Christian God and of the need to secure this divine support. He desired a unified Christian Church as an essential for a united empire, but he failed to settle the conflict between Catholics and the heretic *Donatists in North Africa, and though his efforts seemed rewarded at the Council of Nicaea (325), called to settle the controversy about the *Arian heresy in the East, his success was not lasting. Constantine died in 337, having been baptized a Christian on his deathbed (such a postponement was not unusual at the time). In the Eastern Church he is venerated as a saint. Having put to death in 326 his eldest son Crispus (whose tutor was *Lactantius), he was succeeded by his three remaining sons who each took the title Augustus and divided the empire between themselves.

Constantinople, see BYZANTIUM, BYZANTINE AGE, CONSTANTINE I, and JUSTINIAN.

Constantius, see CONSTANTINE I, and BRITAIN 6.

Constitution of the Athenians (*Athēnaiōn politeia*). **1.** Political treatise by Aristotle; see ARISTOTLE 3 (ii).

2. Short pamphlet attributed in antiquity to Xenophon but probably written in the 420s BC, and so too early to be by him. Its author is an Athenian of oligarchic sympathies who is critical of the policy and system of contemporary Athenian democracy, and hence is often called the Old Oligarch. Despite its evident bias, the pamphlet concedes that as far as democracies go the Athenian version is efficient, and it is useful for its attempt to explain how democracy at Athens worked.

Constitution of the Lacedaemonians (*Lakedaimoniōn politeia*), minor work of *Xenophon, written *c.*388 BC, a largely admiring account of the Spartan way of life. Xenophon attributes the power of Sparta to the traditonal institutions of *Lycurgus which he describes: the marriage system, the physical training of both sexes, the unusual manner of educating the young, the system of eating in public messes, the discouragement of private property, the preference for an honourable death to a disgraceful life, the army system, and the position and function of the kings (see SPARTA). In ch. 14, perhaps written later, he laments the decline of the old ways in the Sparta of his day. Of the actual Lacedaemonian constitution, in spite of the title, he tells us very little.

Consuā'lia, see CONSUS.

consuls (Lat. *consules*), at Rome under the republic, the supreme civil and military magistrates (originally called *praetors, *praetores*, perhaps until the reforms of the *decemvirs in 451 BC), two in number with equal powers (see COLLEGIUM 1). On the expulsion of the kings in 509 BC they received the 'power to command' (*imperium*), namely the military and judicial authority formerly wielded by the kings (but not their religious authority, which passed to the *rex sacrorum* and *pontifex maximus*). Consuls were elected annually by the people in the *comitia centuriata*, but as the candidates were required to be senators their choice was restricted (see SENATE). After about the middle of the fourth century BC one consul was always *plebeian (see ROME 3). The consuls' power was in course of time reduced by the creation of new magistracies, notably the censorship (see CENSORS). The chief functions retained by the consuls were those of military command. Later they received as 'proconsuls' an extension of their authority after the termination of their year of office, to enable them to carry on a military command or govern a province (see PROCONSUL). In the Roman calendar the years were dated by naming the consuls. Under the emperors the consulship increasingly became a mainly honorary office; consuls were generally appointed for no more than two to four months, only those who entered office on 1 January giving their name to the year. The consuls retained some judicial functions and introduced legal cases before the senate. See LAW, AT ROME 2 and CURSUS HONORUM.

A *consul suffectus* was appointed to succeed a consul unable to complete his term of office, or, under the emperors, appointed after the term of *eponymous consul (see above) had expired.

Consus ('storer'), in Roman religion, an ancient god of the granary whose festivals, Consuālia, in August and December, suggest that he was connected with the harvest and the autumn sowing. He had an underground barn and altar in the Circus Maximus which was uncovered only during his festival. The Romans later thought he had something to do with *consilium*, 'counsel', and because they also associated him with horses they sometimes identified him with the Greek god *Poseidon. There were chariot-races at the Consualia; the other horses and asses had a holiday on that day and were garlanded with flowers. For the origin of the games see ROME 2.

co'ntio, public gathering at Rome; see COMITIA.

Contra Rullum ('against Rullus'), or *De lege agraria* ('on the agrarian law'), three speeches delivered by Cicero in 63 BC ; see CICERO (1) 2.

contrōve'rsiae, Latin rhetorical exercises in the oratory of the law-courts; see SENECA (1) and NOVEL.

Cōpa, short Latin elegiac poem doubtfully attributed to Virgil; see APPENDIX VIRGILIANA.

Cōpā'is, lake in *Boeotia.

copper, see MINES.

Corax, of Syracuse (first half of the fifth century BC), said to have been the first Greek teacher of *rhetoric.

Corcȳ'ra (Kerkyra, modern Corfu), an island in the Ionian Sea in north-west Greece, off the coast of Epirus, identified by the ancients with Scheria, the land of the Phaeacians in Homer's *Odyssey* (book 5). It was colonized first perhaps by Eretrians, and then in 733 BC by Corinthians (see COLONIZATION, GREEK 3). In consequence of a quarrel with its mother city in 435 BC it made an alliance with Athens in 433. Serious political strife between oligarchs and democrats in 427 resulted in wholesale massacre, memorably described by Thucydides (3. 69 and 4. 46–8). Corcyra remained an Athenian ally until 410, and rejoined the Athenian League in the fourth century BC.

cordax, comic dance performed in Old Comedy (see COMEDY, GREEK 3), associated with lewdness and drunkenness. Aristophanes claimed to exclude it from his plays (but see WASPS).

Corē ('the maiden'), in Greek myth, *Persephonē.

Cori'nna. 1. Greek lyric poetess from Tanagra in Boeotia, thought in ancient times to be an older contemporary of her fellow-countryman the poet Pindar, and thus of the second half of the sixth century BC. But her spelling of the Boeotian dialect and the lack of early references to her have led to the suggestion that she lived c.200 BC. The question is still unresolved. The fragments of her poetry which survive in quotation have been augmented by the substantial remains of two poems found in a papyrus. One concerns a singing contest between the mountains Cithaeron and Helicon, each traditionally associated with the Muses and so with poetry; the other is a catalogue poem in the manner of Hesiod concerning the genealogies of Boeotian heroes and heroines. The poems are written in regular stanzas using simple lyric metres. According to an ancient anecdote Corinna criticized the absence of myth from one of Pindar's poems; when he thereupon went to the other extreme she remarked that one should 'sow by handfuls, not with the whole sack', an expression which became proverbial.

2. In Ovid, see AMORES.

Corinth (Korinthos), mentioned in Homer's *Iliad*, where it is also referred to by the name Ephyrē, one of the most important cities of ancient Greece, strategically situated on the Isthmus joining north Greece to the Peloponnese, between two important seas (the Ionian and Aegean), and therefore destined to be a great maritime power. Also, it was situated at the focal point of north–south and, more importantly, east–west trade routes, along which came luxury goods from the East and metals from the West, and, eventually, the products of the western colonies. It was easier to drag small ships across the Isthmus (see next entry) or unload from ships on one side and reload on to different ships on the other, than to undertake a long and stormy voyage around the Peloponnese.

Corinth was associated in myth with *Sisyphus and his descendants; *Medea and Jason fled there after the former contrived the murder of Jason's uncle Pelias. It was occupied by the *Dorians c.900 BC. The tradition was that from 747 until 657 BC the city was ruled by the Dorian oligarchy of the *Bacchiadae, under whom Corinth founded *Corcyra and Syracuse in 733, and remains found on the site attest the city's widespread foreign contacts. Corinth became something of a shipping centre for the Greek world. The Corinthian Ameinoclēs was the first Greek shipbuilder known to history, who built ships for Samos in 704, and the first recorded Greek sea-battle took place between Corinth and Corcyra, in 664. In 657 the Bacchiads were overthrown by the tyrant *Cypselus. The disaffected Bacchiad Demaratus was said to have emigrated to Etruria and become the father of Tarquinius Priscus, king of Rome. Under Cypselus and his son *Periander (c.625–585 BC) Corinthian power and prosperity reached their zenith. Three years after Periander died, to be succeeded by his nephew Psammetichus, the tyranny fell and was replaced by an oligarchy which maintained friendship with Sparta and Athens. With the growth of Athenian imperialism in the second half of the fifth century relations with Athens deteriorated, and disputes between Athens and Corinth over Corcyra and *Potidaea (another Corinthian colony) led to the outbreak of the Peloponnesian War in 431. Corinthians naturally took part in the defence of their colony Syracuse against Athenian attack in the Sicilian Expedition, and were one of the most active and persistent opponents of Athens throughout the war, although they suffered severely from loss of trade, colonies, and fleet.

Later, however, Corinth joined Athens, Argos, and Boeotia to make war against the tyrannical rule of Sparta (the Corinthian War, 395–386 BC). Its position at the base of the Isthmus made Corinth's hostility a particular source of danger to the Spartans, threatening their land communications with the north. The war ended with the Peace of Antalcidas (a Spartan general), engineered with the aid of Persia. In the war against Philip II of Macedon, Corinth joined Athens in the cause of Hellenic freedom. After the defeat of the Athenians and Thebans at Chaeronea (338), it was at Corinth that Philip summoned a congress of Greek states to form a confederacy under Macedonian supremacy. Later, Corinth became one of the principal strongholds of the *Achaean League. It afterwards passed into Macedonian control until Flamininus' victory over Macedon in 198–196, when it was declared free like all other Greek cities and became the chief city of the Achaean League. In the course of Rome's operations against the League it was completely sacked by Mummius in 146 BC in revenge for the insults suffered by the Roman ambassadors, and its population slaughtered or enslaved. It was the extinction, as Cicero said, of 'the light of all Greece'. The Greek Anthology contains a moving lament by a contemporary poet (9. 151). After a century's desolation it was refounded by Julius Caesar as a colony (46 BC). When the apostle Paul visited it about a hundred years later it was the capital of the Roman province of Achaea, and a prosperous and populous city.

Corinth is connected with the early history of Greek literature through *Arion and *Eumelus. Its pottery was especially famous from c.650 to 550 BC; and Corinth gave its name to one of the three Greek orders of architecture (see ARCHITECTURE 1 (iii)). It also gave its name to the mysterious 'Corinthian bronze' so-called, an alloy said to be of gold, silver, and copper, employed in costly ornaments. Corinth became notorious for luxury and excessive refinement; the adjective 'Corinthian' was in former times used in English with this connotation.

Corinth, Isthmus of. The Isthmus, 6 km. (4 miles) wide at its narrowest, is the neck of land east of the city of Corinth across which merchandise was transported from one sea to the other and ships were dragged along a portage-road (diolkos), still visible in part, perhaps built by Periander. It was also the site of the Isthmian games. Octavian's fleet was dragged across when Octavian pursued Antony and Cleopatra after defeating them at Actium in 31 BC. The emperor Nero undertook the work of cutting a canal through the Isthmus (as others, from Periander onwards, had contemplated before him), and actually started it with his own hands and a golden pick-axe; but it was discontinued after a considerable amount of excavation had been done.

Corinthian War, 395–386 BC, Corinth, Athens, Argos, and Boeotia against Sparta. See CORINTH.

Coriolā'nus, Gnaeus Ma'rcius, one of the great legendary heroes of Rome. He was a patrician and a general who won his name (cognomen) from the capture of the Volscian town of Corioli in 493 BC. His arrogance towards the people during a corn shortage led to his prosecution by the tribunes on the charge of aspiring to become tyrant, and subsequent exile. He withdrew to his old enemies the Volscians, led them against Rome, and approached within five miles of the city. Moved by the pleas of his mother Veturia and his wife Volumnia (the names vary in the sources), he withdrew his army and returned to the Volscian city of Antium (Anzio), where he was put to death by the Volscians. His story is told by Livy (2. 33). Shakespeare's play *Coriolanus* depends upon the Life written by Plutarch, whose source was Dionysius of Halicarnassus.

Cornē'lia (second century BC), mother of the *Gracchi, famous in her day and after as the ideal Roman matron, distinguished for her virtue and accomplishments. She was the second daughter of *Scipio Africanus, and married Ti. Sempronius Gracchus (d. *c.*153 BC). Among her twelve children were the two famous tribunes Tiberius and Gaius Gracchus, and a daughter Sempronia who married Scipio Aemilianus. After her husband's death she devoted herself to the management of her estate and the education of her children. She remained an important influence on her sons. Tiberius was said to have been urged on to propose his laws by his mother's reproach that she was known as the mother-in-law of Scipio, not the mother of the Gracchi. She was also said to have persuaded Gaius to drop a law directed against Octavius, who had been a colleague of Tiberius in the tribunate. Plutarch tells the well-known story that when a visitor asked to see her jewels she produced her sons, saying 'These are my jewels'. The Romans erected a statue to her inscribed 'Cornelia, mother of the Gracchi'. The authenticity of two fragments of letters from her to Gaius which have survived in quotation has been disputed.

Cornē'lius Gallus, see GALLUS.

Cornē'lius Sevē'rus, Roman epic poet of the late first century BC; see EPIC 2.

Corno'vii, British tribe which occupied what is now Staffordshire, Cheshire, and Shropshire, centred on Viriconium (Wroxeter).

corn supply.
1. *Greek.* Cereals formed the staple part of the Greek diet, and the Greek population from at least the eighth century BC constantly exceeded the number that the country could feed; only a few regions, e.g. Boeotia and Thessaly, were self-sufficient. Colonization was in part a response to this fact. Most states and especially Athens imported corn, at least in wartime when their land was ravaged, mainly from around the Black Sea, Egypt, Cyrene, and Sicily. Safeguarding the corn-route was one of the factors underlying the establishment of the Athenian

empire and always an important political topic (see COLONIZATION, GREEK 3).
At the begining of each *prytany, the corn supply was an item on the agenda of the assembly; the transactions of merchants, millers, and bakers were rigorously controlled by law and supervised by *sitophylakes,* 'guardians of the corn', to prevent irregularities. The corn trade was chiefly in the hands of foreigners and metics, not of Athenian citizens.
2. *Roman.* See ANNONA.

Cornū'tus, Lucius Annae'us, philosopher at Rome in the first century AD. See LUCAN and PERSIUS.

Corōnē'a (Korōneia), in Boeotia, the scene of two battles. 1. In 447 BC, the Athenians, under Tolmidēs, were defeated by the Boeotians and had to surrender the sovereignty they had exercised over Boeotia for the previous ten years. 2. In 394 BC the Spartans under *Agesilaus defeated the Boeotians and their allies, including Athens.

Corō'nis, in Greek myth, mother of *Asclepius.

Corpus Iūris Cīvīlis ('the complete civil law'), a volume of Roman law compiled by *Justinian containing all imperial legislation still in force in his day.

correption, in metre, the shortening of a long vowel or diphthong at the end of a word when the following word begins with a vowel. It occurs frequently in Homer, much less frequently in other poets.

Corsto'pitum, important Roman military post near Corbridge in Northumberland.

Coryba'ntēs, male priests associated with various gods who had orgiastic cults (see ORGIA), and in particular the companions of the Asiatic goddess *Cybelē, whom they followed with wild dances and music. They were often confused with the *Curetes.

Cory'cian cave. 1. In Greece, a celebrated cave on Mount Parnassus above Delphi, sacred to *Pan and the nymphs. The Delphians used it as a refuge in 480 BC during the Persian invasion; it was the scene of one of the miraculous happenings that brought about the Persians' precipitate retreat from Delphi (Herodotus 8. 36).
2. A cave at Corycus in Cilicia (on the southern coast of Asia Minor), the reputed dwelling of the giant *Typhoeus (Typhon), and famous for its saffron-producing crocuses. Corycus was the home of Virgil's *Corycius senex,* 'old man of Corycus', the gardener of *Georgics* 4. 125.

coryphae'us, chorus-leader; see CHORUS.

Cos, one of the south Sporades islands off the SW tip of Asia Minor, opposite Halicarnassus, colonized by *Dorians. It won fame in the Hellenistic age, in the fourth and third centuries BC, as a literary centre under the patronage of the Egyptian kings the Ptolemies, and was the home of the Greek poets Philetas and Theocritus. It was the birthplace of *Hippocrates (fifth century BC), the father of Greek medicine and a member of a famous medical family in that island, reputedly descended from *Asclepius.

cothu'rnus (*kothornos*), 'buskin' or calf-length laced boot of soft leather with a thin sole and turned-up toes worn by actors playing heroic roles in Greek tragedy, and hence the symbol of high tragedy. The famous tragic buskin with a sole several inches high was an invention of the late Hellenistic Age. Since the boot could be worn on either foot, the word was used as a nickname for a politician prepared to support either side, a 'trimmer' (see THERAMENES). See also CREPIDATA and SOCCUS.

Cotta, Gaius Aurē'lius, Roman consul in 75 BC and subsequently proconsul in Gaul, a distinguished orator and one of the interlocutors in Cicero's *De natura deorum. He figures also in the latter's *De oratore.

co'ttabus, the onomatopoeically named Greek after-dinner game, originating in Sicily, in which the diner, reclining on his left elbow, had to throw with his right hand the last drops of wine from his cup into a metal basin, so that none was spilt (the noise as the wine struck the basin giving the game its name). If this proved too easy there were several more difficult variations. In one of the most popular the basin was filled with water, saucers floated on the top, and the wine aimed at each of the saucers so as to sink it. In the simplest form of the game, the thrower might associate his lover's name with the throw, the quality of the sound from the struck basin telling him whether his love was reciprocated.

Cottus, see HECATONCHEIRES.

Coty't(t)o, Cotys, Thracian goddess whose orgiastic cult spread over Greece and Italy. She was associated with the Phrygian goddess *Cybelē.

Crannon, town in Thessaly, the home of the powerful family of the Scopadae (see SIMONIDES). For the battle of Crannon see ATHENS 2 (v).

Crantor, of Soli in Cilicia (on the southern coast of Asia Minor), c.335–275 BC, a Greek philosopher belonging to the *Academy at Athens, who wrote a commentary on Plato's dialogue *Timaeus*. His work 'On grief' was much admired by later writers including Cicero, who used it as a model for his own 'Consolation' written to comfort himself on the death of his daughter Tullia (see CICERO (1) 4).

crāsis, in Greek grammar, the running-together of a vowel or diphthong at the end of a word with a vowel or diphthong at the beginning of the next, the two words being thus joined together. Compare SYNIZESIS, where the spelling of the two words remains unaffected.

Crassus. 1. **Lucius Lici'nius Crassus** (140–91 BC), the outstanding Roman orator of his day, exemplar for Cicero, who makes him the chief speaker in his *De oratore. He was a strong supporter of the aristocracy, and was the teacher of a new generation of ambitious aristocrats, e.g. *Cotta and *Sulpicius Rufus. His speeches have not survived, but a saying has: see AHENOBARBUS.

2. **Marcus Lici'nius Crassus** (115–53 BC), the triumvir, one of *Sulla's lieutenants, who had made a fortune in the *proscriptions. After his praetorship in 73 he was appointed to put down the slave revolt (72–71) led by *Spartacus, who had defeated the consuls in the previous year. This he successfully did, killing Spartacus. He was consul in 70 with *Pompey whom he now felt to be his rival. They greatly modified Sulla's constitution and diminished the power of the senate. In the following years Crassus increased his fortune, and by helping suitably eminent or promising men in need (such as Julius *Caesar) he gained much influence. When Caesar returned from Spain, he, Pompey, and Crassus made an informal coalition, known in modern times as 'the first triumvirate', with the purpose of enabling each man to achieve his particular aim. Crassus helped Caesar to become consul in 59. In 55 Caesar procured the consulship for both Pompey and Crassus, and arranged for Crassus to proceed afterwards to the province of Syria, which the latter reckoned to be the place to acquire wealth and military glory by a victory over the Parthians. In the event the Romans suffered an appalling defeat at Carrhae in 53 and Crassus was subsequently murdered by the Parthians. The Parthian king was celebrating the marriage of his son and entertaining the wedding party with a performance of Euripides' *Bacchae*, when a messenger arrived with the head and hand of Crassus. To the delight of the spectators the actors applied to Crassus' head the lines in the play referring to that of Pentheus.

Crassus sought success through wealth and the influence that wealth could bring him. He enriched himself in many ways: he owned silver mines, and came to possess a large part of Rome. It was said that he kept many slaves to rebuild houses damaged by fire, which he bought for next to nothing from distraught owners.

Crātēs. 1. Writer of Greek Old Comedy; see COMEDY, GREEK 4.

2. Of Thebes, *Cynic philosopher, c.365–285 BC.

3. Of Athens, philosopher, head of the *Academy after the death of Polemon in 270 BC. He died between 268 and 265 BC.

4. Of Mallos in Cilicia (on the south coast of Asia Minor), the head of the library at *Pergamum in the second century BC. He wrote commentaries on the Greek poets, including Homer. He was sent from Pergamum as an envoy to Rome, probably in 168 BC (see ROME 5); being detained there through breaking his leg (by falling in the *Cloaca Maxima), he gave lectures which aroused an interest in literary study.

Crati'nus, writer of Greek Old Comedy; see COMEDY, GREEK 4.

Cra'tylus, dialogue by *Plato on the origin of language, written c.384 BC. Cratylus was a philosopher of the school of *Heracleitus and a friend, or teacher, of Plato. According to the views expressed in the dialogue by Cratylus and Socrates, all words in all languages are by nature appropriate to the things they describe, being imitations of them, but in language there are also elements of chance, of design, and of convention. Cratylus is represented as accepting Socrates' fanciful etymologies.

cremation, see BURIAL.

Crĕ'mera, see FABIA GENS.

Cremŭ'tius Cordus, Aulus, Roman historian who wrote in the first century AD a history of the civil wars. He committed suicide when prosecuted by the emperor Tiberius because, it was said, he called *Cassius (one of Caesar's murderers) 'the last Roman'. His work has not survived.

Crĕon ('prince'), name given to several figures in Greek myth; compare CREUSA, 'princess'.

1. King of Corinth, with whom Jason and Medea took refuge (see ARGONAUTS). Jason abandoned Medea in favour of marriage with the king's daughter, and in revenge Medea contrived the death of father and daughter.

2. Brother of Jocasta, the wife of *Oedipus, king of Thebes. He ruled Thebes on three occasions: after Laius' death, after Oedipus' downfall, and again after the death of Oedipus' son Eteocles (see ANTIGONE). He gave his daughter Megara in marriage to Heracles (see *HERACLES, MADNESS OF*).

crepidā'ta, fa'bula, term applied to a Roman tragedy on a Greek theme, such as the tragedies of Accius and Pacuvius; from *crepida,* the Latin word for the high boot, *cothurnus,* worn by Greek tragic actors.

Crete (Krētē, Lat. Crēta), Mediterranean island to the south-east of Greece and the south-west of Asia Minor. Its position makes it a natural stepping-stone from Europe to Egypt, Cyprus, and Asia. Holding therefore an intermediate position in early times, between the ancient civilizations of the Near and Middle East and barbarian Europe, it was well suited to become the site of the earliest European high civilization.

1. *Minoan civilization.* This was the name given by Sir Arthur Evans to the Bronze Age culture in Crete (c.3000–1000 BC) revealed by his excavations at the beginning of the twentieth century; he named it after Minos, the legendary early king of Crete. Evans divided the civilization into three main phases, Early, Middle and Late Minoan (EM, MM, LM), and each phase into three sub-periods, I, II, and III. Further subdivisions have since been made, e.g. LMIIIA, LMIIIA 1. Sixteen or more successive periods can be recognized by changes in the shape and decoration of Minoan pottery. It is possible to correlate the Minoan phases with the Egyptian dynasties to achieve a rough absolute dating. The chief sites are at *Cnossus, Phaestus, Mallia, and Khania (in classical times known as Cydonia); other smaller sites have also been excavated.

2. The beginning of the Early Minoan period (c.3000–2200 BC), which succeeded a long Neolithic Age, was marked by a striking new style of pottery, indicating the arrival of a new (and non-Greek) people from western Asia, from Anatolia perhaps, or a Semitic people from Syria or Palestine. The end of this period marked the start of the great period of Minoan civilization, c.2200–1450 BC (MMI–LMI). The island seems to have been peaceful (there were few defences) and prosperous; there is much evidence of contact with Egypt, and the population grew considerably, living not only in the cities that grew up around the palaces, the centres of economic and political organization, but also in smaller communities. Writing existed in the form of pictograms on stone seals, out of which developed a simplified script (see LINEAR A) found on clay tablets and in inscriptions and graffiti. This script has not yet been deciphered. In MMII, perhaps at the end of the eighteenth century BC, the great palaces at Cnossus and Phaestus were destroyed, probably by earthquake rather than war. Afterwards they were entirely rebuilt, and the period following the rebuilding is sometimes referred to as the 'second palace period'. Although the art of pottery declined somewhat, the arts generally flourished, particularly those of gem-engraving, jewellery, fine metal working, fresco-painting, and glazing (the glazed objects being usually referred to as 'faience'), and gradually pervaded the Aegean area, especially the Greek mainland. Trade was actively pursued. However, Cnossus and other Cretan sites suffered further destruction c.1500 BC, in consequence, it has been thought, of the great volcanic explosion of *Thera, which caused widespread damage and may have been followed in some places by foreign conquest. After these disasters only

Cnossus seems to have recovered her former prosperity in the succeeding period, LMII (c.1450–1400 BC). During this time a new influence becomes apparent, both in pottery styles and in writing. Clay tablets, mostly at Cnossus but at other sites also, appear late in the period (the dating is uncertain) written in a different script, *Linear B, which is also known from several sites on the mainland of Greece. This has been deciphered as an early form of Greek, different from the language of the earlier scripts and probably indicating that the island rulers were by this time Mycenaean Greeks from the mainland whose power was expanding as that of Crete declined (see MYCENAE).

A final catastrophe, accompanied by fire and looting, overwhelmed Cnossus in the 'last palace' period, c.1375 BC (LMIIIA); there is no clear evidence to show the origin of the catastrophe, whether it was natural or caused by revolution or foreign invasion. Other sites show similar signs, and the populations of some cities may have withdrawn inland to high, defensible hills. By the end of the Bronze Age (towards 1000 BC), Minoan culture was in sharp decline. Cnossus, however, remained an important city into the Early Iron Age, c.1000 BC, and Crete's strategic position ensured its continuing fame. Homer talks of 'Crete of the hundred cities' (more than half of which are known). In historical times Crete was predominantly *Dorian; it was governed by an aristocracy and its important cities were Cnossus (still), Gortyn, and Lyttos, and later Cydonia (Khania). It had a reputation for producing good slingers and archers, and also lawgivers (see GORTYN). During the fifth and fourth centuries BC the island lay outside the mainsteam of Greek history. By the late third century BC, the notoriety of Crete as a refuge for pirates rivalled that of Cilicia. The pirates supported *Mithridates VI, king of Pontus, against Rome, but those in Crete were crushed in 68–67 BC by the Roman general Q. Metellus who captured many cities and destroyed Cnossus. Thereafter Crete became a Roman province. See also RELIGION, GREEK I.

Cretheus, son of *Aeolus (2) and Enaretē, father of Aeson (see ARGONAUTS).

cretic, in metre the sequence – ∪ –; see METRE, GREEK I.

Crĕū'sa, 'princess' (the feminine equivalent of 'Creon'), in myth the name of several heroines of whom the best-known are the following.

1. Daughter of Erechtheus, king of Athens, and mother, by Apollo, of *Ion.

2. Daughter of the Trojan king *Priam and his wife Hecuba, wife of Aeneas and mother of Ascanius; she died in the flight from Troy after its capture by the Greeks. In Virgil's *Aeneid* her ghost warns Aeneas of the adventures that lie before him.

Crīmī'sus, river in the west of Sicily, near which Timoleon of Corinth defeated the Carthaginians in 339 BC. See SYRACUSE 3.

Crīna'goras, born c.70 BC, a Greek elegiac poet of Mitylene who went to Rome; some of his verse is preserved in the Palatine Anthology (see ANTHOLOGY I).

Crīsa (or **Crissa** or **Cirrha**—whatever the original differences, the names were used interchangeably in classical times), in Phocis, one of the most ancient of Greek cities; the territory of Crisa included a fertile plain. The name is often used to denote Delphi, which was situated a few kilometres to the north-east. See SACRED WARS.

Cri'tias (c.460–403 BC), at Athens, an extreme oligarch, from an aristocratic family, a cousin of Plato's mother. He was implicated in the mutilation of the *Hermae, but released on the evidence of *Andocides. After playing a part in the oligarchic revolution of the Four Hundred in 411, he went into exile c.406, but returned when Sparta defeated Athens at the end of the Peloponnesian War (404). Being strongly pro-Spartan he became one of the *Thirty Tyrants (see also ATHENS 2 (iii)); he may have helped to bring about the death of his more moderate colleague Theramenes. He was killed fighting at Munychia in the civil war that ended the tyranny of the Thirty. In his lifetime he associated with the sophists and with Socrates. He wrote elegiac poems and tragedies, some fragments of which survive. Plato, who disapproved of the excesses of the Thirty, nevertheless made him figure in his dialogues *Protagoras, Timaeus,* and *Critias* (see PLATO 2).

Cri'tias, dialogue by Plato; see PLATO 2.

Crīto (*Kritōn*), dialogue by *Plato.

Socrates is in prison, awaiting the time when he must submit to the death penalty by drinking hemlock. His friend Crito comes to him and proposes a means of escape, urging his duty to his children. Socrates replies that the only question is whether an attempt at escape would be a just act; evil must not be done in return for evil suffered. Suppose the laws of Athens should remonstrate with him and ask why he, who was born and has lived under them, should now try to overturn them? Moreover, how will he gain by a life of exile? The requirement of the laws is that he should first act justly, and only afterwards think of life and children: that is what the laws say to him. Crito admits that he has no reply.

Critolā'us, head of the *Peripatetic (Aristotelian) school of philosophy at Athens in the second century BC. Only a few fragments of his writings have survived. Like Plato he was severely critical of rhetoric, but he recognized the outstanding qualities of the orator Demosthenes. See PHILOSOPHY 2.

Croe'sus, the last king of *Lydia, *c.*560–546 BC, son of Alyattes and proverbial for his great wealth. He subdued the Greek cities on the coast of Asia Minor, but in general he showed favour to the Greeks, making rich offerings to Greek shrines, especially Delphi. The rise of Persia as a rival power led him to seek a decisive battle, and emboldened by an oracle from Delphi which in the event proved ambiguous ('If you cross the Halys you will destroy a great realm') he crossed the river Halys, the boundary of his empire, in an expedition against the Persian king Cyrus. Croesus was utterly defeated and his capital Sardis taken. Legends telling of his fate seem to have sprung up soon after: that he set himself on his own funeral pyre, but was saved by Apollo out of gratitude for the gifts to Delphi, or that he was spared after being put on a pyre by Cyrus, who, hearing Croesus recall the warning of Solon about the uncertainty of life, reflected on his own mortality, and repented of his murderous intention (see also CLEOBIS AND BITON).

Crŏnus, in Greek myth, the youngest and most important of the *Titans, the older gods who preceded the Olympian *gods. The Titans were the children of *Uranus and *Gaia, Heaven and Earth. On the advice of his mother Gaia, Cronus castrated his father Uranus, releasing the other Titans from inside Gaia where Uranus had forced them to remain confined. Cronus then took as wife his sister Rhea, and they became the parents of many of the important Greek gods. Because Cronus knew he was fated to be supplanted by one of them, he swallowed them all at birth, but when *Zeus was born Rhea handed Cronus a stone instead and hid the baby in Crete (see CURETES). When Zeus grew up he made Cronus disgorge the stone and all the rest of his children (a stone set up at *Delphi is by tradition the one disgorged). Cronus and the other Titans (with the aid of the *Giants and *Typhoeus) waged war against Zeus and the new gods (who were helped by the *Cyclopes and the *Hekatoncheires), but the Titans were eventually overwhelmed and consigned to *Tartarus. The extraordinary narrative of this succession myth is paralleled by myths current among eastern peoples, notably the Phoenicians and the Hittites, in the second millennium BC, and it is likely that it reached Greece from these sources. The act of castration represents the separation of heaven and earth, a common motif in mythology from many parts of the world. A different group of stories represents the period when Cronus ruled, after he had overthrown Uranus, as a Golden Age on earth. Cronus is mainly a figure of myth (rather than of religion) and rarely the object of a cult. The Romans identified him with *Saturn.

Crŏton (Krŏtōn, Lat. Crŏtōna or Cortōna; modern Crotone), Greek colony on the west coast of the Gulf of Tarentum in south Italy, somewhat south of its rival *Sybaris, settled by *Achaeans from the Peloponnese in 709 BC. It became a large and flourishing city, founding its own colonies, and famous for its doctors and athletes. It won a notable victory against Sybaris at the river Crathis in 510 BC (its army led by its most famous athlete, *Milo), reaching the height of its power as a consequence. *Pythagoras settled there *c.*530 BC and founded his school. The Pythagoreans came to dominate the politics of the city, but were overthrown by a democratic revolution *c.*450 BC. Croton was conquered by Dionysius I of Syracuse and suffered severely in the Roman wars against Pyrrhus and Hannibal. It is ironic that the Greek pastoral poet *Theocritus chose it in Idyll 4 as the scene of tranquil country life at a time when it was being ravaged by war (first half of the third century BC). In 194 BC it was recolonized by the Romans, but without lasting success.

Crown, On the (Peri tou stephanou, Lat. De corona), speech by Demosthenes in reply to Aeschines' general indictment of his policy. See DEMOSTHENES (2) 1 and 4.

Ctē'sias, of *Cnidus in Asia Minor, a Greek physician of the early fourth century BC, who lived for a number of years at the Persian court. He wrote a history of Persia in twenty-three books (Persika), as well as the first book to be devoted entirely to India (Indika). We possess a few fragments of these and synopses made by *Photius (Bibliotheca 72).

Ctesi'bius, see CLOCKS.

Ctē'siphon, see AESCHINES.

cucu'llus, in Roman *dress, a covering for the head, a hood.

Cu'lex ('gnat'), Latin poem in hexameters doubtfully attributed to Virgil (see APPENDIX VIRGILIANA).

cult, the worship of a god or hero with rites and ceremonies. Believing in, respecting, or recognizing the gods was to both Greeks and Romans primarily a matter of observing their cult by performing acts of worship. Worship consisted of correct action rather than intense personal conviction or spirituality. The most important aspect of cult was making an offering to the god by *sacrifice, *libation, or dedication (i.e. gift of an object). The offering was accompanied by prayer, on the principle of do ut des, 'I give (to you) so that you will give (to me)'. See FESTIVALS and RELIGION.

Cūmae (Kȳmē), the earliest and for some time the most distant Greek settlement in Italy, on the coast a little north of the Bay of Naples. It was founded by Euboeans from the cities of Chalcis and Eretria soon after 750 BC (see COLONIZATION, GREEK 2), but it took its name from the city of Cyme in Aeolis in Asia Minor, the home town, it was said, of one of the founders. Having excellent harbours nearby and surrounded by very fertile country it rapidly acquired wealth, the period of its greatest prosperity being 700–500 BC. In the late sixth century, when the Etruscans threatened the city, the leader of the people, Aristodemus, successfully drove them off and afterwards made himself tyrant (c.505 BC). He died c.492. In 474, with the aid of Hieron, tyrant of Syracuse, Cumae crushed the combined fleets of Etruria and Carthage in a famous victory, but c.421 was conquered by the (Italian) Samnites and thereafter ceased to be a Greek city. It came under the control of Rome in 338, and steady decline set in. The cave of the Cumaean *Sibyl was here, and may still be seen, and nearby is Lake *Avernus.

Cunobelī'nus, 'Cymbeline', British king in the first half of the first century AD; see BRITAIN 3. He figures in medieval legends; Holinshed's *Chronicles* (1577) were the source for Shakespeare's *Cymbeline*.

Cupid (Lat. *cupīdo*, 'desire'), the Roman boy-god of love, son of Venus and Vulcan, an adaptation of *Eros, the childlike god of Hellenistic Greece with wings and a quiverful of arrows, and a figure of literature rather than of cult. He is familiar in the Latin poets, and especially in the first book of Virgil's *Aeneid* where Venus sends him to take the place of Ascanius, and to excite the love of Dido for Aeneas. Later he appears in the fairy story of Cupid and *Psychē, set in the narrative of the *Golden Ass,* a Latin novel of the second century AD by *Apuleius. Cupids appear on ancient coffins as a symbol of the life after death promised to initiates of the mystery religions, and hence into churches as winged cherubs.

Cupid and Psyche, see PSYCHE.

Curcu'lio ('weevil'), Roman comedy by *Plautus.

Phaedromus is in love with Planesium, a slave-girl, but lacks the funds to buy her from the pimp Cappadox. Curculio, a *parasite of Phaedromus, steals a seal-ring from the boastful soldier Therapontigonus, who has deposited with a banker a sum of money in order to buy Planesium for himself. By means of a letter sealed with this ring Curculio secures the girl for his master. Therapontigonus is furious at the fraud, but the ring reveals the fact that Planesium is his freeborn sister, and so he gets his money back and Phaedromus marries the girl.

Cūrē'tēs, attendants of the goddess *Rhea. They were thought to be originally semi-divine people inhabiting Crete in mythical times, to whom the infant *Zeus was entrusted by his mother Rhea for protection against his father *Cronus; to conceal the child they danced around him, drowning his cries with the clashing of their weapons (see also AMALTHEA). They are often confused with the *Corybantes, who were properly the attendants of the Asiatic goddess Cybelē, because she was often assimilated to Rhea and to other mother-goddesses.

Cū'ria, originally, one of the groups into which the Roman people was divided in earliest times, thirty in number, ten to each *tribe. They were the basis of the political and military organization of the state, such as it was. Each *curia* had its own meeting-place, whence the word came to mean 'a place of assembly', and in particular denoted the senate-house of Rome, situated on the north side of the *Comitium in the Roman Forum. This was known as the Curia Hostīlia because its erection was ascribed to Tullus Hostilius, king of Rome in the mid-seventh century BC. It was burnt down by the mob in 52 BC when Clodius' body was placed on a pyre made up of its furnishings, and a new one was begun near the site of the old by Julius Caesar in 44 BC. Later rebuildings retained Caesar's plan, namely a rectangular hall with magistrates' dais facing the door and marble benches along the side walls.

Curiā'tii, see HORATII.

Cu'rius Dentā'tus, Mā'nius, famous in Roman times as epitomizing the Roman values of simplicity and severity. As consul in 290 and in 275 BC he defeated first the Samnites, bringing the Samnite War to an end, and secondly *Pyrrhus at Beneventum (Benevento). His triumphal procession was adorned by four elephants, the first ever seen at Rome. He was consul for a third time in 274, and defeated Pyrrhus' Italian allies who were still in arms. When the Samnites had tried to bribe him with costly presents, he replied that he preferred ruling over those who possessed gold to possessing it himself.

cursive (script), name given to fluent, everyday handwriting and in particular to that used in the early centuries of the present era not only privately but by Greek and Roman scribes for official letters and documents. It was an influence in the development of the later book-hand known as minuscule (see BOOKS AND WRITING 6). Some letter forms are unexpected; e.g. in Roman cursive E was written ||, N |||, and M ||||.

cursus honō'rum ('the sequence of magistracies', i.e. political offices), at Rome, a term signifying the various political offices in the order in which they were to be held, and the periods of time which were required to elapse between the tenure of successive offices. It was determined by custom at an early date and first fixed by law in 180 BC, with later amendments, notably by Sulla after 82 BC. The required pattern was service in the army followed by the offices of quaestor, praetor, consul, and censor. If the aedileship was held (which was not obligatory) it came after the quaestorship. The minimum age at which a consulship might be held did not vary much, being in general 42. The minimum interval between magistracies was set at two years, but this requirement varied at different times, and in any case there was always a tendency for these constitutional requirements to be ignored (see e.g. the election of *Scipio Aemilianus to the consulship in 147 and 133 BC). To gain a magistracy 'in one's own year' (*suo anno*) meant at the earliest possible age (see CICERO (1) 2).

Curtius, hero of a Roman legend invented to explain a depression or pit known as Lacus Curtius, 'Curtius' pond', in the Roman Forum, which had dried up and was paved over in Sullan times (beginning of the first century BC). There were three versions of the legend: (i) a Sabine, Mettius Curtius, pursued by Romulus and the Romans, leaped with his horse into the swamp which covered the later site of the Forum; (ii) the consul Curtius in 445 BC had the area enclosed as sacred because it had been struck by lightning; (iii) (most famously) after a cleft had opened in the Forum (supposedly in 362 BC) and an oracle had said that the chief strength of Rome must be thrown into it before it would close, a soldier Marcus Curtius, understanding the oracle's meaning, rode fully armed into the cleft.

Cu'rtius Rufus, Quintus, Roman historian of the first century AD who wrote a history of Alexander the Great in ten books, of which the first two are lost. The extant books start in 333 BC with Alexander's march through Phrygia and the cutting of the Gordian knot. The narrative is dramatic and romantic, with vivid detail, but with little critical sense or grasp of Alexander's place in history.

curule magistracies, in Rome, important magistracies which entitled the holders to use the *sella curūlis*, or 'chair of state', as a symbol of their authority. The 'chair' was in fact more like a folding stool, inlaid with ivory; it originated in Etruria, where it had been used in the royal chariot from which justice was administered. The entitled magistrates were censors, consuls, praetors, and the two 'curule' aediles. It was also the prerogative of a dictator and those immediately under him, and the *flamen dialis.

Cy'belē (Kybelē or Kybēbē), the great mother-goddess of Phrygia associated in myth and cult with a young male consort *Attis. Her fame spread all over the ancient world. The centre of her cult was on Mount Dindymus, at Pessīnus, where she was called Agdistis, and where her image, of stone, was believed to have fallen

from heaven. She was primarily a goddess of fertility, but also a goddess of wild nature, symbolized by her attendant lions. She was said to cure (and send) disease, and protect her people in time of war. By the fifth century she was known in Greece and was soon identified with the local 'mother of the gods' and Demeter. In 204 BC in the stress of the Second Punic War, and in accordance with a prophecy in the Sibylline books and advice from Delphi, the Romans sent a distinguished embassy to Pessinus on the delicate diplomatic mission of taking back to Rome the sacred stone. On its voyage it had an escort of five quinqueremes. The temple built for the goddess's reception stood on the Palatine, but the cult was kept under surveillance until the end of the republic, and participation in priesthoods and rituals was forbidden to Roman citizens (except that they might join in her festival, the *Megalesia); she was kept to her temple and served only by oriental priests (see GALLI) although processions of the priests were allowed (as described by Lucretius, 2. 600). These restrictions were lifted by the emperor Claudius; worship of Cybele and Attis became part of the state religion, and one of the important *mystery religions of the Roman empire.

Cy'clades, group of islands in the southern part of the Aegean Sea, so called because they form roughly a circle (*kuklos*). They include Delos, Ceos, Naxos, Paros, Andros, and Tenos. During the early and middle Bronze Age (which in Greece was *c*.3000–*c*.1000 BC) they enjoyed an independent culture (sometimes called 'Cycladic'). Towards the end of the Bronze Age several of the islands were settled from Minoan Crete and later came under the influence of Mycenean Greece. In about 1000 BC they were occupied by Ionic-speaking Greeks. After the Persian Wars they joined Athens' Delian League.

cyclic poems, see EPIC CYCLE.

Cȳclō'pēs (sing. Cyclops), in Greek myth, one-eyed giants, according to Homer, dwelling on a distant island. *Odysseus visited the cave of one of them, *Polyphemus. In Hesiod they were the sons of *Uranus (Heaven) and Gaia (Earth), three in number, called Brontēs, Steropēs, and Argēs ('thunderer', 'lightener', 'bright'), who made the thunderbolts of Zeus and aided him in his war against the Titans. They often appear as Hephaestus' workmen, and were credited with the construction of ancient walls, such as those of Tiryns and Mycenae. In these cases they have little in common with the Cyclopes of the *Odyssey*. See also ASCLEPIUS, and CYCLOPS below.

Cȳclops, *satyric drama by *Euripides, produced perhaps in 412 BC.

The Greek god *Dionysus having been captured by pirates, Silenus has set out in pursuit, accompanied by his satyrs, and has fallen into the power of the Cyclops *Polyphemus. Odysseus and his crew arrive and bargain with Silenus for food in exchange for wine. Polyphemus returns and makes prisoners of Odysseus and his men. The blinding of the Cyclops and the escape of Odysseus are told much as in the *Odyssey*. The whole subject is dealt with humorously.

Cycnus, see SHIELD OF HERACLES. There are several figures of this name in Greek myth. The best known are the following.

1. Son of Ares, who robbed and killed travellers taking offerings to Delphi, and tried to build a temple to Apollo out of their skulls. He was killed by Heracles when the latter was on his way to fetch the apples of the Hesperides (see HERACLES, LABOURS OF 11).

2. Son of Poseidon, ally of the Trojans in the Trojan War, invulnerable to human weapons but strangled by the Greek hero Achilles when he tried to prevent the Greeks landing at Troy. The story, not found in Homer, was in the *Cypria*.

Cӯlon, Athenian noble who married the daughter of Theagenes, tyrant of Megara, and with his help seized the Acropolis at Athens with a view to setting himself up as a tyrant (*c*.632 BC). The Athenians under the archon Megacles laid siege to the Acropolis, and after Cylon and his brother managed to escape to Megara, killed their associates who had taken refuge at the altar of Athena. Those responsible for this sacrilege, especially Megacles and his family, the *Alcmaeonidae, were said to have incurred *pollution, and this was frequently invoked against them in later political disputes at Athens.

Cӯmē, see CUMAE. See also HESIOD.

Cynēgeʹtica, see OPPIAN and GRATTIUS.

Cynēgeʹticus (ʹhuntingʹ), a treatise by *Xenophon.

After an exordium, exceptional in Xenophonʹs works, tracing the invention of hunting game with hounds to Apollo and Artemis, who handed it on to Chiron, and he to a number of heroes, the author urges all young men to take up hunting, especially of hare and deer on foot, with hounds. He begins by describing the necessary equipment, the nets, the hounds, and their points, but wanders on to the question of scent and the habits of the hare. He then returns to the trappings of the hounds, the proper way to fix the nets, and the actual hunt; here Xenophon shows his enthusiasm. A passage follows on the breeding, training, and naming of hounds (forty-seven names to choose from, all disyllabic for easy calling). The author next describes the hunting of deer (for which hounds and snares were used) and of wild boar (with hounds, nets, javelins, and spears), and gives a short chapter to the hunting of big game in foreign countries. He then enumerates the benefits of hunting, in respect of health, military service, and moral education. The treatise concludes with an attack on sophists as useless and untrustworthy.

*Arrian also wrote a book on hunting, which still survives, in the style of Xenophon and as a supplement to his treatise.

Cynic philosophers, those following the principles of Antisthenes and Diogenes of Sinopē.

Antiʹsthenēs (*c*.445–*c*.360 BC), at Athens, a pupil and friend of Socrates, but differing in his views from the latterʹs most famous follower, Plato; he was considered the founder of the sect, and influenced its best-known exponent Diogenes of Sinope, from whose nickname, *kyōn*, ʹthe dogʹ, the sect derived its name (see below, and CYNOSARGES). Antisthenes believed that happiness is based on virtue, that virtue consists in action, and that it is a practical quality which can be taught; thus to him the life of the mythical hero Heracles epitomized the ideal. Since happiness results only from virtuous action, most pleasures do not contribute to it. The knowledge of virtue, once acquired, cannot be lost; the wise man cannot act unwisely. Antisthenesʹ voluminous writings, except for some fragments, have been lost, but it is known that he was interested in literature, linguistic theory, and dialectic.

Dioʹgenēs (*c*.400–325 BC), after his arrival in Athens, seems to have been attracted by the austere character and way of life of Antisthenes, which perhaps influenced him in his fanatical espousal of the ʹnaturalʹ life, the subject of many anecdotes. While in Athens he was supposed to have lived in a tub (of earthenware) belonging to the Metrōon (temple of the Mother of the gods). It is said that his later life was spent in Corinth, as a result of the voyage in which he was captured by pirates and sold as a slave to a Corinthian. Here he is reputed to have met Alexander the Great. If he in fact wrote any of the works attributed to him, nothing has survived. He rejected all conventional views of what constituted a personʹs happiness; for him it consisted of satisfying oneʹs barest natural needs for things outside oneself, for food and shelter for example, in the cheapest and easiest way, and for the rest living on oneʹs own natural endowments, renouncing all possessions and relationships. This self-sufficiency could be achieved by physical and mental self-discipline, and by losing the conventional sense of shame. It was supposed to be on account of this last characteristic that Diogenes was nicknamed ʹdogʹ. He illustrated his principles in his way of life and in caustic utterances. His philosophy and way of life were spread by his disciple Crates.

Cratēs (*c*.365–285 BC), who came to Athens from Thebes and was won over by the example of Diogenes, became famous for the whole-hearted way in which he embraced Cynic doctrine. Having renounced his large fortune, and restricting himself to absolute necessities, he achieved a high degree of self-sufficiency. Hipparchia, the daughter of a rich family, threatened suicide in order to persuade her parents to let her share his life. (See also ZENO.)

The Cynics developed no elaborate philo-sophical system and were never organized into a school, so in practice they embraced a range of beliefs while maintaining as their central tenet that self-sufficiency could bring contentment in all the vicissitudes of life. Crates originated the type of Cynic philosopher who wandered the Greek world with stick and knapsack, the frequent object of mockery. Cynic beggars of this kind suddenly proliferated in the first and second centuries AD, and still existed in the sixth; the contrast between them and true Cynic philosophers became a literary commonplace. See also STOICS.

Cynosa'rges, a gymnasium outside the city of Athens sacred to Heracles, for the use of those who were not of pure Athenian blood. Anti-sthenes is said to have started teaching there, and on this has been based an alternative explanation for the name 'Cynic' (see CYNIC PHILOSOPHERS).

Cynosce'phalae, in Thessaly, scene of the defeat in 197 BC of Philip V of Macedon by the Roman Q. Flamininus (see MACEDONIA 3). For an earlier battle there see ALEXANDER OF PHERAE.

Cynthia, Cynthius, epithets given to the Greek deities Artemis (equivalent to the Roman Diana) and Apollo, derived from Mount Cyn-thus in their native island of Delos. 'Cynthia' was the name given by the Roman poet *Propertius to his mistress (compare Lesbia, the object of Catullus' love poems, named from the island of Lesbos, and *Delia).

Cy'pria (perhaps 'the epic composed in Cyprus'), a lost poem of the Greek *Epic Cycle. It recounted, in eleven books, the events that led up to the point in the Trojan War at which Homer's *Iliad* begins, including the wedding of Peleus and Thetis, the judgement of Paris, the abduction of Helen, the assembly of the Greek fleet, the rescue of Iphigeneia by Artemis at the moment of sacrifice, the fight with Telephus, and the first engagements at Troy. The epic is sometimes ascribed to Stasinus of Cyprus, hence the title (otherwise unexplained).

Cyprian, Saint (Thascius Caecilius Cypriānus), c. AD 200–58, made bishop of Carthage in 248, born in the Roman province of Africa of a pagan family, the first of the Latin Christian writers to hold high official position in the Church. He fled from the persecutions of the emperor Decius (249–51) but returned in 251. In the persecutions under the emperor Valerian he

was first banished, in 257, and then in 258 put to death. Cyprian's writings, mainly short treatises and letters, have always been popular, and are valuable sources for ecclesiastical history as well as being sometimes of theological importance. His Life, by his deacon Pontius, is the earliest Christian biography. See CHRISTIANITY.

Cȳprus, island in the north-east Mediterranean, about 80 km. (50 miles) south of Cilicia in Asia Minor. In the early Bronze Age it was populated from Anatolia, and a prosperous culture grew up, but influences from Mycen-aean Greece in the late Bronze Age have been detected, and by the end of the thirteenth century BC the native culture seems to have been submerged, perhaps by Mycenaean Greeks fleeing from destruction on the mainland. Modern Enkomi appears to have been the site of the chief Mycenaean city. During this Mycen-aean period the Cypriots used a syllabic script derived from Cretan *Linear A, and now known as Cypro-Minoan, which was the ancestor of a syllabic script used from the seventh to the third centuries BC to write Cypriot Greek (see DIALECTS). The Greek element in the population was not substantially reinforced after Mycenaean times, but settlers came in large numbers from Phoenicia, and their influence grew until in the fourth century BC much of central Cyprus was in their control. In 525 BC Cyprus had fallen to the Persians but it enjoyed a brief period of independence after the efforts of the philhellene *Evagoras in 411. In the late fourth century BC the island came under the control of the Ptolemies of Egypt for nearly two and a half centuries. It was annexed by Rome in 58 BC and attached to the province of Cilicia.

The sanctuaries of *Aphroditē on the island, at Păphos and Amathus, were especially re-nowned, so that the goddess is often called simply 'the Cyprian' (Gk. Kypris, Lat. Cypria). According to one myth, it was at Paphos that she was born from the sea-foam.

Cy'pselus, tyrant of *Corinth, who overthrew the oligarchy of the *Bacchiadae and founded a dynasty of tyrants, ruling himself from c.657 to c.625, when he was succeeded by his son *Periander. Under him Corinth grew in power and prosperity; large quantities of local pottery were exported, especially to the West, and he founded colonies on the route to Italy and Sicily, namely Leucas, Ambracia, and Anacto-rium (see also COLONIZATION, GREEK 2). His name was explained by a story, that his father Eëtion was of humble birth but had managed to marry a Bacchiad wife, Labda, because she was lame. As the result of an oracle prophesying their overthrow the Bacchiads tried to kill the son of the marriage, but his mother had hidden him in a chest, kypselē, and he survived. A magnificent chest of cedar wood carved and decorated with figures in ivory and gold, purporting to be that of Cypselus, was dedicated by the Corinthians at Olympia and was seen there many centuries later by Pausanias. His description suggests that it was not made until the sixth century BC.

Cȳrenā'ic school of philosophy, founded at Cyrene by *Aristippus.

Cyrē'nē, the very important Greek colony in Libya (North Africa), on a high plateau a few kilometres inland, roughly midway between the Egyptian delta and Tunisia. Being cut off from other civilized regions of Africa by deserts and great distances, it looked naturally towards Greece. It was originally colonized from Thera in 630 BC (see COLONIZATION, GREEK 4), but received more settlers from Greece on several occasions. The colony attained great prosperity, its territory (Cyrenāica) being rich in corn, wool, oil, and the mysterious plant silphium, trade in which was a monopoly of the rulers. Unknown today, it was greatly valued in classical times as a universal medicine and was exported on a large scale. Cyrene was unique in that its founder *Battus established a long-lasting royal dynasty, unbroken until it was overthrown some time after 460 BC; the rulers were named Battus and Arcesilaus alternately. It was made a Roman province in 74 BC. Cyrene was the birthplace of Aristippus, Carneades, Synesius, and Callimachus, who was occasionally called 'Battiadēs' (son of Battus) in allusion to his royal descent.

Cȳropaedī'a (*Kyrou paideia*, 'education of Cyrus'), narrative by *Xenophon, in eight books, of the career of *Cyrus the Great, king of Persia, in which characters and historical facts are modified to suit the author's didactic purpose. Writing roughly at the same time as Plato, who in the *Republic* argues for *his* conception of the education of an ideal ruler, Xenophon sets out his own in the *Cyropaedia*, a work which strongly resembles a historical novel with a moral purpose. Cyrus himself is an idealized character, the perfect statesman, ruler, and general, drawn partly from the character of the younger Cyrus who was known to Xenophon and appears in his *Anabasis*. The constitution of Persia, and the method of education described, similarly represent Xenophon's ideals (based in part on the institutions of Sparta). The military precepts and the tactics described are Xenophon's own. There are numerous minor characters, kings, soldiers, and councillors, and among them the Indian tutor of the Armenian king's eldest son, Tigranes, unjustly put to death— a portrait intended to suggest Socrates. The tedium of the work (for most modern readers) is somewhat relieved by the romantic episode of the farewell of Abradatas (who is about to die in battle) to his wife Panthea. After the narrative of Cyrus' military campaigns is concluded with the capture of Sardis and Babylon, the work ends with a description of the organization of the Persian empire and the death of Cyrus. But by the time Xenophon came to write the end of the book it had become apparent that the Persian system was neither efficient nor progressive; the final chapter, describing the confusion resulting from Cyrus' death, was perhaps intended as a counterweight to the earlier admiration.

Cȳrus. 1. Cyrus the Great (559–529 BC), the founder of the Persian empire. He was the son of Cambyses, of the Persian family of the Achaemenids, and the vassal of Astyages, king of Media. He ousted Astyages from his throne and by 547 had extended Persian rule as far west as the river Halys. He then overthrew and captured *Croesus, king of Lydia, and gained control over Asia Minor, Babylonia (thereby liberating the Jews from captivity), Assyria, Syria, and Palestine. He administered a vast empire with wisdom and tolerance; to Xenophon he was an example of the ideal ruler (see *CYROPAEDIA*). His grave is at the Persian city of Pasargadae, near the place where he defeated Astyages. He was succeeded by his son Cambyses.

2. Cyrus the Younger, descendant of Darius I, the second son of Darius II, king of Persia 424–405 BC. His friendly relations with the Spartan general Lysander were fatal for Athens at the end of the Peloponnesian War. After the death of his father he gathered together a mercenary army, which included Xenophon, ostensibly for an expedition against Pisidia, but in reality to oust his elder brother Artaxerxes from the throne. A pitched battle was fought at Cunaxa in 401; Cyrus' army was defeated and he himself killed. The westward march of the Greek mercenaries to the coast is the subject of Xenophon's *Anabasis*.

Cythē'ra, island off the south coast of Laconia in the Peloponnese. Some Greek myths relate that Aphrodite landed there after being born from the sea-foam, hence she is sometimes called 'Cytherean' (but see also CYPRUS).

Cythē'ris, see GALLUS.

D

dactyl (*daktylos*, 'finger'), in metre, the sequence − ∪ ∪. See METRE, GREEK I.

Dactyls, Idaean, in Greek myth, magical smiths, but beyond this fact the subject of obscure and conflicting stories. They were located on either the Cretan or the Phrygian Mount Ida. Hence they are sometimes associated with Rhea, as the beings in Crete to whom the infant Zeus was entrusted (thus being identified with the *Curetes), or with *Cybelē (being then confused with the Corybantes).

da'ctylo-e'pitrīte, see METRE, GREEK 8 (iii).

Dae'dala, in Boeotia, a festival of the goddess *Hera.

Dae'dalus ('cunning worker'), legendary Athenian craftsman and inventor, thought of as living in the age of *Minos, in whom the Greeks personified the development of sculpture and architecture through mechanical inventions; his impossibly ingenious devices provided the plot of many exciting stories. It was said that his statues could move themselves. Being afraid that his nephew and pupil Talōs would outdo him (for the latter invented the saw and the potter's wheel), Daedalus threw him down from the Acropolis (Pausanias saw his reputed grave at Athens in the second century AD) or into the sea (when Athena changed him into a partridge, *perdix*, by which name Talōs was also known). Daedalus was condemned for his crime by the Areopagus and fled to Crete, where he constructed the *labyrinth for king Minos. Afterwards, Minos would not let him go; Daedalus then made wings for himself and his son Icarus out of wax and feathers, and they flew away. But Icarus flew too near the sun; the wax of his wings melted and he fell into the sea and was drowned. Daedalus landed on the island in the Sporades now called Ikaria and buried his son's body. He then escaped to king Cocalus in Sicily, whither Minos pursued him; enticed into Cocalus' palace Minos was scalded to death in a bath of Daedalus' invention. Virgil at the beginning of book 6 of the *Aeneid* describes Daedalus arriving at Cumae in his flight from Minos and dedicating a temple there. *Pausanias (2), in the course of his travels around Greece in the second century AD, saw several statues said to have been sculpted by Daedalus, and accepted that he really existed.

daimon (pl. *daimonĕs*), in Greek, 'divine spirit', commonly interpreted etymologically as 'he who allots'. The word is used loosely in Greek poetry to mean 'god' or 'the gods'; but in general *daimones* did not have this equivalence; there were no images of them and they received no cult, except that the first *libation at a wine-drinking was made in honour of the Good Daimon. In general *daimon* describes an aspect of divine power which cannot be identified with a particular god, and is only rarely used to designate one of the Olympian gods. It is this power which gives a man good or bad fortune at any time, so that he may feel that he has the *daimon* on his side, or else that he is struggling against it; thus *daimon* approximates in meaning to irresistible fate. (Heracleitus declared in a famous utterance that an individual's character is his *daimon*, thereby asserting that a person's destiny is under his own control.) Hesiod says that after death the men of the *Golden Age were transformed by Zeus into *daimones*, able to confer prosperity on mankind. Perhaps this was the basis for honouring great and powerful men when they had died, as for example in the case of the Persian king Darius, who was conjured up as a *daimon* in the *Persae* of Aeschylus; Plato thought those who died fighting for their country should be honoured as *daimones*. The notion of *daimones* as intermediate beings between gods and men may long have existed in popular superstition, but is introduced into literature by Plato. His followers extended the idea to include *daimones* as evil spirits, 'demons'. For Socrates' 'divine sign' (*daimonion*) see SOCRATES. See also EMPEDOCLES.

Dama'stēs, another name for *Procrustēs.

damna'tio memo'riae ('obliteration of the record'), at Rome, punishment for a crime against the state, whereby use of the *praenomen* (see NAMES) of the condemned man was forbidden in his family, every image of him destroyed, and all public mention of him erased.

Da'moclēs, a courtier of Dionysius I, tyrant of *Syracuse (see 2) in the fourth century BC. When he praised to excess the happiness of a tyrant, Dionysius invited him to experience it for himself. He placed Damocles at a banquet where presently the latter observed a naked sword hanging over his head by a single hair, symbolizing the precarious nature of such happiness.

Damon, Pythagorean philosopher from Syracuse, proverbial for his friendship with Pythias (whose name in fact seems to have been Phintias). The latter, condemned to death, left Syracuse in order to arrange his affairs, leaving Damon to stand surety for him, and returned in time to redeem his friend. The tyrant was so impressed by their friendship that he pardoned the criminal.

Dana'ans (Dănăoi), general name for the Greek nation in Homer and later poets; more particularly, a Peloponnesian Greek people inhabiting the region of Argos in early times; thus the name Danaans sometimes signifies Argives. For their supposed origin see DANAUS.

Dă'năē, in Greek myth, daughter of Acrisius king of Argos (brother of Proetus). An oracle foretold that Acrisius would be killed by his daughter's son, and he therefore confined Danae in a bronze tower, so that no man might approach her. But Zeus descended on her in a shower of gold, and she bore a son Perseus. Acrisius placed Danae and the child in a chest and cast them adrift in the sea (for a Greek lyric poem on the subject see SIMONIDES), but they landed on the island of Serīphos, where they were sheltered by Dictys, brother of Polydectēs, king of the island. See also PERSEUS.

Da'naids (Dănăidĕs), in Greek myth, daughters of *Danaus.

Dă'năus, in Greek myth, son of *Belus, king of Egypt, descendant of *Io, and brother of Aegyptus. The brothers' names show that they were regarded by the Greeks as the ancestors of the *Danaans and the Egyptians. Aegyptus had fifty sons, Danaus fifty daughters (the Danaids). Belus gave Aegyptus the kingdom of Arabia and Danaus Libya, but the latter, feeling threatened by his brother's conquest of Egypt, sailed away with his daughters to Argos, the city from which Io had come, and became king, the inhabitants being called in consequence Danaoi. The sons of Aegyptus pursued their cousins to Argos in order to marry them, though they were unwilling. Danaus was forced to consent, but ordered his daughters to stab them with daggers which he provided, on their wedding night. This they all did except Hypermnestra, who spared her husband *Lynceūs. She was imprisoned and put on trial by her father, but the Argive court, perhaps through the intervention of the goddess of love, Aphroditē, acquitted her. Pindar tells how Danaus, in order to select other husbands for his daughters, set these at the end of a race course and let their suitors run for them. After their deaths the other Danaids were punished for their crime in the Underworld by having to try to fill leaky jars with water.

dancing. In the ancient world, dancing was a natural and inseparable part of many everyday activities, religious, social, and even military.

1. *In Greece.* The popularity of dancing is attested by the two hundred or so names for dances that have come down to us. It is frequently mentioned in Homer as a natural entertainment: in the *Odyssey* the suitors of Penelope amuse themselves with music and dancing; Odysseus at the court of Alcinous is impressed by a display of specially skilful dancers. Entertainments of this sort, sometimes verging on the acrobatic (see the anecdote concerning *Hippocleides), sometimes including mimetic dances interpreting a story, might be provided at the end of a dinner-party (*symposium*) by professionals, slaves, or prostitutes hired for the purpose. Xenophon describes how, when he was on campaign, an evening's entertainment was concluded by a soldier's dancing girl performing a war-dance to amuse the Paphlagonian guests. Public religious festivals were accompanied by choruses singing and dancing with simple rhythmical movements (see CHORUS). Plato thought that all dancing should have this religious character. Dancing was also educative, associated with music and poetry in the art called *mousikē* which embraced all three elements and developed grace and beauty. In a more bracing form it was a part of gymnastic training as a preparation for war, especially in Sparta; it trained soldiers to perform their evolutions simultaneously and in order. Most celebrated of the war dances, usually performed with weapons, was the Pyrrhic dance, said to be of Cretan or Spartan origin. Its rapid body movements represented the way in which a soldier evaded blows and missiles. Although people danced at social gatherings such as weddings, harvests, and victory celebrations, grown up men and women did not dance together in modern fashion: the dances were for groups of people. One of the most famous was the Delian dance known as the *geranos* ('crane'), invented according to tradition by Theseus and his companions when they stopped at Delos on the way back to Athens from Crete, its complicated figures commemorating the *labyrinth. Other distinctive dances were those of the Greek theatre, the stately *emmeleia* of tragedy, the lewd *cordax* of comedy, and the coarse and violent *sikinnis* of satyric drama.

2. *In Rome.* Dancing did not pervade civic life to the same extent as in Greece. In early times it was common at religious festivals, the most famous being that of the *Salii. Military dances too existed among the Romans as among the Greeks: the *bellicrepa saltatio* ('dance to the sound of arms') was said to commemorate the capture of the Sabine women by Romulus. But by the first century BC the Romans had a low opinion of dancing, which was not engaged in by a citizen for purposes other than religious:

Cicero observes in a speech that 'no sober man will dance unless he is mad'. Hence the traditionalists' sense of outrage when the emperor Nero danced in public was a natural Roman response. Mimetic dances, however, were developed to such a pitch that they became an independent art-form. See PATOMIME.

Daphnē ('laurel'), in Greek myth, a nymph, daughter of a river-god (generally Ladon in Arcadia but also represented as Pēnēus in Thessaly). She was a huntress and wanted no lovers, but was pursued by Leucippus who joined her hunting companions disguised as a girl. When Daphne and her companions bathed after the hunt Leucippus was found out and killed. She also rejected the love of the god Apollo and fled from him, praying to the river-god Peneus for deliverance; she was thereupon changed into a laurel tree.

Daphnis, legendary Sicilian herdsman, a recurring figure of bucolic (i.e. pastoral) mythology, said to be the originator of bucolic song. His father was sometimes said to be the Greek god Hermes, his mother a nymph who exposed him under a laurel bush (*daphne*), from which his name is derived. He himself was mortal. He was loved by a nymph to whom he vowed eternal fidelity, but he was made drunk and seduced by a princess. Thereupon the nymph blinded him, and he spent the rest of his life composing mournful songs on his unhappy fate, the supposed origin of bucolic poetry. There are variations on this story, notably in *Theocritus where Daphnis appears to die of love. Daphnis epitomizes the musician-shepherd, the ideal inhabitant of the idyllic pastoral world, his life and death powerfully signifying that even in such a world there is no escape from the pangs of unhappy love and death.

Daphnis and Chloe, Greek *novel by Longus.

Da'rdanus, in Greek myth, son of Zeus and Electra, the daughter of the Titan *Atlas. He was the ancestor of the kings of Troy, and was said to have lived in Samothrace (in the north Aegean), from where he went to Phrygia. The local king Teucer welcomed him and gave him his daughter as wife and part of his territory. Dardanus built a city on the slope of Mount Ida (south-east of the future site of Troy) and called it Dardania. Hence the Trojans are sometimes called 'Dardanians'. In the Trojan war, the enmity of Zeus' wife Hera towards the Trojans in part originated from her jealousy of Electra for having won the love of Zeus. See TROY.

Darēs, in Virgil's *Aeneid*, a companion of Aeneas; he figures in the boxing match (book 5).

Darēs Phry'gius, in Homer's *Iliad*, the priest of Hephaestus at Troy. He was thought by later Greeks to have existed in fact and to be the author of a pre-Homeric poem on the destruc-

tion of Troy, a supposed translation of which into Latin prose survives, written no earlier than the fifth century AD. This work was subsequently ascribed to Cornelius *Nepos because it was prefaced by a forged letter purportedly written by Nepos to Sallust, explaining how he had discovered the original in Athens. During the fifteenth and sixteenth centuries the poem enjoyed great popularity because of its subject matter (the *Iliad* does not give an account of the fall of Troy), as did the similar work of *Dictys of Crete.

daric, see MONEY 1.

Darī'us (Dāreios). **1. Darius I,** son of Hystaspes, and king of Persia from 521 to 486 BC. Like Cyrus the Great he was a member of the Persian *Achaemenid family; he succeeded to the kingdom after the death of Cambyses by overthrowing a usurper who was impersonating Cambyses' dead brother. Restoring order after anarchy, he revised the boundaries of the provinces, creating twenty *satrapies, a system which was retained by later kings. In about 514 Darius cut across Europe, marching through Thrace in a north-easterly direction in a show of force against the Scythians, and calling on the Ionian Greek cities to support him: these cities were his vassals, ruled by tyrants under the general control of Persia. In 499 they revolted, but by 494 the revolt was suppressed. The cities of mainland Greece had been implicated and in 491 Darius sent envoys to Greece demanding submission. When this was not forthcoming he sent an army, which was defeated at Marathon in 490 (see PERSIAN WARS). Darius died four years later.

2. Darius III Codomā'nus (c.380–330 BC), the king of Persia overthrown by *Alexander the Great.

Dark Age(s). This term is applied to various turbulent periods of history when civilization was endangered and few records handed down. In the ancient world it refers to the following two periods.

1. In Greece, the period from, very roughly, the twelfth to the ninth century BC. It begins with the invasions that resulted in the final destruction of *Mycenae and ends with the emergence of Athens as a cultural force in Greece, c.875 BC, marked by the new and influential *Geometric style of pottery. See also IRON AGE and PROTO–GEOMETRIC.

2. In the later Roman empire, the period of the barbarian invasions and their aftermath, very roughly from the sixth to the ninth century AD. See ARABIA; BYZANTINE AGE; FALL OF ROME; GOTHS; HUNS; TEXTS, TRANSMISSION OF ANCIENT 3 and 5; VANDALS; VISIGOTHS.

Davus, name of the cunning slave in Terence's *Andria*, and also of the slave who lectures Horace in *Satires* II. 7.

De'a Dīa, a Roman corn-goddess whose cult was promoted by the *arval priests.

De agri cultū'ra or *De re rustica* ('on agriculture'), treatise by M. Porcius *Cato the Censor, the oldest piece of Latin prose of some length to survive. It is a concise, practical handbook, dealing with the cultivation for profit, in Latium and Campania, of vines, olives, and fruit, and with cattle-breeding. Cato discusses the purchase of a farm; the duties of owner, overseer, housekeeper, and slaves; the tilling of the soil; the care of livestock; and a few minor matters, such as a prescription for treating a sick ox, recipes for curing hams and making cheese-cakes, and religious and superstitious formulas. It is written in a curt, abrupt style, without much organization of material, but it was widely read and quoted from in ancient times.

De amici'tia ('on friendship'), also known as *Laelius*, dialogue by *Cicero ((1) 5) composed in 44 BC and addressed to *Atticus. The dialogue is supposed to take place in 129 BC shortly after the death of *Scipio Aemilianus. The interlocutors are *Laelius, the intimate friend of Scipio, and his two sons-in-law, C. Fannius and the augur Quintus Mucius *Scaevola. Cicero in his youth had received instruction in the law from Scaevola and had heard him, he tells us, repeat the conversation. Laelius in his discourse discusses the nature of friendship and the principles by which it should be governed. The conclusion is that friendship is founded on, and preserved by, virtue; for it owes to virtue the harmony, permanence, and loyalty that are its essential features. This is one of the most admired of Cicero's dialogues for its dignity and calm and for the melodious quality of its prose. It was one of the two books in which Dante found consolation for the death of Beatrice.

De architectū'ra ('on architecture'), *Vitruvius' treatise on Roman building, written towards the end of the first century BC.

De be'llo cīvī'li and *De be'llo Ga'llico*, see COMMENTARIES.

De benefi'ciis ('on benefits'), treatise in seven books by *Seneca (2), addressed to Aebutius Liberalis, the first four books of which were issued c. AD 54 and the rest later. The work deals with the nature of benefit, gratitude, and ingratitude, and various problems connected with the conferring and receiving of benefits; it shows considerable insight into human conduct. Some interesting examples are given of heroic self-sacrifice.

De brevitā'te vī'tae ('on the shortness of life'), dialogue by *Seneca (2), addressed to Paulīnus, an official, probably written c. AD 49. Its theme is the value of time and the need for the wise and thrifty use of it on self-improvement, not on vicious pursuits. This is considered one of the best of Seneca's essays.

De causis planta'rum ('inquiry into plants'), treatise by *Theophrastus written towards the end of the fourth century BC.

Decelē'a (Dekeleia), an Attic deme north-east of Athens near the pass east across Mount Parnes. It was about 22 km. (14 miles) from Athens and visible from there; ships entering Piraeus were in its view. Its occupation by the Spartans in 413 BC, during the Peloponnesian War, at the suggestion of the Athenian Alcibiades, put a stranglehold on Athens for the rest of the war. The term 'Decelean War' is sometimes used to describe the last period of the Peloponnesian War, from 413 to 404.

decemviri, decemvirs, 'ten men'. In Rome the name was given to several boards of ten men set up for particular purposes. The most famous were the *decemviri legibus scribundis* (an early form of the classical Latin *scribendis*), 'decemvirs for writing down the laws', appointed in 451 BC. Before that time the laws at Rome remained unpublished and inaccessible to the people, and it was thus easier for the ruling patricians to manipulate justice to their own advantage (see ROME 3). The decemvirs of 451 were patricians appointed in response to the demands of the *plebs* to codify and publish the laws (see TWELVE TABLES). According to Roman legend, the decemvirs acted responsibly for the first year, but behaved arrogantly when re-elected, under the influence of their leader Appius *Claudius. Apart from codifying the laws these decemvirs were credited with a reform of the calendar, the creation of *consuls as the chief magistrates and of *quaestors, and the reorganization of the census as well as of judicial procedure. *Decemviri stlitibus* (an early Latin form of *litibus*) *iudicandis* were 'decemvirs for judging cases'; they acted as a jury to decide whether an individual was a slave or free.

Dě'cius Mus, Publius, one of the Roman consuls in 340 BC during the war with the Latins. According to legend he gained the victory for Rome by 'devoting' himself and the enemy to the gods below (see DEVOTIO), and then charging into the enemy ranks to his death. His son of the same name played a similar part in 295 BC at the battle of Sentīnum (Sentino) against the Samnites. The latter instance of *devotio* is more likely to be historical (see FABIUS MAXIMUS RULLIANUS).

De civitā'te De'i ('city of God'), St *Augustine's monumental demolition of paganism and defence of Christianity, 'a great and arduous work' as he called it, in twenty-two books written between AD 413 and 426. The collapse of Rome and Roman institutions, ending in the capture of Rome by *Alaric in AD 410, was attributed by many pagans to the rise of Christianity and the overthrow of the old gods, and the Christians themselves were confused and demoralized. Some have seen the origin of this book in Augustine's desire to refute pagan charges and hearten the Christians. But the work developed into something far greater, an exposition of the spiritual history of the human race, showing that since the fall of Adam it had always been divided into two *civitatēs*, 'cities', 'Babylon' and 'Jerusalem', inextricably mixed in this world but to be separated at the Last Judgement. The moral qualities of the Romans had made their empire superior to any of its predecessors, but its virtues could only be fully realized in the city of God; for all human glory and ambition are vain. Augustine attacks with ridicule the remains of the old Roman religion; he criticizes the doctrines of the best of the pagan philosophers, the Stoic, Platonic, and Neoplatonic schools, for being incapable of yielding complete happiness because they lacked the promise of eternal life. These attacks are directed against the formidable opposition set up by the highly cultivated and deeply religious pagans of his day, staunchly adhering to the old ways, in comparison with whom Christians seemed to lack intellectual foundation. Finally Augustine sets out the ultimate destiny of the two cities, the heavenly city comprising the righteous on earth and the saints in heaven, living in accordance with God's will; and the earthly city, guided by worldly and selfish principles, doomed to perish.

dēclāmātiō'nēs (Gk. *meletai*, 'declamations'), in Roman oratory (but originating in Greek practice of the third and second centuries BC; see EDUCATION 5), the technical term for the exercises performed by young wouldbe orators in the rhetorical schools. These pupils were required to speak on invented themes (*thesēs*), some highly implausible. For judicial declamations, *controversiae*, and deliberative declamations, *suasoriae*, see SENECA (1) and QUINTILIAN.

De clāris orātō'ribus ('on famous orators'), an alternative title to Cicero's treatise *Brutus*, written about 45 BC.

De clēme'ntia ('on clemency') (AD 55–6), treatise by *Seneca (2) in three books, of which the first and part of the second survive, on the need for clemency in a ruler. It was written in the second year of the emperor Nero's reign. Its theme was suggested by his exclamation when unwillingly signing a death warrant, 'Would that I had never learnt to write!' The praise of Nero that it contains must be judged in relation to the comparative mildness of his rule in the first years.

De compendiō'sa doctri'na ('epitome of learn-ing'), Latin encyclopaedia of the fourth century AD by *Nonius Marcellus.

De consōlatiō'ne ad Ma'rciam, ad Poly'bium, ad He'lviam, three 'consolations' written by *Seneca (2) between AD 40 and 43.

De consta'ntia sapie'ntis ('on the constancy of the wise man'), written by *Seneca (2) after AD 47.

De corō'na (*Peri tou stephanou*, 'on the crown'), title of a speech by Demosthenes (see DEMOSTHENES (2) 1 and 4).

De'cuma. 1. The (early) Latin name for Decima, one of the *Fates. She also presided over the 'tenth' (final) month of a woman's pregnancy.

2. At Roman law, one tenth of the grain harvest paid as tax to the treasury.

De dīvinātiō'ne ('concerning divination'), dialogue by Cicero composed as supplement to his *De natura deorum* ('on the nature of the gods'; see CICERO (1) 5) and published in 44 BC soon after Caesar's murder. It examines *Stoic beliefs about fate and the possibility of prediction. Cicero here shows little sympathy with Stoic views, but affirms his belief in a divine being. The dialogue takes place at Cicero's villa at Tusculum, and the interlocutors are his brother Quintus and himself (Marcus). Quintus expounds, with a wealth of illustration and quotations from the Stoics (and also from Cicero's own writings) his reasons for believing in certain forms of *divination. Marcus explodes the belief in divination in general by this dilemma: future events are either at the mercy of chance or are foreordained by fate. If the former, no one, not even a god, can have foreknowledge of them; if the latter, there is no use in divination (i.e. investigation into the future in order to avoid unpleasant events) because what is foreordained cannot be avoided. Marcus thinks that divination on state matters by official augurs should be maintained for reasons of prudence but ridicules its absurdities, quoting in passing the saying of Cato (the Censor) that he wondered how a soothsayer (*haruspex*; see HARUSPICES) could meet another soothsayer without laughing. Marcus recognizes an art of *augury, but denies a science of divination. He similarly demolishes other methods of prediction based on dreams, omens, astrology, and 'inspired' prophecy. The work contains the much-quoted observation, 'there is nothing so ridiculous that some philosopher won't say it' (*nihil tam absurde dici potest quod non dicatur ab aliquo philosophorum*).

De do'mo sua ('concerning his house'), speech delivered by *Cicero ((1) 3 and 4) before the College of Pontiffs (see PONTIFICES). Its genuineness has been contested, but is now generally accepted.

When Cicero was exiled in 58 BC, *Clodius had his house on the Palatine destroyed, consecrated the site, and erected on it a monument to Liberty. Cicero asks the College of Pontiffs to annul the consecration on the grounds that Clodius' tribunate was irregular, that his law banishing Cicero was unconstitutional, and that the dedication was unjust and impious. The College decided in Cicero's favour. (See also DE HARUSPICUM RESPONSO.)

De falsa lēgātiō'ne (*Peri tes parapresbeias*, 'on the false embassy'), speech by Demosthenes; see DEMOSTHENES (2) 4.

De fāto ('on fate'), treatise by *Cicero ((1) 5) written in 44 BC in which, at the request of Hirtius (consul in 43 BC), he discusses whether or not our actions are predetermined, and decides against *Stoic fatalism. Only part of the work has survived.

De fī'nibus bono'rum et malo'rum ('on the different conceptions of the chief good and evil'), treatise by Cicero in five books, addressed to M. *Brutus, in which he sets out and criticizes the ethical systems of the Epicurean and Stoic schools, before giving the views of the 'Old' *Academy. It was written in 45 BC (see CICERO (1) 5).

The treatise takes the form of three dialogues, each dealing with one of the above systems. In the first, set in Cicero's villa near Cumae in 50 BC, the Epicurean view is put forward by L. *Manlius Torquatus (d. 48 BC). In the second, M. *Cato of Utica (d. 46 BC) puts forward the Stoic view, and the scene is Lucullus' villa near Tusculum in 52 BC. In the third the view of the 'Old' Academy is expounded by M. Pupius Pīso Calpurniānus (consul 61, d. before 47 BC), and the scene is Athens in 79 BC when Cicero was studying philosophy there. In each case the criticism is supplied by Cicero, who was not attracted by the Epicureans but had some sympathy with the ethical doctrines of the Stoics, while chiefly supporting the views of the Academy.

Book 1 opens with a defence by Cicero of the task he has undertaken of reproducing Greek philosophical thought in Latin dress. Manlius Torquatus expounds and defends the view that the chief good is pleasure in the absence of pain. This Cicero demolishes in book 2. In book 3 Cato defends the view that the chief good consists in virtue, which is achieved by living in agreement with nature, whose formative principle is reason. In book 4 Cicero criticizes this as not sufficiently taking into account the lower faculties of the human race. Book 5 opens with a remarkable description of the Athenian scene with its historical and literary associations. The opinion of the 'Old' Academy (as revived by the philosopher Antiochus) is set out, that the chief good is perfection of the whole self, and that

virtue alone gives happiness, a view largely coinciding with that of the Stoics. It is criticized by Cicero on the ground that virtue alone cannot give happiness; for the virtuous man is not always happy, if pain, as is admitted, is an evil. But the last word is left with Piso, who maintains that the virtuous man, if not supremely happy (owing to pain), is yet on balance happy; for virtue outweighs all else.

dēfi'xio (Gk. *katadesis*), 'binding', see MAGIC 5 (ii).

De gente po'puli rōmā'ni ('on the Roman nation'), a lost treatise by *Varro on the prehistory and early chronology of Rome.

De gramma'ticis ('on the grammarians'), book of short biographical sketches by *Suetonius on about twenty-one Roman grammarians, of which some part survives.

De haru'spicum respo'nso ('concerning the response of the soothsayers'), speech delivered by *Cicero before the senate in 56 BC (see (1) 3 and 4).

The soothsayers had attributed some mysterious noises heard near Rome to the anger of the gods aroused by certain impieties, among others the profanation of consecrated sites. Clodius had interpreted this as applying to the rebuilding of Cicero's house on its original site which Clodius had consecrated. Cicero now replies to Clodius, claiming that the impieties referred to were all of them acts of Clodius. (See DE DOMO SUA.)

De histo'ria conscrībe'nda (*Pōs dei historian syngraphein*, 'the way to write history'), by *Lucian, perhaps the best of his critical works.

Dēianei'ra, in Greek myth, the wife of *Heracles.

de'i conse'ntēs, see DI CONSENTES.

Dēidamī'a (Dēidameia), in Greek myth, the mother of Neoptolemus by *Achilles.

De impe'rio Cn. Pompeii ('concerning Pompey's command'), alternative title for Cicero's speech *Pro lege Manilia* in support of the proposal in 66 BC to extend Pompey's command in Asia.

Deina'rchus (*c.*360–*c.*290 BC), a distinguished Greek orator, Corinthian by birth, who lived in Athens. Not being an Athenian citizen he was debarred from addressing the assembly, but he composed a large number of speeches for others, including a speech *Against Demosthenes* connected, like his other two surviving speeches (*Against Aristogeiton* and *Against Philocles*), with the Harpalus affair (see DEMOSTHENES (2) 1). Three other speeches surviving in the manuscripts of Demosthenes have sometimes been attributed to Deinarchus: *Against Boeotus II*, *Against Theocrines*, and *Against Mantitheus*.

De interpretātiō'ne (*Peri hermeneias*, 'on interpretation'), title of a short treatise on logic by *Aristotle (4 (i)).

De inventiō'ne ('on invention'), an early work (*c.*84 BC) on oratory by *Cicero ((1) 4). It explains how the subject matter should be chosen and arranged, how the speech should be divided into sections, and what kind of treatment is appropriate to each section.

Dēi'phobē, name of the Cumaean *Sibyl in Virgil's *Aeneid*.

Dēi'phobus, in Greek myth, son of *Priam, king of Troy, and of Hecuba. He took a prominent part in the fighting at Troy. After the death of Paris he married Helen and was subsequently killed at the fall of Troy. His body disappeared, but Aeneas erected a cenotaph to him on Cape Rhoeteum; on his visit to the Underworld Aeneas heard the story of his death from Deiphobus himself (see AENEID 6).

Deipnosophi'stai, title of a literary work by *Athenaeus.

De ira ('on anger'), treatise in dialogue form by *Seneca (2), addressed to his brother Novātus. Of the three books, the first two may have been written in AD 41, just before Seneca's banishment, and the last at a later date. The work deals with the nature of anger, shows that it can be controlled, discusses the means of restraining it, and refers to instances of the emperor Caligula's furies and cruelties.

De ira Dei ('on the wrath of God'), a Christian work by *Lactantius.

De lau'de Pīsō'nis ('in praise of Piso'), Latin verse panegyric in 261 hexameters by an unknown author sometimes thought to be *Calpurnius Siculus. The Piso of the poem may be Gaius Calpurnius Piso who was executed for plotting against Nero in AD 65.

De lēge agrā'ria ('on the agrarian law'), or *Contra Rullum* ('against Rullus'), three speeches delivered by Cicero in the first days of his consulship (63 BC), the first to the senate, the second and third before the people, against the proposed agrarian law of the tribune P. Servīlius Rullus (see CICERO (1) 2). Cicero appears to have delivered a fourth speech, now lost, on the same subject.

Rullus proposed the appointment of ten commissioners (*decemviri*) authorized to sell all the property of the Roman people acquired outside Italy since 88 BC, and also the remaining property of the people in Italy, and to acquire land in Italy for distribution and for the foundation of colonies. Cicero attacks the proposal as giving the commissioners what were in effect unlimited powers; as being directed against Pompey; as being cruelly unfair to the foreign peoples and allies concerned; and as

likely to bring no benefit to the Roman public. The proposal, of which the real author was probably Caesar, was defeated.

De lē'gibus ('on laws'), dialogue by *Cicero ((1) 4), a sequel to *De republica*, probably begun about 52 BC. The date of its completion (if it ever was completed) is unknown; Cicero seems not to have published it. Most of the first three books survive.

The interlocutors are Cicero, his brother Quintus, and Atticus; the scene is Cicero's estate at Arpīnum. The first book is a discussion of the origin and nature of justice, Cicero expounding a (Stoic) conception of law as based on reason and divinely sanctioned. In the second book Cicero sets out and explains the religious laws of an ideal state, that is, those dealing with the worship of the gods and with priests and augurs, sacrifices, sacrilege, and the rites for the dead. In the third book he similarly sets out and discusses laws relating to the constitution of the state, and the appointment and functions of the magistrates.

Dē'lia, name of the woman celebrated in his poems by the Roman poet *Tibullus. (Compare CYNTHIA.)

Dē'lian League, the modern name given to the alliance of Greek states against the Persians created in 478 BC after the expulsion of the Persian invaders from Greece. The alliance comprised mainly Athens, the Ionian Greek cities on the coast of Asia Minor, the Hellespont, the Propontis, and most of the islands in the Aegean. At the allies' request Athens took over the leadership (see PAUSANIAS (1)). The island of *Delos, sacred to Ionians everywhere, was the venue for meetings of the League and provided the treasury for League funds. Some states with strong navies, e.g. Chios, Samos, and Lesbos, contributed ships; the remainder paid tribute (money) annually, the original contributions being assessed by Aristeides and said to total the large sum of 460 talents. At first the League undertook military operations against the Persians, thereby extending Greek control along the whole coast of Asia Minor. At this time there were nearly 200 League members. One notable expedition was that led by the Athenian *Cimon which defeated the Persians at the river Eurymedon (in Caria) at some time between 469 and 466, but a very large expedition to the Egyptian delta in support of a revolt against Persian domination there ended in complete disaster in 454 (see EGYPT). In 451 an expedition to Cyprus, again led by Cimon, was successful in securing the Aegean area against Persian interference, although Cimon himself was killed. Peace between Athens and Persia was arranged by the Athenian *Callias, after whom the treaty was named. But though the League had thereby lost its original function, it was not dissolved. During this time its character had been changing. In the 460s Naxos and Thasos had wanted to withdraw but had been compelled by force, for reasons of Athenian self-interest, to remain members. After the Egyptian disaster the treasury was moved from Delos to Athens for safety, the arrival of the tribute in the city being associated with the Athenian spring festival of the *Dionysia. By this time most of the allies who had contributed ships to the League had changed to contributing money instead, and Athens was in control of it. The League was becoming an alliance of cities controlled by Athens, i.e. her empire. League funds were spent on Athenian buildings, and during this period (450–446 BC) Athens forced upon the allies the use of her own coinage, weights and measures, and the requirement that they should come to Athens to have important court cases decided. Athenians were also settled in allied territories, partly at least to ensure security (see CLERUCH). Allied troops were called upon to serve with Athenian troops in Athenian battles. When Athens and Sparta made the Thirty Years' Peace in 446 the treaty acknowledged Athens' right to keep her sea-empire. The revolt in 440 of Samos, finally reduced after a long siege, was the last before the outbreak of the Peloponnesian War in 431; in the intervening years Athens was too powerful to resist. When war with Sparta began there was no immediate movement among the allies to revolt, and in 425 Athens was able to raise the tribute assessment to nearly 1,500 talents. It was not until the failure of the Syracusan expedition in 413 BC that revolt spread at all widely, but only Samos remained loyal after the defeat at Aegospotami in 405. With the end of the war came the end of the Athenian empire. (See also ATHENS 2 (ii) and TRIBUTE LISTS.)

De lingua latī'na ('on the Latin language'), treatise by *Varro in twenty-five books of which books 5–10 survive (with gaps).

Dēlos, small island (less than 5 sq. km. (2 sq. miles) in area) in the Aegean sea, in the midst of the Cyclades, according to Greek myth the birthplace of Artemis and Apollo. It was an important centre for the worship of Apollo, who once had an oracle there, which lapsed in classical times. The Homeric Hymn to Apollo attests that already in the eighth century BC Delos was the scene of a festival to the god, with song, dance, and games, attracting Ionians (including Athenians) from the islands and coasts of the Aegean. In later times it was said that the Athenians instituted the festival to commemorate the safe return of Theseus and his companions from Crete. Peisistratus, tyrant of Athens in the sixth century BC, purified Delos (by removing the tombs in view of the temple) in the course of extending his control over the Ionian Cyclades. In the same century Polycrates

of Samos (another Ionian tyrant) took control of the island of Rheneia next to Delos and dedicated it to Apollo by binding it with chains to Delos. After the sixth century the festival declined and the competitions lapsed; in 426 Athens revived the festival, in future to be quinquennial, first purifying the island again, this time removing all tombs and declaring that thenceforth no one should be born or die there. The competitions were reinstated, with the addition of horse-races. In 422 the Athenians decided that the removal of the Delians themselves was essential for the complete purification of the island and banished them elsewhere, but, in obedience to the Delphic Oracle, permitted their return in the following year. Every year, reputedly since the days of Theseus, the Athenians sent a sacred embassy to Delos. During the absence of the state ship on this mission Athens was kept in a state of ceremonial purity, when no criminal might be executed. (It was this which delayed the execution of Socrates.) Delos was also chosen as the centre of the maritime alliance founded in 478 BC and known as the *Delian League.

From early times the island had commercial importance owing to the business transacted there during the festival of Apollo. In the third century BC, with the development of Asia, this importance grew and Delos, no longer controlled by Athens, became a great corn-market. Notable buildings were erected by Hellenistic kings. Its prosperity increased again after 166 BC when Rome, putting Delos under Athenian control, made it a free port (i.e. abolished all duties on the movement of goods) in order to damage the trade of Rhodes, a free city and an object of Roman jealousy. Many Italians settled in the island, and its population became very cosmopolitan. Slaves were one of the chief commodities exchanged on Delos, often provided by pirates, and many were sold for the great estates of Italy. The island was sacked in 88 BC by Mithridates' general and 20,000 inhabitants killed, and it was devastated by pirates in 69 BC. Before the end of the first century BC trade routes had changed; Delos was replaced by Puteoli as the chief focus of Italian trade with the East, and as a cult-centre too it entered a sharp decline.

Delphi (Delphoi), city in the Greek state of Phocis and the site of the famous oracle of Apollo. It was situated on the southern slopes of Mount *Parnassus, enclosed in a narrow valley but occupying the central area of a great natural theatre. Through the wall of rock to the north of the town, dividing it into two, flowed the Castalian stream. These two peaks of rock were often spoken of, erroneously, as the two peaks of Parnassus. There was a small settlement here in Mycenaean times (c.1400 BC) but it seems to have been destroyed in the *Dark Age and a fresh start made in the eighth century BC. The famous crossroads where Oedipus was said to have murdered his father Laius is found on the road from Thebes to Delphi, which was precipitous and difficult in places.

Above the town was the sanctuary and oracle of Apollo, the Sacred Way leading from the Castalian spring up to the principal entrance. Inside the wall surrounding the sanctuary and oracle stood the many statues dedicated by successful athletes in the Pythian games (see GAMES, PUBLIC (1) 3) held at Delphi, and also the treasuries built by various Greek cities to hold their most valuable offerings to Apollo. Only the Athenian treasury, dating perhaps from the 490s, still stands. In front of the temple, in the open air, stood the great altar of Apollo. An archaic temple was destroyed by fire in 548 BC; the Athenian family of the *Alcmaeonidae (see also CLEISTHENES (1)), then living in exile at Delphi, contributed to the building of the new temple, and won fame by using expensive Parian marble to face the temple, where coarse stone had been prescribed in the contract. Euripides' tragedy *Ion*, set in the Delphic temple, vividly describes some aspects of it. On the front of the temple were engraved the maxims ascribed to the *seven sages, *gnōthi sauton*, 'know yourself' (i.e. know your human weakness in contrast with the power of the gods), and *mēden agan*, 'nothing in excess'; also set up was the Greek letter E, the exact significance of which remains obscure (see PLUTARCH 3).

Inside the temple was the hearth beside which the priest of Apollo was said to have killed *Neoptolemus, and beside it the iron chair of Pindar, from which he reputedly sang his hymns to Apollo. On the hearth burned a perpetual fire. Further inside was the *omphalos*, the navel-stone, supposed to mark the mid-point of the earth, determined by Zeus as the place at which two eagles met, after flying one from the eastern and one from the western boundary of the world. In Aeschylus' tragedy *Eumenides* the Pythia (prophetess of Apollo), passing through the temple to the inmost sanctuary (*adyton*), catches sight of Orestes sitting upon the *omphalos*. In the *adyton* the Pythia gave oracular responses to those who came to consult her. It seems to have been quite commonly thought from late antiquity onwards that the Pythia was in an underground chamber, seated over a chasm from which intoxicating gases arose, and induced a prophetic trance, but excavations have produced no evidence whatsoever for a chasm, nor for noxious vapours, and neither of these factors is mentioned in any early classical source.

North of the temple, still in the sacred enclosure, was the tomb of Neoptolemus, and beyond it the stone which, according to Greek belief, *Cronus swallowed in place of his son

Zeus. Here also was the spring (where Apollo slew the serpent Python; see DELPHIC ORACLE), which watered the sacred grove of myrtles and laurels and perhaps provided water for the *adyton*. To the west of this area lay a small theatre where the musical contests in the Pythian games were held, and a little further north the Leschē or public room (dedicated by the Cnidians), famous for its two large paintings by *Polygnōtus, *The Fall of Troy* and *The Descent of Odysseus into Hades*, both crammed with incident. About 10 km. (6 miles) north-east of Delphi was the famous *Corycian cave.

The Alcmaeonid temple was destroyed by an earthquake in 373 BC, the replacement surviving until Roman times; it was repaired by the emperor Domitian at the end of the first century AD. In AD 391 it was closed for ever along with all other pagan temples by the Roman emperor Theodosius, in the name of Christianity.

Excavations at the site have revealed the remains of several famous memorials: the base of the Serpent Column commemorating the Greek victory over the Persians at Plataea in 479 BC (the bronze serpent was taken by Constantine the Great to Constantinople, where it still survives in a public square, the site of a former hippodrome); the bases of the statues dedicated by the Spartan general Lysander after he destroyed the Athenian navy at Aegospotami in 405 BC; the bases of the gold tripods dedicated by Gelon and his brother Hieron, tyrants of Syracuse in the early 470s; the bronze charioteer probably dedicated in 474 BC by Polyzelos, tyrant of Gela; and many notable finds of sculpture.

Delphic Oracle, at *Delphi, the most important *oracle in Greece, belonging to the god Apollo. Delphi may possibly have been a holy place in Mycenaean times, but the cult of Apollo as a god of prophecy seems to have started only in the eighth century BC. The Greeks themselves believed that Apollo was not among the deities originally worshipped by them, but a late-comer, arriving at the end of the *Dark Age, and preceded at Delphi by an earth-goddess whose serpent, Python, he slew before ousting the goddess. An accumulation of female figurines, mainly terracottas of the twelfth century BC, has been found there, which seems to confirm this belief. In Homer the name Delphi does not occur; the site of the oracle was called 'holy Pytho', its temple of Apollo already famed throughout Greece and filled with treasures. In this temple the priestess of Apollo, known as the Pythia, speaking under the inspiration suppos-edly of Apollo, gave oracles to those who consulted her. The Pythia was over the age of 50 when she was appointed, and thereafter lived a secluded and dedicated life; how she was selected is never explained, but the Delphian authorities may have chosen her from among a band of holy women whose task it was to tend the hearth in the temple (see DELPHI). When prophesying the Pythia sat on a tall *tripod similar in style to the cooking utensil (i.e. three metal legs supporting a bowl), said in late antiquity to be placed over a chasm from which fumes were exhaled (but for which there seems to be no archaeological or classical evidence; see DELPHI). Plutarch records that in early times the Pythia gave oracles on only one day a year, in early spring; at a later date, perhaps in the sixth century BC, on one day a month, with the exception of the three winter months which the god spent with the Hyperboreans (see below). The day had to be declared auspicious by the priests, after they had tested the omens. Each enquirer, or indeed anyone who was in Delphi for a religious purpose, was required first to purify himself in the waters of Castalia. Before entering the temple he had to offer a sacred cake on the altar outside, and sacrifice sheep or goats at the hearth inside. Only then was he admitted to the inner sanctuary (*adyton*) where the Pythia was seated. It seems that the enquirer addressed his question to her directly and was answered directly, occasionally in verse, more often in prose. A priest or *prophētēs* ('mouthpiece') may have been in charge of the proceedings, and may even have 'interpreted' the Pythia's response, or put it into hexameter form. An enquirer might have let the priest know his question in advance, especially if bribery of the priests or Pythia was involved; see CLEISTHENES (2). With the reply, the consultation ended.

The impressiveness of the wild scenery at Delphi as well as of the ritual no doubt contributed to the importance of Apollo's oracle. In religion its authority was for many centuries supreme, especially in the matter of cult laws and institutions. Under the authority of the priests and other prominent Delphians it promoted the Olympian gods but also local deities and everything that was 'according to custom'. It also assisted in propagating the worship of Dionysus, who in the post-classical period was said to be present at Delphi during Apollo's three months' annual absence. During the first period of Greek colonization its sanction in the matter of choosing a site and a patron deity was of paramount importance. One of Apollo's most ancient and important functions was that of giving laws to cities; thus Delphi was the source of the laws of *Lycurgus at Sparta, it gave Cyrene her constitution, and nominated Zaleucus to be the Locrian law-giver. Apollo was also the god of purification, especially after homicide (see POLLUTION). As a sign of purification and of a new beginning after the victory at Plataea in 479 BC the Greeks extinguished their fires and new fire was fetched from Delphi. In political matters the oracle was occasionally open to persuasion or other influences. It seems to have favoured *Croesus, king

of Lydia, a generous donor, discouraged Greek resistance to Persia, and taken the side of Sparta in the Peloponnesian War (the priests were Dorian; see DORIAN INVASION). On moral issues its admonitions were strict. The severe consequences for a Spartan, Glaucus, of merely asking the god if he might be permitted to perjure himself for his own financial gain, were quoted (Herodotus 6. 86) by way of moral example. Even if the oracular responses purportedly given in early times are not in fact authentic, in the classical period the belief that they were exerted a powerful influence.

Every four years, at the Pythian games, Delphi was the centre for a panhellenic concourse (see GAMES, PUBLIC (1) 3); the Delphic *Theoxenia was another major festival and widely attended. Delphi was also a member of a powerful religious league of northern Greek states (see AMPHICTYONY). In Hellenistic times its decline began. Some of the functions of Delphi were taken over by defunct oracles in Asia and Europe which were revived after Alexander the Great had destroyed Persian domination. Sharp decline did not set in until the first centuries BC and AD as a consequence of increasing secularism and perhaps because of the rising interest in *astrology. The oracle enjoyed a brief revival under the emperor Hadrian, but by the time of the fervently pagan Julian (emperor AD 360–3), it was beyond resuscitation as its last message to the emperor, reported by a later historian, makes clear: 'Tell the emperor that the finely wrought hall is fallen to the ground; no longer has Phoebus his shelter, nor his prophetic laurel, nor his babbling spring; the water of speech is dried up.'

Dē'mades (*c*.380–319 BC), Athenian politician and orator who realized that in order to survive Athens must come to terms with Philip II of Macedon. After the Athenian defeat at Chaeronea in 338 BC he secured an honourable settlement for Athens. When in 322 BC Antipater, the governor of Macedonia, had put down a revolt against Macedonian rule in which Athens took part, Demades procured the deaths of the politicians opposed to peace with Macedon, Hypereides and (indirectly) Demosthenes. In 319, caught in the political intrigues after the death of Antipater, he was himself executed by *Cassander. Only a few phrases from his speeches survive. See DEMOSTHENES (2) 1.

de'magogue (*dēmagōgos*, 'leader of the people'). This term to describe a leader of the people arose in Athens in the late fifth century BC and it usually had the pejorative sense of an unprincipled mob orator. In the *democracy of fifth-century Athens, when all political actions were decided by the vote of the popular assembly (*ecclesia*), it was always the case that policy could be shaped by influential speakers. For the period from 478 to 431 BC these men were usually *strategoi, 'military commanders', and aristocratic, but during the Peloponnesian War and after the death of Pericles in 429 the strongest influence was exerted by speakers who were populist in manner, played on the volatile emotions of the people, and for the most part did not hold magistracies so that they could not be called to account if any of the actions they had advocated miscarried (see EUTHYNAE). The most notable were *Cleon, *Hyperbolus, *Cleophon, and Androcles.

De mercē'de condu'ctis (*Peri tōn epi misthōi synontōn*, 'on salaried posts'), satirical dialogue by *Lucian.

demes (*dēmoi*), local communities or parishes in Attica, eventually numbering about 170. In the reforms of *Cleisthenes (2), they replaced kinship groups as the basis of the democratic constitution in Athens. Cleisthenes arranged the demes into ten tribes (*phylai*) and each tribe into three *trittyes* (see TRITTYS); in each tribe one *trittys* comprised demes from the city region, another demes from the interior, and the third demes from the coast. In this way each tribe was made representative of the whole. Each deme had its own finances and its demarch (deme leader), elected by its assembly (*agora*) which dealt with local affairs. After Cleisthenes, membership of a deme was hereditary and did not change with change of residence. On reaching the age of 18 every male Athenian citizen was registered in his family deme (see CITIZENSHIP, GREEK).

Demē'ter, in Greek myth, daughter of Cronus and Rhea, sister of Zeus, a corn-goddess, patroness of agriculture in general and goddess of the Eleusinian *mysteries. By Zeus she was the mother of *Persephonē (Lat. Proserpina), and by *Iasion the mother of *Plutus. The Romans identified her with the Italian goddess of the corn, *Cerēs. She was also identified sometimes with the Egyptian Isis and the Phrygian *Cybelē. Most of the myths concerning her relate to the rape of Persephone by Hades, god of the Underworld. Demeter sought her daughter all over the world, fasting, with hair untied, and carrying torches, and the earth became barren as a result of her neglect. To appease her, Persephone was released for part of the year. This myth has always been interpreted as an allegory of nature: Persephone must descend like seed into the earth so that the new corn may germinate. In her wanderings Demeter came to Eleusis where, in the guise of an old woman, she was hospitably received by the king, Celeus, and his wife Metaneira, and tended their new-born son Dēmoph(o)ōn (or *Triptolemus). She was discovered holding the child in the fire, to make it immortal by purging away its mortality. She explained her action by revealing her divinity, and ordered that rites, known thereafter as the Eleusinian mysteries,

should be instituted at Eleusis in her honour. It was at Eleusis that Persephone was restored to her. She also sent Triptolemus about the world teaching the art of agriculture. See also ERYSICHTHON.

Dēmē'trius. 1. Demetrius of Phalērum (*c.*350–*c.*283 BC), Athenian statesman and philosopher. He was pro-Macedonian and favoured *Cassander's cause. When most of the Greek states including Athens surrendered to Cassander in 318, the latter made Demetrius governor of Athens, where he ruled in an enlightened manner for ten years. He went into exile when the Macedonian Demetrius Poliorcetes (see MACEDONIA 2) took Athens in 307, and later joined the Egyptian court of Ptolemy I Soter at Alexandria. He had studied at the Peripatetic school of philosophy in Athens as the pupil of *Theophrastus, and it is probable that he advised Soter about the foundation of the *Alexandrian Library and possibly about the *Museum too. He is thus partly responsible for their being organized in the Peripatetic fashion and spirit, which accounts for the nature and trend of much of the intellectual life of Alexandria. After Ptolemy II Philadelphus became sole ruler in 283 BC Demetrius was exiled to Upper Egypt where he died. He was an outstanding orator and the author of many scholarly works of which only fragments survive. See FABLE.

2. Demetrius Poliorcē'tēs, Macedonian general and ruler; see MACEDONIA 2, ATHENS 2 (v), and RHODES.

3. Greek author of a treatise 'On Style' (*Peri hermeneiās*), traditionally said to be Demetrius of Phalerum (see above), but the style and contents suggest a date at least a century later, and the work perhaps belongs to the first century BC. The author analyses style (*charactēr*) under four headings (rather than the more usual three; compare ORATOR): plain (*ischnos*), grand (*megaloprepēs*), elegant (*glaphyros*), and forceful (*deinos*); the last category is a novelty in this kind of criticism. He also gives an account of style in letter-writing, a literary genre usually ignored by other ancient critics.

Demiu'rge (*dēmiourgos*), in Greek, originally 'skilled workman', later 'creator', 'producer', and so, in Plato (see TIMAEUS), the creator of the visible world, and in Greek Christian writers God the Creator of all things. The Gnostics (see GNOSTICISM) used the term to denote the inferior deity who created the material universe, as distinct from the supreme God. The name *Demogorgon, taken in later times to mean the primeval god of ancient mythology, is probably a corruption of this word.

democracy (*dēmokratia*, 'rule of the people', i.e. of the *demos). Democracy in the sense of government by the majority vote of all male citizens is first known in ancient Greece, and this ideal was most nearly achieved at Athens in the fifth century BC. Democracy at Athens was established in essentials by *Cleisthenes (1) in 508 BC and lasted until Athens' conquest by Macedon in 322 BC. All political decisions were made by the majority vote of a direct, non-representational assembly of citizens (*ecclesia), its business prepared and decisions executed by a council (*boulē) and officials, themselves chosen in the main by lot (see SORTITION). After c.462 BC, under the influence of *Ephialtes and *Pericles, measures were introduced to bring about a radical (i.e. thoroughgoing) democracy. These were to ensure that all decisions were kept in the hands of the people, and to prevent power falling into the hands of those holding office. Thus all offices were decided by lot (except for those few requiring special experience, in practice the generalship; see STRATEGOS); the term of office was brief and not generally open to re-election; officers underwent an examination of suitability before taking office (*dokimasia), and were called to account at the end of it (*euthynae); and the property qualification, where it still existed, was minimal (see SOLON). Similarly with the law-courts: all legal cases were decided by juries drawn by lot from the citizen body. Payment was made by the state to all who might be excluded by poverty from performing their civic duties, including jury service and even, in the fourth century BC, to those attending meetings of the assembly. It was a feature of Athenian democracy that considerable power to influence decisions was wielded by skilful orators who held no official position and exercised this power with varying degrees of responsibility. See, on the one hand, DEMOSTHENES (2), and on the other, DEMAGOGUE.

For the constitution of Rome see REPUBLIC, ROMAN.

Demo'critus, Greek philosopher, with Leucippus founder of the Greek atomic theory. He was born in Abdera (in Thrace) in 460 BC and reputedly lived to a very great age, dying c.357. In his early years he is said to have travelled very widely in Asia. Plato never mentions him by name, but Aristotle refers to him frequently and in several connections, always with respect. He wrote copiously on a wide variety of subjects including natural sciences, mathematics, mechanics, grammar, music, and philosophy, but comparatively little has survived, and all of that in quotation. These few fragments deal mostly with ethics. Since the works of Leucippus, who was said to have been his teacher, have also perished, it is impossible to separate the contribution of each to the atomic theory. The atomists' arguments aimed to explain the perceptible world as it appears to the senses, containing multiplicity and diversity as well as motion and change.

Earlier philosophers, known as the Eleatics (see PHILOSOPHY 1), had argued that 'what exists' (i.e. the cosmos and all that it contains) is single, indivisible, and unchanging, despite appearances to the contrary: the opposite to 'what exists', namely 'what is non-existent', their argument ran, is not there to be thought about and therefore cannot exist. The atomists' answer was that 'nothingness' exists and is as real as 'a thing', and might separate parts of 'what exists' from other parts. 'What exists' is indeed single, indivisible, and unchanging, but it is in the form of particles, indivisible small solids (atoma, 'things which cannot be divided'), differentiated from each other only in shape and size, randomly moving for ever in limitless 'nothingness', i.e. the void. All worlds—ours is not unique—first came into being through randomly colliding atoms causing a rotary movement in which atoms became attached to each other; different arrangements of atoms form different compounds, hence the variety of the world as we perceive it. Our world like every other came into being by accident and developed by necessity; its intelligibility does not depend upon its having been created by some sort of divine intelligence. The gods, if they exist, though superior to the human race are still creatures which have come into being and will eventually perish. People's consciousness and perception are entirely physical, to be accounted for by the arrangements of atoms which are by themselves not capable of consciousness. Consciousness resides in the soul (which is also the cause of life) because the soul is made of particularly fine atoms, though it is as perishable as the body. Perception comes about through the impact made on the soul (mediated through the sense-organs) by fine films emanating from the objects perceived. In his treatise On Cheerfulness (Peri euthymiēs) Democritus states that to achieve cheerfulness the atoms forming the soul must be protected from violent disturbance, thus expressing for the first time the idea (later developed by *Epicurus) that men should aim at the happiness which derives from peace of mind, itself based on knowledge of the physical basis of life. Most later Greek philosophers did not take up the atomic theory of matter; Democritus' most influential followers were Epicurus and (the Roman) *Lucretius. A tradition in the Latin writers represented Democritus as 'the laughing philosopher' unable to restrain his mirth at the spectacle of human life (in contrast with the melancholy Heracleitus).

Dēmo'docus. 1. In Homer's Odyssey, a bard at the Phaeacian court of king Alcinous, who sings of the love of Arēs and Aphroditē.

2. In Virgil's Aeneid (10. 413) a companion of Aeneas.

Dēmogo'rgon. This ominous name (compare GORGON), used by writers from the fifteenth century to denote the primeval god of ancient mythology, seems to have originated with a medieval scribe's miswriting of the name *Demiurge. The Italian poet Boccaccio (1313–75) copied this ghostword from the scholia to *Statius' *Thebaid* 4. 516 (see SCHOLIUM), and thence it entered literature.

Dēmō'nax, of Cyprus (second century AD), a Cynic philosopher known only by the biography of him ascribed to *Lucian.

De mo'rtibus persecūto'rum ('on the deaths of the persecutors'), essay by the Christian *Lactantius on the downfalls of the Roman emperors who persecuted the Christians.

dēmos, in Greece, 'the people'; the term sometimes denoted the whole citizen body (and its assembly), sometimes only the lower classes in contrast with the upper. See DEMOCRACY.

Dēmo'sthenēs. 1. Prominent Athenian general during the Peloponnesian War. After earlier successes in the war his occupation of Pylos in 425 BC led to the capture of a body of Spartan hoplites on the neighbouring island of Sphacteria (see CLEON). In 413 after less successful campaigning he was sent with reinforcements for Nicias in Syracuse, but failed to persuade that general to withdraw from the city until the Athenians lost control of the sea and had to attempt an escape by land. In that retreat he commanded the rearguard but was forced to surrender to the Syracusans and Spartans on the sixth day and was subsequently executed.

2. (384–322 BC), the greatest of the Athenian orators.

1. *Life.* Demosthenes was born at Athens, in the deme of Paiānia, the sickly son of a wealthy father of the same name, who manufactured couches as well as swords and cutlery (hence the orator's nickname *machairopoios*, 'the cutler'). When Demosthenes was 7 his father died, and he was left to the care of three guardians appointed in the will; these so mismanaged the property that Demosthenes at 18 found himself almost without funds. He had already been inspired to become an orator by witnessing as a child the trial of the statesman Callistratus. He now prepared to sue his guardians, and for three years tried unsuccessfully to obtain restitution, during this time studying rhetoric and legal procedure, perhaps under *Isaeus. In 363 he brought an action against his guardians and won it, but probably recovered little (see 2 below). In the political sphere, his early attempts to address the assembly at Athens were said not to have been a success (he could not pronounce his r's and was given the nickname *batalos*, 'the stammerer'); he thereupon made strenuous efforts to improve his delivery (practising with pebbles in his mouth, for example), and studied literature and the orators. He also became a speech-writer (*logographos*) for those who had

to plead private suits in the law-courts, and he taught pupils. His growing reputation brought him employment as a speech-writer for public trials also, and he wrote speeches for the prosecution of Androtion in 355, Leptines in 354, and Androtion's associate Timocrates in 353. Demosthenes himself delivered the speech against Leptines, and it is possible that he was personally opposed to the policy Leptines advocated (see 2 below). This would be consistent with his attitude in the speech *On the Taxation Groups* (*Symmoriai*) in 354 (see 3 below).

It was not until 351 that he became prominent as a politician, eventually earning the admiration of the Greeks by constantly urging resistance to the encroachments of *Philip II of Macedon. In the previous eight years Philip had been extending his mastery over the countries to the north and west of Macedonia, and had gained possession of the most important seaboard cities on the north Aegean coast (including Amphipolis, always coveted by Athens); he had made alliances with Olynthus and the Chalcidic League, and having been invited by the Thessalians into Greece to assist them against the Phocians (see SACRED WARS and PHILIP (1) 2) won a military victory at the battle of the Crocus Field and gained the virtual mastery of Thessaly also. He was checked at Thermopylae by an Athenian force, but then resumed activity in Thrace, threatening the Athenian cleruchy (see CLERUCH) in the Chersonese as well as the Athenian corn-route from the Hellespont. At this juncture Demosthenes delivered his first oration against Philip, the so-called *First Philippic*, in 352, advocating a vigorous policy of resistance. However, the sense of urgency passed and little was done. Meanwhile Olynthus, alarmed by the growing power of Philip, had broken with him and made overtures of friendship to Athens. Philip's attack in 349 was the occasion for Demosthenes' three orations urging help for that city (the *Olynthiacs*), but a faction inside Olynthus betrayed the city to Philip in the following year. With Olynthus gone there was little chance of Athens ever gaining possession of Amphipolis, and it became necessary to make peace. The Peace of Philocrates followed, in which Demosthenes was one of the negotiators. Despite this, as soon as the Peace was agreed Demosthenes became convinced that Philip was breaking it; he set about undoing it, but advised caution in his speech *On the Peace*. In 344 he persuaded the assembly to refuse Philip's offer to renew the Peace (the *Second Philippic*). In 342 Philip intervened more directly in the affairs of Greece and Demosthenes tried to organize a Greek alliance against him; in 341 in his speech *On the Chersonese* (followed by the *Third Philippic*) he defended the aggression in Thrace of the Athenian general Diopeithes, by arguing that Philip's actions were already tantamount to war. The *Fourth Philippic*, if genuine, would have been delivered soon afterwards.

When Philip's activities in Thrace reached *Byzantium, Athens, anxious for the security of her corn-route, sent aid to the Byzantines, and open war with Philip was begun; Demosthenes was the most influential voice in Athens at this time. In 339 Philip moved south and was at Elatea in Phocis before the end of the year. Demosthenes procured an alliance with the Thebans, and both sides met at Chaeronea in autumn 338. Philip won a decisive victory by feigning withdrawal and then turning to overwhelm the pursuing Athenians. His son Alexander (the Great) is said to have led the Macedonian cavalry. Demosthenes, who was also present at the battle, delivered the funeral oration over the dead, a speech which has not survived. There was no need for Philip to impose a direct political settlement on Greece: in most cities pro-Macedonian politicians and policies naturally came to the fore. Despite the defeat at Chaeronea, a battle which Demosthenes had actively sought, Ctesiphon proposed soon afterwards that he should be honoured with a gold crown at the Great *Dionysia for his service to the city. *Aeschines charged Ctesiphon with the alleged illegality of the proposal, but the case did not come to trial until 330. In his speech (*Against Ctesiphon*) Aeschines reviewed Demosthenes' career and blamed on him all the recent misfortunes of Athens, but the latter's reply (*On the Crown*) was a masterpiece and secured an overwhelming vote in his favour; fewer than one fifth of the jury voted for Aeschines (who then retired to Rhodes, where he died). Meanwhile, Alexander had succeeded to the throne of Macedon after Philip's assassination in 336, and had quickly indicated that he did not intend to let Greece slip from Macedonian control.

Demosthenes remained to the fore in public affairs, but the later part of his career was clouded by the affair of Harpalus, the fugitive treasurer of *Alexander the Great (see 6), who decamped to the coast of Attica in 325 with a vast sum of money. Demosthenes seems to have proposed first that Harpalus should be kept prisoner and his money stored on the Acropolis, and later, after Harpalus had escaped, that the *Areopagus should investigate the disappearance of some of it. Demosthenes' actions and motives are by no means clear, but he was accused and found guilty of appropriating a large sum from it for himself and was fined fifty talents (see DEINARCHUS and HYPEREIDES). He retired into exile, but after the death of Alexander in 323 he was active once again in stimulating concerted Greek resistance to Macedon, and returned to Athens in triumph. When the defeat at *Crannon in 322 led to the breakup of the Greek alliance, each state made its own separate peace with Antipater, Alexander's successor. The terms for Athens were that the chief agitators against Macedon should be surrendered; Athens refused, but when the Macedonians marched upon the city Demosthenes and his supporters fled. *Demades' proposal that they should be sentenced to death was carried. Rather than be taken alive from the temple on Calaureia (an island off the east coast of Argolis) where he had sought refuge, Demosthenes took poison. The Greek traveller Pausanias who visited Athens in the second century AD summed up his life: 'Demosthenes loved the Athenians too much, and this is what came of it. It seems to me a true saying that a man who devotes himself unsparingly to his country's affairs and trusts his people never comes to a good end.'

Sixty-one speeches have come down to us under the name of Demosthenes, but the authenticity of some of them, particularly among the speeches relating to civil cases, has been doubted. Among the speeches generally accepted as genuine the following are the most important.

2. *Speeches in the law-courts*. Demosthenes' first private speeches in the law-courts were the three delivered against his fraudulent guardian Aphobus in 363; his last was against Dionysodorus in 322. He won his suit against Aphobus but could recover no more than a fraction of his property. This was followed by further fruitless proceedings, against Onetor, brother-in-law of Aphobus, in which Demosthenes delivered two speeches. The private speeches cover many subjects, including bottomry loans, mining rights, forgery, and trespass. Speeches on behalf of Phormio (350) and against Stephanus (349) concern the wealthy banker *Pasion, whose chief clerk Phormio was. A speech *Against Boeotus* (348) attempts to prevent an illegitimate son from claiming the name of his legitimate half-brother (with implications for his legitimacy). In a speech *Against Meidias* (347), which was never delivered, Demosthenes prosecutes an old personal and political enemy who had slapped the orator's face at a public festival (see DIONYSIA). After long delay the suit was settled out of court, Demosthenes receiving a considerable sum in damages. *Against Conon* (341) is a brilliant and entertaining speech for the prosecution of Conon and his rowdy sons, for assault upon a virtuous young man. The speech *Against Callicles*, of uncertain date, alleges with touches of humour that the defendant has caused the plaintiff's land to be flooded by blocking a watercourse.

Against Androtion is Demosthenes' earliest speech in a public prosecution, in 355. Androtion had proposed that crowns be awarded to the outgoing members of the council (*boulē*); Demosthenes supports a certain Diodorus in raising objections, on the grounds that the navy has not been increased during the year. In *Against Timocrates* (353) Demosthenes again supports Diodorus, in an embezzlement case. *Against Aristocrates* (352) is an attack on the politician Charidemus for his dealings in Thrace. None of these was actually delivered by Demosthenes, but he himself spoke *Against Leptines* (in 354; see 1 above). Leptines had proposed, in view of the financial difficulties of the state, to abolish all hereditary exemptions from taxation granted as a reward to benefactors of the state. Demosthenes argues that the proposal is contrary to good policy and that the saving will be negligible.

3. *Early speeches on public policy.*

On the Taxation Groups (or symmories, Gk. *symmoriai*) (354). The duty of equipping triremes (i.e. warships) had in 357 been laid on the twelve hundred richest citizens, divided into twenty groups, the members of which each paid the same share of the cost, however much property each had. The system worked unfairly, and in this speech Demosthenes proposes its reform. At the same time he opposes war with Persia, proposed by some politicians in Athens, as being inexpedient in the circumstances.

For the Megalopolitans (353). Demosthenes advocates alliance with Megalopolis, the capital, recently founded with Theban help, of a newly confederated Arcadia. While Thebes was occupied with the *Sacred War against Phocis, Sparta was trying to regain her former control over Arcadia. Some of the Athenian assembly, out of hostility to Thebes, did not wish to take any action unfavourable to Sparta. Demosthenes, on the contrary, urges the maintenance of a balance of power between Sparta and Thebes: if Sparta reduces Arcadia she will become too strong. (Subsequent events seem to show that Demosthenes greatly exaggerated Sparta's aggressive power at that time.)

On the Liberty of the Rhodians (351). Rhodes had revolted from the Athenian League at the instigation of Mausolus of Caria (d. 353), a Persian satrap but virtually an independent ruler. Oligarchs were in control in Rhodes and the leading democrats in exile. Demosthenes urges the Athenians to restore the democrats and follow their traditional role of liberators, in spite of possible complications with Artemisia (Mausolus' widow and successor) and the Persians. (Demosthenes may here have underestimated the dangers of becoming embroiled with Persia.)

4. *The Philippics and other speeches on Macedon.*

First Philippic (351). Philip's aggressive policy in Thrace threatened not only Athens' corn-route and the cleruchy in the Chersonese, but also Olynthus, which had concluded a peace with Athens in 352. Demosthenes urges the Athenians to rouse themselves, and details the measures they ought to take: the immediate dispatch of a small expedition and the prepar-

ation of a larger permanent force to meet Philip's rapid movements in whatever direction. The citizens themselves must form part of the force; they must not rely entirely on mercenaries.

Olynthiacs (349). Philip had resumed his threat to Olynthus and had captured some other Chalcidian towns, although not Olynthus itself. The Olynthians appealed to Athens in 349. In the three *Olynthiacs*, speeches delivered in quick succession, Demosthenes urges the fullest support, including the suggestion that the *theoric fund (used to pay for festivals) should be diverted to military purposes. (He wanted to send a citizen-army to attack Philip in the north rather than wait for him to arrive in Greece.) He contrasts the public-spiritedness of the citizens in former days with present-day indolence fostered by public doles distributed without regard to public service. (Three expeditions from Athens were not enough to prevent Olynthus being razed by Philip in 348.)

On the Peace (346). In mid-348 before the fall of Olynthus Demosthenes had successfully defended Philocrates against the charge that the latter's proposal to open negotiations with Philip was illegal. His friendship with Philocrates continued and he took part in the embassies that resulted in the Peace of Philocrates (346). However, soon after that Philip had extended his conquests in Thrace, advanced into Greece, subdued the Phocians, and secured a place on the Amphictyonic Council. Demosthenes, who subsequently did all he could to repudiate the Peace, considered that for the time being resistance was impossible and in this speech advises a pacific policy.

Second Philippic (344). After an interval Philip had resumed his interference in Greece, strengthening his position in Thessaly, and in the Peloponnese supporting the Argives and Messenians against Sparta. Demosthenes went on an embassy to those cities to warn them of the dangers of consorting with Philip, who promptly protested. This speech is his reply to Philip's protests. He exposes Philip's designs for empire and proposes a reply to him (the text of which has not survived).

On the False Embassy (343). There had been serious disagreements between Demosthenes and his fellow ambassadors at the time when the Peace of Philocrates was made. The terms agreed upon were that Athens and Macedon should each retain the territories they possessed to date. As Philip was constantly engaged on fresh conquests it was urgent, when once Athens had accepted the terms, that the second embassy sent to receive Philip's oath of ratification should act with all speed. In spite of Demosthenes' protests the embassy delayed and Philip delayed further, so that by the time the Peace was ratified Philip had subdued Thrace. Moreover, on the embassy's return to Athens

Aeschines gave so favourable an account of Philip's intentions with regard to Athenian interests that the assembly voted to extend the treaty to Philip's descendants, allowed him to occupy Thermopylae, and left Phocis, whose appeal for help Athens had earlier answered (see SACRED WAR), to surrender to him. In 343, when feeling at Athens had been roused by Philip's continuing aggressions, Demosthenes prosecuted Aeschines for the delays which had resulted in Philip's intervention in Phocis, and for giving false reports, suggesting that bribery was the cause of his pro-Macedonian stance. Aeschines' reply (which we possess; see AESCHINES) secured a decision in his favour by a narrow majority.

On the Chersonese (341). Demosthenes in this speech (and in the *Third Philippic*; see below) is seeking to end the Peace by persuading the Athenians that Philip has already broken it. Philip was in Thrace, in dangerous proximity to the Chersonese and projecting an attack on Byzantium. After the Peace of Philocrates Athens had sent settlers to the Chersonese under Diopeithes. The town of Cardia refused them admission, and Philip sent an expedition for the town's protection. Diopeithes, ill-provided with funds by Athens, made piratical raids in various directions, among others into Philip's Thracian territory, and Philip sent a protest to Athens. In his speech Demosthenes urges that Diopeithes should be vigorously supported: Philip, though pretending to be at peace, is in fact at war with Athens, and all his operations are ultimately designed to bring about her destruction; the longer he is tolerated the more difficult he will be to overcome. The speech is distinguished by the passion with which Demosthenes expresses his feelings about Philip's fundamental and implacable ambition.

Third Philippic (also 341, a few months after the previous speech). The threat to the Chersonese and Byzantium was closer and Philip was also interfering in Euboea. Demosthenes wants to unite the Greek cities against Philip and, trying to rouse the Athenians to the imminence of their danger, proposes the immediate dispatch of forces. This is one of the finest of Demosthenes' speeches, marked by gravity and deep anxiety; in one notable passage he contrasts the ancient spirit of Athens with her present degeneracy. (The *Fourth Philippic*, if genuine, would have been delivered soon after the *Third*.)

On the Crown (330). This is Demosthenes' greatest oration. The policy recommended in the *Third Philippic* was in the main adopted and war with Philip was begun in 340, ending in the defeat of Athens and Thebes at Chaeronea in 338. (For the background see 1 above.) On the technical point as to the illegality of Ctesiphon's proposal Aeschines may well have been right. But the case really turned on Aeschines' indictment of the policy of Demosthenes, and

this, from the Peace of Philocrates in 346 to the defeat at Chaeronea in 338, Demosthenes defends in detail, maintaining that his advice has always been in accordance with the honourable traditions of Athens which has never 'preferred an inglorious security to the hazardous vindication of a noble cause'. He includes a virulent attack on Aeschines, ridiculing, perhaps without strict regard to truth, his humble origins, and endeavouring to prove from the facts of his career that he was a traitor, bribed by Philip's money. Two passages are especially famous: the description of the confusion at Athens when the messenger came with the news that Philip was at Elatea (in Phocis) and so on Athens' doorstep (ch. 169), and the invocation of the Athenians who had fought the Persians at Marathon, Salamis, and Plataea a century and a half earlier (ch. 206).

5. Demosthenes' claim to greatness rests on his character as well as his oratory, his sincere and far-sighted patriotism trenchantly expressed in simple language. His speeches are marked by a passionate earnestness expressed in a great variety of tones: anger, irony, sarcasm, invective; pathos and humour rarely appear. A striking feature of his eloquence is that it is at once elevated and practical: there is no fine speaking for its own sake; all is directed to the persuasion of his hearers' minds, but in a form calculated to appeal to a popular audience. He is sometimes criticized for the artificial expression and the sophistic character of some of his arguments. But the development of his arguments and the arrangement of his topics, although often intricate, are lucid and compelling. He writes in pure Attic Greek, with bold metaphors rarely but aptly placed, and likes vivid examples: the Athenians in their warfare with Philip are like barbarians boxing, 'Hit one of them, and he rubs the place; hit him on the other side, and there go his hands; but as for guarding, or looking his opponent in the face, he neither can nor will do it' (*Philippic* 1. 40). The speeches were most carefully prepared but the style aims to conceal this fact, long, periodic sentences often being followed by short, pithy statements, which gives an impression of spontaneity. In all his speeches Demosthenes deliberately avoided hiatus (the placing of a word ending in a vowel before a word beginning with a vowel) except in unavoidable cases, such as those involving the use of 'or' (*ē*) or 'and' (*kai*); in his early speeches he was strict in the observance of this rule. As a further aid to euphony he avoided as far as possible a run of more than two short syllables. (For length of syllables see PROSODY.)

The oratorical method of Demosthenes was much studied by subsequent orators, and by none more than *Cicero (1) 6. 'Philippics' was used by him as the title of his own speeches against Mark Antony, and hence adopted as a general title for speeches of political invective. *Quintilian thought that Demosthenes' speeches should not only be examined but learnt by heart by students of rhetoric; *Longinus admired his intensity and sublimity. In comparatively recent times his works have been used obliquely to stir up political resistance to oppressive regimes.

demotic, see ROSETTA STONE.

dena'rius, a Roman silver coin introduced at Rome probably in the late third century BC, worth ten *asses*; see MONEY 2.

De nātū'ra deo'rum ('on the nature of the gods'), philosophical dialogue in three books by Cicero, written in 45 BC after the death of his daughter, in which he sets out the theological tenets of the three principal Greek schools of philosophy in his day, the Epicurean, Stoic, and Academic. The work is addressed to M. Brutus. (See CICERO (1) 5.)

The scene is laid at Rome in about 76 BC and the interlocutors are C. Vellēius the Epicurean, Q. Lucilius Balbus the Stoic, and C. Aurelius *Cotta the Academic. The first two are known only from Cicero's writings. Velleius, after attacking the cosmogonies and theologies of the ancient philosophers from Thales to Plato, expounds the Epicurean notion of the gods, anthropomorphic beings living a life of blissful inactivity. Cotta replies, ridiculing this conception and criticizing the arguments in support of it. Next Balbus sets out in the second book the Stoic view of a world governed by a divine active and intelligent providence, a universe which in the last resort is itself God. In the third book Cotta in turn criticizes this doctrine, maintaining the Sceptical Academic attitude of suspended judgement. Cicero concludes that in his opinion on this occasion the Stoic argument is nearer the truth. See also DE DIVINATIONE.

Dentā'tus, Mā'nius Cu'rius, see CURIUS DENTATUS.

De offi'ciis ('on [moral] duties'), by Cicero, his last work on moral philosophy, finished in November 44 BC (see CICERO (1) 5), in the form of a letter to his son Marcus then studying philosophy at Athens. It consists of three books of moral advice, based on Stoic precepts and, in the first two books, on the teaching of *Panaetius; the third is based on that of *Posidonius and others.

The first book deals with the four cardinal virtues, wisdom, justice, fortitude, and temperance, develops the various duties that devolve from these, and passes on to their application to individual people who vary in age, position, abilities, etc. The second and third books discuss the application of the above principles to the pursuit of success in life: the reconciliation of expediency with virtue. The two are shown to be in reality identical, even in cases of apparent conflict; for material gain cannot compensate for the loss of the sense of honour and justice. Cicero's doctrine is illustrated throughout with examples from Greek and Roman history. Noteworthy are the highly practical character of his precepts, his condemnation of abstention from public activities (in opposition to the Stoics), and his insistence on the social character of a man and the duty of men to their fellow human beings, something beyond patriotism. This work received high praise in later ages and was a pervasive influence in its exposition of the virtuous political life.

De opifi'cio Dei ('on the handiwork of God'), Christian work by *Lactantius.

De o'ptimo ge'nere ōrātō'rum ('on the best kind of orators'), by Cicero, an introduction to translations of the Greek orations *De corona* of Demosthenes and *Against Ctesiphon* of Aeschines (see CICERO (1) 5), which is only partially preserved. Cicero argues that Demosthenes, who wrote in Attic Greek, had such a command of every oratorical style that it is inappropriate to use the term Atticism to describe a plain style of *oratory (see 1).

De ōrātō're ('on the orator'), work in three books by *Cicero ((1) 4), the most finished of his treatises on oratory, completed in 55 BC after his exile and addressed to his brother Quintus. The dialogues which it comprises are supposed to take place in 91 BC and the chief interlocutors are the eminent lawyers L. Licinius *Crassus and M. *Antonius; Q. Mucius *Scaevola, another great lawyer, is also present; and after the first dialogue Q. *Catulus, consul with the general Marius, and C. Julius Caesar Strabo the orator. The scene of the dialogues is the villa of Crassus at Tusculum. Cicero's aim is to describe the general principles underlying the practice of oratory.

In book 1 Crassus discusses the qualifications of the good orator; these include, in his opinion (and clearly in Cicero's too), a wide knowledge of the sciences and philosophy, and especially of civil law. Antonius thinks such knowledge to be, practically speaking, unattainable, and narrows the orator's requirements to the faculty of pleasing and persuading, without special knowledge. In book 2 Antonius develops in detail the methods of conciliating, instructing, and persuading the judges; Caesar is induced to give a dissertation on the use of wit and humour (of which he was regarded as a master) with many illustrations (interesting as evidence of Roman taste in this respect). In book 3 Crassus discusses styles, ornamentation, and delivery.

Deo'rum conci'lium, satirical dialogue by *Lucian.

Deo'rum dia'logi, short dialogues by *Lucian, making fun of Greek myths.

De ō'tio ('on leisure'), dialogue by *Seneca (2), advocating that leisure should be spent in contemplation.

De philoso'phia ('on philosophy'), lost treatise by *Varro, apparently an outline of the doctrines of the different philosophical schools.

De prŏvide'ntia ('on providence'), dialogue by *Seneca (2), addressed to his friend Lucilius (the Younger), in which he discusses the question why good men meet with misfortune when there exists a providence. The answer is that misfortune serves a useful purpose: it is a school of virtue. Stoicism provides the remedy of suicide when misfortune becomes intolerable.

De prŏvi'nciis consulā'ribus ('on provinces governed by consuls'), speech by Cicero in 56 BC (see CICERO (1) 4), advocating the prolongation of Caesar's command in Gaul.

De re eque'stri (*Peri hippikēs*, '*horsemanship*'), treatise by *Xenophon.

De repu'blica ('on the state'), dialogue in six books on political science by *Cicero ((1) 4), begun in 54 BC and published by early 51 BC. We possess the greater part of the first three books and fragments of the others, including the *Somnium Scipionis*, 'dream of Scipio', which formed the conclusion of the work and is preserved mainly in a commentary by Macrobius.

The dialogue is modelled to some extent on Plato's *Republic*. It is supposed to take place in the course of three days in 129 BC, in the garden of *Scipio Aemilianus, and the principal interlocutors are Scipio and *Laelius. Cicero declares that he had a report of the conversation from P. Rutilius Rufus (who had served under Scipio). After a preface by Cicero, in defence of patriotic statesmanship, the dialogue begins by asserting the superiority of an active over a contemplative career. Then the meaning of the word 'republic' is defined, and Scipio sets out the three typical forms of government, monarchy, aristocracy, and democracy, with their degenerate counterparts, and the ideal form, which is a combination of all three. The Roman republic is an instance of the last. The second book relates the evolution of the Roman republic from earliest times to its contemporary form, and passes to the necessity for justice and harmony in the state. The third book opens with a preface by Cicero of which much is lost. Philus, one of the interlocutors, presents the arguments of the philosopher *Carneades that a man needs to practise injustice if he wants to promote his own welfare. Laelius and Scipio maintain that the state cannot exist without justice. Only fragments survive of books 4, 5, and 6. Book 6 was evidently concerned with the duties and rewards of the statesman in this life, and closed, after the manner of the myth at the end of Plato's *Republic* (the vision of Er, son of Armenius), with an exposition, through the dream of Scipio, of the heavenly life of great souls after death.

De repu'blica Athenie'nsium ('on the Athenian constitution'), short political pamphlet attributed to *Xenophon; see CONSTITUTION OF THE ATHENIANS (2).

De re ru'stica ('on farming').   1. Of M. Porcius *Cato; see DE AGRI CULTURA.

2. Treatise on farming written in dialogue form by M. Terentius *Varro when his eightieth year admonished him 'that he must be packing his baggage to depart this life'. The treatise is in three books and takes the form of conversations, to some extent in a dramatic setting: the first conversation is interrupted by news of a murder, and the third by incidents in an election. Book 1 deals with the farm itself, its buildings and equipment, and the agricultural year in general; book 2 with cattle- and sheep-breeding; book 3 with the smaller livestock on a farm, aviaries, poultry, bees, game preserves, and fishponds. The work is written in a more literary form than that of Cato, and is animated by touches of wit and a feeling for the country life.

3. Treatise by *Columella.

De rerum nātū'ra, philosophical poem by *Lucretius.

Dere Street, see ROADS 2.

De rhēto'ribus ('on the orators'), brief biographical sketches of sixteen Roman orators by *Suetonius, of which some part survives.

Derveni papyrus, the only ancient book to have been found in Greece (see PAPYROLOGY), consisting of the upper half of a papyrus roll of the late fourth century BC, found at Derveni, *c*.9 km north of Thessaloniki where it is on display in the museum. It had been carbonized (and so preserved) from being placed on a funeral pyre. It contains a commentary on an Orphic religious poem.

De senectū'te ('on old age'), dialogue by *Cicero ((1) 5), whose title for it was *Cato Maior de senectute*, probably written just before Julius Caesar's murder in 44 BC. The work is dedicated to *Atticus. The conversation is supposed to take place in 150 BC, when M. Porcius *Cato (the Censor) was in his eighty-fourth year. At the request of his young friends *Scipio Aemilianus and *Laelius, Cato expounds how the burden of old age may best be borne; he describes its compensations and consolations, drawing illustrations from his own experience, from reminiscences of old men he has known, and from his reading (notably of Plato and Xenophon). He concludes with a reasoned statement of his belief in the immortality of the soul. The early part of the dialogue is imitated from the conversation of Socrates and Cephalus in book 1 of Plato's *Republic.

De situ orbis ('the geography of the world'), treatise by Pomponius *Mela.

De sophi'sticis ele'nchis ('refutations in the manner of the sophists'), treatise on logic by Aristotle; see ARISTOTLE 4 (i).

De tranquillitā'te a'nimi ('on tranquillity of the soul'), dialogue by *Seneca (2); see 2.

Deuca'lion, in Greek myth, the son of *Prometheus. When Zeus was so angry at the crimes of men that he decided to destroy them by a flood, Deucalion, warned by Prometheus, built a boat for himself and his wife Pyrrha; they floated in it until the water subsided and they grounded on Mount Parnassus. Advised by an oracle to throw their mother's bones over their shoulder, they realized that this meant the stones of the earth and did so, those thrown by Deucalion becoming men and those thrown by Pyrrha women. The new race was called the Leleges. Subsequently Deucalion and Pyrrha became the parents of *Hellen, the eponymous founder of the Greeks. Another Deucalion, said to be the son of *Minos, was an Argonaut and one of the Calydonian boar-hunters.

de'us ex ma'china, see THEATRE 1.

De verbo'rum significā'tu ('on the meaning of words'), an encyclopaedic work by *Verrius Flaccus.

De viris illu'stribus ('on famous men'), collection of biographical sketches of Roman literary figures by *Suetonius, of which only fragments survive.

De vīta beā'ta ('on the happy life'), dialogue by *Seneca (2), addressed to his brother Gallio (so named after adoption; he was originally called Novatus), in which Seneca discusses what happiness consists of and how it is to be obtained. He finds the answer in the Stoic doctrine that happiness lies in living virtuously and in accordance with nature, but he does not deny that other things, such as health and riches, have their value. The work as we have it is incomplete.

De vīta Cae'sarum ('the lives of the Caesars'), biographies of the Twelve Caesars from Julius to Domitian (d. AD 96) by *Suetonius.

De vīta po'pulī rōmā'nī ('the manner of life of the Roman people'), history of Roman culture and society by *Varro.

dēvō'tio. 1. If a battle was going against a Roman general it was possible for him to dedicate himself and the enemy army to 'Tellus and the Manes', i.e. the gods of the Underworld, by a fairly elaborate ritual. He then sought to be killed among the enemy, on the understanding that if the gods accepted his

'dedication' of himself they must also accept the enemy army. See DECIUS MUS.

2. For *devotio* in the sense of 'curse' see MAGIC 5 (ii).

dia'dochoi ('successors'), the name given to the Greek rulers who succeeded to various parts of the empire of *Alexander the Great after his death in 323 BC. See MACEDONIA 2 and 3 (for Antigonids), ATTALIDS, PTOLEMIES, SELEUCIDS, and EPIGONOI.

diae'resis, see METRE, GREEK 2.

Dia'goras, famous boxer of Rhodes, from a family of athletes. See PINDAR 5 (O. 7).

dia'krioi, in Athens of the sixth century BC the 'men of the hills' organized by *Peisistratus as a revolutionary faction.

dialectic (*dialektikē*), term of Greek philosophy, derived from the verb meaning 'to converse', 'to discuss'; in Plato and others, a method of philosophical inquiry conducted by question and answer. The inventor of dialectic was said to have been the philosopher *Zeno the Eleatic, whose characteristic method was to take an opponent's hypothesis and deduce from it two contradictory conclusions, thereby rendering it absurd. The dialectical method of Socrates (see ELENCHUS), as it appears from the dialogues of Plato, had as its aim the testing of the truth of a proposition by question and answer, in a manner roughly resembling ordinary conversation. It was destructive rather than constructive, in that it demonstrated flaws in a suggested proposition but arrived at no better substitute. Plato's own dialectic is a development from that of Socrates. At its simplest it starts from an assumption taken to be true for the purposes of argument (as did Zeno's), and proceeds through question and answer (as did Socrates') in a methodically rigorous way until a conclusion is reached. It seemed to Plato that his method made it possible to acquire knowledge, and provide explanations for what is known, positively and systematically. For Plato dialectic was the only way to reach the true end of philosophy, knowledge of the Good, and sometimes therefore signified philosophy itself rather than simply a philosophical method. In the logical works of Aristotle, the term dialectic describes reasoning from a hypothesis; as a philosophical method Aristotle thought it inferior to deduction, which starts from premises known to be true. In modern usage, which is sometimes at a considerable remove from the ancient meaning, the term often describes the general arguments or ideas of a work or an author.

dialects. 1. Greek. (For the origins of the Greek language see GREECE.)
1. The evidence of inscriptions (see EPIGRAPHY) and of literary texts shows that in classical times the Greek language existed in a number of

dialects. The differences between them, small enough to allow each Greek city to understand the others, reflect the movement of Greek peoples in early times (see MIGRATIONS) into and within Greece, and into the Aegean islands and the west coast of Asia Minor. They may have developed in a fairly short time, once the various tribes had settled down in their chosen regions. The later predominance of the Attic dialect reflects the ascendancy of Athenian literature and culture generally (see 3 below).

The dialects of Greece in classical times fall into two broad divisions, West Greek and East Greek. These divisions sub-divide further: West Greek comprises North-West Greek, spoken in Phocis, Locris, Elis, and Aetolia, and Doric, spoken throughout the Peloponnese and in the places colonized by Doric speakers, namely the southern group of Aegean islands, Crete, Rhodes, the south-west coast of Asia Minor, and many colonies in Sicily and Magna Graecia (south Italy); see COLONIZATION, GREEK. East Greek subdivides into Ionic, Aeolic, and Arcado-Cyprian. Ionic was spoken in Ionia (on the coast of Asia Minor), Euboea, and the islands in the Aegean colonized by Ionic speakers; its offshoot Attic was spoken in Attica and so by the Athenians. Aeolic was spoken in the island of Lesbos and in the neighbouring part of Asia Minor, and, with an admixture of West Greek, in Thessaly and Boeotia. The name Arcado-Cyprian (invented in modern times) expresses the close relationship between the dialect of Arcadia, in the centre of the Peloponnese, and that of Cyprus, far away in the eastern Mediterranean; for this dialect there are no literary texts. It has been suggested that the Arcadian and Cyprian dialects preserve some of the forms present in the *Mycenaean Greek of earlier times because these parts were difficult of access and relatively isolated. The Dorians were a people of Greek stock who were thought to have arrived from the north-west c.1100 BC (see DORIAN INVASION), and who spoke a dialect not substantially different from that spoken in Greece before they arrived (see GREECE and LINEAR B).

2. The dialect used by a Greek author is not necessarily that of his native speech nor that of the city in which he wrote. It is characteristic of the conservatism of Greek literature in its formal aspects that the dialect in which a literary genre originated remained the dialect of that genre in later times. Thus, because choral lyric poetry originated in a Doric-speaking region, all such poetry is written in a (literary) form of Doric, even when it is composed by a Boeotian (Pindar) or by an Ionic speaker (Bacchylides) or is found in Attic tragedy. All the dialects that appear in literature are modified so as to present their most conspicuous characteristics while avoiding the parochial or undignified; in the choral lyric of tragedy, for example, the Doric

element became a conventional means of enriching and ennobling the diction.

The dialect of Homer's epic is an artificial amalgam of Ionic and Aeolic elements never spoken in conjunction at any one time in any one place. It was the product of a long tradition of epic poetry, the composition of which seems to have passed from an Aeolic- to an Ionic-speaking area. Hesiod, a Boeotian, wrote his poems in hexameters, the metre of Homeric epic, and so his dialect is virtually identical with Homer's, as was that of all later epic, e.g. the *Argonautica* of Apollonius Rhodius. Elegy (whose metre is hexameter followed by pentameter) was the invention of the Ionians, but since the hexameter was also the metre of Homeric epic, the dialect of elegy too is quite strongly epic, but with a larger admixture of Ionic forms. Tragedy and comedy at Athens were written in Attic, the local dialect and a branch of Ionic, except for the choral lyric parts, which were written in a form of Doric (see above). The lyric poetry of Sappho and Alcaeus was written in the native dialect of Lesbos, a branch of Aeolic. Anacreon wrote in his native Ionic, and Corinna in her local Boeotian. Iambic and trochaic poems were written in Ionic, although the Athenian Solon when writing in these metres used many forms taken from his native Attic. Pastoral poetry, a genre created by Theocritus, is mostly written in an artificial Doric made up of a variety of forms, some in general use, some purely local, others made up by false analogies; it also has a sprinkling of Aeolic and epic features. The modern sense of Doric meaning 'rustic' derives from the use of this dialect in pastoral poetry. Because prose literature first arose in Ionia, Ionic became the dialect of historical and scientific works. Even the Athenian historian Thucydides, writing mainly in Attic, avoided using peculiarly Attic forms so as not to depart too obviously from the appropriate dialect.

3. The *koinē* ('common tongue'). The political unification of Greece which began under Philip II of Macedon (reigned 359–336 BC), and the absorption of large tracts of the East into a Greek empire, brought about the decline of separate dialects and the rise of this new, uniform Greek. The Athenian *Xenophon, who spent most of his life abroad, may be considered the first writer of the new *koine*. The basis of it was Attic, officially adopted by Philip II in preference to the semi-barbarous Macedonian dialect (see MACEDONIA 1), and it spread, with the conquests of his son Alexander the Great, throughout the Greek empire. (The poets of the Hellenistic age could reproduce the old dialects only by studied effort.) The *koine* was the language in which the *Septuagint and the Greek New Testament were written. In the first century AD there was an attempt to write Greek prose literature in the classical Attic dialect; of

this revival Lucian is the best example. See SOPHISTIC, SECOND.

2. Italic. The Italic languages (a branch of Indo-European) consist of Latin, Oscan, and Umbrian, as well as the dialects of various mountain tribes of central Italy. When the Latin language was still confined to Rome and Latium, Oscan was the chief language of central Italy. See LATIN LANGUAGE.

dialogue, literary genre, Greek in origin, in which characters, usually real but sometimes imaginary, conduct a conversation, pursuing a single theme but admitting some of the digression and inconsequence found in normal conversation. The *mimes of Sophron of Syracuse (fifth century BC) are an example, said to have been admired by Plato, whose Socratic dialogues may have taken their form from the mimes while their content was based on the actual conversations of Socrates. Xenophon and Aristotle wrote similarly, the latter's dialogues surviving only in fragments. This literary form reappeared in the second century AD in the dialogues of *Plutarch and *Lucian. These were modelled on Plato's but in the case of Lucian served satirical rather than philosophical ends and were a witty and biting form of entertainment. In the *Deipnosophistai* *Athenaeus relates in fifteen books the conversations of learned men meeting over dinner and discussing food in all its aspects.

In Roman literature the chief examples of the dialogue are to be found in Cicero's political, rhetorical, and philosophical treatises and in the *Dialogus de oratoribus* of Tacitus. In these it is the usual pattern for the leading role to be taken by one interlocutor (sometimes the author himself), who expounds his view at length, the other characters' parts being conspicuously less important. In *Seneca's dialogues the dramatic element is reduced to a minimum. The *Noctes Atticae* ('Attic nights') of Aulus *Gellius is an idiosyncratic compilation of learning, some of it purporting to record past conversations.

Dialogues of the Dead, of the Gods, of the Sea-Gods, see LUCIAN.

Dia'logus de ōrātō'ribus ('dialogue on orators'), dialogue attributed to *Tacitus and now generally accepted as by him, in spite of differences in style from his later work, which may be the result of its belonging to a different literary genre. It is no longer thought to be an early work; since it is dedicated to Lucius Fabius Justus, consul in AD 102, it was probably published in that year or soon after. The claims of oratory against other branches of literature are discussed, and the reasons why oratory has declined since Cicero's day. The scene is set in the house of Curiātius Māternus, a poet. The other interlocutors are two distinguished orators, Marcus Aper, an advocate, and Julius

Secundus, both of Gallic birth and both teachers of Tacitus; and Vipstanus Messalla, a man of distinguished birth. The date is supposed to be c. AD 75. The first twenty-seven chapters are introductory. Aper, a practical, utilitarian lawyer, maintains the superiority of oratory over poetry, for the rewards it brings. Maternus, a meditative idealist, disdains wealth and power and prefers a quiet life and the companionship of the Muses. Aper admits no decline in oratory. Messalla, a champion of former times, criticizes the modern speakers. At the request of Maternus he passes to the causes of the alleged decline (ch. 28), which for the purposes of the discussion is to be assumed. These causes Messalla finds in the lax education of the young, contrasted with the careful methods of former days; and in the defective training given to orators in the schools of rhetoric. After this there is a gap of several pages in the manuscript. When the text resumes someone else (probably Maternus) is speaking. He argues that the decline in oratory is due to the changed conditions of public life. Oratory flourished under the republic in times of disorder and revolution, when orators were inspired by political enthusiasm. The calmness of political life under the emperors has removed these incentives, but has brought compensations.

Oratory was seen by Tacitus to be in an inevitable decline, linked as it was to political institutions themselves in decline. It is interesting to compare this work with the near-contemporary *Education of an Orator* (published in the 90s) by *Quintilian, whose concern is rather with the technical and literary aspects of oratory.

This dialogue was discovered in a codex (which contained the other minor works of Tacitus also) in the library of Fulda in Germany by the agency of the Florentine scholar Niccolò Niccoli, in the early fifteenth century. See also TEXTS, TRANSMISSION OF ANCIENT 6.

Dia'na, Italian goddess of woodland and wild nature, protector of women, identified with the Greek *Artemis; her cult was widespread in Italy. From very early times she had a temple at Rome on the Aventine, traditionally founded by the king Servius Tullius (578–535 BC). Catullus' poem 34, *Hymn to Diana*, describes her role. Her most famous cult was at Arīcia, on the shore of Lake Nemi in the Alban hills. Her shrine there stood in a grove where she was worshipped in association with *Egeria and with a male god of the forest named Virbius, later identified with the Greek Hippolytus. The priesthood of this shrine was given to a runaway slave, called *rex* ('king'), after he had broken off a branch from a certain tree in the grove (see GOLDEN BOUGH) and killed his predecessor. Diana may have been thought of as a moon-goddess. From being worshipped (like *Hecatē) at crossroads she derives her title 'Trivia' (*trivium*, 'place where three roads meet').

diatribe (*diatribē*, 'spoken address', 'lecture'), in Greek, the name given to a short, ethical discourse, particularly of the kind composed by Cynic and Stoic philosophers (see EPICTETUS). These popular moral lectures were often polemical in tone, and 'diatribe' soon acquired the modern sense of 'invective'. Many Roman writers produced diatribes, as did Christian polemicists.

Dicaea'rchus (third to second century BC), of Messana in Sicily, Greek scientist and pupil of Aristotle, whose works are lost. He wrote biographies of earlier Greek writers as well as philosophical, political, and geographical works. His most interesting was a treatise on life in Greece (*Bios Hellados*), which was the first universal history of culture from the (imagined) *Golden Age to Dicaearchus' own day, and included a description of the known world. He was an important influence upon Eratosthenes, Cicero, Josephus, and Plutarch. Cicero admired him greatly, and took him as exemplar of the 'practical life' (see DE OFFICIIS).

dicasts (*dikastai*), in Athenian law-courts, the members of the jury; see LAW, AT ATHENS.

dice (Gk. *astragaloi*, Lat. *tali*, 'knucklebones', dice with four sides, numbered 1, 3, 4, and 6, and two rounded ends; or Gk. *cyboi*, Lat. *tesserae*, 'cubes', with six sides, numbered as in modern dice). Playing with dice, including board games with counters, was popular in the ancient as in the modern world. When the dice were *tali*, four were used. The best throw was known as 'Venus', when all four dice showed different numbers; the worst was *canis*, 'the dog', when every die showed the number one. In games with *tesserae* only three were used.

di conse'ntes (perhaps 'the gods that are'), in Roman religion, the twelve great gods, six male and six female; according to two hexameter lines of the poet Ennius,

Juno, Vesta, Minerva, Ceres, Diana, Venus, Mars, Mercurius, Jovi', Neptunus, Volcanus, Apollo.

Dicta Catōnis, see CATO (1), end of entry.

dictator. At Rome, the dictatorship was an *ad hoc* magistracy, admitted to the Roman constitution soon after the expulsion of the kings in 509 BC to allow supreme authority to be entrusted temporarily to one individual in times of grave crisis (compare COLLEGIUM 1). The dictator was appointed by the nomination of a consul on the senate's proposal. He had supreme military and judicial authority, which was not subject to appeal, and he could not be called to account for his actions. The dictator, who was

also known as *magister populi*, 'master of the infantry', immediately appointed as his assistant a *magister equitum*, 'master of the horse'. The other magistrates remained in office but were subordinate to the dictator, who held office for six months at most. This time limit meant that the office was of little use outside Italy, and it declined in importance in the third century BC. However, in 82 BC Sulla was appointed dictator 'to restore the republic', i.e. for an indefinite period. Similarly, Julius Caesar was appointed dictator first in 49 BC for the specific purpose of holding the elections for 48; secondly in 48, perhaps for a year; thirdly in 46 for ten years; and finally in 44, for life. These dictatorships obviously were different in intention from the earlier office. After Caesar's murder the dictatorship was formally abolished, and Augustus refused to revive it.

Dictē, mountain in the east of Crete, an important centre since Minoan times of Zeus' cult; the site of his archaic temple has been found at Palaikastro. There is no good evidence for the existence of the 'Dictaean cave' in which Zeus was said by some writers to have been born or brought up. This seems to be the result of a confusion with the cave, also associated with Zeus, on Mount Ida. Zeus presumably took the place of an earlier Minoan deity. See also DICTYNNA below.

Dicty'nna, '(the goddess) of Mount *Dicte', a (Minoan) Cretan goddess, whose *proper name was *Britomartis; she was later identified with Artemis. The derivation of her name is from the mountain rather than from the Greek *diktys*, 'net', as was sometimes supposed. This gave rise to the story that she fled from King Minos, who was in love with her, but became entangled in fishermen's nets.

Dictys Crēte'nsis, Dictys of Crete, said to have accompanied *Idomeneus (leader of the Cretans) to the Trojan War and to have written a diary of the events. This work, inscribed in Phoenician characters (the earliest alphabet used by the Greeks; see CADMUS), was supposed to have been discovered during the reign of the emperor Nero (AD 54–68), and subsequently transliterated into Greek letters and deposited in a library. (A fragment of the Greek version has been found on papyrus.) It was rediscovered by a certain Lucius Septimius in (perhaps) the fourth century AD and translated into Latin, under the title *Ephemeris belli Troiani*, 'diary of the Trojan War'. This work of fantasy, together with that attributed to *Dares, provided the principal material for medieval writers on the story of Troy.

didactic poetry, poetry designed to give instruction. Before writing came into general use, instruction was conveniently expressed in verse, as being more easily remembered than prose. The Greeks did not recognize didactic poetry as a separate literary genre; since, like epic, it was written in hexameters (see METRE, GREEK 3) they regarded it as a form of epic poetry. For early examples of didactic poetry see HESIOD, EMPEDOCLES, and PARMENIDES. In Greece this kind of composition died out in the fifth century BC with the rise of prose literature, but was revived in the Hellenistic age: see ARATUS and NICANDER. For later works see DIONYSIUS PERIEGETES and OPPIAN.

Didactic poetry found favour in Rome quite early: *Ennius translated from Greek a poem on nature falsely attributed to the Sicilian Epicharmus. In the first century BC there are Lucretius' *De rerum natura* and Virgil's *Georgics*; in the following century Ovid's *Fasti*, the *Astronomica* of Manilius, and the *Aetna* of an unknown author. See also COLUMELLA (book 10).

didasca'lia, at Athens, the 'teaching' of a *dithyramb, comedy, or tragedy to the chorus and actors who were to perform it, by the dramatist (or his representative). The word came to be used to describe the official record of a dramatic performance, giving the name of the festival at which the work was produced and that of the *eponymous archon; in the case of drama, the names of the dramatists in order of success (Greek drama was always a matter for competition; see TRAGEDY 2), and of the plays which each dramatist entered; the names of the protagonists, the best actor, and the *choregos* of the winning play; in the case of the dithyrambic competitions, the name of the victorious tribe (each of the ten tribes provided a chorus) and the best flute-player. This information has in some cases survived on inscriptions. Aristotle in the fourth century BC compiled a book of *didascaliae* which has not survived but which was used by Hellenistic scholars, some of whose records found their way into the manuscripts of extant plays, providing valuable information concerning dates and names.

Dīdo, legendary daughter of a king of Tyre called Belus by Virgil. She is said to have had the name Elissa at Tyre, but subsequently, at Carthage, Dido. She was married to her uncle Sychaeus, who was murdered for his great wealth by her brother Pygmalion when the latter was king of Tyre. Dido fled with some followers to Libya and founded the city of Carthage: Iarbas, a local king, had given her as much land as might be covered by an ox-hide; this she had cut into strips and stretched. To escape marriage with Iarbas she built a pyre as though for an offering and threw herself on to the flames. For Virgil's adaptation of her story see AENEID.

Di'dymus (*c.*65 BC–*c.* AD 10), of Alexandria in Egypt, a notable Greek scholar, nicknamed *Chalkenteros* ('brazen-guts') on account of his enormous industry (he was said to have written four thousand books). None of his works has survived entire, though some fragments have turned up on papyrus, yet the results of his labours can be seen in the learned notes (*scholia) on ancient texts that are found in some manuscripts, in the lexica and etymologies compiled by scholars in later centuries, and in the collections of out-of-the-way learning represented by works such as the *Deipnosophistai* of *Athenaeus. As a compiler and abstracter of earlier researches Didymus has been invaluable in preserving some of the Hellenistic scholarship of the previous two and a half centuries which would otherwise have been completely lost. Perhaps his most important commentaries were on Homer and on Attic comedy, the contemporary background of which needed systematic elucidation, but he also wrote on Pindar, Bacchylides, the tragedians Sophocles and Euripides (there is no certain evidence that he wrote on Aeschylus), and the orators, especially Demosthenes. His many important monographs included one on the classification of Greek lyric poetry and another on proverbs.

di'es fasti, nefa'sti, at Rome, lawful and unlawful days for conducting public business. In the Roman calendar, a day marked F for *fastus* was a day 'of speaking', when it was permitted to transact legal business by speaking the formal words necessary (see LAW, AT ROME 2); conversely, the sign N indicated a *dies nefastus*, 'day of not speaking', when for religious reasons the courts were not open. See FASTI.

Die'spiter, archaic Latin nominative form of *Jupiter, generally replaced by the vocative Iuppiter.

diga'mma, or vau, name given to a Greek consonant equivalent to the English w, in written form resembling F (hence its name 'double-gamma'), a sound originally in use in all the Greek dialects but which gradually disappeared from most of them. It started to disappear from Attic-Ionic before 1000 BC, from the other dialects later. The earliest Greek literature we possess, the *Iliad* and *Odyssey* of Homer, was composed in perhaps the eighth century BC but our text of these poems is based on that established by the Alexandrian scholars in the third century BC. It thus has no written indication of the digamma, but metrical effects indicate that the sound must originally have been present in many words; the most obvious example is *hiatus (where a word ending with a vowel precedes one beginning with a vowel): hiatus is normally very rare in Greek poetry, but appears with unusual frequency in Homer. It was observed (by the English scholar Richard Bentley, d. 1742) that if in these cases the lost initial digamma was restored to the second word, hiatus was removed. The digamma must still have been used in the spoken language when these words were incorporated into Homer's epic poetry, but as it dropped out of the spoken language it disappeared from epic also, with consequences for the metre. Although the sound was lost in Greek, it was preserved in languages cognate to Greek, e.g. English *wine*, Latin *vinum*: Greek (w)*oinos*; English *work*: Greek (w)*ergon*; English *sweet*: Greek (sw)*edus*. See also ALPHABET.

dīge'sta ('system'), in Roman jurisprudence, a body of law arranged systematically; the name was applied especially by the Roman emperor *Justinian to the main part of his codification.

di i'nferi, 'gods of the Underworld' in Roman religion; see RELIGION, ROMAN I.

Dikē ('justice'), in Greek myth, the personification of justice. See ASTRAEA.

di mānēs, pare'ntēs, see MANES, PARENTALIA.

dī'meter, metrical line containing two metra or metrical sequences; see METRE, GREEK I.

Dī'narchus, see DEINARCHUS.

Dindymē'nē, name of the goddess *Cybelē from Mount Dindymon in Phrygia, where stood one of her early shrines.

Dio, see DION.

Dīocle'tian (Gaius Aurēlius Valērius Dioclētianus, originally named Dioclēs), Roman emperor AD 284–305. He was a Dalmatian of humble birth, elevated by the army. His genius was for administration, and many of his measures lasted for centuries. He made the empire into a tetrarchy (i.e. he divided the rule into four), in order to make government more effective and to bring about an ordered succession to the throne (see AUGUSTUS, THE). Many provinces were divided so as to become smaller administrative units, the frontiers were strengthened by fortifications and the size of the army was greatly increased. The financial burdens of these measures led Diocletian to fiscal reform. He instituted a regular system of tax revisions every fifteen years; from these fifteen-year periods, known as 'indictions', a new method of time-keeping arose (see CALENDARS 6). Diocletian was less successful in trying to curb galloping inflation. His anxieties for the unity of the empire made him favour the old Roman ways, and it was probably this which led to his notorious persecution of the Christians, begun in 303 and felt particularly in Palestine and Egypt (see CHRISTIANITY). As a consequence the Coptic and Ethiopian Churches reckon the years of the Christian era from the accession of Diocletian in 284 ('era of the martyrs'). See also EUSEBIUS.

Diodō'rus Si'culus, Sicilian Greek historian who wrote between *c*.60 and 30 BC a world history (*Bibliothēkē historikē*), centred on Rome,

in forty books. Books 1–3 comprise the ancient legends of Asia and North Africa, books 4–6 those of Greece and Europe. All these books are fully preserved except for 6, which is fragmentary. Books 7–17 cover the period from the Trojan War to Alexander the Great; 7–10 survive in fragments, 11–17 are fully preserved. Books 18–40 cover the period from the Diadochoi (successors of Alexander) to Julius Caesar (54 BC); 18–20 are fully preserved, 21–40 survive in fragments. A complete copy is said to have perished in the sack of Constantinople by the Turks in 1453. The work is an uncritical compilation, and confused when Diodorus changes sources, but valuable for preserving the evidence of these sources: for example, his evidence is very important when, for the events in Greece around 400 BC, he draws on the history of which *Hellenica Oxyrhynchia* is a part (see OXYRHYNCHUS HISTORIAN, EPHORUS). In the early books he is a useful source of mythological information. Concerning the gods his view is somewhat euhemerist (see EUHEMERUS).

Dio'genes. 1. Of Sinōpē, see CYNIC PHILOSOPHERS.

2. Of Oenoanda, see EPICURUS.

3. **Diogenes Lāe'rtius** (i.e. of Laertē in Cilicia), the Greek author of *Lives and Opinions of Eminent Philosophers* (generally known as *Lives of the Philosophers*). He probably lived in the first half of the third century AD but about his life nothing is known. His work, in ten books, purports to give an account of the principal Greek thinkers (including in the term such men as Solon, the Athenian poet and reforming politician, and Periander, tyrant of Corinth), eighty-two in number, from Thales (*c*.600 BC) to Epicurus (fourth century BC). Diogenes was industrious, but he compiled his book from the works of earlier biographers and epitomizers of philosophical doctrines, so that he is often at several removes from the works of the philosophers themselves. Fortunately, he usually names his sources, and thus it is to some extent possible to tell when his evidence may be relied upon. He is most valuable in his preservation of the maxims and three epistles of *Epicurus, and he preserves the epigram of *Callimachus upon the death of his friend Heracleitus. Diogenes also wrote (rather bad) poetry, some of which he quotes in the *Lives*.

Diomē'dēs (in English often Dio'mede). 1. In Greek myth, a Thracian, son of Ares and a nymph Cyrenē, king of the Bistones, whose man-eating horses Heracles captured as one of his Labours.

2. In Greek myth, son of *Tȳdeus and of Dēïpylē, daughter of Adrastus. He took part in the expedition of the *Epigonoi against Thebes, and was leader of the men of Argos and Tiryns in the Trojan War. With the help of Athena he wounded Aphroditē and even the war-god

 Arēs, and killed a number of Trojan warriors, but behaved chivalrously to his guest-friend *Glaucus of Lycia although he was on the enemy side. He and Odysseus raided the Trojan camp and killed Rhesus. He plays an important part in the poems of the *Epic Cycle which describe what happened to the Greek heroes after the fall of Troy. With Odysseus he brought *Philoctetes from Lemnos and stole the *Palladium from Troy. When on his return home from Troy he found that his wife Aigialeia had been unfaithful to him, he left again and wandered to Italy where he founded various towns in Apulia; on his death he was buried on one of the 'Islands of Diomedes' (*Diomedeae insulae*; modern Tremiti Is.) near the Apulian coast. In *Aeneid* 11 he is represented as refusing to join in the resistance to Aeneas.

Dīo(n). 1. Ruler of *Syracuse (see SYRA-CUSE 2 and PLATO 1).

2. **Dio(n) Chry'sostom** (*Chrysostomos*, 'golden mouthed'), properly Dio(n) Cocceiānus (*c.* AD 40–after 111), also known as Dio Prūsius, 'of Prusa' in Bithynia, Greek orator and popular philosopher. A member of a wealthy family from Prusa, he came to Rome and fell under the influence of the Stoic philosopher Musonius. Banished from Rome and Bithynia because of opposition to the emperor Domitian, he travelled widely through Greece and Asia Minor preaching Stoic-Cynic philosophy. He was highly thought of by the enlightened emperors Nerva (who succeeded Domitian in AD 96) and his successor (in 98) Trajan. Some of his eighty or so surviving speeches are genuinely political, dealing with real situations in Bithynia, but the rest are 'display pieces' on a variety of popular themes, delivered to inform, improve, and entertain a variety of audiences while he was on his travels. He aims at the style and language of Attic Greek, in the easy manner of Plato and Xenophon, and his philosophy reflects conservative values of virtue and charity towards others. His speeches give a vivid picture of his life and times.

3. **Dio(n) Ca'ssius,** see CASSIUS.

Diō'nē, consort of Zeus at Dodona, the only seat of her cult, and by him the mother of *Aphroditē. The name is the feminine of Zeus.

Diony'sia, name given in Greece to festivals of the god Dionysus, which included dramatic performances (see also LENAEA). Attica celebrated two festivals annually under this name, the Rural (or Rustic) Dionysia in the month Poseideon (December), whose procession is memorably imitated by Aristophanes in the *Acharnians*, and the Great (or City) Dionysia at Athens itself in the month Elaphebolion (March), the sobriquet 'Great' being given because of its importance. This latter festival was instituted, or at any rate considerably

augmented, in 534 BC by the tyrant Peisistratus, who brought the cult to Athens from Eleutherae (on the border between Attica and Boeotia, north of Eleusis). The god's image was placed in the old temple of Dionysus within the precinct of the theatre (see DIONYSUS, THEATRE OF). A day or two before the festival began the image was taken from its temple to another outside Athens near the *Academy, so that by escorting it in a torchlight procession back to the theatre the Athenians might re-enact its original arrival in the city from Eleutherae; it was thus present throughout the dramatic performances staged in the god's honour. The Great Dionysia proper began on the tenth day of Elaphebolion with a spectacular religious procession (in which one conspicuous element was the carrying of phalluses in honour of the god) leading up to the sacrifices and libations poured by the 10 *strategoi* in the precinct of Dionysus' temple. The procession included the *choregoi* of the various dramatic performances, dressed in their robes. One of Demosthenes' charges against Meidias (see DEMOSTHENES (2) 2) was that the latter had partly destroyed the gold crown and gold-embroidered robe which the orator, being a *choregos*, had intended to wear. Except for the period of the Peloponnesian War the festival seems to have lasted for five days, when five comedies were performed, one on each afternoon, preceded on two days by dithyrambic competitions and on three days by tragedies and satyr plays, the activities beginning at daybreak. During the war, to save expense and time, the festival was curtailed by one day and the number of comedies performed reduced to three.

At the time of the Great Dionysia, when the winter was over, the seas were navigable and there might be many visitors in Athens (as there were not at the earlier Lenaea in winter). During the existence of the *Delian League, it was the time when the allies brought their tribute to Athens, to be displayed in the *orchestra* of the theatre; it was also the occasion when foreign ambassadors were received, and children whose fathers had died fighting for Athens paraded in the theatre. The names of citizens awarded a crown because they were public benefactors were announced; it was at the Great Dionysia of 338 BC that Demosthenes, according to the proposal of Ctesiphon, was to be presented with his crown (see DEMOSTHENES (2) 1). The festival thus became for Athenians a patriotic display of the cultural and political superiority of their city.

Diony'sius. 1. **Dionysius I** and **II,** tyrants of Syracuse; see SYRACUSE 2 and 3.

2. **Dionysius the Thracian** (Dionysios Thrax) (*c.*170–*c.*90 BC), of Alexandria, a pupil of *Aristarchus and later a teacher of grammar and literature at Rhodes. His only surviving work is

a Greek grammar (*Technē grammatikē*), which remained a standard work for many centuries. Latin grammar fell under its influence, and through Latin most of the modern grammars of Europe are indebted to it. Its influence spread through Syriac and Armenian adaptations, and a large body of comment grew up around it. The Greek verb *typtō* ('I beat') was used to exemplify voices, numbers, and persons, but the full paradigm with all possible moods and tenses was introduced later.

3. Dionysius of Halicarnassus, Greek *rhetor and historian who lived at Rome for many years from 30 BC. As a literary critic of good judgement he wrote (in Greek) a number of treatises: criticism of the Greek orators Lysias, Isocrates, Isaeus, and Demosthenes, showing in the introduction his preference for the Attic style of rhetoric over that of the Asianic school (see ORATORY 1); some minor works on Deinarchus, Demosthenes, and Thucydides, and a letter on Plato, of whose 'dithyrambic' style Dionysius was very critical; and, the most interesting of his works, a treatise *On the Arrangement of Words* (*Peri syntheseōs onomatōn*), the only surviving ancient work on word-order and euphony. To this we owe the best preserved text of Sappho's *Ode to Aphrodite* and the fragment from the *Danae* poem of Simonides. As a historian Dionysius had a great enthusiasm for Rome, expressed in the twenty books of his *Roman Antiquities* (*Rōmaïkē archaiologia*), of which books 1–9 and large parts of 10 and 11 survive. It went from mythical times down to the outbreak of the First Punic War (264 BC), the point at which the history of Polybius begins, but the surviving part breaks off in 441 BC. It is a painstakingly detailed composition made from the Roman annalists, and a valuable supplement to Livy. It contains the observation, much repeated since the writer's day, that the style is the man (1. 3).

4. Dionysius the Areo'pagite, see NEOPLA-TONISM.

5. Dionysius Periēgē'tēs ('the guide') (probably second century AD), the Greek author of a *Description of the World*, a didactic poem in 1,185 hexameters, repeating the views of the Hellenistic scholar *Eratosthenes, who was by then somewhat out of date. It enjoyed great popularity in later times. *Eustathius in the twelfth century wrote a valuable commentary on it.

Dionȳ'sus, in Greek myth, son of Zeus and Semelē, the daughter of *Cadmus, king of Thebes. When Semele was made pregnant by Zeus, his jealous wife Hera, in human disguise, persuaded her to pray to Zeus to visit her in all the splendour of a god. This he did and she was consumed by his lightning; but he rescued her unborn child from the ashes and placed him in his thigh, from which in due time he was born.

The child was entrusted to Ino, sister of Semele and wife of *Athamas, but Hera, still jealous, punished them by driving them mad, so that Athamas killed his son Learchos and Ino leaped into the sea with her other son Melicertes. Ino was transformed into a sea-goddess Leucothea, and Melicertes became the sea-god Palaemon. Dionysus was now handed over to the nymphs of Mount Nysa (variously located), whence he derived his name, where he was worshipped, and where he introduced the cultivation of the vine. He was persecuted by those who refused to recognize his divinity, but overcame them and extended his conquests far into Asia and into India. The most famous of these persecutions was that of Pentheus, king of Thebes, which forms the subject of the *Bacchae of Euripides. The daughters of Proetus (see BELLEROPHON), king of Argos, also opposed him and were driven mad; their madness was cured by the intervention of the seer *Melampus. For another similar legend see MINYAS. Dionysus is represented as accompanied on his conquests by a host of votaries, male and female, *Satyrs, *Sileni, *Maenads, *Bassarids, dancing about him, intoxicated or possessed. They were known as *Bacchi* (fem. *Bacchae*), sharing with the god his other name, Bacchus. The seventh *Homeric Hymn relates how pirates found and kidnapped him, tying him up on shipboard; but the bonds fell off him, a vine grew about the mast, and the captive turned into a lion. The pirates in terror jumped into the sea, whereupon they were transformed into dolphins. For other myths about Dionysus see ARIADNE and ICARIUS.

Dionysus was the god of wine and of ecstasy. He scarcely appears at all in Homer, and this fact, combined with the stories of his coming to Greece from Thrace and having to overcome resistance before being accepted, has suggested to some that he was a new god, accepted late into the Greek pantheon of Olympians (see GODS 1). However, his name has been found in Greece in the late Bronze Age on *Linear B tablets, perhaps even in connection with wine, and archaeological evidence seems to suggest that he was worshipped in the island of Ceos from the fifteenth century BC onwards; moreover, the Dionysiac festival of wine, the *Anthesteria, predates the Ionian migrations (in about the tenth century BC). This evidence seems to indicate that his name and cult may be Mycenaean in origin. He is a god of an essentially different type from the Olympian deities, a giver of joy and a soother of cares (the latter described by his epithet Lyaios), experienced by the worshipper through intoxication; he is also experienced through ecstasy, felt as intensified mental power and the surrender of everyday identity. But he had another aspect, seen when his ecstatic worshippers seized a wild animal and tore it apart in order to eat it raw (the act known as *sparagmos*) believing that they were then incorporating in themselves the god and his power. This side of Dionysiac possession and the dire results it could lead to are often shown in the myths. Characteristic of the cult of Dionysus is the mask, symbol of the surrender of identity, and a means of transforming identity. At its simplest his image consisted of a mask on a column draped with a piece of cloth. Important in connection with his worship were the *dithyramb (a variety of Greek choral lyric poetry), tragedy, and comedy, all of which were performed at his festivals (see DIONYSIA and LENAEA). Dionysus is frequently represented as a rather effeminate youth, with luxuriant hair, reclining with grapes or a wine-cup in his hand, or holding the *thyrsos, a rod with a bunch of ivy leaves fastened to the top. The Greeks identified him with the Egyptian god Osiris, and the Romans with their wine-god Liber, also called Bacchus. See also DIONYSUS ZAGREUS, IACCHOS, and BACCHANALIA.

Dionysus, Theatre of, at Athens. The theatre at Athens was situated in the open air in a hollow on the southern slope of the Acropolis; it was within the precinct of the old temple of the god Dionysus, who thus gave the theatre its name and whose image watched over the dramatic performances of the Great *Dionysia and of the *Lenaea. An altar of the god (thymelē) stood in the centre of the dancing-floor (orchestra). The oldest remains of buildings on the site go back perhaps to the sixth century BC (the period of the Peisistratids). Construction of the fifth-century theatre has been attributed to Pericles (see THEATRE I).

Diony'sus Za'greus. The myth of Dionysus Zagreus played an important role in the beliefs of the Greeks who practised the mysteries of *Orpheus. Zagreus was the son of Persephonē and Zeus, who came to her in the form of a snake. He gave the rule of the world to the child, sat him on a throne and had the *Corybantes guard him. At the instigation of the jealous Hera (wife of Zeus) the *Titans distracted the child's attention with toys, then seized him, tore him to pieces, and devoured him, all but the heart; this Athena saved and took to Zeus. From the heart Zeus remade his son and implanted him in Semelē (see DIONYSUS), from whom was later born a new Dionysus Zagreus. He punished the Titans by striking them with his lightning, and from the rising soot sprang the human race, rebels against the gods but having in them some portion of the divine. This story is known only from writers of the Hellenistic age, but it seems to have been current earlier. The association of Dionysus with the Underworld (through his mother Persephone, wife of Hades and queen of the Underworld) is significant in the *mystery religions which were primarily concerned with

judgement after death, freedom from punishment, rebirth, and eventual blessedness.

Diosco'ridēs, see DIOSCURIDES.

Dio'scūri (Dios kouroi, 'sons of Zeus'), in Greek myth, Castor and Polydeuces (Lat. Pollux). They were native to Sparta, where they were worshipped. In Homer and in Hesiod they are the twin sons of Tyndareus and *Leda, and the brothers of Helen (of Troy). Later, Polydeuces is represented as the son of Zeus, and immortal. When Castor, the mortal son of Tyndareus, is fatally wounded (see below), Polydeuces chooses to share his immortality with his brother, so that they both spend half their time in the Underworld and the other half with the gods on Mount Olympus. Other accounts make them both sons of Zeus, born like Helen from an egg. They occur in three mythical stories. When *Theseus carried off Helen as a child they made an expedition to Attica, recovered her, and took Theseus' mother Aethra as well to be Helen's slave. Helen's place of concealment had been revealed by the hero Akademos (see ACADEMY), whose land was always spared in consequence by invading Lacedaemonians. In another story they took part in the voyage of the *Argonauts, Polydeuces distinguishing himself in the fight against *Amycus. Finally they carried off the two daughters of a certain Leucippus, Hilaeira and Phoebē, who were betrothed to their cousins Idas and Lynceus. In the ensuing fight (or, in some versions, in a cattle raid) Castor and both opponents were killed. It was on this occasion that Polydeuces gave Castor a share of his immortality (see above). The Dioscuri are often identified with the constellation Gemini (the Twins). They were commonly regarded as protectors of sailors, to whom they appeared during storms as the lights of St Elmo's fire. They were also notable boxers and horsemen, frequently called 'riders of white horses', and therefore the patrons of athletes and athletic contests.

In Roman religion the worship of Castor and Pollux was introduced in early times, Castor always being the more popular. Their temple at Rome (nearly always known as the temple of Castor) was vowed by the dictator Aulus Postumius during the battle of the Romans against the Latins at Lake Regillus (496 BC). The story was that they then fought at the head of the Roman army and after the battle brought the news of the victory to Rome; they were seen watering their horses at the Lacus Iuturnae ('pool of Juturna', a fountain in the Forum) and their temple was erected on that spot, beside that of Vesta. According to another story (related in Cicero, De natura deorum), Publius Vatinius (grandfather of the famous tribune) informed the senate that he had met two youths on white horses who told him of the capture of Perseus of Macedon on that day (168 BC); he was thrown into prison until his statement was confirmed by dispatches. The Roman *equites* regarded the brothers as their particular patrons. The common oaths *mecastor* and *edepol*, based on their names, are evidence of their popularity.

Dioscu'rides (Dioskouridēs) (first century AD), Greek physician who served with the Roman army. He was the author of a *Mäteria medica* (*Peri hylēs iatrikēs*, 'pharmacopoeia') in five books in which he described the medicinal properties of some six hundred plants and nearly a thousand drugs, some produced from minerals. Dioscurides is a careful observer and unsuperstitious, but the herb lore he preserves is irrational and very few herbs seem to have the properties he ascribes to them; nevertheless his work, with the numerous commentaries on it, was the standard text-book of pharmacy for many centuries. The many illustrations make the manuscripts particularly fine.

Dī'philus, see COMEDY, GREEK 6.

diplo'mata milita'ria, see ARMY, ROMAN 3.

Di'pylon ('double gate'), the principal gate of Athens, on the north-west of the city in the Ceramicus (potters' quarter). Through it passed a road leading from the agora to the Academy; bordering it outside the walls were the tombs of those who died in war. Here *Pericles delivered the Funeral Oration. For Dipylon vases see VASE-PAINTING.

Dīrae or **Furiae,** the Roman counterparts of the Greek Erinyes or Eumenides; see FURIES.

Dīrae ('Furies'), Latin poem in hexameters attributed to Virgil; see *APPENDIX VIRGILIANA.*

Dircē, in Greek myth, wife of Lycus, regent of Thebes. She was killed by the sons of *Antiopē in revenge for her treatment of their mother; they tied her to the horns of a bull and she was dragged to death. After her death she was changed into the stream that bore her name, symbolic of Thebes in Greek literature: for example, the 'swan of Dirce' signifies the poet Pindar.

dirge (Gk. *thrēnos*), in Greek literature, lyric poem of lament sung over the dead. The dirges of Simonides and Pindar were famous, but only a few fragments survive. Compare NAENIAE at Rome.

Dis, in Roman religion, the ruler of the Underworld, the equivalent of the Greek god Pluto (another name for *Hades), of whose name Dis (i.e. Dīvēs, 'rich') is perhaps the Latin translation. During the Punic Wars foreign religious rites were from time to time introduced at Rome by order of the senate to hearten the people. In 249 and 207 BC the senate appointed special festivals of appeasement to the Roman equivalents of the Greek Underworld deities Pluto and Persephone, namely Dis and Proserpina. In classical Roman literature Dis has become merely a symbol of death.

Disciplī'nae, lost treatise on the liberal arts by *Varro.

Discord, Apple of, see ERIS.

discus, see ATHLETICS (vii).

Dis exapatō'n ('twice a swindler'), Greek comedy by *Menander, very probably the original of Plautus' *Bacchides. A papyrus fragment from the play is clearly the source of lines 494–562 of *Bacchides*, and is the first passage in Menander of any length which has been found to correspond to a later Roman adaptation.

di'thyramb (*dithyrambos*), in Greek, form of choral *lyric sung to the god Dionysus; the word is of unknown origin, almost certainly not Greek. Its development into a literary genre was the work of the poet *Arion in Corinth in the last quarter of the seventh century BC. From Corinth it was brought to Athens by *Lasus of Hermione, and in 509 BC it became a subject for competition at the festivals of Dionysus (see DIONYSIA). Simonides, Pindar, and Bacchylides all wrote dithyrambs; of the first two only fragments exist, but several of Bacchylides' survive almost entire. The dithyrambic chorus did not wear masks; they danced and sang in a circle (see DIONYSUS, THEATRE OF). Narrative plays a large part in these poems, but its subject-matter is not particularly connected with Dionysus. At the Great Dionysia at Athens each tribe entered two choruses for the dithyrambic competitions, one of boys and one of men, each under the charge of a *choregos* (see CHOREGIA) chosen from the tribe. Lots were drawn to determine the order for selecting poets and flute-players; the *choregos* also needed the services of a good chorus-trainer. The inscriptions preserving the lists of victors in the dithyrambic contests at Athens (see DIDASCALIA) preserve the names of the victorious tribes and their *choregoi* but not the names of the poets, no matter how famous. The successful *choregos* received, as the representative of his tribe, a *tripod, which he erected at his own expense upon a monument, with an inscription. After Bacchylides the musical component of the dithyramb seems to have increased in importance at the expense of the words, but since no music has survived it is hard to discern what happened. Up to this time the dithyramb had been composed in regular form in *strophes and antistrophes, but now this correspondence was abandoned in favour of a freer style of composition, with solo songs, and the language became far-fetched and artificial. The names chiefly associated with these changes are Melanippides of Melos (flourished c.480 BC) who introduced lyric solos, Philoxenus of Cythera (*c.*436–380) who introduced in his *Cyclops* a solo sung to the lyre, *Cinesias of Athens, and *Timotheus of Miletus. After the fourth century BC it seems that the dithyramb was no longer an important form of literary composition, although the competitions survived into the time of the Roman emperors.

Dīus Fī'dius, in Roman religion, a god sworn by in oaths, perhaps a title of Jupiter.

dīver'bium, name given to dialogue in a Roman comedy, as distinct from *cantica*, the parts declaimed by the actors to a musical accompaniment.

Divinatio in Q. Caecilium, see CICERO (1) 1.

divination. The prediction of the future by supernatural means, called by the Greeks *mantikē*, was practised by the Greeks and Romans in many ways. The most important source of our knowledge is Cicero's **De divinatione*. Divination may be divided into two kinds, natural and artificial. The most obvious form of natural divination is based on dreams, which the dreamer might interpret for himself or take to professional interpreters (for an ancient 'dream-book' see ARTEMIDORUS). As the result of a dream the father of the young *Galen directed his son to the study of medicine. The emperor Marcus *Aurelius was thankful to have received advice from a similar source on how to cure his ailments. In the practice of incubation, a sick person would sleep in the temple of a healing god, most usually *Asclepius, so as to receive from the god a dream which would suggest a cure. Another form of natural divination is prophecy from the speech of someone acting as the mouthpiece (*prophētēs*) of a divine power which possesses him. This kind of divination became institutionalized, with a succession of prophets, at the great oracular sites of Delphi, Dodona, Oropus, Ammon, and the various Sibylline sites.

Artificial divination is based on external observations of animals, plants, or objects; the best known form is *augury, observation of the behaviour of birds, which at Rome was entrusted to a college of augurs. Widely used also was observation of the entrails of sacrificial animals (see HARUSPICES). Predictions were sometimes based on certain involuntary human actions, a twitch or a sneeze for example (see OMENS). Exceptional plant growth might also be meaningful. Divination by throwing dice or drawing lots was common, and localized at certain sites. In later times, random consultation of the works of famous poets was favoured, perhaps because they were considered divinely inspired: hence the *sortes Homericae* and *Virgilianae* ('Homeric, Virgilian consultations'); see VIRGIL. Unusual meteorological phenomena were considered significant at all times, and at

Rome were recorded in the *annales maximi* (priestly records; see ANNALS). *Astrology became very popular after increased contact with the East following the conquests of Alexander the Great (second half of the fourth century BC). Necromancy, calling up the spirits of the dead, was practised at all periods but never acquired respectability. See MAGIC 5 (iii).

Most people accepted the forms of divination that had become established by their own day but looked with suspicion upon any new forms. The attitudes of philosophers to divination seem to have varied with the individual, though Epicureans rejected it, as did some Sceptics. Prophecy by inspired utterance was more acceptable. Stoics, by the nature of their beliefs, defended most types. Early Christian writers saw pagan divination as the work of evil demons; the edict of the emperor Theodosius in AD 391, banning all forms of pagan cult, put a formal end to the practice.

division of the Roman empire, into eastern and western halves in AD 395, see BYZANTINE AGE.

Dīvitiā'cus (first century BC), pro-Roman chief of the Gallic tribe of the Aedui, who appealed for Roman help against the invading Germans led by *Ariovistus. He assisted Caesar in his operations in Gaul (see COMMENTARIES 1 (books 1 and 2)).

do'chmius or **do'chmiac,** see METRE, GREEK 1.

Dōdō'na, see ORACLES, GREEK.

dogs. Dogs were kept from earliest times for hunting, for guarding the house and herds, and as companions. Odysseus' hunting dog Argos, at the age of twenty, lifted his head and pricked his ears at the approach of strangers, but dropped his ears and wagged his tail when he recognized his returning master; Odysseus shed a tear to find the dog neglected now that his hunting days were past. Homer also speaks of dogs who fawn on their master when he brings them scraps after a feast (*Odyssey* 10. 216). In the myth of *Icarius it is his faithful hound Maera who leads his daughter Erigone to his body. Xenophon in his treatise on hunting (**Cynegeticus*), written in the fourth century BC, writes with warmth and enthusiasm about the breeding, raising, and training of hounds, their points, and even, at enormous length, their names (disyllabic, for ease of calling). These hounds were used for hunting hares, deer, and wild boar, generally on foot. The Greeks knew several types of dog, the Molossian (from Epirus), which resembled a mastiff, the Laconian hunting dog, divided by Xenophon into the Castorian and a smaller kind which is a cross between dog and fox; the Cretan hound, which was famous for speed and tracking; and the 'Melitaean' terrier (from Malta), a small, long-haired, white dog. All these types were introduced into Italy, which had its own native Umbrian and Etruscan dogs. From Gaul came a type of greyhound used for coursing, and from Ireland the wolfhound.

References to house-dogs are frequent. In Aristophanes' *Wasps* the dog Labēs is put on trial for stealing some cheese. Plutarch relates that *Alcibiades had an unusually large and handsome dog whose chief beauty was his tail, yet Alcibiades had it cut off so that the Athenians would talk of this piece of eccentricity rather than find something worse to say of him. The story was handed down of the dog belonging to Xanthippus (Pericles' father) which swam by his master's ship to Salamis when the Athenians were obliged to abandon their city in the Persian Wars. Among several instances of dogs giving warning of enemy attacks, Plutarch in his Life of Aratus tells how noisy little dogs belonging to a gardener proved a considerable hazard to Aratus in his attempt to gain possession of Sicyon (by contrast see MANLIUS CAPITOLINUS). The Greek Anthology contains several epitaphs on dogs. The dog was also proverbial for its unpleasant characteristics, among others its greed, its fawning, and its shamelessness. The Romans valued the dog as a protector; the figure of a dog stood between the images of the *lares praestites* ('guardian spirits') of the state.

dokima'sia, at Athens, the examination by which the selected candidates for state office (who had already been chosen, primarily by lot but in some cases by vote) were questioned about their eligibility in respect of age, the previous holding of office, legal convictions, and so on.

Dolabe'lla, Publius Cornēlius (*c*.80–43 BC), husband of Cicero's daughter *Tullia, a dissolute and debt-ridden aristocrat, a legate of Julius Caesar in the civil war, nominated by Caesar before his death to stand in for him as consul during his absence in Parthia. After Caesar's murder Dolabella briefly turned republican for his own advantage, but reverted. He was finally defeated by the republican Cassius in Syria and committed suicide.

Dōlon, in Homer's *Iliad* and the *Rhesus* of Euripides, a Trojan spy killed by Odysseus and Diomedes.

Domi'tian (Titus Flāvius Domitiānus) (AD 51–96), Roman emperor from 81 to his death, younger son of the emperor Vespasian, and the last of the Flavian emperors. See ROME 11.

Domus Au'rea, of Nero, see GOLDEN HOUSE.

Domus Pu'blica, official residence at Rome of the *pontifex maximus*.

Donatists, schismatic body in the African Church who became divided from the Catholics because they refused to accept as bishop of Carthage one who had been consecrated by a *traditor*, i.e. a Christian who had surrendered the scriptures when their possession was forbidden in the persecutions of Diocletian (AD 303–5). They took their name from a certain Donatus, who was consecrated by some bishops as a rival. The orthodox position was that the unworthiness of the minister did not affect the validity of the sacraments since their true minister was Christ. *Augustine continued the theological attack upon the Donatists, but the schism persisted until the African Church was destroyed by the Arabs in the invasions of the seventh and eighth centuries.

Donā'tus. 1. **Ae'lius Donatus** (fourth century AD), Latin grammarian, teacher of *Jerome. He wrote two books of Latin grammar which remained in use throughout the Middle Ages, to the extent that 'donat' or 'donet' was used generally to mean 'text-book'. He also wrote a commentary on Terence which survives, combined with the notes of other commentators, in the *scholia on that author; and most valuably a commentary on Virgil. Of this only the preface and the Life, with an introduction to the *Eclogues*, survive entire, but it was extensively used by *Servius in his commentary.

2. **Tiberius Claudius Donatus** (late fourth century AD), the author of a rhetorical and stylistic commentary in twelve books on Virgil's *Aeneid*, which has no connection with the commentary of Donatus (1).

Do'rians, Dorian Invasion. According to Greek myth, it had been the will of Zeus that *Heraclēs should rule over the country of *Perseus at Mycenae and Tiryns. After Heracles' death, however, these cities came into the hands of the descendants of *Pelops, and at the time of the Trojan War Agamemnon ruled at Mycenae. The Greeks believed as historical fact the legend that two generations after the Trojan War, *c*.1100 BC, there was an invasion into Greece from the north by a new, Greek-speaking people known as Dorians (for the name see DORUS). They accompanied the sons of the hero Heracles (see AEGIMIUS), who were returning to the Peloponnese to claim their father's inheritance, first the city of Tiryns and then, by conquest, the whole Peloponnese. By this legend many historical facts were explained; first, how large parts of Greece were occupied by a (Greek) people who spoke in the Doric dialect. The close relationship between Doric and North-west Greek (see DIALECTS) supports the legend that the Dorians came from the north-west, from Epirus and south-west Macedonia, and advanced into Thessaly and Boeotia, and that some of them remained in the small district of central Greece known as Doris, whence they later advanced south (taking the name with them) through Delphi (where the priesthood remained by tradition Dorian in historical times), south-west to Naupactus, and thence into the Peloponnese. Corinth was, by tradition, one of their latest conquests. The fact that the Arcadian dialect remains closest to pre-Dorian Greek (see DIALECTS 1) seems to indicate that the Dorian invaders failed to penetrate the remoter parts of Arcadia. Secondly, it was a peculiarity of Dorian states that every state was divided into the three tribes, Hylleis, Dymanes, and Pamphyli, a fact which suggests a strong sense of identity. Thirdly, the Dorians were apparently unknown at the time of the Trojan War (c.1184 BC) and not mentioned by Homer, yet in later historical times they occupied the territory once held, according to Homer, by Agamemnon and the Achaeans, and in Argos and Sparta they ruled over a serf-like population of non-Dorian Greeks. The Dorian invasion may also account for a historical fact of which the Greeks themselves were scarcely aware, that the cities and civilization of Mycenaean Greece were destroyed in successive attacks in the twelfth century BC, to be succeeded by *migrations overseas to the coast of Asia Minor from c.1050 to 950, and by poverty and deprivation in Greece itself. There is no archaeological evidence for the identity of the people who destroyed the Mycenaean culture, and no positive signs of an influx of new people. This makes sense if the invaders were of related Greek stock from the fringes of the Mycenaean world. It has also been argued that there was in fact no Dorian invasion, that different groups of Greeks had been present in Greece since the beginning of Mycenaean culture, and that the destructions were caused by spasmodic raids or local uprisings of a suppressed population. However, a strong sense of discontinuity following the destructions as well as the legends themselves tell in favour of the essential historicity of the Dorian invasion.

Doric. 1. See DIALECTS, GREEK 1 and 2. **2.** See ARCHITECTURE 1 (i).

Dō'richa, the Egyptian courtesan loved by *Sappho's brother.

Dōrus, in Greek myth, son of *Hellen, the eponymous ancestor of the Hellenes (Greeks), himself the son of *Deucalion. Hellen became, by the nymph Orseïs, the father of the mythical ancestors of the three great branches of the Greek race, Aeolus (of the Aeolians), Xuthus (of the Achaeans and Ionians), and Dorus (of the Dorians). See also AEGIMIUS.

drachma, in Greece, a coin worth six obols (see MONEY 1). The word dates back to the days when Greece had a primitive iron currency; it means 'a handful', i.e. of obols (*oboloi*, 'spits').

Drāco (Drǎkōn), an Athenian legislator, who received special authority to organize and codify the laws in 621 BC, the first time the Athenian laws were put down in writing. Details of his legislation are not now known, but the laws were notoriously harsh (hence the adjective 'Draconian') with nearly all offences (including idleness) punishable by death. When asked why he decreed death as the penalty for most offences he said that small offences deserved death and he knew of no severer punishment for great ones. All his laws were repealed by *Solon except those dealing with homicide (which entrusted trials for murder to the *Areopagus), but although no one at Athens in the fifth and fourth centuries BC doubted that the homicide laws then in force were those of Draco, it cannot be assumed that in fact they had remained unchanged since his day. The constitution attributed to Draco by Aristotle (*Constitution of the Athenians*, ch. 4) and based on the franchise of *hoplites is now rejected as a later compilation.

drama, see CHOREGIA; CHORUS; DIDASCALIA; DIONYSIA; DIONYSUS, THEATRE OF; DRAMATIC COMPETITIONS; THEATRE; TRAGEDY; COMEDY; MIME; and PANTOMIME. For the musical accompaniment of plays see MUSIC. For Roman dramatic performances see also LUDI 1 (ii).

dramatic competitions. At Athens, from the late sixth century BC onwards, tragedies and comedies were performed at festivals, under state supervision, by dramatists in competition with each other to win the prize for the best play. See TRAGEDY 2 and COMEDY, GREEK 1.

Drancēs, in Virgil's *Aeneid* (11. 336), the Italian chief who taunts the Rutulian king Turnus. Virgil is said to have modelled him on Cicero.

dreams, see DIVINATION.

Dreams (Gk. Oneiroi, Lat. Somnia). Dreams are frequently personified in Greek and Latin literature; according to Hesiod, they are the daughters of Night. In Homer's *Odyssey* (24. 12) they live beyond *Oceanus, near the gates of the sun. Later poets wrote of a god of dreams, Morpheus (hence 'morphia' etc.), who made human shapes (*morphai*) appear to dreamers. Virgil says (in *Aeneid* 6. 893) that the spirits of the dead send dreams to men from the Underworld, those which are true through a gate of horn, false dreams through a gate of ivory. He thus adapts what Homer says, very similarly, in *Odyssey* 19. 562.

dress. Ancient dress was in general very simple; garments were usually made at home out of large, rectangular pieces of linen or wool; what was worn during the day as a cloak might serve as a blanket at night. Men's and women's clothing were quite similar and there were no rapid fluctuations of style. The greatest variety of forms, colours, materials, and names is found in footwear.

1. *Greek.* The dress of Greek men and women alike consisted normally of two garments only, the *chitōn* or tunic worn next to the skin and the *hīmation*, which resembled a cloak. The Doric tunic was basically a sleeveless woollen garment, worn to the knees: it consisted of a rectangle of cloth doubled around the body, pinned at each shoulder and held by a girdle at the waist, leaving the arms free. Women also wore the Ionic tunic, a longer, fuller version, usually made of linen, with wide sleeves covering the upper arm. As it was usually longer than the body, part of the length was drawn up to overhang the girdle. Women might also wear a soft band around the body below the breasts. In early times men too might wear the Ionic tunic, but by the mid-fifth century BC they had adopted the Doric tunic. The *exōmis* was a coarse working tunic that fastened on the left shoulder and left the right arm free. The *himation* was worn out of doors by both men and women. It was usually passed over the left shoulder, drawn behind the back and under the right arm, leaving it free, and then thrown over the left shoulder. Aristophanes makes it a sign of the hardiness of Athenian youth in former days that they went in all weathers without a *himation*. On the other hand, to wear the *himation* without the tunic indicated poverty or asceticism, such as was shown by the philosopher Socrates and the soldiers Agesilaus and Gelon (tyrant of Syracuse). Either poverty or the ability to endure hardship was similarly demonstrated by those who wore a cheap and often threadbare *himation* known as a *tríbōn* (or *tribōnion*), notably Spartans and philosophers (Diogenes the Cynic slept and died in his). The term *peplos* seems to have been used in the general sense of 'long robe' and applied to a female garment such as a shawl or to oriental men's dress. Horsemen wore a short cape known as the *chlamys*. The prevailing colours of Greek men's dress were those natural to wool or flax, predominantly white, but with some greys and browns. Dyes were used on more luxurious garments and especially on women's clothes. Hats were not generally worn, except when travelling or hunting. The *petasos* was a broad-brimmed felt hat offering protection from the sun; it was part of the costume of the **ephēboi*. The *pīlos* was a round, brimless felt cap chiefly worn by workmen. Leather sandals, shoes, and boots were worn out of doors (see also COTHURNUS); tanning and shoe-making were active industries in Athens, and women's shoes were often highly decorated.

2. *Roman.* Men's dress in republican times consisted of a tunic (*tunica*), resembling the Greek *chiton* (see above), the usual indoor dress, and an outer garment, the *toga*. Originally men wore only the toga; when tunics became general it was considered effeminate to wear a long tunic with sleeves. Later it became usual to wear two tunics; Augustus wore four in winter. Those of senatorial rank wore tunics with a broad purple stripe, *latus clavus*, stitched to or woven into the fabric, running from each shoulder to the hem, front and back; those of equestrian rank had a narrow stripe, *clavus angustus*. The toga was a heavy white woollen garment, roughly semi-circular, about five metres long and two wide at its greatest width, but its size varied according to the taste of the wearer. The straight edge was placed on the left shoulder from behind, with a third of its length falling in front of the wearer and supported by the left arm; the toga was then drawn across the back (straight edge uppermost, curved edge passing down to the right leg), brought under the right arm and thrown again over the left shoulder so as to hang down at the back. Originally the toga was worn by both sexes but it became the distinctive badge of Roman citizenship for men. The ordinary *toga virilis* ('man's toga') was entirely white. The *toga praetextata* ('bordered toga'), worn by certain priests and magistrates and also by free-born boys until they received the *toga virilis* on reaching manhood, had a purple hem. The toga was an uncomfortable garment and needed frequent cleaning, but it was dignified, and was obligatory dress on formal occasions even in imperial times when more convenient garments had come into use, such as the *synthesis*, a matching set of loose, brightly coloured garments suitable for wearing at dinner-parties.

Roman women customarily wore a tunic and under it could be worn a band beneath the breasts. Over the tunic the married women wore the *stola*, a long, full dress half covering the feet and gathered up by a high girdle; the *stola* came to be as characteristic of the Roman matron (see WOMEN) as the toga was of men. There was a coloured border around the neck of the *stola*, and a flounce around the hem. A *palla*, resembling the Greek *himation* (see above), was worn out of doors. The *lacerna* was a man's rough cloak worn on journeys and against the weather. Similar in use was a *paenula* or cape which had an opening in the middle, with hood, *cucullus*, attached, so that it was put on over the head. The *trabea* was a kind of short toga or cloak worn by the equestrian order on official occasions, by the consul at certain ceremonials, and by augurs and various orders of priests. A round felt cap, *pilleus*, was worn in the country or on journeys, and also during the *Saturnalia, the so-called 'cap of freedom'; otherwise, the Romans sometimes wore a hood or drew their outer garment over the head. Roman footwear was much like that of the Greeks. The *calceus* was the leather shoe worn in the city, the *pero* a boot worn in the country. The *calceus* differed in form and colour according to the rank of the wearer. Senators wore high shoes fastened in front with four black thongs and decorated with a small crescent of ivory. The *calīga* was a hobnailed boot worn by soldiers and peasants. Sandals (*soleae*) were worn indoors, but were taken off when reclining at dinner. To ask for one's sandals was the signal that one was leaving. See also TOILET.

Druids, see GAUL 2 and BRITAIN 1 and 4.

Drūsus. For the various members of the Roman Julio-Claudian family who bore this name see below and see also GERMANICUS.

1. **Marcus Li'vius Drusus,** tribune of the plebs in 122 BC, a supporter of the aristocracy against C. *Gracchus.

2. **Marcus Livius Drusus,** son of (1), grandfather of *Livia, the wife of the emperor Augustus, tribune of the plebs in 91 BC, who proposed, besides various democratic measures, to give the franchise to the Italian allies. His various enemies combined against him, and he was assassinated. His proposals and the consequent upheavals brought about the *Social War.

3. **Nero Claudius Drusus** (38–9 BC), second son of Ti. Claudius Nero and *Livia. Since Livia was later the wife of Augustus he became the latter's stepson. His older brother was Tiberius (Augustus' successor as Roman emperor). He was commonly known as Drusus the Elder to distinguish him from Tiberius' son Drusus the Younger (see below). He married Antonia Minor (daughter of Mark Anthony and Octavia), and was the father of Nero Claudius Germanicus and of the emperor Claudius. He was brilliantly successful in a series of campaigns against Germany during the years 12–9 BC, but died in the latter year from injuries received in a fall from his horse. After his death he was given the cognomen Germanicus; it is rarely used to describe him, but the name passed to his descendants.

4. **Drusus Julius Caesar** (*c.*13 BC–AD 23), Drusus the Younger, son of Tiberius (later emperor) and his first wife Vipsania Agrippina, daughter of *Agrippa. His original name, before the adoption of his father by Augustus, is not known. After the death of Germanicus, in AD 19, he became his father's principal col-laborator and appears to have been designated to succeed him, but he died in 23, poisoned, it was later suspected, by his wife, who had been seduced by *Sejanus (Tiberius' ambitious minister).

drÿads, *nymphs of trees.

Dying Gaul or **Gladiator,** Roman copy of a statue erected by king Attalus I of Pergamum to commemorate his victory *c.*230 BC over the Galatians (or Gauls, a Celtic tribe in central Asia Minor). In more recent times it was wrongly thought to represent a gladiator: hence the poet Byron's famous line describing the statue as of one 'butchered to make a Roman holiday'. See SCULPTURE 1.

Dy'scolus ('bad-tempered man'), Greek comedy by *Menander, produced at the *Lenaea of 317 BC and awarded first prize.

During a hunting-party a rich young man Sōstratus catches sight of a country girl praying to Pan and the nymphs at a shrine, and immediately falls in love and decides to marry her (this happens by the will of Pan, as the god himself reveals in a prologue). Unfortunately the girl's father Cnēmōn is a misanthrope (the *dyscolus* of the title) who lives a deliberately solitary life with only his daughter and a servant for company. His unpleasant nature has driven his wife to leave the house, and she has gone to live on the next farm with her son by a previous marriage, Gorgias. Sostratus now asks him for his help. Gorgias tells him that the only kind of son-in-law Cnemon will contemplate is one like himself. Sostratus tries to impress Cnemon with his hard work on the farm but Cnemon does not see him. Sostratus' mother has a bad dream and proposes a sacrifice at the shrine of the nymphs and Pan. At this juncture Cnemon falls down a well, is rescued by Gorgias, with the help of Sostratus, and emerges cured to some extent of his liking for a solitary life. He takes back his wife and entrusts his property and daughter to Gorgias, who bestows the daughter on Sostratus. The latter then persuades his father to give his sister to Gorgias as wife, and the play ends with the teasing of Cnemon to make him join the feast.

E

ecclē'sia, assembly and sovereign body at Athens, comprising all the adult male citizens over the age of 18, all equally entitled to address the assembly and to vote. It normally met forty times a year on the *Pnyx, with extra sessions as required, and was presided over by the chairman of the *boulē (executive council) who had been chosen by lot for the day. Voting was by simple majority and generally by show of hands. The assembly elected the *strategoi (military commanders) and served as a law court in the matter of grave crimes threatening the safety of the state, but its chief work was the passing of decrees (*psephismata*) dealing in detail with every sphere of government, including foreign affairs, finance, naval and military operations, and the corn supply. The agenda for meetings were prepared by the boule and any citizen might submit a matter for inclusion. No motion might be debated unless it appeared on the agenda and had been duly advertised: snap decisions were thus avoided. To some extent the agenda comprised routine matters which came up regularly, such as the continuation of magistrates in office. On uncontroversial issues the boule produced draft motions, *probouleumata*, so that much formal business could be speeded through, though any citizen could debate or amend a motion. On controversial issues the boule did not normally propose a motion but put the matter directly to the assembly, leaving it open to any citizen to draft the motion during the course of the debate. The only restraint on the powers of the assembly was that of the laws. If a motion proposed was illegal or even inexpedient, the proposer was liable to prosecution. The normal peacetime attendance was well over 5,000, a good proportion of the male citizen-body. Those attending seem to have been fairly representative of the population, possibly with a preponderance of those with only moderate means. From perhaps 403 BC, to ensure that every citizen could exercise his political rights, payment of one obol to those attending was introduced, the rate becoming more liberal in the course of time. During the fifth and most of the fourth centuries the assembly functioned in a fully democratic way (given that women, slaves, and *metics were excluded). The boule exercised no control, and the initiation of policy lay entirely in the hands of the citizens. Continuous policy was achieved only when one man, or a group of men, holding the confidence of the people over a period of time, was repeatedly elected to the office of *strategos. These semi-professional politicians were sometimes aristocrats, sometimes men of no family who were skilled orators, occasionally accepting fees from others in return for promoting certain measures in the assembly. They were the men who by and large proposed motions, were informed about public affairs, were voted into the elective offices, were chosen as envoys, and acted as prosecutors or advocates for the defence in political trials. Certainly by the fourth century they were differentiated from the mass of ordinary citizens who held only the offices that were filled by lot, and they wielded considerable influence in the assembly. See also CITIZENSHIP 1, DEMOCRACY, DEMAGOGUE, SOLON, CLEISTHENES, PERICLES, CLEON, DEMOSTHENES, and EUBULUS.

Ecclēsiazū'sae (*Ekklēsiazousai*, 'women at the assembly'), Greek comedy by *Aristophanes produced probably in 392 BC (the *didascalia has not been preserved). The theme of the play, women taking over the running of the city (from which they were in reality excluded; see DEMOCRACY) and introducing community of property, has something in common with *Lysistrata; both plays depict the women of Athens seizing the political and social initiative under the guidance of a powerful female character, here Praxagora. A remarkable feature of the play, foreshadowing the way drama was to develop in the fourth century, is the greatly reduced role of the chorus, who do not sing a song until the end (see COMEDY, GREEK 5). It is likely that the comic poet was no longer writing his own lyric passages, and these were not now integral to the drama but served simply as entertainment at breaks in the action. There is no *parabasis*, no boisterous attack on politicians, and there is a new style of quiet witty dialogue of the kind found later in New Comedy. The similarity between Praxagora's reforms and Plato's intention for the ruling class in his ideal republic (see REPUBLIC), that they should not possess any private property, has suggested the possibility that Aristophanes is satirizing Plato, but this is unlikely on chronological grounds and in view of the lack of evidence in the text.

As a result of a conspiracy of women led by Praxagora, she and her fellow conspirators, disguised as men, pack the assembly, and carry by a large majority a motion transferring control of the affairs of state from men to women. Praxagora, having been appointed head of the new government, returns to her husband, who has been put to great inconvenience by her having borrowed his clothes. She explains the new social system that is to be introduced: community of property, community of women and children; a fair share in sexual relations for the old and ugly, men and women alike, to be secured by legislation. Then she goes off to the agora to arrange for the reception of all private property and administer the drawing of lots for dinner. A law-abiding citizen hastens to hand in his property; a sceptic waits to see what will come of the new system. The sexual consequences become immediately apparent. A young man arrives to find his girl, but three old women assert their prior rights to him, and one succeeds in carrying him off. The play ends with the chorus hurrying away to a communal dinner (where one of the dishes has a name seven lines long).

Echi'dna, 'snake', in Greek myth, a monster, half woman and half serpent. Her genealogy as found in Hesiod's *Theogony* admits of various interpretations. She was most probably the daughter of Phorcys and Ceto (compare GORGONS) and lived in the Underworld. She bore, by Typhon, Orth(r)us (Geryon's hound), Cerberus, and the Hydra; some would add the Chimaera, and, by Orth(r)us, the *Sphinx and the Nemean lion (see HERACLES, LABOURS OF I).

Echo. 1. Nymph unsuccessfully wooed by the god Pan; in revenge he sent madness upon the local shepherds so that they tore her to pieces and only her voice survived.

2. Nymph who was punished by the goddess Hera for engaging her in talk when the goddess wanted to spy on the amours of Zeus, her husband, with other nymphs. She was deprived of speech except for repeating the last words of her interlocutor. Having fallen in love with *Narcissus and been rejected by him, she wasted away to a voice.

eclogue (Gk. *ekloge*), an occasional poem or passage 'selected' from a larger collection or work; in the plural the word was used to describe any short poems and in that sense was applied to Virgil's pastoral poems (see ECLOGUES below) although having itself no pastoral connotation. Since this title was also given to the later pastoral poems of *Calpurnius and *Nemesianus, it was appropriated by the poets of Charlemagne's court to describe their own pastoral poems written in imitation of Roman models and thence applied to the Latin pastoral poems of the Middle Ages and the Renaissance. Once the identification of eclogue and pastoral had been made, scholars attempted to find an etymological connection. From the ninth century throughout the Middle Ages 'eclogue' was understood by false etymology to mean 'goatish

speech', and in the late sixteenth century when the English poet Edmund Spenser was writing his own pastorals, to mean 'goat-herds' tales' (*aigōn logoi*); but by the middle of that century the scholar J. C. Scaliger in France had already given the correct derivation.

Eclogues (Lat. *Eclogae* or *Būcolica*) of *Virgil, ten unconnected pastoral poems written in imitation of Theocritus, Idylls 1–11, those Idylls which are mainly *bucolic (i.e. pastoral), at the suggestion of *Pollio, Virgil's literary patron at the time. (For the meaning of 'eclogue' see above.) *Eclogues* seems not to have been the title used by Virgil, who apparently called the book (and the poems) *Bucolica*. The ancient authorities state that Virgil began the *Eclogues* when he was 28, i.e. in 42 BC, and that he spent three years in their composition. The second and third Eclogues are generally considered the earliest, written 42–41. However, not all were written between 42 and 39. Eclogue 10 is later, and Eclogue 8 may well be dedicated not to Pollio but to *Octavian and refer to his campaigns of 35 BC. Universal agreement on dates cannot be reached, but Virgil was certainly engaged in the composition of the *Eclogues* from 43 to at least 37, and they probably circulated among the poet's friends before publication. They won immediate popular success; they were recited in the theatre, where their author was publicly acclaimed. Their present arrangement is not chronological but governed by artistic considerations of symmetry and contrast. The odd-numbered poems are dialogues, the even-numbered are narratives for only one speaker. (The following Eclogues are discussed in roughly chronological order.)

In Eclogue 2 the shepherd Corydon laments that his love for the boy Alexis is unrequited. This theme, of 'the passionate shepherd to his love', and much of the detail, are taken from *Theocritus (Idylls 3 and 11). Eclogue 3 is also indebted to Theocritus for its form and characters—an exchange of banter between two rival shepherds, Damoetas and Menalcas, leading to a singing match (see AMOEBOEAN VERSE)—and some of the content: the two pairs of cups, for example, offered as the stake in the contest, recall the description of the cup of Idyll 1. In Eclogue 5, also rich in echoes from Theocritus, two shepherds celebrate in song the death and deification of *Daphnis. The shepherd Menalcas reveals himself as the composer of Eclogues 3 and 4 and the way is thus open to see Daphnis too as an allegorical figure, concealing an identity relevant to Virgil's own times. Since after the assassination of Julius Caesar in 44 BC it had been decreed that divine honours should be paid to him as if he were a god, some scholars, from antiquity onwards, have thought that Daphnis represents Caesar, if not in particular at least in general terms. Eclogue 7, of uncertain date, describes a singing match between Corydon and Thyrsis, two Arcadian herdsmen (the first reference to Arcadia in connection with pastoral poetry); by staging this on the banks of his native river Mincius, Virgil demonstrates the detachment of his pastoral world from any specific landscape. The poem is notable for the grace and beauty of the pastoral songs. Eclogues 1 and 9 are concerned with shepherds whose farms have been confiscated for the settlement of soldiers after the battle of Philippi in 42, when Virgil perhaps lost his own farm. Both poems may have been coloured by the poet's own experiences but they are not autobiographical: his concern is a general one for the sufferings inflicted by war. Eclogue 1 contrasts the good fortune of Tityrus, who made his first journey to Rome under the threat of eviction and was rewarded by being allowed to keep his farm through the intervention of 'a young man', with the enforced exile of Meliboeus who had not left his home. Eclogue 9 depicts a similar situation. Two countrymen fall into conversation on the way to town; Moeris has just been evicted, and Lycidas recalls how Menalcas, a poet, tried to save the district by his poetry but failed.

In Eclogue 4, which owes nothing to any Greek predecessor, the poet looks forward to the birth of a child who will inaugurate a new era. This poem has been more discussed than any other short poem in Latin; throughout the Middle Ages it was accepted as a Messianic prophecy of the birth of the Christ-child given under divine inspiration. St Jerome was exceptional in expressing disbelief. Several contemporary children have also been suggested as the subject: a child of Pollio, an expected child of Mark Antony and Octavia, a child of Octavian and Scribonia, even Octavian himself. The poem can be dated to 40 BC, near the time of the Treaty of *Brundisium. It may well be that the child is for Virgil simply a symbol of the forces which he hoped would bring about the dawn of a new age. Eclogue 8 is dedicated to an unnamed person, usually thought to be Pollio, the campaigns referred to are those of 39; *Servius, however, says that the dedicatee is Octavian, and it has been suggested that the campaigns are his of 35. The Eclogue is modelled mainly on Idylls 1 and 2 of Theocritus, and consists of a singing match between Damon and Alphesiboeus: the first sings a lament for his faithless mistress, the second relates the incantations and magic by which a girl hopes to win back her lover. Eclogue 6 remains obscure to us because we know little of its literary background; it does not have much to do with pastoral and bears little resemblance to Theocritus. It consists of a song sung by *Silenus in which he recounts the creation of the world in the style of *Lucretius as a prelude to some allusively narrated myths. The narrative is interrupted by a description of Virgil's friend and fellow-poet *Gallus accepting his vocation as a poet, in language reminiscent of *Callimachus in the *Aitia*. Eclogue 10, possibly the last to be written, in 37 (but see Eclogue 8 above), has Gallus as the subject, represented as dying of hopeless love for his absent mistress Lycoris. This is the boldest juxtaposition of the Arcadian and the real world that Virgil aspires to, and one that was to have great influence on the style and content of later pastoral poetry (see below).

Virgil extended the character of pastoral in new directions. The *Eclogues* became the models of pastoral poetry and the inspirers of pastoral romance and drama in later ages (for the Idylls of Theocritus were little read until the Renaissance). Unlike Theocritus in general (whose Idyll 7 is the exception) he allowed elements of contemporary reality to intrude into his Arcadian world, using myth and symbolic imagery to allude to recent history. This was an innovation decisive for the later development of pastoral, providing a precedent for the introduction of elaborate *allegory into the genre. Virgil was also the first to use pastoral as a vehicle for moral criticism of the society of his own day. From Petrarch and Boccaccio onwards pastoral became a recognized form for expressing political and ecclesiastical controversy and eulogy.

Virgil created a simple world which is an image of life but distinct from it, and his *Eclogues* derive their haunting quality from the implied relationships between the two. But not many later pastoral poets were content merely to imitate Virgil. *Calpurnius (first century AD) and *Nemesianus (third century) enlarged the scope of this literary mode by using it more enthusiastically than had Virgil as a vehicle for panegyric, and in this they were followed by the eighth- and ninth-century poets of Charlemagne's court. Virgil's *Eclogues* were interpreted as allegory by generations of commentators, and as a result allegory was thought to be an essential feature of the mode. Latin pastoral written in the Middle Ages thus came to have very little to do with shepherds unless they were specifically allegorical (in contrast with an entirely independent vernacular pastoral where the shepherd was the key figure). Petrarch, for example, used the eclogue form to inveigh against the bad government of specific popes and rulers. The richness of English Renaissance pastoral, exemplified by the poets Sir Philip Sidney, Edmund Spenser, Michael Drayton, and Shakespeare, springs from the successful blending of the Virgilian and the vernacular traditions, as well as the poets' own belief in the mode as one that could be taken seriously. But by the eighteenth century pastoral had lost its vitality and degenerated into the witty parodies of John Gay or the saccharine effusions of Alexander Pope's imitators. There was nothing left but for Samuel

Johnson to dismiss it as 'easy, vulgar, and therefore disgusting'.

economic conditions, in Athens and Rome, see ATHENS 4 and ROME 13.

e'cphrăsis, type of rhetorical exercise taking the form of a description of a work of art. The earliest extant collection of ecphrases is the *Eikones* ('Images') of *Philostratus, probably dating to the third century AD.

education

1. Alphabetic writing was introduced into Greece in the second half of the eighth century BC (see ALPHABET and BOOKS AND WRITING 1), but we have no evidence until much later for schools being set up to teach children the rudiments of reading, writing, and counting. Tradition said that the Spartan poet Tyrtaeus, who lived in the mid-seventh century BC, was a schoolmaster, and that the Athenian Solon introduced laws for the regulation of schools in 594 BC.

2. *In Sparta*. At some time in the seventh century BC Sparta adopted a militaristic form of education which subjected Spartan boys to a regime of military training and obedience. From the age of 7 they were entirely under the control of the state, living in barracks away from their families. Priority was given to their physical education so that they might become efficient soldiers, though they were also taught reading, writing, and music (see DANCING). Girls too were educated, especially in gymnastics, as befitted the future mothers of Spartan soldiers. See SPARTA 2 and 6.

3. *In Classical Athens*. It has been thought that the institution of *ostracism, reputedly by Cleisthenes in 508 BC, gave evidence for general literacy at the time, but this may be an overstatement. It is possible that no more than about 10% of male citizens in the fifth century BC were truly literate, though more would have been semi-literate. For evidence of Greek literacy in the writing of Ionian Greek soldiers c.600 BC see EGYPT. The ancient historians refer to schools in existence at the end of the sixth century. Schoolteachers had to be paid by the parents, but the fees were generally low, for teachers as a class were not highly esteemed. Children were generally accompanied to school by a slave known as a *paidagōgos*. Elementary education began at the age of 7 and was in the hands of the *grammatistēs*, who taught reading, writing, arithmetic (with the help of the abacus), and literature, the last consisting of learning by heart and reciting passages from the poets, especially Homer, selected largely for their moral content. (For the early part of the fifth century Athens was still virtually a bookless society; literature was oral and books merely a substitute for recital; see BOOKS AND WRITING 3.) This constituted the minimum of education for Athenian children. The two other main branches of education were *music and physical training. Music played a substantive role in Greek society, and was also considered to have an educative value. Not only was it the case that every educated many expected to be able to play the lyre and sing, skills which he learned from the *kitharistēs* ('lyre-player'), but also, that certain styles ('modes') of music were believed to foster moral virtue. Physical education, directed partly towards military prowess but also cultivated for its own sake, was taught by the *paidotribēs* ('trainer'; see GYMNASIUM and PALAESTRA). To judge from vase-paintings, girls too might sometimes take part, but to a lesser extent. (By the end of the fourth century BC it was established that young men of 18 should spend two years in physical and military training; see EPHEBOI.)

For education in specialist subjects like medicine and *rhetoric the pupil had to seek out an expert in the field who was prepared to teach him. In fifth-century Athens there was no organized form of higher education, and this in part accounts for the success of the *sophists. In the latter half of the fifth century these itinerant teachers went from city to city charging high fees for giving instruction in a variety of subjects, including the new geographical and scientific topics which the recent expansion in knowledge had thrown up, and which had had no place in earlier education. One of these sophists, the polymath *Hippias, listed together in his educational programme arithmetic, geometry, music (a mathematical subject in its theoretical aspect), and astronomy. This combination of sciences was taken up by Plato and subsequently had a long and varied history until *Boethius gave it the name *quadrivium* nearly a thousand years later (see 4 and 6 below). Most sophists, however, concentrated upon literature and especially on language, with the aim of making the pupil expert at public speaking. Thus they fulfilled their claim to teach men how to succeed in political life by equipping them with the skill most needed by politicians in a fully democratic state where power lay with the assembly (see ECCLESIA). Rhetorical teaching was always the area in Greek education where pedagogic skill was most highly developed.

In the fourth century BC schools of higher education came into existence, notably *Isocrates' school of philosophy and rhetoric at Athens founded in the late 390s, Plato's *Academy at Athens founded probably in 385, and Aristotle's *Lyceum outside Athens founded in 335. Isocrates recognized that both philosophy and rhetoric were needed in addition to the other subjects taught by the sophists, but it was rhetoric he judged to be of supreme importance, and it was his educational programme which ultimately became the norm throughout the ancient world. Plato, at least in his early days, was strongly opposed to rhetoric and literature on moral grounds, and though he later allowed rhetoric to be taught in the Academy his curriculum was mainly scientific, mathematical, and philosophical. Most philosophical instruction at the Academy was by Plato's favoured dialectical method (see DIALECTIC), and study of the exact sciences was the necessary propaedeutic to dialectic. According to a later commentator he had on his door the inscription *ageōmetrētos mēdeis eisitō*, 'without knowledge of geometry no one may enter'. Plato aimed to produce true politicians, men trained by dialectic to have philosophical insight who could therefore be just legislators and advisers to those in positions of power. Aristotle's Lyceum, by contrast, was more in the nature of a research institute.

4. *Hellenistic education.* The pattern established somewhat incompletely by Athens was formalized in the Hellenistic period. Elementary education remained unchanged, but now a scheme of secondary education emerged. Most cities had at least one gymnasium, conjoined with a public library, where literature, philosophy, and music were commonly taught as well as physical training. The gymnasium was supervised by a *gymnasiarchos*, a state official elected for a year only. The curriculum now expanded to include literature, mathematics, and science as well, thus forming the ancient ideal of 'general education', the *enkyklios paideia* (the origin of English 'encyclopaedia'), a system ultimately derived through Isocrates from Hippias and eventually becoming the Seven Liberal Arts of the Middle Ages (see 5 and 6 below). Some specialist education in schools was possible even after the age of 18, but for serious study many youths who could afford it went to the great centres of learning—Alexandria, of course, then Athens, Pergamum, and Rhodes for philosophy and rhetoric, and Cos, Pergamum, and Ephesus for medicine. This pattern of education remained largely unchanged until medieval times. See also SOPHISTIC, SECOND.

5. *Roman education.* In early republican times boys' education consisted of parental training and, in noble families, political apprenticeship. A father taught his son to read, write, and use weapons, as well as grounding him in manners, morals, religion, and knowledge of the law. The son accompanied his father to all religious ceremonies and social occasions and even, if his father was a member, to the senate. At the age of 16 a youth of noble family was attached to some prominent figure to gain political experience, and from 17 spent the campaigning season with the army (see CURSUS HONORUM). In some families this kind of education persisted into imperial times. However, from very early times education had a formal aspect as well. Livy attests the existence of elementary schools at an early date, and in the third and second centuries BC under the influence of Greece, education could be had from schools, developed on the Greek models, or from tutors. The teachers

were often slaves or freedmen, frequently Greeks. The *litterator* or *ludi magister* taught reading, writing, and arithmetic to both boys and girls aged about 7 to 11. Girls in Rome had a greater share in education than in Greece. The employment of a *paidagogos* was adopted in imitation of Greek practice (see 3 above) and he sometimes taught his pupil Greek. Secondary education from 12 to 15 was in the hands of the *grammaticus* who taught literary subjects in Latin and Greek both as a general education and as a preparation for rhetoric. Towards the end of the first century BC the works of Virgil and other contemporary poets were introduced as suitable subjects for study.

Higher education for pupils over the age of 16 existed in Rome from the second century BC when Greek rhetoric was first taught. The study of Latin rhetoric began early in the first century BC with the foundation of a Latin rhetorical school. Thus two parallel systems of rhetorical education existed, one Greek and one Latin, and education was predominantly literary though with the aim of inculcating moral principles. Conservative Romans like Cato the Censor looked with disfavour upon the introduction under Greek influence of, in their view, less morally improving subjects such as music and dancing (see PHILOSOPHY 2, CRATES (4), PAULLUS). The Romans also paid far less attention than the Greeks to physical education, except when it was directly aimed at training future soldiers. When under the empire the practice of political oratory declined with the loss of political freedom, the rhetorical schools prepared boys for the career of advocate, again along Greek lines, or for administration in the public services. The themes that the boys expounded in their public declamations (see DECLAMATIONES) have been criticized for their unreality and irrelevance to life, but they encouraged ingenuity and a facility of mind and speech which were valuable assets to an advocate. *Quintilian writes of the practical and moral value of a general education, which he calls *encyclios paedia* in imitation of the Greek term (see 4 above), as a preliminary to specialized study. Pupils who wished to pursue their studies further usually went to Athens or Rhodes. Julius Caesar, Cicero, Octavian, and Horace all studied abroad. State interest in education of a certain kind showed itself in Rome under the republic by the expulsion of teachers from time to time, or on the other hand by measures aimed at attracting them. The emperors and other benefactors sometimes founded professorships and public municipal schools. However, the Roman state never instituted special officials to supervise schools comparable with the Hellenistic gymnasiarchs.

6. Education in both Greece and Rome—the Greek tradition being borrowed and continued by the Romans—was based largely on the

humane study of traditional literature and of the two languages in which it was written, with the aim, constant from beginning to end, of producing informed, cultivated, able, and effective public speakers. The *quadrivium* of Hippias (see 3 and 4 above) preceded by the *trivium* of grammar, rhetoric, and dialectic, derived from the sophists and Isocrates, formed the curriculum of the Middle Ages, designated the *Seven Liberal Arts by *Martianus Capella.

Ēge'ria, in Roman religion, Italian water-nymph, to whom pregnant women sacrificed to secure easy delivery. She was worshipped in association with the goddess *Diana at Aricia in Latium, and with the *Camenae at a grove outside the gate known as the Porta Capena at Rome, where from a spring the *Vestal Virgins drew water daily. She was said to be the consort and adviser of *Numa Pompilius, legendary second king of Rome (715–673 BC), whom she used to meet by night at the Porta Capena and instruct in statesmanship and religion. At his death she was said to have moved to Africa.

Egypt (Gk. Aigyptos, Lat. Aegyptus). For much of its history Egypt was divided into Lower and Upper Egypt, the former being the delta region, the latter the area south from the delta to Syenē (Aswan). Upper Egypt itself was often divided, the area north from Syene to Hermopolis Magna (El Ashmunein) being known as the Thebaid, and that north from Hermopolis to the delta as Middle Egypt. Among the most ancient and important cities of Egypt was Thebes, the capital of Upper Egypt; the modern villages of Karnak and Luxor are on part of its site. It was a city of impressive size; according to Homer (*Iliad* 9. 381) it had 100 gates and 200 war-chariots for each gate. Another ancient city was Memphis, near modern Cairo, the first capital of the united kingdom of Upper and Lower Egypt. It declined in importance after the foundation of Alexandria (see below). Syenē, the southern frontier town of Upper Egypt a little north of the first cataract, was believed in antiquity to be situated on the Tropic of Cancer, where the sun is vertically overhead at the summer solstice (see ERATOSTHENES).

Archaeological evidence testifies to the existence of trading relations between Egypt and the Greek world in Mycenaean times (second half of the second millennium BC). It was in this period that Greece learned ivory-working from Egypt, for example. Greek myth attests closer ties: the Egyptian *Danaus became king of Argos in Greece and the eponymous ancestor of the *Danaans. Literary evidence becomes available in the eighth and seventh centuries. Homer tells the story of Menelaus' visit to Egypt (*Odyssey* 4. 351). Egypt was conquered by Assyria in the eighth century but the conquerors soon withdrew, leaving civil war in their wake. With the

more adventurous attitude to seafaring shown by the Greeks of the seventh century and the establishment of Greek settlements on the North African coast, it was not long before they secured a foothold in Egypt. Herodotus (2. 152) tells us that Carians and Ionian Greeks entered Egypt in the sixties of the seventh century. Psammetichus I (664–610 BC), who was at this time struggling to reunite Egypt, enlisted their aid in setting himself up as sole ruler, and he thereby established the twenty-sixth (Saïte) dynasty. It was his son Necho who, when pharaoh, began the canal from the Nile to the Red Sea which was completed, or reopened, by Ptolemy II Philadelphus (b. 308 BC). It was at Necho's bidding also that Phoenician sailors circumnavigated Africa from the Red Sea south to the Cape, and back by way of Gibraltar. Their report of observing the sun in the north, convincing enough to a modern reader, was disbelieved by Herodotus (4. 42). For a hundred years or more after Psammetichus the pharaohs placed great reliance on their Ionian mercenaries. (Nor were they the only rulers to appreciate the superiority of Greek *hoplites: according to the poet Alcaeus, his brother won a sword of honour for his services to Nebuchadnezzar of Babylon.) Seven Ionian Greek soldiers employed in Egyptian service *c.*600 BC have left their names and the extent of their passage up the Nile, inscribed in Greek writing, on the left leg of the monumental statue of Rameses II at Abu Simbel. At about the same period some Ionian Greek cities, together with Aegina and the Aeolian city of Mitylene, developed *Naucratis on the Canopic mouth of the Nile as a trading centre. Psammetichus was reputed to have been sufficiently philhellenic to have his sons taught Greek. The pharaoh Amasis (570–526), friend of the Greek tyrant Polycrates of Samos, used Greeks as a bodyguard in preference to Egyptians; he also made generous gifts to Greek shrines, and, although Greeks by no means had the freedom of the country, gave concessions to the Greek traders at Naucratis, perhaps wishing to secure Greek aid against the threat of Persia. Amasis died shortly before the Persian conquest of Egypt by *Cambyses in 525 BC, which brought to a close the Saïte dynasty and with it Egyptian independence.

The Greeks were profoundly impressed by the great antiquity of Egypt, as well as by its religion, monuments, and customs. They also thought that Egypt above all other lands was the repository of ancient wisdom. The men of Elis even sent a delegation to ask advice about the best way of administering the Olympian games. Many Greeks proverbial for their wisdom were supposed to have visited Egypt in the seventh and sixth centuries, and some are known to have done so. Solon is said to have visited the pharaoh Amasis, Thales to have invented geometry after studying 'land-measurements' in

Egypt; Hecataeus did in fact travel extensively in Asia and Persia. In 462 a large Athenian fleet assisted in an Egyptian revolt, under the Libyan Inaros, one of several against Persian rule. This was put down, with the almost total destruction of the fleet and considerable damage to a relieving squadron, in 454 (see DELIAN LEAGUE). Soon after, the historian Herodotus visited Egypt, and devoted the second book of his history to giving an account of the country; his evidence suggests that in the second half of the century Greeks were widely tolerated in Egypt, in contrast with the reign of Amasis, when they were restricted to Naucratis. Hence, when the hated Persian monarchy was finally overthrown in 332 BC by Alexander the Great (a Macedonian Greek), the change was not wholly resented. The Macedonian kings who thereafter ruled Egypt were known as the *Ptolemies (and Egypt under their rule as Ptolemaic Egypt). In their time the city of *Alexandria which Alexander founded became a centre of Greek culture. The Greeks were at first the dominant race there, and the native Egyptians were not regarded as full citizens. Later the Greek element became Egyptianized; the official language was Greek, but Egyptian persisted, to emerge in the Christian period as Coptic. (See also ROSETTA STONE.) The Greek gods were known only as names for local deities (see HARPOCRATES).

Greek rule was in turn brought to an end by the Roman annexation of Egypt in 30 BC (after the battle of *Actium) when the country became a province of peculiar status, being governed by the emperor through an equestrian prefect rather than, as in all other important provinces, a senatorial legate (see PROVINCES). This indicates the value Augustus put upon the province and his appreciation of the temptation it presented to a governor ambitious for wealth and independence. No senator was allowed to set foot in Egypt without the emperor's permission. The first prefect was the soldier-poet *Gallus who for reasons which remain obscure was recalled in disgrace by Augustus and committed suicide. Egypt with the rest of North Africa was the granary of Rome, eclipsing Sicily in that respect. It had a monopoly in the production of papyri (see BOOKS AND WRITING 1), and was the starting-point for the Indian trade. A general survey of the Nile valley was made and to this we owe the accurate description of it that appears in book 17 of Strabo's Geography (first century AD). The only serious revolt against Roman rule lasted from AD 162 to 166 before being finally put down. In the reign of Caracalla (early third century) Egyptians entered the Roman senate for the first time, and the worship of the Egyptian goddess *Isis was publicly sanctioned at Rome. Nevertheless, the province was never Romanized, and Greek and native Egyptian elements were united in opposition to Roman

government. The Roman era came to an end with the Arab conquest of Egypt in 640.

Ēhoē'ae or **Ēhoīai,** see CATALOGUE OF WOMEN.

Eido'thea (or Īdothea), in Greek myth, nymph, daughter of *Proteus, a sea-god. In Homer's *Odyssey* Menelaus tells Telemachus that, on the way home from Troy, when his ship was becalmed off the coast of Egypt and he nearly starved, Eidothea showed him how he might secure her father, despite his attempts to escape by assuming different forms, and force him to reveal the cause of the misfortune.

Eileithyī'a(e), the Greek goddess of childbirth, sometimes referred to in the plural (compare PAN and SILENUS); she was a lesser deity, not one of the twelve Olympian gods (see GODS 1). Her name may mean the 'coming', i.e. of the child. Hesiod makes her the daughter of Zeus and Hera, who was herself a goddess of birth and therefore is sometimes given this title. Perhaps a Minoan mother-goddess in origin, her cavern-sanctuary in Crete at Amnisos, mentioned by Homer and appearing on the *Linear B tablets from Cnossus, has been excavated and shows continuous cult from neolithic to classical times. She has no myth of her own but appears in various stories of birth, often in association with Artemis and Hera. The Romans identified her with Lucina (see JUNO).

Eisagō'gē, see PORPHYRY.

e'kphrasis, see ECPHRASIS.

Elaga'balus (incorrectly, Heliogabalus), Roman emperor AD 218–22. His resemblance to the emperor *Caracalla (to whom he was related) caused him to be proclaimed the latter's successor when he was only fifteen, in the belief that he was Caracalla's bastard son. He was a Syrian from Emesa, and he took the name of the Syro-Phoenician sun-god, worshipped in the form of a black conical stone, whose priest he was and to whom he was fanatically devoted. The stone was brought to Rome and passing through streets strewn with gold-dust was installed in a magnificent temple on the Palatine. Elagabalus' ludicrous and obscene excesses outraged the army, and he was murdered by the *praetorian guard. He was said to have been the first man at Rome to wear garments of pure silk.

Elatē'a (Elateia), in Greece, a city of Phocis, three days' march from Athens, of great strategic importance in that it commanded the passes into southern Greece from the north. Philip II of Macedon occupied it in 339 BC, thereby threatening Boeotia and Athens. In the ensuing panic at Athens, described in his *De corona*, Demosthenes proposed and brought about an alliance between Athens and her old enemy Thebes; the two fought together and were defeated by Philip at the battle of Chaeronea in the following year (see ATHENS 2 (v)).

E'lea (Lat. Velia), Greek colony on the west coast of south Italy founded by Phocaea (in Ionia) c.540 BC, when the whole population left the city at the threat of Persian conquest (the story is told by Herodotus, 1. 164). It is chiefly famed for its school of philosophers (see below).

Eleatic School, Greek philosophical school of thought originated by *Parmenides of Elea at the end of the sixth century BC. Parmenides believed that 'what exists', the essential matter of the universe, is single, indivisible, and unchanging, and this monistic theory was subsequently defended by *Zeno and by Melissus, who lived in the mid-fifth century BC and was the last important member of the school.

Ele'ctra. **1.** In Greek myth, daughter of *Agamemnon and Clytemnestra. She does not appear in epic, but in the tragedies of Aeschylus (especially *Choephoroe*; see ORESTEIA), Sophocles, and Euripides she becomes a heroic figure in the story of the House of Atreus (see PELOPS), represented as implacably hostile to Clytemnestra and her lover Aegisthus, faithful to her father's memory and devoted to her brother Orestes, whom she supports in the vengeance he takes on Clytemnestra and Aegisthus. She eventually marries Orestes' faithful friend Pylades. Her supposed tomb was shown in later times at Mycenae.

2. In Greek myth, daughter of the Titan *Atlas, mother by Zeus of Dardanus (see TROY).

Electra. **1.** Greek tragedy by *Sophocles, of uncertain date but very probably produced between 418 and 410 BC. It is disputed whether it preceded or followed Euripides' *Electra* (see below) of perhaps 417. For the myth on which it is based see PELOPS.

Orestes arrives at Mycenae, accompanied by Pylades and an old man, Orestes' childhood attendant (*paidagogos*), to avenge the murder of his father Agamemnon, in obedience to the *Delphic Oracle. The old man is sent on to tell Orestes' mother Clytemnestra that Orestes has been killed in a chariot race, and the others prepare to follow in disguise, taking with them an urn supposed to contain his ashes. Meanwhile Clytemnestra, having had a dream of ill omen, has sent her daughter Chrysothemis to pour libations on the tomb of Agamemnon, the husband she has killed. Her other daughter Electra, who is living a wretched life, bullied by Clytemnestra and Aegisthus on account of her constant mourning for her murdered father, meets Chrysothemis and persuades her to substitute for the polluted offerings of Agamemnon's widow and murderer other more personal offerings from his daughters. Clytemnestra appears and abuses Electra, who retorts in kind, but they are interrupted by the arrival of the old man, and learn, the former with scarcely concealed joy, of the death of Orestes. Electra, on the other hand, is reduced to despair. The announcement of Chrysothemis that she has found a lock of hair on Agamemnon's tomb which is clearly Orestes' seems only to mock her sorrow. She determines, now that the expected help of Orestes is lost, to kill Clytemnestra and Aegisthus herself. The more prudent Chrysothemis refuses to share in the murder. Orestes and Pylades now approach, and Orestes tells Electra by degrees who he is. He and Pylades enter the palace, and the cries of Clytemnestra are heard as they kill her. Aegisthus then approaches. He is lured into the palace to see what he supposes to be the corpse of Orestes, but finds to be that of Clytemnestra. He is driven at the point of a sword to the room where Agamemnon met his death and there killed. The chorus of Mycenaean women rejoice at the final passing of the curse which has rested on the house of Atreus.

The greater complexity of plot and situation open to the Greek tragedians after the introduction, by Sophocles, of the third actor (see TRAGEDY 2) is very apparent in *Electra*. One might note the three-cornered scene where the messenger's false narrative about the death of Orestes has very different effects upon Clytemnestra and Electra, and the action preceding the recognition-scene where Sophocles is able to portray Electra faced by a rapid progression of people and events. It has seemed to many readers that Sophocles has chosen to ignore the moral issue, which is so important to Aeschylus and Euripides, as to how far the matricide is justified.

2. Greek tragedy by Euripides, often dated to 413 BC because of a supposed reference to the Sicilian Expedition, but perhaps a few years earlier (compare the date of Sophocles' *Electra*, above).

The theme of the play is the same as that of (1) above, but there are differences of detail. Aegisthus has married Electra to a poor farmer so that no son of hers may aspire to lay claim to the kingdom of Mycenae. This farmer, though poor, is of noble descent and high character, and refuses to consummate the marriage, considering that her marriage to him is beneath her dignity. Electra takes her share with Orestes in the murder of their mother, an act of justice but morally horrifying. The play is an interesting character study of the exiled Orestes and the haunted Electra. By making the latter the wife of a poor farmer, and by dwelling upon her physical privations and mental suffering, Euripides has brought the myth down from the heroic plane and placed the matricide in a setting of everyday life, where the characters bear the marks of human experience.

Plutarch relates that after the Spartan capture

of Athens in 404 BC, the Spartan admiral Lysander was moved to spare the city by hearing a Phocian singing the opening chorus of *Electra*.

Ele'ctryon, in Greek myth, son of Andromeda and *Perseus, whom he succeeded as king of Mycenae. He became the father of Alcmena (later the mother of Heracles), and six sons. He was accidentally killed by his nephew Amphitryon to whom he had betrothed his daughter. By a Phrygian woman Midea he was the father of a seventh son Licymnius.

elegī'ac, see METRE, GREEK 4.

elegy, in Greek and Latin literature, any poem written in elegiacs (also called elegiac couplets), that is, in alternate lines of hexameter and pentameter (see METRE, GREEK 4). The ultimate derivation of the name is uncertain, but it was perhaps connected with a word for 'flute', an instrument which seems originally to have accompanied its recitation (compare LYRIC). In antiquity the elegiac metre was considered to be primarily the metre of lament, but it was used for a variety of poems, and the earliest lines we possess, written in Greece at the end of the eighth century BC, bear no resemblance to lament. Elegiac poetry was the medium for expressing personal sentiments (as distinct from narrative): for description, for exhortation to war or to virtue, for reflection on a variety of subjects, serious and frivolous, for epitaphs and laments, and for love-poems. The use of elegiacs for inscriptions to commemorate the dead seems to have become popular in the middle of the sixth century BC and persisted throughout antiquity; those attributed to Simonides are the most famous (see EPIGRAM). Among the principal early elegiac poets of Greece were Tyrtaeus, Mimnermus, Solon, Phocylides, Callinus, and Theognis. Love poems in elegiacs are said to have been first written by Mimnermus; they may have been a development from the cheerful symposiac elegies such as were written by Archilochus. The Hellenistic poets in particular used this form for love poetry, and also introduced a number of metrical refinements.

The history of Latin elegy begins in the first century BC when it was developed at Rome under Greek influence chiefly as a medium for love poetry. The Romans gave elegy a new direction by using it for a cycle of short poems centred on the poet's relationship with a single mistress. Almost every individual feature of Latin love-elegy is derived from Greek models, but the whole effect is of something completely original. The principal Roman poets were Cornelius Gallus, whose work has not survived, Catullus, Tibullus, Propertius, and Ovid. Ovid also refined the already strict metrical rules for Latin elegiac still further, and extended the range of subjects to be treated in this metre.

After Ovid, the metre was used chiefly for short occasional poems and for epigrams. Martial is the most famous practitioner of the epigram and he sometimes rivals Ovid in metrical virtuosity.

Only in comparatively modern times, since the sixteenth century, has the term elegy come to denote specifically a poem of lament for an individual or a poem of serious, meditative tone. Several famous elegies in English literature are written using the conventions of pastoral (see BUCOLIC), one of the earliest being Edmund Spenser's *Astrophil* (1586) on the death of Sir Philip Sidney. The origin of the pastoral lament or elegy is to be found in *Theocritus' first Idyll; this poem, however, being written in hexameters and not in elegiacs, is not, in classical terms, an elegy.

ele'nchus, 'cross-examining', a term used to describe *Socrates' method of philosophical inquiry. In his search for knowledge it was his practice to ask for definitions ('what is courage? goodness?' etc.) on the grounds that if one could define or give an account of e.g. goodness one would have clearer ideas about the good life and a basis for further investigation. The answerer's definition was then submitted to rigorous testing by means of question and answer (*elenchus*). This, however, turned out to be a negative process: the answerer's definition was found to be inconsistent with his other assumptions, and was thus revealed as defective or inadequate, while no satisfactory alternative could be arrived at to take its place. The answerer was left in a state of helplessness, *aporia*, but his gain was that he now knew the extent of his ignorance. The method was further developed by Plato, who uses the term *dialectic to describe it.

elephants. Mycenaean Greeks knew about ivory and how to work it, but it was not until the time of Alexander the Great (late fourth century BC) that precise knowledge of the elephant reached the West. Aristotle described one with an accuracy that could only have come from dissection. The ancients knew of two species, the Indian and the African, and of the two sub-species of African elephant it was the smaller kind, the forest elephant, smaller even than the Indian, that was used for war by the Ptolemies and the Carthaginians. Alexander the Great was the first European general to encounter elephants in serious battle when he defeated the Punjab rajah Porus and his (reputed) 200 elephants in 326 BC. Elephants could be a decisive factor on the battlefield by the first shock of their appearance, though defenders soon learned how to ham-string them (Alexander's method) or confront them with ditches or planks of upturned nails. Alexander did not employ elephants himself for battle, but soon after his death his officers were using them to perform useful feats of strength, and it is certainly as a consequence of Alexander's Indian invasion that his successors, the Ptolemies and the Seleucids, used war elephants to the full. Their disadvantages for Mediterranean military service are considerable: they dislike winter cold and are happiest in warm mud; each consumes one hundred pounds of hay and fifty gallons of water a day; wherever they are, males are difficult to control when in musth; and they cannot distinguish between friend and foe. The Romans first encountered elephants, which they called 'Lucanian oxen', when they were defeated by Pyrrhus and his twenty Indian elephants in Lucania in 280 BC, during his invasion of Italy. When the Seleucids gained control of the sources from which Indian elephants came, the Ptolemies, looking elsewhere, created elephant-hunting grounds by the African shore of the Red Sea. The Carthaginians, perhaps like Pyrrhus influenced by the Ptolemies, had built up a force of African war-elephants before 264 BC, capturing them from the foothills of the Atlas mountains. These contributed to their victory over Regulus. Hannibal started with twenty-one elephants when he set out to cross the Alps; many perished, but enough remained to be useful to him at the battle of the river Trebia in 218 BC. By the time of the battle of Zama in 202 the Romans had learnt how to open ranks to allow them to pass through without inflicting damage. The Romans themselves used elephants for war rather rarely, at Pydna in 168, Numantia in 153, and Thapsus in 46 BC. Elephants became instead a symbol of grand pretension—elephants drew Pompey's chariot in a triumphal procession—or a show in the circus. Elephants seemed to the Romans to possess intelligence and many human qualities. Cicero comments in a letter how the spectators were moved by pity for those presented by Pompey at the lavish games inaugurating his new theatre. The Elder Pliny has a story of an elephant which could write a sentence in Greek. In the mid-fourth century AD, when Persian power revived, elephants were included among their armaments of war. With the fall of the Roman empire the elephant largely vanished from Europe.

Eleusi'nian mysteries, see MYSTERIES.

Eleusi'nion, at Athens, a temple below the Acropolis, east of the Panathenaic Way, dedicated to the goddesses Demeter and Persephonē, dating from the time when Eleusis was finally amalgamated with Athens, perhaps at the end of the seventh century BC. Here were kept the sacred objects of the Eleusinian *mysteries.

Eleu'sis, the most important town of Attica after Athens and Piraeus, situated about 20 km. (12 miles) north-west of Athens near the sea. It remained independent of Athens till perhaps as late as the seventh century BC. The myth of *Erechtheus may reflect the Athenian conquest. According to ancient tradition it was at Eleusis that Persephone, who had been snatched away by Hades, god of the Underworld, was restored to her mother *Demeter. Eleusis owed its fame to the *mysteries traditionally instituted by Demeter herself and celebrated primarily in her honour. These attracted visitors from all over Greece and were much venerated. There is evidence that a cult was practised on that site in Mycenaean times; the magnificent *telestērion* ('hall of initiation') dates from the time of Peisistratus in the sixth century BC. There was much building in Roman times, including the great Propylaea ('gateway') finished by Marcus Aurelius (emperor AD 161–80). The sanctuary ceased to function after being sacked by Alaric and the Visigoths in AD 395. See also ELEUSINION.

Eleuthe'ria, a festival instituted at Plataea after the victory over the Persians in 479 BC, and celebrated every five years (see PERSIAN WARS).

Eleven, the (*hoi hendeka*), at Athens, magistrates responsible for the care and management of the public prison, and for seeing that sentences, including the judicial torture of slaves, were carried out. See ATHENS 3.

Elgin Marbles, see PARTHENON.

ēliai'a, see HELIAIA.

Ēlis, Greek state in the north-west Peloponnese, comprising a rich plain in which Olympia is situated; it was famed for horse-breeding. From 471 BC the Eleans presided formally over the Olympian festival and games, a right disputed from time to time in previous centuries with their small neighbour *Pisa (see also OLYMPIA). There is evidence for occupation at Elis since Mycenaean times. Elis was an early and loyal ally of Sparta until 420 BC when, upon Sparta's challenging the independence of her small neighbour Lepreum, she changed allegiance to Athens. For this Sparta severely punished her in 399. Sparta gave the Athenian historian *Xenophon an estate near Olympia to live in during his exile, but Elis in defiance of Sparta obliged him to leave in 371.

elision, in Greek and Latin speech and writing, the 'thrusting out', i.e. dropping, of a vowel at the end of one word before a vowel at the beginning of the next; in Greek this feature was confined mainly to the short final vowels a, e, o, and sometimes i; in Latin it extended to the dropping of long final vowels also, and of syllables ending in m; early Latin writers sometimes elided final s. In Latin poetry the elided vowels are printed but dropped in scansion (compare CRASIS).

Eli'ssa, name by which *Dido, queen of

Carthage, was said to have been known at Tyre, where her father was king.

Elpē'nōr, in Homer's *Odyssey*, companion of Odysseus who fell from the roof of Circē's dwelling and was killed and left unburied. His is the first shade Odysseus meets in the Underworld; Odysseus grants his request to be buried and to have his oar planted on his grave.

Elpinī'cē, daughter of the younger *Miltiadēs and wife of *Callias.

Ely'sium, also known as the *Islands of the Blest (*makarōn nēsoi*), thought of by Homer and Hesiod as a place in the far West beyond the stream of *Ocean where certain favoured heroes are sent by the gods instead of dying, to enjoy a full and pleasant after-life. It has been suspected that this Elysium, at variance with the idea that all the dead dwell together in the Underworld (or *Hades), is a survival from Minoan religion (see RELIGION, GREEK I). It seems probable that the attainment of Elysium was promised to the initiates of the *mysteries of Eleusis. In later myth Elysium was represented as part of the Underworld ruled over by *Rhadamanthys (and Cronus). That is where Virgil locates it in *Aeneid* 6; for him as for Plato it is the place where the good soul temporarily rests before being reborn.

Ema'thion, see EOS.

E'mathus, in Greek myth, son of Macedon and brother of Pierus, from whom Emathia (the Homeric name for Macedonia) was believed to have derived its name. The daughters of Pierus, the Pierides, are sometimes called Emathides. 'The Emathian' is Alexander the Great.

Embassy, On the False (*De falsa lēgātiōne*), political speech by Demosthenes. See DEMOSTHENES (2) 4.

embo'lima, see TRAGEDY 3 (iv).

emmelei'a, see TRAGEDY 2.

Empe'doclēs (*c*.495–*c*.435 BC), Greek Presocratic philosopher of versatile genius, with the reputation of being a statesman, healer, philosopher, mystic, and wonder-worker. After his death he became the subject of a number of apocryphal biographical stories. He was born of aristocratic family at Acragas in Sicily and after the fall of the tyranny *c*.468 BC was offered but declined the kingship, being an ardent democrat. Political upheavals led to his exile, and he travelled to south Italy and Greece. He was an accomplished orator, credited by Aristotle with the invention of rhetoric; *Gorgias is said to have been his pupil. He also won fame as a scientist and healer; Galen called him the founder of the Sicilian school of medicine. However, it is as a thinker of far-reaching importance that he is chiefly known, and like

*Parmenides, by whom he was strongly influenced, he expressed his thought in hexameter verse, much read until late antiquity. Only some 450 lines survive, in quotation in other authors, but this is enough to give a fairly clear idea of Empedocles' meaning. According to *Diogenes Laertius he composed two poems, *On Nature*, addressed to a friend, and *Purifications* (*Katharmoi*), addressed to the people of Acragas. In these Empedocles attempts to explain the world on scientific and rational grounds.

He accepts the thesis of the *Eleatic School that 'what exists' cannot come into being nor pass away, but he denies that it is a unity and unchanging. There are four eternally persisting elements from which all other things are formed, earth, air, fire, and water, and the rearrangement of these elements gives rise to change; Empedocles uses as analogy the painter's depiction of a great variety of objects by mixing a limited number of pigments. He introduces two further principles, Love and Strife, also eternal, but having no perceptible qualities of their own and apprehended only by their effect on the other four. The universe is under their alternate domination: Love maintains a properly balanced mixture in things, but Strife dissolves this mixture into constituents that war against each other; the universe is recurringly brought together and then fragmented in a cosmic cycle. Strife, Empedocles believed, was increasing at the time in which he lived. Part of his work is devoted to cosmogony, the gradual development of the present world, the evolution of animals, and many topics in biology. He relies on metaphor and analogy for giving clarity to his explanations; one of his most vivid passages illustrates the nature of respiration with the analogy of a girl playing with a *clepsydra by putting her hand over the mouth of the vessel, thus preventing the water from dripping through the holes in the bottom. In the fragments which have been attributed to *Purifications* Empedocles gives an account of the primal sin and collective fall of mankind (though not apparently precluding the particular fall of the individual soul) from a state of innocence when Love ruled the universe. The sin appears to be that of bloodshed and meateating. The fallen soul, an exiled god, *daimōn*, is punished by successive incarnations in animal (and even vegetable) forms; it feels a homeless exile until it regains its original purity and rises up the scale of lives to the highest rung, 'prophets, bards, doctors, and princes'— Empedocles himself has been thought to be all these—and thence escapes back to its original incorporeal state of divinity. In some surviving lines Empedocles declares that he has attained this state and is no longer a mortal but an immortal god. Much of this is clearly close to Pythagorean teaching (see PYTHAGORAS) and the Orphic poems (see ORPHEUS).

The Roman poet *Lucretius was inspired by Empedocles to compose his own scientific poem, *De rerum natura*, in which he praises his predecessor for 'the songs of his godlike heart'. Empedocles' death is variously recounted, most notably in the story that he committed suicide by throwing himself into the crater of Mount Etna.

emperors, empire, Roman, see PRINCIPATE, BYZANTINE AGE, and FALL OF ROME.

empire, Athenian, see DELIAN LEAGUE.

Ence'ladus, see GIANTS.

enco'mium (*enkōmion*), Greek choral hymn (see LYRIC POETRY 1) in celebration not of a god but of a man. By derivation the word means a song 'at the *kōmos*', in this context the revel at the end of a banquet, and so suggests a eulogy of the host and guests. The word came to cover eulogies in general; the first poems of a generally eulogistic nature so described were those of Simonides. The *epinikion* or epinician ode, a triumphal ode for victory in the Games, and the *thrēnos*, a funeral dirge, are developments of the encomium.

Endy'mion, in Greek myth, a beautiful young man, famed for his eternal sleep on Mount Latmus in Caria. He was the son of Calycē, daughter of Aeolus, and Āethlius or Zeus, and was king of Elis. He was especially loved by *Selenē (Moon); according to one tradition he came from Elis to Mount Latmus and while he was sleeping in a cave Selene came down to him. His eternal sleep is variously explained, one version being that Selene sent it upon him, wishing to embrace him unobserved. One of his children (not by Selene) was Aetōlus, the eponymous hero of Aetolia.

E'nneads, see PLOTINUS.

enneakrou'nos ('nine springs'), fountain-house at Athens built by the tyrant *Peisistratus.

E'nnius, Quintus (239–169 BC), one of the greatest and most versatile of the early Roman poets, born at Rudiae in Calabria; since that was an area of Italy partly *Oscan and partly Greek, Ennius spoke Oscan and Greek, as well as Latin. He seems to have been in Sardinia (perhaps as a soldier) when he met Cato the Elder, quaestor there in 204, who took him to Rome. There he won a reputation in the 190s for writing tragedy. In 189 he accompanied M. Fulvius Nobilior on his Aetolian campaign (probably in order to celebrate his patron's achievements) and on his return had Roman citizenship conferred on him. He lived in modest style on the Aventine, teaching and writing. Anecdotes told by Cicero connect him with *Scipio Africanus, *Scipio Nasica, and Ser. Sulpicius Galba. It was at this time that he began the *Annales* ('annals'), which, with his tragedies,

constituted his principal work. He died during the *ludi Apollinares* of 169, at which his latest tragedy, *Thyestes*, was being performed. His heir was his nephew, the poet Pacuvius. Ennius also wrote comedies, of which only four separate lines survive; *fabulae *praetextae*; *saturae* (see SATIRE), four books of mixed verse of which seventy lines are extant; *Epicharmus*, a poem on the nature of the universe; the *Hēdyphagētica* ('of sweet eating'), a mock-heroic poem on gastronomy; and a poem in special celebration of Scipio Africanus. The *Euhemerus* was a prose work which adopted the rationalist theory of *Euhemerus on the origin of the gods. Of his tragedies some twenty titles are known, of which perhaps twelve are derived from Euripides, perhaps three from Aeschylus, and one from an obscure contemporary of Euripides. The fragments remaining allow interesting comparison with the Greek originals, particularly in the case of *Medea*. The natural ease of the Greek has been replaced by a rather grand and high-flown style, but Cicero's admiration for it is understandable.

The *Annales*, an epic poem chronicling Roman history in eighteen books, occupied Ennius up to the time of his death. Fewer than 600 lines survive, which do no more than indicate the general scope of the work. The poem inaugurated a new era in Roman literature, being composed not in the saturnian metre used by Naevius and Livius Andronicus (see METRE, LATIN 1) but in the hexameter of Greek epic (see METRE, GREEK 3). To emphasize the connection with Greek poetry Ennius began his work by recounting a dream in which he had been told by Homer that he was the latter's reincarnation. The *Annales* presented the history of Rome from the time of Aeneas, through the regal period (see ROME 2), down to the wars of the poet's own day, including a series of descriptions of great Romans. The First Punic War was omitted, having been dealt with by Naevius. The events of living memory seem to have occupied the second half of the work. It was from reading Ennius that Roman schoolboys learned about the heroes of old and the Roman virtues. The famous line on Fabius Maximus Cunctator: *unus homo nobis cunctando restituit rem,* 'one man by delaying restored the state for us', was much quoted. Clumsy though the hexameters are, the style is grave and sonorous and suited to the poet's grand conception of his subject. Ennius was regarded by the Romans as the father of their literature; Lucretius and Virgil were considerably influenced by him, Cicero admired and quoted him. He enjoyed a long, if not quite unbroken, period of esteem among Roman critics of later times. He reputedly composed his own epitaph:

nemo me lacrumis decoret neu funera fletu
faxit. Cur? volito vivo' per ora virum.

('Let no one honour me with tears or attend my funeral with weeping. Why? I fly, still living, through the mouths of men.')

Enȳ'o. **1.** One of the *Graiae. **2.** Greek goddess of war, secondary in importance to *Arēs. The Roman *Bellona was identified with her.

Ēoe'ae or **Ēoīai,** see CATALOGUE OF WOMEN.

Ē'ōs, in Greek myth, the dawn-goddess (Lat. Aurora), who figures in story rather than in cult, daughter of *Hyperion and Theia (Ovid calls her a daughter of Pallas the Titan or Giant), and sister of Helios (Sun) and Selenē (Moon). She carried off several youths celebrated for their beauty: *Tithonus, by whom she became the mother of Emathion and Memnon; *Orion, whom Artemis killed; Cleitus, son of Mantius; and *Cephalus the husband of Procris.

Epamino'ndas (Epameinōndās), the great Theban general of the fourth century BC who with his friend *Pelopidas raised Thebes (in Boeotia) to be for a time the most powerful city in Greece. Epaminondas was active in the struggles of Athens and Thebes, 379–371, to put an end to Spartan domination in Greece. At the peace negotiations in Sparta in 371, at which Sparta and Athens were reconciled, Epaminondas, representing Thebes, wanted to ratify the peace treaty in the name of all Boeotia, in order to obtain recognition of Thebes' supremacy over all the other Boeotian cities. When this recognition was refused, Epaminondas withdrew Thebes from the treaty altogether, and Sparta sent an army to invade Boeotia which reached Leuctra. Here, under Epaminondas' brilliant command, the Thebans won a decisive victory in 371, bringing Sparta's supremacy in Greece to an end and making Epaminondas famous. He invaded the Peloponnese in 370/69 to help the Arcadians throw off Spartan control (see MEGALOPOLIS), and he established the independence of *Messenia. He invaded again in 369 and in 366, with less effect. In 364 he even challenged Athens' naval supremacy at sea. In 362 he invaded the Peloponnese once more in order to reassert Theban influence there. This time the Thebans and their allies had to face an alliance of Athenians and Spartans. The armies fought at *Mantinea and the Thebans were in fact victorious, but the victory turned into defeat when it was known that Epaminondas had been killed. His creation of independent Arcadia and Messenia survived him, but he left behind no constructive policy for Thebes or Boeotia which others could continue, and he had no successors. His new military tactics of reinforcing the battle line with a deep wedge of men on the left wing, of irresistible weight, to break through the enemy line, met with spectacular success and led to the further innovations of Philip II of Macedon and his son Alexander (the Great).

Epaminondas' greatness lay in his qualities of mind and character which so impressed his fellow-countrymen. See also SACRED BAND.

Epaphrodī'tus, freedman and secretary to the emperor Nero whom he accompanied in his final flight and helped to commit suicide. He was subsequently secretary to the emperor Domitian, by whom he was killed in AD 95. The philosopher *Epictetus was his slave.

Epei'os, maker of the *Trojan Horse.

epeiso'dion, see EPISODE.

ephē'boi ('youths'), in Greek, term normally used of boys of any age between 15 and 20, but in Athens in the fourth century BC used specifically to denote members of the *ephebīa* ('ephebic college'). Founded *c*.335 following the defeat of Athens by Macedon at Chaeronea in 338, this institution gave the young men of 18 to 20 a compulsory and efficient military training, and spread rapidly throughout the Greek world. During their training the youths were excluded from the law courts, paid an allowance of four obols a day, and subjected to strict discipline by their trainers and teachers. They ate together in barracks and carried out guard and patrol duties along the coast and the frontiers. In their characteristic dress of dark mantle and broad-brimmed hat they were during their existence a graceful feature of the Athenian scene. With the end of compulsory military service in about 300 BC and the abolition of the allowance, the *ephebia* became a largely educational institution for a wealthy élite (see EDUCATION 3) and by the end of the second century BC it had been remodelled into a school especially of literature and philosophy.

ephēme'ridĕs, 'diaries', a term especially applied to the diaries of *Alexander the Great (see 8), supposedly kept by his secretary Eumenes and thought to have been consulted by contemporary historians.

Ephesi'aca (or *Habrocomes and Antheia*), *novel by Xenophon of Ephesus.

E'phesus, one of the principal Ionian Greek cities on the west coast of Asia Minor, at the mouth of the Caÿster. It was founded by Ionian Greek settlers under Androclus, son of the Athenian king Codrus (see MIGRATIONS). They were reputed to have found the worship of Artemis (presumably the Asiatic Mother-goddess; see CYBELE) already established there. Ephesus survived the Cimmerian invasions (seventh century BC) but was captured in the mid-sixth century by Croesus, king of Lydia, who contributed to the rebuilding of the great temple of Artemis, the fourth to be built on the site. Fragments of some of the columns dedicated by Croesus are now in the British Museum. The new temple, built in the Ionic style and on a magnificent scale, was designed by Chersiphron of Cnossus and completed by his son Metagenes. Its foundations were bedded on alternate layers of charcoal and fleeces, because of the marshy nature of the site. Unusually the temple faced west (see TEMPLES I), preserving the orientation of the original shrine. In the later sixth century Ephesus, like the rest of the Ionian seaboard cities, passed under the domination of the Persians. In the fifth century, after the defeat of the Persians (see PERSIAN WARS) it became a member of the *Delian League, but revolted from Athens c.412 BC and sided with Sparta. The temple, which had been one of the few to be spared by the Persians at the end of the Ionian Revolt, was burnt down in 356 BC (see HEROSTRATUS), reputedly on the night Alexander (the Great) was born, and it was 220 years before it was finally restored, on the same plan.

In 334 the city passed into the control of Alexander, and in 133 BC, with the kingdom of Attalus III (see ATTALIDS), to the Romans. In Roman times Ephesus became the chief city (although Pergamum was the capital) of the province of Asia, and the seat of the governor. Strabo in the early first century AD describes it as 'the greatest place of trade of all the cities of Asia west of the Taurus' (a mountain range in Cilicia). Acts 19 gives a lively picture of the city in the mid-first century AD. Its famous citizens included the philosopher Heracleitus, the poet Hipponax, and the painter Parrhasius (Apelles too was connected with Ephesus). In AD 391 the emperor Theodosius suppressed all pagan worship, and the temple of Diana (the Roman goddess corresponding to Artemis) was closed. The ruins of the ancient city are still notable.

Ep(h)ia'ltēs. 1. In Greek myth, brother of *Otus; they were the giant sons of Aloeus. It was also the name of the demon of nightmare.

2. Of Trachis, said to have shown Xerxes the path by which the Persians outflanked Leonidas at Thermopylae (see PERSIAN WARS).

3. An Athenian statesman who became the leading politician on the democratic side after about 465 BC and the opponent of the aristocratic *Cimon. He resisted (unsuccessfully) the sending of help to the Spartans during the helot revolt of 462 on the grounds that Sparta was the rival of Athens for power. He took advantage of Cimon's absence in Sparta, or eclipse in popularity following his ignominious return, to put into effect a number of radical reforms necessary for the institution of democracy. In this he was supported by the young Pericles. He persuaded the assembly to pass laws depriving the ancient council of the *Areopagus of all political powers and leaving it only with jurisdiction in cases of homicide and with the administration of sacred property. The functions which it lost he transferred to the *boulē, the *ecclesia, and the popular lawcourts. The *Eumenides of Aeschylus, performed in 458, testifies to some extent to the thoughts and feelings aroused by these new measures. Ephialtes was murdered in 461.

ĕphors, at *Sparta a body of magistrates, by the late fifth century BC five in number, elected annually by the citizens and exercising general control over the kings' conduct; two ephors always accompanied a king on campaign. Every month kings and ephors exchanged oaths, the latter swearing to support the kings, the former to maintain the constitution. The senior ephor gave his name to the year (see CALENDARS 3). The ephors wielded great power which they gradually extended. They controlled the general administration and had certain judicial functions; they could even sentence the kings to be fined or imprisoned, recall generals, and negotiate foreign treaties. Their first proclamation when they entered office, according to Aristotle, was that the citizens should shave their moustaches and be obedient to the laws.

E'phorus, of Cyme, one of the most influential Greek historians of the fourth century BC, the author of a history of the cities of Greece and Asia Minor in thirty books, no longer extant; it began with the 'return of the *Heracleidae' (i.e. the *Dorian Invasion c.1100 BC) and continued to the siege of Perinthus by Philip II of Macedon in 341 BC, including myths and legends, geography and ethnography, political and military history. Ephorus consulted numerous authorities now lost to us, and his work was known to Polybius and extensively used by Strabo and Diodorus, books 11–16 of whose history are almost entirely dependent on him as well as being the main source of our knowledge of him. See also OXYRHYNCHUS HISTORIAN.

Ephy'ra, the name of several cities in Greece in early times, including Corinth and Crannon.

epic (from Gk. *epē*, 'hexameters'; see METRE, GREEK 3). In literature, an epic is a narrative poem on the grand scale and in majestic style concerning the exploits and adventures of a superhuman hero (or heroes) engaged in a quest or some serious endeavour. The hero is distinguished above all men by his strength and courage, and is restrained only by a sense of honour. The subject-matter of epic includes *myth, legend, history, and folk tale. It is usually set in a heroic age of the past and embodies its country's early history and expresses its values. Battles and perilous journeys play a large part, as do gods, the supernatural, and magic; scenes are often set in the Underworld or in heaven. Certain formal features are conspicuous: the narrator vouches for the truth of his story; there are invocations, elaborate greetings, long speeches, detailed similes, digressions, and the frequent repetition of 'typical' elements, for example the stock adjective or *formula, the stock scene such as the hero arming for battle. Epic expresses a delight in the physical world, shown by painstaking descriptions of such things as arms, clothing, or ships.

1. *Greek epic and the Epic Cycle.* Epic poetry in the shape of the *Iliad* and *Odyssey* of Homer is the earliest surviving form of Greek literature; the origins of these poems are lost, but they probably go back to Mycenaean times. From the incident of Odysseus asking the bard Demodocus (*Odyssey* 8) to sing of the ruse of the Trojan Horse it is clear that there was a corpus of sagas on which a bard could draw. What the bard recited (or rather chanted, to the lyre) would be a story taken from an existing body of myth but with no fixed text (and before literacy with no written text at all); rather it was an improvisation made up for each occasion with the help of stylized elements of phrasing or formulae, previously memorized, developed by a long succession of bards. The relationship between the early type of oral epic narrative and the Homeric poems as they now exist is still far from clear, but it is commonly thought that with the advent of alphabetic writing into the Greek world in the second half of the eighth century BC the Homeric poems were committed to writing in something like their present form, perhaps by a bard called Homer. It is at least clear that they embody traditional material of a much earlier date.

The *Epic Cycle* is the name given to a collection of epics (excluding the *Iliad* and *Odyssey*), of which only some 120 lines now survive, written by various poets in the seventh and sixth centuries BC, which could be arranged so as to make a chronological narrative extending from the beginning of the world to the end of the heroic age. Some of these poems were occasionally ascribed to Homer. They seem to have been well known in the fifth and fourth centuries BC but little read later; a writer of the sixth century AD declares that they are no longer to be found, and our knowledge of their contents derives in part from summaries made in antiquity by *Proclus. There was a Trojan cycle completing the story of the Trojan War. The epics comprising it are the *Cypria* (covering the preliminaries of the Trojan War), *Aethiopis, Little *Iliad, *Iliupersis, Nostoi ('home-comings' of the heroes), and the *Telegonia* (concerning Telegonus). There was also a Theban cycle, the narrative of the legends of *Thebes, which included the *Thebais*. These formed the storehouse from which Greek dramatic and lyric poets drew many of their subjects.

The last great epic poet of archaic Greece seems to have been Panyassis, a kinsman of Herodotus, who flourished in the early fifth century BC and wrote an epic on Heracles. By the end of the fifth century Greek epic writing had lost its spontaneity and was becoming allusive and even pedantic, as is clear from the sparse fragments of Antimachus of Colophon and Choerilus of Samos (the latter noteworthy in having composed an epic, the *Persica*, on a historical subject, the Persian Wars). Some later epic still survives. In the third century BC the Hellenistic poet *Apollonius Rhodius wrote the *Argonautica* in four books; in the fourth century AD *Quintus of Smyrna wrote the *Posthomerica* in fourteen books, to fill the gap between the events of the *Iliad* and of the *Odyssey*, and in the fifth century AD *Nonnus wrote the *Dionysiaca* in forty-eight books.

2. *Roman epic.* Epic was introduced at Rome in the third century BC in a Latin version of Homer's *Odyssey* rendered into saturnian metre (see METRE, LATIN 1) by *Livius Andronicus. It seems from the remaining fragments to have been an adaptation rather than a translation of Homer, but it became a famous and influential work. *Naevius in the late second century BC undertook an entirely original piece of work by composing an epic in saturnian metre on the Punic Wars which was justly regarded as his most important composition. The *Annales* of *Ennius, an epic in eighteen books on the history of Rome, was a work in which the dactylic hexameter was applied to Latin epic for the first time. The greatest Roman epic was the *Aeneid* of Virgil, who was influenced in its composition not only by the Homeric Greek epics but also by Ennius and other Latin hexameter poets. In the Silver Age Latin epic became rhetorical in character and seems written with the intention that it should be declaimed. The best epic of that age was Lucan's *Bellum civile* (sometimes entitled *Pharsalia*). Other epic poets of the empire whose works survive in part were *Silius Italicus, *Valerius Flaccus, *Statius, and *Claudian. Among those whose works are lost were Cornelius Severus (praised by Ovid and Quintilian) who wrote historical poems, and Albinovanus Pedo, author of a *Theseid* and a poem on the campaigns of Germanicus.

epice'dion, see DIRGE.

Epicha'rmus, Greek writer of comedy from Sicily, who was active perhaps in the late sixth and certainly in the early fifth centuries BC. He was at the court of Hieron of Syracuse in the 470s. No play survives, but many titles are known, and quotations and papyrus fragments give some idea of the contents. He seems to have enjoyed writing mythological burlesque, with Odysseus and Heracles the favourite heroes. It would appear that he also introduced various types of character, e.g. the *parasite, the sightseer, the philosopher, and an ancient writer asserts that he was the first to bring a drunkard on to the stage. Some of these characters were to appear later in literary *mime as well as in Attic comedy. The plural titles of some plays suggest that he employed a chorus, but there is no firm evidence in the fragments that he did so, nor do we know how many actors he employed, nor how long the plays were. His language is Sicilian Doric, used as wittily as the Attic of Old Comedy (see COMEDY, GREEK 3). Many of the comic aspects of language familiar from Aristophanes are present: parody, word-play, the coining of long words, and the rattling-off of lists of things good to eat. There is no evidence that he used a variety of metres and there are no lyrics among the extant fragments. In antiquity Epicharmus was regarded as the author also of a number of philosophical and quasi-scientific works, but these are no longer thought to be genuinely by him.

Epictē'tus (*c.* AD 50–*c.*120) of Hierapolis, in Phrygia, *Stoic philosopher, born a slave, owned and later freed by Epaphroditus, freedman and secretary of the emperor Nero. He attended the lectures of *Musonius Rufus at Rome and then gave lectures there himself; after Domitian banished the philosophers in *c.*89 he migrated to Epirus in Greece where he spent the rest of his life. His lectures there were attended by the historian *Arrian, who took careful notes of what he said and published them; four books of *Diatribai* ('lectures') survive (see DIATRIBE). Later Arrian published a summary of Epictetus' philosophy, the *Encheiridion* ('manual'). These works strongly influenced the emperor Marcus *Aurelius. The *Manual* is a rather formal statement of Epictetus' views but the *Diatribai*, which are his comments on various Stoic writings, have a vivid informality, enlivened by anecdotes and imaginary conversations, and Arrian reproduces the *koinē* Greek in which Epictetus spoke (see DIALECTS). He taught that the universe is governed for the best by an all-wise Providence, and that all men are brothers. Unlike many Stoics he taught for the many and the humble, rather than for those few to whom Stoicism had an intellectual appeal, thereby continuing a tradition of popular preaching which began with the *Cynics in the third century BC. Only those who knew their own weakness and misery, he said, could benefit from philosophers. Like the other early Stoics he wanted to make men independent of their circumstances and of the vicissitudes of life. Having experienced slavery himself, he lays emphasis on that part of a man over which no one else has control, his mind. He is said (by Aulus *Gellius, 17. 19) to have preached that people should take to heart two words, *anechou* and *apechou*, 'endure' and 'abstain'. He shows a robust faith in the power of the human will to surmount trials, and is more positive than Marcus Aurelius, with whom it is natural to compare him. The nineteenth-century British

general Gordon (of Khartoum) used to present his friends with the works of both.

Epicū'rus (Epikouros) (341–271 BC), Greek philosopher of the Hellenistic age and founder of the Epicurean school of philosophy. He was born in Samos, the son of a schoolteacher who had Athenian citizenship. In his youth he studied and was impressed by the atomist philosophy of *Democritus, and established his own philosophical circles at Mytilene and Lampsacus. He settled in Athens in 307 and bought a house with a garden (*kēpoi*), which gave its name, the Garden, to the school of philosophy which he set up in it. At his death he bequeathed this property to his successor Hermarchus. Epicurus resembled Socrates in the affection and respect he inspired among his friends, who sought out his company. His school, perhaps better called a community, consisted of a group of likeminded people, including women and slaves, who lived with him in austere seclusion. It attracted ridicule and accusations of profligacy because of its communal life and Epicurus' philosophical hedonism (see below), the serious aspects of which were ignored. Although Epicurus wrote prolifically most of his work is lost. *Diogenes Laertius preserves three important letters summarizing his teaching, together with a collection of forty aphorisms, *Kyriai doxai* ('principal doctrines'); some eighty further aphorisms survive in a manuscript. Of the thirty-seven books of his great work *On Nature*, fairly substantial fragments have been recovered from carbonized papyrus rolls found in a villa excavated at *Herculaneum, the study of which is yielding results. For our knowledge of Epicurus' thought we also depend largely on the poem of *Lucretius, *De rerum natura*, which expounds his physical theory and to some extent his moral theory too.

Epicurus' aim was the wise conduct of life, to be attained by reliance on the evidence of the senses, and the elimination of superstition and of the belief in supernatural intervention. He accepted from Democritus that the world consisted of (unchanging and indestructible) atoms and void, change being brought about by the rearrangement of atoms. He gives a strictly mechanistic account of all phenomena: the universe came into being through a chance combination of atoms, and will eventually perish through their dispersal. Gods exist, but have no part in the ordinary processes of nature and take no thought for humankind. The latter is merely an ephemeral compound of atoms, and the human soul, also compounded of atoms, perishes with the body. Epicurus makes atomism serve a moral purpose. Happiness consists in attaining tranquillity of mind, an attainment achieved by a proper understanding of nature. Epicurus' moral theory is summed up in a sentence from one of his letters: 'We say that pleasure is the beginning and end of living happily.' Thus for Epicurus pleasure is identical with the good. It is in the nature of people to seek pleasure; pain, which is a disturbance of the natural state, is caused by unsatisfied desire, and pleasure is experienced when the natural state is restored. Therefore one must satisfy desire, and this is pleasure. But some pleasures bring pain in their wake. Therefore one must satisfy desires which are natural and necessary, but accept as the limit of pleasure the onset of pain. Hence pleasure may lie in limiting desire. (Epicurus is perhaps uniting under the term 'pleasure' both positive enjoyment and the absence of pain.) Mental pleasure is far greater than physical pleasure (as mental suffering is worse than physical suffering), and is found in *ataraxia*, 'freedom from disturbance'. This can be achieved in three ways: by learning the nature of the universe and of death, which removes fear of the supernatural (the worst mental pain), by withdrawing from the turmoils of public life, and by avoiding emotional commitments.

The meaning given in modern times to the word 'epicure' represents widespread hostility to and misunderstanding of Epicurean philosophy (not helped by Horace's ironic description of himself, *Epistles* 1. 4. 16, as 'a hog from the sty of Epicurus'). Particular antagonism was felt by the *Stoics; nevertheless Epicureanism spread, first to Antioch and Alexandria, then into Italy, and for a brief time during the late republic it won the adherence of men like Calpurnius Piso, Cassius, and Cicero's friend Atticus. Naturally the early Christians regarded Epicureanism with abhorrence because it stated that there was no providential God and no survival after death, that the universe had been created by accident, and that the aim of life was pleasure. A remarkable testimony to the continuing vitality of the philosophy was a very large public inscription (of which fragments survive) erected in AD 200 at Oenoanda in the interior of modern Turkey by a certain Diogenes, giving passages of Epicurean doctrine together with a concise summary of Epicurus' teaching: there is nothing to fear in God, nothing to feel in death; good is attainable, evil endurable. Informed interest in Epicurus was not much to be found until the seventeenth century and the dawning scientific enlightenment. In 1685 the English poet John Dryden included some verse translations of Lucretius in his *Second Miscellany* which stimulated interest, and for a short period a popular form of Epicureanism was fashionable in England. By the early eighteenth century the new empiricism needed no further support from Epicurus, and interest in his teaching once more waned.

Epidau'rus, small Greek state on the Argolis peninsula in the north-eastern Peloponnese, chiefly famed for its sanctuary of *Asclepius.

This contained several public buildings, including a great temple built in the early fourth century BC which held a chryselephantine statue of the god. Two other important buildings still survive: a *tholos*, or rotunda, built by the sculptor-architect Polycleitus the Younger in the mid-fourth century BC, notable for its Corinthian columns with very beautiful capitals; and a theatre, also designed by Polycleitus, which is well preserved in its original form. Many inscriptions from the sanctuary also survive, attesting cures effected by *incubation (sleeping in a dormitory attached to the temple) and by following the prescriptions of the priests.

epidei'ctic oratory, the oratory 'of display', that is, speeches for delivery at festivals (panegyrics), and funeral orations; epideictic is distinguished from forensic oratory (of the law-courts) and deliberative (symbouleutic) or political oratory.

Epi'dicus, Roman comedy by *Plautus. The complicated plot turns on the deceits of the slave Epidicus. He tricks his old master out of money, first to pay for a harp-girl to whom the old man's son has taken a fancy; then to pay for a captive whom the son, who has gone off to the wars and transferred his affections, has bought with borrowed money. The fraud is discovered, but as the captive turns out to be the old man's lost daughter, Epidicus is forgiven and freed.

Epi'gonoi ('successors'), in Greek myth, the sons of the *Seven against Thebes who, under the leadership of *Adrastus, the only survivor of the original Seven, took and destroyed Thebes, an event supposed to have occurred shortly before the Trojan War. Their names (with some variations in the sources) were usually given as Alcmaeon and Amphilochus, sons of Amphiaraus; Aegialeus, son of Adrastus and the only one of the Epigonoi to be killed in the expedition; Diomedes, son of Tydeus; Polydorus, of Hippomedon; Promachus, of Parthenopaeus; Sthenelus, of Capaneus; and Thersander, of Polyneices. The term epigonoi was also applied to the officers of Alexander the Great who 'succeeded' to his empire (see DIADOCHOI).

epigram (*epigramma*, 'inscription'), a verse inscription. In Greece, epigrams were written at first in hexameters, later in elegiacs (see METRE, GREEK 3 and 4). The early epigrams (of the seventh century BC) were placed on grave-stones or votive tablets, composed so as to suggest that the dead man or the dedicator was directly addressing the reader, giving him the bare facts in a severely laconic style which became the artistic hallmark of the epigram. The first famous epigrammatist was *Simonides of Ceos, to whom many anonymous epigrams have been falsely attributed. The few which we know to be genuinely his combine intensity of feeling with great simplicity of expression. Quite a few

Greek epigrams purport to survive from the classical period attached to famous names, among them Euripides, Plato, and Aristotle, but they are almost certainly spurious. It was not until the fourth century BC that epigrams were written simply as literature (though real inscriptions in verse were still being composed) and the term was extended to mean a brief poem suggested by a single event, serious or trivial. Thus *Callimachus' epigram on the death of his friend Heracleitus, well known in English poetry through the nineteenth-century translation of William Cory, 'They told me, Heraclitus ...', is a direct address by the poet to the dead man, in which he voices his personal sorrow in a manner very different from the impersonal style of the classic inscriptional epigram. *Asclepiades was one of the earliest and most influential of the Hellenistic epigrammatists. The subjects they treated were very varied, but the themes of love and wine predominated. Whatever the subject matter, brevity and elegance of expression were essential. In the first century BC *Meleager compiled the first large anthology of epigrams written during the previous five centuries, the *Garland*, which was supplemented by later anthologists (see also ANTHOLOGY I). Marcus Argentarius in the first century AD introduced that final refinement of the epigram which is now considered its characteristic feature, an unexpected twist—a pun or a paradox—in the last few words. Epigrams continued to be written in Greek throughout the Byzantine period, sometimes upon Christian themes but often in a markedly pagan spirit; the poets best remembered are *Palladas, *Paul the Silentiary, and *Agathias.

The Romans had their own tradition of funerary epigrams, but their first literary epigrams, written in the late second century BC in elegiacs, were Greek in inspiration and were all on the theme of love. *Catullus wrote epigrams of both love and hate, and after him epigrams were said to have been written by most of the prominent men of the late republic and early empire, but very few have survived. The literary form of the Latin epigram culminated in the work of *Martial, who cultivated especially the witty, paradoxical ending that is imitated by all modern writers of epigrams.

epigraphy, study of inscriptions in respect of both their form and their content, an inscription being taken to mean any writing cut, scratched, or impressed on any durable material such as stone or metal, either in official form or casually by an individual (in the latter case known as a graffito). Coins are excluded, their inscriptions being within the province of the numismatist, and it is usual to exclude painted inscriptions and texts written in ink, on whatever material.

1. *Greek*. The earliest surviving Greek inscriptions are dated to the middle of the eighth century BC. At this time the Greeks, after centuries of apparent illiteracy following the disappearance of the *Linear B script with the collapse of the *Mycenaean civilization, took over the (Semitic) Phoenician script and created from it a simple *alphabet adapted to their own tongue. These early inscriptions consist merely of names or brief personal comments scratched on pots. By the early seventh century inscriptions are of a more formal nature—dedications to gods or names of the dead on gravestones. Like the Phoenicians the Greeks originally wrote from right to left (retrograde); if a second line of writing was required to complete the inscription, it was often written underneath the first line but proceeding in the opposite direction, creating a hairpin-like pattern. This pattern of writing was known as *boustrophēdon, 'as the ox turns', and was helpful for the inexperienced reader whose eye could then continue to read without interruption at the end of a line. It sometimes seems from the inscriptions of the seventh and sixth centuries that the lines of writing need not even be horizontal: the words could apparently be as easily read when written vertically. It was not until the Greeks set up formal inscriptions, as opposed to using words merely to identify, say, figures on a vase, that they adopted a consistent left-to-right direction. In the sixth century the Greeks, and notably the Athenians, adopted a style of inscription which suited their feeling for symmetry and uniformity, in which the letters were exactly aligned both horizontally and vertically (the *stoichēdon*, 'in a line', style). This persisted until the end of the fourth century BC, but had disappeared almost entirely by the end of the third.

Greek inscriptions survive in their tens of thousands, including hundreds of poems of various kinds which would otherwise be unknown to us. They immeasurably enrich our knowledge of Greek history, thought, and speech by being first-hand, contemporary records, in the authentic language of the time, of every aspect of Greek life—political, social, religious, and economic—both important and trivial. Among the more important Greek historical inscriptions are the Athenian *tribute lists, the law-code of *Gortyn in Crete, and the chronological table known as the Parian Marble (see MARMOR PARIUM).

2. *Latin*. Latin inscriptions earlier than the third century BC are rare, and unfortunately so, since those we have provide valuable evidence of linguistic usage at a period earlier than that of most surviving Latin literature. (The earliest inscription was at one time thought to be a craftsman's label on a gold fibula from Praeneste dated to the late seventh century BC, but this has been found to be a forgery.) Most Latin inscriptions date from the early empire, but they continue beyond the collapse of Rome in the

fifth century AD. Inscriptions from the provinces of the empire are of particular historical value. The Latin script was originally very like that of the early Greek alphabet used by the Greek settlers at Cumae (on the coast near Naples, founded c.750 BC), from which the Latin alphabet was ultimately derived. By the first century AD the cutters had developed the beautiful Roman capital lettering, seen at its best on the base of Trajan's Column. Latin inscriptions, like Greek, are an invaluable source of information on politics and law, social, religious, and military administration, and other aspects of Roman life which without them would remain obscure to us. Christian inscriptions throw light on the development of Christian society and religious thought. Important Latin historical inscriptions include the so-called *Monumentum Ancyranum*, the emperor Augustus' official autobiography, written in both Latin and Greek; the emperor Diocletian's *Edict on Prices*; the texts of many early laws and *senatus consulta*, e.g. much of the *s.c. de bacchanalibus* of 186 BC (see BACCHANALIA); and the consular *fasti* which list the principal magistrates for various periods of Roman history and provide a chronological framework for dating many historical events.

Epime'nidēs, semi-legendary Cretan poet, prophet, and wonder-worker, variously dated to between 600 and 500 BC, and credited with remarkable longevity, with wandering out of the body and with a miraculous sleep of 57 years (compare ARISTEAS). He is supposed to have visited Athens in about 600 BC to purify the city after the murder of Cylon's associates (see ALCMAEONIDAE). Tradition ascribed to him a theogony and other poems of a mystical nature. The quotation in Titus 1: 12, 'Cretans are always liars', is said to be from his work.

Epimē'theus ('afterthought'), in Greek myth, brother of *Prometheus.

epinī'kion (Lat. *epinīcium*), epinician ode, a form of Greek choral *lyric composed in the grand manner in honour of a victory in one of the great Games in Greece, and publicly performed usually upon the victor's return to his city. The principal epinician poets whose odes are still largely extant are *Pindar and *Bacchylides. Of *Simonides' epinicians only a few lines survive. Virtually all the odes adhere to a standard pattern: they are usually written in *triads, they eulogize the victor and his family and city, they narrate a myth, and they relate the victory to life in general, often by means of moral reflections and exhortations which may seem sombre in the context of victory and celebration.

epirrhē'ma ('what is said afterwards'), in Greek Old Comedy, passage spoken by the *coryphaeus* (chorus-leader) after the chorus has sung a short lyric at the end of the *parabasis*. It often satirizes various Athenians or admonishes the audience. The metre is trochaic. See COMEDY, GREEK 3 (iv).

episode (*epeisodion*), in Greek tragedy, the dialogue between two choral odes, corresponding to the modern 'act' (see TRAGEDY 3). In Old Comedy, episodes are the brief scenes following the *parabasis*, separated by choral songs and illustrating the consequences of the hero's achievement of his aim (see COMEDY, GREEK 3 (v)).

Epistles (*Epistulae*, 'letters'), of *Horace, two books of Latin hexameter poems of a reflective nature and written ostensibly as letters to friends, a literary genre which had no obvious antecedent in Greek. The first book was probably published in 20 or 19 BC; in the opening poem Horace professes to have abandoned lyric poetry (*Odes* I–III were published probably in 23 BC) and to have turned to philosophy. This 'philosophy' is not that of the professionals, which he treats with irony and humour (for his own description of his Epicureanism see EPICURUS), but is rather a matter of the morals of everyday living—the contentment to be found in a simple life, the dangers of avarice, and above all the advantage of moderation in all things, themes which the form of the *Epistles* enables him to treat conversationally from a personal view-point, with wit and good sense. It is a matter of debate whether the *Epistles* are entirely fictitious, merely providing a convenient framework for composition, or are real letters sent on particular occasions to particular persons.

Book I contains twenty epistles, and is memorable for its many telling passages and felicitous phrases: the comparison of the man who puts off the hour of right living with the countryman who waits for the river to flow by: *dimidium facti qui coepit habet: sapere aude* ('he who has begun his task has half done it; have the courage to be wise', 2. 40); the folly of men who look for peace of mind in a new place: *caelum non animum mutant* ('they change the sky but not their state of mind', 11. 27); *ira furor brevis est* ('anger is a short madness', 2. 62); *naturam expellas furca, tamen usque recurret* ('you may drive nature out with a pitchfork but she will return every time', 10. 24); the 'by-ways of a quiet life', *fallentis semita vitae* (18. 103). Epistle 4 is interesting as addressed to the poet Tibullus; Epistle 6 is a series of reflections on peace of mind, *nil admirari*, 'to wonder at nothing' (the *ataraxia* of Epicurus); Epistle 9 is a letter introducing a friend to the future emperor Tiberius; Epistle 16 contains a description of the poet's farm. Book II contains only two epistles (but see below), the first to the emperor Augustus, written perhaps in 15 BC, and the second to Julius Florus, a young companion of Tiberius with literary aspirations, written in 19 or 18 BC. Both concern literature; in the first

Horace surveys the development of Latin poetry and defends the refinement of contemporary poetry under the influence of Greek literature; in the second Horace gives his reasons for abandoning lyric poetry in favour of philosophy. There are other interesting autobiographical passages and some literary doctrine; unsparing self-criticism in an author is especially recommended. For a third epistle see ARS POETICA, a name it has been known by since Quintilian.

Epistle to the Pisos (*Epi'stula ad Pisōnēs*), see ARS POETICA.

Epi'stulae ex Ponto ('letters from the Black Sea'), four books of elegiac poems written by *Ovid in the latter years of his exile at Tomis. Books 1–3 were published in AD 13; book 4 probably appeared posthumously. Like the poems of books 3–5 of the *Tristia*, these describe the rigours of his exile and plead for leniency; they differ only by being addressed to individuals by name. Ovid's hopes rested largely on the genial character of Germanicus, nephew and adopted son of the emperor Tiberius, who is addressed or mentioned in several places.

epitaphs, see EPIGRAM.

epithala'mium (Gk. *epithalamion*), 'at the bedroom', in Greek and Latin poetry, a marriage-song, sung by young men and girls outside the bedroom on the wedding-night (compare HYMENAEUS). Sappho is the first poet known to have used it as a literary form; only a few lines survive of her epithalamia (which probably made up book 9 of her poems); Theocritus' Idyll 18 is also an epithalamium. The most famous Latin examples of this genre are Catullus' poems 61 and 62, which show the influence of Sappho.

epithets, divine. Particular epithets or adjectives are often applied to Greek and Roman gods, especially in *epic literature. Many of these are purely ornamental or poetic, often joining with the proper name to form a convenient metrical unit, but others are known to have been used in cult. It can be difficult to decide to which category a particular epithet belongs. Some obviously indicate the place where the deity is worshipped; others more interestingly, sometimes more importantly from a historical point of view, indicate an association with another deity. The largest class of epithets refers to the functions of the deity. Thus Zeus has many titles referring to his function as a weather god; he is the cloud-gatherer, loud-thunderer, rain-sender, the god 'who descends' (in lightning and the thunder-bolt). Sometimes the epithet refers not to the characteristics of the god but to those of the worshipper. In one place Hera was addressed as 'girl', 'wife', and 'widow' because she was worshipped by women of all ages and condi-

tions (Pausanias VIII. 22. 2). More rarely deities are described by an epithet referring to their moral or civic qualities (e.g. Apollo Archēgetēs, Apollo in his role as the god who approved schemes of colonization).

For Homeric epithets see HOMER 3, ORAL POETRY, and FORMULAE.

Epitrepo'ntes ('arbitrants'), Greek comedy by *Menander, of which half is preserved intact on several papyri and a further sixth in fragments.

During the absence of her husband Charisios, Pamphilē has borne a child five months after their marriage, and has exposed it with the help of her old nurse Sophronē. Charisios, told of this by his slave Onesimos, leaves home to stay with a friend Chairestratos and invites the harp-girl Habrotonon to join him, to the great indignation of Pamphile's unpleasant father Smikrines. A shepherd Daos finds the child and gives it to a charcoal burner Syriskos whose wife has lost her own baby, but Daos and Syriskos dispute possession of some trinkets found with the child and agree to submit to the arbitration of a passer-by. This chances to be Smikrines, who judges that the trinkets, being evidence of parentage, should accompany the child. Onesimos recognizes one as being his master's ring, and thus Charisios, already repenting of his priggish self-righteousness, is eventually revealed as having himself seduced Pamphile at a festival before their marriage and being the father of her exposed child. With the kindly help of Habrotonon all are reconciled and the play ends with the discomfiture of the objectionable Smikrines who, unaware of the turn of events, arrives determined to remove his daughter.

Terence's *Hecyra* resembles the *Epitrepontes* in plot.

e'pitrīte (*epitrītos*), see METRE, GREEK 8 (iii).

epode ('sung after'). For the *Epodes* of Horace see ODES AND EPODES; see also TRIAD.

E'pŏna, 'great mare', Latin name of a Celtic goddess associated with horses and mules and known from a large number of western European dedications.

eponymous ('that gives his name'), term used both of those who gave their names to places, as the goddess Athena to Athens, and of the chief magistrate of a city (in Athens the principal archon, in Rome the two consuls) who gave his name to the year in which he held office, thereby identifying it (see CALENDARS). When *Cleisthenes divided the Athenians into ten tribes, the Delphic Oracle chose ten Attic heroes to be their eponyms (*epōnymoi*).

epy'llion (Greek diminutive of *epos*, 'epic'), in Greek and Latin literature, a very brief epic, i.e. a narrative poem a few hundred lines long, in hexameters, usually on the subject of the life and especially the loves of a mythical hero or heroine, and popular from the Hellenistic age (Theocritus' Idyll 24 on the infant Heracles is an example) to Ovid. The use of the word as a descriptive term appears to be modern.

equestrian order (Lat. *equēs*, 'knight', pl. *equitēs*), an important social class of Roman citizens, originally enrolled, according to tradition, by the kings of Rome from the wealthiest men in the state to form the cavalry section of the army; each was given a horse from state funds (the so-called 'public horse') and the insignia which later became the distinctive attire of patricians, magistrates, and senators, i.e. the tunic with the *clavus*, the purple upright stripe, and the *trabea*, the short embroidered cloak (see DRESS 2). For the political rights of the equites see REPUBLIC, ROMAN. In the late second century BC they were enrolled by the *censors from all non-senators who possessed a minimum property of 400,000 sesterces (were 'of equestrian census') as well as being deemed physically and morally worthy. Thus the term 'equestrian order' came to denote a wealthy social class. During this century the original *raison d'être* of the equites had gradually disappeared when the cavalry contingents, if needed at all, were raised outside Italy (see ARMY, ROMAN I). From this time on the military function of the equites changed to service as staff officers. In addition, eligibility for magistracies at Rome belonged only to those of equestrian census at least, since those holding public office were unpaid; hence military and civil offices were held by the same class. But it was various legal measures passed in the late second century BC which effectively gave political significance to the equites by handing over to them state responsibilities, such as the manning of certain juries which had been the prerogative of the senatorial class (see LAW, AT ROME I (ii)). By the end of the republic the term equites denoted all well-to-do citizens, *publicani*, bankers, businessmen and administrators, who were of equestrian census and who did not belong to the senatorial class. After the enfranchisement of Italy at the beginning of the first century BC the equestrian order was augmented by men of similar background from the colonies and *municipia*. In social standing the equites were almost equal to senators and shared with them both landed and business interests. They were capable of exerting considerable political force, and were particularly influential in the time of Cicero, who, himself the son of an eques, tried to unite them with the senate in a *concordia ordinum* ('concord between the classes'; see CICERO (1) 3). But although both classes were often united on an important issue, the equites were too disparate in their views and insufficiently interested in politics to form a stable political group. Under the empire the order ceased to be a political force, but individual equites continued to be of importance in the civilian and military administration. When the rights of citizenship were extended to the Roman provinces, many of their wealthiest citizens qualified for and were enrolled in the equestrian order and were thus enabled to take up administrative duties in the empire. By the end of the third century AD almost all the higher military and administrative posts were held by equites. But in the following century the wide diffusion of honours among officials blurred the distinctions of class, and the equestrian order ceased to be a recognizable element in the state.

Erasi'stratus, of Ceos (third century BC), famous physician who may have practised at Alexandria, the leading medical centre of the time, or more probably at Antioch, and a younger contemporary of *Herophilus, the great anatomist, whose anatomical and physiological investigations he continued. He was the first to expound a complete physiological scheme of the body, which he saw as a mechanism. Unlike Herophilus he abandoned the doctrine of humours as an explanation of the origin of disease and instead ascribed the latter to the repletion of the body through undigested nutrition. He added to Herophilus' discovery of the distinction between motor and sensory nerves by distinguishing between cranial sensory and cranial motor nerves. Since it was his view that the heart is the centre and source of both the arterial and the venous systems and that there are very fine interconnections between arteries and veins, he was not far from the conception of circulation; in this he was ahead of all opinion until the English physician William Harvey (1628). His writings were still being read in the fourth century AD, but survive today only in quotation.

E'rato, see MUSES.

Erato'sthenes. 1. At Athens, one of the *Thirty Tyrants, prosecuted by *Lysias.
2. Of Cyrene (b. *c.*285–80, d. *c.*194 BC), head of the Library at Alexandria, the most versatile scholar of his time, styled *pentathlos*, 'all-rounder' (properly, in athletics), and *beta* because he was next best to the (*alpha*) specialist in every subject (for the terms see ALPHABET). From *philologia*, 'love of learning', he coined to describe himself the word *philologos*, 'scholar'; it is apt for one who was philosopher, mathematician, astronomer, chronographer, geographer, grammarian, and poet. Nothing of his work survives except for scattered quotations. Of his literary works the most interesting was his book *On Ancient Comedy*, but his most important works were the *Chronographiae* (for which he was indebted to *Timaeus), the *Geographica*, and *On the Measurement of the Earth*. The *Chronographiae* presented in the form of tables a reasonably clear and accurate chronological system of Greek

history, free from myth, beginning with the fall of Troy (which he dated to 1184 BC) and ending with the death of Alexander the Great (323 BC). The three books of the *Geographica* were the first complete description of the inhabited world, and the work was completed by a world-map of tolerable accuracy on which he projected his measurements, and which may have included two main axes of latitude and longitude. (See also BARBARIANS.)

Aristotle had demonstrated what some, notably, it would seem, Pythagoras, had previously assumed, that the earth was spherical, and his pupil Dicaearchus had established a basic line of latitude (determined by means of shadow-sticks) from Gibraltar to the Himalayas. Establishing longitude without accurate *clocks was a matter of guess-work, but Eratosthenes established a meridian drawn through Alexandria which he employed to make his famous calculation of the earth's circumference in his book *On the Measurement of the Earth*. He discovered that at Syenē (Aswan) in Upper Egypt a vertical stick cast no shadow at noon on the day of the summer solstice, being, he thought, on the tropic (of Cancer; Aswan is in fact 70 km. north of it), whereas at the same time in Alexandria, which he thought to be on the same line of longitude (though in fact he was out by some 3 degrees) and at a distance of 5,000 *stades, a vertical stick cast a shadow of a length which showed the angle of the stick to the sun's rays to be 1/50th of a circle (7.2 degrees). He therefore concluded that the distance from Syene to Alexandria must be 1/50th part of the earth's circumference, which would thus be 250,000 stades. Some say Eratosthenes emended this to 252,000 stades, so that his result might give an exact number of stades to a degree, namely 700. On some estimates of the stade as used by Eratosthenes, his result is within 1 per cent of the modern figure (40,075 km.). The actual difference in latitude between Alexandria and Aswan is about 7.1 degrees, slightly less than 1/50th of a circle.

E'rebus (Darkness), in Greek mythical cosmogony, one of the primeval deities sprung from *Chaos, (Void); the others are Gaia (Earth), Tartarus, Eros (Love), and Nyx (Night). Nyx and Erebus became the parents of Aether and Day, and of the *Hesperides.

Erechthē'um (Erechtheion), at Athens, the temple that housed the most famous cult of Athena, under the title of Athena Polias, 'goddess of the city', erected on the *Acropolis north of the Parthenon; it was probably begun after 421 BC and after a short interruption completed in 406. An inscription of 409 (now in the British Museum) records details of its construction. The architect is unknown but perhaps was Mnesiclēs who built the *Propylaea. Its name reflects the fact that Erechtheus

(see below) was also worshipped there, and this joint cult was known to Homer. The Erechtheum was the last of a series of temples erected on the site, the one immediately preceding having been built by Peisistratus and his sons and burnt by the Persians in 480. The design is very complicated, primarily because it had to incorporate certain spots sacred to the Athenians: the tombs of the mythical kings *Cecrops and Erechtheus; the sacred olive tree which Athena called forth from the earth in her contest with Poseidon for possession of Attica (see POSEIDON), burnt with the previous temple but miraculously surviving; and the well of salt water which Poseidon produced at the stroke of his trident on a rock. It is likely that the cella or chamber (see TEMPLES) contained the Palladium, the most ancient statue of the goddess in Athens, made of olive wood and said to have fallen down from heaven (and referred to in Aeschylus' *Eumenides* when Athena tells Orestes to grasp it in supplication). This was the statue to which the Athenians originally dedicated the *Panathenaic robe (before the erection of the Parthenon); in front of it a golden lamp designed by the sculptor Callimachus burned perpetually. The temple also contained an altar to Poseidon and Erechtheus (the reason for the combination of these two names is obscure), and other altars to Erechtheus' son Butēs and to Hephaestus. The temple was of the Ionic order (in contrast with the Doric order of the Parthenon), built in white Pentelic marble with a frieze of black Eleusinian limestone. The south porch is famous for the six 'maidens', the *caryatid figures supporting the marble roof with their heads, perhaps representing the *arrēphoroi* or maidens who bore in baskets at the Panathenaea the secret symbols of Athena. One of those now seen is a copy, the original being in the British Museum together with one Ionic column. The porch was reproduced in the design of the London church of St Pancras.

Ere'chtheus, mythical king of Athens, sometimes confused with the hero Erichthonius, and like him said to have sprung from the earth and to have been nurtured by Athena. According to Homer, Athena installed him in her temple, the Erechtheum, at Athens and made him her companion. The chief myth concerning him relates that when the Eleusinians and Eumolpus the Thracian, son of Poseidon, invaded Attica, Erechtheus, having enquired of the Delphic Oracle and been told that victory would be his only if he sacrificed one of his daughters, performed the sacrifice and duly defeated the Eleusinians, killing Eumolpus. Poseidon in anger caused the death of Erechtheus and all his house. The story was the subject of a popular tragedy by Euripides, now lost.

erga'stula, barracks which housed gangs of

slaves employed in agricultural labour in Italy. See SLAVERY 2.

Erichtho'nius, Attic hero and mythical king of Athens, usually said to be the son of *Hephaestus, whose semen fell upon the earth as he struggled to ravish Athena. Gaia (Earth) gave birth to the child and Athena took him and hid him in a chest which she gave to the daughters of *Cecrops, king of Athens, to guard, instructing them not to open it. They disobeyed, and terrified by what they saw (either the child in serpent form or attended by serpents), leaped from the Acropolis to their deaths. Erichthonius became king of Athens and received from Athena two drops of the *Gorgon's blood, one of which poisoned and the other healed. He was later worshipped at Athens in the form of a serpent. In some stories his son and successor is *Pandion.

Eri'danus. 1. Legendary amber-bearing river, vaguely located by the Greeks in the far north-west, into which *Phaethon supposedly fell, the amber being the tears wept by his sisters who were transformed into poplar trees. Herodotus reported that he had heard of it as the source of amber but did not believe it existed. Later Greeks identified it with the river Po (Lat. Padus) in north Italy, and the Roman poets and occasionally prose writers adopted the name.
2. Name of a small tributary of the river Ilissus at Athens.

Eri'gonē. 1. In Greek myth, daughter of *Icarius of Attica who was killed by his drunken fellow-countrymen after introducing them to wine. When Erigone, aided by their dog Maera, found his body she hanged herself for grief. She was loved by *Dionysus.
2. In Greek myth, daughter of Aegisthus and Clytemnestra.

Eri'nna, Greek poetess of the island of Tēlos near Rhodes, probably of the fourth century BC, who died at the age of 19. She was famous for a poem of 300 hexameter lines, *The Distaff* (*Ēlakatē*), which has not survived except for a few quotations and papyrus fragments; it was written in memory of her friend Baucis from whom she had been separated by the latter's marriage and death.

Erī'nyes, see FURIES.

Eriphy'le, in Greek myth, sister of Adrastus and wife of *Amphiaraus.

Eris, in Greek myth, the personification of strife. She is said to have thrown an apple, the 'Apple of Discord', among the goddesses at the wedding of Peleus and Thetis, for the most beautiful to pick up, thereby leading to the judgement of Paris and the Trojan War (see PARIS, JUDGEMENT OF).

Ermine Street, see ROADS 2.

Eros, in Greek myth, the god of love, the Roman Cupid. He does not appear in Homer, but Hesiod includes him as one of the first created gods (see EREBUS), signifying the power of love over gods and men. Eros in this cosmogonic sense sometimes figures in the thought of the early Greek philosophers. In the lyric poets however he is the personification of physical desire, cruel and unpredictable, but embodying those qualities that inspire love, and hence young and beautiful. This Eros is the companion, often the son, of Aphrodite. His bow and arrows, first mentioned by Euripides, and later his torch, figure prominently in his role of mischievous boy assigned to him by the Hellenistic poets and artists. Quite often he is expanded into a plurality of Erōtes. Eros was not, however, simply a literary conceit; he was also an object of worship in several ancient cults. See also IRIS.

Eryma'nthus, range of mountains in Arcadia, famous as the haunt of the fierce boar destroyed by Heracles (see HERACLES, LABOURS OF 3).

Erysi'chthon, in Greek myth, man who cut down a grove sacred to Demeter, by whom he was punished with insatiable hunger which ruined all his household. See CALLIMACHUS (Hymn 6).

Eryx, mountain above Drepana in west Sicily, the site of a famous temple of Aphroditē built according to some by Eryx, a son of Aphrodite, but according to Virgil by Aeneas. From Sicily the worship of Aphrodite (Venus) Erycina was introduced at Rome.

E'squiline (Lat. Esquiliae or later Mons Esquilinus), one of the *seven hills of Rome, on the eastern side of the city; it gave its name to one of the four regions (with the Suburbana, Collina, and Palatina) into which the republican city was divided.

E'teoclēs, in Greek myth, the elder son of *Oedipus and Jocasta, brother of Polyneices, Antigonē, and Ismenē.

Etesian winds, winds blowing steadily and often strongly from the north over the Aegean Sea from mid-June for up to three months, making northward navigation difficult.

Ether, see AETHER.

Ethiopia, the land of the 'burnt-faced men' (Aithiŏpĕs) according to the Greeks, situated with vague delimitations in north Africa, between the equator, the Red Sea, and the Atlantic, but especially describing the lands south of Egypt. Aeschylus had the Ethiopians extend to India, and Herodotus distinguishes between straight-haired (Asian) and curly-haired (Libyan) Ethiopians. Neither Greeks nor Romans penetrated further south than Meroë, and consequently their accounts of the various Ethiopian tribes are scanty and confused.

Etna, see AETNA.

Etrū'ria, in Italy, the country of the Etruscans (see below).

Etruscans, called Tyrrhenians by the Greeks, Tusci or Etrusci by Latin speakers, a pre-Roman people of central *Italy and in early times Rome's principal rivals for the control of that area. Etruscan culture came into being c.700 BC, apparently as a development from that of the early Iron Age Villanovans, which flowered briefly in that region. Politically the Etruscans made up a loose confederation of independent cities, and at the height of their power, from c.620 to c.500 BC, they controlled an empire reaching from the Po in the north to Campania in the south, including early Rome. The Roman king Tarquinius Priscus was said, probably rightly, to have been of Etruscan origin. After the expulsion of the Tarquins from Rome at the end of the sixth century, the Etruscans gradually lost their southern territory, suffering a famous defeat at Aricia c.504, and had perhaps already surrendered their northern lands to invading Celts. Their naval supremacy was destroyed in a sea-battle off Cumae in 474 when they were defeated by a fleet of Cumaeans and Syracusans under Hieron, tyrant of Syracuse. By the end of the third century BC Rome held the whole of Etruria.

The origin of the Etruscans was already a subject for antiquarian speculation in the middle of the first century AD when the emperor Claudius wrote their history (which has not survived). The Greek historian Herodotus thought they came from Lydia in Asia Minor (and the language might well be Anatolian; see below); but others (including Dionysius of Halicarnassus) have thought them indigenous to Italy. Their culture seems rooted in a development from that of the Villanovans, although the richly decorated and furnished tombs for which they are famous show Greek and oriental influences and appear on the scene so suddenly as to suggest (probably wrongly) the arrival of new cultural stock, and their religion and astrology likewise seem to contain oriental elements. There exist thousands of inscriptions written in a Greek alphabet, mostly epitaphs, dating from the seventh century to the time of the emperor Augustus, but their language seems not to be Indo-European, nor directly related to any other, and it remains largely undeciphered, although the phonetics and morphology are understood. The Etruscans are known to us chiefly through their tombs, shaped like houses, dating from the seventh century onwards, magnificently decorated with wall-paintings of their occupants at their everyday pursuits or with sculptures of lifelike immediacy, and

containing portraits of the dead realistically modelled. Their metal-work was outstanding and widely exported. The Capitoline Wolf and the Chimaera of Arretium (Arezzo) are both Etruscan bronzes. The Etruscans were celebrated in antiquity for the way in which every aspect of their public and private life was regulated by a code of religious practice, the so-called *Etrusca disciplīna*. They were particularly famed for their skill in augury based on scrutiny of the entrails, especially the liver, of sacrificial animals (see HARUSPICES). In this as in art, architecture, and engineering, Rome was deeply indebted to Etruria.

Eubū'lus (Euboulos) (c.405–c.335 BC), an important Athenian statesman who greatly influenced Athenian financial policy to the city's advantage, and was an advocate of peace with *Philip II of Macedon in opposition to *Demosthenes and the war-party. See also ATHENS 2 (v) and ISOCRATES 5.

Euclid (Eukleidēs), Greek mathematician, who lived in Alexandria c.300 BC, but of whose birthplace and life nothing reliable is known. His fame rests on his great textbook, *Stoicheia* ('elements'): books 1–4 and 6 on plane geometry, 5 on proportion, 7–9 on arithmetic and the theory of rational numbers, 10 on irrationals, 11–13 on solid geometry; books 14 and 15 are not by Euclid. This work caused the name 'Euclid' to become almost synonymous with 'geometry'. One of the few anecdotes told about him says that when Ptolemy I of Alexandria asked him if there was a shorter way to understand geometry than that of the *Elements*, he replied that there was no 'royal road' to geometry. His work drew extensively on the discoveries of his predecessors, but its great value lies in its rigorous exposition of the geometrical knowledge acquired by the Greeks from the time of Pythagoras, arranged systematically and in logical sequence. The seeming inevitability of the arrangement is illustrated by the apocryphal story told of the seventeenth-century French philosopher and mathematician Pascal, that as a boy he discovered geometry for himself and proceeded by the light of nature to the thirty-second proposition of the first book; the inventor of the story assumed that geometrical knowledge was bound to develop in the same order as in the *Elements*. As soon as it was published Euclid's textbook became the subject for study and comment, and the edition (or reworking) of *Theon (fourth century AD) was widely used; most valuable is the commentary of *Proclus (fifth century AD) on book 1.

In western Europe Euclid's work suffered the common fate of Greek science and mathematics, being known only to the Arabs until in the first half of the twelfth century an Englishman, Adelard of Bath, translated the Arabic version of the *Elements* into Latin. (See TEXTS,

TRANSMISSION OF ANCIENT 7.) In the next century Roger Bacon quoted Euclid, and from then on knowledge of the *Elements* was widely dispersed. The original Greek was not generally known until a text was printed at Basle in 1533. The vernacular translations date from the middle of the sixteenth century; although in Europe geometrical textbooks gradually incorporated modern advances in the subject, in Britain the *Elements* held their ground more or less unadulterated until the end of the nineteenth century. Euclid seems to have been the source of the words put at the end of mathematical proofs, in Greek, *hŏper edei deixai*, 'which was to be proved', but usually known in the Latin version, *q(uod) e(rat) d(emonstrandum)*. He wrote a number of other mathematical works, some of which survive in Greek and others in the Arabic translations only. He also wrote a treatise on music, still extant.

Euclī'dēs (Eukleidēs), of Megara (c.450–380 BC), associate of Socrates and present at his death; founder of the Megarian school of philosophy and, apparently in the tradition of the *Eleatic school, identifying the single principle of the latter with moral good.

Eu'clio, the old miser in the *Aulularia*, a Roman comedy by Plautus.

Eudē'mus (second half of the fourth century BC), friend and pupil of *Aristotle; his writings have not survived. He used to be regarded as the author of the *Eudemian Ethics*, preserved among the works of Aristotle, but this work is now usually attributed to Aristotle himself (see 4 (iv)).

Eudo'xus, of Cnidus (c.400–c.350 BC), outstanding mathematician in the half-century before Euclid, a younger contemporary of Plato and an associate of his in the Academy. His writings are lost but their contents are fairly well known from later writers. He is largely responsible for the discovery of the theory of proportion between incommensurables (covered by Euclid in *Elements*, book 5) and, in showing that a proportion could be established between any magnitudes, for removing the check given to geometry when irrational numbers were discovered. In solid geometry he showed that the volume of a pyramid was one third of that of a prism of equal height on the same base, and correspondingly that the volume of a cone was one third that of its containing cylinder. In astronomy his work marks the beginning of a new epoch, for he was the first to give a mathematical account of the movements of the heavenly bodies that tried to explain the fact that the planets occasionally appear to interrupt their movement eastward (relative to the fixed stars) along the zodiac, and for a time to move backwards from east to west (retrogression). (He is also the first Greek who we can be sure knew the five planets of the ancient world; see ASTRONOMY.) Eudoxus suggested that the paths of the sun and moon and planets were produced by the circular movements of concentric spheres, rotating at different speeds and about different axes with the earth at rest at their common centre. The system showed great mathematical skill and managed to account fairly successfully for a wide variety of phenomena. It was modified by Callipus to remove the most obvious inconsistencies with observable fact, and in this form it was accepted by *Aristotle, though no amount of modification could account for the noticeable variations in the brightness of the planets, which suggested that their distances from the earth were not constant. Eudoxus' astronomical calendar of the risings and settings of the constellations formed the basis of *Aratus' astronomical poem the *Phaenomena*.

Euhē'merus (Euēmeros), of Messene, author c.300 BC of a fantasy travel novel in Greek, *Sacred Scripture* (*Hiera anagraphē*), now surviving only in fragments, but influential in its day. In it he describes an imaginary voyage to an island Panchaia in the Indian Ocean where he found documentary evidence that the gods of mythology were originally great kings, deified by their grateful people, a theory known to the modern world as 'euhemerism'. The idea was very relevant to the contemporary Hellenistic world where rulers might demand worship from their subjects, and where a rationalizing atheism was part of the new view of life. *Ennius wrote in Latin a prose work based on the *Sacred Scripture*, impugning the majesty of Jupiter Optimus Maximus. That likewise has not survived but it is quoted extensively by the Christian apologist *Lactantius, who used it as evidence of the fraudulent nature of the Greek gods.

Eumae'us, in Homer's *Odyssey*, the faithful swineherd of Odysseus; he entertained Odysseus in his hut when the latter returned to Ithaca and afterwards helped him to destroy the suitors. His story is told in *Odyssey* 15.

Eumē'lus, of the Bacchiadae of Corinth, Greek epic poet of the second half of the eighth century BC, author of an epic on the mythical and heroic history of Corinth (and perhaps other epic poems). He also wrote a famous *prosodion* (procession-song; see LYRIC POETRY I) for the Messenians to sing at the festival of Apollo at Delos. The small fragment which survives in quotation is interesting as a very early specimen of lyric.

Eu'menēs, Eu'menids, see ATTALIDS.

Eume'nidēs, 'the kindly ones', euphemistic name for the *Furies and the title of a Greek tragedy by Aeschylus (see *ORESTEIA*).

Eumo'lpus, in Greek myth, a Thracian, the son of Poseidon, who while in exile from Thrace as punishment for rape visited Eleusis where he founded, or became connected with, the Eleusinian *mysteries. He succeeded to the throne of Thrace, but was sent for by the Eleusinians to help them against *Erechtheus, king of Athens, in which campaign he was killed. He was the eponymous ancestor of the family of the Eumolpidae, who officiated at the mysteries.

Eunū'chus ('eunuch'), Roman comedy by *Terence adapted from a Greek comedy of the same name by *Menander, with the characters of the *parasite and the soldier added from Menander's *Colax*. It was performed at the Roman *ludi Megalenses in 161 BC with great success, well-earned by its varied action and lively dialogue.

Phaedria, a young Athenian, is in love with the courtesan Thāis, who is also loved by the boastful soldier Thraso (always attended by the parasite Gnatho). Thraso wants to give her as a bribe a young slave-girl bought in Rhodes whom Thais, knowing her to be of Athenian birth and stolen in childhood, wishes to own so as to restore her to her family. She therefore persuades Phaedria to let her pretend to give in to Thraso. Phaedria, meanwhile, has himself bought a present for Thais of a eunuch, but his brother Chaerea, having seen and fallen in love with the Rhodian slave-girl on her way to Thais' house, exchanges clothes with the eunuch and assumes his character in order to gain access to her. In this he succeeds, and when Thais reveals the girl's Athenian birth they are betrothed. Thraso, repulsed by Thais as soon as she has gained possession of the slave-girl, tries unsuccessfully to carry her off, but a compromise is reached by which both he and Phaedria share her favours.

The prologue contains a line which subsequently became well known, *nullumst iam dictum quod non dictum sit prius*, 'nothing is said which has not been said before'. The play was imitated by Nicholas Udall (headmaster successively of Eton and Westminster) in the later scenes of *Ralph Roister Doister* (*c.*1554), the earliest known English comedy.

Eupa'tridae ('well-born'), the aristocracy at Athens, i.e. those born into one of the sixty or so named *genē* (see GENOS) or families which each claimed descent from a heroic ancestor who was himself the son of a god. They were generally rich landowners who could muster political support from their own territory. Until the end of the sixth century BC they monopolized the offices of government (see CLEISTHENES (2)). Even when the city became more democratic they were still influential. Certain priesthoods remained their prerogative (e.g. the priests of the Eleusinian mysteries (see MYSTERIES) were

from the *gene* of the Eumolpidai and Ceryces). See also SOLON.

Eupho'rion. 1. Son of the Attic tragedian Aeschylus, who is said to have won victories in the drama festivals with tragedies written by his father but not produced in his lifetime. In 431 BC he defeated both Sophocles and Euripides (one of whose plays was *Medea*), but with what plays is not known.

2. Of Chalcis in Euboea, a Hellenistic Greek poet of the third century BC who lived most of his life in Antioch in Syria where he was librarian. The scantiness of his surviving work makes it difficult to assess, but he seems mostly to have written epic-style poetry on mythological subjects. He exercised a considerable influence on later poets; at Rome his *epyllia were greatly admired by Catullus and his contemporaries (hence Cicero's description of these poets as *cantores Euphorionis*, 'those who sing the praises of Euphorion') but he did not write love elegies in the Roman manner, as used to be thought. Probably the *Ciris* reproduces his manner most closely (see APPENDIX VIRGILIANA).

Euphrā'nor (flourished *c.*360 BC), a native of Corinth famous both as a sculptor and as a painter. Three of his paintings, *Cavalry Battle before Mantinea* (fought 362 BC), *The Twelve Gods*, and *Theseus with Democracy and Demos* ('the people'), stood in the stoa of Zeus Eleutherios at Athens. He said of his *Theseus*, in contrast with the *Theseus* painted by *Parrhasius, that he had been fed on meat. His famous statues, some of them more than life-size, included one of Paris of which a copy exists, and others of Alexander the Great and Philip II of Macedon riding in chariots. His cult statue of Apollo Patrōos has been excavated from its temple in the Athenian agora. His books on symmetry and on colours have not survived.

Eu'polis, one of the trio of famous Athenian writers of Old Comedy, the others being Cratinus and Aristophanes (see COMEDY, GREEK 4). He was contemporary with the latter, producing his first play in 429 BC and dying at some time after 415. None of his plays survives in manuscript, but we have nineteen titles and numerous quotations as well as some papyrus fragments. His comedies are similar in subject-matter and style to those of Aristophanes. In *Marikās* (a non-Greek word meaning 'catamite') he attacked Hyperbolus much as Aristophanes did Cleon in *Knights*; in *Demoi* ('demes') great Athenians of the past were brought up from the Underworld to give the city good advice, and in *Taxiarchoi* ('corps-commanders') he represented the god Dionysus undergoing hard military training, recalling themes in Aristophanes' *Frogs* and showing that he and Aristophanes, as well as being rivals, were imitators of each other's work.

Euri'pidēs (*c*.485–406 BC), the youngest of the three great Athenian tragedians. We have little reliable information about his life, most of the anecdotes told about him being ultimately derived from the hostile jokes of the comic poets, such as the references to his mother selling herbs in the market. The story that he wrote his plays in a cave on Salamis confirms other reports of his solitary disposition, and he was not prominent in politics. He was associated in people's minds with the *sophists, whose influence is discernible in his work, and said to be acquainted with Anaxagoras, Socrates, and Protagoras; it was supposed to have been at his house that Protagoras gave the first public reading of his sceptical work *On the Gods*. Euripides won the dramatic competitions with the trilogy containing *Hippolytus* in 428, and posthumously with the trilogy containing *Bac-chae* and *Iphigeneia in Aulis*, produced probably in 405, and on only two other occasions. In about 408, embittered, it was said, by his unpopularity, he withdrew from Athens to the court of Archelaus, king of Macedon. There he died, allegedly torn to pieces by Archelaus' dogs, not long before the Dionysia of 406, at the *proagon* of which Sophocles commemorated his death by presenting his own tragic chorus ungarlanded.

We possess nineteen of the ninety-two plays Euripides is said to have written, and know the titles of about eighty. The plays we possess are of two classes:

(i) a selection of ten plays perhaps made *c*. AD 200 and transmitted with *scholia, consisting of *Alcestis* (438, second prize), *Medea* (431, third prize), *Hippolytus* (428, first prize), *An-dromache* (date not known; *c*.426), *Hecuba* (date not known; *c*.424), *Trojan Women* (415, second prize), *Phoenician Women* (see PHOENISSAE; between 412 and 408), *Orestes* (408), *Bacchae* (405; the scholia are lost), and *Rhesus* (perhaps not genuine);

(ii) part of an alphabetic arrangement of his work comprising plays whose (Greek) titles begin with the Greek letters E to K, namely, *Helen* (412), *Electra* (date not known; *c*.417), *Children of *Heracles* (Heracleidae) (date not known; *c*.430), *Madness of *Heracles* (date not known; *c*.417), *Suppliant Women* (see SUPPLI-ANTS 2; date not known; *c*.422), *Iphigeneia in Aulis* (405; produced with *Bacchae*), *Iphigeneia in Tauris* (date not known; *c*.414), *Ion* (date not known; *c*.410), and *Cyclops* (a satyric drama, probably late). In this second group we therefore have some plays of Euripides that may be considered a representative selection of his work rather than plays selected for a purpose, such as a school curriculum. Very fragmentary remains of several lost plays have turned up on papyri in the twentieth century.

Euripides' tragedies derive their characteristic tone from the author's departure from the

orthodoxies of Aeschylus and Sophocles, his giving prominence to unconventional and un-traditional views and to socially insignificant people like women and slaves, as well as his reappraisal of old stories in the light of late fifth-century scepticism. His mythical heroes and heroines, clothed in garments appropriate to their sufferings—the Athenians never forgot that in the *Telephus* he depicted the hero dressed in rags—describe their misfortunes in contem-porary language and human terms, while a slave may reveal an inherent nobility of mind at odds with his status. Aristotle, in the *Poetics*, quoted in this connection Sophocles' saying that he, Sophocles, represented people as they should be, Euripides as they are. Euripides was often censured in antiquity for making his characters, and especially his women, unnecessarily bad. He was clearly attracted by stories of violent and bizarre passion—Phaedra falling incestuously in love with her stepson Hippolytus, Medea taking vengeance on her husband by murdering their children, Heracles' madness; but what interested him also was the conflict that arose in the minds of such people. Nineteenth-century critics liked to call him a rationalist because of his sceptical attitudes to traditional religion and morality, but in more recent times he has been called, no less justly, an irrationalist, because he depicts people struggling with powerful irrational forces within themselves. In construction the plays sometimes seem awkward. Characters speak what is rhetorically appropriate, especially in the set debates of which Euripides was so fond, or raise questions relevant to the thought and events of the late fifth century (and in particular to the Peloponnesian War), but the speeches often seem incongruous in the context and the characters themselves less credible therefore. Eleven plays are brought to a conclusion by 'a god in a machine' (*deus ex machina*; see THEATRE 1). Aristophanes parodied Euripides brilliantly in· *Frogs*, and to a lesser extent in *Acharnians* and *Thesmophoriazusae*. Aristotle called him 'the most tragic of the poets' (i.e. best at arousing pity and fear; see POETICS), a description particularly apt to his depiction of the horrors of war. It was said that some Athenian prisoners after the Sicilian Expedition won their liberty by reciting pas-sages from his plays. (See also ELECTRA 2.)

Eurī'pus, in Greek, word meaning any strait where the flow of the tide is violent, the name in particular of the strait separating Euboea from Boeotia.

Eurō'pa ('broad-browed'), in Greek myth, daughter of Agenor, king of Tyre. Zeus loved her and so took the form of, or sent, a beautiful bull which swam to the sea-shore where she was playing and seemed so mild that she climbed upon its back. Thereupon it swam away with her to Crete, where to Zeus she bore *Minos,

*Rhadamanthys, and, in post-Homeric accounts, *Sarpedon. The bull became the constellation Taurus. Europa was identified with a Cretan goddess and worshipped on the island.

Europe. The continent of Europe was said to have been named from the mythical *Europa, although Herodotus (4. 45) found this implausible since she was from Phoenicia and never entered mainland Europe. The name as used by the ancients does not correspond with the modern continent. Not mentioned by Homer, it is first found in the *Homeric Hymn to Apollo (seventh century BC) where it is an unspecified area (around Greece) distinct from the Peloponnese and the Greek islands. Herodotus and his contemporaries in the mid-fifth century BC considered the whole of the known earth as one continent divided into three main parts, Asia, Libya, and Europe. The last was naturally bounded by the Mediterranean and the Atlantic; its western boundary was signified by the Pillars of Hercules (the Straits of Gibraltar) beyond which the Greeks rarely penetrated, while in the east Europe was divided from Asia first by the river Phasis (modern Rioni) which flows to the eastern shore of the Black Sea, and later by the Tanais (modern Don). The northern boundary was the mountain-chain which runs north of Thrace, Italy, and Spain. The Greeks hardly explored beyond south Russia; central and northern Russia and Scandinavia were unknown and fabulous regions. The land exploration of Europe was chiefly accomplished in the first centuries BC and AD by the Roman army surveyors under Julius Caesar and the generals of the emperor Augustus.

Eurōʹtās, the chief river of Laconia.

Eurus (Gk. *euros*), in Latin literature, the east or south-east *wind.

Euryʹalē, one of the three *Gorgons.

Euryʹalus, in Virgil's *Aeneid*, the friend of *Nisus.

Eurycleiʹa, in Homer's *Odyssey*, the old nurse of Odysseus.

Euryʹdicē, the name of several women in Greek myth, including the wife of Creon, king of Thebes (see *ANTIGONE* of Sophocles). The best-known was a nymph and the wife of *Orpheus. While pursued by Aristaeus she was bitten by a snake and died. Orpheus followed her to the Underworld where the charms of his lyre suspended the tortures of the damned and persuaded Hades to allow him to bring her back, provided that he did not look round at her before he reached the upper world. He broke this condition and thus lost her forever. Through Virgil (*Georgics* 4. 453) and Ovid (*Metamorphoses* 10. 1) the story became well known to the Middle Ages. The story was

sometimes given a happy ending as in Gluck's opera, where Eurydice was restored by the gods' forgiveness. The theme easily lent itself to a variety of symbolic interpretation, in ancient as well as modern times.

Euryʹmedon, one of the principal rivers of Pamphȳlia (in the south of modern Turkey), at the mouth of which the Athenian general Cimon destroyed a Persian fleet and then won a victory on land in or about 467 BC (see DELIAN LEAGUE). The ruins at Aspendus (modern Belkis), some 12 km. (7 miles) upstream, include a well-preserved Roman theatre and aqueduct.

Eurypoʹntid, the name of the junior branch of the royal house at Sparta, descendants of Eurypon, grandson of Procles (see HERACLEIDAE). (The senior branch was the *Agiad.)

Euryʹstheus, in Greek myth, king of Tiryns in Argos, son of Sthenelus and Menippē, a descendant of *Perseus. When Zeus swore on oath that the first descendant of Perseus to be born on a certain day would rule the surrounding peoples, intending that it should be his son Heracles, Hera in jealousy contrived that Eurystheus was born first. In the usual version of the myth, after Heracles in madness had killed his wife and children, the oracle at Delphi ordered him to live at Tiryns and serve Eurystheus for twelve years in expiation. Eurystheus imposed upon him many dangerous tasks, known later as the Twelve Labours (see HERACLES, LABOURS OF).

Euryʹtion. 1. In Greek myth, the herdsman of Geryon (see HERACLES, LABOURS OF 10).
2. In Greek myth, the *centaur whose misbehaviour at the wedding-feast of Pirithous, king of the Lapiths, began the quarrel between centaurs and Lapiths.

Euʹrytus, in Greek myth, king of Oechalia and father of Iolē; see HERACLES.

Euseʹbius (*c.* AD 260–*c.*340), Greek Christian writer, bishop of Caesarea in Palestine. His most important work, for which there was no precedent, is the *Ecclesiastical History*, which has earned him the title of father of Church history. It is divided into ten books, and is the main source for the history of the early Church in the East from its foundation to 324 (in the final version). It survives in the original Greek and also in Latin, Syriac, and Armenian versions. Among his other works is 'The Martyrs of Palestine', an eyewitness account of the persecutions (from 303 to 310) of the emperor *Diocletian. The *Praeparatio evangelica* ('preparation for the gospel'), in which he shows that the Greek tradition is inferior to the Hebrew and that the best of Greek philosophy merely coincided with or was derived from biblical teaching, is incidentally valuable in that it includes many quotations from classical authors now lost. Of importance for the study of ancient history are the two books of the *Chronikon* ('chronicle'), of which the first is an outline history of several ancient nations, and the second consists of synchronical tables with catalogues of rulers and striking occurrences from the birth of Abraham (reckoned as 2016 BC) to AD 328. It is a valuable adjunct to, and sometimes the only source for, our knowledge of dates and events in Greek and Roman history. The original Greek text survives only in a few fragments, but we have a Latin adaptation by Jerome and (since 1818) an Armenian translation.

Eustā'thius (latter half of the twelfth century AD), a native of Constantinople, archbishop of Thessalonika, the most learned man of his age, whose commentaries on ancient Greek writers embody much valuable scholarship which has not survived elsewhere. His classical commentaries consist of an *Introduction* to Pindar, a *Paraphrase* of Dionysius Periegetes, and *Commentaries* on Homer's *Iliad* and *Odyssey*; these last are of great length and deal with the history, geography, language, and mythology of the two works, incorporating much ancient learning not found elsewhere. Eustathius is regarded as a saint by the Orthodox Church.

Eute'rpē, one of the *Muses, in late authors specified as the muse of flute-playing.

Euthydē'mus, title of one of the earlier Greek dialogues of *Plato, taken from the name of the sophist of Chios.

Socrates narrates to his friend Crito, who is pondering how best to educate his son, a recent debate in the wrestling school, in which Cleinias, an aristocratic Athenian youth in danger of being corrupted unless properly educated, is presented with two opposing principles of education, the sophistic (see SOPHISTS), represented by Euthydemus and Dionysodorus, and the Socratic. The sophist would teach 'virtue', *aretē*, understood as meaning success in public life; Socrates expresses doubt as to whether *arete* can be taught at all. Crito, reinforced by an anonymous bystander who concluded that philosophy was worth nothing, doubts whether he should entrust his son to any of them.

euthȳ'nae, at Athens, the examination conducted by the public auditors, *logistai*, of the accounts of every magistrate at the end of his term of office. It was primarily an examination of the officer's handling of public money, but complaints of other kinds could be brought against him.

Eu'thyphrō (*Euthyphrōn*), title of an early Greek dialogue by *Plato.

Socrates, awaiting his trial for impiety, meets outside the court house Euthyphro the seer, who some years earlier had prosecuted his own father for unintentional homicide in order to clear himself of the pollution attendant on being connected with a murder. Socrates, appropriately, asks him for a definition of piety, but can only elicit the answer that piety is what is pleasing to the gods, and this turns out to be a matter of asking the gods for things and giving things to them. The dialogue is a gentle satire on an unworthy conception of religion.

Eutro'pius, Roman historian who published during the reign of the emperor Valens (AD 364–378) a survey of Roman history (*Breviarium ab urbe condita*) in ten books, from the time of Romulus to the death of the emperor Jovian in 364, ending with events of which the historian had personal knowledge. The early books are based on the epitome of Livy. The work is concise, well-balanced, and impartial.

Euxine, the 'hospitable' sea (Gk. *euxeinos*; originally *axenos*, 'inhospitable'), the euphemistic Greek name for the stormy Black Sea. It was opened up in the seventh century by explorers from Miletus and other Ionian Greek cities, an event perhaps reflected in the legends of the voyage of the Argonauts to Colchis, at the eastern end. By 600 BC its shores were dotted with Greek colonies (see COLONIZATION, GREEK), founded largely for the sake of trade. The earliest surviving description of it is given in the history of Herodotus, book 4.

Eva'dnē (Euadnē). **1.** In Greek myth, daughter of *Poseidon, by Apollo mother of Iamus, ancestor of the prophetic clan of the Iamidae who performed priestly functions at Olympia.

2. In Greek myth, wife of Capaneus, one of the *Seven against Thebes, who threw herself on his funeral pyre.

Eva'goras (Euagoras) (*c*.435–374 BC), king of Salamis in Cyprus, reputedly descended from *Teucer (2). He was friendly towards Athens and received many Athenian exiles at the end of the Peloponnesian War. His Hellenism brought him into conflict with Persia, by whom he was finally defeated. He died by assassination in a palace intrigue.

Eva'nder (Gk. Euandros, 'good man'), in Greece a minor deity associated with Pan and worshipped in Arcadia, especially at Pallantion. In Roman legend he was regarded as the first to make a settlement on the site of the future city of Rome. He was the son of Hermēs (or of a human father) and a nymph, identified with the Roman goddess Carmentis, and he led a small colony from Arcadia to the future site of the city on a hill called, after his native city, Pallanteum. This became known as the Palatine, and there he instituted the festival of the *Lupercalia, connected with the worship of Faunus, in reminiscence of the Arcadian festival of the Lycaea, which was connected with Pan. Hercules visited him on one occasion and killed the monster *Cacus. In commemoration Evander established the cult of Hercules at the Ara Maxima. Virgil in the *Aeneid* represents Evander as still alive when Aeneas arrives in Italy and as forming an alliance with him against the Latins. His son Pallas was killed fighting Turnus; it was to avenge him that Aeneas refused to spare Turnus. The story of Evander illustrates how the Romans created a connection in legend between Greece and Rome which included place-names and cults.

Exe'mpla ('examples'), a lost work of Cornelius *Nepos consisting of a collection of anecdotes from Roman history.

exile, a form of penalty for criminal offences used in Athens and Rome. In Athens it was imposed for unintentional homicide and sometimes for treason, but not for other offences, though it was permissible to go into voluntary exile in order to escape the death penalty. (*Ostracism, which meant banishment for ten years, was a political expedient and not a penalty for an offence.) Exile could be augmented by other penalties—the loss of property and of the right to be buried in Attic soil, the destruction of one's house, for example—but most of those who had committed unintentional homicide could keep their property and live abroad in freedom provided they avoided the great religious festivals and games, so as not to be a *pollution. If a man suffering penal exile was found in Attica, he ran the risk of imprisonment and perhaps execution, but as long as he remained in exile he had some protection under Athenian law. However, a man who had gone into voluntary exile to avoid the death penalty, or had been outlawed, had no legal protection while living abroad and was liable to summary execution if he appeared in Attica. Exile lasted for life unless the sufferer obtained pardon.

In Rome, as in Athens, a defendant on trial for a capital crime might choose to go into exile (*exsilium*) before judgement was pronounced. However, in the last century of the republic exile became a substitute for the death penalty when magistrates were obliged to allow a condemned person time to escape before executing sentence, after which he was deprived of all legal protection and threatened with death ('denied fire and water') if he returned. There were varying degrees of voluntary and prescribed banishment, from the mild *relegatio* up to the severe *deportatio* (introduced by the emperor Tiberius), a perpetual banishment to a certain place, confiscation of property, and loss of citizenship. The term 'exile' came to be applied to them all.

e'xodos, in Greek drama, the final scene; in *tragedy, it is the action following the final *stasimon* (choral ode); in comedy it is the final rejoicing following the last *episode.

exō'mis, tunic with one sleeve, leaving one shoulder bare, worn in Greece by slaves and the poor.

exo'rdium, in *rhetoric, the introduction (or proem) of a speech.

ex Ponto, Epi'stulae, see EPISTULAE EX PONTO.

F

Fa'bia, gens, one of the most ancient patrician clans at Rome which traced its origins to *Hercules and *Evander. The *gens* came to prominence in the fifth century BC when three brothers are said to have held seven succesive consulships from 485 to 479 inclusive. Its greatest fame derives from an exploit in 479 when the *gens* offered to pursue the war against the Etruscan town of Veii entirely on its own. 306 men withdrew from Rome and built a fortress on the Cremera (Fosso Valchetta), a small stream which falls into the Tiber a few miles above Rome. They were caught in an ambush and all perished with the exception of one youth, from whom all later members of the *gens* were descended. The later battle at the *Allia was generally believed to have occurred on the same day of the year (18 July). See ROME 4.

Fa'bius Ma'ximus Rulliā'nus (or Rullus), Quintus, the first Fabian to bear the *cognomen* Maximus, a famous Roman general of the Samnite wars (see ROME 4), five or six times consul, dictator in 315 BC and perhaps again in 313, censor in 304. He celebrated *triumphs over Samnites, Etruscans, and Gauls. His first feat was in 325 when as master of the horse he defeated the Samnites, having been forbidden to attack by the dictator L. Papirius Cursor. Livy's account of his numerous exploits in books 8–11, based on Fabius Pictor and the later annalists, is untrustworthy and introduces incidents from the life of his great-grandson, Fabius Cunctator (see below). When consul for the fifth time in 295 he and his colleague P. *Decius Mus defeated an alliance of Samnites, Gauls, and others at Sentinum (Sassoferrato) in the decisive battle for the supremacy of Italy.

Fa'bius Ma'ximus Verrucō'sus, Cunctā'tor, Quintus (*c*.275–203 BC), the famous Roman general and consul of the Second Punic War, dictator in 221 and again in 217 after Hannibal destroyed the consul Flaminius and the Roman army at the battle of Lake Trasimene. During the six months of his second period of office he fought a defensive war against Hannibal (see PUNIC WARS 2), and was called in consequence Cunctator, 'delayer', by doggedly following Hannibal's movements while avoiding a direct encounter. He once trapped Hannibal and his men in a valley, but they escaped behind a herd of oxen driven with blazing faggots tied to their horns. Rome soon came to distrust Fabius' policy of exhaustion, especially since it allowed Hannibal to ravage Campania unchecked, and Fabius was made to share his command with his *magister equitum* (master of the horse), Minucius Rufus. Tradition says that Minucius subsequently had to be saved from defeat by the timely arrival of Fabius. After Rome ventured on a pitched battle at Cannae in 216 and was disastrously defeated, Fabius' evasive strategy had to be resumed. The name derisively given to him took on an honourable connotation, and was incorporated in a famous line by the poet Ennius: *unus homo nobis cunctando restituit rem* ('one man by his delaying restored the situation for us'). Fabius was consul (and leader of the senate) for the fifth time in 209 when he recovered Tarentum (Taranto) from the Carthaginians. He strenuously opposed the plans of Scipio (Africanus), who had driven the Carthaginians out of Spain by 205, to take the war into the enemy's country by invading Africa; he died in 203, at about the time of Hannibal's departure from Italy, before the favourable conclusion of the war. Fabius was rightly called the Shield of Rome and was admired by later generations for his (perhaps unimaginative) courage and his old-fashioned patrician virtues. An anecdote is told which exemplifies the Roman approval of strict adherence to the proprieties. In 213 he served as legate to his son Q. Fabius, who was consul. On entering the latter's camp the father advanced on horseback to greet him and passed the *lictors, but was sternly told to dismount by his son. The father gladly complied, with the words 'I wished to see if you remembered you were consul'. In British politics 'Fabianism' describes a socialist policy of cautious advance, as opposed to immediate revolution.

Fa'bius Pictor ('painter'), **Quintus,** the earliest Roman historian, whose work survives only in quotations in later writers. (The family name derives from his grandfather who painted a temple *c*.302 BC.) He was a senator, fought in the Second Punic War (218–202 BC), and was sent to consult the Delphic Oracle after the Roman defeat at Cannae in 216. His history of Rome, which began with its foundation (dated by him to 748 BC) and continued to his own day, was written in Greek partly because Latin prose was not yet a literary medium but also with the purpose of justifying Roman policy to the Greeks. His work probably used pontifical records (see FASTI) and lists of magistrates. He was reliable, and used by Livy and Polybius.

fable, in literature, an anecdote with a moral in which the characters are animals behaving as men. The fable was a popular literary genre in Greece, as in other countries, at all times. Quintilian observes that it appeals particularly to the simple and uneducated. It is not found in Homer, but occurs in Hesiod (see WORKS AND DAYS) and *Archilochus. By the end of the fifth century BC Greek fables were generally attributed to *Aesop (said to have been a slave in Samos in the sixth century BC); they were probably written in prose. A collection of 'Tales of Aesop' was made by *Demetrius of Phalerum. The earliest surviving collection of fables is that of *Babrius, probably of the second century AD, written in choliambic verse (see METRE, GREEK 5 (iii)). It enjoyed wide popularity.

Latin authors frequently refer to fables which we know from Aesop. The earliest Latin collection was that of *Phaedrus, of the first century AD, written in iambic verse (see METRE, GREEK 5).

Fabri'cius Luscī'nus ('blind in one eye'), **Gaius,** a hero of the Romans' war with *Pyrrhus (280–272 BC), a *novus homo* who was twice consul and was admired in later times for his old-style virtues of austerity, high principle, and incorruptibility. He refused bribes from Pyrrhus when he was sent to him by the Romans in 280 to negotiate an exchange of prisoners; and in the campaign of 278 when he was consul and in command of the Roman forces, he sent back to Pyrrhus the latter's treacherous doctor who had offered to poison him. This generous act paved the way for Pyrrhus' withdrawal from Italy. Fabricius was a notably strict censor in 275. At his death he left no money to provide his daughters' dowry, which was given by the senate.

fā'bula, besides meaning 'story', the general Latin word for 'play', frequently combined with an adjective defining the subject. The commonest types were the *fabula* *Atellāna,* farce, *f.* *crěpidāta,* Roman tragedy on a Greek theme, *f.* *palliāta,* adaptation of a Greek comedy, *f.* *praetexta,* a serious play on a Roman historical subject, and *f.* *tŏgāta,* a Roman comedy with a native theme concerning low life in Rome.

Fali'sci, an Italian Iron Age people (see ITALY) closely related to the Latins, who lived on the right bank of the Tiber north of Latium.

Fall of Rome. Between AD 395 (when the Visigothic leader *Alaric began to ravage inside the Roman imperial frontiers in Thrace and Macedonia) and 495 (when Theodoric the Great, king of the Ostrogoths, was proclaimed king of Italy), the Roman empire in the West was no longer capable of resisting barbarian incursions. Italy and the western provinces were gradually occupied by Germanic peoples mostly migrating under pressure from the advancing Huns. In 401 and again in 403 Alaric invaded Italy but was forced to withdraw by *Stilicho. After the latter's death in 408 there was no general able to defeat the Visigoths, and on 24 August 410 they entered Rome and sacked it, the first time the city had fallen to a foreign enemy since its capture by the Gauls in 390 BC (see ROME 4). In 452 the Huns devastated parts of Italy, but their king Attila (known as the 'Scourge of God') was persuaded by Pope Leo I, the Great, to withdraw without entering Rome. Three years later the city fell to Gaiseric, king of the Vandals, who stayed for a fortnight in the city to plunder its treasures. The last Roman emperor in the West was the young Romulus Augustulus who reigned briefly 475–6. He was deposed and banished by Odo(v)acer, German commander of the imperial guard, who was proclaimed king of Italy by the army and accepted the emperor in the East as his overlord. With him the Roman empire in the West came to an end. (For the division of the empire into two halves see BYZANTINE AGE.)

fascēs, 'bundle of rods', bound together by red thongs and carried on their shoulders by *lictors before important Roman magistrates as a symbol of their power. The practice seems to have been of Etruscan origin. Under the kings each bundle enclosed an axe, symbolizing the king's right to scourge and execute, but from the early republic onwards only dictators were allowed axes in Rome; other magistrates retained the axe when outside Rome and at the head of an army. In the case of a general who had won a victory and been saluted as Imperator by his soldiers, his *fasces* were always crowned with laurel. From the Italian equivalent *fascio* the Italian Fascist party took its name, with the *fasces* as its symbol.

fasti, the name given to the old Roman *calendar which originally indicated *dies fasti and nefasti, the days on which it was or was not permissible to transact legal and public business. Later were included lists of consuls (*fasti consularēs*), priests (*fasti sacerdotalēs*), and records of triumphs. They were published in 304 BC by Gnaeus *Flavius. Some fragments survive in inscriptions. (Compare ANNALS.)

Fasti, *Ovid's poetical calendar of the Roman year, with its various observances and festivals, written in elegiacs. It was incomplete at the time of his exile in AD 8, and we have only the first six books (January to June), partially revised at Tomis. Ovid's models were Hellenistic poems, for astronomy the *Phaenomena* of *Aratus, and for his explanations of the origins of Roman history and religion the *Aitia* of *Callimachus, though he may also have been influenced by

*Propertius' last book of elegies which contains a large number of Roman legends.

Ovid's design, as stated in the preface to the poem, is to study the calendar in the light of old annals, and to show what events are commemorated on each day and the origins of the various rites. It accordingly records day by day the rising and setting of the constellations (not without mistakes), and explains the origins of the fixed festivals and the rites noted in the calendar, such as the *Lupercalia on 15 February. It also relates the legends connected with particular dates, such as that of the founding of Rome on 21 April, and that of the expulsion of the Tarquins on 24 February. The scheme provides opportunity for telling afresh some of the old Greek myths, such as the tale of Proserpine; and for excursions on a multitude of customs and beliefs, such as those connected with New Year's Day, the unluckiness of marriages in May, and the casting of straw men into the Tiber (see ARGEI).

fate (Gk. *moira* or *aisa*, 'apportionment'; Lat. *fātum*, 'what is said', probably deriving from a belief in spoken magic), in Greek and Roman religion, a person's apportionment or lot which governs what happens to him in life but most often refers to his death, since death is everyone's portion. In Homer, Moira or Aisa is a goddess who allots to everyone his apportionment, but the heroes often speak as if she and the gods together did this. At other times fate and the gods appear to be independent of each other: a god relinquishes his own desire in the face of opposing fate, or Zeus contemplates overthrowing fate by averting a hero's death; but the apparent conflict is more of a dramatic device than a religious dilemma (see ZEUS). Certainly for the poets Hesiod, Pindar, and Aeschylus, fate and Zeus together govern the world, though Apollo, being the god of prophecy, was sometimes thought to be able to influence fate. In Homer a man's fate is spun around him like a thread; hence the concept of *Fates, Moirai, as divine spinners, in Hesiod three in number. Good or ill fortune in a man's life was sometimes attributed by the Greeks to his personal *daimon, which in this context has a sense very close to 'fate', but is more like a personal agent, to whom a man could attribute e.g. his hard lot. During the fourth century BC the word *moira* was felt to be poetic and was replaced by *heimarmĕnē*. At the same time there arose a somewhat different view of fate: many people, affected by the new influences of astrology and scientific determinism, came to believe that the world in general and individuals also were entirely governed by an unavoidable fate, which could be described as necessity (Gk. *anankē*). Some sought escape from the oppressive power of fate in mystical religions (see MYSTERIES), which set up god and the spirit in opposition to fate, now becoming identified with matter, and offered their adherents a happy after-life.

Fates (Gk. Moirai; Lat. Fāta or Parcae). The Greek Fates, to which the Latin Parcae (so called from *parĕrĕ*, to bring forth) were in all respects assimilated, were represented from Homer onwards as old women spinning, three in number according to Hesiod, the children of Nyx (Night) or, somewhat allegorically, of Zeus and Themis (Righteousness). The three were called Klōtho ('spinner'), who held the distaff, Lachĕsis ('apportioner'), who drew off the thread, and Atropŏs ('inflexible'), who cut it short, Milton's 'blind Fury with th'abhorred shears'. The Parcae were named Nōna, Decuma, and Morta, meaning respectively, a nine-months' birth (premature, by Roman inclusive reckoning; see CALENDARS), a ten-months' (full-term) birth, and a still-birth. They could have been in origin birth-goddesses who became abstract powers of destiny only later. Their spinning may be thought of as completed at the moment of birth or continuing throughout life until all the thread is drawn off the distaff. They may also weave; the images in the poets are various. They are present at all great beginnings, as at the marriage of *Peleus and Thetis, where they also sang. The Moirai could be worshipped as birth-goddesses—Athenian brides offered them locks of hair, and women swore by them.

Faunus, in Roman myth, son of Pīcus, grandson of Saturn, and father of Latīnus, king of the Latini when Aeneas arrived in Italy. He was an Italian pastoral god, connected with the *Lupercalia, a hunter and promoter of agriculture, whose festival on 5 December was celebrated by cheerful celebrations in the countryside. He was also an oracular god (hence his title Fātŭus, 'the speaker') who revealed the future by dreams or supernatural voices in sacred groves, of which there was one near Tibur and another on the Aventine. The spectral appearances and terrifying sounds he was believed to make in wooded places caused him to be visualized as a monster with the legs and horns of a goat. Hence he was identified with the Arcadian god Pan and, as in the case of the latter, the idea grew up of a plurality of Fauni (fauns), who were identified with the Greek satyrs but usually thought of as more gentle.

Faustī'na, A'nnia Gale'ria. 1. The Elder, aunt of the Roman emperor Marcus *Aurelius and wife of Antoninus Pius, emperor AD 137–61. She died in 140; Antoninus named after her a charity for the maintenance of poor children.

2. The Younger, daughter of (1) above, who married her cousin M. Aurelius, emperor AD 161–80, in 145, and bore him at least 12 children. She accompanied her husband during his northern campaign in 170–4 and to the East, where she died in 175. She too, like her mother, was said by ancient writers to be faithless and disloyal, but it seems from his *Meditations* that she was loved by her husband, who also founded a charity in her memory.

Fau'stŭlus, in Roman legend, the herdsman who found Romulus and Remus in the she-wolf's den (see ROME 2), and whose wife Acca Larentia brought them up.

Favō'nius, in Latin, the west wind, also known as Zephyrus, and associated with spring-time. See WINDS.

Favorī'nus, orator and teacher of Greek rhetoric in the second century AD (see SOPHISTIC, SECOND); born at Arelatē (Arles) in Gaul he learned Greek at Massilia (Marseilles), and always seems to have written and spoken it in preference to Latin. Two of the speeches handed down in the works of Dion of Prusa (37 and 64) are probably by him, and a fragment of his treatise *On Exile* survives. His powers of oratory and his philosophical knowledge brought him high distinction in Greece and Rome, and for a time he enjoyed the favour of the Roman emperor Hadrian. He was banished to Chios c.130, but Hadrian's successor Antoninus Pius allowed him to return to Rome where he remained until his death in about the middle of the century. He used to boast of three things: that being a (natural) eunuch he had been charged with adultery, that being a native of Gaul he wrote and spoke Greek, and that he continued to live despite having offended the emperor.

federal states, in Greece, city-states in alliance with each other (in English usually called a confederacy or a league). When states formed a *symmachia* ('alliance in fighting'), each kept its individual freedom but they were all under the general leadership of one state; when they formed a *sympoliteia* ('alliance in political life'), perhaps under the leadership of a general, a state surrendered some of its independence to a central government, and the citizens had double citizenship and allegiance. Federal states first appeared in the fifth century BC and were most numerous and influential in the Hellenistic age when they created political units larger than the city-state.

Fēlī'citās, the Roman goddess of good luck, unknown until the mid-second century BC, when L. Licinius *Lucullus dedicated a temple to her; another was planned by Julius Caesar and was erected after his death. She was important in official cult under the emperors.

Fērā'lia ('commemoration of the dead'), in the Roman calendar, the festival of the dead held on 21 February, the last day of the *Parentalia, when food was carried to tombs for the use of the dead.

fē'riae, Latin term for a festival or holiday which involved visiting temples and making sacrifice to the gods. Holidays were either public, observed by the state, or private, observed by a family to celebrate e.g. a birthday. Some of the former were fixed by the calendar (*stativae*), others were movable festivals held annually on days appointed by priests and magistrates (*conceptivae*). Abstention from work, including legal and political business, was obligatory during public holidays (which were thus *dies nefasti), so that the sacred time should not be polluted. There exist interesting decisions made by the pontiffs as to what kind of work might be permissible; the pontiff Scaevola permitted any work in which delay might cause injury or suffering, such as rescuing an ox which had fallen into a pit (compare Luke 14: 5). See FERIAE LATINAE below; and also COMPITALIA, FERALIA, FORDICIDIA, FORNACALIA, LEMURES, LIBER, LUPERCALIA, LUDI, MEGALESIA, PAGANALIA, PALES, QUINQUATRIS, SATURNALIA, and VESTA.

fē'riae Lati'nae ('Latin festival'), a joint religious celebration of the Romans and the Latins in honour of Jupiter Latiāris, in his role as god of the *Latin League, held on the Alban Mount annually, usually at the end of April, on days appointed by the magistrates (*feriae conceptivae*), under the presidency of Rome. It dated back to the period when *Alba Longa and not Rome was the chief city of Latium. The flesh of the sacrificial victim (a white heifer) was eaten in a communal meal by representatives from all the cities of the League. It was an important occasion, attended by all the magistrates; the festival was still celebrated in the third century AD.

Fērō'nia, an Italian goddess of widespread cult; of her functions and the etymology of her name nothing is known.

Fesce'nnine verses (*versus fescennīni*), in Latin, one of the earliest kinds of Italian poetry, ribald songs or dialogues in extempore verse, produced for amusement at festivals and also sung at weddings; they were of the same nature as the abusive songs sung by soldiers at triumphs and the term was used of scurrilous verse in general. Livy and Horace thought the original Fescennine verses were a crude form of metrical repartee exchanged extempore between rustics, and the origin of Italian drama, perhaps in imitation of the Aristotelian theory of the origin of drama in Greece (see COMEDY, GREEK 2; TRAGEDY 1). The ancients derived the name either from Fescennium, a town in Etruria (which has no obvious connection), or from *fascinum* ('enchantment', the 'evil eye'), which the songs, like the phallic emblem worn by children (also called *fascinum*), were supposed to ward off.

festivals, in the ancient world, a day or days set aside by a city, state, or country for the worship of gods. Although festivals were always in some aspect religious and never purely secular, no rigid distinction was made between religious and secular activities, and they were frequently occasions of general merry-making. Feasting, athletics, play-acting, and bawdiness were all considered appropriate constituents of certain festivals.

Greek festivals. The Greek word for festival, *panēgyris*, signifies a meeting of a whole people for worship at a common sanctuary. The festival could be of local interest only, or be open to the whole population of Greece, as were the great panhellenic games (Olympian, Pythian, Nemean, and Isthmian); they were repeated annually or at regular intervals of a certain number of years, usually at the time of full moon. Most of those held in the countryside were ancient and agrarian in origin, and gradually came to include dramatic, musical, and athletic competitions. Orators sometimes amused the crowds with a festive oration or 'panegyric', which later acquired the sense of 'speech of praise'. In towns, the magistrates arranged the festivals and performed the religious rites. Almost every god had his festival day. The procession and the sacrifice gained in importance, particularly since the flesh of the slaughtered animals was shared among the people. In early times the colonies sent embassies to the festivals of the mother-city, and the cities sent embassies to the panhellenic games. The Athenians urged their colonies and allies to attend the Panathenaea and Great Dionysia at Athens, and these became occasions for expressions of patriotic sentiment.

For individual festivals, see the following. For the Olympian, Pythian, Nemean, and Isthmian games: GAMES, PUBLIC I (i–iv). For Athenian festivals: PANATHENAEA, DIONYSIA, LENAEA, AN-THESTERIA, OSCHOPHORIA, THESMOPHORIA, SCIRO-PHORIA, THARGELIA, PYANEPSIA. For Apaturia see PHRATRIAI. For Spartan festivals: GYMNOPAEDIAE and CARNEA. For Argos: HERAEA. For Boeotian Daidala see under HERA. See also ELEUTHERIA, LYCAEUS, and MYSTERIES.

For Roman festivals see FERIAE.

Festus, Sextus Pompē'ius, see VERRIUS FLAC-CUS.

fētiā'lēs, *college of Roman priests, selected for life from among the nobles, who represented the people in their dealings with other nations; the origin of their name is uncertain, but it may be connected with words meaning 'ordinance'. They were concerned particularly in the rituals of making a treaty and declaring war. In the former case a fetial would pronounce a curse on Rome in the event that she should break the treaty first, and confirm it by killing a pig with a flint; in the latter case the fetial cast a specially

hardened spear across the border into the offending country, if it was a neighbour, or into a special piece of land near the temple of Bellona that by a legal fiction was constituted as enemy territory. The office seems to have lapsed in the last century of the republic but to have been revived under Augustus.

finance

1. *Greek.* The ordinary income of the Athenian state in the fifth century BC and that of other similar states was derived as a rule not from direct taxes, though these were paid by resident aliens and some minority groups, but from indirect taxes: customs dues, royalties and concessions from the silver mines, rents of public and sacred land, and fees, fines, and confiscations exacted by the law-courts. Direct taxation was imposed only in time of war, when a property tax (*eisphora*) was levied on the richest citizens, who numbered around 6,000 and therefore made up a quarter to a third of the (adult male) citizen-body. Some of the very richest were made trierarchs, in which capacity they had to maintain a trireme (warship) in seaworthy condition for one year. In peace as well as war the rich were also subject to another form of tax, the *liturgy, by which they met the expense of certain costly public functions out of their own pocket. The usual expenditure of the state covered the cost of the police, army, navy, and defences, ambassadors, the *palaestrae* and gymnasia, religious festivals, public buildings, payment of those with official duties, and allowances to the poor (see THEORIC FUND).

Some expenditure was statutory, certain sums being allocated by law to certain departments for their own purposes. Thus the assembly received ten talents a year to pay for engraving inscriptions, entertaining foreign envoys, feting ambassadors, etc. In hard times the allocations might be cut; in 348 BC when Euboea was in revolt against Athens the law-courts were suspended because insufficient money had been allocated to pay the jurors.

The complications of finance were administered with surprising efficiency by a multiplicity of boards (constituted of citizens chosen annually by lot) under the supervision of the *boulē. These inexperienced citizens could handle complicated business because duties were minutely subdivided, so that an individual's area of responsibility was small. Moreover, the money and accounts passed through so many hands that peculation was difficult. In the latter half of the fourth century BC certain important financial offices were filled by election and the holders exercised great political influence (see EUBULUS and LYCURGUS).

When Athens possessed an empire in the second half of the fifth century BC she derived from it an annual income of 600 talents as well as profiting incidentally from being the capital city. This wealth made her a powerful city with resplendent public buildings, and enabled her to support a larger than average citizen population at a higher standard. See DELIAN LEAGUE.

2. *Roman*. The income of the Roman state during the early republic was derived from rents paid for the use of public lands and pastures (*ager publicus*). The only direct tax paid by Roman citizens was the land and property tax, *tributum*, levied in times of emergency to cover the expenses of war, and sometimes repaid. (See PROLETARII.) During the century preceding the end of the Third Macedonian War in 167 BC the treasury was so enriched by overseas conquests that it had no further need to levy *tributum* on land in Italy; but it continued to be paid by all inhabitants of conquered territories (which became Roman provinces), whether Roman citizens or not, and during the last century and a half of the republic this became the most important source of revenue. It took the forms of a land-tax (*tributum soli*) and a poll-tax (*tributum capitis*). Revenue was also raised indirectly from customs dues (*portoria*), salt works, and mines, and from taxes levied on the sale of slaves and other property and on the value of manumitted slaves. Provincial governors received a grant from the state for their own expenses and those of their staff, and thereafter were responsible for revenue and expenditure in their province. The *tributum*, either a fixed sum of money (*stipendium*) or a tithe paid in kind (*decumae*), was collected by *publicani*, a system that gave opportunity for the enrichment of individuals, including the governor (fully illustrated in Cicero's *Verrines*). Under the empire the system by which *publicani* contracted for *decumae* died out, and the fixed *tributum* based on the *census and collected by local magistrates became almost universal.

All public money was paid into the *aerarium ('treasury') at Rome, which was under the general supervision of the two urban quaestors. The quaestorship was the first magistracy held by someone embarking on a senatorial career (see CURSUS HONORUM) and hence the quaestors were men of little experience; they acted entirely under the direction of the senate, who made all decisions about public finance. The *censors superintended the collection of all revenues, usually by leasing the collecting rights to the *publicani* for a fixed sum and for a certain number of years. They also superintended all public buildings and works, for which the senate voted them a sum of money every five years, and were in charge of expenses connected with religious worship. The most costly objects of public expenditure were always the army and the corn supply (see ANNONA); the cost of government was small since magistrates were unpaid. Rome's deficiency in trained administrators during the later republic is most apparent in the area of finance. The senate drew up no detailed budget

and did not scrutinize closely the accounts of the magistrates, while the censors and quaestors exercised only perfunctory control. Augustus transferred the management of the *aerarium* to the more experienced men of praetorian rank, and under the empire a large, competent, paid bureaucracy grew up. The effective power of decision in financial matters was transferred from the senate to the emperor.

Augustus and his successors preserved the immunity of Italy from direct taxation. But while retaining the harbour dues and the tax on the manumission of slaves, Augustus introduced new indirect taxes, death duties of five per cent on inheritances of over 100,000 sestertii (payable by Roman citizens both in Italy and in the provinces), a tax of one per cent on sales at auction and by contract, and a tax on the value of slaves sold. The senate continued to manage the public *aerarium*, but under the early empire an imperial treasury, *fiscus*, was instituted, in which were deposited the emperor's own considerable funds, the sources of which, whether the imperial provinces or elsewhere, are still a matter of debate. These funds were increasingly spent on public needs, so that by the third century AD there was little distinction between public and imperial monies or between the terms *aerarium* and *fiscus*. During this century the maintenance of a large regular army, without the help of large quantities of booty, and a greatly augmented bureaucracy produced financial strain which brought about a rapid inflation of prices. The government drastically depreciated the coinage and then refused to accept its own coin from taxpayers, so that the greater part of the state's revenues, as well as the transactions of ordinary people, was in kind. Reforms by *Diocletian and *Constantine the Great led to a slow revival of confidence and the resumption of a money economy in the fourth century.

fiscus ('basket', 'money-bag'), the term which came to denote the funds of the Roman emperor, as opposed to the public *aerarium*; it was instituted as a separate treasury in the first century AD (at what point exactly is not known), and possessed certain rights in law. The source of the fiscal income is still disputed, but probably in the main it was formed by the revenues of the imperial provinces supplemented by gifts and inheritances, especially of land and property. The funds it contained were thus very considerable and were used to pay for public needs, such as the corn supply and the army. See also FINANCE 2.

Five Thousand (at Athens), see FOUR HUNDRED.

Flaccus, Ve'rrius, see VERRIUS.

flamen (apparently meaning 'priest' or 'sacrificer'), at Rome, a priest appointed to the service of one particular god from among the most ancient Roman deities, further distinguished by an epithet derived from the god's name. Fifteen in number, the flamens were part of the college of pontiffs (see COLLEGIUM) under the authority of the *pontifex maximus*. The most ancient and dignified (*maiorēs*) were the *flamen dialis* of Jupiter, *martialis* of Mars, and *quirinalis* of Quirinus, all chosen from among the patricians, the rest (*minorēs*) being plebeian. They were nominated by the people and elected for life. Their characteristic dress was the conical white leather hat (*apex*). The *flamen dialis* was held in great reverence and was subject to an elaborate system of taboos and rules designed to keep him from pollution and in constant attendance on his duties, and which even regulated the conduct of his wife. Originally he was precluded from holding any magistracy, but this prohibition lapsed in later times. The municipal towns (see MUNICIPIUM) also had their flamens; the notorious murder of *Clodius by Milo took place while the latter was on his way to Lanuvium, of which he was dictator, to declare the election of a flamen. After the deification of the emperors, starting with Julius Caesar in 42 BC, flamens were appointed in Rome and in the provinces to superintend their worship also.

Flāminī'nus, Titus Qui'nctius, consul 198 BC, sent in 197 to Macedonia where Rome was engaged in the Second Macedonian War against Philip V of Macedon (see MACEDONIA 3). The latter was fighting to maintain his supremacy in Greece against many Greek states which were aided by Rome. Flamininus won a pitched battle against him at Cynoscephalae in Thessaly, and by this victory the Romans found themselves responsible for the settlement of a newly-liberated Greece. In 198, when Philip had tentatively sued for peace, Flamininus had required him to acknowledge the independence of all the Greek states; in 196, when the senate was dictating the settlement, it was influenced by Flamininus to establish a protectorate over autonomous Greek city-states, though moved also by motives of expediency. When Flamininus announced the liberation of Greece to the crowds gathered at Corinth for the Isthmian games of 196, he was honoured as no one had ever been before for what seemed to the Greeks an act of extraordinary generosity. In 194 he left Greece, where, however, peace was short-lived; further unrest brought a Roman army back in 192, and eventually in 146 Rome put an end to Greek freedom by imposing a strict settlement on the cities and constituting Macedonia a province under a governor. In his philhellenism Flamininus was comparable with *Scipio Africanus; he died in 174.

Flavian emperors, the emperors of Rome from AD 71 to 96 who belonged to the *gens Flāvia*; they were *Vespasian (71–9), his elder

son *Titus (79–81), and his younger son *Domitian (81–96).

Flā'vius, Gnaeus, secretary to Appius *Claudius Caecus (censor 312 BC), aedile in 304 BC, famous in the annals of Roman law for having been the first to publish and therefore make known to the people the rules of the calendar (see FASTI) which determined what legal acts might be done on which days, and probably also the *formulae* or form of words which had to be used to state a claim or make a defence (see LAW, AT ROME 2). This knowledge had formerly been the monopoly of the pontiffs, who were patrician, and the patricians were indignant to see it broken. Flavius had been made a senator by Appius Claudius, who may have been the instigator of the publication. Flavius' election to the aedileship was secured in spite of his humble origins and unpopularity in senatorial circles.

Flōra, an Italian goddess of flowers and spring whose antiquity is proved by the assignment to her of a *flamen floralis*, but who was not given a temple until 238 BC. At this temple, near the Circus Maximus, cheerful and ribald celebrations in her honour were held every April, reaching their climax on the first of May. Ovid tells the story of Chlōris who, when pursued by Zephyrus, changed into Flora and breathed out flowers which spread over the countryside; this myth is depicted in Botticelli's *Primavera*. For the festival of the Floralia see LUDI I (vii).

Flōrus, author of the Latin history known as the 'Epitome of all the Wars during Seven Hundred Years', an abridgement of Roman history up to the age of Augustus with special reference to the wars, and designed as a panegyric of the Roman people. Some manuscripts describe it as an epitome of Livy, but it is sometimes at variance with that historian while it draws on the work of Sallust and Caesar and perhaps Virgil and Lucan. The style is markedly rhetorical, and the author is sometimes brief to the point of obscurity. Florus' identity and other names are not known for certain, though he is commonly called Lucius Annaeus. He lived in the second century AD and is variously identified with the Florus who was poet-friend of the emperor Hadrian and with the author of a dialogue, imperfectly preserved, entitled 'Is Virgil an orator or a poet?'

flute (Gk. *aulos*, Lat. *tibia*), see MUSIC.

food and drink. The earliest meals mentioned in classical literature, in Homer, are of a kind fit for heroes, who after fighting devoured quantities of roast meat—oxen, sheep, goats, or pig—washed down with draughts of *wine. This is in strong contrast with the comparative rarity of meat in later Greece (except after sacrifices or at public banquets) and the abundance of fish: as Plato observed, the heroes never eat fish. However, Homer recognized that the staple drink was wine and the staple food bread; barley meal and wheaten flour remained throughout the ancient world 'the marrow of men'.

The Greeks and Romans typically ate two light *meals during the earlier part of the day and took their main meal at about sunset. A common Greek meal consisted of bread eaten with a 'relish'—cheese, *honey, or, very often, fish (fresh, dried, or pickled). Although meat in general was a rarity compared with fish, pork was favoured, especially by the Romans, and there were also various kinds of sausage, as well as domestic fowl, game, and wild birds. Vegetables formed an important part of the diet—beans and lentils, beets, cabbage, lettuce, onions, and garlic. Several varieties of cake were eaten and the Romans in particular had many kinds of tarts and sweetmeats. Figs and grapes were the commonest fruits, but apples, pears, mulberries, and dates were also well known. Olive oil was the main source of fat; butter, 'cow-cheese', was considered a food for barbarians. Milk, usually goats' or ewes', was kept mainly for cheese; like beer, it was drunk only by those beyond the pale of civilization (e.g. the Cyclopes), though its medicinal value was well known. The only important beverage was wine, usually diluted with water. Honey was used for sweetening. Both Greeks and Romans were generally frugal in their diet, despite the contrary impression given by descriptions of banquets in imperial Rome. The Spartans were notable for their austerity, and their local broth was considered by other Greeks to be particularly nasty. The Romans had a greater range of dishes available—for example, more shellfish, (particularly oysters from artificial beds), fish bred in ponds, and more varieties of birds, the latter a consequence of the intensive breeding methods which they practised (see AGRICULTURE). They also prized snails and dormice, specially bred for the table. They liked to disguise the natural taste of food with highly spiced sauces (their fish-sauce *garum* was famous), a taste which seems to have survived in Mediterranean cuisine to the present day.

Fordicī'dia, at Rome, a religious festival held on 15 April, at which a pregnant cow (*forda*) was sacrificed in each of the thirty wards (*curiae*) of the city. The intention was to promote the fertility of the cattle and fields. The unborn calves were removed from the womb and burnt, and the ashes subsequently used in a purificatory rite at the festival of the Parilia (see PALES).

Fo'rmiae (Formia), an ancient Volscian town on the Appian Way, identified by the Roman poets with Lamus, the city of the Laestrygonians in Homer's *Odyssey*. In the classical period it became a fashionable pleasure resort where many Romans had villas, including Cicero, who was killed nearby.

Forms, Platonic, see PLATO 4.

formulae, Homeric and formulaic verse. Homeric epic is in its origin *oral composition, and every performance was an improvisation. In order to facilitate improvisation within the strict constraints imposed by the metre, the bard memorized what have been called in modern times 'formulae', groups of words of various metrical patterns which express a commonly repeated idea or action and can fit into many contexts. Formulae may vary in length from a noun plus adjective—'swift-footed Achilles', 'wily Odysseus'—to several lines, such as those describing a hero arming for battle. The use of formulae accounts for the repetitive nature of Homeric verse.

Fornācā'lia, at Rome, religious festival celebrated by the wards or *curiae,* held in early February on a day to be decided by the leaders of the *curiae.* Its purpose was in some way to prosper the ovens, *fornacēs,* which parched the grain.

Fortū'na or **Fors Fortuna,** Italian goddess, perhaps originally the 'bringer' of fertility (Lat. *ferre,* 'to bring'), but identified with the Greek *Tychē and so the goddess of chance or luck. She had an ancient temple in the Forum Boarium at Rome. Her cult was said to have been introduced into Rome by *Servius Tullius; she was not, therefore, one of the most ancient deities, a fact confirmed by her not having a *flamen. She was worshipped at Antium and at Praenestē, where she had an oracular shrine. At Rome her festival on 24 June was a popular holiday, and large crowds including slaves (see SLAVERY 2) flocked to her shrine, near the river Tiber about 2 km. (1 mile) downstream from the city, to witness the sacrifices. The Romans addressed her by a variety of epithets expressing either particular kinds of good luck or the kinds of people to whom she granted it.

Forty, the, at Athens, the magistrates (four picked by lot from each of the ten tribes) responsible for deciding private law-suits if the amount of money involved did not exceed ten drachmas. See LAW, AT ATHENS 1.

forum ('market-place'), a levelled rectangle of ground in the centre of every large Roman town and a constant feature of Roman town-plans even in the provinces. Although there was a tendency over the years for trade to be transferred to shops in other quarters, the forum remained the focus of the town's political, social, and commercial life, and was surrounded by the chief civic buildings. It sometimes gave a town its name, e.g. Forum Julii (Fréjus). The various fora in Rome itself are described below.

Forum Augu'stum, at Rome, a forum that was also the very large precinct (110 m. by 83 m., 360 ft. by 270 ft.) of the temple of Mars Ultor ('avenger'). The temple was dedicated in 2 BC by the emperor Augustus, having been vowed by him during the battle of Philippi in 42 BC. The forum was surrounded by a very large wall, considerable parts of which survive, as a protection against fire and the shabby neighbourhood. In the sixteenth century wooden dowels were found in it so well preserved that they could be used again. The forum was built to provide additional room for the law-courts and to meet other needs of the increasing population. Augustus placed in it bronze statues of all successful Roman generals, many of whose inscriptions have been found. It was from here that provincial governors ceremonially set off, and here they were received upon their return.

Forum Boā'rium, the 'cattle-market' of ancient Rome and also an important centre for traffic, situated between the Palatine hill and the river Tiber. In time this large open space was encroached upon by buildings, but the name was still applied to the whole district. The crowded area which resulted was often devastated by fire.

Forum Ju'lium or **Cae'saris**, a forum at Rome, dedicated by Julius Caesar in 46 BC as a centre for business. In it he erected a temple to Venus Genetrix, mythical ancestress of the *Julian gens*, which he had vowed at the battle of Pharsalus in 48, and in front of it placed an equestrian statue of himself. There was also a fountain surrounded by statues of nymphs, called Appiadēs.

Forum Rōmā'num, the ancient market-place and later the political, commercial, and religious centre of Rome, occupying what was originally a marshy valley which served as one of the defences of the first city on the Palatine hill and separated it from the Capitoline and Quirinal hills (see SEVEN HILLS OF ROME). It is this which is normally referred to as 'the forum' at Rome. The memory of its original state long survived in Roman tradition. The area was drained in the sixth century BC by the *Cloaca Maxima and became the market place. For early features of the forum see JUTURNA, REGIA, and VESTA. Its earliest monuments were the first temples to Saturn (497 BC), Castor (484), and Concordia (336). The speaker's platform (*rostra) was in existence by 338 BC. During the second century BC the forum acquired sufficient civic importance for the *concilium plebis*, assembly of the people, to be transferred here from the Campus Martius (see COMITIA). Tradesmen and shopkeepers were relegated to special markets and replaced by bankers and usurers. Basilicas were erected—large covered halls in which law-courts sat and business was transacted. The first

overall plan of the forum is in large part due to Sulla who at the beginning of the first century BC paved much of the area, built a new basilica, and restored the Rostra. Julius Caesar's further designs for it were largely carried out by the emperor Augustus, who transformed it, and most of the surrounding buildings have come down to us much as he left them—the rebuilt temples of Saturn, Castor, and Concordia, the temple of Julius Caesar, two basilicas, and the restored Rostra. Among the minor monuments erected by Augustus was the *miliarium aureum*, 'golden milestone'. Later monuments in the forum include the temples of Vespasian (AD 81) and of Faustina (141), and the arch of Septimius Severus (203).

Forum Trāiā'ni (sometimes called the Forum Ulpium), a forum at Rome built by the emperor Trajan in AD 113 between the Capitoline and Quirinal hills, the last and most magnificent of the Roman fora erected by the emperors. It contained the Basilica Ulpia (a law-court), the Bibliotheca Ulpia (a library comprising two halls, one for Greek and the other for Latin books), and Trajan's Column. After Trajan's death Hadrian erected in the forum a temple dedicated to him. Trajan's Column, 38 m. (125 ft.) high and hollow, with a spiral staircase leading to the top, still stands in a good state of preservation. It is decorated with a spiral frieze illustrating the events of the Dacian Wars and once contained Trajan's ashes in a golden urn. An inscription seems to say that the column was designed to show the depth of excavation necessary to construct the forum on the extreme eastern shoulder of the Quirinal hill.

Foss(e) Way, see ROADS 2.

Four Hundred, the, at Athens, a council of their own members which oligarchs set up to rule Athens in 411 BC (see OLIGARCHY). It was believed by some Athenians that if democratic rule at Athens were replaced by an oligarchy the king of Persia would support Athens in the *Peloponnesian War. In an atmosphere of distrust and fear arising in part from the murder, presumably by the oligarchs, of several prominent democrats, the assembly was intimidated into passing a measure suspending the democratic institutions and magistrates and electing 'officials' to choose a council of four hundred (replacing the democratic council of five hundred, the *boulē*) who were to have absolute authority to govern as seemed best to them. Their claim to govern was based on their assertion that they would prosecute the war more efficiently. It was also agreed that there should be a new-style assembly of five thousand, to meet whenever the new council convened them, but in fact this hypothetical body never met. The Four Hundred seized power before the agreed date by entering the council chamber and summarily expelling the *boule*. They governed the city for three months, but then the Athenian fleet at Samos rebelled against their oligarchic commanders and negotiated with Athens; the Four Hundred, who were themselves split into moderate and extreme oligarchs, the latter being very unpopular, were deposed in September 411 after the fleet had been defeated by the Spartans. An assembly of Five Thousand was properly established, consisting only of those who could afford to furnish themselves with arms (i.e. the hoplites). In 410, after a naval victory at Cyzicus, the democratic party was sufficiently encouraged to be able to restore the democracy, with its old council of five hundred and unrestricted franchise. See ATHENS 2 (iii), ANTIPHON, and THERAMENES.

François Vase, see VASE-PAINTING, GREEK.

Franks (Franci, 'free men'), a coalition of small German tribes on the Lower Rhine who took this name in the third century AD. In the fourth century they were permitted by Rome to occupy a large area in the region of modern Belgium. They expanded further into Gaul in the fifth century, and in 486, led by their king Clovis, of the Merovingian family, they defeated Syagrius, the last Roman ruler in Gaul. Clovis, who became a convert to Christianity, and his descendants succeeded in uniting under their rule the whole area of modern France (Francia).

fratres arva'les, see ARVAL PRIESTS.

freedmen (Lat. *liberti, libertini*), slaves who had been freed ('manumitted') by their masters, and a class of people who figured much more prominently in Roman society than in Greek. In Athens manumission required no formal procedure; a manumitted slave was registered as a metic (resident alien) with his former owner as sponsor. This meant that he was not a citizen and could not normally become one (see CITIZENSHIP I), and that he was liable to certain taxes and restrictions of privilege. He was also obliged by law to fulfil certain obligations imposed by his former owner as a condition of freedom, such as paying his owner retrospectively for his freedom, as well as other duties the nature of which is unknown. Freedmen in Rome have been regarded as almost comprising a middle class in the society of the late republic and early empire, and they included many people of intelligence, energy, and ambition.

It was an extraordinary feature of Roman law that a slave manumitted in proper legal form by a Roman citizen owner became himself a Roman citizen, though with certain disabilities because he was not himself free-born (which his children would be). He could not serve in the regular legions (until the first century BC), aspire to senatorial or equestrian rank or even, perhaps, to a local magistracy. A freedman whose former owner or his children still lived owed obligations to the family which were enforceable at law (see CLIENT), and the family had some rights in the freedman's property after his death. Romans liked to think of the relationship between freedmen and patron as filial, and certainly bonds of affection existed, as for example between Cicero and his family and their freedman *Tiro. The fact that freedmen were regularly accepted into the family grave is further evidence of the solidarity of the relationship. During the republic slaves could also be manumitted informally, for example by an announcement among friends; they would have their freedom protected by the praetor, but were not free in the eyes of the law. Under the early empire such freedmen were legally recognized but their rights were severely restricted; their chief disability was that at their death all their property reverted to their former owners. They were not Roman citizens; their status was comparable with those who had *Latin rights, and they were known as 'Junian Latins', but they could acquire citizenship in several ways.

By the end of the republic freedmen constituted a large proportion of the Roman citizen body; the distinction between citizens of servile birth and those of free birth became blurred, and was replaced by the distinction between the rich and the poor. *Petronius' imaginary freedman Trimalchio is an extravagant satire on the characteristics of the class. Many of the higher posts in the bureaucracy during the first century AD were held by freedmen, who were ineligible for the *curule magistracies. These men often came to exercise great power, and incurred widespread hatred.

Frogs (*Batrachoi*, Lat. *Rānae*), Greek comedy by *Aristophanes which won the first prize at the *Lenaea in Athens in 405 BC and earned its author a crown of sacred olive, as well as the right to produce it a second time. It gives expression to the city's literary attitudes and political plight at that time. The great tragic poets, Aeschylus, Sophocles, and Euripides, are all dead, the last two only recently; Athens, despite her victory in the sea-battle at Arginusae the previous year, is exhausted; she badly needs sound advice such as might be given by the best poets. The play opens with the patron god of tragedy Dionysus, characterized as possessing the human failings of the Athenian people—he is weak, conceited, credulous, and has a passion for Euripides—setting off for Hades disguised as Heracles in order to bring back Euripides. The journey in Charon's boat across the lake is accompanied by the croaking of a (secondary) chorus of frogs, who give their name to the play; the main chorus comprises initiates in the Eleusinian mysteries (see MYSTERIES). After arriving in Hades Dionysus has various adventures in consequence of being mistaken for Heracles, but is finally identified and asked to judge a dispute between Aeschylus and Euripides for possession of the throne of tragedy, Sophocles having relinquished his claim in favour of Aeschylus. Aeschylus represents his plays as superior in grandeur and moral purpose, Euripides his as more realistic and human, but each produces telling criticism of the other. Both agree that the duty of the poet is to make men better; Aeschylus says his heroes were models to be imitated, Euripides that he made the audience think; but Aeschylus objects that Euripides' depraved characters are the cause of the decline in morals. The poets then attack the construction of each other's plays, their language, metre, and music. The final test whereby each poet speaks a line into a pair of scales to determine whose poetry is the weightier is easily won by Aeschylus. Dionysus, still undecided as to which poet he prefers, asks each for advice on how to save the city. Euripides makes a characteristically enigmatic reply, and Dionysus chooses Aeschylus as representative of the old Athenian spirit.

Frontī'nus, Sextus Julius (*c.* AD 30–*c.*104), consul in 73 or 74, after which he was sent as governor to Britain (where he preceded Agricola, the father-in-law of Tacitus). He was also an augur, succeeded after his death by the Younger Pliny. He subdued the Silures in southeast Wales and established a legionary fortress at Isca (Caerleon on the Usk). Of his writings there survive the *Stratēgēmata* in four books, a manual of Greek and Roman strategy for the use of officers; fragments of a work on land-surveying; and his most famous work, *De aquis urbis Romae* ('on the waters of Rome'), in two books written after he was appointed curator of the Roman water-supply (*curator aquarum*) in 97. He describes for the benefit of his successors the aqueducts and their history, the regulations governing them, and technical details concerning the quality and distribution of supply. Frontinus' writings have a straightforward style in keeping with their subject matter. See AQUEDUCTS.

Fronto, Marcus Cornelius (*c.* AD 100–*c.*176). Born in North Africa, Fronto went to Rome where he became an influential figure in literature and was regarded as the foremost orator of his day. His political importance was negligible although he was consul in 143 (with *Herodes Atticus the Greek sophist). An inscription describes him as tutor to the future emperors Marcus *Aurelius and Lucius Verus. Very little of his work was known until a collection of his letters (partly in Greek) was discovered in the early nineteenth century at Rome and Milan. Disappointing as historical sources, despite being written to and including letters from the leading figures of the day, they

are more revealing on personal and literary matters. A cordial friendship between Fronto and M. Aurelius is apparent, although the latter ultimately rejected rhetoric as being unworthy of serious pursuit. Fronto's interest in rhetoric is largely confined to matters of language and style, and he was attracted by old Latin words no longer in use. His most admired models of life and speech were the old Romans down to Cicero and Sallust; he disliked Seneca. The few rhetorical exercises of his which survive are in a vigorous and straightforward Latin. From the casual mention in one letter of *elocutio novella* it has been assumed that this is a technical term meaning a 'new style' which was being advocated by Fronto and his friends, but it may mean no more than 'novelty of expression' which Fronto valued highly and reproved M. Aurelius for not using.

Fu'lvia, first wife (by 45 BC) of Mark *Antony (she had previously been the wife successively of P. Clodius and C. Scribonius Curio), who played an important part in the political struggles after the death of Caesar in 44 BC. She is said to have taken an active part in the proscriptions and gazed with delight at the corpse of Cicero, who had attacked her in his speeches. In 41 BC she tried to promote Antony's interests by encouraging his brother Lucius, who was consul, to support the cause of those dispossessed by Octavian's settlement of his veterans, and in the ensuing civil war joined him in holding Perusia (Perugia) until Octavian captured it. She was allowed to escape to Greece, where she met Antony in Athens. He meanwhile had been entertaining himself with Cleopatra, and is said to have been so angry at Fulvia's action in causing the Perusine War by promoting discord between himself and Octavian that she lost all interest in life and died in 40. Her death was opportune for a reconciliation between Octavian and Antony, who then married Octavian's sister.

funeral games. In Greek epic poetry, the deaths of heroes were marked with athletic competitions, as were those of great men in early historical times. At such an occasion the poet Hesiod won a tripod in a competition for a funeral song.

Funeral Oration, see PERICLES.

Fu'riae or **Dīrae,** Roman equivalent of the Greek Erinyes or Eumenides (see FURIES). There is no proof that they were ever the object of cult in Italy.

Furies (Gk. Erīnўĕs), also known by the propitiatory names of Eumĕnidĕs, 'kindly ones', and Semnai, 'the holy ones', in Greek myth, spirits of punishment avenging without pity wrongs done to kindred and especially murder within the family. According to Hesiod they were the daughters of Gaia (Earth), conceived from the drops of blood spilt when Cronus castrated his father *Uranus (Heaven), i.e. they were born of a crime committed by a son against a father. Authorities differ as to their parentage, but they are always represented as more ancient than the Olympian gods and not under the rule of Zeus, although they honour him. They also punished perjurers and those who had violated the laws of hospitality and supplication, and came to assume the character of goddesses who punish crimes after death and seldom appear on earth. They were represented as carrying torches and scourges, and wreathed with snakes. Later writers make them three in number with the names Tīsiphŏnē, Megaera, and Allecto. Their cult was rare, but they had a sanctuary at the foot of the Acropolis.

Fūrī'na, see FURRINA.

Fu'rius Cami'llus, Marcus, see CAMILLUS.

furniture, see HOUSES AND FURNITURE.

Furrī'na or **Fūrīna,** ancient Italian goddess whose nature and function had, by Cicero's day, become a matter of conjecture. Nevertheless she possessed a grove on the slopes of the Janiculum near the Pons Sublicius, a *flamen, and an annual festival (Furrinalia, 25 July), although in classical times this was celebrated only by the priests connected with the cult. It was in the grove of Furrina that C. *Gracchus had his slave kill him in 121 BC.

G

Gadēs (Cadiz, Gk. Gadeira), colony founded by the Phoenicians from Tyre, traditionally in 1100 BC, on a small island off the Spanish mainland north-west of the Pillars of Hercules (Gibraltar), and for a long time the westernmost point of the world known to the Greeks and Romans. It was sometimes identified with and sometimes said to be near the mythical island of Erytheia, where *Geryon grazed the cattle which were later carried off by Heracles (see HERACLES, LABOURS OF 10). Occasionally it was confused with the region of southern Spain known as Tartessus. For a long time it was dependent on Carthage, and from 237 BC was *Hamilcar Barca's base in his Spanish campaigns. In 206 BC during the Second Punic War it surrendered to Rome on favourable terms, and was later made a Roman *municipium* by Julius Caesar. For a long time it was the most important commercial shipping port in the West, and enjoyed considerable wealth.

Gaia, in Greek myth, the Earth, personified as a goddess, the daughter of Chaos, the mother and wife of *Uranus, Heaven; their offspring included the Titans and the Cyclopes. On the advice of Gaia, Cronus, the youngest of the Titans, castrated his father; fertilized by the blood, Gaia became the mother of the Giants and the Furies. Later she bore Typhon to her son *Tartarus. Her cult can be traced in many places in Greece, but for the most part it was superseded in classical times by that of later gods; at Delphi she seems to have been thought of as the original holder of the oracular shrine, before Apollo seized it by killing the serpent Python. Her characteristic function was to be a witness to oaths, as one who knows all that is done on earth.

Gaiseric, see VANDALS.

Gaius (second century AD), one of the most distinguished Roman jurists, who lived in Rome and wrote extensively but whose full name and origins are unknown; he was never quoted by contemporary or near-contemporary jurists. It is likely therefore that he was a teacher rather than a practical jurist, and did not in his lifetime have *ius respondendi*, 'the right to give a legal opinion', i.e. his opinions could not be cited as authority for subsequent legal decisions (see LAW, AT ROME 3). This prerogative was granted posthumously in AD 426 when his writings were given equal authority with those of *Papinian, *Paulus, and *Ulpian. His best-known, though perhaps not wholly original, work is the *Institutiōnēs* ('institutes'), which was taken by *Justinian, the Roman emperor at Constantinople, as the basis of his own *Institutiones* in AD 533 and thereby exerted immense influence on later legal thought. This work was known only in an abbreviated version until its discovery on a palimpsest at Verona in 1816, the Letters of St Jerome having been written over it. It is the only classical legal work to have come down to us in substantially its original form.

Gaius Caesar, properly Gaius Julius Caesar Germanicus, popularly known as Caligula (AD 12–41), Roman emperor, the son of *Germanicus and Agrippina. In AD 14–16 he was on the Rhine with his parents, where he was nicknamed Caligula ('little boot') because of the military boots he wore. After the death of his brother Drusus in 33 he became next in succession to the principate, being the only surviving son of Germanicus. Soon after his accession in 37 at the death of Tiberius, he fell seriously ill; *Philo the Jew, who went on an embassy to Rome in 40, suggests that the illness affected his mind. Certainly his behaviour afterwards became increasingly despotic and mad, marked by wild extravagance, arbitrary executions, and aspirations towards deification. He was murdered in 41. For his reign see ROME 10.

Galatē'a (Galateia, 'milk-white'), Greek sea-nymph, daughter of *Nereus and Doris. The story of her wooing by the ugly *Cyclops Polyphemus was frequently told, by the bucolic poets (Theocritus, Idyll 11; Virgil, Eclogue 9; Ovid, *Metamorphoses* 13); and by the early eighteenth-century English poet John Gay in his libretto to Handel's *Acis and Galatea.* Ovid tells how she loved a young shepherd Acis but was discovered by Polyphemus who hurled a rock at him. As it fell Galatea turned Acis into a river which henceforth bore his name. A later story made her bear a son to Polyphemus who became the eponymous ancestor of the Gauls ('Galatians'; see below).

Gala'tians (Galătae), a Gallic people (i.e. *Celts) who crossed the Hellespont from Europe into Asia Minor in the third century BC and settled in Phrygia, in the area surrounding modern Ankara in central Turkey. In a Greek-speaking part of the world they maintained their tribal system and language for several centuries. A warlike people, they terrorized western Asia for more than a century. Attalus I of Pergamum inflicted a notable defeat on them some time before 230 BC (commemorated by a monument that included the statue of the *'Dying Gaul'), and they were finally subdued in 188 BC by the Roman proconsul Manlius Vulso. The emperor Augustus created the province of Galatia in 25 BC by adding adjacent territories to Galatia proper. The apostle Paul passed through the latter region on his second missionary journey, but it is uncertain whether his Epistle was written to the inhabitants of Galatia proper or to churches in the whole province.

Galba, Se'rvius Sulpi'cius (*c.*3 BC–AD 69), Roman emperor for about six months in 68–9 in succession to Nero (see ROME 11). He came from a patrician family and had enjoyed the favour of previous emperors. After a distinguished military career he was from AD 60 governor of eastern Spain, until Vindex, governor of western Gaul, rebelled against the emperor Nero in 68 and invited Galba to replace him. Vindex was soon defeated, but then the praetorian guard, after bribery, deserted Nero and declared for Galba. Encouraged, he took the title of Caesar and slowly marched to Rome with Otho, governor of Lusitania, who hoped to be named as Galba's heir. Disappointed in this hope, Otho took advantage of the unpopularity Galba had incurred by his severity and meanness, to conspire with the praetorian guard, and they murdered Galba in AD 69 and proclaimed Otho emperor. Tacitus describes Galba's career and character in book 1 of his *Histories*.

Galen (Gălēnos), of Pergamum (AD 129–99), Greek physician, whose outstanding influence on medicine in ancient and modern times has not been equalled. As a young man he studied and travelled widely, but he spent most of his life at Rome as physician to the emperor Marcus Aurelius, his son Commodus, and Septimius Severus. He was the most learned scientist of his day, satisfying the popular taste of the time with anatomical displays, lectures, and handbooks on medical topics. He was a voluminous writer; almost all his extant works are medical and cover every branch of health and disease, especially physiology and anatomy, but he believed that there was a close connection between medicine and philosophy and wrote a number of commentaries on works of Plato, Aristotle, and Theophrastus as well as on general philosophical and philological topics. He wrote in elegant if somewhat prolix Greek, and was in many ways typical of the cultural life of his time (see SOPHISTIC, SECOND and ATHENAEUS). In his day the medical profession was divided into several mutually antagonistic sects, but Galen was eclectic; he professed allegiance to none and preferred to take from each what seemed to him

to be true. After his death his influence caused the various sects to die out. He was a profound admirer of *Hippocrates whose doctrines he professed to be merely reinforcing and augmenting. Much of his physiology was traditional, but his discourses on anatomy and physiological processes reveal his close observation which brought to light many new facts. He followed *Herophilus in maintaining that the arteries contained blood, not air. It appears that he seldom, perhaps never, dissected human bodies, for which opportunities were rare, but used animals of various kinds, preferably apes.

Galen's writings formed the basis of all later medical works. After the ninth century, and the translation of his works into Arabic, he became the standard of medical perfection. His fame in Europe in the Middle Ages probably derived from the influence of the Arabic medical writers, and his opinions and his name were universally invoked even when his writings were little read.

Gale'rius, see CONSTANTINE I.

Galli (Galloi), the eunuch priests of *Cybelē, supposedly named from the river Gallus in Galatia, which flowed near the original temple of Cybele and whose waters were said to madden anyone who drank from them. The priests were thought to castrate themselves in imitation of the act of *Attis, Cybele's cult-partner.

galliambic, see METRE, LATIN 3 (iii).

Gallic, see GAUL, GALATIANS, and CELTS.

Gallic War, the campaigns in which Julius Caesar completed the conquest of Gaul between 58 and 51 BC, and the name by which his commentary on the conquest (in seven books) is commonly known. The narrative is one of the best examples we have of unadorned Latin prose (see *COMMENTARIES* 1).

Gallus, Gaius Cornelius (*c.*69–26 BC), soldier and poet, friend of the emperor Augustus and of Virgil. Born at Forum Julii (Fréjus), possibly of a Gallic family, he went to Rome at an early age and rose to equestrian rank. He fought in the civil war on Octavian's side and was one of the commissioners appointed by him in 41 to confiscate land in north Italy and distribute it among his veterans (see VIRGIL). Octavian made him the first prefect of Egypt in 30 BC but after four years he was recalled in disgrace for an offence which remains obscure; Octavian (now called Augustus) formally renounced his friendship, and Gallus committed suicide. Virgil is said to have rewritten the latter half of the fourth Georgic which had formerly contained a eulogy of Gallus.

His poetry, of which only one pentameter line and perhaps tiny papyrus fragments survive, included four books of love-elegies centred upon the poet's mistress, the famous actress Cytheris (also loved by Mark Antony), under the pseudonym of Lycōris. This was a genre which he appears to have originated (see ELEGY). His poetry was influenced by the Hellenistic Greek poets Callimachus and Euphorion, and the Roman *neoterics. Virgil in his tenth Eclogue worked some of Gallus' own lines into his poem.

games, private

Greek and Roman children appear to have been much like the children of more recent times in their amusements. They had rattles, balls, tops, hoops, swings and see-saws, dolls and toy animals, knucklebones (see ASTRAGALOI), *dice and board games, and played guessing-games, such as 'odd and even' and 'how many fingers?'

The Greeks attached high importance to physical development, and *athletics formed a prominent part of Greek education. Apart from public competitions (see below), athletic sports of an organized nature—wrestling and boxing, running, jumping, javelin- and discus-throwing—took place at gymnasia and wrestling schools (*palaestrae*) where young men went to train and meet their friends. Other games of an informal nature were popular with Greeks and Romans; ball games played with balls of ranging size and weight were thought to provide healthy exercise for all ages. The Campus Martius at Rome was described by Strabo as allowing people not only to race in chariots and engage in every kind of equestrian activity but to take exercise by playing with balls and hoops and by wrestling. The later Greeks, but more particularly the Romans, had special courts built for ball games. There are no certain references in literature to bats, but a famous early fifth-century marble relief shows men playing ball with something that bears a remarkable resemblance to the modern hockey stick. There is very little to suggest that the ancients ever played any kind of football. Young men as well as children bowled hoops. The Greeks were great swimmers, but there is not much to suggest that they looked on swimming as a sport, though they and the Romans enjoyed it as well as boating and boat races. Older men enjoyed dicing and board games resembling draughts and backgammon; chess, invented probably in India, did not reach Mediterranean countries until after the classical period. Women were said to be fond of playing with knucklebones.

games, public. 1. In Greece

1. In the eighth century BC, during the period of colonization, when the great religious *festivals of Greece arose out of consciousness of the unity of all Greeks, athletic and equestrian contests came to be a feature of these festivals. This was partly because the Greeks felt that as they enjoyed these contests so also would their gods,

partly because the large festival crowds provided spectators. Thus the connection of sport with religious festivals was to some extent accidental.

There were two categories of public games, those in which prizes of money were offered and those which were primarily religious festivals, where the victors won crowns only. The former could be established by any city able to afford it, and during Hellenistic and Roman times many cities founded such games in honour of kings and emperors. In the second category were the original four great panhellenic festivals, all in existence by the mid-sixth century BC and attended by visitors from all over the Greek world, the Olympian, Pythian, Isthmian, and Nemean games. Later they were known simply as 'the circuit' (*periodos*). These games were held in high esteem, so that competition was severe and the material rewards subsequently given to the victors by their grateful cities were considerable. Judges and umpires were sometimes treated as disrespectfully as their modern counterparts. Plutarch says that in his day (second century AD) Spartans were the only athletes who did not hurl abuse at the umpire. Most festivals also became the occasion for a great fair, at which poets and orators could earn themselves widespread fame by reciting their works.

2. The *Olympian games* were the most important part of a festival held every four years in honour of Zeus at *Olympia in Elis (in the north-west Peloponnese) from 776 BC. They were always supreme in the ancient world. Because of their universal prestige the Olympian programme and rules were accepted as the norm for games everywhere, and the four-year period between festivals, known as an *Olympiad, was used by the Greeks as a dating system (see CALENDARS 6). The victor's prize was a wreath of wild olive from a sacred tree growing in the precinct of Zeus, but he would also receive substantial rewards from his city. The games were held without a break from 776 BC until at least AD 261, and finally abolished as a pagan cult by the Christian Roman emperor Theodosius in 391. In the eighth century the contests consisted only of the three foot-races, the pentathlon, and wrestling, but during the seventh century they were extended to include the *chariot- and the *horse-race, boxing, and the pancration. The last important innovation was the race in armour (520 BC). For the various events see also ATHLETICS. The chariot- and horse-races were highly esteemed events and victory in them much coveted by the aristocrats who could afford to compete. The mule-car race was introduced in 500 BC and the mysterious 'trotting-race' (*kalpē*) in 496, but both were abandoned after 444, the former at least being thought too undignified for Olympia. In 408 BC the two-horse chariot-race was introduced, and the next

two centuries saw the institution of corresponding races for colts. By 256 BC the Olympian programme was complete, but there had been little significant change since 520. Athletic events were held in the *stadium, except perhaps for wrestling, which seems to have taken place in the empty space around the altar of Zeus. Equestrian events took place in the hippodrome, south-east of the stadium. From 472 the festival occupied five days. The Olympic truce, proclaimed for a stated period before and after the games, was intended to prevent war from disrupting them and to ensure safe passage for all participants. In this it was successful.

3. The *Pythian games*, next in importance after the Olympian, were held in honour of Apollo at *Delphi, where from early times there had existed a musical competition of hymns to the god. In 582 BC the festival was reorganized and thenceforth celebrated every fourth year, in the third year of each Olympiad. Extended musical competitions still took pride of place, but athletic contests and horse races were added on the model of the Olympian games. The prize was a wreath of laurel cut in the valley of Tempē.

4. The *Isthmian games* were celebrated on the Isthmus of Corinth in the first and third years of each Olympiad, in honour of Poseidon. They were said to have been founded by *Sisyphus in honour of his kinsman *Melicertes or, according to Athenian tradition, by Theseus as a monument to his exploits on the journey from Troezen to Athens, but their historical existence dates from the 580s. It was at these games in 196 BC that Flamininus proclaimed the independence of Greece from Philip V of Macedon (see ROME 5). When the poet Pindar was writing odes for the victors at the Isthmian games, in the first half of the fifth century BC, the victors were crowned with wreaths of (dry) wild celery, although at other periods the crown was made of pine branches.

5. The *Nemean games*, held in the sanctuary of Zeus at Nemea in Argolis, were according to tradition founded either by Heracles after he had killed the Nemean lion, or by the Seven against Thebes to commemorate the accidental death of an infant, Opheltēs (see HYPSIPYLE). The first official Nemean games were probably celebrated in 573 BC, and thereafter in the second and fourth years of each Olympiad. The victor won a crown of (fresh) wild celery.

2. At Rome
Athletic contests of the Greek type were never popular at Rome. At best they became another form of entertainment, but in popular appeal they never rivalled gladiatorial shows; the competitors were for the most part Greek. The term *ludi* was used to describe a variety of theatrical performances, games, and contests held at Rome on various occasions but chiefly at the festivals of the gods; games and contests took place in the *circus. Emperors founded new festivals with games in the Greek East and frequently encouraged their establishment in Italy. Domitian established at Rome the Capitoline games (at which *Statius failed to win the poetry prize); the athletic events included races for girls. Nero founded the short-lived Neronian games.

Ga'nymēde (Ganymēdēs), in Greek myth, son of Tros (or Laomedon), king of *Troy, carried off by the gods or the eagle of Zeus or Zeus himself because of his beauty, to be the cup-bearer of Zeus, who gave in exchange to his father a pair of divine horses. In later times he was thought to be immortalized as the zodiacal sign Aquarius. From the Latin version of his name (Catamītus) is derived the word 'catamite'. For the Middle Ages he typified homosexual love, but during the Renaissance his ascent to Zeus symbolized for some the soul's ascent to the absolute.

Garden, the, see EPICURUS.

Gates of Dreams, see DREAMS.

Gaugamē'la, small village east of the river Tigris in Assyria, the scene of the final victory of Alexander the Great over Darius III, king of Persia, in 331 BC.

Gaul (Gallia)
1. *Cisalpine Gaul.* This is the name which the Romans before 42 BC gave to the region of north Italy that lies between the Apennines and the Alps, denoting 'Gaul this side (i.e. south) of the Alps' (as opposed to Transalpine Gaul, or 'Gaul beyond (i.e. north of) the Alps'). The Romans gave the name Galli to the Celtic invaders (see CELTS) who, originating perhaps in the Upper Danube, moved westwards across Europe in the eighth and seventh centuries BC and passed into north Italy c.400 BC. Though they were successfully resisted by the Veneti who lived in the north-east of Italy, in general their marauding bands terrorized the country and in 390 BC even captured Rome (see ALLIA). They were a constant menace to Italian security until in the latter part of the third century BC, after a particularly dangerous incursion of a coalition of four Gallic tribes, Rome decided to put an end to the danger by annexing Cisalpine Gaul. This was largely effected by the campaigns of 224–2 but the area was mostly lost again through Hannibal's invasion of 218. It was regained in the 190s and by 150 few Gauls remained in the Cisalpine plain. The name Gallia Togata was often applied to this area after it was settled by the Romans, indicating the numerical superiority of the togati ('those who wear the toga', i.e. Romans) over the Gallic population. Those inhabitants north of the river

Padus (Po) were sometimes called Transpadani. Cisalpine Gaul was constituted a Roman province by Sulla in his settlements of 82 BC, with the river *Rubicon as its southern boundary. In 42 BC the province was incorporated into Italy. Under the emperor Augustus the tribes of the Alpine foothills were conquered, and the Alps thus became the frontier of Italy.

2. *Transalpine Gaul.* This is the area that is commonly denoted by the single word 'Gaul', i.e. modern France. It was occupied by a population predominantly Celtic advancing from the Upper Danube (see 1 above), superimposed upon a race of earlier inhabitants generally known as Ligurians. Gaul first came into contact with the Mediterranean civilization through the foundation in about 600 BC of the Greek colony of Massilia (Marseilles); see COLONIZATION, GREEK 2. This city became an important source for the spread of Hellenism inland and along the coast. Rome's first interest in Transalpine Gaul arose from the need to secure communications with her trading ally Saguntum (Sagunto) in Spain. Communication was usually safeguarded by Massilia but when, in the second century BC, that city was threatened first by Ligurian invaders and then by the Celtic tribes of the Allobrogēs and the Arverni, the Romans themselves fought and finally defeated them. These campaigns gave Rome possession of the Gallic territory between the Alps and the Rhone as far north as Geneva; in 121 it was formed into a province, at first called simply Provincia (modern Provence). Its territory was subsequently extended westwards when in 118 the Roman colony of Narbo (Narbonne) was established, and the province was then called Gallia Narbonensis; the Romans thereby commanded the road into Spain through the eastern Pyrenees. Narbo became a commercial rival to Greek Massilia, which remained nominally independent.

The next threat came from incursions of Northmen, the Cimbri and Teutones, who caused terrible devastation in Gaul at the end of the second century BC. These were finally crushed by Marius in 101, after which there was no great movement of peoples until 58. In this year Julius Caesar, after the expiry of his consulship in 59, obtained Cisalpine and Narbonese Gaul for his province at a time when Transalpine Gaul had already suffered an invasion of Germanic peoples under Ariovistus, and an invasion from the Helvetii was threatening. For the events of the next few years see *COMMENTARIES* I. By 51 Caesar had finally subjugated the whole of Transalpine Gaul, a country twice as large as Italy, and given it the structure of a province. He divided the country into three parts (excluding Narbonese Gaul, a fourth), namely Aquitania, Celtica, and Belgica. The final settlement of Gaul was the work of Augustus: between 27 and 13 BC Narbonese

Gaul became a senatorial province; the other three parts, often known collectively as Gallia Comata ('long-haired'), became one imperial province which was eventually redivided into three, the divisions deliberately cutting across ethnic boundaries. Celtica disappeared and the division known as Lugdunensis came into being, named after the new settlement at Lugdunum (Lyons).

Even before the Romans arrived in their territory, the Gauls were at a fairly civilized stage of development. A considerable amount of land was already under cultivation; vines were grown, cattle and pigs raised, and horses were reared in the plentiful pasturage to supply the formidable Gallic cavalry. The country was populous and communications seem to have been easy, with a number of good roads and bridges. The network of rivers facilitated trade, including trade with Britain whence tin was imported. The Gauls were familiar with metalworking and had their own iron mines. They had a flourishing pottery industry, and some tribes used coined money. Gaul before the Roman conquest was made up of numerous independent states, the most powerful continually contending for supremacy. None the less, there was some approach to national unity owing to the predominance of certain tribes such as the Arverni, and to the Druids who acted as arbitrators. The government was aristocratic, the leaders both political and military being of the nobility; the Druids were a powerful priestly corporation possessing extensive rights of jurisdiction. Their fanatical nationalism led to their suppression by the emperor Claudius.

Romanization was very rapid; long contact with the Greeks of Massilia may have helped. New towns were built in place of hill-forts and public buildings and roads were constructed, and the Gauls were quick to realize the advantages. Roman ideas and (later) the cult of emperor-worship were also introduced, and a provincial government set up at Narbo. From the second century AD Christianity began to gain a hold and was firmly established by the fourth century. Since the language of the Church was Latin, Christianity led to the extinction of the Gallic language. In the late empire Gaul produced several interesting Latin writers, including *Ausonius, Paulinus of Nola, and *Sidonius. The Roman empire in Gaul came to an end in the fifth century with the withdrawal of the garrisons and the gradual development into separate kingdoms of those settlements made by the barbarian invaders of the fourth and fifth centuries. See FALL OF ROME and FRANKS.

Gē, alternative form of *Gaia.

geese, sacred, see MANLIUS CAPITOLINUS.

Gēla, Greek city on the south coast of Sicily founded in 688 BC by Cretans and Rhodians, itself colonizing *Acragas a century later. Under the tyrants Cleander and Hippocrates it became the most powerful city in the island, but in 485 its tyrant *Gelon transferred himself and a large proportion of the population to Syracuse, leaving his brother Hieron in control at Gela. It was repopulated in 466 and prospered; Aeschylus died there in 456. It supported Syracuse during the Athenian expedition to Sicily (see PELOPONNESIAN WAR). After being sacked by the Carthaginians in 406, together with Acragas and Camarina, it was abandoned by the tyrant of Syracuse, Dionysius I, and in 280 BC the remaining inhabitants departed to a new foundation. One remarkable surviving monument is the fortifications built by *Timoleon, the great Corinthian general of the fourth century BC and liberator of Sicily.

Ge'llius, Aulus (*c*. AD 130–perhaps 180), the (Latin) author of *Noctes Atticae* ('Attic nights'), in twenty books, of which all survive except the beginning of the preface and book 8 (for which we have chapter headings). His birthplace is unknown, but he studied literature at Rome before proceeding to Athens where he visited *Herodēs Atticus. His book is a random collection of short essays, based on the Greek and Latin books he had read and the conversations and lectures he had heard, and deals with a great variety of topics: philosophy, history, law, grammar, literary and textual criticism, antiquarian knowledge, and many other subjects. He began collecting his material during the winter nights in Attica and arranged it in later life for the amusement and instruction of his children. It contains thousands of curious and interesting passages from works no longer extant, and is a mine of information on Greek and Latin authors; we are particularly indebted to him for the preservation of many passages from early Latin literature, and, among many good stories, for that of Androclus and the lion (5. 14).

Gelon (*c*.540–478 BC), tyrant of *Gela and subsequently of Syracuse, in (Greek) Sicily. He had been cavalry-commander under the Geloan tyrant Hippocrates and became guardian of the latter's sons *c*.490, but usurped the tyranny himself. In 485 he seized Syracuse and transferred his power there, leaving his brother Hieron in control at Gela. During his tyranny Syracuse became the leading Hellenic power of the time; the mainland Greeks sought his aid against Persia (see PERSIAN WARS), but withdrew on his making it a condition that he should have supreme command. In alliance with *Theron, tyrant of Acragas, he defeated at Himera in 480 a great Carthaginian expedition, traditionally on the same day as the Greeks defeated the Persians at Salamis. He died two years later.

Gemō'niae, Scalae, see SCALAE.

gems, gem-engraving. Precious stones were valued in antiquity for their magical and medicinal properties, as ornaments, and as seals when engraved. Mycenaean gems are particularly rich in the variety of their designs. Greek gem-engraving reached its peak in the late fifth and the fourth centuries BC; the conquests of Alexander the Great introduced to Greece new stones such as garnets. Alexander employed the gem-cutter Pyrgotelēs to engrave his portrait.

In Rome, gems of the later republic were used for signet rings and show a wide range of subjects. Engraving was in the form of the *intaglio*, where the design is sunk and so is appropriate for seals, and the cameo, where it is engraved in relief and is for ornament only. Larger examples include a fine portrait of Augustus in the British Museum, the *gemma Augustea* at Vienna representing Augustus, Tiberius, Germanicus, and a group of deities, with a military scene below, and the *grand camée* in Paris showing Tiberius, Livia, and Germanicus, with various symbolic figures. The gem-cutters were probably Greek or from the Hellenistic East. The most famous of the Augustan age was a certain Dioscorides.

gē'nius, literally 'the begetter', in Roman belief a man's guardian spirit, which enabled him to beget children; the marriage-bed, *lectus genialis*, was its sphere. A household worshipped the *genius* of the house on the birthday of the *paterfamilias*, head of the family, in whom it was thought to reside. Its symbol was the house-snake; by many it was identified with the *lar. The idea was extended so that places and even corporations might be said to have their own genius (see RELIGION, ROMAN 3). We hear of a *genius populi Romani*, 'genius of the Roman people', and a *genius urbis Romae*, 'genius of the city of Rome', and the practice of slaves venerating the genius of their master led in imperial times to the cult of the emperor's genius. Although in the post-classical period the word sometimes refers to 'talent' or 'inspiration' in literature, it seems not to have had the senses it usually has in modern English, intellectual power of a very high order, or the person possessing it, or the prevalent spirit of a nation, age, language, etc. The corresponding spirit in women was known as *Iuno* (Juno).

gĕnos (pl. *genē*), in the Greek social system, a 'clan' or group of families claiming descent in the male line from one ancestor; it was narrower than a *phratry. Naturally most is heard about noble families whose ultimate ancestor was reputedly a hero or god; their family name was usually in patronymic form (see NAMES), meaning 'the descendants of . . .'. Not all citizens were members of a *genos*; the Athenian *gene* were probably entirely aristocratic. Powerful *gene* at Athens were the Philaidae (the clan of Miltiades and Cimon) and the *Alcmaeonidae. The *genos* could come together as a body for the specific function of worshipping the ancestor; it generally met at least once a year to elect officials, pass decrees, and enrol new members, who had to be the lawful (including adopted) sons of existing members. At Athens the *gene* were often referred to as the *Eupatridae.

genre, in literature, a class or type of literary work, such as epic, lyric, tragedy, or comedy. In classical literature the genres were carefully distinguished from each other not only by subject matter but also by formal aspects such as dialect (in Greek), vocabulary, and metre, and the conventions of each genre were strictly adhered to. Ignorance of these has sometimes resulted in misplaced criticism, as when Samuel Johnson found 'inherently improbable' the poet Milton's pastoral elegy *Lycidas*.

gens (pl. *gentēs*), in the Roman social system, a 'clan' or group of families bearing a common name or *nomen* (see NAMES) and descended in the male line from one ancestor whom, in distinction from the Greeks, they neither recorded nor worshipped (compare *genos*). Originally the *gentes* were aristocratic, *patrician families, but in early times the wealthiest *plebeian families organized themselves also into *gentes* and some probably gained admission to the patrician *gentes*. This supposition, if correct, would explain the existence of both patrician and plebeian families within the same *gens*. A *gens* had certain common property (including a burial ground), held meetings of its members, and performed religious rites in common.

Geogra'phica, see STRABO.

geography, (*geōgraphia,* 'description of the earth'). For Homer and Hesiod the earth was a plane land mass of circular contour around the Mediterranean basin, surrounded by the stream of Ocean, and the first world *maps drawn by Anaximander and Hecataeus in the sixth century BC largely supported this view. The Greeks and Romans knew of three continents, *Europe, *Asia, and *Africa (Libya), but of none of them fully. It was generally believed that the distance from east to west was twice that from north to south. *Hecataeus wrote a *Periegesis* ('guide') to illustrate his map, a description of the countries and people to be met on a coastal voyage round the Mediterranean and Black Sea, with some excursions inland, and his work extended as far as India, Persia, and Scythia. Unfortunately only scanty fragments survive. During the fifth century works of descriptive geography began to be more specialized. Herodotus' *Histories* contain much geographical and ethnological material. *Ctesias wrote a geographical treatise and the first

separate work on India. Two fourth-century historians, *Ephorus and *Timaeus, devoted several books to descriptive geography. The conquests of Alexander the Great in the second half of the fourth century BC stimulated the composition of many treatises on the East, and the opening up of western Europe by the Romans in the second and first centuries BC had a similar effect. The most notable work of descriptive geography to survive is that of the Greek *Strabo (first century BC to first century AD) who combined physical, historical, political, and mathematical geography. This last had been made possible by Aristotle's proof (*c.*350 BC) of the earth's sphericity and his introduction of the general principle of dividing the globe into zones. *Eratosthenes (*c.*275–194 BC) established mathematical geography as a science and *Ptolemy applied its principles in the first half of the second century AD. Unfortunately the scientific geographers did not oust the traditional and erroneous beliefs of older writers, which were perpetuated in the compilations of late antiquity. (See also POMPONIUS MELA.)

Geometric age, name given to one of the five periods of the Greek era (based on the differences in pottery styles; see POTTERY I (iv)), denoting very roughly the period 875–750 BC. (Compare PROTO-GEOMETRIC, ORIENTALIZING, ARCHAIC, and CLASSIC. See also IRON AGE.)

Georgics (*geōrgica,* 'husbandry'), *Virgil's didactic poem (in four books and over 2,000 hexameter lines) written in imitation of the *Works and Days* of the early Greek poet Hesiod. Virgil spent seven years (36–29 BC) on its composition and dedicated it to his patron Maecenas. His debt to the *Works and Days* is relatively small. The *Georgics* are much more sophisticated in thought and in technique, and owe something to the polished versification of the later Greek didactic poets such as *Aratus of Soli and *Nicander. The poet derived some factual information from *Varro's prose handbook *De re rustica* ('on farming') published in 37 BC (and he was perhaps also influenced by its moral and patriotic tone). However, Virgil resembles Hesiod in that his intention is not to compose a handbook of instruction for those who wish to be farmers; rather he is presenting a picture of the (Italian) farmer's life as the ideal: it is frugal and austere, prone to setbacks and not free from suffering, but, lived in harmony with nature and with the divine scheme of things, it is morally satisfying and it brings the reward of peace and contentment (2. 458 ff.); it is also the basis of Italy's greatness. For Virgil, as for Hesiod, hard work, *labor improbus,* is essential; he sees the individual as an oarsman rowing upstream whom the current will carry backwards if he slackens his effort (1. 199). Virgil's greatest debt is perhaps to *Lucretius, to whom he alludes obliquely in 2. 490. He recalls that poet not only in phrasing and in style but also in the passion with which he expounds his subject. Nevertheless the *Georgics* are a rebuttal of Lucretius' Epicureanism which asserted that the gods did not intervene in the world; Virgil reasserts divine providence, and dwells affectionately on the gods of the countryside. It was Virgil's deep sympathy for all living things and his sense of the need for men to co-operate with nature that led his English translator John Dryden (1631–1700) to call the *Georgics* 'the best poem of the best poet', a judgement also supported by Virgil's mature mastery of expression. The poem must therefore be seen as far more than a practical guide to farming, which its omissions and inaccuracies could not allow it to be, and to which the philosophical 'digressions' are irrelevant. Ancient critics soon observed that Virgil's aim was to give pleasure rather than instruction.

Book 1 deals with the raising of crops and the signs of the weather, ending emotionally with a description of the horrors suffered by Italy as a consequence of the murder of Julius Caesar; book 2 covers the growing of trees, chiefly the olive and the vine, and also contains magnificent praise of Italy (136 ff.); book 3 deals with the rearing of cattle (concluding with the notable description of the cattle-plague in the Alps); in book 4 Virgil describes bee-keeping, treating the bees with affectionate irony as exemplars of the ideal citizen body, 'little Romans' (*parvi Quirites*). The work ends with the episode of *Aristaeus together with the story of Orpheus and Eurydicē. The reason for this latter inclusion is hard to discern; the ancient commentator Servius implausibly suggests that it was written to replace an earlier panegyric of the Roman poet *Gallus which had to be excised after the latter's disgrace. Whatever the reason, it contains some of Virgil's most haunting poetry, and the effect of the highly individualized, hapless love of the poet Orpheus for his beautiful wife Eurydice, following after the description of the busy, orderly, useful, and sexless lives of the bees, is deeply moving.

Geō'rgos ('farmer'), Greek comedy by *Menander, a fragment of which has been recovered from a papyrus. The plot revolves around two neighbours, one a poor widow, Myrrhinē, with a son and a daughter, the other a rich man with a son, by a previous marriage, and a daughter. The rich man's son wishes to marry Myrrhine's daughter, who is already pregnant by him, but his father is arranging to marry him to his half-sister. The farmer of the title, Kleainētos, apparently also wishes to marry the widow's daughter. Presumably in the end it is the rich neighbour's son who succeeds in doing so.

Germā'nia ('Germany'), the name commonly given to a monograph by *Tacitus on the origin, geography, institutions, and tribes of the

Germans, published in AD 98. It describes the various tribes north of the Rhine and the Danube, their appearance, political and social customs, and dress; the organization of their army; their religion and land tenure; their sloth alternating with warlike activity; their intemperance and gambling; the exemplary morality of their family life (sarcastically contrasted with the laxity prevailing at Rome). Tacitus then passes on to the geography of the area and the particular characteristics of the several Germanic tribes (including the Swedes and ending with the Finns). As an ethnological work it is somewhat incoherent and some of the material was out of date when Tacitus wrote it, but there seem to be other motives underlying its composition, a desire to point out the corruption of Rome by contrast with the purer morals of the barbarian, and to emphasize the threat Germany posed to Rome's security: 'Germany has afforded more triumphs than victories to Rome'.

Germa'nicus, *cognomen* (see NAMES) borne by various members of the Julio-Claudian family in Rome. It was originally bestowed by the senate as a title of honour upon Nero Claudius *Drusus (38–9 BC) and his descendants for his victories over the Germans. He was the son of Tiberius Claudius Nero and Livia, and brother of the future emperor Tiberius; he is usually known as Drusus the Elder. The name Germanicus by itself commonly designates Nero Claudius Germanicus (15 BC–AD 19), the elder son of the above Drusus and Antonia Minor (daughter of Mark Antony and Octavia), who was adopted by his uncle Tiberius in AD 4 when the latter was himself adopted by Augustus. Germanicus thus became a member of the Julian *gens*, in line to succeed to the imperial throne, and took the name Germanicus Julius Caesar. Emulating his natural father he too waged successful wars against the Germans (AD 14–16) and won his troops' affection, on which he was able to rely when he quelled the mutiny of the Rhine army in 14. He was not allowed by Tiberius to undertake a final campaign that he was sure would bring lasting victory because the more sceptical Tiberius could not sanction a further drain on Roman resources, or perhaps feared his popularity. In 17 he was given command over all the eastern provinces, but Tiberius appointed Cn. Piso as governor of Syria with the open intention of having him as a restraining influence on Germanicus. The two quarrelled and Germanicus ordered Piso to leave his province. Soon after Germanicus died in mysterious circumstances and his friends accused Piso and his wife Plancina of having poisoned him with the connivance of Tiberius. The death of so admired and popular a leader—he was commonly compared with Alexander the Great—caused widespread grief and resentment in Rome (see Tacitus' vivid description in *Annals* 2. 82). By his wife Agrippina (the Elder) he had nine children who included the future emperor *Gaius (Caligula) and Agrippina (the Younger), the mother of the emperor Nero. He had literary tastes; he is said to have written comedies in Greek, but all are lost; fragments of his Latin translation of the *Phaenomena* of *Aratus still survive, with a few epigrams.

Germany, for the Romans an undefined area east of the Rhine (Rhenus) and north of the Danube (Danubius or Ister). In the north it comprised what are now Denmark, Sweden, and Norway. The German tribes originated in south Scandinavia and Jutland, and from about 1000 BC they expanded southwards and westwards and eventually came into contact with the Celts who resisted their advance. The third century BC saw the German tribes crossing the Rhine and pressing south and west. According to Tacitus one of the tribes was called Germani, and this name was first used by the Gauls to designate the whole race. It was not until shortly after 120 BC that they entered Roman history, when the tribes of the Cimbri and the Teutones, invading south-east Gaul and, later, northern Italy, inspired great terror at Rome; they were finally destroyed by Roman armies under Marius. Early in the first century BC another German tribe, the Suebi, moved south-west to the area of the rivers Main (Moenus) and Rhine. Their inroads into Gaul in 58 BC led Julius Caesar, after fruitless attempts to come to an understanding with their chief Ariovistus, to drive them back across the Rhine (as related in the first book of Caesar's *Gallic War*), which river became a frontier of the Roman empire. Later, under Augustus, Roman invasions of German territory were systematically undertaken. From 12 BC Drusus the Elder (see GERMANICUS) and after his death in 9 BC his brother Tiberius, the future emperor, fought successful campaigns between the Rhine and the river Elbe (Albis); but the Roman ascendancy in this region was brought to an end in AD 9 when the Roman forces under P. Quinctilius Varus were destroyed by the German chief Arminius. After this disaster Augustus abandoned all attempts to establish a frontier beyond the Rhine, although in the east he established the river Danube as a frontier against tribes from the north. The emperor Tiberius felt obliged in 16 to put an end to the attempts of his adopted son Germanicus to reconquer north-west Germany. Around AD 90 Domitian formally established the two provinces of Germania Superior (Upper Germany) in the south and Germania Inferior (Lower Germany) in the north. During the reign of Marcus Aurelius (AD 161–80) there occurred a dangerous invasion across the Danube by the Marcomanni, a German tribe who advanced even into Italy and besieged Aquileia (near the coast at the head of

the Adriatic Sea). The resulting war continued to the end of the emperor's life, and his successor Commodus had to make a compromise peace with the Germans. During the next three centuries the German tribes, especially the Alemanni and *Franks, harassed Gaul by frequent invasions and finally crossed in great numbers over the Rhine, the Danube, and the Alps, conquering Gaul, Italy, and Spain and even penetrating into Africa. Other tribes such as the Angli and the Saxons had by that time crossed over into Britain. Nearly the whole of western Europe was thus overrun by German tribes. (See also FALL OF ROME.)

According to Tacitus the Germans in his day were an agricultural and pastoral people. Among some tribes there were permanent chieftains, but among others military leaders were elected for special campaigns. Important decisions were taken by the warriors in their assemblies, but the business of the assembly was first considered by a council of *principes* ('chieftains'). Their gods included those known to us as Woden, Freia, Thor, and Nerthus, usually worshipped in the open air, in groves and forests. The Germans were virtually illiterate; they had no alphabet of their own, and may have borrowed a form of runic script. In the course of time they adopted the Latin alphabet.

gerou'sia, at *Sparta, the council of elders composed of the two kings and twenty-eight other members over 60 years of age, elected for life from certain aristocratic families by measuring the acclamation of the citizens (a method which Aristotle thought childish). As a deliberative body they prepared business for the assembly (see APELLA); as a judicial body they heard cases involving death, exile, or disenfranchisement and could even put the kings on trial.

Ge'ryon (Gēryōn, Gēryonēs, or Gēryoneus), in Greek myth, son of *Chrysaor and Callirrhoë, a three-headed or three-bodied giant living in the far West on an island, Erytheia, in the stream of *Ocean beyond the Pillars of Hercules; there he pastured a herd of magnificent cattle, aided by his herdsman Eurytion and his dog Orthrus. It was one of the labours of Heracles to steal the cattle and drive them back to Greece (see HERACLES, LABOURS OF 10).

Giants (Gigantēs), in Greek myth, monstrous beings of vast size, according to Hesiod sons of Gaia (Earth), conceived from the blood of *Uranus that fell upon the earth when he was castrated. In post-Homeric legend they rebelled against Zeus and the Olympian gods, who, learning that they would not win unless they were assisted by a mortal, called in Heracles. The Giants were defeated at Phlegra (Pallēnē, the westernmost prong of Chalcidice), and were believed to be buried under volcanoes in various parts of Greece and Italy. The Battle of Gods and Giants was a very popular myth in Greece, especially among sculptors, and was sometimes thought of as symbolizing the fight of civilization against barbarism. The events of the three attacks on the Olympian gods made respectively by the *Titans, the Giants, and *Otus and Ephialtes were often confused by the poets. See also HECATONCHEIRES.

gladiators, men who fought with one another in Roman amphitheatres for the amusement of the spectators. Gladiatorial combats were said to have originated in Etruria. They were introduced at Rome in 264 BC, and were at first confined to public funerals, until the games held by Julius Caesar in 46 BC which were only partly commemorative (of his daughter Julia). Under the empire the passion for this amusement reached its height and contributed to the decline of drama at Rome; five thousand pairs fought in the games given by Trajan to celebrate the conclusion of the Dacian War in AD 107. Gladiators were selected from prisoners of war, condemned criminals, slaves bought for the purpose, or volunteers who took part for a fee. In late republican times large numbers were trained in gladiatorial schools and retained by private individuals, becoming a danger to law and order (see MILO). It was from a school in Capua that *Spartacus escaped to lead a slave revolt in 73 BC. Cicero, in a letter to Atticus (7. 14) speaks of five thousand gladiators at Capua. After the time of Domitian (emperor AD 81–96) gladiatorial shows could be given in Rome only by emperors, and outside Rome they required official sanction. There were several types of gladiator: the *murmillo*, who fought with helmet, oblong shield, and sword, and had a fish for crest on his helmet; he usually fought a *retiarius*, who was lightly clad and armed only with a net and trident; there were also the Samnite, armed with oblong shield, visored helmet, and sword, and the Thracian, with round shield and curved scimitar. The poet Statius mentions women and dwarves among the combatants. A repeatedly successful gladiator might receive by favour of the people a wooden sword (*rudis*), a token of his discharge from service. A wounded gladiator raised his forefinger to ask for the mercy of the spectators. They signified their decision either by pressing the thumb against the forefinger (*premere pollicem*) as a sign of good omen (apparently), thereby sparing his life, or by turning the thumb upwards or towards the breast (*vertere pollicem*) to signify the death-stroke. See also VENATIONES.

glass. The art of glazing stone or clay was known in pre-dynastic Egypt, in Crete in the second millennium BC, and in archaic Greece. Objects made purely of glass appeared in Egypt about 1500 BC. Glass beads and inlay have been found at Mycenae from a slightly later period. Greeks in the fifth century BC knew of monochrome and polychrome moulded glass vessels, usually from Syria or Egypt, although they did not become popular until the second and first centuries BC, together with the striped ware known as *millefiori*. Towards the end of the first century BC moulded glass was being made in Italy; the *Portland Vase is an example of moulded glass in two layers, the outer layer being carved like a cameo. Knowledge of glass-blowing (invented probably in Syria in the first century BC) arrived at the beginning of the first century AD, and what had hitherto been a luxury became a commodity capable of mass-production. Under the Roman empire glass came to replace pottery to a considerable extent. Glass window panes, made by a primitive process of rolling, have been found at Pompeii and Herculaneum. Mirrors continued to be made of metal—gold, silver, or bronze—or of natural volcanic glass throughout antiquity. The first glass mirrors were made of dark glass; backed glass mirrors, their backs covered with sheet lead, did not appear until the third century AD. The ancient world knew of burning glasses and of magnifying lenses, probably used for gem-engraving, but spectacles were a very much later invention. Glass lamps are not mentioned until the fourth century AD.

Glau'cia, Gaius Servi'lius, Roman politician. As tribune (101 BC) and praetor (100) he co-operated with Marius and *Saturninus, and passed a law restoring the *repetundae* court to the equites (see LAW, AT ROME I (ii)). He hoped to be consul for 99 BC but his candidature was disallowed. He fled with Saturninus, but the senate had them arrested and they died in prison.

Glaucus. In Greek myth, the name of several characters, including the following.
   1. A fisherman from Anthedon in Boeotia who saw a fish which he had caught and laid on a certain herb come to life. He ate the herb, sprang into the sea, and became immortal, turning into an oracular god of the sea. He figured in some versions of the story of the *Argonauts.
   2. Son of Sisyphus and Meropē and (usually reputed to be) father of *Bellerophon. He inherited his father's kingdom of Corinth but kept a team of mares at Potniae in Boeotia. These he did not allow to breed, but the goddess Aphroditē, angered, drove them mad (or they went mad because Glaucus fed them on human flesh, or for some other reason); they killed Glaucus when he lost the chariot race at the funeral games of Pelias, and ate him. His ghost, known as Taraxippus, was supposed to haunt the stadium and frighten the horses at the Isthmian games (held near Corinth). Aeschylus' tragedy *Glaucus Potnieus* ('Glaucus of Potniae') was one of the trilogy that included the *Persae*, produced in 472 BC. Only fragments survive.
   3. In Homer's *Iliad*, a grandson of Bellero-

phon and leader (after *Sarpedon) of the Lycian allies of the Trojans. During the battle he confronted the Greek Diomedes, but when they found that their grandfathers were bound by ties of hospitality they exchanged armour, Glaucus giving Diomedes his equipment, made of gold and worth a hundred oxen, and receiving the other's of bronze, worth nine. He was killed by Ajax, son of Telamon.

4. A son of *Minos of Crete who was drowned in a vat of honey, and eventually restored to life by the Argive seer Polyidos (descended from Melampus); this complex story was the subject of lost tragedies by Sophocles and Euripides, and according to Lucian represented in mimic dances.

5. The Spartan who was punished by Apollo at Delphi for premeditating perjury in his presence.

glyco'nic, see METRE, GREEK 8 (i).

Gnātho, the parasite in the *Eunuchus* of Terence.

gnō'mē, gnōmic verse. *Gnōmē*, in Greek, literally 'expression of opinion', is used to describe the pithy expression of an acknowledged truth. The most famous *gnomai* are those inscribed on the temple at Delphi, *gnōthi sauton* ('know thyself') and *mēden agan* ('nothing in excess'). They are frequent in the poetry of Hesiod and Euripides. Gnomic poetry, usually written in elegiacs and embodying popular wisdom, can be traced back to *Phocylidēs and *Theognis in the mid-sixth century BC.

gno'sticism, the name (derived from the Greek *gnōsis*, 'knowledge') given to a complex religious movement based on a myth of redemption. It was perhaps pre-Christian in origin, but it became prominent in the second century AD and had Christian as well as pagan forms. Gnosticism distinguished between a remote and unknowable divinity and a *Demiurge descended in some way from the former, who was the (imperfect) creator and ruler of the world, his imperfect creation. Some individuals, however, possessed a spark of the divine spiritual substance and these might hope, by correct observances in this world, to return to the divinity after death. A redeemer was sent, perhaps Christ (or there might be another redeemer still to come), from the divinity, who brought *gnosis* and temporarily inhabited the body of a human being. Gnosticism in various forms persisted for many centuries; much light has been thrown on the movement by the discovery and publication in the twentieth century of some early gnostic texts belonging to the Mandaeans, a quasi-Christian sect still existing in Iraq.

gods

1. *Greek.* The Greeks thought of their most important gods as living on Mount *Olympus and numbering twelve. The number was fixed, although some slight variation of names was possible. The Olympian gods who appear as the central group on the east frieze of the Parthenon are Zeus, Hera, Poseidon, Athena, Apollo, Artemis, Aphroditē, Hermes, Demeter, Dionysus, Hephaestus, and Arēs. It is likely that Hestia was originally one of the canonical twelve and that she was included on the Altar of the Twelve Gods erected by the Peisistratids in the agora at Athens. In the Parthenon she has been replaced by Dionysus. Lesser gods who were sometimes important in cult include Asclepius, Cabeiri, Charitēs, Cybelē, Eileithyia, Enyalios, Eros, Hadēs, Hecatē, Helios, Leto, Leucothea, Muses, Pan, Thetis, Titans, and various sea-gods (Glaucus, Nereus, Pontus, and Proteus). For each of these, see under the name; see also RELIGION, GREEK.

2. *Roman.* See DIANA, FLORA, JANUS, JUNO, JUPITER, LARES, MAIA, MARS, MERCURY, MINERVA, PENATES, QUIRINUS, TERMINUS, VENUS, VESTA, and VULCAN; see also RELIGION, ROMAN.

gold, see MINES.

Golden Age. The Greek poet Hesiod was the first to describe earlier races or generations of men who lived in happier times than we, and the earliest, whose life was most idyllic, was the Golden race, who lived at a time when the ruling god was not yet Zeus but his father *Cronus (Saturn at Rome). This race was succeeded by progressively inferior races, those of silver, bronze, and iron, the last being our own; the deterioration was interrupted by the race of *heroes (those who fought in the Theban and Trojan wars) who immediately preceded us. The Roman poets Horace, Virgil, and Ovid all borrowed the idea, but the Romans, in translating the Greek word *genos*, 'generation' or 'race', by the Latin *saeculum*, incidentally introduced the additional meaning of the latter, namely 'age' or 'long period of time'. Hence there came about the idea of a Golden Age.

The term 'Golden Age' has also been used by literary critics to describe the *Ciceronian and *Augustan ages of Latin literature.

Golden Ass, see APULEIUS.

Golden Bough. In Virgil's *Aeneid,* book 6, Aeneas is told by the Cumaean Sibyl that he must find and pluck a 'golden bough' for Proserpine before he can enter the Underworld. This idea seems to be an invention of Virgil's own; Servius, the fourth-century commentator on Virgil, associated it with the cult of the goddess *Diana at Aricia, where there was a sacred tree from which a branch had first to be broken off by the runaway slave who wished to kill the priest and take his place. This legend of ritual killing can be paralleled in other societies, and from this starting-point Sir James Frazer developed his great work on the evolution of religious beliefs and institutions, the *Golden Bough* (1890–1915).

Golden Fleece, the fleece of the ram that had carried away Phrixus and *Hellē, sought by Jason and the *Argonauts.

Golden House (Domus Aurea), the vast palace built by the emperor Nero in Rome after the great fire of AD 64, covering, it is calculated, about 50 hectares (125 acres) between the Palatine and Esquiline hills; the centre-piece was an ornamental lake in the valley later occupied by the Colosseum. Uncompleted at Nero's death and damaged by fire in AD 104, its remains were covered over by the emperor Trajan; as a consequence the ruins which have been excavated are in a fair state of preservation, the paintings being particularly fine.

Golden Milestone, see MILIARIUM AUREUM.

Gordian knot. Alexander the Great, on his arrival at Gordium in Phrygia, found in the acropolis there an ox-cart of which the pole was fastened to the yoke by a knot of cornel-bark. According to legend, in ancient times a Phrygian peasant called Gordius, his wife, and son *Midas chanced to arrive in this cart at an assembly of the Phrygians, who had just been told by an oracle that a cart would bring them a king to put an end to the civil disturbances. The Phrygians at once made Gordius king, and he dedicated to Zeus in the acropolis at the town subsequently named Gordium his cart and the yoke to which the oxen had been fastened. A further oracle declared that whoever could untie the knot, which had defeated all attempts to undo it, should reign over Asia. Alexander cut the knot with his sword and applied the oracle to himself. 'To cut the Gordian knot' thus signifies drastic action to solve a difficulty.

Go'rgias, of Leontini in Sicily (*c.*483–*c.*385 BC), one of the most influential of the Greek *sophists whose particular expertise was the teaching of rhetoric, based less upon systematic treatment of the subject-matter than upon mannered, poetic, and effective expression. He made his pupils learn typical passages by heart. He appears in one or two of Plato's dialogues (see below), where he is treated with a certain amount of respect (although Agathon's speech in the *Symposium* is a telling parody of his style). His speeches delivered in Athens in 427 when he headed an embassy from his home-town stunned the Athenians with the brilliance and novelty of their style (see RHETORIC). His extant *Encomium of Helen* and *Defence of Palamedes* illustrate both his confidence that the well-taught orator could with ingenuity find arguments to support any case and also his remarkable prose style, with its short symmetrical clauses, rhythmically balanced antitheses,

verbal echoes, and play on words. Part of a funeral oration also survives, and a fragment on the paradoxical theme that 'nothing exists'. Gorgias later travelled about Greece giving lectures, dying at a great age at Larisa in Thessaly. His influence has been detected in Antiphon, Thucydides, and especially in the speeches of *Isocrates.

Go'rgias, dialogue by *Plato named after the famous sophist (see above). Socrates opens the dialogue by asking Gorgias to define rhetoric. The latter replies that it is the most important of human concerns because successful statesmanship depends not upon knowing what should be done and advising accordingly, but upon having the knack of persuasive speech. A successful orator can therefore act as he pleases, justly or unjustly. When Gorgias retires his pupil Polus takes up the argument; Socrates makes him agree, against his will, that it is better to suffer injustice than to do it, and that when one has done evil it is better to be punished than to go unpunished. When Polus retires his place is taken by a certain Callicles (otherwise unknown to us), who in a manner foreshadowing Nietzsche argues that virtue and happiness are to be found in the exercise of lawless self-will, for those who are capable of it. The issue of the dialogue is suddenly seen to be the choice a man has to make between a life of action of the kind Callicles stands for and a life of philosophy represented by Socrates. Socrates reinforces his own choice of philosophy with a passionate denunciation of the 'great' Athenian statesmen of the past, Pericles, Cimon, and Miltiades, and emerges himself as the only true statesman because he alone improves his fellow citizens. At the climax of the dialogue there is a myth, the earliest in Plato, of the judgement of the soul after death, perhaps as an additional incentive to avoid injustice.

Gorgons (Gorgonēs), in Greek myth, female monsters. Homer seems to know only one Gorgon: in the *Iliad* her head adorns the *aegis of the goddess Athena and inspires terror. According to Hesiod there were three Gorgons, Sthen(n)o ('mighty'), Euryalē ('wide-wanderer'), and Medusa ('queen'), living in the far West, by the stream of Ocean, daughters of the sea deities Phorcys and his sister Ceto, and sisters of the Graiae. They are often given monstrous features such as serpents in their hair and glaring eyes. Medusa, who alone was mortal, and whose head was so fearful that anyone who looked at it was turned to stone, was loved by Poseidon and pregnant by him when *Perseus killed her. At the moment of her death she gave birth to Pegasus and Chrysaor ('golden-sword'). The head of Medusa was said to be buried under a mound in the agora of Argos, where it was probably thought to have apotropaic power, and the representation of the head or

Gorgoneion was often carved as a protective figure on armour and walls. In the art of the fifth century BC the head is humanized, and later is often shown as beautiful in death.

Gortyn, an ancient and important city of Crete. Much has been excavated and among the many inscriptions found is the famous 'code of Gortyn', dating from *c*.450 BC, which enumerates many of the laws of the city at that time, and is the most important source of prehellenistic Greek law. The code includes many older laws, some of which are also preserved in other inscriptions, and is a mixture of primitive and more advanced conceptions. The laws deal with the family and family property, the rights of slaves, mortgages, procedures in trials, and other items.

Goths, a Germanic people originating in the Baltic area who moved southwards and settled to the north of the Black Sea, whence in the third century AD they attacked the territory of the Roman empire. Around 370 the Ostrogoths (East Goths) of the Ukraine were overwhelmed by the *Huns, as later were the *Visigoths (West Goths) on the river Tyras (Dniester). The latter subsequently moved into Italy; the former migrated in the fifth century, and eventually, in 489, under their leader Theodoric the Great, reached Italy also, having been ordered by the emperor in the East to 'secure' it from the first barbarian king, *Odo(v)acer. Peace was made between the two in 493; Theodoric was proclaimed king of Italy and took *Ravenna as his capital. He appears in the thirteenth-century German poem the *Nibelungenlied* as 'Dietrich von Bern' (i.e. Theodoric of Verona). See also FALL OF ROME.

The Gothic language is the most primitive Germanic language known to us. See ANTHIMUS.

Gracchi, the, at Rome, the two brothers Tiberius Sempronius Gracchus (*c*.164–133 BC) and Gaius Sempronius Gracchus (d. 121 BC). They were among the twelve children of Tiberius Sempronius Gracchus, the censor, who as praetor completed the reduction of the Celtiberians in Spain and by his generous settlement brought peace there for a generation. He was a man of high character and liberal thought, famous for his austerity. He married *Cornelia, the daughter of Scipio Africanus, and died in *c*.153 BC.

1. Tiberius Sempronius Gracchus first came into prominence when serving in Spain as quaestor to the consul Mancinus. When the latter was threatened with the annihilation of his army by the Numantines, Tiberius was able to negotiate a peace through his father's reputation. The senate, however, urged on by Scipio Aemilianus, Tiberius' cousin and brother-in-law, refused to accept the concessions made to the Numantines and rejected the peace, which,

because it had saved many Roman lives, had brought Tiberius great popularity with the people. Scipio was on campaign against the Numantines when Tiberius was elected tribune in 133. The latter, on the advice of Ap. Claudius, whose daughter he had married, together with the support of a powerful minority in the senate who were hostile to Scipio, proposed an agrarian law aimed at alleviating poverty and increasing the number of men with sufficient property to qualify for military service. This law reaffirmed a previous but long-ignored law that limited the amount of public land an individual might hold (thus striking at occupiers of large tracts of land); the surplus land was to be redistributed in small lots to poor citizens by a commission consisting of Tiberius, his brother Gaius, and Ap. Claudius. The law was passed, but in haste and by unconventional means that included deposing a hostile tribune, M. Octavius. When Tiberius further proposed that the property of Attalus III of Pergamum, bequeathed to Rome, should be used to finance the new allotment-holders, before the senate had decided whether or not to accept the bequest, thus ignoring the senate's traditional control over such decisions, and when he unconstitutionally sought re-election, the senate was persuaded that he was aiming at a tyranny. His friend the consul Scaevola refused to resort to force but Scipio Nasica led a mob of senators and their clients against Tiberius, killing him and many of his supporters on the Capitol. Although the consul of the following year, 132, punished many of his adherents the land commission continued its work. Tiberius' tribunate marks the advent of violence upon the Roman political scene, and the beginning of the disintegration of the senate's power under the attacks of its own members who supported the people.

2. Gaius Sempronius Gracchus, the younger brother of Tiberius, was with Scipio Aemilianus in Spain in 133 when news of Tiberius' murder arrived. He returned to Rome, where he was already a member of the agrarian commission, but he seems not to have been very active in public life until he gained the quaestorship in 126 and was sent to Sardinia. After two years there he returned to Rome and was elected tribune for 123 and again for 122. The first laws he proposed were aimed at taking vengeance on his brother's enemies; he then passed a series of laws aimed at alleviating poverty as well as winning the support of the people. The most important were: (i) providing for the sale of corn at a fair and stable price; (ii) authorizing the foundation of colonies; (iii) reviving his brother's laws on land distribution; (iv) relieving some of the hardships caused by army service. Other laws aimed at protecting provincials from senatorial oppression and limiting the power of senators by transferring some of their prerogatives to the richest non-senators (see

EQUITES). He enacted that the rights to collect the (lucrative) tithes in Asia should be sold by the censors in Rome, and also that the jury of the *repetundae courts should be composed entirely of the richest non-senators. Since these rights would be so greatly sought after that they would be bought only by the richest men, i.e. the same class as were to man the *repetundae* courts, he was in effect giving this class far-reaching power in the state. Finally, in 122, he proposed but failed to pass a bill to give Roman citizenship to the Latins, and the former Latin rights to the Italians (i.e. rights of trade and intermarriage with Rome). He had proposed to establish a number of colonies, mainly in Italy, but including one on the site of Carthage, and had set out for Africa to supervise the settlement of this. During his absence the tribune Livius Drusus (who enjoyed senatorial support) managed to turn the people against him. Opposition to him had been growing not only from the senatorial class but also from the Roman people who grudged his championship of the Italians. Drusus outbid him in the liberality of his offers to the people and thus weaned away his popular supporters. Gaius failed to obtain re-election for 121, and violence broke out between the Gracchans and their enemies. The senate declared a public emergency (the first recorded use of the *senatus consultum ultimum*), and Gaius, finding himself cut off, ordered a slave to kill him (see FURRINA).

Gaius was the more able of the Gracchi; an astute politician and impassioned orator (some fragments of his speeches survive), he used his skills to promote the radical reforms he saw were necessary, but which his enemies' success nullified, with results disastrous for Rome.

Graces, the (Gk. Charitěs, Lat. Gratiae), in myth, minor goddesses, usually said to be daughters of Zeus and to be three in number, called by the Greek poet Hesiod Euphrosynē, Aglaia (sometimes said to be Hephaestus' wife), and Thalia. They are the personification of the grace and beauty that enhance the enjoyment of life. Thus they accompany the Muses, and the most perfect works of art are called the work of the Graces; they give wisdom its charm, they moderate the exciting influence of wine, and they accompany Aphroditē and Eros. For later Romans they were also the symbols of gratitude. They had cults of their own in various parts of Greece (notably an ancient one at Orchomenus in Boeotia; see PINDAR 5, O. 14), and are often made attendants on other gods. In early times they were portrayed clothed, but later always naked.

Gradi'vus, see MARS.

Graiae, in Greek myth, Pemphrēdo, Enȳo, and Deino, daughters of Phorcys and Ceto and sisters of the *Gorgons, the personification of

old age, grey-haired from birth, with one eye and one tooth between them. *Perseus stole their eye and so made them tell him where to find the Gorgons.

Gra'ttius (less correct Grātius), Augustan poet mentioned by Ovid, the author of a Latin poem on hunting (*Cynēgetica*) of which 536 hexameters survive.

Greece. In the ancient world Greece comprised an area of the Balkan peninsula comparable with that of modern Greece. It may be divided into three parts: (i) the peninsula south of the Isthmus of Corinth, known as the Peloponnese; (ii) the land north of the Isthmus roughly as far as the Ambracian Gulf in the west and the river Peneius in the east, which includes Thessaly and is in many contexts known as Greece proper (or mainland Greece); and (iii) the northern regions comprising Epirus, Macedonia, and Thrace, whose inhabitants were regarded as scarcely Greek by the states in the southern regions. For the main ethnic divisions of the Greek people in historical times, see HELLEN. To a large extent the north of Greece was cut off from the rest by the mountain ranges in that area, and Greece itself from the rest of Europe by the high mountain chain that runs from Thrace to Italy. Greece is a land dominated by mountains, which have been held to be the reason for the political development of the country into a scatter of independent states each centred on a pocket of arable land. The country is bare and the soil mostly thin and poor; it is almost rainless in the height of summer, when most of the rivers run dry. The main ploughing and sowing were done in the autumn, with harvest in May. The farmer was free in early summer, until the grain was winnowed in July; then there was another brief respite until the grape harvest and olive picking (see AGRICULTURE). This alternation of hard work and leisure has been seen by some as exerting a significant influence upon the Greek character. The food supply could be overtaxed by a slight rise in population in a country where only the olive crop produced a surplus for export; and overpopulation was at least part of the cause for the colonizing movements of the eighth and seventh centuries BC (see COLONIZATION, GREEK). Metals too were in short supply. The silver mines at Laurium in Attica and the iron mines near Sparta played their part in the rise to power of these states. Thrace had some gold, silver, iron, and copper, as did Macedonia, and more copper came from Cyprus, but tin (needed for the alloy bronze) was mostly imported from western Europe.

The origins of the Greek language go back to migrations into Greece of an *Indo-European people towards the end of the third millennium BC, probably over a protracted period of time. An invasion c.2200 BC brought to an end the Early Bronze Age in Greece and introduced a new culture. Three centuries later came another but less destructive incursion, when the Indo-Europeans seem to have brought with them *horses and a new kind of *pottery (see I (ii)). These invaders flourished in the settled conditions of their new home, and their culture was gradually influenced by the advanced Minoan civilization of Crete. The influence of the indigenous inhabitants on their culture and language is uncertain, but during the seventeenth and sixteenth centuries BC the Greek language took shape: the language written on clay tablets during the *Mycenaean period (*c.*1600–1125 BC), the so-called *Linear B, is recognizably Greek. In *c.*1450 the Mycenaeans seem to have gained control of Minoan Crete, including the powerful city of Cnossus, and their civilization was at its height. The century 1250–1150, however, was a period of destruction throughout the eastern Mediterranean, initiated by the collapse of the Hittite empire and widespread movements of peoples. Troy was one of the cities to fall, her destruction perhaps being Mycenae's last military exploit. Migrating peoples invaded Greece, first Epirus and Thessaly, *c.*1150 BC. Mycenae was herself burnt, with many other cities. Greece's whole political and economic system, the civilization of the Bronze Age, collapsed, and among much else even the knowledge of writing disappeared. The following *Iron Age was marked by depopulation of the mainland, accompanied by emigration to the remoter parts of the Greek world. This period, often known as the Greek *Dark Age, lasted for about 300 years, during which time the Greeks lost all but a dim memory of the splendours of the Mycenaean age and all knowledge of how that culture was organized and how it came to disappear.

Surviving legends seem to indicate some memory of events associated with the Dark Age: one event, which may have hastened the collapse of Mycenaean Greece, was known as the 'Return of the sons of Heracles' (see HERACLEIDAE), or more prosaically the *Dorian Invasion; a second was the subsequent migration of Greeks across the Aegean to the coast of Asia Minor to become the Ionian Greeks (see MIGRATIONS and IONIA). The historicity of these events is largely supported by the distribution of *dialects in historic Greece. By 800 BC the population of Greece was already distributed much as it was going to be in the classical age, and in communities that were somewhat different in organization from those of Mycenaean Greece, being small independent cities, which owed no allegiance to a higher authority. During the following century the art of writing was rediscovered (see ALPHABET), and there was a resumption on a large scale of communication and trade with the East, and the start of exploration and colonization in the West. Greece was now about to enter the period for which documentation exists. For her subsequent history see ATHENS, SPARTA, THEBES, MACEDONIA, and HELLENISTIC AGE.

Despite the fact that Greece was made up of a large number of independent communities, the Greeks formed a single people, with one and the same civilization (see HELLAS); they spoke the same language and were distinguished thereby from the '*barbarians'; there was a broad similarity in their political institutions (government in city-states, normally under oligarchic or democratic constitutions); they had a common religion and respected the same oracular shrines; they had a common heritage of literature from Homer onwards and their art, despite certain diversities, had unity; many of the Greek colonies were founded in common by emigrants from more than one state. Ionia was the first centre of this common civilization; in the early fifth century, after the defeat of the Persian invasions, the intellectual leadership passed to Athens, which already in the previous century, by the liberal policy of the Peisistratids and Cleisthenes, had welcomed strangers, in particular poets and artists, from all parts of Greece. The social unity of Greece manifested itself in the common festivals and games; and some degree of political unity was shown in the combined resistance to Persia. But the various attempts, such as that of Pericles, to consolidate this unity always collapsed before the jealously independent spirit of the different states.

The Greeks called their country Hellas and themselves Hellenes (originally the name of a tribe in south Thessaly). Graii, the local name of a tribe in west Greece, became the Latin name for the Greeks in general; Graeci and Graecia ('Greeks' and 'Greece') are derivatives from Graii. It has been suggested that the Graii took part in the colonization of Cumae, the oldest Greek colony in Italy, and from them the name was applied more widely. When the Romans created the province of Greece in 27 BC they called it Achaea.

The phrase 'Greek world' describes that part of the world at the time in question in which Greek was, or had become, the principal language, or was the language of the rulers and the administration. Apart from Greece and the Peloponnese, together with Epirus, Macedonia, and Thrace, it might include Magna Graecia and Sicily (during the Greek classical period; both were slowly Romanized), Egypt and Cyrenaica (see CYRENE), Asia Minor, and to a varying extent lands to the east and south: Syria, north Arabia, and even Mesopotamia (Iraq) and beyond. Rome began to take over the Greek world in the second century BC and had done so before the end of the first century BC.

griffin or **gryphon** (Gk. *gryps*), fabulous animal with the body of a lion and the head and wings of an eagle, supposed to dwell in the far north between the Hyperboreans and the one-eyed Arimaspians, guarding the gold of the north. The conception would seem to be eastern in origin.

groma'tici, Roman land-surveyors (Lat. *groma*, a measuring rod). During the empire several Latin authors wrote on surveying, including *Frontinus and *Hyginus; the former's treatise is known to us only in extracts.

guilds, see COLLEGIUM.

Gyas, in Virgil's *Aeneid*, a companion of Aeneas; he figures in the boat-race (book 5). Also, the name of a Latin slain by Aeneas (*Aeneid* 10. 318).

Gy'es, see HECATONCHEIRES.

Gygēs, king of Lydia (*c*.685–*c*.657 BC); he founded the dynasty of the Mermnadae by killing the king Candaules (called Myrsilus by the Greeks). According to Herodotus he was the favourite officer of Candaules who, being proud of his wife's beauty, insisted that Gyges should see the queen naked while remaining himself hidden. The queen, however, sensed his presence, and later summoned Gyges to offer him the choice of dying himself or murdering the king and taking the kingdom, with her as his queen. He chose the latter course. Plato in *Republic*, book 2, tells the story that Gyges won the queen and the kingdom by means of a magic ring of invisibility, to illustrate the view that men are not virtuous when they need not fear the consequences of their actions. 'Gyges' ring' subsequently became proverbial, as did 'the riches of Gyges'. He reputedly sent rich gifts to Delphi in gratitude for an oracle which established his right to the throne. He was the first Lydian king to try to extend his rule over the Greek cities of the Ionian coast.

Gyli'ppus, Spartan general sent in 414 BC to help the Syracusans against the Athenians (see PELOPONNESIAN WAR). Under his leadership the Athenian fleet and army were utterly destroyed. He was convicted at Sparta in 405 of embezzling public funds and went into exile.

gymnasia'rchia, see GYMNASIUM and LITURGY.

gymna'sium (Gk. *gymnos*, 'naked'), in Greece, a (gymnastic) school, its name derived from the practice among Greek boys and men of exercising naked (see also ATHLETICS). Education to the Greeks meant a training both intellectual and physical (in preparation for war), and the gymnasia catered for both. While intellectual training ceased after youth, gymnastics were practised at all ages. In Sparta there were no gymnasia since all male citizens from the age of 7 were engaged exclusively in military training. At Athens, on the other hand, three gymnasia, the *Lyceum, the *Academy, and the *Cynosargēs, became famous schools of philosophy. By the Hellenistic age the gymnasium had become an essential element of Greek life, and a hallmark of Hellenism. Essentially it consisted of an open court for wrestling and similar sports, and a running track, but refinements were often added—jumping pits and throwing ranges, a colonnaded walk (*stoa*), and a variety of rooms: cloakrooms, oiling rooms, dusting rooms where the gymnasts powdered themselves, rooms for ball-games, bathrooms, lecture-rooms. It was a public institution, the upkeep and the trainers paid for by the city. The gift of a gymnasium was a favourite act of charity by rich individuals in Hellenistic and Roman times. The management was in the hands of a gymnasiarch, a state official elected for a year, whose office was one of the regular *liturgies and involved the holder in considerable expense, since he might be expected to subsidize the costs and above all to provide free oil. See also ATHLETICS, EDUCATION, and PALAESTRA.

Gymnopae'diae, an annual festival 'of the naked youths' at Sparta, instituted soon after Sparta suffered a crushing defeat at the hands of the Argives at Hysiae in 669 BC. It was held in July, lasted for several days, and included displays of gymnastics and dancing by boys and men; hymns were sung in honour of the gods and Spartan heroes.

Gymno'sophists, see ALEXANDER THE GREAT 6.

H

Habro'comēs and Anthei'a (or *Ephesiaca*), *novel by Xenophon of Ephesus.

Hādēs (Haidēs, Ăidēs, or Ăidōneus), also known as Plūto (the Latin form of the Greek Ploutōn, 'the wealth-giver'), or Dis (the contracted form of Latin *dives*, 'rich'); in Greek myth, one of the three sons of Cronus and Rhea, and brother of Zeus and Poseidon. When the three cast lots for their domains (see ZEUS), Hades obtained the Underworld. He and his wife *Persephonē are the rulers of the dead. Although he is therefore a grim and dreaded god, he is not an enemy to mankind, nor to his brothers. Plato observes that out of fear people prefer to call him by the euphemistic name of Plouton because all metals are found under the earth. The etymology of Hades is uncertain; it may mean 'the unseen one'. The name in Greek nearly always designates the god, not his kingdom, to which it was later extended by natural usage: the dead were said to go 'to (the house of) Hades'. His kingdom was thought of as underground, despite the tendency of Greeks to locate the abode of the dead in the West. The two ideas were reconciled by supposing the entrance to be at some locality in the West. In Homer's *Iliad* it is in the far West beyond the stream of *Ocean (which was believed to encircle the earth). Later it was thought to be approached by various natural chasms. Details in the description of the realm of Hades also vary. It contains the dreary Plain of Asphodel, where the ghosts of the dead lead a vague, unsubstantial life. A few fortunate ones escape this fate and are taken to *Elysium, while those who have been enemies of the gods are removed to *Tartarus for punishment (see also AFTERLIFE). Generally the realm of the dead is separated from that of the living by one of the rivers of Hades, *Styx or *Acheron. Across this the dead, provided they have been duly buried, are ferried by *Charon. At the entrance of the Underworld stands the watch-dog *Cerberus who prevents any of the dead from going out again. Within sit the judges of the dead, *Minos, *Rhadamanthys, and *Aeacus, who assign to each ghost its appropriate abode. Besides Styx and Acheron, three other rivers intersect the Underworld, Phlegethon or Pyriphlegethon ('the fiery one'), *Cocytus, and (in Latin poetry) *Lēthē. John Milton (1608–74), *Paradise Lost* 2. 575 ff., speaks of

> four infernal Rivers that disgorge
> Into the burning Lake their baleful streams:

> Abhorred *Styx* the flood of deadly hate;
> Sad *Acheron* of sorrow, black and deep;
> *Cocytus*, nam'd of lamentation loud
> Heard on the ruful stream; fierce *Phlegeton*
> Whose waves of torrent fire inflame with rage.
> Farr off from these a slow and silent stream,
> *Lethe* the River of Oblivion roules
> Her watrie Labyrinth.

When Hades was in his kingdom nothing reached his ears except the oaths and curses of men. When men invoked him they struck the earth with their hands. Black sheep were sacrificed to him, and those who offered the sacrifice kept their faces averted. Hades had very little cult, and few statues of him exist. He figures little in myth except for the story of his rape of Persephone.

Hadrian (Publius Aelius Hādriānus), Roman emperor AD 117–38. He was born in 76 in Spain, and when left fatherless entered the household of Trajan, to whom he was distantly connected. He won favour and held significantly high offices, but his adoption by the childless emperor Trajan on the latter's deathbed surprised and displeased some; nevertheless the senate sanctioned his succession. He passed the years 120–31 in touring the provinces, visiting *Britain in 121 or 122 (see 5) and spending at least two years in Athens, a city he greatly loved. While he was in Egypt in 130 his favourite companion *Antinŏus, then aged about 20, was drowned. These travels reinforced his intention to aim at peace and sound defences in his foreign policy—hence the Wall across Britain; he renounced those eastern conquests of Trajan which could not be secured. A revolt in Judaea, 132–5, led by Bar-Cochba, was the only serious war of his reign, precipitated perhaps by his misjudgement in proposing to found a (pagan) colony on the site of Jerusalem, and (it is said) by the prohibition of circumcision. The revolt was finally suppressed by Julius Severus, a general sent from Britain, with great devastation and heavy loss of life: when the colony was established, the Jews were in effect deprived of their homeland Judaea.

Hadrian made reforms in administration: men of equestrian rank replaced freedmen in the high posts of the imperial bureaucracy (see FREEDMEN), there was reorganization in the army, provincial extortion became rarer, and the conditions of slaves were improved. In the sphere of law, four circuit judges, of consular rank, were appointed to administer law in Italy, and private law was codified, so that thereafter it could not be altered except by the emperor, a measure which put an end to legal innovations by magistrates. Hadrian was the most intellectual and cultivated of all the emperors, and a generous patron. Most places he visited benefited from his liberality. Athens received a library, a gymnasium, and a colonnade, as well as seeing the completion of the temple of Olympian Zeus begun by Peisistratus nearly 700 years before (see OLYMPIEUM). In Rome he founded the Athenaeum, an institute for lectures and recitations, built the *Pantheon, the temple of Venus and Rome, and his mausoleum (modern Castel S. Angelo) together with the bridge, Pons Aelius, by which it was approached. He also built an extensive villa at Tibur (Tivoli), which has been a rich source of art treasures. His attitude towards Christianity was tolerant as far as was consistent with good order. Hadrian died reputedly with a poem addressed to his soul on his lips, 'animula, vagula, blandula' ('little soul, wandering, pleasant . . .'). His other works, which include speeches, letters, and an autobiography, are lost.

Hadrian's Wall, see BRITAIN 5.

Haedui, see AEDUI.

Haemon, son of Creon; see OEDIPUS.

Halicarna'ssus, city in *Caria on the south-west coast of Asia Minor near the island of Cos, the birthplace of Herodotus and Dionysius. In classical times its culture was Ionian. The strength and beauty of its position led *Mausolus, king of Caria in the fourth century BC, to make it his capital. See also MIGRATIONS.

Halieu'tica. 1. Latin poem wrongly attributed to *Ovid, of which a fragment survives.
   2. Greek didactic poem in five books of hexameters by *Oppian.

hamadry'ads, *nymphs of trees, whose lives were co-terminous with their trees.

Hami'lcar. 1. Carthaginian general at the battle of Himera (480 BC) in which he was defeated and killed by *Gelon, tyrant of Syracuse. He was a son or grandson of the great Mago, who founded the fortunes of the family in the mid-sixth century and was the first to organize the Carthaginian army.
   2. **Hamilcar Barca,** general appointed at a young age to command the Carthaginian forces in Sicily during the First *Punic War against Rome in 247 BC. Nothing is known of his family. He seized Herctē on the north coast of Sicily in the midst of enemy territory and held it for three years while raiding the Italian coast as far as Cumae. In 244 he abruptly left and took the town at the foot of Mount Eryx, where he defied the Romans for another two years. After the Carthaginian naval defeat at Aegates Insulae

in 241 he negotiated the terms of peace and resigned his command. After putting down with great bloodshed a revolt of mercenaries, he was sent in 237 with his young son Hannibal to Spain, where the Carthaginians do not appear to have had any great dominion up to this time. He conquered southern and eastern Spain, and perhaps intended to form there a new empire for Carthage, to compensate for the loss of Sicily and Sardinia, and to provide wealth and manpower for a new onslaught against the hated Romans. He was drowned during the siege of a Spanish town in 229, leaving three sons, *Hannibal, *Hasdrubal, and Mago, all of whom distinguished themselves in the Second Punic War.

Ha'nnibal (247–183/2 BC), eldest son of *Hamilcar Barca and the great leader of the Carthaginians against Rome in the Second *Punic War. Hamilcar took him to Spain in 237, after making him swear eternal hatred to Rome, a story told by Hannibal himself. When *Hasdrubal (1) was assassinated in 221, the army elected Hannibal commander-in-chief. For two years he extended Carthaginian power in Spain and then in 219 besieged Saguntum, a city in alliance with Rome, thus, as he expected, precipitating war with Rome. His bold plan of invading Italy before Rome was ready nearly succeeded; after sixteen years of continuous warfare in Italy he was ordered in 203 to withdraw his undefeated army and return to Africa in order to defend Carthage from the invading Romans. Finally defeated by *Scipio Africanus at Zama in 202 he escaped to Carthage and urged an immediate peace. After the conclusion of the treaty in 201 he carried out constitutional and administrative reforms at Carthage, weakening the power of the oligarchs. When his enemies informed Rome that he was conspiring with Antiochus of Syria, Hannibal left to join Antiochus, who was on the verge of war with Rome. Hannibal was defeated in a naval engagement at Sidē, and subsequently fled to Crete and thence to king Prūsias of Bithynia. The Romans were uneasy as long as he remained alive, and eventually demanded his surrender. Hannibal, seeing all ways shut to him, took poison in 183 or 182. Acknowledged to be one of the world's greatest soldiers, Hannibal excelled in many areas: he was a bold strategist as well as a skilful tactician, who learned how to combine infantry and cavalry so as to surround the enemy. Most of all he could retain the loyalty of mercenary troops even in defeat and hardship, and his character survived accusations of treachery and cruelty from the Roman side.

Harmo'dius and Aristogei'ton, two lovers who killed Hipparchus, the younger brother of the Athenian tyrant Hippias, at the festival of the Panathenaea in 514 BC. The story was that Hipparchus had arranged a public insult to

Harmodius' sister after he had made advances to Harmodius and been rejected. The two then made an attempt to overthrow the tyranny but failed and were killed. The tyranny lasted until 510 BC, but they were later honoured by the Athenian people as if they had succeeded. A statue to them was erected in the agora with an epigram by Simonides inscribed on the base, fragments of which have been found. See ALCMAEONIDAE and PEISISTRATUS 3.

Harmo'nia, necklace of. Made by the god Hephaestus, it was given as a wedding present to Harmonia, daughter of Ares and Aphroditē, by her husband Cadmus. It did harm to all who subsequently possessed it. (See CADMUS, AMPHIARAUS, and ALCMAEON.)

harmony or **music of the spheres,** a Pythagorean concept (see PYTHAGORAS), harmony having cosmic significance for the Pythagoreans. It seemed to them, as to others, that the heavenly bodies (the spheres) must, like other large bodies moving at speed, produce a sound as they whirl through space, and that since the bodies move at different speeds they must each produce different (but harmonious) notes. Plato's version of this idea, expounded in the Myth of Er (*Republic*, book 10), is that on each of the eight concentric circles in which the bodies rotate stands a *Siren uttering a note of constant pitch, the eight notes together making up a scale. Because the sound is with us constantly from birth and there is no contrasting silence we are unaware of it.

ha'rmosts (*harmostai*, 'regulators'), name given to Spartan military governors abroad, especially to those sent to the cities occupied by Sparta after the latter defeated Athens at the end of the Peloponnesian War in 404 BC.

Ha'rpalus, unreliable treasurer of *Alexander the Great (see 6); see also DEMOSTHENES (2) 1 and DEINARCHUS.

Harpies (harpūīai, 'snatchers'), in Greek myth, the daughters of Thaumas (son of Pontus, Sea) and Electra (daughter of *Oceanus). They appear to have been regarded by Homer and Hesiod as personifications of violent winds which carried off the daughters of Pandareus, Cleothera and Meropē, to be slaves to the *Furies. Among their names were Aёllo ('storm-wind'), Ōcypetē ('swift-flying'), Podargē ('fleet-of-foot'), and Celaino ('dark'). They are represented as birds with the faces of women. In the story of *Phineus the Harpies carry off or defile all his food. Virgil makes Aeneas encounter them at the islands of the Strophades (*Aeneid* 3. 225). The famous Harpy relief in the British Museum is from the frieze of a monument discovered at Xanthus in Lycia.

Harpo'cratēs, Greek name for the Egyptian god *Horus.

haru'spicēs (sing. *haruspex*), name given in Rome to Etruscan diviners, believed to be interpreters of the will of the gods, who were sometimes sent for on important occasions not only by private individuals but also by the senate. They came to rival in importance the official diviners at Rome, the augurs (see AUGURY), though they possessed no religious authority in the state and it is not until the empire that we hear of their being organized into a *collegium*. Their art, known as the *Etrusca disciplīna* ('the Etruscan study'), was practised far into Christian times. It interpreted the will of the gods as conveyed through the state of the entrails (*exta*) of sacrificial animals, or through *monstra*, 'prodigies' (unusual births or growths), or *fulgura*, 'lightning', the two last categories being considered as sent from the gods as warnings. Significant for the *exta* were the size, shape, colour, and markings of the liver and gall-bladder. Lightning was interpreted by its frequency and the precise region of the sky in which it was seen. See DIVINATION and also CICERO (1) 4 and *DE HARUSPICUM RESPONSO*.

Ha'sdrubal. **1.** Carthaginian general and son-in-law of *Hamilcar Barca, upon whose death in 229 BC he became the commander in Spain. He extended the Carthaginian empire in Spain to the boundary of the river Ebro, but in 221 was murdered by a Celtic slave, and was succeeded in the command by Hannibal.

2. Son of Hamilcar Barca and brother of Hannibal, left in command of the Carthaginians in Spain when Hannibal invaded Italy in 218 BC (Second Punic War). From 218 to 208 he fought in Spain against the Roman generals Publius Cornelius *Scipio and his son Scipio Africanus. Having evaded the Roman army he then marched to Italy to the relief of Hannibal (207), but he was intercepted in the valley of the river Metaurus, defeated, and killed, in a significant victory for the Romans.

Heau'ton timōrū'menos ('self-tormentor'), Roman comedy (with Greek title) by *Terence, adapted from a Greek comedy of the same name by *Menander, and produced at Rome in 163 BC.

The self-tormentor is an Athenian father, Menedēmus, who imposes hardships on himself in penitence for the harshness which has driven his son Clīnia out of the country on account of his love for Antiphila, supposed to be the daughter of a Corinthian woman of small means. His neighbour Chremēs, perplexed by his behaviour, intervenes: *homo sum; humani nil a me alienum puto* ('I am a man; I reckon nothing human to be foreign to me'), he says in explanation, and somewhat officiously lectures Menedemus on a parent's duty of indulgence. Clinia returns to Athens, making his home with his friend Clītipho, son of Chremes, who, unknown to his father, is spending his money on the prostitute Bacchis. It is arranged that Bacchis shall come to the house of Chremes, in the character of Clinia's friend, bringing with her Antiphila as a companion. By a trick of the slave Sўrus, Chremes is cheated out of some money for the benefit of his son's extravagant mistress, and when Chremes discovers this and what has been going on in his house, he angrily disinherits the boy, repudiating his own doctrine of parental duty. His wife intercedes for their son, and Clitipho is let off on condition of a suitable marriage (not, however, with 'the red-headed, cat-eyed girl' first proposed to him). Meanwhile Clinia has been restored to his repentant father, and Antiphila has been discovered to be the daughter of Chremes, who gives her in marriage to Clinia.

Hebdo'madēs ('sevens'), lost work by Marcus Terentius *Varro, an illustrated biographical dictionary of famous Romans and Greeks, containing seven hundred portraits.

Hēbē, in Greek myth, daughter of Zeus and Hera, the cup-bearer of the gods and wife to *Heracles after his death and translation to Olympus. She is the personification of the Greek word for youth. The Roman goddess Juventas was identified with her.

He'calē, *epyllion by the Hellenistic Greek poet *Callimachus, describing how Theseus was once hospitably entertained by a poor old woman of this name while on his way to kill the bull of Marathon. The poem was intended to explain the name and cult of the Attic deme of Hecale.

Hecatae'us, of Miletus (an Ionian Greek city in Asia Minor), one of the earliest composers of Greek prose history and geography (see LOGO-GRAPHERS). He lived around 500 BC, when he advised the Ionians against revolting from Persian rule, knowing well the extent and resources of the Persian empire. He seems to have survived the Persian Wars and to have died *c*.476. The results of his extensive travels in the Persian empire, Egypt, Greece, and around the coasts of the Mediterranean and Black Sea were embodied in a map of the world, showing a flat, circular earth with a hole in the middle, representing the Mediterranean, and the stream of *Ocean running like a river around the outside. (This was said to be the second map made in Greece: see ANAXIMANDER.) Makers of this style of map were much derided by Herodotus for their ignorance. Hecataeus wrote in (Ionic) Greek a *Periēgēsis* (or *Periodos gēs*, 'guide') to illustrate his map, many fragments of which survive in quotations mostly too short to be illuminating. Herodotus seems to have made extensive use of this work without acknowledgement. Hecataeus also wrote a work entitled the *Histories* or *Genealogies*, the few surviving fragments of which show that he was tracing

back to mythical times the families (including, apparently, his own) of those who claimed a god or hero as their ultimate ancestor. The first sentence is famous for embodying a new critical approach: 'I write these things as they seem to me; for the stories of the Greeks are many and ridiculous in my opinion.'

He'catē, an ancient and somewhat mysterious Greek goddess, unknown to Homer, but according to Hesiod the daughter of the *Titans Persēs and Asteriē (sister of Leto). Hesiod described her as the source of innumerable blessings for men—wealth, victory, wisdom, good luck to sailors and hunters, and so on, and as uniquely honoured among the Titans for being allowed to keep her powers under Zeus' rule. She was frequently confused with Artemis (at Rome, Diana), whose functions overlap hers to some extent. But generally in Greece she was associated with the ghost world, an attendant upon *Persephonē, queen of the Underworld, and so in some sense herself a ruler over the souls of the dead. At night she sent ghosts and demons into the world, and wandered about with the souls of the dead, her approach signalled by the howling of dogs. She was associated with sorcery and black magic, and is invoked by Medea in Euripides' play and by Simaetha in the second Idyll of Theocritus. She was worshipped at cross-roads (i.e. wherever one road meets another), where dishes of food were put out for her at the end of every month as a purificatory rite; the usual sacrifice to her was of dogs. In statues she was often represented in triple form (perhaps looking along three roads).

he'catomb, in Greece, originally the sacrifice of a hundred oxen (*hekaton bous*); the term came to be used even in Homer of any great sacrifice of animals; see SACRIFICE. *Hekatombaion* was the name of a month at Athens, 'the time when hecatombs are offered'.

Hecato'mpedon (the 'hundred-foot temple'), name given to an earlier temple built on the site of the present *Parthenon (the temple of Athena Polias) on the Acropolis at Athens. The Parthenon is occasionally given the title of the Hecatompedon in order to distinguish it from the other temple of Athena Polias on the Acropolis, the so-called *Erechtheum. The Hecatompedon is usually identified with the temple built of *poros* (limestone) and dedicated in 566 BC, some remains of which are to be found in the Acropolis Museum, notably the painted pediment sculpture. It was intentionally demolished *c*.488 BC to make room for the present Parthenon's immediate predecessor, the Older Parthenon.

Hecatonchei'res ('hundred-handed'), in Greek myth, monstrous *giants, Briareus, Cottus, and Gyēs, sons of Uranus (Heaven) and Gaia (Earth), who helped Zeus in his war against the Titans.

Hector, in Greek legend, the eldest son of *Priam, king of Troy, and of his wife Hecuba, the husband of Andromachē and father of Astyanax, the leader and the bravest of the Trojans during the siege of Troy (see ILIAD). In the early books of the *Iliad* he takes a prominent part in the fighting and arranges the single combat between Paris and Menelaus. In book 6, having left the fighting to advise the Trojan women to supplicate the gods, he sees Andromache and Astyanax for the last time in a memorable scene of farewell. After his return to battle his challenge to single combat is taken up by Ajax, son of Telamon, who is his superior though the fight is inconclusive; in the battles that follow, while Achilles is absent from the field, Hector plays the leading part in the Trojan successes which culminate in his slaying of Patroclus. When Achilles returns to battle and the Trojans are routed, Hector alone awaits Achilles before the walls of Troy. Achilles pursues him around the city but eventually Hector halts, deceived by the goddess Athena into thinking that his brother Deïphobus has come to his aid. When he realizes the deception he knows that he must die. Achilles kills him and mutilates the body by dragging it behind his chariot to the Greek ships. In a moving scene Priam calls upon Achilles in order to ransom his son's body, and Hector's funeral ends the *Iliad*.

Hector is the greatest hero on the Trojan side; on his life alone the survival of Troy depends. He is always inferior to the Greek hero Achilles, but noble and chivalrous, regarded by his countrymen as god-like. He dies gloriously defending Troy, and his death not only portends the complete destruction of the city but is in itself an event of extreme pathos as the hero shorn of his god-like qualities to become merely a mutilated corpse. It is significant for the Homeric conception of Hector that later poets add nothing to his history, though Pausanias has the story that the Thebans removed his body from Troy and buried it at Thebes in response to an oracle.

He'cuba (Hekabē), in Greek myth, the (chief) wife of Priam, king of Troy, and mother of nineteen of his children including Hector, Helenus, Troilus, Paris, Cassandra, Creusa, and Polyxena. In the *Iliad* she remains in the background fulfilling the role of the bereaved queen destined to survive the sack of Troy and the loss of her husband and nearly all her children. In Greek tragedy this latter part of her life becomes a favourite subject, being rich in dramatic possibilities. In the *Trojan Women* of Euripides she is allotted as spoils of war to Odysseus, and has to endure the sacrifice of her daughter Polyxena on Achilles' tomb and the murder of Hector's only son Astyanax. In the *Hecuba*, also by Euripides, she discovers the murder of her last remaining son Polydorus (see

below), and the prophecy is made that she will be metamorphosed into a bitch. Later legend elaborated upon this topic.

He'cuba, Greek tragedy by *Euripides written perhaps in 424 BC.

Troy has fallen to the Greeks, the women of Troy have been apportioned to the victors, but the return home of the Greek fleet is delayed by contrary winds. The ghost of the Greek hero Achilles has demanded the sacrifice to him of Polyxena, daughter of Hecuba and Priam, king of Troy. The Greek hero Odysseus comes to lead her away. He is unmoved by Hecuba's despair and by her reminder that he once owed his life to her. But Polyxena, a striking figure, prefers death to slavery, and willingly goes to her sacrifice. As Hecuba prepares for the burial, she suffers a further sorrow. Her youngest son Polydōrus had been sent for safety to Polymēstor, king of the Thracian Chersonese (where the Greek fleet is now detained), with part of the treasure of Priam. When Troy fell, Polymestor had murdered the boy in order to secure the treasure for himself, and had thrown his body into the sea. It has now been washed up and is brought to Hecuba. She appeals to the Greek leader Agamemnon for vengeance; but he, though sympathetic, is timid. Hecuba thereupon takes vengeance into her own hands. She lures Polymestor and his sons to her tent, where her women put out his eyes and kill the sons. Agamemnon orders the blinded king to be left on a deserted island; he then prophesies that Hecuba will turn into a bitch, and that the site of her tomb will be commemorated by the name Cynossēma ('dog's tomb'), on the east coast of the Thracian Chersonese.

He'cyra ('mother-in-law'), Roman comedy by *Terence adapted from the Greek original by Apollodorus of Carystus, a writer of New Comedy (see COMEDY, GREEK 6). The plot also resembles that of Menander's *Epitrepontes*. The *Hecyra* lost its audience at its first two productions, first in 165 BC to the rival attractions of rope-dancers and a boxing match, and secondly in 160 to a gladiatorial combat, and was successfully performed only at its third attempt in the same year. It has never been a popular play.

Pamphilus has been reluctantly persuaded by his father to give up the prostitute Bacchis and to marry. Soon after the marriage he is sent away by his father on business. During his absence his wife leaves her mother-in-law's house on a pretext and returns to her own mother's house. There she gives birth to a baby conceived before her marriage, having been seduced by an unknown man under cover of darkness. This man had taken from her a ring, subsequently discovered in the possession of Bacchis. With the latter's help it is discovered that the wife's seducer was Pamphilus himself, who is after all the father of his wife's child. Pamphilus, who had reluctantly felt that he must separate from his wife, therefore returns to her. The title of the play is derived from the carefully drawn characters of the two mothers-in-law.

hektē'moroi, see SOLON.

Helen. In Greek myth, Leda, the wife of Tyndareus king of Sparta, bore four children, the twins Castor and Polydeuces, Clytemnestra, and Helen, of whom the last at least was fathered by Zeus. According to the usual story, Zeus visited Leda in the form of a swan, Leda laid an egg, and from this Helen was hatched. Helen and her brothers were worshipped as important deities in Sparta, but in the literary tradition, starting with Homer, she is the entirely human wife of King Menelaus of Sparta, the younger brother of Agamemnon, the latter being married to Helen's sister Clytemnestra. Of outstanding beauty, Helen was said to have been carried off in her youth by Theseus to Attica; but during Theseus' absence in the Underworld her brothers rescued her and took her back to Sparta together with Theseus' mother Aethra. She was subsequently wooed by all the leading men in Greece; at the suggestion of Odysseus she was allowed to choose whom she pleased, and the rest swore to abide by her choice and support her husband's rights. She married Menelaus and bore him a daughter Hermione, but while he was absent in Crete Paris arrived in Sparta, and either persuaded Helen to flee with him or carried her off by force to Troy. (The goddess Aphrodite had promised him the most beautiful woman in the world as his wife; see PARIS, JUDGEMENT OF.) On his return Menelaus and his brother Agamemnon raised an expedition against Troy. Another tradition, apparently as old as the poet Stesichorus (sixth century BC), has it that Helen was carried for safe keeping to King Proteus of Egypt, while Zeus and Hera allowed only a phantom resembling her to accompany Paris to Troy, thus providing a pretext for the Trojan War, which Zeus had already decreed should take place so as to reduce the wickedness and the multitude of men. After the war Menelaus found Helen in Egypt and took her home.

In the *Iliad* Helen is a tragic figure, compelled by Aphrodite to be the wife of Paris and aware that her wrong-doing has caused suffering for everyone. She reproaches herself, but is not generally reproached by the Trojans and never, as she says, by Priam or Hector. In a memorable scene on the battlements of Troy the old men, seeing her, observe that such beauty puts her beyond blame. In the *Odyssey* she lives peacefully in Sparta reconciled with her husband, but is an enigmatic figure. She tells how once in Troy she alone recognized Odysseus when he entered in disguise, and of her delight when he

slew many Trojans. Menelaus on the other hand recalls how she tempted the Greeks in the Wooden Horse to reveal themselves by imitating the voices of their wives. Later writers, Greek and Roman, were generally hostile to Helen, and the speeches in her defence composed by *Gorgias and *Isocrates are little more than rhetorical demonstrations of how to defend the patently guilty.

Helen, Greek tragedy (with a happy ending) by *Euripides, produced in 412 BC. The plot is based on the legend (see above) that it was not the real Helen but her phantom which accompanied Paris to Troy.

Helen herself has been magically conveyed by the god Hermes to the court of Proteus, king of Egypt, where she awaits the return of her husband Menelaus from Troy. But Proteus is now dead, and his son Theoclỹmenus is trying to force her to marry him. She has taken refuge at the tomb of Proteus. The Greek hero Teucer, the brother of Ajax, arrives and tells her of the fall of Troy seven years previously, and of the probable death of Menelaus. While she is lamenting, Menelaus himself appears. He has been shipwrecked on the Egyptian coast, has left the 'Helen' whom he was bringing from Troy in a cave, and has come to the palace for help. A curious scene of reconciliation follows, for Menelaus is puzzled by the two Helens and is convinced of the reality of the 'Egyptian' Helen only when he learns that the other has disappeared into the air after revealing the deception. Helen now devises an escape for both of them from Egypt, a difficult matter, for Theoclymenus not only is determined to marry her, but will kill any Greek whom he finds in the land. With the help of Theonoē, a priestess and the sister of the king, Theoclymenus is fooled with a pretence of a funeral ceremony at sea for a supposedly dead Menelaus, and Menelaus and Helen escape on the ship provided for the purpose. Castor and Polydeuces, Helen's deified brothers, appear at the end to avert the king's wrath against Theonoe for her complicity. The chorus consists of Helen's attendants, captured Greek maidens.

The poet does not fail to point out the grim humour of the situation: the ten years' siege of Troy has all been for nothing; and the lore of seers is not worth much, for *Calchas and *Helenus gave no indication whatsoever of the deception.

Helen, Encomium on, see GORGIAS and ISOCRATES.

He'lenus, in Homer's *Iliad*, son of Priam, king of Troy, and his wife Hecuba, gifted with prophecy. According to later legend (not in Homer) he was captured by Odysseus and revealed that the Greeks would take Troy only if *Philoctetes was brought there with his bow and arrows. After the fall of Troy, Helenus became the captive of Neoptolemus, and after the latter's death married Andromachē and became king of Chāonia, a part of Epirus. *Aeneas, in the course of his wanderings, visited him there and received advice on the direction he should follow (see AENEID 3).

hēliai'a or **ēliai'a.** In Greek this word appears to mean originally 'assembly'. *Solon in his constitutional reforms at Athens in the sixth century BC seems to have established the right of a citizen to appeal against the magistrates' judicial decisions (formerly absolute) to the people assembled as a jury, and to this court the name *heliaia* was given. It would appear that appeals became so common that the assembly did not have time to deal with all the cases referred to it. By the mid-fifth century BC the *heliaia* had been subdivided into a number of juries of varying size according to the importance of the case, and the magistrates' function reduced to presiding over the juries. These smaller courts, usually known as *dikastēria*, heard almost all cases in the first instance. The word *heliaia* was then often used to denote the whole body of jurors, and a juror would be called *hēliastēs* or *dikastēs*. More commonly, however, the name *heliaia* was given to the particular court presided over by the six junior archons known as the *thesmothetai*. (See LAW, AT ATHENS.)

He'licon, largest mountain of Boeotia in Greece, celebrated as one of the two favourite haunts of the Muses (the other is Pieria) who had an ancient sanctuary there. On its slope was the village of Ascra, the home of the poet Hesiod, who tells how he met the Muses while tending sheep on the mountainside. The fountains of Aganippē and Hippocrēnē on the mountain, which supplied the streams Olmeios and Permessos, were believed to inspire those who drank from them; see PEGASUS.

Hēliodō'rus, of Emesa in Syria, author of the Greek novel the *Aethiopica* (or *Theagenes and Charicleia*). Nothing certain is known of his life, which is dated variously in the third and fourth centuries AD, but he has been identified with a Christian bishop in Thessaly of that name. See NOVEL 1.

Helioga'balus, see ELAGABALUS.

Hē'lios, in Greek myth, the Sun, personified as a god, son of the *Titans Hyperion and Theia, brother of Selēnē (Moon) and Eōs (Dawn), and the father of Aeētēs, Circē, and *Phaethōn. (Homer occasionally calls him Hyperion, a practice imitated by other poets.) He is generally represented as a charioteer driving daily from east to west across the sky, and floating back to the east during the night in a golden cup on the stream of Ocean, the cup that Heracles once borrowed (see HERACLES, LABOURS OF 10). He

had cattle and sheep in the island of Thrinacia (see ODYSSEY (book 12) and SICILY). His cult was not widespread in Greece, although he is often appealed to as a witness because he sees and hears everything. This aspect perhaps contributed to his occasional identification with Apollo, the all-knowing god, after the fifth century BC. In Rhodes, however, he appears to have been the chief national god, who chose the island as his own before it rose above the surface of the sea. The famous *Colossus erected by the harbour entrance was a statue of him.

Hellani'cus, of Mitylene in Lesbos, a Greek *logographer of the fifth century BC. He was a prolific writer, of whose books some fragments survive. His most important works were a *History of Attica* (see ATTHIS), a list of the priestesses of Hera at Argos, which he used as a chronological basis for his history, and a list of victors at the Carnea.

Hellas, Hellenes, names used by the Greeks in classical times to denote Greece and the Greeks. Homer (who did not have a comprehensive name for the Greeks, calling them Achaeans, Argives, or Danaans) used these names to denote a small region of south Thessaly and its inhabitants; by 'Panhellenes' he seems to mean the northern, as opposed to the southern, Greeks. Hesiod, however, uses Hellas in the general sense of Greece, and from about the seventh century onwards the Greeks called themselves and their country by these names, deriving them from a mythical ancestor *Hellen. How this came about remains obscure, but perhaps the name spread with migrating tribes (see DORIAN INVASION). Herodotus (1. 57; see also 8. 144) uses the term Hellenes to describe the (immigrant) Greeks as distinct from the ancient indigenous non-Greek-speaking population (from whom the Athenians were sprung) whom he calls Pelasgians. In classical times the name Hellas embraced all lands inhabited by Hellenes, including not only the mainland of Greece, the Peloponnese, and the Greek islands, but also the colonies and the Greek cities on the coast of Asia Minor. Hellas was thus the land of the Hellenes, who shared a common language, religion, and social customs, in distinction to the land of the barbarians. From the fourth century AD onwards the Greeks of the eastern Roman empire called themselves *Rhōmaioi* ('Romans'); by that time the name 'Hellenes' denoted pagans. (See also GREECE.)

Hellē, in Greek myth, sister of Phrixus. While she and her brother were flying through the air on the back of the ram with the golden fleece to escape from their father *Athamas and step-mother Ino, Helle fell off into the sea and drowned. In consequence the sea was called the Hellespont, 'sea of Helle'.

Hellēn, in Greek myth, the eponymous ancestor of the Hellenes, usually described as the son of Pyrrha and *Deucalion. He was the father of Dorus, Aeolus, and Xuthus, whose sons were Ion and Achaeus; thus he engendered the ancestors of the main ethnic divisions of the Greeks in historical times, Dorians, Aeolians, Ionians, and Achaeans. (Some regions of Greece, e.g. Phocis, Elis, and Arcadia, lay outside these divisions.)

Hellē'nica. **1.** History of Greece from 411 to 362 BC by *Xenophon, who lived through the events he describes. The work was not conceived as a unity, but was written in instalments which were probably published together but without revision. Xenophon begins his narrative at the point in the Peloponnesian War where Thucydides' history stops, and books 1–2 cover the years 411 to 403, the rule and overthrow of the Thirty at Athens. After leaving a gap for the events of 402 to 400, he covers the years 399 to 379 in books 3–5: the Spartan war against the Persians (399–387); the attempt of various Greek states to check the growing power of Sparta (the Corinthian War, 394–387, ended by the Peace of Antalcidas); the rivalry of Sparta and Thebes. The second half of book 5 and books 6 and 7 take the reader from 379 to 362, and cover the triumph of Thebes at the battle of Leuctra (371) and her supremacy under the general Epaminondas, ending with his death at the battle of Mantinea in 362. See ATHENS 2 (iii).

2. History by *Theopompus, of which only fragments survive.

Helle'nica Oxyrhy'nchia, see OXYRHYNCHUS HISTORIAN.

Hellenism, the national character and culture of the (ancient) Greeks; see HELLAS.

Hellenistic, term used to denote the civilization, language, art, and literature of the Greek world from the late fourth to the late second centuries BC. (For the Greek world see GREECE; for the term 'classical' referring to the fifth and fourth centuries BC in Greece, see CLASSIC.) See also HELLENISTIC AGE, below.

Hellenistic age

1. The Hellenistic age was that period of Greek culture which may be said to start from the death of Alexander the Great of Macedon in 323 BC and which ended with Rome's absorption of Greece and the Greek East in the latter part of the first century BC, notable stages in this process being Rome's victory over the Achaean Confederacy in 146 BC and the creation of the province of Asia out of the kingdom of Pergamum in 133 BC. Before Alexander, Greek culture had little influence outside *Hellas; after his conquest of the Persian empire, important centres of Greek civilization and economy were to be found in Egypt and Asia, and the dominant culture of the East was Greek. The new city of Alexandria in Egypt was its focus,

whence the period is sometimes known as the Alexandrian age, but the cities of Pergamum (north-west Asia Minor), Antioch (in Syria on the river Orontes), and Athens were cultural rivals.

2. *Historical background.* After Alexander's death there was no one successor to hold together his vast empire, and his conquests were divided among the leading Macedonian generals (for the struggles among Alexander's successors, known as the *diadochoi*, see MACEDONIA 2). By 275 BC, following a series of internal wars, three dynastic kingdoms had emerged, stemming from the generals Ptolemy, Seleucus, and Antigonus. That of the *Ptolemies contained Egypt, south Syria, and some coastal strips of Asia Minor with the adjacent Greek islands; that of the *Seleucids had its capital at Antioch in north Syria but extended across Asia from the coast of Asia Minor as far as the frontier of India, including what had been the Persian empire; the *Antigonids ruled Macedonia and controlled the city-states of mainland Greece without attempting outright conquest. Later in the third century BC a fourth dynasty arose, the *Attalids, who with the help of Rome acquired a large part of Seleucid territory; their capital Pergamum became one of the greatest and most beautiful of all Greek cities. At the end of the third century began the expansion of Rome into the Greek world, and Roman conquest was completed within the next two centuries.

The Hellenization of the Seleucid and Ptolemaic domains came about by colonization on a grand scale: Greek and Macedonian settlers founded a large number of cities, even east of the Tigris where hitherto scarcely a city had existed. Alexander had often planted colonies of mercenary soldiers to hold down strategic points; he may also have intended to relieve the over-population of Greece by founding cities for the landless adventurers in his army, and he, like his successors, was probably interested in the expansion of trade with the East. But he also had higher aspirations: his aim had been to spread Greek culture throughout the world and to obliterate the distinction between Greek and barbarian: both were to live together on equal terms in the new colonies. The notion of the brotherhood of humankind was also spread by the Stoic philosophy which flourished during this period (see 5 below). Alexander died before it became clear how his aim was to be achieved, and his successors seem not to have pursued the ideal: Greeks and Macedonians still comprised the citizen body and the governing minority wherever they settled. They brought to these new cities the largely democratic political systems of the Greek city-states, admitting resident aliens to share their city but not their government, to which outsiders gained admittance only gradually and in small numbers. The land was worked by native peasant labour.

Despite the appearance of democracy the fact remained that the cities were contained within kingdoms that were absolute monarchies, their independence ultimately dependent on the will of the king. Cities often called on the help of the king in an attempt to avoid war, or indeed a king might interfere to help prevent one. The avoidance of unnecessary war, and the mitigation of the sufferings of war, now became a priority of city policy. It became common to settle disputes by *arbitration. War itself tended to become more humane (for example, in the treatment of the conquered) and was subjected to restrictions; certain cities and places claimed immunity from war or reprisals (*asylia*). The old isolation of Greek cities was broken down and mutual grants of citizenship and other rights became frequent. Distant territories were united by the common culture of the ruling class and its 'common tongue', the *koinē*, a simpler form of Attic Greek (see DIALECTS) which was spoken all over the Greek world by Egyptians, Jews, Romans, and the rest alike. The practice grew of entrusting the trial or arbitration of cases to commissions of one or more judges from other cities, thus securing greater impartiality than was possible under the old system of the jury courts. As the bond of the city on the individual weakened, there were formed a large number of professional associations, often centred on a cult. There was a growing interest in *mystery religions involving initiation ceremonies and promises of individual salvation (e.g. those of the *Cabeiri on Samothrace). The cult of *Asclepius at Epidaurus reached a peak during this time (see 5 below).

The third and second centuries were in most parts of the Greek world (though not in Athens and Sparta) a period of material prosperity for the upper classes. There were great extremes of poverty and wealth, and in the cities of Greece itself this led to the threat of social revolution. The number of actual revolutions was not large, which perhaps indicates that the city authorities were fairly successful in the use of palliatives such as cheap or free corn; private individuals too came forward with gifts and assistance to their cities. But during the third century BC there were temporarily successful revolutionary movements at Sparta led by the kings Agis IV and Cleomenes III (see SPARTA 5).

3. *Alexandria*. The most important propagators of Hellenistic culture were the first three of the Ptolemies, Macedonian kings of Egypt, whose reigns extended from 323 to 221, centred on their capital *Alexandria. The wealth and scale of the city, and the requirements of the huge bureaucracy that administered it, attracted large numbers of Greeks from all parts of the Greek world. Most of the intellectual and artistic stimulus of this period derived from the patronage of the Ptolemies. Literary patronage was no new phenomenon in the Greek world:

democratic Athens had offered no scope for it, but before that the *tyrants had encouraged and supported many poets—as did other monarchies such as that of *Macedonia (see 1). The difference in the case of the Ptolemies lay in the scale and disinterestedness of the support: they did not in general expect repayment by eulogy. The foundations they established, such as the *Museum ('the Muses' sanctuary') and the Library, attracted scholars, scientists, and writers from all parts. Writers in particular found stimulus in Alexandria. For them the conditions differed from any which had prevailed before: they were no longer addressing a homogeneous citizen body; in so cosmopolitan a city there was no single unifying tradition apart from the Greek language. They were therefore free to follow their inclinations; their works are markedly individualistic, and were often intended for a small circle of like-minded friends. After the rise of Pergamum, scholars were sometimes tempted to migrate there; occasionally others left Alexandria to return to their native countries, in many cases maintaining contacts that were to be a valuable bridge between East and West. When Archimedes returned to his native Syracuse his correspondence with Alexandrian mathematicians was fruitful for the further development of mathematics.

4. *Literature*. What remains of Hellenistic literature is only a small and unrepresentative fraction of the vast amount produced by the age. Out of hundreds of histories only five books of Polybius survive entire; important histories such as those of Timaeus, Hieronymus of Cardia, and Posidonius survive only in fragments. Such literature as survives is largely in verse. Even so, almost nothing remains of the scores of tragic poets, not even of the so-called *Pleiad whose title was borrowed in emulation of antiquity by the more celebrated French poets of the sixteenth century. Comedy retained its vigour at Athens in the early years of the Hellenistic age, in the so-called New Comedy of Menander and Philemon (see COMEDY, GREEK 6); although it cannot be said to have survived in manuscript to the present day, our knowledge of it has been considerably enhanced by substantial papyrus discoveries made in the twentieth century (see PAPYROLOGY). Among other poetry which has perished are the works of poets who considerably influenced later Latin literature, like Philetas of Cos and Euphorion; but they seem to have resembled, in small scale and exquisite refinement, the surviving works of their contemporaries Callimachus and Theocritus. By contrast Apollonius of Rhodes wrote an epic about the voyage of the Argonauts (which survives), and there is a tradition that Callimachus quarrelled violently with him over his use of this genre, outdated in its large scale. Didactic poetry was popular on a variety of topics such as geography, astronomy, and

fishing; the *Phaenomena* of Aratus is the chief example of the class. A novel Greek literary form, the mime, came to light when eight of these miniature dramas by Herodas turned up on a papyrus discovered at the end of the nineteenth century.

In the second and first centuries BC the rise of Rome, accompanied by constant wars and widespread destruction in the Greek world, brought about the decline of science and literature. But early in the first century BC the poet Meleager published an anthology of epigrams from Archilochus (seventh century BC) to his own day, called 'the Garland' (*Stephanos*), the first large critical anthology of poems of which we have knowledge; each of the fifty or so poets represented was likened to a flower. By now the oratory of the city-state, which largely depended on political stimulus, had died (with the exception of a few political speeches), but rhetoric, outliving it, had become the chief tool of education. It flourished in Greek Asia, where particularly exaggerated importance was attached to form and to a mannered and florid style ('Asianism'; see ORATORY 1) against which later Greeks (and some Romans; see BRUTUS) were to react.

5. *Philosophy and religion*. One of the most important contributions of Hellenistic civilization was in the sphere of philosophy. The old Greek ethical philosophies, culminating in Aristotle, had been concerned with the ethical ideals of people who were members of a city-state. With the decline of the city-state and the loosening of the bond which united its citizens, philosophies arose that gave support to people as individuals and aimed to bring them peace of mind. The Hellenistic age saw the rise of two new systems, that of Epicurus and that of Zeno and the Stoics; the doctrine of the latter exerted an immense influence not only on the Greek world but later on Rome and ultimately on Christianity. The other schools occupied from now onwards a secondary position. After Aristotle's death the Peripatetics under Theophrastus and his successor Strato continued his interest in problems of natural science, but their importance thereafter came to an end. Plato's Academy was likewise eclipsed, until under Arcesilaus and Carneades it resumed some prominence by its adoption of Scepticism. City cults no longer had their former significance, and the old religion with its Olympian gods had decayed; there was a readiness to accept the deities of Asia and Egypt, and a tendency to see in them various forms of a single god; more significantly, there was a marked decline in rationalism and a rise in mystical cults. See RELIGION, GREEK 3 and 4.

6. *Science and scholarship*. The Hellenistic age saw a striking advance in scholarship and scientific knowledge. The Museum was a research institute devoted to the systematic study of language and literature. The great names in this area were Zenodotus, Aristophanes of Byzantium, and Aristarchus of Samothrace. Hellenistic achievements in the fields of *mathematics, *astronomy, biology, and *medicine are known to us mainly through the works of later writers. The great names in mathematics and astronomy are Aristarchus of Samos, Archimedes, Hipparchus, Euclid, and the polymaths Eratosthenes and Posidonius. Much of the knowledge of astronomy acquired by the Babylonians now became available to the Greeks. Among many important discoveries were the precession of the equinoxes and the length of the solar year (Hipparchus), and the circumference of the earth (Eratosthenes). The geometrical knowledge presupposed by the latter discovery was largely the legacy of Euclid, who lived in the reign of Ptolemy I (323–283). Aristarchus advanced the hypothesis that the earth and the planets revolved round the sun, though the suggestion was not taken up by his successors. Archimedes was distinguished for his work on astronomy too, but in particular for his contributions to optics, statics, hydrostatics, and the design of machines. In biology and medicine the two great names were Herophilus and Erasistratus, who between them greatly extended Greek knowledge of the brain, the eye, the liver, the reproductive organs, the digestive tract, and the vascular system.

7. *Art*. Hellenistic art showed a change of character from that of the fifth and fourth centuries BC, especially a loss of restraint and repose and a striving for theatrical effect. But masterpieces were produced including the Aphrodite of Melos (Venus de Milo) of the second century BC, based on the statue by Praxiteles; the Winged Victory of Samothrace, of the third century BC; and the Dying Gaul (a monument of the late third century BC from Pergamum). The famous paintings of Apelles (of Colophon, late fourth century BC) are now known only by descriptions. The coins of the period represent some of the finest Greek portraiture. See also ART.

He'llespont, the Dardanelles; the strait which connects the Aegean Sea in the north-east to the Propontis (Sea of Marmora), and divides Europe from Asia. For the name see HELLE. In 1810 the English poet Lord Byron swam the Hellespont from Abydus to Sestus, in emulation of the mythical lover *Leander, at roughly the place where the Persian king Xerxes had built his bridge of ships (see PERSIAN WARS).

helots (*heilōtĕs*), word of uncertain derivation applied to the serfs at Sparta, the descendants of the original inhabitants whom the incoming Dorians had conquered (see DORIAN INVASION). The helot system was extended to *Messenia after the Spartan conquest in the seventh century BC. Helots belonged to the state which alone had the right to manumit them (see MANUMISSION), but they were assigned to particular citizens to do the work required on the land and in the house (or act as servant to the master when he was on campaign); they were obliged to provide their masters with a fixed amount of produce, keeping the surplus for themselves. They lived in families and were self-perpetuating. They had no political rights and were kept in subjection both by individuals and by the state. When the *ephors took office they always declared war upon the helots (so that the latter might be killed as an enemy without bringing *pollution upon the murderer; see KRYPTEIA). Manumission was rare, though occasionally shortage of manpower compelled the Spartans to enrol helots into the army; after manumission they were known as *neodāmōdes*.

Helve'tii, Celtic tribe which tried to settle in Gaul in the first century BC by moving from its territory roughly north-east of Lake Geneva through the Roman province of Narbonese Gaul to settle in Gaul proper. They were halted by the Romans and the remnants driven back to their old territory. See COMMENTARIES I (book I).

Helvi'dius Priscus (first century AD), son-in-law of Paetus *Thrasea, whose political views he shared, a member of the Stoic and republican opposition to the emperor Nero. He was exiled in AD 66, but returned to Rome two years later. He became violently opposed to the emperor Vespasian and after being again exiled was put to death (perhaps in 75). Helvidius' son (of the same name) by his first marriage was a friend of Tacitus and Pliny the Younger.

hendecasy'llable, see METRE, GREEK 5.

Hēphae'stion. 1. Macedonian, son of Amyntor, military commander and closest friend of Alexander the Great. He died suddenly in 324 BC.
2. Of Alexandria, second century AD, a Greek metrist. He was the author of a treatise on Greek metres in forty-eight books, of which only an epitome survives; he analysed metres into feet and cola (see METRE, GREEK I and 8 (i)). Much of his value lies incidentally in his quotations from many otherwise lost Greek poems.

Hēphae'stus, Greek god of fire and of crafts, particularly those in which fire is employed. His origin, like his name, may be non-Greek, and perhaps Asian. In Greek myth he was the child of Zeus and Hera, or of Hera alone, and because he was lame from birth Hera threw him out of Olympus. He fell on Lemnos, an important centre of his cult. According to another version, he intervened on his mother's side in a quarrel between Zeus and Hera, whereupon Zeus seized him by the foot and hurled him down to earth:

from Morn
To Noon he fell, from Noon to dewy Eve,
A Summers day; and with the setting Sun
Dropd from the Zenith like a falling Starr,
On Lemnos th' Aegaean Ile.

Milton, *Paradise Lost* I. 742 ff.

Hephaestus revenged himself on Hera by ensnaring her in an ingeniously constructed throne where she had to remain until Dionysus made him drunk and brought him back to Olympus to release her. This episode became a favourite subject for vase-painters. With a net of his own devising he also trapped his unfaithful wife Aphroditē with the god Arēs. His many famous works of craftsmanship include the armour of Achilles and the necklace of *Harmonia. Hesiod has him create the first woman, Pandora. In Athens, where he was the father of the first king *Erichthonius and so in a sense the ancestor of the Athenians, he had a special cult and a temple above the Ceramicus (see ATHENS I), where the shops of the smiths and braziers (as well as the potters) were to be found.

Hēra, with whom *Juno was identified by the Romans, in Greek myth, the daughter of *Cronus and Rhea, and the sister and wife of Zeus, from which position she derived her authority as queen of the gods. Her children by Zeus were *Hephaestus, *Arēs, *Hēbē, and *Eileithyia. She is essentially the goddess of marriage and of married women; but she is never invoked as a mother and never represented as a mother with a child. Her depiction in myth is often as the jealous wife outraged by her husband's infidelities and pursuing with vindictive hatred his children by other mothers, e.g. Dionysus and Heracles, as well as the other women he loved, e.g. Io. For her part in the Judgement of Paris see PARIS, JUDGEMENT OF. Her principal temples were at a sanctuary between Argos and Mycenae, and at Samos, where she was said to have been born, and where her sixth-century temple remained one of the largest in Greece. At the Heraeum 3 km. (2 miles) from Mycenae was a statue of Hera enthroned, made of gold and ivory by Polycleitus, very famous for its grandeur and beauty, now familiar only from its representation on Argive coins. But she was worshipped all over Greece, and the earliest and most important Greek temples are dedicated to her. In Boeotia a curious festival known as the Daidala was said to be celebrated in her honour every fifty-nine years. The *daidala*, 'intricately worked', were wooden images, one of which was dressed as a bride and carried in procession to the top of Mount Cithaeron, where a sacrifice was performed and a great bonfire made of the several *daidala*. The aetiological myth which explained the ritual stated that Hera and Zeus quarrelled, and afterwards Zeus had a wooden doll dressed as a bride and announced that he was about to make a new marriage. Thereupon Hera rushed out of hiding on Mount Cithaeron to attack her rival, but on discovering the trick was happily reconciled with her husband. Nevertheless, the 'bride' had still to be burnt.

Heraclei'dae, the children or the descendants of *Heracles, who was father by Deianeira of several sons, of whom Hyllus was the eldest, and of one daughter Macaria. For their story see HERACLES, CHILDREN OF. The phrase 'Return of the Heracleidae' was often used by the Greeks to refer to the *Dorian Invasion; the Dorians claimed connection with Heracles through their kings who were descended from him, and his son Hyllus became a Dorian by adoption: see AEGIMIUS. Hyllus consulted the Delphic Oracle to ask how he and his brothers should claim their father's kingdom of Tiryns in Argos (or, according to the Dorians, the whole Peloponnese; in this way they legitimized the Dorian Invasion). He was told to await 'the third fruit'. Misunderstanding this to mean the third harvest he duly made his attack on Tiryns three years later but failed and was killed in single combat by Echemus the Tegean. It was subsequently learnt that 'third fruit' meant 'third generation', and when this was reached Tēmenus and the other Heracleidae conquered the Peloponnese. The territory was divided into three portions: Cresphontēs (see MEROPE) took Messenia, Temenus took Argos, and the sons of Aristodemus, Eurysthenēs and Proclēs, received Lacedaemon, thus founding the dual kingship of Sparta; the line of the elder twin Eurysthenes had seniority and greater honour. The Spartan kings traced their ancestry back in the male line to *Perseus (whose father was Zeus). Perseus' mother, however, was *Danaē, descendant of the Egyptian Danaus. Herodotus (6. 52) speaks as if the Egyptian element was well known.

Heraclei'tus. I. (*c*.540–*c*.480 BC), Greek philosopher who was born and lived his life at Ephesus. He came from a royal family but surrendered his hereditary privileges to his brother. He was notorious for misanthropy, and for arrogance towards the reputations of those who were generally admired for wisdom: Homer, Hesiod, Archilochus, Hecataeus, Xenophanes, Pythagoras. Although he is said to have written a book entitled 'On Nature', many of the eighty or so fragments that survive in quotations rather suggest a collection of aphorisms, striking and paradoxical, but, lacking a context, difficult to interpret. The Greeks themselves complained of the obscurity of his writings. He believed that it is impossible to comprehend fully the reality of things and that appearances are unreliable, but nevertheless that some sort of knowledge is attainable. Wisdom lies in understanding that the world has an underlying coherence and is a unity; this unity depends upon a balance between opposites; change in one direction leads to change in the other. Therefore 'all things are in a state of flux'

(*panta rhei*). The essential stuff of the universe is pure fire, of which some is always being kindled and some being extinguished to form sea and earth; the soul too is composed of fire, and after death the souls of the virtuous join the cosmic fire. In Roman times Heracleitus became known as 'the weeping philosopher' (in contrast with 'the laughing philosopher' *Democritus), weeping at the spectacle of human life.

2. Of Halicarnassus, a poet and friend of the Hellenistic poet *Callimachus, who wrote a famous epigram on his death.

He'raclēs (Hēraklēs, Lat. Herculēs), son of Zeus and Alcmena, and most famous of the Greek heroes; his exploits were known and his cult was observed throughout the Greek world. He was descended from *Perseus and through Perseus' mother *Danaē from *Danaus. Famous for his strength, courage, endurance, good nature, and compassion, he was also known for his appetites, gluttony and lust. Being considered the universal helper, he was invoked on every occasion, and commonly called *Alexikakos*, 'averter of evil'. He later became an ideal of human behaviour: as the noble ruler who acts for the good of mankind and is finally elevated to the gods (Alexander the Great stamped the image of Heracles on his coins), and the ordinary mortal who, at the end of a life of toil, may hope to join after death the company of the gods. The Stoics and Cynics saw him as an exemplar of fortitude, to the neglect of his other qualities. At all times he caught the popular fancy, and myths, some of them transferred from less-known heroes, accumulated about him, including those of the Labours (see HERACLES, LABOURS OF, below). For the story of his birth at Thebes see AMPHITRYON.

In his cradle Heracles strangled two snakes which Hera had sent to kill him; for she, always roused to jealousy by Zeus' union with other women, human or divine, pursued him with implacable anger throughout his life. (It is inexplicable why he should have a name that seems to mean 'glory of Hera'.) He was instructed in the various arts by all the greatest experts: by Eurytus, grandson of Apollo, in the use of the bow; by *Autolycus in wrestling; by Polydeuces (see DIOSCURI) in the use of arms; by *Linus in music. When the last tried to correct him, Heracles killed him with his own lute. Amphitryon then sent Heracles to tend his flocks on Mount Cithaeron, and there, when eighteen, he killed a huge lion. Cithaeron was also the setting of 'The Choice of Heracles': as he was pondering which course of life to follow, two women appeared before him, Pleasure and Virtue, one offering a life of enjoyment, the other a life of toil and glory; he chose the latter. On his return to Thebes, he relieved the city of a tribute it had been forced to pay to Orchomenus, and *Creon, king of Thebes, in gratitude gave him his daughter Megara to marry. Creon's younger daughter married Iphicles (Heracles' twin brother) who already had a son Iolāus. The latter became Heracles' faithful companion and charioteer. After some years Hera sent a fit of madness upon Heracles, so that he killed Megara and his children under the delusion that they were his enemies. After this calamity he went into exile and sought advice from the Delphic Oracle on how he might be purified. He was told to go to Tiryns and serve Eurystheus, king of that city, for twelve years, and win immortality by performing the labours that Eurystheus imposed. There are many different versions of the events of Heracles' life: Euripides' version of Heracles' madness, for example, makes it come upon him after the performance of the Labours; and various reasons are given why Heracles served Eurystheus. Eurystheus is sometimes represented as a coward who would take refuge in a bronze tub when Heracles returned with some monster or other. Subsequently Heracles married Dēianeira, daughter of Oeneus of Calydon, winning her by defeating the river-god Achelōus in wrestling. When he and Deianeira departed, they came to the flooded river Evēnus (in Aetolia). A centaur, Nessus, carried Deianeira across and tried to rape her, whereupon Heracles shot him with a poisoned arrow. As he lay dying the centaur advised Deianeira, apparently with friendly intention, to keep some of his blood, which, smeared on a garment, would win back the love of Heracles if he was ever unfaithful to her; this Deianeira did.

The adventures ascribed to Heracles are too numerous to relate more than a few. He accompanied the *Argonauts (see also HYLAS) on the early part of their voyage. He rescued Alcestis, wife of *Admetus, from Death. He fell in love with Iolē, daughter of Eurytus, king of Oechalia, but her father and brothers would not give her to him. One of these brothers, Iphitus, who had come to Tiryns in search of some lost cattle of his father's, was thrown by Heracles, in a fit of madness, from the walls of the city. For this murder the Delphic Oracle sent him into slavery for a year, and he was sold to Omphalē, queen of Lydia. There he was set to do a woman's work, in woman's dress, while Omphale took over his lion's skin and club. When his period of servitude was over he led an expedition against *Laomedon, king of Troy. Poseidon at an earlier time had sent a sea-serpent against Troy, and Laomedon had promised Heracles his famous horses if he would kill it, but when the feat was done had refused the reward. Heracles now gathered an army, which included Telamon (father of Ajax) and Peleus (father of Achilles), attacked the city, and captured it. Heracles gave Laomedon's daughter Hēsionē to Telamon, by whom she became the mother of Teucer.

Finally Heracles attacked Oechalia and carried off Iole. Deianeira, to win him back, followed the advice of Nessus and sent Heracles a robe smeared with the centaur's blood. But this blood had been poisoned by the blood of the Hydra, in which Heracles dipped his arrows (see HERACLES, LABOURS OF 2); the robe clung to Heracles' flesh and caused terrible suffering. To escape from it he had himself carried to the summit of Mount Oeta and placed on a pyre. He gave Iole to his son Hyllus (see HERACLEIDAE) and persuaded Poias, father of *Philoctētēs, by the gift of his bow and arrows, to light the pyre. He was then carried up to Olympus, reconciled to Hera, and married to her daughter Hēbē.

Among the numerous opponents of Heracles at one time or another were Cycnus, a son of Arēs, who robbed Apollo of the hecatombs intended to be sacrificed to him at Delphi (the subject of the poem The *Shield of Heracles attributed to Hesiod); Busiris, king of Egypt, who in order to avert a drought sacrificed strangers who came to his country and attempted to sacrifice Heracles too while the latter was on his way to the Hesperides (see HERACLES, LABOURS OF 11); and Eryx, the legendary king of the mountain of that name in Sicily, whom Heracles wrestled with and killed while searching for one of Geryon's cattle which had wandered into his territory. See also PROMETHEUS, ANTAEUS, CHIRON, and CERCOPES.

The legends of Heracles connected him with both Thebes and Tiryns. For the claim of his descendants to the latter (extended to the whole Peloponnese) see HERACLEIDAE.

Heracles, Children of (*Hērakleidai*), Greek tragedy by *Euripides, perhaps produced in the early part of the Peloponnesian War (i.e. *c*.430 BC), possibly intended to remind the audience of the gratitude due to Athens for saving the children of Heracles (the founders of the Dorian race) from the persecution of *Eurystheus, king of Argos.

The children of Heracles, who is now dead, with his nephew and former comrade-in-arms Iolāus, now an old man, have taken refuge from the unremitting persecution of Eurystheus at the altar of Zeus at Athens. The herald of Eurystheus demands their surrender, and, on the refusal of Dēmophōn, king of Athens and son of Theseus, declares war. The soothsayers announce that the sacrifice of a nobly-born maiden is necessary to secure the success of the Athenian army, and Macaria, daughter of Heracles, voluntarily offers herself as the victim and is sacrificed. As the army of Eurystheus approaches, Hyllus, eldest son of Heracles, comes to the aid of Athens, and Iolaus, miraculously made young again, joins in the fight and captures Eurystheus. The captive is brought before Alcmēna, mother of Heracles, is reviled by her, and ordered off to his death.

Heracles, Labours of. The number of Labours seems to have been canonized as twelve by the scholars working at Alexandria in the third century BC, but Euripides had already spoken of twelve, and twelve were depicted on the metopes of the temple of Zeus at Olympia (c.460 BC). They were imposed on Heracles by *Eurystheus and according to the most commonly accepted list were as follows.

The Peloponnesian Labours

1. The Nemean Lion, an invulnerable monster, the offspring of *Echidna and *Typhon or Orthrus, sent to Nemea in Argos by Hera, to destroy Heracles. Heracles choked the monster in his arms, and clothed himself with its skin, using the beast's own claws, by which alone the skin was penetrable, to separate it from the body.

2. The Hydra, the offspring of Echidna and Typhon; it was a poisonous water-snake which lived in the marshes of Lerna near Argos. It had numerous heads; when one was cut off another grew in its place. Moreover Hera sent a huge crab to help it, hence the proverb 'Not even Heracles can fight two', spoken by the hero as he summoned his comrade-in-arms Iolaus. The latter, as Heracles cut off the heads, seared the stumps with burning brands. Heracles then dipped his arrows in the Hydra's blood, which made their wounds incurable (fatally for himself, as it proved; see HERACLES). There were various elaborations of the legend, as that the Hydra had one immortal head, which Heracles buried under a rock. The crab, which Heracles killed by crushing it under foot, became the constellation Cancer.

3. The Erymanthian Boar. Heracles' labour in this case was to catch alive the boar that lived on Mount Erymanthus in Arcadia. He drove it into a snowfield, tired it out, and caught it in a net. It was while searching for the boar that he was entertained by Pholus the centaur, to whom he gave wine. The other centaurs, lured to the cave by the smell of wine, got drunk and attacked Heracles; in defending himself he killed many of them with his poisoned arrows.

4. The Cerynitian Hind. In the usual version Heracles captures the hind alive after a year-long chase which takes him to the land of the Hyperboreans. Though female and therefore by nature hornless, this creature was said to have gilded horns and to be sacred to Artemis. According to some it lived in the woods of Oenoë in the Argolid. Its connection with the Achaean town Ceryneia or river Cerynitēs is obscure.

5. The Stymphalian Birds, which infested the woods round lake Stymphalus in Arcadia. Various reasons are given about the need for their destruction, e.g. they used their bronze-tipped feathers as arrows and killed and ate men and beasts. Heracles scared them by means of a bronze rattle (made by Hephaestus), then shot some with his arrows and drove the rest away.

6. The Augean Stables. Augeas, king of Elis, had enormous herds of cattle, like his father Helios, and Heracles was required to clean in one day their stables which had never been cleaned before. This he did by diverting the river Alphēus so that it flowed through the yard.

Labours outside the Peloponnese

7. The Cretan Bull, either the bull with which Pāsiphaē (see MINOS) fell in love, or the one which bore *Europa to Crete. Heracles caught it alive, brought it back to show Eurystheus, and let it go. It wandered throughout Greece and finally settled down near Marathon (see THESEUS).

8. The Horses of Diomēdēs. Diomedes was the son of Arēs and a nymph Cyrēnē, and king of the Bistones in Thrace. His horses were fed on human flesh. Heracles killed Diomedes and fed his body to the horses, whereupon they became tame and Heracles brought them to Argos.

9. The Girdle of the Amazon. The girdle given to Hippolytē, queen of the Amazons, by her father Arēs, was desired by the daughter of Eurystheus, and Heracles was sent to procure it. Hippolyte would have handed it over, but Hera stirred up war; in the ensuing battle Heracles killed Hippolyte and removed the girdle from her dead body. In another version he captured Hippolyte's second-in-command Melanippē who handed over the girdle as the price of freedom.

10. The Cattle of Geryon. In order to obtain the cattle Heracles had to travel to the extreme west where they were pastured on the mythical island of Erytheia ('red island') in *Ocean. Helios (Sun) so much admired Heracles' boldness in drawing his bow on him when annoyed by the heat that he gave him his golden cup in which to sail to Erytheia. At the end of the journey Heracles erected two pillars (Calpē and Abyla), the Pillars of Hercules, one on each side of the Straits of Gibraltar. Having reached the island Heracles killed the dog Orthrus, the herdsman Eurytion, and lastly Geryon himself, who was a three-headed ogre, and brought away his cattle either in the golden cup, or by a long overland route through Spain, France, Italy, and Sicily, reaching even the Black Sea, and thus having opportunity for many more adventures (see CACUS, and ARA MAXIMA) before he reached home safely.

11. The Golden Apples of the Hesperides ('daughters of Night'). These were the apples given by Gaia to Hera as a wedding present, and kept in a garden at the edge of the world. Heracles, who had to bring back the apples, had much difficulty in finding the way and forced *Nereus to give him directions to the garden. Having killed Ladon, the dragon that guarded it, he carried off the apples. According to another version he induced *Atlas to fetch the

apples, holding up the sky in his place while he did this. Some say that Atlas then refused to resume his burden, and had to be tricked into doing so.

12. The Descent to the Underworld for *Cerberus (Heracles' last labour and the only one explicitly mentioned in Homer). Heracles, after preliminary initiation into the Eleusinian mysteries, and with the help of the gods Hermes and Athena, descended to the Underworld near Cape Taenarum in Laconia. While there he freed Theseus, but was unable to free Pirithous. (See also HERACLES, MADNESS OF, below.) This may have been the occasion on which Heracles wounded Hades himself with an arrow, as Homer mentions. Heracles captured and bound the dog Cerberus, brought him to Eurystheus, and then returned him to the Underworld. This myth perhaps suggests that by conquering death Heracles earns his final immortality (see also ALCESTIS). For Heracles at Rome see HERCULES.

Heracles, Madness of (*Hēraklēs mainomenos*, Lat. *Hercules furens*), Greek tragedy by *Euripides, of uncertain date but perhaps produced *c*.417 BC. It was originally called simply *Heracles*.

Heracles, engaged on the last of his twelve labours, has gone down to the Underworld to bring up the dog *Cerberus. During his long absence Lycus, supported by a faction of Thebans, has killed Creon, king of Thebes and father of Heracles' wife Megara, and seized power. He threatens with death Megara and the three young sons of Heracles (fearing their vengeance in the future) and Heracles' reputed father the now aged Amphitryon. They have taken sanctuary at the altar of Zeus, but Lycus threatens to burn them to death there, and they prepare themselves. At this point Heracles returns, rescues his family, and kills Lycus. But his persistent enemy the goddess Hera sends Lyssa ('madness') who reluctantly seizes on Heracles and drives him to kill his own children (under the impression that they are the children of Eurystheus) and his wife. Upon recovering from his madness, Heracles is filled with despair. Thereupon Theseus (whom Heracles brought back from the Underworld in his final Labour) arrives upon the scene, helps to restore his courage, and takes him away to Athens to be purified. For the *Hercules furens* of Seneca see that entry.

He'raclids, see HERACLEIDAE and *HERACLES, CHILDREN OF.*

Heracli'tus, see HERACLEITUS.

Hērae'a, Greek festival held at Argos every four years in honour of Hera, and celebrated with a procession to the *Heraeum, the priestess riding in a chariot drawn by oxen (see CLEOBIS AND BITON); there was a hecatomb, and athletic contests in the stadium near the temple, for which the prize was a bronze shield.

Hērae'um, 'temple of *Hera', the most famous being that in Argos, 3 km. (2 miles) south-east of Mycenae. An early wooden temple there was destroyed by fire in 423 BC; the new temple, containing the famous gold and ivory statue by *Polycleitus, was built *c*.416 BC.

Herculā'neum, ancient Italian town built on a spur projecting from the lower slopes of the volcano Vesuvius and to the west of it, about 8 km. (5 miles) from Naples. In the first century AD it was a small and wealthy residential town. The eruption of Vesuvius on 24 August AD 79, which also destroyed *Pompeii, overwhelmed it with a mud-flow (rather than volcanic ash). As a result, although the buildings are more collapsed than at Pompeii, the furnishings, being completely sealed in, are better preserved. But the mud set hard so that the town is buried beneath solid rock on which is built the modern town of Resina. Excavation, or rather treasure-hunting, began in the mid-eighteenth century, but poisonous volcanic gas drove out the excavators in 1765. More systematic excavation has been carried out since 1987. In one of the luxurious villas nearby, excavated in the eighteenth century, and now known as Villa dei Papyri, a fine collection of sculpture was found (now in Naples museum) and a small library of carbonized papyrus rolls containing works on Epicurean philosophy, mainly by Philodemus (fl. 75–35 BC), the influential Epicurean teacher of philosophy, but also by Epicurus himself. See PISO CAESONINUS.

He'rculēs, the Roman adaptation of the Greek hero *Heracles. His was perhaps the earliest foreign cult to be brought to Italy by colonists of Magna Graecia. His altar, the *Ara Maxima, stood in the *Forum Boarium ('cattle market'); here he was worshipped as the god of victory and of commercial enterprise. Two patrician families, the Potitii and the Pinarii, had for many generations charge of his cult. The *gens* *Fabia traced its origin to him. The myth of Hercules and *Cacus, which Virgil makes *Evander narrate (*Aeneid* 8), is probably of Roman origin, perhaps invented to explain the presence of his altar in the Forum Boarium.

Hercules furens, Roman tragedy by *Seneca (2), based on Euripides' play *Heracles* (see *HERACLES, MADNESS OF*). There are differences of detail: Lycus, instead of threatening to kill Heracles' children, demands his wife in marriage; and Heracles' murder of her and the children forms part of the actual drama.

Hercules Oetae'us ('Hercules on Mount Oeta'), Roman tragedy by *Seneca (2), based on the *Trachiniae of Sophocles. The play is of great length (part of it is thought to be spurious) and shows variations from the original, presenting Dēianeira not as a gentle and attractive figure but as fiercely jealous, and adding a scene showing Heracles' death and deification on Mount Oeta in Thessaly.

Here'nnium, Rheto'rica ad, Latin treatise on oratory; see RHETORICA AD HERENNIUM.

Hermae ('herms'), at Athens especially (but also elsewhere in Greece), quadrangular stone pillars bearing an erect phallus and surmounted by a bust of the god *Hermēs (later other gods as well) depicted with old-style pointed beard, set up as boundary-marks at crossroads, by the roadside, near public buildings, and in front of houses; some acted as signposts. They replaced the heaps of stones which were the customary ancient boundary marks. Being phallic they were intended to be apotropaic, i.e. to avert evil influences. At Athens some were set up c.520 BC by Hipparchus, son of the tyrant Peisistratus, with moral maxims engraved on them. They were regarded with reverence; hence the indignation and alarm felt at Athens when in the course of a night shortly before the departure of the Sicilian Expedition in 415 BC the herms were mutilated (see ALCIBIADES and ANDOCIDES).

Hermaphrodī'tus, in Greek myth, son of Hermēs and Aphroditē, who was loved by Salmacis, the nymph of the fountain in which he bathed, near Halicarnassus. She closely embraced him and prayed to the gods to make them one body, which they did. Art of the fourth century BC portrayed Hermaphroditus accordingly, as a beautiful youth with developed breasts.

Hermēs, in Greek myth, son of Zeus and *Maia. He was born on Mount Cyllēnē in Arcadia. By noon on the day that he was born he had left his cradle and invented the lyre, killing a tortoise and making the instrument from its shell. The same day he drove off fifty cows belonging to Apollo, making them walk backwards so that they should not be traced, and then returned to his cradle. When Apollo, informed by an old man, arrived in a rage, he was mollified by the gift of the lyre and allowed Hermes to keep the cattle he had stolen and gave him in addition various divine powers. This story is told in the fourth *Homeric Hymn. The name Hermes, which appears in the *Linear B tablets, appears to be derived from *herma*, a pile of stones set up to mark a boundary (see HERMAE). He was the god of roads and boundaries, the messenger or herald of the gods, and conductor of the souls of the dead to the Underworld, *psychopompos*; he was also the god of sleep and dreams. Furtiveness and trickery were his attributes as well: he was the god of luck, particularly in the matter of making money, the patron of merchants and thieves; every lucky find was a *hermaion*, gift of Hermes. He was the patron of athletics, and his statue was commonly erected in gymnasia. In many parts of Greece he was the god of herdsmen and of the fertility of herds. Successful communication with enemies and strangers was due to Hermes, hence the Greek word for interpreter, *hermēneus*; and he gives his name to the art of interpretation, 'hermeneutics'. For this reason he was regarded as the patron of oratory with an interest in literature generally. He is represented with wings on his sandals, a winged cap or a broad-brimmed felt hat (the *petasos* characteristic of the *ephebos*), and the herald's staff (*kērykeion*, Lat. *cādūceus*) on which two serpents are twined in a broken figure-of-eight shape. Hermes was identified by the Romans with their god *Mercury. See also PAN and HERMAPHRODITUS.

Hermēs Trismegi'stus ('thrice-greatest'). This name was given by the *Neoplatonists and the devotees of mysticism and alchemy to the Egyptian god Thoth (who was identified with the Greek god Hermes), the father and protector of all knowledge, who was believed to be the author, under this name, of a collection of Greek and Latin religious and philosophical writings, dating probably from the first to the third centuries AD. The aim of this mystical teaching was the deification of humankind through knowledge of God.

Hermī'onē, in Greek myth, daughter of Menelaus and *Helen (of Troy), wife of *Neoptolemus and later of *Orestēs.

Hermo'genēs, of Tarsus, b. c. AD 160, Greek rhetorician, author of several treatises, the most important of which is *Peri ideōn* ('on types of style'). He finds that authors have many different qualities of style, and distinguishes between them with considerable subtlety. Demosthenes is the outstanding exemplar of all qualities. Compare DEMETRIUS (3) and LONGINUS ON THE SUBLIME.

herms, see HERMAE.

Hero, heroine of a love story known to us from Ovid but perhaps of Hellenistic origin. For her story see LEANDER.

hero-cult, etc.; see HEROES and CULT.

Herod (Hērōdēs). **1.** Herod the Great (c.73 BC–4 BC), the son of Antipater, the local governor of Idumaea, a country south of Judaea. Because of his friendship with Rome, Antipater was made a Roman citizen and procurator of Judaea. Herod was himself a Roman citizen from 47 BC. After Antipater's death by poison in 43 BC Herod obtained from the Roman triumvirs the title king of Judaea; in 37 BC a Roman force stormed Jerusalem for him and the foundation of his authority was secured. He ruled Judaea on the lines of a Hellenistic kingdom, built and adorned cities, and gave peace and prosperity. But he was tyrannical and unscrupulous, and though by his loyalty he retained Augustus' confidence for many years, his high-handed behaviour and his cruelty to his family—he put to death his wife, her two sons, and his own eldest son—lost him Rome's support. Not even his magnificent rebuilding of the Temple won him the affection of the Jews, who hated him for being a foreigner among other things. He is said to have ordered the slaughter of the male children in Bethlehem in order to procure the death of the infant Jesus.

2. The erroneously called 'Herod' of Acts 12, M. Julius Agrippa (10 BC–AD 44), grandson of Herod the Great, friend of the Roman emperors Caligula and Claudius, who was granted by these emperors territories in Palestine which eventually comprised all the land his grandfather had ruled over. He was a popular ruler; on his death Claudius annexed the whole kingdom. It was before his son, Agrippa II, that the apostle Paul was brought (Acts 25).

Hērō'das or **Herondas** (c.300–250 BC), native of Cos or Miletus, a Greek writer of literary *mimes, mimiambi, in the Ionic dialect and in scazons (see METRE, GREEK 2). Only a few fragments existed in quotation until the publication in 1891 of a papyrus found in Egypt to which other fragments were later added. There now exist mimes 1–7 complete, and 8 and 9 in a fragmentary state. These are short, dramatic vignettes, probably intended for private reading rather than for solo performance, and present with vividness and humour scenes typical of mime, drawn from city life: the bawd, the pimp, the schoolmaster, the women worshippers, the jealous mistress, the private conversation, the shoemaker, the dream, women entertaining.

Hērō'dēs A'tticus (L. Vibullius Hipparchus Tiberius Claudius Atticus Herodes, AD 101–77), Athenian *sophist and rhetorician, born at Marathon, consul at Rome (with Fronto) in 143. His fame as an orator, teacher, and public benefactor won him the friendship of powerful men: he enjoyed the support of the emperors Hadrian and Antoninus Pius, and was the instructor of the emperor Marcus Aurelius and his co-emperor Lucius Verus. He came of an ancient family which was reputed to trace its descent from the Greek hero *Aeacus. The basis of his fortune was said to have been his father's discovery of a treasure buried on his land, probably concealed there by his grandfather to escape the depredations of the emperor Domitian. With prodigious generosity he endowed public buildings on a grand scale: at Athens most notably the stadium (in Pentelic marble), the Odeum, and a temple to Fortune; he also built at Corinth a theatre, at Olympia an aqueduct, at Delphi a race-course, and at Thermopylae a hospital, as well as restoring many towns that had fallen into decay. Aulus *Gellius has left an account of pleasant days spent with him at his villa among the woods of Cephissia (in Attica), which was a literary centre. None of his writings has survived except for one speech doubtfully attributed to him and a Latin translation of another by Aulus Gellius.

Hērō'dian. 1. Aelius Hērōdiānus, son of *Apollonius Dyscolus the Greek grammarian, who lived at Rome under Marcus Aurelius (emperor AD 161–80) and wrote in Greek on a number of grammatical subjects. His principal work was a treatise on Greek accents in twenty-one books, of which only excerpts survive. Two other small works are extant.

2. Of Syria (fl. c. AD 230). He wrote in Greek a history of the Roman emperors in eight books, from the death of Marcus Aurelius in AD 180 to the accession of Gordian III in 238, being a contemporary observer. His authority is generally preferable to that of the *Historia Augusta.

Hero'dotus (c.490–c.425 BC), Greek historian, author of the 'Histories' (historiai, 'inquiries') of the Persian Wars, son of Lyxēs, of a distinguished family in *Halicarnassus in Caria, at that time a city of Ionian Greek culture. He was a kinsman (nephew or cousin) of the epic poet *Panyassis, who was put to death by Lygdamis, tyrant of Halicarnassus, in the political troubles of the 460s. Herodotus withdrew or was exiled to Samos and then travelled widely in Egypt and the Greek world. He visited Athens in the mid-440s, where he is said to have become acquainted with Pericles, before (reputedly) joining the Athenian colony at Thurii (founded 443) near Sybaris in south Italy. He mentions Greek events of 430 but none later, and is presumed to have died before 420.

Herodotus has been called by Cicero and others 'the father of history' because in his account of the Persian Wars he was writing on a scale and with a comprehensiveness that had never been attempted before, and with a grasp of the decisive importance these wars had for the future development of the Mediterranean world. He describes the scope of his work in the opening sentence: it is an investigation, historiē, undertaken so that the great achievements of Greeks and *barbarians (in this case, the people of Asia) may not be forgotten, and in particular, to show how they came to fight one another. He was writing a generation after the wars, and facts were hard to come by. His sources were for the most part not written down; he himself emphasized that his work was based on what he had seen and what he had heard and the conclusions he had drawn. On this basis, he was trying to make a true and systematic record. He sought out those who had the information he needed: aristocrats who preserved their family history (information particularly liable to distortion for political or other reasons), and priests and officials who had access to written records;

but in foreign countries where he did not know the language he had to rely on interpreters. His history was shaped in subtle ways by many influences. He may have learned from Homer to divide the world into Greeks and barbarians and to see his purpose as akin to that of epic, namely to preserve the memory of great deeds. He certainly understood the events of history to originate in the characters and actions of individual great men. In this respect he may have been influenced by folk tales which preserved, embroidered upon, and shaped the events in the lives of such men. These stories also had a moral slant. Herodotus saw an inexorable moral providence underpinning his whole history: the gods bring it about that overweening pride eventually ends in ruin; the gods intervene in human affairs; their oracles cannot be disregarded. But as well as divinely operated cause and effect Herodotus understood that on a different, non-moral level, scientific cause and effect operated. His search for rational explanations of things and his interest in natural causes reveal his own cast of mind, as well as the influence of earlier Ionian scientists and *logographers, 'those who write accounts of stories', especially *Hecataeus. Herodotus' digressions from the main theme of his history, from mere anecdotes to a whole book on Egypt, for example, may be in the manner of such writers, but the boundless scientific curiosity they display is entirely Herodotus' own. These digressions diversify Herodotus' work so that parts of it are, rather than history, studies in anthropology, ethnography, and archaeology.

The History comprises the struggle between Greece and Asia from the time of Croesus (mid-sixth century BC) to Xerxes' retreat from Greece (478 BC). It has been regarded as unfinished but it is not clear that Herodotus intended to cover events later than the capture of Sestus, which concludes the ninth and last book; the last episode, indicating Persian degeneracy at the end, has a final ring. The division of the work into nine books each named after a Muse is probably the scheme of Alexandrian editors; Herodotus himself divided his work into logoi, 'episodes'. So improbable did some of his stories seem to later Greeks that he had the reputation of being a liar: Plutarch accused him also of unfairness and uncharitableness (Plutarch came from Boeotia whose chief town, Thebes, was the bitter enemy of Athens). In modern times Herodotus' attempts to use oral tradition in describing other societies have been better understood and his reputation for veracity restored. His style is simple, clear, and graceful, and his narrative has great charm. He wrote in his native Ionic dialect, using also archaic and poetic forms; the manuscripts, however, include forms that it seems unlikely Herodotus could ever have written, the text having been compiled perhaps by later Greek editors ignorant of the correct usage. The following are the principal subjects of the several books:

Book 1. Blame for the conflict between Greeks and barbarians is attributed to Croesus, whose attack on Cyrus of Persia ruined his own kingdom of Lydia. A digression explains why neither Athens nor Sparta helped Croesus. The conquest of the *Medes by Cyrus is followed by his subjection of the Greeks of Asia Minor, and then an account of the Persian empire under Cyrus, and of Babylon; the book ends with the war of Cyrus against the Massagetae.

Book 2. This book is devoted to a description of Egypt, the pretext for which is furnished by the invasion of that country by Cambysēs, Cyrus' son and heir (the story of Rhampsinītus is in chapter 121).

Book 3. The conquest of Egypt by Cambyses, the story of the Persian usurper, the false Smerdis, and the accession and reforms of Darius (anecdotes of Polycratēs, tyrant of Samos, and his seal-ring, 40, and of Zōpyrus and the capture of Babylon, 153).

Book 4. The expeditions of Darius in Scythia and Libya (145), with an account of their peoples.

Book 5. The operations of the Persian general Megabazus with a detachment of troops against the Thracians, and an account of the latter; the Ionian Revolt (28) and the burning of the Persian city of Sardis by the Ionians (101).

Book 6. The suppression of the Ionian revolt; the march of the Persian general Mardonius to Macedonia and the wreck of the Persian fleet off Mount Athos (43); the second Persian expedition to Greece under Datis and Artaphernes (94); the Greek victory at Marathon (102); Pheidippidēs' run from Athens to Sparta (105); anecdote of Cleisthenes and Hippocleidēs (126). Events on the Persian side are alternated with events at Sparta and Athens.

Book 7. The death of Darius; preparations by Xerxes, his son and heir, and invasion of Greece; defeat of the Greeks at Thermopylae (201).

Book 8. Victories of the Greeks at Artemisium and Salamis (56); the withdrawal of Xerxes (97).

Book 9. The victory of the Greeks at Plataea and the retreat of the Persians; the victory of the Greeks at Mycalē (98); the capture of Sestus (previously held by the Persians; 114).

heroes (Gk. hērōĕs). In archaic and classical Greece the Greeks thought that in times past there was living in Greece a race of men and women who were bigger, stronger, braver, and more beautiful than the men and women of their own day. These were heroes and heroines, the offspring or descendants of unions between gods and mortals, but still essentially human. The age in which they lived, the Heroic age, was quite short, embracing no more than two or three generations, and not wholly remote; it was the period of the Theban wars (see SEVEN AGAINST THEBES) and the siege of Troy, the latter dated to the early twelfth century BC by the Greeks, who believed both events to be historical. The exploits of the heroes at Thebes and Troy was the stuff of epic poetry, often called in consequence 'heroic' poetry. The fact that Greek myths are dominated by stories about them rather than about gods makes them different from the myths of other cultures and gives them their human scale and interest. The close association of heroes and gods and the latters' interventions in the heroes' lives often give a moral significance to heroic myths and to the characters of the heroes. From the eighth century BC onwards, when the Homeric epics became widely popular (see HOMER), ancient burial sites came to be thought of as the graves of Homer's heroes, and, since they had been superhumanly powerful, sacrifices and rites were performed by the graves in the hope that in return for cult the heroes would actively defend their own locality, rising from the dead when the need arose. Only *Heracles, exceptional in this as in other respects, was both hero and god, his apotheosis following upon his death. Any community would be glad to have its own hero; aristocratic clans often claimed descent from one. The poet Hesiod, in his myth of the five ages of humankind (see WORKS AND DAYS and GOLDEN AGE), described the heroes as constituting the glorious race that existed before this present sadly degenerate age of iron. In practice, however, not all so-called heroes belonged to the heroic age or were the offspring of gods: ordinary men who were outstanding in some way were sometimes paid heroic honours after death as being the possessors of power that might be channelled to good use: the Spartan general Brasidas was so honoured after his death in battle in 422 BC.

Heroic age, see HEROES above.

Heroic poetry, see EPIC POETRY.

Hērō'idēs (or *Hērōidum epistulae*, 'letters of heroines'), Latin amatory poems in elegiacs by *Ovid, in the form of letters purporting to be addressed by heroines of legend to their lovers or husbands, though they read rather like dramatic monologues. In the first fourteen letters women address men (the authenticity of the fifteenth letter, from Sappho to Phaon, is doubted); letters 16–21 are in pairs, the woman answering the man's letter. It used to be thought that this last group was not by Ovid. The first group was published between the two editions of the *Amores*, i.e. towards the end of the first century BC; the second group perhaps in the earliest years of the first century AD, before Ovid's exile in AD 8. He claimed that they constituted a new literary form, invented by him.

The letters of the heroines are studies of love from the woman's point of view, based perhaps on observation but also on rhetorical training in character-drawing; the sentiments and moral standpoint are those of contemporary Rome. This technique Ovid applies to the characters of Greek epic and drama, and of the Hellenistic poets, as well as of those depicted by the Roman poets, Virgil's Dido and Catullus' Ariadne (poem 64). The heroines are represented in various situations: betrayed or deserted (Dēianeira, Phyllis, Medea, Ariadne, Oenonē, Dido), neglected (Brisēis), bound in a hateful marriage (Hermione), punished for their love (Hypermnestra, Canacē), the victim of unlawful passion (Phaedra), or anxious for their husbands' safety (Penelope, Laodamia). Compare CATALOGUE OF WOMEN.

Hērondas, see HERODAS.

Hēro'philē, most ancient of the legendary *Sibyls.

Hēro'philus (first half of the third century BC), from Chalcedon, one of the great founders (with *Erasistratus) of medicine at Alexandria. He made his mark primarily for his study of human anatomy based on human dissection; he is alleged to have practised vivisection on criminals. His writings (which survive only in quotation) included an account of the liver; he correctly opposed the orthodoxy of his day that the veins originated there. His studies of the genital organs, the eye, and the brain were famous; his names for some of the main sections and chambers still survive in their Latin form (the term 'duodenum' is his also, a translation of the Greek *dōdekadaktulos*, 'twelve fingers long'). He established that the brain and not the heart was the centre of the nervous system (as did Hippocrates, *On the Sacred Disease*, ch. 6), maintaining for the first time the distinction between motor and sensory nerves. The vascular system was not understood by the physicians of his day, and no connection was seen between heart beat and pulse beat. Herophilus probably accepted that the arteries contained blood (not air, as was generally thought), and certainly believed that pulse beat was caused by the normal contraction and dilation of the arteries, though he did not understand that the blood circulated through the arteries because of the pumping action of the heart. He invented a portable water-clock (*clepsydra) to measure pulse beat. He also made increased use of drugs, calling them 'the hands of the gods'. His pathology however showed no advance on that of his predecessors; having no knowledge of bacteria, he believed, as did almost everyone else, that disease was caused by an imbalance of humours. The information about him that survives attests a man of great intellectual ability, wit, and wisdom.

Hērōs ('hero'), Greek comedy by *Menander.

Hēro'stratus, the man who burned down the temple of *Ephesus in 356 BC 'to make his name immortal', according to *Valerius Maximus.

Hē'siod (Hēsiodos) (lived *c*.700 BC), one of the earliest known Greek poets, and with Homer representative of early Greek *epic poetry. He tells us himself something of his life: his father gave up his livelihood of sea-trading as being unprofitable and moved from Cymē in Aeolis (on the coast of Asia Minor) to Ascra in Boeotia, where Hesiod was born, to become a farmer. As Hesiod was tending the sheep on Mount Helicon he heard the Muses calling him to become a poet and sing of the gods (*Theogony* 22). He once took part in a poetic contest at Chalcis in Euboea and won a tripod. On his father's death the estate was divided between Hesiod and his brother Perses; the latter claimed more than his share and a dispute ensued in which Perses bribed the authorities to favour him. Hesiod is said to have died in Locris, but his tomb was shown at Orchomenus in Boeotia. The story of his meeting and contest with Homer is certainly untrue. Two genuine poems of his survive, the *Theogony* and the *Works and Days*. A third short poem, the *Shield of Heracles*, is not genuine. The *Catalogue of Women*, thought by the ancient Greeks to be by Hesiod, exists only in fragments. Among other works attributed to him, of which only small fragments survive, are the *Precepts of Chiron*, the *Melampodia* (stories of famous seers), and an *Astronomy*. In the *Works and Days* Hesiod sought his subject from outside the field of myth (see DIDACTIC POETRY), and much of the poem seems to derive from his own experience and to reveal his own character. He wrote in the same oral tradition as Homer, using the epic dialect (see DIALECTS), but perhaps at a later stage of its evolution.

Hēsi'onē, in Greek myth, daughter of *Laomedon, wife of *Telamon, and mother of *Teucer.

Hespe'ria, in Latin, 'the western land', from Greek *hespera*, 'west'. From the Greek point of view the term often denotes Italy; from the Roman, Spain.

Hespe'ridĕs, in Greek myth, the daughters of Night (Nyx) and Darkness (*Erebus) who lived in the extreme West on the edge of Ocean, guarding a tree that produced golden apples (see HERACLES, LABOURS OF 11), a present given by Gaia to Hera when the latter married Zeus. The tree was also watched by the dragon Ladon (whom Heracles killed). From the same tree came the apples thrown down before *Atalanta.

He'sperus (Lat. Vesper), the evening star.

He'stia ('hearth'), in Greek myth, the virgin daughter of *Cronus and Rhea, goddess of the hearth and symbol of the home and family. The goddess was never developed, hardly an-thropomorphized, and has virtually no mythology; Homer never mentions her. When a new baby was accepted into the family and received its name, someone ran with it round the hearth. A hearth with ever-burning fire was consecrated to her in the chief public building (*prytanēum*) of every capital city (and at Delphi and Olympia); fire from this was taken to every new colony of that city. Sacrifices began with libations to Hestia and she was mentioned first in prayers; the beginning of a meal was marked by small offerings being thrown on to the fire. The Romans worshipped her as *Vesta, and accorded her considerably more importance than the Greeks did Hestia. See GODS 1.

hestiā'sis, see LITURGY 4.

Hēsy'chius (probably fifth century AD), Alexandrian Greek lexicographer, whose lexicon is known from one badly preserved fifteenth-century manuscript, itself a considerable abridgement of the original work. Even so it is a valuable aid for the study of Greek dialects and inscriptions, and it often preserves correct readings which have been replaced in Greek literary texts by easier synonyms.

hetae'rae (*hetairai*, 'female companions'), in Greece, a euphemistic name for prostitutes and courtesans. They enjoyed certain legal safeguards but had to pay a tax, whether living privately or in brothels. They were virtually never of citizen status but were slaves, or aliens, or freed women. Many were musicians or dancers, hired to entertain at dinner parties. Some of them were highly accomplished and became known as the mistresses of distinguished men, as, for example, *Aspasia (mistress of Periclēs), Lais (who loved Diogenēs the Cynic), *Phrynē, and Leontion (who loved Epicurus). *Hetaerae* figured prominently as characters in New Comedy (see COMEDY, GREEK 6), where they inspired infatuation in young men, and are often credited with hearts of gold.

hexa'meter, see METRE, GREEK 1.

He'xapla, the six parallel versions of the Old Testament compiled by *Origen.

hiā'tus ('gap'), in Greek and Latin poetry, a break in a line when a vowel at the end of one word is not elided before a vowel at the beginning of the next, as it would be by normal scansion (see ELISION). If the earlier vowel is long it may retain its length or be shortened (for an explanation of 'long' and 'short' in metric see METRE, GREEK 1). Hiatus is common in Greek epic verse (see DIGAMMA), rare in Latin epic.

Hibe'rnia (Gk. Hiernē), the Latin name for Ireland. The Greeks knew of Ireland from *c*.500 BC, and Eratosthenes, writing *c*.235 BC, placed it correctly on his map; Strabo, writing at the end of the first century BC, had heard that its savage inhabitants were cannibals; *Agricola in the first century AD reconnoitred the coast, meditating conquest; Solinus in the third century is the first to observe that there are no snakes in Ireland. Ptolemy a century earlier shows fair knowledge of the whole coast and even mentions seven inland towns; some of his names are still current, e.g. Liboius (Liffey), and Eblana (Dublin).

Hī'eroclēs, probably of Alexandria, *Stoic philosopher of the early second century AD, author of *Elements of Ethics (Ēthikē stoicheiōsis)* of which a large part has survived.

Hī'eron I and **II** (unrelated), rulers of Syracuse. See SYRACUSE I and 3.

Hi'eron, one of the minor works of the Athenian *Xenophon (428–c.354 BC), a dialogue between Hieron I, tyrant of Syracuse (see SYRACUSE I), and *Simonides, in which the lot of the tyrant and that of the private citizen are compared; Hieron points out the disadvantages of the former, while Simonides shows how a tyrant, by ruling well, may make himself popular and so acquire happiness.

Hiero'nymus. **1.** Of Cardia (third century BC), the contemporary and trustworthy historian of the period from the death of Alexander the Great (323 BC) to the death of Pyrrhus, king of Epirus, in 272 BC, or perhaps as far as 263. He served as general and statesman under Eumenes of Cardia (secretary to Philip II of Macedon and his son Alexander), Antigonus I (one of Alexander's generals), his son Demetrius and his grandson Antigonus Gonatas, and thus had first-hand knowledge of the events he related. His history is lost but is the most important source behind Arrian and Diodorus (books 18–20), and was used by Plutarch for his Lives of Eumenes, Pyrrhus, and Demetrius.

2. See JEROME.

hills, see SEVEN HILLS OF ROME.

hīma'tion, see DRESS I.

Hī'mera, town on the north coast of Sicily, founded *c.*648 BC by colonists from Zanclē in the east of the island, itself a Euboean colony founded in the previous century (see COLONIZATION, GREEK 2). Its most famous citizen was the poet Stesichorus. It was the scene in 480 BC of a spectacular defeat of the Carthaginians by Gelon, tyrant of Syracuse, and Theron of Acragas.

Hīme'rius (AD *c.*310–*c.*390), Greek rhetorician from Bithynia, twenty-four of whose ceremonial speeches survive, incidentally valuable for their quotations from Greek lyric poetry otherwise lost. His pupils at Athens included the Christian Fathers St Gregory of Nazianzus and St Basil.

hippale'ctryon ('cock-horse'), monster mentioned by Aristophanes and occasionally portrayed on vases; it had the head and forelegs of a horse, and behind these the legs, tail, and body of a cock.

Hippa'rchicus, see CAVALRY COMMANDER.

Hippa'rchia, see CYNIC PHILOSOPHERS: CRATES.

Hippa'rchus. **1.** Younger son of Peisistratus, tyrant of Athens, who ruled Athens jointly with his brother Hippias after the death of their father in 527 BC. He was a patron of literature and art. He was murdered by *Harmodius and Aristogeiton in 514 BC. See PEISISTRATUS 3.

2. (*c.*190–after 126 BC), the greatest of ancient astronomers, a Greek born at Nicaea in Bithynia but living mostly in Rhodes. His only surviving work is his commentary on the *Phaenomena* of *Eudoxus and *Aratus; Hipparchus criticizes the accuracy of Aratus' source, Eudoxus. Most of our knowledge of his other work comes from the *Almagest*, the astronomical textbook of *Ptolemy (second century AD). His principal work was his catalogue of more than 800 fixed stars arranged in categories of magnitude and brightness, their positions fixed by latitude and longitude in relation to the ecliptic (the geocentric path of the sun). He is famous for his discovery of the precession of the equinoxes (i.e. the slight change in timing in each successive year), achieved by comparing his observation of the position of a particular star with the observation made 160 years earlier; his figure differs by only ten seconds from the modern estimate. He calculated more accurately the length of the natural year (from one equinox to the same equinox again), but his retention of the erroneous geocentric theory (as opposed to *Aristarchus' heliocentric theory) made his calculations on the relative size and distance of the sun and moon inaccurate. He is the first person known to have made systematic use of trigonometry, and was probably the inventor of stereographic projection. His researches on the sphere led him to criticize the geographical procedures of *Eratosthenes; he himself applied more rigorous mathematical methods to specify location, and again was apparently the first to use latitude and longitude systematically.

hippeis ('knights', 'the cavalry'), at Athens, one of the names of the top social class; under *Solon, the second of his census-classes, those sufficiently wealthy to keep a horse. See HORSES and ARMY, GREEK I, and HOPLITES. For Aristophanes' play see *KNIGHTS*.

Hi'ppias. **1.** Eldest son of Peisistratus, tyrant of Athens, and himself tyrant from 527 to 510 BC. At first a mild ruler, he became harsher as his reign progressed. His brother *Hipparchus was assassinated in 514 BC; during his reign the Spartans invaded and were repulsed, but a second invasion in 510 forced him to withdraw from Athens to the colony of Sigeum (see COLONIZATION, GREEK 3) and thence to the court of the Persian king Darius. He was with the Persian forces when they were defeated by the Greeks at Marathon in 490 BC. See PEISISTRATUS 3.

2. Of Elis, a *sophist of the later fifth century BC, a contemporary of Socrates, whose vast range of learning included grammar, poetry, mathematics, and astronomy. He is vividly depicted in two of Plato's dialogues, *Hippias Minor* and *Major* (the latter less certainly by Plato). He is commonly said to have compiled a list of victors at the Olympian games for chronological purposes (see CALENDARS 6).

hi'ppikēs, Peri, see HORSEMANSHIP.

hippoca'mpus, in Greek art, a monster on which sea-gods often rode; it had a horse's body and a fish's tail.

Hippoclei'dēs, Athenian who won immortality through an anecdote in Herodotus. He had become the favourite with Cleisthenes, tyrant of Sicyon, to marry the latter's daughter. At the feast at which Cleisthenes' choice was to be made known Hippocleides ordered the flute-player to play a dance and 'probably danced to his own satisfaction', concluding by standing on his head and gesticulating with his legs, but he gravely displeased his intended father-in-law. 'Son of Teisandros, you have danced away your marriage', he was told; his reply, 'Hippocleides doesn't care', became proverbial. (The daughter Agaristē later married Megacles of the family of the Alcmaeonidae: their son was Cleisthenes, the great reformer of the Athenian constitution.)

Hippo'cratēs. 1. The most famous name in Greek medicine, belonging to a Greek physician who was born in the island of Cos about 460 BC and lived to at least 370; he is said to have died at Larisa (in Thessaly). Scarcely anything is known about his life; yet the attitudes apparent in the writings that go under his name as well as the medical practice they describe are attributed to him personally. The former still express the ethical ideal of a doctor, and the latter too has exerted a very strong influence until comparatively recent times. The collection of medical writings known as the Hippocratic Corpus consists of some sixty treatises, all in the Ionic Greek *dialect, most of which were compiled between c.430 and 330 BC. There is no evidence that Hippocrates wrote any of them personally. The collection as a whole seems to have been made in the third century BC. It may represent the contents of the library of the Hippocratic school of medicine associated with the healing shrine of the god *Asclepius on Cos. The works cover surgery, epidemiology, pharmacology, embryology, and anatomy, including treatises on prognosis and general health care. In some

cases they propound widely differing medical doctrines. Nevertheless the collection as a whole reflects the spirit of Greek science in its insistence on the permanence of the relation of effect to cause, and the necessity for careful observation of medical facts.

Of two fifth-century works, *On Airs, Waters and Places* and *On the Sacred Disease* (epilepsy), the former discusses the effect of climate, water supply, and region on people, and compares the geophysical conditions of life in Europe and Asia; the latter attacks popular superstitions about the disease and demonstrates that, no differently from any other disease, it arises from natural causes. The *Epidemics* contain the interestingly detailed case-book studies of over forty patients with serious illnesses (of which most of the patients died); books 1 and 3 appear to date from the fifth century. The *Aphorisms* or collection of medical sayings contain the famous dictum: 'Life is short, science (*technē*) long, opportunity fleeting, experiment dangerous, judgement difficult.' The Hippocratic Oath seems to have originated in a particular group of medical practitioners, but most of the ideals it expresses are common to all. In the Middle Ages 'Ypocras' became a favourite subject with European story-tellers in tales of magic and intrigue, as was 'Bokrát' among Arabic writers, who represented him as studying in a garden near Damascus.

2. Of Chios (c.470–400 BC), Greek mathematician whose writings are lost. He was the first to collect together an *Elements of Geometry* (the forerunner of Euclid's *Elements*), which must have contained the propositions known to the Pythagoreans, and presumably contained a certain amount of the geometry of the circle since Hippocrates was well-known for his quadrature of lunes. He also contributed to solving the problem of doubling the cube.

Hi'ppocrēne (Hippokrēnē), fountain sacred to the Muses on Mount *Helicon in Boeotia (see PEGASUS), supposedly with the power to inspire with poetry those who drank from it.

Hippodamei'a. 1. In Greek myth, daughter of Oenomaus and wife of *Pelops.

2. In Greek myth, wife of Pīrithŏus, king of the Lapiths (see CENTAURS and THESEUS).

Hippoda'mus, of Miletus (fifth century BC), the most famous Greek town-planner. In the mid-fifth century he planned the town of *Piraeus around the original sea-port, substituting broad straight streets intersecting at right angles in place of crooked, narrow streets. He was also the architect of the Athenian colony of Thurii (near Sybaris) in 443 BC and, according to one tradition, of the city of Rhodes, founded in 408 BC. See also POPULATION 1.

hi'ppodrome, in Greece and Rome, track for *horse- and *chariot-races.

Hippo'lytē (or Hippolyta). **1.** In Greek myth, queen of the Amazons, sometimes called Antiopē; see HERACLES, LABOURS OF 9 and THESEUS.
2. In Greek myth, wife of Acastus, sometimes called Astydameia; see PELEUS.

Hippo'lytus, in Greek myth, the son of *Theseus and the Amazon queen Hippolytē; after the latter's death Theseus married *Phaedra, the sister of Ariadne. During his absence Phaedra fell in love with Hippolytus who, being honourable, rejected her advances. Moreover, as a devotee of the goddess Artemis he led a life of perfect chastity. Phaedra subsequently hanged herself, after writing a letter to Theseus denouncing Hippolytus as her seducer. Theseus, not believing his protestations of innocence, banished him, and also used against him one of the three curses which he had been given by the god Poseidon. As Hippolytus drove away from the palace along the shore a monster or bull sent from the sea by Poseidon terrified the horses; Hippolytus was thrown from the chariot and dragged to his death. Theseus learned of his error from Artemis too late. Hippolytus had a cult at Troezen (north-east Peloponnese), the scene of his death, which included laments for him and offerings of hair from girls about to marry. Virgil and other authors relate that Hippolytus was brought back to life by *Asclepius and was conveyed by *Diana (the Roman equivalent of Artemis) to the grove of the nymph Aricia at Nemi in Latium, where under the name of Virbius (vir bis, 'a man twice') he lived out his days. His son by Diana, also called Virbius according to Virgil, was among the heroes who resisted the settlement of Aeneas in Latium.

Hippo'lytus, Greek tragedy by *Euripides produced in 429 BC. For the story see above. Euripides makes Phaedra a virtuous woman trying to resist her passion, her feelings betrayed to Hippolytus by her nurse. The false accusation Phaedra makes in the letter to Theseus was motivated, according to Euripides, by shame and anger at Hippolytus' scorn. See also PHAEDRA, the Roman tragedy of Seneca. The subject is treated by the French dramatist Jean Racine in his tragedy Phèdre (1677).

Hippō'nax, of Ephesus (mid-sixth century BC), Greek poet of satirical, often scurrilous, verse. He invented his own version of the iambic trimeter, making it end with a spondee, the so-called 'limping iambic' or scazon; see METRE, GREEK 5 (iii). He was banished from Ephesus and moved to Clazomenae, another Ionian city, where according to one of his poems he lived in great poverty. His poems survive only in fragments, but enough remain to show his mordant wit, his realism, and his vigorous use of earthy Greek laced with colloquialisms and words from local dialects. He attacked his

enemies with gusto. The best known (apocryphal) story about him relates his quarrel with the sculptor Bupalus and his brother Athēnis, who made a statue caricaturing the features of the poet. He retaliated with such offensive verse that they both hanged themselves. Hipponax is sometimes credited, not impossibly, with the invention of parody.

Hi'rtius, Aulus, one of Julius Caesar's lieutenants in Gaul and consul with Vibius Pansa in 43 BC after Caesar's assassination; in the subsequent fighting Cicero persuaded him to take arms against Mark Antony, who was besieging Mutina. The two consuls, together with Octavian, raised the siege but were both killed (see ROME 7 and BRUTUS (3)). Hirtius added the eighth book to Caesar's Gallic War (see COMMENTARIES I) and probably wrote the *Bellum Alexandrinum as well.

Hispa'nia, see SPAIN.

Histiae'us, tyrant of the Ionian Greek city of Miletus at the time of the first expedition of the Persian king *Darius into Europe c.514 BC (see PERSIAN WARS). He guarded the bridge of boats when Darius crossed the Danube, and resisted the proposal to destroy the bridge when his return was delayed, thus enabling him to retreat safely with his army. For this service Darius rewarded him with a district in Thrace where he built the strategically important city of Myrcinus; but Darius, growing distrustful, recalled him to Susa (the Persian capital). Meanwhile Histiaeus' son-in-law Aristagoras ruled Thrace. They were both involved in the Ionian Revolt (499 BC), but Darius, trusting Histiaeus, allowed him to proceed to Ionia nominally to crush the rising. He was unsuccessful, and distrusted now by both sides, took to piracy, at one time occupying Byzantium. In 494/3 he was captured by the Persian satrap Artaphernēs and crucified.

Histo'ria Animā'lium ('inquiry into animals'; the usual English title is 'History of Animals'), treatise by *Aristotle; see 4 (iii) (e).

Histo'ria Augu'sta, name given by the Swiss scholar Casaubon in the early seventeenth century to a collection of biographies of Roman emperors, and certain heirs and claimants to the empire, from Hadrian to Numerianus (AD 117–284); there is a gap between 244 and 259. The biographies are attributed to six authors: Aelius Spartianus, Julius Capitolinus, Volcatius Gallicanus, Aelius Lampridius, Trebellius Pollio, and Flavius Vopiscus. Nothing is known of the authors. Of the Lives by the first four, some are addressed to Diocletian, some to Constantine the Great, and it was long assumed that they were written in the reigns of these emperors in the early fourth century. However, study of the style has led some to believe that the collection is the work of only one author, perhaps writing at the very end of the fourth century; the author's purpose in compiling this forgery has been variously described, as intended to entertain readers with sensational stories or even as a veiled pagan attack on Christianity. To others it still seems to be the work of more than one hand. It is clear that the documents cited in the *Historia* are mostly forgeries, and the historical value of the narrative is doubtful.

Histo'riae Phili'ppicae ('Philippic histories'), history of the world by *Trogus.

Historians

1. *Greek*. The following ancient historians wrote in Greek (some on Roman history): Apollodorus, Appian, Arrian, Callisthenes, Cassius Dio, Ctesias, Diodorus, Dionysius of Halicarnassus, Ephorus, Eratosthenes, Eusebius, Herodian, Herodotus, Josephus, Onesicritus, Plutarch, Polybius, Posidonius, Theopompus, Thucydides, Timaeus, Xenophon, and Logographers.

2. *Roman*. The following names include ancient historians who wrote in Latin, and the titles of Latin histories: Ammianus Marcellinus, *Annales*, Caesar, Cremutius Cordus, Curtius, Eutropius, Festus, Florus, Hirtius, *Historia Augusta*, Jerome, Justin, Livy, Nepos, Orosius, Sallust, Sisenna, Suetonius, Tacitus, Trogus, Valerius Maximus, Velleius Paterculus. See also HISTORIOGRAPHY.

Histo'ria planta'rum ('inquiry into plants'), treatise by *Theophrastus.

Histories, The (*Historiae*), a work by the Roman historian *Tacitus. Originally twelve or fourteen books long, they dealt with the period AD 69–96, from Galba to Domitian, but only the first four books and part of the fifth survive, covering the events of the 'Year of the Four Emperors', 69, and the first nine months or so of 70. They were published, perhaps in instalments, between AD 105 and 108, and were written before the *Annals*. Portions were revised by the Younger Pliny, who sometimes furnished Tacitus with material, e.g. the account of the eruption of Vesuvius in AD 79 which caused the death of Pliny's uncle and namesake.

Book 1 opens with a survey of how, after the prosperous security of the Julio-Claudian dynasty, the empire is shaken by palace conspiracies, sudden murders, the armies moving on Rome from the frontiers, the frontiers themselves overrun by barbarians, the times 'rich in tragedies, terrible with battles, torn by civil strife'; even the Capitol is set on fire by citizens. It describes the brief reign of Galba, his adoption of Piso Licinianus, and the intrigues of Otho with the military which brought about the murder of Galba and Piso and his own accession (69). Tacitus brilliantly portrays the emperor Galba, his mediocrity, 'rather free from vices than endowed with virtues', the stinginess which was his undoing, his high birth and military reputation thanks to which he would have been judged 'equal to the imperial office had he not held it', *capax imperii nisi imperasset*. The narrative passes to the mutinous conduct of the legions in Germany, their adoption of Vitellius as emperor, the movement of his forces under Valens and Caecina, the negotiations between Otho and Vitellius, the shifting allegiances of provinces and legions, and the outbreak of civil war.

Book 2. Tacitus turns to the important role that the commanders Vespasian and Titus were playing in the East, where, except for the resistance of Jerusalem, the war against the Jews had been concluded. Vespasian and Mucianus, governor of Syria, decide to await developments. Tacitus then returns to events in Italy, the fighting around Bedriacum (on the road between Verona and Cremona), and the suicide of Otho, death seeming the only honourable course open to him. The reign of Vitellius is described, the emperor's sloth and gluttony, the disorder in the legions, the wasteful administration, and the threat of the advance of Vespasian's forces under Mucianus.

Book 3 describes the operations of Vespasian's generals against Vitellius, the siege and the terrible sack and burning of Cremona, the fighting in Rome between partisans of the opposing forces, which leads to the burning of the Capitol, the final capture of the city and the end of Vitellius, discovered wandering forlornly in the deserted palace and put to death (December 69). The author's gift for sombre depiction is seen at its best in this book.

Book 4 and the surviving portion of book 5 are occupied with the reign of Vespasian, the rising of the Batavians under Civilis, and the expedition of Titus against Jerusalem (the account of the siege is lost).

historiography

1. *Greek*. Greek prose history was first written in the late sixth century BC in Ionia. Coinciding with the development of early science and philosophy in that part of the Greek world, a rational and systematic approach was applied not only to local traditions and the more widespread myths of epic poetry, but also to the information gathered by seafaring people about the coastline and harbours, people, customs, and local history of the Mediterranean. These historians were the so-called *logographers, 'prose writers', of whom the most influential was *Hecataeus of Miletus (*c.*500 BC), but their work survives only in fragments. They wrote both local and general (not necessarily Greek) history. Local histories continued to be written throughout the fifth and fourth centuries; those of Attica for example (see ATTHIS) form much of the basis of Aristotle's *Constitution of Athens*.

Lists of annual magistrates and similarly regular recurrences were also compiled with the aim of establishing a chronological framework, e.g. of eponymous archons at Athens, priestesses of Hera at Argos, and victors in the footrace at Olympia.

Greek history proper begins with the full-scale *historiai*, i.e. 'inquiries', of *Herodotus (b. *c*.490 BC); the word soon acquired its more restricted meaning. Herodotus' work established the scale of history, and his all-embracing curiosity, which made him include in his work, as well as history in its restricted sense, archaeology, ethnography, geography, religion, and a fair amount of anecdote, might well have established also its scope. He applied proper standards in evaluating evidence where they seemed to him appropriate, but he does not always manifest a strictly rational approach, and it is difficult to categorize his thought or even to discern what its foundation is. His intellectual successor is in some sense Aristotle, writing treatises over a wide range of historical and scientific subjects. *Thucydides (b. *c*.460 BC) writing a generation later than Herodotus, and choosing to write on contemporary history in which he himself had played some part, was able to apply much more rigorous standards of factual accuracy than had been possible for the latter. He criticizes his immediate predecessors (left unnamed but certainly including Herodotus) for writing what is merely entertaining to listen to for the moment, rather than what is true and has permanent value. He did not only aim to relate what actually happened; his passion for generalization led him to write on such large matters as the underlying cause of the Peloponnesian War, the behaviour of oligarchs and democrats, and the dynamics of imperialism. His influence narrowed the scope of history, turning it in the direction of politics almost before it had set off along the path Herodotus had indicated. Thucydides' combination of generalization with factual accuracy was difficult to sustain and no later Greek historian made the attempt. The nearest approach to his analytical style is that of *Polybius (b. *c*.200 BC).

In the fourth century BC a new type of history evolved under the direct influence both in style and moralistic outlook of *Isocrates (b. *c*.436 BC), but affected too by Plato's preoccupation with moral education. History became the vehicle of moral instruction and political prejudice, and style became more important than content. Isocrates' pupil Ephorus (b. *c*.405 BC) wrote a universal history, now lost, in which he appears to have regarded it as one of his chief functions to apportion praise or blame. This school of thought had great influence on the Roman historians.

In the Hellenistic age (from *c*.300 BC), historians generally aimed less at being accurate than at being readable. Careful historians like *Hieronymus of Cardia are the exception; the favoured style was rhetorical and romantic, and because history in this style gave prominence to outstanding individuals, it was the source for later biographers and ultimately Plutarch. Monographs on particular subjects continued to be written, along with histories of cities, memoirs, and other topics similarly limited in scope.

2. *Roman*. The earliest Roman historians, of whom *Fabius Pictor is the most celebrated, working at the beginning of the second century BC, wrote in Greek, both because they wished to glorify Rome's foundation and justify her institutions and policy to the Hellenistic world, and because Latin prose had not yet developed as a literary medium. Thus they are primarily political writers in intent, within the tradition of Hellenistic Greek historiography; Polybius (b. *c*.200 BC) worked along the same lines to explore the rise of Rome, and this aim was further pursued but, for the first time in a work of this kind, in Latin, by *Cato (1) in his *Origines*, a history of Rome from its foundation, written between 168 and 149 BC. This great work, which survives only in fragments, inspired further historical study in Rome. The 'old' annalists (see ANNALS), Cassius Hemina and Calpurnius Piso, began the systematic study of Roman institutions which led to the publication after 130 BC of the *annales maximi* ('the most important records'). Later writers who depended on this work for their chronological framework also tended to follow its method, describing events as they happened year by year. This basic form was elaborated by historians of the early first century BC, including Valerius Antias and Claudius Quadrigarius, who established in Rome the moralistic tone and especially the rhetorical style of writing history that harked back to Isocrates; this was the style accepted by Livy. On the whole the Romans were more interested in the literary merits of their histories than in giving an accurate report of what actually happened.

The various other kinds of historiography current in Hellenistic times had taken root in Rome by the beginning of the first century BC (see end of 1 above). This was the background against which Sallust and Cicero wrote, and the same tradition was later followed by Tacitus. *Sallust's political thought is intensely moralistic, in the Isocratean manner, but his chief exemplar was Thucydides; his portraits of individuals go back through the biographical tradition to Thucydides, whose severe style he also imitated. He was influenced too by the concise and abrupt style of Cato, and he rejected the amplitude of the oratorical style of his own day. In marked contrast, *Cicero ((1) 5), in his writings on the history of philosophy and oratory, kept to Isocratean standards, and although sincerely aiming at accuracy declared that his merits as a stylist compensated for his lack of philosophical knowledge, and that writing history was the province of orators. *Tacitus (b. *c.* AD 56) in style and content resembled Sallust; and both have been criticized for political bias and inaccuracy. Tacitus, however, united the various traditions of historical writing into work of great power. The biographical tradition was continued with the *Lives* of *Suetonius (b. *c.* AD 69), but degenerated after him into the *Historia Augusta* (fourth century AD). Tacitus' history was continued (from AD 96) and imitated by *Ammianus Marcellinus (b. *c.* AD 330), a Greek writing in Latin for Roman readers. He is considered accurate in general and relatively free of bias, but his work was done in isolation. This was the age of epitomes and outlines of history, and, with the addition of Jewish history to that of Greece and Rome, the start of a tradition of Christian chronicles (see EUSEBIUS).

Homer (Hŏmēros) (probably eighth century BC), Greek epic poet.

1. Homer was regarded in antiquity as the author primarily of the *Iliad* and the *Odyssey*; other *epic poems were sometimes attributed to him, most popularly *Margites* and *Batrachomyomachia*, but the best authorities rejected these. The Greeks themselves knew no certain facts about his life; various dates were suggested, ranging from the Trojan War (beginning of the twelfth century BC) to five hundred years later. Herodotus dated him to about 850 BC. Modern scholars, using the evidence of history, archaeology, and language, generally date the poems to the end of the eighth century, long after the events of the Trojan War and its aftermath that they describe. Many cities claimed to be Homer's birthplace, most plausibly Smyrna and Chios, the home of the *Homeridae. The ancient Greeks thought of Homer as a blind minstrel, suffering poverty and hardship in the course of a wandering life before his eventual death and burial on the Aegean island of Ios.

2. The view of some Hellenistic scholars, the 'separatists' (*chōrizontĕs*), that the *Iliad* and the *Odyssey* were not written by the same person, has been adopted by some modern scholars, who argue on the basis of the language, the social customs, and the attitude to the gods, that the *Odyssey* was composed perhaps a generation later than the *Iliad*. Other modern scholars (the 'unitarians'), thinking that the differences between the two poems can be accounted for by their very different subjects, believe, as the ancient Greeks themselves believed, that both poems are the work of one man. Whether two poets or one, it is clear that both poems were composed in an Ionian-speaking part of the Greek world, that the *Odyssey* was intended as a sequel to the *Iliad*, the events of which it presupposes, and that the characters appearing in both have recognizably the same individuality.

3. Not only has it been suggested that there were two poets, it has been doubted whether there was even one. Since the end of the eighteenth century Homeric scholarship has been dominated by the problem of defining the authorship, the so-called 'Homeric question'. It had always been observed that the language of the poems is an artificial amalgam drawn from different parts of the Greek world and from different periods (see DIALECTS and DIGAMMA) and, to a lesser extent, that Homeric society and institutions similarly lack authenticity; now more attention was paid to the serious (it was felt) discrepancies in the narratives themselves. It was therefore suggested that each poem was created out of a compilation of shorter ballad-type poems, 'lays', and brought to its present length by natural accretions and collective effort, or, it might be, by the editorial activity of one man, whose individual contribution it would be impossible to assess. In fact, extensive study of comparable epic material such as that surviving in Yugoslavia into the twentieth century seems to have established that the poems are the culmination of a centuries-old tradition of *oral poetry, and this may account for the disparate elements and for discrepancies which may become apparent to readers able to turn back the pages of a book but which would not be noticed during a recitation. It also accounts for one of the most distinctive features of Homer, the fact that his language is highly '*formulaic', i.e. repetitive; the poet constantly repeats not only epithets and phrases but lines and passages; even scenes are repeated, for example those describing such 'typical' activities as preparing a meal or arming for battle. The poet, by already having in his memory a large repertoire of traditional formulae, would be able to deliver extempore a sizeable narrative, improvising a story which he may previously have rehearsed in his mind.

4. Some of the traditional elements in the poems may go back, as is often alleged, to the Mycenaean period of Greek prehistory (say 1400–1200 BC), but these are not very numerous. Perhaps the poems recall a war that was the last concerted effort of Mycenaean Greece against a foreign enemy; archaeology confirms that Troy was in fact destroyed between *c.*1250 and 1200 BC. Shortly afterwards the Mycenaean civilization itself collapsed, perhaps in the wake of the *Dorian Invasion. The poems vaguely hark back to the glories and the practices of that palace society, but the formative period of Homeric epic and the society it by and large reflects is that of the late Dark Age, the ninth and eighth centuries BC (see HOMERIC AGE).

5. It has been thought likely that the apparent reintroduction of writing into Greece towards the end of the eighth century (see ALPHABET) was the crucial factor in determining the form of the poems, giving an exceptional poet—Homer—

the opportunity to meditate and perhaps dictate to a scribe a longer and vastly more complex poem (or poems) than he could otherwise have composed or delivered. The resulting poems were intended for oral delivery (epic was in fact sung or chanted, the poet accompanying himself on the lyre); on the other hand the continuous narrative shows that they were designed to be heard in their entirety, the *Iliad* in particular being difficult to break up into episodes. Their length, however, precludes their being performed at a sitting: uninterrupted recitation of the *Iliad* would take roughly twenty hours, and perhaps would only have been possible at one of the great festivals. It is therefore probable that in general the poems were sung in excerpts by *rhapsodes.

6. The indications, then, are that the poems were each conceived as a unity and composed by an individual poet (or two poets) working in the Ionian tradition of oral composition; it is generally felt that the cohesion and subtle artistry that each poem shows could not have been achieved by mere editorial activity; Aristotle in the *Poetics* singles out Homer's grasp of artistic unity for special praise. Moreover, ancient Greek unanimity about the existence of 'Homer' should not be discounted. A story of doubtful authenticity tells how the sixth-century Athenian tyrant *Peisistratus, finding the Homeric texts in confusion, was responsible for having them put in order and recited at the Panathenaic festival (see also ONOMACRITUS). The Athenian element in a few episodes, and perhaps even traces of the Attic dialect, indicate that at some stage Athens played a part in the transmission of the text. Indeed, an Athenian version of the text would appear to be the source of all our manuscripts of Homer; it may even be the origin of the division of the poems into 24 books each. At the end of the sixth century BC quotations from and references to Homer begin to appear in fair quantity; from these and subsequent quotations, as well as from papyrus fragments, it is clear that texts at that time contained considerable if superficial variations; for some centuries there was probably an oral transmission maintained by the rhapsodes as well as a written transmission. However, it is upon the editorial labours of the scholars at Alexandria from the third century BC onwards, *Zenodotus, *Aristophanes of Byzantium, and above all *Aristarchus, that the modern text is based.

7. The Homeric poems have been read continuously, first in Greece and then in Europe generally, ever since their creation. Homer was regarded with reverence by most Greeks, the source (with Hesiod) of their knowledge of the gods, the formulator of the heroic code of conduct, a touchstone of wise behaviour; and he was constantly quoted. Passages were frequently imitated or translated by Latin poets (e.g.

Lucretius and Virgil); the *Odyssey* was translated into Latin saturnians by *Livius Andronicus. A much-imitated stylistic feature is the Homeric simile which, once the point of comparison is made, develops into an independent vignette; it may be descriptive or it may have an emotional effect or relieve tension, particularly in the *Iliad* where it often introduces into an epic of war a glimpse of ordinary, peaceful life. Homer has since earliest times been regarded as a poet beyond all others: 'in the serious style the poet of poets', 'unequalled in diction and thought', Aristotle claimed in the *Poetics*. Homer, he further says, has taught poets the true art of illusion, keeping himself in the background and leaving his characters to reveal themselves. In a famous sentence the nineteenth-century English poet and critic Matthew Arnold, in *On Translating Homer*, gave as the dominant characteristics of Homeric style, rapidity, plainness, directness, and nobility; he adds that what Homer has in common with the poet Milton, namely the noble and profound application of ideas to life, is the essential part of poetic greatness. But the English scholar Richard Bentley, writing in the early eighteenth century, protested against the notion that Homer 'designed his poems for eternity to please and instruct mankind': 'Take my word for it, poor Homer had never such aspiring thoughts. He wrote a sequel of songs and rhapsodies, to be sung by himself for small earnings and good cheer … The *Iliad* he made for the men and the *Odyssey* for the other sex.'

8. The first printed edition of Homer appeared at Florence in 1488, prepared by Chalcondyles of Athens, an immigrant scholar who taught Greek in Italy. Another landmark in Homeric studies was the publication in 1795 of F. A. Wolf's *Prolegomena ad Homerum* ('introduction to Homer') in which he tried to prove that the *Iliad* and the *Odyssey* were not the work of a single author but the blending of a number of poems handed down by oral recitation and unified by subsequent treatment. Famous English verse-translations of Homer were written, in the Elizabethan age, by George Chapman (inspiring Keats's sonnet, 'On first looking into Chapman's Homer'), and, in the 1720s, by Alexander Pope. Bentley's judgement on Pope's translation is well-known: 'a very pretty poem … but he must not call it Homer'. Pope's *Odyssey* contains a line that soon became famous, 'Welcome the coming, speed the parting guest' (15. 74). The late-Victorian prose translations, of the *Iliad* by Lang, Leaf, and Myers, of the *Odyssey* by Butcher and Lang, written in a deliberately archaic and dignified English, keep closely to the original. The translations by E. V. Rieu, racy and colloquial and often rather free, were very successful.

For medieval legend connected with the *Iliad* see TROJAN WAR. See also HEROES.

Homeric age. The age which Homer's epic poems, the *Iliad* and the *Odyssey*, dimly reflect is that of Mycenaean Greece in the period before the fall of Troy in the early twelfth century, but the formative period of the epics was the subsequent Dark Age, from about 1000 BC. Many obvious features of Dark Age society have been clearly incorporated into the two poems, but other events of that age which might have been thought to be well known, for example the *Dorian Invasion and the *migrations to Ionia, have been excluded, it would seem deliberately. In some ways, therefore, the political, social, and economic conditions depicted are an artificial conglomeration (see HOMER above). Nevertheless, the elements belong to real societies even if their combination is in some aspects unreal: to a large extent Homer presents a coherent portrait of Greek society towards the end of the Dark Age.

In Homer, the government of a community is aristocratic rather than monarchical, in the hands of a group of hereditary nobles, the 'kings' (*basilēes*), one of whom may preside over them and lead the people in war. Each noble is the head of his own family (*gĕnos*) and household (*oikos*). On his death his property is divided between his sons, who then set up their own households; a bastard son may have some share of the property. Marriages are arranged for sons with brides from the same social class (but perhaps outside the community), who bring dowries with them when they join their father-in-law's household, but also expect bride gifts in return. Women in Homer enjoy a high social status and considerable freedom, even being present at banquets in the hall; they also supervise most of the domestic activities of the household. Homeric society is, in contrast with classical Athens, markedly heterosexual (see HOMOSEXUALITY). The estate is worked by slaves and occasionally hired labour. Women slaves are relatively common, usually acquired (with children) at the sack of a city when the menfolk have been killed; male slaves, acquired by raiding and warfare, are less common; these have a recognized position in society; are often reared as members of a household and are highly valued; they are put in charge of farms and allowed families of their own. Hired labourers (*thētĕs*) are the least fortunate members of the population. They lack the security of the slave and when unemployed revert to the position of beggars, without the latters' call upon the protection of Zeus.

Apart from the specialized professions of bards, diviners, physicians, and heralds, Homeric society includes four kinds of artisans: woodworkers, metalworkers, leatherworkers, and potters. Commerce is limited: there is some trade with Phoenicia, Egypt, Cyprus, Lydia, and Caria. Precious metals are in use, but the finest pieces of gold and silver work are imported; these form the luxury items given and received by guest-friends; silver probably comes through Phoenician traders. The population is largely supported by agriculture. The scenes portrayed on the shield of Achilles include ploughing, reaping, and the vintage. Fruit is cultivated in orchards; in that of Alcinous grow pears, pomegranates, apples, figs, and olives, and there is a vegetable garden as well. The olive has not yet achieved its position as a staple. It was observed in ancient times that while the Greeks of the classical period ate mostly cereals, fish, and dairy products, and meat only at festivals, the Homeric heroes were meat-eaters and measured wealth in terms of cattle. If there was a change in agriculture during the Dark Age, away from animal husbandry to arable farming, it may be that Homer recalls the more extravagant practice of an earlier age.

The house of a 'king' consists of a courtyard (*aulē*) with stables, in the centre of which is the hall (*megaron*), with seats round the walls and a central hearth, and an inner chamber (*thalamos*) for the women, used also as a store for possessions, and perhaps a porch or antechamber (*prodomos*) where guests may sleep. Not all such houses were in the country; Alcinous' house is within the city walls. The feasting of male companions in the hall wins repute for a king (or noble) and enables him to obtain support in the community and, through ties of mutual obligation, 'guest-friendship', outside it. A relationship established by such entertainment was under the protection of Zeus Xenios ('of strangers') and sustained the power of the noble through his travels beyond his immediate locality. Poems like Homer's were originally sung at such entertainments, where there might also be dances and athletic contests. The noble's principal occupation is cattle-raiding or piracy, booty being shared among his supporters in proportion to their standing. The picture of Homeric warfare seems basically confused. The noble still rides to battle in a chariot (see CHARIOT-RACES and HORSES), which disappeared from warfare at the end of the Mycenaean age, but has forgotten how to use it, preferring to dismount and fight on foot. He fights with a jumble of weapons from different periods which are all made of bronze, although iron is known and used for implements of peace (in historical fact iron seems to have been used for weapons first).

The aristocratic style of life that underlies Homeric society, based on the ethos of the warrior band, never entirely disappeared from Greek society, nor did its morality, with emphasis on competition and on excelling. The influence of the aristocratic clans, with their ramified bases of power, is seen in the success of such families as the Alcmaeonidae at Athens; the comradeship of the Homeric feast survives in the *symposium of classical Athens, and the gifts of guest-friendship in the reciprocal ties of obligation that bound Greeks to each other in later times.

Homeric Hymns (composed during the period from the eighth to the sixth centuries BC), a collection of thirty-three Greek hexameter poems in epic style addressed to gods and minor deities, commonly attributed to Homer in antiquity but denied Homeric authorship by the Alexandrian scholars. It is not known when the collection was put together. The authors were evidently *rhapsodes; the author of the third Hymn describes himself as 'a blind man living in rocky Chios' (thus suggesting Homer). Many of the Hymns are only a few lines long and are preludes to the recitations from epic often given at festivals, invoking the gods whose festivals were being celebrated. Others narrate at length some episode relating to the god. The most notable are: the Hymn to Demeter (hymn 2), which relates the famous myth of the seizing of Persephonē by Hadēs and Demeter's search for her, and ends with the founding of the Eleusinian mysteries; the Hymn to Apollo (3, attributed to Homer by Thucydides and Aristophanes), the first part of which describes the god's birth on Delos and the second the establishment of his oracle at Delphi (the whole may be constituted out of two hymns); the Hymn to Hermes (4), a lively and amusing account of the god's achievements as a baby; the Hymn to Aphroditē (5), which depicts the goddess of love herself yielding to the power of love and marrying Anchisēs; and the Hymn to Dionysus (7), which briefly tells the story of the god's capture by pirates and the subsequent miracles he performed.

Homeridae ('sons of Homer'), name, from the sixth century BC if not earlier, of a clan (*genos*) of *rhapsodes in Chios who claimed descent from Homer and the prerogative of reciting Homer's poems 'by right of succession'. They later developed into a guild by admitting rhapsodes not claiming to be related to Homer.

homosexuality. In Greece, at some time during the archaic period, the heterosexual society known to Homer (see HOMERIC AGE) changed. For the aristocracy of this period marriage was concerned not with love but with property, inheritance, and the practicalities of life, and it cemented political and social ties; the care taken by Cleisthenes, tyrant of Sicyon, to find a suitable son-in-law (see HIPPOCLEIDES) was not untypical. The segregation of upper-class women (at least in an urbanized society), who were consequently not much seen in public, meant that they could hardly inspire romantic love; those women who were seen, professional entertainers at dinner parties or prostitutes, were merely the object of sexual desire (see also HETAERAE). In this society positive encouragement to homosexuality was given by the social institutions of the aristocracy: the cult of athletic prowess and physical beauty in the gymnasium, where men exercised naked, the all-male dinner party or drinking party (see SYMPOSIUM) with its entertainments and love poetry, and the comradeship of war (see SACRED BAND). The accepted relationship was between an older man, the lover (*erastēs*), and an adolescent of the same social class, 'the loved one' (*erōmenos*). The proper behaviour of the latter was to appear oblivious of or indifferent to the advances of the lover. The lover was expected to win the love of the younger boy by his own virtues and by the care he took for the latter's education and well-being. The relationship might be as much romantic as physical; it gradually developed into one of friendship: the indefinite prolongation of a love affair was not approved. Male prostitution or open enjoyment of the passive role was abhorrent to the right-thinking Greek male. The virtues of homosexual love were exemplified by the behaviour of the (would-be) tyrannicides *Harmodius and Aristogeiton, who were greatly admired by the Athenians. The large number of Attic black- and red-figure cups inscribed 'so-and-so [a boy] is beautiful' testifies to the accepted place of homosexuality in the late seventh and sixth centuries BC. Towards the end of the fifth century these cups are not so numerous.

Female homosexuality is less in evidence; its strongest expression is found in the poems of Sappho, who enjoyed a freer life on Aeolian Lesbos than was permitted to most women on the Greek mainland. Evidence for physical relationships is doubtful; the language of the poems in which she addresses other girls justifies the observation of a late Greek commentator that her relationship with girls was like Socrates' relationship with handsome youths (i.e. ardent but chaste). A fragment of another commentary describes her, perhaps plausibly, as a teacher of girls.

honey, favourite sweetening agent of the ancient world, used in cookery and medicine and as a preservative. Hymettus honey (from Attica) was particularly famous for its flavour and its pale colouring. It was credited with mystical qualities, and sometimes symbolized the natural blessings men enjoyed in the *Golden Age. The production of honey was relatively small and it was always expensive. Cheap substitutes included the juice of dates and grapes, and secretions from trees, 'manna'. In Roman times sugar from canes, *sacc(h)aron*, was imported from Lydia, but cane sugar from India is not mentioned before the seventh century AD.

ho'plites (*hoplītai*), in Greece, the heavy-armed infantry of the city-states, citizens who could not maintain horses but could afford to equip themselves with armour (see ARMY, GREEK 1) and to provide for their families while they were away on campaign. The style of fighting with hoplites in phalanx formation spread throughout Greece from *c*.700 to *c*.650 BC, giving a sense of cohesion to the middle class with important political consequences: the *hippeis*, 'knights', lost their prestige as battle-winners, and as the new battle-winners hoplites claimed a greater share in the government.

Hoplite armour spread to Etruria and Rome by the end of the seventh century BC. This was later modified, so that the hoplite shield (*clipeus*) was replaced by the longer *scutum* (see ARMY, ROMAN 1), and the kind of spear known as the *pilum* was introduced, perhaps *c*.400 BC by Camillus at the time of the siege of Veii.

Horace (Quintus Horātius Flaccus) (65–8 BC), Roman poet, all of whose published work survives. A great deal is known about his life from a biography by *Suetonius and the poet's own testimony. He was the son of a freedman from Venusia (Venosa, near the river Aufidus in Apulia, south Italy), a Latin colony which had joined the rebellion of 90 BC that started the Social War and had subsequently been granted the citizenship. He was five years younger than Virgil. His father was a collector of payments at auctions, and had acquired a small estate. He gave his son the best education available, first at Rome under *Orbilius, and later at Athens. The civil war following Caesar's murder in 44 BC broke out while Horace was in Greece; in 44–42 he served in Brutus' army (the republican side) as military tribune, and fought on the losing side (and, he says, ran away) at the battle of Philippi in 42 BC. After that he returned to Italy, obtained a pardon from the victors, and purchased a secretaryship in the office of a quaestor. But he had been stripped of his family property, and poverty drove him to write poetry. About 38 BC he was introduced by Virgil and *Varius Rufus to *Maecenas, who after some delay took him under his protection and patronage, and in about 33 BC gave him a villa in the Sabine hills beyond Tivoli which was to be the source of much happiness to him and which he often celebrated in his poetry. Augustus offered him a post as private secretary, but this offer was politely refused.

During the thirties Horace wrote the *Epodes* (see ODES) and *Satires*; the two books of the latter were perhaps published together in 30 BC, after the defeat of Mark Antony at Actium. The first three books of the *Odes, composed gradually in the course of some ten years and reflecting the political events of 33–23, were probably published together in 23; the first book of the *Epistles perhaps in 20. The *Carmen Saeculare is a long ode written for the Secular Games of 17 BC and commissioned by Augustus, a sign of continuing imperial favour. Book IV of

the *Odes* was published in perhaps 13 BC. There remain three literary essays, two of which form Book II of the *Epistles*, while the third is known as the *Epistle to the Pisos* or, more usually, the *Ars poetica* ('art of poetry'). These are generally assigned to the last years of the poet's life, but their exact date is uncertain: Epistle II. 1 may be dated to *c*.16 BC, and II. 2 and the *Ars poetica* are sometimes placed as early as 19 BC. Horace died in 8 BC, a few months after Maecenas, with whom he had maintained a friendship of thirty years. He was never married. Suetonius describes him as short and stout; Horace speaks of himself as (prematurely?) grey.

Horace's position as one of the greatest of Roman poets rests on the perfection of form shown by his poetry and on the depth and detail of his self-portraiture: he shows himself to be one of the most likeable of men, urbane, humorous, tolerant, observant, a lover of the good things of life, a lover of his country. In the *Odes* particularly, his gentle irony and subtle choice of words caused Petronius to refer to his *curiosa felicitas* or 'studied felicity'; Quintilian called him *felicissime audax*, 'most felicitously bold' (in expression). He has been the most quoted of Latin poets, giving lovers of the apt phrase a multitude to choose from. In his lifetime his works were appreciated by his fellow-countrymen, and the *Odes* had become a school text-book before he died. He had few successors to imitate his lyric forms; the *Odes* themselves were not much read in the Middle Ages, though an inventive German scholar lecturing on Horace in the late fifteenth century induced a composer to set nineteen of them to music so that the students might sing them daily at the end of the lectures. They found particular favour in the Renaissance (as did the *Ars poetica*, accepted as a complete guide to poetry) and again in the eighteenth century, when Horace's philosophy of moderation had particular appeal.

horae, see SEASONS.

Horā'tii and Curiā'tii. According to Roman legend, the struggle between Rome and Alba Longa (in Latium) in the reign of Tullus Hostilius (seventh century BC; see ROME 2) was decided by the single combats of three Roman brothers, the Horatii, against three Latin brothers, the Curiatii. Two of the former were killed but the survivor killed the three latter. As he returned to Rome he met his sister weeping for the death of one of the Curiatii whom she was to marry. He stabbed her to death, was tried for murder, and eventually acquitted on appeal to the people.

Horā'tius Coclēs, Roman hero of the sixth century from the same family as the Horatii above; see COCLES.

Horolo'gion of Androni'cus, also known as the Tower of the Winds, at Athens, the water-clock built by Andronicus of Cyrrhus early in the second half of the first century BC and still in a good state of preservation. Varro mentions it in his *De re rustica* (of 37 BC) and Vitruvius gives important information about it. Built of Pentelic marble, the tower is octagonal, with its faces to the points of the compass, each bearing a sundial. At the top is a frieze decorated with relief sculptures of figures symbolizing the *winds. The tower was surmounted by a weather-vane in the shape of a bronze Triton. In the interior was an elaborate mechanism for a twenty-four hour clock, operated by water which was supplied from a cistern in a turret on the south side. See also CLOCKS.

Horolo'gium of Augustus, the huge 'shadow-clock' or sundial constructed in 9 BC by the emperor Augustus in the Campus Martius at Rome. Its gnomon (the 'finger' of the sundial which casts the shadow) was the first of the city's obelisks, one hundred Roman feet high (about 30 m.), brought from Heliopolis in Egypt. Still standing perhaps as late as the eleventh century, it was repaired in 1792 and re-erected in the Piazza Montecitorio where it may be seen today. The horologium, which must have transformed the difficult business of time-keeping at Rome (see CLOCKS), served also as a calendar; the date was shown by the length of the shadow cast by the obelisk at noon each day along a graduated line. Pliny the Elder, who described the horologium in some detail, observed that by his day the gnomon had shifted from its correct position, perhaps because of natural disturbances, and was failing to keep the right time.

Horse, Trojan, see TROJAN HORSE.

Horsemanship (*Peri hippikēs*, Lat. *De re equestri*), treatise by *Xenophon. The author, himself a keen and experienced horseman, gives advice to his younger friends on the management of horses, under the following heads: buying a colt, the points, beginning with the feet and working upwards; breaking a colt; buying a horse that has already been ridden, age, mouth, behaviour etc., of the animal; stable and yard; duties of a groom; instructions to the rider, mounting, seat, exercises, jumping, dismounting; treatment of a spirited horse; bits; horses for parade; armour for man and horse and arms for the rider. See also Xenophon's treatise the *CAVALRY COMMANDER*, and HORSES.

horse-races. The horse-race was introduced at the Olympian games of 648 BC and thereafter became an event at many games. It was held, like the *chariot-race, in the hippodrome, and the horses raced for one lap (about 800 m. or 900 yds.). They were unshod, and the riders rode bare-back and without stirrups.

horses. Domesticated horses were introduced into the Mediterranean world soon after the beginning of the second millennium BC, perhaps by invading *Indo-Europeans. They are much in evidence in *Mycenaean Greece from the sixteenth century BC onwards, and two skeletons of horses have been found near Marathon in Attica arranged at the entrance to a tomb of this period. In Italy evidence for their use in riding is found in the horse-bits buried in Iron Age tombs of the tenth and ninth centuries. Horses were both ridden and used for chariots. The chariot figures prominently in the *Linear B tablets of Greece and Crete, drawn by a pair of horses and carrying a charioteer and a passenger. (For a description of a chariot see CHARIOT-RACES.) In the *Iliad* it is merely a means of transport to and from battle, but the Greek hero Nestor describes a charge of a hundred massed chariots happening in his father's day, which may be an instance of the poet's faintly recalling the battle tactics of the earlier Mycenaean age, though most of the terrain of Greece is not suitable for such a deployment. It may be that it was the chariot as a novel instrument of war that brought success to the Indo-Europeans in their invasion of Greece soon after the beginning of the second millennium BC. By 1200 BC in Greece, and at the latest by 700 BC in Italy, chariots for warfare had been superseded by cavalry (see ARMY, GREEK I, ROMAN I), which was used much less by Greek armies (except for Thessaly and Macedon) than by Roman. In Greece, with its hard and hilly terrain, cavalry was not very efficient; control over unshod horses ridden without saddle (until Roman times) or stirrups (unknown to the entire classical world) was difficult, and made possible largely by the use of harsh bits. Cavalry was used mostly for scouting and for harassing the enemy. Because good pasture-land was rare in Greece and fodder expensive, horses were the possession of the very rich; membership of the cavalry (see HIPPEIS) was a social asset, and the cavalry played an important part in ceremonial, in the procession of the *Panathenaea, for example, which is depicted on the Parthenon frieze. For the development of the role of the cavalry in Rome see EQUITES.

The aristocratic pride that possession of horses represented especially in Greece was most apparent in the keen competition for the equestrian events in the panhellenic *Games, the horse- and chariot-races. It was considered typical of the ostentatious pride of Alcibiadēs, the Athenian aristocrat, that he entered more chariots for the Olympian games (probably in 424 BC) than anyone else had ever entered (and won first, second, and fourth places). To the Greeks and Romans horses were for riding, racing, and fighting; they were never used as draught-animals, this function being performed by mules and oxen. The types of horse known in the ancient world may be seen illustrated in their art, especially sculpture. The small, fine-headed horses of Greece and Etruria may be contrasted with the massy, heavy-headed Persian horses that appear in sculpture from Persepolis. See also Xenophon's treatises the *CAVALRY COMMANDER* and *HORSEMANSHIP*.

Horte'nsia, daughter of Quintus *Hortensius Hortalus, famous as having made, in 42 BC, contrary to custom, a speech in the Roman Forum against a proposal of the triumvirs to impose special taxation on the property of wealthy women. Her plea was successful.

Horte'nsius, title of a lost dialogue by *Cicero ((1) 5), composed in 45 BC after the death of the orator after whom it was named (see below). It was an introduction and an exhortation to the study of philosophy, which Cicero defended against Roman prejudices. It was based on the *Protrepticus* of Aristotle (of which only fragments survive). Reading it inspired St *Augustine to seek the 'wisdom' of God (*Confessions* 3. 7).

Horte'nsius Ho'rtalus, Quintus (114–50 BC), generally known as Hortensius, a distinguished Roman orator, consul in 69 BC, eight years older than Cicero and the latter's chief rival in the law-courts. He won fame on his first appearance in 95 BC pleading on behalf of the province of Africa which was accusing a Roman governor of corruption. He was eclipsed by Cicero as the leading orator of the day after Cicero's success in 70 BC at the trial of Verres, whom Hortensius was to defend (see CICERO (1) 1); he had no opportunity to speak since Verres prudently retired after Cicero's opening attack. Hortensius was consul-designate at the time. After Cicero's own consulship of 63 BC he and Hortensius were friends rather than rivals, though Cicero never quite trusted him, and avoided dedicating a work to him until the latter was dead; he praises Hortensius' oratory during the latter's lifetime in *De oratore* (53 BC), and after his death in *Brutus* (about 45 BC). Many stories are told of Hortensius' wealth and of his flamboyance, which extended to his oratorical performances: the pains he took in arranging his toga, and his theatrical deliveries (so that he was called Dionysia after a well-known dancer of the day), were keenly observed by the tragic actors Aesopus and Roscius, as was his florid ('Asianic') style of language (see ORATORY). He also possessed a prodigious memory.

Hōrus, Egyptian god, the child of *Isis, usually called by the Greeks Harpocratēs, corresponding to the Egyptian Harpechrat, i.e. 'Har (or Horus) the child'. After the death of his father Osiris he succeeded in overcoming many obstacles and killing the wicked Set (Typhon to the Greeks). He became popular in Hellenistic times, and is represented as a child holding a finger to his lips, taken to indicate mystery and secrecy; among the Romans he was regarded as

the god of silence. Herodotus identified him with Apollo, others with Heracles and Eros.

houses and furniture

1. *Greek.* For the Homeric house see HOMERIC AGE. Greek houses of the fifth and fourth centuries BC were constructed out of sun-dried brick and presented a plain façade to the street broken only by a door and perhaps a few small windows. The door led through a porch (*prothyron*) into a courtyard (*aulē*), with an altar to Zeus Herkeios ('of the courtyard') in the middle. There might be a simple colonnade (*prostōon*) along one or more sides. Various rooms led off the courtyard: in a fair-sized house, a dining room (*andrōn* or *andrōnītis*, 'room for the men'), an important and better decorated room than most, a room or rooms set apart for the women (*gynaikōnītis*), bedrooms, a kitchen, a small bathroom, work- and storerooms. In houses with two storeys the women's rooms were often on the first floor with the bedrooms (reached by an external staircase). The same basic plan served for shops and workshops as well. There might be some decoration of walls with paintings and tapestry but usually they were left in bare brick; there was no heating apparatus (such as the Romans used) beyond a stone hearth set in the floor or a movable charcoal brazier; smoke escaped through holes in the roof. The floors were of beaten earth, and though floor coverings were known to Homer and became common in Hellenistic times, their use in the fifth century was considered effeminate. There was no drainage; water was provided by wells and rainwater cisterns. Furniture was simple and austere, the principle kinds being the chair or stool (*diphros, thrēnys*), the table (*trapeza*), always three-legged, small, and portable, the couch (*klinē*) used both for dining and sleeping, and the chest (*kibōtos, larnax*) in which clothes and bedding were stored. Utensils were piled on the floor or hung on the wall; lamps stood on shelves or in niches.

2. *Roman.* At Rome, the house (*domus*) of the well-to-do family was centred on a rectangular hall, the *ātrium*, with an opening in the tiled roof to admit light and rain (the latter flowing into a tank in the floor known as the *impluvium*) and to allow the exit of smoke from the hearth. The arrangement of rooms leading off it was more or less stereotyped. Originally these rooms derived their light from the atrium. At the further end opposite the entrance was the *tablīnum*, a room or alcove which contained the family records and archives (*tabulae*), and, if the family was aristocratic, the *imāginēs* or portrait-masks of ancestors. The *atrium* was originally the only room in the house, and in retaining many of its original functions it remained the most important. It was a reception room, the place where the women of the house carried on their spinning and weaving; the marriage bed

(*lectus geniālis*) of the master and mistress was placed here, and here also was the hearth (*focus*) sacred to the family *lares.

From the late second century BC, under Greek influence, a garden (*peristylium*) was added at the back of the *atrium*. This was a court open to the sky, enclosed by a colonnade and decorated with flowers and shrubs. Beyond the colonnade could be found various rooms including dining rooms, sleeping apartments, living rooms, kitchen, and store rooms. The *atrium* now served only as the official reception-room; see also TRICLINIUM.

By the end of the republican period the mass of the population at Rome lived in large tenements called *insulae* ('islands') four or more storeys high, let in single rooms to lodgers. They soon acquired a bad reputation for being overcrowded and unsafe, and their construction of timber and sun-dried brick entailed the constant risk of fire and collapse. Strabo says that to reduce the risk Augustus limited the height of houses on streets to 70 feet (about 21 m.). The *insulae* provided no 'home' in the sense of a family hearth as the focus of domestic religion. They were owned by capitalists such as *Crassus; Cicero had a share in one, and M. *Caelius Rufus had apartments in one, suggesting that not all were unsavoury.

Under the empire, the houses of the rich had their walls decorated with marbles or frescoes, and the floors with mosaics. There were skilful arrangements for warming the rooms from a central furnace (see HYPOCAUST), and elaborate bathrooms. Houses had an abundant supply of water, sometimes even in the upper storeys (see AQUEDUCTS). Some of the very rich possessed spacious country houses (see VILLA), by the sea or on the spurs of the Apennines, designed especially to suit the changing seasons or to command beautiful views. *Glass was in use, and some windows might be glazed.

Etruscan and Roman furniture is modelled on Greek but became more luxurious and used costlier materials. The Etruscans introduced a new style of chair with rounded back; they also had metal lamp stands which could hold clusters of candles and were movable. Once the olive began to be extensively cultivated (from *c*.200 BC), oil lamps began to be substituted for candles and were common in the first century BC, made of clay or bronze, holding more than one wick; these were placed on metal stands or sometimes adapted for hanging from the ceiling. The Roman chair (*cathedra*), stool (*sella*), and couch (*lectus*) follow Greek models, the couch sometimes being provided with a back rest, like a sofa; feather mattresses and cushions were introduced. Under the empire new kinds of furniture appear, including sideboards (on which valuable plate might be displayed) and cupboards with drawers, sometimes used for holding papyrus-rolls. Tables became heavier; those made of rare woods or expensively inlaid were greatly admired. At that period the houses of the wealthy contained many decorative objects, statues, vases, and carpets from the East.

Hundred-handers, see HECATONCHEIRES.

Huns, nomadic people, formidable horsemen, originating in central Asia, described by the contemporary historian *Ammianus Marcellinus as savages who drank the blood of their slaughtered enemies. Their advance westward in the fourth century AD to the area north of the Black Sea caused terror and the widespread migration of *barbarian peoples across the frontiers of the Roman empire; see FALL OF ROME, GOTHS, VANDALS. The Huns subsequently occupied the area of modern Hungary, Rumania, and south Russia. Under their leader *Attila they sacked Italy in 452, but spared Rome. After Attila's death in 453 his empire was broken up among his sons and thereafter ceased to play an important role in history.

hunting. For the treatise on this subject attributed to Xenophon see CYNEGETICUS. The huntsman usually pursued on foot, using dogs and nets. The commonest quarry was hares and deer. In the case of boar-hunting, a dangerous sport, a large company of huntsmen was recommended, with Laconian hounds (see DOGS) and a full complement of nets, javelins, spears, and caltrops. The Romans appear not to have been greatly addicted to hunting except for philhellenes like Scipio Aemilianus (the emperors Trajan and Hadrian were keen hunters, but they were Spaniards). It was, however, regarded as good training for war. When the younger Pliny hunted he took his writing materials with him. The frequency of hunting incidents in the elegiac poets and Virgil is due to Greek sources or Greek influence. The Roman writers on hunting, *Grattius and *Nemesianus, are largely influenced by the poetical tradition, and give no true picture of Roman conditions.

Hyaci'nthus, in Greek myth, a beautiful youth of Amyclae (an ancient city near Sparta, in pre-Dorian times the seat of a royal palace). He was loved both by the god Apollo and by Zephyrus (the west wind), and preferred Apollo. Zephyrus, out of jealousy, blew a discus thrown by Apollo so that it struck and killed Hyacinthus. From his blood sprang a flower bearing his name, perhaps a kind of iris, with markings interpreted as reading *aiai*, 'alas, alas'.

Hy'adĕs ('raining ones'), in Greek myth, five daughters of *Atlas, the nymphs who supplied moisture to the earth, and were nurses of Dionysus. They were placed by Zeus as a group of stars between the *Pleiades and Orion. The start of the season of rainy weather was marked by their setting just before sunrise at the beginning of November.

Hyda'spēs, river of the Punjab ('land of five rivers'), now the Jhelum. The classical name is derived from the Sanskrit Vitasta. It was the scene of the defeat of Porus by *Alexander the Great (see 6) and so is used by the poets to indicate the distant and romantic East.

Hȳdra, see HERACLES, LABOURS OF 2.

Hygiē'a (Hygieia), the Greek goddess of health, daughter of *Asclepius.

Hygī'nus, Gaius Julius (c.64 BC–AD 17), Spanish *freedman of Augustus, friend of Ovid, one of the greatest scholars of his day. His writings, now lost, covered a wide range of subjects, including a commentary on Virgil, a treatise on agriculture, historical and archaeological works, and works on religion. Under his name, though not in fact by him, two works have survived, a handbook of mythology, *Genealogiae* or *Fabulae*, compiled from Greek sources probably in the second century AD, and a manual of astronomy, also based on Greek sources. A work on land-surveying and the laying-out of camps, probably of the third century AD, is attributed to a certain Hyginus *Gromaticus.

Hȳlas, in Greek myth, son of the king of the Dryopēs. Heraclēs, having killed the father, carried off the son to accompany him on the expedition of the *Argonauts. When the Argo touched at Cios on the coast of Mysia (Heracles having broken his oar), Hylas was sent for water. The water-nymphs, falling in love with him, drew him into the spring and he was lost. The Argonauts went on their way, but Heracles remained to look for him. The Mysians held a ritual search for him every year, in obedience to Heracles' orders, even in Hellenistic times.

Hyllus, eldest son of *Heraclēs by Dēianeira; see also HERACLEIDAE.

hymenae'us, wedding-song sung by the bride's attendants as they escorted her to the groom's house (see EPITHALAMIUM). The name was derived from the custom at Greek weddings of calling out, *Hymen o Hymenaie*, supposedly an invocation to a deity, Hymen, who presided over weddings.

Hyme'ttus, mountain in Attica overlooking Athens on the coast, famous for its *honey and its marble. The honey is mentioned by Strabo and Pausanias; the marble is of a bluish-grey colour. It was when the glow of sunset appeared on Hymettus that Socrates drank the hemlock.

hymns, in Greece, songs sung in honour of a god or hero. In earlier times the word had not acquired its later specialized meaning and included hexameter poetry that was mainly narrative, e.g. the *Homeric Hymns. Of true cult hymns very little remains; there are a few fragments of those by Alcman, Alcaeus, Pindar, and Bacchylides. The clearest indications of their style are given by some of the choruses in tragedy which are hymnal in form. The cult form consists of an invocation of the god under his several names and titles (clearly the aim was to be comprehensive), and a recital of his deeds, followed by a short prayer. The Latin hymns of Catullus (see poem 34) and Horace were probably modelled on Greek hymns and written to be read rather than performed (but see *CARMEN SAECULARE*). Horace's hymn to a wine-jar (*Odes* III. 21) is an amusing parody. The greatest Latin hymn, in effect if not in form, is the invocation to Venus at the beginning of the *De rerum natura* of *Lucretius.

Hȳpā'tia (d. AD 415), Alexandrian Greek mathematician and Neoplatonist philosopher, daughter of the mathematician Theon; she was murdered by a Christian mob. See NEOPLATONISM.

hype'rbaton, figure of speech in which words are transferred from their usual order, commoner in poetry than in prose.

Hype'rbolus (d. 411 BC), an Athenian *demagogue during the Peloponnesian War, reputedly a lamp-maker by trade, detested by Thucydides and Aristophanes. After the death of *Cleon in 421 he became a leader of the people. A few years later, perhaps in 417 BC, an *ostracism took place in which he expected to effect the removal of *Nicias or *Alcibiades, but he was outmanœuvred and was himself ostracized. He went to Samos, where he was murdered by revolutionary oligarchs.

Hyperbo'reans ('dwellers beyond the north wind'), a fabulous people believed by the Greeks to live a blessed existence in the distant and inaccessible north, worshippers of Apollo, who traditionally spent the three winter months with them (see DELPHIC ORACLE). Offerings supposed to be from them arrived at Apollo's shrine on Delos in classical times, passed from city to city. Those specially-favoured by the gods might spend their afterlife with the Hyperboreans.

Hyperei'dēs (389–322 BC), distinguished Athenian orator, a contemporary of Demosthenes. At first he was a professional speech-writer, but becoming involved in politics he made a name as an accuser of prominent men; early in 343 he successfully prosecuted Philocratēs (see PHILIP (1) 2). He supported Demosthenes in the latter's attacks on Philip II of Macedon and proposed a decree to honour him, but in 324 BC at the time of the Harpalus affair (see DEMOSTHENES (2) 1) Hypereides appeared as one of his prosecutors. He was one of the principal promoters of the war of revolt against Macedon (the Lamian War) after the death of Alexander the Great in

323 BC and pronounced the funeral oration (which survives) on the Athenian dead. After the defeat of the Greek alliance, when the Macedonian ruler demanded the surrender by Athens of those hostile to Macedon, he was seized and put to death, along with Demosthenes and others.

Hypereides' works were lost in antiquity and virtually nothing was known of them until in the mid-nineteenth century papyri were discovered containing extensive remains of six speeches, including fragments of *Against Demosthenes*. He was a pupil of *Isocratēs but in general avoids his florid and rather articificial style, resembling *Lysias rather in the grace and simplicity of his language, and using a slightly colloquial vocabulary. One of the best preserved speeches is *Against Athenogenēs* which was found in a papyrus of the second century BC and is therefore one of the most ancient of all classical manuscripts. This speech was praised in the treatise *Longinus on the Sublime*. In it Hypereides makes a lively and urbane speech for a client about a contract for the purchase of a perfumery (in order to free a slave, a youth with whom the client was in love). In his speech *For Euxenippus* (which survives complete) he defends a man accused of reporting a dream falsely after he had slept in the shrine of Amphiaraus in order to ascertain from a god-sent dream the ownership of a piece of land (see DIVINATION). In *For Lycophron* he defends an aristocratic cavalry commander on a charge of adultery, complicated by other issues. In his defence of the famous hetaera Phrynē (whose lover he was), to procure her acquittal he had her uncover her breasts at the climax of his speech. The speech has not survived. The ancients ranked Hypereides second to Demosthenes. Longinus compared him with the pentathlete who wins the whole competition by being second-best in every particular.

Hȳpe'rion, in Greek myth, one of the *Titans, husband of his sister Theia and father by her of *Helios (Sun), Selēnē (Moon), and Eōs (Dawn). Homer and the poets occasionally give his name to Helios.

Hyperm(n)e'stra, in Greek myth, one of the daughters of * Danaus.

Hypnos, in Greek myth, the god of sleep, the (fatherless) son of *Nyx (Night) and brother of Thanatos (Death) with whom he is usually linked, especially in vase-paintings. He lives in the Underworld, but is kindly to men.

Throughout antiquity he is thought of as a winged youth who pours sleep-inducing liquid from a horn, or touches the tired with a branch.

hypocaust (*hypokauston*, Lat. *hypocaustum*), in ancient architecture, a system for heating rooms with warm air, invented at Rome *c*.100 BC, originally in order to produce a vapour bath. The floors were raised on pillars and the air underneath heated by a furnace and piped through flues. By the end of the first century BC its use had spread to private houses.

hyporchē'ma (pl. *hyporchēmata*, 'dance-song'), form of Greek choral *lyric in which dance, with mimetic movements, was prominent. The very few surviving fragments of *hyporchemata* by Pindar and Bacchylidēs give little indication of form or content.

hypo'theses, the ancient term used to describe the introductory notes found in the manuscripts of Greek tragedy and comedy. These notes are derived ultimately from Alexandrian scholarship and give basic information about the plays, the outline of the plots and details of production. See DIDASCALIA.

Hypsi'pylē. According to Greek myth, the women of the island of Lemnos, in consequence of neglecting the rites of Aphroditē, were inflicted by the goddess with a foul smell and so were deserted by their husbands who preferred to have concubines from Thrace. The women jealously killed all the men on the island, except that Hypsipyle spared her father, king Thoas, son of the god Dionysus, and aided his escape. When the *Argonauts came to Lemnos they spent a year there and married the women, fathering the next generation of Lemnians who were known in consequence as Minyae. Hypsipyle bore twin sons to Jason, called Euneōs and Thoas. Some time after, she was driven away from Lemnos when it was discovered that she had saved her father; she was captured by pirates and sold to Lycurgus, king of Nemea. When the Seven were marching against Thebes (see SEVEN AGAINST THEBES) and their army halted near Nemea, Hypsipyle, who was nurse of the king's infant son Opheltēs (or Archemorus), laid the child on the ground in order to lead them to a spring. During her absence the child was killed by a serpent. The Seven gave him a splendid funeral and founded the Nemean games in his honour. Hypsipyle was saved from the anger of Lycurgus by the army and finally rescued by her sons who arrived and recognized her. The story is told in the *Thebaid* of Statius.

I

Ia'cchus. At Athens, during the celebration of the Eleusinian *mysteries, the main public event was the procession from Athens to Eleusis along the Sacred Way, in which the crowd shouted *Iakch' o Iakche*, it was presumed in invocation of a deity Iacchus who was being celebrated together with Demeter and Persephonē. He was variously said to be the son of Demeter or of Persephone, or to be Dionysus by another name, because of the similarity between his name and Bacchus (i.e. Dionysus). Herodotus recounts that after the Persians had conquered the Greek mainland shortly before the battle of Salamis a great cloud of dust 'as if caused by thirty thousand men' was seen coming from the direction of Eleusis, and the Iacchus shout was heard proceeding from it. The cloud moved towards Salamis, where the Greek army was stationed; the festival prevented by war was being celebrated supernaturally, with good omen for the Athenians. In Italy Iacchus was occasionally identified with *Liber, as in the temple of Cerēs on the Aventine.

ī'amb (*ĭambos*, Lat. *ĭambus*), **īa'mbic;** see METRE, GREEK 1, 2, 4, and 5.

Ia'mbē, see MYSTERIES.

īa'mbic poetry, that poetry in which the iambic metre prevails (see METRE, GREEK 2). The Greek word *iambos* is of unknown derivation but seems to be Asiatic in origin. It is the metre in which the dialogue parts of Greek tragedy and comedy are written. Aristotle thought that it was nearest in rhythm to ordinary speech and for that reason was used in satirical and abusive verse. The poet *Archilochus was apparently the first to use the term, and applied it to his own satiric verse written in the iambic metre. *Semonidēs and *Hipponax who also wrote iambic poetry were, like Archilochus, Ionian Greeks. *Solon the Athenian may have imitated them in writing his political poems in iambics, the metre suiting the controversial and prosaic nature of the subject matter, although the poems were not abusive. The *Iambi* (a book of iambic poems) of *Callimachus are miscellaneous in character, though many are satirical. Iambics were not much used in Latin for personal invective. The iambic trimeter occurs in only three poems of Catullus, though its variant, the scazon (see METRE, LATIN 3 (i)), is used in eight poems. Not all of these poems are abusive. When Catullus refers to his 'iambi' he is

probably referring to the satirical nature of his poetry, not to the metre. Horace's claim to have been the first to introduce 'Parian (i.e. Archilochian) iambics' into Latin is probably justified, for his largely iambic *Epodes* contain the elements of Archilochus' poetry—abuse, satire, moralizing, themes of friendship.

Ia'mblichus. **1.** (d. *c.* AD 330), Neoplatonist philosopher with an interest in magic, born in Syria, who studied under *Porphyry in Rome or Sicily. Later he founded his own school in Syria. Among his surviving writings are an 'Exhortation to Philosophy' (*Protreptikos logos*) largely comprising extracts from earlier philosophical works and valuable as a source-book, a work on Pythagoreanism, and a defence of ritualistic magic, *De mysteriis* ('on mysteries'), interesting for the light it throws on fourth-century superstition. A number of his commentaries (now lost) on Plato and Aristotle are much quoted by *Proclus.

2. Author of a Greek novel (of the second century AD), which has not survived.

iambo'graphers, in Greek, writers of *iambic poetry.

Ia'mus, in Greek myth, son of the god Apollo and the mortal Evadne, the mythical ancestor of the prophetic clan of the Iamidae in Greece. Seers from this clan made prophecies from the evidence of the sacrifices on the altar of Zeus at Olympia. The famous seer Teisamenus employed by the Spartans during the Persian Wars was of this clan. See OMENS.

Iani'culum, see JANICULUM.

Ia'petus, in Greek myth, one of the *Titans (children of Gaia and Uranus), and father, by Clymenē the daughter of *Oceanus, of Prometheus, Epimetheus, and Atlas. From the Renaissance he was identified with Japhet, son of Noah.

Ia'sion, in Greek myth, brother of Dardanus and lover of *Demeter. He met Demeter at the wedding of Cadmus and Harmonia, and lay with her in a thrice-ploughed field; the offspring of this union was the god *Plutus (Gk. Ploutos, Wealth).

Ībē'ria (or Hibēria), one of the ancient names for *Spain.

Ībis, said to be the title of an abusive poem by *Callimachus, addressed to a certain 'Ibis' who was supposed to have been the poet *Apollonius Rhodius. The poem has not survived. The Latin poet Ovid, while in exile at Tomis, also wrote a poem, in elegiacs, with this name, in the form of a curse directed at an unknown enemy, in which he expresses indebtedness to Callimachus' 'brief poem'. Ovid's poem is full of abstruse mythological learning.

I'bycus, Greek lyric poet of the sixth century BC from Rhegium (in south Italy). It is said that he refused to become tyrant there and withdrew to Samos, where he worked at the court of the tyrant *Polycrates. The Alexandrian scholars arranged his works in seven books; to judge from the surviving fragments his poems seem to have consisted largely of narrative choral *lyric in the style of *Stesichorus. They also included *encomia of which an interesting specimen, to Polycrates, has turned up on papyrus, and personal love poems. The small fragments of his poems that have survived in quotation show that he had a taste for the colourful and picturesque, and wrote vividly on the power of love.

According to legend Ibycus was attacked and killed by robbers. A flock of cranes was passing overhead and Ibycus exclaimed, 'Those cranes will avenge me'. Soon after, one of the robbers in a crowded theatre, seeing a flock of cranes hovering overhead, said to his companion, 'There go the avengers of Ibycus'. This was overheard, and the murderers brought to justice.

Ica'rius. **1.** In Greek myth, inhabitant of Attica who entertained the god Dionysus and received from him the gift of wine. He gave some to his neighbours, who, feeling the effect and concluding that they were poisoned, killed him (see ERIGONE). He gave his name to an Athenian deme.

2. In Greek myth, of Sparta, father of *Penelope (wife of Odysseus).

Icaromeni'ppus, see LUCIAN.

I'carus, see DAEDALUS.

I'celus, a god of *dreams, who sent to men dreams in the form of monsters.

Ice'nī, a British tribe inhabiting East Anglia; see BRITAIN 4.

Ichneu'tae, see SOPHOCLES.

Ictī'nus, one of the three Greek architects who worked at Athens in the time of Pericles under the direction of Pheidias. He designed the *Parthenon in collaboration with Callicrates.

ictus, a term in metric, 'beat' or stress. See also ARSIS.

Ida (Idē). **1.** Range of mountains in southern Phrygia, the southern boundary of the Troad. It was there that the Trojan *Paris was said to have

been exposed and brought up by shepherds, and to have fallen in love with Oenonē. From its summit Zeus watched the Trojan War.

2. Mountain in the centre of Crete. In a cave on this mountain (or on Mount Dictē) Zeus is said to have been born.

Idae'an Dactyls, see DACTYL, IDAEAN.

Īdas, see LYNCEUS and MARPESSA.

Ideas, Platonic, see PLATO 4.

Ides, see CALENDARS 5.

Ido'meneus, in Greek myth, grandson of *Minos and leader of the Cretans at the siege of Troy. In a storm on his way home he vowed to sacrifice the first living creature that met him, if he returned safe. This proved to be his son. He fulfilled, or tried to fulfil, his vow; in consequence a plague broke out and Idomeneus was driven into exile by the Cretans (and settled, according to Virgil, on the south coast of Italy).

Īdo'thea, see EIDOTHEA.

idyll (apparently from the Greek *eidyllion*, 'little form'), the name given in Roman times to the poems of *Theocritus, which describe some episode or scene from idealized rural life. Hence 'idyllic' is used to describe an idealized state or scene of tranquil happiness, particularly of a pastoral nature.

Īleithyī'a, see EILEITHYIA.

Ī'lia (or Rhea Silvia), according to Roman legend, the daughter of the Roman king Numitor, a *Vestal Virgin, who became by Mars the mother of Romulus and Remus (see ROME 2), and was thrown into the river Tiber by order of her uncle Amulius. The river-god took her as his wife (see Horace, *Odes* I. 2).

Ī'liad (*Īlias*), Greek epic poem by *Homer in twenty-four books (for this division see HOMER 6). The title is derived from Ilion, another name of *Troy, which was so called from Ilus, its legendary founder.

The subject is the 'wrath of *Achilles', arising from an affront to his honour given by *Agamemnon, leader of the Greek army at the siege of Troy, and the tragic consequences of his wrath. This is an episode in the history of the siege, occupying no more than a short part of its tenth and final year, and yet its action in effect encapsulates the whole war, with the final death of the Trojan hero *Hector symbolizing the fall of Troy that will soon follow. The gods in Olympus are divided in their sympathies and intervene on one side or the other, or even fight among themselves. Their mixture of sublimity and frivolity makes a remarkable contribution to the character of the *Iliad*. The events of the epic are as follows.

Books 1–8: A plague has broken out in the Greek camp, and the seer Calchas declares that it has been brought about by the anger of Apollo on behalf of his priest whose daughter, Chrysēis, has been taken prisoner and given to Agamemnon as a gift of honour; if Agamemnon surrenders her the plague will cease. Agamemnon angrily consents but takes in her place Brīsēis, a slave-concubine belonging to Achilles. The latter, angry at this high-handed act, retires to his tent with his Myrmidons (see AEACUS) and his friend Patroclus and refuses to take further part in the fighting. The Greek army, deprived of his powerful support, suffers serious losses and is driven away from the plain of Troy and back to the camp.

Book 9: Being now hard-pressed, Agamemnon recognizes the wrong that he has done, and sends an embassy to Achilles offering to make handsome amends if he will lay aside his anger. But Achilles has been nursing his grievance and is disillusioned with war and fame; he rejects Agamemnon's offers and announces that he will not fight until Hector fires the Greek ships.

Books 10–17: As a result, he sees the Greeks suffer further losses. His friend Patroclus is stung to shame and regret by their reverses, and obtains Achilles' permission, when the Trojans are actually setting fire to the Greek ships, to join in the fight; moreover Achilles, himself moved by the danger to the Greeks, lends his armour to Patroclus and summons the Myrmidons. The Trojans are driven back, but Patroclus is killed by Hector, and retribution for his anger thus comes to Achilles.

Books 18–22: Achilles, maddened with grief, puts aside his anger with Agamemnon and reveals himself unarmed to the Trojans, who retreat from Patroclus' body. His mother Thetis brings him new armour forged by the god *Hephaestus, and he goes out to avenge the death of his friend. He kills Hector and treats the dead body with gross outrage, tying it by the heels to his chariot and dragging it through the dust.

Books 23–4: The body of Patroclus is then buried and the event marked by funeral games. Priam, the aged king of Troy, comes to Achilles to beg the body of his son and save it from the threatened fate of being thrown to the dogs. Achilles' passion has now spent itself: he feels his common humanity with Priam, pities him, and returns the body. The poem ends with the funeral of Hector.

Side by side with this tragedy we have a picture of life in Troy under the shadow of impending disaster: Priam and *Hecuba bereaved of many of their sons, and finally mourning their dearest, Hector; Hector talking to his wife *Andromachē, his helmet frightening their young son; Helen, conscious of her guilt and the trouble she has brought on Troy, despising Paris, wishing that she had died at birth, and kindly treated by Hector, Priam, and the other Trojans.

A host of other warriors are presented, some of them sharply characterized (see entries for Aeneas, Ajax, Diomedes, Menelaus, Odysseus, Nestor, Sarpedon, Glaucus). Notable passages are the following: the Catalogue of Greek ships, 2. 484–785; the Catalogue of Trojan forces, 2. 786–877; the *Teichoscopia* (the 'viewing from the walls' of the Greek chiefs by Helen and Priam), and the duel of Menelaus and Paris, book 3; the *Epipōlēsis* (Agamemnon's 'review' of his forces), 4. 223–421; the exploits of Diomedes, 4. 422 ff. and book 5; the meeting and recognition of Diomedes and Glaucus, 6. 119–236; Hector's farewell to Andromache, 6. 370–529; the *Doloneia* (the night expedition of Odysseus and Diomedes, the slaying of the spy Dolon and of the Thracian *Rhesus, and the capture of the latter's horses), book 10; the *Diŏs apatē* ('deception of Zeus' by Hera), 14. 153–362; the forging of the arms of Achilles, 18. 468–617; the fight of Achilles with the river Scamander, 21. 211–382; the funeral games for Patroclus, 23. 257–897. The principal events, from the beginning of the fighting to the death of Hector, occupy four days.

For medieval legend connected with the story of Troy see TROJAN WAR.

Iliad, Little (Lat. *Ilias parva*), title of a lost poem of the *Epic Cycle, attributed to Leschēs of Pyrrha or of Mitylene in Lesbos, a sequel to Homer's *Iliad*, in four books. The events it is said to cover are the awarding of the arms of Achilles to *Odysseus; the madness and suicide of *Ajax; the ambushing of *Helenus and his prophecy about the capture of Troy through the agency of *Philoctetes, who kills Paris; the arrival at Troy of *Neoptolemus (Achilles' son); the secret entry of Odysseus into Troy and his stealing of the *Palladium; and the entry of the Wooden Horse. See *ILIUPERSIS*.

Īlias Latīna ('Latin *Iliad*'), Latin version of Homer's *Iliad* in 1,070 hexameters by an unknown author, perhaps of the first century AD: on internal evidence the author's name may be Baebius Italicus and the date not later than AD 68. The work seems to have been a popular school text.

Īli's(s)us, one of the two streams which water the Athenian plain (the other being the Cephisus). It has its source in springs on Mount Hymettus and descends through the stony plain of Attica past Athens on the south-east and south. In the neighbourhood of the city the river-bed is generally dry, but its shady banks and spreading plane trees have been immortalized in Plato's dialogue *Phaedrus*.

Ī'lium, see TROY.

Iliūpe'rsis (*Īliou persis*, 'sack of Troy'). **1**. Title of a lost poem of the *Epic Cycle attributed to Arctīnus of Miletus, a sequel in two books to the

Little *Iliad*. The events are said to be the following. The Wooden Horse enters Troy; two snakes destroy *Laocŏon and one of his sons; Sinon (see TROJAN HORSE) signals to the departed Greek army to return to Troy, and the Greeks take the city; *Neoptolemus kills Priam, Menelaus finds Helen, and *Ajax son of Oileus tries to carry off Cassandra, pulling over the statue of Athena in the attempt; Odysseus murders *Astyanax, son of Hector, and Neoptolemus takes Hector's wife *Andromachē as prize; the Greeks set fire to the city, sacrifice *Polyxena at the tomb of Achilles, and sail home, with the goddess Athena planning vengeance for Ajax' violation.

2. See STESICHORUS.

Illy'rii, group of tribes, *Indo-European in origin, who occupied a region to the east of the Adriatic Sea bordering on Macedonia and Epirus.

Īlus, see TROY.

Īlȳthī'a, see EILEITHYIA.

imā'ginēs, wax masks of Romans who had held *curule office; they were kept in cupboards in the *atrium* of the family *house. They received religious cult and, on the death of a member who had held similar office, were worn by actors in the funeral procession, who were clad in robes such as the ancestors would have worn, e.g. those of a consul.

Ima'ginēs, dialogue by *Lucian.

Ima'ginum libri XV, see VARRO.

imperā'tor (Gk. *autocratōr*), originally a Roman military title given by acclamation of the soldiers to a general after his victory. He kept the title after his name until he celebrated his *triumph. The first properly attested *imperator* was L. Aemilius *Paullus in 189 BC. The increasing importance of the army in the late republic made the title the symbol of military authority, and Julius Caesar used the title permanently. After 38 BC Octavian (later the emperor Augustus) used the title as a *praenomen* (see NAMES), i.e. Imperator Caesar, not Caesar Imperator. Thus it came to signify the supreme power of the emperor. The use of the title as *praenomen* did not prevent its being applied in the original manner, after the emperor's name, when he had won a victory. The formula *imperator Caesar* was sometimes extended to members of the imperial family who shared the emperor's power (compare AUGUSTUS, THE).

impe'rium, in the Roman constitution, 'power to command', the supreme administrative authority vested in certain individuals, involving command in war and originally the interpretation and execution of the law (including the power to impose the death penalty); later, Roman citizens could not be executed without

trial, and had the right of appeal to the people. *Imperium*, originally the authority of the king, was possessed under the republic by consuls, military tribunes with consular power, praetors, dictators, and *magistri equitum* ('masters of the horse'), and by proconsuls and propraetors in their provinces. Sometimes a private citizen was granted *imperium* for a specific purpose. Very occasionally there was conflict between holders of *imperium* in the same territory (as in 67 BC between Pompey in pursuit of pirates and Metellus, proconsul of Crete). In a comparable situation in 43 BC Cicero proposed, successfully, that Brutus and Cassius should be granted *imperium maius* ('superior authority') over that of the other governors in the East. When Augustus in 23 BC resigned the consulship (see ROME 9), his *imperium* was made 'superior' (*maius*) to that of every other provincial governor.

imports and exports, see ATHENS 4 and ROME 13.

I'nachus, see IO.

In Catili'nam, see CICERO (1) 2 and CATILINE.

incubation, practice common among Greeks and Romans of sleeping when ill in the temple of a god, most usually of *Asclepius, so as to receive from the god in a dream information about a remedy. The god was sometimes approached in this way for help in other troubles, finding a lost article for example. Before sleeping in the temple the patient observed three days of ritual purity, followed by various sacrifices, a gift of money, and finally an offering of three cakes, to Success, Recollection, and Right Order (Themis). The patient slept in a chamber in the temple precinct, wearing a laurel-wreath. Such a cure is described by Aristophanes in his comedy *Plutus*. See also ARISTEIDES (3) and DIVINATION.

Index rērum a se gestā'rum, epitomized 'summary of the deeds of Augustus by (the emperor) himself', inscribed on bronze in his mausoleum. Copies were placed in various temples of the empire; one of these survives (imperfectly) on the temple of 'Rome and Augustus' at Ancȳra (Ankara), besides fragments of others; see MONUMENTUM ANCYRANUM.

indictions (Lat. *indictio*). Under the Roman empire the word denoted the compulsory purchase of food and other goods for the army and the court; from the time of Diocletian (emperor AD 284, d. 316) it was applied to the annual assessment of all levies in kind. From 287 indictions were numbered serially in five-year cycles; from 312, in fifteen-year cycles. Thus the number of the indiction came to be used for dating financial years (which began on 1 September) and then as a general system of dating. See CALENDARS.

Indi'getēs, indigitame'nta, respectively, a class of Roman gods and a list of religious formulae used in invoking gods, taken from the books of the *pontifices* ('priests'). The meaning of the terms is obscure.

Indo-European. In the nineteenth century it became known that many past and present European languages, including Greek and Latin, are more or less closely related. (European languages outside this class include Basque, Estonian, Finnish, Hungarian, Lapp, and Turkish.) It has proved possible to reconstruct from them many features of their common proto-language, known as Indo-European, and also to group the various branches of Indo-European into families. The family from which Greek eventually developed was spoken by peoples living in the third millennium BC in an area of south Russia, the Greek branch being around the western shores of the Black Sea, whence they eventually migrated into Europe, including the Balkans and Greece, perhaps *c.*2200 BC (see GREECE). It had been thought in the mid-nineteenth century that many place-names and plant-names in Greece belonged to the early non-Indo-European population, as, for example, those ending in *-nth(os)* and *-ss(os)*, such as Corinth, Tiryns (Tirynthos), Parnassos (compare Cnossos in Crete), hyacinth, and narcissus. It is now thought that they are Indo-European but from a different family, and they indicate that earlier Indo-European speakers took possession of Greece before the arrival of those speaking the language that was eventually to develop into Greek, at the end of the third millennium. It has proved difficult, if not impossible, to distinguish between pre-Indo-European elements in Greece and the superimposed layers of Indo-European, and to separate the characteristics of the former.

To some extent the vocabulary of the Indo-Europeans provides evidence for the structure of their life and society and even for their religious ideas. It may be inferred that they were a pastoral people, to whom cattle and horses were important, agriculture less so, and that they were ignorant of the sea and sea-faring. Their society was patriarchal; they were organized in large kinship groups or *tribes, each tribe ruled by a king aided by a council, and with an assembly of free men. All of this suggests that they were a warlike, semi-nomadic race, becoming the masters of the developing civilizations on which they imposed themselves. Attempts have been made to identify as pre-Indo-European an essentially matriarchal religion with a Mother goddess and Mistress of Animals (in *Crete especially), but the evidence is far from clear (see RELIGION, GREEK I).

The Indo-Europeans, on the other hand, had a developed, polytheistic religion with cult of the gods and a poetry concerned with heroes and gods. Originally Indo-European is the male Sky-Father of Greeks and Romans, Zeus Pater (Diespiter, Iuppiter), and so are Helios, the sun-god, and Eos (Aurora), the dawn-goddess, although in Greek religion these last are not among the important Olympian *gods. Parallels between Greek and Vedic (Sanskrit) poetic forms suggest that the Indo-Europeans had a tradition of oral poetry composed in measured lines, relating the exploits of gods and heroes (perhaps the remote origin of Homeric epic). Similarities between Greek and Indian or Iranian cult practice also suggest an Indo-European origin for the Greek cult of the dead and the pouring of libations, *choai,* as well as for animal sacrifice.

See also LATIN LANGUAGE.

i'nferi, di ('gods of the Underworld'), in Roman religion; see RELIGION, ROMAN I.

Inō, in Greek myth, a daughter of *Cadmus and Harmonia, and wife of *Athamas. See also DIONYSUS for her death and transformation into a sea-goddess. It was she who saved Odysseus when his raft was wrecked, giving him her scarf to keep him afloat (Homer, *Odyssey* 5).

In Pisō'nem, see CICERO (I) 4.

inscriptions, see EPIGRAPHY.

Institutes, see GAIUS and JUSTINIAN.

Institūtiō'nēs, see GAIUS and JUSTINIAN.

Institūtiō'nēs dīvī'nae, see LACTANTIUS.

Institū'tiō ōrātō'ria ('education of an orator'), treatise in twelve books by *Quintilian.

Book 1 deals with the early education of the future orator; the influence of nurses, parents, slaves; the superiority of school education over education at home; the importance of a thorough study of language as a foundation; and the need for Greek and various other subjects. The subject-matter should not be dictated by commercial consideration.

Book 2, which begins with the boy's entry to the school of rhetoric, is on the general method and aim of training in rhetoric, on the qualifications of a good teacher and the proper treatment of pupils, and on the need in an orator for moral character as well as wide knowledge.

Books 3–7 pass on to technicalities: the three kinds of oratory (judicial, deliberative, laudatory), the parts of a speech (exordium, narrative, etc.) and the arrangement of matters to be dealt with. These are principally related to speeches in the courts, and are illuminating when read in conjunction with the speeches of Cicero.

Books 8–11 deal with style and delivery. Of these book 10 contains the famous discussion of those authors, Greek and Latin, who are to be studied as 'particularly suitable to those proposing to become orators', and Quintilian's judgements on them; it should be remembered that these are made solely from a rhetorical viewpoint. Of the Greeks he places Homer first for his many qualities and in particular his oratorical skills. Pindar is by far the greatest of the lyric poets, especially for his flood of eloquence; Aristophanes, Eupolis, and Cratinus are the greatest of the writers of Old Comedy, Menander of New. Sophocles and Euripides are the most accomplished of the tragedians, for Aeschylus, in spite of his dignity, is often uncouth. In history he sets far above the others Thucydides ('compressed and concise and always pressing on') and Herodotus ('delightful, clear, and discursive'). He discusses Demosthenes and his lesser rivals. He praises Plato's acuteness, and his 'divine and Homeric' gift of eloquence, Xenophon's unaffected style, and Aristotle's knowledge and penetration. Of the Romans he places Virgil first, as most nearly approaching Homer. The style of Lucretius he thinks difficult. Ennius he compares with those ancient sacred groves whose mighty oaks are admired less for their beauty than for their sanctity. Ovid is too much an admirer of his own genius. Satire, for the Roman Quintilian, is 'all our own'; he places Horace as a satirist before Lucilius, and mentions Persius favourably. Horace is also the only lyric poet in Latin worth reading (he mentions Catullus only for the invective of his iambics). He thinks the (now lost) *Thyestes* of Varius the equal of any Greek tragedy, and commends the (also lost) *Medea* of Ovid, but makes no high claim for Roman tragedy. Comedy is Rome's weakest point. In history he regards Sallust as equal to Thucydides, Livy to Herodotus. Cicero is a match for any Greek orator: Quintilian compares his style with that of Demosthenes, and though scrupulously fair to the merits of both cannot conceal the pleasure he feels at Cicero's overall brilliance. Caesar might have been his rival had he devoted himself to the subject; as it is he equals Cicero in force, acumen, and vigour. Quintilian is critical of Seneca's style and bad influence but admits the value of his subject matter. Book 11 discusses the manner of delivery.

Book 12 sums up Quintilian's view of the ideal orator, not a speaker merely, but a man of highest character, properly trained in morals as well as in taste; in the words of Cato, *vir bonus dicendi peritus*, 'a good man who knows how to speak'.

interce'ssio, at Rome, the veto which a magistrate might impose upon a motion carried by another magistrate of equal or lower rank. Only the *dictator could not be obstructed by a veto since he had no equal or superior. With this exception, tribunes of the plebs could veto the official acts of all magistrates, including each other.

interrex, at Rome, originally an individual appointed by the senate at the death of a king to hold temporary power until a new king was appointed. Under the republic, if both consuls should die or resign, *interreges*, who had to be senators and patricians, were appointed until new consuls were elected. The last known example of such an event was in 43 BC when both consuls were killed.

In Vati'nium, see CICERO (1) 4.

Īō, in Greek myth, daughter of Inachus, mythical first king of Argos. When Zeus fell in love with her she suffered disturbing dreams. Inachus, in response to oracles he had consulted, then turned her out of the house. Zeus (or his wife Hera) changed her into a heifer, for purposes of deception; Hera set the herdsman Argus, who had eyes all over his body, to watch over her, and sent a gad-fly to sting her continuously, so that she would not rest long enough for Zeus to make love to her. Zeus sent Hermēs to kill Argus, but Io, now constantly haunted by the herdsman's ghost, was forced by the gad-fly to wander far and wide. Part of the Adriatic Sea was thenceforth called Ionian (Gk. Iŏnios, not derived from Iōnia, for which see ION), and the Bosporus, 'ox-ford', was named after her crossing. When she passed by *Prometheus bound to his rock he prophesied to her what was to come. Eventually she reached Egypt where Zeus changed her back to human form, touched her with his hand, and thus begat his son Epaphus ('he of the touch'). According to one version she was worshipped there as the goddess Isis (Epaphus being identified with the bull-god Apis). Epaphus was the ancestor of Danaus and Aegyptus.

Io'batēs, see BELLEROPHON.

Ioca'stē, see JOCASTA.

Iolā'us, see HERACLES and *HERACLES, CHILDREN OF.*

I'olē, see HERACLES and *TRACHINIAE.*

Īōn. 1. Eponymous ancestor of the Ionian Greeks (Gk. Iōnes or Iāŏnes). According to Greek myth (as preserved by Euripides; see below), Crĕūsa, daughter of *Erechtheus, king of Athens, was loved by the god Apollo and bore him a son Ion, whom for fear of her father's anger she left in a cave under the Acropolis. Hermes carried the child to Delphi, where he was reared as a servant of the temple. Creusa afterwards married Xuthus (see HELLEN), but as they remained childless they went to Delphi to ask for offspring. At the order of Apollo, Xuthus accepted as his son the first person he met on coming out of the shrine, and this was Ion. Creusa, angered at the adoption of one whom she supposed to be a bastard son of her husband, attempted to kill the boy, but being detected, and in danger of death, took refuge at the altar of Apollo. By the intervention of the priestess, who produced the swaddling clothes in which the infant Ion had been wrapped, Creusa recognized her child, and the goddess Athena revealed what had happened. Ion returned to Athens with Xuthus and Creusa to become, according to Athena's prophecy, the ancestor of the Ionian race.

2. Of Chios (b. *c.*490 BC, d. before 421), Greek poet famed chiefly for his tragedies, which were studied and admired by the Alexandrian scholars and by *Longinus on the Sublime*. None of them has survived. It is possible that he wrote a comedy as well, thus being the exception to the rule that no Greek wrote both (see COMEDY, GREEK 1). Interesting anecdotes link Ion with many of the famous names of the fifth century: he heard Cimon speak in the assembly, met Aeschylus at the Isthmian games and Sophocles when he was *strategos* in 441/40, and was defeated in the tragic contests at the Great Dionysia of 428 when Euripides won with *Hippolytus*. A long quotation by *Athenaeus (*Deipnosophistai* 603), from Ion's prose work *Epidemiai* ('visits'), in which he vividly describes an evening spent with Sophocles, gives cause for regret at the loss of his writings.

Ion. 1. Greek tragedy (with a happy ending) by *Euripides, probably written a little after 412 BC. It deals with the story of Ion as in (1) above. The essential features of the plot—a woman seduced, her child exposed, the subsequent recognition, and happy consequences—became typical of New Comedy (see COMEDY, GREEK 6; also MENANDER).

2. Dialogue by *Plato (see 2) named after a *rhapsode of that name.

Iō'nia, Ionians. The country of Ionia comprised a portion of the west coast of Asia Minor, roughly from Smyrna to Miletus (in the south), as well as the adjacent islands, and was inhabited by Ionian Greeks who had migrated there from mainland Greece *c.*1000 BC (see MIGRATIONS and ASIA MINOR). Ionians as a Greek people are mentioned once by Homer, the Ionian cities not at all. Ionia was the region in which early Greek literature and *philosophy were principally developed (see also HOMER and HISTORIOGRAPHY 1). For the legendary origin of the name see ION (1). All who traced their origin from the city of Athens and kept the festival of the Apaturia were reckoned as Ionians (see PHRATRIAI). Athens could not claim to be the mother-city of all Ionians, but she may have some claim to have organized the first migrations: the four ancient tribes of Attica, the Geleontes, Aigikoreis, Argadeis, and Hopletes (supposedly named after the sons of Ion), are found among the Ionians also. For their dialect see DIALECTS.

Ionian Revolt (499 BC), see PERSIAN WARS 1.

Io'nic verse, see METRE, GREEK 8 (i)

Īphiana'ssa, the name under which *Iphigeneia appears in Homer.

Ī'phiclēs, half-brother of *Heraclēs.

Ī'phiclus, in Greek myth, son of Phylacus. He imprisoned for a year the seer *Melampus, who discovered the reason for Iphiclus' childlessness and cured him. Iphiclus subsequently became the father of Podarcēs and *Protesilaus.

Īphi'cratēs (*c.*415–353 BC), Athenian general; see ARMY, GREEK 4.

Īphigenei'a, in Greek myth, a daughter of *Agamemnon and Clytemnestra, whom Agamemnon was forced to sacrifice. The Greek fleet, when about to sail to Troy, was held by contrary winds at Aulis (see TROJAN WAR). The seer Calchas declared that Artemis required the sacrifice of Agamemnon's daughter (authorities vary on the reason), and Agamemnon sent for Iphigeneia on the pretext that she was to be married to Achilles. In Aeschylus' *Oresteia the belief is that she was actually killed; the version of the *Cypria, followed by Euripides in *Iphigeneia in Tauris* (see below), describes how, when she was about to be sacrificed, Artemis carried her off to be her priestess in the land of the Tauri (the Crimea), substituting a deer for her at the altar. The Tauri had a savage rite by which all strangers coming to their land were sacrificed to Artemis, and Iphigeneia was required to consecrate the victims.

Iphigeneia's brother *Orestes, in order to expiate the blood-guilt incurred by his murder of Clytemnestra, was ordered by Apollo to secure the image of Artemis of the Tauri and bring it to Attica. He had been separated from Iphigeneia since he was a child and believed her dead. He and his friend Pyladēs were captured by the Tauri and ordered to be sacrificed, but Iphigeneia discovered her brother's identity and was persuaded to escape with him from the country, carrying off the image of the goddess. The latter was set up in a temple in Attica—both Halae and Brauron in historical times claimed the distinction—where Iphigeneia became the perpetual priestess of Artemis. Other stories tell that she was married to Achilles on Leucē or in Elysium.

Iphigenei'a at Aulis (*Īphigeneia hē en Aulidi*), Greek tragedy by *Euripides, produced posthumously, perhaps in 405 BC. The text may have been completed by another hand after Euripides' death. The play deals with the story of the sacrifice of *Iphigeneia at Aulis. The poet has Agamemnon wavering and in despair. After sending for Iphigeneia, on the urging of his brother Menelaus and on the pretext of her marriage to Achilles (of which the latter knows nothing), he cancels the summons, but the second messenger is stopped by Menelaus. Clytemnestra and Iphigeneia arrive. Menelaus repents of his interference and offers to give up the expedition, but in vain; Agamemnon now dreads the anger of the army if the expedition is called off. Achilles learns that he has been used in a deception and boldly tries to save the girl. But Iphigeneia, after pleading for her life, changes her mind; resolving to be sacrificed in order to save the Greek expedition, she acquiesces.

The tragedy shows important developments: it is concerned almost exclusively with the interplay of the various characters, and the role of the chorus is insignificant.

Iphigene'ia in Tauris (the Latin title, meaning 'Iphigeneia among the Taurians'; Gk. *Īphigeneia hē en Taurois*), Greek tragedy by Euripides, produced probably a little before 412 BC. The play deals with that part of the legend of *Iphigeneia which relates to her life in the land of the Tauri as the priestess of Artemis. The heroine is represented as a woman who has long brooded over her grievances, bitter against the Greeks who sought to murder her, but longing for home. The coming of Greeks to the Tauric Chersonese (Crimea) for the first time during her priesthood and the discovery that she is required to sacrifice her own brother arouse her natural affections. A plan of escape is devised. Thoās, king of the Tauri, is fooled; Iphigeneia, Orestes, and Pylades escape with the image of the goddess.

Ī'phitus, see HERACLES.

Ipsus, battle of, see MACEDONIA 2.

Iris, in Greek myth, the goddess of the rainbow. She was the daughter of Thaumās (son of Pontus, Sea) and Electra (daughter of Oceanus), and consequently sister of the *Harpies. Iris is not only a personification of the rainbow but also a messenger of the gods, particularly of Hera. In Virgil the rainbow is the path along which she travels. According to the early Greek poet Alcaeus she is the mother by Zephyrus of Eros. She had no cult.

iron. During the Mycenaean age, iron in Greece was as costly as gold. In Homer the predominant metal is bronze; iron appears incidentally, as something valuable: Achilles offered as a prize a 'mass of unwrought iron', such as might be used for ploughshares. In the thirteenth century BC iron was mined in the north-east of Hittite Anatolia. From the tenth century BC it replaced bronze as the metal in everyday use. Greece had a few sporadic iron deposits, notably in Laconia, and a few islands, but in the early period of *colonization Greeks may have gone west in search of iron from Elba and Etruria, where the Etruscans started mining c.900 BC. The main source for the Greeks, however, was the south-east coast of the Black Sea, an area associated with the semi-legendary Chalybes, known to the Greeks as the first

workers in iron (compare DACTYLS, IDAEAN and TELCHINES). By the seventh century BC iron was the most widespread form of currency, in the form of iron spits (*obeloi*; see MONEY 1). Under the Roman republic iron was brought from Spain, and later from Gaul. British iron seems to have been used locally. Cast iron was not used in the ancient world. Iron statues were made by chasing pure wrought iron. Weapons were made of mild steel, hardened by quenching in water. The Romans seem to have known how to relieve brittleness by tempering. See also MINES.

Iron Age, the period succeeding the *Bronze Age. In *Greece it lasted from c.1050 to c.850 BC; see also DARK AGE, PROTO-GEOMETRIC, and GEOMETRIC. In *Italy it was the period c.1000–600 BC.

Īrus, in Homer's *Odyssey*, book 18, the beggar with whom Odysseus fights.

Īsae'us (c.420–after 353 BC), an Athenian orator of whose life little is known. He is represented as either Athenian or Chalcidian by birth, a pupil of *Isocrates and a teacher of *Demosthenes. He was a *logographos* (see LOGOGRAPHERS (2)): all his speeches were composed for others to deliver, and he took no part in political life. Of some fifty speeches with which he was credited, eleven and part of a twelfth have survived. The eleven all deal with cases of inheritance and are important as illustrative of Athenian testamentary law. He was considered 'clever in elaborating pleas for the worse cause' according to Dionysius of Halicarnassus. He is comparable with *Lysias in plainness and simplicity of language but more elaborate in setting out his (sometimes complex) logical proofs, and more vigorous in controversy. In these latter characteristics it may be thought that he influenced Demosthenes.

Īsagō'gē, see PORPHYRY.

Isidore of Seville (bishop AD 602–636), an important link between the learning of classical antiquity and the Middle Ages; he tried to keep knowledge of the ancient world alive at an unpropitious time. The most famous of his writings was an encyclopaedia of arts and science in twenty books, *Etymologiae* ('etymologies') or *Origines* ('origins'), a work of the same sort as, but superior to, that of *Martianus Capella. It was in widespread use for the following 600 years, and dealt with the seven liberal arts as well as geography, law, medicine, natural history, food and drink, and many lesser topics. Some of the sections are valuable in preserving the contents of authorities now lost.

Isis, great Egyptian goddess, sister and wife of *Osiris and mother of Hōrus. She represented the female productive force of nature: Herodotus identified her with Demeter, but in the early Hellenistic age she is identified with Aphroditē and also with the Ptolemaic queens. Her symbol was the cow. She was also, with Osiris, thought of as ruler of the Underworld. In Greece, her worship was established in Piraeus by the fourth century BC, by Egyptians living there. Her cult, which in some respects was akin to a mystery religion (see MYSTERIES), spread to Rome in the second century BC. See also RELIGION, ROMAN 3.

Islands of the Blest, in Greek myth, islands in the stream of *Ocean in the fabulous far West beyond the Pillars of Hercules (see HERACLES, LABOURS OF 10), where after their death specially favoured mortals, notably the *heroes and the first generation of humankind, the men of the *Golden Age, spent a blissful afterlife, ruled over, it was often said, by *Cronus. Many other fabulous beings were thought to live in the same region: Chrysaor, Callirhoē, the Gorgons, the Hesperidēs, the Hecatoncheires, and the Sirens (see individual entries). See also ELYSIUM.

Ismē'nē, see OEDIPUS and ANTIGONE.

Īso'cratēs (436–338 BC), Athenian orator.
1. Hampered by physical weakness, Isocrates played no direct part in the political affairs of his city, but his written speeches no doubt influenced public opinion and provide a valuable commentary on the issues of the day. He was the son of a wealthy Athenian, Theodorus, and fell under the influence of Socrates. (Plato in the *Phaedrus*, writing when Isocrates had become famous, represents Socrates at an earlier period prophesying the young man's future greatness either as an orator or as a philosopher.) He studied under Prodicus, Gorgias, and Teisias (see ORATORY 1 and SOPHISTS) and the moderate oligarch *Theramenēs. His family lost its fortune in the latter part of the Peloponnesian War, and Isocrates appears to have fled from the tyranny of the Thirty (see ATHENS 5) to Chios, where he taught rhetoric, and to have returned to Athens on the restoration of democracy. For a period he wrote speeches for others to use in the courts. (Orations 16–21 belong to this period.) In about 392 he opened a school at Athens and also began to write political discourses. The school was distinguished from those of the sophists by the greater breadth of education it gave and by its emphasis on morals (see EDUCATION); also by its method, which relied greatly on the efforts and hard work of the pupils themselves. It became famous, and pupils from all parts of the Greek world came to it, including the historians *Ephorus and *Theopompus, Androtion the atthidographer (see ATTHIS), the orators *Hypereidēs and *Isaeus, and the politician *Timotheus (2).

The political writings of Isocrates were chiefly devoted to the cause of Greek unity. When his appeal in the *Panegyricus* met with no

success (see 5 below), his panhellenism took another form: he sought a strong man to assume the leadership of a united Greece in an expedition against Persia, and hoped to find him first in the Spartan king Agesilaus, then in Dionysius I of Syracuse, followed by Alexander tyrant of Pherae (in Thessaly), and later perhaps by Archidamus III of Sparta. But his chief hope lay in Philip II of Macedon (see *Philippus*, 5 below). His political speeches (or rather, essays cast in the form of speeches, for they were intended to be read) also include other topics of a more limited scope. Isocrates died at a great age shortly after the Athenian defeat by Philip at Chaeronea in 338 BC, it is said by starving himself to death when his third appeal to Philip failed.

2. Isocrates was the first orator of significance to treat rhetorical prose as a work of art (compare GORGIAS). His rhetoric is of a literary character rather than practical oratory. His sentences are long and flowing, the periods complex and highly wrought so that clarity is sacrificed to form; his avoidance of hiatus and of dissonance is almost total. This is Attic prose at its most elaborate. Owing to the popularity of his school, his influence on literature, Latin as well as Greek, was long-lasting, extending to Cicero. Nine letters (some of which may not be genuine) and twenty-one of his speeches survive.

3. Of the epideictic pieces, the *Busiris* (c.390) and the *Encomium of Helen* (written in the 380s), are criticisms of the works of other rhetoricians, in which he shows how the themes should have been handled; the *Evagoras* is an *encomium on a king of Salamis (in Cyprus) who had recently died (374); the *Panathēnāicus*, begun when he was ninety-four and completed three years later, perhaps for delivery and publication at the time of the Panathenaic festival of 342, is mainly a laudatory historical review of the deeds and constitution of Athens.

4. Of the two essays on education, *Against the Sophists* (391 or 390) and *On the Antidosis* (353), the first is a protest against what he feels to be the narrow and futile instruction given by the sophists and an exposition of his own principles of teaching. The second is a defence of himself and his educational method, and the chief source of our knowledge of his system of education. Isocrates had been challenged, as a wealthy citizen, by a certain Megacleidēs, to undertake a trierarchy (see LITURGY) or accept an exchange of properties (see ANTIDOSIS). The matter had come to court and Isocrates had been defeated. *On the Antidosis* is a self-vindication.

5. The political writings are his most important. The *Panegyricus* ('festival oration'), his version of a conventional subject treated by Gorgias and Lysias (see 1 above), was published in 380 after ten years of composition. It is in structure and expression perhaps his greatest work. Its

theme, a plea for the union of the Greek city-states under the joint hegemony of Athens and Sparta, is supported by a historical review. The *Philippus*, written in 346, is generally considered the most important of his works. It was written after the voting of the Peace of Philocratēs between Athens and Philip and before the latter's intervention in Phocis (see PHILIP (1) 2), and is an appeal to Philip as a *Hellene and descendant of Heracles to unite the Greek states under his leadership and undertake an expedition against the Persians. The *Platāicus*, written in 373 after the seizure and destruction of Plataea by the Theban Nīcoclēs, is a plea for Athenian retaliation purporting to be spoken by a Plataean to the Athenian assembly. *On the Peace* (Lat. *De pace*), written shortly before the Social War ended in 355 with Athens' failure to retain her League, is a denunciation of an imperialist policy as a way to bankruptcy; Isocrates urges, in place of the limited peace being made with the allies, a Common Peace, and the foundation of colonies in Thrace as a way out of economic difficulties. It is inspired by strong feeling, and is the most vigorous of Isocrates' speeches, a companion piece to the *Revenues* of Xenophon. Both works illuminate the policies of *Eubulus. The *Archidamus* (366) purports to be spoken by the future Spartan king (Archidamus III) on the Theban proposal that, as a condition of peace, Sparta shall recognize the independence of Messenē. In the *Areopagīticus*, probably written in 355, Isocrates contrasts the degenerate Athenian democracy of his day with the earlier democracy of Solon and Cleisthenes, with particular reference to the function, formerly exercised by the *Areopagus, of censor of public morals. (John Milton's *Areopagitica* of 1644 deals with state censorship of publications.) This uncharacteristic outburst on the ills of Athenian democracy may have been occasioned by the financial and moral impoverishment of Athens after the Social War.

6. The forensic speeches (see 1) are of less importance. They were written for private litigants and include one for the son of (the famous) *Alcibiadēs. An Athenian citizen alleged that the elder Alcibiades had robbed him of a team of horses, and sued his son for their value. The speech is interesting for the defence it contains of the father's character.

Isthmian festival, games, see GAMES, PUBLIC, IN GREECE 1 and 4.

Italy (Italia), a word perhaps meaning 'land of calves' (as if from Vitelia; Lat. *vitulus*, 'calf'); the name appears to have been originally applied to the southern half of the toe of Italy. By 450 BC it meant all of the south-west peninsula (now Calabria), subsequently inhabited by the Bruttii, and by 400 it also included Lucania (the mountainous district of south Italy north of Calabria). By the third century BC it meant the whole Italian peninsula south of Liguria and Cisalpine Gaul. After the death of Julius Caesar in 44 BC Cisalpine Gaul too became part of Italy.

By the end of the Italian Neolithic period, *c.*2000 BC, there were several different, pre-*Indo-European cultures in what is now Italy. The Italian Bronze Age, which lasted from *c.*1800 to 1300 BC, was heralded by the arrival of Indo-European invaders. One important early group, apparently from central Europe, settled in the Po valley; their villages and culture are known as *terramare*, from the local name for deposits of rich 'black earth' which have accumulated on the sites. Other groups spread their Indo-European (later, Italic) dialects as they came. In *Sicily and Sardinia, however, Bronze Age culture seems to have arrived from Crete and the Greek mainland earlier than in the peninsula, and Sicily enjoyed for some time greater prosperity and a higher cultural level. It was during this time that the massive stone fortresses, *nuraghi*, were built in Sardinia. Transition to the Iron Age, which occurred at the beginning of the second millennium as a result of contact with the Aegean and Danubian areas, was slow, and not completed until *c.*900 BC in Sicily and a century later in the peninsula. As in the case of the Bronze Age, the Iron Age culture had its regional characteristics. The most important region at this time was that stretching west and south from Bononia (Bologna) to Etruria and Latium, called Villanovan (from Villanova, a town near Bologna); it played a significant part in the development of the *Etruscan civilization, of which it may be an early stage. Migrations to Italy across the Adriatic ceased by about 800 BC, and were succeeded by the arrival of settlers from Greece, who moved into Sicily and south Italy between the mid-eighth and mid-sixth centuries (see COLONIZATION, GREEK 2). Their arrival brought Italy into contact with the more advanced Greek and Asian cultures of the eastern Mediterranean, and introduced a more civilized, even luxurious, life-style than had hitherto been possible.

During the Italian Iron Age (down to *c.*600 BC) many peoples rose to prominence who were subsequently to play an important part in the early history of the peninsula. The Ligures lived in the north-west corner of (modern) Italy and in Corsica, descendants of the original pre-Indo-European population but speaking an Indo-European dialect in historical times. The Veneti, also speaking an Indo-European dialect, occupied the territory in north-east Italy between the Po and the Alps, and eastwards towards Illyria. The *Etruscans had already spread northwards from Etruria on the west coast and had overrun an area north and east of the Apennines. The area south of the Tiber was held by the Latins, who were to become the leading people in Italy in early historical times (see LATIN LEAGUE, LATIUM, and ROME 4). The valleys of the central southern Apennines were occupied by a large group of tribes known as Umbro-Sabellians, the most important of which were the Umbri, Sabini, Aequi, Marsi, Volsci, and the Samnites or Sabelli. They seem to have been of mixed stock, descended from Indo-European invaders from across the Adriatic and from the previous population. All these peoples except for the Ligures and the Etruscans are known as Italic, as are their (Indo-European) dialects. Chief among the latter were Umbrian in the north and Oscan, with variations, in the south, as well as Latin (see LATIN LANGUAGE). See also CAMPANIA and SICILY. Thus at the beginning of historical times, at the end of the sixth century BC, the Italian peninsula as a whole was inhabited by a variety of races: *Celts in the north, Etruscans south of these, Greeks in the south of the peninsula, and in the centre an agglomeration of kindred tribes, Umbrians, Sabellians, Oscans, and Latins. These peoples differed from each other to a greater or lesser degree in race, language, and culture. The physical characteristics of the country are no less varied, from the Apennines and other mountain ranges, which produced a hardy, frugal mountain people, to the warm southern seaboard, where Greeks led an easy and luxurious life, e.g. at Sybaris and Croton. The achievement of *Rome during the republican period was to conquer and absorb all the inhabitants of the peninsula, receiving from them in return influences which are clearly reflected in Roman literature.

I'thaca (Ithakē), one of the loveliest islands in Greece, but one which played no part in classical Greek history. It is situated off the west coast of Greece, east of the island of Cephallenia. It was the island-kingdom of Odysseus, according to Homer, 'lying low, furthest up the sea-line towards the darkness', 'a rugged island'.

Ithō'mē, Mount, isolated and easily fortified mountain in the plain of *Messenia (in the Peloponnese), the rallying point of the Messenians in their struggles for independence against Sparta. In the Third Messenian War, after the great earthquake of 464 BC, the Messenians, having revolted, took refuge there. They were blockaded but did not surrender for a number of years. In 369 BC, when Messenia recovered its independence with the help of the Theban general Epaminondas, a new capital Messenē was founded on the slopes of Mount Ithome.

itinerā'ria ('itineraries'), lists of stations on the Roman roads and of the distances between them, with other relevant information. These were common under the Roman empire, and copies were kept in libraries or engraved on stone. The most important of those which have survived is the *Itinerarium Antoninianum*, of the late third century AD, a collection of routes perhaps used for moving troops. The fourth-century Jerusalem (or Bordeaux) Itinerary, which gives the routes from the one place to the other, by way of Arles, Milan, Constantinople, and Antioch, is one of many guides for Christian pilgrims.

I'tylus, see AEDON.

Itys, see PHILOLEMA and AEDON.

Iuba, see JUBA.

Iugu'rtha, see JUGURTHA.

Iu'lia, Iu'lius, see JULIUS.

Iūlus (or Ascanius), the son of Aeneas; see *AENEID*.

Iu'ppiter, see JUPITER.

iūs trium libero'rum ('the right of three children'). In an effort to check the falling birth rate the emperor Augustus granted certain privileges, referred to by this title, to parents of three (or more) children. The mother was freed from some of the restrictions of guardianship, and the father had a prior claim to magistracies and exemption from certain taxes. Later the privileges were extended as a mark of the emperor's favour to individuals not strictly qualified to receive them, e.g. Martial and the Younger Pliny.

Iutu'rna, see JUTURNA.

Iuve'ntas, see JUVENTAS.

Ixī'ōn, in Greek myth, a Thessalian, the ruler of the Lapiths, who married Dia, daughter of Dēioneus (or Ēioneus); their son was Pirithŏus (see CENTAURS). He was traditionally the first Greek to murder a kinsman. When his father-in-law came to fetch the bride-price that had been promised, Ixion contrived that he should fall into a pit of burning coals. For this murder he could obtain purification only from Zeus. When Zeus invited Ixion to Olympus for the rite, Ixion tried to seduce Zeus' wife Hera. Hera complained to Zeus who, to trap Ixion, formed a cloud in the likeness of Hera, and by this cloud, Nephelē, Ixion became the father of the centaurs (or of Centaurus, a monster, who mated with the mares on Mount Pelion to produce the centaurs). As a punishment for his crime Zeus had him bound to a fiery wheel, constantly revolving, in the Underworld.

J

Jāni'culum, the hill on the west bank of the river Tiber opposite Rome (but not one of the seven hills); the name is connected with the early king Janus (see below), who was said to have had a citadel here. From early times it was a defensive outpost of Rome. A flag flew from the hill when assemblies were held in the Campus Martius (see COMITIA 1); its removal was a sign that an enemy was approaching and public business was abruptly ended. The removal of this flag by the praetor Q. Metellus Celer brought to a close the trial of Rabirius in 63 BC (see PRO RABIRIO). The grove in which C. *Gracchus died was on the Janiculum.

Jānus, in Roman religion, the god of gates and doorways and subsequently of beginnings in general. The word properly means an archway or gateway, free-standing rather than set in a wall, and used originally for ceremonial purposes. Janus was originally one of the principal Roman gods: the 'god of gods' in the hymn of the *Salii, the first to be named in any list of gods in a prayer, even before Jupiter, and the first to receive a portion of the sacrifice. The first month of the Roman *calendar was named after him, and his priest was the *rex sacrorum. His symbol was a double-faced head, looking in opposite directions. A statue of Janus Bifrons ('with two faces') stood with that of Saturnus in the palace hall of King Latinus (Virgil, *Aeneid* 7. 180). In Rome his temple was a small bronze shrine in the Forum, the Janus Geminus, 'double Janus', consisting of an arched passage with doors at its eastern and western ends. The doors were closed only in time of peace. Livy records that from the time of Numa to his own day the shrine had been closed only twice, after the First Punic War (241 BC) and after the victory of Octavian at Actium (31 BC). The emperor Augustus in the *Monumentum Ancyranum* says that it had been closed on three occasions in his principate. Janus rarely figured in myth. According to one Roman tradition he was an early king of Latium; his son Tiberinus was drowned in the river Tiber, so giving it his name.

Jāson (Iāsōn). 1. In Greek myth, son of Aeson and leader of the *Argonauts.

2. **Jason of Pherae,** tyrant (c.385–370 BC) of the Greek Thessalian town of Pherae who sought control over the whole of Thessaly; he achieved his object in 374, winning over the last important city, Pharsalus, by diplomacy.

Ancient sources have suggested that he may have aimed at becoming the dominant power in Greece and even at leading a Greek expedition against Persia. After the defeat of Sparta by Thebes at the battle of Leuctra in 371 (see SPARTA 4) he mediated between these two, perhaps not wishing to see Thebes unduly aggrandized, and he ordered to be destroyed the Spartan fort at Heraclea which commanded the pass at Thermopylae, to prevent anyone approaching his own territory by that route in future, but also to allow himself free passage into Greece. In 370 he alarmed Greece by his plan to display the strength of his army at the next Pythian festival, and to preside at the games, but he was assassinated before he could carry out his plans and his further intentions remain unknown.

javelin-throwing, see ATHLETICS (vi).

Je'rome, Saint (c.347–420), Eusebius Hieronymus (his name in English being a version of the latter), Latin father of the Church. Born at Strido near Aquileia (near the Adriatic coast in north Italy) of a well-to-do Christian family, he was educated at Rome (as a pupil of *Donatus) where he was baptized but continued to enjoy a life of dissipation, and then travelled in Gaul before returning to Aquileia and devoting himself to an ascetic life. In about 374 he went to Antioch, where he started upon theological studies and learned Greek, but remained devoted to classical Latin literature. It was here that he had a nightmare in which he found himself facing the Judgement Seat and, upon being asked his condition and answering that he was a Christian, heard the reply, '*mentiris; Ciceronianus es, non Christianus*' ('You lie; you are a Ciceronian, not a Christian'). From 375 to 378 he lived in the desert of Chalcis on the frontier of Syria, where he learned Hebrew with much difficulty. But interference by the other hermits made life there intolerable for him. He returned to Antioch (c.377), where he was ordained priest, but theological disputes there made him decide to go back to Rome. Making his way westwards he stayed at Constantinople (c.379), where he attended the lectures of the great Greek theologian Gregory of Nazianzus. From 382 to 385 he stayed at Rome, acting as secretary to Pope Damasus and preaching asceticism. The Christian women who enthusiastically embraced his teaching included Marcella, Paula, and her daughter Eustochium. His advocacy of asceticism and his suspected aspiration to become Pope aroused hostility, and, accompanied by Paula and Eustochium, he left Rome. He travelled first by way of Antioch to Jerusalem, then to Egypt, and subsequently to Palestine; he settled finally at Bethlehem, where Paula founded a monastery over which he presided, and three convents for women which she herself directed. He spent the rest of his life there in intense scholarly activity and vigorous, often virulent, controversy, and died in 420.

Jerome's scholarship was unsurpassed in the early Church. His Latin is classical in its purity; he had absorbed the works of Cicero (as his nightmare suggested), Virgil, Horace, and others to such an extent that constant echoes of them are to be found in his writings. His most important work was his translation of most of the Bible from the original languages into Latin, the so-called *Vulgate (i.e. the 'common text'). This work had originally been suggested to him by Damasus when he stayed at Rome in the 380s. The purpose of the work was to construct an authoritative text to supersede the Old Latin manuscripts with their serious textual variants which were circulating at the end of the fourth century (Latin texts of the Bible earlier than Jerome's Vulgate are known as the 'Old Latin' versions). He published a revision of the Gospels in 383, using as well as Old Latin texts a Greek manuscript closely related to the *Codex Sinaiticus. It is a matter of dispute whether or to what extent he revised the remaining books of the New Testament. Soon after, he produced a revision of the Psalter. After he had settled in Bethlehem he worked on another text of the Psalter, using as a basis *Origen's Hexapla. After this he turned to Job and other books of the Old Testament, but he soon became convinced that he needed to work directly from the Hebrew original and to ignore the unsatisfactory Greek translation (the *Septuagint). His Latin translation from the Hebrew occupied him for about fifteen years. There was at first considerable opposition to Jerome's translations from those who remained faithful to old and familiar versions, but the excellence of his work was gradually realized, and his were the translations chosen when (probably in the sixth century) the various books came to be collected into a single Bible.

His other principal works were the *Chronicle*, a Latin translation from the Greek of *Eusebius, with a supplement covering the period 324–78, one of the most important documents for dating events in the ancient world; *De viris illustribus* ('concerning famous men'), a series of notices of 135 Christian writers, modelled on the work of *Suetonius which has the same title, and closely following Eusebius where the latter had dealt with the same authors; and at least 63 biblical commentaries. There is also a collection of 150 letters (including a number of forgeries), some of which are letters to Jerome and include ten from St *Augustine. These are of great interest and historical importance. Jerome had a passionate nature, and his letters reflect his tender affection for his friends, his hatreds and combative nature in controversy, his attacks on hypocrites and heretics, and his condemnation of himself. In his twenty-second letter he recounts how, when he separated himself from his home and family, he could not separate himself from his library; he would fast, but then afterwards commit the sin of reading the pagan Cicero. In art he is often depicted with a lion at his feet.

jewelry, see GEMS and TOREUTIC ART.

Joca'sta (Iokastē, Epikastē in Homer), the mother and wife of *Oedipus.

Jōsē'phus, Flāvius (AD 37–after 93), Jewish historian, of priestly descent and a Pharisee. He visited Rome in early adulthood, returning to Jerusalem in 66 on the eve of the Jewish Revolt against Roman domination (Judaea having been a province since AD 6; see HEROD). He tried to persuade the nationalist leaders that war with Rome could lead only to disaster, but without success. When the revolt broke out in the same year, Josephus was given command of Galilee by the Sanhedrin. He survived the siege of Jotapata and was captured; his life was spared when he prophesied to the Roman commander Vespasian that he would become emperor, but he was kept in captivity until his prediction was fulfilled in 69. After the fall of Jerusalem in 70 he did what he could to help his Jewish friends. Subsequently he settled in Rome, where he received Roman citizenship, a house, and a pension. His first work, *Bellum Iudaicum* ('history of the Jewish War against the Romans'), in seven books, was originally written in Aramaic for circulation among the Jews who settled in Mesopotamia after the Diaspora, and later translated into Greek. The rest of his works are in Greek (Jerome called him 'the Greek Livy'). The first part of the *Bellum Iudaicum* deals with the history of the Jews during the two hundred years or so before the revolt; the rest is devoted to the events of the war, many of which he witnessed in person. It ends with a moving description of the self-slaughter by the defenders of Masada. His next work was *Antiquitates Iudaicae* ('Jewish archaeology') in twenty books, a history of the Jews from Adam to AD 66, giving a fuller account than the *Bellum Iudaicum* of the events covered by the latter work. Josephus' third work was his *Vita* ('life'), not a full autobiography but a reply to the allegations of his enemy, Justus of Tiberias, that he had instigated and organized the Jewish Revolt in Galilee, a dangerous charge against one who lived in Rome by the favour of the emperor (Domitian at this period). His last work, in two books, was entitled 'Concerning the Antiquity of the Jews' but widely known under the title given it by Jerome, *Contra* (or *In) Apionem* ('against Apion', an Alexandrian Greek scholar); this is an eloquent defence of Jews, their religion, law, and customs, against anti-Semitic detractors personified in Apion.

Juba. 1. King of Numidia in North Africa from 60–46 BC, notorious for his cruelty. He sided with Pompey in the civil war and defeated and killed Caesar's ally Gaius Scribonius Curio in 49 BC. He escaped after the republican defeat at Thapsus in 46, but, rejected by all sides, committed suicide.

2. **Juba II,** son of Juba (1), who while still an infant was led in Julius Caesar's triumph in 46 BC; he was brought up in Italy, and when grown up reinstated in Numidia, receiving in addition the kingdom of Mauretania. He married Cleopatra, the daughter of Mark Antony and the Egyptian queen Cleopatra, and died *c.* AD 23, being succeeded by his son Ptolemy. Juba was a man of great learning who sought to introduce Greek and Roman culture into his kingdom, and made a remarkable collection of artistic treasures. He wrote many books, in Greek, which are frequently cited by the Elder Pliny: they include a treatise on the medicinal plant euphorbia which he discovered growing on the slopes of Mount Atlas and named after his physician Euphorbus (brother of Antonius Musa, physician to the emperor Augustus).

Judgement of Paris, see PARIS, JUDGEMENT OF.

judicial procedure, see LAW.

Jugu'rtha, Numidian king and enemy of Rome. An illegitimate grandson of Masinissa, king of Numidia, as a young man he served at the siege of *Numantia in Spain (134–3 BC) under Scipio Aemilianus, hereditary patron of the Numidian royal house, and on his recommendation was adopted by King Micipsa (who succeeded Masinissa in 149) and regarded as his likely successor. After Micipsa's death in 118 he first put to death one of Micipsa's sons and then attacked the other, who fled to Rome. When the kingdom was divided into two Jugurtha launched another attack to gain the whole kingdom, rather than half of it, and killed the remaining son after besieging Cirta. In the sack of that city some Italian businessmen died, which led to agitation at Rome to declare war. In spite of Jugurtha's lavish bribery (according to *Sallust), the Romans decided to crush him. After two unsuccessful campaigns (111–110) Metellus, consul of 109, was sent against him. Metellus repeatedly defeated Jugurtha, but found it impossible to subdue him. His legate *Marius, profiting by this, gained the consulship in 107, on the promise of a quick end to the war. Success eluded him too, but the war was ended when Sulla, Marius' quaestor, persuaded Bocchus, king of Mauretania and Jugurtha's

father-in-law, with whom Jugurtha had taken refuge, to surrender him to the Romans. Jugurtha was taken to Rome and after Marius' triumph in 104 was put to death. The story of the war, with its many exciting incidents, is vividly told in the *Bellum Iugurthinum* ('Jugurthine war') of Sallust.

Ju'lia. Some of the famous women of the *gens* *Julia* (who therefore had this *name) were the following.

1. Wife of Marius and sister of Julius Caesar's father.

2. Sister of Julius Caesar and mother of Atia, who was the mother of the emperor Augustus.

3. Daughter of Julius Caesar and his first wife Cornelia, and wife of Pompey. She died in childbirth in 54 BC.

4. Daughter of Augustus and Scribonia; she married her cousin, Augustus' nephew, M. Marcellus, in 25 BC, and after his death in 23 married in 21 M. Agrippa, by whom she became the mother of Gaius and Lucius Caesar, Julia, Agrippina, and Agrippa Postumus. Her third marriage, after Agrippa's death, to Tiberius, took place in 11 BC. In 2 BC Augustus finally learned of her adulteries and banished her to a small island; in AD 4 she was allowed to move to Rhegium. Scribonia, who had been divorced from Augustus since 39 BC, voluntarily shared her exile. She died in AD 14.

5. *Livia, the wife first of Ti. Claudius Nero and afterwards of Augustus. Under the latter's will she was adopted into the Julian *gens* and renamed Julia Augusta.

Ju'lia, gens, distinguished patrician *gens* ('clan') at Rome, which claimed descent from Iulus (Ascanius) the son of Aeneas, and through them from the goddess Venus. To this *gens* belonged Julius Caesar and the emperor Augustus (distantly through his mother, properly through being adopted by Caesar and made his heir).

Ju'lia Domna, of Emesa in Syria, the second wife of Septimius Sevērus, Roman emperor AD 193–211, and mother of *Caracalla, reputedly a woman of great intelligence and character who gathered about her a circle of cultivated and learned men, including *Galen and *Philostratus (2). After Severus' death she tried unsuccessfully to reconcile her two sons Caracalla and Geta (Caracalla stabbed Geta to death in her arms). She died or committed suicide at Antioch in 217 on learning of Caracalla's death. See also ELAGABALUS.

Julian (Flavius Claudius Juliānus), Roman emperor AD 360–3, named by Christian writers 'the Apostate' because of his 'renunciation' of belief in Christianity. He was the son of Julius Constantius, half-brother of Constantine the Great. Constantine's son Constantius II put to death all rival members of the imperial family except for his young cousins Julian and his brother. They were brought up in captivity in Cappadocia and given a Christian education, but Julian acquired a passion for the classics and the pagan gods. In 351 he went to complete his education at Ephesus, where he was influenced by the *Neoplatonist philosopher Maximus, and thence to Athens (where a fellow student was the later Greek Father of the Church, Gregory of Nazianzus). After his brother's murder Julian reluctantly gave up his studies when Constantius II, who had no male heirs, summoned him and proclaimed him Caesar, putting him in charge of Gaul and Britain. He was a successful general and very popular with his soldiers, whose hardships he shared. When Constantius demanded some picked troops to be sent to the eastern empire Julian's men mutinied and proclaimed him Augustus (360). Before Julian could reach Constantinople, Constantius died. Julian became sole emperor, openly professed his paganism, proclaimed general religious toleration (but not without some persecution of Christians), and reinstated pagan cults and temples.

Soon after his accession he set out in 361 for Antioch, where he went to make preparations for the invasion of Persia. He met there the pagan orator *Libanius, but found the city hostile, it being both Christian and opposed to his taste for austerity. As a result of his stay there he wrote his Mīsopōgōn ('enemy of the beard'), an attack on the high-living, anti-philosophical inhabitants, who shaved, and ridiculed him for allowing his beard to grow. He also wrote a comic satire on the Roman emperors entitled Caesars or The Banquet, much approved of by the English historian Edward Gibbon. Eighty letters, containing much historical material, eight speeches, and a few poems also survive. The Commentaries on his Gallic campaigns are lost, and so too is his important work in seven books 'Against the Christians', refuting the Christian religion. All available copies of this work were destroyed by order of the Christian emperor Theodosius II, and it would have perished entirely but for the many extracts quoted by Cyril of Alexandria in a counter-refutation. Julian embarked on his campaign against Persia early in 363 but was mortally wounded in battle later in the year. The story (in the Church History of the fifth-century bishop Theodoret, with later embellishment) that he was murdered by a Christian and died exclaiming, vicisti, Galilaee! ('You have conquered, Galilean') is picturesque but unfounded. After his death the pagan revival collapsed. See also CHRISTIANITY and DELPHIC ORACLE.

Julio-Claudian emperors, see ROME 10.

Julius Caesar, see CAESAR.

Julius Capitoli'nus, see HISTORIA AUGUSTA.

Julius Pollux (second century AD), Greek scholar and rhetorician of Naucratis in Egypt, and teacher of the Roman emperor Commodus. He was a lexicographer and the author of an Onomasticon, a list of Attic words and technical terms, a much abridged and interpolated version of which is extant, descended from an epitome possessed by Arethas c. AD 900 (see TEXTS, TRANSMISSION OF ANCIENT 3). The arrangement of terms is not alphabetical but according to subject. In its explanation of terms it supplies incidentally a great deal of information on a very wide range of topics in antiquity, perhaps most valuably on music, the ancient theatre, and the Athenian constitution. Its collection of thirty-three terms of abuse for a tax-collector deserves to make it more widely known.

Julius Vale'rius (third to fourth century AD), translator, from the Greek of Pseudo-*Callisthenes, of the romantic history of Alexander the Great, Res gestae Alexandri Macedonis, in three books: birth; acts; death. The work is important in connection with the transmission of the Alexander story in the Middle Ages.

jumping, see ATHLETICS (viii).

Jūno, in Roman religion, the wife of *Jupiter; she was an ancient and important Italian goddess, resembling the Greek *Hera with whom she was identified, closely associated with the life of women, hence sometimes connected with the moon, with fertility, and with the sanctity of marriage. She had many distinctive names indicating her various attributes, e.g. Lucīna, 'she who brings [the child] to light', as the goddess presiding over child-birth, or Opigena, 'who brings help to women in childbirth'. But she also became a goddess of the state; as Juno Regina ('queen') she forms one of the Capitoline triad with Jupiter and Minerva. She had one Roman myth related by Ovid: being annoyed at the birth of *Athena without a mother, she determined to produce a child without a father; at the touch of a herb produced for her by Flora, she became pregnant and bore Mars, the god of war. (In Greek myth Hera, the wife of Zeus, is also the mother of Arēs, the god of war, but Zeus is the father; the child she produces without male assistance is Hephaestus.) The Roman story may have been invented to explain the important festival of the *Matronalia, confined to women, on the first of March, the month dedicated to Mars. There was also an interesting festival of women in honour of Juno Caprōtīna, so called from the date, the Nonae Caprotinae, 'the Nones of the wild fig' (caprificus), i.e. 7 July; the festival seems to have been the celebration of an old fertility rite, in later times confined to slaves. The Kalends of every month were sacred to Juno. 'Moneta' was another of her titles, perhaps meaning 'remembrancer' (i.e. the goddess should remember her previous favours to Rome). The temple of Juno

Moneta stood on the northern summit of the Capitoline hill; it had been vowed during a war in 345 BC and dedicated in the following year, and was said to have replaced an older shrine where the sacred geese had been kept (the geese perhaps being originally kept for divination); see MANLIUS CAPITOLINUS. An adjoining building contained the Roman mint: thus from *moneta* is derived the word 'money'. See also LIBRI LINTEI. There was a temple to Juno in the Campus Martius and another on the Aventine. The latter was dedicated in 392 BC by M. Furius Camillus, the conqueror of Veii, who placed in the temple a wooden statue of Juno brought from the captured city. For Juno in the sense of a woman's tutelary spirit see GENIUS.

Jū'piter (Lat. Iuppiter; in English, often Jove), sky-god and supreme god of the Romans, the name probably derived from an original vocative *dieu-pater* (compare the Greek vocative, *Zeu pater*, 'Father Zeus'), where *dieu* is akin to *dies* ('day') signifying the bright sky (see INDO-EUROPEAN and DIESPITER). He appears to have been originally the power (**numen*) of the sky, responsible for the weather, especially rain and lightning. He was worshipped at the rural **Vinalia* (grape-harvest) on 19 August, when the **flamen dialis* offered a ewe-lamb to him and cut the first grapes. As Jupiter Lapis ('stone') he was associated with the stones used in taking oaths and presumably thought of as thunderbolts, by which the perjurer may be struck down. Hence he seems to be connected with Fides, the personification of 'good faith', whose temple was near that of Jupiter on the Capitol at Rome (see below).

The Etruscan kings were thought to have introduced the cult of Iuppiter Optimus Maximus (i.e. the 'best and greatest' of all Jupiters) in which the god, in his temple on the Capitol said to have been founded by Tarquinus Superbus, was associated with Juno and Minerva, the three together known as the Capitoline triad. This was Jupiter in his aspect of god of the Roman state. In this temple the magistrates offered sacrifices on entering their year of office, and generals brought their spoils after victorious campaigns. Here every year the first meeting of the senate was held.

Jupiter Feretrius was also worshipped on the Capitol, in a temple reputedly founded by Romulus (see ROME 2). The derivation of the epithet is uncertain; it has been plausibly thought to be connected with Latin *fero*, 'I bring', in reference to the institution of dedicating to the god arms taken in war. The original act of dedication was supposed to have been made by Romulus, who hung his **spolia opima* on a sacred oak-tree on the Capitol. The temple may have dated from the seventh or sixth century BC; it had no cult statue but a sceptre (symbolic of military success) and the *silex*, 'rock' (probably a meteorite) used in the ritual

connected with the declaration and conclusion of wars.

Jupiter was also worshipped as Jupiter Stator, in his aspect of 'stayer of rout', the protector in battle and giver of victory. Tradition related that Romulus vowed a temple to him in the midst of a battle in which the Romans were being driven back by the Sabines. The temple, which stood near the highest point of the Via Sacra, appears not to have been built until much later, 294 BC, and then in consequence of a vow made at a critical moment in a battle against the Samnites, so the Romulus story appears to be a later invention. In it was held the meeting of the senate at which Cicero delivered his first oration against **Catiline.

For the worship of Jupiter as Jupiter Latiāris see FERIAE LATINAE.

Justin (Marcus Juniānus Justīnus), Roman historian of uncertain date (second or third century AD), who wrote in Latin an abridgement of the universal history (*Historiae Philippicae*, now lost) of **Trogus. It consists of largely unaltered (or apparently unaltered) excerpts joined together by colourless résumés; there are a few striking passages, such as the description of the multitude of Athenians pouring out to see **Alcibiadēs on his return from exile (5. 4), and of **Brennus and his army of Gauls at Delphi (24). Since Trogus' work has not survived Justin's book is valuable for the history of Macedon and the Hellenistic kingdoms. It was widely read in the Middle Ages.

Justi'nian (Flavius Petrus Sabbatius Justiniānus), Roman emperor at Constantinople AD 527–65. He was born *c*.482 near the border of Thrace and Illyricum, and took the name Justinianus upon his adoption by his uncle Justin, who had himself risen from obscurity to become emperor in 518 by the favour of the army. After 518 Justinian was rapidly promoted, becoming consul in 520. In 522 he married the actress and courtesan Theodora despite the scandals of her early life, and remained devoted to her until her death in 548, making her an equal and independent colleague in his imperial office. There are contemporary portraits of them both in the magnificent mosaics of San Vitale at Ravenna. It was thanks to Theodora's persuasive powers that Justinian survived the city riots of 532 which originated among the circus factions (see CHARIOT-RACES) and were called the Nika riots from the (Greek) battle cry *nika* ('conquer') used by the participants. The revolutionaries were subdued by the general **Belisarius. Justinian was determined to restore the Roman empire by recovering the lost provinces of the West, by codifying and rationalizing the legal system, and by reforming the administration. All this, he thought, depended upon God's favour, and this he resolved to win by suppressing heresy and paganism. His first aim was achieved through his great general Belisarius, who recovered Africa from the Vandals, occupied Rome, and overthrew the Ostrogothic kingdom in Italy (see GOTHS); finally, part of Spain was freed from the Visigoths. In his reorganization of Roman law, which he began upon as soon as possible, Justinian was assisted by *Tribonian, who rose to the high rank of quaestor of the palace. In 528 a commission was set up to codify all imperial constitutions still valid, i.e. the enactments of the emperors and their 'rescripts' or answers to legal questions submitted to them, and the first Code (*Codex*) of Justinian was published in 529. In the following year another commission was set up under Tribonian to codify the work of previous jurists, an enormous task, in which the codifiers employed nearly 2,000 different books. In 533 they published the Digest or Pandects (*Digesta seu pandectae*), in seven parts or fifty books. The work consists of extracts, grouped under subjects from the writings of jurists of authority (see LAW, AT ROME 3). At the same time a commission of three under the direction of Tribonian wrote an elementary work of instruction for beginners in the law, the Institutes (*Institutiones*), in four books. In 534 a new edition of the Code was produced. Throughout his reign Justinian promulgated many new laws himself, and he promised that a collection of these *Novellae constitutiones* ('new constitutions') would be made, but no collection of these, often known as the Novels, seems to have been published before his death. The complete collection of Justinian's legal work is known by the title *Corpus iuris civilis* ('the complete civil law'). Justinian carried out many reforms of the provincial administration and kept a careful watch on financial expenditure.

In the matter of religion Justinian reinforced the penalties against heretical Christian sects, Jews, and pagans, and strove to achieve orthodoxy throughout the empire. In accordance with this policy and to put an end to *Neoplatonist doctrines, in 529 he closed the schools of Alexandria and even of Athens, where philosophical teaching had been carried on at the Academy since the foundation of the school by Plato in the early fourth century BC.

Justinian perpetuated his name by the erection of hundreds of churches, aqueducts, and other public buildings, often of considerable splendour, throughout the empire; in Constantinople and its suburbs alone he caused to be built twenty-five churches in addition to the magnificent St Sophia. Less momentous but of some importance was the introduction of the silk-worm to Constantinople, brought back by monks who had visited fellow-Christians in China.

jūs trium libero'rum, see IUS.

Jutu'rna, an Italian goddess of fountains. It was at her spring in the Roman Forum that Castor and Pollux were said to have watered their horses after the battle of Lake Regillus (see DIOSCURI). A temple was dedicated to her at Rome in the Campus Martius by C. Lutatius Catulus, vowed in 241 BC during the notable sea-battle off Sicily in the First *Punic War. She is said to have been loved by Jupiter, who rewarded her with immortality and with rule over springs and rivers. Virgil in the *Aeneid* makes her the devoted sister of Turnus, who disguised herself as his charioteer Metiscus, and restored to him his lost sword made by Vulcan. She was compelled by a Fury, sent from Jupiter, to give up her brother to his fate, and returned lamenting to her spring.

Ju'venal (Decimus Junius Juvenālis, flourished early second century AD), the greatest of Roman satirical poets. He was a native of Aquinum (on the Via Latina in Latium) but beyond that fact very little is known of his life. Two inscriptions from that town were found (but are now lost), which may possibly have referred to him, and if so may indicate that he served in the army (as the first step on an official career) and held a local magistracy. The poet *Martial, his elder contemporary, addressed three epigrams to him. The various ancient Lives of Juvenal which survive are of late date, somewhat contradictory, and probably not reliable. They mostly agree in referring to a period of banishment, in consequence of an offence to a favourite (the actor Paris) of the emperor Domitian; it is also stated by one that he practised declamation until middle age (Martial calls him *facundus*, 'eloquent'). Acceptance of what Juvenal says in his *Satires as literally true would require one to believe that he was at one time poor, but later acquired a farm at Tibur (Tivoli), that he could offer hospitality in his house at Rome, and that he had visited Egypt. His sixteen satires, of which the last breaks off short, are arranged in five books (for a resumé of each see SATIRES). Internal evidence suggests they were published between *c.*110 and shortly after 127, in the peaceful reigns of Trajan and Hadrian which followed Domitian's death in 96.

The Satires are notable for their bitter, ironical humour, power of invective, grim epigrams, sympathy with the poor, and a narrow pessimism. Juvenal claims Lucilius and Horace as his masters, but he has none of the latter's mellow humour or gentle irony. The extravagance of his wholesale hatreds and condemnations is effective as rhetoric, but taken as the expression of personal feelings it indicates a man deeply embittered. His gift is for the vivid evocation of scenes of Roman life with a few economical phrases.

Juvenal found many admirers among English satirists, notably Samuel Johnson. Chaucer in *Troilus and Criseyde* (4. 197) appeals to his authority on the subject of wise objects for prayer (Satire 10), and in the Wife of Bath's Tale (*Canterbury Tales*) paraphrases an epigram in the same Satire. Juvenal was a favourite of John Skelton (?1460–1529), and influenced Joseph Hall (1574–1656) and John Donne (1572–1631). John Dryden had a high regard for him, translated the Satires, and prefaced them with an essay on the Roman satirists; Alexander Pope too came under his influence. The satire of Jonathan Swift, with its own *saeva indignatio* ('savage resentment'), is perhaps closest to the spirit of Juvenal.

Juve'ntas, the Roman goddess of youth, identified with the Greek *Hebē.

K

For Greek names with initial K see under C.

Kalends, see CALENDARS 3.

kalos ka'gathos (pl. *kaloi kagathoi*), Greek adjective of strong social and moral approval, used to describe men (and actions). It had approximately the meaning and connotations that 'gentlemanly' had in Victorian English; it implied not only that a man so described was of good birth and looks, education, and high position in society, but also that he was active in war and politics, and was expected to be brave, just, and honourable.

King's Peace, see ATHENS 2 (iii).

knights, at Rome, see EQUESTRIAN ORDER; at Athens, see HIPPEIS.

Knights (*Hippeis*, Lat. *Equites*), Greek comedy by *Aristophanes, produced at the *Lenaea of 424 BC and awarded first prize. It was the first occasion on which Aristophanes produced one of his plays himself. The demagogue *Cleon, the object of attack, was at the height of his fame after his victory at Pylos the previous year. The play is in some sense an allegory; the master of the house is called Dēmos ('the people'), and his slaves Demosthenes and Nicias (the Athenian generals) are terrorized by a new slave, a Paphlagonian (i.e. Cleon; compare *paphlazein*, 'to bluster').

Demosthenes and Nicias are lamenting their ill-treatment at the hands of the Paphlagonian, a spying flatterer of their master, and contemplating desertion as the only remedy. They learn from a collection of oracles that the Paphlagonian is to be ousted from favour by a sausage-seller. One of this trade appears on his way to the market, is told of his destiny to rule over the whole Athenian empire, and has his terror at the prospect of conflict allayed by the assurance that the knights (*hippeis*) will support him against the Paphlagonian. The latter enters threateningly, but the chorus of knights is called and comes charging on to the stage uttering their battle-cry, *paiĕ, paie* ('strike! strike!'). The Paphlagonian and the sausage-seller contend with each other for the favour of Demos by flattery, bribes, interpretation of oracles, and mutual abuse. Then they both go off to the *boulē* ('council') to do the same there, the sausage-seller returning to announce his victory. He is immediately followed by the Paphlagonian, and the competition in flattery of Demos continues. The sausage-seller is preferred in this, and in the competition of oracles, and in the final competition to settle who does more for Demos. After this the Paphlagonian discovers that the sausage-seller fits the description of the man fated to overthrow him, and retires in despair; the sausage-seller wins the day, and it is revealed that his name is Agorakritos, 'choice of the assembly', and that he is to be the reformer and saviour of the state. Demos confesses his past gullibility and promises to behave better in future.

koinē, the Greek 'common dialect'; see DIALECTS (1) 3.

kommos, in Attic tragedy, lyric dirge or lament sung by the chorus and one or more of the actors alternately.

Korē ('daughter'), see PERSEPHONE.

krypteia, at *Sparta, the equivalent of a secret police force in which selected young Spartan men were authorized by the ephors to patrol the Laconian countryside and murder any supposedly dangerous *helots. It has been suggested that it was the rationalization of an ancient initiation rite for young men approaching manhood (compare EPHEBOI at Athens). Aristotle ascribed the institution to *Lycurgus.

L

La'beō. 1. Marcus Anti'stius Labeo (d. AD 10 or 11), an eminent jurist of the time of the emperor Augustus. Of republican views, he is said to have refused the consulship from Augustus. He was a man of great learning, reputed to have written about 400 books, which are known from quotations by other jurists, from an epitome, and from the Digest of *Justinian. He was the founder of a progressive school of lawyers, in distinction from that of his contemporary, the jurist Ateius *Capito, which was conservative.

2. A'ttius Labeo (first century AD), author of translations of Homer's *Iliad* and *Odyssey* into Latin hexameters, which have not survived.

Labe'rius, De'cimus (c.105–43 BC), Roman knight and a distinguished writer of *mimes. According to Macrobius, his outspoken criticism of Julius Caesar brought upon him the humiliation (perhaps in 45 BC) of being required to appear on stage in his own mimes in competition with *Publilius Syrus. Several anecdotes are told of this famous occasion. It is said that at one point all eyes turned towards Caesar when a character said, 'He needs must fear many whom many fear'.

Labie'nus, Titus, Julius Caesar's most senior and trusted officer during a great part of the latter's campaigns in Gaul from 58 to 49 BC. He had been tribune of the people in 63 (the year of Cicero's consulship), and had prosecuted Rabirius (see PRO RABIRIO), who was defended by *Cicero (see (1) 2), in order to please Caesar, under the pretence of avenging the death of his uncle Quintus who had died with Saturninus in 100. At the outbreak of civil war in 49, he joined Pompey and fought against Caesar until he was defeated and killed at the battle of *Munda in 45. His home seems to have been at Picenum, where Pompey's father had large estates and many *clients, and may have had personal ties with the family.

labyrinth (*labyrinthos*), the complicated building or maze said to have been built by *Daedalus for king *Minos of Crete, where the Minotaur was kept, and from which no one could escape (see THESEUS). The word may be of pre-Greek origin (see INDO-EUROPEAN), perhaps derived from *labrys* which, according to Plutarch, is the Lydian word for 'double-headed axe', the royal or religious symbol frequently found represented in the palace remains of Minoan Crete (see RELIGION, GREEK 1). The original labyrinth was supposed to have been at *Cnossus; the idea was perhaps suggested to later Greeks by the complex ruins of the Bronze Age palace. The complicated figures of the Greek 'crane dance' were supposed to represent the convolutions of the labyrinth (see DANCING).

Lacedae'mon (Lakedaimōn, Lat. Lacōnica, also Lacōnia), the ancient Greek name for Sparta, used by Homer both for the country (in the south-east of the Peloponnese) and its capital. Later Greek writers often called the country Lakōnikē (from *Lakōn*, 'a Spartan', a shortened form of *Lakedaimonios*), although the name Lacedaemon continued to be used. See SPARTA.

Lacedaemo'nians, Constitution of the, a work by Xenophon; see CONSTITUTION OF THE LACE-DAEMONIANS.

lace'rna, rough cloak worn by Romans; see DRESS 2.

Lachēs, dialogue by Plato; see PLATO 2.

La'chesis, see FATES.

Lacō'nia or **Lacōnica** (Gk. Lakōnikē), the Latin name for Sparta. See LACEDAEMON and SPARTA.

Lacta'ntius, Lucius Caeci'lius (or perhaps Caelius) **Firmiā'nus,** c. AD 245–c.325, Latin author and Christian apologist, a native of North Africa, pupil of the African rhetorician Arnobius. His fame was such that he was summoned by the (pagan) Roman emperor Diocletian (284–305) to teach Latin rhetoric at Nicomedia (a Greek city in Bithynia and Diocletian's eastern capital). It is uncertain when he was converted to Christianity, but at the beginning of the Great Persecution of the Christians (303–313) he seems to have been without employment, probably on that account. In his old age he was summoned to Gaul by the emperor Constantine the Great to become tutor (c.317) to the latter's son Crispus. Only his Christian works survive. Chief among these are *De opificio Dei* (303–4), ('on God's handiwork'), an attempt to prove the existence of divine providence based on the evidence of design in the human body; *De ira Dei* ('on the wrath of God'), arguing against some philosophers that anger is a necessary part of the character of God, who must deliver just punishment against evil-doers; and the *Institū-tiōnes dīvīnae,* ('divine institutions') in seven books, written between 305 and 313, of which he later produced an epitome. This last is a work of wide scope, a defence of Christian doctrine as a harmonious and logical system; it is addressed to cultivated pagan readers and appeals not to the scriptures but to the testimony of pagan writers themselves. The first three books are a criticism of polytheism and of Roman philosophers; book 4 turns from criticism to constructive argument, demonstrating that the Christian faith alone provides true unity of philosophy and religion; this is followed by an exposition of the faith, the Christian idea of justice and morality (in book 5), the manner in which homage ought to be paid to God (book 6), and an investigation of the chief good, the purpose of creation, and the immortality of the soul (book 7), concluding with an exhortation to the Christian life. Lactantius has been criticized by Christians for unorthodox beliefs, but he has a grasp of what seem to be the essential principles of the Christian religion. He writes in an oratorical Ciceronian prose (he has been called the Christian Cicero), in a persuasive rather than a polemical tone, seeking to justify faith by reason rather than by authority. An exception to this manner is found in his *De mortibus persecutorum*, ('on the deaths of the persecutors'), written in Gaul *c*.318, shortly after the triumph of Christianity (see CONSTANTINE), a bloodcurdling description of the successive fates of the emperors who persecuted Christians, particularly in Lactantius' time. Being written by an eyewitness the book has considerable interest; it includes a description of Constantine's vision before the battle of the Milvian Bridge. There also survives a poem generally believed to be by Lactantius, the *Phoenix*; it relates the well-known story of the mythical bird and treats it as a symbol of the resurrection of Christ. See also EUHEMERUS.

Lādas, runner employed by Alexander the Great, famous for his speed.

Ladē, battle of (494 BC), see PERSIAN WARS.

Lādōn. 1. River of Arcadia, tributary of the Alpheus.

2. River of Elis, tributary of the Peneus.

3. In Greek myth, the dragon that guarded the golden apples of the *Hesperides.

Lae'lius, Gaius, consul at Rome in 140 BC, and close friend of *Scipio Aemilianus. He was a good soldier and led the decisive assault on Carthage as a legate under Scipio in the Third Punic War (149–146 BC). He was a prominent member of the intellectual, philhellenic circle of Scipio and his friends; Cicero (in *Brutus*) considered him the outstanding orator of his day, and he was given the name Sapiens, 'the wise', for his wide learning and philosophical attainments (or, according to Plutarch, for dropping his proposal for agrarian reform in the face of senatorial opposition). It was said that the comedies of *Terence, who was also a friend of Scipio, owed much to Laelius. Cicero makes him the principal speaker in *De amicitia, and an interlocutor in *De senectute* and *De republica*. In *De oratore* Cicero tells how Laelius and Scipio liked to go on holiday to the seaside 'where they became incredibly childish and used to collect shells and pebbles on the beach'.

Laelius, see DE AMICITIA.

Lāe'rtes, in Homer's *Odyssey*, the father of Odysseus.

Laestrygo'nians, see ODYSSEY (book 10).

Lae'vius 'Meli'ssus' (flourished *c*.100 BC; the *cognomen*, sometimes added, depends on an identification in Suetonius), Roman poet of whom little is known except that he wrote *Erōtopaegnia* ('diversions of love'), love poems in a great variety of lyric metres. He was never mentioned in the succeeding two centuries but was discovered by the literary circles of the second century AD who were attracted by his idiosyncracies. He is important as a pioneer of *Alexandrianism at Rome, as an experimenter in metres, and as a predecessor of Catullus in lyric poetry. Only fragments of his work survive.

Lā'ius, in Greek myth, legendary king of Thebes, father of *Oedipus, son of Labdacus, and great-grandson of *Cadmus. See also ANTIOPE.

La'machus, Athenian general of the time of the *Peloponnesian War; he had been *stratēgos* *c*.435 BC and so was well known by 425 when he was caricatured by Aristophanes in his comedy *Acharnians*. In 415 he was appointed with Alcibiadēs and Nicias to command the Sicilian Expedition, and he pursued an energetic policy until killed in a skirmish in 414.

La'mian War (323–322 BC), the war that followed the revolt of the Greek states against Macedonian rule after the death of Alexander the Great. Athens joined with the states of northern Greece, and under the Athenian general Leōsthenēs the Greeks were successful for a time and besieged Antipater, regent of Macedonia, in Lamia, a Thessalian town. But after Leosthenes was killed the war ended with a Macedonian victory at the battle of Crannon. The Macedonian fleet played an important part in the war and put an end to the sea-power of Athens. Antipater imposed on Athens a change of her democratic constitution, and the franchise was restricted to citizens possessing more than 2,000 drachmas. He placed a Macedonian garrison at Piraeus and demanded the surrender of *Demosthenes (see (2) 1).

lampadēdro'mia, see TORCH-RACE.

Lampri'dius, Ae'lius, see HISTORIA AUGUSTA.

Lānuvī'nus, Lu'scius, see LUSCIUS.

Lāo'cŏon, Trojan prince, brother of Anchises; for his story see TROJAN HORSE. Laocoon is best known through his depiction with his two sons in a statuary group carved in Rhodes in about 25 BC (by Hagesandros, Athanodoros, and Polydoros) and brought to Rome. There it was seen and ranked by the Elder *Pliny as the greatest work of art in the world; his description enabled it to be recognized when it was found in the ruins on the Esquiline hill (possibly from Nero's *Golden House) in 1506 and bought by Pope Julius II for the Vatican Museum, where it still stands despite having been looted by Napoleon. The German critic Gotthold Lessing (1729–81) made this sculpture the basis of his essay *Laokoon* analysing the different media of poetry and the fine arts.

Lāodamei'a. 1. In Greek myth, wife of *Protesilaus.
  2. In Greek myth, daughter of *Bellerophon and mother of *Sarpedon.

Lāo'medon, in Greek myth, king of *Troy, father of Priam. When the gods Apollo and Poseidon were doomed to serve a mortal for wages (a punishment for revolting against Zeus), Laomedon employed them to build the walls of Troy; when they had finished, however, he refused to pay them. Poseidon then sent a sea-monster against Troy, the danger from which could be averted only if Laomedon sacrificed his daughter Hesionē to the monster. Heracles happened to arrive at Troy and undertook to kill the monster if Laomedon would give him his famous horses (originally a gift from Zeus in exchange for *Ganymede), but Laomedon defrauded him as well. After many years Heracles returned with an army, captured the city, killed Laomedon and all his sons except Priam, and gave Hesionē to *Telamon, who had distinguished himself in the attack. There was a story that Laomedon was buried above the Scaean Gate at Troy, and ensured the safety of the city as long as he was undisturbed (the gate was dismantled to admit the Trojan Horse). When the Trojans were called 'sons of Laomedon' it was a hint at possible treachery.

La'pithae, Lapiths, in Greek myth, a Greek tribe inhabiting the north of Thessaly; Pirithous, son of *Ixion, was their king. See CENTAURS.

lārēs, in Roman religion, spirits (*numina*; see NUMEN) whose original character is disputed. The *lares compitālēs* were worshipped at the agricultural festival of the *Compitalia. At a cross-roads (*compitum*) where the boundaries of three or four farms met, a small shrine would be erected, open in all four directions to allow free passage to the *lar* that presided over each farm. At the Compitalia the farmers hung up a plough

at the shrine, and also a woollen doll for every free person in the household and a woollen ball for every slave. The purpose of the offerings remains obscure; if the intention was that the *lares* should take these objects and spare the living, it suggests that they were thought of as dangerous spirits. It would seem likely that the *lares* were originally deities of the farm-land, invoked (in the words of Tibullus) to 'give good crops and wine', and that the household *lar familiāris* ('of the servants') was introduced into houses at a later time by the farm-slaves. The *lares familiārēs* were sometimes thought of, it has been argued, as the deified spirits of dead ancestors, good and beneficent so long as they were treated with respect. By classical times the *lares familiares* were guardian spirits who had the special care of the house and household, and were worshipped at the domestic hearth on the Kalends, Nones, and Ides of the month (see CALENDARS 5) and on occasions of importance to the household, such as a wedding. Every household had its *lararium* or shrine, often like a cupboard, containing small images of the *lares*, standing in a corner of the *atrium*. The *lares familiares* had their counterpart in the *lares praestitēs* ('guardians') of the state. These had a temple at the head of the Via Sacra; the figure of a dog stood between their images, symbolic of their faithful guardianship. In later times the *lares* were identified with the *Dioscuri. They have no mythology. See also GENIUS and PENATES.

Lars Po'rsena, see PORSENA.

larvae, see LEMURES.

Lāsus (b. *c.*548 BC), of Hermionē in Argolis, an early Greek *lyric poet, celebrated as the founder of the Athenian school of *dithyrambic poetry (he is said to have instituted dithyrambic contests) and as the teacher of Pindar. He was a contemporary of Simonides, and like him he lived at Athens under the patronage of Hipparchus (brother of Hippias the tyrant). According to Herodotus he revealed *Onomacritus as the forger of oracles supposedly by Musaeus. Virtually nothing of his poetry survives.

latifu'ndia, in Italy, large agricultural estates originating in distributions by lease of *ager publicus* ('state-owned land') in the early second century BC. Each had an extensive farm-house (*villa*) with a large staff of slaves (*familia*) providing plentiful cheap labour. Such estates had the capital to produce new crops and breeds while exploiting the land for profit. In consequence a large number of peasant farmers in Italy (and also in the provinces) were compelled to sell their smallholdings. The small-holder, with his mixed farming and need to make a living, could not compete in the markets, especially since so much land was turned into pasture tended by slave herdsmen. *Columella actually regarded the system as uneconomical; the Elder *Pliny believed the *latifundia* were the ruin of Italy. When slave labour ceased to be cheap, the *familia* was replaced by tenant-farmers, *coloni*. See AGRICULTURE.

Latin, Latini, Latins. Latini, 'Latins', was the name of a people in Italy who in the early *Iron Age were occupying the southern part of the lower valley of the river Tiber (between, to the south, the Greek culture of Magna Graecia and, to the north, the Etruscan culture of Etruria). They gave their name to this territory, *Latium. See LATIN LEAGUE and ROME 4. For a later use of the name 'Latins' see BYZANTIUM. See also ITALY and LATIN LANGUAGE.

Latin language
1. Latin was the language of the city of Rome and the territory of *Latium to the south; it spread with the power of Rome until it became the language of most of western Europe. It is known to have been one of several related dialects which formed the Italic group in the *Indo-European family of languages, but it is not at all close to Greek, although the latter is also Indo-European. Its nearest Italic relative is *Faliscan, and it is markedly different from the other main branch of Italic, Osco-Umbrian (*Oscan was spoken in the Samnite territories, and *Umbrian in central Italy to the north-east of Rome; both are known only from inscriptions, proper names, and the writings of early grammarians). It is possible that both Latin and Osco-Umbrian developed separately out of one common Italic language, but it is perhaps more likely that Latin resulted from the fusion of one Italic-speaking people with a pre-existing population of Latium. Exactly how and when Italic speakers came into Italy is not clear, nor are the reasons for the development of their different dialects (see ITALY). Other languages spoken in Italy in early historical times were Greek in the south, Celtic in the north, and the (non-Indo-European) language of Etruria, all of which exercised some influence upon Latin. The Latin *alphabet seems not to have been derived directly from the Greek but to be partly of Etruscan origin.

In the course of its long history, Latin has undergone considerable change. Scholars of the late republic and early empire did not find archaic Latin easy to understand or attractive (see LIVIUS ANDRONICUS, SALII, and TWELVE TABLES). Polybius, writing in the second century BC of the 'first Carthaginian treaty' (perhaps 509 BC), says that even the best scholars after much study had difficulty in interpreting some of it.

The following periods can be distinguished: early Latin, up to about 100 BC; classical (or 'Golden Age') Latin, from 100 BC to the death of Livy, occurring soon after the death of the emperor Augustus in AD 14 (the literary activity of Cicero and Caesar gives special importance to the years 81–43 BC; see also CLASSIC); 'Silver Latin', the term which describes the post-classical period up to about AD 150, and marks a falling off from the preceding Golden Age; and late Latin, from AD 150, which merges into medieval Latin.

2. *Silver Latin*. The period of Silver Latin, broadly from the time of the deaths of Livy and Augustus, say AD 14, to about 150, is a period of what can generally be considered a decline from previous greatness. It is characterized by the development of *rhetoric, which led to a striving for novelty and effect, over and above meaning, and is marked by exaggerated emphases, antitheses, and epigrams. These trends are seen most clearly in the prose of Tacitus and the poetry of Lucan.

3. *Spoken or colloquial Latin*. These terms cover the easy 'everyday speech' (*sermo cotidiānus*) of educated people. The plays of Plautus and Terence provide the best evidence for this style, but also important are the letters of Cicero, especially those to his intimate friend Atticus, with their very free syntax. In similar vein, although poetic, are Horace's Satires and Epistles, and parts of Catullus. Interesting in this respect is the *Satyricon* of *Petronius, which ranges from cultured urbanity to coarse vulgarity.

4. *Vulgar Latin*. Vulgar Latin is the spoken Latin of the uneducated classes in Rome, Italy, and the provinces. It is known from inscriptions and especially graffiti, a few texts such as the *Satyricon* of Petronius (see 3 above), and the early development of the Romance languages. It is marked by slurred or confused pronunciation, resulting in different spellings, a standardization of originally diverse word forms, a break-down of declensions leading to an increased use of prepositions, a much simpler syntax, and a more natural word-order.

Latin League, in Italy, the association of *Latin towns, from the seventh century BC onwards, for, among other things, the joint worship of deities widely recognized among all the Latins. Most important was the celebration of the festival of the Latin Jupiter (Jupiter Latiaris) on the Alban Mount (see FERIAE LATINAE). *Alba Longa traditionally led a Latin League, but the leadership allegedly passed to Rome when she destroyed Alba *c*.600 BC. The military reforms of the Roman king *Servius Tullius in the early sixth century probably made Rome the leading military power in Latium and gave her the hegemony. After the expulsion of the kings (509 BC) the other Latin cities took advantage of Rome's temporary weakness to challenge her leadership. The result was the battle of Lake *Regillus, traditionally in 496 BC, in which Rome, although barely victorious, was nevertheless established as the leading city in the League. After the Latin War of 340–338, in which the Romans were completely victorious, the Latin League was dissolved and the individual cities had to accept Rome's terms, of incorporation into the Roman state for some (the smaller), and of becoming Roman (subject) allies for the rest. See ROME 4.

Latin rights (see also NOMEN LATINUM), rights held by Latin cities that remained unincorporated in the Roman state (such as Tibur and Praeneste) and by Latin colonies. The Latins by their origin (see LATIUM and ROME 1 and 2) and special position among Rome's allies (see LATIN LEAGUE above and ROME 4) occupied from the Roman point of view an intermediate position between Romans and other Italian allies; they shared many material privileges with Roman citizens including the important rights of *commercium* (the right of transacting business and conducting law-suits at Rome on the same footing as Roman citizens) and *cōnūbium* (the right of intermarriage with Romans). This was largely because of the continuous tradition of social and political equality between the Latin cities. The Latins remained loyal to Rome until abuses of their *imperium* by Roman commanders led to the Latins demanding the right of appeal, which may have been granted them in 122 BC. They took no part in the Social War (see ROME 6), and in 89 BC were granted Roman citizenship along with all the Italian allies.

Latī'nus, in Roman legend, eponymous hero of the Latins, king of *Latium and, according to Virgil, son of the god *Faunus and of the nymph Marīca; thus through Faunus' father *Picus he was descended from Saturn. He was the father of Lavinia whom Aeneas married (see AENEID). A certain Latinos was known to Hesiod, who makes him a son of Odysseus and *Circē (there is a hint in Aeneid 12 that Circe was Latinus' mother).

La'tium, originally a small area of land in western Italy around the Alban Mount (about 20 km. or 13 miles south-east of Rome), lying between the Apennines and the Tyrrhenian Sea, whose boundaries were gradually extended north to the river Tiber and south to Sinuessa. In historical times Latium was inhabited by Latini (see LATIN), a people formed by a fusion of *Indo-European invaders and the previous inhabitants. See ROME 4.

Lātō'na, Latin name for the Greek goddess *Leto.

Laudā'tio Tu'riae, see WOMEN, POSITION OF 2.

Lau'rium, see MINES and ATHENS 4.

Laus Pisō'nis, see DE LAUDE PISONIS.

Lausus. 1. In Virgil's Aeneid, the son of *Mezentius. While trying to save his father he is killed by Aeneas.

2. Name of a son of Numitor, king of *Alba Longa, killed by his uncle Amulius.

Lavi'nia, in Virgil's Aeneid, daughter of *Latinus; she is betrothed to *Turnus but is given by her father in marriage to Aeneas.

Law. 1. At Athens
For legislation at Athens before the fifth century BC see DRACO and SOLON. Once democracy was established at Athens by Cleisthenes (2) in 507 BC, laws were made by a vote of the *ecclesia ('assembly'). They were called nomoi, 'laws', or psēphismata, 'decrees' (lit. 'votings'). In general usage nomos seems to refer to a law that was regarded as more fundamental and perhaps more permanent than a psephisma, but there is no hard and fast distinction. The laws were inscribed in various public places, accessible to everyone. See AXONES.
Judicial procedure
1. In the course of the fifth century BC the administration of justice passed almost entirely into the hands of the people. The boulē ('council') and ecclesia dealt with misdeeds of officials and grave crimes against the state. The *Areopagus retained its ancient jurisdiction in cases of murder, malicious wounding, and arson. Some trivial cases were disposed of by judges known as the *Forty. All other cases fell within the jurisdiction of the popular courts, developed from the earlier *heliaia.

Law-suits were either public, where some offence against the state was involved, or private. In public suits the charge might be made either by a magistrate or by a private citizen, but in essentials there was no difference between public and private procedure. The case usually came before one of the thesmothetae (see ARCHONS), unless it fell within the province of another magistrate. The magistrate prepared it for trial and subsequently presided over the court where it was held. He was not called a judge nor did he fulfil the function of a modern judge; he did not sum up or give guidance to the jury. All judicial decisions were made by the jurors independently; they had to interpret the law for themselves and judge for themselves what was or was not evidence, and what were valid arguments. Thus they played the part of judges as well as jury, and in English are frequently referred to as 'judges' as well as 'jurors'. Their Greek name was dikastai, 'dicasts', or, less commonly, heliastai, 'heliasts'. In the present context all four names are synonymous.

2. The jurors who made up the courts were taken from a list of 6,000 volunteers drawn up at the beginning of each year; they were (male) citizens over 30 not disqualified in any way, distributed in ten sections, with every *tribe represented in each. From these the courts (or juries), dikastēria, were selected, varying in size according to the type of case, but numbering usually several hundred (to prevent bribery or

intimidation), again with each tribe represented. In the fourth century a jury was composed of an odd number of jurors, 201 for example, to avoid a tie in the voting, but there is no evidence for odd numbers in the fifth century. If there was a tie, the accused was acquitted (see ORESTEIA (*Eumenides*)). Each juror received a payment (introduced by *Pericles) of two obols, raised to three before 425. Since an able-bodied man would hope to earn more than that by a day's work there was a preponderance of old men on the juries. It is not known what method was used in the fifth century for allocating jurors to courts. By the early fourth century a system of lot was used, developed into a more complicated arrangement later in the century. The aim was to prevent bribery by avoiding prior allocation. The jurors decided the verdict by vote, in the fifth century by placing a pebble or shell in an urn; there was one urn for condemnation, another for acquittal. In the fourth century each dicast was given two bronze discs, one with a hole pierced in it signifying condemnation, one without a hole signifying acquittal; he placed his vote in a 'voting' urn and the other disc in a 'spare' urn. In this way it was hoped to ensure that the voting was secret, and that each dicast cast only one vote. If the accused was convicted, accuser and accused proposed a penalty (except in cases where it was fixed by law), each man speaking in support of his proposal, and the dicasts decided by vote between the two proposals. The penalty might be death, imprisonment, banishment, disfranchisement, confiscation of property, or a fine. Long terms of imprisonment were not imposed. Fining was the commonest penalty, the amount varying from a few drachmas to very large sums. Demosthenes was once fined twenty talents, Timotheus a hundred. The prosecutor was liable to a fine of 1,000 drachmas if he withdrew before the trial or failed to obtain one fifth of the votes. The fines (and fees of the litigants) went to supply the fund from which the dicasts were paid. There was no appeal from the decision of the court.

3. The majority of private suits (on rights of property, debts, contracts, etc.) came first before the Forty (see 1 above), who, if the matter in dispute exceeded the very small amount of ten drachmas, referred the case to arbitration by one of the public arbitrators (*diaitētai*), Athenians in their sixtieth year. Once accepted by both parties the decision of the arbitrator was legally binding, but before then appeal against it could be made to a lawcourt. In the lawcourt, accuser and accused were sometimes allowed two speeches each, sometimes only one. The accuser spoke first, and the length of the speeches, fixed according to the importance of the case, was measured by a water-clock (see CLOCKS). No advocate was allowed: the parties had to conduct their own cases and address the court in

person, unless incapacitated in some way; however, they were normally allowed to consult others more experienced in the law for advice or even to have their speeches written (see LOGOGRAPHERS (2)); *Antiphon was the first to acquire fame as a speech-writer. A slave's testimony in a law-suit was admissible only if given under torture (see SLAVERY 1).

4. This judicial system gave security against intimidation or corruption of the jurors, but the latter could easily be swayed by skilful speakers, since presiding magistrates did not give them the guidance expected of a modern judge (see 1 above). Aristophanes in *Wasps* attacks the system on the ground of the ferocity of the juries towards the rich and their tendency to be swayed by irrelevant factors. Yet on the whole the system worked effectively.

2. At Rome

The law interpenetrates Roman life and thought to an exceptional degree, and the body of material relating to Roman law and its procedures is vast. The basis of Roman *ius civilē*, 'civil law', was custom. Civil law, in its widest sense, was the law applicable to Roman citizens (and to some extent to their close allies; see LATIN RIGHTS). It was codified when the *Twelve Tables were published, according to tradition in the mid-fifth century BC. (For the circumstances see ROME 3 and DECEMVIRI.) According to Livy the Twelve Tables were 'the fount of all public and private law at Rome'. (Public law is constitutional and criminal; private law, which is civil law in its limited sense, relates to the rights of individuals and deals with family relations, property, and contract.) The Twelve Tables were never abolished, but later developments made much of their content obsolete.

During the republic, legislative proposals originated in the *senate and had to be ratified by the political assembly of the people, the *comitia centuriata*. Laws were named after the magistrates who proposed them, e.g. *lex Calpurnia*, 'the law of Lucius Calpurnius Piso'. In addition, the edicts of magistrates with *imperium* had the force of law and did not require the approval of the assembly. The magistrate with particular responsibility for the administration of the law was the *praetor urbanus* (see PRAETOR).

1. *Judicial procedure, criminal.*

(i) Criminal jurisdiction, originally in the hands of the king, passed in republican times to magistrates who possessed *imperium*. Their power of punishment was limited from early times by the right of the condemned prisoner to make an appeal (*provocatio*) against the death sentence to the people meeting in the *comitia centuriata* ('assembly'). In effect this meant that jurisdiction, first in capital cases, then in all important criminal cases, passed from the magistrates to the assembly. Any person might act as prosecutor, provided that he was not for some reason disqualified; the state encouraged the prosecution of criminals by offering rewards, but an unsuccessful accuser might in turn be prosecuted. The power of veto (*intercessio) could be used against the sentence in a criminal court. During the conflict of the orders (see ROME 3), the jurisdiction of the *tribunes of the plebs in criminal matters was established, and they became the chief prosecutors in cases concerned with political offences and abuses on the part of patrician magistrates.

(ii) From time to time, when a serious political case came up, the senate set up a special court (quaestio extraordinaria), whose members were senators. In 149 BC, by the Calpurnian law (lex Calpurnia), the first permanent court was set up, the quaestio perpetua de repetundis (see REPETUNDAE), to try cases of extortion by provincial governors. The members of this court were senators, until C. Gracchus (122 BC) transferred the membership to the *equestrian order. In the next forty years several other quaestiones perpetuae ('permanent courts') were set up to deal with particular crimes of frequent occurrence, certainly for cases of death by poisoning and for treason (veneficia and maiestas), probably for bribery at elections (ambitus) and embezzlement of public money (peculatus). Sulla in 81 BC further developed the system of quaestiones, establishing at least seven to try various specified offences, to be composed entirely of senators. Thus criminal jurisdiction passed out of the hands of the people.

By the Aurelian law (lex Aurelia) of 70 BC, by which time Sulla's juries had proved themselves to be unsatisfactory, three jury-panels (decuriae) of 300 each were established, one consisting of senators, one of equités, and the third of *tribuni aerarii. From these panels juries for individual cases were chosen by lot, one-third from each decuria. The size of juries varied according to the importance of the case. Both accuser and accused were allowed within certain limits to reject jurors. From the second century BC voting had been secret, by means of tablets placed in an urn. There was no public prosecutor: prosecutions before the quaestiones, as before the comitia, were undertaken by private individuals, or in political cases by tribunes. The accused might have an advocate, a patrōnus (see PATRON), or several patroni to speak on his behalf; the prosecutor, except in cases of repetundae (see above), or where a woman or child was the nominal prosecutor, had to conduct his case in person, but might be supported by other men equally interested in bringing the prosecution who were also 'signatories to the indictment' (subscriptores). Authority to bring a case before a court was sought from the magistrate in charge at a preliminary hearing known as a divinatio. The length of the speeches, at first unlimited, was later regulated by the water-clock (see CLOCKS). At the end of the trial the jury gave its

verdict by a majority vote. The presiding magistrate did not vote but pronounced the verdict and the sentence, against which there was no appeal (see (iii)). It was not possible to prosecute anyone who was absent on state business.

(iii) After the changes of 70 BC the system of quaestiones remained unchanged but decline eventually set in. Special quaestiones were still occasionally set up to try special cases, e.g. *Clodius for the Bona Dea affair of 62 BC and Julius Caesar's assassins in 43 BC. The emperor Augustus added a fourth jury-panel whose members were of lower census (i.e. poorer) than the previous bottom class, the tribuni aerarii. He also reorganized some of the quaestiones and added one for adultery. However, under the later emperors the quaestiones gradually declined, and in the third century seem to have ceased to exist. Their functions were taken over by others: the emperor might try any case that he thought fit; the senate was constituted as a criminal court to try important cases, which usually involved its own members; the *praefectus urbi had criminal jurisdiction in Rome and for 100 (Roman) miles (148 km.) around, and by the third century AD the *praefectus praetorio had criminal jurisdiction in the rest of Italy (both the prefects acting as delegates of the emperor). During both republican and imperial times many minor cases must have been dealt with by magistrates such as the tresviri capitālēs (see VIGINTISEXVIRATE).

(iv) Towards the end of the republic appeals to the popular assemblies (comitia) became obsolete (see (ii) above). Under the empire the emperor had the power to interfere with a decision of a magistrate presiding at a trial (or to renounce the power himself in favour of his delegates) by reason of his 'tribunician power' (tribunicia potestas); see TRIBUNES OF THE PLEBS. During the first century AD the criminal jurisdiction of provincial governors was limited by the right of Roman citizens to appeal to a court at Rome or to the emperor. Thus the apostle Paul's claim to 'appeal to Caesar' against the procurator of Judaea was allowed.

(v) The death penalty was rarely inflicted in practice, but it might, in republican times, be pronounced by the comitia centuriata; it was usually replaced by exile from Roman territory. In the last century of the republic the quaestiones were obliged to allow a condemned person time to escape (see EXILE) before executing the death sentence. After his escape a decree was passed which forbade his return on pain of death (aquae et ignis interdictio, 'denial of water and fire'). Such executions as took place were generally the result of exceptional circumstances, e.g. a *senatus consultum ultimum. The death penalty was more frequent under the empire.

Fines, or some diminution of civil status (such as infamia, 'disgrace'), were the most common penalties under the republic. In later times punishment became more varied and more severe, including deportation to some desolate island, confiscation of property, penal servitude (e.g. in the mines), and scourging.

2. *Judicial procedure, civil.* The civil jurisdiction, like the criminal, passed from the king to the magistrates. In 366 BC the magistracy of *praetor urbanus* ('city praetor') was constituted and he was given special responsibility for the administration of justice in Rome. Around 242 BC Rome's extended relations with foreign countries led to the appointment of a *praetor peregrinus* ('foreign praetor') to deal with lawsuits in which either one or both parties were foreigners.

When the *praetor urbanus* entered office, although he was formally obliged to do no more than apply the existing *ius civile*, 'civil law', he issued an edict, as did all the important magistrates at Rome, proclaiming the new actions and remedies he was going to institute during his year of office. Thus in effect he created a mass of new rules. Legally an edict ceased to be binding when the magistrate left office. But as it was obviously impracticable for the new praetor each year to change all the existing rules or re-enact them, the previous edict was customarily continued by the succeeding praetor, with occasionally such amendments as the jurists of the time advised. The edict which remained continuously valid was known as the *edictum tralaticium* ('traditional edict'). These edicts, issued annually, grew into the great code of civil law.

Under the republic there were two principal kinds of procedure in a civil law-suit. The first was the archaic system known as *legis actio*, which dated from early times, and of which comparatively little is known; it began to die out in the third and second centuries BC, though certain aspects of it may have persisted to the end of the republic. It was characterized by a rigid formalism; a claim could be instituted in only one of a limited number of ritual ways recognized by statute, and the slightest mistake in performing the ritual meant disaster for the litigant. The second procedure was introduced *c.*150 BC; it proceeded *per formulam* ('through written direction') and was more elastic. There was a first stage, before the praetor, who declared the law, and a second stage before a judge (*iudex*, an individual appointed to decide a case at law) or the standing courts of the *decemviri* or *centumviri* who decided the issue on the facts (these courts existed before the formulary system). When the case was before the praetor it was said to be *in iure*, 'at law'; before the *iudex* it was said to be *sub iudice* or *apud iudicem*, 'with the judge'. After discussion before the praetor, the legal issue was defined and summarized by him in a written direction (*formula*) to the judge as to what judgement to

pronounce. In this way the praetor acquired the power to grant new remedies and thereby to 'support, supplement, and correct the civil law'. The *edictum tralaticium* contained the *formulae* of actions, and in the last century of the republic was the main instrument for the development of the law. This process came to an end, and the praetor's edict took its final form, with that issued by Salvius Julianus under the emperor Hadrian. The praetor's importance in the development of Roman law increased greatly as a result of the formulary system.

3. *Responsa iurisprudentium.* Since neither magistrate nor judge was necessarily or even normally familiar with the law, laymen with legal knowledge (*iurisprudentes, iurisconsulti, iurisperiti*) came into prominence, especially in the matter of advising the praetor. The *responsa iurisprudentium* were the 'answers (opinions) of the legal experts' to questions concerning the interpretation of the law put to them by their clients. These answers were recorded and edited by the pupils of the expert concerned, and had authority proportionate to his reputation as a lawyer. Such a person was not normally an advocate, but he was usually a man of standing whose legal expertise was only one aspect of a public career, as for example *Scaevola under the republic, and under the empire *Papinian, *Paulus, and *Ulpian. Giving *responsa* resulted in the acquisition of power, which Augustus may have tried to bring under control to some extent by limiting the right to give *responsa* to certain jurists. (But the extent to which *responsa* were binding on a judge remains obscure.) Similarly the praetor's edict came under imperial control in as much as the emperor exercised influence over the appointment of the praetors. After the edict of Julianus (see 2 above) jurisprudence was developed mainly in the writings of the above-named jurists.

4. *Ius gentium and ius naturālē.* The question arose early as to the principles on which disputes should be adjudicated where one or both the parties were foreigners, an ever-increasing number of whom were brought to Rome by trade or business. The large number of such cases is shown by the appointment *c.*242 BC of a special praetor, *praetor peregrinus*, to deal with them. The most general solution seems to have been found in the idea of a *ius gentium*, 'universal law', the universal element to be found in the laws of all nations, but how this idea came to develop is not clear. In a practical sense the *ius gentium* came to denote especially the law of contract, and presumably embodied the customs generally observed by the Mediterranean peoples in their commercial dealings. After AD 212, when by the *constitūtio Antoniniāna* Roman citizenship was conferred upon all free inhabitants of the empire, there was no effective difference between *ius gentium* and *ius civile* (see 5).

Under the influence of Greek theory, the *ius gentium* in the last century of the republic became identified for most practical purposes with the *ius naturale*, 'natural law', a set of precepts dictated by reason and universally valid. Only in the case of slavery did the Romans distinguish between natural law, by which all men are born free, and universal law, by which some men might be enslaved.

5. *Diffusion of Roman law.* Alongside the process of evolution described above came a process of diffusion by which Roman law spread gradually over a large part of the civilized world. The diffusion was at first by conquest. In the territories conquered by Rome and governed as provinces the system applied varied according to the degree of social organization prevailing among the natives, and the state, developed or otherwise, of their own laws and institutions. In the provinces cities were often granted the right, and even more often were allowed in practice, 'to have their own laws', *suis legibus uti*. The edict which the governor of a province, like the praetor at Rome, issued when entering office, appears to have included regulations applying to the various categories of disputes dealt with in the governor's court, between Roman citizens, between these and aliens, and probably between one alien and another. The experience of the *praetor peregrinus* at Rome supplied a body of rules applicable between parties whose native laws were not the same, and these no doubt would serve as a model for provincial courts. But the natural tendency was to Romanize the law of the province, while Roman law itself was becoming permeated with the *ius gentium*, especially in the fields of property and contract.

A further stage in the process of diffusion was reached in AD 212 (see 4), when Roman citizenship was extended by the emperor Caracalla to all freeborn subjects of the empire, and Roman law in consequence became applicable to a great variety of foreigners, to some of whom, particularly the peoples of the East with their well-established institutions, it was not suited. As a consequence local law and native customs still persisted, and Roman law was modified to accommodate them. After the transfer by the emperor Constantine of the centre of government to Constantinople (AD 330), Roman law was naturally subjected to Greek as well as Christian influences. As expressed in its final form, the *Corpus iuris* ('body of law') of Justinian, it includes the effect of non-Roman influences, but nevertheless it is in the main the creation of the Roman mind. The main development of law in this period was by imperial constitutions (see JUSTINIAN), which were issued in the names of the western and eastern emperors jointly and were normally valid throughout the empire. The Theodosian Code, issued by Theodosius II in AD 438, was a collection of those issued from Constantine

onwards. The principal forms of Roman legal writings are: commentaries, particularly on the praetors' edicts; collections of *responsa* ('opinions'); discussions of hypothetical or actual cases (*quaestiones*); systematic collection and arrangement of cases (*digesta*); monographs on particular topics; and text books, known as *institutiones*. All Roman legal writings are marked by frequent reference to cases and thus by much richness of detail.

The later spread of Roman law was effected chiefly by peaceful diffusion, radiating from two centres, Italy and Constantinople. After the Dark Ages a great impulse to its extension was given by the revival of legal study at the University of Bologna towards the end of the eleventh century. Thence the study of the *Corpus iuris* of Justinian spread to the universities of France, England, Spain, and Germany. The development of Canon law for the regulation of ecclesiastical affairs, largely based on Roman law, was a further stage in this diffusion. By the definite adoption of Roman law or by the codification on Roman principles of local customs, much of Europe is still governed by what is essentially Roman law.

law courts, see LAW above.

Laws (*Nomoi*), dialogue by *Plato, his last and longest work (in twelve books), probably left unrevised at his death. It lacks the vigour and charm of the earlier dialogues; the style is tortuous and the sentences very long. The interlocutors are three elderly men, an unnamed Athenian, Cleinias a Cretan, and a Spartan Megillus. The dramatic situation is fully revealed only at the end of book 3. The Cretans have decided to refound a deserted city, and the task has been entrusted to ten commissioners, of whom Cleinias is chief. Cleinias and Megillus have met an Athenian and are walking on a midsummer's day from Cnossus to the cave and temple of Dictē, the traditional birthplace of Zeus. Their conversation turns to the merits of the traditional lawgivers of Sparta and Cnossus, Lycurgus and Minos, whom the Athenian criticizes for directing their laws towards superiority in war, whereas peace not war is the business of the legislator. The Athenian stranger seems to have had experience of life in a city under a tyrant, and to represent the views of an organized group of scientific thinkers (such as Plato's Academy at Athens), being knowledgeable about jurisprudence and constitutional theory. The conversation therefore develops into a complete outline of a constitution and code of laws for the new city, and the Athenian lays down for Cleinias the number of its citizens and their distribution, its organization in respect of magistrates, marriage, property (including slaves), and the material conditions of life generally, education, festivals, and other regulations. The last three books are mainly concerned with criminal offences and their expiations. The general purpose of the *Laws* seems to be to provide a model of procedure for those members of the *Academy who at this time were often called upon to assist in drawing up a written constitution and laws for some newly founded city.

Lea'nder (Leandros), youth of Abȳdus (on the Asiatic side of the *Hellespont) who, according to legend, was in love with Hero, the beautiful priestess of Aphroditē at Sestus on the opposite (Greek) shore. Leander used to swim across to Hero every night, his course guided by a light in a tower. One stormy night the light was extinguished and Leander was drowned. When his body was washed up Hero, in despair, threw herself into the sea. Lord Byron, the English poet, swam from Abydus to Sestus in 1810. See MUSAEUS 2.

lectiste'rnium, Roman version of the Greek *theoxenia, in which a god or gods were invited to partake of a sacrificial feast, a couch (*lectus*) or couches being prepared for them as for ordinary banqueters. The ceremony was first held in 399 BC, after consultation of the Sibylline books, because Rome was struck by plague, and repeated later at times of similar emergency (see Livy 5. 13).

lē'cythus, oil-flask; see TOILET.

Lēda, in Greek myth, daughter of Thestius, king of Aetōlia, the wife of Tyndareus, king of Sparta, and mother of *Clytemnestra, *Helen of Troy, and of Castor and Polydeucēs (the *Dioscuri). She was loved by Zeus, who approached her in the form of a swan (a favourite subject in ancient art). Stories vary as to which children were fathered by Zeus; usually Helen is so described, and either both the Dioscuri, or Polydeuces alone. Leda is often said to have laid an egg, from which Helen (or Helen and Polydeuces) was hatched. Homer does not mention the egg, and later Greeks disbelieved the story or made fun of it.

legā'ti, during the late Roman republic, senatorial members of a provincial governor's staff, often made military commanders of a detachment or legion.

legend, see MYTH.

legion (*lĕgio*), see ARMY, ROMAN 2.

Lela'ntine war, see CHALCIS.

lemma, see TEXTS, TRANSMISSION OF ANCIENT 2.

Lemnos, large island in the north-east Aegean Sea, where *Hephaestus is said to have fallen when thrown out of heaven; its extinct volcano, which made the island fertile, was said to be the forge of Hephaestus. To its uninhabited shore the hero *Philoctētēs was banished. For the

story of the Lemnian women and the Argonauts see HYPSIPYLE. Herodotus relates that when the *Pelasgian (pre-Greek) population was driven out of Attica they occupied Lemnos, and later carried off a number of Athenian women. The Pelasgians afterwards became suspicious of the children of these women (for they banded together and spoke the Attic language), and therefore murdered them and their mothers; so that 'Lemnian deeds' became proverbial in Greece for atrocious acts. Lemnos was seized by *Miltiadēs *c.*500 BC when he ruled the Thracian Chersonese, subsequently received Athenian colonists, and was under Athenian domination for much of its later history.

le'murēs or **larvae,** in Roman religion, spirits of the dead, ghosts; dead members of the household were believed to haunt the house on 9, 11, and 13 May, the festival of the Lemuria, the most terrifying being those who had died young and were therefore thought to bear a grudge. Ovid gives an account of the ritual which every householder carried out privately at this time. To exorcize the ghosts he rose at midnight and walked barefoot through the house, spitting out (as he went) nine black beans for the ghosts to eat, in order to ransom the living members of the family whom otherwise the ghosts would carry off. (Beans were among the things that the *flamen dialis* might not touch.) After performing other rites he succeeded in driving the ghosts away (Ovid, *Fasti* 5. 419 ff.). Contrast the *Parentalia, when the ghosts were of immediate relatives, and regarded as beneficent.

Lēnae'a, at Athens, festival in honour of *Dionysus Lenaios, the epithet meaning either 'of the *lenōs*' ('wine-vat'), or 'of the *lēnai*' ('maenads'); it was celebrated on the twelfth day of the month named Lenaion among the Ionian Greeks, from the festival, but known as Gamelion at Athens, roughly January. There was a procession, but very little is known of the rites. Its chief importance lies in the dramatic competitions held in the Theatre of Dionysus which were inaugurated *c.*440 BC and in which comedy was particularly important.

Leo'nidas. 1. King of Sparta, who succeeded after the death of his half-brother Cleomenēs, and was commander of the Greeks at the battle of Thermopylae in 480 BC (see PERSIAN WARS).

2. Of Tarentum (first half of the third century BC), Greek writer of *epigrams, one of the best poets of the Greek *Anthology. His verse is highly finished, densely expressed, and often melancholy.

Leō'sthenēs, the Athenian general in the *Lamian War (323–322 BC). See also HYPEREIDES.

Le'pidus, Marcus Aemi'lius, the triumvir. As praetor in 49 BC he supported Julius Caesar, and was consul in 46 and Caesar's *magister equitum* in 46–44. After Caesar's death he joined forces with Mark Antony and in 43 planned the triumvirate with Antony and Octavian (see ROME 7). His importance to the triumvirate gradually diminished: in 36 his troops left him for Octavian, and he was compelled to retire to an Italian municipality. He died in 13 or 12 BC. His wife Junia was a sister of M. Brutus.

Leptinēs, Against, speech in a public prosecution by Demosthenes; see DEMOSTHENES (2) 2.

Lernae'an Hȳdra, see HERACLES, LABOURS OF 2.

Le'sbia, see CATULLUS.

Lesbos, largest of the Greek islands off the coast of Asia Minor, occupied by Aeolian Greek immigrants at the time of the *migrations. Its chief cities were Mytilēnē and Methymna. The poets Terpander, Arion, Sappho, and Alcaeus were born there. The poet Anacreon (mid-sixth century BC, a generation after Sappho) maliciously alludes to the island in a way that suggests that it was already known for the practice of female homosexuality, to which it has given its name. Lesbos formed part of the *Delian League but (except for Methymna) revolted from Athens in 428 BC during the Peloponnesian War. It was subdued by an Athenian expedition in 427, and under the influence of *Cleon the assembly at Athens voted that the whole population of Mytilene should be put to death or enslaved. On the following day the matter was reopened, and on the proposal of Diodotus the edict was revoked and a fast trireme sent to overtake the one already sent to carry out the decision. It arrived at Lesbos just in time to prevent the massacre; only the leaders of the revolt were put to death, and the land of the island (except for Methymna) was distributed among Athenian *cleruchs.

Leschēs, see ILIAD, LITTLE.

Lēthē ('forgetfulness'), in the Greek poet Hesiod the personification of forgetfulness, the daughter of Eris (Strife); in later Greek literature a place of oblivion in the Underworld, and in the myth at the end of Plato's *Republic* a plain which contains the 'river of unmindfulness' (*ameles potamos*). In the Latin poets it is one of the five rivers of the Underworld (see HADES); in Virgil's *Aeneid* 6 its water was drunk by souls about to be reincarnated, so that they forgot their previous existence. Ovid, *Metamorphoses* 11, has it as a river flowing around the Cave of Sleep where its murmuring induces drowsiness. The name was borne also by a spring in the oracular cave of the god *Trophonius.

Lēto (Lat. Latōna), in Greek myth, goddess, one of the *Titans, daughter of Coeus and Phoebē. She is one of the few Titans to have had a cult in Greece in historical times. Her chief importance is as the mother of the twin gods Apollo and Artemis, whose father was Zeus. For fear of the anger of Hera, Zeus' wife, no land would receive Leto when the time of their birth approached, until she came to the island of Ortygia (identified later with Delos), then a floating island, but thereafter secured to the seabed. There she gave birth to Artemis and Apollo, after some delay, because Hera would not allow *Eileithyia (goddess of childbirth) to go to her. While giving birth she leaned against Mount Cynthus, or a palm tree (later identified and regarded as sacred).

letters
1. *Greek.* Letters attributed to famous Greeks which have survived from ancient times are almost all spurious. The most important surviving collections are those attributed to *Isocrates, *Plato, and *Demosthenes. It is possible that none is genuine.

2. *Latin.* The Romans were great letter writers and important men in Cicero's time had among their slaves couriers (*tabellarii*) to deliver and collect letters, who might cover 80 km. (50 miles) a day (see POSTAL SERVICE). Cicero's voluminous correspondence seems to have been preserved in various ways. Atticus, Cicero's most intimate friend, to whom Cicero wrote in his own hand, kept the letters he received, as did Cicero's brother Quintus. His secretary Tiro appears to have kept copies of the letters Cicero sent to his various other friends, and these copies were collected and published after Cicero's death (see CICERO (1) 7 and TEXTS, TRANSMISSION OF ANCIENT 8). Nearly a hundred letters received by Cicero have also been preserved, providing an interesting contrast of styles. The letters of the Younger *Pliny, of which we have ten books, are more self-consciously composed for publication; only those of the tenth book, exchanged between Pliny as a provincial governor and his emperor, seem to have been written for practical purposes, without publication in mind. See also SENECA (2).

Leuci'ppē and Clei'tophon, see NOVEL.

Leuci'ppus. 1. Atomist philosopher; see PHILOSOPHY 1.

2. In Greek myth, son of Oenomaus; see DAPHNE.

Leucothe'a, Greek goddess of the sea; see DIONYSUS.

Leuctra, village in the territory of Thespiae in Boeotia, the scene of a battle in 371 BC, in which the Thebans under Epaminondas defeated the Spartans, thus bringing to an end the period of Spartan hegemony in Greece which had followed the Peloponnesian War. See SPARTA 4.

Liba'nius (AD 314–c.393), of Antioch (in Syria), Greek rhetorician. He studied at Athens

(336–40), and afterwards taught rhetoric at Constantinople (until 346) and at Nicomedia (in Bithynia, on the shores of the Propontis). Having declined a chair of rhetoric at Athens, in 354 he accepted instead a chair at Antioch, and remained there for the rest of his life. Although he remained a pagan, deeply attached to old ways, he had many distinguished Christian pupils, including John Chrysostom, and perhaps Basil the Great and Gregory of Nazianzus. Among his voluminous writings, his sixty-four speeches, which include his autobiography (Oration 1) and his funeral oration on the emperor Julian, and some sixteen hundred letters, are of considerable historical importance.

Libation Bearers (Choephoroe), see ORESTEIA.

libations (Lat. *libationes*, Gk. *loibai* or *spondai*), offerings to the gods, usually of unmixed wine, but sometimes also of milk, honey, and other fluids, including pure water, poured on the ground. At the beginning of a drinking-party (*symposium*), a little unmixed wine was poured on the floor to the Good *Daimon. The wine was usually mixed in three wine-bowls (*craterĕs*), and in Athens at least a libation was poured from each, to Zeus and the Olympian gods, to the heroes, and to Zeus Sōtēr ('saviour'). Libations always accompanied the sacrifice which was offered at the conclusion of a peace treaty; in Greece the treaty itself was called *spondai*, 'libations'.

Līber, Italian god of fertility, commonly identified with the Greek god Dionysus, although Liber seems not to have had any connection with wine. He had no temple in Rome but an important cult on the Aventine hill with his female counterpart Libera and with Ceres. His festival, the Liberalia, was on 17 March, characterized by crude songs and the use of masks, apparently hung on trees (see Virgil, *Georgics* 2. 385 ff.). This festival was a popular time for boys to put on the *toga virilis* ('man's toga'); see DRESS 2. The Romans connected his name with *libertas* ('liberty').

liberal arts, see SEVEN LIBERAL ARTS.

Liber spectāculo'rum, see MARTIAL.

lībe'rtus, freed man, see SLAVERY 2.

Libitī'na, Italian goddess of funerals, in whose temple at Rome registers of the dead were kept.

libraries. The first considerable collection of books of which we are reliably informed is that of Aristotle, although the tyrant Polycrates of Samos was said to have collected books, and the Athenian tyrant Peisistratus is even said to have founded a public library at Athens. Euripides is also credited with a collection of books. It seems to have been the arrangement of Aristotle's library that provided a model for the Ptolemies of Egypt; the library which the first two Ptolemies created at Alexandria in Egypt was the greatest in antiquity (see ALEXANDRIAN LIBRARY and HELLENISTIC AGE 3). The Attalid kings of Pergamum also formed a great library at about this time, said to have contained 200,000 volumes when Mark Antony presented it to Cleopatra. The Seleucid king Antiochus the Great (223–187 BC) had a library at Antioch of which the poet *Euphorion had charge. Perseus of Macedon (king 179–168 BC) also possessed a library. Athens did not have a public library until the second century BC, the gift of a Ptolemy. This Ptolemaion, as it was called, was visited by Cicero and Pausanias.

At Rome we hear of private libraries formed by Aemilius *Paullus, *Sulla, and *Lucullus, all of whom brought to Rome collections of Greek books which they had captured in their wars in the East. Cicero and his friend Atticus both had considerable collections of books. Julius Caesar had the intention of setting up a public library at Rome, and of placing *Varro in charge of it, but the credit for achieving that seems to belong to C. Asinius *Pollio, in the reign of the emperor Augustus. It contained Greek and Latin books, was adorned with portraits of authors, and was housed in the Atrium Libertātis ('hall of liberty'), the site of which is not known with certainty. Augustus founded two other libraries, one in the Campus Martius (the Octavian) and the other on the Palatine. The Bibliotheca Ulpia ('Ulpian library') of the emperor Trajan (AD 98–117) was the most famous of those set up at Rome by the later emperors. Under the empire the gift of a library to a provincial town was a recognized form of public munificence. For an example of a private library see HERCULANEUM.

libri linte'i ('books written on linen'), lists (now lost) of magistrates at Rome from 509 BC, the foundation of the republic, onwards, although they seem upon occasion to have been defective. Supposed to have been of great antiquity, they were probably not compiled before the mid-second century BC. They were stored in the temple of *Juno Moneta, and were consulted by Livy and other Roman historians.

libu'rna, liburnica, see SHIPS.

Libya, see AFRICA.

Licinian–Sextian laws (Licinian rogations), in Roman history, according to tradition, proposals originally made in 376 BC by the tribunes of the *plebs* P. Licinius Stolo and L. Sextius Laterānus and after a long struggle passed in 367 BC, enacting that one consul might be a plebeian and reducing in other areas the political inequalities between patricians and plebeians. Other measures were said to have aimed at relieving poverty by limiting individual tenancies on public land (*ager publicus*) to 500 *iugera* (310 acres), and restricting the number of animals which an individual might graze. However, this tradition may merely be anticipating the legislation of the *Gracchi.

lictors (*lictorēs*), attendants who always walked before Roman magistrates having *imperium*, and before certain priests; they proceeded in single file, each carrying the *fasces* on his left shoulder, symbolizing the magistrate's right of arrest, summons, and, in early times, execution. Their function was to announce the magistrate's approach and clear the public out of the way, except for Vestals and Roman matrons. The number of lictors varied with the importance of the office: a dictator had twenty-four; consuls had twelve, praetors six when outside Italy and at the head of an army. The custom seems to have been of Etruscan origin.

Ligurēs, see ITALY.

Linear A and B. During the second millennium BC there developed in *Crete first a pictographic form of writing, found on seal-stones and incised on clay tablets and other objects, and then out of it a simplified script known as Linear A. This seems to have been used throughout Crete from *c.*1750 to *c.*1450 BC but comparatively few specimens are known and no suggested decipherment has yet won general acceptance. The contents seem to be lists of men, women, and produce. The Linear B script was first found incised on small clay tablets at Cnossus in Crete, originally sun-dried but preserved because they had been baked in the fire which destroyed the building. They were first thought to be a form of Linear A, but subsequent discoveries on the Greek mainland at Thebes, Mycenae, Tiryns, and Pylos (in Messenia) show that it is the script of Mycenaean Greece; its use in Crete seems to indicate that the rulers there were by that time from mainland Greece. Some tablets at Cnossus may date from the fourteenth century; those on the mainland certainly date to a little before the final destructions of about 1200 BC (see MYCENAE), but the form of the writing probably evolved several centuries earlier. The Linear B script is quite similar to Linear A and is an adaptation of it; many of the signs are identical or virtually so; but whereas the language of Linear A is unknown, that of the Linear B texts, the language of the Mycenaeans, has been shown to be an early form of Greek. The script consists of about ninety signs, each of which represents a syllable; this syllabary is not well adapted to show Greek noun inflexions, so that there are ambiguous cases; there are also many words which cannot be matched with words known in later Greek. Nevertheless, the script was adequate for the day-to-day accounts and inventories which are all that the thousands of clay tablets so far discovered seem to record. It is possible that other records were kept on more perishable material, but the evidence so far suggests that writing was not used by private individuals but was merely a bureaucratic tool. The tablets are valuable for the light they throw on economic conditions and the nature of the administration; those concerned with temple property have been particularly interesting for the gods they name (see GODS). See also ALPHABET and GREECE.

Līnus, in Greek literature, an ancient and apparently mournful song containing the refrain *ailinon, ailinon* which was interpreted as *ai, Linus* or 'alas for Linus!'. The history of Linus was variously told in different parts of Greece; according to one version, he was a music teacher killed with his own lyre by Heracles, whom he had reprimanded. The 'song of Linus' was sung at harvest and vintage time from Homeric times onward. Compare LITYERSES.

literacy, see ALPHABET, BOOKS AND WRITING, and EDUCATION.

literary criticism, Greek and Roman. See ARS POETICA, DEMETRIUS (3), DIONYSIUS OF HALICARNASSUS, *LONGINUS ON THE SUBLIME*, POETICS, QUINTILIAN, RHETORIC, and ORATORY.

Little Iliad, see ILIAD, LITTLE.

liturgy (*leitourgia*), at Athens in the fifth and fourth centuries BC, a public service involving considerable expense compulsorily required of the richer citizens and *metics. Exempted were *archons and members of the *boulē during their year of office, and descendants of *Harmodius and Aristogeiton. There were some sixty liturgies a year in Athens alone, apart from the rest of Attica. The most important were the following. (i) The *chorēgia (provision of a chorus) for one or other of the various lyric and dramatic contests (at the Panathenaea, Thargelia, Dionysia, and Lenaea; see also TRAGEDY 2 and COMEDY, GREEK 1). This was a particularly costly service, and the *choregoi* (those undertaking it) rivalled one another in lavish expenditure. A client of Lysias spent 15,000 drachmas on eight of these liturgies. (ii) The *gymnasiarchiā*, the management (with nine others) of the *gymnasia and everything connected with them as well as the financing of the trainers and of those preparing for the games and public festivals; the gymnasiarch was also responsible for selecting and training one of the ten teams that took part in the torch-race. Lysias records the cost of this last duty as reaching twelve hundred drachmas. (iii) The *architheōria*, the leadership of a public embassy to one of the panhellenic festivals. (iv) The *hestiāsis*, the provision of a banquet for the members of a tribe or deme at a festival (the cost might be seven or eight hundred drachmas). In the fifth century there were some twelve hundred citizens liable to be called upon in rotation.

Individuals were nominated to the various liturgies by a magistrate or by the tribes, the heavier burdens being laid on the wealthier citizens. The only method of escaping one's turn was to challenge another who, in the opinion of the challenger, was better able to bear the expense. The person challenged might accept the liturgy, exchange properties with the challenger, or appeal to the courts (see ANTIDOSIS).

In addition to the regular liturgies there was the occasional charge of the *trierarchia*, for the equipment of a trireme (i.e. a warship). This was imposed only or principally in time of war, and only on the wealthiest citizens. The state provided the hull, mast, and sails, together with the pay and food of the crew; the trierarch, who was also the captain, bore all the expense of maintenance and repair. The cost of the service totalled nearly one talent, and after 411 BC it became necessary to allow the expense to be shared between two or three trierarchs. In 357 BC, *symmoriai* or companies of sixty citizens were set up to divide the expense, and later in 340 Demosthenes' naval law transferred this burden to a panel of 300. Service in the cavalry, entailing the provision of a horse and servant, was a lighter form of occasional liturgy.

Litye'rsēs, in Greek legend, son of *Midas, king of Phrygia. It is said he used to require all comers to help in the harvest, and if they did not surpass him in activity would kill or beat them, until a mightier hero (some say Heracles) arrived and killed him. It is also said that 'Lityerses' is the Phrygian reapers' song; it would seem therefore to be a traditional song with a story to explain it (compare LINUS).

Lī'via. 1. Later known as Julia Augusta (b. 58 BC), wife, first of Tiberius Claudius Nero (Cicero's first choice as husband for his daughter Tullia), and mother by him of the emperor Tiberius and of Claudius Drusus, father of the emperor Claudius; and secondly of the emperor Augustus. In 39 BC when she was pregnant with her second son, Nero was obliged to divorce her because Octavian (later the emperor Augustus) wished to marry her himself. Although she had no children by Augustus she retained his affection and high regard throughout their long marriage (she survived him, dying in AD 29). She was a woman of intelligence, dignity, great beauty, and tact, and she ruled over an orderly, well-regulated household. It is impossible to tell how much influence she exerted in matters of state, but Augustus valued her counsel, and she won the reverence of the Roman people. Under Augustus' will she was adopted into the *Julian *gens* and renamed Julia Augusta; she was the link between the Julian and the Claudian houses in the Julio-Claudian dynasty. After the accession of her son Tiberius, discord arose between them. At her death he refused to execute her will or allow her to be deified (as Julius Caesar and

Augustus were deified after their deaths); the emperor Caligula later carried out the former, and her grandson Claudius, when emperor, the latter. Some believed her to have acted ruthlessly to promote her own wishes (such as the succession of her son Tiberius) and to have had a hand in the deaths of *Marcellus and of Augustus' grandsons C. and L. Caesar (see JULIA), as well as of *Agrippa (2) and of her grandson *Germanicus (son of Claudius Drusus).

2. Livia or Livilla, b. *c.*13 BC, the daughter of Claudius Drusus who was the son of Livia (1) above, the sister of Germanicus (see above), and wife first of C. Caesar, Augustus' grandson, and secondly of Drusus, son of Tiberius. In league with *Sejanus, Tiberius' prefect of the praetorian guard, she caused her husband Drusus to be poisoned. In AD 25 Sejanus proposed to marry her but Tiberius refused. In 31 she was accused of misconduct and put to death.

Lī'vius Androni'cus, Lucius (*c.*284–204 BC), Roman writer. He was probably by origin a Greek of Tarentum, taken as a prisoner of war, after the fall of that city, to Rome in 272 (see ROME 4). (An alternative chronology in antiquity made him come to Rome in 209 after the Romans recaptured Tarentum from Hannibal.) He probably became tutor to the family of the father of M. Livius Salinātor, from whom he took his name when he was manumitted (see MANUMISSION). It can be claimed that he is the father of Roman literature. He seems to have wanted to introduce Greek literature to the Romans, and translated Homer's *Odyssey* into the long-established Italian saturnian metre (see METRE, LATIN I). His translation remained a school text-book for more than two centuries; forty-six lines of it survive. He is credited by Livy with introducing plot into the hitherto plotless Roman stage performances (see COMEDY, ROMAN I); he did so for the first time in 240 (according to the earlier chronology), producing a tragedy and a comedy at the *ludi Romani ('Roman games'), probably based on a classical Greek tragedy and a play of New Comedy (see COMEDY, GREEK 6); the *ludi* of that year were of special magnificence to celebrate the end of the (First) Punic War. He continued as a playwright; the titles of at least eight tragedies are known, but very few lines; even less is known of the comedies. In 207 BC he was commissioned to compose a 'maiden-song' to Juno (see LYRIC POETRY 2). This does not survive; Livy considered the words too 'unpleasing and graceless' to quote, though good enough for the time at which they were written. As reward the temple of *Minerva on the Aventine was set aside as a place where writers and actors might meet and make dedications as a *collegium ('guild'). His work was regarded by Cicero as antiquated and not worth reading, but his historical importance is considerable; he introduced to Roman literature Greek epic, drama, and lyric. Horace tells us that he used to learn Livius' *Odyssey* by heart, under threat of beating by *Orbilius.

Livy (Titus Livius) (59 BC–AD 17), Roman historian. He was born at Patavium (Padua) in north-east Italy, probably of a well-to-do family, but little is known of his life. The evidence suggests that he did not come to Rome until his adulthood. There he gave readings of his work, and won and retained the friendship of the emperor Augustus, who respected his republican sympathies, and encouraged the future emperor Claudius in his historical studies. He had at least two children, a son and a daughter. Livy appears never to have held any public office, but to have devoted his life to literature and history. He began his great 'History of Rome from its Foundation' (*Ab urbe condita libri*) in or shortly before 29 BC, and published it in instalments; it immediately brought him fame. He survived Augustus by three years, and is said to have died at Patavium.

The history consisted of 142 books, of which the last twenty-two dealt with the events of his own day from the death of Cicero in 43 BC. An epitome of it was written as early as the first century AD, and from this were compiled *periochae* or short abstracts of each book, of which there were perhaps two versions. Of the original work there survive books 1–10, 21–45 (41 and 43 incomplete), and a palimpsest fragment of book 91. The epitome is lost except for the parts covering books 37–40 and 48–55, which have been found on an Egyptian papyrus in the twentieth century; the *periochae* survive for all the books except 136 and 137. Books 1–5 describe the legendary founding of the city, the period of the kings, and the early republic down to its conquest by the Gauls in 390 BC. Books 6–15 deal with the subjugation of Italy (the Samnite Wars) before the conflict with Carthage, 16–30 with the first two Punic Wars; 31–45 with the Macedonian and other eastern wars down to 167. Of the subsequent books, now lost, 46–70 covered the succeeding period to the outbreak of the Social War; 71–90 to the death of Sulla; 91–108 to the Gallic War; 109–16 the civil war to the death of Caesar; 117–33 to the death of Antony; 134–42 the rule of Augustus down to 9 BC. The whole survived to late antiquity, but the Middle Ages knew no more books than are known today.

The work opens with an introduction in which Livy explains his purpose, to commemorate the deeds of the leading nation of the world, to describe the men and the mode of life that had raised Rome to greatness, and the decline of morals which brought about the troubles of the first century BC, so that his readers might thereby learn important lessons. His general purpose is thus ethical and didactic. His methods

were those of the fourth-century Greek Isocrates (see HISTORIOGRAPHY): it is the duty of the historian to tell the truth and be impartial, but the truth must be elaborated and given literary form. Livy's attitude to the early legends which he relates is that he neither affirms nor denies their truth, but regards it as of no great importance: if the legends are not true, they resemble the truth. They illustrate those aspects of Roman character which led to Rome's imperial greatness, as well as the true traditions to which Livy hoped, in the early Augustan period, that Rome might return from the moral decay, luxury, and indiscipline of the recent past. Livy used as his sources the earlier *annalists, then *Polybius (in books 31–45), and for the latest books *Posidonius, Julius Caesar, and Augustus' own *Memoirs*. He relied on written histories and made comparatively little use of original records, nor does he criticize his source material; he lacked the scientific method and the insight of Thucydides and Polybius. His inexperience of military affairs makes his descriptions of battles, and of the phalanx in particular, unrealistic; he has little understanding of political institutions, and throws little light on economic conditions or social life in Rome. He sometimes confuses his sources or misunderstands them so that his narratives are inconsistent; they are often given an anachronistic or implausible slant because of his ignorance of conditions at different times and in different places, e.g. in early Rome or in the East. But significant events are treated dramatically and memorably: the action is set against what Livy imagines its background to be in time and place; previous deliberations, changes of mind and heart, the characters of the protagonists, all such circumstances are explored and explained, so that the reader is presented with a story fully comprehensible in the way in which Livy wishes it to be comprehended, whatever its relation to actuality. Livy's prose is eloquent, clear, orderly, and full, developed from that of Cicero. Asinius *Pollio saw in it an element which he humorously called 'Patavinity', i.e. provincialism.

Livy was much praised by his immediate successors, Tacitus, the Senecas, and Quintilian, and drawn upon by Plutarch and Lucan. He is little heard of in the Middle Ages, but the Renaissance adopted him with enthusiasm. Dante speaks of him as the historian 'who errs not'. Among the many famous narratives found in the extant books are the following.

Book 1. Romulus and Remus (chapters 4–7); the rape of the Sabines (9–13); the fight of the Horatii and Curiatii and the death of Horatia (24–6); the coming of Lucumo (Tarquinius Priscus) to Rome (34); the accession of Lucius Tarquinius and the crimes of Tullia (46–8); the rape of Lucretia by Sextus Tarquinius and the revenge of Brutus (57–60).

Book 2. The execution of the sons of Brutus by their father (5); 'how Horatius kept the bridge' (10); Mucius Scaevola's attempt to kill Porsena (12); Cloelia swimming the Tiber (13); Menenius Agrippa and the parable of the belly and the members (32); the meeting of Coriolanus and his mother outside Rome (40); the 306 Fabii marching out against the Veientes (49).

Book 3. The summoning of Cincinnatus from the fields to be dictator (24); Appius Claudius and Verginia (44–58).

Book 4. The fight between Cossus and the Etruscan king, in which the former won the *spolia opima* (19).

Book 5. The siege of Veii, and the Greeks in Rome.

Book 6. The execution of M. Manlius Capitolinus (20).

Book 7. M. Curtius leaping into the abyss (6).

Book 8. T. Manlius Torquatus ordering the execution of his son who, in defiance of orders, had fought and killed an enemy chief (7); P. Decius Mus 'devoting' himself to death (see DEVOTIO) for the victory of his army (9); the anger of Papirius Cursor against his *magister equitum*, Q. Fabius Maximus Rullus (30).

Book 9. The disaster of the Caudine Forks (1); and the unexpected digression on what would have happened had Alexander the Great encountered the Romans (17).

Book 21. The character of Hannibal (4), the siege of Saguntum (12), Hannibal's crossing of the Alps (30), the battle of the Trebia (52).

Book 22. The battle of Lake Trasimene (4); the conflict of Q. Fabius Maximus (grandson of Fabius above) with his impetuous *magister equitum*, Minucius (14); the defeat at Cannae (44). Maharbal's criticism of Hannibal's delay, that he knew how to conquer but not how to use his victory (51).

Book 23. Hannibal at Capua, the debilitating effect of Capuan luxury on his army (45), and the turning point of the war.

Book 24. The siege of Syracuse by Marcellus and the defensive devices of Archimedes (34).

Book 25. The capture of Syracuse (24) and the death of Archimedes (31).

Book 26. Hannibal's approach within three miles of Rome (10; the land on which his camp stands is sold in the city at its full price, 11); Scipio Africanus appointed commander in Spain at the age of 24 (18), and capturing Nova Carthago (46); his generosity and restraint in the treatment of a beautiful Spanish captive (50).

Book 27. The interception and defeat of Hasdrubal.

Book 30. The romantic story of *Sophonisba, Syphax, and Masinissa (15); the battle of Zama (32).

Book 33. The defeat of Philip V of Macedon at Cynoscephalae (7); the notable speech of Flamininus on making peace with a defeated enemy (12); the proclamation of Greek freedom at the Isthmian games (32).

Book 34. The repeal of the Oppian sumptuary law (1).

Book 35. The conversation of Scipio and Hannibal at Ephesus about great military commanders (14).

Book 38. The proud reminder by Scipio Africanus when tried for embezzlement that the day was the anniversary of his victory at Zama (51).

Book 39. The discovery and suppression of the Bacchanalian orgies (8); the character of Cato the Censor (40).

Book 44. The victory of Pydna (40).

logo'graphers (*logographoi*). 1. Early Greek prose writers who were forerunners of historians proper (see HISTORIOGRAPHY 1), and who lived mostly in Ionia (Greek Asia Minor) in the sixth and fifth centuries BC. None of their works has survived, but there are numerous references to them and quotations in later authors. The earliest are said to have been Cadmus and Dionysius, both of Miletus, but very little is known of either. *Hecataeus, also of Miletus, was one of the most famous. Pherecȳdēs of Athens, active in the first half of the fifth century BC, wrote *Histories* (i.e. 'inquiries') in ten books, both mythical and genealogical. Charōn of Lampsacus, Xanthus of Lydia, and *Hellanīcus of Lesbos were a little earlier than, or contemporary with, Herodotus. Of these, Hellanicus, who outlived Herodotus, was a prolific author, writing on mythological topics (systematic genealogies of heroic families), on regional history (e.g. *Lesbiaca, Persica*), and on local history and chronology; his *Atthis* was criticized by Thucydides for its inadequate chronology of the fifth century.

2. Name given at Athens to persons who were hired to write speeches for litigants to deliver in a court of law (see LAW, AT ATHENS 3). *Antiphon was said to have been the first of these; *Lysias and *Demosthenes (2) were also very successful at this practice. Since many trials were political, speech-writing sometimes laid the foundation for a later political career.

Lo'llius U'rbicus, Quintus, governor of Britain from AD 139 until after 142; see BRITAIN 5.

Longī'nus, Ca'ssius (*c.* AD 213–73, to be distinguished from the supposed author of the treatise 'On the Sublime'; see below), an eminent Greek rhetorician and philosopher. A *Neoplatonist, he taught at Athens, and was the teacher of *Porphyry. In the last few years of his life he became the principal counsellor of Odaenathus and *Zenobia, the rulers of Palmyra. For his loyal support of Zenobia he was executed when the city fell to the Roman emperor Aurelian. Fragments of his works survive.

Longī'nus on the Sublime (*Peri hypsous*), Greek literary treatise (a third of which is lost) of unknown authorship and date. Its manuscript attribution to Longinus (above) is contradicted on chronological grounds by internal evidence indicating a date in the first century AD. The author says that his work is a reply to a similarly entitled treatise of the first century BC by Caecilius of Calactē, who gave what 'Longinus' considers to be an inadequate account of 'sublimity', failing in particular to attach sufficient importance to the emotional element in this concept. It is addressed to a friend, Postumius Terentianus (of whom nothing is known but who is presumed from his name to be Roman), and is on the subject of what constitutes sublimity in literature. It has greatly appealed to later readers by its enthusiasm, sage criticism, apt illustrations (mostly from Greek literature), and clarity of expression. The author analyses the constituents of sublimity, and finds them in elevated thought ('sublimity is the echo of a noble mind', 9. 2); strong emotion; certain kinds of figures of thought and speech; nobility of diction ('truly beautiful words are the very light of the spirit', 30. 1); and composition, i.e. word-order, rhythm, euphony. He lists the faults to be avoided: turgidity, puerility, false emotion, frigidity; discusses the part played by imagination and various figures of speech; and illustrates his points by a wealth of quotation. There are interesting observations on successful and unsuccessful ways of representing supernatural beings and of exciting awe, and comparisons of Homer's *Iliad* and *Odyssey*, and of Demosthenes and Cicero, which are very rewarding. The author finds the chief examples of sublimity of style in Homer, Plato, and Demosthenes, of whom he speaks with appreciative enthusiasm. At one point (in a section on selection and organization of material) his quotation preserves an ode of *Sappho, translated by the Roman poet Catullus (see poem 51). There is a notable passage (9. 9) in which the author points out, as an instance of grandeur in representing the divine, the first verses of Genesis. No other pagan writer uses the Bible in this way, and one must presume that the author had, unusually, both Roman (in the case of his addressee) and Jewish contacts.

This is a critical work of great importance; the writer is able to transcend the rhetorical tradition within which he worked and contribute to our understanding of true literary greatness.

long jump, see ATHLETICS (viii).

Longus, see NOVEL.

Long Walls. At Athens, the two Long Walls connecting Athens with her ports to the south-west at Piraeus and Phalerum were built between 461 and 456 BC. Around 445 BC after the Thirty Years' Peace (see ATHENS 2 (ii)) and at the prompting of Pericles, a third wall was built parallel to the Piraeus wall and about 170 m. (190 yds.) south of it, the original Phaleric Wall being allowed to fall into ruin. The two walls to Piraeus were each about 6 km. (4 miles) long. The main road from Athens lay outside these parallel walls, the road between them being primarily military. The effect of the walls during the Peloponnesian War was to turn the whole territory between Athens and the ports into a fortress, victualled from the sea. After the Spartan victory at the end of the Peloponnesian War (404 BC) the walls were dismantled, to the sound of flute music. They were rebuilt by *Conon after his victory at Cnidus in 394 BC, but were in ruins when Philip V of Macedon attacked Athens in 200 BC. Today there is virtually no trace of them to be seen.

lot, see SORTITION.

Lotus-eaters (Lōtophagoi), in Homer's *Odyssey* 9, a fabulous people whose land Odysseus visits. They live on the lotus-fruit, whose property is to make those who eat it forget their home and desire to remain for ever in Lotus-land.

Lūcan (Marcus Annaeus Lūcanus) (AD 39–65), Silver Latin poet, born at Corduba (Cordoba) in Spain. He was grandson of Seneca the Elder, and his father was the brother of Seneca the Younger (and the brother of Gallio of Acts 18). He was educated at Rome, studying philosophy under the Stoic Cornūtus, whose tuition he is said to have shared with the satirist *Persius. He continued his studies at Athens but was recalled by the emperor Nero, who admitted him to his circle, made him quaestor and augur, and greatly admired him for a time. In AD 60 at the first celebration of the games called Neronia he won a poetic competition. In 62 or 63 he published three books of his epic *Pharsalia (on the civil war between Caesar and Pompey). However, he incurred the enmity of Nero, for which various reasons are given; it is possible that the emperor was jealous of Lucan's literary success, having himself some claim to being a poet. Lucan was forbidden to write further poetry or to plead in the courts. He took to lampooning the emperor and even joined the conspiracy of *Piso (64–5). When this was discovered Lucan, in spite of confessions and abject pleas, was compelled to commit suicide (as were his father and both uncles). There is a biography of him by *Suetonius.

Lucan was a voluminous and precocious writer, but all his works apart from the *Pharsalia* are lost, among them an address to his much-loved wife Polla Argentaria. The *Pharsalia* is the greatest Latin epic after the *Aeneid*, and Lucan's brilliant style won him the admiration of his contemporaries. One of them, Quintilian, while recognizing its qualities, adds that it is 'a safer model for orators than for poets'.

Lucā'nia, see ITALY.

Lū'cerēs, see RAMNES.

Lu'cian (Lūciānus, Gk. Loukiānos) (c. AD 115 to after 180), born at Samosata on the Euphrates in Syria, the author (in Greek) of some eighty prose pieces in various forms, essays, speeches, letters, dialogues, and stories, mainly satirical in tone. His native language was Syriac, but he received a good Greek education in rhetoric and became first an advocate and then, like many of his day, a travelling lecturer, although he was a satirist rather than a sophist (see SOPHISTIC, SECOND). The details of his life are known only from his own writings; no contemporary or near-contemporary mentions him. He travelled through Asia, Greece, Italy, and Gaul, but in middle age he moved to Athens and abandoned rhetoric for philosophy. It may have been after that that he developed the dialogue form (familiar from Plato) which made him famous, although it is impossible to date his works securely. His writings were influenced by Attic Old Comedy (see COMEDY, GREEK 3), the dialogues of Plato, and especially the satires of the Cynic *Menippus, and he scathingly, if humorously, indicts the follies of his day. In later life he was appointed to a minor post in the Roman bureaucracy in Egypt.

1. Among his writings on literary and quasiphilosophical subjects are the following: (i) *The Vision* or the *Life of Lucian* (*Somnium* or *Vita Luciani*), a chapter of his early life, telling how he abandoned sculpture (to which his parents had apprenticed him) for learning; (ii) *Nigrīnus*, which contains an interesting picture of the simplicity and peace of contemporary Athens contrasted with the turbulent and luxurious life of Rome; (iii) *The Literary Prometheus* (*Ad eum qui dixerat, 'Prometheus es in verbis'*: 'to him who said, "you are like Prometheus in your language"*'*), in which he describes the basis of his satires, namely a blend of comedy and Platonic dialogue; (iv) *The Way to Write History* (*De historia conscrībenda*), an entertaining criticism of the eccentricities of contemporary historians, followed by an acute exposition of the qualities required in a history and its author; (v) *Dēmōnax*, an account of the character of that Cynic philosopher, Lucian's teacher, praised for his austere virtue; (vi) *Imāginēs (Eikonĕs)*, a dialogue with interesting references to the chief works of some of the great Greek artists, Pheidias, Praxitelēs, Polygnotus, and Apellēs; and (vii) *True History* (*Vērae historiae*), a parody of travellers' tales, including Homer's *Odyssey* and *Ctesias' Indica*, which Lucian begins with the assertion that he tells the truth only when he says that it is all lies. The adventures related in this last work are of the most extravagant and

ingenious kind, involving a voyage to the moon and to the Isles of the Blest, where the travellers meet Homer and hear him condemn his critics, and assert, among other things, that he began the *Iliad* with the anger of Achilles merely from chance, without any settled plan. When the travellers arrive at the Underworld they find Herodotus and Ctesias there paying the penalty for their falsehoods. Both Rabelais in the sixteenth century and Jonathan Swift in the eighteenth found inspiration in this work.

2. Lucian's satirical dialogues are numerous, and together with his fantastic tales are his most characteristic works, showing his wit and inventiveness as well as his hatred of cant, hypocrisy, and fanaticism, especially in religion and philosophy. Among the best-known of these dialogues are the following. (i) *Dialogues of the Gods* (*Deorum dialogi*) and *of the Sea Gods* (*Marīnorum dialogi*), short dialogues making fun of the myths about e.g. the birth of Athena, Apollo's love affairs, the Judgement of Paris, and the story of Polyphemus and Galatea. (ii) *Dialogues of the Dead* (*Mortuorum dialogi*), short dialogues set in the Underworld, the interlocutors being such characters as Pluto, Hermēs, Charon, Menippus, Diogenēs, Heraclēs, Alexander the Great, and Achilles. Death shows up the vanities and pretences of living men (including the arguments of philosophers), and defeats the intrigues of expectant heirs. The irony, at the expense of all humankind, is grim and tinged with melancholy and resignation. (iii) *Menippus* (also called *Necyomantia*); Menippus, the Cynic philosopher, exasperated by the contradictions of philosophy, visits the Underworld to consult Teiresias as to the best life to lead, and is told merely to do, with smiling face and taking nothing too seriously, the task that lies to hand. Similar themes are treated in the *Charon*, where Charon, the ferryman from the Underworld, visits the upper world to see what life is like and what it is that makes men weep when they enter his boat (i.e. life seen from the point of view of death); this is the most poetic of Lucian's dialogues, with its comparisons of cities to bee-hives attacked by wasps, and of human lives to bubbles. The whole is a picture of the pettiness of mankind; Charon himself observes, 'This is all laughable'. (iv) *The Voyage to the Underworld* (*Kataplous*), describing a boat-load of the dead and their attitudes. Only the cobbler Micyllus eagerly accepts his summons to the Underworld. (v) *The Dream* or *The Cock*, concerning Micyllus the cobbler again, who threatens to kill a cock which has woken him from a happy dream of riches. The cock reveals himself to be Pythagoras, in one of his incarnations (a previous one had been *Aspasia), and argues that Micyllus is much happier than many rich men. To prove the point the cock and Micyllus, rendered invisible by the former's magic tail feathers, visit

the houses of several rich men and observe their miseries and vices. (vi) *The Sale of Lives* (*Vitarum auctio*), an entertaining piece in which the chief proponents of various philosophic creeds are put up for sale, Hermes being the auctioneer: Diogenēs the *Cynic goes for two obols, useful as a house dog; Heracleitus is unsaleable; Socrates (apparently identified with Platonic philosophy), after considerable ridicule, fetches the enormous sum of two talents, bought by Dion of Syracuse; Pyrrhon the *Sceptic is disposed of last, and even after he is in the hands of the buyer is still in doubt as to whether he has been sold or not. (vii) *Icaromenippus*, very Aristophanic in its fantastic plot: Menippus (see (iii) above), disgusted with the disputes of the philosophers, resolves to visit the heavens himself to find out the truth, cutting off the wings of an eagle and a vulture as a mechanical aid. He finds *Empedoclēs in the moon, carried there by the vapours of Aetna. He is civilly received by the gods, and watches Zeus receive human prayers, through ventholes in the floor of heaven; he attends a banquet and hears the gods decide to destroy all philosophers as useless drones. Returned to earth Menippus hastens with malicious pleasure to the *Stoa Poikilē to announce to the philosophers their impending doom. (viii) *The Cross-examination of Zeus* (*Zeus confutātus*), on the conflict between the doctrine of fate and that of divine omnipotence. (ix) *Meeting of the Gods* (*Deorum concilium*), in which Momus complains of the admission among the genuine deities of a number of foreigners, mortals, and others of doubtful credentials, from Dionysus and his hangers-on to the Egyptian Apis and Anubis. (x) *Dependent Scholars* (*De mercēde conductis*), written to dissuade a Greek philosopher from accepting a place in a Roman household, with its attendant hardships and humiliations, for a pittance; it is an excellent example of Lucian's witty good sense. (xi) *Peregrine* (*De morte Peregrīni*), a satirical narrative of the career of a fanatical Cynic and apostate Christian (a historical character) who, in pursuit of notoriety, had himself burnt alive on a pyre. (xii) *Lucius or the Ass* (*Lucius sive asinus*), a short novel doubtfully ascribed to Lucian; it is perhaps an abbreviated form of an earlier Greek romance which was also the basis of the Latin novel 'The Golden Ass' of *Apuleius. See also TIMON (1).

Lūcī'lius, Gaius (*c.*180–102 BC), Latin satirical poet, born at Suessa Aurunca in Campania, a member of the literary circle of *Scipio Aemilianus, and famous as the creator of that purely Roman form of literature, (poetical) satire. Lucilius established hexameters as the standard metre for Roman satire and in it wrote thirty books of informal discourses, mainly autobiographical, greatly influenced by Greek literature and Stoic philosophy. The subjects he

dealt with included incidents in the lives of himself and his friends, travels, literary subjects, public and private morality, and popular philosophy. Some of his satires included outspoken criticism of authors and men in public life. Of these works some 1,300 lines survive, but no single substantial passage. The satires served as a model for later satirists, especially Horace, whose celebrated 'Journey to Brundisium' (*Satire 1. 5) was modelled on one, and they were read until the end of the Roman empire.

Lūcī'na, see JUNO.

Lucius or the Ass, see LUCIAN.

Lucrē'tia, in Roman history, the wife of L. Tarquinius Collatinus, nephew of Tarquinius Priscus (see ROME 2). According to legend she was raped by Sextus, son of Tarquinius Superbus, and having revealed this to her husband took her own life. This incident led to the insurrection headed by Junius *Brutus and the expulsion of the Tarquins from Rome. The story is told by Livy and is the subject of Shakespeare's poem *Rape of Lucrece* (1594).

Lucrē'tius. 1. **Titus Lucretius Cārus** (98–*c.*55 BC), Roman poet and philosopher, author of *De rerum natura* ('on nature'), his only known work. Of his life virtually nothing has come down to us. *Jerome, in his translation of the *Chronica* of Eusebius, states that he was born in 94 BC, was poisoned by a love-philtre, wrote in the intervals of madness some books which Cicero later 'emended', and took his own life at the age of 44. There is no other evidence for his madness, and the story has the appearance of Christian polemic. Cicero, writing to his brother in 54 BC, mentions Lucretius in a way which suggests both brothers had read some of his poetry. The poem, though in a finished state, was clearly not finally completed, and it must be concluded that it was published as it stood after the author's death, probably near the middle of the first century BC. The poem is dedicated to the aristocrat C. Memmius, the patron of Catullus and Cinna (whom Catullus accompanied to Bithynia during Memmius' propraetorship of 57). The description Lucretius gives of Memmius in the proem to Book 1, as excelling in all graces and helping his country in her hour of need, is likely to antedate his disgrace and banishment in 53 for corrupt practices in the elections of 54.

De rerum natura is a didactic poem in six books of hexameters, and is the fullest exposition we possess of the physical system of *Epicurus, in which Lucretius was a convinced and ardent believer. The purpose of the poem is to free men from a sense of guilt and the fear of death by demonstrating that fears of the intervention of gods in this world and of punishment of the soul after death are groundless: the world and everything in it are material and governed by the mechanical laws of nature, and the soul is mortal and perishes with the body. Thus most of the poem is devoted to an exposition of the atomic theory which Epicurus had adopted from the philosophers *Democritus and Leucippus: that an infinite number of atoms moving about in infinite space collide and combine with each other to bring into existence the world in all its variety, and there is nothing in the world that is not material. However, Lucretius allows that men possess free will, and accounts for it by stating that atoms occasionally swerve from their path out of their own volition. He also touches upon Epicurus' moral theory that pleasure is the aim of life.

Book 1 opens with a superb invocation of Venus, goddess of creative life, to grant to the poet inspiration and to Rome peace. It proceeds to the demonstration that the universe consists of void and small particles of matter, atoms, which are solid, indivisible, and indestructible. In passing Lucretius refutes the physical systems of *Heracleitus, *Empedocles, and *Anaxagoras, and demonstrates that the universe is infinite in extent.

Book 2 starts with a passage on the blessings of philosophy. It then deals with the motion of atoms which, endlessly falling through space by their own nature, may swerve a little from their path (the swerve being Epicurus' rejection of a determinist universe) and, colliding with other atoms, form into masses; from these masses the universe is built up by chance arrangement. The atoms possess only size, shape, and mass, other qualities being secondary. The book concludes with a demonstration that the universe contains many other worlds similar to ours.

Book 3 starts with praise of Epicurus and then proceeds to a demonstration that the soul too is made of atoms, of an extremely rarefied nature, and, with a long series of proofs, that it is mortal. The book ends triumphantly with an eloquent exposition of the foolishness of fearing death.

Book 4 deals mainly with the Epicurean theory of vision, sensation, and thought, and with various biological processes, digestion, sleep, and the meaning of dreams, and ends with a vigorous denunciation of the physical passion of love which destroys the Epicurean ideal state, peace of mind.

Book 5 begins with an extravagant eulogy of Epicurus, holding him to be partly divine because of his god-like peace of mind. Lucretius attacks the theological view of the world. He shows how the world had a beginning and will have an end, and discusses some problems of astronomy. He then traces the origin on earth of plant and animal life, including human life, and with remarkable insight describes the development of primitive man and the birth of civilization.

Book 6, whose introduction is one more laudation of Epicurus, is the loosest in composition and shows signs of being unfinished. It deals with unusual meteorological and terrestrial phenomena, earthquakes, volcanoes, the magnet, etc., concluding with pestilence and a horrific account of the plague at Athens (see PELOPONNESIAN WAR).

There is no specific treatment of the subject of moral conduct, but it is clear from various passages that Lucretius accepted the view of Epicurus. Pleasure and pain are the only guides to conduct, but by pleasure he understands the calm that proceeds from absence of pain and desire, and freedom from care and fear. He is deeply moved at the thought of Epicurus' great contribution to the alleviation of human suffering by banishing superstitious fears, introducing peace of mind, and teaching men how to face all the disasters of life with serenity, and he speaks of the philosopher with religious awe. Although he describes Epicureanism with the fervour of a religious convert, he has at the same time a firm grasp of his intellectual arguments, and writes with intelligent understanding of the issues as well as with emotion. Much of the subject matter does not lend itself easily to poetic treatment, and there are parts that make for tortuous reading, and others where the versification is heavy and clumsy; but the work as a whole is suffused with an intense awareness of the world about him, especially of the beauty of the countryside, with warm sympathy for all living things and a compassionate, even painful, understanding of humanity. His strong moral sense, lightened by a lively feeling for the ridiculous, often leads naturally to satire, while his close observation of the world makes it easy for him to illustrate his arguments with vivid but homely images and similes which drive them home. His hexameters have weight and dignity, though admitting metrical practices that later poets preferred to avoid. The style shows the influence of the old Latin poets, *Ennius (particularly), *Naevius, *Pacuvius, and *Accius. He freely uses alliteration, assonance, and even rhyme, as well as repetition, and archaic forms and constructions; and he does not hesitate to invent new words including such compound adjectives as terriloquus ('uttering frightening words') and horrisonus ('making a terrifying noise'), complaining of the poverty of his native tongue. He is aware of his own originality and the difficulty of treating such a subject in poetry at all, let alone in Latin with no tradition of writing philosophy in verse. But poetry is important as the 'honey on the rim' of the cup containing the bitter draught of philosophy.

Lucretius aroused the admiration of Virgil (felix qui potuit rerum cognoscere causas, 'happy the man who was able to understand the causes of things'; see GEORGICS), of Statius (who speaks of the docti furor arduus Lucreti, 'the towering frenzy of the learned Lucretius'), even of Ovid. But in the Middle Ages he appears to have been almost completely forgotten; the text is still based upon only two primary manuscripts. It is through Lucretius that the atomic theories of Epicurus are best known today.

2. **Quintus Lucretius Vespi'lio** (consul 19 BC), who was concealed by his wife Turia during the proscriptions of 43–42 BC until his pardon was obtained. He has been thought to be the author of the remarkable *Laudatio Turiae* ('eulogy of Turia'); see WOMEN, POSITION OF 2.

Lūcu'llus, Lucius Lici'nius (*c.*114–57 BC), member of a noble but impoverished family, nephew of *Metellus Numidicus, for whose return from exile he pleaded. He showed ability as a general in the Social War under *Sulla, and as quaestor in 88 BC was the only officer who supported Sulla's march on Rome. He was Sulla's most reliable officer, entrusted with the diplomatic side of his dealings in the East, and became his literary executor. He governed Africa as propraetor in 77 with honesty and humanity. Consul in 74, he obtained the command against *Mithridatēs, king of Pontus, and carried out a series of brilliant campaigns in the Third Mithridatic War until his troops, kept under strict discipline, began to mutiny. He settled the taxation of Asia fairly, thereby offending business interests at Rome, and in 66 he was replaced by Pompey under the Manilian law (see PRO LEGE MANILIA) and returned to Rome, where he had to wait until 63 for a *triumph. He then led the senate's opposition to the eastern settlement of his rival Pompey, but after unpleasant experiences of Caesar's consulate (59) retired and gave himself up to the indulgence of his hedonist tastes, having acquired great wealth in Asia. His luxury became proverbial: 'Lucullan' has been applied as an epithet to good food. He was an ardent philhellene, a lover of literature and the arts. The books of the Pontic kings, booty from the war, remained his private property, but he was always ready to lend them, and his library became a centre for literary Greeks at Rome (see PRO ARCHIA). He wrote an account in Greek of the Marsian War (90–89 BC; see ROME 6). He is said to have introduced the cherry into Italy from Cerasus in Pontus. He lapsed into insanity before his death.

lūdi, the public games at Rome, a term used to describe a variety of theatrical performances, sports, and contests which took place on the occasion of festivals of the gods, and were instituted to win their favour or avert their anger, or to comply with some oracular command. They were usually annual but sometimes were held for a specific occasion. They followed an exact ritual, any deviation from which entailed a repetition (*instaurātio*) of the proceedings. Unlike the Greek games they did not for the most part include an element of athletic contest: this was first introduced in imperial times in what were known as *agōnēs*, such as the *agon Neroniānus* and the *agon Capitōlīnus* (see 2 below).

1. *Republican period.*
(i) The earliest *ludi* appear to have been *chariot-races, *ludi circenses*, held in honour of Mars or Consus, under the control of magistrates. Then came gladiatorial and other displays in the forum and in amphitheatres, a survival perhaps from Etruscan funeral games. The first permanent site for the games was constructed in 329 BC. There were also games under the control of the priests, like the dances of the *Salii. The *ludi Romani* or *magni* were also of early date, given annually by the *curule aediles in September and probably originating in the return of a general with his army after a victorious campaigning season, when he carried out the vow he had made to give a festival to Jupiter if successful. From being 'votive' in origin these games became annual after 366 BC and their duration was extended from one day to fifteen (5–19 September). They included a great procession to the temple of *Jupiter (Optimus Maximus) on the Capitol, in which images of the great gods were carried, as well as chariot-races and military displays. They were similar to, but distinct from, the *ludi Capitolini*, very ancient games held on the Ides of October.

(ii) *Ludi scaenici,* consisting in the performance of plays, were added to the *ludi Romani* in 240 BC when *Livius Andronicus produced the first adaptations from Greek drama. (However, this was not the occasion of the first public dramatic performances at Rome, for Livy states that in 364 BC pantomimic dances by Etruscans were exhibited to appease divine anger at a time of plague: see COMEDY, ROMAN 1.) From 214 BC four days were devoted to stage-performances at the *ludi Romani* and later these were also included in the *ludi plebeii* (from 200 at the latest), *Apollinares* (from at latest 169), and *Megalenses* (in 194–191): see below. It is probable that at first only two tragedies and two comedies were produced annually. In the later republic there were fifty-five days in each year on which *ludi scaenici* took place, and the number was further increased under the empire.

(iii) *Ludi plebeii* were instituted by 214 BC at the latest and held in November, the first of several festivals intended to cheer the citizenry in the dark days of the Second Punic War. They may have devoted a day to drama from their inception, although the first recorded performance is that of Plautus' *Stichus* in 200. The games may have been a repetition of the *ludi Romani*, but little is known about them.

(iv) *Ludi Apollinārēs,* in honour of Apollo, were also instituted in the Second Punic War, at a dangerous time (212). They were shortly afterwards made annual on the proposal of the *praetor urbanus* at a time of epidemic. They were extended from one to eight and then to nine days (5–13 July); there is no evidence for the presentation of plays before 169 BC, but this may be chance. One day was given to games in the Circus.

(v) *Ludi Megalenses* (4–10 April), in honour of the Magna Mater ('great mother', *Cybelē), again established in the Second Punic War, in 204 BC, celebrated the arrival from Phrygia of the sacred stone of the goddess. Drama was probably a feature from the beginning, with only one day occupied with games in the Circus. See also MEGALESIA.

(vi) *Ludi Cereālēs* (12–19 April), established in at latest 202 BC, were a plebeian festival in honour of Ceres (the tutelary goddess of the plebs). On the last, most important, day there were games in the Circus, and under the empire dramatic performances.

(vii) *Ludi Flōrālēs* (28 April–2 May), instituted in 240 or 238 BC at the command of the Sibylline books because of a prolonged famine, and restored or regularized in 173 BC, were designed to secure the protection of the goddess Flora for the new blossom. It was a time of general festivity without much restraint; theatrical and mimic performances constituted the first part of the celebrations; the last day was occupied with *venationes*, the hunting of animals in the Circus.

All these games were provided by the state, but their cost might be supplemented by the magistrates concerned (the aediles except in the case of the *ludi Apollinares*, which were under the *praetor urbanus*). The magistrates used the opportunity to increase their popularity and chance of election to higher magistracies by putting on lavish shows.

Displays and hunting of large animals, first mentioned as occurring in 186 BC, became a popular feature of the public games (see VENATIONES); in a letter to Cicero when he was governor of Cilicia M. *Caelius Rufus begged the former to send him some panthers. *Gladiators were apparently not introduced in the official games till the end of republican times, though gladiatorial displays given by private individuals had by then become very popular. See also NAUMACHIAE (mimic sea-fights).

2. *Imperial period.* The games mentioned above were continued under the empire and others were added, of which the most important are the following.

(i) *Ludi saeculārēs*, though strictly speaking of republican origin, came into prominence only in imperial times. They were originally introduced at an unknown but early time as games and sacrifices performed in order to end some national danger or distress from plague or for some other cause (the stories vary widely), and were supposedly held at intervals of a hundred years (*saeculum*). Soon after the emperor

Augustus had established himself as the supreme power in the state it was announced by the *quindecimviri* (see VIGINTISEXVIRATE) that, according to their books, *ludi saeculares* ought to be held; the celebrated jurist and antiquary Ateius *Capito was asked by the emperor to determine what the ceremony should be, and the poet Horace was requested to compose a festival hymn (*Carmen Saeculare*), which survives. These games were celebrated from 31 May to 2 June 17 BC, and the ceremonies and performances of plays and of the hymn are recorded in detail in an inscription which survives, the *acta sacrorum saeculārium* of 17 BC. The *ludi saeculares* were celebrated again by the emperor Claudius in AD 47 (on the eight hundredth anniversary of the foundation of Rome) and by the emperor Domitian in AD 87 (as being roughly a century after the celebration by Augustus). On the latter occasion Tacitus the historian was one of the *quindecimviri* in charge of the ceremonies; the celebration is referred to by the poets Martial and Statius. They were celebrated for the last time with unprecedented magnificence on 21 April AD 248 by the emperor Philip the Arab, for the thousandth anniversary of the founding of Rome.

(ii) *Ludi Martiālēs* in honour of Mars were celebrated every year on 1 August under Augustus. The *ludi Augustālēs* (or Augustalia, from 14 BC) commemorated the return of Augustus from the East (on 12 October 19 BC); after his death they were celebrated with greater solemnity, and under the emperor Claudius the festival lasted from 3 to 12 October.

(iii) The *agon Nerōniānus* was instituted by Nero in AD 60 in partial imitation of the Olympian games. It was to be held every five years and to include chariot-races, athletic contests, and contests in music and poetry.

(iv) The *agon Capitōlīnus* was instituted by Domitian in AD 86, also in imitation of the Olympian games. It was held every four years and included athletic and musical contests (see STATIUS (2)).

See also GAMES, PUBLIC.

lūdus Trō'iae ('game of Troy'), at Rome, apparently of ancient origin, a kind of shamfight performed by young men of aristocratic rank on horseback, said to have been invented by *Aeneas, and often exhibited by Augustus and later emperors. The significance of *Troiae* is obscure; Virgil (*Aeneid* 5. 596) describes the event and connects it with the games celebrated at the tomb of Aeneas' father Anchisēs.

Lupercā'lia, very ancient Roman festival held every year on 15 February, originally a shepherd-festival; it was in honour of *Faunus, worshipped under the name Lupercus (and presumably had some connection with driving away wolves, *lupi*, from the flocks). Its primary purpose was to secure fertility for the fields, the flocks, and the people. The worshippers gathered at the Lupercal, a cave on the Palatine hill where Romulus and Remus were supposed to have been suckled by a wolf. Here the Luperci (a priestly *collegium, 'college', drawn from particular patrician families) sacrificed goats and a dog, and two youths of noble family were then smeared with the blood of the sacrifice, a ceremony which was probably a symbolic purification of the shepherds. The Luperci then clad their naked bodies in part of the skins of the sacrificed goats and with the rest cut into thongs they and some of the magistrates ran through the streets of the old Roma Quadrata (see ROME 1), striking with the thongs all whom they met, especially women, who put themselves in the way of blows in order to be rendered fertile. The act of running was a symbolic purification of the land, the thongs were called *februa*, 'means of purification', and the month in which the ceremony took place *februarius*, the time of purification. Mark Antony ran as one of the consuls of 44 BC and in his course mounted the Rostra and offered Julius Caesar a diadem twined with laurel, which Caesar refused. The ceremony survived into Christian times, and was finally suppressed in AD 494. See also LYCAEUS.

Lu'scius Lānuvī'nus, writer of Latin comedies in the early second century BC, whose criticisms of *Terence are rebutted by the latter in several of his prologues. His works have not survived.

lustrā'tio ('lustration'), in Roman religion, a ceremony designed to effect purification and protection from evil influences, and to invite good luck into the purified place (compare LUPERCALIA). It consisted in the solemn procession of a beneficial object, e.g. an animal to be sacrificed, around what was to be purified, whether city, fields, army, or flocks, and the offering of prayer and sacrifice at certain points. A lustration after the funeral rites for Mīsēnus is described by Virgil in *Aeneid* 6. 229 ff.

Lyae'us, epithet of the Greek god *Dionysus.

Lycae'us, name of a mountain in the west of Arcadia, near Bassae, from where there is a view of a large part of the Peloponnese. It was one of the chief centres of the worship of Zeus, who is sometimes given the epithet Lycaeus as a consequence. On the summit was a grove and altar of Zeus, and also a hippodrome and stadium where games in honour of Zeus, the Lycaea, were celebrated. (The Roman *Lupercalia were sometimes said to have originated with the Greek Lycaea, imported into Rome from Arcadia, the Roman god Faunus then being identified with Pan; as in the case of the Lupercalia, the Greek name appears to be connected with the word for wolf, *lykos*.) Plato in the *Republic* mentions as well known a story that in the worship of Zeus Lycaeus a man is

sacrificed and whoever eats his flesh becomes a wolf (see next entry). On Mount Lycaeus was also the birthplace of the god *Pan, who had a sanctuary near the hippodrome.

Lycā'on, in Greek myth, son of Pelasgus and king of Arcadia, who founded the cult of Zeus *Lycaeus. He sacrificed a child on the altar and was thereupon turned into a wolf. From that time onwards, every time sacrifice was made at that altar a man turned into a wolf; the creature might revert to human shape in the ninth year if it had not tasted human flesh. Another story said that when Zeus and Hermes visited Arcadia, Lycaon, to test Zeus, served him human flesh. Zeus as punishment blasted all Lycaon's sons except one, turned Lycaon into a wolf, and sent a great flood (see DEUCALION). The story seems to represent a belief that the weather-god (*Zeus) could be moved by human sacrifice.

Lycei'us, epithet of *Apollo.

Lȳcē'um (Lȳkeion), grove and gymnasium near Athens, sacred to Apollo Lyceius, where Aristotle taught. The name is sometimes used to signify the philosophy school of Aristotle. The Lyceum lay to the east of the city near the river Ilissus.

Lȳ'cophron. 1. The younger, talented son of *Periander, tyrant of Corinth, exiled by his father to the west Greek island of Corcyra (then under Corinthian control) on account of his bitter hostility. In his later years Periander proposed to hand over his kingdom to Lycophron, and to go himself to Corcyra. To prevent this the Corcyreans murdered Lycophron, whereupon Periander seized three hundred youths from the leading Corcyrean families and sent them off to be made into eunuchs at Sardis; they were saved from this fate by the Samians. (The story is told in Herodotus 3. 48–53.)

2. (b. *c.*320 BC), Hellenistic poet from Chalcis in Euboea. When a young man he went to Alexandria and became one of the *Pleiad of tragic poets (see HELLENISTIC AGE 4). The only work of his to survive is the *Alexandra*, a dramatic monologue in 1,474 lines of iambic trimeters (see METRE, GREEK 5) in which the slave set to watch Alexandra (i.e. *Cassandra) reports her prophecies to her father Priam, king of Troy. They concern the destruction of Troy and the crime of *Ajax, the return of the Greeks and their fate, Aeneas' arrival in Latium, the eventual struggles between Europe and Asia, and the rise of Roman power. These last passages, which concerned events of Lycophron's own lifetime, raised doubts even in antiquity as to whether he could really be the author. The whole poem is written in an extremely obscure and allusive style. Lycophron ·was also the author of a prose treatise on comedy (which has not survived).

Lycō'ris, see GALLUS.

Lȳcu'rgus (Lȳkourgos). **1.** Legendary king of the Ēdōnēs, a Thracian people; he persecuted the youthful *Dionysus when he came with his nurses seeking refuge, and was consequently struck blind, or driven mad, so that he killed his own son Dryas; he was then eaten alive by wild horses.

2. Legendary legislator of *Sparta, about whom nothing certain is known, not even when he lived. He is said to be the founder of the Spartan constitution and the social and military systems, and so of the *eunomia*, 'good order', the name generally applied to these. It has been suggested that most of the Spartan institutions existing in historical times were a result of ancient practice gradually modified over a period of time and not the work of one man, but it may be that at some time between 800 and 600 BC, perhaps in the seventh century, a single legislator was responsible for the formalization of Sparta's institutions.

3. (*c*.390–*c*.325 BC), distinguished Athenian orator and statesman, pupil of Isocrates, and a member of the Eteobutadae *genos* (a noble family, one branch of which held the hereditary priesthood of Poseidon Erechtheus, another the priesshood of Athena Polias). Lycurgus was in charge of Athens' finances from the time of her defeat by Philip II of Macedon at Chaeronea in 338 BC until 326, successfully raising the revenue to 1,200 talents a year. The increase in the size of the navy at this time is attributed to him, and he embarked on an extensive building programme, including the reconstruction in marble of the temple of Dionysus. He won the confidence of his fellow-citizens to such a degree that they refused to surrender him to Philip's son Alexander the Great in 335 when the latter demanded the arrest of those hostile to Macedon. Lycurgus had statues erected of the tragic dramatists Aeschylus, Sophocles, and Euripides, and an official copy made of all their works (later borrowed by Ptolemy II Philadelphus, king of Egypt, for the library at Alexandria). Of his fifteen orations known to the ancients one survives, the indictment for treason of a certain Leōcratēs, for having allegedly fled from Athens at the news of the defeat at Chaeronea. It was said that after his death Lycurgus was accused of having left a deficit in the city treasury, and that when his sons were unable to repay the money they were imprisoned, in spite of a defence by *Hypereidēs; after an appeal by Demosthenes they were released.

Lȳcus, see ANTIOPE and *HERACLES, MADNESS OF.*

Ly'dia, country occupying the centre of western Asia Minor, bordered by Mysia in the north, Phrygia in the east, and Caria in the south. The river Hermus and its tributaries flowed through it, and its capital was Sardis. It contained much natural wealth including gold (see PACTOLUS) and, being traversed by two main routes from the west coast to the interior, it gained wealth from trade and contributed greatly to the material prosperity of western Asia Minor, including the Greek cities. Under the dynasty of the Mermnadae, which was founded by *Gyges early in the seventh century BC and ended with *Croesus in the middle of the sixth, a Lydian empire was formed, extending north to the Troad and west to the territories of the Greek cities on the coast. It is clear from the poems of Alcaeus and Sappho that Lydia was not regarded as *barbarian but enjoyed great esteem as a semi-Hellenic state. After Croesus was defeated by the Persian king Cyrus, Lydia became the chief Persian satrapy in the west, with its headquarters at Sardis, and was often a threat to the autonomy of the Greek cities. It was closely connected with Greek history during the classical period. After its conquest by Alexander the Great in 333 BC it was settled by Greek colonists, eventually becoming part of Attalid territory (see ATTALUS) and passing into Roman control in 133 BC with the rest of the Attalid kingdom. Lydia was influenced by and herself influenced Greece (see ASIA MINOR). It was said to be the first country to use coined money, and was regarded by the Greeks as the source of some of their musical modes. The Lydian language, which seems to be a branch of *Indo-European, is found on some inscriptions. Maeonia was an ancient name of Lydia (whence perhaps 'Maeonidēs', i.e. *Homer).

Ly'dia, Latin poem of unknown authorship, probably incomplete, consisting of eighty hexameters, and included in the *Appendix Virgiliana*. It is a lament by a lover for the loss of his mistress.

Ly'gdamus, see TIBULLUS.

Ly'nceus. 1. In Greek myth, son of Aphareus, king of Messenia, and the younger brother of Idas. The two brothers were inseparable, and both sailed with the *Argonauts. Lynceus' eyesight was so keen that he could see for great distances and even through the earth. In a fight with Castor and Polydeucēs (see DIOSCURI) both brothers were killed, as also was Castor.

2. In Greek myth, a son of Aegyptus, the only one to be spared by his bride, Hypermnestra, on their wedding night (see DANAUS). He became king of Argos and was succeeded by his son *Abas.

lyre, see MUSIC 1.

lyric poetry

1. *Greek.* Lyric poetry, meaning poetry 'sung to the lyre', existed in Greece from earliest times. Although it was, strictly speaking, song, the words were of primary importance and are now

all that remain, knowledge of the accompanying music having been lost in antiquity (see MUSIC 1). The Alexandrian scholars of the third century BC drew up a *canon of nine great lyric poets: Alcman, Sappho, Alcaeus, Stesichorus, Ibycus, Anacreon, Simonides, Pindar, and Bacchylides. Some added a tenth, Corinna. Lyric poetry is also found in the Attic drama of the fifth century BC, in the choruses (so-called; see CHORUS), but towards the end of the fifth century the chorus was relegated to a subordinate role (see COMEDY, GREEK 5). In relatively modern times, Greek lyric poetry outside drama has been divided into two kinds, choral lyric (also known as choral odes) and monody (Gk. *monōdia*, 'solo song'). Both kinds of lyric were written in a great variety of metres; for examples of possible kinds see METRE, GREEK 8. Elegy and iambic poetry, written in their own particular (non-lyric) metres, are both occasionally included with lyric poetry (strictly speaking erroneously and despite incompatibility of metre) when the subject-matter seems to suggest this grouping.

Choral lyric was sung (and often danced) by a chorus (or by a leader answered by a chorus) to a musical accompaniment usually played on the lyre, occasionally on the flute (*aulos*, a wind instrument like the oboe). It was composed from earliest times and throughout Greek history for public religious ceremonies. To this fact are attributable the predominantly elevated tone and the inclusion of myth and moralizing. Homer mentions many varieties of choral lyric: *dirges, *hymns, *hyporchemata, maiden-songs (see PARTHENEION), and wedding-songs (see EPITHALAMIUM and HYMENAEUS). The procession-song (*prosodion*) is another very ancient form. Later developments were the *dithyramb (accompanying the worship of Dionysus), the *nome, and the *encomium and *epinikion, the two last written in praise of men, and indicative of the increasing secularization of this form of poetry. The earliest choral ode of which a substantial part survives is a *partheneion* by *Alcman (seventh century BC) which seems to be composed in metrically corresponding stanzas known as *strophes and antistrophes. In later choral lyric the form became triadic (see TRIAD), reputedly the innovation of *Stesichorus, and of an increasing metrical complexity which reached its culmination in the odes of *Pindar. The material of a choral ode was relatively standardized and included praise of the gods, mention of the occasion and the personalities involved, moral maxims, and mythical narrative, this last providing the main subject-matter.

The development of choral lyric is associated with the Doric-speaking Peloponnese, especially Sparta, and with the names of *Thaletas, *Eumelus, and *Arion, whose works are all but lost. The association is indicated by the ancient convention that choral lyric was written in the Doric *dialect; Doric elements were retained even in the choral lyric of Attic tragedy. The great poets of choral lyric, some of whose works survive, are Alcman, Stesichorus, *Ibycus, *Simonides, Pindar, and *Bacchylides. For choral lyric as an element in Attic drama see CHORUS, TRAGEDY 1, and COMEDY, GREEK 2.

Of monody relatively little survives. It was sung to the accompaniment of a lyre. The intimate nature of the subject-matter—friendship, love, and hate—suggests that it was performed by a single individual on private occasions, for example after a banquet among friends (see SYMPOSIUM and SCOLIA). The surviving lyric of *Sappho, *Alcaeus, and *Anacreon is mostly monody. The fact that a poem is triadic in form is usually taken as an indication that it is a choral rather than a monodic ode; monody is generally simpler than choral lyric in form, metre, and expression. Attic tragedy contains a small amount of monody in the lyrics occasionally sung by individuals (rather than by the chorus). See also ARCHILOCHUS.

2. *Latin.* Comparatively little lyric poetry was written by the Romans. There exist in Latin some fragments of folk-songs, hymns, and religious incantations which indicate the existence in early times of an indigenous lyric poetry, but the earliest Latin lyric deserving of the name was modelled on Greek forms, mostly the simpler forms of monody, and it was entirely a literary product, not rooted in social practice, and intended to be read and not sung. Two notable exceptions are, first, the maiden-song composed for Juno at a time of crisis in 207 BC by *Livius Andronicus, based presumably on Greek models; and, secondly, Horace's elegant *Carmen Saeculare* which survives, composed for a chorus of youths and maidens to sing at the *ludi saeculares* of 17 BC (see LUDI 2 (i)). *Laevius was another early writer of lyrics (probably at the beginning of the first century BC), but only fragments of his work have survived. The two chief writers of literary lyric were *Catullus and Horace. Catullus experimented with lyric metres in poems of great verve (11, 17, 30, 34, 51, and 61), and wrote other equally lively poems in hendecasyllables and scazons (see METRE, LATIN 3 (iii)) which it is natural to regard as lyrics, even if the metres are not strictly speaking those of song (see 1 above); their style and subject matter both recall the manner of Greek monody. Horace in the *Odes* uses a fair variety of lyric metres found in Greek monody, frequently combining lines of different metres into couplets or four-line stanzas; he also expresses a range of sentiments, from deep seriousness in Pindaric vein (though not attempting the complexities of Pindar's triadic structure), to love poems and drinking songs in a more subjective style (exquisite, but lacking the spontaneity of Greek monody). The iambic

metres of the *Epodes* (see *ODES*) do not strictly belong to lyric, although the subject matter in most cases makes them close to it. Horace's technical mastery seems to have deterred later poets from attempting to follow him, and lyrical subjects tended to be treated in the elegiac metre. *Statius' *Silvae* include two lyrics (4. 5 and 4. 7), *Martial occasionally used lyric metres, and *Seneca (2) included choral lyrics in his tragedies. The note of true inspiration is not heard again until the Christian hymns of *Prudentius and *Ambrose (to which should perhaps be added the emperor Hadrian's poem to his soul).

Lÿsan'der (Lÿsandros) (d. 395 BC), Spartan naval commander towards the end of the *Peloponnesian War (431–404 BC), who won a great victory over the Athenian fleet at Aegospotami in 405. He blockaded Piraeus and after the surrender of Athens in the spring of 404 BC supported the establishment of the Thirty Tyrants (see ATHENS 5). He subsequently became estranged from the Spartan government and lost power and influence. At the outbreak of the Corinthian War (395–386; see CORINTH), in which an alliance of Greek states opposed Sparta's tyrannical rule, he invaded Boeotia but was killed there at the siege of the city of Haliartus in 395. He was among the ablest Spartan leaders, but unpopular because of his arrogance. His Life was written by Nepos and Plutarch.

Ly'sias (*c*.458–*c*.380 BC), Attic orator, son of Cephalus, a wealthy Syracusan, whom Pericles persuaded to settle as a metic (resident alien) in Athens, and brother of Polemarchus and Euthydemus. The family owned a prosperous shield-making business; it is the house of Polemarchus, the eldest son, at Piraeus, that provides the setting for Plato's *Republic, in which Cephalus and Polemarchus take part in the opening discussion. At some time Lysias went with his brothers to *Thurii in south Italy and is said to have studied rhetoric under *Teisias of Syracuse. The defeat of the Athenian expedition to Sicily (see PELOPONNESIAN WAR) led to the expulsion of Lysias from Thurii in 412 and the brothers returned to Athens, where they lived until the tyranny of the Thirty in 404 BC (see ATHENS 2 (iii)). These, to procure funds, arrested the wealthy, among them Lysias and Polemarchus; Lysias escaped to Megara but Polemarchus was put to death and their property was seized. While in exile Lysias spent what was left of his fortune in aiding the democracy; as a consequence, on his return in 403 an attempt was made to confer citizenship upon him, but it was defeated by a technicality. Being now rather poor he became a professional speech-writer (see LOGOGRAPHERS (2)) and proved outstandingly successful, reputedly composing over 200 forensic speeches. As a metic he could not appear in

court in person. However, the first speech of his career he delivered on his own behalf, perhaps to a court of inquiry. The speech was 'Against Eratosthenēs' (speech 12), the defendant being allegedly the murderer of Lysias' brother, and it contains a vivid description of the writer's experiences under the Thirty.

Of his speeches thirty-five survive, some spurious and only twenty-three entire. They include a funeral oration (*epitaphios*) on those who died in the Corinthian War (395–386; see CORINTH) and a fragment of an epideictic ('display') speech delivered at the Olympic festival of 388 (*Olympiakos*), in which he urges the Greeks to end internal discord and unite against the two great enemies, the Persian king and Dionysius, tyrant of Syracuse. Lysias' speeches cover a range of cases, from murder and treason to adultery and embezzlement. Among the most interesting are: 'For Mantitheus' (a young man accused of having served in the cavalry under the Thirty); 'For the cripple', a defence of a man charged (perhaps justifiably) with receiving a state pension under false pretences; 'Against Alcibiadēs' (son of the famous Alcibiades, for dereliction of military duty; 'On the murder of Eratosthenes' (speech 1, not to be confused with 12; see above), a speech for a husband who had murdered his wife's seducer, fascinating for its glimpse of the life and conversation of an ordinary Greek household.

Lysias was admired in antiquity for the simplicity and naturalness of his style. His precise use of language, avoidance of all affectation and extravagance, and moderation of tone—he is rarely passionate, and pathos is not his strong point—could lead to monotony, but this is avoided by his gift of putting himself in his client's place and preparing for him a persuasive speech such as only he could have made according to his own circumstances, age, and temperament. Without resort to rhetorical devices, the speeches are clear and vivid, and orderly in arrangement (preface, narrative, proof, conclusion). It is said that he wrote a defence for Socrates to speak at his trial, but that Socrates refused it. The *Phaedrus of Plato contains what purports to be a speech by Lysias on love. It is probably a Platonic parody.

Lÿsi'machus, see MACEDONIA 2 and SELEUCIDS. This was also the name of the father of *Aristeides (1).

Lÿsi'ppus, of Sicyon, a famous and prolific sculptor in bronze, active in the second half of the fourth century BC. The literary sources ascribe to him the invention of a new system of proportions, confirmed by the Roman marble copy of his bronze statue of an athlete scraping the dust and oil from his body (the *Apoxyomenos*): the head is smaller, the legs longer, so that the whole figure looks taller and more slender. His statues are also noted for appearing to catch the action of a moment, and for their advance in three-dimensional representation. His portraiture was famous: his Socrates, known from a Roman copy, seems to have been a masterpiece of characterization. He made many statues of Alexander the Great, whose edict, that no one should paint him but *Apelles, and no one make his statue but Lysippus, is well known. One statue showed Alexander in characteristic pose, with head inclined and tilted upwards. An epigrammatist suggested that he was saying 'I have subdued the earth; you, Zeus, may keep Olympus'.

Lȳsis, see PLATO 2.

Lȳsi'strata (*Lȳsistratē*), Greek comedy by *Aristophanes, produced in the spring of 411 BC (probably at the *Lenaea rather than the Dionysia; it is not known whether the play won first prize). This was an alarming time for Athens: the Athenian expedition to Sicily had ended in disaster in 413 BC (see PELOPONNESIAN WAR), a large part of her empire was in revolt, and her enemy Sparta had made an advantageous alliance with the Persian satrap Tissaphernēs. Yet though Athens was seriously weakened there was no immediate danger of collapse; for the time being she could hold on. The play is an expression of a natural desire for peace, so long as it can be achieved by compromise, without putting Athens in real danger. It contains no *parabasis*, and in this represents the beginning of a change in the form of Old Comedy (see COMEDY, GREEK 3 (iv) and 5).

The men having failed to bring the war to an end, it occurs to Lysistrata ('disbander of armies') that the women should take over control of affairs and force a peace, first by refusing sexual relations, and secondly by getting possession of the Acropolis and the state's reserve of money in the Parthenon, without which the Athenian war-effort would collapse. She gets the women together, including Lampito from Sparta and women from other enemy states. After some reluctance they fall in with her scheme and swear to carry it out. The foreigners depart to their own countries and Lysistrata with the Athenian wives occupies the Acropolis, which has already been seized by a band of old women. A chorus of old men tries to recapture it, but is driven off by a second chorus of old women with pails of water. An elderly *proboulos is also routed, together with his band of Scythian archers (the Athenian police force). In place of a *parabasis* the two choruses exchange insults. Then Lysistrata has to encourage the women, who are trying to slip away, to keep to their resolve. An anxious husband Cinesias arrives to recover his wife Myrrhinē, is tantalized by her, and finally cheated as she returns to the Acropolis. A herald from Sparta, similarly distressed, arrives to announce his country's intention to sue for peace, and a conference of both sides follows. Lysistrata scolds them all and urges reconciliation; peace is made, and Athenians and Spartans go to the Acropolis for a banquet.

M

Maca'ria, see HERACLES, CHILDREN OF.

Maccabees, see SELEUCIDS.

Macedon, Macedonia; in general the former is used to describe the political entity, the latter the geographical area. Geographically, Macedonia is intermediate between the Balkans and the Greek peninsula. In early times it was the country around the western and northern shores of the Thermaic Gulf, from Mount Olympus in the south to the river Strymon, forming the boundary with Thrace, in the north; but its territory was much enlarged by king Philip II in the fourth century BC.

1. *Early history to Alexander the Great.* In the centuries after the *Dorian Invasion (*c.*1100 BC) many new peoples entered Macedonia. In historical times the royal house traced its descent from the mythical Temenus, king of Argos, who was one of the *Heracleidae, and more immediately from Perdiccas I, who left Argos for Illyria, probably in the mid-seventh century BC, and from there captured the Macedonian plain and occupied the fortress of Aegae (Vergina), setting himself up as king of the Macedonians. Thus the kings were of largely Dorian Greek stock (see PHILIP (1)); they presumably spoke a form of Dorian Greek and their cultural tradition had Greek features. Whether or not the Macedonian people spoke a Greek dialect or a foreign tongue is still a matter of debate, but such evidence as exists suggests that they spoke a distinctive dialect of Greek, perhaps related to Aeolic. However, other Greeks persisted in saying that the Macedonians were not full *Hellenes (see below and also INDO-EUROPEAN). The kings were chosen by the assembly from those of the royal line who showed ability to command; they ruled directly over the Macedonian people of the coast; to some extent they controlled the Illyrian hill-tribes of the west and north, but never brought them completely under direct rule.

During the reigns of Amyntas (late sixth century) and his son and successor Alexander I (who was a contemporary and to some extent ally of Xerxes, king of Persia, and played an ambiguous role in the *Persian Wars), considerable territorial gains were made. Friendly relations were established with *Peisistratus and his sons, tyrants at Athens, and the process of Hellenization began. The Greeks competing at the Olympian games *c.*500 BC attempted to prevent this Alexander from competing with them on the grounds that he was a *barbarian, but the stewards gave permission, accepting his Argive descent. Alexander's successor Perdiccas II (king *c.*452–413) played as shifty a role in international politics as Alexander, vacillating between Athens and Sparta during the Peloponnesian War. He was succeeded in 413 by Archelaus, memorably portrayed by Plato in the *Gorgias* as a monster of cruelty. Nevertheless, he did most to ensure that his country was part of Greece proper by making his new capital at Pella a centre for Greek artists and poets, entertaining among others Euripides, Agathon, Choerilus of Samos, Timotheus, and Zeuxis. Many Macedonian customs which seemed un-Greek, like tattooing, had lapsed by this time, but one or two lingered; by the time of Aristotle it was no longer traditional for a Macedonian who had not 'killed his man' to wear a cord round his waist, but until a very late date no one was permitted to recline at table (having instead to sit upright) who had not killed a wild boar without nets. (At the age of 35 *Cassander was still sitting up to the table.) The country was wild, and as late as classical times contained lions and bears, and perhaps even panthers and leopards.

The importance of Macedonia in Greek history begins with the accession to power of Philip II and culminates in the reign of his son Alexander the Great; for this period of Macedonian history (359–323 BC) see PHILIP (1) and ALEXANDER (2).

2. *The struggle for Alexander's succession, 323–280 BC.* The death of Alexander the Great in 323 left an empire stretching from the Adriatic to the Punjab, and from north Afghanistan to Libya, and no competent successor in the family. Alexander's half-brother, Philip Arrhidaeus, chosen to succeed by the assembly, was mentally unfit; he was executed by Alexander's mother Olympias in 317. Alexander's son by his wife Roxana, also called Alexander, was not born until after his father's death; in 316 he fell into the power of Cassander (see below) and was ultimately put to death, the last of the Temenid line. Although both had been made joint successors to the kingship, they were from the outset merely pawns in the power-struggle between Alexander's generals. On Alexander's death, it was decided by the Macedonian army at Babylon that *Antipater, Alexander's representative in Europe, 'general of Europe', and governor of Macedonia, should be confirmed in

his position; that Perdiccas, Alexander's senior cavalry officer, should be regent of the empire (the most important position); and that the satrapies should be allotted to various generals, Egypt to Ptolemy, western Asia Minor (including Great Phrygia, Lycia, and Pamphylia) to Antigonus, Thrace to Lysimachus, Cappadocia and Paphlagonia to Eumenes.

There followed for nearly half a century a complicated struggle for fragments of Alexander's empire. Perdiccas was overthrown by a coalition of satraps, and was murdered while attacking Egypt in 320. The coalition met and a new settlement was negotiated at Triparadeisos (near Hermel) in north Syria (320), by which Antipater was made regent of the empire and the satrapies were redistributed, Seleucus (one of Alexander's lesser generals) receiving Babylonia. Antipater died the next year, and Antigonus, from a Macedonian noble family, became the leading figure for the next nineteen years (320–301), aspiring to rule all the empire. In 319, on hearing that Antipater before his death had appointed as regent Polyperchon, one of Philip II's officers, Antigonus organized the coalition, including Antipater's son Cassander, against him. Thus began many years of manœuvring and fighting; in 311 peace was made between Cassander, Ptolemy, Lysimachus, and Antigonus on the basis of the status quo, a peace which Antigonus regarded as a breathing space before his next move. In 307, during the absence of Cassander (now in control of Greece), Demetrius I Poliorcetēs, son of Antigonus, sailed to Athens, expelled the governor (Demetrius of Phalerum) and set up a democracy. In 306 Antigonus proclaimed himself and his son Demetrius kings, and in 305 Ptolemy, Seleucus, Lysimachus, and Cassander also proclaimed themselves kings of their various satrapies. This marks the dissolution of Alexander's empire. The exact significance of the royal title to the individuals who claimed it is difficult to assess. It seems to indicate the holder's view of his personal high achievement rather than to designate a particular claim to territory; for many years Demetrius, for example, was a king without a kingdom.

In 301 a coalition of Cassander, Lysimachus, and Seleucus (together with 500 elephants which Seleucus had acquired through his Indian campaign) forced Antigonus and his son Demetrius, whom he had summoned from Europe, to battle at Ipsus in Phrygia. Antigonus was killed and Demetrius fled; the former's eastern territories were divided between Seleucus and Lysimachus. Antigonus' role in Greece was taken over by Demetrius who, after Cassander's death in 297, became king of Macedonia and master of nearly all Greece. Already in his father's time he had captured Athens (in 307, see above) and ousted Demetrius of Phalerum, Cassander's governor. He received his additional name

Poliorcetes, 'besieger', in consequence of a prolonged siege of *Rhodes (304), which he failed to take. From 289 onwards his position deteriorated. He lost his Aegean possessions and Athens to Ptolemy (now Ptolemy I Soter of Egypt) and was expelled from Macedonia by the combined forces of Lysimachus and *Pyrrhus, king of Epirus (related to Ptolemy II by marriage). His career ended in an unsuccessful invasion of Asia; he was taken prisoner by Seleucus in 285 and died two years later. There remained Ptolemy I, Seleucus, and Lysimachus. The possession of Macedonia was still undecided. Lysimachus first divided it with Pyrrhus and then annexed the whole, but incurred the hostility of Seleucus, who invaded Asia Minor, defeating and killing Lysimachus at Corupedium (near Magnesia in Lydia) in 281. But Seleucus was himself assassinated treacherously by his ally Ptolemy Ceraunus (son of Ptolemy I and Eurydicē, but excluded from the throne of Egypt), who then usurped the throne of Macedon. With the death of Seleucus (in 281) the possibility of the union of Alexander's empire under one ruler came to an end. He was the last survivor of Alexander's generals, for Ptolemy I had died in 283 (see HELLENISTIC AGE). For the later *diadochoi*, 'successors', to the empire of Alexander the Great, see ATTALIDS, PTOLEMIES, and SELEUCIDS.

3. *The Antigonids and the struggle with Rome.* In 279 Macedonia was invaded by a Celtic people known as Gauls (or Galatians), part of a large-scale migration. They broke into several groups: one swept over northern Greece and reached Delphi, but was driven back; another established a kingdom in Thrace; a third passed into Asia Minor and settled into what was henceforth to be known as *Galatia. In resisting this invasion Ptolemy Ceraunus was killed. He was succeeded on the throne of Macedon by Antigonus Gonātas, son of Demetrius I Poliorcetes, who inflicted a notable defeat on the Gauls at Lysimacheia in 276; he was named Gonatas, it seems, because born at Gonnos (or Gonnoi) in Thessaly. Gonatas was interested in poetry, philosophy, and history, and drew literary men to his court. He proved a vigorous and successful ruler (277–239) and established the Antigonid dynasty in Macedonia. This dynasty maintained a partial control over Greece until 168 BC, varying in extent from time to time as a result of such incidents as the Chremonidean War (c.267–262) against Sparta and Athens (see ATHENS 2 (vi)), the interventions of the Ptolemies and of Pyrrhus, and the activities of the *Aetolian and *Achaean Leagues. Control was exercised in some states by means of Macedonian garrisons; in others Gonatas set up his own supporters as tyrants.

After Gonatas, the most prominent of the Antigonids was his grandson Philip V (221–179), a man of remarkable energy and misplaced ambition, largely responsible for bringing Greece under Roman domination. The operations undertaken by Rome against Illyrian pirates in 229 and 219 (see ROME 5), in which Rome had the support of the Greek cities Apollonia and Epidamnus (both in Illyria), brought nearer the prospect of a collision between Rome and Macedonia. In 216, when Rome was in the crisis of the Second Punic War, Philip embarked upon naval attacks against Roman fleets off Illyria, in the Roman sphere of influence, and in the following year offered an alliance to Hannibal. By this embroilment with Rome, together with his ruthless piratical expeditions against Greek states of the Aegean, he alarmed the senate and brought about two successive Macedonian wars (the first in 214–205; the second 200–197), as a result of which Rome assumed the position of arbiter in the affairs of Greece. The first war was inconclusive; in the second Philip was defeated by Q. Flamininus at Cynoscephalae in Thessaly in 197, and his rule thereafter was limited to Macedonia proper. He died in 179. In the course of the Third Macedonian War (172–168/7), when Philip had been succeeded by his son *Perseus, the Macedonian army was practically annihilated at the battle of Pydna (in Macedonia) by the Roman consul Aemilius *Paullus; this was followed by the dethronement of the Antigonids and the break-up of the Macedonian kingdom into four federal republics. The end came twenty years later, when an attempt by a pretender to reunite Macedon was defeated by Caecilius Metellus, and the country became a Roman province (146). Those cities, like Athens and Sparta, which had taken Rome's side, remained Roman allies; the rest were made subject and tributary. Greece became a Roman protectorate (not a province until the time of Augustus).

4. *The Macedonian princesses.* The Macedonian kings married several notable women, with character and ability, who played a large part in public affairs. Outstanding was *Arsinoë II, who as the wife of her brother Ptolemy II Philadelphus (married *c.*276) was the effective ruler of Egypt, and brought her country triumphantly out of an unpromising war with Antiochus I, king of Syria and Asia Minor. She was deified in her lifetime and her head appears with her husband's on the coinage. Cleopatra Thea, daughter of Ptolemy VI Philometor and wife of the Seleucid king Demetrius II of Syria (reigned 145–139 and 129–125), was a powerful queen who coined in her own name. *Berenicē II, wife of Ptolemy III Euergetēs (reigned 246–221), was another important queen, celebrated by the Hellenistic Greek poet *Callimachus in a poem written at her death. Finally there was *Cleopatra VII, queen of Egypt, the last ruler of her line, famous for her beauty, her unscrupulousness, the part she played in Roman history, and her tragic end.

Macedonian Wars, of Rome, see MACEDONIA 3 and ROME 5.

Macer. 1. **Gaius Lici'nius Macer** (d. 66 BC), Roman orator and annalist, the father of the poet *Calvus. His annals have not survived, but they were used by Livy for large parts of his books 4 and 5. Macer claimed to have consulted the *libri lintei* ('linen books'), an ancient list of magistrates.

2. **Aemi'lius Macer,** Roman poet of Verona, d. 16 BC, the author of Latin didactic poems, *Ornithogonia* on birds, and *Thēriaca* on snake bites. These works have not survived. He was a friend of Virgil and of Ovid.

Machā'on and Podalei'rius, in Homer's *Iliad*, sons of *Asclepius and Epionē and doctors to the Greek army at Troy. Machaon was a surgeon, Podaleirius a physician.

Macrō'bius,   Ambro'sius   Theodo'sius (flourished around AD 400, known to his contemporaries as Theodosius), Roman writer and philosopher. He was probably African by birth, and is generally identified with the praetorian prefect of 430, but little else is known of his life.

Macrobius wrote the *Saturnalia*, a dialogue in seven books dedicated to his son; it is supposed to represent a conversation at a banquet during the *Saturnalian festival, between a number of eminent Romans, at the house of Vettius Praetextatus, praetorian prefect in 384 and the leading pagan intellectual of his time. In form the work is very similar to that of *Athenaeus and of Aulus *Gellius (who is used as a source, though nowhere mentioned). Among those who are purported to be present are *Avienus, *Symmachus (the orator and administrator), *Servius (the Virgilian commentator), and a certain Euangelus, sceptical and rather bitter, who speaks disparagingly of Virgil and Cicero. The discussion covers a multitude of subjects, but the central topic is criticism of Virgil. Book 1 is occupied with the subject of ancient religion, and Praetextatus expounds the theory of the solar origin of mythology, all the gods being ultimately identified with the sun under one or other of its aspects. Book 2 contains a number of anecdotes on the religious and political changes at Rome, including mention of *Laberius, who after taunting Caesar was compelled by him to suffer the humiliation of acting in his own mime, and books 3–6 are devoted to Virgil. He is discussed from various points of view which cover his knowledge of ritual, his power of expressing emotion, his debt to Homer and other Greek authors, his debt to Ennius and other ancient Romans; and he is gradually built up to be the unique scholar and poet in a way which foreshadows the medieval view of him as a wonder-working magician. This section throws light on the history of Virgilian scholarship at the time. Book 7 proceeds to a discussion of various physical, physiological, and psychological questions, in general on the way the brain influences the workings of the body.

The second work of Macrobius is a *Neoplatonist commentary, also dedicated to his son, on the *Somnium Scipionis* ('dream of Scipio') from the sixth book of Cicero's *De republica* ('on the republic'): the successive passages of Cicero's narrative were set out (and were thus preserved when other parts of the *De republica* now known to us were still undiscovered). Macrobius' commentary was attentively studied in the Middle Ages. It depends largely on *Porphyry's (Greek) commentary on Plato's *Timaeus*, either directly or through a Latin intermediary. In it Macrobius examines the enigma of the soul and its destiny in the light of Neoplatonism and of the astronomical and mathematical sciences of the day. Its tendency is to reinforce the doctrine put forward in the *Somnium* of the immortality and divine quality of the soul, from a pagan rather than a Christian standpoint.

A quotation from Macrobius was the sole contribution to the conversation made by an otherwise silent Samuel Johnson (1709–84) on his first evening in Pembroke College, Oxford.

Maecē'nas, Gaius (d. 8 BC), the most famous Roman literary patron, descended from a distinguished Etruscan family, an equestrian by birth. He was the trusted counsellor of the emperor Augustus and the enlightened patron of a literary circle which included Virgil, Horace, Propertius, and Varius. The rewards for these protégés were great: Horace owed his Sabine farm and Virgil his independence to him, and both poets addressed him in terms of admiration and gratitude; they made a substantial return by supporting the imperial regime in their poetry. Maecenas is said to have suggested to Virgil the subject of the *Georgics* (3. 41). Only fragments survive of his own poetry and prose. He wrote a *Prometheus*, perhaps a tragedy, and a *Dialogue*, perhaps in the style of Menippean satire (see MENIPPUS). Seneca regarded him as typical of the adage that the style is the man, perhaps indicating a complex personality. After the conspiracy and execution of his brother-in-law Varro (or Licinius) Murena in 23 BC a coolness developed between Maecenas and Augustus and his political career came effectively to an end. He was a man of luxurious tastes and habits (he is said to have introduced heated swimming-baths at Rome), and spent the closing years of his life in the enjoyment of a cultivated leisure. See also AUGUSTAN AGE.

maenads (*mainadĕs* (also referred to as *bacchae* and *thyiadĕs*), 'mad women'), women inspired with ecstatic frenzy by the god *Dionysus. See BACCHANTS.

Mae'nalus, mountain in Arcadia. See PAN.

Maeo'nidēs, name sometimes applied to Homer, either because Maeonia was an ancient name for *Lydia where, according to some, Homer was born, or because he was said to be the son of one Maeon.

Maera, the dog of Icarius, set in the heavens by the god Dionysus as the Dog-star. See ERIGONE.

Mae'vius, see BAVIUS.

magic

1. Magic is the practice of incantations, spells, charms, curses, and other rites in order to influence and control the natural course of events by these means. It may be contrasted with religion in that the latter uses prayers not in order to constrain but in order to supplicate. Magic was encouraged and developed by the widespread belief in the existence of spirits which permeated the universe and intervened in natural processes, and which it was believed could be influenced by appropriate spells and acts. Belief in certain kinds of magic gradually declined as some Greeks came to regard the world as knowable by rational means and an object of scientific study, and as knowledge of physical laws increased. Some doctors, for instance, discarded incantations and charms (see 5 (i) below), and the writer of the Hippocratic treatise 'On the Sacred Disease' vigorously denies that epilepsy is any more sacred than any other disease and that it should be treated by magic (see HIPPOCRATES). Nevertheless, magical practices continued at all levels of society, both of harmful kinds ('black') and beneficial ('white').

2. The earliest references to magical practices are found in Homer. When Odysseus is wounded by a boar the flow of blood is stopped with a song of healing (*epaoidē*; *Odyssey* 19. 457). *Circē (*Odyssey* 10. 276), an enchantress, 'knowing many drugs and charms' (*polypharmakos*) works transformations with a wand, aided by drugs (*pharmaka*, a word used both of healing and of harmful drugs). She also teaches Odysseus how to summon ghosts from the Underworld. On the other hand Hesiod's *Works and Days* gives us glimpses of magic of an agricultural and everyday kind.

3. Greek myths provide examples of people who work magic, the *Telchinēs and the Idaean *Dactyls, *Orpheus, *Musaeus, *Melampus, and the most famous of all, *Medea, niece of Circe. In the myth of the Argonauts (known to Homer: *Odyssey* 12. 69), her magic powers put the dragon at Colchis to sleep, made Jason impervious to fire-breathing bulls, and restored the aged Aeson to youth. Later myth made her a priestess of *Hecatē, who came to be regarded as the divine patroness of witches and was invoked by magicians (as in Theocritus, *Idylls* 2.12 and in a fragment of Sophron; see MIME), although in Hesiod's *Theogony* she is

represented as all beneficence. Thessaly was from early times regarded as the special home of witches. Jason and Medea were supposed to have lived there for a time, and the Thessalians claimed that Medea lost her box of wonder-working plants there, which took root and grew again in their fertile soil. The Thessalian witches had a reputation for brewing poisons and working wonders, such as bringing the moon down from the sky (Aristophanes, Clouds 749; Canidia in Horace, Epodes 17. 77 made the same claim). Lucan's description of Thessalian witchcraft is outstanding as a horror story (Pharsalia 6. 452). In a later age Thessalian witches figure large in *Apuleius' novel, The Golden Ass.

4. In historical times in Greece and Rome a distinction must be drawn between magical practices in official religion and the popular uses of magic. Conscious magic was a matter for individual and private performance. In public cult, magical rites turned into ritual appropriate to the particular god, e.g. weather-magic into the ritual of Zeus, rites designed to produce fertility into that of Demeter, and the rites preparatory to making war became symbolic and lost their original meaning (at Rome, see FETIALES). In ritual the use of fire and water was magical, as were the offerings to the dead. There are traces of magic also in the Greek belief that the *pollution of blood-guilt could be washed away by water or the blood of sacrificial victims or burned away with fire. However, as with apotropaic ceremonies, i.e. those to avert danger, which also had an obviously magical element, these public rituals also had a private aspect. At certain Greek festivals the hair might not be tied into a knot and rings might not be worn because they were thought to obstruct the magic. Similarly at Rome the *flamen dialis was not allowed to wear knots or rings. In Rome at the *Lupercalia, the touch of the thong was believed to remove sterility.

5. The discovery in Egypt in the nineteenth and twentieth centuries of many papyri relating to magic has given much greater insight into the techniques of magic in ancient times, its incantations and the belief it presupposes in demons and demonic powers. Through these it has been possible to compare the presentation of magic in literary texts with the practice of it in real life. Among its purely popular uses the commonest are the following.

(i) Medical and love charms. Magic and medicine were inextricable in early times. Pindar (Pythian Odes 3. 91) represents *Chiron as treating his patients either with soothing incantations (malakais epaoidais) or with potions. The poems of *Nicander and the works of *Dioscurides illustrate the connection thought to exist between the two. Plutarch refers to the amulet hung about Pericles' neck when he caught the plague (see PELOPONNESIAN WAR), though Pericles himself thought it nonsense. Incantations were among the remedies recommended by Cato (De re rustica) in certain cases. The use of these, and of love charms by lovers, is illustrated in Theocritus (Idyll 2), Virgil (Eclogue 8), and Horace (Epode 5). There is more information on magical concoctions in Apuleius (Apology 30–1 and 42). The fascinum, a representation of the phallus, was employed as an amulet to protect children from witchcraft. The strange use in love-charms of the bird known as the wryneck is referred to by Pindar and Theocritus. The bird may have been credited with magical powers because of the writhing motions of its neck in the mating season, by which it was perhaps thought to attract a mate. It was spreadeagled on a wheel and the wheel made to revolve, thereby attracting the person chosen. (The wheel was also used by itself with no bird attached.) This kind of charm is not mentioned by the papyri and may have dropped out of use in early times.

(ii) The use of images and names. It was a doctrine of magic that an effect could be produced on a person by corresponding action on his image (sympathetic or homoeopathic magic) or on something that belonged intimately to him (contagious magic). Both in Greece and in Rome it was commonplace to make an image in wax of someone whose illness or death or love was desired: if the image was pierced with a nail or melted in a fire the subject suffered pain or melted with love accordingly. If, while the image was being burned, a snippet of the victim's hair or garment was thrown into the fire, use was being made simultaneously of contagious magic. There are references to these beliefs in Plato, Laws 933b, Theocritus, Idyll 2, and Ovid, Heroides 6. 91–2. At Rome the practice was known as devotio. Not only the image but the name of a person, thought of as being in some sense identical with him, might be used for similar purposes. The name would be inscribed on a lead tablet and a nail driven through it, with or without a written indication of the desired result. Since the gods of the Underworld were invoked to carry out the curse, the tablet was buried in the ground, and in tombs especially, or thrown down a well. This practice was known in Greek as katadĕsis, in Latin as defixio, 'binding', 'nailing down'. Many of these tablets have been discovered in modern times. They were sometimes used, with appropriate inscriptions, for other purposes, for example to effect the recovery of lost or stolen property, or a departed lover, or the 'binding' or hindering of chariots in races.

(iii) Evocation of spirits (necyomantía). The earliest example of this is found in Odysseus' summoning of the ghosts in the Underworld (Odyssey 11). That it was practised in Greece in historical times is shown not only by the story of Periander, after he had mislaid some property, summoning up a ghost to tell him where he had put it (Herodotus 5. 92), but also by the statement in Plutarch, *Cimon*, that there was a temple at Heraclea in Elis where it was customary to consult the spirits of the dead. Magicians who practised this, necromancers (*psychagōgoi*), were popular also in Etruria. Cicero refers several times to necromancy practised in his day, and the emperors Nero and Caracalla are said to have had recourse to it. It was also a skill possessed by Horace's Canidia, and there are further references to it in Ovid (*Metamorphoses* 7. 206 and *Remedia amoris* 253).

6. Since harmful magic was magic practised privately, it came to be repressed by law both in Greece and in Rome. Plato recommends that the abuse of magic should be punished, as did the writer of a speech erroneously ascribed to Demosthenes (*Against Aristogeiton* 79). According to Pausanias a witch named Lamia was executed in Demosthenes' day. In Rome the *Twelve Tables made provision for the punishment of anyone who uttered a harmful incantation and there were later penal laws against magic practices. In the time of Alexander the Great, with the introduction of foreign gods and foreign demons, interest in magic and a wide range of superstitious practices became widespread, and ever more complicated in thought and act. The attempts to suppress magic were due not to disbelief on the part of the enlightened in its genuineness and efficacy but to the fear of its dangerous consequences (compare ASTROLOGY). Magic received considerable impetus under the empire from the speculations of the *Neoplatonists, especially in the direction of rites to conciliate or exorcize the good and evil spirits supposed by them to people the universe. New laws to some extent repressed the conspicuous practice of magic, which was also energetically condemned by the early Fathers of the Church, not as a delusion, but as impious. Authors such as Juvenal and Lucian who showed a sceptical spirit were very few.

See also ASTROLOGY, AUGURY, and HARUSPICES.

magi'ster e'quitum ('master of the horse'), at Rome, the assistant of a *dictator.

magistrates, name given to officers of state in Greece and Rome. For Athens see ARCHON, POLEMARCH, and STRATEGOS. For Rome see AEDILE, CENSOR, CONSUL, CURSUS HONORUM, CURULE MAGISTRACIES, DICTATOR, PRAETOR, and QUAESTOR.

Magna Graecia (Megalē Hellas), collective name for the Greek cities of southern Italy founded by *colonization from the mainland of Greece and from the Greek cities of Asia Minor. They became prosperous through trade and the fertility of their land, and developed a flourishing culture and even their own schools of philosophy (see PYTHAGORAS and ELEA). Mutual hostility brought about the destruction of *Sybaris by *Croton, and decline set in *c.*400 BC. By 300 BC most of the cities needed Roman protection, and the Roman wars against Hannibal and Pyrrhus completed their ruin (see ROME 4). See also PAESTUM, THURII, and TARENTUM.

Magna Mater ('great mother'), a mother goddess worshipped in Asia from ancient times and introduced into Greece; see CYBELE.

Magnēs, see COMEDY, GREEK 4.

Maia. 1. In Greek myth, eldest of the *Pleiadēs, daughters of the Titan *Atlas; she was the mother by Zeus of the god Hermes, and lived in a cave on Mount Cyllenē in Arcadia.

2. Obscure Italian goddess associated with Vulcan; on 1 May the *flamen volcanalis* sacrificed to her. She seems to have been connected with the growth of living things, and the name of the month is probably derived from her name. By confusion with (1) she was associated with Mercury, the Roman equivalent of Hermes.

maiden-song, see PARTHENEION.

Ma'mertines (Māmertīni; 'Mamers' is the name of the Roman god Mars in the *Oscan dialect), Italian mercenaries from Campania, settled in Syracuse by the tyrant Agathoclēs who had hired them to fight for him against Carthage (see SYRACUSE 3). When he died they seized Messana (between 288 and 283 BC), and terrorized north-east Sicily. After a defeat, in fear of the Syracusans, they requested the Carthaginians to install a protective garrison in Messana, but at the same time they also asked Rome for help. The resulting clash of interest between Rome and Carthage precipitated the First *Punic War.

Māmu'rra, of Formiae, Caesar's chief engineer in Spain and Gaul, where he acquired much wealth. He was the first at Rome to face his mansion with marble. He is prominent in Catullus' invectives against Caesar.

mānēs, in Roman thought, the spirits of the dead, named euphemistically the 'kindly ones' (from the old Latin adjective *mānus*, 'good'). From a sense of their collective divinity they were worshipped as the *di manes* ('the divine dead') at the festivals of the *Feralia, *Parentalia, and Lemuria (see LEMURES). By extension the name *manes* was applied by the poets first to the realm of the dead, the Underworld, and secondly to the gods of the Underworld (*di inferi*), Dis, Orcus, Hecatē, and Persephonē. Later the *di manes* were individualized and identified with the *di parentes*, the dead of the family. The individual tomb led to the conception of each dead person having an individual spirit, and *manes*, although a plural noun, came to be used of a single spirit. Graves were originally dedicated to the dead collectively and were inscribed *dis manibus sacrum* ('sacred to the divine dead'); under the empire it became customary to add the name of the dead person, as if the meaning was 'sacred to the divine spirit of so-and-so'. See MUNDUS.

Ma'netho, priest of Heliopolis in Egypt in the third century BC who wrote in Greek a history of Egypt from mythical times to 323 BC, claiming to have consulted the chronological lists of kings. Portions of his history have been preserved by later writers such as *Eusebius and are of great value in establishing biblical chronology.

Mānī'lius. 1. **Gaius Manilius,** tribune for 67/6 BC, who carried a law conferring on *Pompey the command against Mithridates, with *imperium* over all the provinces of Asia Minor.

2. **Marcus Manilius** (flourished at the beginning of the first century AD), author of a Latin didactic poem in hexameters in five books entitled *Astronomica*, dealing with astrology. The work as it stands appears unfinished, the fifth book breaking off abruptly. Unlike Lucretius the author sees design and 'heavenly reason' in the organization of the universe. The subject matter is not universally appealing, but the non-technical parts of book 1, describing the creation and the arrangement of the stars in the heavens, and of book 5, describing the risings of signs, other than those of the zodiac, and their effect on children born on each occasion, contain interesting and eloquent passages. The text of Manilius is of incidental interest as being the subject of some of the best work of the three great Latin scholars Joseph Scaliger, Richard Bentley, and A. E. Housman.

maniple, in the Roman army, a sub-division of a legion, containing two centuries; see ARMY, ROMAN 2.

Ma'nlius Capitōlī'nus, Marcus, according to Roman tradition, a commander who held the Capitol against the Gauls when they sacked Rome *c.*390 BC (see ROME 4). It is said that, awakened by the cackling of the sacred geese while sleeping in his house on the Capitol, dogs having failed to give warning, he summoned the guards and repulsed a surprise attack by the Gauls. Thereafter the feeding of the sacred geese, contracted for by the censors and their responsibility, was a charge on the state. In an annual commemoration geese were carried on litters with purple and gold cushions, and dogs were crucified on stakes of elder (a ritual which survived into Christian times). In the political crisis that followed the withdrawal of the Gauls, Manlius, though a patrician, supported the poor who were suffering under the stringent laws of debt. He was accused of attempting to make himself tyrant and was thrown to his death from

the Tarpeian rock (see TARPEIA). He was supposed to have acquired the *cognomen* Capitolinus (see NAMES) from his earlier exploit, but the name existed in the family before that time and arose because they lived on the Capitol. After his death and disgrace no other member of the family received the *praenomen* Marcus.

Ma'nlius Torquā'tus (Titus Manlius Imperiōsus Torquātus), Roman hero who, in resisting an invasion of Gauls in 361 BC, reputedly killed in single combat an enormous Gaul and earned his *cognomen* (see NAMES) by taking from him an ornamental neck-chain, *torquēs*. He also exemplified Roman *pietas* ('dutifulness') in saving his father from prosecution. In the Latin War of 340 BC the consuls, of whom Torquatus was one, forbade single combats with the enemy. When the son of Torquatus nevertheless engaged and killed a Latin champion his father had him executed for disobedience. In later times the expression *Manliana imperia*, 'Manlian orders', became proverbial for commands of extreme severity.

The L. Manlius Torquatus of Cicero's *De finibus* was one of Pompey's supporters who, after Pompey's defeat at Pharsalus in 48 BC, went to Africa and was killed in the fighting there.

Mantinē'a, small city-state in the south-east of Arcadia, north of Tegea, created by the unification of five villages *c.*500 BC. In the fifth century BC it was friendly to Sparta, not taking part in the war of the other Arcadians against Sparta *c.*470 BC, and it rendered the Spartans great help in the Helot revolt of 464. In *c.*450 BC Mantinea became a moderate democracy, and during the *Peloponnesian War entered into alliance with Athens, Argos, and Elis (*c.*420). It was the scene of a decisive Spartan victory in 418 BC in a battle against Athenians and Argives.

In the fourth century BC Mantinea was attacked by Sparta and broken up into villages (387–386). After the battle of *Leuctra (371) the city was restored and took part in the pan-Arcadian confederacy founded at this time. It was the scene of another battle in 362 BC between Sparta and Thebes (in which Thebes was victorious but Epaminondas killed; see SPARTA 4). Gryllus, the son of Xenophon, fighting with the Athenian contingent on the Spartan side, was killed in a cavalry engagement at Mantinea shortly before the main battle.

Manto, see MOPSUS.

Ma'ntua (modern Mantova), on the river Mincius in Cisalpine Gaul, seldom mentioned in ancient literature but famous as the town near which the Roman poet Virgil was born.

manumission, at Rome, the act of freeing a slave; it might be formal (before a magistrate) or informal (before friends). In the commonest form, the master brought the slave before a magistrate and after declaring that he wished the slave to be free turned him round and 'let him go' (*manu misit*). A slave could also be freed with his master's consent at the *census, where he was registered as a citizen, having acquired or been given sufficient property. Slaves could be given their freedom after their master's death by direction in his will. By formal emancipation the Roman freedman, unlike the Greek freedman, acquired the full rights of a Roman citizen, except that he was not eligible for political office or (until the first century BC) military service (see FREEDMEN).

maps. The Greeks attributed the earliest map, of the inhabited world, to *Anaximander in the sixth century BC, and it was revised or improved upon by *Hecataeus. This may have been the map, engraved on a bronze tablet, which was shown in 499 BC to the Spartan king Cleomenes by Aristagoras of Miletus (Herodotus 5. 49). Contemporary maps were derided by Herodotus for showing a land mass surrounded by *Ocean, drawn as if with a compass, in which the known regions were shown in roughly equal segments. A map of the world is mentioned in Aristophanes' *Clouds* (produced in 423 BC) as if it were not a complete novelty. The foundation for scientific map-making was established when Aristotle confirmed that the earth was a sphere (a fact apparently assumed but not proved by Pythagoras), and opined that it has a circumference of 400,000 *stades. *Dicaearchus, a pupil of Aristotle *c*.320 BC, laid down from the evidence of shadow-sticks a main line of latitude from the Straits of Gibraltar to the Himalayas and the assumed eastern Ocean. *Eratosthenes (*c*.275–194 BC) made a quite accurate calculation of the circumference of the earth; his world map was the first to achieve a reasonable degree of accuracy. *Hipparchus (*c*.190–after 126 BC) corrected this in descriptive and especially mathematical details. Cratēs of Mallos (second century BC) made a terrestrial globe.

At Rome under the empire maps were relatively commonplace, mentioned by Propertius (IV. 3. 37), Pliny the Elder, Seneca the Younger, Suetonius, and Vitruvius. To the Greek discoveries was added information from Roman road-makers. An official map of the empire was prepared in the reign of the emperor Augustus from a geographical work by *Agrippa (1), and (after the latter's death) publicly displayed on the Porticus Vipsania so that the full extent of the Roman empire could be seen at a glance. Geographical knowledge was by this time widespread. *Strabo discussed the principles of map-making. *Ptolemy the mathematician and geographer constructed a world-map which survives in his manuscripts; it extends from *Thule in the north to Africa south of the equator. Other surviving maps are a

street-plan of Rome of *c*. AD 200, various road maps (see ITINERARIA) and the Peutinger Table (*Tabula Peutingeriana*), so called from the name of the sixteenth-century scholar who first published it; it is a strip over 6 m. (20 ft.) long and some 30 cm. (1 ft.) wide, showing the course of Roman roads (in a distorted form). See also GEOGRAPHY.

Ma'rathon, large Attic *deme on the north-east coast of Attica, commanding a long fertile plain lying along a deep bay, sheltered at its northern end, and connected with Athens by a main road running south of Mount *Pentelicus. It was the scene of a defeat inflicted by the Athenians and Plataeans under Miltiades on the invading Persians in 490 BC. (See PERSIAN WARS and, for the Marathon race so-called, PHEIDIPPIDES.) *Herodes Atticus was a native of Marathon.

Marcelli'nus, Greek author of a valuable biography of Thucydides, perhaps a *rhetor of the fifth century AD.

Marce'llus, Marcus Claudius. 1. Famous Roman general of the third century BC. As consul in 222 BC he campaigned successfully against the Gauls, winning the *spolia opima* by killing the Gallic chief in single combat. He fought with distinction in the Second Punic War, showing great determination after the disaster at Cannae in 216 BC, and capturing *Syracuse (see 3) in 211 after a long siege. He was killed in an ambush by Carthaginian forces when consul for the fifth time in 208.

2. Son of Gaius Claudius Marcellus and of Octavia, sister of the emperor Augustus. He was born in 42 BC. In 25 BC he was married by Augustus' wish to the latter's daughter Julia, and in 24 Augustus showed his favour towards him as possible heir by accelerating his progress through the magistracies (see CURSUS HONORUM). In 23, as aedile, Marcellus celebrated particularly magnificent games, but died later that year. He was a youth of great promise, and was lamented by Virgil in a famous passage of the *Aeneid* (6. 861–87), the reading of which was said to have so affected Octavia that she fainted.

Marcus Aure'lius, Roman emperor; see AURELIUS.

Mardo'nius, nephew and son-in-law of the Persian king Darius; see PERSIAN WARS.

Margī'tēs ('madman'), title and hero of a lost Greek epic poem, of unknown date and authorship, but an early work, attributed to Homer in antiquity; it was written in hexameters irregularly interspersed with iambic trimeters (see METRE, GREEK 5 (i)). Margites was an ancient Simple Simon, proverbial for his stupidity. He could not count beyond five, nor did he know whether his father or his mother had given birth to him. A tattered papyrus fragment describing a bedroom scene comes from the poem; otherwise only some five lines survive. Aristotle, who believed the author to be Homer, saw in *Margites* the germ of comedy, as the same poet's *Iliad* and *Odyssey* seemed to him to contain the germ of tragedy.

Mā'rius, Gaius (*c.*157–86 BC), born near Arpinum (Arpino, the birthplace also of Cicero) of an equestrian family; he served under *Scipio Aemilianus at the siege of *Numantia in Spain in 134–133 BC, became tribune of the *plebs* in 119, and in 114 made an important connection by marrying the patrician Julia (later aunt of Julius Caesar). In 109 the consul *Metellus (2) took him to Numidia in the war against *Jugurtha, but after being insulted by Metellus when the latter learned of his desire to stand for the consulship he intrigued against Metellus and secured election for 107. He was able to end the war thanks to the diplomacy of his quaestor *Sulla, and brought Jugurtha to Rome as a prisoner, celebrating a *triumph in 104. But his greatest achievement was the overthrow in 102 and 101, at Aquae Sextiae (Aix) and Vercellae (Borgo Vercelli), of the Teutones and Cimbri, German tribes who were invading Gaul and Italy and had inflicted severe defeats on Roman armies.

Marius won these victories with a reorganized army (see ARMY, ROMAN I), remedying the long-standing shortage of manpower by converting the old Roman citizen army recruited on a property basis to a professional army of volunteers recruited from all classes including the *proletarii*. Thus, without realizing it, he created a new type of client-army which was dependent on its general for its reward, paving the way for the political domination of successful generals and ultimately for the empire. From 104 to 100 Marius was consul every year, although he was from a family which had never before held high office (see NOVUS HOMO). In 100, when consul for the sixth time, he made close ties with *Saturninus, who as tribune in that year brought forward various measures on Marius' behalf. But when Saturninus appeared to be building up independent power Marius broke with his ally, joined with the *optimates, and supported the passing of a *senatus consultum ultimum*, causing Saturninus to surrender. He thus alienated Saturninus' supporters, as he did the *optimates* also by renewed opposition to them. He prudently withdrew on a mission to Asia Minor (99–97) and his influence declined.

Although he had favoured Italian enfranchisement Marius was probably against the proposals of Drusus (tribune in 91; see ROME 6), and mobilized his Italian clients against the latter. He served as *legatus* (deputy commander) in the North with some success, but the *optimates* now turned to Sulla as military commander. Sulla was elected consul in 88, but Marius schemed to secure the command of the war in the East against *Mithridates, and by popular resolution (of the *concilium plebis*) and some degree of violence he achieved his aim. Sulla refused to admit the legality of the resolution and marched on Rome; Marius had to flee, arriving in Africa after many dramatic adventures (later much embroidered). After Sulla's departure for the East early in 87 Marius returned to Italy, joined the popular leader Cinna (who, although consul in 87, had been illegally expelled by his colleague), marched on Rome and captured it late in 87. Marius was consul for the seventh time in 86, thus fulfilling, it is said, a prediction. He then embarked on indiscriminate massacre of all those who might be considered his enemies, until Cinna, now his colleague, intervened. His health failed and he died before he could take up the Eastern command which had been voted to him.

Mark Antony, see ANTONY, MARK.

Marmor Pa'rium (the 'Parian Marble'), an inscribed marble slab originally set up in the Greek island of Paros and containing a chronological table of events from the beginning of the reign of Cecrops, the mythical first king of Athens (taken to be 1580 BC), down to 263 BC. Two substantial fragments survive; one came from Smyrna into the possession of Thomas Howard in 1627 (so becoming one of the 'Arundel Marbles'), of which the upper part was lost in the seventeenth century during the English Civil War; the other was discovered in 1897 at Paros, where it remains. The events selected for inclusion are a mixture of political, military, religious, and literary history. Other inscribed tablets found in the nineteenth and twentieth centuries on Paros, relating events in the life of the local poet *Archilochus, are not included under this name.

Māro, *cognomen* (see NAMES) of the poet *Virgil, by which he is occasionally called.

Marpe'ssa, in Greek myth, daughter of the river-god Evēnus. She was loved by Idas (see LYNCEUS) and carried off by him in a winged chariot given him by the god Poseidon (in some accounts his father). They were pursued by Apollo, who also loved Marpessa, and Idas prepared to fight the god, but Zeus intervened and asked the girl to choose: she chose Idas, since, being mortal, he would grow old with her. Marpessa had a daughter Cleopatra who married *Meleager (in consequence Idas and Lynceus took part in the Calydonian boarhunt). After Idas died Marpessa killed herself; his father Aphareus, king of Messenia, being left without an heir, bequeathed his kingdom to Nestor of Pylos (or Nestor's father Neleus).

marriage

1. *Greek.* Polygamy was not practised in Greece in general, and it was not permitted at Athens.

Alexander the Great allowed his Macedonian soldiers to take as wives the captive women they were living with in Persia while retaining their wives in Macedonia, and polygamy was certainly practised by the ruling house to ensure a plentiful supply of heirs. Philip II had seven wives, none of whom did he apparently divorce.

At Athens the law required that marriage should be preceded by a betrothal agreement, formally made, with witnesses present from both sides. The giving of a dowry by the bride's father or guardian was universal, and was one of the conditions of the marriage agreed upon at the betrothal. It was the wife's share of the paternal estate and was intended for her maintenance. It remained under her husband's control but might pass to her children at her death. Widows also received a dowry if they remarried. In early times at least, bridegifts were sent to the bride by the family of the bridegroom. Marriage was arranged for prudential reasons (often to a relative; see WOMEN, POSITION OF) by the parents of the bride and groom, and a daughter at any rate would have very little say in the matter. Plutarch records as a matter of interest that Cimon's sister or half-sister Elpinicē married *Callias for love and, it would appear, without a dowry. Men married at about 30; women were usually married by the time they were 16. At the wedding the bride was taken to the groom's house and joined his family (see MARRIAGE CEREMONIES below). Living together established the fact of marriage, and its object was the procreation of children. The marriage was registered with the husband's phratry (see PHRATRIAI), as were subsequently the children of the marriage, so as to establish their citizen-status. Divorce was equally easy for both husband and wife, marriage being ended by the fact of ceasing to live together; the wife might have to give written notice of divorce in court in order to ensure the return of the dowry to her guardian. To some extent a large dowry was a deterrent to divorce.

2. *Roman*. Only in the case of *confarreatio*, an ancient and exclusive form of marriage from which it was almost impossible to obtain divorce, was a Roman marriage celebrated with religious rites. The various other ceremonies which normally accompanied a marriage were merely civil acts and had no legal force; the marriage contract had been signed by both parties some time previously, and marriage was constituted by the living together of a man and a woman with the intention of forming a lasting union. Marriage at Rome was a part of 'personal' law, i.e. the law that regulated the family, for example by establishing the succession following a death; thus only a marriage where both parties were citizens or enjoyed Roman marriage rights could be bound by such regulations as that of *patria potestas*, 'power of a father' (see PATERFAMILIAS). Roman marriage entailed different rights at different times for different classes of people; e.g. patricians could not marry plebeians until 445 BC (for the historical background see ROME 3), nor could a free person marry a freedman or freedwoman until the marriage legislation of the emperor Augustus in 18 BC and AD 9 made it permissible for all except the senatorial class. But Augustus introduced new restrictions on marriage in the interests of morality (e.g. concerning the remarriage of an adulteress), and this gave impetus to the institution of *concubinatus* ('concubinage'), a recognized form of permanent union that lacked the social consequences (and avoided the legal requirements) of full marriage.

In early times, a formal betrothal usually preceded marriage, and was binding. Later, betrothal, where it existed, was informal and not binding. Also in early times a bride passed into the control (*manus*) of her husband, who had power over her comparable with that of *patria potestas*. But by the end of the republic she usually remained under her father's authority or her own (*sui iuris*), as she was before marriage, and retained the ownership of her property if she had any. Husband and wife each kept control of their own property, but the dowry (which was not legally necessary but a social duty for a father to provide) was to a limited extent under the control of the husband. Since the essence of marriage was consent, divorce was easily obtained by the dissent of either party, and though rare in the earlier republic became common in the first century BC; however, the rules governing the return of the dowry acted as a deterrent. See also CITIZENSHIP.

marriage ceremonies. Our knowledge of marriage ceremonies in the ancient world is based on descriptions in literature, which are generalized and probably idealized.

1. *At Athens*. The favoured time for marriage was in winter, the month Gamelion (January) deriving its name from *gamos*, 'marriage'. (This was the time in the agricultural year when least work was required.) The ceremony started with a sacrifice to the gods of marriage, Zeus and Hera, and the bride might make a dedication of a lock of hair. Both bride and groom would each take a ritual bath, the water being brought from the spring *Callirhoē. A feast would be held at the bride's father's house (or perhaps later at the groom's house), the bride sitting veiled with the women, the men sitting apart. In the evening the bridegroom and his best friend took the bride away from her father's house to the groom's house in a carriage, preceded by a torchlight procession of friends uttering the wedding cry of *Hymen, o Hymenaie* (see HYMENAEUS). Upon arrival the bride, still veiled, was conducted by the groom's mother

with a lighted torch into the house, where she and the groom were showered with sweets. After they entered the bedroom the *epithalamium or wedding hymn was sung outside the closed door.

2. *At Rome.* The favoured month for marriage was June. The bride's dress and appearance were prescribed by custom. Her hair was arranged in six locks, divided by the point of a spear, and bound with woollen fillets; she wore a white woven tunic fastened at the waist with a girdle, and a veil and shoes of flame-colour. Friends gathered at the bride's father's house; a married woman linked the bride's and groom's right hands; a sacrifice was made, and if, as under the empire, a marriage contract was made, it was signed now. A wedding feast was held at the bridegroom's expense and might take place at this point, at the bride's father's house. Then the bride was torn with apparent violence from the arms of her mother and escorted in procession to the groom's house, accompanied by three young boys, she herself carrying a distaff and spindle with wool. She was carried over the threshold of her new house to avert an ill-omened stumble, and was received by her husband with fire and water which she had to touch; she greeted him with the words, *ubi tu Gaius, ego Gaia* ('where you are Gaius, I am Gaia'). She was conducted to the *lectus genialis* (marriage-bed) in the *atrium* (see HOUSES AND FURNITURE, ROMAN), undressed by women who had known only one husband, and her husband admitted. Meanwhile the epithalamium or wedding-song might be sung.

Mars, Italian god of war and the most important god after Jupiter, equated with the Greek god *Arēs and consequently regarded as the son of Juno (the equivalent of the Greek goddess Hera). He was also connected with agriculture; the Elder Cato, in his handbook on agriculture, quotes an elaborate prayer to be addressed to Mars by the farmer at the *lustratio* of his fields. Since the month named after the god, March (originally the first month of the Roman year; see CALENDARS), saw both the rebirth of the agricultural year and the start of the campaigning season, it may be that his combination of functions was natural to an agricultural people often engaged in war. Mars had his own priest at Rome, the *flamen martialis*; his altar was in the Campus Martius, and his sacred animals were the wolf and the woodpecker. A succession of festivals in March was dedicated to Mars the god of war and the protector of growth, including, on 14 March, horse-racing in the Campus Martius, and on 23 March the purification of the sacred trumpets, originally used in war (the Tubilustria). On several days in March the *Salian dancers (see SALII) performed a sort of war-dance wearing ancient armour and bearing his sacred shields

(*ancilia*), and sang their traditional hymn. All these occasions suggest preparation for war. There were also festivals in October slightly resembling those of March and marking the fact that this is the time of year when farmers and soldiers lay aside their tools and weapons. A great two-horse chariot-race, held on the Ides (15th) of October, was connected with the cult of Mars, for the right-hand horse of the winning team was sacrificed to him. On 19 October there was a purification of arms, and again during this month the Salian dances were performed.

At the quinquennial purification that accompanied the census, the people were drawn up round the altar in the Campus Martius, and the sacrifice of the *suovetaurilia* (pig, sheep, and ox) was offered to Mars to secure military success. The name Grādīvus, often applied to him, probably signifies 'he who marches forth' to war. A temple of Mars, probably dedicated during the Gallic War of 390 BC, stood on the Appian Way outside the city. Here was celebrated annually the victory of Lake Regillus. The emperor Augustus promoted the worship of Mars in the god's capacity as father of Romulus, founder of Rome, and under his title of Ultor ('avenger'). As early as 42 BC Augustus vowed a temple to Mars 'in vengeance of his father' (i.e. Julius Caesar), and again in 20 BC he ordered a temple of Mars Ultor to be built in the Forum: here were laid the standards lost by Crassus and by Antony and recovered by Augustus from the Parthians; it was eventually dedicated in 2 BC. Both Horace (*Odes* I. 2) and Ovid (*Fasti* 5. 561) glorify the new cult. Mars' love for Venus was early established as a favourite subject for artists.

Marsian or **Marsic War,** alternative name for the Social War (see ROME 6), from the central Italian tribe the Marsi who precipitated the war by taking the initiative in demanding Roman citizenship.

Ma'rsyas, in Greek myth, a *satyr or silenus associated with the river of that name (a tributary of the Maeander in Asia Minor), who picked up the flute which the goddess Athena had invented but had thrown away because it distorted the player's face. He became so proficient a player that he challenged Apollo to a musical contest (Apollo playing the lyre), with the Muses as judges. It was agreed that the victor should do what he pleased to the other, and when Apollo was judged victor he tied Marsyas to a tree and flayed him alive. The river sprang from his blood or the tears of his mourners. Marsyas picking up the flute discarded by Athena was represented in a mid-fifth century bronze group by *Myron, known from Roman copies, and the story was a popular subject with vase painters. In later times it was interpreted in several symbolic ways. See also MIDAS.

Ma'rtial (Marcus Valerius Martiālis) (*c.* AD 40–103/4), Roman poet, given his *cognomen* (see NAMES) to commemorate his birth on 1 March. He was a native of Bilbilis in Spain and claimed Iberian and Celtic ancestry. He went to Rome in AD 64, where his association with his fellow Spaniards Seneca the Younger and Lucan was cut short by their deaths as a result of the conspiracy of *Piso (2). Little of his early career is known and that mostly depends on what he tells us himself. He was poor and lived in a third-floor lodging, but later had a cottage at Nomentum (in Latium, about 20 km. or 13 miles from Rome) and a small house on the Quirinal hill at Rome. He wrote poetry for his living, depending on the sale of his books and on patrons who did not make very generous return for his complimentary verses. Gradually his reputation, if not his wealth, increased. He was granted the (honorary) rank of military tribune and, though he never married, the *ius trium liberorum*; he took no part in public affairs. His first known work was a *Liber spectaculorum* ('book of spectacles') to celebrate the opening in AD 80 of the Colosseum; of this work thirty-three poems survive, interesting for what they reveal of the shows given on that occasion. In 84–5 were published the collections of elegiac couplets which later appear as books 13 and 14 of the *Epigrams* (see below): they consist of mottoes to accompany *xenia*, guest-gifts (mostly of food and drink), or *apophorēta*, gifts taken home from banquets at the festival of the *Saturnalia (which are of the most varied kind, stationery, clothing, furniture, toys, works of art, food, pets, even slaves).

Martial's more important work, the first twelve books of the *Epigrams*, began to appear in 86. Between that year and 98 eleven of these books were issued. In 98 he returned to Bilbilis (his travelling expenses paid by the Younger Pliny), to a quiet country life on a farm given him by a patroness. From there he issued his twelfth book of epigrams in the winter of 101. The Younger Pliny in a letter of 104 mentions his death. Among Martial's friends, or addressees at least, besides Pliny (who speaks of him as 'talented, subtle, penetrating, witty, and sincere') were Juvenal, Quintilian, Silius Italicus, and Valerius Flaccus.

The *Epigrams*, which number well over 1,500, are short poems each expressing concisely and pointedly some single idea. By far the most are written in elegiac couplets; about a sixth are in hendecasyllables, some eighty in choliambics, a few in iambics and hexameters (see METRE). Many consist of a single couplet; the rest rarely exceed twenty lines. Several of the books are preceded by an interesting preface in prose defending the author's work against criticism, actual or anticipated. The epigrams are for the most part addressed to some individual, but the name may be imaginary; Martial does not give the real names of those he satirizes: *parcere personis, dicere de vitiis*, 'spare the sinner but denounce the sin', is his aim. He depicts with realistic detail the most diverse characters of contemporary Rome, fortune-hunters, gluttons, drunkards, debauchers, hypocrites of various kinds; he includes a few devoted wives, faithful friends, true poets, and honest critics. Many of the pieces are complaints about the meanness of patrons, or requests for gifts or loans. Some are invitations to a simple hospitality, some take leave of a parting guest or greet his return. Many give vivid glimpses of the Roman scene: the vendor of hot sausages on his round, the Gaul who has sprained his ankle in the street and gets a lift home on a pauper's bier, the far-from-perfect guest who arrives too late for breakfast and too early for lunch. Those addressed to the emperor Domitian are markedly adulatory and often frigidly contrived; adulation was no doubt necessary for survival, and his role as suppliant for patrons' favours does not appear to have struck Martial as humiliating. Many are obscene (Martial defends this in the preface to book 1 and in 1.35, appealing to the precedent of Catullus among others), but none of these are in book 5, addressed to *matronae puerique virginesque* ('mothers, youths, and maidens'), or book 8. As a rule he feels amusement rather than indignation at the vices he reveals, a trait which has been better received in some ages than in others.

Against this may be set his pride in his Spanish homeland, his admiration for the heroism of Romans in the days of the republic, his delight in country life, his affection for his friends, his occasional tenderness. His poems include some epigrams in the original sense of the word (i.e. 'inscriptions', see EPIGRAM), some touching epitaphs, including three laments for the poet Lucan, and notably that for the young girl Erōtion on whom he bids the earth press lightly, 'for she pressed light on thee': these lines were parodied in a later age in the mock epitaph on Vanbrugh, the architect of Blenheim Palace,

> Lie heavy on him, earth! for he
> Laid many heavy loads on thee.

Martial generally writes straightforwardly and without mythological allusion. By giving his poems wit and pointedness, and especially by putting the sting in the tail, he changed the form of the epigram, giving that term the meaning which it bears in modern times, in marked contrast with the Greek epigram, which did not aim to have a pointed conclusion. But he does not merely aim at wit; his view of life is essentially humorous. Some of his lines have become well known, such as that frequently seen on sundials, *soles ... qui nobis pereunt et imputantur* ('the days that perish and are charged to our account'). A plea that his epigrams are more serious than some authors' tragedies ends with the line, *laudant illa, sed ista legunt* ('*Those* they praise, *these* they read'). A couplet (1. 32) directed against a certain Sabidius acquired a wide circulation in its seventeenth-century English translation by Thomas Brown, 'I do not love you, Dr Fell . . . '.

Martiā'nus Cape'lla, of Carthage, Latin writer, the author, probably between AD 410 and 439, of *De nuptiis Mercurii et Philologiae* ('on the marriage of Mercury and Philologia'), an elaborate allegory in nine books, in Latin prose interspersed with verse (in the manner of Menippean satire or Petronius' *Satyricon*). Mercury, the god of eloquence, having decided to marry, consults the god Apollo, who commends to him the learned virgin Philologia, who possesses all learning. Two books are devoted to the married couple, and one to each of the *seven liberal arts who, personified as handmaids, are given to the bride as a wedding present; thus Grammar, Rhetoric, Logic (or Dialectic), Arithmetic, Geometry, Music, and Astronomy each expound their discipline. The work therefore forms an encyclopaedia of these, in which pedantry and fantasy are mingled. It owes something to the *Disciplinae* of *Varro. Amongst much trivial information there are passages which preserve ancient and curious learning that is otherwise lost. The Middle Ages accepted this work as an authoritative description of the seven liberal arts, and it was the subject of several commentaries.

Masā'da, Jewish fortress by the Dead Sea, seized by Jewish extremists in the revolt against Rome of AD 66; it held out until 73, three years after the fall of Jerusalem; see JOSEPHUS.

Masini'ssa, see SOPHONISBA.

Massi'lia (Gk. Massalia; Marseilles), colony founded *c.*600 BC by *Phocaea, an Ionian Greek city, on the Mediterranean coast of France, east of the river Rhône (see COLONIZATION, GREEK 2). In the civil war between Caesar and Pompey, after a resolute stand in favour of the latter, the city surrendered to Caesar in 49 BC.

master of the horse, *magister equitum,* see DICTATOR.

mathematics. Greek tradition ascribed the invention of geometry to the Egyptians and its introduction into Greece to *Thalēs and *Pythagoras. The first Greek mathematician of whose work there is clear evidence is *Hippocratēs (2) (late fifth century BC). See also APOLLONIUS OF PERGE, ARCHIMEDES, ARCHYTAS, ARISTARCHUS OF SAMOS, CONON (2), ERATO-STHENES, EUCLID, EUDOXUS, HIPPARCHUS (2), HYPATIA, METON, PROCLUS, PTOLEMY, THEON, and NUMBERS.

Mātrā'lia, the matrons' festival at Rome, celebrated on 11 June, centred on the goddess *Matuta.

Mātrōnā'lia, in Roman religion, the festival of *Juno on 1 March (the old New Year's Day; see CALENDARS), when prayers were offered to her and her son *Mars. It was called by the poet Martial the 'Saturnalia of women', when wives received presents from their husbands, and mistresses feasted their female slaves.

Mātū'ta, in Roman religion, a goddess of the dawn, having some connection apparently with young growth. She developed into a protectress of childbirth, and was worshipped at the Matralia. Later she was identified with the Greek goddess Ino, also called Leucothea.

Mausō'lus (Maussōllos), native of Caria (in south-west Asia Minor) who in 377 BC succeeded his father Hecatomnus as ruler of that country and was recognized as its satrap by the king of Persia. However, he ruled in virtual independence of Persia and extended his rule over the Greek cities of the coast and over Lycia, plotting to get control of the neighbouring islands. For this purpose he fomented the revolt of Rhodes, Cos, and Chios from the Athenian League in 357 BC (the Social War; see ATHENS 2 (iv)) in order to bring them under his control. In this he was successful; but he died in 353 and was succeeded by his widow (and sister) Artemisia. His tomb, the Mausoleum, built by Pythius and regarded as one of the *Seven Wonders of the ancient world, included the over life-size statues of Mausolus and Artemisia, other figures, human and animal, and some fine friezes. It was excavated in the mid-nineteenth century.

Maxe'ntius, see CONSTANTINE I.

meals. *Greek.* In early times meals consisted of an early breakfast (*ariston*), followed by the main meal at midday (*deipnon*), and supper (*dorpon*) in the evening. In classical Athens it seems to have been usual to take only two meals, *ariston* in the morning and *deipnon* in the evening. From the fourth century BC an earlier breakfast, *akratisma*, was added.

Roman. In early times, dinner (*cena*) was eaten at midday, and supper (*vesperna*) in the evening. Gradually *cena* was taken later, an earlier meal, a light lunch, *prandium*, was introduced, and supper was omitted. Breakfast, *ientaculum*, when taken, was little more than a piece of bread.

measures, see WEIGHTS AND MEASURES.

Mēdē'a (Mēdeia), in Greek myth, daughter of Aeētēs, king of Colchis, and like her aunt *Circē an enchantress (see MAGIC). When Jason and the *Argonauts arrived at Colchis in pursuit of the Golden Fleece, Aeetes consented to surrender it to Jason if the latter would perform certain apparently impossible tasks. These included the sowing of a dragon's teeth from which armed men arose whose fury was turned against Jason. With the help of Medea's magic the tasks were successfully accomplished, and Medea finally enabled Jason to take the fleece by killing or drugging the serpent that guarded it. She engineered the Argonauts' escape from Aeetes; in one version of the story she murdered and cut into pieces her young brother Apsyrtus, scattering the fragments so that her father might be delayed in his pursuit of the Argonauts by gathering up the body; in other versions Apsyrtus is grown up and leads the pursuit until Medea contrives his murder. At Iolcus Medea took vengeance on Pelias (Jason's uncle) for the wrong done by him to Jason's family. First she restored Aeson, Jason's father, to youth by boiling him in a cauldron with magic herbs, and then persuaded the daughters of Pelias to submit their father to the same process. But on this occasion she deliberately gave them ineffective herbs, and the daughters were unwittingly the cause of their father's death. Acastus, their brother, then drove Jason and Medea from Iolcus and they took refuge in Corinth. For the rest of the story, see MEDEA below. Medea was the subject of tragedies by Aeschylus, Sophocles, and Euripides, but only that of Euripides survives. Seneca the Younger and Ovid (see (2) and (3) below) also wrote tragedies about her; she receives a more romantic treatment by Apollonius Rhodius, and by Ovid in *Heroides* and *Metamorphoses*.

Mede'a. 1. Greek tragedy by *Euripides, produced in 431 BC. Despite its later fame it won only third prize in the dramatic competition. It deals with the later part of the story of Jason and Medea (see MEDEA above). These two have fled to Corinth after Medea has murdered Pelias for Jason's sake. Jason, ambitious and tired of his barbarian princess, has arranged to marry the daughter of Creon, king of Corinth, for prudential reasons he alleges. The desertion and ingratitude of her husband arouse savage anger in Medea and she openly declares her feelings. Creon, fearing her vengeance upon himself and his daughter, pronounces instant banishment on Medea and her two children. Medea coaxes him into allowing her one day's respite, and by a poisoned robe and diadem contrives the deaths of Jason's bride and her father. Then she kills her own children, partly to make Jason childless, partly because, since they now must surely die, it is better that it should be by her hand than by that of her enemies, who would thus triumph over her. Finally, taunting Jason in his despair, she escapes to Athens where she has secured asylum from king Aegeus (who appears earlier in the play).

2. Roman tragedy by *Seneca (2), based on that of Euripides, with variations of detail. Medea's children are not sentenced to banishment; she asks for them to be allowed to accompany her into exile, but Jason's love for them prevents it. Medea thus learns where Jason is vulnerable and kills them to revenge herself

on him. The play contains a famous passage in which Seneca seems to prophesy the discovery of a New World (374 ff.):

> venient annis
> saecula seris quibus Oceanus
> vincula rerum laxet, et ingens
> pateat tellus Tethysque novos
> detegat orbes, nec sit terris
> ultima Thule.

(In later years a new age will come in which Ocean shall relax its hold over the world, and a vast land shall lie open to view, and Tethys shall reveal a new world, and *Thulē will not be the last country on earth).

3. Roman tragedy by *Ovid, of which only two lines have survived. It was praised by *Quintilian.

Medes. Media, mountainous country southwest of the Caspian Sea, was for a century the heartland of a Median empire whose capital was at Ecbatana (Hamadan). The Medes, who were related to the Persians, were the first Asian people to revolt against the dominant Assyrians. The founder of their empire was Deiocēs in the early seventh century BC, who was succeeded by his son Phraortēs and then by Cyaxarēs, his grandson. Cyaxarēs (615–585 BC) conquered surrounding territories and in alliance with (probably) the father of Nebuchadnezzar, king of Babylon, captured the Assyrian capital Nineveh in 612. During the war between the Medes and the Lydians, under their king Alyattēs, there occurred the eclipse of the sun (585 BC) which the Ionian Greek philosopher *Thalēs is said to have predicted for that year. Cyaxares was succeeded by his son Astyagēs (585–549), who was defeated and captured by his vassal *Cyrus, king of the Persians, and from 549 the Persians became the ruling race.

Me'dia, see MEDES.

Medicā'mina faciē'i fēminē'ae ('cosmetics for the female face'), Latin poem in elegiacs by *Ovid; only one hundred lines survive.

medicine, see ERASISTRATUS, GALEN, HEROPHILUS, and HIPPOCRATES.

medi'mnus, see WEIGHTS AND MEASURES I (iii).

Medū'sa, in Greek myth, one of the three *Gorgons, the only one who was mortal. Anyone who looked at her head, even after her death, was turned to stone. She was killed by *Perseus.

Me'gaclēs, name of several prominent members of the aristocratic *Alcmaeonid *genos* at Athens.

1. Archon, 632/1 BC, responsible for the murder of *Cylon.

2. Grandson of (1), married to Agaristē, daughter of Cleisthenēs, tyrant of Sicyon.

3. Nephew of *Cleisthenes (2) who was the founder of Athenian democracy (and who was

himself the son of (2) above), ostracized in 486, winner of the Pythian chariot-race in the same year (see GAMES, PUBLIC, GREEK), and celebrated in Pindar's seventh Pythian Ode. He was the uncle of Periclēs.

Megae'ra, see FURIES.

Megalē'sia or **Megale'nsia,** festival and games at Rome in honour of Magna Mater ('great mother'), a Phrygian goddess, also known as *Cybelē, introduced to Rome in 204 BC; the festival was celebrated on 4 April.

Megalo'polis (Gk. *hē megalē polis,* 'the big city'), city in Arcadia founded between 369 and 362 BC by *Epaminondas, the Theban general, after his victory over the Spartans at Leuctra (371). It was founded to be the capital of the Arcadian League and was one of the largest cities in the Peloponnese; Plato is said to have been invited by Epaminondas to draw up the constitution and code of laws, but to have declined. In the fourth century BC it always took the side of Macedon. In 234 it joined the *Achaean Confederacy, but was subdued and its inhabitants expelled by Sparta under Cleomenes III. The city was restored by Philopoemen, the general of the Confederacy, after he had defeated the Spartans at Sellasia (222). It was the birthplace of Philopoemen and the historian Polybius.

Megalopo'litans, For the, political speech by the Greek orator Demosthenes. See DEMOSTHENES (2) 3.

Me'gara (Gk. *ta megara,* 'the temples'), Dorian city at the eastern end of the Isthmus of Corinth overlooking Salamis, originally known as Nisa, according to one story, from its first king *Nisus; the name was preserved in that of the harbour, Nisaea. The city reputedly became Dorian when Dorian invaders, repelled from Athens by the self-sacrifice of the king Codrus, settled at Megara. It was of some importance as a land passage between central Greece and the Peloponnese. Between 730 and 550 BC it showed considerable colonizing enterprise, founding Chalcedon and Byzantium on the Bosporus, Heraclea Pontica in Bithynia, and Megara Hyblaea in Sicily. In about 600 BC it fell under the rule of the tyrant Theagenes, and the tyranny was followed by political struggles reflected, according to some critics, in the poems of the Megarian poet *Theognis (but see the discussion of dates for that poet). It lost its western region to Corinth and Salamis to Athens. Shortly before 500 BC it joined the Peloponnesian League and was active in the Persian Wars. After these ended, the Megarians, having become involved in boundary disputes with Corinth, left their Peloponnesian allies and placed themselves under Athenian protection (460); the Athenians then sent an occupying garrison. After the Athenian defeat by the Boeotians at Coronea in 447, the Megarians revolted and massacred the garrison. Subsequently the Athenians passed a decree excluding them from all the harbours and ports of the Athenian empire, and this 'Megarian decree' (there may have been others) became a contributory cause of the *Peloponnesian War. Megara suffered severely in the war, but escaped capture by Athens through the prompt arrival of the Spartan general Brasidas with a relieving force in 424. In the fourth century it remained relatively detached from operations of war, although it allied itself with Athens against Philip. See also MEGARIAN SCHOOL below.

Mega'rian School of philosophy, founded by Eucleidēs of Megara (flourished *c.*390 BC), a pupil of Socrates. It adopted the doctrines of the *Eleatic philosophers. Its members developed a reputation for skill in dialectical argument (compare ZENO (1)).

Mei'dias, Against, speech prepared by Demosthenes but not delivered. See DEMOSTHENES (2) 2.

Mēla, Pompō'nius, see POMPONIUS.

Mela'mpus (Melampous), in Greek myth, famous seer, son of Amythāon (a grandson of *Aeolus), and supposed ancestor of the prophetic clan of the Melampodidae, who produced famous seers in historic times. He took care of some young serpents whose parents had been killed by his servants, and these one day licked his ears while he was sleeping. Thereafter he understood the language of all creatures. His brother Bias sought to marry Pēro, daughter of *Neleus, but the latter demanded as bride-price the cattle which *Iphiclus had taken from Neleus' mother. Melampus undertook to get them for Bias but was caught and imprisoned. Hearing from the wood-worms that the roof was about to fall in, Melampus warned the gaoler. When Iphiclus heard this he was so impressed he promised to hand over the cattle if Melampus could tell him why he was childless. This Melampus was able to do by questioning a vulture, and Bias was thus enabled to marry Pero. Another feat of Melampus was curing the daughters of *Proetus of their madness. According to Herodotus it was Melampus who introduced the name of the god *Dionysus into Greece. Among his mythical descendants who were also seers were *Amphiaraus and Theoclymenus (see Homer, *Odyssey* 20).

Melani'ppidēs, see DITHYRAMB.

Meleā'ger (Meleagros). **1.** In Greek myth, son of Oeneus, king of Calydon, and his wife Althaia. He married Cleopatra, daughter of Idas and *Marpessa. The *Fates appeared at his birth and declared that he should live as long as a brand that was on the fire was not consumed. Althaia snatched the brand from the fire and carefully preserved it. Later, when Meleager was a young man, Oeneus omitted to sacrifice to Artemis and the goddess in anger sent a great boar to ravage Calydon. Oeneus collected a band of heroes to attack the beast, offering the boar's skin to whoever should kill it. *Atalanta, the virgin huntress, was the first to wound it, and when Meleager finally killed it he gave her the spoils, being in love with her. His mother's brothers tried to take them from her and Meleager killed them. When Althaia heard of her brothers' deaths she took out the brand and burned it, and Meleager died. In the version of the myth told by Homer, he is cited as an example of a valiant but misguided warrior of a past generation who refused to aid his people when they were attacked (by the *Curetes) because he was angry (having been cursed by his mother for killing one of her brothers). Although he was finally persuaded and drove off the enemy, he received no reward because he changed his mind too late. He was sometimes said to have been one of the *Argonauts. Later writers add that after his death the women who mourned him were turned into guinea-fowl (*meleagrides*). The hunt of the Calydonian boar, Meleager leading, was a favourite subject in art.

2. Of Gadara in Syria, Greek poet who lived *c.*100 BC. He wrote short elegiac poems on love and death, about a hundred of which survive in the Greek *Anthology. They are technically very accomplished and often moving. He was also the compiler of an early anthology of poetic epigrams (which has not survived intact), calling it his 'Garland' (*stephanos*) and likening each poet to a flower.

Melēsi'genēs, name sometimes applied to Homer in allusion to his alleged birthplace Smyrna, on the river Melēs.

Melē'tus, nominal accuser of Socrates in 399 BC, probably son of the tragic poet of the same name who is mocked by the comic poets; probably not identical with the Meletus who prosecuted *Andocidēs for impiety in 400.

Mēlian dialogue, in *Thucydides 5. 84 ff., the discussion between Athenian envoys and the magistrates of Mēlos, a (Dorian) Greek island, the most southerly of the Sporadēs. During the *Peloponnesian War Melos was friendly to Sparta and refused to surrender to Athens. The dialogue took place in 416 BC when the Athenians proposed to subdue the island, and the speeches of the Athenians are an exposition of their ruthless imperial policy. Melos was taken by the Athenians shortly afterwards and the inhabitants put to death or enslaved.

Melice'rtēs, see DIONYSUS. According to Greek myth, the body of the drowned Melicertes (who was deified and known as Palaemon) was washed up on the Isthmus of Corinth, where the Isthmian games (see GAMES, PUBLIC, 1) were founded in his honour. There was a temple of Palaemon at Corinth.

Meli'ssus, of Samos, commander of the Samian fleet which defeated the Athenians in 441 BC, the last important member of the *Eleatic School of philosophy.

Mēlos, Greek island, with Thera the most southerly of the Sporadēs. See MELIAN DIALOGUE.

Melpo'menē, the Muse of tragedy; see MUSES.

Me'mmius, Gaius, dedicatee of *Lucretius' poem *De rerum natura*, minor poet and orator, and patron of poets; nothing of his work survives. Catullus and Helvius *Cinna accompanied him to Bithynia where he was propraetor in 57 BC. In 53 he was banished for dishonesty in the elections of the previous year. He married *Sulla's daughter, who later married Milo, and died before 46 BC.

Memnon, in Greek myth, son of *Tithonus and *Eos (Dawn), king of the Ethiopians and brother of Emathion, king of Egypt; he fought on the Trojan side at the siege of Troy. Memnon killed Antilochus and was later killed by Achilles. His story was related in the *Aethiopis* (by Arctinus), a poem of the *Epic Cycle, according to which Zeus made him immortal. His final battle and his body carried away by his mother are favourite subjects for vase-painters. A tradition arose that a colossal statue of Memnon which stood before a temple in Egyptian Thebes used to sing at dawn when struck by the sun (but the statue is engraved with the name of an Egyptian king).

Memorābi'lia (*Apomnēmoneumata*), reminiscences of Socrates by *Xenophon, in four books, which describe his character and some of his opinions, chiefly by means of more or less imaginary conversations between Socrates and various persons (including Xenophon himself).

The first part is a refutation of the particular charges on which Socrates was tried and sentenced to death (that he did not believe in the gods of the state, but introduced other new deities, and that he corrupted the youth). This part is based on a literary exercise by a certain Polycratēs. Xenophon then proceeds to illustrate the character and opinions of Socrates, his helpfulness to his friends, his piety, and his views on education and various philosophical questions, probably derived in part from Xenophon's own recollections, in part from other sources. The opinions attributed to Socrates, do not always accord with those attributed to him by Plato. The work concludes with a peroration on the virtues of Socrates.

Menae'chmi, Roman comedy by *Plautus. A merchant of Syracuse had twin sons so much alike as to be indistinguishable. One of these, Menaechmus, was stolen when seven years old. The other, Sōsiclēs, had his name changed to Menaechmus in memory of his lost brother. When he is grown up Sosicles-Menaechmus sets out in search of his brother, and finally arrives at Epidaurus where his brother is living. Comic misunderstandings arise when he successively encounters the lost brother's mistress, wife, and father-in-law. Wife and father-in-law conclude that he is insane, but owing to a further confusion it is the original Menaechmus, their real husband and son-in-law, whom they attempt to lock up. Finally the twins confront each other and the puzzle is solved.

This play, directly or indirectly, furnished the main idea for Shakespeare's *Comedy of Errors*. The *Menaechmi* was performed at the marriage of Lucrezia Borgia to Alfonso d'Este, before Pope Alexander VI and the cardinals, in 1500.

Mena'nder (Menandros) (342–*c*.292 BC), the greatest writer of Attic New Comedy (see COMEDY, GREEK 6). He was said to be related to, perhaps a nephew of, the comic poet Alexis (see COMEDY, GREEK 5), a pupil of the philosopher Theophrastus, and a companion in military service of another philosopher, Epicurus. He was also a friend (and fellow pupil) of *Demetrius of Phalerum, the anti-democratic governor of Athens. He was said to have died by drowning in the harbour of Piraeus. Nearly one hundred titles of his plays are known, although some may be alternatives. The plays themselves were lost in the seventh and eighth centuries AD, but in the twentieth century numerous finds of papyri have brought to light one complete play, *Dyscolus* ('bad-tempered man'), and sizeable fragments of *Aspis* ('shield'), *Geōrgos* ('farmer'), *Dis exapatōn* ('twice a swindler'), *Epitrepontes* ('arbitrants'), *Cōlax* ('flatterer'), *Misumenos* ('hated man'), *Perikeiromenē* ('shorn hair'), *Samia* ('woman from Samos'), and *Sicyonios* ('man from Sicyon'). There are shorter fragments of many others including *Heros* ('hero'), *Theophoroumenē* ('woman possessed'), *Kitharistēs* ('flute girl'), and *Phasma* ('ghost'). *Orgē* ('anger'), which has not survived, is said to have been his first play, and some authorities say that it won the dramatic competition; on the whole Menander was unlucky at the competitions, winning only eight victories. Quintilian commented that he enjoyed more fame after his death than in his lifetime, and the Latin poet Martial has the line (5. 10), *rara coronato plausērĕ theatra Menandro*, 'the theatre applauded Menander but he rarely won the crown'. The number of papyri found of his works is exceeded only for Homer and Euripides. The loss of his plays is due to their exclusion from the Greek school curriculum of the fifth and subsequent centuries AD, largely because they were written not in classical Attic Greek but rather in the *koinē* (see DIALECTS).

Before the discovery of the papyri Menander was known from a large number of quotations, many of them highly sententious, so that a false impression was given of moral earnestness. Even St Paul quoted him (1 Corinthians 15: 33), 'Evil communications corrupt good manners.' In fact many of these famous lines are now seen to have been spoken ironically: 'Whom the gods love die young', to an old man; 'I am a man, and I think nothing that is human to be outside my interest', by a busybody.

His plays are set in contemporary Greece, usually in Athens or the surrounding countryside. The plots are concerned with the private lives of well-to-do families, with a love-entanglement as an important but not always central feature: thus in *Dyscolus* Cremon and his misanthropy are more important than his son's love-affair. The plays contain many features that were commoner in the theatre of the time than in real life: abandoned or kidnapped children, recognitions by means of trinkets, seductions of well-brought-up girls at night festivals (where it was too dark to see their faces), amazing coincidences. Characters too are often conventional, the talkative, self-important cook, the bragging soldier, the angry father, the cunning but cowardly slave, the kind-hearted prostitute. Yet they are given other traits that conventional portraits lack and consequently seem more lifelike. Their speech, too, is apt and appropriate. The plots are often complicated but always skilfully put together and exciting, and the dialogue is fast moving, often pointed and witty. A frequently cited apostrophe from the Alexandrian scholar Aristophanes of Byzantium, 'O Menander and Life, which of you copied the other!' indicates that for all their contrivance the actions and the characters seem natural, and the underlying sentiments real. Menander's attitude to his creations is one of sympathy and gentle irony; resolution of the difficulties is achieved through the virtues of generosity and understanding.

The plays are written in verse, for the most part in iambic trimeters (see METRE, GREEK 4), which contrive to give the effect of natural speech. The Roman rhetor *Quintilian warmly recommended the study of Menander's plays even to students of rhetoric, regarding him as supreme among the writers of New Comedy. Through the adaptations of the Roman comic writers *Plautus and *Terence he deeply influenced the development of European comedy, notably in Molière, the Restoration dramatists, and Sheridan.

Menelā'us (Menelāos, Meneleōs), in Greek myth, king of Sparta, son of Atreus, younger brother of *Agamemnon, and husband of *Helen, whom Paris carried off to Troy, thus bringing about the expedition of the Greek chiefs to recover her. In Homer's *Iliad* he agrees to settle the war by a duel with Paris and would have killed him but for the latter's rescue by Aphroditē. Menelaus acquits himself well in the fighting over the body of Patroclus, but he is usually overshadowed by Agamemnon, the leader of the Greek army. He reappears in the *Odyssey* living at Sparta, reconciled with Helen, and visited by Odysseus' son Telemachus; he had returned to Sparta when Orestēs killed Clytemnestra and Aegisthus. He appears also in Sophocles' *Ajax* and Euripides' *Helen, Andromachē*, and *Trojan Women*.

Menēnius Agri'ppa, consul at Rome in 503 BC; he is said to have induced the plebeians who had seceded from Rome to return to the city (see ROME 3) by relating to them the parable of the belly and the members (Livy 2. 32).

Mene'xenus, dialogue of *Plato (see 2).

Meni'ppus, of Gadara in Syria (third century BC), a *Cynic philosopher who satirized (in Greek) the follies of men and philosophers in a serio-comic style, using a mixture of prose and verse. He was a slave who later acquired his freedom. His writings are lost, but they were imitated in Latin by *Varro in his *Saturae Menippeae* and by *Lucian in his dialogues. Menippus himself figures frequently in the latter's 'Dialogues of the Dead', and one of Lucian's satires bears his name.

Mēno (*Mĕnōn*), a dialogue by *Plato. Socrates is represented as conversing with a young Thessalian aristocrat Meno on the question of whether virtue can be taught. When attempts to define virtue meet with no success, the origin of knowledge is discussed; Socrates propounds his theory that knowledge is acquired before birth by the soul, which is immortal, and that knowledge is in fact recollection, which it is the purpose of teaching to bring out. Socrates demonstrates how this can be done by eliciting from Meno's slave, through careful questioning, the solution to a geometrical problem. But there are no teachers of virtue; it is not teachable; virtue is at most 'right opinion' (*orthē doxa*), and it arises from an irrational 'divine possession' (*theia moira*). It cannot be stated with certainty how virtue arises until it is known what exactly virtue is.

The historical Meno was a Thessalian general in the expedition of the Ten Thousand, whose treacherous conduct is related by Xenophon in the *Anabasis*.

Mentor. 1. In Homer's *Odyssey*, an old Ithacan friend of Odysseus, to whom the latter, when he left Ithaca for Troy, gave charge of his house. He acts as an adviser to Telemachus, Odysseus' son; hence the use of his name to describe a trusted counsellor.

2. The most celebrated Greek silver-engraver, of uncertain date but perhaps flourishing

c.100 BC. Many of his small cups were highly prized at Rome in the first centuries BC and AD. See TOREUTIC ART.

Mercā'tor ('merchant'), Roman comedy by *Plautus adapted from a Greek comedy by Philemon (see COMEDY, GREEK 6). A young man, sent abroad on a trading venture by his father, falls in love with a girl at Rhodes and brings her back to Athens, pretending that she is a present for his mother. His father discovers her and himself falls in love, with consequent complications.

Mercury (Mercurius), in Roman religion, son of *Maia and Jupiter, the god of trade (*merx*), particularly of the corn-trade, introduced at an early date from a Greek or Graeco-Etruscan source and identified with the Greek god *Hermēs, whose attributes he shared. His temple was on the Aventine overlooking the Circus Maximus; it was dedicated in 495 BC at a time of economic crisis (compare the introduction of Ceres, goddess of growth, in 496 and Apollo, god of healing, before 450). Like Hermes he was the god of eloquent speech and was often represented carrying a herald's staff, *caduceus*, with two entwined snakes, and winged hat and shoes. His name was later given to the element mercury (quicksilver) because of his imagined quickness of movement. Under the influence of astrology he assumed considerable importance in the Middle Ages, symbolizing the constant activity of the human intellect (compare English 'mercurial', which properly describes someone born under Mercury). He was also seen as mediator between divine and human wisdom. The fact that he does not have a *flamen* indicates that he was not a deity worshipped at Rome from earliest times.

Me'ropē, name of several heroines in Greek myth.

1. Wife of Cresphontēs (see HERACLEIDAE). Cresphontes, king of *Messenia, was killed by Polyphontēs (another descendant of Heracles), as were two of his sons. A third son, Aepytus, was saved by Merope and sent out of the country. Merope was then forced to marry Polyphontes, but when Aepytus was grown up he returned, killed Polyphontes, and recovered the throne.

2. One of the *Pleiadēs, the seven daughters of Atlas and the Oceanid Pleionē.

3. The wife of *Sisyphus.

4. Also known as Polyboea, the wife of Polybus, king of Corinth, who brought up *Oedipus.

Messalī'na, Vale'ria, great-granddaughter of Octavia (sister of the emperor Augustus). She married at the age of 14 in AD 39 or 40 her second cousin the emperor Claudius, then aged 48, as his third wife, and bore him two children, Octavia (later the wife of the emperor Nero) and Britannicus. She was notorious for her promiscuity (pilloried by Juvenal in Satires 6 and 10) to which Claudius alone was blind. In AD 48, though still apparently married to Claudius, she went through the formalities of a marriage with the consul designate C. Silius. While Claudius was still irresolute his freedman Narcissus had the pair killed.

Messa'lla Corvī'nus, Marcus Vale'rius (64 BC–AD 8), Roman patrician and distinguished orator, soldier, and patron of literature. He fought on the republican side at Philippi (42 BC) and then supported Antony, but disillusioned by the latter's conduct with Cleopatra transferred his allegiance to Octavian, fighting against Sextus Pompeius and taking part in the defeat of Antony at Actium in 31. He was employed in Roman administration, and proposed the title 'Pater Patriae' ('father of the country') for the emperor Augustus (2 BC). He was a great patron of poets, notably of Ovid and Tibullus, and was regarded, with Asinius Pollio, as the greatest orator of his time; he was also famous for his linguistic knowledge. See also AUGUSTAN AGE.

Messā'na (modern Messina), on the north-east tip of Sicily opposite the toe of Italy, founded as Zanclē by Euboean colonists c.730 BC (Zancle itself colonizing Himera in 648). Later it received immigrants from Messenia in the Peloponnese who changed its name to Messēnē; the Doric form of this name, Messana, seems to have been used from the first half of the fifth century. See also MAMERTINES. After 241 BC Messana became a prosperous city in alliance with Rome. Compare MESSENE below.

Messē'nē, city founded in 369 BC to be the capital of an independent Messenia in the Peloponnese (see below). See also EPAMINONDAS.

Messē'nia, south-west region of the Peloponnese. In mythology it was the kingdom of Aphareus who gave refuge, and later bequeathed his kingdom, to *Neleus, when the latter was driven from Thessaly. Subsequently it was ruled over by Neleus' son Nestor. After the *Dorian Invasion Messenia was ruled by Cresphontēs, and then by his youngest son Aepytus, who gave his name to the Messenian royal line. After the First and Second Messenian Wars against Sparta in the eighth and seventh centuries BC, the land was seized by the Spartans and the Messenians reduced to the status of helots (see SPARTA 1). Their bid for independence after the earthquake of 464 BC, the Third Messenian War, ended with the surrender of their stronghold at Ithōmē after a long siege. During the Peloponnesian War the Messenians were encouraged by the Athenians to revolt, and the threat increased the anxieties of the Spartans. In 369 BC the Theban general *Epaminondas achieved independence for Messenia. In the second century BC it came with the rest of Greece under Roman control.

metals, see MINES.

Metamorphō'sēs ('transformations'). 1. Latin epic-style poem in fifteen books of hexameters by *Ovid, his longest and his only surviving work in this metre. (It is longer than Virgil's *Aeneid.*) The poem is essentially a collection of stories from classical and Near-Eastern legend and, although it purports to tell of miraculous transformations into another form undergone by characters drawn mostly from Greek and Roman myth and legend, the transformation is sometimes of minor importance in the story. A deeper meaning and more significant unity than the poet's desire to entertain are often looked for in the *Metamorphoses*, but no suggestion has won general agreement. The stories are linked together, often tenuously and in a far-fetched manner, by devices of association and contrast. There is a chronological progression starting with the transformation of Chaos into the ordered universe, and after a succession of stories about gods and heroes drawn from Greek mythology the subject matter passes to what was thought of as history, Aeneas and Dido, Numa and Egeria, the doctrines of Pythagoras, and to Ovid's own times, ending with the death and deification of Julius Caesar. The Eastern tale of the Babylonian lovers, Pyramus and Thisbe, goes beyond the range of classical legend. The poem is composed with great care, and is the work to which Ovid pinned his hopes of immortal fame. It seems to have been composed from c. AD 2 onwards, and had not been finally revised when the poet was banished in AD 8. The model for this kind of composition was to some extent the *Aitia* of *Callimachus, but there the stories are unconnected. It is a work of great inventiveness, charm, and originality. Among the narratives usually thought to be best are (book 2) Phaethon driving the chariot of the sun; (book 3) Echo and Narcissus; (book 4) Pyramus and Thisbe, Perseus and Andromeda; (book 5) the rape of Proserpine; (book 6) Pallas Athena and Arachnē; (book 7) Jason and Medea, Cephalus and Procris; (book 8) the flight of Daedalus, Philemon and Baucis; (book 10) Orpheus and Eurydicē, Venus and Adonis; (book 11) Midas, Ceyx, and Halcyonē; (book 13) Polyphemus and Galatea.

2. See APULEIUS.

Metanī'ra (Metaneira), see DEMETER.

Metaphysics, group of treatises by *Aristotle on the nature of existence. Aristotle does not himself use the word 'metaphysics'. See ARISTOTLE 4 (ii).

Mete'lli, name of a noble family at Rome, belonging to the plebeian *gens Caecilia*. The Metelli first came to prominence in the First

Punic War and thereafter became one of the most distinguished of the Roman families, always supporting the *optimate cause. (For an anecdote about them see METRE, LATIN 1.) Members include the following.

1. Lucius Caeci'lius Metellus, consul 251 BC, *pontifex maximus* 243, died 221. In 250 BC, during the First Punic War, he won a notable victory against the Carthaginians in Sicily, capturing many war-elephants, hitherto considered invincible. As a consequence the elephant was the symbol used on coin-issues of later members of the family. In 241 he rescued the *Palladium when the temple of Vesta was on fire, and lost his sight as a result.

2. Quintus Caecilius Metellus Numi'dicus, consul in 109 BC at a critical time in the war against *Jugurtha. His immediate success earned him his *cognomen* Numidicus, 'of Numidia', but he failed to bring the war to a conclusion and was superseded in 107 by his former subordinate C.*Marius. In 100 he was the only senator not to swear to observe an agrarian law of Saturninus, and went into exile. His recall (probably in 98) was a victory for the senate.

metics (*mĕtoikoi*), in the Greek city-states, voluntary resident aliens who had acquired a recognized status in the community; those at Athens, where very large numbers were resident, are best known. Metics enjoyed full civil rights (as opposed to political rights, which they did not possess) except that they could not own land or contract legal marriages with citizens. They paid property tax (*eisphora*) at a slightly higher level than citizens, and a poll-tax in addition, as well as being subject to all the ordinary duties of citizenship, including naval and military service (usually in their own divisions; the right to serve alongside citizens was granted as a privilege) and the performance of *liturgies (except the trierarchy). As a class they concentrated on commercial and industrial activities, and carried on important businesses as bankers, shipowners, importers, and contractors. Some were physicians, philosophers, sophists, and orators (e.g. Aristotle, Protagoras, Lysias); the comic poets Antiphanēs and Philemon were metics.

Mētis ('counsel'), in Greek myth, daughter of *Tethys and *Oceanus, the first wife of Zeus and the wisest of gods. Zeus was warned by Gaia and Uranus that his children by Metis would be dangerously clever. He therefore swallowed her when she became pregnant, and the goddess *Athena was subsequently born from Zeus' head. By swallowing Metis, Zeus also acquired her practical wisdom.

Mēton, Athenian astronomer of the fifth century BC. He suggested a system of regularly intercalating lunar months (seven in a period of nineteen years, the Metonic cycle) to correlate the lunar month and the solar year, with the purpose of providing a fixed system of reckoning for astronomical observations (the civil calendar, it appears, remained unaffected). Since, by Meton's system, the sun and the moon were out of step by one day after seventy-six years, the nineteen-year cycle was superseded a century later by the corrected seventy-six year system of Callipus (fourth century BC), which was used by *Hipparchus (2) and *Ptolemy. Meton appears in Aristophanes' *Birds* as a comic 'town-planner'.

meto'nymy ('name-change'), figure of speech where a thing is called not by its own name but by the name of one of its attributes, e.g. 'the throne' stands for the monarchy, 'the stage' for the theatrical profession. Compare SYNECDOCHE.

me'tope (Gk. *metopē*, the space between two beam-ends), in Greek architecture, originally the panels of brick wall between the holes left for the ends of the ceiling beams; a term subsequently applied to the sunk panel between the triglyphs (the ornamental panels representing the original beam ends). See ARCHITECTURE.

Metre. 1. Greek

1. In English verse the metre (rhythm) of a poem is determined by the particular arrangement of stressed and unstressed syllables in the line. In Greek verse stress accent played no part; the metre of a poem depended on the number of syllables in a line and on their 'quantity', i.e. whether they were long or short. Hence Greek verse (and also Latin; see LATIN 1 below) is often described as 'quantitative', the quantity of a syllable being determined by a number of factors which governed the length of time it took to pronounce (for the rules of quantity see PROSODY). A line of Greek verse is thus composed of words which fit a pattern of long and short syllables, indicated for the purposes of analysis (scansion) by the signs – and ᵕ respectively. At certain places in the line the pattern might allow a syllable to be either long or short; these places are indicated by the sign × (some metricians prefer ≚) and the position is said to be *anceps*, Latin for 'ambivalent'. In general, a line of Greek verse is formed by the repetition several times of a short sequence of syllables, each sequence being known as a metron or a foot. A line of verse containing two metra is known as a dimeter, three metra a trimeter, four a tetrameter, and so on. In some metres (e.g. the dactylic hexameter; see 3 below) there is no difference between the foot and the metron and either term may be used; in others (e.g. the iambic trimeter) there are two feet to each metron, and in this case it is sometimes more satisfactory to analyse into metra because there are features which occur in each metron but only in every other foot.

Resolution and contraction. Two short syllables

are roughly equivalent in duration to one long syllable, and so in many cases two short syllables may be substituted for a long, a feature known as resolution, or two short syllables contracted into a single long; these possibilities may be indicated by the signs ⏑⏑ or ⏡.

The principal feet and metra are the following:

(i)	dactyl ('finger')	– ∪ ∪
(ii)	spondee (from a word meaning 'libation', a metre suitable for solemn ceremonies)	– –
(iii)	anapaest ('reversed', a reversed dactyl)	∪ ∪ –
	the anapaestic metron is	∪ ∪ – ∪ ∪ –
(iv)	iamb(us) (of uncertain derivation)	∪ –
	the iambic metron is	× – ∪ –
(v)	trochee ('running', sometimes, but rarely, called a choree, *chorēus*)	– ∪
	the trochaic metron is	– ∪ – ×
(vi)	tribrach ('three shorts')	∪ ∪ ∪
(vii)	crētic ('Cretan')	– ∪ –
(viii)	paeon (from *Paean)	– ∪ ∪ ∪
		or ∪ ∪ ∪ –
(ix)	bacchīus or bacchīac (from 'Bacchus')	∪ – –
(x)	choriamb (choree + iambus)	– ∪ ∪ –
(xi)	epitrite ('divided in the ratio of 4 : 3')	– ∪ – –
(xii)	dochmius or dochmiac ('aslant', from a word meaning 'a hand's breadth')	∪ ⏑⏑ ⏑⏑ ∪ ⏑⏑

It will be seen that a paeon is a resolved cretic, ⏑⏑∪ – or – ∪⏑⏑, and a tribrach a resolved iambus, ∪⏑⏑ or trochee, ⏑⏑∪. An anapaest may sometimes occur in the form – – or even – ∪∪, but in these cases it is usually clear from the metrical context that it is neither a spondee nor a dactyl.

2. *Caesura and diaeresis.* In some metres it is the practice to have word-end coincide with the end of a particular metron in the line, so that at this point a word never runs over into the next metron. This feature is known as *diaeresis*. For *bucolic diaeresis* see 3 below. In other metres it is the practice for word-end to occur regularly within, rather than at the end of, a particular metron. This is known as *caesura*, 'cut'. Both diaeresis and caesura are indicated by a broken line, thus ⋮.

3. *The hexameter.* The hexameter established itself at a very early date as the metre of epic and didactic poetry, besides being used for some hymns, for bucolic poetry, and for satire. It consists of six metra or feet, each of which is a dactyl or, its metrical equivalent, a spondee. A spondee might replace a dactyl in any foot; when this happened in the fifth foot the line is known as a 'spondaic' hexameter, but it was rare except in the Hellenistic poets and their Roman imitators, the *neoterics. The sixth foot was always a spondee, of which the last position was anceps, the pause at the end of the line making good the deficiency if the syllable was naturally short. Thus the hexameter pattern is

$$– ⏑⏑ \mid – ⏑⏑ \mid – ⏑⏑ \mid – ⏑⏑ \mid – {}^{\backprime}⏡{}^{\prime} \mid – \times$$

As a rule, every line had a caesura, regularly occurring at one of the two alternative places in the third foot, either – ⋮ ⏑⏑, the 'masculine' or penthemimeral ('after the fifth position') caesura, or – ∪ ⋮ ∪, the 'feminine' or 'weak' or 'trochaic' caesura. The latter is commoner. Occasionally the caesura occurred instead after the first syllable of the fourth foot, the hephthemimeral ('after the seventh position') caesura, when a long word extended across the whole third foot and to that point.

The hexameters of Theocritus (and of other Hellenistic poets) often have, in addition to the normal caesura, word-end at the end of the fourth foot, the so-called *bucolic diaeresis*. For dactyls in lyric see 8 (ii) below.

4. *The elegiac couplet* or *elegiacs*. This was a very popular metre, widely diffused by the seventh century BC. It was used for epitaphs, verse inscriptions, and epigrams generally. It consists of two lines, a hexameter (see 3 above) followed by a so-called 'pentameter' which in fact does not contain five metra or feet in sequence, as the name suggests, but apparently two and a half followed by two and a half, thus:

$$– ⏡ – ⏡ – \mid – ∪ ∪ – ∪ ∪ \times$$

Spondees are excluded from the second half of the line. The position of the caesura is invariable. The sequence – ∪ ∪ – ∪ ∪ – is often described as a *hēmiepēs*, 'half a hexameter'.

5. *Iambic metres.* (i) The principal example is the *iambic trimeter* (or *senarius*). This metre was used for occasional poems, sometimes political, often scurrilous, and also for inscriptions. The earliest surviving iambics may be those of the poem *Margitēs* ascribed to Homer; Archilochus in the seventh century BC also employed iambic metres. In particular it was the metre of the spoken parts of drama, of tragedy and (with more metrical freedom) of comedy. As the name indicates, the iambic trimeter consists of three iambic metra (it is sometimes analysed less satisfactorily into six feet). A caesura regularly occurs after the first or third position of the second metron. Thus the pattern of the iambic line is

$$\times ⏑⏑∪⏑⏑ \mid \times ⋮ ⏑⏑∪ ⋮ ⏑⏑ \mid \times ⟨⏑⏑⟩∪ \times$$

in which the broken lines indicate the alternative positions of the caesura. Resolution of the first four long syllables is fairly common. The fifth long syllable is resolved rather rarely, and only when the preceding anceps is short. Occasionally the first anceps is resolved into two short syllables and followed by an (unresolved) long syllable; this feature is often described as an 'anapaest in the first foot'. When the line ended with a word forming a cretic $(- \cup -)$, the preceding anceps had to be short (Porson's Law). Prepositives, i.e. words that can stand only before another word or words, such as the article and prepositions, are considered for metrical purposes to be part of the following word. Thus Porson's Law would not be broken if a noun of cretic form was preceded by its article, e.g. tās sy̆mphŏrās.

(ii) In Attic comedy a much freer form of the iambic trimeter is used. The main features which distinguish the trimeters of comedy from those of tragedy are these:

(*a*) many lines have either no caesura at all in the second metron, or a caesura that occurs in the middle of the metron (i.e. at the end of the third foot);

(*b*) 'anapaestic feet' are admitted freely, especially in the first, second, and fourth feet; i.e. the first anceps and the first and second short syllables become double short syllables;

(*c*) Porson's Law is ignored;

(*d*) in general, resolution is very common.

(iii) The *'limping' iambic trimeter, choliambic*, or *scazon* was invented by, or at any rate frequently used by, Hipponax; it has the form of the tragic iambic trimeter (see (i)) except that the penultimate syllable is always long, and the preceding anceps is often long also.

(iv) In *pure iambics* the anceps is always short. This metre is rather rare.

6. *Trochaic metres*. The principal trochaic metre is the *trochaic tetrameter catalectic*, used like the iambic trimeter for political or scurrilous verse, but also found in tragedy and, most commonly, in Attic comedy. It consists of four trochaic metra of which the last is catalectic, 'stops short', i.e. a syllable in the last metron (usually, as in trochaics, the final syllable) is omitted; catalexis is indicated by a caret mark at the end of the metron. There is normally diaeresis at the end of the second metron. Thus the pattern of the line is

$$\underset{\smile\smile}{} \cup \underset{\smile\smile}{} \times \mid \underset{\smile\smile}{} \cup \underset{\smile\smile}{} \times \mid \underset{\smile\smile}{} \cup \underset{\smile\smile}{} \times \mid - \cup - \wedge$$

(A line that does not lack a final syllable, when a distinction is needed, is known as acatalectic.)

7. *Anapaestic metres*. No doubt because of their marching rhythm these are found in drama, and principally in the *parodos* or entrance song of the chorus, in the form of groups of anapaestic dimeters (i.e. lines containing two anapaestic metra), closing with a catalectic line. There is normally diaeresis after each metron in the dimeters. Thus a sequence of lines may end

$$\cup\cup - \cup\cup - \mid \cup\cup - \cup\cup -$$
$$\cup\cup - \cup\cup - \cup\cup - - \wedge .$$

In tragedy these entrance songs are chanted rather than sung. Sung (i.e. lyric) anapaests, with greater metrical freedom, also occur in tragedy, in monodies and in dialogues where an actor sings his lines. They are distinguished from marching anapaests by not having diaeresis between the metra and by frequent contraction and resolution. Aristophanes uses anapaests in the form of the anapaestic tetrameter catalectic, i.e. four anapaestic metra, with the final metron in the form $\cup\cup - - \wedge$. The anapaestic dimeter catalectic is usually known as the *paroemiac*, a name which suggests that it was the metre in which proverbs were often couched (*paroimia*, 'proverb'). It has the form

$$\underset{\smile\smile}{} - \cup\cup - \cup\cup -$$

8. *Lyric metres*. These are the metres of poetry that was sung rather than chanted or recited.

(i) *Aeolic metres*. These are the metres in which Sappho and Alcaeus wrote most of their poetry, and they are known as aeolic after the poets' homeland, *Aeolis. They are also found elsewhere in lyric poetry, in Anacreon, Pindar, Bacchylides, and many of the lyrics of Greek tragedy. They are analysed not into feet or metra but into *cola* of various kinds; a *colon* is a metrical sequence of not more than about twelve syllables with a recognizable recurring pattern. Sometimes a line of poetry consists of one colon; at other times two or three cola are put together to form a line or a stanza (*strophe). It is characteristic of aeolic metres that the number of syllables in a given colon is always the same; there is no resolution (- into $\cup\cup$) or contraction ($\cup\cup$ into -). Some cola begin with two syllables which may be either long or short ($\times \times$), although it is rare for both to be short. This feature is known as the 'aeolic base'. The commonest aeolic cola are:

$\times \ \times - \cup\cup - \cup -$	glyconic
$\times \ \times - \cup\cup - -$	pherecratean
$\times \ \times - \cup\cup - \cup - -$	hipponactean
$\times - \cup\cup - \cup -$	telesillean
$\times - \cup\cup - -$	reizianum
$- \cup\cup - \cup - -$	aristophanean
$- \cup\cup - -$	adonean
$- \cup - \times - \cup -$	lecythion
$- \cup - \cup -$	ithyphallic
$- \cup\cup - \cup -$	dodrans A
$- \cup - \cup\cup -$	dodrans B
$\cup\cup - - \cup\cup - -$	ionic dimeter
$\cup\cup - \cup - \cup - -$	anacreontic

In the last two pairs of cola, the one colon differs from the other only in the exchange of middle syllables. Such an exchange within a colon or metron is known as *anaclasis*. It will also be seen that several cola differ from each other by having one syllable more or less at the beginning or the end. Other cola can be produced by the internal addition of $-\cup\cup$ or $-\cup\cup-$. The *asclepiad*, for example, is a glyconic extended by $-\cup\cup-$, thus:

× × $-\cup\cup--\cup\cup-\cup-$

or even

× × $-\cup\cup--\cup\cup--\cup\cup-\cup-$

The *sapphic* stanza or strophe (used by both Sappho and Alcaeus) combines aeolic cola in the following way:

$-\cup-$ × $-\cup\cup-\cup--$
$-\cup-$ × $-\cup\cup-\cup--$
$-\cup-$ × $-\cup\cup-\cup-$ ×
$-\cup\cup--$

Lines three and four should properly be run together as one, but since there is usually caesura at the end of what is printed as the third line, it has been common since antiquity to show the sequence as four lines.

The *alcaic* stanza or strophe (perhaps not used by Sappho) combines the following cola:

× $-\cup-$ × $-\cup\cup-\cup-$
× $-\cup-$ × $-\cup\cup-\cup-$
× $-\cup-$ × $-\cup-$ ×
$-\cup\cup-\cup\cup-\cup--$

As in the sapphic stanza, lines three and four should properly be run together as one line. These two stanza forms are also familiar from the *Odes* of Horace (see LATIN 3 (iii) below).

(ii) *Dactylic metres.* Some lyric poetry, especially that of Stesichorus, Ibycus, and Alcman, makes use of dactylic sequences having irregular numbers of metra or feet, sometimes ending with dodrans A, $-\cup\cup-\cup-$. Contraction of the double short of $-\cup\cup$ into $--$ is fairly common. The particular sequence $-\cup\cup-\cup\cup-\cup-$ was used so often by Ibycus that it came to be known as the 'ibycean'. Occasionally these dactylic sequences are preceded by an initial long syllable or a double short, e.g. $\underset{\smile}{-}-\cup\cup-\cup\cup--$. Sometimes the metre is described as dactylo-anapaestic since it can be analysed either as anapaests ($\overline{\cup\cup}-\cup\cup-$) with a catalectic final metron, or as dactyls with an extra syllable at the beginning, or ending with a dodrans ($-\cup\cup-\cup-$) or a spondee ($-\cup\cup--$).

(iii) *Simonides, Bacchylides, and Pindar.* (What follows refers mainly to Pindar and Bacchylides; relatively little of Simonides survives.) The poems of these three were mostly *triadic and the metres of two main kinds, aeolic and dactylo-epitrite. With a few exceptions these two metres were not mixed; a poem was written either in the one or in the other. The aeolic poems employ the cola described in (i) above but in a large variety of abbreviated, headless ('acephalous') and catalectic forms, and in unusual combinations, so that it is difficult to identify the cola. Some of the aeolic poems also contain admixtures of iambic metra.

The dactylo-epitrite poems are composed mainly of the sequences $-\cup\cup-\cup\cup-$ (the *hemiepes*; see 4 above) and $-\cup-$ in various combinations, these two sequences often linked by an anceps syllable, usually long. It has become customary to analyse dactylo-epitrite in the following notation:

D $-\cup\cup-\cup\cup-$ e $-\cup-$
d¹ $-\cup\cup-$ d² $\cup\cup-$
E $-\cup---\cup-$ (that is $e-e$).

Of these, D, e, and E are very common, d¹ and d² relatively rare forms.

(iv) *Dochmiacs.* This metre occurs in sequences in tragedy, at moments of excitement or high emotion. Although the normal dochmiac metron is described as $\cup--\cup-$, it is not in fact the commonest form, which is $\cup\cup\cup-\cup-$. Analysis is made difficult by the large number of possible variants. In theory, any of the three long syllables of the normal dochmiac may be resolved, and the two short syllables replaced by longs, so that the metron may be represented thus:

$\overline{\cup}\;\underset{\cup\cup}{}\;\underset{\cup\cup}{}\;\overline{\cup}\;\underset{\cup\cup}{}$

In practice only about two thirds of all theoretically possible forms are found. Dochmiacs often occur in association with iambic metra, cretics, and bacchiacs.

2. Latin

1. Spoken Latin had a stress accent which classical Greek apparently did not have, yet the metres of classical Latin poetry were quantitative, as in Greek (see GREEK 1 above); on the whole, ·Latin poets avoided conflict between stress accent and quantity. All Latin metres were borrowed from Greek (except perhaps the saturnian metre), with adaptations to make them fit the different sound pattern of Latin or to suit the individual poet's technique.

The *saturnian metre*, the oldest Latin verse form, was so named by later poets to suggest its origin in a remote past (such as the Golden Age, when Saturn was king of the gods). It was the metre used by *Livius Andronicus for his translation or adaptation of the *Odyssey* into Latin, by *Naevius for his original Latin epic poem on the First Punic War, and is also found in the hymn of the *arval priests. Later poets expressed repugnance for it. There is no agreement about its metrical form, except that each line fell into two parts, roughly iambic and trochaic respectively. The most frequently quoted example is a line supposedly uttered by one of the family of the Metelli, responding to attacks on them by Naevius: dăbūnt mălŭm Mĕtēllī | Naēviŏ pŏĕtaē ('the Metelli will get their own back on Naevius the poet'), which seems to have a rhythm resembling 'The queen was in the parlour, eating bread and honey.' To some the rhythm appears to be merely stressed or accentual, as is the case with early prayers, epitaphs, oracles, incantations, and maxims. Others suppose that the rhythm is basically quantitative (though with many changes from its original pattern) like that of all other Greek and Latin classical poetry, and that the metre reached Rome ultimately from a Greek source. Probably both influences were at work. Alliteration too seems to have played a part in saturnian verse.

2. *The metres of Latin drama.* Livius Andronicus and Naevius, as well as writing in saturnian metre, used Greek metres in drama, but *Ennius is the first Roman dramatist of whose tragedies sufficient fragments remain to show that he certainly adopted the Greek quantitative scansion. Plautus and Terence adopted a wide range of quantitative metres, and show a compromise between stress accent and quantity, the latter being frequently modified to fit the former. This was made possible by the *brevis brevians tendency of popular Latin pronunciation, which allowed a naturally long syllable to be scanned short, and by *synizesis, which allowed two syllables to be conflated into one. Also, when two short syllables occurred through resolution of a long, the first of them often carried a stress accent which sustained the rhythm.

The dialogue of the plays was usually written in *iambic senarii* (i.e. lines of six iambic feet, equivalent to iambic trimeters in Greek drama). The Latin senarius, unlike the Greek trimeter, is best analysed into feet. The various possibilities can be indicated thus:

$$\genfrac{}{}{0pt}{}{\cup}{\cup\cup}\; \cup\cup \;\Big|\; \genfrac{}{}{0pt}{}{\cup}{\cup\cup}\; \cup\cup \;\Big|\; \genfrac{}{}{0pt}{}{\cup}{\cup\cup}\; \overset{\cdot}{\underset{\cdot}{}}\; \cup\cup \;\Big|\; \genfrac{}{}{0pt}{}{\cup}{\cup\cup\;\cdot}\; \overset{\cdot}{}\; \cup\cup \;\Big|\; \genfrac{}{}{0pt}{}{\cup}{\cup\cup}\; \cup\cup \;\Big|\; -\,- $$

Caesura (see GREEK 2 above) usually occurs in the third foot but sometimes in the fourth; *hiatus is allowed at the caesura. Porson's Law (see GREEK 5) does not apply. Although resolution is common, a sequence of four short syllables is generally avoided.

Iambic and trochaic *septenarii* (i.e. catalectic tetrameters; see GREEK 6) are also common in the dialogue of comedy, with diaeresis at the end of the fourth foot. The pattern of resolutions is the same as in senarii.

The lyric songs (*cantica*), common in Plautus, rare in Terence, include a variety of lyric metres; they are written in iambic, trochaic, anapaestic, bacchiac, and cretic dimeters and tetrameters, with occasional admixtures of choriambics, glyconics, and ionics.

3. *Later Latin metres.*

(i) The *(dactylic) hexameter*, introduced by Ennius and perfected by Virgil and Ovid, is similar to the Greek hexameter (see GREEK 2 above). A spondaic fifth foot $(-\,-)$ is frequent only in Catullus, who copied the Hellenistic Greek poets in this respect. Except for Ennius, shortening by *brevis brevians and conflating two syllables into one by *synizesis are rare. The frequency of *elision varies from poet to poet; it

is common in Lucretius and Virgil (especially in the *Aeneid*), rarer in Ovid. The caesura occurs most commonly after the first long syllable of the third foot (the masculine or penthemimeral caesura), less often after the first short syllable (the trochaic or feminine caesura), as was commoner in Homer. After Ennius, monosyllables at the end of the line became rare, although in Horace's *Satires* monosyllabic adverbs and particles placed in the final position impart a casual, conversational tone to the verse. The *bucolic diaeresis* (see GREEK 2) sometimes occurs. In general, if there is conflict between stress accent and quantity it happens in the first half of the hexameter, and there is harmony in the second half.

(ii) The *elegiac couplet* or *elegiacs*, also introduced by Ennius, and perfected by Tibullus, Propertius, and Ovid, was based on the Greek (see GREEK 4). A monosyllable immediately before the central caesura of the pentameter was avoided unless it followed another monosyllable or a word consisting of two short syllables. Usually the final syllable of the line was naturally long. Ovid normally ended the line with a disyllabic word; earlier elegists admitted a word of five syllables. Except in Catullus, elision was usually avoided in the second half of the line.

(iii) *Lyric metres.* Latin lyric poetry is less in quantity and not generally as complex as Greek. The chief writers of Latin lyric were Catullus and Horace, but Martial also used lyric metres (hendecasyllables and choliambics; see (*a*) and (*b*) below), as did Seneca in his tragedies.

Horace used especially the sapphic and alcaic stanza forms (see GREEK 8 (i)), and combinations of asclepiads, glyconics, and pherecrateans, in all of which he bound himself by restrictions unknown in Greek. Thus, in sapphics, in the first three lines he made the fourth syllable long (anceps in Greek), and normally had word-end after the fifth syllable. In alcaics he made the fifth syllable long in the first three lines, and in the first two lines normally had word-end after the fifth syllable. In his asclepiads, glyconics, and pherecrateans he always began with a spondee (with one apparent exception at *Odes* I. 15. 36), whereas in Greek the first two syllables were anceps.

(*a*) The *hendecasyllable* metre (having a line 'of eleven syllables') was originally Greek; it has the form:

$$\times\;\times\;-\,\cup\cup\,-\,\cup\,-\,\cup\,-\,-$$

Catullus keeps the aeolic base (see GREEK 8 (i)); in Martial the first two syllables are always long.

(*b*) The *scazon* or *choliambic* metre, also adopted from Greek by Catullus and Martial, was a 'limping' iambic trimeter in which a long syllable appeared in place of the short expected in the penultimate position (see GREEK 5 (iii)).

(*c*) *'Pure' iambics* (i.e. where every anceps syllable is short) are found in Catullus 4.

(d) The *ionic* metre (see GREEK 8 (i)) is used by Horace in *Odes* III. 12. The *galliambic* metre, a variety of ionic scarcely known apart from Catullus 63, reproduced the peculiar rhythm of the chants used in the worship of Cybelē (whence its name; see GALLI). The basis of the metre is four ionic metra, admitting resolution and contraction, the last metron being catalectic. In Catullus the first half of the line appears as an anacreontic, by anaclasis (see GREEK 8 (i) above). There is diaeresis after the second metron:

∪∪ − ∪ − ∪ − − ⫶∪∪ − ⏕ ∪∪ ×

Mētrō'on, at Athens, the sanctuary of the Mother (*mētēr*) of the gods (see CYBELE), in the agora (see ATHENS I). The original small temple may be dated to the beginning of the fifth century BC. After the destructions of the Persian invasion of 480 BC (see PERSIAN WARS) this temple was not rebuilt, and the cult seems to have been transferred to the neighbouring (old) Bouleutērion, council-chamber of the *boulē.* It was no doubt here that the famous cult statue stood, which was ascribed to Pheidias but is now thought to be (as stated by the Elder Pliny) the work of Pheidias' pupil Agoracritus. After the new Bouleuterion was built at the end of the fifth century the old building came to be called the Metroon from the fame of the statue. The building served also as a public record office. In the precinct stood the large earthenware tub in which Diogenēs the *Cynic philosopher is said to have lived.

Me'vius (or Maevius), see BAVIUS.

Mēze'ntius, in Virgil's *Aeneid,* a cruel atheistical tyrant, of Caerē in Etruria (the name is Etruscan), who has been expelled by his people and joins *Turnus in opposing Aeneas and the Trojan settlement in Italy. In contrast his son Lausus is made an attractive figure. Both are killed by Aeneas, Lausus in defence of his father. Mezentius has a horse called Rhaebus. Mezentius and Turnus both figured in the Aeneas legend as known to Cato the Censor.

Mīdas, legendary king of Phrygia who, having hospitably entertained *Silenus, the companion of Dionysus, when he had lost his way, was given a wish, and wished that all he touched might turn to gold. On discovering that this applied to his food also he asked to be relieved of the gift. He was told to wash in the river Pactolus, which ever since has had sands containing gold. Midas is also said to have captured Silenus, who used to visit his garden, and curious to learn his wisdom made him drunk by mixing wine with the water of the spring. What he told Midas seems to have been a matter of conjecture among the ancients, but according to one version he said that it was best

for a man not to be born at all, or once born to die as soon as possible.

On another occasion, having to judge a musical contest between Apollo and *Pan (or *Marsyas), Midas had the indiscretion to decide against Apollo, who thereupon gave him ass's ears to indicate his stupidity. These Midas concealed with his head-dress but was obliged to tell his barber. The latter, unable to keep the secret but afraid to reveal it publicly, whispered the news into a hole in the ground which he then filled up. But reeds grew over the hole and repeated the story whenever the wind blew.

Middle Platonism, the philosophy deriving from the work of Plato in the period between the time of Antiochus of Ascalon, d. *c.*68 BC, to *Plotinus (b. AD 205). Following Antiochus in rejecting the Scepticism of the New *Academy, it turned towards a positive philosophy that included doctrines from several schools and led eventually to *Neoplatonism.

migrations, Greek. Greek legends that have to do with the *Dark Age of Greek history (very roughly from 1150 to 900 BC, 'dark' as a consequence of the fall of the *Mycenaean civilization and the upheavals of the *Dorian Invasion) attest during this period a series of migrations, in which Greeks left the mainland from *c.*1050 to *c.*900 BC to sail east and settle in new cities built along the coast of Asia Minor. These cities are not mentioned by Homer, since they were not yet founded in the time of the heroes. (Thucydides writes as if the migrations coincided with the first period of Greek *colonization, whereas in fact they preceded colonization, which did not start until the eighth century.) These legends (largely the foundation legends of individual cities) are in some respects confirmed by archaeology and by the distribution of Greek *dialects in Asia Minor.

According to tradition, the migrations began when the Ionians (one of the main ethnic divisions of the Greeks; see HELLEN) were driven out of their ancestral home in the northern Peloponnese by the Dorians and settled temporarily in Athens. Under Athenian leaders (often called 'the sons of *Codrus', an Athenian king) they sailed off to find new homes, a process which in fact probably lasted for generations. The immigrants were not solely Ionian (they included several Greek nationalities), but the Ionian dialect, which was spoken in Attica, prevailed amongst them, and they had enough in common with Athens in the matter of religious cults, civic institutions, and, notably, the four ancient 'tribes' of Attica, to justify the claim of Athens to be their mother-city and their own sentimental attachment to her. In time they gave their name to the territory they settled, Ionia, the central part of the coast of Asia Minor.

During the same period the region of Asia Minor north of Ionia was settled by Greeks said to be 'the children of *Orestes'. In historical times they claimed kinship with the Boeotians, and the dialect they spoke, known as Aeolic, was related to the dialects of Thessaly and Boeotia. Their territory came to be known as Aeolis; it included the large island of Lesbos, with its five cities, and some settlements further south.

The Dorians also followed this example of overseas migration c.900 BC. They occupied the island of Cythera and the southern Cyclades, settled in Cos and Rhodes off the Carian coast and then in western Caria itself. They founded two new cities at Cnidus and *Halicarnassus (which later had a mixed population and declared itself to be Ionian). The Dorian cities of Asia Minor joined in a joint festival of Apollo at Triopion (in Caria; it corresponded with the Ionian festival at Panionium, near Mount Mycalē). Thus by c.800 BC the three main branches of the Greek race were established in Asia Minor, Greek possession of the whole coast-line was complete, and the cities and territories mapped out. The Lydian kings, who ruled over most of central Asia Minor at this time (see LYDIA), seem not to have set a limit to the Ionians' frontiers until the early seventh century BC.

Mīlēs glōriō'sus ('the boastful soldier'), Roman comedy by *Plautus; there is reason for thinking it was produced c.204 BC and is therefore an early work. It is uncertain from what Greek comedy it was adapted; *Menander's *Ephesios* ('the Ephesian') has been suggested, this title being in that case a variant for *Alazon* ('boaster') which Plautus gives as the name of his original.

The boastful captain Pyrgopolynicēs (a name recalling Polyneicēs from the Greek myth of the *Seven against Thebes, with the addition of *pyrgos*, 'tower') carries off the girl Philocōmasium from Athens to Ephesus while her lover Pleusiclēs is absent at Naupactus. Pleusicles' slave sets off to inform his master but is captured by pirates and given as a present to Pyrgopolynices at Ephesus. The slave then writes a letter to Pleusicles, who comes to Ephesus and takes up residence with an old family friend next door to the soldier. By the ingenuity of the slave and the kindness of Pleusicles' host, Pleusicles and Philocomasium meet by passing through a hole in the party wall between the two houses. It is given out that the girl's twin sister has arrived, and this explains Philocomasium's appearance now in one house, now in the other. Pyrgopolynices is fooled into believing that Pleusicles' host has a young wife who is dying for love of him; he is therefore induced to dismiss Philocomasium in order to pursue this new love, and is lured into the neighbouring house, where he is well beaten as an adulterer, while Pleusicles and his mistress sail off to Athens.

The *miles gloriosus* was a stock character in Roman comedy (see the prologue to Plautus' *Captivi*); he is the prototype of Ralph Roister Doister and Bobadil and other swaggering soldiers of the English Elizabethan stage.

Mīlē'sian Tales (*Milēsiaka*), by Aristeidēs of Miletus, a Greek writer of the second century BC, probably short stories of love and adventure; only one fragment survives, but the type may be seen in the tale of the Ephesian widow in the *Satyricon* of *Petronius Arbiter. They were translated into Latin by L. Cornelius *Sisenna. Their generally erotic and titillating character may be inferred from the fact that the Parthians were greatly shocked by a copy found among the spoils after the Roman defeat at Carrhae in 53 BC. They were forerunners of such medieval collections of tales as the *Gesta Romanorum*, the *Decameron* of Boccaccio, and the *Heptameron* of Marguerite of Navarre. 'Milesian Tales' became the name given to this kind of literature.

milestones, see MILIARIUM AUREUM and ROADS.

Mīlē'tus, Ionian Greek city with a fine harbour, on the coast of Asia Minor near the mouth of the river Maeander. Excavations have revealed *Minoan and *Mycenaean settlement, a fact which has been taken to support the perhaps over-optimistic identification of Miletus with the 'Milawanda' that appears in Hittite records of the thirteenth century BC as the name of a city belonging to the king of 'Akhkhijava' (perhaps Achaea). During the seventh and sixth centuries BC Miletus founded many colonies on the Black Sea (see COLONIZATION, GREEK) and was an important sea-power. It attained great brilliance at the end of the seventh century under the tyrant Thrasybulus, but after the expulsion of the tyranny it suffered from bitter civil conflict, settled finally by arbitrators from Paros who put government in the hands of the landowners. During the sixth century it produced the philosophers *Thalēs, *Anaximander, and *Anaximenēs, and a little later *Hecataeus the logographer and *Phocylidēs the poet. *Histiaeus was tyrant at the time of the first Persian expedition into Europe. Later his son-in-law Aristagoras ruled in his place, and both seem to have promoted from Miletus the Ionian Revolt of 499 against Persia (see PERSIAN WARS I). Miletus was captured after a siege and burnt by the Persians in 494; its inhabitants were carried off to the Persian capital Susa (see PHRYNICHUS). It was refounded in 479, joined the *Delian League, and revolted against Athens in 412. Famous Milesians of this period were *Aspasia, the *hetaera of Pericles, *Hippodamus the town-planner of the Piraeus, and the poet *Timotheus. In the fourth century Miletus came under the control of *Mausolus, but in 334 it was captured and liberated by Alexander the Great. It was a manufacturing town and the centre of the wool industry, its wool being regarded in antiquity as the finest in the world.

mīliā'rium au'rĕum (the 'golden milestone'), erected by the emperor Augustus at the head of the Forum at Rome, as the point from which roads radiated to various parts of Italy. It seems to have been a column covered with gilt bronze, inscribed with names of places and their distances from Rome.

Mīlō, Titus A'nnius, tribune at Rome in 57 BC and notorious as the rival of *Clodius in the political violence of 57–52. In the hope of achieving consular office and so being able, after governing a province as *proconsul, to pay his huge debts, he attached himself to Pompey and promoted the recall from exile of Cicero, who had been banished by the design of Clodius in 58. For the ensuing five years Milo and Clodius organized street violence against one another with rival gangs of hired gladiators, thereby contributing to the general collapse of law and order at this time. Milo broke with Pompey and aimed to become consul in 52, but at the beginning of the year his killing of Clodius in one of their affrays led to an unprecedented outbreak of rioting and the election of Pompey as sole consul to restore order. Milo was brought to trial by Pompey; Cicero was to defend him, and some of the senate supported him out of jealousy of Pompey. The latter however had filled the area with soldiers to suppress the violence of the Clodian faction, who were obstructing the proceedings; Cicero was intimidated, withdrew perhaps without delivering his speech, and Milo was condemned and exiled. In 48 he joined M. *Caelius in an abortive rebellion against Caesar and was killed in south Italy. See CICERO (1) 3 and 4.

In 54 BC Milo married Fausta, daughter of Sulla and divorced wife of C. *Memmius.

Mī'lō(n), of Croton in south Italy, a famous wrestler who lived towards the end of the sixth century BC and of whose strength many stories were told, even by Pausanias (VI. 14. 5) who lived some seven hundred years later. He was victorious six times at the Olympian and seven times at the Pythian games. He is reputed to have led the army of Croton against Sybaris in 510 BC.

Miltī'adēs, name held by several members of the noble (*Eupatrid) family of the Philaïdae at Athens. A certain Miltiades was *archon in 664/3 BC and again in 659/8, and it was his great-grandson (the elder Miltiades) who took settlers to the Thracian Chersonese, a local tribe having invited them to be their king (see COLONIZATION, GREEK 3). He accepted the invitation allegedly (and improbably) because he would not live at Athens under the tyrant Peisistratus. A story connecting him with Croesus of Lydia suggests that this happened before 546, when Croesus was defeated by Persia. His death, c.525 BC, was honoured by funeral games. The younger Miltiades (c.550–489), nephew of the former, was sent out to the Thracian Chersonese c.524 by Peisistratus' son Hippias to regain possession of his uncle's dominion when it had fallen again into Thracian hands. This Miltiades was a vassal of the Persian king Darius and accompanied him on the Scythian expedition c.514 BC (see PERSIAN WARS); it seems that he later claimed to have proposed the destruction of the bridge of boats over the Danube (see HISTIAEUS). After the suppression in 494 of the Ionian Revolt, which he had supported, he returned to Athens in 493, perhaps fearing the Persians. He survived a prosecution for 'tyranny over Greek subjects' in Thrace and became an influential politician in spite of the opposition of the *Alcmaeonidae. As *strategos ('military commander') under the polemarch Callimachus he persuaded the Athenians to adopt his strategy at Marathon and was therefore the architect of that victory. An unsuccessful attempt to capture Paros in 489, for which the Athenians had entrusted him with seventy ships, led to his being impeached (on the accusation of *Xanthippus) and fined fifty talents. Soon after he died in prison of wounds received in the attack.

Miltiades married Hegesipylē, a Thracian princess, who became the mother of *Cimon and (probably) other children including *Elpinicē. He had at least one son by a previous Athenian marriage.

Milvian bridge, battle of. See CONSTANTINE I.

mime (Gk. *mīmos*, Lat. *mīmus*). Originally a Greek word meaning 'a mimic', the term came to be applied in Greece to a dramatic sketch presenting a scene from daily life ('the quack doctor') or myth ('Dionysus and Ariadne'). In the fifth century BC Sophron of Syracuse wrote mimes in some kind of rhythmic prose and popular (Doric) language; a papyrus fragment and some quotations survive. Sophron was perhaps the first to give mime a literary form, was admired by Plato, and probably influenced *Herodas and *Theocritus.

At Rome the name was applied to a kind of dramatic performance introduced there before the end of the third century BC, perhaps from Magna Graecia. The actors included both men and women, who acted in bare feet and without masks scenes from everyday life or from romance, spoken in prose. Mime gradually ousted the *Atellan farce as a tail piece or finale (*exodium*) after tragedies. It developed into licentious farce, with stock characters of husband, faithless wife, her lover, and the maid. A popular feature of the *ludi Floralēs was the appearance of actresses, *mimae*, naked. The mime took a literary form in the first century BC. The principal writers then were D. *Laberius and *Publilius Syrus, who included elements of social and political criticism. Under the empire, mimes contributed to the decline in stage performances of comedy, being patronized by the emperors and highly popular with the people, who loved their farcical nature, indecency, and topicality. They were finally suppressed in the Roman world in AD 502.

Mime in the ancient world should not be confused with 'mime' in the modern sense, which signifies a play in which the parts are performed by gesture and action alone, without words, and to the accompaniment of music. For this see PANTOMIME.

Mimne'rmus (second half of the seventh century BC), of Colophōn in Ionia, Greek poet. He wrote chiefly love poems in elegiacs which were collected in two books, one of which was called *Nanno* after the flute-girl he is said to have loved. His most memorable poems are concerned with the pleasures of youth and love and the horrors of old age, but he seems also to have written a *Smyrnēis* or historical poem on Smyrna, which may have formed part of the *Nanno*. Other fragments suggest that he wrote on a variety of themes: a description of the Sun sailing in his cup over the Ocean through the night to his rising (see HELIOS), an account of the foundation of Colophon, and another of the war between Smyrna and *Gygēs of Lydia. He is admired for the musical qualities of his verse, and for the hedonism, tinged with melancholy, that he expresses.

mina (*mnā*), Greek weight or sum of money, in both cases equivalent to a hundred drachmas: see MONEY.

Mine'rva, Italian goddess of crafts and trade guilds, probably a native deity rather than an early borrowing from Greece. She was one of the great Capitoline triad, together with *Jupiter and Juno. She was worshipped in a shrine on Mons Caelius and also had a temple on the Aventine, outside the city wall. Here the guild of flute-players held a festival on the Ides (13th) of June, in the evening of which they dressed in masks and long robes and roamed the streets (see LIVIUS ANDRONICUS). Minerva's festival was the *Quinquatrus, on 19 March, the date of the dedication of the temple. She was identified with the Greek goddess Athena and seems to have taken over the martial characteristics of Athena Promachos ('champion'). Certainly her worship spread at the expense of that of Mars, the Quinquatrus having originally been his festival. Virgil presents her both as a goddess of handicrafts and as a goddess of war.

mines. Mining for the extraction of metals was widespread in the ancient world; from the beginning of the Bronze Age, the copper and tin required to make bronze had to be mined as ores. Iron-mining was not an important industry in Greece since deposits there were small (see IRON), but in Italy the Etruscans were mining iron around 900 BC. Lead, silver, gold, and mercury were also mined. The silver mines of Laurium in Attica were famous. Worked from Mycenaean times, they were leased by the Athenian state to contractors and were the source of great wealth to fifth-century Athens (see THEMISTOCLES). Their importance declined from the time of the Spartan occupation of Decelea (413 BC) during the Peloponnesian War, which prevented Athenian access. Activity was resumed later, and they were worked until the first century AD (probably having been in Roman control since the subjugation of Greece in the second century BC), by which time there were around 2,000 shafts, some of them a hundred metres deep or more. The gold and silver mines of Mount Pangaeus in Macedonia were taken over by Philip II of Macedon in the fourth century BC and provided him with funds for his campaigns. They were closed by the Romans after their subjugation of Macedonia in 168 BC, partly in order to avoid a possible source of discontent; apparently reopened in 158 BC, they were later abandoned.

Spain, especially the Sierra Moɪena, had mines for gold, silver, and copper from early times, and was the most important source for these metals in the first centuries BC and AD. Spanish mines also produced tin, lead, and iron, and were a source of great wealth to Rome after the conquest of the Peninsula. Copper, the first of the useful metals, was mined very widely from early times; much of it came from Cyprus, from which island the metal takes its name (Lat. *aes Cyprium*, 'Cyprian metal'). The Romans exploited mines throughout their provinces: the iron-mines of Noricum (or Carinthia, a region south of the Danube, roughly that of Austria and Hungary) were notable; Britain provided not only tin from Cornwall (see CASSITERIDES) but also lead and silver from the Mendips and gold from Wales as well as some copper and iron. In Italy itself the principal mining district was Etruria, which furnished copper, iron, tin, silver, and lead. Elba was an important source of iron, Sardinia of silver and lead.

For the most part, and especially in early classical times, mining was carried out by slave labour; fetters and stone blocks with rings have been found in ancient workings. The frequently harsh conditions caused a high mortality rate: Diodorus Siculus said of the Spanish silver mines that the strongest workers were the least fortunate, being the slowest to die; the mercury mines in Cappadocia were also notably unhealthy. The horror felt by Agatharchidēs (Greek historian and geographer of the second century BC) at the sufferings of the men, women, and children working in the Nubian gold mines under the Ptolemies is vividly conveyed even in the excerpts and paraphrases of his work made by Photius (*Bibliotheca* 250. 25).

In later republican times Rome tried to check the development of mining in Italy by limiting the number of workmen allowed in the mines, probably from fear that the concentration of large numbers of slaves might encourage revolt. There appears to have been no legal monopoly of mining of any kind in the Roman empire, but in fact most mines came sooner or later into the hands of the state, either through having belonged to a head of state before annexation, or by confiscation. The copper-mines of Cyprus, for example, were royal under the Ptolemies and passed directly to the Roman government; some silver-mines in Spain, on the other hand, were still in private ownership under the emperor Tiberius and were confiscated by him. Mines might be leased to large companies or leased shaft by shaft to small contractors (lessees of both kinds are called *conductōrēs*). Government officials (*prōcūrātōrēs*) might supervise the *conductores* or exploit the mines directly.

Mīnō'an, the name given by the British archaeologist Sir Arthur Evans to the Bronze Age civilization of *Crete (*c.*3000–1000 BC), first revealed by excavations at *Cnossus; the name is derived from that of the mythical Cretan king *Minos.

Mīnos, in Greek myth, a king of Crete. The stories told about him faintly reflect the historical importance of the Cretan civilization known as *Minoan, and 'Minos' may have been a dynastic name, or a title like 'pharaoh', so that contradictory stories told about Minos may relate to more than one character. He is represented in the *Odyssey* (book 11) as a just ruler who became a judge of the dead in the Underworld (together with, in later authors, his brother *Rhadamanthys and the hero *Aeacus). Minos, Rhadamanthys, and *Sarpedon were the sons of Zeus and Europa, whom Zeus carried off by assuming the form of a bull. To settle the question of who should be king of Crete, Minos prayed to the sea god Poseidon to send him a victim he might sacrifice, and the god sent a bull from the sea. Thus Minos took the kingdom, but he could not bring himself to kill the magnificent bull. Poseidon thereupon caused Minos' wife *Pasiphaē to fall in love with it, and the result of their union was the Minotaur ('Minos' bull'), which had the body of a man with a bull's head. *Daedalus constructed the *labyrinth, a maze, in which to hide it (and in which he was himself imprisoned).

Minos is said to have been close to his father Zeus, who received him every nine years on Mount Ida and gave him laws to impose on his Cretan subjects. He is said to have possessed a powerful navy, and in the course of his reign he made war on Megara and Athens. For the story of the former conflict see SCYLLA. In Athenian legend he is made the villain of a story in which *Theseus is the hero. Minos laid siege to Athens in the time of king Aegeus because of the city's involvement in the death of his son Androgeos,

and for its deliverance the city had to agree to pay an annual or nine-yearly tribute of seven youths and girls, who were shut up with the Minotaur. One year Theseus, king Aegeus' son, contrived to be included, and succeeded in killing the Minotaur. Herodotus (7. 170) relates that Minos met a violent death during his pursuit of Daedalus, who had escaped to Sicily. By Pasiphae Minos was the father of many children, including *Phaedra, *Ariadnē, and *Deucalion (and through Deucalion the grandfather of Idomeneus, who fought at Troy). See also BRITOMARTIS.

Mī'notaur, see MINOS, DAEDALUS, and RELIGION, GREEK 1 (i).

Minū'cius Felix, Marcus (flourished AD 200–40), early Latin Christian apologist of whose life virtually nothing is known. He wrote *Octavius*, a dialogue between Octavius Januarius and Minucius, two Christian converts, and Caecilius Natalis, an educated pagan. The setting is imitated from Cicero: the three interlocutors are walking by the sea at Ostia. Caecilius is reproved for saluting an image of *Serapis, and a discussion on Christianity results. Caecilius criticizes the Christians for (*a*) their dogmatism, on the grounds that the human intelligence is incapable of grasping the mystery of the universe, (*b*) their rejection of the ancient religion of Rome, and (*c*) their immoral life. Octavius replies, establishing the existence of God and Providence by the testimony of the pagan writers themselves (those expressing Stoic views, notably Cicero and Seneca the Younger), attacking the Roman mythology, and repudiating the charges brought against the manner of life of the Christians, of which he depicts the virtue and heroism. Caecilius declares himself converted, and the friends separate. Christ is referred to only indirectly in the dialogue, and the defence is rather of the moral and philosophic side of the Christian religion than of its specific dogma. It is addressed in fact to the cultivated Roman pagan and is intended to dissipate his prejudices, as much perhaps by its cultivated tone—the elegant Latin and ironic wit—as by argument. Its urbanity is in strong contrast with the imperious vehemence of *Tertullian's *Apologeticum*, on which it very probably depends.

minuscule script, see BOOKS AND WRITING 6.

Mi'nyans (Minyai), an ancient people, a legendary race of heroes, living in Greece, whose chief branches appear from the *Iliad* to have lived at Orchomenus in Boeotia and Iolcus in Thessaly. As most of the Argonauts were descended from the Minyans they are often called by that name.

The fine grey pottery of soapy texture known as 'grey Minyan ware' (see POTTERY 1(ii) and GREECE) was so called by the German archaeologist *Schliemann because he first found it at Orchomenus. It is dated to soon after 2000 BC, and has no connection with the Minyans of legend. See MINYAS.

Mi'nyas, legendary ancestor of the *Minyans and founder of Orchomenus in Boeotia. His reputed 'treasury' seen at Orchomenus by Pausanias was excavated by the German archaeologist *Schliemann and shown to be a Mycenaean tomb. He was the father of *Clymenē and other daughters. Of these it is told that they resisted the cult of Dionysus, were driven mad, and tore in pieces Hippasus, the son of Leucippē, one of their number. They were turned into bats.

Mīsē'nus. According to Virgil, *Aeneid* 6, Cape Misenum in the Bay of Naples was named after the Trojan trumpeter Misenus who had followed Aeneas from Troy but, having aroused the jealousy of the sea-god Triton, was dragged into the sea by him and drowned when the Trojans landed at Cumae.

Misū'menos ('the hated man'), Greek comedy by *Menander; in antiquity it was very popular but only a fragment of it survives from a papyrus, and not sufficient to reconstruct the plot. Thrasonidēs, a professional soldier, holds captive a girl Crateia, with whom he is madly in love, but refuses to force himself upon her because of her hatred for him. Her father Demeas seems to have ransomed her; more than that cannot be ascertained. The chief interest of the play must have lain in the relationship between Thrasonides and Crateia, both of whom are made sympathetic.

Mithras, ancient Indo-Iranian god of light and truth, in the Zoroastrian religion the ally of the good power Ahuramazda. His cult came to Rome in the second half of the first century BC in the form of a mystery religion, confined exclusively to men, which offered a happy life to its devotees, with secret rites and various stages of initiation. It was attractive to merchants and soldiers, and soon spread through the Roman empire, flourishing in the important cities and sea-ports of the western Mediterranean. The cult included a form of baptism and a communal meal. Mithras was depicted with a bull which he was said to have captured and sacrificed; the temples of Mithras were built underground in artificial caves recalling the cave in which Mithras had originally killed the bull. *Taurobolium,* bull-slaying, was part of his ritual, as it was of *Cybelē. Mithras seems to have been identified with the sun.

Mithridā'tēs or **Mithradates VI, Eu'pator** (reigned 120–63 BC), the sixth of the kings of Pontus (on the south shore of the Black Sea) bearing this name, an indefatigable enemy of Rome, and during his lifetime a permanent threat to her control over client kingdoms in Asia Minor. The kings of Pontus were of Persian noble birth, claiming descent from *Darius; the population was Hellenized. Mithridates shared the throne with his brother for about six years under his mother's regency; he then imprisoned his mother, murdered his brother, married his sister Laodicē, and proceeded to extend his power around the Black Sea area. After occupying the north shore he took possession of eastern Pontus, Lesser Armenia, and Colchis. While Rome was occupied with the menace to Italy of the German tribes, the Cimbri and Teutonēs, Mithridates was largely left alone, but his repeated attempts between 112 and 92 to seize Cappadocia were foiled by the Romans. In 91 he dispossessed Nicomedes IV, king of Bithynia, a country which lay between Pontus and the Roman province of Asia, but was again forced to withdraw. When Roman commissioners encouraged Nicomedes to raid Mithridates' territory at a time when Rome was too occupied with the Social War to lend assistance, Mithridates made elaborate preparations and, finding Rome preoccupied, attacked late in 89, beginning the First Mithridatic War (89–85). He quickly overran Bithynia and most of Asia, and his large fleet was active in the Aegean. Many provincials, exploited by Roman governors and tax-gatherers, welcomed him as a deliverer. On a set date in 88 he had Roman and Italian residents in Asia put to death (the number killed was said to have been 80,000). Mithridates received the support of some of the Greek states, including Athens, where the oligarchic government set up by Rome was overthrown. On his way to Athens one of the king's generals exterminated the Italian banking and commercial community at *Delos. These events precipitated a political crisis at Rome (see MARIUS) before Sulla obtained the command in the East and embarked for Greece early in 87. He laid siege to Athens, and finally captured and sacked the city in 86. Mithridates was defeated at Chaeronea and again at Orchomenus. He withdrew from Europe and a negotiated peace was concluded in 85 by which he gave up his conquests and paid an indemnity but kept Pontus intact.

Mithridates consolidated his kingdom and prepared to renew the struggle with Rome. He was attacked in 83 and 82 by Lucius Murena, proconsul of Asia (Second Mithridatic War) but easily repelled the attacks and again Sulla made peace. Mithridates renewed the war in 74 (Third Mithridatic War) by invading Bithynia, which had been bequeathed to Rome by Nicomedes in 75. Mithridates was defeated and driven back from his conquered territory first by Lucullus, then by Pompey, and took refuge eventually in the Crimea. Here he failed to raise a new fleet and army, and a revolt against him was led by his son Pharnacēs. He preferred death to captivity, but found that, having taken so many antidotes, he was immune to poison, and had to get a slave to stab him (63 BC). In indomitable courage and powers of organization he was Rome's most formidable antagonist in the East.

Mityle'nē (or, officially, Mytilēnē), see LESBOS.

Mnēmo'synē, in Greek myth, a *Titan goddess, a personification of Memory, and the mother, by Zeus, of the *Muses.

Mnē'siclēs, Athenian architect of the *Propylaea. See TEMPLES 1.

mo'dius, see WEIGHTS AND MEASURES.

Moerae, see FATES.

Moira, see FATE.

mola salsa, in Roman religious practice, a cake, or perhaps loose meal, of spelt (a particular kind of wheat) gathered, roasted, and ground by the *Vestal Virgins and mixed with salt. It was used for sacrificial purposes (see SACRIFICE).

Molio'nes, in Greek myth, the twin sons of Actor (or Poseidon) and Molionē, named Eurytus and Cteatus; in some accounts (but not in Homer) Siamese twins. They were enemies of the Pylians, and also took part in the Calydonian boar-hunt (see MELEAGER). They fought against Heracles on behalf of their uncle Augeas (see HERACLES, LABOURS OF 6), killing Heracles' brother Iphiclēs; later they were themselves ambushed and killed by Heracles.

Mōmus ('blame'), in Greek myth, a divine personification, and according to Hesiod a son of Night (*Nyx). He had no cult.

Monē'ta, see JUNO.

money and coins

1. *In Greece.* Coinage in the sense of marked metal pieces of standard weight is now generally agreed to have been first used in Asia Minor, in the second half of the seventh century BC. These first coins were made of electrum, a mixture of gold and silver found naturally in the river-beds of Lydia, and were roughly the shape of small flat pebbles. In the sixth century BC Lydia and some Greek states were minting electrum coins. Which state in Greece itself was the first to have coinage is a matter of dispute (see PHEIDON) but it may well have been Aegina c.595 BC. Athens may have followed c.575 and Corinth very soon after that. Many of the Greek states had adopted a·coinage by the end of the sixth century; silver coinage was struck in the last quarter of the sixth century, while electrum continued to be used.

Before coinage proper, the Greeks had a primitive currency based on the iron cooking-spit, *obelos*; from this derived the names and equivalences of the Greek silver coinage. The smallest silver coin, the obol, had the value of one spit; six obols constituted the *drachma*, 'handful', a coin worth as many spits as could be held in the hand, reckoned to be six. (In Sparta, spits continued to be the only permitted currency long after all other states had coinage.) Common coins in circulation represented multiples of these, for example, the two-drachma and four-drachma pieces, the didrachm (pronounced *dīdram*) and tetradrachm. A common coin circulating in the Greek world was the Lydian *stater*, 'weight' or 'standard' (compare Hebrew 'shekel'), which in silver generally had the value of two drachmas (sometimes three). Large sums of money were represented by weights in silver. The Greek standards of weight varied somewhat between states: the principal systems were the Euboic (adopted by Athens and Corinth) and the Aeginetan. The relative values, however, remained constant. Thus a hundred drachmas was the equivalent of a mina (Gk. *mnā*) in silver, and sixty minas of a talent (Gk. *talanton*; about 26 kg. (57 lb.) in the Euboic–Attic system: see WEIGHTS AND MEASURES). The terms stater, mina, and talent could also on occasion signify weights of gold, with a correspondingly higher monetary value (in the heroic world of Homer a talent always means that weight of gold). Although currency in mainland Greece was mostly based on silver, the availability of gold elsewhere resulted in its use for coins in some areas. In Lydia the king *Croesus replaced the electrum stater with both gold and silver staters, of the same weight but of different values. The gold staters which continued to be minted there under the Persian and, later, the Macedonian kings, were often named accordingly (e.g. 'daric' after Darius, 'philippeius' after Philip). Some of the Gallic and British coinage, before the Roman conquest, was based, at a great remove, on the gold stater of Philip II.

The use of different metals for nominally the same coins meant that their relative values, weight for weight, were important. These values varied according to the availability of the metals: gold was worth ten times its weight in silver at Athens during the Peloponnesian War (twelve times at Rome under the emperor Augustus); silver had about 110 times the value of bronze in Greece in the fifth century BC (56 times in Italy from 89 BC to perhaps the third century AD). A bronze coinage was introduced in Greece in the late fifth or early fourth century BC, with twelve *chalkoi* ('coppers') to the obol.

Greek money values may be summarized as follows.

12 chalkoi	= 1 obol
6 obols	= 1 drachma
(1 stater	= 2 or 3 drachmas)
100 drachmas	= 1 mina
60 minas	= 1 talent.

By the sixth century BC Greece had already produced coins of high quality, but in the fifth and fourth centuries coins of remarkable design and execution were produced not only in Greece itself but also in colonies as far apart as Lampsacus (on the Sea of Marmora), Panticapaeum (on the Black Sea), and the cities of Sicily, which produced some of the most beautiful coins ever minted. Athenian coins retained an archaïc design, on the obverse a head of the goddess Athena, on the reverse an owl, a crescent and a sprig of olive, and the first letters of the name of the city. These, especially the tetradrachm, were noted for their reliable character, and were used throughout the Mediterranean. By a famous 'Coinage Decree' (probably to be dated to the period 450–446 BC), the use of Athenian coinage and weights and measures was supposedly enforced throughout Athens' empire (see DELIAN LEAGUE) and the minting of an independent silver coinage by allied cities forbidden. The coinage of Philip II of Macedon and, especially, of his son Alexander the Great had world-wide circulation; Alexander and his successors introduced portraits of themselves, some of them very fine, on their coins.

For the value of Athenian money in real terms see ATHENS 4.

2. *At Rome*. The cities of Magna Graecia in south Italy issued splendid series of silver coins as early as the sixth century BC, and in Etruria, to the north of Rome, coinage began in the fifth century BC. But in the rest of Italy at this time coinage, such as it was, consisted of rough lumps of bronze (*aes rudē*) of irregular weight and without any mark of standard value. The Latin word for money, *pecunia*, is probably derived from the use of livestock, *pecus*, as units of exchange. Later, bronze was in circulation in the form of rectangular bars, but not until the beginning of the third century BC were these issued in a roughly standard weight, equivalent to about 1.5 kg. (3.3 lb.), marked with a design (e.g. an elephant or a pig) on two sides (*aes signatum*). The appearance of these bars probably coincided with the appointment of Rome's first mint-masters, the *tresviri monetalēs*, 'the three moneyers', traditionally ascribed to 289 BC. The earliest Roman coins proper were issued twenty years later. They were heavy bronze pieces of circular form and standard weight (*aes gravē*); each was known as an *aes* or *as* (pl. *asses*) and weighed one Roman pound (twelve Roman ounces or 327 g.); it had a distinctive mark on each side and carried a value-sign. The series stemming from the *as* consisted of the *sēmis* (half-*as*), *triens* (third of an *as*, four ounces), *quadrans* (quarter-*as*, three ounces), *sextans* (sixth of an *as*, two ounces), and the *uncia*, ounce. In the financial stress of the Punic Wars the as was reduced in weight until it was worth only a third of its original value, and after *c*.155 BC only a twelfth, known as the 'uncial as' or 'the uncial standard'.

In the first part of the third century BC Rome

introduced silver coins based on the weight standard of the Greek cities in the south; it was not until the end of that century that Rome introduced a new system based on the silver *denarius*, roughly equivalent in value to the Greek drachma. At the time when the as weighed a sixth of the Roman pound or slightly under 55 g. (2 oz.), the denarius had the value of ten asses, the *quinquarius* five asses, and the *sestertius* two and a half. The denarius weighed 4.5 g. (0.16 oz.) which implies a ratio of about 120 in the value of silver to that of bronze. The Romans commonly expressed sums of money, even very large sums, in sestertii (*sestertius* is a contraction of *semis-tertius*, 'the third time, half', i.e. two and a half times the unit; it was written in abbreviated form HS, that is II + S(emis)). As the value of bronze coinage fell so did that of the denarius; but when the as was reduced to one twelfth of its original weight (the 'uncial as') the denarius was valued at sixteen uncial asses instead of ten, and the value-sign on the coin changed from X to, first, XVI, then to ✕. Roman coins were minted near the temple of *Juno Moneta at Rome, and also at Capua; other mints were used later as Roman influence expanded.

Gold was first issued by the Romans as currency in order to defray the costs of the Second Punic War, in three denominations of sixty, forty, and twenty asses. Sulla, Pompey, and Julius Caesar struck gold pieces, *aurei*, of various weights, and they continued to be struck under the empire. The minting of gold and silver was monopolized by the emperor. Bronze (or copper) was struck by the senate at Rome, and nearly all eastern cities struck their own bronze or copper coins down to the mid-third century AD. In Nero's reign (in AD 64) there was a debasement of the gold and silver currency; both the aureus and the denarius were lightened (the former to one forty-fifth of the pound, the latter to one ninety-sixth). There was further tampering with the currency during the third century, until a state of confusion existed under the emperors Aurelian (AD 270–4) and Diocletian; the monetary reform of the latter in 295–6 was a great landmark and established a new system of coinage, including an aureus struck at sixty to the pound, a silver coin struck at ninety-six to the pound, and a reformed bronze coinage. From Aurelian's time all currency was issued by the emperor. Further reforms by Constantine (emperor AD 306–37) put the currency on a sound footing. In 312 he introduced a new gold piece, the *solidus*, but the eastern mints continued to produce the heavier aureus until 324.

The early silver coins (from the late third century BC) sometimes bear the name or other indication of the magistrate who struck them. Julius Caesar was the first to have his own head represented on Roman coins, and we have a series of portraits of the emperors on their coins. On the reverse side of Roman gold and silver coins appeared symbols of Rome, such as Janus, four-horse or two-horse chariots, and Castor and Pollux.

While the coinage of the Roman republic was uniform throughout the Roman territories, the independent Italian communities in early times had their own coinage. Their coins reached Rome in course of trade, as did at a later date the currencies of the East. Hence arose the need for the services of *argentārii* or money-changers.

monism, monistic theory, see ELEATIC.

monody, monodic poetry, see LYRIC POETRY I.

Mons Grau'pius, see BRITAIN 4 and AGRICOLA.

months, see CALENDARS.

Monume'ntum Ancȳrā'num, inscription in Latin (with Greek translation) found in 1555 at Ancyra (Angora, modern Ankara) in Galatia, engraved on the walls of the temple of Rome and Augustus. It contains the text of one of the four documents written by the emperor Augustus and read in the senate after his death, a 'record of his enterprises', *index rerum a se gestarum*, which, in accordance with his wish, was then engraved on bronze tablets and placed outside his mausoleum. The text is not preserved on manuscript, nor has the original inscription survived, but copies were set up in the provinces, of which this is one. The inscription sets out the offices Augustus held and the honours he received, including the title of Pater Patriae, 'Father of the Country' (see MESSALLA); his victories and conquests (and his clemency to the conquered); his political measures and, incidentally, his attempt to revive the ancient Roman virtues; the closing upon three occasions in his reign of the temple of *Janus, and the celebration of the Secular Games (see LUDI 2 (i)); his benefactions and his grants to veterans; the public buildings he erected or restored; the games and spectacles he provided.

Fragments of two other copies have been found at Apollonia and at Antioch, both in Pisidia.

Mopsus, in Greek myth, a seer, son of Manto, who was herself a prophetess, the daughter of *Teiresias. He encountered *Calchas after the Trojan War, and caused his death by outdoing him in a contest of divination. There was also a seer of this name who accompanied the *Argonauts and is therefore contemporary with the generation before the Trojan War. He died on the journey, bitten by a serpent in Libya. (Mopsus is also the name of a shepherd in Virgil's fifth and eighth Eclogues.)

Mōrā'lia, see PLUTARCH.

Morē'tum ('salad'), see APPENDIX VIRGILIANA.

Mo'rpheus, son of Hypnos (Sleep), the Greek god of *dreams.

Morta, see FATES.

Mortuo'rum dia'logi ('dialogues of the dead'), see LUCIAN.

mosaic. Mosaic work of the late eighth century BC has been found in houses in Phrygia; in Greece, the technique of making mosaic pavements out of coloured pebbles (mostly black and white at first, but later in various colours) seems to have originated in the North *c.*400 BC with white-on-dark, two-dimensional, geometric designs, and passed to southern Greece, Sicily, Asia Minor, and Alexandria. Pavements made of small, squarish pieces (*tesserae*) of naturally coloured stone, marble, or tile, ground to a flat surface, seem to have been first created in Sicily in the middle of the third century BC. Pictorial mosaics including human figures, often three-dimensional in effect, appear to date from about that time. Hieron II of Syracuse in that century is said to have sent to the reigning Ptolemy of Egypt a shipload of mosaics representing the whole narrative of the *Iliad*. From the second century BC this art form spread to Rome and other Italian cities. The Hellenistic mosaicist Sosus of Pergamum is said to have originated the two famous and much-copied designs of an unswept floor strewn with the debris of a meal and of two doves drinking from a bowl. In the West the favoured design was for an entire floor to be covered with figures or abstract shapes in many colours. Mosaics began to be applied to walls and vaults in the first century AD, and since they were not subject to wear and tear were often made of fragile materials such as glass or gold. In the Byzantine period this art form became popular as church decoration.

Moschus (flourished *c.*150 BC), Greek poet of Syracuse whose extant poems include five hexameter pieces, one of which is *bucolic (comparing the pleasures of the countryman with the hard lot of the fisherman), and an *epigram on Eros as a ploughman; there are also an *epyllion *Europa* in 166 hexameters on the rape of Europa by Zeus, and the *Megara*, a hexameter dialogue between Heracles' wife (who gave her name to the poem) and his mother Alcmena, who bewail their misfortunes caused by Heracles' long absence. Also attributed to Moschus, but improbably since *Bion (2) lived at least a generation after him, is the beautiful (bucolic) *Lament for Bion*.

Mostellā'ria ('ghost'), Roman comedy by *Plautus, probably adapted from a Greek comedy by Philemon (see COMEDY, GREEK 6).

The plot depends on the effrontery and resourceful lying of the slave Trānio. Philolachēs, during his father's absence abroad, purchases from a pimp and then frees a girl whom he loves, borrowing money for the purpose from a moneylender, and brings her to live in his father's house. The father returns unexpectedly. Tranio, to prevent him entering the house and discovering what is going on, pretends that the house is haunted by the ghost of a murdered man and has consequently been vacated. But the moneylender appears and demands his money. Tranio tells the father that Philolaches has borrowed it to buy the house of their neighbour Simō, and Simo is induced by further lies to allow it to be inspected. In the end Tranio's lies are exposed, and the father is appeased.

Mother-goddess, see CYBELE.

Mu'lciber, name of the Roman god *Vulcan meaning 'smelter' of metals.

mule-car race, see GAMES, PUBLIC (1) 2.

Mu'mmius Acha'icus, Lucius, consul 146 BC. He succeeded *Metellus as the Roman commander against the *Achaean Confederacy in that year, and was responsible for the sack of *Corinth, and for shipping Corinth's art treasures to Italy. He was censor with *Scipio Aemilianus in 142.

Munda, town in Spain, and scene of a battle won by Julius *Caesar in 45 BC, after a revolt by Pompey's sons and Labienus (Caesar's own former legate in the Gallic War). Caesar is reported to have said it was his hardest victory.

mundus, according to Plutarch, a pit in Rome dug by Romulus (traditionally sited in the *Comitium) in which he put first fruits and earth from each country from which his followers came, afterwards filling it up and putting an altar on it. In other Italian cities it was the name given to a pit dug to give access to the *manēs (of the Underworld). The Roman mundus was closed with stone except for three days of ill omen, 24 August, 5 October, and 8 November, when mundus patet, 'the pit is open'. This pit seems to have been called mundus Cereris or Cerealis, 'pit of Cerēs'.

mūnici'pium ('municipality'), term describing originally the towns of Etruria, Latium, and Campania, and indicating their status; the inhabitants had the duties of Roman citizenship, including serving in the army and paying taxes, but only the private rights of Roman citizens, not the public rights: they had civitas sine suffragio, 'citizenship without the vote'. The municipia retained much local independence and had their own officials, but in their foreign relations they were under the jurisdiction of higher Roman magistrates. This status was willingly embraced by Rome's early allies but later, having been given to conquered peoples, notably the Sabines and the people of Picenum,

it came to be regarded as inferior (compare SOCII). After the Social War (90–88 BC) all Italian communities had the right to vote and their inhabitants became full Roman citizens; henceforth municipium meant an Italian borough (see ROME 6).

Mūny'chia (Mounychia), or Munichia, the acropolis (citadel) of *Piraeus and a small harbour adjoining it.

Mūsae'us (Mousaios).   **1.** Mythical Greek poet, said to have come from Thrace and to have been a pupil of *Orpheus; a collection of oracles was attributed to him. See also ONOMACRITUS.

2. Greek poet of uncertain date but perhaps late fifth century AD; he wrote an epic poem on the love of Hero and *Leander.

Muses (Mousai, Lat. Musae), in Greek myth, daughters of Zeus and *Mnemosynē (Memory), the goddesses of literature, music, and dance, later of all intellectual pursuits. The early Greek poet Hesiod is the first to name them (and perhaps coined their names himself). According to him they were nine in number, and his famous description at the opening of the *Theogony of their gift to him of song and knowledge of the past influenced later poets when they came to give an account of how they were inspired to compose poetry. The original seats of the Muses' worship were Pieria, near Mount Olympus in Thessaly, and Mount Helicon in Boeotia (whence they are often spoken of as Pierian or Heliconian), but smaller cults existed throughout Greece. In late Roman times, each Muse presided over one particular art: Calliopē, epic poetry; Clīo, history; Euterpē, flute-playing (and lyric poetry accompanied by the flute); Melpomenē, tragedy; Terpsichorē, (choral) dancing (and the song that goes with it); Eratō, the lyre (and the lyric poetry, often erotic, accompanied by it); Polyhymnia, hymns to the gods, and later, pantomime; Urania, astronomy; Thalia, comedy and bucolic poetry. Their numbers, names, and attributes vary considerably at different times. A few myths are associated with them: the Thracian poet Thamyris competed against them and lost his sight and power of song; the *Sirens competed against them, but were defeated, lost their wings, and jumped into the sea; in one version of the story describing the contest between Apollo and *Marsyas, the Muses are made the judges. Artists of all kinds felt a personal bond with the Muses, who seemed to them to be the source of their gifts. See MUSEUM below.

musē'um (Gk. mouseion), in Greece, originally a place connected with the *Muses, sometimes in a religious sense but more usually as a place where the arts and learning were cultivated. Thus 'museum' came to mean a place of education, connected with the Muses. Euripides describes the places where birds sing as *mouseia*. The most famous museum was that of *Alexandria in Egypt, founded by Ptolemy I Soter (ruled 323–283 BC) possibly on the advice of the Athenian *Demetrius of Phalerum. It was distinct from the Library, and housed scholars who were supported by the Ptolemies and, after Egypt came under Roman control, by the emperors. There is no evidence that there was provision for formal teaching, but lectures were given and there were many discussions which even the kings might attend; Cleopatra, the last independent ruler of Egypt, is reputed to have done so. After the foundation of Constantinople in AD 324 many of the Museum scholars are said to have retreated there to avoid the theological controversies of Alexandria. The last member of the Museum to be mentioned explicitly is Theon the mathematician, father of Hypatia, *c.* AD 400. Dinners with clever conversation were a characteristic institution of the Museum; a poet of the third century BC described it as the 'hencoop of the Muses'.

music (Gk. *mousikē*, 'art of the Muses').
1. *In Greece*. Music was an integral feature of Greek life, an essential ingredient of all public religious occasions and of banquets and social gatherings; competitions in music were a component of many of the great Games, most notably the Pythian games, which incorporated solo flute competitions from 590 BC and solo lyre from 558 BC. Nearly every form of Greek poetry was traditionally accompanied by some form of music: the Homeric epics were chanted or recited to the lyre, '*lyric' poetry was sung to the lyre, and choral lyric was sung to the accompaniment of music and dancing. In classical times instruction in singing and playing the lyre (and less often the flute) was part of every well-bred boy's education. Thus the citizen body of a Greek city contained a large number of people capable of participating in civic and religious musical performances.

The principal musical instruments were the lyre, *lyra* or *cithara* (the latter a more elaborate version of the former), and the so-called flute, *aulos*. The lyre was used mostly to accompany lyric poetry; Pindar's lyric odes, however, were sometimes accompanied by the flute as well. The flute was the usual instrument for accompanying the *dithyramb and for the choruses of tragedy and comedy. It was also played at banquets, sacrifices, and funerals, and was used to mark time for dancers. The lyre was considered the superior instrument both socially (playing the flute distorted the face) and for education, and it was also important in military music; both were used in religious music.

The lyre and cithara were instruments with vertical strings of equal length (thereby differing from the harp) which were plucked, bowing being unknown in Greece. Pitch was regulated by the tension, and perhaps the thickness, of the strings; each string provided one note only, although finger pressure may have been used occasionally to shorten the string and change the pitch. The strings of gut or sinew stretched upwards from a holder, over a bridge, to a cross-bar at the top of the instrument, which joined the two slender, curved, side pieces of horn or wood. At the cross-bar there were pegs for tuning. The sound-box at the bottom of the lyre was originally provided by the shell of a tortoise, often replaced by a similarly shaped wooden frame, with a piece of ox-hide stretched over its concave side. The *barbitos* (or *barbiton*), the kind of lyre used by Sappho and Alcaeus, had longer strings than the usual Greek lyre and therefore a lower pitch overall. The *phorminx* or *citharis* used by Homer seems to have been a simple instrument with three to five strings only. The introduction of seven strings is ascribed to *Terpander in the seventh century BC (although the much earlier Minoan and Mycenaean citharas had seven strings or more), and this number became almost invariable. The player rested the instrument against his body as he played, plucking (and perhaps dampening) the strings with his left hand directly, and with his right hand plucking the strings with a device made for that purpose, the *plectrum*. The exact function of each hand is not clear.

The translation 'flute' for Greek *aulos* is misleading since the instrument, having a reed and being blown down, was more akin to the clarinet or oboe. Its invention was attributed to the goddess Athena (see also MARSYAS). The pipe, made of reed, wood, bone, or ivory, was cylindrical or slightly conical, and was in early times pierced with three holes, increased by the early fifth century BC to six, one of which may have been a vent-hole. By the late fifth century the pipe was longer and the number of holes was increased to as many as sixteen. Both double and single vibrating reeds may have been used in the mouthpiece at different periods. Auloi were generally played in pairs, the pipes often being held in position by a cheek-band worn by the player. It is not known whether the two pipes were played separately and provided an extended scale or whether they were played together, a rudimentary harmony thus being achieved; possibly both techniques were used. The pipes were not always of the same length. In early times a separate instrument was probably needed for each 'mode' (or scale; see below). Later, for an instrument with sixteen or so holes, a device was invented for closing the holes not needed for a particular mode, so that several different modes could easily be played on one pair of auloi. The *syrinx* (or Pan-pipes; see PAN), consisted of about seven pipes (more and fewer are known) bound together and blown directly without the aid of a mouthpiece. In Greece the pipes were of equal length but were stopped internally; the syrinx with a 'stepped' shape, familiar in art, is the Etruscan and Roman variety.

Ancient Greek music was based on a large number of scales or 'modes' (*harmoniai*). The modes roughly resembled modern octave scales, but they differed from each other in the sequence of musical intervals (as a modern major scale differs from the corresponding harmonic minor by the flattening of its third and sixth notes). In Greek modes the intervals could be both larger than the tones and smaller than the semitones of a modern scale. Classical writers refer to the different modes by ethnic names, Ionian, Aeolian, Lydian, Dorian, and Phrygian, sometimes with the modifying prefixes 'mixo-' ('mixed') or 'hypo-' ('sub-'). Further names were used to indicate the pitch (*tonos*) of a scale, i.e. how high or low it was. In the case of the lyre, each mode probably required its own tuning.

For the Greeks music had an ethical dimension. Plato thought that music not only aroused the emotions temporarily but permanently influenced a man's character. Thus when he describes his ideal state (in the *Republic*) he says that it will contain no modes that are plaintive (his example is Mixolydian) or effeminate (Ionian and Lydian), but will have only the Dorian and the Phrygian, because they represent courage and moderation. Aristotle too accepts that music expresses moral qualities and thus has an effect on the soul: for education (though not for relaxation, for which all kinds of music are suitable) he would admit only the Dorian. Clearly the Greeks associated the different modes with distinct feelings and emotions, although some (e.g. Epicureans and Sceptics) did not believe that they had direct moral influence.

Concerts of solo lyre playing and duets of lyre and flute are attested, but on the whole Greek music was thought of as an accompaniment to song (or song and dance). Pericles built a special theatre at Athens, the *Odeum, for the musical contests of the Panathenaic festival. At the festivals of the *Dionysia and the *Thargelia the ten tribes competed, each with a choir of fifty voices. They sang chiefly *nomes. Greek music was almost entirely melodic, without harmonization. Choruses sang in unison (or in octaves if men and boys were performing together), and to the same melody as the accompanying instrument. (There is some slight evidence that a professional accompanist might occasionally deviate from the melody being sung.) In the case of lyric, the rhythm of the music was identical with the metre in which the poem was written (see METRE, GREEK I). The melody probably extended over a colon at a time, and since the cola sometimes varied in the number of syllables they contained (see METRE, GREEK 8 (i)), and the syllables themselves varied

in the length of time they took to pronounce (i.e. they differed in quantity), there was in Greek rhythms nothing like the regularity of a fixed number of beats in a bar, which the modern western ear has come to expect. In the fourth century BC the words of a lyrical performance tended to become subordinate to the musical effect; the music itself became elaborate, full of contrasts and embellishments, and the melodic range was extended. This was a change vigorously condemned by the more conservative Athenians, including Plato, and mocked by Aristophanes. Similarly in tragedy the songs of the chorus gave place to mere musical interludes.

A few small fragments of Greek music survive, on papyri, on stone, and in manuscripts. It is apparent that the Greeks used two kinds of alphabetic notation, one for the voice and another for musical instruments. Interpretation of the fragments is very uncertain. The most interesting (papyrus) fragment contains the music for Euripides' *Orestēs*, lines 338–44. Since the papyrus dates from *c.*200 BC the music may well be that composed by Euripides himself, since the poet's own score was apparently still in existence 200 years after his death. The most extensive fragments on stone were excavated at Delphi and represent two lyrics, perhaps paeans of the second century BC.

See TIMOTHEUS (1) and CINESIAS.

2. *At Rome*. In contrast with Greece, music did not figure at Rome as an essential part of an aristocratic education, and on the whole music as an art, and musicians, were regarded with mild contempt, the latter organizing themselves into guilds (*collegia*) at an early stage for mutual protection. However, the importance of the flute (*tibia*, like the Greek single *aulos*) in religious ceremonies is shown by the dismay felt at a strike of flute-players in Rome in 311 BC, described by Livy (9. 30), although the tone of the narrative indicates the author's lack of respect for the musicians themselves. Music on the tibia accompanied prayers, sacrifices, triumphal marches to the Capitol, processions to the Circus Maximus, and funeral processions. The number of flute-players at a funeral was limited to ten by the *Twelve Tables. Music for the sung portions of dramas (*cantica*) was also played on the tibia. Etruscan influence probably accounts for the use of horns and trumpets in ritual connected with the dead. The trumpets, *tŭbae*, were 'purified' at the annual festival of the Tubilustria on 23 March (see MARS). Stringed instruments were introduced from Greece, and under Greek influence musical contests were occasionally held at Rome in later republican times and were continued under the emperor Augustus and developed by Nero (emperor AD 54–68) in the *agon Neronianus* (see LUDI 2 (iii)). Domitian (emperor 81–96) built an odeum ('music hall') for the musical contests held at the

agon Capitolinus (see LUDI 2 (iv)). Under the empire there was a development of music as an accompaniment of the *pantomime; concerts by large instrumental ensembles were also performed in the theatres, and music became a regular feature of dinner-parties.

music of the spheres, see HARMONY OF THE SPHERES.

Mūsō'nius Rūfus, Gaius, Roman *Stoic philosopher of the first century AD who probably taught in Greek. Among his pupils were Pliny the Younger, Epictetus, and Dio Chrysostom. He was banished by the emperor Nero for being involved in the conspiracy of *Piso (AD 65), but subsequently recalled. Some of his sayings have been preserved by a pupil, and these show him to have been a humane and attractive figure. They include the remark that marriage is a very good thing, and even a philosopher should accept it gladly. Musonius believed that girls and boys should receive the same kind of education.

Mu'tina (Modena, near Bologna), prosperous town of Cisalpine Gaul famous for its successful resistance to Pompey in 78 BC and to Antony in 43 BC (the *bellum Mutinense*, 'war of Mutina'). On the latter occasion it was held by the republicans under D. Brutus (see ROME 7).

My'calē, mountainous promontory in Asia Minor, opposite the island of Samos, the scene of the last battle of the *Persian Wars (479 BC), where the Greeks destroyed the Persian army and fleet.

Mȳcē'nae (Mȳkēnai, Mykēnē), **Mycenae'an civilization.** Mycenae was a very ancient Greek city situated on a hill in the north-east corner of the plain of Argos in the Peloponnese. According to Greek myth it was founded by *Perseus and was subsequently the kingdom of the Homeric hero *Agamemnon who led the Greek army during the Trojan War. Homer calls it 'rich in gold' but its greatness did not survive the heroic age (see below), and it was eclipsed by the rise of Argos. Eighty Greeks from Mycenae were present at the battle of Thermopylae in 480 BC, but in 468 BC the city was destroyed by Argos and never reinhabited. The very considerable ruins were visited in the second century AD by Pausanias, who commented upon the graves, the massive walls, and the Lion Gate, all still to be seen today. All knowledge of the people who had built this remarkable city had disappeared long before the classical period, and the Mycenaeans were known to later Greeks only in the vaguest outlines through myth and legend. Their late Bronze Age civilization was first revealed to the world by the excavations in 1876 of Heinrich *Schliemann, a retired German merchant and archaeologist, who wished to prove that My-

cenae was indeed the city of Agamemnon. His uncovering of the shaft-graves, later known as Grave Circle A, with their fabulous treasures, in gold predominantly but also in silver, ivory, bronze, and pottery, and above all with the remarkable gold masks covering the faces of some of the dead, seemed to him confirmation that he had discovered the graves of Agamemnon and his followers: 'I have looked upon the face of Agamemnon.' In fact Schliemann had discovered the tombs of kings who reigned some four hundred years or more before the popular date for the fall of Troy (1184 BC), and in so doing revealed a splendid civilization, the background and basis of later stories of the heroic age (see HEROES and HOMER 4). After Schliemann, further discoveries revealed that Mycenae was already inhabited during the third millennium BC by a pre-Hellenic population akin to that of Minoan *Crete at the same time. When *Indo-European invaders entered Greece *c.*2200 BC, bringing with them a new, proto-Greek language and culture, they occupied the site but apparently did not change its earlier name (see GREECE).

The Greek Bronze Age as a whole is referred to for chronological purposes by the name Helladic; what is known as the Mycenaean period, lasting roughly from 1600 to the final collapse of the city and its culture *c.*1125, covers that part which is defined as Late Helladic (LH), following on from Middle Helladic (MH) and subdivided as follows:

LH I	*c.*1600—1500
LH II	*c.*1500—1400
LH III	*c.*1400—1125

Further sub-divisions can be indicated by the addition of letters, e.g. LH IIIB. LH I was essentially a continuation without noticeable break of the previous period, MH III, but by this time Mycenae and other cities in central and southern Greece, including Thebes, Orchomenus, Pylos, and Tiryns, showed a great increase in wealth and importance as well as considerable influence from the Minoan civilization of Crete. A unified Mycenaean culture spread throughout the Aegean area, in the East reaching to the coasts of Asia Minor and Syria, in the West to Sicily and southern Italy. Minoan influences at Mycenae continued to be strong until the middle of LH II, and thereafter declined while native elements re-emerged; nevertheless they are apparent to the end.

Our knowledge of LH I and II comes chiefly from the amazingly rich deposits of grave goods of these periods, starting with the earliest shaft-graves at Mycenae. The discoveries made by Schliemann in Grave Circle A, usually dated to 1500 BC, were supplemented by further finds from Grave Circle B, usually dated to 1600 BC, which was first excavated in 1951. Concurrently with the later shaft-graves, tombs of a radically different kind were constructed, clearly for the rulers of Mycenae. These are known as beehive or *tholos* ('circular chamber') tombs, cut into the hillside and approached by special runways (*dromoi*), each chamber roofed over by a vault or dome constructed with diminishing rings of stones, and the whole structure sealed and covered with earth. Such tombs continued to be built to the end of the Mycenaean period. The best-known, at Mycenae the so-called Treasury of Atreus and Tomb of Clytemnestra, and at Orchomenus the Treasury of Minyas, were all erected after 1300 BC. Very few *tholos* tombs have been found intact, most having been plundered in ancient times; nevertheless, the treasures remaining have been considerable and show advanced techniques of metal-working, precious stone-work, and jewellery, often indistinguishable from Minoan work of the same period. Beautiful pottery was also produced at this time, with geometric and naturalistic plant decoration. During LH II, vases painted in the exuberant and florid 'palace style' are common in Crete as well as on the mainland. Apart from the royal *tholos* tombs, chamber tombs, very similar to them but made without masonry, have been discovered, some undisturbed. These seem to have belonged to individual families of some importance and to have been used for multiple burials over a period of time.

The high period of Mycenaean civilization was from *c.*1400 to 1200 BC (LH IIIA and B). It was during this time that the palaces and citadels were constructed, the best-known being at Mycenae, Tiryns, and Pylos. The sites were enclosed by massive 'Cyclopean' walls (see CYCLOPES), still visible in part at Mycenae, where they reach a width of over 6 m. (20 ft.); their height was perhaps 12 m. (40 ft.). The famous Lion and Postern Gates were erected at Mycenae towards the middle of the thirteenth century BC. The palaces were built around the *megaron* or hall, familiar from Homer (see HOMERIC AGE and ARCHITECTURE 1), with corridors and other apartments arranged around it, and were decorated with frescos in the manner of the Minoan palaces. Towards the end of the thirteenth century storage rooms were constructed at Mycenae within the thickness of the walls. During this period metalwork and jewellery continue to display the outstanding skill of the craftsmen; blue paste and glazed objects (usually described as 'faience') are more in evidence, and ivory carving, known in the earlier periods, becomes much more common and reaches new heights of brilliance. In LH IIIB (1300–1200) vases were produced in abundance and show greater uniformity of style; clay tablets inscribed with the script known as *Linear B begin to appear, and show that the language of the Mycenaeans was an early form of Greek.

The second half of the thirteenth century witnessed successive destructions in the eastern Mediterranean. It has been suggested that the destruction *c.*1250 of Troy VIIa (numbered according to the succession of occupation levels on that site) is the reality behind Homer's *Iliad* and the myth of the Trojan War, and that the siege of Troy by the Greeks under Agamemnon, king of Mycenae, was the last united effort of the Mycenaean Greek world. In about 1200 BC Mycenae, Pylos, and other cities in southern Greece were burned. The period LH IIIC, *c.*1200–1125, also known as sub-Mycenaean, is one of upheaval, destruction, and decline. Some attempt at recovery was cut short by the final destruction of the large citadels of Mycenae and Tiryns *c.*1125, perhaps by a wave of Dorian invaders (see DORIAN INVASION). Some areas, notably Attica, seem not to have suffered at the hands of invaders, and their prosperity received no sudden check; but eventually they too declined into the *Dark Age.

My'rmidons, see AEACUS.

Mȳron, of Eleutherae in Attica, one of the most celebrated early classical sculptors of Greece, active *c.*480–440 BC and thus an older contemporary of Pheidias and Polycleitus. He made statues of athletes victorious in 456 and 448. His two famous bronzes, now known only from marble copies, belong to the late part of his career: Discobolus, ('discus-thrower'), and Athena and *Marsyas, the original of which stood on the Acropolis at Athens; both catch a single moment of the action without trivializing the event. In the latter group Athena looks round at the satyr with a warning gesture as he uncomprehendingly moves to pick up her discarded flute which will bring about his death. Myron's 'Cow in the market-place of Athens' excited great admiration and is celebrated by no fewer than 36 epigrams in the Greek Anthology. It eventually found its way to Rome, where it was still to be seen in the sixth century.

Myrrha (or Smyrna), see ADONIS and ZMYRNA.

My'rsilus. 1. Name by which Candaulēs, king of Lydia, was known among the Greeks; see GYGES.
2. Tyrant of Mytilenē; see ALCAEUS.

My'rtilus, charioteer of Oenomaus; see PELOPS.

Myrtis, Boeotian poetess, said to have been the teacher of *Corinna and Pindar. In a surviving fragment from one of her poems Corinna reproves her for competing with the far more brilliant Pindar. Apart from the summary Plutarch gives of one of her poems, nothing of her work survives.

Mȳs, see TOREUTIC ART.

mysteries, mystery religions. These were secret forms of worship, in contrast with the very public nature of most Greek and Roman religious observances, and available only to individuals who had been specially initiated (Gk. *myein*, to initiate; *mystēs*, an initiate; *mysteria*, the whole proceedings; Lat. *initia*). Their common element seems to be a guarantee that the initiate will enjoy a happy existence in another world after death; but if the chance of initiation is let slip in this life it cannot be retrieved in the afterlife. Initiation involved the revelation of secrets; it was often open to all, women and non-citizens included. Many mystery-cults are known to have existed in Greece, but the details are usually far from clear. In contrast, the best-known mysteries, those of *Demeter and Persephonē at *Eleusis (some 20 km., or 12 miles, from Athens) are more extensively documented throughout their thousand-year history than any other Greek cult, from the earliest testimony in the Homeric Hymn to Demeter to the suppression of the cult by the Roman emperor Theodosius in AD 393. Three years later the sanctuary at Eleusis, which had been a sacred site since Mycenaean times, was destroyed by Alaric and the Visigoths. From historical times until its destruction the administration of the mysteries was in the hands of two Athenian Eupatrid families, the *Eumolpidae and the Ceryces, the former providing the initiating priest. Most, but not all, Athenians seem to have been initiated.

The Eleusinian mysteries were celebrated in the month Boedromion (September–October), at the time of sowing. The priest opened the festival by declaring that those should keep away who 'are not of pure hands and speak an incomprehensible tongue', i.e. murderers and *barbarians. Those participating, having gathered at Athens, bathed in the sea for purification, and then each sacrificed a piglet. After the initiation ceremony for new initiates in the *Eleusinion above the agora, the sacred and secret objects, which had been brought a few days earlier by *epheboi from Eleusis to Athens and placed in the Eleusinion, were taken back to Eleusis in a great procession of initiates along the *Sacred Way. The ritual re-enacted in part the myth of Demeter and Persephone (or it may be the case that myth explained the ritual). Thus on the day following the sacrifices the initiates remained at home fasting, as Demeter fasted when mourning the loss of Persephone. Like Demeter the initiates broke their fast with a special drink, *kykeon*, of barley-water flavoured with pennyroyal. During the procession, at a certain place on the route to Eleusis, obscenities were shouted, in imitation of the abusive joking of a woman, Iambē (a name connected with the iambic metre in which abusive poetry was often written; see METRE, GREEK 5 (i)), who according to the myth had made Demeter smile. The

rhythmic shout of *Iakch' o Iakche* (see IACCHUS) was also regularly raised during the procession; it was regarded by many as referring to the god Dionysus. In the Telesterion, ('hall of initiation') at Eleusis, built to hold several thousand people, the initiating priest showed the sacred objects to the initiated. The details are not known: it appears that after the hall had been in darkness for some time, a bright light suddenly shone, the birth of a divine child (his identity uncertain) was announced, and gloom gave way to general rejoicing. Demeter and Korē ('daughter', i.e. Persephone), Iacchus-Dionysus, Pluto, and Triptolemus, the mythical hero of agriculture, all had their role. The Eleusinian mysteries claimed to take away the terror of death by guaranteeing to initiates a happy afterlife.

Bacchic mysteries, *orgia*, associated with *Bacchus (Dionysus) are also very ancient in Greece, although direct evidence is available only for the later periods. They seem not to have been associated with particular cult-sites but appeared wherever adherents might be found, who were mainly but not entirely, it would seem, women (Herodotus has a story of the Scythian king being initiated, and Euripides in the *Bacchae* has the aged king Cadmus and the seer Teiresias joining in the rites). Liberation and surrender to Bacchic frenzy in order to achieve a sense of freedom and well-being seem to have been the aim of the Bacchic mysteries, but initiates were also given promises about the afterlife. Other mysteries were associated with the name of *Orpheus over which Plato in the *Phaedrus* has Dionysus preside, and which were apparently performed according to the writings of Orpheus. They too aimed to free from guilt and give better hopes for the afterlife to those who practised their rites, and were based on the myth of *Dionysus Zagreus. See also RELIGION, ROMAN 3.

mythology. The term 'mythology' is used to denote either the study of myths or, loosely, myths themselves. Myths are traditional tales, and they have become so because they possess some significance or enduring quality. When stories of this general kind are based on some great historical or purportedly historical event (the Siege of Troy, the Return of the Children of Heracles) they are often loosely described as saga. On the other hand, when they are short narratives which are fictional but attached to a real person or place and given a fairly realistic setting, as for example the stories of the early kings of Rome, they may be termed legends. Myths of these two kinds constituted all the Greeks knew of their early history, and pervaded all aspects of Greek life. A third variety of myth is folk-tales, simple narratives of adventure, often containing elements of ingenious trickery and of magic, perhaps involving superhuman creatures, e.g. monsters and giants; they are characterized by recurring features of character and plot, lost sons seeking their rightful inheritance, princes slaying monsters to win princesses; the stories of *Perseus contain many such. Myth can include any of the features of saga, legend, or folk-tale, but its particular characteristic is that it is a serious story about the gods (and in Greece about *heroes too) and their relations with one another and with men and women.

There is no touchstone to enable one kind of myth to be clearly distinguished from another, nor can the characteristics of myth be isolated: the same elements may occur in all types, and a given narrative may be categorized differently by different critics. There are myths which explain the origin of the earth, natural phenomena, human (and animal) behaviour, religious practices (see MYSTERIES, concerning the myth of Demeter and Persephonē), and human institutions in general. Another feature of mythical narrative is its fluidity, admitting of endless variations on its general storyline (see HELEN). But Greek myths in general, as we meet them in poetry from Homer to Attic tragedy and beyond, are stories of some complexity and subtlety, and they are the form in which the poets choose to express their ideas. A striking thing about Greek myth is the importance attached to it by the Greeks up to the end of the fifth century. But in the course of that century, the medium for serious thought came to be prose. Out of the mythical genealogies of gods and heroes arose the concept of history (see HISTORIOGRAPHY I); similarly, the cosmological myths shaped the speculations that led eventually to the rise of science and philosophy (see PHILOSOPHY I). Both history and philosophy were written in prose. Myth continued to be of significance in poetry and art as long as it was of religious importance for cult and ritual, but as Greece moved into the *Hellenistic age it became more of a decorative element and less intellectually and emotionally charged.

It is noteworthy that many of the principal Greek myths are connected with *Mycenaean centres, e.g. the stories of Perseus and Atreus with Mycenae itself, that of Oedipus with Thebes, that of Heracles with Thebes and Tiryns, a fact which suggests that the stories are of great antiquity. The sources of our knowledge of Greek myths are in the first place Homer and Hesiod, then the classical Greek poets, in particular Pindar and the dramatists. Further material is provided by the Hellenistic poets, notably Callimachus, and by compilers such as Diodorus Siculus and the author of the *Bibliothēkē* attributed to Apollodorus; also by the Roman poets, especially Ovid. Finally the scholiasts, in their commentaries on the classical authors, frequently furnish mythological information. Naturally the stories drawn from these various sources do not always agree, local traditions and the fancies of the narrators being freely incorporated.

Roman and Italian myths which antedate contact with Greek literature can hardly be said to exist. That of Romulus (see ROME 2) is the best-known (see also CACUS). The old Italian gods (see RELIGION, ROMAN I) are vague personalities, and barely anthropomorphic; they are not actuated by human motives, they do not marry or fight or have love affairs with mortals. The myths that the Roman poets and antiquarians attached to them were borrowed from Greece (e.g. by the process of identifying Roman deities with Greek), or invented, largely under Greek influence. Such native Italian traditions as there were have been lost or, where they survive, lack imaginative richness: imagination comes into play only to explain some old custom, ritual, or name.

Mytilē'nē or **Mitylene,** see LESBOS.

N

nae'niae or **neniae,** at Rome, funeral poems or songs sung by female relatives of the deceased or by hired singers. They gave place in later times to funeral orations.

Nae'vius, Gnaeus (*c*.270–190s BC), Roman tragic and comic dramatist and epic poet from Campania. He fought in the First Punic War (264–241 BC), and started producing his own plays in 235. As well as writing tragedies on themes taken from Greek originals he wrote on subjects drawn from Roman history, *fabulae* **praetextae,* and was the first Roman to do so. Of these, very few fragments or titles survive. However, it seems to have been in comedy that he excelled; again, the surviving fragments are very scanty, but some thirty titles are known. These seem to have been based on models from Greek New Comedy, *fabulae *palliatae,* but it is possible that Naevius also wrote comedies with an Italian setting, *fabulae *togatae.* His outspokenness offended the powerful family of the *Metelli: one line in particular became notorious (written in iambics, the metre of spoken drama, and so presumably delivered in a play), *fato Metelli Romae fiunt consules* ('by fate the Metelli become consuls at Rome') implying lack of ability. (For the alleged reply see METRE, LATIN I.) Naevius may have gone into exile as a consequence; he is said to have died at Utica in North Africa. He is supposed to have composed his own epitaph, claiming that the Latin language died with him. It is quoted by Aulus Gellius (I. 24. 2) but may not be authentic. His most important work, written in old age, was the epic *Bellum Punicum* ('Punic War'), written in saturnian metre (see METRE, LATIN I) and later divided into seven books. Only about sixty lines survive; the work seems to have contained mythological digressions, including descriptions of the departure of Aeneas from Troy, the founding of Rome, and perhaps that of Carthage also. In some respects it was an influence on Virgil's *Aeneid.*

nai'ads (naiadēs), *nymphs of springs, rivers, and lakes.

names, personal

I. *Greek.* One personal name only was the rule, given at birth for men and women alike; women did not change their name upon marriage. There was a very wide variety of names, many of which were compounds of two common nouns with a flattering meaning; Megaclēs, for example, means 'of great fame'. Others incorporated the name of a god, e.g. Apollodorus, 'gift of Apollo', or reflected personal characteristics (Plato, 'broad-shouldered'), or circumstances (Didymus, 'a twin'). Choice of name was entirely free, although it was quite customary for the eldest son to be named after his paternal grandfather. In Homer it is common for a hero to be called on occasions not by his own name but by a form of his father's name, his 'patronymic': thus Agamemnon is sometimes called Atreidēs, meaning 'son of Atreus'. By classical times the patronymic had ceased to be used in its original sense; a name in patronymic form, e.g. Miltiadēs, was sometimes chosen as an ordinary personal name; occasionally a patronymic was added to indicate the subject's *genos (clan); for example, someone called additionally 'Philaidēs' would belong to the *genos* of the Philaidae, the descendants of Philaios. If an additional name was necessary to aid identification, the father's name was added in the genitive case: thus 'Cimon, (son) of Miltiades'. In some contexts indication of the person's *deme is added, in adjectival form: thus 'Cimon, (son) of Miltiades, Lakiadēs (from the deme of Lakiadai), or Periclēs, (son) of Xanthippus, Cholargeus (from the deme of Cholargos)'. These additional names were not used as a form of address. It is the practice of the historians Herodotus and Thucydides to identify a person by adding the father's name; in Aristophanes' comedies, on the other hand, characters introduce themselves by name and deme, and this is usually the practice in the fourth-century orators.

2. *Roman.* Among the Italian peoples, including the Etruscans, every man and woman had two basic names, the *praenōmen,* 'forename' or personal name, of which there were relatively few, and (more importantly) the *nōmen,* the 'name' of the *gens or clan. In addition they usually had a *cognōmen* (see below). The *praenomen* was commonly written in abbreviated form as follows:

A.	Aulus
Ap(p).	Appius
C.	Gaius (see ALPHABET 2)
Cn.	Gnaeus (see ALPHABET 2)
D.	Decimus
L.	Lūcius
M.	Marcus
M'.	Mānius

N.	Numerius
P.	Publius
Q.	Quintus
Ser.	Servius
Sex.	Sextus
Sp.	Spurius
T.	Titus
Ti.	Tiberius

For Roman women, at least in the upper classes, the *praenomen* was virtually abandoned, and they were usually known by the feminine form of their *nomen* or clan name, e.g. 'Cornelia', 'Claudia'. A person's *nomen* was of course the same as that of the (legal) father; women did not change their name upon marriage. The *nomen* very often ends in -*ius* (Cornelius, Claudius); the (masculine) endings -*a*, -*as*, -*anus*, and -*enus* are characteristic of names from the north of Italy.

The *cognomen* was an extra personal name added after the *nomen*, and functioned originally rather like a nickname, indicative of the bearer's personal characteristic: Rūfus ('red-head'), Brutus ('idiot'), Nāso ('big-nose'), Pictor ('painter'), Scipio ('stick', originally given to a Cornelius who acted as a 'stick' to his blind father). Often, as in the case of Scipio, the *cognomen* was also handed down from father to son, and thus came to designate a sub-division within the clan, a family. Some clans, even distinguished ones such as that of the Antonii, admitted *cognomina* only rarely (Mark Antony, for example, had no other name; and compare C. *Marius, whose lack of *cognomen* has sometimes been attributed to alleged humble origins). Further *cognomina* (sometimes called *agnomina*; sing. *agnomen*) could be added: thus the Cornelii Scipiones Nasicae were a subdivision of the Cornelii Scipiones.

An adopted son took his adoptive father's names but might add as *cognomen* the adjectival form of his own original *nomen*: thus the elder son of L. Aemilius *Paullus, when adopted by P. Scipio, became P. Scipio Aemilianus; C. Octavius, when adopted by C. Julius Caesar, became C. Julius Caesar Octavianus (Octavian). Slaves were usually called by their own (single) name. Freedmen took their original owner's *praenomen* and *nomen*, adding their own (slave) name as a *cognomen*: thus Cicero's faithful slave *Tiro became M. Tullius Tiro.

In informal surroundings a man might be addressed intimately by his *praenomen*; by friends he might be called by his *nomen* or his *cognomen* alone. In formal circumstances he was addressed by *praenomen* and *nomen* (and perhaps *cognomen* as well).

Under the empire, with the use of a plurality of names and reversal of the usual order, the system broke down, and there was eventually a reversion to the ancient use of a single name.

Nanno, see MIMNERMUS.

Na'rbonese Gaul, see GAUL.

Narci'ssus. 1. In Greek myth, a beautiful youth, son of the Boeotian river god *Cephisus and the nymph Līriopē. The nymph *Echo fell in love with him, but was rejected. Aphroditē punished him for his cruelty by making him fall in love with his own image reflected in water. His fruitless attempts to approach his beautiful reflection led to his despair and he wasted away until he died. The gods changed him into the flower that bears his name.

2. Freedman and private secretary to the emperor Claudius (d. AD 54), who exercised great political influence and gained enormous wealth. He did not favour Claudius' marriage to Agrippina (mother of Nero), and after the emperor's death and the succession of Nero he was arrested and compelled to commit suicide. See also MESSALINA.

Nāso, *cognomen* of the Roman poet *Ovid, by which he always refers to himself. It is derived from *nasus*, 'nose', and probably means 'big nose'.

Naturā'lēs Quaestiōnēs, see SENECA (2) 3.

Naturā'lis Histo'ria, see PLINY THE ELDER.

Nau'cratis, Greek town in the Delta of Egypt, about 50 km. (30 miles) from the sea on the Canopic (western) branch of the Nile. Archaeological remains seem to show that it was founded *c*.620 BC under Psammetichus I, when Greek trade with *Egypt began in earnest, as an *emporion* or trading settlement. By the time of the pharaoh Amasis (570–526), the trade there was important enough to come under royal control, and the Greeks were restricted to Naucratis as their commercial and industrial centre. The town contained separate quarters for Aeginetans, Samians, and Milesians, and a temple, the Hellenium, was set up for all Greeks in common. The chief export (to Greece) was corn. Naucratis was the principal port of Egypt until the foundation of Alexandria in 332 BC by Alexander the Great. It was famous for its prostitutes, who included *Rhodopis, Doricha, with whom Sappho's brother Charaxus fell in love when he travelled there on business, and a certain Archidicē, said by Herodotus to be 'known by song the length and breadth of Greece'. It was the birthplace of Athenaeus and Julius Pollux.

nauma'chiae, mimic 'sea-fights', held as a popular spectacle at Rome in the flooded arena of an amphitheatre, or in specially constructed lakes, also known as *naumachiae*. The first display of this kind was given by Julius Caesar on an artificial lake in the Campus Martius in 46 BC, and simulated a sea-battle between Tyrians and Egyptians. The emperor Augustus constructed a lake in 2 BC on the right bank of the Tiber, and performed a re-enactment of the battle of Salamis, cited by Ovid in the *Ars* *amatoria* as a good occasion for meeting girls. In AD 52 the emperor Claudius gave a famous *naumachia* on the Fucine lake (in Samnium), an engagement between two fleets, each of twelve triremes, representing Sicilians and Rhodians. Prisoners of war and condemned criminals did the fighting, often to the death unless spared by the emperor.

Nau'plius, in Greek myth, an Argonaut, and the father of *Palamedēs. The town of Nauplia was named after his ancestor, another Nauplius, son of the god Poseidon and *Amymonē.

Nausi'căa or **Nausicā'a,** in Homer's *Odyssey* (book 6) the daughter of the Phaeacian king, Alcinŏus. On the night of Odysseus' shipwreck, the goddess Athena, appearing to her in a dream, tells her to go down to the river-mouth next day and do the household washing. This she does, with her maids, and they all play ball. Odysseus, woken by their cries, emerges from some bushes, frightening away the maids. Nausicaa receives him with dignity and offers to show him the way to the city, requesting him to walk the last part alone, so as to avoid giving rise to gossip. The hero is then entertained and sent on his way by Alcinous, who, like Nausicaa herself, had rather hoped that Odysseus might prove a suitable bridegroom. This is one of the most charming and touching episodes in the *Odyssey*. It was dramatized in the lost *Nausicaa* of Sophocles. The English writer Samuel Butler (d. 1902) believed that Nausicaa was a self-portrait by the authoress, as he supposed, of the *Odyssey*.

Naval Boards (*symmoriai*), **On the** (or, *On the Taxation Groups*), political speech by Demosthenes. See LITURGY and DEMOSTHENES (2) 3.

navy, see SHIPS.

Nea'rchus, of Crete, friend of *Alexander the Great (see 7 and 8). Nearchus wrote an account of his voyage along the coast from the mouth of the river Indus to the Persian Gulf, of which only fragments survive. See ONESICRITUS.

nectar, see AMBROSIA.

Necyomanti'a (*Nekyomanteia*), see LUCIAN.

Nēleus, in Greek myth, a son of the god Poseidon and *Tyro, and king of Pylos (see MESSENIA). He married Chloris, the only daughter of *Niobē to survive. *Heracles, after he had killed Iphitus, sought purification from Neleus, who refused it. Thereupon Heracles killed him and all his sons except *Nestor.

Ně'měan games, see GAMES, PUBLIC (I) 5.

Ně'měan Lion, see HERACLES, LABOURS OF I.

Nemesiā'nus (Marcus Aurelius Olympius Nemesianus), North African Latin poet of the third century AD, author of four pastoral poems in hexameters, long ascribed to *Calpurnius Siculus, by whom, as well as by Virgil, he was strongly influenced. He also wrote *Cynegetica,* a hunting manual in verse which breaks off after 325 lines, at the beginning of the hunt.

Ne'mesis, in Greek myth, a daughter of *Nyx (Night) and the personification of righteous anger, especially that of the gods at human presumption. According to some versions she and not Leda was loved by Zeus and laid the egg out of which Helen (of Troy) was hatched. She provides one of the rare instances where an apparent personification of an abstract quality is the object of an ancient cult. She was worshipped at Rhamnus in Attica, where a magnificent temple was built for her in the fifth century BC.

nē'niae, see NAENIAE.

Neobu'lē, see ARCHILOCHUS.

Neopla'tonism, the dominant philosophy of the ancient pagan world from the time of *Plotinus, mid-third century AD, to the closing of the schools of philosophy at Athens (because they were pagan) by the Christian emperor Justinian in AD 529. It exerted a strong influence on medieval and Renaissance thought. Plotinus is the greatest philosopher of Neoplatonism and is usually considered to be its founder, but there is much that foreshadows his thought in the philosophy of Antiochus of Ascalon (d. c.68 BC; see ACADEMY), *Posidonius (d. c.50 BC), *Philo the Jew (d. AD 45), and others nearer to Plotinus' own time. They all aimed at a comprehensive Greek philosophy, one that incorporated into Platonism the best of Aristotle, Pythagoras, and the Stoics, so as to make a synthesis of the collected wisdom of the ancient world. But Neoplatonism was not only a philosophy; it also met a religious need by showing how the individual soul might reach God. Thus it presented with traditional Greek rationalism a scheme of salvation comparable with those schemes offered by Christianity and the *mystery religions. No one before Plotinus could either achieve the desired philosophical synthesis or convey as he did the inner mystical experience of the merging of the self into some larger life. After Plotinus and his pupil *Porphyry the next notable Neoplatonist was the early fourth-century Syrian *Iamblichus. He introduced into Neoplatonism the idea that the unity of the soul with the One could be achieved not by a man's own mystical efforts but by acts of magic correctly performed and by the power of symbols comprehensible only to the gods. The intellectual content of Plotinus' brand of mysticism was thus rejected.

During the fourth century Neoplatonism became the favoured pagan creed; Latin Neoplatonists included *Macrobius. It also began to influence Christian thinkers, notably Augustine.

It was widely taught, but its intellectual centres were Athens and Alexandria. In the latter school the mathematician *Hypatia and her pupil Synesius of Cyrenē (c. AD 370–413) were both Neoplatonists. Synesius was a poet and orator rather than a thinker; he has left a collection of hymns and letters and a discourse entitled *Diōn*, a defence of learning and the cultivated life both against extreme forms of Christian asceticism and against the superstitious theurgy of the pagans. Nevertheless his Neoplatonism took the form also of an interest in the occult. In 410 he became bishop of Ptolemais in Libya somewhat reluctantly, not wishing to relinquish his wife, his country pursuits, and his philosophical beliefs, or to profess doctrines which seemed to him more symbolic than actual. The last important Neoplatonist at Athens was *Proclus (AD 411–85), born at Constantinople. Many of the later Neoplatonists carried metaphysical speculation into the realm of fantasy, mingling magic with eastern superstitions. Demonology in particular was highly developed by them, and a complete hierarchy was devised of good and evil demons who were thought to pervade the universe and were the object of semi-religious, semi-magical rites. The teaching of Neoplatonism, ended at Athens by Justinian in 529, continued at Alexandria until the end of the sixth century.

Proclus' writings survived to influence early medieval thought by virtue of being reworked and Christianized soon after his death by someone unknown, who aimed to achieve a synthesis of Neoplatonism and Christian dogma. They were then promulgated under the name of 'Dionysius the Areopagite', who four centuries earlier had been a convert of the apostle Paul (see Acts 17: 34). Although their authenticity was challenged by some, in general they were accepted as the work of Dionysius and the texts commented upon by a succession of eminent theologians. They were translated into Latin by Erigena in the ninth century and became one of the bases of medieval theology, second only to the writings of St Augustine. Their authenticity was not finally disproved until the nineteenth century.

Neoplatonism itself was revived by the Byzantine scholar Psellus in the eleventh century and taken up by some humanists at the time of the Renaissance.

Neopto'lemus, in Greek myth also named Pyrrhus ('red-haired'), son of *Achilles and Dēidamīa. Odysseus was sent as messenger to summon him to the siege of Troy from Scyros after his father's death because his presence was one of the conditions necessary for taking the city. He went also with Odysseus to bring *Philoctētēs to the siege; he was one of the warriors concealed in the Trojan Horse, and it was he who killed the Trojan king Priam, in some versions incurring the wrath of Apollo thereby (and as a consequence being himself killed later, by attendant priests at Delphi). He also killed the Trojan princess Polyxena at the tomb of his father Achilles. His prizes from the sack of Troy were Andromachē, widow of Hector, and Helenus, the latter's brother. In Homer Neoptolemus returned home safely, and Menelaus sent his own daughter Hermionē to marry him. There was another tradition which said Neoptolemus accompanied by Andromache went to Epirus to rule over the Molossians. The kings of Epirus claimed descent from him and were often named after him (see PYRRHUS). In the *Andromache* of Euripides, Neoptolemus marries Hermione but is murdered by Orestes, who carries off his widow.

neoterics (*neoterikos*, 'modern'), Greek term often used to describe the 'modern school' of poets at Rome, in imitation of Cicero, who, writing in 50 BC, called them sarcastically in Greek *hoi neōteroi* ('the young ones'); elsewhere he referred to them as *novi poetae*, 'new poets'. Of their writings only the poems of *Catullus survive. They avoided epic and drama as old-fashioned, and turned for their models to *Callimachus and the Hellenistic Greek poets (see EUPHORION), aiming at perfection in miniature, and experimenting with new metres (see METRE, GREEK 3), different kinds of language, new words (often Greek), new themes (romantic, exotic, some bizarre), and a mannered style. Apart from Catullus the neoterics included *Calvus, *Cinna, Bibaculus, and Cornificius. Virgil felt their influence but their style lived on chiefly in the works of the elegiac poets Cornelius Gallus, Tibullus, Propertius, and Ovid.

Nēpos, Cornēlius (c. 100–c. 25 BC), Roman biographer; his *praenomen* is unknown. He was a native of Cisalpine Gaul like Catullus who dedicated his book of poems to Nepos (see CATULLUS, poem 1), with a touch of irony at the expense of the latter's 'laborious and learned' universal history in three books, *Chronica* (which has not survived). Nepos was also a friend of Cicero and, especially, *Atticus. His writings included love poems, a book of anecdotes and other information (*Exempla*), and a series of 'Lives of Famous Men', *De viris illustribus*, in at least sixteen books, of which one survives on foreign generals (nineteen of them Greek). The Lives include Themistoclēs, Miltiadēs, Epaminondas, Pausanias, Hannibal, Hamilcar, and Datamēs the Persian. They are biographical sketches designed to eulogize their subjects and point a moral rather than relate the historical events of their lives. From a historical point of view they are marked by many inaccuracies and omissions and by lack of proportion (the battle of Leuctra, for example, is barely mentioned in the biography of Epaminondas). Of the Greek Lives the most interesting character portrayal is that of Alcibiadēs. There also survive a short Life of the elder Cato, and a longer one of Atticus, of whom Nepos can speak with intimate knowledge, and whose stance of political neutrality Nepos understood and shared. Both of these Lives show greater talent.

Neptune (Neptūnus), ancient Italian god of water, of whom in his original form hardly anything is known. He was worshipped at the festival of the Neptunālia on 23 July; of the ritual it is known only that arbours of foliage were erected, and the object may have been to obtain sufficient water at this hot and dry time of year. Under Greek influence he became a sea-god and was identified with *Poseidon. Owing to Poseidon's connection with horses, and because horses were associated with the Roman god *Consus, the latter was identified with Neptune.

Nē'reïds, see NEREUS below.

Nēreus, in Greek myth, a sea-god, represented as very old, son of Pontus, husband of the Oceanid Doris, and father of the Nereids, the sea-maidens. He is praised by Hesiod and Pindar for his benevolent justice, and like other 'old men of the sea' he had great wisdom and the gift of prophecy (see HERACLES, LABOURS OF 11), and could transform himself into various shapes (compare PROTEUS). Two of the Nereids were famous, Thetis (see PELEUS) and *Galatea.

Nēro (AD 37–68), Roman emperor 54–68, son of Cn. Domitius *Ahenobarbus and *Agrippina (3), who was later the fourth wife of the emperor *Claudius; the latter adopted Nero as son and heir. Originally named Lucius Domitius Ahenobarbus, he assumed on his adoption the name of Nero, a *cognomen* in the Claudian *gens* (see NAMES) first held by a son of Appius *Claudius Caecus the Censor, from whom the emperor was descended. It is said to be a Sabine word meaning 'brave and energetic'. For the chief events of his reign see ROME 10; see also Suetonius, *Lives of the Caesars*. Nero possessed considerable talent. He drew, painted, made models, sang, and composed poetry. His patronage of the arts and encouragement of musical and dramatic contests (in which he himself sometimes performed) scandalized the senatorial classes and were responsible for much of his unpopularity. The disastrous fire which destroyed one half of Rome in 64 was probably not started on his orders but he made the Christians scapegoats for the misfortune; he also showed zeal in ordering relief measures for the city. He made the destruction of his own house in the fire the pretext for building himself a remarkable palace, the Domus Aurea (*'Golden House'), the ruins of which have been excavated. His last words, before his suicide, are reputed to have been, *qualis artifex pereo!* ('What

an artist dies in me!'). Suetonius describes him as having pleasant features but a spotty complexion, yellow hair, spindly legs, and a prominent belly, and as being careless of his appearance.

Nerva, Marcus Cocce'ius, Roman emperor AD 96–8. He had come to the fore while aiding Nero in the suppression of the Pisonian conspiracy in 65 (see PISO and ROME 10). Nero also admired his verse composition. He was chosen by the emperor Vespasian as his colleague in the consulship of 71, and was similarly the colleague of the emperor Domitian in 90. After the latter's assassination in 96 the senate chose Nerva as emperor. In his short reign he avoided serious problems, propitiating the army by the adoption of Trajan as heir.

Nessus, see HERACLES.

Nestor, in Greek myth, son of *Neleus and king of Pylos. He lived to a great age, and in Homer's *Iliad* is represented as having outlived two generations, while retaining considerable mental and physical vigour. He fulfils the role of an elder statesman, full of long-winded advice and inclined to be anecdotal. In the *Odyssey* he is shown as having returned safely from Troy to Pylos, where he entertains Odysseus' son Telemachus. For the death of his son see ANTI-LOCHUS. The Mycenaean vase of beaten gold known as the 'cup of Nestor' is so called because it resembles (in simpler form) the great gold cup, brought by Nestor from Pylos, described in *Iliad* 11.

Nica'nder (Nikandros), of Colophōn (an Ionian Greek city in Asia Minor), Hellenistic Greek didactic poet of the second century BC, of whose numerous works there survive only the hexameter poems the *Theriaca* ('on poisonous animals') and the *Alexipharmaca* ('antidotes to poison'). He also wrote the *Georgica*, on farming, which had some influence on Virgil, and a mythological poem which apparently influenced Ovid when the latter composed the *Metamorphosēs*. His poems are not inspired but contain some interesting and out-of-the-way pieces of folklore.

Ni'cias (c.470–413 BC), Athenian politician and general. After the death of Periclēs at the beginning of the *Peloponnesian War, he became one of the political leaders at Athens in opposition to Cleon; his opinions were moderate and he did not favour the aggresive imperialism of the extreme democrats, preferring to aim for peace with Sparta as soon as possible. He was largely responsible for the Peace of 421 that bears his name, by which the war was for a short time suspended. Despite his disapproval of the ambitious Sicilian Expedition, he was appointed one of its generals, with Lamachus and Alcibiadēs, in 415. After the recall of Alcibiades and the death of Lamachus he was left in sole command. He was now seriously ill and, despite the arrival of Demosthenēs in 413 with reinforcements, the Athenians were in grave difficulties. He refused to withdraw by sea until too late (convinced that an eclipse of the moon was an ill omen); in a desperate attempt to escape overland his troops were overwhelmed and he with many others was forced to surrender and later executed. The disaster may have been largely the result of his irresolute leadership.

Nicias was one of the richest men at Athens, his great wealth deriving at least in part from owning a large number of industrial slaves. He was admired by his contemporaries, including the historian Thucydides, for his virtuous and upright life.

Nico'machus, son of *Aristotle; according to an ancient source, Aristotle dedicated to him the *Ethics* that bear his name (see 4 (iv)), but the name may be owing to his having edited the work.

Night, see NYX.

Nigrī'nus, see LUCIAN.

Nīkē, in Greek religion, the (female) personification of victory. She became especially popular after the Persian Wars, the Athenians dedicating a statue to her at Delphi after the victory against the Persians at Salamis (480 BC). She was often depicted with wings. The Hellenistic Nike of Samothrace (the 'Winged Victory' now in the Louvre), by a Rhodian sculptor of the third or early second century BC, is shown alighting on the prow of a ship, and indicates how she caught the imagination of Greek artists.

Nī'obē, in Greek myth, daughter of *Tantalus and wife of Amphion, mother of six (or seven) children. She boasted of her superiority to the goddess *Leto, who had only two children, Apollo and Artemis. Thereupon Apollo and Artemis killed all Niobe's sons and daughters with their arrows. Niobe wept for them until turned into a column of stone on Mount Sipylus in Lydia (visited by the Greek traveller Pausanias in the second century AD, and still to be seen).

Nīsus, in Greek myth, son of Pandion and king of Megara, whose life and his city's safety depended on a lock of red hair on his head. His daughter *Scylla cut it off and Nisus was turned into a osprey. The port of Nisaea was named after him. Megareus, the husband of Nisus' daughter Iphinoē, gave his name to the city.

Nīsus and Eury'alus, in Virgil's *Aeneid*, devoted friends and companions of Aeneas, who figure in the foot-race in book 5. They are killed in a sortie from the Trojan camp in Italy.

nō'bilēs, 'nobles', i.e. the 'well-known'; at Rome, those families, whether *patrician or *plebeian, whose members had held *curule magistracies (later, the consulship only), and were therefore allowed to have images (*imāginēs*) of their ancestors. They enjoyed high status. Although all families at Rome which had a relatively recent ancestor in the senate were 'senatorial' and thus belonged to a fairly closed governing class, within this class the *nobiles* became, towards the end of the republic, increasingly exclusive, believing that only the consulate conferred this entitlement (see the family history of *Octavian). At all times it was possible, though rare, for a man not of a noble nor even of a senatorial family to achieve the consulship, usually with the backing of noble families; if he succeeded he was known as a *novus homo,* 'new man', 'recruit' (see CATO (I), MARIUS, and CICERO (I) 2). These men were then absorbed into the nobility, which was thus revitalized. Under the empire the *nobiles* were those descended (on either side) from republican consuls.

Noctēs A'tticae, see GELLIUS.

nome (*nomos*), in Greek music, originally 'tune', 'melody'; the word was applied especially to a type of melody invented, it was said, by *Terpander as a setting for texts taken from epic poetry, which could be played on the flute or on the lyre. In the late fifth century BC it was applied to a kind of choral lyric poetry approximating to the *dithyramb, composed astrophically (see STROPHE), like *Timotheus' *Persae*.

nōmen, cognō'men, etc., see NAMES.

nōmen Latī'num ('Latin name'), term used in the Roman republic to describe the status and rights, in relation to Rome, of communities in Latium and of Latin colonies; see ROME 4 and LATIN RIGHTS.

Nōme'ntum (Mentana), in Italy, town on the edge of the Sabine hills 23 km. (14 miles) northeast of Rome, with which it was connected by the Via Nōmentāna, the latter crossing the river Anio by a bridge which still stands. There Atticus had a farm, Seneca a country house, and Martial a cottage. Martial told a friend he went there because the noise in Rome made sleep impossible.

Nōna, see FATES.

Nones, see CALENDARS 5.

Nō'nius Marce'llus, a Numidian of the first half of the fourth century AD who, during the reign of the emperor Constantine, wrote in Latin an encyclopaedia in twenty books for his son, *De compendiosa doctrina* ('handbook of instruction'), of which book 16 is lost. The first twelve books deal with the diction and grammar of the older

Latin writers, and the later books with their subject matter. For many fragments of early writers, Varro and Lucilius especially, Nonius is the main source.

Nonnus (fifth century AD), from Panopolis in Egypt, the author of a Greek epic poem *Dionysiaca*, in forty-eight books, on the adventures of the god Dionysus, of which books 13–48 deal with his expedition against the Indians. Nonnus' metrically strict style is of interest to metricians. The poem contains a large fund of mythological learning.

Nostoi ('returns'), lost poem of the *Epic Cycle dealing with the adventures of various heroes on their return from the Trojan War.

Notus (Gk. Notos, Lat. Auster), the south wind; see WINDS.

novel, romantic narrative in rhetorical prose.
1. *Greek.* Five complete novels survive (together with two summaries and a number of papyrus fragments): *Leucippē and Cleitophon* by Achilles Tatius; *Chaereas and Callirrhoē* by Chariton; *Aethiopica* or *Theagenēs and Chariclea* by Heliodorus; *Daphnis and Chloē* by Longus; and *Habrocomēs and Antheia* by Xenophon of Ephesus. The novel as a literary genre seems to have developed in the Hellenistic age, but flourished especially from the second century AD onwards. It was poor in characterization but strong in plot. Its antecedents may be seen in the *Milesian Tales*, a text of which scandalized the Parthians when discovered in the booty after the Roman defeat at Carrhae. An impetus to the novel's development may have been given by the rhetorical schools, where the themes set for declamation were often imaginary situations well suited for elaboration as romances—young lovers, harsh fathers, pirates, seductions, shipwrecks, and so on. But there are many other possible origins. The characteristics of the plot are the separation of two lovers, hair-breadth escapes from a series of appalling perils and adversities, and final reunion and a happy ending. The best known of the novels is *Daphnis and Chloe* (mid-third century AD) by Longus (about whom nothing is known), a charming pastoral romance in which adventures give way to descriptions of sentiment and scenery. The innocent lovers were the inspiration for the French novel of Saint-Pierre, *Paul et Virginie* (1787). The *Aethiopica* of Heliodorus is the story of Chariclea, a priestess of Delphi, with whom Theagenes, a Thessalian, falls in love. He carries her off to Egypt. After a long series of adventures Chariclea is on the point of being sacrificed to the gods in Ethiopia when she is recognized as being the daughter of the king, and the lovers are then happily married.
2. *Latin.* The *Satyricon* of *Petronius is the first Latin work that can properly be called a novel; enough survives to show that it contained a continuous narrative of considerable length. It is itself partly a parody of romantic novels. In about the middle of the second century AD appeared *Apuleius' *Metamorphosēs* (also known as 'The Golden Ass'), a series of tales attached to the hero's adventures in the form of an ass. This novel has a surprising and serious ending in the description of the hero's initiation into the *mysteries. Apart from these two great works very little is known about the Latin novel. The anonymous *History of Apollonius, King of Tyre*, may have been written originally in Greek in the third century AD; in about the sixth century it was translated into Latin and given a Christian slant. It is the ultimate source of Shakespeare's *Pericles*.

novels (*novellae*), see JUSTINIAN.

No'vius, see ATELLAN FARCES.

novus homo ('new man', 'recruit'), term used at Rome to describe the first man in a family to obtain a *curule magistracy, and in particular the consulship. See NOBILES.

Numa'ntia, an important town on the upper Douro in Spain, which resisted Rome with great success throughout much of the second century BC, finally falling after siege to Scipio Aemilianus in 133 BC. This event effectively ended Spanish resistance to Rome (see ROME 5).

Numa Pompi'lius, in legendary Roman history, successor of Romulus as second king of Rome (see ROME 2). He had, according to tradition, a long and peaceful reign (715–673 BC), regarded in later times as a sort of Golden Age, and to him the Romans attributed many of their religious institutions: festivals, sacrifices and other rites, the *pontifices*, the Vestal Virgins, and the Salii. He is said to have constructed the Regia ('palace') near the Forum, the Temple of Vesta, and other temples; also to have reformed the *calendar, adding January and February to a primitive ten-month year. (See also ANCILIA.) Later legends say that he received counsel from the nymph *Egeria, and make him a disciple of the Greek philosopher and mystic *Pythagoras (in defiance of chronology) to account for similarities between early Roman religion and Greek cults in south Italy (where Pythagoras lived). Most of the reforms attributed to him were probably the result of a long process of cultural development and religious change.

numbers
1. *Greek.* The Greek names for the numbers 1 to 10 are: *heīs, duo, treīs, tessarĕs* (or *tettares*), *pentĕ, hex, hepta, octo, ennĕa, deka*. The system commonly found in papyri and manuscripts for

writing numbers is based on the *alphabet and is as follows:

1–5		α–ε
6		ς (the minuscule, i.e. small-letter, version of the digamma)
7–9		ζ–θ
10–80	(by tens)	ι–π
90		ϙ (koppa, not in the Attic Greek alphabet)
100–800	(by hundreds)	ρ–ω
900		ϡ (sampi, in the Carian alphabet, equivalent to σσ or ττ)

It is customary to add a stroke above the line when writing numbers up to 999, e.g. α′, β′, etc. Higher numbers are written as follows:

| 1,000–9,000 | (by thousands) | ͵α–͵θ |
| 10,000 | | Μ |

Multiples of 10,000 are indicated by writing the multiplier on top. Thus (e.g.):

$$21{,}527 \qquad \overset{\beta}{M}{,}\alpha\phi\kappa\zeta$$

(For Archimedes' system of expressing very large numbers see ARCHIMEDES.)

A different system, of acronyms, was used on inscriptions, usually to express sums of money, thus: Γ = 5 (pentĕ); Δ = 10 (deka); Η = 100 (hekaton); Χ = 1,000 (chilioi); Μ = 10,000 (myrioi). Units were represented by single strokes. Characters were repeated if necessary; e.g. ΔΔΔ = 30.

2. *Roman*. The Latin names for the numbers 1 to 10 are: *unus, duo, tres, quattuor, quinque, sex, septem, octo, novem, decem*. Roman numerical signs, originally special characters, gradually developed into letters of the alphabet as follows: I = 1; V = 5; X = 10; L = 50; C = 100; D = 500; M = 1,000. Horizontal lines were often used to denote thousands; thus V̄ = 5,000. A notation was constructed by conventions for adding or subtracting according to the following rule: when two figures stand side by side, if the right-hand figure is the larger, the left-hand figure is to be subtracted from it; if the left-hand figure is the larger, the right-hand figure is to be added: e.g. IX = 9; XI = 11; MCM = 1,900. When, as in this last example, a smaller numeral occurs between two larger, it is subtracted from the numeral on the right.

In about AD 800 Arab scholars at Baghdad adopted Hindu numbers, which we know as 'arabic numerals', together with a sign for zero. This had been lacking in Greek and Roman numerical systems, although our sign 0 seems to have originated in Greek astronomical works and is found in Ptolemy's *Almagest*. The use of arabic numerals greatly simplified arithmetical calculations, and by the fifteenth century had been widely adopted in Europe.

numen, in ancient Roman religion, divine power, a god; the word is derived from *nuĕrĕ* 'to nod' (a god is thought to nod to indicate his will). See RELIGION, ROMAN 1.

numerals, see NUMBERS.

Nu'mitor, see ROME 2.

nu'ndinae, in the Roman calendar, 'every ninth day', a market-day occurring at regular intervals of eight days according to the Roman inclusive method of reckoning. The days of this eight-day 'week' were marked in the calendar by the letters A to H, and *nundinae* had the letter A assigned to it. It was a day of rest from agricultural labour, and a day on which country people would come into Rome.

Ny'cteus, see ANTIOPE.

nymphs (*nymphē*, 'maiden'), in Greek myth, female personifications of various natural objects, rivers, trees, mountains; they were vague beings, young and beautiful, fond of music and dancing, long-lived but not immortal, usually gentle, occasionally formidable. They possessed some divine gifts, such as that of prophecy. The nymphs of trees, especially oak trees, were called dryads (*drys*, originally 'tree', but commonly 'oak tree'). Hamadryads were tree-nymphs whose life depended on that of their tree. Nymphs of springs, rivers, and lakes were naiads; those of mountains oreads. Before the battle of Plataea against the Persians (479 BC), the nymphs of Mount Cithaeron were among the deities to whom the Athenian commander Aristeidēs was told to pray by the Delphic Oracle.

Nyx, Night, in Greek myth, one of the earliest deities to come into existence, the child of *Chaos. Her children included Death (Thanatos), Sleep (*Hypnos), and the three *Fates.

O

o'belos, o'bolos (Lat. *obelus*). **1.** At Athens, an obol, an iron spit, used also as currency in early times; from the sixth century BC a small silver coin of equivalent value, one-sixth of a drachma. An obol was also used as a small measure of weight; see MONEY AND COINS 1 and WEIGHTS AND MEASURES 1 (i).

2. Critical sign used in the annotation of texts by Alexandrian scholars of the Hellenistic age, a horizontal stroke in the left-hand margin, originally indicating a spurious line in Homer; see ZENODOTUS. The modern equivalent is the obelus, 'dagger'.

Ōce'anus (Ocean), in Greek myth, a *Titan, son of Uranus (Heaven) and Gaia (Earth), husband (and brother) of Tethys; his daughters are the Oceanids and his sons the river-gods. Like Uranus and Gaia he also has a cosmological significance in early Greek thought as the wide river encircling the whole plain of Earth (see MAPS). All the rivers of the earth are thought of as having their origin in Ocean through subterranean connections and his waters are therefore fresh. Everything in the world that is strange and fabulous is situated by the 'stream of Ocean', the Aethiopians, Cimmerians, and Pygmies, Geryon and the Gorgons, and the Gardens of the Hesperides. The sun and stars rise and set in the Ocean; a fragment of a poem by *Mimnermus describes the sun sailing over the stream of Ocean from west to east during the night.

Ocnus ('sloth'; but see below), in Greek myth, a symbolic figure in the Underworld, famously depicted by *Polygnotus in his painting in the *Leschē* or public room at Delphi (seen by Pausanias). The story was that Ocnus was an industrious man with an extravagant wife who spent everything he earned, so that he came to symbolize useless effort; in the Underworld he endlessly plaits a rope which a she-ass standing behind him continually eats. His name indicates lack of achievement rather than laziness.

Octa'via. 1. Sister of *Octavian, later the emperor Augustus; she was married first to C. Claudius Marcellus by whom she had three children including a son, M. Claudius Marcellus, who married Augustus' daughter Julia (see MARCELLUS (2)). In 40 BC her husband died and she was married at once to Mark Antony to seal the Treaty of Brundisium (see ROME 7). She was divorced by him in 32 BC but brought up not only their two daughters but also all his surviving children by Fulvia and Cleopatra, as well as her three children by Marcellus. Her Roman virtues of nobility and loyalty as well as her kindness won her general admiration. She died in 11 BC. One of her daughters by Antony was the mother of the emperor Claudius; the other married Lucius Domitius Ahenobarbus (consul 16 BC) and their son Gnaeus was the father of the emperor Nero.

2. b. AD 40, daughter of the emperor Claudius by his third wife *Messalina, and sister of Britannicus; she married the future emperor *Nero in 53. Nero divorced her in 62, banished her, and had her murdered in 63.

Octa'via, Roman tragedy, the only surviving *fabula *praetexta*, a dramatization of the fate of the emperor Nero's first wife (see (2) above). It has been handed down in the manuscripts of the plays of Seneca the Younger, who is included as a character to protest against Nero's cruelty, but it cannot be by him: the 'prophecy' uttered by the ghost of Nero's mother about her son's fate is so true to fact that it shows the play was written after Nero's suicide (and Seneca's death) in 68. The true author is unknown. The play contains too much lamentation and mythological display to be dramatically successful.

Octa'vian (Gaius Octavius, 63 BC–AD 14), later known as *Augustus, the first of the Roman emperors; see also ROME 7, 9. He was the great-nephew and adopted son of Julius *Caesar (on adoption he took the name Gaius Julius Caesar Octavianus); his mother Atia, who married the wealthy equestrian C. Octavius, was the daughter of Caesar's sister Julia and her husband M. Atius Balbus. The Octavii, a plebeian *gens*, had acquired nobility in 205 BC when an ancestor was elected to the praetorship (see NOBILES). This man's son, when propraetor in 167, earned a *triumph for his capture of *Perseus as well as great wealth from captured booty, and was consul in 165. After that, other Octavii held the consulship upon several occasions. The members of Octavian's own branch were very wealthy, but lived quietly; his great-grandfather was one of the few to survive the defeat at Cannae (216) in the Second Punic War. His father, who had a reputation for quiet integrity and won the approval of Cicero, was praetor in 61 (as a *novus homo*), but died in 58 before he could attain the consulship. For the life and work of Octavian as the emperor Augustus see ROME 9 and AUGUSTUS.

Octa'vius, dialogue by *Minucius Felix.

Odaena'thus, see ZENOBIA.

ode (Gk. ōdē, 'song'), in Greek or Latin, a *lyric poem in stanza form (see STROPHE and TRIAD).

Odes and **Epodes,** of Horace, short Latin poems in various lyric metres. For the dates when they were written and published see HORACE. The *Epodes*, which Horace referred to as *iambi*, 'iambics', were professed imitations of *Archilochus. They consist of seventeen poems, eleven in iambic metre (where Horace does not observe Porson's Law; see METRE, GREEK 5 (i)), and six in a combination of iambics and dactyls. Their name denotes the form of the metres: an epode is, metrically speaking, the second, shorter, line of a couplet, and thence is applied to short poems written in this way. Horace tells us himself (*Epistles* I. 19. 23) that he followed the metres and spirit of Archilochus but not the latter's subject matter or words. Some of the Epodes are on political themes (notably 16, a lament over the fate of Rome, now apparently about to be destroyed by civil strife), some are lampoons on personal enemies, some on love and miscellaneous subjects. Epodes 1 and 9 are notable poems expressing the poet's feelings at the time of the battle of *Actium (31 BC), when Octavian defeated Antony and Cleopatra. Epode 13 is a fine poem on a theme—drink as a remedy against bad weather, with symbolic undertones—that was to become familiar with the *Odes*.

Horace declares that his models for the four books of *Odes* were the early Greek lyric poets Sappho and Alcaeus. Books 1–3 comprise eighty-eight poems; book 4, published later, comprises another fifteen. Thirty-seven poems are in the alcaic metre (see METRE, GREEK 8 (i)), twenty-five in the sapphic, and the rest in a variety of asclepiads and other forms. The first six odes of book 3 are sometimes referred to as the Roman Odes, written in stately alcaics in elevated style on patriotic themes. These grander odes owed something to the inspiration, if not the form, of the Greek poet Pindar, who also had had to evolve a style in which he could address powerful rulers intimately. There are many odes which touch on political themes, as did the lyrics of Alcaeus. They reflect the transition of Roman feeling from anxiety for the safety of the state to security and triumph under the guidance of Augustus, whom Horace sincerely admired.

Overall the *Odes* cover a variety of subjects, private as well as public, incidents in the poet's own life or the lives of his friends, their departures on voyages or happy returns, their love affairs and his own, the changing seasons, the joys of the countryside and of wine; the poet sometimes treats these last subjects as symbolic of the brevity of human life with its ephemeral pleasures. Mostly the poems address individuals, as did early Greek lyric poetry, or start out with a personal reference. Many of them show Horace's keen sense of situation and his sharp observation of the human comedy; they are full of wit and charm and cleverness, often with a surprise at the end. The *Odes* are the product not of immediate, intense emotion, but of meditation, not lyric in a modern sense nor yet in the original Greek sense (see LYRIC POETRY). They are characterized by faultless economy of phrasing, perfect control, balance and harmony of thought and expression; their euphony and intricate word order have proved inimitable. The moderation and urbane good sense they express, in an often ironic and self-deprecating tone, have endeared them to readers of all periods.

ōde'um (Gk. ōdeion, Eng. odeon), in Greece, a theatre built for musical performances and, unlike other Greek theatres, provided with a roof. An odeum was built by Pericles east of and near to the theatre of Dionysus at Athens c.444 BC for concerts and the musical contests of the *Panathenaea. The *proagon also took place here. The interior is described in ancient authors as having many seats and columns; the exterior was thought to have been an imitation of the tent of the Persian king Xerxes and probably had a pyramidal roof. The Athenians themselves set fire to this odeum before the invasion of Sulla in 86 BC so that the enemy would not find in it a ready supply of wood for the siege of the Acropolis. Another odeum was built in the agora c.15 BC by M. Vipsanius *Agrippa, but by AD 150 it had ceased to serve its original purpose and a third was built between 160 and 174 by *Herodes Atticus. This was a magnificent building seating 5,000 spectators, its interior walls lined with marble slabs and its roof made of cedar. This, like the earlier odeum and many other buildings, was burnt down in the sack of the city by the Herulian (Germanic) invaders of AD 267. Much of it has now been reconstructed and is used again for concerts and plays.

Odo(v)acer, first barbarian king of Italy, AD 476–93; see FALL OF ROME.

Ody'sseus (or Ulyssēs; Lat. Ulixēs), in Greek myth, the son of Lāertēs, king of Ithaca, and Anticleia, daughter of Autolycus. Odysseus was one of the suitors of *Helen but had no hope of being chosen because he was poor. It was he who advised Helen's father Tyndareus to make the suitors swear to support the chosen bridegroom. He then married Penelope, daughter of Icarius, king of Sparta. When Helen was carried off to Troy, Odysseus, bound by oath like the other suitors, joined in the Greek expedition to recover her, having failed to escape his obligation by pretending to be mad (see PALAMEDES). Odysseus figures prominently in Homer's *Iliad*, notably in the embassy to Achilles (book 9) and the night expedition with Diomēdēs (book 10). After the death of Achilles, a quarrel arose between Ajax, son of Telamon, and Odysseus in the contest for Achilles' armour. Since Odysseus was much the better speaker he easily persuaded the army that he had best served the Greek cause, and won their vote. Ajax, mortified, committed suicide. It was Odysseus who with Neoptolemus brought *Philoctētēs to Troy from Lemnos. Homer's *Odyssey* relates his adventures on the way home to Ithaca from Troy. After his safe return to Ithaca, and his killing of the suitors of Penelope who had thought him dead, he appeased his last enemy the god Poseidon, founding a shrine in his honour so far inland that an inhabitant mistook the oar he was carrying for a winnowing fan. There he fixed the oar in the ground, and sacrificed a ram, a bull, and a breeding boar to Poseidon. Odysseus met his death at the hands of Telegonus, his son by *Circē, who had come to Ithaca to make himself known to his father and killed him unwittingly. See also PALLADIUM and TROJAN HORSE.

In the *Iliad* Odysseus is represented as good in counsel no less than in battle, cool, energetic, tactful, and at times cunning. Subsidiary stories lay great emphasis on this last trait. In the *Odyssey* his chief characteristics are his longing for home, his endurance of suffering in order to reach it, and his self-control until the moment is ripe for him to destroy Penelope's suitors. He is less favourably depicted in some of the Attic tragedies; Euripides in particular makes him heartless and unscrupulous.

O'dyssey (*Odysseia*), epic poem by *Homer, divided into twenty-four books (for this division see HOMER 6). It is the story of the return of *Odysseus from the siege of Troy to his home in *Ithaca, and of the vengeance he took on the suitors of his wife *Penelope. Various indications in the text suggest that the *Odyssey* is a later work than the *Iliad* (see also HOMER 2), but that they both belong to the same general period. The gods do not take sides, as in the *Iliad*, though Poseidon and Helios exact punishment for offences committed against them personally; Athena, hostile to the returning Greeks in the early stage of the story, later protects Odysseus and takes an active part in promoting his return. The events of the poem occupy six weeks.

When the story opens, ten years have elapsed since the fall of Troy to the Greeks. All the Greek leaders have returned to their homes, or are dead, except Odysseus, who is in the island of *Ogygia where the goddess *Calypso has detained him for seven years. Odysseus' wife Penelope has had no news of him but, hoping that he is still alive, has put off choosing a second husband from her many suitors among the island princes, by insisting that she must first finish weaving a shroud for Odysseus' father Laertes; but each night she has secretly unravelled what she had woven during the day. The trick has now been discovered and she must come to a decision. Meanwhile the suitors are staying at Odysseus' palace lavishly entertaining themselves at his expense. In the hope of hearing news his son Telemachus goes to visit *Nestor at Pylos and Menelaus and Helen at Sparta; the suitors plot to ambush and kill Telemachus on his way home (books 1–4). Calypso is ordered by Zeus to release Odysseus; the latter builds a raft and sails on it for seventeen days until within sight of *Scheria, the land of the Phaeacians. The god Poseidon, who hates Odysseus because he has blinded Poseidon's son *Polyphemus, raises a storm and destroys the raft. Odysseus, after two days in the sea, buoyed up by a scarf given him by the sea-goddess Ino, is washed up on the shore of Scheria (book 5). He is found by *Nausicaa, daughter of the Phaeacian king Alcinous, and by her help is hospitably received in the palace (books 6 and 7). Here he is entertained by the songs of the bard Demodocus (which include the quarrel of Odysseus and Achilles, book 8, 75–82; the love of Arēs and Aphroditē, 266–366; the Trojan Horse, 499–520) and by the athletic contests of the Phaeacians.

Odysseus reveals his name and tells of his adventures since leaving Troy, first of his piratical raid on the Cicŏnes at Ismarus (on the south coast of Thrace), then of his visit to the land of the Lotus-eaters, and afterwards to that of the Cyclōpēs, where he encountered Polyphemus (book 9). Next he tells of his entertainment by *Aeolus and the gift of the bag containing the adverse winds (which his companions released), of his adventures with the Laestrȳgonēs, cannibal giants who destroyed eleven of his twelve ships, and of his coming to the island of Aeaea, where the enchantress Circē turned his companions into swine; he himself was protected by the herb moly, given him by the god Hermēs, and he obtained the restoration of his companions. After a year Circe released him and directed him to consult *Teiresias in the Underworld (book 10). Odysseus recounts his visit there, where he saw the ghosts of many dead heroes, their wives and daughters, and conversed with some of them, including his mother Anticleia; Teiresias then prophesied to him the manner of his return (book 11). Odysseus tells of his sailing past the *Sirens and between *Scylla and Charybdis, and of his coming to *Thrinacia, where, in spite of Teiresias' warning, his company killed the cattle of the sun-god Helios. This sacrilege brought about the destruction by Zeus' thunderbolt of the ship and its crew. Odysseus alone was carried on the wreckage to Ogygia, where Calypso received him kindly but refused to let him go (book 12). This brings him to the situation at the opening of the first book.

After finishing his tale (which became proverbial among later Greeks for a long story) Odysseus is carried in a Phaeacian ship to Ithaca (on its return to Scheria the ship is turned into a rock by the god Poseidon). The goddess Athena disguises Odysseus as an old beggar (book 13). He learns of the insolent and extravagant behaviour of Penelope's suitors from the faithful swineherd Eumaeus. He reveals his true identity to Telemachus, when the latter returns safely from Sparta, having escaped the ambush. Together they plot the destruction of the suitors (books 14–16). Odysseus now goes to his house where he is recognized by the old dog Argus, but in his beggar's disguise is beaten and insulted by the goatherd Melanthius and the suitors Antinoüs and Eurymachus, and fights with the beggar Irus (books 17 and 18). Odysseus is recognized by his former nurse Eurycleia, who is ordered to keep her knowledge secret. Penelope reveals her decision to marry the man who the next day will string the bow of Odysseus and shoot an arrow through a line of twelve axe-heads (book 19). The seer Theoclymenus has a vision of the doom of the suitors (book 20). Odysseus alone is able to bend and string the bow, and he shoots an arrow through the axes. He then shoots Antinoüs, and aided by Telemachus, Eumaeus, and another faithful servant, kills the rest of the suitors. Those women servants who have been their lovers are hanged. Penelope is at last convinced, by the hero's knowledge of the peculiar construction of the bedstead, that he is her husband (books 21–3). Odysseus makes himself known to his father Laertes. The relatives of the suitors attempt revenge, but are repulsed, and the goddess Athena stops the blood-feud (book 24).

Oecono'micus ('household management'), treatise by *Xenophon on the management of a household and estate, in the form of a dialogue between Socrates and Critobulus, in the course of which Socrates recounts an earlier conversation (occupying most of the work) which he had with a certain Ischomachus (who seems to represent Xenophon). Chapter 4 describes the horticultural activities of the younger *Cyrus (the Persian king), and the latter's conversation with the Spartan general Lysander on the subject of gardens (imitated by Cicero in *De senectute* ('on old age'), ch. 17). The conversation with Ischomachus is an interesting and humane account of the latter's relations with his very young wife, of the wife's equal but separate role in marriage, and of the running of a house. This is the most charming of Xenophon's treatises.

Oe'dipus (Oidipous, 'swollen-foot'), in Greek myth, the son of *Laius, king of Thebes. When Amphion and Zethus gained possession of Thebes (see ANTIOPE), Laius had taken refuge with *Pelops, but had carried off his host's son Chrysippus. The god Apollo warned him that, as punishment, if he fathered a son that son would kill him. Laius recovered his kingdom after the death of Amphion and Zethus, and married Jocasta (Epicastē in Homer). Accordingly, when a son was born, he was given to a servant to expose on Mount Cithaeron, his feet having been transfixed by a spike. Instead the servant gave him to a shepherd who brought him to Polybus, king of Corinth, and Meropē, his queen. These two, being childless, brought him up as their own son, naming him Oedipus from the deformity of his feet.

When Oedipus was grown up, being taunted with being no true son of Polybus, he went to Delphi to enquire about his parentage. He was told only that he would kill his father and marry his mother. Deciding therefore never to return to Corinth he wandered in the direction of Thebes and by chance encountered Laius (whom he did not know) at a place where three roads met. A quarrel ensued in which Oedipus killed Laius. He went on to Thebes, which was at that time terrorized by the *Sphinx, a monster who destroyed those who could not answer the riddle she posed. Creon, brother of Jocasta and regent of Thebes, offered the kingdom and Jocasta as wife to whoever should overcome this pest. Oedipus guessed the answer to the riddle and the Sphinx killed herself. He married Jocasta and they had two sons, Eteoclēs and Polyneicēs, and two daughters, Antigonē and Ismenē.

According to Homer, when it was discovered that Oedipus had married his mother, the latter hanged herself, but Oedipus continued to rule in Thebes. In Sophocles' tragedy *Oedipus Tyrannus*, discovery was precipitated by plague and famine, and the pronouncement of the Delphic Oracle that these could be averted only if the killer of Laius was expelled from the city. Oedipus' attempts to discover the truth revealed that he himself was Laius' son and killer; Jocasta hanged herself and Oedipus blinded himself. Oedipus was deposed and went into retirement, at first shut up in Thebes; later he went into exile, wandering, attended by Antigone, to Colonus in Attica, where he was protected by *Theseus and where he died (see OEDIPUS AT COLONUS). His sons having quarrelled about who should succeed to the throne, Oedipus before he died put a curse on them that they should each kill the other. When they first took the throne they agreed to divide the inheritance, ruling in alternate years. Eteocles ruled first, but when his year of kingship had elapsed he refused to make way for Polyneices. The latter had spent his year of absence from Thebes at the court of Adrastus, king of Argos, and had married his daughter Argeia. Adrastus supported his son-in-law and gathered an army, headed by seven champions, the *Seven Against Thebes (see also GAMES, PUBLIC (1) 5). Their names (as usually given) are: Adrastus, Polyneices, Tӯdeus (the other son-in-law of Adrastus), Capaneus, Hippomedon, Parthenopaeus, and *Amphiaraus. Each champion was stationed at one of the seven gates of Thebes, and Eteocles similarly assigned a Theban defender to each gate, deciding to confront Polyneices himself. The Argive army was routed and all the champions killed except Adrastus. The brothers Eteocles and Polyneices both died.

Creon, now king of Thebes, ordered that the bodies of the enemy, including that of Polyneices, should not be buried (thus preventing their spirits from entering the Underworld, according to traditional belief). What followed is variously told. One version is given by Euripides in the *Suppliants. Sophocles, in *Antigone, tells how Antigone, rebelling against Creon's decree, contrived secretly to perform the burial rite for her brother. For this Creon had her placed alive in a stone tomb, although she was to marry his son Haemon. There she hanged herself, and Haemon stabbed himself beside her body. The story was related in the lost poem of the *epic cycle Thebāis. See also EPIGONOI.

Oe'dipus, Roman tragedy by *Seneca (2), based on Sophocles' play *Oedipus Tyrannus, but with long descriptions of the plague at Thebes, and of necromantic and sacrificial rites. Jocasta's suicide takes place on stage.

Oe'dipus at Colō'nus (Oidipous epi Kolōnōi, Lat. Oedipus Colōneus), Greek tragedy by *Sophocles written not long before his death in 406/5 BC, produced in 401 BC by his grandson Sophocles the Younger.

*Oedipus, blind and banished from Thebes, has wandered, attended by his daughter Antigonē, to Colonus, a deme of Attica a little north of Athens. He is warned by the inhabitants to leave, but having learnt that this is the locality foretold in an oracle as the place where he will die, refuses to go. Theseus, king of Athens, is appealed to, and assures Oedipus of his protection and of a burial place on Attic soil; in this way his spirit will be a protection to Athens (see HEROES). Oedipus' second daughter Ismenē arrives and tells him of the quarrel between his sons Eteoclēs and Polyneicēs for the throne of Thebes, arousing his anger against them. Creon, regent of Thebes and brother of Oedipus' dead wife Jocasta, arrives to seize Oedipus so that Thebes and not Athens may have his body; his guards carry off Ismene and Antigone, and Creon himself is about to lay hands on Oedipus when Theseus intervenes and rescues him and his daughters. Meanwhile Polyneices has arrived and with professions of repentance asks for his father's favour in his struggle with Eteocles.

Oedipus turns on him with bitter anger and places on his sons a curse that they may die by each other's hand. Peals of thunder warn Oedipus that the time of his death is approaching. He withdraws, and a messenger reports that he blessed his daughters, withdrew to a lonely spot, and in the presence of Theseus alone met his end, the exact form of which remained unknown to the messenger.

Oe'dipus Tyra'nnus (Oidipous Tyrannos, Lat. Oedipus Rex, 'Oedipus the king'), Greek tragedy by *Sophocles, of unknown date; some tenuous indications suggest it may have been written in the years following 430 BC. The tetralogy (see TRAGEDY 2) of which it was part is reputed to have come only second in the dramatic competition, yet Oedipus Tyrannus itself is regarded by many as Sophocles' masterpiece, and was particularly admired by Aristotle (in the Poetics). It deals with that portion of the story of *Oedipus in which he is king of Thebes and husband of Jocasta. When the discovery is made that he is the son of the same Jocasta and of the previous king Laius (whom he has murdered), Oedipus blinds himself and Jocasta commits suicide.

Oedipus learns from the Delphic Oracle that a plague which has fallen on the city is due to the presence there of the murderers of king Laius. He calls upon all who have any knowledge of the matter to come forward. Teiresias, the blind seer, is first summoned. He knows the truth but at first refuses to divulge it. Accused by Oedipus of plotting with Creon, Jocasta's brother, against him, he then speaks the truth but it sounds too far-fetched for Oedipus to entertain it as true. Oedipus next turns against Creon whom he charges with trying to oust him from the throne. He is deeply disturbed by Jocasta's description of the scene of Laius' death and of the retinue he then had with him, which matches the circumstances in which Oedipus himself had once killed a man. On one point he seems now to receive enlightenment: a messenger comes from Corinth to announce the death of the king Polybus and the election of Oedipus to succeed him, and Oedipus, still dreading that he may unwittingly marry his mother in fulfilment of the oracle, expresses reluctance about returning to Corinth. But the messenger then reveals that Oedipus is not in fact the son of Polybus; he himself had given Oedipus as a baby to the king and his wife Meropē, having received the baby from a shepherd on Mount Cithaeron (near Thebes). Whose son then is he? Jocasta guesses the truth and retires. An old shepherd who has been sent for as the only surviving member of Laius' retinue at the time of the latter's death now completes the disclosure. It was he who had carried the infant Oedipus, son of Laius and Jocasta, to Cithaeron, and had from pity given him to the Corinthian.

Oedipus rushes into the palace, to find that Jocasta has hanged herself, and blinds himself with her brooch. Creon takes over the government and Oedipus, though begging to be sent away from the city, remains in Thebes.

Oeneus, see MELEAGER.

Oeno'măus, in Greek myth, king of Pisa and father of Hippodamīa; see PELOPS.

Oenō'nē, in Greek myth, nymph of Mount Ida near Troy, who was loved by *Paris before he knew that he was a Trojan prince. Later she tried to persuade him not to sail to Greece, where the beautiful *Helen lived, having prophetic powers and foreseeing the outcome. Failing to persuade him she promised to heal him if he was wounded. When, towards the end of the Trojan War, he was shot by the poisoned arrow of *Philoctētēs, he sought her help but she refused because he had deserted her. Soon after she repented, but he had already died; in her grief she hanged herself.

Oeno'phyta, place in Boeotia where the Athenians, under the general Myronidēs, defeated the Boeotians in 457 BC; see ATHENS 2 (ii).

Ogy'gia, in Homer's *Odyssey*, the island of Calypso. It is described by Homer as being far away to the west beyond Scheria (generally identified in antiquity with Corcyra), and as the 'navel of the sea'; but it is not clear whether it was thought of as being in the Mediterranean or in the Ocean further west.

Old Comedy, see COMEDY, GREEK 3.

Old Oligarch, see *CONSTITUTION OF THE ATHENIANS* (2).

oligarchy (*oligarchia*, 'rule of the few'), the limitation of political power to a portion of the community, such as a few families or individuals (the oligarchs). It was characteristic of oligarchs that they possessed greater wealth and influence than the rest of the community; high birth was not a necessary condition (compare ARISTOCRACY), but in Greece it commonly happened that the oligarchs were a section of the old nobility which had excluded from power the poorer nobles. There were various kinds of oligarchy (discussed by Aristotle in the *Politics*): the two main kinds were, first, that in which a very large property qualification was required, so that power was kept in the hands of a few rich men or families who might rule arbitrarily, according to no fixed law; and secondly, where the property qualification was not large, so that a considerable number shared equal political rights, although perhaps only a few were eligible for the highest magistracies. In this latter kind, the government was based on a code of law rather than the arbitrary whim of a few individuals, but it was still the case that magistrates were not likely to be brought to account for their actions. Even during the second half of the fifth century BC, when Athenian ascendancy promoted democratic forms of government, there were still many oligarchic states in Greece, the most notable perhaps being at Corinth and at Thebes. For oligarchic rule at Athens (the Four Hundred and the Thirty) see ATHENS 2 (iii). The government at Rome under the republic is often described as 'oligarchical'; see NOBILES and REPUBLIC.

Oly'mpia, the main sanctuary of Zeus in Greece, near the west coast of the Peloponnese on the north bank of the river Alpheus. The festival of Zeus held here in ancient times included the Olympian (or Olympic) games: see GAMES, PUBLIC (I) 2. (The location is quite separate from Mount Olympus, which is some 275 km. or 170 miles to the north.) Olympia was on a well-watered site in a fertile region among gentle hills, a fairly unusual landscape for Greece and particularly appealing to Greek sensibility. It was in marked contrast with its rival in religious importance, the main sanctuary of Apollo in the dramatic setting of Delphi. In historical times Olympia was part of Elis, and the games were under Elean control, formally from 471 BC; in earlier centuries possession of Olympia and responsibility for the festival had been disputed by the small territory of Pisa, which Elis finally overcame and absorbed. The name Pisa is sometimes used in poetry to denote Olympia.

The early history of Olympia is obscure. The 'mound of Pelops', supposed in historical times to be the burial mound of the hero *Pelops, is Mycenaean and goes back to the second millennium BC, but no Mycenaean votive offerings have been found on the site to provide evidence of a religious cult. It was believed by the Greeks that before the ascendancy of Zeus the deities in possession of the site were Gaia (Earth), Cronus, the Mother of the Gods, and Eileithyia. But at some point during the Dark Age (roughly 1150–900 BC), after the fall of Mycenae, the worship of Zeus was established perhaps by Greeks infiltrating from the northwest, and the new cult was combined in some way with that of the local hero Pelops, in whose honour the games may originally have been held. In accordance with Greek ways of thought the games were given a mythical origin; local legend said that they were started by Pelops after he defeated Oenomaus, king of Pisa; the general Greek view was that they were founded by Heracles, who introduced the wild olive to Greece, planting the sacred tree at Olympia to shade the *stadium, and using its leaves to crown the victor.

Away from myth, the first Olympian games were reckoned to have been held in 776 BC, a fact roughly confirmed by archaeological finds at Olympia of eighth-century *tripods, presumably dedicated to Zeus as thank-offerings by victorious athletes. From at latest 776 BC until AD 391 or soon after the festival was held every four years. (For the system of dating based on the sequence of festivals see OLYMPIADS.) Most victors in the early years seem to have come from the western Peloponnese (to judge from their home-towns as recorded in the surviving fragments of the Olympian victor-lists), but by the end of the eighth century tripods begin to appear from Athens (whose first recorded victory was in 696 BC); clearly by 700 the fame of the festival was spreading throughout Greece.

The foot-race at the games in its earliest form had as its goal the altar of Zeus, a vast structure (almost 7 m. (23 ft.) high when *Pausanias saw it) composed entirely of the ash from the burnt thighs of oxen sacrificed to Zeus (see also IAMUS). The sacred precinct of Zeus, a walled enclosure which included the mound of Pelops, was known as the Altis (the local dialect form of *alsos*, 'precinct'). In the seventh century BC permanent buildings began to be erected, first the famous temple of Hera, built mid-century in the precinct; it was about 19 m. (62 ft.) wide by 50 m. (164 ft.) long, and originally the columns were of wood (some of them still standing in the second century AD when they were seen by Pausanias), replaced from time to time by stone as the wood decayed. The walls are thought to have been of sun-dried brick. The limestone head of the cult-statue of Hera has been found. Here too was discovered in 1877 the famous statue by *Praxiteles of the god Hermes holding on his arm the infant Dionysus; this also was noted by Pausanias, and he reports having seen a magnificent carved cedarwood chest said to have been that in which *Cypselus (later tyrant of Corinth) had been hidden by his mother.

The other famous temple in the precinct was that of Zeus himself, designed by Libon of Elis and completed by 457 BC. It was large, about 28 m. (91 ft.) wide by 64 m. (210 ft.) long, and over 20 m. (65 ft.) high, of the Doric order (see ARCHITECTURE I (i)) with columns more than 2 m. (7 ft.) in diameter. Its great glory, one of the *Seven Wonders of the ancient world and the masterpiece of the Athenian sculptor *Pheidias, was the great seated statue of Zeus, made of gold and ivory ('chryselephantine') over a core of wood. It was probably dedicated in 448 BC. The god's head rose more than 12 m. (39 ft.) above the pedestal; Strabo observed that the statue was out of proportion to the temple, which had not been planned for it, since it gave the impression that if the god were to rise he would lift the roof off. In front of the pedestal was a sunken pavement enclosing a shallow basin in which oil was kept to treat the ivory and perhaps to prevent the wooden core from swelling in the damp atmosphere of the Olympian plain. The statue deeply impressed all who visited the temple, including the Roman general Aemilius *Paullus. The emperor Caligula (AD 37–41) intended to convey it to Rome and substitute his own head for that of the god, but the ship built to carry it was struck by lightning. It was finally destroyed in a palace fire in Constantinople during the fifth century. There survive a few moulds that appear to have been used in making some of the folds in Zeus' robes. These were found in Pheidias' workshop, which has been excavated at Olympia from under the ruins of the Byzantine church west of the precinct.

As well as the temples, the precinct contained very many statues of athletes and race-horse owners who had been successful at the games, and of other distinguished men, scholars, statesmen, and kings, who were often generous benefactors. Certain states had treasuries at Olympia (as at *Delphi also). Excavations have shown that the archaic stadium was constructed in a more permanent form before the mid-fifth century BC, and that this was replaced about a century later by the stadium still visible (and now restored). The festival with its games was suppressed as a pagan cult by the emperor Theodosius in AD 391 or soon after; in the sixth century the whole site was covered with debris from an earthquake, an event to which is owed the burial and hence preservation of many objects.

Oly'mpiacus, see LYSIAS.

Oly'mpiad (*hē Olympias*), the four-year period between two Olympian festivals (see GAMES, PUBLIC (1) 2). Greek writers of the post-classical era often date an event by ascribing it to a particular Olympiad, each Olympiad being numbered in sequence from the first recorded games of 776 BC. The first list of Olympian victors, which such a dating system presupposes, is thought to have been published by the sophist *Hippias (2) in the late fifth century BC; the Athenian historian Thucydides twice relates an important event to the year of a significant Olympian victory. According to ancient sources the numbering system was introduced either by *Timaeus or by *Eratosthenes. The years within an Olympiad were numbered (by Eratosthenes) one to four. Thus by this reckoning the battle of Marathon (490 BC) occurred in Olympiad 72, 3 (for strict accuracy it must be remembered that the Olympian year, like the Attic year, began in the summer). From Eratosthenes onwards all Greek dating was based on, or synchronized with, Olympiads. There was some difficulty in Roman times in relating Olympiads to the Roman consular year, which from 153 BC began on 1 January and so included parts of two Olympian years. See also CALENDARS.

Olympian festival, games, see FESTIVALS and GAMES, PUBLIC (1) 2.

Olympian gods, see GODS 1.

Oly'mpias, wife of *Philip II of Macedon and mother of Alexander the Great. In 331 BC she left Macedon for Epirus, which she virtually ruled by herself for a number of years; after Alexander's death in 323 she returned to Macedon, where she made Alexander's posthumous son Alexander IV sole king. Her violence brought back *Cassander, who condemned her to death, and she was finally killed by relatives of those she had murdered.

Olympië'um (Olympieion), name given to the temple of Zeus Olympius (Olympian Zeus) at Athens, situated south-east of the Acropolis. According to the Athenian historian Thucydides this shrine was of great antiquity; Pausanias in the second century AD attributed the first building to the mythical *Deucalion. The first important temple (to be of the Doric order: see ARCHITECTURE 1) was begun on the site of an earlier temple at the end of the sixth century BC. With the fall of the Peisistratid tyranny in 510 BC, work on the temple was discontinued and was not resumed until 174 BC when Antiochus IV Epiphanēs, the *Seleucid king of Asia (176–165), undertook to rebuild it at his own expense, from plans drawn up by the Roman architect Cossutius. It was now to be of marble and in the Corinthian order, but was again left unfinished at Antiochus' death and remained so for three centuries. In 86 BC Sulla removed some of the columns to Rome. It was finally completed, still to Cossutius' plans, by the emperor Hadrian in AD 132, making it one of the largest of Greek temples, 108 m. (354 ft.) long by 41 m. (135 ft.) wide. Fifteen of the columns are still standing.

Oly'mpus (not to be confused with *Olympia), the highest mountain in Greece, situated at the eastern end of the chain of mountains which forms roughly the northern boundary of Greece proper, overlooking the Vale of Tempē. In Greek myth it was believed to be where the twelve Olympian gods had their houses, built for them by the god Hephaestus, with Zeus' house occupying the summit. (The gods could also be thought of as dwelling in the heavens above Olympus.)

Oly'nthiacs, three political speeches by Demosthenēs. See DEMOSTHENES (2) 5.

Oly'nthus, Greek city north of Potidaea on the mainland of Chalcidicē. It was a city of mixed race, and after 433 BC became the capital of a Chalcidian confederacy (see CHALCIDIC LEAGUE). Sparta, suspicious of its power, captured it in 390 and disbanded the confederacy, which reformed after the Spartan defeat at Leuctra in 371. When Amphipolis fell to *Philip II of Macedon in 357, Olynthus and the confederacy went over to him, but becoming alarmed by his

increasing power turned to Athens. Athens, however, failed to save the city. It was betrayed to Philip in 348 and completely destroyed.

omens. An omen, in Greek and Roman thought, was a phenomenon or circumstance signifying good or ill fortune in the future, a message sent from the gods. Almost any occurrence which was not entirely a matter of course might be a sign: *dreams especially, but also a celestial phenomenon—lightning, comets, eclipses, even a drop of rain; or a sneeze, a stumble, a name or phrase heard in passing. When it was being debated whether or not to abandon Rome, in ruins after the Gallic invasion of c.390 BC, it was not *Camillus' oratory that prevented an exodus but the chance remark of a centurion marching his men through the Forum, overheard in the senate: 'We might as well stop here.' Superstitious fear following an eclipse delayed the Athenian retreat in Sicily during the *Peloponnesian War (see 5, and NICIAS), with fatal consequences for Athens. The Romans, on the other hand, warned before the battle of Pydna (168 BC) that an impending eclipse was in the course of nature, remained unmoved, whereas the Macedonians, thinking that it signified the overthrow of their kingdom, were frightened and subsequently defeated.

Observation of the flight of birds was particularly important (see AUGURY); the sight of a bird of prey, vulture or eagle, was significant, as was the direction, left or right, from which it appeared (for the Greeks right was good, left bad); the omen had greater weight if the viewer was facing north. Xenophon in 401 BC heard the cry of an eagle perched on his right, which was interpreted to him as being on the whole favourable. At a *sacrifice every stage was ominous: the Greeks regarded as significant the reluctance or willingness of the victim to approach the altar. Inspection of the entrails of the sacrificial victims was the most important duty of the seers who accompanied armies in times of war (see HARUSPICES). Before the battle of Plataea in the *Persian Wars both Greeks and Persians remained inactive for ten days because the omens on both sides were unfavourable for attack. For an army to have a good seer, whatever 'good' might mean, was of great importance. In the Persian Wars the Spartans went to considerable trouble to procure the services of Teisamenus, who was reputedly descended from the mythical seer *Iamus, and under his seership the Spartans and their allies achieved five victories. See also DIVINATION and ORACLES.

The Romans, besides deriving omens from birds, lightning, and sacrificial victims, attached importance (as did the Greeks) to a significant word or phrase casually spoken. When L. Aemilius *Paullus (the victor of Pydna; see above) heard his small daughter say that their dog Persa was dead, he took it as a good omen for his campaign against the Macedonian king Perseus. Contrary to the Greeks the Romans generally regarded signs on the left as favourable, on the right as unfavourable, but under Greek influence they sometimes reversed this interpretation.

O'mphalē, see HERACLES.

O'mphalos, see DELPHI.

Onēsi'critus, Greek historian with Alexander the Great in India, who with *Nearchus explored the sea-route from India to the Persian Gulf. The longest surviving fragment from his narrative of Alexander's Indian campaign describes an interview between the author and some Indian sages. His reputation in antiquity was of being a great liar.

Ōnē'tōr, see DEMOSTHENES (2) 2.

Onoma'critus, an Athenian who lived at the court of the tyrant *Peisistratus and his sons at Athens in the late sixth century BC. He was engaged to collect and edit the oracles of *Musaeus and is said to have been detected by *Lasus of Hermione in inserting a false one (that the island of Lemnos would disappear into the sea). When the Peisistratids had been overthrown, they employed him to give oracles to the Persian king Xerxēs which favoured his planned invasion of Greece. Onomacritus was later believed to have been the author of some of the poems ascribed to *Orpheus, and was also said to have been given the task by Peisistratus of editing Homer's *Iliad* and *Odyssey*.

onomatopoe'ia, the formation and use of words to imitate sounds. A famous example occurs in a line of the early Roman poet Ennius: *at tuba terribili sonitu taratantara dixit* ('the war-trumpet with terrifying sound blew *taratantara*'). The word is used also, in a wider sense, of the formation of whole phrases or sentences which suggest in sound what they describe, such as Virgil's dactylic hexameter, *quadrupedante putrem sonitu quatit ungula campum* ('the horses' hooves with four-fold beat shake the crumbling plain'). For an interesting ancient discussion see Dionysius of Halicarnassus, *De compositione verborum* 14–20.

Opeconsī'va or **Opiconsī'via,** see OPS.

opi'sthograph, see BOOKS AND WRITING 1.

O'ppian (Oppiānos, early third century AD), of Cilicia in south-east Asia Minor, writer of Greek didactic poetry in hexameters. His *Halieutica* ('on fishing') is in five books; the *Cynegetica* ('on hunting'), in three books, is also ascribed to him but seems to be the work of a different poet, a native of Syria, though perhaps of the same

name. Both poems contain passages of power and beauty, despite the unpromising material.

Ops, Roman goddess of abundance. Her festivals, Opalia on 19 August and Opiconsivia on 25 August, were close to festivals of *Consus, the god of the granary. Because her December festival was also close to the *Saturnalia she was usually associated with Saturn, and since he was identified with the Greek *Cronus she was identified with Rhea, the consort of Cronus. Her oldest place of worship was a small shrine in the Regia or ancient royal palace, where her harvest ceremony was performed, attended only by the *pontifex maximus* and the Vestals, symbolizing the storage of the state crops by the king and his daughters.

optimā'tēs ('the best class'). In Roman politics, until the time of the Gracchi (*c.*133 BC) there was no serious challenge to the overwhelming predominance of the noble families in the ruling oligarchy (see NOBILES). In response to the rise of the *populārēs*, political leaders 'on the side of the people', the Roman upper class called themselves *optimates*, understanding the term socially and morally on the model of the Greek *kaloi kagathoi*; thus in the late republic the name was applied to the senatorial party and their supporters, those who acted in the interests of the *optimi*, the 'best men'.

oracles. An oracle (Gk. *manteion, chrēstērion*, Lat. *orāculum*) was an answer given by a god to a question asked him by a worshipper; it usually took the form of a command or a prediction or a statement of fact. An oracle may also mean the shrine itself where the answers were given. In each of the many oracular shrines in the ancient world the god was consulted in his own particular way. The most famous were those of Zeus at Dodona in Epirus, and of Apollo at Delphi. The former dates from very ancient times and is mentioned in Homer's *Iliad* and *Odyssey*; there the oracles seem to have been extracted in some manner from a sacred oak-tree, perhaps by the rustling of its leaves (late legends say by the sound of a sacred spring or brazen gong), and interpreted by priests known as Selloi, 'of unwashed feet and sleeping on the ground'. Zeus had another oracular shrine at Olympia (see IAMUS). At Delphi a priestess, the Pythia, seated on a tripod and under the inspiration of Apollo, answered the question put to her by the enquirer (see DELPHIC ORACLE). Apollo had many oracles of similar type in Greece and Asia Minor. The healing god *Asclepius had a shrine at Epidaurus particularly famed for sending curative visions to the sick through *incubation. The shrine of the hero *Amphiaraus at Oropus was similarly credited with healing properties. One of the most famous hero-oracles was that of *Trophonius in a cave at Lebadea in Boeotia. Among foreign oracles that of Zeus *Ammon at Siwa in the Libyan desert, consulted notably by Alexander the Great, had a high reputation among the Greeks. Very many oracular responses to questions are known, and mostly they direct the questioner to perform some religious act, such as a sacrifice to a particular god. It seems probable that the famous replies said to have been given on notable historical occasions are not in fact genuine. From at latest the sixth century BC (see ONOMACRITUS) collections of oracles were made and peddled.

There were no oracular shrines in Italy comparable in importance with those in Greece. During the Roman republic oracles, apart from the Sibylline books (see SIBYL), were not consulted by the state. However, under the empire, and with the increased worship of Greek and oriental divinities, more attention was paid to oracular predictions. As in Greece, the collection of oracles at Rome must have begun quite early. In 213 BC at a critical time in the Second Punic War the senate made the praetor Acilius seize and suppress several collections in circulation. With the similar purpose of arresting panic the emperor Augustus had 2,000 books of prophecies burnt. The most important oracle in Italy was at Cumae, where the Sibyl's cave was situated under the temple of Apollo. At Praenestē there was an ancient and famous temple of Fortune (see FORTUNA), where oracles known as *sortēs*, 'lots', were given: tablets, each inscribed with its own oracle, were shuffled by a child who drew one and gave it to the questioner. *Faunus was regarded as a prophetic god, as was the nymph *Carmentis (mother of Evander); both are referred to by Virgil. At the temple of Faunus at Tibur incubation was practised; a sheep was killed and the enquirer slept in its skin. The use of oracles as an aid to decision-making became particularly apparent in the second century AD with the popularization of the *sortes Virgilianae* (see VIRGIL), a practice said to have originated with the emperor Hadrian, by which the enquirer opened Virgil's works and chose a line at random to be a guide to the future. Copies of the *Aeneid* were deposited in temples for that purpose. See also DIVINATION and OMENS.

oral poetry, poetry composed and transmitted without the aid of writing. The term is usually applied to narrative poetry composed in preliterate societies, since there is very little evidence for other kinds of poetry. The Greek epic poems of *Homer, the *Iliad* and *Odyssey*, are generally believed to be in origin oral compositions. It is characteristic of oral poetry that it contains '*formulae', repeated words, especially 'stock' epithets and phrases, even whole lines and paragraphs describing typical scenes, which enable the poet who has already committed them to memory to deliver a poem extempore when required. It is generally felt that if a poem is the product of oral composition, disproportionate significance should not be given to, for example, epithets which fit the metre but not the context, or slight discrepancies between one typical scene and another. See EPIC.

Ōrā'tōr, Latin treatise by *Cicero written in 46 BC and dedicated to M. Brutus, which describes the ideal orator and outlines a scheme for his education. He must be a master of the three styles, the plain, the grand, and the middle. In declaring that *Demosthenes, his great Greek exemplar, is uniquely eminent in all three styles, Cicero defends himself against the charge that he is an Asianist rather than an Atticist (see ORATORY) by showing that the best Attic oratory embraced more than the simple plainness of *Lysias (compare the *BRUTUS*). The qualifications of the orator in technical respects (invention, elocution, style, for example) are set out, together with his functions (to teach, to please, to persuade), and the branches of knowledge which he must have mastered (including philosophy and physics). The treatise ends with a discussion on euphony and rhythm. As in the *Brutus*, there are interesting references to works of art taken as illustrations, e.g. the Aphroditē of *Apellēs, the Zeus and Athena of *Pheidias.

oratory. Although in general usage the two terms oratory and *rhetoric are virtually synonymous, in what follows a distinction is made between them: rhetoric is taken to denote the theoretical art of speaking, oratory its practical application. Both were exhaustively studied in the ancient world, for mastery of the spoken word was the key to success in the fields of politics and law, and successful careers in either field (though both were generally associated) brought power, prestige, and wealth.

1. *Greek.* Attic Greek oratory, in its period of splendour (from *c*.460 BC to the suppression of political freedom at Athens at the end of the fourth century BC), produced a large number of people who professed to be able to teach it, known as *rhetors. The earliest teachers, Corax and Teisias, were active in Sicily in the middle of the fifth century BC when the rule of tyrants gave place to democracy; the lawsuits which followed this change of constitution are said to have given Corax the idea of systematizing and writing down the rules for speaking in a lawcourt. According to Aristotle, *Empedoclēs too played some part in this development. *Gorgias of Leontini (in Sicily) brought this new style of public speaking to Athens in 427 BC, adopting in particular a poetic style, although it is clear from the earlier plays of Euripides that oratory was already a developed art in the city. Gorgias' influence has been detected in the speeches of Thucydidēs and Isocratēs. The teaching of

rhetoric was part of the stock-in-trade of many *sophists, some of whom specialized in particular aspects of the subject, such as semantics or figures of speech. The sophists and rhetors laid emphasis on the techniques necessary for winning over an audience. The teaching of this kind of rhetoric aroused the hostility of Socrates and especially of Plato, who thought that persuasive speech should be based on knowledge of the truth, and thus introduced the idea of an opposition between rhetoric which aimed to persuade and philosophy which aimed to know the truth (see GORGIAS). The theoretical study of rhetoric was further developed by *Aristotle (see 4 (v)), who was probably the first to divide oratory into three kinds, judicial (or forensic), political (or deliberative), and *epideictic (the oratory of display), each with its own particular style.

No speech by any of the great political figures of the fifth century survives, though the Funeral Speech of Pericles as it is reproduced by *Thucydides (2. 35–46) may possibly give some idea of his lofty style. The earliest and only truly fifth-century Attic orator whose speeches in part survive is *Antiphon (c.480–411 BC); he was followed by *Andocides (at the very end of the fifth and beginning of the fourth century), and the great fourth-century orators *Lysias, *Isocrates, *Isaeus, *Demosthenes, and *Aeschines. Of the remaining Attic orators the most important were *Lycurgus, *Hypereides, and *Deinarchus (see CANONS). After the end of the fourth century BC the political situation in Greece did not give much scope for the practice of political oratory (see ATHENS 2 (iv) and HELLENISTIC AGE); but its importance in education did not decline and the study of oratory was still pursued at Athens and also among the Greeks of Asia Minor, at Rhodes and Pergamum, where oratory of a rich, exuberant, and declamatory kind developed, the so-called Asianic style, in contrast with the simple lucid Attic style modelled on Lysias. The former term arose, according to a grammarian, when the Greek language spread into Asia (from the late fourth century BC) and the Asians used Greek circumlocutions when they did not know the precise words. Quintilian's view is that the style reflected the bombastic and boastful nature of the Asians, compared with Attic speakers who despised vapid and redundant speech.

2. *Roman.* At Rome, as in Greece, oratory was recognized as an art from early times. Even in the fourth century BC Appius *Claudius Caecus the Censor had a high reputation as an orator. In the survey that Cicero gives in his *Brutus* of the great Roman speakers, the principal names are those of *Cato the Censor, the *Gracchi (especially Gaius, described by Cicero as wise, lofty, and weighty, but lacking the final polish), M. *Antonius (grandfather of Mark Antony), L. Licinius *Crassus (consul in

95 BC, whose speeches were deliberately built up in accordance with the rules of Greek oratory), Julius *Caesar, C. Licinius *Calvus, an exponent of the pure Attic style, and *Hortensius, noted, on the contrary, for his luxuriant Asianism. Cicero found himself under attack as an Asianist by admirers of Calvus who thought his periodic and rhythmical style over-elaborate; he defended himself in the *Brutus* and *Orator*.

From the second century BC onwards Roman orators were a product of Greek schools or of Greek teachers who had migrated to Rome. Handbooks such as the *Rhetorica ad Herennium* were based on Greek models. But Greek theory was subordinate to Roman practice: it was the institutions of the law-courts and above all the senate, where affairs of state were debated before an intelligent, educated, and trained audience, that moulded the dignified Roman oratorical style. Of this wealth of eloquence only the speeches of Cicero survive.

As in Athens in the late fourth century BC, so in Rome under the empire oratory as a living art declined when the political decisions were taken by the emperor and no longer followed public debate. But rhetoric still remained the fundamental element in *education, though now it was taught only for the law-courts or display purposes, and exercised in consequence a strong influence on all forms of literature. Professorships of rhetoric were set up in all the large cities of the empire, and for as long as the empire lasted higher education was almost entirely rhetorical. *Quintilian was the first professor of rhetoric at Rome and, like Cicero, saw rhetoric as providing the finest literary discipline. In the second century AD *Dio Chrysostom and Aelius *Aristeides in the eastern empire could draw large audiences to hear performances of their epideictic oratory. Orators or teachers of rhetoric in the West included many of the greatest figures of their time, e.g. St *Augustine, St *Ambrose, and *Ausonius. True understanding of much of classical literature and ancient literary criticism requires appreciation of the large role of rhetoric and oratory in ancient life and culture.

Orbi'lius Pupi'llus, Lucius (c.112–c.17 BC), of Beneventum, a grammarian, famous as the schoolmaster of Horace, who calls him *plagosus*, 'whacker', from beatings inflicted during lessons on *Livius Andronicus' version of Homer's *Odyssey*. There is an account of him in Suetonius.

orchestra ('dancing-floor'), see DIONYSUS, THEATRE OF, and ATHENS I.

Orcho'menus, name of several Greek cities but especially of that in Boeotia on the north of the Copāic plain (known locally as Erchomenus), apparently the principal Boeotian city until it was eclipsed by Thebes; the site, originally settled in neolithic times, became particularly important in the Mycenaean period, when the rulers were buried in a magnificent tholos-tomb, known as the Treasury of *Minyas when Pausanias visited it in the second century AD. Orchomenus was proverbial for its wealth and associated in legend with the *Minyans. It has been suggested that its wealth depended upon the fertility of the Copaic plain after the lake was drained, and that its decline is reflected in the story that Heracles, hero of the rival city of Thebes, broke down the drainage system and flooded the plain. Orchomenus was the site of an ancient and famous cult of the Graces. The city was destroyed by a confederacy of Boeotian towns in 364 BC.

Orcus. In Roman religion Orcus is apparently a synonym of *Dis, the god of the Underworld, or the Underworld itself.

orders, at Rome in the early republic, the two hereditary estates or broad social divisions of the Roman people, namely patricians (the rich) and plebeians (the poor); each had its own privileges and disabilities sanctioned by law, religion, and custom. For the 'conflict of the orders' from 494 to 287 BC see ROME 3. The practical distinctions between patricians and plebeians largely disappeared after 366 BC. In the first century BC the term 'order' denotes only the senatorial or equestrian order. Cicero's *concordia ordinum*, 'harmony of the orders', was the union of senators and equestrians; see CICERO (1) 3.

orders, of architecture, see ARCHITECTURE I and VITRUVIUS.

o'rĕads (Gk. *oreiadĕs*, Lat. *orēades*), *nymphs of the mountains.

Orestei'a, the collective name given to the three Greek tragedies (trilogy) by *Aeschylus on the story of *Agamemnon, Clytemnestra, and Orestēs, produced at Athens in 458 BC when it won the dramatic competition. It is the only trilogy that survives complete. The plays are *Agamemnon, Choēphoroe* ('libation bearers'), and *Eumenidēs* ('kindly ones', a euphemism for the *Furies).

The story is taken from the mythical history of the descendants of *Atreus in which crime led to further crime through several generations. The *Agamemnon* opens in an atmosphere of hope mingled with foreboding, as the watchman on the roof of Agamemnon's palace in Argos looks out for the signal beacon to announce the fall of Troy. After the signal is seen, the news is confirmed by the arrival of a herald. Agamemnon's wife Clytemnestra appears jubilant, but the chorus of Argive elders recall Agamemnon's sacrifice of his daughter Iphigeneia to enable the Greek fleet to set sail, and brood over the possible consequences. Agamemnon arrives, bringing with him the captured Trojan princess

Cassandra, his concubine. Clytemnestra treacherously welcomes him and then leads him into the palace. Cassandra, who has not spoken up to this point, is now moved to frenzied prophecy, foresees Agamemnon's murder and her own, as well as having a vision of the past crimes of the house, and utters a lament. She too enters the house, knowingly going to her death. The cries of the dying Agamemnon are heard. The interior of the palace is revealed, with Clytemnestra exulting over the bodies of the two victims. She answers the elders' reproaches by citing as justification Agamemnon's sacrifice of Iphigeneia. *Aegisthus, her lover, appears, and subdues the elders with threats of force. The latter can only hope that one day Agamemnon's son Orestes will avenge him.

In the *Choephoroe*, Orestes, the son of Agamemnon, after years of exile, returns to Argos with his friend Pyladēs, to avenge his father on the god Apollo's instructions; he comes to his father's tomb and dedicates on it a lock of his hair. The two draw aside while Electra, Orestes' sister, and a chorus of Argive women approach to pour libations on the tomb by order of Clytemnestra, who has been disturbed by ominous dreams. Electra recognizes the lock of hair and footprints nearby as strikingly similar to her own; her brother reveals himself and a reunion takes place (a scene thought by some to be mocked by Euripides in his *Electra*, where Electra rejects these proofs of identity). Electra and Orestes join in an impressive invocation of their father's dead spirit, calling upon his aid in their pursuit of vengeance. Orestes and Pylades, disguised as travellers bringing news of the former's death, enter the palace. Aegisthus is summoned and on his arrival is killed by Orestes. Clytemnestra pleads with her son for her life, and for a moment Orestes falters; but Pylades, in his only speech, reminds him of Apollo's command, and Orestes drags her into the palace and kills her. While he is justifying his action he sees avenging Furies arrive to haunt him, and he flees from them.

Eumenides opens to show Orestes as suppliant at the shrine of Apollo in Delphi. The Furies, forming the chorus, are asleep around him. Orestes is promised protection by Apollo, who tells him to go to Athens to seek justice from the goddess Athena. After he leaves, the ghost of Clytemnestra stirs up the Furies to pursue him. The scene changes to the front of Athena's temple on the Acropolis at Athens. Athena, having heard the pleas and justifications of the Furies and of Orestes, refers the judgement to a tribunal of Athenian citizens acting as judges (i.e. the historical Areopagus court for judging cases of homicide, of which this episode was the legendary foundation). The Furies prosecute, and Orestes defends himself. Athena votes with the other judges, and the votes are found to be equally divided. Athena therefore declares that in future, when the votes are equal the defendant is to be acquitted (as was Athenian practice; see LAW, AT ATHENS 2). The Furies are indignant, but are conciliated by Athena's promise of a permanent home in her city and honour in their new role as beneficent powers.

For Stesichorus' poem *Oresteia* see STESI-CHORUS.

Ore'stēs, in Greek myth, son of *Agamemnon and Clytemnestra, and brother of Iphigeneia and Electra. See PELOPS, ORESTEIA, and the articles on the tragedies *Orestes* (below), *Electra*, and *Iphigeneia in Tauris*. For his marriage with Hermionē (daughter of Menelaus and Helen) see NEOPTOLEMUS.

Ore'stēs, Greek tragedy by *Euripides produced in 408 BC. For his story see ORESTEIA above.

Orestes, having killed his mother Clytemnestra and her lover Aegisthus, has been driven mad by the Furies and is tenderly nursed by his sister Electra. The citizens of Argos are about to pass judgement on them for their crime, and a sentence of death is expected. At this point Agamemnon's brother *Menelaus appears, on his way home to Sparta from Troy, together with his wife Helen, but is too cowardly to help, although Orestes appeals to him. Sentence of death is passed on Orestes and Electra who now, urged on by *Pyladēs, plan to kill Helen, the source of all their troubles, and to seize Menelaus' daughter Hermionē as a hostage. Helen mysteriously disappears. They then threaten to kill Hermione unless Menelaus intervenes to save their lives. However, in this confused situation Apollo appears and dictates a general pacification, explaining that Helen has been carried off to heaven, and that it is Orestes' destiny to be brought to trial at Athens and, after being freed, to marry Hermione and become ruler of Argos.

O'rganon, see ARISTOTLE 4 (i).

orgy, from the Greek *orgia* meaning 'secret rites', used of the worship of the gods of the *mystery religions, such as Demeter (at Eleusis) or Bacchus.

Orientalizing age, name given to one of the five periods of the Greek era (based on the differences in pottery styles; see POTTERY I (v)), denoting very roughly the period from 720 to 620 BC (compare PROTO-GEOMETRIC, GEOMETRIC, ARCHAIC, and CLASSICAL).

O'rigen (Ōrigenēs) (AD 185–254), the successor of *Clement as head of the Christian (catechetical) school of Alexandria, the first great scholar among the Greek Fathers of the Church. He was a pioneer in the textual criticism of the Bible, and is chiefly famous for his *Hexapla*, an edition of the Old Testament containing in six parallel columns the Hebrew text, the same transliter-

ated into Greek letters, the *Septuagint, a revision of the Septuagint, and two other Greek translations. Only fragments of the work survive. Many of Origen's voluminous theological writings have also been lost, but we still have *First Principles*, the first work of Christian dogma to be produced, and *Against Celsus*, a work of Christian apologetic. Origen exerted considerable influence, but his speculations were often considered heretical and were condemned by the Church.

Orīgines ('origins'), of the Italian cities, a work by *Cato the Censor.

Orī'on, in Greek myth, a giant and a hunter of Boeotia, and also the name of a constellation; the two were known to Homer (see SIRIUS). He was the subject of various stories. He pursued the *Pleiades, and both he and they were turned into constellations. He was deprived of sight by the god Dionysus, or killed by Artemis (either because he challenged her to throw the discus against him or from jealousy because he was loved by Eos, Dawn), or stung to death by a scorpion sent by Gaia (Earth), because he boasted that he would kill all wild beasts. Ovid (*Fasti* 5. 495) relates the curious story of how he was created from the urine of three gods (based on the false derivation of his name Orion from *ouron*, 'urine').

Orni'thes, see BIRDS.

Orō'pus, town on the borders of Attica and Boeotia, near the sea, for a long time a subject of contention between the two states. For the oracular shrine there see AMPHIARAUS.

Oro'sius, Paulus (early fifth century AD), a Christian historian from Spain, who took refuge with St *Augustine in North Africa from the barbarian invaders of his homeland. At Augustine's request he composed in AD 417 a *History against the Pagans* in seven books, a history of the world down to his own day, to counter the pagan view that the conversion of the Roman empire to Christianity was the cause of recent disaster (which he does by citing disasters that occurred before the rise of Christianity). The final part of the last book, covering the events of Orosius' own time, is a valuable historical source. During the Middle Ages his work was the standard history of the ancient world.

Orpheus, in Greek legend, a pre-Homeric poet, dated by the Greeks to a generation before the Trojan War and associated with the expedition of the *Argonauts, by his singing helping them to resist the lure of the *Sirens. He was said to be a Thracian, a follower of the god *Dionysus, the son of a *Muse, perhaps Calliopē, and so marvellous a player on the lyre that he could charm wild beasts and make even trees and rocks move by his music. His story is well known from the Roman poets Virgil and Ovid. He married Eurydicē, a *dryad. While being pursued by *Aristaeus, Eurydice trod on a snake, was bitten and died. Orpheus went down to the Underworld to recover her and by his music induced the goddess Persephone to let her go, but on condition that he should not look back at her as she followed him. When they approached the world of the living, Orpheus forgot the condition and looked back, and Eurydice immediately vanished for ever. Later Orpheus was torn to pieces by women, either Thracians who were jealous of his love for Eurydice, or by *maenads because he did not honour their god Dionysus (this story was the subject of a lost play by Aeschylus). His severed head, floating down the Thracian river Hebrus, and in some versions still speaking, reached the island of *Lesbos, the home of lyric poetry, where it was buried.

From perhaps the middle of the sixth century onwards the authorship of several poems that referred to mystery cults (see MYSTERIES) was attributed to Orpheus. These poems dealt with purifications and initiations; secret rites that were supposed to free participants from ancient guilt, and impart to them better hopes for the afterlife, were performed according to the books of Orpheus and *Musaeus (see also ONOMACRITUS). The name of Orphism is sometimes used to describe the beliefs and practices of those who took part in mystery cults based on the poems attributed to Orpheus, or who engaged in ascetic practices. However, it is uncertain to what extent Orphism can be thought of as a unified spiritual movement. Interesting information has come from the *Derveni papyrus, which contains an ancient commentary on the theogony of Orpheus. Orphic myth, now known mostly from references in Plato and the Neoplatonists, explained the mixture of good and evil in human nature by the myth of *Dionysus Zagreus. It departed from normal Greek beliefs in making the guilt and punishment of the individual after death the centre of its doctrine; it would seem that, according to Orphic myth, men bear the guilt for the death of Dionysus Zagreus, and they have to pay the penalty after death to Persephone before she allows them to rise to higher existence. It also taught the transmigration of souls (having much in common with Pythagoreanism); after the soul has been reincarnated three times and has each time lived a virtuous life, it dwells in the Isles of the Blest for ever. But as well as a virtuous life, ritual purity and correct knowledge as prescribed by Orphic doctrine are necessary. Evil doers, and the uninitiated, risk punishment after death. Tombs have been found in south Italy and Crete containing gold leaves, dating from the Hellenistic age, on which are inscribed verses to be spoken like passwords upon arrival in the Underworld. The high ethical tone and ascetic practices of some of the followers of Orpheus became debased into the superstition and charlatanism of others, and although Pindar and Plato were attracted by some of the docrines, to others of the fifth century BC 'Orphic' was a term of contempt. There was a revival of belief under the Roman empire.

Orth(r)us, in Greek myth, the dog of *Geryon and the offspring of the monsters *Typhon and *Echidna. See HERACLES, LABOURS OF 10 and SPHINX.

Orty'gia, see LETO and SYRACUSE 1.

Oscan, Oscans. The Oscans (Gk. Opikoi) were an early Italic (*Indo-European) people of southern Italy who established themselves principally in Campania. When *Sabelli replaced them in Campania and elsewhere their name survived and in due course was used to describe the newcomers' very similar language: Samnites, Frentani, Campanians, Lucanians, Bruttians, Mamertines, and Apulians all spoke Oscan-type languages. Oscan and *Umbrian form one group of Italic languages, Latin and *Faliscan the other (see LATIN LANGUAGE). After the Social War of 90–88 BC (see ROME 6) Oscan was gradually replaced by Latin, but it was still being spoken at Pompeii in AD 79. The *Atellan farces were in origin an Oscan literary form.

Oschopho'ria, at Athens, the festival of the vintage, celebrated in October, which had as its central ceremony the carrying of vine-branches with clusters of grapes from a sanctuary of Dionysus in Athens to the shrine of Athena Skiras at Phalerum, by two young men dressed in female robes. They were followed by a choir singing special hymns. The festival was popularly associated with the myths of *Theseus.

Osī'ris, most widely worshipped of the Eygptian gods, representing male fertility in nature and incarnated in the sacred bull Apis. According to myth he had been a pharaoh of Egypt who had civilized and educated his people but had been murdered and his body cut in pieces by his brother Set (identified with the Greek *Typhon). *Isis, his sister and wife, collected and buried his mangled remains, and with her son Horus took revenge on Set, the author of all evil. Thereafter Osiris was regarded as the god of the dead, but the source, through Horus (the Sun), of renewed life. The Greeks identified him with *Dionysus. See also SERAPIS and HARPOCRATES.

Ossa, mountain in Thessaly; see PELION and OTUS.

Ostō'rius Sca'pula, Publius, see BRITAIN 3.

o'stracism (*ostrakismos*), at Athens in the fifth century BC, an institution traditionally ascribed to *Cleisthenēs in 508/7 BC whereby a prominent but unpopular citizen might be banished without loss of property for ten years. Each year the *ecclesia voted on whether an ostracism should be held that year. If an ostracism was agreed upon, every citizen who wished to vote scratched on a potsherd (ostrakon; see OSTRAKA below) the name of the person whose banishment from the state seemed to him necessary for public well-being. Provided there was a total of 6,000 votes cast in all, the person whose name appeared most often was banished. The first man ostracized, in 487 BC, was one Hipparchus, a relation of the former tyrant *Hippias, followed in 486 by *Megaclēs (3), one of the Alcmaeonidae, and in 485 by another supporter of Hippias: it was probably feared that they supported the restoration of the tyranny and the Persian invaders (see PERSIAN WARS). Other prominent men known to have been ostracized are *Xanthippus, *Aristeidēs, *Themistoclēs, *Cimon, and *Thucydidēs son of Melesias. *Hyperbolus, perhaps in 417, is the last known victim. Afterwards ostracism was found to be not the most convenient way of dealing with politicians. Many hundreds of ostraka have been excavated at Athens, some containing the names of people otherwise entirely unknown. A cache of about 200 has been found all inscribed with the name of Themistocles by only a few different hands, presumably for distribution by his political enemies. Ostracism existed in a few other Greek states. At Syracuse the institution was called 'petalism' because the names were written on olive-leaves (petala).

o'straka ('potsherds'), broken fragments of pottery used as writing material, especially in Egypt after the Greek conquest at the end of the fourth century BC. Ostraka were not greatly used for writing in Greece except as voting tablets (see OSTRACISM above). Most of the early ostraka found in Egypt are tax-receipts; later examples often contain lists, school exercises, magical spells, and religious texts. Their chief value lies in the light they throw on social history. Latin ostraka have been found near Carthage.

O'strogoths, see GOTHS and JUSTINIAN.

Otho, Marcus Sa'lvius (AD 32–69), friend of the emperor Nero and husband of Poppaea Sabina, whom the emperor loved and later married (see ROME 10). He was governor of Lusitania from 58 until the emperor's death in 68. In an attempt to become the succeeding emperor he organized a conspiracy among the praetorian guard and was hailed as emperor by part of the army, but was defeated by Vitellius and his legions and committed suicide. See also GALBA.

Ōtus and Ephia'ltēs, in Greek myth, giant sons of Alōeus (whence they are called Alōĭdae), or of Poseidon and the wife of Aloeus. They attacked the gods and tried to pile Mount Ossa on Olympus, and Mount Pelion on Ossa, in order to reach the heavens themselves and attack the gods there. They were destroyed by Zeus. A passage in Homer's Iliad tells how they imprisoned Arēs, the god of war, in a bronze jar for thirteen months, where he would have perished if Hermēs had not released him. A different tradition makes them beneficent heroes who founded cities and the worship of the Muses. Ephialtes was also the name of the demon of nightmare among the Greeks. See also GIANTS.

ovā'tio, see TRIUMPH.

Ovid (Publius Ovidius Nāso, 43 BC–AD 17), Roman poet. He was born at Sulmo, in a valley of the Apennines east of Rome, on 20 March. He tells the story of his life in one of his own poems, Tristia IV. 10. His family was of equestrian rank, and he was educated at Rome; by his father's wish he studied rhetoric with a view to practising law, but his taste for poetry asserted itself. According to the Elder Pliny he applied himself to the emotional rather than the argumentative side of rhetoric. He travelled, and visited Athens, Asia Minor, and Sicily. For a time he held some minor official posts in Rome, but soon abandoned public life for poetry. He was one of the group of poets around *Messalla and stood slightly apart from the Augustan circle centred on *Maecenas. Horace and Propertius were among his friends, but his warmest feelings were expressed in his elegy for *Tibullus (Amores III. 9), also a member of Messalla's circle. Virgil he only saw. He was three times married and had one daughter, probably by his second wife. His third wife remained devoted to him, and loyal during his exile.

Ovid's poetry had made him a leading figure in the social and literary circles at Rome, when in AD 8 he was suddenly banished by Augustus to Tŏmis on the western shore of the Black Sea and his books removed from the public libraries. (He suffered only relegatio, which meant that he retained his property and civic rights at Rome, not the more severe exsilium.) According to Ovid himself the grounds for this sentence were two, carmen and error, that is, a poem and a blunder; the poem was the Ars amatoria, published eight years before. The error, which Ovid refers to only obliquely, but insists was not scelus, 'a crime', was connected with the Julian family to which Augustus belonged; Ovid seems to have been present when something culpable was done, perhaps being involved in one of the adulteries of Augustus' granddaughter Julia, also banished in AD 8. The error must have provided the occasion for the emperor to satisfy his resentment at the poem, which ran counter to his moralistic legislation and had been published and won enormous success soon after Augustus discovered his daughter *Julia (see (4)) to be a notorious adulteress (2 BC). Ovid has described in a famous poem (*Tristia* I. 3) his last sad night at Rome and the hardships of his voyage to Tomis, and many of the poems of the *Tristia* and the *Epistulae ex Ponto* (see below) attest the tedious years of boredom, deprivation, and even danger (from barbarian attack) he had to endure, as well as the rigours of the climate, in that bleak land. There he died after ten years of unbroken exile. He eventually became reconciled to its inhabitants: they were kind and considerate and won his esteem. Though the city was a Greek foundation, half the population was Getic and either spoke Greek with Getic accent or used the local language. Ovid not only learned the language but wrote in it a poem (which has not survived) in honour of Augustus and Tiberius.

The order in which Ovid wrote his works is difficult to establish but is roughly as follows (see under each name): *Amores*, of which the first edition may have appeared as early as 20 BC, the second shortly before the *Ars amatoria*; *Heroides*, published between the first and second editions of *Amores*; *Medicamina faciei femineae*, written before the third book of the *Ars amatoria*, i.e. perhaps before I BC; the first two books of the *Ars amatoria* (published not before I BC, the third book was added later); *Remedia amoris*, AD I; *Metamorphoses* and *Fasti* contemporaneously, from AD 2 onwards; *Tristia*, AD 9; *Ibis*, c. AD 11; *Epistulae ex Ponto* I–III, AD 13 (book IV probably appeared posthumously). A tragedy, *Medea*, was praised by Quintilian and Tacitus, but only two lines survive. The poems *Halieutica*, of which only a fragment survives, *Nux*, and *Consolatio ad Liviam*, all attributed to Ovid, were probably not by him. All Ovid's works are in elegiac couplets except for *Metamorphoses* (and *Halieutica*), in hexameters (see METRE).

Ovid was born in the year after the murder of Julius Caesar, too late to experience the horrors of civil war and so to welcome the policies of the Augustan regime. He was single-mindedly devoted to poetry, and his virtuosity, linguistic as well as metrical, was considerable. He refined even more strictly the rules of composition for the elegiac couplet. His wit and inventiveness make him the most consistently entertaining of the Roman poets, and a brilliant, sometimes over-exuberant, epigrammatist. Frivolous and irresponsible his poetry may sometimes seem, but when, as not infrequently happens, his imaginative sympathy is aroused, he can write movingly and simply, without artificiality or straining for effect. He is a gifted story-teller, skilful at focusing upon the telling scene or significant moment in a narrative, and with a sensitivity to natural beauty rare in the ancient world. The Elder Seneca has preserved a story

illustrating Ovid's fondness for verbal extravagance. He was once asked by his friends if they might choose three lines to be excised from his works. He agreed, on condition that he might choose three lines that were on no account to be sacrificed. The lines chosen on each side turned out to be the same. One of them was (of the Minotaur), *semibovemque virum semivirumque bovem*, 'a man half bull and a bull half man'.

As a story-teller and guide to Greek myth and Roman legend Ovid was very influential on later Roman writers and was read, quoted, and adapted during the Middle Ages. He was the favourite Latin poet of the Renaissance, and there were many translations of his works into English. Chaucer drew largely on him in the *Book of the Duchess, House of Fame, Legend of Good Women*, and, to a lesser extent, the *Canterbury Tales*. John Gower's *Confessio Amantis* (1390) has a multitude of Ovidian tales; Spenser's *Faerie Queen* contains many allusions to him. Marlowe's Faustus (*Dr Faustus*, pub. 1604) in his last speech movingly quotes the *Amores*: *O lente, lente, currite noctis equi* ('run slowly, slowly, horses of night'). Shakespeare knew the *Metamorphoses* in Golding's translation. The critic Francis Meres in his *Palladis Tamia* (1598) made the well-known observation that 'the sweet witty soul of Ovid lives in mellifluous and honey-tongued Shakespeare, witness his *Venus and Adonis*, his *Lucrece*, his sugared sonnets among his private friends'. *As You Like It* (III. 3. 9) has a reference to Ovid's exile 'among the Goths'. The line in *Romeo and Juliet*, 'At lovers' perjuries they say Jove laughs' (II. 2) is a translation from the *Ars amatoria*. The *Taming of the Shrew* (III. 9) gives two lines from the *Heroides*.

Oxyrhy'nchus (El Bahnasa), place in Upper Egypt, south of the Faiyum, where many ancient papyri, some of literary importance, have been found from the last decade of the nineteenth century onwards. Very little is known of the history of the town. See PAPYROLOGY.

Oxyrhy'nchus historian, the, Greek historian, unknown by name, fragments of whose work were discovered at *Oxyrhynchus in 1906 on papyri containing about 900 lines of prose. These covered in detail and in a style commanding considerable respect events in the Greek world from 396 to 395 BC. The close agreement between *Diodorus Siculus and the Oxyrhynchus historian, where the two can be compared, shows that the latter was used by Diodorus' source *Ephorus himself. This fact has led to the realization that Diodorus is a more reliable source at this point than had hitherto been thought.

P

Pactō'lus, tributary of the river Hermus in Lydia; its sands contained gold. See MIDAS.

Pacu'vius, Marcus (220–*c*.130 BC), Roman writer of tragedies (and also a painter), nephew of the poet Ennius, born at Brundisium. There exist the titles and fragments of twelve tragedies, based on Greek originals, and of one *fabula* *praetexta (a drama having its subject in Roman history) on Paullus (probably L. Aemilius *Paullus). Of the titles, only *Antiopa* (Gk. *Antiopē*), his most famous work, indicates an original by Euripides (contrast *Ennius and *Accius); the original of *Niptra* ('the foot-washing', of Odysseus by his old nurse) was probably by Sophocles; other titles suggest post-Euripidean originals. The poets *Lucilius and *Persius ridiculed certain peculiarities of his diction, especially compound adjectives, but his work showed command of pathos and passion, and impressive character drawing. He was known as *doctus*, 'learned', a term of high praise, probably on account of his Grecisms and his familiarity with lesser-known stories of Greek legend. Varro and Cicero looked upon him as the greatest of Roman tragedians; the latter in his *De amicitia* testifies to the popular enthusiasm with which a scene in Pacuvius' *Orestes* was received.

Paean (Paiān or Paiōn). In the *Linear B tablets and in two passages in Homer's *Iliad*, Paian (Paion) appears as the name of a healing god. Also in Homer, and in later Greek literature, the name is given to the Olympian god *Apollo in his aspect of a god of healing who drives out pestilence, averts evil, and brings about victory. The cult hymn of Apollo is called a paean, from the cry *iē, ie Paian*, which came to be used as a refrain. Literary sources say that the paean was introduced to Sparta from Crete as a healing hymn and dance at the beginning of the seventh century BC, and was particularly associated with feasts of Apollo in Sparta. Later the paean could be addressed to other gods also: Sophocles is said to have composed one to Asclepius, and Xenophon in his *Anabasis* describes the Greeks singing a paean to Zeus. Several paeans by Pindar have been discovered, in a rather fragmentary condition, on papyri. For the metrical term *paeon* see METRE, GREEK I.

paedagō'gus, in Greece, a slave employed to take boys to and from school. See EDUCATION I.

Paeli'gni, central Italian tribe inhabiting the high valleys of the Apennines east of Rome. They were allies of Rome before 300 BC and remained loyal until the Social War (see ROME 6) when their chief town, Corfinium, became the capital of the Italians. They were rapidly Romanized after 90 BC. In their territory lay Sulmo, birthplace of Ovid.

paeon, see PAEAN and METRE, GREEK I.

Paestum (Gk. Poseidonia), Roman name for a coastal town of Lucania in south Italy, originally a Greek colony founded by *Sybaris *c*.600 BC. Rome made it a Latin colony in 273 BC. It is famous for its Greek temples, of which the fine ruins still remain. Virgil speaks of its roses flowering twice a year.

Paetus, see ARRIA.

Pāgānā'lia, at Rome, the celebration in the *pagi* (hamlets) of the sowing, a festival associated with the earth-goddesses Ceres and Tellus, who according to Ovid were then invoked to protect the seed. The date for its celebration was not fixed.

pāgā'nus ('pagan'), the inhabitant of a *pagus*, 'hamlet', the smallest division of the community in the Italian countryside. By the first century AD it had acquired the contemptuous sense of 'one who stays at home' (i.e. a civilian, in contrast with a soldier), and hence in Christian writers 'one who is not a soldier of Christ', 'a heathen'. It has also been suggested that its last meaning is derived from the sense of 'rustic', 'uncultured'.

painting. Palaces in Minoan Crete and in Mycenaean Greece during the second millennium BC were decorated with large fresco paintings (that is, paintings on wet plaster), but, like much else, knowledge of the art of painting disappeared in Greece in the subsequent *Dark Age. Figure-painting reappeared on vases in the eighth century BC (see VASE-PAINTING, GREEK). Apart from vases, the surviving remains of Greek painting are very few, and none of the first rank; it is a measure of how much has been lost that the Roman critics thought as highly of Greek painting as of Greek sculpture. From the seventh century BC there are some painted slabs of stone and terracotta (fired after being painted), from the sixth century BC a few wooden plaques, and from the early fifth century the wall paintings of the underground tombs from (Greek) Etruria in Italy. There is also the indirect evidence from vase-painting, which as well as occasionally copying actual pictures imitated the techniques of large-scale painting, and there are some later Roman copies of Greek originals which have survived (notably the mosaic in the House of the Faun at Pompeii depicting the battle between Alexander the Great and Darius III at Issus, derived from a contemporary Greek painting by Philoxenus).

Most painting was done on walls or on wooden panels first coated with white paint, and from the seventh century BC a good range of colours was available. For the techniques used we depend largely on the statements of the Elder Pliny, Pausanias, and Lucian: for walls, there were fresco-painting and tempera (which used some sticky medium); for wood and marble, tempera and encaustic. In the encaustic method, which is not fully understood, the colours were mixed with wax, applied to the surface, and then burnt in with a red-hot rod; this imparted some of the richness of tone associated with oil-painting, a medium unknown to the Greeks.

*Polygnotus of Thasos (first half of the fifth century BC) was the first great master, much of whose work was done in or near Athens and was still to be seen 600 years later. His figures were celebrated for their representation of character (*ēthos*) and simple dignity. He represented depth by setting figures at different levels and showed them thrusting backwards or forwards out of the plane of the surface. (See under DELPHI for his paintings in the Cnidian Leschē described by Pausanias.) Another well-known painter and sculptor of this period was Micon of Athens. There was at this stage no use of perspective; the technique was to make outline drawings with economical linear detail and cover them with flat washes of colour. Modelling by hatching or by gradation of colour seems to have come slowly, but by the middle of the fifth century such shading was used for rounded objects, while folds were depicted with thickened lines to suggest depth. In the late fifth century Apollodorus was called 'shadow painter' (*skiagraphos*) which suggests that he was the first to use shadowing to any extent. His younger contemporary *Zeuxis is said to have gone further in this respect. Cast shadows appear in the late fourth century BC but were not much found until the third. The most popular subjects in the early period were mythological figures, arranged in small groups: Perseus rescuing Andromeda, for example. Some large compositions, especially battle pieces, were executed. *Parrhasius, another painter of the late fifth century, was famed for his sketches. Caricature appeared at the end of that century, still-life painting certainly by the next, and portraiture in the mid-fourth century (see APELLES). It is not clear when perspective was understood: Attic vase-painters were content with occasional foreshortening of furniture.

In the first century AD the architectural vistas painted at Pompeii show that a rudimentary perspective was understood by then.

Greek traditions of painting continued into Hellenistic and Roman times. It has been conjectured that landscape painting first appeared in Hellenistic times, perhaps in the second century BC at Alexandria, as part of the new appreciation of nature evident in, for example, the *Idylls* of Theocritus. In Italy soon after 100 BC there appeared frescos, decorating the interior walls of houses, which aimed to give an illusion of three-dimensional space. The subjects were often taken from Greek myths, either whole scenes or single figures such as Orpheus or a centaur, and put in an architectural setting of great splendour and fantastic complexity. Part of a frieze depicting scenes from Homer's *Odyssey* has been found from a house on the Esquiline hill at Rome, dating from the middle of the first century BC. A large number of wall-paintings has been recovered from Pompeii, Herculaneum, and Stabiae (about 6 km. or 4 miles south of Pompeii and buried in the same eruption of AD 79); they include scenes of contemporary life, and many show great beauty of colour, line, and expression. A notable painting of the Augustan period is the so-called Garden of Livia from Livia's villa at Prima Porta, showing a park beyond a low wooden fence, the dark green trees glittering with brilliantly coloured birds and fruit. Roman artists also produced some pleasing still-life paintings, arrangements of fruit and eggs with domestic tableware, showing interest in the minutiae of simple domestic life, in a manner again reminiscent of Hellenistic Greece.

By the fourth century AD technical standards were falling. The same styles lasted for the next 300 years, but by AD 700 the characteristic Byzantine style was becoming established in the East, while in western Europe the barbarian invasions had more or less destroyed the art of painting in the tradition originated by the Greeks.

Palae'mon, in Greek myth, a sea-god. See DIONYSUS.

Palae'mon, Quintus Remmius, at Rome, in the first century AD, a former slave who became a famous grammarian and teacher, mentioned by Juvenal. His pupils included Persius and Quintilian. Martial refers slightingly to his poetry. His book on Latin grammar, now lost, was the basis of subsequent grammars.

palaeo'graphy. Palaeography is the study of manuscripts or their equivalent (e.g. papyri and wax tablets) in respect of their handwriting, and includes the study of variations in the latter which help to establish date and place of writing. It is also concerned with the layout of the writing on the page and with the form of the book. See also BOOKS AND WRITING.

palae'stra ('wrestling school'), in Greek cities, the place where boys were instructed in wrestling and gymnastics (see ATHLETICS (ii)). It was generally in private ownership (in contrast with the municipally owned *gymnasium). In essentials it consisted of a central courtyard, the ground covered in fine sand, surrounded by changing rooms.

Palamē'dēs, in Greek myth, a proverbially ingenious hero, son of Nauplius, said to have invented some of the letters of the alphabet and the game of draughts. When *Odysseus tried to avoid his obligation to join in the expedition to Troy by pretending to be mad, Palamedes exposed his deceit. In revenge Odysseus forged a letter purporting to come from king Priam of Troy arranging for Palamedes to betray the Greeks in return for gold. Palamedes, in whose tent Odysseus hid the gold, was consequently stoned to death by the army. Nauplius avenged his son by luring the Greek fleet, returning from Troy, on to the rocks of Euboea by false beacons.

Pa'latine (Palātīnus mons), chief of the seven hills of Rome and traditionally the site of the first Roman settlement (see ROME I). Traces of Iron Age occupation have been found. It was here that Aeneas was shown by Evander (*Aeneid*, book 8) the cave of Lupercal (see LUPERCALIA). From 330 BC at the latest many famous Romans chose to build their houses on the hill, including in their day Hortensius, Cicero, Crassus, Milo, and Mark Antony. The house of Hortensius was acquired by the emperor Augustus and became the nucleus of a group of buildings known as *palatia* (pl.), from which the English word 'palace' is derived. Nero made important additions before and after the great fire of AD 64. After the conquest of Italy in the sixth century AD by the Byzantine emperor Justinian, the palace became the seat of the Byzantine governor.

Pa'latine Anthology, see ANTHOLOGY I.

Pālēs, in Roman religion, a deity of flocks and shepherds, similar to Pan among the Greeks, male according to Varro and others, female according to Virgil and Ovid. The festival of Pales, the Parilia, took place on 21 April, the traditional 'birthday' of Rome (and still regarded as such). It seems to have been a ritual purification of shepherds and flocks, firmly connected (for reasons which remain obscure) with the foundation of Rome. The sheep pens were cleaned and decorated with greenery, and sulphur was burnt on bonfires so that the smoke purified the sheep; offerings of cake and milk were made to Pales. The shepherd washed himself in dew, drank milk, and leaped through the bonfire. At the urban celebration of the festival the ashes of the calves burnt at the *Fordicidia were sprinkled on the fire. Ovid believed that the Parilia were older than Rome itself.

palimpsest (*palimpsēstos*, 'scraped again'), manuscript in which the text has been written over an effaced earlier text. The practice of writing on the renovated surface of an old manuscript was frequent among the monks of the Middle Ages, and since perfect removal of the original writing was seldom achieved, it has proved possible to recover valuable old texts of e.g. the Bible, Cicero, and Plautus.

Palino'dia, see STESICHORUS.

Palinū'rus, in Virgil's *Aeneid* (books 5 and 6), the helmsman of Aeneas, who, overcome by the god of sleep, fell overboard, was washed up on the shore of Italy and there murdered by the inhabitants. Aeneas, visiting the Underworld, met his ghost; it had not crossed the river Styx because his body remained unburied. A tomb was subsequently erected to Palinurus, and a cape (on the west coast of Italy) named after him.

palla, at Rome, a woman's mantle; see DRESS 3.

Pa'lladas, Greek writer of *epigrams who lived at Alexandria *c.* AD 400. About 150 of his poems are in the Greek *Anthology. He was a schoolmaster embittered by poverty, and a pagan, or at least agnostic, in an age of expanding Christianity. His bitterness, vigorously expressed, and his cold pessimism recall the manner of classical Greek poetry, but sound a wholly individual note.

Pallā'dium, an image of the Greek goddess *Pallas Athena, identified by the Romans with Minerva, said to have been sent down from heaven by Zeus to *Dardanus, the founder of Troy (or to his son Ilus). Since Troy could not be captured while it contained this image, legend related that the Greek heroes Diomedēs and Odysseus carried it off and thus made it possible for the Greeks to sack Troy. It is variously said to have found its way to Athens, or Argos, or Sparta, or Rome. The Romans believed that an image in the temple of *Vesta, thought to have saved Rome from the attack of the Gauls in 390 BC, was the Palladium, either brought safely to Rome by the Trojan Aeneas after the sack (Diomedes having succeeded in stealing merely a copy) or else surrendered by Diomedes. When the temple of Vesta caught fire in 241 BC the image was rescued by the *pontifex* L. Metellus at the cost of his eyesight. Whatever its origin, it seems clear that such a talismanic object was kept in Rome. For the Palladium at Athens see ERECHTHEUM.

Palla'dius (Palladius Publius Rutilius Taurus

Aemilianus), author in the fourth century AD of a Latin treatise on agriculture (*De re rustica*) in fourteen books, with an appendix in elegiacs on grafting trees. The first book contains general directions on the choice of a site, on farm buildings, the management of poultry, and agricultural implements. The next twelve books deal with the work to be done on the farm in each month. The fourteenth book, published for the first time in 1926, is on veterinary medicine. The work was quite well known in later times and a translation was made into Middle English.

Pallăs, title of the Greek goddess *Athena (who is often called Pallas Athena); suggested meanings include 'maiden' and 'brandisher' (of weapons). A late legend says that Pallas was the friend of Athena whom the goddess accidentally killed. See PALLADIUM.

Pallās, in Greek myth, the name of (i) a Titan, (ii) a giant, (iii) an Attic hero; none is of particular importance. It was also the name of (iv) an Arcadian hero, founder of the city of Pallanteion, the grandfather of Euandros (see EVANDER) who figures in the story of the founding of Rome; and (v) the son of Evander, who accompanies Aeneas to the war against the Italians and is killed by Turnus.

palliā'ta, fā'bula, in Latin literature, term applied to Roman comedies adapted or imitated from Greek comedies, for instance the plays of Plautus and Terence. The name is derived from *pallium*, a Greek cloak. Compare PRAETEXTA.

Palmy̆'ra, oasis-city between Syria and Babylonia, whose trade it organized. In Roman imperial times it was an independent city between the Roman and Parthian empires, and in the early third century AD supported Rome. For its rise to prominence thereafter see ZENOBIA.

Pan, Greek god of shepherds and of flocks, for whose fertility he is responsible. Native to Arcadia, where he was born on Mount *Lycaeus, he has a human torso and arms but the legs, ears, and horns of a goat. He is generally thought to be the son of *Hermēs (the only other Arcadian god of importance), but his mother is variously named; she is generally a nymph, often *Callisto, but some stories say she is Penelopē. Pan has little mythology; a late story tells how he invented the musical pipe of seven reeds which he named *syrinx* in honour of the nymph of that name whom he loved and who was changed into a reed in order to escape from him. Other stories describe how he also loved the nymphs Pitys and Echo, who when they fled from him were changed respectively into a pine tree and a voice that can only repeat the last words spoken to her. Generally he loves mountains, caves, and lonely places; he was reputed to be the cause of sudden groundless fear, 'panic', especially that which may be felt in such remote surroundings. His cult began to spread beyond Arcadia in the early fifth century BC. Herodotus (6. 105) tells how in 490 BC Pan appeared to the Athenian runner *Pheidippidēs and promised help against the Persians, as a consequence of which the Athenians gave him after the battle of Marathon (490 BC) a cave-shrine on the Acropolis, still to be seen on the north slope.

A famous story narrated by Plutarch tells how, in the reign of the Roman emperor Tiberius (AD 14–37), the passengers in a ship sailing along the west coast of Greece heard a great voice shouting from the direction of the islands of Paxi that the god Pan was dead. In Christian legend this story was associated with the death and resurrection of Christ, which entailed the death of the pagan gods. Since his name is also the Greek word 'all', and the classical Greeks themselves sometimes understood the name to have this meaning, in later times speculations concerning a universal god were attached to his name. Sometimes a collection of Pans is found, the god's individuality submerged in a generalized representation of pastoral nature. By the Romans he was identified with *Faunus.

Panae'tius (*c*.185–109 BC), of Rhodes, Greek *Stoic philosopher. In *c*.144 he went to Rome and joined the circle of P. *Scipio Aemilianus, whom he accompanied on a mission to Egypt and Asia. After his return *c*.138 he divided his time between Rome and Athens; in 129 he succeeded Antipater as head of the Stoic school in Athens, and there he died. He adapted Stoic doctrine to fit Roman ideals, dwelling on the active virtues of magnanimity and benevolence rather than the passive virtues of indifference to misfortune and danger and of avoiding wrong-doing; he emphasized the subordination of private ambition to the good of the state, conformity to the same standard of virtue in public and private life, and the suppression of self-indulgence. The most important of his works was *On Duty* (now lost), on which Cicero modelled his own *De officiis*. He was a powerful influence on Roman thought.

Panathēnae'a, ancient Athenian festival supposedly founded in the time of *Theseus in honour of the birth of Athena, the patron goddess of the city, and held every year at the end of July. For three out of four years it was held on 28 and 29 Hekatombaion (July) and called the Lesser Panathenaea, but starting from the archonship of *Hippocleidēs in 566/5 BC it was celebrated with particular splendour every fourth year, when it lasted from 21 to 28 Hekatombaion and was called the Great Panathenaea. The augmented festival included games, horse-races, and musical contests, to which the Peisistratids added poetical recitations by *rhapsodes. The equestrian events were held on that part of the Panathenaic Way (from the Dipylon Gate to the Acropolis) which crossed the agora. Pericles extended the musical contests and built a special theatre, the Odeum, for them. The prizes at the athletic contests were beautiful vases (some of which still survive, the earliest dated 570–560 BC) filled with olive oil; as many as 140 of them were given as the principal prize. The festival culminated on the last day in a magnificent procession along the Panathenaic Way and up to the Parthenon, in which Athena's new robe, a *peplos* (see DRESS 1), was carried to her statue (see ERECHTHEUM). This peplos was a costly garment, woven by Athenian girls of good family and embroidered with a representation of the struggle between Athena and the Giants. Living personages were sometimes represented in the embroidery, and it was a signal honour for a girl to be thought 'worthy of the peplos'. It was carried on a great ship on wheels, followed by girls known as *arrēphoroi* bearing baskets with the implements of sacrifice, by groups of boys bearing pitchers and old men with olive branches, by chariots, and finally by a cavalcade of young men on horseback (as depicted on the frieze of the Parthenon). The feast was completed with a *hecatomb of oxen, the flesh distributed among the people. In the fifth century BC the Panathenaea had not only a civic but a political character, being held in honour of the patroness not of the city alone but of the *Delian League also; the part taken by the allies in the sacrifices was regulated by decrees.

Panathēnā'icus, late work by *Isocratēs in praise of Athens.

pancra'tion, see ATHLETICS (iv).

Pa'ndarus, in Homer's *Iliad*, son of *Lycaon and leader, in the Trojan War, of the Trojans who lived about the foot of Mount Ida. He breaks the truce and wounds Menelaus with an arrow, and is eventually killed by Diomedēs. The story of his relations with Troilus and Cressida as told by Chaucer and by Shakespeare is derived ultimately from the work of *Dictys Cretensis and *Darēs Phrygius. His name survives in the English 'pander'.

Pandects (*pandectae*, 'digests'), one of the four parts of the corpus of Roman law drawn up by the emperor *Justinian.

Pandi'on, legendary king of Athens, variously described as grandson or great-grandson of *Erechtheus, or son of Erichthonius. He was father of *Philomela and Procnē.

Pandō'ra, in Greek myth, the first woman; see PROMETHEUS.

panegyric (*panēgўris*), see FESTIVALS.

Panegy'rici. 1. For the panegyric of Isocratēs see ISOCRATES.

2. For the panegyric on Trajan by Pliny see PLINY THE YOUNGER.

3. A collection of eleven complimentary speeches in Latin by rhetoricians, ranging in date from AD 289 to 389, in honour of the emperors of this time, chiefly Maximian, Constantius, Constantine I and II, Julian, and Theodosius. The collection also contains Pliny's panegyric (see 2 above) on which the later speeches were modelled. They were composed in the rhetorical schools of Gaul and have little literary merit, except as examples of pure Pliny-like Latinity, but throw much light on the history of fourth-century Gaul.

panhellē'nic, involving all the Greek states and colonies.

Paniō'nium, see POSEIDON.

Panthe'on or **Pa'ntheon,** at Rome, a magnificent temple consecrated, as the name implies, to all the gods, built by Hadrian (emperor AD 117–38) to replace that of M. Agrippa built 27–25 BC in the Campus Martius. It consists of a rotunda with a pedimented portico of granite columns in the Corinthian style; the interior was richly decorated in marble, and there were niches for statues of various gods. The walls and ancient bronze doors still survive. It was dedicated as a Christian church by Pope Boniface IV in AD 609.

pantomime, form of dramatic entertainment among the Romans in which a single actor/dancer (*pantomimus*) mimed a story in dumb show, playing all the parts himself, supported by a chorus of singers and a small orchestra. The stories chosen were almost entirely mythological. Pantomime in this form was introduced to Rome in 22 BC by Pyladēs of Cilicia (in southeast Asia Minor) and Bathyllus of Alexandria; hitherto in Rome dumb shows had been enacted by individuals, but it was Pylades' innovation to introduce chorus and orchestra. Bathyllus was so popular in this form of drama that his name came to be used for any pantomime actor. Performances took place on the public stage and privately. The actor wore a graceful silk costume and a mask with closed lips. The songs of the chorus were of minor importance; surviving fragments are in Greek. Pantomime and *mime, the delicate sophistication of the former contrasting with the coarseness of the latter, came to dominate the Roman stage, and contributed to the decline of serious drama there.

Panya'ssis, of Halicarnassus, older kinsman of Herodotus and the last great epic poet of archaic Greece (i.e. of the period before 480 BC), who lived in the early part of the fifth century and was put to death for his political activities by Lygdamis, tyrant of Halicarnassus, in the 460s or early 450s. He wrote two works: on Heraclēs, the *Heracleia* (9,000 lines in fourteen books), of which a few fragments remain, and on the Ionian colonial settlements, the *Ionica* (7,000 lines, and perhaps written in elegiacs: see METRE), of which poem, as far as is known, nothing survives. Panyassis' language appears to be basically Homeric, but includes some unusual words. The fragments of the *Heracleia*, few as they are, still provide valuable information about Greek myths and legends.

Paphos, city near the south-west coast of Cyprus, where according to tradition Aphroditē was born from the sea-foam, and the site of an ancient and widely famed temple to that goddess. This temple seems to date originally from the twelfth century BC, when the Mycenaean Greeks settled there (traditionally, the Arcadian contingent on their way back from Troy, led by Agapenor). Already in Homer's *Odyssey* Paphos is the home of Aphrodite. See also CYPRUS.

Papi'nian (Aemilius Pāpiniānus), d. AD 212, famous Roman jurist during the late second and early third centuries, the 'classical' period of jurisprudence. His origins are unknown: he may have come from Syria or Africa. He accompanied the emperor Severus to Britain and took part in the imperial tribunals held at York. In 203 he became praetorian prefect (see PRAEFECTUS PRAETORIO), assisted by the equally brilliant jurists *Paulus and *Ulpian (see LAW, AT ROME 3). After the death of Severus the latter's son Caracalla succeeded to the throne; it is said that, having murdered his brother Geta, he asked Papinian to defend his action before the senate. Papinian replied that fratricide was not so easy to defend as to commit, whereupon Caracalla put him to death. His principal works were thirty-seven books of *Quaestiōnēs* (discussions of hypothetical or actual cases), and nineteen books of *Responsa* (collections of opinions); there are many excerpts from them in the Digest of *Justinian.

papyro'logy, the decipherment and elucidation of anything written on papyrus, and the study of the papyrus roll as a form of book. For the manufacture and uses of papyrus see BOOKS AND WRITING 2. Most papyri discovered in modern times come from Egypt where the rainless climate favours their survival. Some few have come from other places where particular circumstances have ensured their preservation (see DERVENI PAPYRUS and HERCULANEUM). After its conquest by Alexander the Great in 332 BC Egypt became a Greek-speaking region, a fortunate circumstance for the survival of Greek literary texts; many of these were read in Egypt and their remains have been among the papyri discovered. Some of the Egyptian papyri have been found in tombs and in mummy-casings, but most come from the rubbish heaps of towns

abandoned when the irrigation levels dropped. Serious excavations began in the nineteenth century, and at *Oxyrhynchus in particular. The earliest papyrus book we have, the *Persae* of *Timotheus, dates from the fourth century BC. Since many of the papyri are of school texts, and the *education available was the traditional Greek one, more than half of the several thousand surviving literary papyri are of Homer. Of the rest, fragments of works hitherto unknown slightly outnumber the fragments of works already familiar. New texts discovered include several plays of Menander (mostly incomplete), much of Bacchylidēs, some poems of Sappho, Pindar, and other lyric poets, much of Callimachus, the mimes of Herodas, the *Ichneutae* of Sophoclēs, and several other sizeable fragments of tragedy; and, in prose, Aristotle's *Constitution of Athens*, the *Hellenica Oxyrhynchia* (a history continuing that of Thucydides), and several speeches of Hypereidēs. Other papyri contain fragmentary scientific and medical texts, and works on astrology and magic, important as social documents. Discoveries of Christian literary papyri have been equally important, adding further testimony to works already known, most valuably in the case of the New Testament text, and revealing hitherto unknown works, for example the *Sayings of Jesus* (part of the Gnostic *Gospel of Thomas*).

Most of the papyri discovered are not literary but documentary: private letters and accounts, legal and administrative documents. These have greatly illuminated the social and economic life of Egypt throughout several hundred years, when it was under the rule first of the Ptolemies, then of Rome, and finally of Byzantium, and thus under Hellenistic Greek followed by Roman law, and under different administrative systems. A great deal has been learnt about the Greek language at various periods, in its most educated and in its semi-literate forms; in particular, the language of contemporary documents has thrown new light on the syntax, vocabulary, and idiom of the New Testament.

Latin papyri have been found in Egypt and a few other places but are comparatively rare. After Egypt had been incorporated into the Roman empire in 30 BC, because of its wealth it remained under the private control of the emperor, and for the first two centuries AD few Romans other than the military visited it. It may be that one of the latter owned the near-contemporary papyrus of the poems of *Gallus, of which a tiny scrap has preserved what are, if genuine, almost the only lines of the poet now known. Also near-contemporary is a fragment of Cicero's speeches against Verrēs (see CICERO (1) 1). In the late third century AD the emperor Diocletian opened up Egypt, making it equal in status to the rest of the empire and encouraging all the eastern provinces in the use of Latin, knowledge of which was essential for a public career. Most of the Latin papyri date from the centuries following this reform; they are largely legal documents and military archives, and occasionally private letters. Nearly all papyrus fragments of Latin literary texts belong to prose works, but there are important papyri of Juvenal and of Terence's *Andria*. Some fragments of Christian texts have been found, including one of a trilingual phrase-book in Greek, Coptic, and Latin, presumably of use to those intending to visit the monasteries.

para'basis, see COMEDY, GREEK 3.

pa'raloi or **para'lioi** ('coastmen'), see PEISISTRATUS.

Pa'ralos, name of one of the two warships kept by the Athenians for ceremonial and exceptional purposes, in which none but citizens might serve. (The other was *Salaminia*.)

parasang, Persian unit of length, very roughly equivalent to 3 miles (see WEIGHTS AND MEASURES I (ii)).

parasite (*parasītos*), in Greek, originally 'fellow-diner', 'guest'. In the Old Comedy of the fifth century BC it had acquired the pejorative sense of 'sponger', one who earns a meal by flattering and humouring his host. To judge from surviving titles, the parasite often played a leading role in Middle Comedy; in New Comedy he is a stock character, the companion of another of the same, the boastful soldier, whose vanity he flatters in return for being kept. The names of notorious parasites in real life appear in some comedies. See COMEDY, GREEK.

Parcae, see FATES.

Parentā'lia, at Rome, the festival of the dead (13–21 February), on the last day of which was a public ceremony, the *Feralia; the rest of the time was reserved for private commemorations at family graves. During this period magistrates did not wear the insignia of office, temples were closed, and marriages forbidden. Some of the days, however, were *comitialēs* (days on which public assemblies might be held; see CALENDARS, 5). Immediately after the Parentalia, on 22 February, the Caristia were celebrated, a family reunion and worship of the *lar familiaris* (see LARES), and an acknowledgement of the relationship existing between the dead and living members of the family.

Parian Chronicle or **Marble,** see MARMOR PARIUM.

Parī'lia, see PALES.

Paris. I. In Greek myth, a son of *Priam king of Troy and his wife *Hecuba, also called Alexander (Alexandros). He was exposed when he was born because his mother had dreamed that she would bear a firebrand which would destroy the whole city, and a seer foretold that he would bring destruction on Troy. However, he was rescued and brought up by shepherds, and passed his youth pasturing sheep on Mount Ida, wedded to the nymph *Oenōnē. He had a favourite bull which Priam's servants carried off to be the prize at some funeral games. Paris, determined to win back the animal, entered for the games, won every event, and was identified by Priam's daughter Cassandra and restored to the family. Priam sent Paris on an embassy to Menelaus, king of Sparta, whose wife Helen fell in love with him (see PARIS, JUDGEMENT OF). They fled together to Troy, thus bringing about the Trojan War, in which Paris, a skilful archer, took part. Homer represents him as affectedly bold and self-consciously martial in appearance, but unable to withstand the onslaught of Menelaus. In the single combat between the two, to decide the war, Paris was dragged off by Menelaus and had to be rescued by Aphroditē. It was his arrow, guided by Apollo, which finally killed Achilles. At the fall of the city he was fatally wounded by a poisoned arrow from *Philoctētēs' bow (which had belonged to Heraclēs) and sought, in vain, a cure from the nymph Oenone whom he had deserted.

2. The name of two popular *pantomime dancers, one of whom was executed by order of the emperor Nero (AD 67), the other by Domitian (AD 87). For one of them the poet *Statius wrote his libretto *Agavē*.

Paris, Judgement of. In Greek myth, at the marriage feast of *Peleus and the goddess Thetis, Eris (Discord) threw down a golden apple (the 'apple of Discord') inscribed 'for the most beautiful'. The goddesses Hera, Athena, and Aphroditē all claimed it, and they applied to Paris, the most handsome of mortal men, then a shepherd on Mount Ida near Troy, to settle the dispute. Each goddess offered him a reward in return for the apple: Hera greatness, Athena success in war, and Aphrodite the most beautiful woman in the world as his wife (compare the 'choice of *Heraclēs'). Paris awarded the apple to Aphrodite, and with her help carried off *Helen. It was ultimately this judgement which brought about the Trojan War, but it is not an aspect of the story used by Homer: he retains the hostility of Hera and Athena for Troy, but leaves it unexplained.

Parme'nidēs (*c.*515–after 450 BC), Greek philosopher from Elea (Lat. Velia) in south-west Italy, a Greek colony founded in 540 BC by Phocaea, the most northerly of the Ionian Greek cities in Asia Minor. He is said to have given laws to his city. According to tradition he was a pupil of, but did not follow, the Ionian philosopher *Xenophanēs, preferring to associate with Pythagoreans. He is said to have visited Athens late in his life and to have met Socrates (see PLATO 2 for the dialogue *Parmenides* in which he is one of the chief interlocutors). He was the founder of the so-called *Eleatic school of philosophy, and the first Greek philosopher whose doctrines survive fairly intact; they are found in a coherent series of quotations from the (lost) didactic poem in which he set out his thought. Written in hexameters, the poem consists of a prologue and two sections called the *Way of Truth* and the *Way of Seeming*.

The prologue opens with an allegory describing Parmenides' journey by chariot through the gate that leads from Night to Day, i.e. from false reasoning to true reasoning, the latter represented by a goddess who proceeds, in the *Way of Truth*, to tell the philosopher the truth of things as they really are. She begins by defining the two possible ways of enquiry, each contrary to the other: either a thing 'is, and cannot not-be'; or it 'is not, and must not-be'. The latter way is rejected on the grounds that it is impossible to conceive of the non-existent: one can only think or speak about 'what is'. There is a third way which combines the two others: ordinary mortals, deluded by their sense perceptions, believe that a thing both is and is not ('what is' can become something different, i.e. what it hitherto was not, by means of change). This too is rejected, on the grounds that it is self-contradictory. Once the premiss 'a thing is' is established by elimination as the only possibility, Parmenides (in the person of the goddess) deduces all that follows from it: 'what is' is not subject to birth or decay; it is single and not divisible; it is complete in itself and unchanging. All of these conclusions are reached by reason alone, without appeal to the senses.

This section is followed by the *Way of Seeming*, in which the goddess, starting from an acceptance of the opposites light and darkness, builds up a cosmology which apparently represents the erroneous beliefs of men, based on the senses. Since Parmenides rejects these, believing only in the *Way of Truth*, and since in any case his cosmology had little apparent influence later, it hardly matters that the text of this part is too fragmentary to permit reconstruction. But in describing a self-consistent cosmology Parmenides seems here to be admitting the possibility of structure and pattern in the world of the senses. The mutually exclusive nature of the two Ways may indicate that Parmenides considered the world as explained by the senses and the world as explained by reason to be utterly different and unrelated constructions, only the latter representing reality. The interest of the *Way of Seeming* lies also in the incidental fact that Parmenides here implies, for the first time in Greek thought, the requirements of a scientific theory, that it should account for and correspond with all the observed phenomena, and should be coherent and systematic. The doctrines of Parmenides (and of his formidably brilliant disciple *Zeno) offend against experience and common sense, but he was the most

influential of the Presocratic philosophers; he had shown that even what men regard as fundamentally true was open to question. (For the answer of the atomists to Parmenides see DEMOCRITUS.)

Parme'nidēs, dialogue by Plato (see PLATO 2).

Parna'ssus, in Greece, a mountain a few miles north of Delphi, rising to about 2,460 m. (8,070 ft.). The towns of Phocis lie on its eastern flank, and the plain of Crisa with the high valley of Delphi on the south. On it were the *Corycian cave and the Castalian spring (see CASTALIA), and the whole mountain, as well as the spring, was sacred, associated with the worship of Apollo and the Muses. The two peaks between which the Castalia flows were sometimes spoken of as the two peaks of Parnassus, but the summit is in reality hundreds of metres above them.

pa'rodos, see TRAGEDY 3 and COMEDY, GREEK 3.

parody. Burlesquing serious poetry for comic effect was known in Greek literature from very early times. It might have been possible to see the *Margitēs* (perhaps *c*.700 BC) as a parody of Homeric epic had more of it survived. One tradition ascribes the invention of parody to *Hipponax (mid-sixth century BC); Aristotle in the *Poetics* attributes its invention to Hegemon of Thasos, who was later than Hipponax and may have been the first to win a contest for parodies. In surviving Greek literature the most notable parodists are Aristophanēs, Plato, and Lucian. The first has a wide range, but mostly parodies tragic style in general and that of Euripidēs in particular, exploiting the comic possibilities in the latter's idiosyncracies of style and thought. Plato's parodies, of the style and manner of his interlocutors, are more subtle and have more than humorous ends in view; those of the participants in the *Symposium* are the most obviously funny; scholars still debate whether the speech purportedly by *Lysias in *Phaedrus* really is by him or by Plato. Lucian's parodies, often at the expense of the Olympian gods as they are depicted in mythology, are very funny in an obvious way.

In Latin literature parody occurs less often. Roman comedy burlesques in the Aristophanic manner the linguistic pomposities of Ennius and Pacuvius, but to a much lesser degree. The only sustained Latin parody is in the tenth poem of the *Catalepton* (see APPENDIX VIRGILIANA), in which Catullus' address to his yacht (poem 4) is turned into an address to an officious magistrate.

paroe'miac, see METRE, GREEK 7 (at the end).

paronoma'sia, in figures of speech, a play on words, a pun.

Parrha'sius, of Ephesus, a famous Greek painter who lived *c*.400 BC and practised mostly at

Athens. According to Pliny his chief merits lay in his accurate drawing, truth of proportion, and power of expression. Among his famous pictures were the *Athenian People* (apparently showing their various qualities, anger, injustice, mutability, leniency, mercy, pity, etc.), and the *Theseus* (of this it was said by *Euphranor that Theseus must have been fed upon roses). The story of his contest with the younger painter *Zeuxis in producing illusion is well-known. Zeuxis painted some grapes so perfectly that birds came to peck at them, and victory seemed to be his. He then asked Parrhasius to draw back the curtain concealing the latter's picture, but the curtain turned out to have been painted by Parrhasius, and Zeuxis declared himself defeated.

parthenei'on ('maiden song'), form of Greek choral *lyric, a processional hymn sung by a choir of girls, upon a religious, but not a solemn, occasion. Partheneia were composed by Alcman, Simonidēs, Bacchylidēs, and Pindar. Fairly substantial fragments of some by Alcman and Pindar have been found on papyri.

Parthe'nius, of Nicaea (first century BC), Greek poet taken as a prisoner-of-war by the Romans and sent to Rome in 73 BC. Freed there, he exerted great influence on the Roman poets of the day (see ALEXANDRIANISM, LATIN). His poetry, mostly in elegiacs, was highly thought of, but very little of it survives. Extant are the prose outlines he made (in Greek) of love stories found in Greek poetry and fictional literature, intended for use by his poet friend *Gallus to ornament either epic or elegy; they provide evidence about the Greek novel.

Pa'rthenon ('temple of the maiden'), the temple of Athena Parthenos built on the highest part of the *Acropolis at Athens and still standing, erected under the administration of Periclēs, begun in 447 BC and dedicated with the cult statue of Athena in 438. A temple had been begun on the site before the Persian invasion of 480 BC, and its foundations were used for the new building. The architect was Ictinus assisted by Callicratēs, and the work was supervised by *Pheidias. In the Parthenon the Doric order (see ARCHITECTURE I) is seen in its most perfect proportions and refined detail. The material is fine marble from the quarries of Mount *Pentelicus, a few kilometres north-east of Athens, as in most of the important buildings of this period. The temple was surrounded by a colonnade of forty-six columns (eight at each end), almost 11 m. (35 ft.) high. The platform measured about 70 m. (230 ft.) by 31 m. (102 ft.). The *cella* or chamber faced east and contained the great statue of the goddess in gold and ivory by Pheidias; it was about 30 m. long and had a porch of six columns at the eastern end. Behind it was a smaller room serving as a treasury; it opened off the back (west) porch which also had six columns.

The adornment of the temple with sculptures continued, almost certainly under the direction of Pheidias, until 432. These sculptures were more elaborate, more relevant to the cult, and more unified in theme than most temple sculptures. The ninety-two *metopes, which must have been made first, before the frieze, represented in high relief on the east the battles of the gods and the giants, on the west the victory of the Greeks over the Amazons, on the south the struggle of the Centaurs and the Lapiths (these now the best preserved), and on the north the Trojan War. The last sculptures to be made, the eastern and western pediments, showed in the east the birth of Athena from the head of Zeus, and in the west the contest of Poseidon and Athena for the possession of Attica. These figures are carved in the round. The Ionic frieze, in low relief, 160 m. (524 ft.) long, which ran high around the inner building, is unique in apparently showing a contemporary scene, the procession at the *Panathenaea, although the figures may also make symbolic reference to the Persian Wars. This frieze, some of the metopes, and figures from the east and west pediments are now in the British Museum; there they are known as the Elgin Marbles, having been acquired by the seventh Earl of Elgin when he was envoy to Constantinople (from 1799 to 1803), and later purchased by the British Government.

Fragmentary inscriptions survive giving the accounts for the Parthenon and the statue of Athena; the Athenians seem to have spent the accumulated reserve of the *Delian League on its construction. In the treasury of the temple (see above) was kept not only the treasure of Athena but also the public funds of Athens and of the Delian League.

The temple was subsequently converted into a church, then into a mosque. It remained almost intact until 1687 when, in the course of a siege of the Acropolis by a Venetian force, it was partially destroyed by an explosion of gunpowder stored there by the Turkish garrison.

Parthenopae'us, in Greek myth, one of the *Seven against Thebes; his mother was *Atalanta and his father either Meleager or Milanion. His son Promachus, fighting among the Epigonoi (sons of the Seven), avenged his death.

Parthe'nopē, in Greek myth, one of the *Sirens. Parthenope was also the name of a Greek colony from Cumae on the site of modern Naples.

Pa'rthia, originally a small district of western Asia which gave its name to the Parthians, a semi-nomadic military aristocracy, who spoke a north-Iranian dialect but seem to have claimed a Scythian origin. The Parthians occupied this territory in 247 BC, but later they ruled an empire extending from the Euphrates to the Indus. Their king Arsacēs I threw off Seleucid domination and established the Arsacid dynasty. They fought a long series of wars against the advancing Romans (see CRASSUS), who did not succeed in conquering the greater part of the country until the reigns of the emperors Trajan, Antoninus, and Caracalla (second and early third centuries AD). The Arsacid dynasty came to an end c.226. The Parthians were famous for their cavalry; the nobles wearing coats of mail and armed with enormously long spears were mounted on magnificent horses; their men, also on horseback, wielded bows and arrows. Their peculiar skill was the ability to shoot backwards when retreating (the 'Parthian shot').

Partitiō'nēs orato'riae, see CICERO (1) 4.

Pa'sion (c.430–370 BC), in Athens, at the time of his death the richest banker and manufacturer of his day. He began his career as a slave in a banking firm, and later acquired his freedom, becoming an Athenian citizen by decree of the assembly. Several speeches of Demosthenēs and a speech by Isocratēs, *Trapeziticus* ('speech against the banker'), give much information about his business dealings.

Pāsi'phăē, in Greek myth, wife of *Minos king of Crete, daughter of Helios (Sun), mother of Ariadnē and Phaedra. When Minos refused to sacrifice to Poseidon, as he had promised, a fine bull, Poseidon punished him by inflicting on Pasiphae a passion for the bull. Enabled by the help of *Daedalus to gratify her passion she became the mother of the Minotaur, part bull and part man.

pastoral poetry, see BUCOLIC.

paterfami'lias, at Rome, the (male) head of the family; in the early republic he had very large powers (*patria potestas,* 'power of a father') over his family: he was the sole owner of the property, including his wife's dowry, and he had complete power over his children including that of life and death, not merely at birth, to say whether they should live or not (as in Greece), but at any time. By the late republic adult sons were often 'emancipated', i.e. freed from the absolute power of the *paterfamilias,* and adult women, though still after marriage nominally in the power of a *paterfamilias* who might be a guardian, were allowed considerable freedom in the management of their property. See also GENIUS.

pater pa'triae ('father (i.e. saviour) of one's country'), honorific title given at Rome to those who had given outstanding service to the state. Cicero was so addressed in the senate after his consulship of 63 BC, and likewise the emperor Augustus in 2 BC.

patrēs conscri'pti, see SENATE.

patri'cians, at Rome, members of certain families, a privileged class, distinguished from the *plebeians, the rest of the citizen body. (It is not certain whether the distinction between patricians and plebeians existed under the kings of Rome, nor is the nature of the original distinction known.) Their name is probably connected with *pater* in the sense of 'member of the *senate'. If, as may be the case, the right to membership of the senate became hereditary in early times, that would have distinguished certain families from the rest of the citizen body. In the patriciate itself a distinction was gradually made between the 'lesser clans' (*gentes minores,* those of later creation) and the 'greater clans' (*gentes maiores,* those longer established). Until 445 BC patricians were not allowed to marry plebeians. Under the early republic they held the magistracies and the important religious offices: only a patrician could become *rex sacrorum,* *interrex,* and perhaps *princeps senatus*; for the struggle of the plebeians to win social and political equality with the patricians see ROME 3 and 6. The diminution of their political strength corresponds to some extent with the reduction in their numbers: about fifty patrician clans are known in the fifth century, but only fourteen at the end of the republic. Patricians could renounce their status by a special public act or simple adoption (compare CLODIUS). Julius Caesar and Octavian admitted new members to the patriciate.

Patro'clus (Patroklos or Patroklēs), in Homer's *Iliad,* son of Menoetius and the favourite companion of Achilles. For his story see ILIAD.

patron (Lat. *patrōnus*), at Rome, a powerful man who agreed to protect another by making the latter his *client. In the early republic the custom grew up of poor citizens attaching themselves to rich and influential men who gave them financial and legal assistance in return for their political support and social attentions. It became a matter of prestige for a patron on his public appearances to be attended by a crowd of respectful clients. The relationship between the two was felt to be a binding obligation. Slaves who acquired their freedom became the clients of their former masters, who retained certain legal rights over them. Sometimes Roman commanders exercised a general patronage over the peoples they conquered which was transmitted to their descendants. Pompey's son Sextus was able to get support from his father's clients in Spain and Asia.

patronage, literary. In Greece, literary patronage was exercised among others by the tyrants of Corinth (see CYPSELUS), Athens (see PEISISTRATUS), Samos (see POLYCRATES), and Sicily (see HIERON), who supported at their courts the poets Alcman, Anacreon, Bacchylidēs,

Pindar, and Simonidēs. Archelaus, king of Macedon at the end of the fifth century BC, invited Agathon, Timotheus, and Euripidēs to his court. In the same century the city of Athens itself with its musical festivals and commissions for temple decoration and other works of art offered the advantages of patronage, and there were wealthy Athenian aristocrats giving hospitality to philosophers and teachers (see SOPHISTS). Similarly, in the Hellenistic age the kings of Egypt, the Ptolemies, were great supporters of all the arts, rivalled by the Attalids, kings of Pergamum.

At Rome, literary patronage was an extension of the relationship between *patron and client, and even included Greek writers. Under the empire Augustus and many later emperors were patrons of literature, as were wealthy individuals such as Maecenas and the Younger Pliny. Among those benefiting were Virgil, Horace, Statius, and Martial.

patrony'mic, see NAMES.

Paullus, Lucius Aemi'lius (c.230–160 BC), given the *cognomen* Macedonicus, son of the consul Aemilius Paullus who was killed at the battle of Cannae in 216 BC. He was consul in 182 and again in 168, when the Macedonian War had been going badly for Rome (see MACEDON 3); he at once brought the war to a successful conclusion at the battle of Pydna, a monument to which can be seen at Delphi. When Epirus was sacked on instructions from the senate the enormous proceeds of the booty were scrupulously paid into the Roman treasury. Paullus kept for himself only the books which had belonged to the Macedonian king (see PERSEUS), thereby forming the first private library at Rome. The triumph that he celebrated at the end of 167 BC was the most spectacular that Rome had until then seen, but marred for the victor by the deaths at that time of his two younger sons. His two older sons were Quintus Fabius Maximus Aemilianus (adopted by the family of the Fabii Maximi) and Publius *Scipio Aemilianus Africanus, adopted by Publius Scipio son of Scipio Africanus. A daughter married Cato's son. Censor in 164, Paullus died in 160. He combined the traditional Roman virtues of integrity and devotion to duty with admiration for the culture of ancient Greece, and was a strong influence on his circle of friends as well as on Roman public life. (See also PACUVIUS.)

Paul the Silentiary (Paulus Silentiārius, d. c. AD 575), an officer of the imperial household of the Roman emperor Justinian, responsible for maintaining peace and quiet in the palace; he wrote an elaborate poetical description of the restored church of St Sophia at Constantinople, which has considerable architectural as well as

poetic interest. He is also the author of some hundred epigrams in the Greek *Anthology.

Paulus, Julius (flourished c. AD 210), one of the greatest Roman jurists. Together with *Ulpian he assisted *Papinian when the latter was praetorian prefect (see PRAEFECTUS PRAETORIO). Banished by Elagabalus (emperor AD 218–22) he was recalled by the latter's successor Alexander Severus, and may himself have shared the office of praetorian prefect with Ulpian. His voluminous writings survive in short excerpts in the Digest compiled by the emperor *Justinian.

Pausa'nias. 1. In Sparta in the early fifth century BC, son of the king Cleombrotus I, nephew of Leonidas and regent of Sparta in 479 BC when he commanded the Greek forces at the battle of Plataea (see PERSIAN WARS). In further Greek operations against the Persians in 478 he captured Byzantium but his arrogant misuse of authority provoked the allies into declaring that they preferred the leadership of Athens (the first step in the creation of the *Delian League). Since Pausanias was also suspected of treasonable negotiations with the Persian king Xerxēs, the Spartans recalled him in 477. He was tried but escaped conviction and returned to Byzantium, apparently still with Sparta's approval. Expelled by the Athenian *Cimon c.475 BC he went to live at Colōnae in the Troad. Reports that he was continuing to negotiate with Persia led to his being recalled to Sparta, but again he was acquitted, in about 470 BC. He now became suspected of fomenting a revolt by the helots (the Spartan serfs), and at about the same time the evidence of a letter revealed his dealing with the Persians. To escape arrest he took refuge in a sanctuary, only to be walled up there. At the point of death he was taken out, to die on unconsecrated ground (467/6 BC).

2. (flourished c. AD 160), Greek traveller and geographer, the author of an extant 'Description of Greece' (*Periēgēsis Hellados*), who appears from passages in it to have been born in Lydia. What he tells us is based on his own travels; his historical information appears to be mostly reliable, and his general accuracy is attested by the extant remains of the monuments he describes. The work is in ten books, namely: 1, Attica and Megara; 2, Corinth and Argolis; 3, Laconia; 4, Messenia; 5 and 6, Elis (with Olympia); 7, Achaea; 8, Arcadia; 9, Boeotia; 10, Phocis (with Delphi). Pausanias generally outlines the history and then the topography of important cities, followed by their religious cults and mythology. Only occasionally does he refer to the scenery and natural products of the regions he describes, for instance, the honey of Hymettus, the bustards around the river Cephisus in Phocis, the white blackbirds of Mount Cyllenē, and the oaks, cork-trees, and great tortoises of Arcadia. He is most interested in

objects and places of historical and religious interest, as at Athens, Olympia, and Delphi, and especially in artistic monuments; the paintings of Polygnotus and the statues of Myron and Pheidias attract his interest, but he has less to say of Praxitelēs and the later sculptors. He admires the Propylaea at Athens, the theatre of Epidaurus, and the temple of Bassae, the ruins of which enable modern visitors to approve his judgement. He is honest about reputed marvels, such as the spotted fish of the river Aroanius; these he admits did not, as was supposed, sing like thrushes, although he waited by the river till sunset. Of the two stories accounting for the presence of a pickled Triton (perhaps some sea-creature) in a temple at Tanagra, he thinks it more credible that the creature was lured ashore by a bowl of wine and decapitated as it lay drunk on the beach, than that it was killed in single combat by the god Dionysus. His style is simple and unpretentious.

Peace (*Eirēnē*, Lat. *Pax*), Greek comedy by *Aristophanēs, produced at the Great *Dionysia in 421 BC, where it came second in the dramatic competition.

The *Peloponnesian War between Sparta and Athens is in progress; the Athenian demagogue and general *Cleon and the Spartan general *Brasidas have been killed in the summer of 422 at Amphipolis, and Aristophanes anticipates the successful outcome of negotiations for the Peace of Nicias (concluded some ten days after the performance). Trygaios, an Attic vine-grower, who with his family is suffering from the food-shortage, decides to imitate the mythical hero Bellerophon on his winged horse Pegasus, and ride to heaven on a dung-beetle, fattening it up to gigantic size for the purpose. The voyage is successfully accomplished, but Hermēs who answers the door tells him that Zeus and the other gods have moved house so as to be further away from the war down below, and War (Polemos) is in charge; he has cast Peace into a deep cave, from which, perhaps, she will never emerge, and is preparing to pound all the states in a mortar. While War looks for a pestle (failing to borrow one from Athens or Sparta because their 'pestles of war', Cleon and Brasidas, are lost), Trygaios and the Attic farmers (the chorus) whom he has summoned, having bribed Hermes with extravagant promises of festivals and a gold cup, draw Peace out of the cave with her two attendants Opōra ('harvest') and Theōria ('holiday'; literally, 'attendance at festivals'), and return with them to Greece. General jubilation follows (except on the part of arms manufacturers), and preparations are made for the wedding of Trygaios and Opora.

Peace, On the, title of speeches by *Isocrates and Demosthenes (see DEMOSTHENES (2) 4).

Peace of Nicias, see NICIAS and PELOPONNESIAN WAR.

pederasty, see HOMOSEXUALITY.

Pe'gasus, in Greek myth, a winged horse who, with his brother Chrysaor, was sprung from the blood of the *Gorgon Medusa, pregnant by Poseidon, when she was killed by Perseus. The fountain Hippocrene on Mount Helicon in Boeotia, sacred to the Muses, was said to have been produced by a stamp of his hoof. With divine aid *Bellerophon was able to catch this horse when it was drinking at the fountain Peirēnē in Corinth, and bridle it. Mounted on it he succeeded in killing the *Chimaera, but was thrown when he attempted to fly to Olympus on its back. Pegasus appears on a handsome series of Corinthian coins, symbolizing the city.

Peirae'us, see PIRAEUS.

Peirē'nē, celebrated fountain at Corinth; see PERIANDER and PEGASUS.

Peiri'thŏus, see CENTAURS and THESEUS.

Peisi'stratus (*c*.600–527 BC) and the **Peisistra'tidai** ('Peisistratids', family of Peisistratus). At Athens, Peisistratus, son of Hippocratēs (who claimed descent from the mythical Neleus, father of the Homeric hero Nestor), and related to Solon on his mother's side, won popularity as *polemarch *c*.565 BC by seizing Megara's port Nisaea when the Megarians still held Salamis (see SOLON). During the struggles for political power that developed following the reforms of Solon in the early sixth century (see ATHENS 2 (i)), Peisistratus emerged as leader of the poorer 'hillsmen' (*diakrioi* or *hyperakrioi*), because of the situation of his family's land at Brauron on the east coast of Attica beyond Mount Hymettus. By *c*.561 he had won enough popularity to get the assembly to vote him a bodyguard when he appeared there wounded after an attack, so he said, by his enemies. He soon used his bodyguard to seize the Acropolis and make himself tyrant. The other two parties (the plainsmen and the coastmen) eventually united to drive him out of Athens, but he soon returned (in the mid-550s), accompanied in his chariot by a tall and beautiful girl (Phȳē, from the country deme of Paiania) dressed in full armour, who, he said, was the goddess Athena come to restore him to her city. This time he had the assistance of Megaclēs (an *Alcmaeonid), leader of the coastmen (*paraloi*), who wanted a powerful alliance against the plainsmen (*pedieis*). To cement the alliance Peisistratus married Megacles' daughter, but marriage and alliance both collapsed (Peisistratus being unwilling to have children by a wife from a polluted family) and he once more went into exile.

During the following ten years Peisistratus built up his influence in the Aegean area, and in 546 landed at Marathon with money and a force of mercenaries. Many Athenians joined his cause. Those who did not were decisively defeated at Pallēnē; Megacles and his followers went into exile and Peisistratus became tyrant until his death in 527. He maintained the form of Solon's constitution but saw to it that the archonship was held by his supporters. (Under his son Hippias archons were elected from families formerly opposed to his rule, e.g. the Alcmaeonids.) He strengthened his position by a skilful policy of foreign alliances. He recovered Sigeum at the mouth of the Hellespont (founded by colonization c.610), and apparently with his approval the Athenian *Miltiadēs became tyrant of the Thracian Chersonese, at the request of the inhabitants; as a result access to the Black Sea was made easier for Athenian merchants. Peisistratus emphasized Solon's claim for Athens as the mother-city of Ionia by purifying the chief Ionian shrine, that of Apollo on *Delos, reburying elsewhere on the island all the dead whose graves were in sight of the precinct. He was friendly with Sparta, Thessaly, and Argos (his third wife was an Argive).

Peisistratus was still firmly in control when he died in 527. His eldest son Hippias succeeded him, and associated his brother Hipparchus in the tyranny; but the powerful families of Athens were hardly likely to tolerate a succession of Peisistratids, and Hippias had no authority from the city to succeed his father. Moreover, Hipparchus was unpopular because of his dissolute arrogance, and Peisistratus' bastard son Hegesistratus, tyrant at Sigeum, was loyal to Persian authority. Hippias linked the family more closely with Persia by marrying his daughter Archedicē to the Greek tyrant of Lampsacus, also under the control of Persia. (Her epitaph describes her as not haughty despite being the daughter, sister, wife, and mother of tyrants.) In 514 *Harmodius and Aristogeiton killed Hipparchus at the start of the Panathenaic procession; Harmodius was instantly struck down by the guard, and Aristogeiton died after torture. The two assassins were remembered as martyrs for the democratic cause. After this the rule of Hippias became harsher. His fall was brought about chiefly by the Alcmaeonids (see CLEISTHENES (2)), who with the assistance of the Delphic Oracle induced Sparta to invade Attica. Hippias, besieged in the Acropolis, capitulated and retired to Sigeum in 510. Here he negotiated with the Persians in order to secure their help in his restoration. He was present at the battle of Marathon in 490 (see PERSIAN WARS), assisting the Persians with his advice. His hopes frustrated, he subsequently died at Lemnos.

Tradition said that Peisistratus was a moderate and benevolent ruler. It is not always possible to distinguish his work from that of his sons. He created a citizens' property tax which provided subsidies to poor farmers, enabling them to avoid debt (which Solon had failed to achieve). Under him the commercial importance of Athens greatly increased; her wine, oil, and pottery reached all the surrounding countries. Under his sons better roads were built between the city and country demes, and milestones were set up to measure distances from the demes to the Altar of the Twelve Gods, also set up by the Peisistratids, in the agora (see HERMAE). Law suits in the demes were heard by travelling judges, so that country people did not need to travel to the city to have their cases heard. Athens was provided with a good water-supply; the famous spring-house (Enneakrounos, 'nine-jets') was built in the agora, the water channelled in clay pipes from the spring Callirrhoē. The Peisistratids beautified the city with new temples (remains of the buildings have been found on the *Acropolis, as well as many marble statues) and they encouraged art and literature: for instance, *Simonidēs of Ceos and *Anacreon of Teos were invited to Athens. The *Panathenaic festival was celebrated with greater splendour from 566 onwards, with the addition of contests in athletics, music, and poetry; recitals of Homer by rhapsodes were said to have been introduced by the Peisistratids (see HOMER 6). Peisistratus is also credited with the creation of the state festival of the City *Dionysia in 534, and with encouraging the cult of Demeter at *Eleusis.

Pelasgians, apparently a north Aegean people scattered throughout Greece by the migrations of the Bronze Age and preserving a common, non-Greek language. The Greeks used the name to describe the original pre-Greek inhabitants of Greece and the Aegean area, with whom they sometimes included the Tyrrhenians (Etruscans). See GREECE and HELLAS.

Pela'sgus, early king of Argos, father of *Lycaon.

Pēleus, in Greek myth, son of *Aeacus (mythical king of Aegina); he became king of Phthia, in Thessaly. His name may mean 'man of Pelion' (a mountain in Thessaly). When he and his brother *Telamon killed their half-brother Phocus, Aeacus banished them; Peleus went to Phthia, where the then king purified him of his crime and gave him his daughter in marriage and a share of his kingdom. Peleus took part in the Calydonian boar-hunt (see MELEAGER), where he accidentally killed one of the participants and was again banished. He went to Iolcus in Thessaly where Acastus, son of Pelias, purified him, and he took part in Pelias' funeral games where he wrestled with Atalanta. Acastus' wife, Astydameia, fell in love with

Peleus. When he rejected her she sent a message to his wife saying that he was about to marry another woman; at that his wife hanged herself. Astydameia told her husband that Peleus had made advances to her; Acastus then took Peleus hunting on Mount Pelion, hid his sword as he slept, and left him to be attacked by the centaurs. The centaur *Chiron, however, restored his sword; Peleus then captured Iolcus and took his vengeance on Astydameia by killing her and marching his army between the pieces of her severed body. He was given as wife the goddess Thetis (see NEREUS). Zeus had previously fallen in love with her, but when told by Prometheus that she was fated to bear a son more powerful than his father, decided to give Thetis to a mortal so that her son should be mortal also. It is said that Peleus had to wrestle with her in order to win her. Thetis' child was Achilles, whom Peleus took to Chiron to be brought up.

Pe'lias, in Greek myth, son of Poseidon and *Tyro, and the usurper king of Iolcus in Thessaly, the rightful king being his half-brother Aeson, father of Jason; see ARGONAUTS.

Pē'lion, high wooded mountain in (Magnesian) Thessaly, famous as the home of the centaur *Chiron. In Greek myth, the Giants *Otus and Ephialtēs, in an attempt to scale the heavens and overthrow the gods, piled Pelion upon Ossa (another Thessalian mountain) and Ossa upon Olympus.

Pella, capital of Macedonia c.400–167 BC (i.e. from the time of king Archelaus until the conquest by Rome). It became the largest Macedonian city until overtaken by Thessalonika in 146 BC. Pella was later a Roman colony.

Pelo'pia, daughter of Thyestēs and mother of Aegisthus. See PELOPS.

Pelo'pidas (c.410–364 BC), great Theban general who first came into prominence when in the winter of 379/8 he overthrew the oligarchy and restored democratic rule at *Thebes. (Plutarch says that he and his fellow conspirators used to meet in the house of Simmias, one of the interlocutors in Plato's *Phaedo*.) With six confederates dressed as women he killed the pro-Spartan generals who, with the support of a Spartan garrison, were tyrannizing Thebes. At the battle of Leuctra in 371 BC Thebes drove the Spartans out of central Greece; Pelopidas won great fame for his leadership of the *Sacred Band both at this battle and the earlier battle at Tegyra (375 BC). He accompanied *Epaminondas on his first invasion of the Peloponnese (370/69), but after that looked northwards to Thebes' other enemies, *Alexander of Pherae (in Thessaly), and Macedon. He brought the city of Larisa and the north of Thessaly under a Theban protectorate and arbitrated in favour of Alexander of Macedon against a rival, Ptolemy. But these settlements did not last for long. Alexander was killed and Ptolemy succeeded to the throne; the latter came to terms with Pelopidas and surrendered hostages who included the future king Philip II of Macedon. In 364, in an expedition against Alexander of Pherae, Pelopidas, although victorious, was killed at the battle of Cynoscephalae. Together with his friend and colleague Epaminondas, he had brought Thebes to the zenith of her power.

Pe'loponnese (Peloponnēsos, 'island of Pelops'), the southern part of Greece, connected with central Greece by the Isthmus of Corinth. Its chief political divisions were Argos, Laconia (Sparta), Messenia, Elis, Achaea, and Arcadia.

Peloponne'sian League, the earliest and longest-lived Greek alliance, dating from the sixth century BC when Sparta negotiated treaties with Peloponnesian states (see above) whereby Sparta could expect the support of all members in war if a majority vote favoured such a course, each state having one vote. *Chilon, one of the Seven Sages, is credited with its creation. The League was dissolved in 366 BC.

Peloponne'sian War (431–404 BC), between Sparta and Athens. For the war between Athens and the Peloponnesians from 460 to 446, sometimes known as the First Peloponnesian War, see ATHENS 2 (ii).

1. The war was in the main a struggle between Athens, a democratic state and a sea-power, which had converted the *Delian League (designed to resist the Persians) into an empire under her own rule, and Sparta, an oligarchical and conservative power, whose land army was the most efficient military force of the day, and who headed most of the Peloponnesian states together with Boeotia. The real reason for the conflict, according to the Athenian historian *Thucydidēs, was the rise of Athens to greatness, which made the Spartans fear for their own position. The events that precipitated it began in 433, when a quarrel arose between Corinth and her colony Corcyra (Corfu, off the coast of Epirus in north-west Greece) which enabled Athens to secure Corcyra as an ally and have the advantage of her large fleet. Athens had already acquired an important western naval base with the seizure in 456 of Naupactus at the western entrance to the Corinthian Gulf, and relations between Athens and Corinth were deteriorating. In 432 Potidaea, a Corinthian colony on the neck of the western prong of Chalcidicē in north-east Greece, but a member of the Delian League, revolted from Athens, which thereupon sent a besieging force while Corinth sent help to her colony. There were other sources of friction, including Athens' infringement of the

autonomy of Aegina and her decrees against Megara, with economic consequences for the latter, in ostensible punishment for the cultivation of sacred land. Technically Sparta and the Peloponnesian League were the first to decide for war, and in the summer of 431 invaded Attica.

2. Of the two sides, Athens was inferior in land forces; the hoplites of Sparta and Boeotia were the best in Greece, and in any case Athens had less than half their number. For the Athenians, pitched battles were evidently to be avoided. The enemy could therefore ravage Athenian territory; but the defences of the city could withstand assault, and it could not be starved into surrender because it was connected by the *Long Walls to the port of Piraeus. At sea Athens was overwhelmingly the superior side in number of ships and the skill of her sailors. She could import supplies almost with impunity and harry her enemies' shipping, and she had sufficient finances to buy supplies and pay the fleet (and army). This was the assessment of the situation made by *Pericles, the Athenian leader, and his strategy was based upon it. He persuaded the country population to move themselves and their possessions into the city and into the space between the Long Walls, temporarily sacrificing their farms.

3. The first ten years of the war, known as the Archidamian War from the name of the Spartan king who led the incursions into Attica, were indecisive. The Peloponnesians who invaded and ravaged Attica in 431 found it deserted, and after about a month returned home; this was to be, in general, the pattern for the next six years. In 430 a devastating plague broke out in Athens and the city lost more than a quarter of her population. Pericles died as a result of it in 429, his death depriving Athens of the only man who could impose a single policy on the Athenians. Nevertheless in 430 Potidaea was forced to capitulate to Athens, in 429 Phormio won two naval victories off Naupactus, in 428/7 the revolt of *Lesbos from the Delian League was crushed, and in 426 *Demosthenes (1) defeated the Peloponnesians in Amphilochia, in north-west Greece. But Athens' chief success was the capture of Pylos on the west coast of Messenia in 425, together with the death or capture of 420 Spartan hoplites on Sphacteria (the island that almost blocks the bay of Pylos, famous in later times as the scene of the battle of Navarino, 1827). This gave Athens a permanent outpost in enemy territory. Sparta gave up her annual invasions of Attica and made overtures for peace.

4. *Cleon persuaded the Athenians to reject the Spartan offers. Then *Brasidas, a brilliant Spartan general, first saved Megara from capture by the Athenians, then won over to his side a number of cities in Thrace including the important *Amphipolis; the historian Thucyd-ides, at that time a general in Thrace, arrived with a squadron of ships but was too late to save the city. For his failure he was exiled for twenty years. At the same time an attempt by the Athenians to regain control over Boeotia (lost in 446) ended in their defeat at Delium in 424. In 422 Cleon led an expedition to recapture Amphipolis; he was defeated and killed, but Brasidas was also fatally wounded, and thus the two chief opponents of peace were removed (the 'pestles of war' as they were called in Aristophanes' *Peace*). The Peace of *Nicias was concluded in 421. It was in the main a victory for Athens, especially since she kept her empire intact while her enemies were divided, Corinth and Boeotia refusing to sign the Peace.

5. The lack of unity in the Peloponnese induced the Athenians, under the influence of *Alcibiades, to enter into alliance with Argos (which had taken no part in the Archidamian War, having a treaty of neutrality with Sparta which ran out in 421) and with Elis and Mantinea; the allies attacked Epidaurus and advanced on Tegea, and Sparta moved against them. A hoplite battle fought at Mantinea in 418 resulted in a great victory for Sparta. Argos abandoned the Athenian alliance and was once more isolated. In 416 Athens attacked and destroyed the island of Melos (see MELIAN DIALOGUE), which had been neutral but friendly to Sparta. This is the last event of the precarious 'Peace' of 421–415, as described by Thucydides. In 415, again under the influence of Alcibiades, Athens undertook the Sicilian Expedition, opposed by Nicias. It was designed to curb the growing power of *Syracuse, to win a footing in Sicily, and to obtain complete control of the sea. While the expedition was being prepared, the Athenians were thrown into painful excitement by the discovery one morning that nearly all the *Hermae in the city had been mutilated. The sacrilege was regarded as ominous for the expedition and Alcibiades' complicity was suspected. Nevertheless the expedition sailed under the command of Nicias (despite his opposition), Alcibiades, and *Lamachus. Alcibiades was recalled soon after to answer charges, brought by his political enemies, of profaning the (Eleusinian) Mysteries (see MYSTERIES), but escaped to Sparta where he gave the Spartans the sensible advice to fortify *Decelea (in northern Attica); this they did in 413. In Sicily, Lamachus was killed and Nicias left in sole command. The arrival in Syracuse of Gylippus, an energetic Spartan general, alarmed the Athenians into sending a relief force under Demosthenes, but the expedition ended in 413 with the defeat of the Athenian fleet and army and the exhaustion of their finances.

6. Athens now began to rebuild her fleet although she no longer had trained crews. Her allies in the Aegean, at the instigation of the island of Chios, began to revolt (412).

Nevertheless Athens built a new fleet and the war continued for another eight years, a consequence of the incapacity of the Spartan generals and the amazing resilience of the Athenians, especially under the leadership of Alcibiades who played (on both sides) a part of great importance in the war. During this time the Spartan occupation of Decelea caused great hardship at Athens. Sparta obtained assistance from Persia (money for a fleet, for example) by agreeing that the Greek cities of Asia Minor should be surrendered to Persia. The north-east Aegean became the chief theatre of war, the Spartans hoping to deprive Athens of her main source of food supply. Athenian naval victories at Cynossema (411) and Cyzicus (410) for a time prevented the Spartans from attaining this end.

In this period there was civil strife in Athens: the oligarchic revolution of the Four Hundred in 411 (see ATHENS 2 (iii)) was a serious but short-lived movement which collapsed six months before Cyzicus. The naval victories restored Athenian morale and, according to Diodorus, caused the Spartans to sue for peace. However, in 407 *Cyrus the Younger was appointed Persian satrap of Asia Minor, and his friendship with the Spartan regent *Lysander, commanding the fleet, led him to give the Spartans every assistance. The Athenian fleet was defeated at Notium, and Alcibiades, who had been appointed *strategos* with full responsibility for the war, retired into exile. Even so, the Athenians won one more victory in the following year, 406, when Lysander was no longer commanding the Spartans, at *Arginusae. (This battle was long remembered for the subsequent trial and illegal execution of the victorious Athenian generals, for failure to recover the survivors.) In 405 the last of the Athenian fleet was surprised and destroyed at Aegospotami in the Hellespont. After a siege, left without ships, money, or allies, in April 404 Athens was obliged to accept Sparta's terms and become virtually the subject-ally of the victor.

The principal literary authority for the Peloponnesian War up to 411 is Thucydides; for 411 to the end, Xenophon in the *Hellenica*; see also DIODORUS SICULUS.

Pelops, in Greek myth, son of the Lydian king *Tantalus; his mother is usually said to be Dione, daughter of Atlas. He was the founder of the Pelopid family after whom the Peloponnese is named. According to the usual story he was expelled from Sipylus in Lydia by Ilus, an early king of Troy, and brought his great wealth to Pisa in Elis, where he became king. There are two main stories about Pelops. In the first, his father Tantalus killed him when a child and served his flesh to the gods at a banquet, to see if they could tell it from that of

some animal. *Demeter, absorbed in her grief for Persephonē, ate part of the shoulder; but the other gods detected the nature of the dish, brought Pelops to life again, and replaced the missing shoulder with one of ivory. Tantalus was punished in Hades. The other story tells how Pelops, grown up, sought to marry Hippodameia, daughter of Oenomaus king of Elis. The condition of winning her was that he should outdistance Oenomaus in a chariot-race. If he was caught, Oenomaus would spear him. Pelops bribed Myrtilus, the king's charioteer, to take out the lynch-pin of a wheel on his master's chariot; the wheel fell off, Oenomaus was thrown and killed, and Pelops carried off his bride. But he refused to give Myrtilus the promised reward and threw him in the sea (hence, perhaps, the name of the Myrtoan Sea, east of the Peloponnese). The dying Myrtilus (or Oenomaus) cursed Pelops, which is the origin of the curse upon his house. For the time being Pelops flourished and fathered six sons. He was supposed to be buried at Olympia, where he was worshipped as a hero and sometimes said to be the founder of the Olympian games.

Two of Pelops' sons were Atreus and Thyestēs, in whom the curse was manifested. Atreus became king of Mycenae, and Thyestes seduced his brother's wife Aëropē; thereupon Atreus banished Thyestes but later recalled him on pretence of being reconciled and prepared a banquet for him consisting of the flesh of his two sons. When Thyestes realized what he had eaten, he fled in horror, calling down a curse on the house of Atreus. He now became, by his own daughter Pelopia, the father of Aegisthus, who was exposed at birth by his mother but brought up by shepherds; when Atreus heard of the boy's existence he sent for him and brought him up as his own child. When Aegisthus was grown up, Atreus sent him to kill Thyestes, but the latter recognized him as his own son and the two contrived the death of Atreus instead. Atreus was the father of *Agamemnon and Menelaus. When Agamemnon led the Greek expedition to Troy and left the kingdom of Mycenae in the care of his wife Clytemnestra, his cousin Aegisthus seduced her and joined with her in murdering Agamemnon on his return. Later, Agamemnon's son Orestēs, with the help of his sister Electra, avenged their father by killing Aegisthus and Clytemnestra. The curse on the house was not finally expunged until the purification of Orestes. (See also ORESTEIA, ORESTES, and ELECTRA.)

This legend (Agamemnon's murder excepted) is not known to Homer, for whom the kingdom of Mycenae passes naturally from Pelops to Atreus, Thyestes, and Agamemnon. A simple genealogy may be constructed as follows, but there are very many variations of relationship in the sources.

House of Pelops

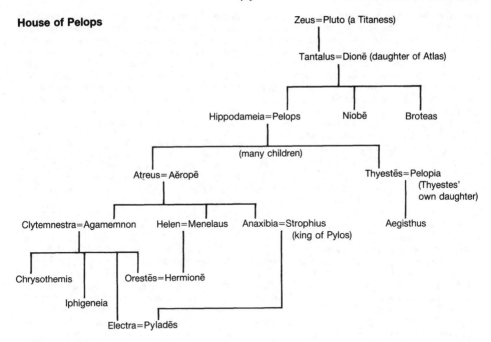

Zeus=Pluto (a Titaness)

Tantalus=Dionē (daughter of Atlas)

Hippodameia=Pelops   Niobē   Broteas

(many children)

Atreus=Aёropē   Thyestēs=Pelopia
                                    (Thyestes'
                                    own daughter)

Clytemnestra=Agamemnon   Helen=Menelaus   Anaxibia=Strophius   Aegisthus
                                                        (king of Pylos)

Chrysothemis   Orestēs=Hermionē

Iphigeneia

Electra=Pyladēs

peltasts (peltastai), in the Greek army, light-armed troops; see ARMY, GREEK I.

penā'tēs, di, in Roman religion, 'the gods dwelling in the store cupboard' (*penus*, 'provisions'), who had their images in the atrium of every Roman house and were regarded together with the *lares* as protectors of the house. There were also state *penates* (*penates publici*, protectors of Rome); their cult was attached to the temple of Vesta. According to Virgil, Aeneas had brought these to Italy from Troy. For Virgil, not only Rome and Troy had their *penates* but even Carthage, the city of a hated enemy; similarly in the fourth Georgic the bees, the most human-like of the animal creation, 'have their *penates* and their fixed abode'. The worship of the domestic *penates* and *lares* centred on the family meal: a portion was set aside and thrown on the flames of the hearth for the gods, and the table always held a salt-cellar and small offerings of first-fruits for them. A member of the family, returning after an absence, would greet the *penates* as living members of the household, the traveller's stick perhaps hung up beside their images. Generally speaking, every notable event of family life involved a prayer to the *lares* and *penates*.

Pēne'lopē (also Pēnelopeiā), in Homer's *Odyssey*, daughter of Icarius (brother of Tyndareus) of Sparta and wife of *Odysseus. She faithfully awaits her husband's return during his twenty years' absence (ten years at the siege of Troy, ten years in his wanderings afterwards), although wooed by numerous suitors among the local nobles. She pretends she cannot remarry until she has woven a shroud for Odysseus' father, Laërtes. This she unravels every night, so that the work is never completed, but her deception is revealed by one of the maids and she is compelled to finish it. She then promises to marry the suitor who can bend the bow of her absent husband. Odysseus returns in disguise at this juncture, wields the bow against the suitors and, when he reveals to her his knowledge of the construction of their bed, is finally accepted by Penelope as her husband.

An entirely different tradition makes Penelope the mother of Pan by the god Hermēs.

pene'stae, see THESSALY.

Pēnē'us (Pēneios), principal river of Thessaly in Greece; it flows through the vale of Tempē between Mount Olympus and Mount Ossa.

pentakosiomedi'mnoi, see SOLON.

penta'meter, in Greek and Latin, line of verse containing five metrical units (*metra*); see METRE, GREEK I and 2. In practice the term almost always refers to the elegiac pentameter.

pentāthlon, see ATHLETICS (v).

Pentēkontaё'tia, in Greek history, the 'period of fifty years' (roughly) between the end of the Persian and the beginning of the Peloponnesian Wars (479–431 BC). It was described (but not so called) by the historian Thucydides (1. 89–118), with some omissions and some doubtful chronology. This was the period in which Athens developed her empire (see DELIAN LEAGUE) and produced some of her greatest works of art and literature. It was the age of the statesman Pericles, the tragedians Aeschylus and (for the first half of their productive lives) Sophocles and Euripides, the philosopher Anaxagoras, the sophist Protagoras, and the artists Polygnotus and Pheidias; the Parthenon was built during this time, and Socrates, Thucydides, and Aristophanes grew up. Thucydides represents Pericles as describing the Athens of his day as 'the school of Greece'. In other parts of Greece it was the period of Pindar, Bacchylides, Herodotus, Parmenides, Zeno, Empedocles, and Polycleitus.

Pente'licus, mountain, about 1,100 m. (3,610 ft.) high, which bounds the Athenian plain on its north-east side, 16 km. (10 miles) from Athens. In earlier times called Mount Brilessus, its later name is derived from the famous marble quarried in the deme of Pentelē on its side. Pentelic marble is of a pure white colour, hard and fine-grained, but not easy to work owing to the particles of quartz and flint embedded in it; it weathers to a beautiful golden brown. It was used freely by the second quarter of the fifth century; 22,000 tons of it were used to build the Parthenon at Athens (finally completed in 432 BC). From the fourth century BC marble from Paros was preferred for sculpture and architecture.

Penthesilē'a (Penthesileia), in Greek myth, queen of the *Amazons who came to the aid of Troy after the death of Hector. She fought with distinction but was eventually killed by Achilles, who grieved over her body.

Pentheus, in Greek myth, son of Echion and of Agavē, daughter of Cadmus king of Thebes. See BACCHAE.

peplos, see DRESS 1 and PANATHENAEA.

Pe'rdiccas, name of several notable Macedonians. The king Perdiccas II was active in the Peloponnesian War, changing allegiance several times from one side to the other in his own interest. Another Perdiccas was second-in-command to Alexander the Great and became in effect regent of the empire after Alexander's death; soon after that he was killed in a mutiny. See MACEDONIA 1 and 2.

Perdix, see DAEDALUS.

Pe'regrine (Peregrīnus), see LUCIAN.

Pe'rgamum (Pergamon). 1. Name of the citadel of Troy.
2. City of Mysia in the valley of the Căïcus in the north-west of Asia Minor, originally a hillfortress founded by Greeks in mythical times, according to local tradition (see ANDROMACHE). In the third century BC it became the capital of the *Attalids, the fourth and last of the dynastic kingdoms which emerged after the death of

Alexander the Great and among which his empire was divided (see HELLENISTIC AGE). Under the Attalids, Pergamum became a splendid and beautiful city with a famous school of sculpture and a library second only to that of Alexandria in size. For its importance as a literary centre and place where parchment was first used extensively for books, see BOOKS AND WRITING 3. It was an important cultural centre during the Second *Sophistic.

Peria'nder (Periandros), tyrant of *Corinth from about 625 to 585 BC who succeeded his father *Cypselus and brought Corinth to the height of fame and prosperity. According to Herodotus, Periander asked Thrasybulus, tyrant of Miletus, how he might rule securely. The latter replied by taking the messenger into a field of corn and cutting off the ears that were rather taller than the rest. Periander was probably a stern ruler, and is reputed to have killed his wife and quarrelled with his sons; he was certainly a powerful and energetic man, and his practical good sense led to his being included by some among the *Seven Sages of Greece (his court is the scene of Plutarch's dialogue, the *Banquet of the Seven Sages*). His public buildings enhanced the city, in particular the temple to Apollo and the building for the Peirēnē fountain, and he was a patron of the arts: *Arion the dithyrambic poet stayed at his court. In his day Corinthian pottery was the most widespread in the Mediterranean until the mid-sixth century, prized for its painted decoration (in the so-called Ripe Corinthian style). Periander and his father founded in north-west Greece the colonies of Leucas, Anactorium, Ambracia, and further north Apollonia and Epidamnus, which opened up trade in the interior and lay on the important route to Italy and the west; in the north-east, on the western prong of Chalcidicē, Potidaea was founded and became one of the most powerful cities in the area. Periander arbitrated in a dispute between Athens and Mitylenē (favouring the former) in the matter of *Sigeum. He was probably responsible for the construction of the *diaulos* or portage way across the Isthmus of Corinth (see CORINTH, ISTHMUS OF).

Pe'riclēs (c.495–429 BC), Athenian statesman, an *Alcmaeonid, son of *Xanthippus and of Agaristē, niece of Cleisthenēs (1) and granddaughter of Agariste (see HIPPOCLEIDES) and *Megaclēs. He was *choregos when Aeschylus' *Persae* was produced in 472. In politics he supported the *democracy and came into political prominence as one of the state prosecutors of *Cimon in 463. In 462/1 he and *Ephialtēs joined in reducing the powers of the *Areopagus, and after the latter's murder and Cimon's *ostracism, both in 461, he became the most influential man in Athens. His policies commended themselves to most of the citizens (who liked, for example, the small payment of two obols for jury service). In 451 at his instigation the citizenship was restricted to those whose parents were both Athenian citizens. From this time until his death he dominated Athenian politics, being elected *strategos fifteen times in succession. Under his guidance Athens adopted an imperialistic policy, and the *Delian League, created to keep the Persians out of Greece, was converted into an Athenian empire. Pericles extended its influence to the Hellespont by planting cleruchies there (see CLERUCH), and he established an important colony at *Thurii in 443 to spread Athenian influence in Italy. He appears to have tried to call a congress of all Greek states to consider the rebuilding of temples destroyed by the Persians, and some measure of political union, but nothing was achieved owing to the opposition of Sparta. In 437 he founded a colony at *Amphipolis, and at about this time led an expedition to establish Athenian influence in the Black Sea area, first having reduced Samos in 439 after the island had revolted from the Delian League.

To what extent Pericles was responsible for the policy that involved Athens in war with Sparta, Corinth, Aegina, and Boeotia during the period 459–446 is not known, but in the Thirty Years' Peace (so-called: war broke out again in 431) which followed he won Sparta's recognition of the empire (see ATHENS 2 (ii)). He was responsible for the building of the *Parthenon (begun in 447) and the Propylaea and other important buildings of this time. Cimon's political heir and Pericles' bitter enemy, who attacked Pericles for misappropriating Delian League funds for the building programme, was *Thucydidēs son of Melesias, whose ostracism, perhaps in 443, left Pericles with a free hand. It is likely that Pericles foresaw war with Sparta well in advance, and he resisted all *Peloponnesian demands. When war started in 431, Pericles dictated a policy for Athens calculated to neutralize Spartan superiority on land, but it involved considerable hardship for the population of Attica. Nevertheless his authority was undiminished until the ravages of the plague in 430 broke Athenian morale. He was then removed from office, tried for embezzlement, and fined. Soon after, he was again elected strategos, but he too had caught the plague, and he died six months later. No other Athenian ever achieved Pericles' unchallenged ascendancy. The historian Thucydides, his great admirer, says that under him Athens, though nominally a democracy, was in fact ruled by its first citizen. He was a man of powerful character, incorruptible, grave and reserved in manner, dignified in speech. He associated with the cultivated men and intellectuals of the day, Pheidias, Anaxagoras, Sophocles, Herodotus. His first marriage ended in divorce, but he formed a lasting union with Aspasia, a celebrated and cultivated *hetaera. The Funeral Oration which he delivered over the Athenian dead after the first year of the war (Thucydides 2. 35–46) expresses his high concept of Athens and the Athenian democracy, although his ideals included undisguised imperialism. Pericles' younger son by Aspasia, also called Pericles, though illegitimate was granted citizenship out of respect for his father; he was put to death after the battle of *Arginusae in 406.

Peri hi'ppikēs, see HORSEMANSHIP.

Peri hy'psous, see LONGINUS ON THE SUBLIME.

Perikeiro'menē ('shorn hair'), Greek comedy by *Menander, of which about half has been discovered on papyrus.

A poor merchant Pataecus has exposed his twin children, a boy and a girl. The boy Moschion is adopted by a rich woman who subsequently marries Pataecus, and the latter adopts Moschion, not knowing that he is really his own son. The girl Glycera, now the mistress of a soldier Polemon, is discovered kissing Moschion, whom she knows to be her brother, although he is still ignorant of this fact. In jealousy Polemon cuts off her hair (hence the title of the play), whereupon she takes refuge in the house of the now wealthy Pataecus. Some trinkets left with her when she was exposed reveal her identity, and Moschion also discovers his identity by eavesdropping. Thus all are reconciled and Glycera is able to marry Polemon.

Pe'rillus, see PHALARIS.

Pe'riochae ('summaries'), see LIVY.

perioi'koi ('dwellers around', i.e. around Sparta), in Laconia (the south-east district of the Peloponnese), the free inhabitants of such small towns and villages as were not subjugated to *Sparta (see 1 and 2). They were, however, under Spartan supervision, served in the army and paid taxes on a par with Spartan citizens although they had no political rights in the Spartan state. They carried on what industry and commerce there was, from which Spartans were excluded. It is impossible to tell what proportion of the population was Dorian and what pre-Dorian (see DORIAN INVASION).

Peripate'tic School, the Aristotelian school of philosophy in Athens (see ARISTOTLE 1). Aristotle taught in the groves and gymnasium of the *Lyceum; one of the buildings (either in his day or in that of his successor Theophrastus) had a covered walk, peripatos, from which the school derived its name. Another explanation given in ancient times for the origin of the name was that Aristotle was accustomed to 'walk about' (peripatein) while lecturing.

peripetei'a, in Greek tragedy, a 'surprising turn of events'; see POETICS.

Pe'riplus (*Periplous*, 'voyage of exploration'); see ARRIAN and SCYLAX.

Pe'riplus maris Erythrae'i ('voyage of exploration around the Red Sea'), the work of an anonymous Greek traveller of the first century AD, describing the coasts of the Red Sea and the Arabian Gulf. It shows knowledge of part of India, and of East Africa as far south as Zanzibar.

pēro, in Roman dress, a thick boot of raw hide.

Pēro, daughter of Neleus; see MELAMPUS.

Persa ('the Persian'), Roman comedy by *Plautus. The subject is the deception of a pimp, to whom a Persian sells a beautiful Arabian captive. But the Persian is in fact the *parasite Saturio and the captive is his daughter; he has agreed to the deceit for the sake of a good meal.

Persae. **1.** Greek tragedy by Aeschylus; see PERSIANS. **2.** A nome by *Timotheus (1).

Perse'phonē (Lat. Prōse'rpina), also known as Korē ('daughter'), in Greek myth, the daughter of Zeus and Demeter, snatched away to be queen of the Underworld by *Hadēs while she was picking flowers in the meadows of Enna in central Sicily, remembered in Milton's lines from *Paradise Lost* as

> that faire field
> Of Enna, where Proserpin gathring flours
> Her self a fairer Floure by gloomie Dis
> Was gatherd, which cost Ceres all that pain
> To seek her through the World.
>
> (4.268–72)

For Demeter's search for her daughter see DEMETER. Zeus yielded at length to her lamentations, but Persephone could not be entirely released from the Underworld because she had eaten some pomegranate seeds (as was revealed by Ascalaphus, son of Acheron, river of the Underworld, whom Demeter thereupon turned into an owl). It was arranged that she should spend eight (or six) months of the year on earth and the remainder with Hades. The myth is told in the *Homeric Hymn to Demeter, by Ovid in his *Fasti* and *Metamorphoses*, and by Claudian in *De raptu Proserpinae*. Persephone was understood in ancient times to symbolize the seed corn that must descend into the earth so that from seeming death new life may germinate; she later came to symbolize death. Cicero visited Enna and tells in his Verrine orations (see CICERO (1) 1) how he found the priestess and inhabitants griefstricken because Verres had stolen their statue of Demeter.

Perse'polis, in Persia, the residence and the burial place of the Achaemenid kings (Cyrus, Darius, Xerxēs, etc.). In 331 BC Alexander the Great captured and looted it and set fire to the palaces. The bas-reliefs which survive are among the finest extant examples of Achaemenid art.

Perseus. **1.** In Greek myth, the son of Zeus and Danae. See DANAE for the story of his birth, of the prophecy that he would kill his grandfather Acrisius, and of the casting away of mother and child and their arrival on the island of Seriphos, where Polydectēs was king. Polydectes fell in love with Danae, but his love was not returned. Perseus was now a young man, and Polydectes, finding him an obstacle to his designs on Danae, persuaded him to undertake the dangerous venture of obtaining the head of Medusa (see GORGONS), thinking that he would be destroyed. But the gods favoured him: although accounts vary as to which gods gave him which gifts, they commonly say that Pluto lent him a helmet which would make him invisible, Hermes wings for his feet, Athena a mirror (so that he need not look directly at Medusa, whose gaze turned people to stone), and the nymphs a wallet to put the head in. Directions for finding Medusa were given him by the *Graiae. On his return, having killed Medusa, Perseus rescued *Andromeda from where she was chained to a rock, and married her, after turning Phineus, another suitor, to stone when he attempted to carry her off. It is also said that with the Gorgon's head he turned *Atlas into a mountain, because Atlas had been inhospitable to him on his travels. Perseus then returned to Seriphos, just in time to save Danae from the violence of Polydectes, whom he turned to stone. Leaving his brother Dictys there as king Perseus now went to his native Argos, but found that his grandfather Acrisius had gone to Larisa in Thessaly. There Perseus, taking part in some games, accidentally killed him when throwing a discus and thus fulfilled the prophecy. He refused to take his grandfather's kingdom himself, to which he was heir, but withdrew to Asia, where his son Persēs became ruler of the Persians, supposedly named after him; or, according to another version, took Tiryns in exchange for Argos and founded Mycenae.

2. King of Macedon 179–166 BC, elder son of Philip V. He devoted his energies to consolidating Macedonian power and prestige in Greece at a time when Greece, while nominally independent, was under the protection (and will) of Rome. When in 171 Perseus refused to accede to Roman requests that infringed his liberty, Rome sent an army which through indiscipline and incompetence failed to make headway (the Third Macedonian War). Finally the Roman general Aemilius *Paullus was sent; he restored morale and utterly defeated the Macedonians at Pydna in 168. Perseus was taken to Rome and died there two years later (see MACEDONIA 3).

Persians (Gk. *Persai*, Lat. *Persae*), Greek tragedy by *Aeschylus, produced in 472 BC. Pericles was *choregos.

The chorus of Persian elders express their

anxiety for the fate of Xerxēs' expedition of 480 against Greece (see PERSIAN WARS), and Atossa, mother of Xerxes, tells of ominous dreams and portents. A messenger arrives and announces the disaster of Salamis, giving a vivid account of the battle and the destruction of the Persian fleet. The chorus call up the spirit of the dead Darius (father of Xerxes), who sees in the catastrophe the accomplishment of oracles and the punishment by the gods of excessive pride. He foretells the defeat at Plataea. Xerxes himself arrives and the play ends in general lamentations. The author displays a certain compassion for the vanquished, mingled with pride in the great victory of the Greeks.

Persian Wars, fought by Greece 490–479 BC. The Assyrian empire in *Asia Minor had collapsed with the capture of Nineveh in 612 BC by the Medes (in alliance with the Babylonians), who under their kings Cyaxarēs and Astyagēs (585–549 BC) became the most powerful people in that part of the world. But their empire in turn passed to the Persians, their kinsmen, when Astyages was challenged and defeated by his Persian vassal Cyrus in 549. Cyrus extended his dominion over large territories: he conquered Lydia (where Croesus was then king) and the Greek cities of Asia Minor, and carried his rule far eastwards. His son Cambysēs (king 529–522) conquered Egypt, and the Persian empire thus encircled the eastern Mediterranean. *Darius (king 521–486) succeeded Cambyses, consolidated the empire (as he recorded in the famous Persian inscriptions at Bisotun), and established a beneficent despotism over its provinces. He next sought to make his northern frontier secure by an expedition, in about 514, through Thrace into Scythia. This almost ended in disaster (see HISTIAEUS), but Darius had obtained a footing in Europe. His further operations in this direction were delayed by a revolt in 499 of the Ionian Greek cities of Asia Minor, restive under Persian rule exercised through Greek tyrants. In this *Aristagoras of Miletus took the leading part; seeking help in Greece, he failed to obtain it from Sparta but won support at Athens and Eretria (in Euboea). An Ionian force, with a body of Athenian hoplites, reached Sardis and burned it in 498. Despite further Greek successes in Caria and Cyprus the Persians recovered their losses, invaded Ionia, and crushed the Greek fleet at Ladē (an island off Miletus) in 494. Miletus and other Greek cities were sacked (see PHRYNICHUS), but democratic local government in Ionia was thereafter permitted.

Darius, not forgetting the part played by Athens and Eretria in the revolt, now turned his attention to Greece. He set about his preparations methodically. In 492 Mardonius, his nephew and son-in-law, reduced Thrace and the island of Thasos, and made Macedonia submit. In 490 Datis and Artaphernēs sailed with a Persian army to Euboea, destroyed Eretria and landed in Attica at Marathon (probably on the advice of the former Athenian tyrant *Hippias). An Athenian appeal to Sparta for help was delivered in record time by the runner *Pheidippidēs (see also in this connection PAN), but the Spartans were celebrating the Carnea and refused from religious scruples to start before the new moon; in consequence the Athenians, numbering some ten thousand, had to face a far stronger enemy with help only from Plataea, who sent all her hoplites, a thousand men. (This act of loyalty was long remembered.) The sequence of events is not altogether clear, but it seems that both sides delayed battle, the Persians perhaps waiting for Athenian traitors sympathetic to Hippias to make a move. The polemarch Callimachus commanded the Athenians, but *Miltiadēs was one of the *strategoi* and he was responsible for the plan of campaign. When the Persians had withdrawn part of their troops, perhaps to sail to Athens, Miltiades, whose force was stationed on the heights overlooking the narrow plain of Marathon, fell upon and utterly routed the remainder. According to Herodotus, 6,400 Persians were killed, and 192 Athenians, including the polemarch. The Spartans arrived in time to inspect the battlefield. Some of the Persians sailed to Athens (in response to a signal, a shield gleaming in the sun on Mount Pentelicus, said to have been given by traitors) but Athenian troops anticipated them by a forced march and the Persians retreated. This was the end of the First Persian War, in reality a minor affair aimed only at Athens and Eretria, but in popular estimation soon acquiring mythical status. The burial mound of the dead is still visible at Marathon, and traces of hero cult have been found there. It has been pointed out as perhaps significant that the number of the Greek dead is equal to the number of mounted figures on the *Parthenon frieze. For Aristophanes and others sixty years later the 'men who fought at Marathon', *Marathōnomachai*, epitomized the stubborn virtues of the old soldier. The epitaph of Aeschylus the tragedian claimed as his only glory that he had fought in the battle.

Darius at once set about measures for a new invasion. But a revolt broke out in Egypt, and before this was subdued Darius died (485); he was succeeded by Xerxēs, his son by Atossa. Xerxes devoted three years to extensive diplomatic and military preparations. By preliminary diplomacy, the states of Thessaly, Boeotia, and Argos were won over, as well as the oracle at Delphi. It is not impossible that, as one historian claimed, the Carthaginian expedition of 480 against Sicily and Magna Graecia was the result of an agreement between Persia and Carthage made in the hope that Greek power would be destroyed simultaneously in the East and the West, to their mutual advantage. A canal was cut across the promontory of Mount Athos to spare the Persian fleet a dangerous piece of navigation; a bridge was built across the Strymon, and two bridges of ships across the *Hellespont (when these were destroyed by a storm, others were constructed in their place and Xerxes had the sea whipped and fetters thrown into it to symbolize his mastery; he also had the engineers beheaded). In 480 the Persian army, after being reviewed by Xerxes at Abȳdus, crossed over to Europe. The Persian fleet set out at the same time. The numbers given by Herodotus for the size of the Persian forces are fantastic; the real numbers are a matter of conjecture: estimates suggested are 200,000 men for the army and 600 ships for the navy. At Athens *Themistoclēs had come to power: under his guidance the city had devoted its efforts to strengthening its naval power. At a Panhellenic congress held at the Isthmus in autumn 481 the Greeks agreed to end internal feuding for the common good, to send spies to Asia Minor, and to send ambassadors to win over powerful uncommitted cities (an attempt which failed). They also agreed to give the command of the land and sea forces to Spartans, namely *Leonidas and Eurybiadēs.

A second congress was held in the spring of 480, to determine strategy. The Greeks abandoned an attempt to resist the Persian advance in Thessaly, but seem to have decided to use their army and fleet in concert. First they posted their army in the narrow pass of Thermopylae on the Gulf of Malia, with the Greek fleet near it, close to the headland of Artemisium at the northern end of Euboea. For two days Leonidas and his contingent (the main body of the army again delayed by the festival of the Carnea) held back the Persians at Thermopylae and inflicted heavy losses on them. Then Ephialtēs, a Malian, showed the Persians a mountain path by which they could turn the Greek position. When Leonidas heard what had happened he dismissed his allies but remained with his 300 Spartans to die heroically in an impossible last stand. Their famous epitaph was written by Simonides:

> Tell them in Lacedaemon, passer-by,
> That here obedient to their words we lie.

Meanwhile the Persian fleet, advancing south along a dangerous coast, suffered heavy losses in late-summer gales and had had a series of indecisive engagements with the Greek fleet. The latter, on receiving the news of Thermopylae, withdrew to Salamis, perhaps to reinforce a second line of defence at the Isthmus of Corinth as advocated by the Peloponnesians, since all central Greece was now lost. The civilian population of Athens was evacuated (to Aegina, Troezen, and Salamis), in accordance with the meaning, Themistocles said, of a second, more ambiguous, oracle from Delphi, the first having counselled flight to the West; the 'wooden wall'

in which the oracle told the Athenians to trust was, according to Themistocles, the navy. Only the treasurers and priestesses remained behind on the Acropolis to guard the possessions of the gods. The Persians, reinforced by the Boeotian cavalry, immediately advanced into Attica and ravaged it; the Acropolis was captured and the buildings on it burnt.

The Peloponnesians meanwhile were engaged in building defences across the Isthmus. By the persuasion of Themistocles, Eurybiades and the Greek fleet forced a battle in the narrows of Salamis; under the eyes of Xerxes the Persians were decisively defeated. A force which they had landed on the little island of Psyttaleia, to deal with any shipwrecked Greeks, was massacred. Xerxes at once returned to Persia with the remnant of his fleet, leaving Mardonius with a picked force to winter in Thessaly and continue the campaign by land. In the following year (479) Mardonius, after two vain attempts to negotiate a separate peace with Athens, returned to the attack. His superior cavalry forces severely harassed an oncoming army of Peloponnesian and Athenian hoplites. The opposing armies met near Plataea, the Greeks being under the command of the Spartan *Pausanias and the Athenian contingent under *Aristeidēs. The Greeks won a complete victory, largely owing to the courage and discipline of the hoplites, and Mardonius was killed. The Persians retreated to their entrenched camp, but this was taken and the defenders massacred. On the same day (it was said) the Greek fleet under Leotychidas attacked the Persians, who had withdrawn to Mycalē (on the Ionian coast opposite Samos) and beached their ships. The Greeks landed, captured the Persian camp, and destroyed their ships. The Ionian Greek troops in the Persian army deserted, the beginning of a new revolt by the Greeks of the islands and mainland of Asia Minor. The Peloponnesians now returned home, but the Athenian squadron under *Xanthippus (Pericles' father) proceeded to the Hellespont and there freed Sestus from the Persians (478). For Sparta's withdrawal from operations against Persia and Athens' succession to the Greek leadership see PAUSANIAS (1) and DELIAN LEAGUE.

As a result of the Persian Wars, Greeks in general became increasingly conscious of their own nationality and superiority, and the Athenian city-state in particular gained enormously in pride and self-confidence. Our knowledge of these wars is derived mainly from Herodotus. Of contemporary evidence there are inscriptions, some epigrams of Simonides, and Aeschylus' tragedy the *Persians*. The Persian side of the story is unknown.

Pe'rsius Flaccus, Aulus (AD 34–62), known generally as Persius, Latin satirical poet. Born at Volaterrae in Etruria, he belonged to an equestrian family and was a relative of the famous *Arria, wife of Paetus. He was educated at Rome, and became the pupil of the *Stoic Cornutus, who exercised a strong influence on him; a fellow pupil was the Roman epic poet Lucan. He joined the group of Stoics around *Thrasea Paetus, the senator who was married to the younger Arria. He bequeathed his books and a part of his large fortune to Cornutus, who accepted the books but not the money. Persius is said to have been a modest and gentle man. He took no part in public life, died young, and left only a small amount of literary work: six satires (650 hexameter lines) modelled on Lucilius and Horace, and a prologue (in scazons; see METRE, LATIN 3 (iii) b). Except for the first satire, these poems are homilies rather than satires in the strict sense, preaching an uncompromising Stoic morality as it could be applied to private life, and only incidentally touching on public life. He uses an incongruous mixture of styles and his language is obscure, but his moral sincerity is unforced and scarcely priggish when considered against the background of Nero's Rome.

Satire 1 is a criticism of the poets at Nero's court and the contemporary fashion for elegant, unrealistic poetry, which Persius finds significant of the corruption of Roman virtue and hardihood. Satire 2 is concerned with the right use of prayer, mocking those who ask for external goods rather than virtue. Satire 3 is a diagnosis of the damage done to sick souls by sloth and vice. Satire 4 urges a young statesman (Nero?) to disregard public admiration and pursue virtue by examining his own character. Satire 5 is a eulogy of Cornutus, describing the simple and studious life the poet leads when in the philosopher's company; its subject is the rarity of true freedom—we are all the slaves of our passions or superstitions. Satire 6 is addressed to Caesius Bassus (a lyric poet commended by Quintilian) who edited Persius' satires after his death and is said to have died in the eruption of Vesuvius in AD 79; it expounds the wisdom of living comfortably, but not covetously.

Perusine War. When in 41 BC relations between Octavian and Mark Antony deteriorated (see ROME 7), Antony's wife Fulvia and brother Lucius Antonius began open war against Octavian on Antony's behalf and without his consent in a campaign known as the Perusine War. Lucius was besieged in the Etruscan hill-city of Perusia (Perugia) during the winter of 41/0 (one of the besieging commanders being the young *Agrippa (1)) until starved into surrender. Octavian executed the Perusine senate but forgave Lucius.

Pervigi'lium Ve'neris ('eve of Venus'), a poem preserved in the Latin Anthology (see ANTHO-LOGY 2) written in trochaic tetrameters (see METRE, GREEK 6), ninety-three lines long; the author and date are unknown, but it was written after the second century AD, perhaps as late as the fourth century. The setting is Sicily, on the eve of the spring festival of Venus; the poem celebrates the triumph of spring, the resurgence of life in the world, and the next day's festival, its spirit summed up by the passionate refrain, *cras amet qui nunquam amavit, quique amavit cras amet* ('tomorrow he who has never loved and he who has loved, let them both love'). The poem ends on a poignant note: *illa cantat; nos tacemus; quando ver venit meum?* ('[the nightingale] sings; we are silent; when will my own springtime come?'). The poem is unique in Latin for its sensuous beauty here enhanced by the strong beat of the trochaic rhythm and by assonance, both characteristic of later Latin accentual poetry.

pe'tasos, broad-brimmed felt hat; see DRESS 1 and HERMES.

Peti'llius Ceri'ālis, Quintus, see BRITAIN 9.

Petrō'nius A'rbiter (d. AD 65), Latin satirical writer, author of the *Satyricon* ('tales of satyrs'), usually assumed to be the voluptuary of that name at Nero's court, whose life and death are memorably described by Tacitus (*Annals*, 16. 18). He was at one time governor of Bithynia and later a consul, and was subsequently admitted by the emperor Nero to the inner circle of his intimates and chosen by him, in Tacitus' words, as his 'arbiter of taste', *elegantiae arbiter*, a play on his name. Tigellinus, prefect of the praetorians, whose jealousy he aroused, falsely accused him to the emperor as implicated in the conspiracy of Piso (see ROME 10); he committed suicide, but not before he had smashed a valuable wine-ladle to prevent it falling into the emperor's hands, and written a letter detailing the latter's vices. Tacitus describes Petronius as devoted to the refined pursuit of pleasure, indolent in his ordinary life, but energetic in public affairs.

Of his long picaresque novel, the *Satyricon*, only parts of books 14, 15, and 16 survive. Like the Menippean satires (see MENIPPUS) it is in prose interspersed with verse, and describes the disreputable adventures of two young men Encolpius (the narrator) and his friend Ascyltus, and the boy Giton who plays the others off against each other, as they wander through the low haunts of the semi-Greek cities of southern Italy. The three are completely devoid of morals but have a quick intelligence which sees them through their escapades, narrated with dispassionate realism. The principal episode in the surviving portion of the work is the *Cena Trimalchionis*, 'Trimalchio's dinner-party' (it appears in only one manuscript, not found until the seventeenth century). Trimalchio is a freedman, a vulgar *nouveau-riche* to whose dinner-party the adventurers obtain admission. He and his wife Fortunata present an ostentatious display of wealth in the decoration of the house and in the profusion of fantastic dishes set before the guests; there are grotesque incidents during dinner—a drunken brawl and a dog-fight—and ridiculous conversation; Trimalchio's absurd conduct as he becomes more and more drunk finally reaches a maudlin stage in which he describes the contents of his will and his future monument. Two good ghost stories round off the episode, one about a werewolf, the other about witches substituting a changeling made of straw for a boy. The whole is told with amazing vitality and panache.

A further character in the remaining incidents is a disreputable old poet named Eumolpus with whom the adventurers travel to Croton in south Italy to advance their fortunes by fraud. The sea-voyage ends in shipwreck, and the extant portion of the work ends with various amorous adventures and misfortunes. In the course of these Eumolpus expounds his views on epic poetry (in chapter 118 he refers, in a phrase that has since become famous, to *Horatii curiosa felicitas*, 'Horace's studied felicity'). As illustration of the kind of inspirational poetry of his own day that he deplores, he recites sixty iambics on the fall of Troy and some 300 hexameters on the civil war of 49 BC. It is Eumolpus who, at an earlier stage (111), relates the story of the widow of Ephesus who, watching inconsolably in the vault where her recently dead husband has been laid, is induced by a kindly soldier to take food, and presently to accept him as her lover. This is a story very similar in type to the *Milesian Tales*. Petronius' characters, while thoroughly disreputable, are not wholly unlikeable. The racy, vivid, colloquial Latin in which the *Satyricon* is written reveals a great deal about the popular speech of the time, as does the Rabelaisian humour about tastes and attitudes. A few lyric and elegiac poems by the same author have also survived.

pets. Animals were kept as pets from early times, but, the evidence suggests, less by the Greeks than by the Romans. Epitaphs (written as literature rather than for inscription on graves) attest the affection in which pet animals were held. *Dogs were popular, especially the small, white, long-haired Maltese dog: Publius' dog Issa was probably a Maltese (see Martial 1. 109). The Romans kept tamed birds, especially starlings, magpies, ravens, and crows, which could be taught to imitate speech. Lesbia's 'sparrow' was probably something a little more colourful, perhaps a bullfinch. Nightingales and blackbirds were kept for their song, cocks and quails for fighting; parrots were kept more rarely. The Romans occasionally had pet monkeys. Greeks and Romans both knew a creature with cat-like characteristics, but it was not the domestic cat as known today, which seems not to have been found in Europe until the first century AD and did not become

common until many centuries later. Other animals were kept outside the house, such as pond fish, murenas and mullet which might be trained to eat from their masters' hands.

Peu'tinger Table, see MAPS.

Phaeā'cians (Phaiākes), in Homer's *Odyssey*, the magical sea-faring people of the island of Scheria on which Odysseus was cast ashore. Their king was Alcinōus.

Phaedo (Phaidōn), of Elis, in the north-west Peloponnese (b. *c.*418 BC), founder of the philosophical school there. He came to Athens as a young man, perhaps brought as a slave and later set free, and became one of Socrates' most devoted pupils. Plato named after him the dialogue in which Socrates' last hours are described. After the latter's death Phaedo returned to Elis.

Phaedo (see above), dialogue by *Plato in which Phaedo narrates the discussion that took place between Socrates and his friends during the last hours of his life, and the manner of his dying. The dialogue starts from the remark of Socrates that the genuine philosopher is one who is willing to die because it is his affirmation of the principles by which he has lived; the philosopher will be convinced that after his death the soul of the just man will be under the care of good and wise gods no less than before —and perhaps in the company of the best men of the past; moreover, death is the release of the soul from the body, and it has been the philosopher's aim during his lifetime to make the soul independent of bodily vicissitudes. Cebes' objection that the soul may not survive death leads to the series of arguments which make up the core of the dialogue and which, as they develop, are intended to vindicate Socrates' belief in the immortality of the soul. The reader is presented with the argument that learning is recollection of knowledge possessed in a former existence (an argument prominent in *Meno also) and therefore the soul must have existed before its present incarnation. The reader also meets the theory of Ideas or Forms by which a particular thing is what it is (e.g. by which a beautiful thing is beautiful) by partaking of the Idea of e.g. beauty. It is also argued that soul, which imparts life to the body, cannot admit death, and is therefore immortal. Socrates introduces this last section by giving an account of his intellectual history, memorably describing his conceptual difficulties with the kind of explanation of the physical world offered in the natural sciences (including the explanation of Anaxagoras; see PHILOSOPHY I) and the evolution of his own method of enquiry based on the formulation of successive hypotheses. The argument is rounded off with a myth which gives a speculative picture of the afterlife and the judgement of departed souls. Belief in 'either this or something like it' is said to be a noble risk. The dialogue ends with the moving description of Socrates' fearless acceptance of the cup of hemlock. This is the work from which *Cato (of Utica) is said to have drawn strength on the night before he committed suicide.

Phaedra, in Greek myth, daughter of *Minos, king of Crete, and Pasiphaë, and sister of Ariadnē; she married Theseus, king of Athens. For her story see HIPPOLYTUS.

Phaedra, Roman tragedy by *Seneca (2), based on the *Hippolytus* of Euripides with certain variations. Here it is Phaedra herself (not the nurse on her behalf) who declares her love to her stepson Hippolytus; she then in person (not in a posthumous letter) slanders him to Theseus; and finally it is she herself who discloses her guilt, before she dies (not the goddess Artemis after her suicide).

Phaedrus, a dialogue by *Plato in direct speech between Socrates and his friend Phaedrus, in a pleasant spot on the banks of the river Ilissus a little outside Athens. Socrates claims (only in this dialogue, and perhaps ironically) to be moved by the beauties of nature, to the extent that he ascribes the exalted tone of his second speech to their influence. The dialogue begins with Phaedrus reading a speech purporting to be by the Attic orator *Lysias (see also PARODY) expounding a paradoxical view of love, that it is better for a boy to accept as a lover a man who is not truly in love with him than to accept one who is, which Socrates counters with a cleverer speech on the same theme. However, Socrates is then prevented from departing by his 'divine sign' (see SOCRATES) which convinces him that he has been blasphemous to associate love only with physical passion: he recants in another speech. The true lover is worthy of respect; he is mad with a madness that comes from the gods. To understand this it is necessary to understand the nature of the soul, and Socrates first establishes that the soul is immortal. He then describes its nature and destiny by the analogy of a charioteer driving a pair of winged horses. These represent the three parts of the soul: reason, in control of man's sensual and spiritual appetites. The true lover may be at first attracted physically to a like-minded person, and if his love is reciprocated, and the sensual appetites overcome, both lovers may leave behind love of physical beauty for the common pursuit of that beauty which is to be finally found only in the Idea (or Form) of the Good. After this the conversation returns, with an abrupt change from the poetic to the prosaic, to a discussion of rhetoric based on the three speeches just made; rhetoric should have as its foundation knowledge of the truth, which can be obtained only by those passionate in its pursuit. The ancients debated whether the dialogue was concerned primarily with love or with rhetoric.

Phaedrus, Gaius Julius (*c*.15 BC–*c*. AD 50), Thracian slave who came to Rome and became a freedman in the household of Augustus, the author (in Latin) of a collection of fables in five books containing some hundred stories, published probably in the thirties of the first century AD. There is also an appendix of another thirty-two fables, probably also by Phaedrus. The collection includes fables proper, a number of anecdotes (e.g. about Aesop, Socrates, and Menander), and defences of the author against detractors. The fables are based on those of *Aesop and on beast-stories from other sources which had come to be attributed to Aesop. They are written in verse, in iambic senarii (see METRE, LATIN 2), and their object is two-fold, to give advice and to entertain. They are generally serious or satirical, dealing with the injustices of life and social and political evils, but occasionally they are light and amusing. In general they express patient resignation. Phaedrus observed in the prologue to the third book that the fable was invented so that a slave might say obliquely what he dared not speak openly. Their political allusions, intentional or imagined, offended *Sejanus, and Phaedrus suffered some unknown punishment. Many of the stories are well known to us, having been handed down (often through the Greek collection of *Babrius) through medieval times to the present day. They include 'The Wolf and the Lamb', 'The Fox and the Sour Grapes' and 'King Log and King Water-snake'. One book is dedicated to Eutychus, the celebrated chariot-driver of the Greens (see CHARIOT-RACES) in the reign of Caligula. The fables are inferior to those of the French poet La Fontaine in dramatic sense and poetry, but the style is clear and simple. Phaedrus is the source of the expression 'adding insult to injury', *iniuriae qui addideris contumeliam* (v. 3. 5).

Phaeno'mena, astronomical poem of *Aratus.

Phaestus, ancient city of south Crete, the site of a Minoan palace (see CRETE) destroyed in about 1400 BC. The clay tablet found there in 1908, known as the Phaestus disc, apparently dates from early in the second millennium and is inscribed on both sides with pictographic writing, otherwise unknown but almost certainly syllabic, running from left to right. The script does not seem to relate to *Linear A or B, and it is not known whether the disc originated in Crete or what its purpose was. The number of different signs employed is 45. These were impressed on the wet clay by individual stamps or punches. The fact that no other object impressed with these stamps has been found at Phaestus suggests a foreign origin.

Phä'ethon, in Greek myth, son of *Helios (Sun) and Clymenē (2). When he grew up he sought out his father who recognized him and offered him his choice of gift. Phaethon asked to be allowed to drive his father's chariot for one day. In spite of Helios' warning he attempted to do so, but soon proved unequal to controlling the horses. They bolted from their course and the earth was in danger of being burnt up, when Zeus intervened and hurled a thunderbolt at Phaethon, who fell into the river *Eridanus. His sisters wept for him until they were turned into poplars; their tears, oozing from the trees, hardened into amber.

phalanx, generally, Greek heavy infantry (*hoplites) arranged in battle formation, but the name is specifically applied to the Macedonian infantry formation after the reform ascribed to Philip II of Macedon in 359 BC, based on that of *Epaminondas of Thebes. This phalanx owed part of its great success under Philip, and later under his son Alexander the Great, to the fact that Macedonia could produce as many as 25,000 men to serve in such formations. In contrast with the hoplite battle-line of about eight rows, the phalanx consisted of sixteen ranks of infantry (famously deepened to fifty by Epaminondas when he defeated Sparta at the battle of Leuctra in 371 BC); the soldiers were armed with unusually long pikes (*sarisai*, about 4 m. or 13 ft. long), so that they presented *en masse* an impenetrable thicket of shafts. The phalanx had comparatively little flexibility but prevailed by sheer weight and perfect drill. Its vulnerable flanks and rear were guarded by cavalry. Inside the phalanx the tactical unit was the brigade (*taxis*: about 1,500 men), subdivided into companies (*lochoi*) and sections (*dekadĕs*). Under Alexander, Macedonian manpower began to decline, and towards the end of his career Alexander planned a mixed phalanx of Greeks and light-armed Persians with bows and javelins. Weaknesses in the phalanx gradually became apparent; its inferiority in flexibility to the Roman maniple (see ARMY, ROMAN 2) was shown by the Roman defeat of Philip V at the battle of Cynoscephalae in 197 BC and of Perseus at Pydna in 168 BC.

Pha'laris, tyrant of Acragas in Sicily in the mid-sixth century BC, soon after the foundation of that city (*c.*580 BC). He was remembered for his cruelty, supposedly roasting his enemies to death in a brazen bull with a fire underneath, their cries sounding like the roar of the bull. This was the invention of a certain Perillus, who was its first victim. The so-called 'Letters of Phalaris' were proved by the English scholar Richard Bentley, writing at the end of the seventeenth century, to be a forgery; they were written in Attic, not Sicilian Doric Greek, and several towns mentioned in them were in fact founded long after the time of Phalaris. The real author was a sophist of perhaps the second century AD.

Phalē'rum, modern Phaleron, the principal harbour of Athens until the early fifth century BC, i.e. before the Persian Wars and the development and fortification of *Piraeus, east of which it lies. It is an open roadstead, offering little protection to ships. For the Long Wall connecting it with Athens see LONG WALLS.

phallus, model of the male genital organ, the symbol of fertility carried in procession in many ancient religious ceremonies in order to stimulate the fruitfulness of the earth, the flocks, and the people, and so prevent weakness of the race. In Greece the phallus was especially associated with the worship of Dionysus, the god of fertility (hence its connection with comedy; see COMEDY, GREEK I and 2); of Hermēs, the god of pastures, crops, and herds (see also HERMAE); of Pan, the protector of flocks; and of Demeter, the earth-goddess. Occasionally a god Phalēs was invoked, the personification of the phallus. In the Roman festival of the Liberalia (comparable with the Greek Dionysia) the phallus was similarly carried in procession (see also PRIAPUS and MAGIC 5 (i)).

Phāon, legendary boatman of Mytilenē (in Lesbos), to whom Aphroditē gave youth and beauty because he had carried her (in the guise of an old woman) across the sea without taking payment. See SAPPHO.

Pharos, the white marble lighthouse built probably in the reign of Ptolemy II Philadelphus on the island of Pharos at *Alexandria (hence its name), and one of the *Seven Wonders of the ancient world. It was polygonal, built in three sections, and said to have been 113 m. (370 ft.) high. The light came from a fire burning in the top, projected by some arrangement of mirrors. The Pharos stood until the fourteenth century.

Pharsā'lia or **Pharsā'lus,** in Thessaly, the scene of the decisive defeat of Pompey by Caesar in the summer of 48 BC (see ROME 7). Pharsalus was the name of the town, Pharsalia of its territory.

Pharsā'lia, Latin epic poem by *Lucan (AD 39–65) in ten books of hexameters, on the civil war between Pompey and Julius Caesar (the title in the manuscripts is *De bello civili*, 'on the civil war': the name *Pharsalia* stems from a mistranslation of 9.985). The poem was apparently not completed and ends abruptly in the tenth book with Caesar at war in Egypt. Lucan probably intended to continue the narrative to the death of Caesar, if not further. His main source was Livy, but it was not his purpose to give a full, historical account of the war (for which see CAESAR), and apart from omissions there are a few notable departures from historical truth, as when he portrays Cicero haranguing Pompey on the eve of the battle of Pharsalus: in fact Cicero missed the battle because of illness. The poem is written with strong sympathy for the cause of Pompey and the republic.

Book 1 first touches on the sources of the war and gives a vivid sketch of the characters of the two leaders; then proceeds to Caesar's crossing of the river Rubicon into Italy. A striking passage shows Caesar confronted by the spirit of Rome, which challenges his right to advance. The dismay at Rome is described, and the flight of citizens and senators.

Book 2 continues the relation of events in Italy (with a long digression on the massacres of Marius and Sulla; see ROME 6), the resolution of Cato (2) and (Marcus Junius) Brutus to resist Caesar, the episode of the resistance of Corfinium (under the command of the senator Lucius Domitius Ahenobarbus), Pompey's withdrawal to Brundisium and his escape to Epirus.

Book 3 is concerned with the occupation of Rome by Caesar and with the fighting on land and sea about Massilia (Marseilles): there is a notable description of the sacred Druid grove in the neighbourhood of the town which Caesar had felled. The book ends with the horrific description of a sea-battle.

The first part of *book 4* deals with Caesar's campaign in Gaul. The narrative then passes to Illyricum (in the north-west of Greece) and includes the incident of the attempted escape of some Caesarian soldiers on three rafts; one of these is stopped and the soldiers on board, Gauls from Opitergium (Oderzo), kill each other rather than surrender. There follow the expedition of Curio, Caesar's commander, to Africa, and his defeat and death at the hands of Juba. There is a digression on the legend of Hercules and Antaeus.

The most interesting parts of *book 5* describe the Delphic Oracle, which Appius, a Pompeian, goes to consult, receiving an ambiguous reply; and Caesar's attempt to cross the Adriatic Sea in a small boat on a stormy night.

Book 6 is occupied with the fighting around Dyrrhachium (Epidamnus, in Illyria) and Caesar's withdrawal to Thessaly. The fight to the death of Caesar's centurion Scaeva is graphically described. (In reality he survived, with, according to Caesar, 120 holes in his shield.) To Lucan's disgust, Sextus Pompeius (Pompey's younger son) consults the Thessalian witch Erichtho, who employs necromancy to foretell the destiny of the Pompeians.

Book 7 describes Pompey's deceptively happy dream before the battle of Pharsalus, the battle itself, and the ensuing scenes.

Book 8 deals with Pompey's flight first to Lesbos to join his wife and then to Egypt, and his murder there by the order of Pothinus, the pharaoh's chamberlain.

In *book 9*, Pompey's spirit is borne to heaven and Cato pronounces a splendid panegyric on the dead leader. Cato resolves to continue the war and marches with his troops to Mauretania (in North Africa). Confident in his Stoic faith and in the rightness of the course that he has chosen, he refuses to consult the oracle of Ammon. This book is largely praise of Cato. There is a digression on Egyptian serpents, their legendary origin in the blood of Medusa, the Gorgon, and their varieties. The Egyptians present Pompey's head to Caesar, who hypocritically laments his fate.

Book 10 describes Caesar's actions in Egypt, and his affair with Cleopatra. He is besieged by the troops of Pothinus and Achillas. At this point the poem ends abruptly.

Lucan had a difficult task in writing epic about events only a century before his own day. As a Stoic he discarded the epic convention of divine interventions to direct human actions, substituting an impersonal Fate or Fortune. He introduced a number of digressions, often displaying seemingly irrelevant learning (see *book 9* above). In general his work is often absurdly rhetorical and his straining for effect grotesque (e.g. his description of Caesar enjoying his breakfast among the corpses after Pharsalus, and of the wild beasts devouring the dead). But it is carried through with great vigour and brilliance; the sensational scenes are interspersed with passages of considerable power and pathos, such as that describing Pompey's farewell to Italy. The author's gift for incisive epigram is evident, and some lines have achieved fame: *victrix causa deis placuit sed victa Catoni* ('the conquering cause pleased the gods, the losing cause pleased Cato'); of Caesar, *nil actum credens cum quid superesset agendum* ('believing that nothing had been done if anything remained still to do'); and of friendship, *nulla fides unquam miseros elegit amicos* ('nobody ever chooses to be the faithful friend of those already unfortunate'). Lucan's feelings for his subject were sincere: he detested Caesar and all he stood for, while admitting his greatness; he makes Pompey a tragic figure and evokes sympathy for him and his cause. The verse is somewhat monotonous in technique and lacks flexibility, but at its best the rhetoric is vigorous and carries the reader along.

Phēgeus, in Greek myth, father of Arsinoē, wife of *Alcmaeon.

Phei'dias (*c*.490–432 BC), son of Charmidēs and one of the greatest of Athenian artists, famous especially as a sculptor but also as an architect and painter. An early work was the bronze statue of the goddess Athena on the Acropolis at Athens later called Promachos ('champion'), erected *c*.456 BC. It was about 10 m. (33 ft.) high, and when the bronze spear-tip and helmet crest caught the sun, they were said to be visible to sailors as they rounded Cape Sunium. Part of the base survives on the Acropolis. Another early statue which won a wide reputation for its remarkable beauty was the Lemnian Athena, given to Athens by the people of Lemnos, probably Athenian colonists, as a thank-offering, and known from a copy. Pheidias was responsible for the adornment of Athens in the mid-fifth century BC, under the direction of his friend *Pericles, and in particular for the construction of the *Parthenon. One of his two most famous cult statues of gold and ivory ('chryselephantine') was the very large statue of Athena in the Parthenon; the Greek traveller Pausanias (I. 24. 5) gives a description of it, from which several Roman copies have been identified. The other, considered Pheidias' masterpiece, was made for the temple of Zeus at *Olympia, and is known only from its representation on coins of Elis. It is said that when asked what model he was going to use for the likeness of Zeus, Pheidias replied that he would model it on Homer's lines in the *Iliad*, 'Cronion [Zeus] spoke, and nodded his dark brow, and the ambrosial locks waved from the king's immortal head; and he made great Olympus quake' (I. 528). The sculptures of the Parthenon, if not actually executed by the master, were no doubt designed by him, and he exerted a lasting influence on all Greek sculpture. His workshop at Olympia has been found, and a drinking cup inscribed with his name. In 432 enemies of Pericles, trying to attack him through his friends, accused Pheidias of embezzling gold intended for the statue of Athena, but he was able to prove his innocence. He was then charged with impiety and sent to prison, where he seems to have died in that same year.

Pheidi'ppides (or Philippides), the Athenian runner who, according to Herodotus (6. 105–6), was sent to request help from Sparta before the battle of Marathon in 490 BC (see PERSIAN WARS, also PAN). He arrived there the day after he left Athens, covering in that time a distance of 200 km. (125 miles) or more. On his way back he is said to have met the god Pan. The basis of the modern Marathon race (introduced at the first modern Olympic games at Athens in 1896) is a legend, which has no authority, that he ran the 42 km. (a little over 26 miles) from Athens to Marathon in order to join in the battle against the Persians, then ran back to Athens and, having announced the victory ('Greetings, we win!'), dropped dead.

Pheidon (perhaps first half of the seventh century BC, possibly nearly a century earlier), king of *Argos; he was a Heraclid, descended from *Temenus. According to Aristotle he exceeded his hereditary powers and made himself tyrant. He was clearly an important figure, but his dates and activities are obscure. He was remembered for three achievements: his recovery of the 'lot of Temenus', i.e. his unification of the Argolid; his standardization of weights and measures; and his seizure of the

management of the Olympian games from Elis. Evidence suggests that he was a very successful military leader, perhaps responsible for Argos succeeding Chalcis (in Euboea) as the greatest military power in Greece, which may have been the consequence of his introducing the hoplite phalanx into Argos. In particular he may have been responsible for the defeat by Argos of invading Spartans, at Hysiae, on the Argive side of the border between the two countries, in 669 BC. His standardization of weights and measures may have been the reform which governed the weight of the iron spits (*obeloi*) which were the precursors of coinage (see MONEY AND COINS).

pherecratē'an, see METRE, GREEK 3 and 5.

Phere'cratēs, see COMEDY, GREEK 4.

Pherecȳ'dēs, of Leros and Athens, a logographer of the early fifth century BC who spent most of his life at Athens and is sometimes confused with Pherecydes of Syros (an island in the Cyclades), who was a philosopher, reputedly the teacher of Pythagoras. His great work was a mythological history in ten books which began with a theogony and then gave an account of the heroic age and of the great families of that time whose descendants were contemporaries of the author. Only fragments survive. See LOGOGRAPHERS.

Phi'dias, see PHEIDIAS.

Phidi'ppidēs, see PHEIDIPPIDES.

Philē'bus, dialogue of Plato; see PLATO 2.

Philē'mōn, one of the chief writers of Greek New Comedy; see COMEDY, GREEK 6.

Philē'mōn and Baucis, an old man and his wife, in a story told by Ovid, who entertained Zeus and Hermēs in disguise as hospitably as their poverty would allow, after the gods had been repulsed by the rich. For this Philemon and Baucis were saved from a deluge that overwhelmed the land where they lived, and their dwelling was transformed into a temple of which they were made the first priest and priestess. They were also granted their request to die at the same time, and were then turned into trees whose boughs intertwined.

Philē'tās (or, perhaps more correctly, Philītas) of Cos (born not later than 320 BC), Greek poet and grammarian of the Hellenistic age, tutor of the (subsequent) king of Egypt Ptolemy II Philadelphus. His other distinguished pupils were said to include the scholar Zenodotus and the poet Theocritus. He was a writer of amatory poems, and particularly famed for his elegies, mentioned by Ovid and Propertius as their model. Only fragments of his work survive.

Philip (Philippos). 1. **Philip II,** king of *Macedon 359–336 BC, born in 383 or 382, youngest son of Amyntas, king of Macedon 393–369. The royal house of Macedon was descended from the Argive *Temenus, one of the *Heracleidae. When Philip's ancestor Alexander I competed in the Olympian games *c.*500 BC, he had to prove to the judges that he was not a barbarian but was of true Greek descent. Philip's mother Eurydicē was connected with another Macedonian royal house, the Lyncestae, descended from Bacchis (see BACCHIADAE). Philip laid the foundations of Macedon's rise to power in Greece.

1. *Early years.* As a boy Philip was sent to *Thebes for three years by the Theban commander *Pelopidas as security for the maintenance of Theban influence in Macedon. While in Thebes he met and learnt much from the great general *Epaminondas. He took over the government of Macedon in 359, his twenty-fourth year, after his brother Perdiccas III had been killed in battle, perhaps in the first instance as regent for his nephew Amyntas. The first years of his rule he devoted to consolidating his position, reorganizing the Macedonian army on the basis of the *phalanx, and crushing the Paeonians and the Illyrians who had defeated his brother. By a combination of diplomacy and military aggression Philip in 357 gained possession of the independent and strategically important city of *Amphipolis, a city which Athens had long wished to possess, and in 356 took the Athenian possession of Pydna (on the Thermaic Gulf). *Potidaea fell to Philip in 356 and Methone in 354 (when he lost an eye); Athens was gradually being ousted from all her positions in this area, and the control of the gold mines in Macedonia and Thrace may have enabled Philip to supplement diplomacy with bribery on a large scale. In time they produced for him over 1,000 talents a year. By now he had set his nephew aside and assumed the title of king. He married as his third wife Olympias, a Molossian princess from Epirus where the royal house traced its descent from the Greek hero Neoptolemus; their son Alexander (the Great) was born in 356. In the course of time Philip married seven wives, polygamy being thought desirable for a king whose duty it was to beget heirs. Only two of Philip's sons outlived him.

2. *Interference in Greece 353–346.* By 353 Philip had secured Macedon against Illyria, Paeonia, and Thrace; he had a marriage tie with Epirus; he had secured outlets to the north Aegean Sea, and he was allied to the remaining Greek power in that area, Olynthus and the *Chalcidic League. In this year the Thessalian League invited his assistance against the tyrants of Pherae (where Lycophron was now in control) and their allies the Phocians. After an early defeat, the only one of his career, Philip defeated and killed Onomarchus, the leader of the

Phocians, and his allies at the battle of the Crocus Field (as it is now known), by the coast south of Pherae, in 352. (See also SACRED WARS.) This gave him the mastery of Thessaly, and he suppressed the tyranny at Pherae and took possession of the Thessalian port of Pagasae. Only by the prompt action of Athens was he prevented from capturing Thermopylae in order to take the war into Phocis. He began to build a fleet and with this harassed the trade of Athens. Returning north he marched against Thrace and forced its three kings, one by one, to accept his overlordship. His dominion over the sea-coast of the Aegean now extended north and east from the neighbourhood of Thermopylae to the Propontis, with the exception of the Thracian Chersonese and Chalcidicē. The interests of Athens were gravely threatened, and *Demosthenes ((2) 4) in his speech known as the *First Philippic* called upon the Athenians to prepare to fight. But Athenian policy was at this time guided by *Eubulus, a cautious statesman and prudent advocate of peace (although he had commanded the forces that checked Philip at Thermopylae). In 349 Philip attacked Chalcidice, and Olynthus sought and obtained an alliance with Athens. But Euboea, perhaps encouraged by Philip, threw off Athenian domination, forcing Athens to divide her efforts between the two places. Philip reduced the cities one by one; Olynthus, left to last, fell in 348, was razed to the ground, and its inhabitants sold into slavery. Chalcidice was incorporated into Macedonia, and Athens had to recognize the independence of Euboea.

The exhaustion of the Athenian treasury, coupled with the news that Philip, at the request of Thebes, was about to march south into Greece to undertake the subjugation of the Phocians, brought home to Athens the necessity for peace with Philip, who also wished for it. What is known as the Peace of Philocratēs (after one of the Athenian negotiators) was concluded in 346, on the basis that Athens and Macedonia should then retain the territories of which each was then in possession. (For the story of the embassies that negotiated the Peace see DEMOSTHENES (2) 1.) Athens thus retained the Thracian Chersonese, but surrendered her long-standing claim to Amphipolis. Philip resisted a last-minute attempt by Athens to get Phocis included in the Peace. Philip appears to have wanted an alliance with Athens, perhaps needing the Athenian fleet for a projected Persian war, but any possibility of a friendly understanding between the two, though not unwelcome to Eubulus, would have been vehemently opposed by Demosthenes. By this Peace, Athens in effect abandoned the Phocians to their fate. Philip advanced south, Thermopylae was surrendered to him by its Phocian garrison, the Phocians were ousted from Delphi, and Macedon replaced Phocis on the Amphictyonic

Council (AMPHICTYONY). Philip demonstrated his new position by presiding over the Pythian festival in the same year, 346.

3. *Philip's further conquests and death (345–336).* From 346 Demosthenes tried every means to bring the Peace of Philocrates to an end. In 344 he persuaded the assembly to rebuff an offer of renewal. Meanwhile Philip was closely involved in the affairs of Euboea and was campaigning in Thrace. In 342 he made the latter a tribute-paying province of Macedonia, and founded several cities there including Philippopolis. This extension of his dominion to the immediate neighbourhood of the Thracian Chersonese was another threat to Athenian interests, and Demosthenes in the *Third Philippic* (delivered in the summer of 341) emphasized the necessity for military preparations. Various acts of hostility in 341 developed into open war in 340: Philip's attack on Byzantium (which had revolted from the Macedonian alliance), provoked Athens, whose corn supply was thereby threatened, to send a fleet; after a few months Philip abandoned the siege and retreated into Thrace. He decided to meet Athens where she was most vulnerable, on land. A pretext was furnished by the Amphictyonic Council, which resolved to proceed against the Locrians of Amphissa for sacrilegiously cultivating the sacred plain, and in 338 invited Philip to lead once more a Sacred War. Philip at once marched through Thermopylae and took possession of Elatea (in Phocis, commanding the passes into southern Greece). Although it is not certain that he had any real intention of invading Attica, the threat to do so, and his attempt to lure the Thebans on to his side, caused Demosthenes to promote an alliance between Athens and Thebes, despite their inveterate hostility; for the subjugation of Athens by Philip would have posed a menace to Thebes itself. The alliance gave the Greek hoplites approximate numerical parity with the Macedonian phalanx at the decisive battle of Chaeronea (on 22 August 338), 'fatal to liberty' as the English poet John Milton called it. The battle was won by Philip's feigning a withdrawal and then routing the over-pursuing Athenians; his son Alexander is said to have led the Macedonian cavalry.

The leadership of Greece passed to Macedonia, but Philip still wanted the co-operation of his opponents. He did not try to impose pro-Macedonian regimes in the cities (where in fact pro-Macedonian parties were now in the ascendancy without Philip's interference), except in the case of Thebes, which had to accept a Macedonian garrison (and to give up Oropus). Nor did he break up the local confederacies in the Greek states, although Athens lost most of her naval league. In 337 a Hellenic congress was summoned at Corinth, in which the Greeks made peace with Philip and the League of Corinth was established for waging a Greek war

against Persia, with Philip as general. Preparations were made for the invasion, and his commander Parmenio was sent to secure a footing in Asia Minor; but while walking in procession during the celebration of his daughter's marriage to the king of Epirus Philip was murdered by an assassin, Pausanias, apparently in pursuit of a private grievance, although it has been alleged that it was the result of a plot by Olympias, his now deposed wife, of which his son *Alexander was aware. To the latter, now aged 20, the succession passed smoothly. Excavations at Aegae (Vergina) in Macedonia have uncovered the tombs of Philip and his family, with magnificent grave goods and wall-paintings. Tests on bones have identified Philip's body beyond reasonable doubt.

2. **Philip V** (238–179 BC), king of Macedon; see MACEDONIA 3.

philippei'us, see MONEY AND COINS 1.

Phi'lippi, city in Macedonia east of the river Strymon on the border with Thrace, refounded under this name by Philip II of Macedon in 356 BC, the scene of the defeat in 42 BC of the republican forces of (Marcus Junius) Brutus and (Gaius) Cassius by those of Mark Antony and Octavian, and of the death of the two former (see ROME 7). Brutus and Cassius held a strong position and were kept well supplied by sea. It was to their advantage to avoid a decisive battle with a force larger than theirs, but whose supplies were precarious. Antony did what he could to provoke an engagement and at last Cassius and Brutus made a sortie. In the inconclusive battle which followed Antony drove back Cassius' wing, and Cassius committed suicide; but Brutus' troops routed those of Octavian, who was ill at the time. Some days later Brutus was forced by his impatient officers to renew the engagement; now he in turn was completely routed, and committed suicide.

Phili'ppica, see THEOPOMPUS.

Phili'ppics, four political speeches by *Demosthenes (see (2) 4) attacking Philip II, king of Macedon. The title was adopted by *Cicero ((1) 6) for the fourteen speeches that he delivered against Mark Antony.

Phili'ppides, see PHEIDIPPIDES.

Phili'ppus, title of a discourse by *Isocrates.

Phili'tas, see PHILETAS.

Philo. 1. **Philo of Lari'sa** (159–80 BC), head of the *Academy at Athens in 109 BC, like Carneadēs a moderate Sceptic.

2. **Philo Jūdae'us,** 'Philo the Jew' (*c.*30 BC–*c.* AD 45), a member of a prosperous Jewish family in Alexandria, who took part in an embassy sent to Rome in AD 39–40 to seek exemption

for Jews from the obligation to worship the emperor (at that time Caligula). Except for this event nothing is known of his life. He was the most important Hellenistic Jew of his age and a prolific author of philosophical and exegetical writings. His religious outlook was eclectic, but his lasting achievement was the development of the allegorical interpretation of scripture, enabling him to find a great deal of Greek philosophy in the Old Testament. His works were a strong influence on later Greek Christian thought as helping to mediate between philosophy (including *Neoplatonism) and Christianity. A considerable portion survives.

Philo'chorus, of Athens, an atthidographer; see ATTHIS.

Philo'cratēs, Peace of, between Greece and Philip II of Macedon, 346 BC; see PHILIP (1) 2, DEMOSTHENES (2) 1, and AESCHINES.

Philoctē'tēs, in Greek myth, son of Poeas; the father had been persuaded, by the gift of *Heracles' bow and arrows, to light the pyre on which the latter was burnt alive. These descended to Philoctetes, who led seven ships from Methonē and other towns of that region in the expedition to Troy. On their way to Troy the Greeks sacrificed in Tenedos, and there Philoctetes was bitten in the foot by a serpent. The stench from his wound, which would not heal, and his terrible cries and curses caused the Greeks, persuaded by Odysseus, to abandon him on the solitary coast of the island of Lemnos, where he supported himself by the bow and arrows which never missed their mark. After many years the Trojan seer Helenus, captured by Odysseus, revealed that Troy would never fall unless Philoctetes could be persuaded to come and fight with his bow and arrows. Accordingly Odysseus and Neoptolemus (or Diomedēs) went to Lemnos and brought him back. *Machaon healed his wound and Philoctetes, by shooting Paris, helped to conquer Troy. According to the *Odyssey* Philoctetes returned home safely. He is mentioned in the *Iliad* and is the subject of a play by Sophocles.

Philoctē'tēs, Greek tragedy by *Sophocles, produced in 409 BC.

*Philoctetes is living wretchedly on Lemnos, suffering from his wound, supporting himself by shooting birds with his beloved bow of Heracles. Odysseus and Neoptolemus arrive to carry him off to the siege of Troy. Odysseus reveals his plan to Neoptolemus: the latter is to pretend that he has quarrelled with the leaders of the Greek army and is on his way home; he is to heap abuse on Odysseus, and to try to get possession of the bow. Neoptolemus is at first unwilling to join in this deceit, but eventually agrees. He meets Philoctetes and tells his story. Philoctetes makes a pitiful appeal to be taken to Greece, and Neoptolemus agrees. But Philo-

ctetes is seized with a paroxysm of pain, after which he falls asleep. Before sleeping, however, he entrusts his bow to Neoptolemus. When he wakes up, Neoptolemus, stung with remorse, confesses the plot. He is on the point of returning the bow when Odysseus appears and takes it. He and Neoptolemus depart with it to the ships; Philoctetes is left lamenting his loss, while the chorus of sailors try to persuade him to join them. They are about to leave him when Neoptolemus returns, determined to give back the bow but pursued by Odysseus. Philoctetes, having regained the bow, tries to shoot Odysseus but is prevented by Neoptolemus who again tries to persuade Philoctetes to accompany him to Troy. He fails, and reluctantly decides to abide by his promise and take Philoctetes home to Greece. At this point Heracles appears from the dead; he reveals Zeus' plan for Philoctetes, that he is to go to Troy with Neoptolemus; Philoctetes yields to the voice of one whom he cannot disobey.

Philodē'mus, see HERCULANEUM.

Philomē'la and Procnē, in Greek myth, daughters of Pandīon, a legendary king of Athens. Procne was married to Tereus, king of Thrace. The latter fell in love with Philomela, and after raping her cut out her tongue and hid her in a lonely fortress so that she could not reveal what had happened. But Philomela managed to depict her sufferings on a tapestry which she sent to Procne by a servant. Procne then went to her sister disguised as a *Bacchant during the festival of Dionysus, and smuggled her into the palace similarly disguised. Seeking revenge Procne stabbed her son Itys to death, to deprive Tereus of an heir, and served up his flesh to her husband. When, after the meal, Philomela brought in the boy's head so that Tereus understood what had happened, he drew his sword to kill the sisters, but was changed into a hoopoe; Philomela was changed into a swallow (since, having no tongue, she could merely chatter like one) and Procne into a nightingale (or, according to Latin authors, Philomela into a nightingale and Procne into a swallow).

Philopoe'men (*c.*250–182 BC), of Megalopolis in Arcadia, the bold and vigorous general of the *Achaean Confederacy, 'the last of the Greeks' according to a quotation in Plutarch. He first distinguished himself at the battle of Sellasia (near Sparta) in perhaps 221, where the Spartans under Cleomenēs were defeated by Antigonus, the Macedonian king, and the Achaeans. He was subsequently elected general of the Confederacy eight times, in which post he reorganized its army and repeatedly defeated the Spartans. It is recorded that after one of his victories Philopoemen was present at the Nemean games when Pyladēs, the most famous singer of his day, was singing part of the *Persians* of *Timotheus. At the words, 'who gives to Greece the glorious crown of freedom', the people rose and gave an ovation to the general. In 183 BC, when he was about 70, he took part in an expedition against Messenē, which had revolted from the Confederacy. He was captured by the Messenians, thrown into prison, and forced to drink poison. His remains were brought back to Megalopolis, his urn being carried by the young *Polybius.

philosophy (Gk. *philosophia*, 'love of knowledge').

1. *Greek*. For the Greeks, 'philosophy', the pursuit of knowledge by rational enquiry, was an elastic term; it began with scientific speculation but it also included speculation as to the conduct of political and social life, and this last was one of the main concerns of philosophers in the fifth and fourth centuries BC. Later Greek philosophy dealt with moral and religious questions, the concept of virtue and the individual's relations with the divine; it had then become not merely a mental activity but a way of life, to be followed in accordance with philosophical beliefs. Greek philosophy had its origins in the sixth century BC among the Ionian Greeks of Asia Minor. It was then mainly occupied with speculation about the cause of the universe, and associated with the name of *Thales of Miletus, whose chief successors (also sixth-century Milesians) were *Anaximander and *Anaximenes. These sought the material principle of the universe in some single uncreated and imperishable substance which underwent various modifications to produce the multitude of phenomena in the world: Thales thought that it was water, Anaximander something indeterminate, without specific qualities, and Anaximenes air. *Heracleitus of Ephesus (writing in about 500 BC), standing apart from this school and rejecting the notion of a permanent substance underlying the variations of matter (though he thought the essential stuff of the universe to be pure fire), saw all things in a state of flux, and matter itself constantly changing.

*Pythagoras (last quarter of the sixth century BC), an Ionian Greek from Samos who migrated to Croton, an Achaean colony on the toe of Italy, founded there a second school of philosophy which in some ways resembled a mystical sect, having secret doctrines not to be revealed to the uninitiated. The Pythagoreans saw in numbers and their relations the basis of the universe. The third school was that of Elea (also in Magna Graecia), founded by *Parmenides (early fifth century BC) and continued by *Zeno. This school distinguished between the true stuff of the universe, single, eternal, and unchangeable, and the unreal phenomena of change, diversity, and motion which are apparent to the senses. *Empedocles of Acragas in Sicily, *Anaxagoras of Clazomenae in Ionia,

and Leucippus (perhaps Ionian also), all working in the fifth century BC, evolved fresh hypotheses about the physical basis of the universe, assuming not one single basic stuff but plural constituents.

Empedocles was the first to propound the theory of the four elements, earth, air, fire, and water, out of which everything is composed in varying proportions. Anaxagoras believed in an original mixture containing 'seeds' of every substance; more significantly, however, he introduced the important concept of an intelligence (*nous*) as a principle of force and order distinct from matter. Leucippus was said to be the originator of the school of atomist philosophy, which rested on the doctrine that the universe is composed of a vast number of atoms, mechanically combined. This doctrine was developed by *Democritus, and found its most eloquent exponent in a later age at Rome, in Lucretius. During the sixth century the Ionian polymath and philosopher *Xenophanes, relying on logic, constructed a rational theology.

Greek philosophy culminated in *Socrates, in the second half of the fifth century, and *Plato and *Aristotle, in the fourth. The conquests of Alexander the Great, however, towards the end of the fourth century, swept away the context of their moral teaching, the independent city-states, the continued existence of which they had not doubted; and the later philosophies, those in particular of the *Stoics and Epicureans (see EPICURUS), reveal a change of outlook: in them, interest has shifted from the theoretical problems of the nature of reality and the scope of knowledge to the practical problems of everyday behaviour. They are to some extent philosophies of resignation; they seek a road to peace and happiness in the state of mind of the individual, by making him independent of external circumstances. See also SCEPTICS, CYNICS, MEGARIAN SCHOOL, PERIPATETIC SCHOOL, ARISTIPPUS (founder of the Cyrenaic School), THEOPHRASTUS (the successor of Aristotle), ACADEMY, and NEOPLATONISM.

2. *Roman*. Rome came into close contact with Greek civilization, including philosophy, with the conquest of Magna Graecia in the third century BC and the occupation of Sicily, Greece, and part of Asia Minor in the second (see ROME 4 and 5). At first Rome regarded Greek philosophy with some suspicion, and fears of its possibly subversive effects led to the temporary banishment of Greek philosophers in 173 and again in 161 BC. In 155 *Carneades, Diogenes, and Critolaus, the heads respectively of the Academic, Stoic, and Peripatetic schools of philosophy in Athens, were sent on an embassy to Rome (to appeal against a large fine imposed by the Romans on Athens), and, giving lectures there, made a great impression. A little later *Scipio Aemilianus received into his household the Stoic philosopher *Panaetius of Rhodes; and

in the early part of the first century BC a successor of the latter, *Posidonius, became the friend and teacher of Varro in Rome and of Pompey and Cicero in Rhodes. The Romans were not interested in theories as to the constitution of the universe, nor in elucidating the processes of thought and knowledge; and they produced no great original speculative philosophers or metaphysicians. *Lucretius alone, in his poem De rerum natura ('on nature'), expounded with enthusiasm the atomic theory put forward by Leucippus and Democritus.

The attention of the Romans was chiefly concentrated on ethical principles, and here they were mainly divided between Epicureans and Stoics, the latter prevailing. Stoic notions of duty and fate appealed to Roman severity. Cicero, who did much to make Greek philosophical thought known to his countrymen, was himself a follower of the New Academy (the Platonic school), with leanings towards the Stoics; he was in fact an eclectic, that is, he did not accept wholly the teaching of any one particular school, but picked out from their various doctrines those which commended themselves to him. *Seneca (2) was the principal Roman Stoic author, and his writings had considerable influence on Christian ethics. The most famous of the later Roman Stoics were Marcus *Aurelius (who wrote his Meditations in Greek) and *Epictetus (who also wrote in Greek). The satirist Persius, under the influence of his teacher Cornutus, and the poet Lucan were followers of the same school. Under the influence of Seneca and his successors, the general tendency of Stoics was to become more practical and human. The tranquillity which the earlier Greek Stoics thought was the exclusive attainment of the sage who lived in detachment from the world was now seen to be attainable by men living fully in the world, through the exercise of fortitude and self-control. See also BOETHIUS.

Philo'stratus, the name borne by four writers, members of a family belonging, according to the Suda, to Lemnos, who lived in the second and third centuries AD. The most important works (in Greek) which have come down under this name are: (i) (by Flavius Philostratus) Lives of the Sophists, that is, of the *sophists and rhetoricians from Protagoras (in the fifth century BC) to the author's own times; (ii) (written for *Julia Domna) a life of Apollonius of Tyana, the wandering Pythagorean mystic and miracle worker of the first century AD (which furnished material for anti-Christians who wanted a pagan narrative to set against the Gospel life of Jesus); (iii) Eikonĕs ('images'), two sets of descriptions in prose of pictures which the author purports to have seen (the first set far superior to the second); (iv) Herōicus, a dialogue in which the ghosts of heroes of the Trojan war appear; and (v) a collection of Letters (sophistical exercises for the most part), chiefly noteworthy as containing in Epistle 33 the source of Ben Jonson's 'Drink to me only with thine eyes'.

Philo'xenus, of Cythera (436–380 BC), Greek dithyrambic poet at the court of Dionysius tyrant of Syracuse. His most famous *dithyramb was the Cyclops, in which he introduced the Cyclops singing a solo to the lyre.

Phily'ra, in Greek myth, daughter of *Oceanus and Tethys, loved by *Cronus. When Rhea (his wife) found them both together, Cronus changed himself and Philyra into horses. Philyra's child was the centaur *Chiron; she was so horrified to see the baby's shape that she prayed to the gods to change her shape also, and she was turned into a lime tree (Gk. philyra) from which her name is taken.

Phīneus. 1. In Greek myth, a Thracian king, plagued by the *Harpies who stole or defiled all his food. When the *Argonauts arrived at his land he agreed to prophesy to them their future adventures in return for deliverance from the Harpies. The sons of Boreas (Calais and Zetes) drove them away, turning back at the islands afterwards known as Strophadĕs ('islands of turning'). Phineus' original offence is variously described. The best known version says that he married Cleopatra, daughter of Boreas, and had sons, but at her death remarried; their stepmother so slandered his sons that Phineus blinded them (or let their stepmother do so). Thereupon Zeus gave him the choice of death or blindness; he chose the latter, and Helios (Sun), who sees all, angry at Phineus' choice, sent the Harpies.

2. See PERSEUS.

Phle'gethon (or Pyriphlegethon), one of the rivers of the Underworld; see HADES.

Phōcae'a, most northerly of the Ionian Greek settlements on the coast of Asia Minor, slightly north of Chios. It was founded by emigrants from *Phocis (a state in central Greece) under the leadership of two Athenians (see MIGRATIONS). Because of its two excellent harbours it soon became famous as a maritime city; according to Herodotus the Phocaeans were the first Greeks to sail far west, visiting Tartessus in southern Spain. In about 600 BC it founded the colony of Massilia (Marseilles), giving the Greeks access to southern Gaul. When Ionia was conquered by the Persian king Cyrus in 540 BC, most of the citizens preferred emigration to submission and finally settled at Elea (Velia) in Lucania, south Italy; Phocaea never recovered its former prosperity. A Phocaean, Dionysius, commanded the Greek fleet at the battle of Ladē (494 BC) during the Ionian Revolt (see PERSIAN WARS), but his city contributed only three ships.

Phō'cion (fourth century BC), Athenian general and statesman during the time of Philip II of Macedon and his son Alexander the Great. He commanded universal respect and was elected *strategos* forty-five times. In politics he was an advocate of peace with Macedon, being convinced that Athens was no longer a match for her in military strength, and supported Eubulus, Aeschinēs, and Demadēs against Demosthenes and Hypereides (see ATHENS 2 (v)). After Athens' defeat at Chaeronea in 338 he assisted Demades in preserving peace with Philip and Alexander, and sought to prevent Athens from joining in the *Lamian War (to throw off Macedonian rule after Alexander's death in 323 BC). When democratic rule was (briefly) restored at Athens in 318, Phocion was put to death on a charge of treason. Plutarch's *Life of Phocion* portrays him as a patriot, with a stern and stoical sense of duty.

Phōcis, small country of central Greece, to the west of Boeotia, important in Greek history as containing Delphi, of which she occasionally lost control, becoming involved in the *Sacred Wars. Her bid for independence in the Third Sacred War ended in her subjugation by Philip II of Macedon (346 BC).

Phocus, see TELAMON.

Phōcy'lidēs, of Miletus (mid-sixth century BC), Greek poet famous for composing *gnomic couplets in elegiacs and hexameters in which he embodied moral observations and precepts; a few of these survive. In each he introduced his own name.

Phoebē (Phoibē, 'the bright one'), in Greek myth, according to Hesiod, a Titaness (see TITANS), daughter of Uranus (Heaven) and Gaia (Earth); she became the wife of Coeus and mother of *Leto, and is thus grandmother of Apollo and Artemis. In later mythology her name was frequently used for Selenē (Moon).

Phoebus Apo'llo, see APOLLO.

Phoeni'cia (Phoinīkē, the biblical Canaan), country forming a narrow strip along the coast of Syria and including the towns of Tyre and Sidon (the former not known to Homer, for whom Sidon is the great city of Phoenician craftsmen and traders). Probably before 1000 BC the Phoenicians, a Semitic people, invented their *alphabet (on which the Greek alphabet was based), and at about the same period earned their reputation as a great sea-faring people; the traditional dates for their foundations of Cadiz in Spain (1100) and Utica in North Africa (1087) may be too early, but Phoenicians were certainly in the West, and in the area of the

Black Sea also, by 900 BC. *Carthage was founded by the Phoenician queen *Dido in about 814 BC. One element in their trade was the *purple dye. After the time of Alexander the Great (late fourth century BC) they were incorporated into the Hellenistic world.

Phoeni'ssae (Phoinissai, 'Phoenician women').
   1. Greek tragedy (which has not survived) by *Phrynichus.
   2. Greek tragedy by *Euripides, produced between 412 and 408 BC. The play derives its name from the chorus of Phoenician maidens dedicated by the citizens of Tyre to the temple of Apollo at Delphi, who happen to be at Thebes on their way to Delphi and witness the events while having no connection with them. The subject is the same as Aeschylus' *Seven against Thebes. It is the longest Greek tragedy in existence and covers the greatest stretch of story.
   The drama takes up the legend of *Oedipus at the start of the quarrel between his two sons: Polyneicēs has been refused by his brother Eteoclēs his share of their alternating rule of Thebes, and has come with Adrastus, king of Argos, and the five other leaders of the Argive army, to enforce his rights. Jocasta, wife of Oedipus, endeavours to reconcile their two sons, but her efforts fail and the attack on Thebes becomes inevitable. The seer *Teiresias predicts the victory of Eteocles and Thebes if a son of Creon (brother of Jocasta and friend of Eteocles) is sacrificed. Accordingly Menoeceus, Creon's younger son, gives his life heroically for his city, in spite of his father's resistance. The Argives are driven back in the first onset, and it is arranged that the quarrel shall be settled by a single combat between the brothers. In this each kills the other, and Jocasta in despair takes her own life with one of their swords; their sister Antigonē brings the news to Oedipus. Creon takes over the government and proclaims that Polyneices' body will lie unburied and that the blind Oedipus will be expelled; moreover, Antigone will marry Creon's son Haemon. Antigone refuses, and accompanies her father into exile, announcing that she will return and secretly bury her brother.
   3. Roman tragedy by *Seneca (2), which survives in an imperfect condition. It appears to combine material from *Oedipus at Colonus by Sophocles (the blind Oedipus wandering under the guidance of Antigonē), with a situation derived from other sources (Antigone at Thebes with her mother Jocasta, who tries in vain to reconcile her two sons). The surviving portions may be fragments of two distinct plays.

Phoenix. 1. In Greek myth, son of Amyntor, a king in Thessaly. His mother persuaded him to seduce his father's concubine, out of jealousy. When his father found out he cursed him with childlessness; Phoenix left home and went to Phthia, where he was kindly received by Peleus and put in charge of the young *Achilles (Peleus' son). In the Trojan War he was one of the ambassadors sent to bring Agamemnon's offer of reconciliation to Achilles, whom he had accompanied to Troy.

2. The *eponymous ancestor of the *Phoenicians, son of Agenor, king of Tyre, and brother of Cadmus and Europa.

Phoenix, Latin poem in elegiacs, 170 lines long, on this mythical Arabian bird, whose resurrection to life from death appealed to Christians and to pagan believers in mystery religions. The poem is usually ascribed to *Lactantius. The phoenix is described by Herodotus (2. 73), Tacitus (*Annals* 6. 28), and others with varying details. In general it was thought to resemble an eagle but with red (*phoinix*) and gold plumage; every 500 years it makes a nest and dies; from the nest arises a new phoenix which carries its parent's body to Heliopolis in Egypt for funeral in the temple of Helios (Sun). The version that has become popular in modern times has the new phoenix arising from the funeral pyre which the old phoenix has made for itself.

Phōlus, *centaur by whom Heracles was entertained when in pursuit of the Erymanthian Boar (see HERACLES, LABOURS OF 3). Pholus died after the fight between Heracles and the centaurs; while inspecting one of Heracles' arrows he dropped it on his foot and was killed by the poison. . .

Phorcys, Greek sea-god, son of Nereus or of Pontus (Sea) and father of the *Graiae, the *Gorgons, and *Scylla.

phorminx, see MUSIC 1.

Pho'rmio, see DEMOSTHENES (2) 2.

Pho'rmio, Roman comedy by *Terence, based on a Greek play of the third century BC, 'The Claimant', by Apollodorus of Carystus, a writer of Greek New Comedy (see COMEDY, GREEK 6). It was produced at Rome in 161 BC.

Antipho, a young Athenian, while his father Demipho is out of the country, has fallen in love with a girl whom he found weeping for her recently dead mother, whose funeral she must arrange, being now alone in the world. Phormio, a resourceful *parasite, taking advantage of the law that orphan girls must be married to their next-of-kin (within the permitted degree), has pretended, in collusion with Antipho, that the latter is the girl's nearest relative and obtained a court order that he is to marry her, and the marriage has taken place. Meanwhile Antipho's cousin Phaedria is desperately in love with a slave girl, a lute-player, but lacks the money to buy her from the pimp who owns her. His father Chremes, Demipho's brother, has been away in Lemnos. Both fathers return at this juncture. Demipho is furious at his son's marriage and determined to put an end to it.

Phormio offers the father, for a sum of money, to take the bride away and marry her himself. Having obtained the money he hands it over to Phaedria who now purchases his lute-player. Meanwhile it has been discovered through a nurse that the girl Antipho has married is in fact the daughter of Chremes, who has bigamously kept a wife on Lemnos; daughter, wife, and nurse had come to Athens to look for him, and there the wife had died. Chremes wishes above all else to keep from his legitimate wife in Athens all knowledge of his liaison. To avoid trouble the two fathers decide to recognize Antipho's marriage, but their attempt to recover the money paid to Phormio leads to the exposure of Chremes to his wife. She is mollified, however, and all ends happily. The play is aptly named: Phormio dominates it, and no other character in Roman comedy quite reaches his commanding position. (The proverb, 'to have a wolf by the ears', is first found in this play, l. 506.)

Phō'tius (*c.* AD 810–*c*.893), patriarch of Byzantium 858–67 and 878–86 and a very important figure for the survival of Greek studies in the *Byzantine age. Among other works he compiled a lexicon of Attic Greek prose usage, which survives. After his day many manuscripts of ancient Greek literature were destroyed, and he was able to read more than anyone since. His fame rests on the *Bibliothekē* ('library'), also known as the *Myriobiblos* ('vast compendium'), consisting of 280 accounts of books read (usually called codices); the accounts range in size from a couple of lines to seventy or so pages of detailed comment, but most give a synopsis of the text. Slightly more than half the books are theological. The rest are Greek prose authors, ranging from the classical to the early Byzantine; quite a few of these works are known to us only through Photius (some twenty of the thirty-three historians, for example).

phrā'triai ('brotherhoods', phratries), at Athens and other Greek cities, groups of related families (or at least in theory related), in existence from earliest times, found as divisions of the *tribes (*phylai*). In historical times each phratry consisted of a noble family and its dependants who all shared in the family cult and claimed descent from a common ancestor, often calling themselves by a name formed from his. The phratries were a major political force until the end of the sixth century BC, when their power in that sphere was broken by the reforms of *Cleisthenēs (2). After this the phratries seem to have covered the whole citizen body, chiefly as religious and social organizations; their great festival was the Apaturia, held in the month of Pyanepsion (October to November). On the last day babies, young adult men, and newly married wives were enrolled in their respective categories in the phratry. See also GENOS.

Phrixus, see ATHAMAS.

Phry'gia, territory in the west of Asia Minor, including part of the central plateau, conquered towards the end of the second millennium BC by a European people, the Phrygēs. The kingdom was associated in Greek legend with the names of Gordius (see GORDIAN KNOT) and *Midas. It was conquered by *Lydia and was never again independent. In the third century BC it was overrun by *Galatians; in 116 BC most of the territory was absorbed into the Roman province of Asia.

Phrȳnē, famous *hetaera of the fourth century BC from Thespiae in Boeotia, whose outstanding beauty gave rise to some notable works of art, including the painting of Aphroditē Anadyomenē by Apellēs and Praxitelēs' Aphroditē of *Cnidus. There was a gilded statue of her at Delphi dedicated by herself (according to Pausanias) or by her admirers (according to other authorities). See also HYPEREIDES (at the end).

Phrȳ'nichus. 1. Of Athens, a tragedian, coupled with *Thespis by some ancient authorities as both being the originators of tragedy; Phrynichus first won a competition for tragedy between 511 and 508 BC. Of his plays only scanty fragments survive. He produced, probably in 492, with Themistoclēs as *choregos*, a play dealing with the capture of *Miletus by the Persians in 494 during the Ionian Revolt (see PERSIAN WARS), and was fined by the Athenians because, Herodotus said, he had reminded them too vividly of the misfortunes of a kindred people. His *Phoenissae* ('Phoenician women') celebrating the Greek victories over the Persians in 480–79, with the chorus composed of the wives of the enemy's Phoenician sailors, was also famous. This may have been produced in 476, a year in which Themistocles was again his *choregos*. Aristophanes seems to have admired his lyrical passages particularly, while mocking his dramas' deficiency in action.
2. One of the extreme oligarchs at Athens at the time of the revolution of the *Four Hundred in 411 BC, towards the end of the Peloponnesian War. After his return from Sparta, where he had gone to negotiate peace, he was assassinated in the agora.

phylae, in Greek, *tribes.

Phy'sica (*Physikē akroāsis*, 'Physics'), treatise by *Aristotle (see 4 (iii)).

Pīcu'mnus and Pīlu'mnus, in ancient Roman religion, two brothers, perhaps agricultural deities, the beneficent gods of matrimony and the protectors of women in childbirth. Pilumnus was thought to be the inventor of the pestle

(*pilum*) for grinding corn; Virgil makes him the ancestor of *Turnus.

Pīcus ('woodpecker'), Italian god of agriculture, sometimes described as a son of *Saturn and as the first king of Italy, possessed of prophetic powers and usually taking the form of Mars' sacred bird, the woodpecker. This bird was of great importance in augury; omens were drawn from the sight of it and from its note. It was said that it helped to feed Romulus and Remus. There was a story that Picus was turned into a woodpecker by Circē ('hawk'), whose love he had spurned. Virgil makes him the father of *Faunus and grandfather of Latinus.

Pīe'ria, in Macedonia, district on the northern slopes of Mount *Olympus, whence, according to tradition, a colony migrated south to Mount *Helicon in Boeotia in prehistoric times. The cult of the *Muses was said to have been brought from Pieria (the birthplace of the Muses and of Orpheus) to Helicon; hence they are sometimes described as Pierian (or Pierides).

Pīe'ridĕs, see MUSES and PIERIA.

pi'etas, see RELIGION, ROMAN 2.

Pillars of Hercules, see HERACLES, LABOURS OF 10.

pi'llĕus, see DRESS 2.

pīlos, see DRESS 1.

Pīlu'mnus, see PICUMNUS.

Pi'nakĕs, see CALLIMACHUS.

Pīnā'rii and Potī'tii, see HERCULES.

Pinax, see CEBES.

Pindar (Pindaros) (518–after 446 BC), Greek lyric poet, born at the village of Cynoscephalae near Thebes in Boeotia, famous for his Epinician ('victory') Odes written in honour of the victors at the four great panhellenic *Games. These odes are accordingly grouped as Olympian, Pythian, Nemean, and Isthmian, commonly abbreviated to O., P., N., I.
1. Very little is known about Pindar's life. In the fifth Pythian ode he appears to claim that he is a member of the Aegeidae, an ancient aristocratic clan with important connections in several Dorian states, and he expresses an especial sympathy for Dorian institutions. Legend relates that he received instruction in composition from the Boeotian poetess *Corinna, and that he went to Athens for his musical education. His devotion to the god Apollo was rewarded by special privileges at *Delphi; his Epinician Odes seem to show a particular affection for the Dorian island of Aegina and its heroes, *Aeacus and his descendants. Pindar's early reputation as a poet is shown by the fact that in 498, when he was only 20, he was

commissioned by the powerful Thessalian family of the Aleuadae to compose an ode (*P.* 10) for a victor in that family (see below). In the following year he won a dithyrambic competition. His attitude to the great historical events of his time was panhellenic rather than narrowly bound by local loyalties; thus he saw the Persian invasions as a threat to Greece as a whole and her deliverance as a blessing. His personal feelings about the consequences to Thebes of her pro-Persian policy cannot be ascertained, though he laments the sorrow and loss that war brought her; his admiration for Athens seems to have been unaffected by the mutual animosity of the two cities. It is said that he was fined by his countrymen for his praises of Athens, but that the Athenians paid him the amount of the fine twice over; they also erected a statue of him (which the Greek traveller Pausanias saw in the agora) but probably long after his death. Pindar travelled widely in the Greek world. Some of his greatest odes were for the Sicilian tyrants, particularly Hieron 1 of *Syracuse (see 1). He is said to have died in Argos at the age of 80 (i.e. in 438; his last dated poem was written in 446). He attained great fame in his lifetime, and was soon quoted as an authority (e.g. by Herodotus and Plato). In the destruction of Thebes in 335 (a punishment for her revolt against Macedonian rule) Alexander the Great ordered Pindar's house to be spared; its ruins were still visible when Pausanias visited Thebes *c.* AD 150.

2. Pindar's numerous poems, which included all the chief forms of choral *lyric, were grouped by the Alexandrian scholars into seventeen books according to their types: epinicians (four books); encomia, dirges, hymns, paeans (one book each); dithyrambs, prosodia, hyporchemata, partheneia (two books each); and of a different type of partheneia another book. Of these only the four books of Epinician Odes survive, virtually entire, in manuscript. The rest are known mostly from quotations, although discoveries of papyri in the late nineteenth and twentieth centuries have greatly augmented our knowledge, especially of the paeans.

3. Pindar wrote in the literary Dorian *dialect but used epic forms as well, particularly for mythical narratives. Of the Epinician Odes, half are written in the metre known as dactyloepitrite, the other half in a syncopated variant of it known loosely as 'aeolic' (see METRE, GREEK 8 (iii)). The structure of nearly all of them is triadic (see TRIAD); a few are in stanza form. No two odes (except *I.* 3 and 4 for special reasons) are metrically identical. Close analysis of the odes reveals that they follow a conventional pattern of praise; there are certain elements that must be included: the name of the victor, his victory, any earlier victories he has won; praise of his family and homeland; perhaps praise of the craft of poetry which has the power to immortalize the victor; and a mythical narrative

which obliquely reinforces the other elements of praise. The poet's skill succeeds in intertwining these rather disparate elements into an artistic whole, and the reader's attention is distracted from the technical aspects of the composition by the rapid and varied flow of the poetry. The essentially repetitious nature of the subject matter is not particularly obvious even when the forty-four odes are read in sequence, as their author can hardly have supposed they would be; the reader marvels rather at the variety. Pindar has complete control over his medium, and his technique is distinguished by constant variation, complexity, and vitality. Some of his sentences are long and periodic, the stopping places arranged to occur at metrically emphatic moments, at the beginning of a new strophe, for example; others are arrestingly short. Sometimes (especially in the later odes) the language seems almost stark, stripped of ornament, and the word order simple and prosaic; in other odes the language is rich and magnificent, the word order intricate. The poet is skilful at building up climaxes within the ode. Transitions from one topic to another are sometimes made abruptly for rhetorical effect, sometimes unobtrusively. Metaphors and metonymies (e.g. the variety of words used to express 'victory') abound.

4. The Epinician Odes are written from an essentially religious standpoint; it is this background that imparts grandeur to Pindar's themes and language. Men are nothing by themselves: success is god-given; but men attain an almost divine happiness at the moment of success. The poet himself has a skill that is god-given and cannot be taught; he is 'the mouthpiece of the Muses'. Zeus and Apollo are the gods most often invoked. The gods favour those who have struggled hard for their victory, but the victors are those whose breeding makes them worthy of it; Pindar admires aristocratic qualities, the beauty and strength fostered in the gymnasium, wealth and standing, courage and preparedness, the aristocratic institution of guest-friendship, traditional worship of the gods, devotion to family and homeland; and he warns against the unjust use of power and the envy from lesser men which success brings in its train. The qualities which he admires he sees exhibited in the heroes of old, and especially Heracles, the hero most often cited in the Odes. Pindar treats myth with freedom and with sensitivity to its appropriateness, always in a way that comports with the dignity of the occasion. Some of his most notable odes are described below.

5. *Olympian Odes. O.* 1, to Hieron tyrant of Syracuse, celebrating the victory of his horse Pherenikos ('bringer of victory') in 476 BC. The Olympian Odes were placed first of the epinicians by the Alexandrian editors because of the pre-eminence of the Olympian games, and this ode first among Olympians perhaps because of the powerful position of Hieron among the

Sicilian tyrants, or perhaps because this is the most splendid of all Pindar's odes. Its opening line is the arresting, 'Water is best'. The ode begins with praise of Hieron and his horse; passes to the myth of Tantalus, his son *Pelops, and the latter's winning of Hippodameia for bride by his defeat of her father Oenomaus in a chariot-race; then returns to praise of Hieron, and a hope that he will win a greater triumph in the Olympian chariot-race, which Pindar will worthily celebrate (a vain hope: that victory, which came in 468, was celebrated by Bacchylides, in Ode 3). This victory of Pherenikos was also celebrated in Ode 5 of Bacchylides.

O. 2, to Theron (Hieron's brother) tyrant of Acragas (also in Sicily), on his victory, also in 476, in the chariot-race. This ode is notable for its doctrine (unique in the Epinician Odes) of reincarnation and of judgement after death, doctrines associated with *Orphic poems.

O. 3, to Theron, on the same victory as O. 2, delivered on the occasion of a *Theoxenia. It contains an interesting myth of Heracles bringing the wild olive to Greece from the land of the *Hyperboreans, thought of as being in the region of the Danube.

O. 6, to Hagesias of Syracuse, victor in the mule-cart race (see GAMES), a competition felt by some to be undignified but treated by Pindar with all seriousness. Some lines (92–4) of this ode, bidding men remember Syracuse or Ortygia, realm of the wise Hieron, have been found stamped on an ancient brick at Syracuse.

O. 7, to Diagoras of Rhodes, winner of the boxing competition in 464, famous in Rhodian politics, and a brilliant athlete, a *periodonikes*, i.e. victorious in all four of the great Games. He lived to be carried through the throng at Olympia on the shoulders of two victorious sons, congratulated on having reached the summit of human happiness. Statues of him, his three sons, and two grandsons, all Olympian victors, stood in a group at Olympia. This ode was engraved in letters of gold in the temple of Athena at Lindos in Rhodes.

O. 14, to Asopichus of Orchomenus, an early ode, brief but exquisite, and interesting for its invocation of the Charitēs (*Graces) who were worshipped especially at Orchomenus.

6. *Pythian Odes and other poems. P. 1*, to Hieron tyrant of Syracuse, winner in the chariot-race in 470 BC. The ode is a glorification of Hieron's new city of Aetna (see SYRACUSE I) and is of interest for its historical allusions (Dorian Invasion, victories of *Cumae and *Himera, etc.), for its description of the eruption of Aetna in 474, and for its exhortation to righteous conduct in a ruler.

P. 3, exceptional in that it seems in content not so much a victory ode (no victory is mentioned) as a poem of sympathy and consolation addressed (c.470) to Hieron on his illness. The illness may have prompted Pindar's narrative of

the myth of the healing deity *Asclepius, child of Apollo and Coronis, blasted by Zeus for restoring the dead to life. There is no cure for human mortality; the greatest men can, however, achieve a kind of immortality in poetry.

P. 4, to Arcesilaus, king of Cyrenē, winner in the chariot-race of 462. It is by far the longest of the odes, a glorification of *Cyrene, tracing its origin, through Battus its first king, Arcesilaus' ancestor, back to Euphemus, one of the *Argonauts. This brings up the story of Jason and Pelias and the Golden Fleece, stirringly told. The ode, which has comparatively little of the epinician character, ends with a petition, by parable and myth, for the restoration from exile of Damophilos, a Cyrenean noble, a recent guest-friend of Pindar.

P. 10, to Hippocleas of Thessaly, boy victor in the double foot-race, a poem commissioned by the powerful family of the Aleuadae. This is the earliest of Pindar's surviving works; see 1 above.

N. 1, to Chromios, governor for Hieron of the city of Aetna (see *P.* 1 above), victor in the chariot-race perhaps in 473. A vivid ode, it contains what is apparently the first account in literature of Heracles as a baby strangling the two serpents sent by Hera to destroy him.

Pindar's links with Aegina are evident in several odes for Aeginetan victors; in every case (except for *P.* 8) with episodes relating to heroes, Aeacus and his descendants: *O.* 8, *P.* 8, *N.* 3–8, *I.* 5, 6, 8. Also interesting are the odes relating the marriage of Apollo and Cyrene (*P.* 9), and the mythical glories of Pindar's native Thebes (*I.* 7). Notable among the many fragments of poems that have been preserved are the hymn to Zeus, written for the Thebans, relating the marriage of Zeus and Themis; the paean for Thebes (Paean 9), an appeal to Apollo on the occasion of the total eclipse of the sun in 463 BC; the fragment of an ode of unknown class that begins, 'Custom is king'; and the second partheneion. The fragments of the dirges (*thrēnoi*) throw light on Pindar's apparent beliefs about the fate of the soul after death.

7. Horace, in the opening stanzas of *Odes* IV. 2, praised Pindar's rushing eloquence, bold originality in metres and diction, and admirable use of myth, and believed that his own odes could never reach such heights. Quintilian shared the general view that Pindar was by far the greatest of the Greek lyric poets. In modern times poets have tried to imitate his free-flowing, vigorous style with varying degrees of success. Of English odes, those of the seventeenth-century poet John Dryden, *Song for St Cecilia's Day* and *Alexander's Feast*, and of the eighteenth-century poet Thomas Gray, *Progress of Poesy* and *The Bard*, capture something of the true feeling.

Pīrae'us (Peiraieus or Peirāeus), chief port of Athens, on a promontory 8 km. (5 miles) southwest of the ancient city, fortified by *Themistocles from the time of his archonship (493/2 BC, a little before the first Persian invasion) in order that the growing Athenian fleet might have a safer anchorage than that provided by the open roadstead of *Phalerum. For the Long Walls connecting Piraeus (and Phalerum) with Athens see LONG WALLS. Piraeus had three harbours, Zea and Munychia on the east, both used for warships, and the great harbour Cantharus on the west. This last became a thriving market. All three harbours were narrowed by moles and fortified, and could be closed by chains drawn across the mouths. The city was laid out on a grid plan by *Hippodamus in the mid-fifth century. The fortifications were demolished by the Spartan Lysander in 404 BC, at the end of the Peloponnesian War, but replaced by the Athenian admiral Conon in 393. The inhabitants, many of them sailors, were always staunch supporters of democracy. Many foreigners settled here, thereby introducing foreign cults, e.g. that of *Bendis. The Roman general Sulla laid siege to Piraeus and subsequently destroyed it in 87–86 BC. It may have been on this occasion that the inhabitants buried the large bronze statues which were unearthed there in 1959.

Pīrē'nē, see PEIRENE.

Pīri'thŏus (Peirithoos), king of the Lapiths, friend of Theseus; see CENTAURS and THESEUS.

Pisa, name of the small district around Olympia in the western Peloponnese, presumably centred on a city (now disappeared); the name was frequently used in Greek poetry to refer to Olympia itself. It was destroyed by *Elis some time before 471 BC, but the date is uncertain; the two were frequently in conflict about the control of the Olympian festival and games (see OLYMPIA). In Greek myth, Oenomaus and Pelops had their home here.

Pīsi'stratus, see PEISISTRATUS.

Pīso. 1. Lucius Calpurnius Piso Caesonī'nus, at Rome, consul in 58 BC; his daughter Calpurnia married Julius Caesar. He refused to support Cicero against Clodius, and was rewarded by the latter with the governorship of the province of Macedonia. His administration there (57–55) was attacked by Cicero in two speeches, *De provinciis consularibus* and *In Pisonem* (see CICERO (1) 4). After Caesar's assassination in 44 BC he tried to prevent civil war, but died within a short time. He was an Epicurean and a friend and disciple of the Greek Epicurean philosopher Philodemus, whom he very probably made a resident of his own magnificent villa at *Herculaneum. The villa excavated there which contained charred rolls of Philodemus' writings may be Piso's.
2. Gaius Calpurnius Piso (d. AD 65), the figurehead of the great conspiracy against the emperor Nero. Exiled during the reign of

Caligula (AD 37–41), consul under his successor Claudius, Piso was a rich and popular figure at Rome, and a great orator. He proved ineffective in the conspiracy to assassinate Nero and to put himself on the throne; the conspiracy was betrayed and he, with many others, including Lucan, Petronius, and Seneca the Younger, were condemned to death. See ROME 10.

Pi'ttacus (mid-seventh century–*c*.570 BC) of Mytilenē in Lesbos, statesman, included among the *Seven Sages. He commanded the Mytilenaeans in a war against Athens for the possession of Sigeum at the mouth of the Hellespont (a matter in which Periander, tyrant of Corinth, arbitrated), and killed in single combat the Athenian general and great athlete Phrynon. He appears by name in the poetry of his younger contemporary *Alcaeus; the latter savagely attacks him as a former comrade-in-arms in overthrowing tyranny at Mytilene, who has now broken with his old friends. The political struggles of the city remain unclear, but the citizens elected Pittacus *aisymnetēs* ('dictator') for ten years to restore order. He did not alter the constitution, but reformed the laws. One reform prescribed a double penalty for offences committed under the influence of drink: one for the crime and one for the drunkenness that caused it. After his period of office Pittacus laid down the dictatorship and retired to live quietly. Many sayings were attributed to him. His answer to the question 'What is best?' was 'To do the present thing well'. One of his sayings, 'It is hard to be good', was the starting point of a poem by Simonidēs discussed in Plato's *Protagoras*.

Pitys, see PAN.

Plague, the, at Athens, see PELOPONNESIAN WAR.

Planu'dēs, see ANTHOLOGY and AESOP.

Platae'a, in Boeotia on the border with Attica, the scene of the great battle of 479 BC in which the Greeks under the Spartan Pausanias defeated the Persian army under Mardonius (see PERSIAN WARS).

Plataea, alone of the Boeotian cities, became allied to Athens when threatened by her Boeotian rival Thebes in the late sixth century BC. At Marathon in 490 the Plataeans were the Athenians' only allies in the battle (a fact long remembered at Athens); both cities were sacked by the Persians in 480. After the defeat of the Persians in 479 the Plataeans were given a guarantee of independence. But Plataea's loyalty to Athens led Thebes, to whom she had remained hostile, to attack her in 431 in what was the first engagement of the Peloponnesian War. After a brave defence the garrison was starved into surrender by the Peloponnesians in 427 and its members put to death, except those who had escaped to Athens during a daring sortie. The town was then razed to the ground.

Platā'icus, see ISOCRATES.

Plato (Plătōn) (427–347 BC), Greek philosopher, founder of philosophical idealism and one of the greatest of Greek prose-writers.

I. Plato was born of a noble family which claimed descent from Codrus, an early king of Athens. His life and writings show the enormous influence upon him of *Socrates' life and the manner of his death. At first he wrote poetry (probably none of the epigrams attributed to him is genuine) but meeting Socrates in about 407 BC turned his attention to philosophy. He was ill at the time of Socrates' execution in 399 and was not present during his last moments. Shortly afterwards Plato retired to Megara with other disciples of Socrates; he travelled widely in the next twelve years, visiting Egypt and making the acquaintance of the Pythagoreans in Magna Graecia, in particular Archytas of Tarentum. In c.387 he visited Sicily where he met (and soon fell out with) Dionysius I tyrant of Syracuse and, most importantly, the young Dion, whose sister was married to Dionysius and who later married their daughter, his niece (see SYRACUSE 2). Dion became Plato's pupil and absorbed his teaching.

After a while Plato returned to Athens and there founded a school near the grove of the hero Academus, from which is derived the name subsequently used for the school of Platonic philosophy, the *Academy. Here Plato and his pupils, who included Aristotle, engaged in mathematics, dialectic, and all studies that seemed relevant for the education of future statesmen and politicians; and in this activity Plato spent the remaining forty years of his life. According to his Seventh Epistle (see 6 below) he had twice made some attempt to enter politics: at the end of the Peloponnesian War in 404, under the Thirty Tyrants (among whom were numbered Critias, his mother's cousin, and Charmides, his maternal uncle), and after the restoration of the democracy in 403 (see ATHENS 2 (iii)); but he had been repelled by the criminal acts of the former and by the condemnation of Socrates under the latter. He was driven to the conclusion that there was no hope for cities until philosophers became rulers or rulers philosophers. He made two more visits to Syracuse, one when Dionysius I died in 367 and was succeeded by his son Dionysius II; Dion summoned Plato to try to create in his nephew Dionysius II, then aged about 30, the Platonic philosopher-king. But Dionysius banished Dion, whose motives he suspected, and Plato returned to Athens. Another visit at Dionysius' request in 361 had no better outcome, and many of Plato's Epistles are devoted to explaining his very unsuccessful role in the affairs of Syracuse. Plato died at Athens in 347.

2. *Philosophical writings.* Plato published perhaps twenty-five philosophical dialogues (the authenticity of some is disputed) and the *Apology* (not a dialogue but a reproduction of Socrates' defence at his trial), written over a period of fifty years, and they all survive. There are also thirteen letters (the Epistles) whose genuineness is much debated. Plato himself thought that the spoken word was superior to the written (see PHAEDRUS and the Seventh Epistle), and Aristotle makes reference to doctrines not found in the dialogues; hence it may be that only Plato's lectures would have given the authentic statement of his views. The precise chronological order of the dialogues is not known, but the evidence of style and the evaluation of doctrine allow a rough division into three periods. The early period includes *Apology, *Charmides, *Crito, *Euthyphro, Hippias Minor, Ion, Lachēs, and perhaps Lysis (which may be later). In these Socrates is the principal figure, examining and demolishing the views put forward by his interlocutors. The second period includes *Protagoras, *Gorgias, *Meno, Menexenus, Euthydemus, *Phaedo, *Phaedrus, *Cratylus, Parmenidēs, *Republic, *Symposium, and *Theaetetus. In these Socrates is still the foremost figure, and now puts forward positive doctrines which may be regarded as Plato's own, or at least Plato's interpretation and development of the views of Socrates. The third group, the work of Plato's later years, includes the Critias, Philebus, Politicus, *Sophist and *Timaeus; the *Laws, Plato's longest and last work, was published after his death, probably unrevised.

Of the dialogues, *Charmides, Laches,* and *Lysis* are concerned with the nature of, respectively, temperance, courage, and friendship. In the *Hippias Minor,* a discussion with the Elean *sophist of that name, Socrates shows by a sophistic argument that he who does evil intentionally is less blameworthy than he who does it unintentionally. *Ion* is the genial mockery of a rhapsodist who is shown to possess no knowledge of his art. *Euthydemus* is a humorous satire on the sophists. In the *Menexenus,* which some have hesitated to ascribe to Plato, Socrates recites a funeral oration (after the style of Pericles' Funeral Oration in book 2 of Thucydides' history) which he says was composed by the hetaera Aspasia (see PERICLES) and which is apparently satirical. In *Parmenides,* the young Socrates meets the older Eleatic philosophers Parmenides and Zeno, defends rather naïvely the theory of Ideas (see below) and receives some telling criticisms; it is a difficult dialogue. The *Critias* is an unfinished dialogue, a sequel to the *Timaeus.* It includes the legend of the Athenian victory over the people of the lost island of Atlantis. The *Philebus* is a discussion of the relative merits of pleasure and wisdom as ingredients in the good life. In the *Politicus* ('statesman') the nature of the Platonic ideal of king or statesman is investigated; in the absence of the ideal ruler, the best practical course is for the citizens to frame the laws with care and make them inviolable.

Much of the charm of Plato's dialogues consists in their dramatic setting, the description of the scenes in which they take place, the amusing and interesting characters whom he stages, and the genial irony of Socrates.

3. It is difficult to know in the early dialogues how far Plato is reproducing Socrates' views and to what extent he has moved beyond them, but in the later dialogues it is reasonable to think that Plato is propounding his own doctrines. His primary concern is with moral education. Plato believes that on the one hand it is possible to be a good man without properly knowing what it means to be a good man or what goodness is. This is to have right opinion (*orthē doxa*); as one might think correctly that a road leads to Larisa (Plato's example in *Meno*) without having been along it and reached Larisa oneself. But on the other hand only to have right opinion is to be in a precarious state: meeting a new idea about goodness might throw one into confusion so that one could not judge its value. True knowledge is needed, which is different from right opinion in that with it one is able to define or give an account of what one knows. The early dialogues portray Socrates seeking definitions of particular virtues, of courage in *Laches*, temperance in *Charmides*, piety in *Euthyphro*, or virtue in general in *Meno*, but without reaching positive conclusions. Virtue is a matter of knowledge. Both Socrates and Plato were attracted by the notion that knowledge of virtue is similar in kind to knowledge of how to practise a craft, such as cobbling shoes. It followed for Socrates and Plato (though not for many others) that wrongdoing is the result of ignorance; if people truly knew the good they were bound to do it. In any case knowledge of what goodness is would enable people both to be good themselves and to lead others to knowledge of goodness. A man having such knowledge would constitute the ideal ruler. Only philosophical enquiry, that is, the practice of *dialectic, can lead to true knowledge, and it must be preceded by the study of mathematics and of abstract thinking in general, including logic, as well as of the science of government. Only a select few may be capable of gaining this kind of true knowledge; the rest must be content with having the right opinions.

4. For Plato all objects of knowledge, abstractions such as 'beauty' as well as concrete things, were real entities, but like the objects of mathematical knowledge, the ideal triangle or circle, they did not exist in our world of the senses. Plato postulated another world, the world of Ideas or Forms (of things), leaving the relationship between Ideas and the material things of this world somewhat vague; but the things we see now in this world remind us of the Ideas that they imitate and in some sense partake of. Knowledge of the world of Ideas is attainable in this world only by thought (as is true of the objects of mathematical knowledge; see 5 below) and true knowledge can only be of these Ideas, because they are eternal and unvarying whereas the objects of this world are forever changing. (Aristotle's criticism of this doctrine was that ideas only had reality in so far as they were embodied in particular objects.)

5. Plato believed in a dualism of immortal soul and mortal body. The soul before birth (that is, before its incarnation) was acquainted with the world of Ideas; knowledge of the Ideas in this life is achieved through the soul's recollection of what it has previously known, a recollection which is brought about by the practice of philosophy (i.e. dialectic). Life should therefore be devoted to the cultivation of the soul and the suppression of the body (which may hinder the soul's activities). Beyond all other Ideas is that of the Good (which in some way that is never explained is the cause of things), knowledge of which it is the soul's ambition to attain. Love of what is good and beautiful in this world can lead by stages, through philosophy, to the soul's contemplation of the Idea of Goodness in another world, for which it yearns.

Plato once advertised a lecture on the Good. A large audience collected expecting to hear about the good things they valued—health, wealth, and material happiness. When they found themselves listening to a discourse on mathematics in which they were told that the Good is Limit (*peras*), they went away contemptuous and angry. This was a favourite story of Aristotle, who drew from it the moral that a prospective audience should always be told in advance what a lecture is really going to be about.

6. Thirteen Epistles attributed to Plato have come down to us. They were regarded as genuine in antiquity and are quoted by Cicero and Plutarch. They are addressed to correspondents in Sicily, and all relate to Plato's dealings with Dion and Dionysius, which they were intended to defend. Perhaps none of them was written by Plato himself, but it is generally accepted that the Seventh Epistle, which is addressed to the friends of Dion after the murder of the latter in 353 BC, is a reliable record of the events of Plato's life even if not written by him. It contains a defence of Plato's political ideals and is a passionate lament for his friend Dion.

7. In the disciplines and methods of philosophy, and the rigour of their application, Plato's immediate heir was Aristotle, but ultimately his intellectual heirs are all those who have tried to think systematically about morals and politics, science and mathematics. Plato has exerted an enormous influence on subsequent philosophic

and religious thought by his theory of Ideas, his sense of an unseen and eternal world behind the changing unrealities of the world of the senses, his conception of God, and his connection of morality with religion. In Judaism his influence is felt in the Book of Wisdom and in the system of *Philo. Among the Romans his philosophy appealed to Cicero in particular, as it did to all who revolted against materialism. In the third century AD Plotinus and others provided systematic exegesis of the dialogues as well as reinterpretations, which together made *Neoplatonism the dominant pagan philosophy of that time. Christian thought was infused with Platonic notions from the time of (the Greek) Clement of Alexandria and Origen (second century AD), and Latin Christianity too was influenced indirectly by Platonic teaching from a variety of sources including *Boethius and (from the ninth century) translations of (pseudo)-Dionysius the Areopagite. At the beginning of the Renaissance, reaction by humanists against scholasticism took the form of disparagement of Aristotle and enthusiasm for Plato. Latin translations of his works were made in the fifteenth century by the Italian humanist Marsilio Ficino (1433–99). Knowledge of Plato came to England in the sixteenth century and Platonism was embraced enthusiastically by the seventeenth-century Cambridge Platonists, so-called, who were in this as in much else opposed to the thought of their age. Although nowadays a Platonist philosophy is not usually thought to be tenable, Plato remains a source of philosophical inspiration.

Platonism, see ACADEMY, MIDDLE PLATONISM, and NEOPLATONISM.

Plautus, Titus Ma'ccius (or Maccus) (c.250–184 BC), Roman writer of comedies. He was born at Sarsina in Umbria, reputedly in humble circumstances. Twenty of the 130 plays that were attributed to him have survived, all included in the twenty-one named by Varro as authentic. Of the twenty-first, the Vidularia ('wallet'), only one hundred or so lines exist in a *palimpsest. The plays are all adaptations from Greek New Comedy (see COMEDY, GREEK 6) of the fourth and third centuries BC, now lost (but see DIS EXAPATON); three or four are known to be from Menander, two from Diphilus, two from Philemon, and one apparently from Alexis, and they reproduce Greek life and, with humorous exaggeration, Greek character, as presented by the Greek originals. They were known among the Romans as fabulae *palliatae. They contain no satire on public affairs. Plautus' success in winning the approval of his uncultivated audience lay in the freedom and liveliness with which he handled the Greek originals. In practice he completely recreated these works, simplifying or abridging the plot and making its progress clear, and at the same time introducing other elements, some incongruous and anachronistic, aimed at appealing to his contemporary Roman audience: short stock scenes where characters exchange threats or insults; stock motifs such as that of the 'running slave' entering to deliver a message ostensibly in a hurry but with a great deal of by-play; the slave in the role of popular entertainer, daringly outspoken and insolent in what the Romans may have felt was the Greek fashion, sometimes contrasted with a loyal slave expressing sentiments towards his masters likely to win the approval of slave-owners in the audience; coarse jokes, a great deal of alliteration, puns, and general word-play. As well as this, instead of having plays consisting almost entirely of spoken dialogue (diverbium), Plautus greatly increased (to about two-thirds of the play) the element of song and recitative (cantica), so that the plays resembled musical comedy. The spoken part was written chiefly in iambic senarii (see METRE, LATIN 2), but the scansion was far less regular than in later authors, and was based in great part not on quantity but on stress accent, probably in accordance with colloquial pronunciation. The sung portion was written in a number of lyric metres.

The plays show variety of manner: sentimental comedy in Captivi, domestic in Trinummus, romantic in Rudens, burlesque in Amphitruo, and farcical in Miles gloriosus. Most plots centre on the tricks of a resourceful slave to forward the love-affair of his young master who is being thwarted by a rival, a pimp, or a stern father. The girl in question is usually a slave-prostitute who is eventually discovered to be free-born and so able to marry her Athenian lover. Often the heroine was kidnapped in childhood and her recognition forms the climax of the play. Among the stock characters may be included a boastful soldier, a *parasite, and a cook. For descriptions of the plays see the entries under their titles. The best-known are: Amphitruo, Aulularia, Bacchides, Captivi, Menaechmi, Mostellaria, Miles gloriosus, Pseudolus, Rudens, Trinummus. Less popular are: Asinaria, Casina, Cistellaria, Curculio, Epidicus, Mercator, Persa, Poenulus, Stichus, Truculentus. (For Vidularia see above.)

These plays are almost the only evidence we have for the Latin language at that period. They were greatly admired in the late republic and under the early emperors, but dropped out of favour later because of the difficulty of the language. Plautus was rediscovered and widely translated in the Renaissance, and his influence is traceable in much sixteenth-century English comedy. Henry VIII had two of the comedies performed to entertain the French ambassador in 1526. Shakespeare used the plot of the Menaechmi in The Comedy of Errors (1594), and Molière's Harpagon in L'Avare (1668) is taken from Euclio in Aulularia.

plebei'ans, plebs (Lat. sing. noun, 'the common people'), name given to the body of Roman citizens other than the privileged *patricians. The nature of the original distinction between the two classes is not clear, but perhaps it arose in part through the self-creation of a separate (patrician) class by richer and more powerful families. In the early republic the plebeians were excluded from religious *collegia*, magistracies, and perhaps from the senate, and from inter-marriage with patricians by a law of the *Twelve Tables. For the 'conflict of the orders' in the fifth and fourth centuries BC, by the end of which the *plebs* had achieved its political objectives, see ROME 3. See also TRIBUNES OF THE PLEBS.

Pleiad, the, name given to a group of eight or more Greek writers of tragedy who lived in Alexandria in the reign of Ptolemy II Philadel-phus (285–246 BC). None of their tragedies survives. Their name, derived from the constel-lation (see below), was later taken over by a group of seven sixteenth-century French poets including Ronsard and du Bellay. See LYCOPHRON 2.

Plei'ădĕs (Eng. Pleiades), in Greek myth, the seven daughters of the Titan *Atlas and Pleionē. Their names were Maia (the mother of Hermēs by Zeus), Tāygetē, Ēlectra, Alcyonē, Asteropē, Celaeno, and Meropē. They were pursued by *Orion and he and they were turned into constellations (as were their sisters the *Hyadĕs). The Pleiads, a cluster of seven stars, have special significance for marking the seasons, in particu-lar the time for sowing and planting. In Hesiod, the first rising of the Pleiads before sunrise (early May) marks harvest-time, their setting just before sunrise (at the beginning of November) marks the time for ploughing and sowing. The name is very old, perhaps Indo-European, and of uncertain meaning.

Pliny. 1. **Pliny the Elder** (Gaius Plinius Secundus) (AD 23/4–79), Roman writer on natural history. He was born at Cōmum (Como) in north Italy of an equestrian family and probably educated at Rome. He knew and was influenced by *Pomponius Secundus who was both a writer of tragedies and a successful military commander and whose biography Pliny subsequently wrote. He spent the first twelve years of his active life in military service, mostly with the armies of the Rhine, being at one time the comrade-in-arms of the future emperor Titus. It may have been after his return to Italy in 57 or 58 that he was active as an advocate at the bar. After the accession of the emperor Vespasian in AD 69 his fortunes im-proved and he held a succession of procurator-ships in Gaul, Africa, and Spain which he discharged 'with the utmost scrupulousness' according to Suetonius. He became a counsellor

(*amicus*, 'friend') of Vespasian and then of Titus who succeeded in 79, and was appointed commander of the fleet at Misenum (near Naples). It was from there that he sailed on 24 August 79 to observe the eruption of Vesuvius from the neighbourhood of Stabiae (south of Pompeii). His nephew Pliny the Younger (see (2) below) describes in a letter to Tacitus (6. 16) how his uncle had his attention drawn to the column of smoke rising above the nearer moun-tains and set off in a light vessel to invest-igate; how he dictated his observations under a hail of stones and the next day went out on the shore despite the darkness and explosions, with a pillow around his head for protection against falling debris, and was suffocated by the fumes.

Pliny was a man of extraordinary industry and thirst for knowledge. He slept little, had books constantly read to him, and took an immense quantity of notes. He wrote works which are now lost on cavalry tactics, oratory, grammar, and history (twenty books on Rome's wars against the Germans, thirty-one books continuing the Roman history of Aufi-dius Bassus, who lived in the time of the emperors Augustus and Tiberius). His greatest achievement, which has survived, is the *Natur-alis Historia* ('natural history') in thirty-seven books, dedicated to Titus in 77 and published posthumously. Pliny tells us in the preface that it consists of 20,000 important facts obtained from 100 authors, but the total of both is much higher. Book 1 consists of a table of contents and list of authorities; book 2 deals with the physics of the universe, and its constituent parts; books 3–6 are on the geography and ethnology of Europe, Asia, and Africa; book 7 on human physiology; books 8–11 on zoology (land animals, sea animals, birds, insects); books 12–19 on botany; books 20–7 on the medicinal properties of plants; books 28–32 on medicines derived from animals; books 33–7 on metals and stones, including the use of minerals in medicine, art, and architecture, with a digres-sion on the history of art.

In spite of many errors and much carelessness, credulity, superficiality, unscientific arrange-ment, and the tedium of dry catalogues, the work is remarkable for the vast labour and the boundless curiosity of the author that it repres-ents; it contains much that is interesting and entertaining, and much unique information about the art, science, and civilization of the author's day. It is full of stories, such as that about the skeleton of the monster by which Andromeda had been menaced, brought from Joppa (Jaffa) and exhibited at Rome (9. 11; Joppa evidently traded on the legend, for the marks of the chains with which Andromeda was fastened were also shown there, 5. 69); the tricks that elephants were taught (8. 4–8); the anec-dote of Lysander permitting the funeral of Sophocles (7. 109); the perils to which sponge divers were exposed (9. 151–3); the coracles of the British (7. 206); the introduction of barbers into Italy (7. 211). Roman life is illustrated by passages such as those about the variety of mattresses and woollen cloths in use (8. 190–3); about hedgehogs' quills used for carding wool, and the senate's decrees to prevent their being monopolized (8. 135); the price of a cook (9. 67); Lollia Paulina's jewels (9. 117–18); ostrich feathers worn in military helmets (10. 2); *foie gras* and pillows of goose-feathers (10. 52–4); wrinkles removed with asses' milk (28. 183). The chapters on the history of painting in book 35 and of sculpture in book 36 are especially interesting, telling us much about the Greek painters *Zeuxis, *Parrhasius, and *Apellēs, and about the sculptors *Pheidias, *Praxitelēs, and *Scopas, and showing the estimation in which they were held at Rome. His discussions of amber (37. 32–5) and coal (37. 99) are also particularly informative.

Like Seneca the Younger, Pliny is a believer in a beneficent deity, a spirit pervading the world. He is an enthusiastic admirer of nature, and a vigorous critic of his times, which he saw as marked by folly, luxury, inhumanity, and ingratitude. He has a sturdy Roman dislike of the Greeks and distrust of their influence.

2. Pliny the Younger, Roman administrator known through his letters. He was called Gaius Plinius Caecilius Secundus after being adopted by his maternal uncle Pliny the Elder (see (1) above). He was 17 at the time of the eruption of Vesuvius in AD 79 and so was born in AD 61 or 62; he inherited his uncle's estate, and died in 113. He was born at Comum (Como) in north Italy, and studied at Rome under *Quintilian, whose influence may be detected in the simplicity and restraint of his pupil's prose. Another of his teachers was the Stoic philosopher Musonius (who also taught Epictetus). He was three times married, his first two wives dying young; his letters show that his marriage to Calpurnia, the third wife, was a very happy one. He had no children, but received from Trajan the privileges granted to fathers of three children (see IUS TRIUM LIBERORUM). He began a career at the bar at the age of 18, specializing in cases of inheritance. He passed through the regular series of magistracies (see CURSUS HONORUM) and succeeded by his discretion in avoiding (though he stood in some danger) Domitian's persecution of the Stoic opposition (see ROME 11), in spite of his sympathy with its views. Under Trajan (AD 98–117) he became one of the officials in charge of the state treasury; he was *consul suffectus* in 100, then a curator of the river Tiber at Rome, responsible for keeping its banks in repair to prevent flooding and for maintaining the sewers. He became augur in 103 (succeeding *Frontinus) and finally governor of the disorderly province of Bithynia–Pontus along the south coast of the

Black Sea (in about 110), where he apparently died in office in 113. Calpurnia had travelled out with Pliny: his last letter, to Trajan, explains that he authorized her return to Italy by the imperial postal service to deal with her grandfather's death.

Pliny was very rich and owned estates in various parts of Italy which he administered with efficiency. He was notably considerate to his slaves, and munificent. He founded a library at Comum and made many large gifts and charitable bequests. He practised in the courts and was proud of his oratory. His only surviving speech is a revised edition of the *Panegyricus* which he delivered to Trajan on entering on his consulship in AD 100, an expression of the relief felt under the new reign after the oppression of Domitian, and a document which throws light on Trajan's reforms. Among other important speeches that Pliny delivered was one on behalf of the Africans, impeaching Marius Priscus, who had been proconsul of Africa. In this he was associated with Tacitus, who, according to Pliny, spoke eloquently and with majesty.

Pliny's fame rests on his ten books of letters. The first nine books of personal letters were carefully selected and published at intervals by Pliny himself before he went out to Bithynia. In general the letters are not dated, and Pliny professes to have arranged them haphazardly. Book 10 was published posthumously; it begins with fourteen short official letters to Trajan, and is followed by correspondence relating to Bithynia. The first three books deal with the events of 97–102, and are closed by a letter on the death of the poet Martial in 103/4; these were published c.107. Books 4–7 refer to the events of 103–7; in the last letter of book 7 Pliny expresses the hope of being included in the *Histories* of his friend Tacitus. Books 8–9 cover the years 108–9, and show Pliny enjoying a leisurely time on the estate of his Tuscan villa at Tifernum (Città di Castello), reading and writing to his friends. Twice he speaks of being recognized and linked with Tacitus as a famous author (see below). His appointment to Bithynia ended this period of cultivated leisure.

The letters resemble short essays on a wide variety of subjects: public affairs (especially the prosecutions of officials, with which he was concerned), descriptions of his villas or of scenery, or of how he spends his day (sometimes in hunting, but he takes his writing materials too), reproof of a friend who fails to come to dinner, literary or rhetorical points, interpretation of a dream, ghost stories, the purchase of a statue or an estate, a murder. He writes movingly of his new marriage, his grief at his wife's miscarriage, and his hopes for further children (not to be fulfilled). Several of his letters are addressed to his friends Tacitus and Suetonius. Among the former is the famous letter (6. 16) describing the eruption of Vesuvius and his uncle's death. Other interesting letters are those containing eulogies of the poets Silius Italicus and Martial (3. 7 and 21), that relating the heroism of *Arria, wife of Paetus (3. 16), and that containing a bibliography of the works of the Elder Pliny (3. 5). The style of the letters is adapted to the subject, serious or light-hearted, and in general strikes a mean between the amplitude of Cicero and the brevity of the Younger Seneca, but the letters are more studied and artificial than those of Cicero to Atticus. Apart from the charm they derive from the agreeable nature of their author, they are interesting for their depiction of the life of a wealthy Roman during a happy period of the empire, and help to correct the unfavourable impression left by the bitter satire of Juvenal and the sombre pessimism which Tacitus retained even when writing under Trajan. The senate is seen, for instance, deliberating on matters of importance within its restricted sphere, punish-ments are inflicted on dishonest officials, and family life pursues its course with a degree of loyalty and decency.

The correspondence with Trajan in the tenth book throws valuable light on the administra-tion of an imperial province. It displays Pliny as an honest but timid governor, referring to Rome such small matters as the absence of a fire-brigade and water-buckets at Nicomedia. The emperor's replies are precise and clear and show him encouraging an extraordinary degree of centralization. The most famous of these letters are Pliny's submission of the question how the Christians should be treated, and the emperor's answer (see CHRISTIANITY).

Pliny prided himself not only on his oratory but on his poetry, and published two volumes of poems. Some rather bad specimens are included in his letters. His pleasure in his literary fame appears when he tells (9. 23) how a Roman *eques*, sitting next to Tacitus at the Circus and conversing with him, asked him who he was, and being answered, 'You know me from your reading', enquired, 'Are you Tacitus or Pliny?'

Plōtī'nus (*c.* AD 205–270), greatest Greek philo-sopher of late antiquity, the chief exponent of *Neoplatonism, probably born at Lycopolis in Egypt. He settled in Rome in 244, after having accompanied the expedition of the emperor Gordion to Mesopotamia in order to learn something of eastern thought. He was admired for his extreme spirituality, mysticism, and ascet-icism. 'He seemed ashamed of being in a body', says his biographer and disciple *Porphyry. Plotinus wrote philosophical essays arising out of discussions and intended for circulation among his pupils. These were collected by Porphyry and arranged in six books of nine essays each, called *Enneads* ('the nines'). Ennead 1 deals with ethics and aesthetics; Enneads 2 and 3

with physics and cosmology; Ennead 4 with psychology; Enneads 5 and 6 with metaphysics, logic, and epistemology. Because of his weak sight Plotinus never read through what he had written; the writings read like oral discourse and are brief, elliptical, and allusive, with abrupt transitions, and are therefore very difficult to understand.

Plotinus' philosophy may be summarized as follows. The universe is to be explained as a hierarchy of realities (or hypostasēs), a great chain of being, in which the higher reality is the cause of and gives existence to whatever is immediately below it; this process Plotinus calls emanation, an 'overflowing' from a higher to a lower level. In this process there is a gradual diminution, so that every existent is slightly inferior to its cause. At the top of the hierarchy are three divine realities, the One (*Hen*), Mind (*Nous*), and Soul (*Psȳchē*). At the very summit is the One, supreme goodness, which can to a large extent be identified with Plato's Idea of the Good (see PLATO 5). Mind, which comes imme-diately below the One, and derives its form from contemplating its source, is a fragmented image of the One, and corresponds to intuitive thought. The Platonic Ideas (see PLATO 4) are to be found in Mind. Soul, which derives from Mind, can only contemplate its objects in succession, moving from one to another, and so it creates time and space. It generates the next reality, Nature (*Physis*), the principle of life and growth. Beyond Nature, at the lowest level of reality, exist material things (matter). Human beings are microcosms, containing within them-selves parts of Matter, Nature, Soul, and Mind. What a human being becomes depends on the level to which he directs his consciousness. By intellectual discipline a person may hope to rise to the level of Mind. It is even possible to rise beyond that and be identified, by ecstasy, with the supreme unity of the One (an experience which Plotinus says came four times to him). In ethics Plotinus enjoined purification by self-discipline, with a view to ascent, impelled by love and enthusiasm, towards the One. His writings are based on personal experience and are a classic of mysticism. He makes no explicit reference to Christianity, and unification with the One is not thought of as attainable by divine grace. Plotinus also makes an important contri-bution to aesthetics: whereas Plato had argued that art imitates natural objects, Plotinus pro-pounds the view that art and nature alike both impose a form on matter in accordance with an inward vision of archetypal Forms or Ideas.

Plūtarch (Ploutarchos) (*c.* AD 46–*c.*120), Greek biographer, historian, and moral philosopher.

1. Plutarch was born at *Chaeronēa in Boeo-tia, of a wealthy and cultivated family, and spent most of his life there. He studied philosophy at Athens under the Platonist *Ammonius, a man

of practical as well as philosophical ability. He visited Egypt and Italy, lecturing and teaching at Rome, and had a wide circle of influential and cultivated friends. But the last thirty years of his life were centred on Chaeronea and Delphi; he was a citizen of both, and served them with devotion for many years. Neither Pliny the Younger nor Tacitus (his contemporaries) mentions him. Plutarch is one of the most attractive and readable of ancient prose authors, writing with charm, geniality, and tact. An ancient catalogue of his works exists, ascribed to Lamprias. His surviving writings (half his complete works) consist of (i) a series of fifty biographies known as *Parallel Lives* (*Bioi parallēloi*) in which he relates the life of some eminent Greek (statesmen or soldier) followed by the life of some similar Roman offering some points of resemblance, and then adds a short comparision of the two; and (ii) seventy-eight miscellaneous works now known as the *Mōrālia* (Gk. *Ēthika*).

2. *Parallel Lives*. These consist of twenty-three pairs of lives, nineteen of them with comparisons attached, and also four single lives. They include lives of Solon, Themistocles, Aristeides, Pericles, Alcibiades, Nicias, Demosthenes, Philopoemen, Timoleon, Dion, Alexander, Pyrrhus, Marius, Sulla, Pompey, Mark Antony, Brutus, Julius Caesar, and Cicero. Of the Roman emperors, only the lives of Galba and Otho survive. Plutarch's object is to bring out the moral character in each case, rather than to relate the political events of his time; hence his full treatment of the subject's education and natural disposition, and his relation of anecdotes calculated to reveal the nature of the man, 'a light occasion, a word, or some sport' which 'makes men's natural dispositions more plain than the famous battles won, in which ten thousand men may be killed'. Although Plutarch distorts the truth in order to exemplify virtue or vice, in general he is as reliable as his sources, and sometimes very valuable. He shows no bias or unfairness in his treatment of Greeks and Romans, no flattery of the now dominant power of Rome or vanity in the past glories of his own nation. He believed in the compatibility of Rome the ruler and Greece the educator.

The *Lives* contain, besides interesting anecdotes, many memorable historical passages: the catastrophe in the Peloponnesian War of the Athenian expedition to Syracuse (*Nicias*), Pompey's defeat by Caesar and subsequent murder, the death of the younger Cato, and the suicide of Otho. There are also great battle-pieces: the victory of the Roman general Marius over the German Cimbri, the victory of the Corinthian general Timoleon over the Carthaginians at the river Crimisus, the siege of Syracuse (when Archimedes was there) by the Roman Marcellus; and striking descriptions of a quite different kind, of the happy state of Italy under Numa, of Sicily pacified by Timoleon, and of Cleopatra

sailing up the river Cydnus in her barge to visit Antony. The most famous translation of the *Lives* into English was that of Sir Thomas North (1579) made not from Greek but from the French version of Amyot (1559). It was closely followed by Shakespeare in his three Roman plays *Julius Caesar*, *Antony and Cleopatra*, and *Coriolanus*.

3. *Moralia*. These treatises are usually referred to by their Latin titles and their subjects are varied. There is one group of rhetorical works and another on moral philosophy (treated in a popular style) on themes such as 'On Busybodies' (*de cūriōsitāte*), 'On Garrulity' (*de garrulitāte*), 'On the Restraint of Anger' (*de cohibenda ira*), 'How to Distinguish a Flatterer from a Friend' (*quomodo adūlātōr ab amico internoscatur*). Plutarch's warm and sympathetic personality is apparent in his 'Advice to Married Couples' (*coniugalia praecepta*) and 'Consolation to My Wife' (*consolatio ad uxorem*) on the death of their infant daughter. There is a religious group, in which Plutarch appears as the interpreter and defender of the old beliefs. It includes the treatise 'On Superstition' (*de superstitione*), in which he regards superstition as the opposite extreme to atheism, and piety as the mean between the two. Plutarch was a (not altogether orthodox) Platonist and was opposed to some of the doctrines of the Stoics, and still more to the Epicurean school and its encouragement of withdrawal from the duties of social life: see his treatises on 'The Unnoticed Life' (*an recte dictum sit latenter esse vivendum*), 'Advice on Public Life' (*praecepta gerendae reipublicae*), and 'Not Even a Pleasant Life is Possible on Epicurean Principles' (*non posse suaviter vivi secundum Epicurum*). There is an interesting treatise 'On the Delays of Divine Justice' (*de sera numinis vindicta*) in which he explains the puzzle of the apparent prosperity of the wicked, and another 'On the E at Delphi' (*de E apud Delphos*), i.e. on the letter E inscribed in the temple of Apollo there (for which he offers a Pythagorean explanation, that it is the Greek for 'Thou Art', identifying the one eternal principle of the universe); also interesting is 'On the Cessation of Oracles' (*de defectu oraculorum*), which contains a discussion of demons (see DAIMONES), beings intermediate between gods and men, and refers to the legend of the genii of the British Isles.

Plutarch used the *dialogue form extensively and often to great effect. The nine books of 'Table Talk' (*quaestiones convivales*) are dinner-party conversations of wise men (rhetoricians, physicians, etc., some of them historical characters) on a multitude of subjects. The treatise 'On Socrates' Sign' (*de genio Socratis*) combines many elements: exciting narrative (the liberation of Thebes), philosophical conversation, and an elaborate myth, in the manner of Plato, on the fate of the soul after death. A different kind of treatise is that 'On the Face in the Moon' (*de facie quae in orbe lunae appāret*), a speculation on the cosmos. Several important antiquarian works have also survived: the 'Greek' and 'Roman Questions' (*quaestiones Graecae, Romanae*) are a mine of information about religious antiquities. Plutarch wrote some literary criticism, including a comparison of Aristophanes and Menander, and an essay 'On the Malignity of Herodotus' (*de malignitate Herodoti*; see HERODOTUS), in which Plutarch's complaint seems to be that Herodotus did not conceal the pro-Persian sympathies of the Boeotians. It is noteworthy that Plutarch, in spite of his familiarity with Roman society, history, archaeology, and religion, almost completely ignores Roman literature (his knowledge of Latin appears to have been limited). In his Life of Lucullus he gives a Greek version of a passage from Horace, but never mentions Virgil or Ovid.

4. Among the *Moralia* have survived several slightly later works not written by Plutarch but of great importance: 'On the Education of Children' (*de liberis educandis*) was very influential in the Renaissance; 'On Fate' (*de fato*) is valuable as a work of Middle Platonist philosophy; 'The Lives of the Ten Orators' (*vitae decem oratorum*) is an important source for ancient knowledge of the Attic orators from Antiphon to Deinarchus; 'The Doctrines of the Philosophers' (*de placitis philosophorum*) is another important source book; and 'On Music' (*de musica*) is one of the principal sources of modern knowledge about the history of Greek music and lyric poetry.

5. Plutarch's *Moralia* were widely read in medieval times and studied by many later authors, notably Montaigne (1533–92), who modelled upon them the form of his Essays, Jeremy Taylor (1613–67), and Francis Bacon (1561–1626). They were translated into French by Amyot in 1572, and into English by Philemon Holland in 1603. These and the *Lives*, perhaps more than the work of any other ancient writer, transmitted to Europe knowledge of the moral and historical traditions of the classical world, and influenced immeasurably its ways of thought.

Pluto, Latin form, commonly used in English, of Ploutōn, in Greek myth, a name of *Hades, god of the Underworld, meaning 'the wealth-giver' (Gk. *ploutos*, 'wealth'), because wealth comes from the earth. Compare *Plutus* below. It is also the name of a Titaness, mother of *Tantalus.

Plūtus (*ploutos*, 'wealth'), in Greek myth, the personification of wealth, the son of *Demeter and *Iasion, whom Homer regarded as a mortal. He was originally connected with abundance of crops and became a figure of popular rather than literary mythology. He was worshipped with Demeter at Eleusis. There was a tradition that Zeus blinded him in order to make him indiscriminate in the distribution of riches. See the Greek comedy *Plutus* by Aristophanes, below.

Plūtus (*Ploutos*, 'wealth'), Greek comedy by *Aristophanes produced in 388 BC; at what festival and with what success is not known. It is the last of Aristophanes' extant plays. An earlier play of the same name, now lost, had been produced by him in 408 BC. The lyrics to be sung by the chorus are very scanty in this play, but provision appears to have been made at various places for choral interludes which had no particular connection with the plot (for the diminishing role of the chorus in the latest plays of Aristophanes see COMEDY, GREEK 5).

Chremylus is so indignant at seeing bad men grow rich while honest men like himself remain poor that, accompanied by his slave Carion, he has been to consult the Delphic Oracle as to whether he should bring up his son to be good or bad if the latter is to succeed in life. The god advises Chremylus to accost the first person he meets on leaving the shrine and induce him to enter his house. This is a blind old man; pestered by Chremylus and Carion he reveals that he is Plutus, god of wealth, whom Zeus has blinded out of ill-will to men so that, being unable to distinguish good men from bad, he will reward them indiscriminately, without regard to their virtue. Chremylus decides that the sight of Plutus must be restored so that he may associate only with honest men. Plutus is terrified of the vengeance of Zeus but is persuaded that he himself is more powerful than that god: he can put a stop to Zeus' sacrifices by not providing men with the money to buy them. He therefore consents to be taken to the temple of Asclepius to be cured. The goddess of Poverty intervenes and tries to deter Chremylus, pointing out the disastrous effects of what he proposes to do, for it is Poverty, the source of all virtue and effort, that has made Greece what she is. But Chremylus remains unconvinced, and he and Carion go off to the temple with Plutus. Carion returns to tell Chremylus' wife of the successful cure, with much entertaining detail; presently Plutus returns and enriches Chremylus' house. Then come a series of visitors: an honest man who has long been poor and is now prosperous; an informer, indignant at being impoverished; an old woman who has lost her young lover now he no longer needs her money; the god Hermēs, who is desperately hungry, now no one bothers to sacrifice to the gods, and is looking for a job; and finally the priest of Zeus who is also hungry now he cannot get his share of the sacrifices. Chremylus seems to identify Plutus and Zeus, and suggests that they install Plutus in the Treasury on the Acropolis. A procession for that purpose ensues.

pnīgos, see COMEDY, GREEK 3 (iv).

Pnyx, hill at Athens a little way west of the Acropolis, where from the time of *Cleisthenēs (end of the sixth century BC) the assembly of the Athenian citizens (the *ecclesia*) used to meet. At the end of the sixth century the area was levelled and a retaining wall built to the north; the citizens stood or sat on the side, facing the city, as Aristophanes describes at the opening of *Acharnians*. There were stone or wooden benches to sit on, but they were apparently never used. At the end of the fifth century the site of the *bēma* (speaker's platform) was changed (according to Plutarch, at the time of the Thirty Tyrants, i.e. 404/3 BC) so that the citizens had their backs to the city. The Pnyx was again remodelled and enlarged in the period 330–326 BC. In Roman times (i.e. after 146 BC) the Pnyx lost its importance and the assembly met in the Theatre of Dionysus.

Podalei'rius, see MACHAON.

Poe'nulus ('little Carthaginian'), Roman comedy by *Plautus. The two daughters of Hanno, a Carthaginian, who were stolen from him in their childhood, have been bought by a pimp and taken to Sicyon (in Greece). In the same place is living Agorastoclēs, son of Hanno's cousin (and the 'little Carthaginian' of the title); he likewise was stolen in infancy and has been adopted by a wealthy citizen of Sicyon. He has fallen in love with the elder of the sisters, not knowing of their kinship to him. He and his slave devise a plot for ruining the pimp in order to free the girl. Meanwhile Hanno, who has been searching every country for his daughters, arrives at Sicyon; he discovers them and his relative Agorastocles, recovers the girls, and bestows the elder on her lover. Some of Hanno's speeches appear to be in the Carthaginian language.

Poetics (Gk. *Peri poiētikēs*, Lat. *Poetica*), treatise by *Aristotle on poetry, primarily a philosophical work of aesthetic theory. Like all Greeks, Aristotle believed that art is essentially representational. In the *Poetics* his fundamental belief is that imitation is the basis of the pleasure derived from all forms of art, not only poetry but also music, dancing, painting, and sculpture. The artist, by pointing out similarities, gives us the pleasure of understanding things better.

Aristotle divides poetry according to whether it imitates people above or below the average state of humanity (tragedy represents good characters, comedy bad) and according to whether it is narrative (epic) or dramatic. He traces the special origins and development of *tragedy and *comedy. An analysis of tragedy follows: its constituent elements are plot, the imitation of character, verbal expression, the imitation of intellect, spectacle, and song-writing; the plot (the pre-eminent part of tragedy) should represent a single action of a certain magnitude; the poet's aim is to produce pleasure in the spectator by eliciting from the representation the emotions of pity (for others) and fear (for oneself). Plato had attacked tragedy for stimulating the emotions a good man tries to suppress; Aristotle seems to suggest that the *catharsis* (purging) of these emotions may incidentally be beneficial. He discusses the construction of the plot, including the complex (as opposed to the simple) plot which contains 'reversal of fortune' (*peripeteia*) and recognition (*anagnōrisis*). This part includes the notable saying that poetry is more like philosophy and more worthwhile than history, because it tells general truths while history tells particular facts, 'what Alcibiades did and what happened to him'. There follow sections on characterization, poetic imagination, and diction.

Aristotle proceeds to discuss epic poetry, the rules to which it should conform, and its metre. Finally he deals with criticisms of Homer and how they may be met, and ends with a comparison of tragedy and epic.

The *Poetics* became the most influential book on poetry ever written. It has, however, the peculiarity that the genuine views of Aristotle contributed no more to its influence than the misinterpretation of these views arising from the author's compressed and elliptical style. The dramatic unities of time, place, and action, for example, which were so rigidly adhered to by the French classical dramatists, find their origin in Aristotle's observations on the practice of his day (he insisted only on the necessity for unity of action) but took their absolute nature from the elaborations of Italian Renaissance scholars and in particular from the widely read *Poetics* (1561) of Julius Caesar Scaliger.

po'lemarch (*polemarchos*), at Athens, one of the nine *archons appointed annually, originally the commander-in-chief of the army; after 487 BC when the archons were appointed by lot the chief command was transferred to the *strategoi and the polemarch's powers were limited to certain judicial and ceremonial functions. He conducted certain sacrifices, and dealt with those legal cases which involved persons who were not Athenian citizens.

Po'lemon, head of the *Academy 313–270 BC.

police. Athens in the fifth century BC had a corps of Scythian archers, slaves belonging to the state, keeping order in assemblies and law courts. The magistrates responsible for them were known as *astynomoi*. Sparta and Syracuse under the fifth-century tyrants had notorious secret police forces; that in Sparta operated only against helots (see KRYPTEIA). At Rome every magistrate was empowered to enforce obedience through his attendants, the *lictors, and the *tresviri capitalēs* ('three magistrates'), minor officials, were responsible with their staff for maintaining nocturnal peace in the city. Urban cohorts of soldiers were used for keeping order, and in the country, stations of legionary detachments were set up at key points along the roads. From the early second century AD special corps resembling secret police developed under the harmless name of *frumentarii*, 'foragers'; they were abolished by the emperor Diocletian but reappeared under the vague name of *agentes in rebus* ('agents').

polis, 'city' (pl. *poleis*), the Greek city-state, the small self-governing community which emerged at the end of the Dark Age and was the characteristic political unit of the Greek world. There were several hundreds in Greece and the colonies. A *polis* consisted of only one city, with its citadel (*acropolis*) and market-place (*agora*), and the surrounding countryside. The citizens (see CITIZENSHIP, GREEK) lived in city or country, but the government of the state was entirely concentrated in the city, and in the hands of those citizens empowered by the constitution to exercise it (see ARISTOCRACY, OLIGARCHY, DEMOCRACY). The government was carried on by an assembly (see ECCLESIA), council (see BOULE), and magistrates (see ARCHONS). Citizens had certain obligations towards the city: to worship the state gods and take part in their cult, perform military service, pay taxes, and obey the laws. There was also a large non-citizen population of slaves and perhaps of resident foreigners also (see METICS). Political struggles mostly centred on the kind of constitution the city possessed (e.g. between supporters of oligarchy and supporters of democracy) and on social and economic conditions; civil war (*stasis*) was frequent. The large number of independent city-states was the chief reason for the endless internal wars in Greece and the infrequency of any panhellenic action. The *poleis* lost much of their vital life when they lost their independence after the conquests of Alexander the Great and the emergence of the Hellenistic kingdoms in the late fourth century BC, but for Aristotle the *polis* 'belongs to the class of objects which exist by nature, and man is by nature a political animal (*politikon zōon*)', i.e. one whose nature it is to live in a *polis* (*Politics* 1235a).

Politics, title of a treatise on political science by *Aristotle (see 4 (iv)).

Poli'ticus ('statesman'), dialogue by *Plato (see 2).

Polity of the Athenians (Athenaiōn politeia, 'The Athenian Constitution'), treatise by *Aristotle (see 3 (ii)).

Po'llio. 1. **Gaius Asi'nius Pollio** (76 BC–AD 4), Roman historian, literary patron, statesman, and supporter of the emperor Augustus. In his youth he was an associate of the poet Catullus, and a supporter first of Julius Caesar in the civil war against Pompey and later of Mark Antony, whose legate he was in Transpadane Gaul (see ROME 7). He was consul in 40 BC, when he helped to bring about the treaty of Brundisium between Antony and Octavian. In 39 he obtained a triumph for his victory over an Illyrian tribe. He refused to fight against Antony at Actium, but became a supporter of the Augustan settlement. It was he who first recognized the genius of Virgil, and came to his assistance when Virgil's farm near Mantua was confiscated after the battle of Philippi in 42. The poet celebrated him in his fourth and eighth Eclogues. His history of the civil wars, from the consulship of Metellus in 60 BC (when Caesar and Pompey made their original pact) to the battle of Philippi in 42 BC (and perhaps continued to the end of the 30s), has unfortunately not survived but was used by Appian and Plutarch; it receives high praise from Horace in *Odes* II. 1. Pollio also wrote tragedies and erotic poems, and won a reputation as an orator. A sharp critic, he ventured to correct Cicero, Caesar, and Sallust, and to criticize Livy for his provincialism (which he calls *patavinitas*). He founded the first public library in Rome, and is said by the Elder Seneca to have introduced the practice of reciting his own works to an audience.

2. **Trebellius Pollio**, see HISTORIA AUGUSTA.

pollution. The Greeks, in common with many races at all times, believed that people were defiled or polluted by close contact with impurity, by breaking a religious rule, or by committing a crime that had religious overtones. The effect of pollution might be similar to the consequences of divine anger; a polluted city, for example (such as Thebes as described at the opening of Sophocles' *Oedipus Rex*), might be struck by sterility and plague; the source of the pollution had to be found and expelled, and purity restored by religious acts of purification. Impurity was abhorrent to the gods, and a polluted person was excluded from temples and all religious occasions. Like *Oedipus, the unwitting perpetrator of parricide and incest, he was contagious and might infect others with his pollution, and therefore his company was shunned.

Pollution could result from contact with something itself unclean, a corpse for example. (At Athens, trials for murder always took place in the open air.) Birth and death were the two commonest natural pollutions, both shunned by the gods. In Euripides' *Hippolytus* the goddess Artemis has to leave her favourite Hippolytus when he is at the point of death, and in Sophocles' *Antigone* the gods refuse to accept men's sacrifices because their altars are polluted by the unburied corpse of Polyneices. Birth and death within a temple were sacrilegious and polluting (see PAUSANIAS (1)); the sacred island of *Delos, by a decree of the Athenians, had to be kept untainted by both, and all tombs were removed. Households in which a birth or death occurred had to be purified.

Pollution might be caused by a quite minor act of impiety or infringement of a religious rule—performing a sacrifice with unwashed hands, for example. The most notable cause of pollution was murder, requiring ritual purification of varying degrees of elaboration to get rid of the victim's blood, thought of as clinging to the murderer's hands. Blood shed in battle could be simply washed away, and similarly the blood of a villain could be easily removed by a straightforward ritual. At the other extreme, the *Alcmaeonidae in the fifth century BC were still dogged by accusations of pollution arising from a particularly sacrilegious murder committed in the seventh (see CYLON). Epilepsy and madness were commonly regarded as if they were the result of pollution, and were treated by rites of purification (but see HIPPOCRATES (I)). Occasionally, as if to mark a new beginning, scapegoats carrying a community's impurities were expelled from a city (see THARGELIA). After the final expulsion of the Persian invaders from Athens in 479 BC (see PERSIAN WARS), all the fires in the city 'polluted' by the Persian presence were extinguished and rekindled from the hearth of Apollo's shrine at Delphi (Rome too was purified after the expulsions of the Tarquins and the Gauls).

Pollux, see DIOSCURI.

Pollux, Julius, see JULIUS POLLUX.

Polyae'nus, (second century AD), Macedonian, author of *Stratēgēmata* (in eight books), a collection of 'ruses in war', written in Greek and dedicated to the emperors Marcus Aurelius and Verus to aid them in the latter's Parthian war (AD 162).

Poly'bius (c.200–after 118 BC), Greek historian of Rome's rise to power, born at Megalopolis in Arcadia, the son of Lycortas, who was a prominent member of the *Achaean Confederacy and friend of its general *Philopoemen. Polybius was given the honour of carrying the ashes of Philopoemen to burial in 182. In 181 he was chosen, with his father, to serve on an embassy to Egypt, but this was cancelled when the king there died suddenly. Nothing more is known of his life until 169, when he was made *hipparchos* (cavalry commander) of the Confederacy. Since 172 Rome had been at war with Perseus of Macedon (son of Philip V) and was suspicious of Greek attitudes and of the Confederacy in particular for its neutral stance (see MACEDONIA 3). After defeating Perseus at Pydna in 168 the Romans instituted a political purge. Polybius was among a thousand Achaeans sent to Rome for examination and kept there for sixteen years without accusation or trial. He was

fortunate to become tutor to the sons of Aemilius *Paullus (who had commanded the Roman army at Pydna), the younger of whom became by adoption Publius *Scipio. Polybius' enduring friendship with the latter, and his consequent connections with two of the leading philhellenic families in Rome, allowed him on several occasions to intercede between Greece and Rome. The Achaean exiles were permitted to return to Greece in 150, and Polybius went with them, but in 147–146 he accompanied Scipio to the siege of Carthage and witnessed the capture of that city. When war suddenly broke out between Rome and the Achaean Confederacy, leading to a Greek defeat and the sacking of Corinth by Mummius in 146, Polybius acted as intermediary and was entrusted with organizing many details of the new administration. In this difficult task he earned the approval of the Romans and the gratitude of the Greek cities. Little is known of the last twenty years of his life, which must have been largely occupied with his literary work, of which only the *History* survives (in part), written in Greek. According to one source he died as a result of a fall from his horse at the age of 82.

Polybius declares the original aim of his *History* in the introduction: '[to relate] by what means and under what system of government the Romans succeeded in less than fifty-three years [from 220 BC, the start of the Second Punic War, to 168 BC, the end of the Third Macedonian War] in bringing under their rule almost the whole inhabited world'. Subsequently he extended his scheme to cover the preliminary period from the beginning of the First Punic War (264) to the destruction of Carthage and Corinth in 146 (see above). In this extended form the history consisted of forty books, of which only the first five survive complete. Of the rest we have only excerpts and quotations, some quite substantial. Book 6 includes a sketch of the Roman constitution in Polybius' day and a comparison of this with the constitutions of Athens, Thebes, Crete, Sparta, and finally Carthage.

Polybius attributed the greatness of Rome to the perfection of the Roman constitution, as an even blend of monarchical, aristocratic, and democratic elements. His history was addressed primarily to Greeks but also to the upper-class Romans of his own day who were familiar with the Greek language. His chief aim was to be useful, to give good advice to the politicians, and to teach all his readers, by examples, how to bear the vicissitudes of fortune. He describes his work as *pragmatikē historia*, a factual history of events in war and politics with careful avoidance of the emotional and sensational (unlike the Greek historians of the Hellenistic age; see HISTORIOGRAPHY I). His history was breaking new ground (only Ephorus had anticipated him) in being not a monograph, a popular form of historical writing but very limited in the moral lessons it could teach, but a universal history which offered wide scope for exemplifying the various truths that Polybius wanted to communicate, and in particular the significant role that fortune played in the rise of Rome (see TYCHE). Polybius attributed to her intervention the rise of Rome, while at the same time indicating that Rome deserved her good fortune through her own merits, an attitude of mind exemplified by Terence's observation that 'fortune favours the brave'.

Polybius is unusually revealing about the qualities needed by one who would write 'pragmatical history': such a one should have studied the writings of others, must know the countries he is writing about, and have personal experience of political life (which includes warfare). A historian should be first of all a man of action (as Polybius was). Polybius envisages history as being for the most part about events which can be recalled by those still alive; the interrogation of eye-witnesses is regarded as supremely important; most of his own history fell within living memory or within the lifetime of the previous generation. Above all a historian must have a passion for the truth. Polybius systematically seeks the causes of events ('nothing whether probable or improbable can happen without a cause'), tracing the evolution of nations and their decline. He does not shrink from exposing the reasons for the decadence of Greece. His narrative is clear and simple, without rhetorical artifice, written in the *koinē* or 'common dialect' of Greek which prevailed from 300 BC (see DIALECTS), and without the elegance of the Greek prose writers of the classical period. It is somewhat monotonous; Dionysius of Halicarnassus included Polybius' history among the works no one ever managed to finish. Polybius himself is severely critical of the methods of other historians.

Po'lybus, in Greek myth, the childless king of Corinth (or Sicyon), who with his wife adopted the infant *Oedipus to rear him as their own child.

Polyclei'tus (second half of the fifth century BC), of Argos, one of the most celebrated Greek sculptors of antiquity. The bases have been found at Olympia of a number of his statues of athletes which were dedicated there. Through the detailed description of the Elder Pliny it has been possible to identify Roman copies of his celebrated *Doryphorus*, 'youth holding a spear', and gain some sense of the harmony of the proportions and careful finish of detail for which Polycleitus was famous. His *Diadūmenus*, 'youth tying a band around his head', has been similarly identified. His most famous work was the very large statue of Hera in gold and ivory made for her temple (*Heraeum) at Argos.

Poly'cratēs, tyrant of Samos in the second half of the sixth century BC. He made Samos a strong naval power and supported the Persian king Cambysēs (see PERSIAN WARS) in his expedition against Amāsis of Egypt, although he had himself previously formed an alliance with Egypt. The Samians he had dispatched to Egypt returned intent to overthrow him with Spartan help, but failed. In *c*.522 he was lured to the mainland of Asia Minor by the Persian satrap Oroetēs, who pretended to be plotting against the Persian king Darius, and was crucified there.

Polycrates had many beautiful buildings erected and maintained a sumptous court where the poets Anacreon and Ibycus enjoyed his patronage. He is popularly credited with the construction of the great temple of Hera and the tunnelled aqueduct on Samos, but these works were probably begun earlier. Herodotus relates that Amasis, alarmed by the constant good fortune of Polycrates, advised him to throw away something that he valued highly so as to avert the jealousy of the gods. Polycrates accordingly threw into the sea a beautiful seal-ring, his most prized possession, but a few days later the ring was returned to him in the belly of a fish which a fisherman had presented to him. Amasis, concluding that Polycrates was marked down for destruction, renounced his friendship.

Polydeu'cēs (Lat. Pollux), brother of Castor; see DIOSCURI.

Polydō'rus. 1. In Greek myth, the youngest son of Priam, king of Troy, and his wife Hecuba, murdered by Polymestor, king of the Thracian Chersonese (for the story see HECUBA). In Virgil's narrative (*Aeneid* 3. 22), Aeneas, landing in Thrace, pulls up some cornel bushes and finds the roots dripping with blood. He hears groans and a voice from the mound telling him that the murdered Polydorus is buried there. Aeneas performs funeral rites and the spirit of Polydorus then rests in peace.

2. In Greek myth, one of the *Epigonoi.

Polygnō'tus (active 475–447 BC), of Thasos, later a citizen of Athens, a famous Greek painter. The Greek traveller Pausanias describes his celebrated paintings in the Cnidian Leschē (public room) at *Delphi, of the 'Capture of Troy' (*Iliupersis*) and the 'Descent of Odysseus to the Underworld' (*Nekyia*), large mural paintings each containing about seventy figures. Polygnotus decorated with mural paintings part of the *Stoa Poikilē at Athens; other works at Athens and other cities were attributed to him. He represented people as serious and dignified in character, but showed advance on earlier art by the life and expression of the faces; for this he is praised by Aristotle and Lucian. His subjects were chiefly mythological. See also PAINTING.

Polyhy'mnia, see MUSES.

Polynei'cēs, see OEDIPUS.

Polyphē'mus, in Greek myth, a Cyclops (see CYCLOPES), son of *Poseidon. He is represented in Homer's *Odyssey* as one of a race of savage, one-eyed giants, rearing sheep and goats on an island identified in later literature with Sicily. Odysseus with twelve of his men enters Polyphemus' cave. The latter, having returned with his flocks and closed the mouth of the cave with a huge rock, discovers the intruders and kills and eats two of them. The next evening Odysseus, who has been kept imprisoned in the cave during the day and has seen four more of his men devoured, makes Polyphemus drunk with wine and destroys his eye with a pointed stake. He has told the Cyclops that his name is No-man (Outis), and when the other Cyclopes come on hearing his cry Polyphemus replies to their enquiries that No-man is killing him; they therefore go away. Next morning Odysseus lashes the rams together in threes, and under each three conceals one of his comrades. When the blinded Polyphemus releases his flocks, they thus escape, Odysseus hiding himself under the shaggy belly of the largest ram. He thereafter taunts Polyphemus, who hurls rocks at Odysseus' departing ship and nearly destroys it. See also Euripides' play CYCLOPS.

In the sixth and eleventh Idylls of the Hellenistic poet *Theocritus the boorish Polyphemus is represented as falling in love with the nymph Galatea and being repulsed by her. According to Ovid he crushed Galatea's young lover Acis with a rock; this is the version adopted by John Gay in his libretto to Handel's opera *Acis and Galatea* (*c.*1718).

Poly'xena (Polyxenē), a daughter of Priam, king of Troy, and his wife Hecuba. See ACHILLES.

pōmē'rium, at Rome (and other cities), the strip of land demarcating the formal, religiously constituted boundary, often understood as the strip of land outside or inside a city wall.

Pōmō'na, Roman goddess of fruit (*pōma*), the wife of Vertumnus. For the story of his wooing of her under various shapes see under his name.

Pompe'ii, prosperous port and market town in Italy about 8 km. (5 miles) south-east of Vesuvius, having some 20,000 inhabitants when it was suddenly destroyed by the volcanic eruptions of 24 August AD 79 (described by the Younger Pliny in his Letters 6. 16 and 20). The city was buried in pumice and ash to a depth of more than 5 m. (16 ft.); about 2,000 people are thought to have died (including the Elder Pliny). Since the site was not built over later, being forgotten in the Middle Ages and not rediscovered until 1748, it has been possible to dig freely, and most of it has now been excavated. The thriving city life that has been

revealed is comparable with that depicted in the *Satyricon* of *Petronius. See also HERCULANEUM.

Pompe'ius. 1. **Gnaeus Pompeius Magnus,** see POMPEY below.

2. **Sextus Pompeius** (*c.*67–36 BC), younger son of Pompey the Great who spent his life in fighting for his father's cause, on the republican side, against the Caesarians. He was defeated in 36, captured, and put to death by one of Antony's officers whom he had once spared.

3. **Pompeius Trogus,** see TROGUS.

Pompey (Gnaeus Pompeius Magnus, 'the Great', 106–48 BC), Roman general, son of Pompeius Strabo who was consul in 89 and prominent in the Social War. Pompey first came into prominence by winning victories for *Sulla in 83 BC with three legions composed of his father's veterans and clients in Picenum, and by distinguished service against the Marians (see MARIUS) in Sicily and Africa. He was allowed a triumph by Sulla in 81 or 80, although he was technically ineligible by not having held a high magistracy, and was granted the honour of the *cognomen* Magnus. In 80, after the death of his wife Aemilia, Sulla's step-daughter, he married Mucia of the family of the Metelli. Despite his youth and the fact that he had not held the usual magistracies he was sent to Spain in 77 with the authority (*imperium*) of a proconsul to suppress *Sertorius, who was in revolt against the Sullan faction then dominant in the senate, and so successful that Pompey had to ask for reinforcements in 75. After Sertorius' murder in 72 the revolt was broken and Spain pacified; Pompey returned to Italy in 71, and co-operated with *Crassus in putting an end to the slave revolt led by *Spartacus. Again he was granted a triumph, and sought to become consul, with Crassus as his colleague. His candidacy was technically illegal because he was below the required age and had not previously held the quaestorship and praetorship (see CURSUS HONORUM), but it could hardly be alleged that he lacked experience; the rules were suspended, and Pompey and Crassus were both elected consuls for 70. (This year was notable for Cicero's successful prosecution of Verrēs, an event which established Cicero as Rome's leading advocate. The trial took place before the passing of the Aurelian law revising the composition of juries and decreasing to one third the number of senators serving. See CICERO (1) 1.) Pompey took no province after his consulship, but in 67 the Gabinian law gave him unprecedented authority to expel pirates from the Mediterranean, which he successfully accomplished in three months. In the following year the Manilian laws (supported by Cicero in his first political speech) gave Pompey the command against *Mithridates, king of Pontus. Pompey's eastern campaigns were his greatest achievement; he utterly defeated Mithridates, made provinces of Bithynia, *Pontus, and Syria (capturing Jerusalem after a siege), and laid the foundation for the subsequent Roman settlement of the East. In 62 he returned to Italy, disbanded his army, and celebrated a *triumph, entering the city on his birthday (30 September) in 61. The triumph was the most spectacular that Rome had ever yet seen, and lasted for two days. But the senate refused to ratify his eastern settlement or to provide land-grants for his troops: they insisted on examining his acts in detail. Julius *Caesar returned from Spain in 60, and Pompey, breaking with the senate, formed with Caesar and Crassus, together the three most powerful men in Rome, a close alliance (called in modern times 'the first triumvirate') so as to attain their individual aims. Caesar, with the support of the other two, was elected consul for 59 (his colleague being Bibulus, the nominee of the faction in the senate hostile to Pompey). Pompey was able to fulfil his promises to his veterans, and to have his acts in Asia ratified. Having divorced Marcia he married Caesar's daughter Julia. In 57 he supported Cicero's recall from exile, and in 55 he and Crassus were consuls. Julia died in 54, but Pompey declined another marriage tie with Caesar. In 53 Crassus was killed in Parthia; in the following year, after the murder of Clodius by Milo, Pompey was appointed sole consul, with some senatorial backing. For his reconciliation with the senate, Cicero's reluctant support, his struggle with Caesar in the civil war beginning in 49 BC, his final defeat at Pharsalus, and his death in Egypt, see CAESAR, CICERO (1), and CATO (2). There is a Life of Pompey by Plutarch.

Pompō'nius. 1. Lucius Pomponius, of Bonōnia, see ATELLAN FARCES.

2. Pomponius Secu'ndus, Roman tragic dramatist of the mid-first century AD who incurred the suspicion of the emperor Tiberius but survived to attain consular rank and military command in Germany after the latter's death. Pliny the Elder served under him against the Germans and wrote his Life, and mentions having seen in his possession papers written by the *Gracchi about 200 years previously. Quintilian regarded him as the best tragic poet of his day. Only the title of one of his plays, Aeneas, a fabula *praetexta, survives.

3. Pomponius Mēla, of Tingentera (in Spain, near Gibraltar), the author c. AD 43 of the earliest surviving Latin work on geography, De chōrographia (or De situ orbis), 'on places', in three books. The work is intended for general readers and is based on earlier accounts. After a summary description of the earth and the three continents Europe, Asia, and Africa, he describes in greater detail the countries around the Mediterranean, starting from Mauretania and working round to Spain; then passing to Gaul, Germany, Scythia, the islands (including the

British Isles), India, and the Persian Gulf. He occasionally preserves information not found elsewhere, as, for example, on the Druids. He enlivens his account by descriptions of national characteristics and customs, scenery, and natural phenomena, and by references to birthplaces, battle-fields, and historical and legendary associations. He offers explanations of the tides (the action of the moon is one of them) and of the midnight sun; he writes of the earth as if it were a disc.

Pons Subli'cius ('bridge on wooden piles'), the oldest bridge, and for several centuries the only bridge, at Rome, famously defended by Horatius *Coclēs against the Etruscans (and described in one of the 'Lays of Ancient Rome' by Lord Macaulay). In consequence of the difficulty on that occasion of breaking it down it was rebuilt exclusively of wood (so as to be easily taken apart) by the *pontifices, 'priests', from which fact they were said by Varro to derive their name; any repairs to it were accompanied by religious rites. See also ARGEI. It was swept away in a flood in AD 69.

Pontic Epistles, see EPISTULAE EX PONTO.

po'ntifex ma'ximus, at Rome, the head of the college of pontiffs (pontificēs, 'priests'; see below), exercising disciplinary function over them as well as over the *Vestal Virgins, whom he appointed, together with the *flamens and *rex sacrorum. He also published the decisions (decreta, without the binding force of laws) of the college of pontiffs. He had his official headquarters in the *Regia, and an official residence (Domus Publica). The position was one of great dignity and importance, exercising control over the whole state religion; it was held by Julius Caesar and by all the emperors down to Gratian (who dropped the title after AD 381).

ponti'ficēs, pontiffs, at Rome, the most important college of priests (see COLLEGIUM), who had supreme control in matters of state religion. Under the kings, they were appointed to assist the king in the duties of the state cult, forming his religious council and being the embodiment of religious tradition. Under the republic they, and especially their head, the *pontifex maximus, became responsible for the organization of the state religion. They seem originally to have numbered three, but were successively increased in number until finally (under Julius Caesar) they reached sixteen. The origin of the name is not known with certainty, but the obvious derivation from pons, 'bridge', and facere, 'to make', has been accepted by authorities ancient and modern though doubted by some (Plutarch, Numa 9. 2, ridicules it); see also PONS SUBLICIUS. The pontifices had technical knowledge in the matter of the calendar (see CALENDARS) and determined the dates of festivals and the days that were fasti and nefasti. They also kept a record of the principal events of each year (see ANNALS, ANNALISTS). They had no more than a general supervision of private worship; they were present at the solemn form of marriage known as *confarreatio*, for this was regarded as a state ceremony. They were not precluded (like the *flamens) from taking part in public affairs. Originally they were all patricians, but after 300 BC half the number was chosen from the plebeians. They wore the *toga praetexta* when officiating (see DRESS 2), and had certain privileges, such as exemption from taxation and military service. Like the holders of political offices, they were unpaid.

Pontus. 1. Sea; in Greek myth, according to Hesiod, son of Gaia (Earth) and father of *Nereus and *Phorcys.

2. (Gk. *pontos*, 'sea'), in particular, in Greek and Latin, the Black Sea, and by extension the region around it. The name was especially applied to the region of Asia Minor south of the Black Sea, between Bithynia and Armenia, the centre of the empire of *Mithridates VI. In 63 BC at the end of the Mithridatic wars Pontus was broken up; Pompey added the western part to the province of Bithynia (now known as Bithynia and Pontus), and in AD 64 Nero incorporated the eastern portion in the province of Galatia. See also Ovid's *EPISTULAE EX PONTO*.

Popi'lius Laenas, Gaius, see SELEUCIDS.

Poppae'a Sabi'na, wife of Otho (friend of the emperor Nero and emperor himself briefly in AD 69), and Nero's mistress. At her instigation, it was said, Nero murdered his mother Agrippina in AD 59 and in 62 divorced, banished, and executed his first wife Octavia. Nero now married Poppaea, and she bore a daughter Claudia, who died at four months. Poppaea is said to have died (in 65), when she was pregnant again, from a kick given her by Nero in a fit of temper.

popula'res ('on the side of the people'). The republican government of Rome was in the hands of an *oligarchy drawn from a limited number of families (see NOBILES). *Populares* was the name adopted at Rome from the time of the Gracchi (i.e. about 133 BC) by those Roman political leaders who, working through the people (*populus*) rather than the senate, challenged the political predominance of this oligarchy. Some were motivated by concern for the people; others by the belief that they could promote their own career in this way. Their political opponents called themselves in consequence *optimātēs*, 'the best men'. See REPUBLIC, ROMAN, and MARIUS.

population. Such information as has come down to us about the size of populations at various periods in the ancient world is very incomplete and garbled as well as often inaccur-

ate to start with, and there is much disagreement in modern times on the interpretation of the evidence.

1. For Athens in the fifth and fourth centuries BC the figures are based on those given by Herodotus and Thucydides on the size of the troop musters during the Persian and Peloponnesian Wars. The figures indicate that during the *Pentekontaetia (479–431 BC) there was a steep increase in the size of the population at Athens, at least among the more prosperous, probably as a result of the general increase in wealth at that time. The number of male citizens eligible to serve as hoplites (i.e. the relatively prosperous, aged 20–60) was about 10,000 in 480, suggesting that the population of male citizens of fighting age and strength numbered 30,000, and thus the total citizen population amounted to about 120,000 people. By 431 the number of hoplites had apparently risen to 20,000, and since the number of poorer male citizens (*thētĕs*) was at least maintained, and probably somewhat increased, this suggests a total citizen population of about 180,000. In the course of the Peloponnesian War which followed there was a sharp fall in the population owing to casualties, the plague, and serious impoverishment. The numbers eligible to serve as hoplites dropped to 9,000, and the male citizen population sank to 21,000, well below its size in the Persian Wars. Despite increased prosperity in the fourth century, the hoplites still numbered only 9,000 in 322 BC.

The population of metics (resident aliens) at Athens seems to have varied considerably; evidence suggests that the proportion of metics to citizens was 1 : 6 at the time of the Persian Wars, and at the end of the fourth century BC a surprising 2 : 5. For the size of the slave population see SLAVERY 1; for the number of Spartiates (Spartan citizens) see SPARTA 2. In the view of the town-planner Hippodamus of Miletus, the ideal city would have a population of 10,000 male citizens, a third of them being soldiers.

2. Figures for the population in Rome and Italy derive from census returns (thirty-seven during the republican period) which give the numbers of all adult male citizens. Since the returns had to be made at Rome itself it is doubtful whether all citizens living at a distance actually made their declarations. Thus the total for 70/69 BC was only 900,000, whereas in 28 BC when a more efficient system had been devised the total of all adult male citizens was recorded as 4,063,000. The estimate by the Greek historian Polybius of the fighting strength of Italy in 225 BC suggests a total free population of about 3,000,000. During the first half of the first century AD the population rose steadily. There were 4,937,000 adult male Roman citizens throughout the empire in AD 14, nearly 6,000,000 in AD 47 according to the historian

Tacitus, but nearly 7,000,000 according to later writers. It has been estimated in modern times that at the death of the emperor Augustus in AD 14 the total population of the whole empire was 54,000,000.

populus ('people'), at Rome, the citizen-body. The 'Roman people', *populus Romanus*, meant the body of those eligible to be soldiers (see below), to participate in public religious rites, and attend meetings of the popular assembly, together with their families. It seems originally to have denoted the citizens as a military body (in contrast to *Quirites*), hence the title *magister populi*, 'master of the infantry' (see DICTATOR). During the struggles of the *orders between patricians and plebeians (see ROME 3) *populus* continued to denote the whole community and not 'people' in the sense of 'plebeians'; however, at a later period (see ROME 6) *populus* designated the classes supporting the *populares* in their opposition to the senate. In the phrase, 'The senate and people of Rome', *senatus populusque Romanus*, *populus* denotes the people as the sovereign body.

Porch, the, name for the Stoic school of philosophy, derived from the alternative translation of *stoa (usually 'colonnade').

Po'rcia (in Shakespeare's *Julius Caesar*, Portia), daughter of *Cato (2) of Utica and wife of, first, Calpurnius Bibulus (consul with Julius Caesar in 59 BC) and secondly Marcus *Brutus. Like her second husband and her father she was an ardent supporter of the republican cause, and is said to have inflicted a wound on herself in order to show that she was worthy to share in the secret of the plot against Caesar's life. After Brutus sailed for the East she became ill and in the early summer of 43 committed suicide, it is said by inhaling fumes from a brazier.

Poroi, treatise by Xenophon; see REVENUES.

Po'rphyry (Porphyrios) (AD 233–c.305), Neoplatonist philosopher originally from Tyre. He is known by the Greek version of his original Phoenician name Malchus, 'king'. He studied philosophy at Athens and was converted to *Neoplatonism by *Plotinus whom he met at Rome in 262. He was particularly hostile to Christianity. His work *Against the Christians* was burnt in the fifth century, and is now known only through quotations. He was the author of numerous philosophical works including a history of philosophy down to Plato, from which a life of Pythagoras survives. His most important work was the editing of the lectures of Plotinus under the title *Enneads*, and the composition of Plotinus' biography. His 'Introduction' (*Īsagōgē*) to the 'Categories' of Aristotle was later translated into Latin by *Boethius and became very influential in the medieval schools.

Po'rsen(n)a, Lars, probably an Etruscan title

misinterpreted by the Romans as the name of an Etruscan chieftain, prince of Clūsium at the end of the sixth century BC and head of the united forces of Etruria. According to tradition he was summoned by the exiled king of Rome *Tarquinius Superbus to lay siege to Rome in order to restore him to the throne. In the campaign that followed occurred the feats of Horatius *Coclēs, Mucius *Scaevola, and *Cloelia. Repulsed in his attack, Porsena made peace with Rome. One tradition implied by Tacitus and the Elder Pliny seems to have made Porsena at one time master of Rome.

Portland Vase, celebrated Roman vase of dark blue *glass, about 25 cm. (10 in.) high, with a cameo-style relief showing scenes from the wedding of *Peleus and Thetis. It probably dates from the early first century AD and may have been made in Rome by Alexandrian craftsmen. In the seventeenth century it was in the Barberini Palace in Rome; in 1787 it was bought by the Duke of Portland, who lent it to Josiah Wedgwood to copy its cameo style in his jasper ware. In 1810 the Portland family deposited the vase on loan to the British Museum, where in 1845 a deranged visitor deliberately smashed it into more than 200 pieces; it was repaired and eventually bought by the Museum in 1945.

portō'ria, see FINANCE, ROMAN.

portraiture. Individualization in Greek sculpture began perhaps in the fourth century BC with the very large statue of Mausolus, now in the British Museum, showing unmistakably the features of an actual person. Portraits of Alexander the Great later in the same century show similar individuality. It was the Romans from the third century BC to the third century AD who developed the art of portraiture to a degree that has not been surpassed, depicting with unflattering accuracy the features of men and women from a wide range of social classes. The art was perhaps promoted by the early custom of preserving death-masks or busts of ancestors in the family *atrium* (see HOUSES AND FURNITURE 2) so that they might be carried in funeral processions, to give the impression that the whole family, covering several generations, was present. One of the most magnificent examples of Roman portraiture at its most dignified is to be found on the reliefs of the *Ara Pacis ('altar of peace'). The screens surrounding the altar are carved with life-size figures of Augustus' family and Roman magistrates and senators, some with wives and children, who are depicted as walking in procession to the altar, just as they did in real life on 4 July 13 BC. All Roman portraiture concentrates upon the verisimilitude of the head. The apparently deliberate portrayal of the features in an unflattering light, the harsh facial lines, give an arresting glimpse of the ruthlessness of the Roman approach to life.

Portū'nus, originally the Roman deity protecting doors, later the protector of harbours as well. Virgil in *Aeneid* 5. 241 makes Portunus give one of the galleys in the boat-race a shove 'into port'. He was represented with a key in his hand. His festival, the Portūnālia, was on 17 August. He had a special **flamen, the flamen portunalis.*

Pōrus, see ALEXANDER THE GREAT 6.

Posei'don, in Greek myth, the god of earthquakes and later of the sea, and associated with horses. He was the brother of Zeus and Hades and son of *Cronus and Rhea; his wife was Amphitritē, by whom he had a son, *Triton. The derivation of his name is uncertain; it has been explained as 'lord of the waters' and 'lord of earth' (i.e. husband of Earth). He is an ancient and important god; in the *Linear B tablets he appears as the principal god at Pylos. As god of the sea his cult was widespread throughout Greece, as is attested by the city names Potidaea in Chalcidicē and Poseidonia in south Italy. He was worshipped on all occasions connected with the sea and navigation. The Isthmian games were held in his honour near his sanctuary on the Isthmus of Corinth; no doubt Corinth's strategic position, commanding the seas to east and west, made her cult of Poseidon particularly appropriate. His usual representation is with a trident (probably a fish spear). As the god of earthquakes his common epithet is 'earth-shaker' (Enosichthōn, Ennosigaios). Perhaps he is to be thought of as the embodiment of elemental forces. Bulls were sacrificed to him. The Greeks also thought of him as the tamer of horses: the cult of Poseidon Hippios ('of horses') was widespread and has been seen as connected with the introduction into Greece from Anatolia of horses and (war) chariots early in the second millennium BC. In mythology he is sometimes represented as the father of the first horse or of magical horses (see PEGASUS and ARION (2)); he is also made the father of the monsters Chrysaor and Antaeus. He does not have a large mythology, but important myths connect him with Attica: one relates his contest with Athena for ownership of Attica in which he struck a spring of salt water from the Acropolis; Athena with her offer of the olive was adjudged the victor by the Athenians, or *Cecrops; another makes *Theseus his son, and he was worshipped at Athens as Poseidon Erechtheus (see ERECHTHEUM). In the Trojan War he was the enemy of the Trojans because he was cheated by *Laomedon, king of Troy, when he and Apollo built the city walls, but he persistently sought the destruction of the Greek hero Odysseus because the latter had blinded his son, the Cyclops Polyphemus. The great temple

dedicated to him at Mount Mycalē (in Asia Minor, between Ephesus and Miletus) was the religious centre of the Ionians of Asia Minor, the Panionium.

His temple of the late fifth century BC on the promontory of Sunium in Attica is still a landmark to sailors. The Romans identified Poseidon with the water-god *Neptune.

Posīdō'nius (Poseidonios) (*c.*135–*c.*50 BC), of Apamea in Syria, historian, scientist, and philosopher, who spent most of his life at Rhodes and became head of the *Stoic school there. He was a polymath who epitomized the learning of the Hellenistic age and transmitted some part of it to the Roman world. For several years he studied philosophy under *Panaetius at Athens. His fifty-two books of history were a continuation of the history of Polybius, from 146 BC to the dictatorship of Sulla (81 BC). Very few fragments survive, but Sallust, Caesar, Tacitus, and Plutarch all made use of it in different ways. The wars of Pompey, of whom Posidonius was a great admirer, seem to have been dealt with in an appendix. His history was strongly biased in favour of the *optimatēs* and hence was hostile to the Gracchi. He had great influence on the development of Stoic philosophy: he saw the Roman empire as embodying the Stoic view of the kinship of all humanity, since it was intended to cover all the peoples of the world. It also reflected the divinely ordained after-life to which philosophers and statesmen might belong after death, a Stoic idea expounded by Cicero in his **Somnium Scipionis* ('dream of Scipio'). He made considerable modifications to the Stoic doctrines of his day. He did not, for example, think that virtue was sufficient for happiness; it needed to be accompanied by external, bodily good. He also tried to banish contradictions from philosophy and religion, to harmonize the doctrines of Aristotle and Plato and the Stoicism of Zeno, and as far as possible reconcile the Stoic principle of divine reason animating nature with the Graeco-Roman religion of his day. Thus he prefigured and influenced later *Neoplatonism. He was also an eminent geographer, ethnographer, and astronomer, and wrote on tides and volcanoes. Nothing of these works has survived. He visited Rome as an envoy from Rhodes at the end of 87 BC to appease *Marius, for whom he personally felt great dislike. In 78 Cicero was taught by him in Rhodes, and often paid tribute to him in his writings. In different ways Cicero, Lucretius, Virgil, Manilius, Seneca the Younger, and the Elder Pliny, as well as the historians mentioned above, were all indebted to him. He was a most important figure, and the loss of his works a particular misfortune.

postal service. Classical Greece had no postal system as such; cities had their own ships and fast messengers for official business (see PHEIDIP-PIDES). In the Persian empire there was a relay system, with couriers and horses stationed at intervals along the royal roads, linking the furthest parts of the empire with the capital Susa. It continued under the *Seleucids and under the Romans. In the Roman republic freedmen or slaves were employed as *tabellarii* ('letter-carriers') by the state and by important private citizens. For confidential letters it was essential for correspondents to have their own letter-carriers. Under Augustus a system of relay stations known as the *cursus publicus* ('public transport') was organized, providing horses and carriages for transporting people on urgent journeys, as well as letters. Though the main purpose was military it could also be used for other official business. Letters were carried by imperial *tabellarii* or trusted soldiers. In the second century AD the service was taken over by the *frumentarii* and later by the *agentes in rebus* (see POLICE). The posting-houses were known as *mansiones*. Licences to use the service were strictly controlled. The last letter of the Younger Pliny was written to the emperor Trajan to explain and apologize for the fact that without waiting for the emperor's permission he had sent his wife home by this service to deal with a family bereavement. Couriers travelled on average 80 km. (50 miles) a day, but urgent news, and people in a hurry, could be carried at very high speeds. Suetonius records that Julius Caesar once travelled in a carriage 160 km. a day for eight successive days. The news that the legions on the Rhine had refused the oath of allegiance to Galba, on 1 January AD 69, reached Vitellius 160 km. away that night, and Rome on 9 January: the courier must have averaged more than 200 km. (125 miles) a day. See also ROADS.

Post re'ditum, two speeches probably delivered by *Cicero (see (1) 4) after his return from exile in 57 BC, one addressed to the senate, the other to the people, thanking them for his recall, reviewing the incidents of recent years, and attacking his enemies. Their authenticity has been questioned.

Potidae'a, Corinthian colony founded *c.*600 BC (see PERIANDER) on the western prong of Chalcidicē in north-east Greece for the purpose of trade with Macedonia. It joined the (Athenian) *Delian League, but the fact that Corinth supplied its annual chief magistrate meant that it was inevitably involved in any hostility between Athens and Corinth. It revolted from Athens in 432 BC but was retaken in 430 after a siege (see PELOPONNESIAN WAR). Athenian *cleruchs held it until 404 when it passed to the Chalcidians. It was recovered by Athens in 363, but in 356 fell into the hands of *Philip II of Macedon (see also DEMOSTHENES (2) 1). Perhaps destroyed in the Olynthian War (348), it was refounded *c.*316 by Cassander under the name of Cassandreia.

Potī'tii, see HERCULES.

pottery

1. *Greek.* Greek pottery includes what are commonly referred to as Greek vases; see also VASE-PAINTING.

(i) In Greece the potter's wheel was introduced, probably from Asia, at the end of the third millennium BC. The indigenous pottery at the beginning of the second millennium and the following centuries had in general a light buff ground simply decorated with dark matt paint, known as 'matt-painted ware'.

(ii) Soon after 2000 BC a new style of pottery appears all over Greece, named 'Minyan ware' by *Schliemann who found it first at Orchomenus (in Boeotia), the traditional home of the *Minyans. It is a striking type of pottery, distinguished by a matt grey burnished surface of high quality which was produced by a method of firing under reducing conditions, the shapes suggesting imitation of metal vessels. It seems likely that it was introduced by the invading *Indo-Europeans (see also GREECE).

(iii) At the start of the *Mycenaean period, *c.*1600 BC, pottery appeared which was enlivened by fresh designs, with naturalistic decoration. After 1400 BC this Mycenaean pottery was predominant, strongly influenced by the styles of Minoan Crete. Most striking were the 'palace style' jars, large elegant storage jars covered with somewhat flamboyant floral and marine motifs.

(iv) After 1200 BC and the collapse of the Mycenaean civilization, the 'sub-Mycenaean' pottery styles were much impoverished and the naturalistic designs simplified and stylized, heralding the geometric style and known as protogeometric. Out of this developed the geometric style, from *c.*900 BC onwards, with bands of decoration in meander or zig-zag patterns, and later with scenes containing highly stylized, abstractly portrayed human figures. During this period Athens became an important centre for the production of pottery, there being a plentiful supply of good clay from nearby Phalerum. The finest examples are found in the amphoras of the Dipylon Master (*c.*760–750 BC).

(v) In the late eighth century a so-called orientalizing style developed as a result of renewed contacts with the East and the influence of eastern art. The geometric bands of decoration were replaced by motifs based on flowers and animals real and imaginary, winged monsters for example, and human figures appeared naturalistically portrayed. Scenes from mythology also began to be depicted. During this period Corinth became an important producer of fine pottery and the first city to export it throughout the Greek world.

(vi) The Attic vases known as 'black-figure' were first produced under the influence of Corinth from *c.*610, and between 570 and 525 the vases reached a peak of perfection. The figures or designs were executed in a brilliant black glaze on the Attic red-buff clay, hence the name 'black-figure'. The inner lines of the designs were incised; white paint was used for women's flesh. Attic pottery was esteemed not only for the careful execution of its figure drawing but also for its fine clay, beautiful shapes, and thinness.

(vii) From about 530 BC there was a change of style in Attic vases; black-figure gave way to red-figure decoration. The figures were left in the ground colour of the clay, the details drawn in by brush, and the background covered in black glaze. A subsidiary style was 'white-ground' pottery, commonly used for tomb offerings, in which the background was coloured white and the design was in black glaze, later painted on in different colours. During the black-figure and red-figure periods pottery continued to be produced with a plain black glaze or with bands of glaze.

(viii) By 300 BC, the start of the Hellenistic age, Attic red-figure vases were no longer made, although small black vases were still produced. Decoration on vases was now mainly moulded, not painted.

2. *Roman.*

(i) Although there was a guild of potters at Rome from early times, fine-quality Roman household ware was at first imported from the Etruscans. Wheel-made pottery in dark clay (*bucchero*) was produced in Etruria from 700 BC. It had a polished black surface and incised decoration; later the decoration was in relief. Painted pottery in imitation of Greek appeared as early as 700, and by 525 the pottery found is for the most part Greek; the local pottery, from Apulia, was very crude. Italian red-figure vases were produced in south Italy in the mid-fifth century BC. By the fourth century BC there were four types of Italian pottery, Apulian, Lucanian, Campanian, and Paestan; there was also Sicilian. All of these were dark-body pottery with light-coloured decoration or applied reliefs. In Roman times the characteristic standardized fine pottery was that known as *terra sigillata* ('pottery with decoration in relief'); it had a glossy red surface resembling glaze, and was made both in moulds and on the wheel. For a time (from c.30 BC to mid-first century AD) the most famous kind of *terra sigillata* was Arretine ware, made at Arretium (modern Arezzo) and popular around the Mediterranean and in Gaul. See SAMIAN WARE.

(ii) Bricks baked in a kiln, replacing sun-dried bricks, and tiles were first extensively used by the Romans, enabling them to erect buildings several storeys high. The brick walls were often covered with stucco or marble. Roman bricks were of high quality and are found in many parts of the Roman empire. Earthenware water-pipes and sewage-pipes were also made.

The manufacture of bricks, tiles, and other pottery including lamps became an important industry under the empire, often in the hands of rich capitalists, including members of the imperial family.

3. Throughout classical antiquity small clay figures, sometimes of gods, were produced. These moulded clay figures, painted after baking, became popular, for ornament and as playthings. The high degree of art attained is shown by the Hellenistic terracotta figurines of women and groups engaged in the activities of daily life, found in graves at Tanagra (in Boeotia), whence they are known as Tanagra figures.

praefec'ti Ca'puam Cūmas, see VIGINTISEX-VIRATE.

praefe'ctus, at Rome, 'officer in charge' of a military unit or branch of administration, etc., and in particular of the administration of justice in provincial towns; he was appointed by a higher authority. Under the empire *praefecti* were officers of equestrian rank. See also EGYPT.

praefe'ctus anno'nae ('prefect of the corn-supply'), at Rome under the empire, an officer of equestrian rank in charge of the supply of corn, the regulation of its price, and distributions to the poor. See ANNONA.

praefe'ctus praetō'rio ('prefect of praetorians'), at Rome under the empire, an officer of equestrian rank who commanded the praetorian cohorts, the emperor's praetorian guard (see PRAETORIANS). First appointed by Augustus in 2 BC, they were usually two in number, occasionally one or three. Their position sometimes gave them great influence over the emperor (see SEJANUS). A few were well-known jurists (see PAPINIAN, PAULUS, and ULPIAN), as was appropriate to the extensive judicial powers they acquired in the second and third centuries (responsibility for criminal jurisdiction in all Italy except Rome), but for the most part they were soldiers. Being responsible for supplies to the armed forces they became under Diocletian (emperor AD 284–305) the most important financial officers of the state. When the praetorian guard was disbanded by Constantine the Great in AD 312, the prefects lost their military authority and became governors of the four divisions of the empire: the Gauls, Italy, Illyricum, and the East. The father of St Ambrose was the prefect of the Gauls.

praefe'ctus urbi ('prefect of the city'), at Rome under the empire, a magistrate instituted by Augustus; he was an officer of senatorial rank responsible for maintaining order within the city boundaries, for which purpose he had *imperium and the command of three urban cohorts (see POLICE). He also presided in his own court of justice which by the third century had taken over the courts of the regular magistrates.

praefe'ctus vi'gilum ('prefect of the fire-brigade'), at Rome under the empire, an officer of equestrian rank in command of the cohorts of *vigiles* forming the fire-brigade, instituted by Augustus.

Praene'stine fi'bula, see EPIGRAPHY 2.

praenō'men, see NAMES.

praete'xta, fa'bula, in Roman literature, a drama which derived its subject from Roman history. The name is derived from the *toga praetexta* (see DRESS 2), the bordered toga which the famous Romans who were presented in the plays were entitled to wear by reason of holding high office. (See also TOGATA.) The invention of the *fabula praetexta* is attributed to *Naevius. Only one complete *praetexta* survives, the tragedy *Octavia*, and fragments of or references to eleven others, such as the *Clastidium* of Naevius (on the exploits of M. Claudius Marcellus, winner of the *spolia opima* in single combat against a Gaul in 222 BC), the *Rape of the Sabines* of *Ennius, the *Brutus* of *Accius, and the *Aeneas* of *Pomponius Secundus.

praetor, at Rome, originally the generic term for the holders of *imperium*, or executive authority, and the name of the two *eponymous magistrates who replaced the king (see ROME 2); later (perhaps as a result of the constitutional reforms of the *decemviri in the mid-fifth century BC) they were called consuls. The Greek translation of praetor was *strategos*, 'general', showing the close connection of the office with military command (see also PRAETORIANS and PRAETORIUM below). In 366 BC a third magistrate was introduced, the *praetor urbanus*, 'city praetor', who was not eponymous and who administered justice between Roman citizens. He sometimes held military command, but as the only praetor so called after the others became designated consuls he was subordinate to them and was attended by only six *lictors as opposed to their twelve. Rome's closer contact with foreign states led to the appointment c.242 BC of a second praetor, *praetor peregrinus*, who administered justice where foreigners were involved. In 227 BC the number of praetors was increased to four for the government of the provinces of Sicily and Sardinia, and to six in 197 BC to include Spain. Sulla increased their number to eight and decreed that they should not proceed to their provinces until the year following a term of office in Rome, as propraetors. The special courts of law (*quaestiones*, see LAW, AT ROME 1) were ordinarily presided over by praetors. The praetors were elected annually by the people (in the *comitia centuriata*), and according to tradition the office was thrown open to *plebeians in 337 BC. For the importance of praetors' edicts in the development of civil law see LAW, AT ROME 2.

praetorians, praetorian guard. Under the Roman republic it was customary for a general to have a bodyguard or *cohors praetoria* ('praetorian cohort'; see PRAETOR above for the connection of the term with military command). The emperor Augustus in 27 BC, for the protection of Italy (where no legion was stationed), formed a permanent corps of nine cohorts (generally thought to be each 1,000 strong) composed of his bodyguard and of veterans; three were billeted about the city, and the remainder stationed in nearby Italian towns. These Augustus kept under his direct control, not until 2 BC appointing two commanders, the *praefecti praetorio*. Thus originated the famous praetorian guard, who played at certain moments a very important part in the history of the empire. Their concentration by *Sejanus in AD 23 into one large barracks on the north side of Rome initiated their political importance. The praetorians attended the emperor and his family at home and abroad. Their length of service was first fixed at twelve years but soon raised to sixteen. They received generous pay, with large and frequent donatives, and were granted *diplomata* when discharged (see ARMY, ROMAN 3).

praetō'rium, in a Roman *camp, the general's tent.

Pratī'nas, Greek poet of the early fifth century BC from Phlius (in Arcadia), reputed to have been the first to compose satyr plays (see SATYRIC DRAMA). He also wrote tragedies, *dithyrambs, and *hyporchemata*.

Praxi'telēs, one of the most famous Greek sculptors, born at Athens c.390 BC. One statue which still exists, almost intact, is thought to be his original work (although some would argue that it is a Hellenistic copy); it was discovered in the Heraeum at Olympia in 1877 and represents the god Hermes with the infant god Dionysus on his arm. Apart from that, two heads by him exist, and it is possible that a bronze of a boy found in the twentieth century in the sea near Marathon may also be by him. Other celebrated works now known only from copies were the Aphroditē of *Cnidus, statues of Eros, and a boy Apollo Sauroctonus ('lizard-slayer'). A statue of a resting satyr has survived in more copies than any other ancient Greek statue. Praxiteles showed, at its best, the tendency of the Greek sculptors of the fourth century to leave behind the strong and dignified style of the fifth century for the expression of softer and finer shades of form and feeling.

prefect, see PRAEFECTUS.

Presocratics, early Greek thinkers with a

rational interest in science and philosophy, who lived not later than the time of *Socrates (469–399 BC). Their way of thinking gradually brought into existence the concepts of science and philosophy as fields of study separate from each other and from all other subjects. Their works survive only in fragments. See individual entries on the following (in roughly chronological order): Thalēs, Anaximander, Anaximenēs, Heracleitus, Pythagoras, Anaxagoras, Parmenides, Zeno (1), and Democritus.

Prīam (Prīamos), in Greek myth, son of *Laomedon, king of Troy at the time of the *Trojan War and husband of *Hecuba. He was the father of fifty sons and many daughters, some by Hecuba, the rest by other wives or concubines. His children include Hector, Paris, Polydorus, Cassandra, and Creusa. In Homer's *Iliad* he is already an old man, and a pathetic figure, lamenting the death of many sons and the sufferings of his people, but loyal and kindly to *Helen, the cause of these misfortunes. After Hector's death he goes to the Greek camp secretly, aided by the god Hermēs, to ransom his son's body with rich treasures for Achilles. The *Iliupersis* told how, at the fall of Troy, he took refuge in the palace at the altar of Zeus Herkeios (see HOUSES AND FURNITURE I) and was there killed by *Neoptolemus. The best-known version is that of Virgil in *Aeneid* 2. His name became almost proverbial for a man who had known the extremes of good and bad fortune.

Priāpe'a (or *Priapeia*), collection of eighty Latin poems in honour of the god *Priapus written in the time of the emperor Augustus and collected in the first century AD. Two other poems of this kind are attributed to Tibullus, and three others are found in the *Catalepton* (see APPENDIX VIRGILIANA). The poems are mainly written in hendecasyllables and elegiacs (see METRE, LATIN 3 (iii) *a*); they are lively, sometimes witty, and, as befits their subject, of varying degrees of obscenity.

Priā'pus, god of fertility, originally worshipped at Lampsacus on the Hellespont and in that area, where his cult was important; he was said to be the son of Dionysus and of either Aphroditē or a local nymph. His cult spread to Greece during the Hellenistic age (after *c.*300 BC) and thence to Italy, but he seems never to have been taken very seriously. His symbol was the phallus; in Lampsacus asses, thought of by the ancients as symbolizing lust, were sacrificed to him. In Italy he was adopted as a god of gardens, where statues of him were often placed, showing him as a small misshapen creature with an enormous phallus, scaring off thieves and birds, a combined scarecrow and guardian. It was customary to compose short humorous poems or epigrams purportedly (or in fact) to be inscribed on his statues (see previous entry).

prices and cost of living, see ATHENS 4 and ROME 13.

priests

1. *In Greece.* Priests and priestesses were appointed (by the assembly, as with political appointments) to the service of particular gods and goddesses, to perform *sacrifices and other rites, and to lead and instruct worshippers in the ritual. They had no hierarchy, initiation, or special sacerdotal authority, nor (except in the case of the priests attached to the *mysteries) special religious knowledge. A priest was not usually kept from secular activities because of his office; on the other hand a magistrate often carried out the duties of a priest as part of his official functions (see ARCHONS). There was normally no division between the secular and religious life of a community. The priesthood was not a profession or a way of life, but a part-time office which brought prestige. In the theatre at Athens seats of honour were reserved for the priests. Priests might be appointed for life, but a fixed period was more usual. A priest received the perquisites of his office, a share of the sacrifices and sometimes money. At Athens the priestess of Athena Nīkē was appointed for life and received 50 drachmas a year beside the perquisites. In general, life-long celibacy was scarcely ever required; in Athens the priestess of Athena Polias was not a virgin but a mature woman who had put sexual relations behind her. Ritual purity (e.g. avoiding contact with death) would have been required upon occasion. Some priesthoods were hereditary in certain ancient families (a survival from earlier times; it was characteristic of aristocracy to lay importance on a knowledge of correct ritual): in Athens the Eteobūtadae provided the priest of Poseidon *Erechtheus and the priestess of Athena Polias; thus the family was responsible for the most important cults on the Acropolis. The mysteries at Eleusis remained throughout antiquity in the hands of the Eumolpidae and Ceryces.

2. *At Rome.* See FLAMENS, PONTIFICES, and VESTAL VIRGINS.

princeps ('chief', 'leader'), title taken by the emperor *Augustus (and adopted by his successors) to indicate his constitutional position. In the late republic the word had been used in the plural, *principes*, to signify 'the chief men in the state', and the singular had been applied to important individuals like Pompey and Julius Caesar. It was not an official title, and was chosen to indicate the civil nature of Augustus' primacy, not carrying connotations of dictatorship or monarchy.

princeps senā'tūs ('the leader of the senate'), at Rome, the senator placed by the censors at the head of the list of members of the senate and ranked as the senior member. When decisions had to be taken by the senate he was the first to be asked his opinion.

principate, at Rome, the term often used in preference to 'empire' to describe the rule of the Roman emperors after 31 BC from *Augustus (see also ROME 9) until (usually) the accession of Diocletian in AD 284. The word designates the period during which the forms at least of republican government were maintained under the *princeps. In the words of the English historian Edward Gibbon it was 'an absolute monarchy disguised by the forms of a common-wealth'. With the accession of Diocletian the senate lost all independent authority and no longer was any attempt made to disguise the monarchical nature of the empire. The period from 284 onwards is often known as the Later Roman Empire. There is no general agreement as to when the empire may be deemed to have ended. Some speak of the Roman empire as continuing until the capture of Byzantium (Constantinople) by the Ottoman Turks in 1453; others prefer to use the term 'Byzantine empire' to describe the continuation of the Roman empire in the East, putting its beginning at various points between the reign of Justinian (527–65) and the death of Heraclius in 641 (see BYZANTINE AGE). The latter date has the advantage of taking into account the Arab conquests of Mesopotamia, Syria, and Egypt in the 630s and 640s.

Pri'scian (Priscianus Caesariensis), native of Caesarēa in Mauretania and a grammarian at Constantinople under the emperor in the East, Anastasius (AD 491–518). He wrote in Latin an *Institutionēs grammaticae* ('grammar') in eighteen books, rich in quotations from the classical Latin authors and also from earlier republican writers, and founded largely on the (Greek) grammatical works of *Apollonius Dyscolus. It became famous in the Middle Ages: more than a thousand manuscripts of it are still in existence.

proa'gōn, at Athens, a day or two before the dramatic competitions at the Great *Dionysia and the *Lenaea, the ceremonial appearance of *choregoi, poets, actors, and choruses, when the names and subjects of the plays were announced. It was at the *proagon* of 406 BC after the death of Euripides that the audience was greatly moved by the appearance of Sophocles in mourning, with his actors and chorus not wearing the usual garlands.

Pro A'rchia pōē'ta, speech by *Cicero (2) delivered in 62 BC in defence of the claim of the Greek poet Archias to Roman citizenship.

Archias, a literary figure and known to Cicero, was attached to the household of the general L. Licinius *Lucullus. His claim to Roman citizenship was based on his citizenship of Heraclea in Lucania, which had been obtained for him by Lucullus in 93 BC, and the fact that in 89 BC the Plautian–Papirian law offered Roman citizenship to all members of Italian communities who claimed it within 60 days. Archias' claim had been doubted through lack of documentary evidence of his enrolment. Cicero meets this by producing witnesses of it. He also appeals to the sentiment of the jury by an eloquent panegyric of literature, which later became famous: *Haec studia adulescentiam acuunt, senectutem oblectant, secundas res ornant, adversis perfugium ac solacium praebent, delectant domi, non impediunt foris, pernoctant nobiscum, peregrinantur, rusticantur* (7. 16). 'These studies sharpen youth and delight old age; they enhance prosperity and provide a refuge and relief in adversity; they enrich private life and do not interfere with public life; they are our companions at night, on journeys, and in our country retreats.'

Pro Balbo ('for Balbus'), see CICERO (1) 4.

probou'loi ('commissioners'), in Greece, in particular those appointed at Athens in 413 BC after the failure of the Sicilian Expedition (see PELOPONNESIAN WAR), to oversee affairs of state. They comprised ten men over the age of 40 (and included the poet Sophocles).

Prŏbus, Marcus Vale'rius (late first century AD), the outstanding Latin grammarian and scholar of his age, from Berytus in Phoenicia, who gathered together a large number of manuscripts and worked on the texts of the classical Latin authors including Virgil, Horace, and Lucretius. He used critical signs in the manner of the Alexandrian scholar Aristarchus (see TEXTS, TRANSMISSION OF ANCIENT 1). Some of his notes survive in the scholia to Terence and Virgil, and there are references to Plautus and Sallust; later grammarians quote him, but it is difficult to establish exactly the scope of his work.

Pro Cae'cina ('for Caecina'), see CICERO (1) 1.

Pro Cae'lio ('for Caelius'), see CICERO (1) 4.

Pro Clue'ntio ('for Cluentius'), speech by *Cicero ((1) 1) delivered in 66 BC in defence of Aulus Cluentius Habitus. In 76 BC Cluentius had accused his stepfather Oppianicus and others of attempting to poison him, and Oppianicus had been condemned and exiled, after notorious bribery on both sides. It had become a *cause célèbre* and an instance of the corruption of senatorial juries, a point which Cicero frequently made in his speeches against Verrēs in 70. In 66 the case was reopened by Oppianicus' son, who charged Cluentius with having murdered Oppianicus by poison while he was in exile, and of having bribed the jury at the first trial. Cicero, defending Cluentius, had to change his tune on the matter of the bribery. The speech is one of Cicero's best pieces of advocacy in a criminal trial, and illumines some curious aspects of domestic relations at Rome.

Proclus (AD 412–85), Neoplatonist philosopher (see NEOPLATONISM). He was born in Lycia but spent most of his life at Athens, succeeding to the headship of the Academy. He was a prolific writer and a scholar of vast learning, so much so that it has been doubted whether all the works that have come down under his name can be genuinely his. Writing as a Neoplatonist (and influenced by the superstitions of his time), he gives in his *Elements of Theology* a concise summary of Neoplatonist metaphysics; he wrote commentaries on several Platonic dialogues as well as on the works of earlier mathematicians including Euclid. His literary works include a book of hymns, scholia on Hesiod's *Works and Days*, and a *Chrēstomathia* ('summary of useful knowledge'), a handbook of literature, of which only an epitome exists. It has been thought that this last work, important for preserving summaries of six poems of the *Epic Cycle dealing with the Trojan War, may be the work of an earlier Proclus.

Procnē, see PHILOMELA.

proconsul. At Rome, the *imperium* of a consul or a praetor could be prolonged for a further year following his year of office whenever necessary for military purposes, the magistrate concerned being deemed to hold his imperium 'in place of a consul (or praetor)', *pro consule* (or *praetore*). The nouns 'proconsul', 'propraetor' are derived from the prepositional phrase. After 146 BC, when Rome had an increased number of provinces to govern, such prolongation of office (*prorogatio*) became the usual procedure to allow magistrates a further year as governors of provinces. A praetor's *imperium* might be raised to rank *pro consule* if the importance of the command seemed to require it.

Procō'pius (*c.* AD 500–after 562), of Caesarea in Palestine, Byzantine Greek historian and secretary to *Belisarius (the famous general of the Roman emperor Justinian) whom he accompanied on his early campaigns in Africa and Italy. He returned to Constantinople (then the capital of the Roman empire) in 542, and was made prefect of the city in 562. His *History of the Wars of Justinian* in eight books, covering the years 527–53, is a clear and reliable account of the events of his own times and is our main source for the first two-thirds of Justinian's reign. His account of the Nika riots of 532 (see JUSTINIAN) is famous. His chief praise is reserved for Belisarius; Justinian and his empress Theodora are treated with much less enthusiasm. He also wrote a work on the buildings and works of art in Constantinople and the empire, a panegyric of Justinian clearly commissioned by the latter and a valuable source of information about the art and architecture of the time. Procopius is also the author of a remarkable supplement to his *History*, a *Secret History*

(*Anecdota*), covering the same period but making a virulent attack on the whole policy of Justinian. On the basis, apparently, of court gossip he also makes scurrilous comments on the dubious morals of the empress Theodora. It cannot have been published in the author's lifetime, and was perhaps not known until the tenth century; *Photius appears not to have known it, but it is referred to in the *Suda*.

Procris, see CEPHALUS.

Procru'stēs (or Damastes), legendary brigand said to be the son of Poseidon, who lived beside the road between Athens and Eleusis. He ensnared strangers with hospitality, then seized them and fastened them to a bed which he then made them fit, cutting short their limbs if they were too long for it, or racking them if they were too short. *Theseus applied the same treatment to Procrustes and cut off his head.

procura'tor, at Rome under the empire, in general, an employee of the emperor in civil administration. Most procurators were of equestrian rank. In particular, procurators might oversee the revenues in the imperial provinces, and also, independently of the governors, in the senatorial provinces. They could also govern some of the minor provinces. Under Claudius and his successors certain high officials at Rome were known as *procurator a rationibus* ('minister of finance'), *ab epistulis* ('principal private secretary'), etc. (see ROME 12).

Pro'dicus, see SOPHIST.

Proetus, in Greek myth, son of Abas and Aglāia and twin brother of Acrisius (father of *Danaē). The two brothers had a life-long feud; when Abas left them his kingdom of Argos jointly they fought each other for its possession. Acrisius drove Proetus out, but was himself ousted in turn. See BELLEROPHON and DIONYSUS.

Pro Flacco ('for Flaccus'), see CICERO (1) 3.

Pro Fontē'io ('for Fonteius'), see CICERO (1) 1.

Pro legĕ Manī'lia ('in support of the Manilian law'; also known as *De imperio Cn. Pompeii*, 'on the command of Pompey'), speech by *Cicero in 66 ((1) 1) delivered before the people when Cicero was praetor, in support of the proposal of the tribune Manilius to extend Pompey's command in Asia to Bithynia, Pontus, and Armenia so as to enable him to take over the command in the war against *Mithridates. This was Cicero's first speech on purely public affairs, and was delivered in order to promote the interests of the equestrian order (who, being the businessmen of Rome, were suffering severe financial losses because of the disturbed condition of the rich province of Asia Minor). Although this command was against the wishes of the senate the proposal was carried.

prolē'psis ('anticipation'), figure of speech in which a person or thing is referred to by name or epithet which will be later, but is not yet, appropriate; e.g. *submersas obrue puppes*, 'overwhelm the sunken ships'. The word is also used to describe, in a speech, the forestalling of objections that an opponent may raise.

prōleta'rii, at Rome, the citizens placed in the lowest property-class who because of their poverty were exempted from compulsory military service and from the *tribūtum* or property-tax, and served the state only with their children (*prōlēs*).

Pro Ligā'rio ('for Ligarius'), see CICERO (1) 4.

prologue (*prologos*), see TRAGEDY 3 and COMEDY, GREEK 3.

Pro Marce'llo ('for Marcellus'), see CICERO (1) 4.

Promē'theus ('forethinker'), in Greek myth, a *Titan, son of Iapetus and Themis (or Clymenē, daughter of Oceanus). He was thought of as the champion of humankind against the hostility of the gods. In some stories he himself created men out of clay (from Panopea, near Chaeronea in Boeotia, visited by Pausanias (x. 4. 3) in the second century AD). When Zeus, having no love for men, deprived them of fire, Prometheus stole a spark from heaven (or from the forge of Hephaestus) and brought it to them in a stalk of fennel (*narthex*). He also taught them all kinds of arts and sciences, thus improving their brutish lives. In the apportionment of sacrificed animals between men and the gods, he induced Zeus by a trick to choose the less desirable portion (bones covered with fat), the meat being left for men. (This story is obviously meant to account for the fact that it was usually the inedible parts of a sacrifice which were allotted to the gods.) To avenge himself Zeus caused Hephaestus to create a woman, Pandora, fashioned out of clay. Athena breathed life into her, and the other gods endowed her with every charm (whence her name, 'all gifts'), but Hermes taught her flattery and guile. This woman was sent not to Prometheus, who was too cunning to accept such a dangerous gift, but to his brother Epimetheus ('he who thinks afterwards'), who gladly received her, although warned by his brother not to take any gifts from Zeus. She brought with her a jar containing all kinds of evils and diseases from which men had hitherto been free; this she opened, and they all flew out, leaving only Hope inside, under the lid, as a consolation for men. Pandora's jar seems to have become a 'box' in post-classical times by a confusion with the box which *Psyche was forbidden to open in the story in Apuleius' *Golden Ass*.

Prometheus also knew the secret concerning the marriage of Thetis (see PELEUS and *PROMETHEUS BOUND* below), but refused to reveal it to Zeus, who wished to marry Thetis himself. To punish him Zeus had him chained to a lonely rock usually said to be in the Caucasus, where an eagle daily fed on his liver which grew again each succeeding night (being a Titan, Prometheus was immortal). This torture continued for long ages until Prometheus was released either by Heracles shooting the eagle with his bow, or by his submitting and revealing the secret about Thetis. Prometheus was worshipped in Attica as a god of craftsmen; he was the father of *Deucalion by a wife variously named.

Promē'theus Bound (Gk. *P. desmōtēs*, Lat. *P. vinctus*), Greek tragedy attributed to *Aeschylus, though perhaps completed or even written by another after the former's death in 456 BC. No one in antiquity doubted that it was by Aeschylus, but in several respects the style is markedly different from that of his six other surviving plays. It is the only one of his plays for which there is no didascalic information (see DIDASCALIA) about production, date, and trilogy. It is possible that it was the second play of a connected trilogy, followed by *Prometheus lyomenos* ('P. Unbound'), of which a few fragments survive, and preceded by *Prometheus pyrphoros* ('P. Fire-carrier'), of which only one line exists, but the order of plays, and even the existence of a connected trilogy, are very uncertain.

*Prometheus the Titan, who in the past has aided Zeus to set up his rule over Cronus and the other Titans, has incurred Zeus' anger by becoming the champion of mankind and giving them fire and the arts. In the opening scene of the play, the god Hephaestus, at the order of Zeus, together with Kratos (Power) and Bia (Force), reluctantly nails Prometheus (possibly represented by a huge dummy figure behind which the actor spoke) to a high rock in the Caucasus, to suffer torment for as long as Zeus pleases. The chorus of Oceanidĕs, the daughters of the Titan *Oceanus, come to grieve with him and comfort him. Oceanus himself also comes, offering to intercede with Zeus if Prometheus will moderate his attitude. Prometheus scornfully rejects his offers, and then enumerates to the chorus all his benefactions to mankind. Another victim of Zeus' tyranny arrives, *Io, a mortal whom Zeus has loved and whom Hera, out of jealousy, has made partly cow-like in form. She is doomed to long wanderings pursued by a gad-fly and haunted by the myriad-eyed *Argus. Prometheus tells her about her sufferings, about her descendant Heracles who will eventually release Prometheus, and about the fatal marriage which Zeus will one day make unless Prometheus warns him. After Io departs Hermes enters, sent by Zeus to demand from Prometheus the revelation of his secret; although Hermes predicts increased torments for him Prometheus haughtily refuses and is plunged into the abyss with the Oceanides, who decide to share his fate.

If a reconciliation between Prometheus and Zeus took place in a following play, it is impossible to say how the author devised it. From the fragments of *P. lyomenos*, it seems that the play opened with Prometheus restored to the light after thirty thousand years, and that the chorus was composed of Titans.

As a suffering god, the creator of mankind, and also as the champion of the oppressed and an independent thinker, Prometheus has had a wide appeal to people of various religions and political beliefs. The English poet Shelley (1792–1822) in his 'Prometheus Unbound' could not accept Prometheus' apparent defeat at the end of the play: in his poem Prometheus is released and it is Jupiter (i.e. Zeus) who is vanquished.

Pro Milō'nĕ ('for Milo'), see CICERO (1) 4 and MILO, TITUS ANNIUS.

Pro Murē'na ('for Murena'), speech by *Cicero in 63 BC ((1) 2) when he was consul, in defence of Lucius Murena, who had been elected consul for the following year and was accused at the instigation of Cato of bribery in the election. The charge was brought at the height of the crisis due to Catiline's conspiracy; if Cato had succeeded in overturning the election of Murena, a man of proved courage and military ability, it would have been beneficial to the cause of Catiline. The speech is a good example of persuasive pleading; Cicero almost condones electoral corruption provided the best man is elected consul, and jokes at the formalism of Roman lawyers and the rigid creed of Stoics such as Cato.

Prope'rtius, Sextus (*c.*50 BC–after 16 BC), Roman elegiac poet. He was born at Asisium (Assisi) in Umbria, deprived of his estate when young by the confiscations of Octavian in 41–40 BC (after the defeat of the republicans at Philippi), was educated at Rome for the practice of law, but turned to poetry instead. He left four books of elegies, of which the first, published probably in 29 or 28 BC, shows Propertius as a member of a small and intimate group of poets who included Ovid (*Tristia*, IV. 10. 45). The book's great success admitted him to the wider circle around *Maecenas, but he seems to have admired the older poets (e.g. Virgil, in 2. 34) rather than known them well. Horace, whom he does not mention, refers to him with some contempt as aping Callimachus and Mimnermus (*Epistles*, II. 2. 90). His first book of poems, known in antiquity as the *Cynthia monobiblos* ('the single volume called *Cynthia*'), consists almost entirely of elegant and witty love poems to his mistress 'Cynthia' so-called, a Greek pseudonym for, reputedly, a certain Hostia

(compare 'Lycoris' of the poet Gallus and 'Delia' of Tibullus).

Book 2 is improbably long and may be a conflation of two books; no poem in it is later than 25 BC. The text is particularly disordered in the manuscripts, which in many cases give no indication of where individual poems begin and end. In style this book is similar to book 1 though now are included some poems on imperial themes pleasing to the new regime (see ROME 9), and the book does not quite have the lyrical freshness of its predecessor. Book 3, published soon after 23 BC, shows a wider range of subject matter, but also a greater degree of generalization and abstraction. Although the influence of the Hellenistic Greek poets was perceptible in the earlier books, it is with this book that Propertius begins to think of himself as the Roman *Callimachus, writing small-scale poems in a refined style, and no longer confines himself to love poetry; only about a third of the poems in this book are concerned with love, and the final poem is a farewell to Cynthia. Book 4 appeared after a longish interval, not before 16 BC, perhaps constructed around two commissioned and honorific poems, 6 and 11. Some of the poems are antiquarian in subject, in the manner of Callimachus' *Aitia*; the rest are miscellaneous, and include two of his most brilliant on Cynthia (7 and 8). Poem 11, an epicedium (a song sung in mourning over a corpse) for the nobly born Cornelia (daughter of Scribonia, the first wife of Octavian), is written as if spoken by the subject herself, and is a touching expression of the virtues of a Roman matron.

Propertius is perhaps the most fascinating of the Roman poets. He has an intense visual imagination which colours everything he writes: the setting of a poem must first be grasped and its implications understood if the reader is to make sense of the poet's abrupt changes of mood and his train of thought. Corruptions of the original text add to the difficulties of interpretation. No other Roman poet shows such strong personal characteristics, the recurrent melancholy, the passionate but objective, occasionally obsessive, self-observation, as he records his ecstasy, torment, and humiliation. His passion appears in a great variety of moods, inspired by Cynthia's beauty, or her venality, or her dangerous illness, and by the vicissitudes of his relations with her. The self-absorption, the striking imagery, the bold and difficult language, mark a new spirit in Latin literature.

Pro Pla'ncio ('for Plancius'), see CICERO (1) 4.

Propo'ntis, now the Sea of Marmora, an intermediate sea between the Aegean and the Black Sea. Its principal cities were Byzantium and Chalcedon at the mouth of the Bosporus.

Propylae'a, at Athens, the great roofed gateway and entrance to the *Acropolis, on the western side, built of Pentelic marble, designed by Mnesiclēs, and erected as part of Pericles' building programme between 437 and 432 BC, after the completion of the Parthenon. Much of it is still intact. It consisted of a central building approached from the ramp up which the Panathenaic procession climbed, having Doric porticoes to the east and west and five doorways through which the procession passed on its way to the great altar of Athena. The central doorway was about 4 m. (13 ft.) wide by 7 m. (23 ft.) high and led to a vestibule whose ceiling was supported by six Ionic columns (see ARCHITECTURE 1). Two wing buildings were constructed, one on each side of the central building and lower in height, the south wing being merely a portico, the north a dining-room. The latter, known as the Pinakothēkē, 'picture gallery', contained dining-couches for visitors to the Acropolis shrines and was decorated with wall-paintings by Polygnotus and others. The Propylaea was partially destroyed c.1656 by an explosion of gunpowder stored there by the Turkish garrison, and was further damaged in 1687 by the bombardment which damaged the Parthenon.

Pro Qui'nctio ('for Quinctius'), the first extant speech of *Cicero, delivered in 81 BC ((1) 1); in it he refers to earlier speeches which have not survived. He defends his client Publius Quinctius against a certain Servius Naevius, whose advocate is the great orator *Hortensius, in an action arising out of their partnership in a farm in Gaul. The result of the action is not known. The contrast of the solemn exordium with the comparative triviality of the matter in dispute was parodied by the seventeenth-century French dramatist Racine in *Les Plaideurs*.

Pro Rabi'rio ('for Rabirius'), speech by *Cicero in 63 BC ((1) 2) delivered when he was consul and defending (together with *Hortensius) Rabirius for allegedly killing Saturninus in 100 BC (when Cicero was 6). The speech was probably delivered in the *comitia centuriata; the proceedings were brought to an end and Rabirius in effect discharged when the praetor lowered the flag on the Janiculum hill. There was something farcical about the prosecution (though not about the serious intentions of the prosecutors) which was intended as an advertisement for Caesar and the *populares*. See also LABIENUS.

Pro Rabi'rio Po'stumo ('for Rabirius Postumus'), see CICERO (1) 4.

Pro Regĕ Dēio'taro ('for king Deiotarus'), see CICERO (1) 4.

Pro Ro'scio Ameri'no ('for Roscius of Ameria'), speech by *Cicero in 80 BC ((1) 1) in defence of Sextus Roscius (not the actor of the same name, for whom see below) on a charge of murdering his father. This was Cicero's first speech in a criminal case; it involved an attack on *Sulla's influential freedman Chrȳsogonus at a time when Sulla was all-powerful.

The father of Sextus Roscius, a well-to-do citizen of Ameria, said by Cicero to have favoured Sulla's cause, was murdered in Rome by neighbours and kinsmen who had a grudge against him. Chrysogonus conspired with these to have the victim's name added after the event to the list of those proscribed (see PROSCRIPTIONS) although the lists were by then closed. The victim's property was accordingly put up for sale and bought by Chrysogonus at a nominal price. A movement in favour of the victim's son, who was now expelled from his father's estate, sprang up in Ameria, and made the conspirators uneasy. They tried to have him murdered, and when that failed they prosecuted him for the murder of his father, hiring witnesses. Cicero shows the accusation to be baseless, throws suspicion upon one of the associates of Chrysogonus of being the true criminal, and finally attacks Chrysogonus himself, while being careful to dissociate Sulla from any knowledge of his freedman's activities.

The speech gives incidentally the origin of the expression *cui bono* ('who profits?'). If Sextus did not kill his father, says Cicero, who did? He then quotes this expression as being the frequent saying of an illustrious judge, L. Cassius Longīnus, in trials of this kind, and proceeds to show that the accusers of Roscius had themselves profited.

Pro Ro'scio comoe'do ('for Roscius the comic actor'), speech by *Cicero ((1) 1) on behalf of the great actor, of uncertain date, but possibly 77 BC.

A certain C. Fannius had a slave Panurgus, of such acting ability that Roscius entered into a partnership with Fannius by which the slave became their joint property; Roscius was to train him as an actor, and the partners were to share the profits. Panurgus became a promising actor, but was murdered by a certain Q. Flavius. Flavius agreed to pay damages to Roscius, in the shape of a derelict farm. This farm improved in value under the management of Roscius, and now Fannius claimed from Roscius half the value of the farm. The outcome is not known.

Pro Scauro ('for Scaurus'), see CICERO (1) 4.

proscriptions. At Rome, a *proscriptio* was a published list of Roman citizens who were declared to be outlaws and whose property was confiscated and auctioned by the state. Those proscribed could be killed by soldiers with impunity; rewards and punishments were used to encourage their friends and families to betray them. This procedure was employed by Sulla from 82 to 1 June 81 BC (see *PRO ROSCIO AMERINO*), and by the triumvirs Antony, Lepidus, and Octavian during the civil war in 43–42 BC as a means both of getting rid of enemies and of acquiring funds. Sulla's proscriptions are said to have named over forty senators and 1,600 *equites*. The sons and grandsons of the proscribed were excluded from public life, but were restored to their rights by Julius Caesar in 49 BC. It was greatly feared that whoever was victorious in the civil war between Caesar and Pompey would reintroduce proscriptions. In the event Caesar was merciful, but the triumvirs (see above) less so. Their lists included about 300 senators and 2,000 *equites*, among them Cicero, but many escaped, to be restored later to their full rights.

prose
1. *Greek.* Prose as a means of literary expression was developed in Greece as in other countries long after poetry. In early times when writing was in its infancy and literary compositions survived by being committed to memory, those written in metrical form were easier to memorize (in Greece, writing was reintroduced at the end of the eighth century; see ALPHABET). The earliest writers of Greek prose appear to have been the chroniclers (see LOGOGRAPHERS (1)) and philosophers (see PHILOSOPHY) of Ionia in the sixth century BC. From this time onward the development of prose was rapid. Heracleitus in about 500 BC was already writing prose of subtlety and style. By the middle of the fifth century BC a technical prose had been developed which was adequate to express all that was needed for a scientific or philosophical treatise. Democritus (*c.*460–*c.*357 BC), to judge from his fragments, was a competent prose writer, and the earliest works in the Hippocratic Corpus (see HIPPOCRATES) show at least the capacity for accurate and concise statement.

The first fully developed prose work that has survived in its entirety is the history of Herodotus (*c.*490–*c.*425 BC). Attic prose reached its height in the dialogues of Plato (*c.*429–347 BC) and the speeches of Demosthenes (384–322 BC). The sophist Gorgias (*c.*483–*c.*385) developed a very mannered oratorical style which did not have a long-lasting influence. Isocrates (436–338) on the other hand exercised through his school a deep influence on later Greek prose, in the direction of greater elaboration and ornament. With the end of the fourth century BC came the close of the classical period of Attic literature, the dialect of Athens then giving place to a common Greek dialect, the *koinē* (see DIALECTS), less subtle, varied, and accurate in expression. Greek prose was influenced by 'Asianism' (see ORATORY I), the florid style favoured by the rhetoricians of the third century BC. There was an energetic reaction against this, and an Attic revival, at Rome in the

Augustan age; of this Dionysius of Halicarnassus is the best example. In the second century AD Lucian wrote in a very good imitation of classical Attic prose. See also NOVEL and SOPHISTIC, SECOND.

2. *Latin.* Latin prose was developed, in its characteristic features, out of public speech, though it originated partly in the *Annales* of the pontiffs (their records of traditional ritual and events of religious importance) which were the origin of written history at Rome. Roman law, published and often learnt by heart, was also a formative influence. Latin prose, unlike Latin poetry, owed little to Greek influences, for it already possessed, before the advent of these, the essential qualities of clarity, precision, and conciseness. In a community like Rome where politics played so great a part, these qualities were naturally esteemed in oratory. We hear of Appius Claudius Caecus and Cato the Censor as noted speakers; and oratory was further developed, with a great variety of appeal, by Gaius Gracchus. Latin prose reached its highest point in the speeches and writings of Cicero. Thereafter it tended to become artificial, epigrammatic, and poetical, under the influence of the poets and of the prevailing education in rhetoric and through the practice of declamation (see DECLAMATIONES). Seneca's prose is typically epigrammatic; that of Tacitus is marked by its excessive compactness and its poeticisms. The Younger Pliny also shows the influence of the rhetorical schools. Quintilian opposed the artificiality of his day and wrote in a style free from conceits and studied effects; but although a professed follower of Cicero he did not recapture the amplitude and symmetry of Cicero's prose.

Pro'serpine (Proserpina), perhaps an original Italian goddess of the earth, or perhaps an adaptation of the Greek *Persephonē*, with whom Proserpina in Roman religion was identified. For her cult at Rome see DIS.

Pro Sestio ('for Sestius'), see CICERO (1) 4.

proso'dion, see LYRIC POETRY I.

pro'sody, the study of versification; in Greek and Latin in particular, the study of the rules which govern the quantity (i.e. length) of syllables in verse (see METRE, GREEK I). Syllables are classified according to the length of time they took to pronounce and are called long, short, or anceps ('ambivalent', i.e. either long or short). A syllable is long or short 'by nature' according as it contains either a long vowel or diphthong, or a short vowel. The general rules of Greek and Latin prosody (to which there are exceptions) are the following.

1. *Greek*
(i) By nature the vowels η and ω are long, ε and ο short; α, ι, and υ are sometimes long by nature, sometimes short. Diphthongs are long (i.e. αι, αυ, ει, ευ, ηυ, οι, ου, υι, ᾳ, ῃ, ῳ), except

that οι and αι, which appear to have been of shorter duration, are sometimes scanned short.

(ii) A syllable long by nature is sometimes shortened if it comes immediately before another vowel. This happens most often at the end of a word (i.e. before another word beginning with a vowel). The shortening is known as *correption (and see (iii) below).

(iii) A syllable that is short by nature is lengthened in pronunciation, and so becomes long 'by position', if the vowel is immediately followed by two (or more) consonants or by a so-called double consonant, ζ (= sd), ξ (= ks), or ψ (= ps), whether or not the consonants are in the same word. There is an exception to this general rule: in Attic poetry (which includes tragedy and comedy), a naturally short syllable usually remains short if it is followed by one of several combinations of two consonants, the first a so-called 'mute' (for this purpose one of π, β, φ, τ, δ, θ, κ, γ, χ), and the second a 'liquid' or 'nasal' (λ, ρ, μ, ν). This phenomenon is known as Attic correption.

2. *Latin*

(i) The vowels a, e, i, o, u (and y) are sometimes long by nature, sometimes short. Diphthongs (ae, au, ei, ou, oe) are long. A vowel which immediately precedes another vowel in the same word but is not part of a diphthong is generally short.

(ii) Correption of a final long syllable (see 1 (ii) above) is rare.

(iii) A syllable that is short by nature is lengthened in pronunciation, and so becomes long 'by position', if the vowel is immediately followed by two (or more) consonants, or by a double consonant, x (= ks) or z (= Greek ζ). (When the 'semi-consonants' i and u are equivalent to English j or v they are counted as consonants; h is discounted; qu is counted as a single consonant.)

(iv) An exception to (iii) is that short syllables remain short before certain combinations of so-called 'mute' and 'liquid' consonants (compare 1 (iii) above), i.e. b, c, d, f, g, p, t followed by l or r. This licence does not occur when the two consonants belong to different words or to different parts of a compound verb (e.g. ābrumpere).

See also BREVIS BREVIANS.

Pro Sulla ('for Sulla'), speech by *Cicero ((1) 3) in defence of P. Cornelius Sulla (elected consul for 65 but convicted of bribery and so disqualified; he was a relation of the famous Sulla, in whose *proscriptions he amassed great wealth). Sulla was accused of having participated in the conspiracy of *Catiline in 65 BC. The prosecutor had attacked Cicero himself in the matter of his proceedings against the conspirators, and in this speech Cicero takes the opportunity of defending his own actions.

protagonist, see TRAGEDY 2.

Prŏta'goras, of Abdēra (in Thrace), born c.485 BC, one of the earliest and most famous of the *sophists. His teaching career began c.455 and in his lifetime he made a great deal of money. What he professed to teach was aretē, 'virtue', by which he meant worldly success achieved through practical good management of public and private afairs. He appears as the opponent of Socrates in the dialogue by Plato named after him (see below), Socrates attaching a somewhat different meaning to 'virtue'. He was a friend of Pericles, and was said to have been prosecuted and expelled from Athens for atheism (compare ANAXAGORAS). His best known works (which have not survived) were *On Truth* and *On the Gods*. Sceptical about any claim to absolute and universal truth, he taught the doctrine of the relativity of all knowledge, summed up in the dictum quoted in Plato's *Theaetetus*, 'a person is the measure of all things' (usually rendered, 'man is the measure'). He also adopted an agnostic attitude towards the gods: 'Concerning the gods I have no means of knowing whether they exist or not, or what they are like in form. Many things prevent knowledge: the obscurity of the subject and the brevity of human life.' When *Thurii was founded by the Athenians in 433 BC Protagoras was appointed to draw up a code of laws for the new colony.

Protagoras, dialogue by *Plato in which the interlocutors are, besides Socrates, the sophists Protagoras (see above), Hippias, and Prodicus. It is a dialogue on the nature of 'virtue' (or 'goodness'; see above), what it is and how it is to be acquired. Protagoras argues that virtue (in his sense) is something that can be taught just as well as any other subject. The dialogue reaches the conclusion that all the virtues are essentially one, founded upon knowledge of the good, and that virtue is in fact knowledge. In the course of the dialogue a poem of *Simonides is analysed, an encomium on 'the good man'; this dialogue remains its only source (see PITTACUS).

Protagoras is presented as a reasonable man, sincere in his arguments and of equable temperament, not provoked by Socrates' sometimes biting irony at his expense. His arguments are thoughtful and based on common sense; those of Socrates more searching and also paradoxical. The dialogue contains a noteworthy declaration by Protagoras that under a rational system criminals are punished to deter them from doing wrong again, not as retribution for past misdeeds.

Prŏtesilā'us, in Greek myth, Thessalian prince, son of Iphiclus. Soon after his marriage he left to take part in the Greek expedition against Troy. When the Greek fleet reached the Trojan coast he was the first to leap ashore, and was subsequently the first to be killed (some said in conscious fulfilment of an oracle that the first to

tread on Trojan soil would be the first to die).
His wife Laodameia was plunged into such grief
at his death that the gods allowed her husband
to return to her for three hours, but when he left
her again she killed herself.

Prōteus, in Homer's *Odyssey* (4. 351), a minor
sea-god, who herds the seals, knows all things,
and has the power of assuming different shapes
in order to escape answering questions; this he
will do if held until he resumes his true shape. In
Herodotus and in Euripides' tragedy *Helen* he is
a virtuous king of Egypt who keeps *Helen safe
throughout the Trojan War.

proto-geometric, name given to one of the
five periods of the Greek era (based on the
differences in pottery styles; see POTTERY I (iv)),
denoting the early part of the Greek *Iron Age,
very roughly 1050–875 BC. (Compare GEOMET-
RIC, ORIENTALIZING, ARCHAIC, and CLASSICAL.)

Pro Tu'llio ('for Tullius'), see CICERO (1) 1.

provinces, Roman. The Latin word *provincia*,
originally (up to the time of the First Punic
War, 264–241 BC) meaning the sphere of action
of a magistrate possessing *imperium* (the right to
command), came to mean in later republican
times a territory outside Italy, subject to the
Roman people, obliged to pay tribute to Rome,
and governed by a resident Roman magistrate.
Except in special circumstances a province did
not have to provide military service. The earliest
Roman provinces, acquired from motives of
defence, Sicily (241 BC) and Sardinia and Corsica
(238 BC), were administered through magistrates
in Rome, but, this proving unsatisfactory, they
acquired Roman governors in 227 BC when the
number of *praetors was increased to four to
allow two to leave Rome for this purpose. The
number of praetors was increased to six in
197 BC to provide governors for Hither and
Further *Spain (which comprised at first only a
relatively small portion of the peninsula). No
more praetorships were instituted for later
provinces: from 146 BC the practice was established of appointing as governor an ex-consul or
ex-praetor (see PROCONSUL). In the next thirty
years occurred the acquisition as provinces of
Africa (some of the most fertile territory of
Carthage, in 146), Macedonia (146), Asia (annexed 133, organized as a province in 129–8),
and Gallia Narbonensis (Narbonese Gaul, 121).
In roughly the first half of the first century BC
Rome acquired Cilicia on the south coast of
Asia Minor (added *c.*102 BC to enable Rome to
deal with pirates), Bithynia in north-west Asia
Minor (bequeathed to Rome in 74; Pompey
added western Pontus to it to make the province
of Bithynia and Pontus in 65), Cyrene (74; Crete
was added to it in 67), Syria (64), and Cyprus
(58, added to Cilicia), while Caesar secured Gaul
(Gallia Comata) by his campaigns of 58–50.
Augustus reorganized the provinces in the years

following 27 BC, dividing Gaul into three
provinces, separating Achaea from Macedonia
and Lusitania from Further Spain (once the
whole peninsula had been pacified) and making
them distinct provinces. During his reign
further provinces were added: Egypt (30 BC,
after the defeat at Actium and the deaths of
Antony and Cleopatra), Galatia (in central Asia
Minor, 25 BC), Raetia (south Germany north of
Switzerland, 15 BC), Nōricum (between Raetia
and Pannonia, also *c.*15 BC), Moesia and
Pannonia (south and west of the Danube, after
AD 9). The list was increased under later
emperors: Tiberius added Cappadocia in AD 17,
Claudius the two Mauretanias (*c.* AD 42), Britain
(43), Lycia-Pamphylia (43), and Thrace (46).
Trajan added Arabia (106) and Dacia (107), and
Septimius Severus added Mesopotamia (199).

After 146 BC the senate decided which provinces should be governed by proconsuls and
which by propraetors, but the actual allocation
of provinces to individuals was determined by
lot. The organization of each province was
settled by the edict (*lex provinciae*) of the
commander who annexed it assisted by ten
senatorial commissioners. Under the overall
control of the governor the provincial
communities (cities or tribes) enjoyed varying
degrees of self-government and usually their
own constitutions and laws, but most had to pay
tribute to Rome, sometimes in accordance with
an already existing system of taxation. The
governor's duties were military, administrative,
and judicial. Upon entering his province he
published an edict stating what legal principles
he would enforce during his term of office.

Under the republic grave abuses were possible. The governor was in fact an autocrat: he
did not share his appointment with a colleague,
no official was empowered to question his
decisions, his capital sentences were not subject
to appeal. Moreover he was not experienced in
the administration of non-Italians and his tenure
of office for one year (not often extended) was
too short to allow him to become so. Finally, he
had strong inducement to make his office a
source of personal enrichment. As a consequence of this we hear repeatedly of cases of
oppression and extortion (*repetundae* laws
could easily be evaded by the rich and well-
connected). Electoral bribes could be recouped
by the successful candidate for office at Rome
when he went to his province at the end of his
year of tenure. Pompey in 52 BC enforced a
disregarded senatorial enactment that five years
should elapse before a governor went to his
province so as to prevent reckless bribery. The
best known example of oppression is that of
*Verres, but Cicero writes eloquently to Atticus
of the excesses of his predecessor in Cilicia,
Appius Claudius Pulcher, 'not a human being but
some sort of savage beast', and of the province
'forlorn and virtually ruined for ever'. Of

Cyprus Cicero writes, 'While I am governor, not a penny will it be asked for'. Yet Cicero, taking only the legitimate profits of office, amassed during his year's governorship 2,200,000 sesterces, by his estimate over three times the annual income required for a life of luxury. The system of farming out the (indirect) taxes of the provinces to *publicani remained a source of serious abuse.

Conditions changed under the empire. Augustus divided the provinces into two classes: the first comprised the more settled and richer provinces, such as Sicily and Africa, where no legions were required; these remained under the direction of the senate and their governors were called proconsuls even when they were of praetorian rank. The second group comprised the imperial provinces, on the frontiers, where legions were quartered, such as Syria; these were under the direct control of the emperor, who appointed senators as legati Augusti ('legates of Augustus') to the command of the more important, and equestrians as prefects, later procuratorēs, of the less important. *Egypt was a special case and was governed by an equestrian prefect. These men became experts in provincial administration, and won promotion by efficiency. Augustus' maius imperium granted in 23 BC gave him power superior to that of all other proconsuls.

Other reasons for the improvement of provincial administration under the empire are to be found in the *census and the regulation of taxation (the publicani virtually disappeared), in the payment of a fixed salary to the governors, improved communications, and the wide extension of Roman citizenship among the provincials. In consequence the provincial administration was generally sound and free from oppression under the early emperors, even the worst. There was considerable centralization, as can be seen from the correspondence of the Younger Pliny with the emperor Trajan. Provincial municipalities were administered under a great variety of conditions; in the West they enjoyed self-government, under somewhat aristocratic constitutions, with a curia or senate, duumvirs (boards of two chief executive officers), aediles, and quaestors.

pro'xenos, in a Greek state, a local citizen chosen to look after the interests of citizens from another state, a sort of consul (in the modern sense). Pindar at Thebes was proxenos of the Athenians staying in that city; Demosthenes at Athens was proxenos of the Thebans. The proxenoi received privileges and distinctions from the states which they represented.

Pro'xenus, Boeotian friend of Xenophon, at whose invitation he took part in the expedition of Cyrus related in the *Anabasis.

Prude'ntius Clemens, Aurē'lius (AD 348–after

405), Christian Latin poet, native of Spain; some of his hymns composed in classical metres are still sung. Other poems are on Christian dogma or tell of the martyrs. His Psychomachia ('battle for the soul'), an allegory of the spiritual struggle in the human soul, set in epic form, was well known in the Middle Ages and was a strong influence on medieval poetry.

prytanē'um, in the chief city of a Greek state, the common 'home' of the whole state, containing the hearth (see HESTIA) where a fire was kept continually burning and from which fire was taken to a new colony. Here also were the offices of the local magistrates; it was the place where ambassadors were entertained and distinguished citizens were rewarded by the provision of meals at the state's expense. The prytaneum at Athens was in the agora. See PRYTANY below.

pry'tany (prytaneia, 'presidency'), **prytanēis** ('presidents'). At Athens, after the political reforms of *Cleisthenes (1) in 508/7 BC, each of the newly constituted ten tribes chose by lot every year fifty of its members to serve on the boulē ('council'). Each group of fifty served as the executive committee of the boule for one-tenth of the year, when they were known as prytaneis, and the period as a prytany. (For the working of the prytany or bouleutic calendar see CALENDARS.) The prytaneis were on duty every day, preparing the day-to-day business of the state and organizing the meetings of the boule and ecclesia. Their office, built in the agora soon after the Persian Wars, was familiarly known as the *tholos ('rotunda') because of its circular shape. There they dined every day at the state's expense. Each day one of the prytaneis, picked by lot, acted as foreman (epistatēs), remaining on duty in the tholos for twenty-four hours, presiding over any meeting of the boule or ecclesia held on that day. No one could act as foreman more than once, so that a large proportion of the citizen-body came to hold this office.

Pseu'dolus, Roman comedy by *Plautus produced in 191 BC. The title is taken from the name of a character in the play.

A Macedonian captain has bought a girl, Phoenicium, from a pimp for 20 minae, paying 15 down. The girl is to be delivered to his messenger when he sends the 5 minae still owing and a certain token. Calidōrus, a young Athenian, is in love with her. The play deals with the trick by which his father's slave, Pseudolus, having intercepted the captain's letter and token, cheats the pimp and carries off Phoenicium for Calidorus. (The part of the pimp Ballio was chosen by *Roscius, the great comic actor of Cicero's day.)

Psȳchē ('soul'), the name of the heroine in a tale, told in books 4–6 of the Golden Ass of *Apuleius, the narrator being an old woman who is trying to amuse a girl captured by robbers. Psyche was so beautiful that Venus became jealous of her and sent Cupid to make her fall in love with some unsightly creature; however, Cupid himself became her lover. He placed her in a palace but only visited her in the dark, and forbade her to attempt to see him. Her sisters, out of jealousy, told her he was a monster who would devour her. One night she took a lamp and looked at Cupid while he slept, but a drop of hot oil woke him. Thereupon the god left her, angry at her disobedience. Psyche, solitary and remorseful, sought her lover all over the earth, and various superhuman tasks were required of her by Venus. The first was to sort out before nightfall an enormous heap of various kinds of grain. But the ants took pity on Psyche and arriving in hordes did the task for her. By one means or another all the tasks were completed except the last, which was to descend to the Underworld and fetch a casket of beauty from Persephonē. Curiosity overcame Psyche and she opened the casket, which contained not beauty but a deadly sleep, to which she succumbed. Jupiter, at Cupid's entreaty, at last consented to their marriage, and Psyche was brought to heaven. This fairy-tale has often been interpreted as an allegory of the soul's journey through life and its final union with the divine after suffering and death.

Pto'lemies (Ptolemaioi), Macedonian Greek dynasty that ruled Egypt from the death of Alexander the Great in 323 BC until the Roman conquest in 30 BC (see DIADOCHOI). For the foundation of the dynasty by one of Alexander's generals see MACEDONIA 2. Its principal members were Ptolemy I Sōter, son of Lagus, b. c.367, who ruled 323–283 BC; his son Ptolemy II Philadelphus, b. 308, who ruled 285–246 BC, for the first two years joint ruler with his father; and Ptolemy III Euergetēs, born between 288 and 280, who ruled 246–221 BC and won for a time a large part of Seleucid Asia.

These first Ptolemies constantly endeavoured, with varying success, to extend their dominions to include Syria and Asia Minor, and to obtain a footing in Greece itself. They were thus in frequent conflict with the *Seleucids. They held southern Syria fairly continuously until 200 BC, and coastal possessions around Asia Minor until a few years later. Cyrenē in North Africa they retained until c.98 and Cyprus until 58 BC, both being annexed by Rome. Judaea remained under their rule until 200 BC. The book of Ecclesiastes in the bible, which dates from the end of that period, reflects the despondency of part of the Jewish aristocracy there at being under Ptolemaic rule and their preference for the Seleucids; but according to Polybius the common people were favourable to the Ptolemies. Their attempts on Greece were defeated by the Antigonids (see MACEDONIA 3). The

Ptolemies owed the control of their dominions outside Egypt in great part to their naval power; but their fleet lost its supremacy in a severe defeat by Antigonus off Andros in 246 or 245 BC.

Under the later Ptolemies Egypt entered a period of great confusion owing to domestic strife within the dynasty, civil wars, and mobrule. The last chapter of Ptolemaic history opened when Ptolemy XII Aulētēs died in 51 BC leaving the throne to be shared by his daughter *Cleopatra VII and his 12-year-old son, Ptolemy XIII, whom Cleopatra married in the same year. During the discord that followed she was driven out by her brother's party. Julius Caesar, who after the battle of Pharsalus in 48 was in Egypt in pursuit of Pompey, was involved in a difficult war against Ptolemy XIII and the Alexandrians, being besieged for a time in the palace at Alexandria, but finally defeated his assailants and established Cleopatra in power. Cleopatra followed Caesar to Rome in 46 and lived with him there until his death in 44, when she returned to Alexandria. She bore to Caesar a son *Caesarion. For her relations with Mark Antony see ANTONY. After the defeat of Actium and Antony's death in 30 BC, Cleopatra, having failed to beguile Octavian, took her own life, and the dynasty of the Ptolemies came to an end.

The Ptolemies needed money, to pay and equip armies for defence and to buy the many essentials that Egypt lacked, metal and timber for example. This need was met by a kind of mercantilism: by control of all areas of production and by the collection of rents and taxes, all administered by a highly controlled centralized bureaucracy. The Ptolemies claimed the ownership of the entire soil of Egypt. Part of it was farmed for them by their own peasants, who were practically serfs. The use (but not the ownership) of the rest was granted, on various terms, to different categories of holders. All corn-land paid a tax in corn which ultimately found its way to the great King's Barn in Alexandria where it was sold. Vineyards, orchards, and gardens were also taxed. Later, land was made over in gifts to temples and individuals and some land came to be privately owned. In addition to exacting heavy taxes, the Ptolemies imposed many monopolies, most importantly on all oil-producing crops, but also on mines, quarries, and salt-production. They also had near-monopolies on linen, papyrus, and beer (the universal drink of Egypt). They had shares in certain businesses, and licences had to be purchased to carry on others, such as bee- and pig-keeping, fishing, and most kinds of trade. In fact practically every business was owned either in part or in whole by the king, taxed or subject to licence. This vast system of exploitation, much of which existed before the Ptolemies arrived in Egypt and which they took over, offers a striking contrast to the policy of the Seleucids in Asia. It was carried on by a highly organized army of officials. The condition of the fellahin (the Egyptian peasants) was miserable; resistance and even strikes were frequent. The army consisted of mercenaries, Greeks, Macedonians, and Anatolians; under the first three Ptolemies no native Egyptian was admitted to it. Ptolemy IV recruited native troops, and with these defeated the army of the Seleucid king Antiochus III, who had invaded Palestine, at Raphia in 217 BC. (The Egyptians, their national consciousness thus aroused, revolted for decades afterwards, and the supremacy of the Greeks was weakened.) A mixed Greco-Egyptian race gradually evolved. Meanwhile serious abuses developed in the Ptolemaic system of administration, which depended on the honesty and efficiency of the officials, and only the energetic reforms of Ptolemy VIII (Euergetes II, 182–116 BC) enabled it to survive until the Roman annexation in 30 BC.

The Ptolemies were immensely enriched by their exploitation of Egypt, and they raised their capital *Alexandria to great wealth and magnificence. By their patronage of art and literature, and especially by the establishment of the *Museum or literary academy of Alexandria, and the *Alexandrian Library, the first Ptolemies made the city a centre of Hellenistic culture. Ptolemy I himself wrote the best of the histories of Alexander the Great (now lost) based on his own recollections and using much official material. It was used by the historian *Arrian. Greek settlements were planted in many parts of Egypt, most extensively in the reclaimed land of the Faiyum. To these Greek settlers we owe numerous papyri, discovered in modern times in places where physical conditions have been suitable for their preservation, and on these many fragments of Greek literary works have been discovered (see PAPYROLOGY). See also EGYPT.

Pto'lemy (Claudius Ptolemaeus, c. AD 100–c.178), Greek astronomer, mathematician, and geographer, born at Ptolemais Hermiou in Upper Egypt; later he lived in Alexandria. He summed up the astronomical knowledge of the age in his Mathēmatikē syntaxis ('system of mathematics'), translated later into Arabic and, to distinguish it from another syntaxis, called by the Arabs 'the Greatest' (Almagest, compound of the Arabic article and the Greek adjective megistē). The work contains thirteen books. In it Ptolemy developed a theory to explain the relative movements of the sun, moon, and planets around the stationary earth, a system which his predecessors had almost universally believed in (for the exception see ARISTARCHUS). This theory (with modifications) was accepted until the time of Copernicus and Kepler in the sixteenth century. Ptolemy himself constructed

the first viable theory of the five planets, and his fixed-star table is based on his own fresh observations (see ASTRONOMY). The Almagest soon became the standard work on the subject and remained so until the end of the Middle Ages, not only in the Greek but also in the Arab world, passing thence into medieval Europe (see TEXTS, TRANSMISSION OF ANCIENT 7). It is an important source for knowledge of earlier works.

Ptolemy also wrote a number of other scientific treatises, including one on optics surviving only in a Latin translation from the Arabic, and one on the mathematical theory of musical harmony. Regarded as authoritative for as long as the Almagest was his 'Outline of *Geography' (Geōgraphikē hyphēgēsis) in seven books, followed by an eighth book containing his famous *maps. After a general introduction the first book has a discussion of maps, with instructions on how to make them; the following six books are devoted to lists of some 8,000 places, located by latitude and longitude. The surviving maps in the eighth book are probably not as Ptolemy originally drew them but later reconstructions. Among numerous errors which the work contained was the notion that Asia stretched much further to the east than is in fact the case. It was this that misled Columbus into thinking that he had reached Asia when he was in fact in the Caribbean. Ptolemy's work on astrology, in which he attempts to find a scientific basis for the various astrological practices, also exerted great influence. Chaucer's Wife of Bath in his Canterbury Tales quotes a proverb from Ptolemy, calling him 'the wise astrologe'.

publica'ni ('publicans', i.e. tax-collectors). In Rome, the collection of taxes was normally farmed out, i.e. sold by public contract to the highest bidder, who then recouped with as much profit to himself as possible. Other public works were sold by contract in the same way and to the same people, who were usually of the *equestrian order, since men of senatorial rank were not permitted to engage in trade of this sort. Julius Caesar restricted the activities of the publicani, in particular depriving them of a highly profitable source of income by abolishing tax-farming in Asia. Under the empire this method of collecting taxes was gradually superseded by direct collection by the government through quaestors and procurators.

Publi'lius Sȳrus (first century BC), writer of Latin *mimes who was brought to Rome as a slave, possibly from Antioch, and manumitted. He is known by a collection of moral maxims made for school use which purport to have been selected from his plays. One of his maxims, iudex damnatur cum nocens absolvitur ('When the guilty man is let off the judge stands condemned') was adopted by the Edinburgh Review

(1802) to express its stern attitude in literary criticism.

punctuation. Punctuation existed in Greek texts from at least the fourth century BC, but its use was sporadic (as it was later in Latin texts). What it consisted of can be inferred from the papyri (see PAPYROLOGY) and early manuscripts, and from explicit statements by Dionysius Thrax. In practice scribes of Greek and Latin texts rarely used more than two marks, the equivalent of the full-stop and the comma. Only for Homer was there a more sophisticated system, invented by Nicanor in the second century AD. See also BOOKS AND WRITING.

Pūnica, see SILIUS ITALICUS.

Punic Wars, three wars in which Rome successfully fought *Carthage for dominance in the western Mediterranean. Rome, having by 270 BC won control of the Italian peninsula and become a Mediterranean power, found herself confronted across the Straits of Messina by the rival power of the Carthaginians (Poeni, adj. Punicus), who now ruled not only the north and west of Sicily but also the greater part of North Africa, Sardinia, Corsica, and the cities on the coast of southern Spain. In 264 the Carthaginians occupied Messana (modern Messina) in north-east Sicily, in response to an appeal for help against Syracuse made first to Carthage and then to Rome by the Messanians (see MAMERTINES). Rome was now the ally of the Greek cities of south Italy, who felt, as did Rome, that trade and security would be threatened if Carthage encroached further. While the senate hesitated, the people decided to accept an alliance with Messana which led directly to war.

1. The First Punic War lasted from 264 to 241 BC. The scene of the first campaigns was Sicily. In 263 the Romans under M. Valerius won a victory which resulted in Hieron II, tyrant of Syracuse, entering into alliance with Rome. As a consequence Valerius earned a triumph for himself and his family and the *cognomen* Messalla (from the name Messana). In 262 the Romans won Segesta and Agrigentum, but realized that to drive the Carthaginians out of Sicily they needed to overcome the latters' superiority at sea. They built a fleet which defeated the Carthaginians at Mylae near Messana in 260, largely thanks to using grapnels (*corvi*). When the situation in Sicily remained indecisive they sent a force to Africa in 256 under *Regulus, one of the consuls. After some early successes the Romans were defeated and Regulus, who had been left in command of a diminished army, was taken prisoner (255). They lost the greater part of their fleet in a storm, and after further naval disasters confined their efforts to Sicily. From 247 they were confronted there by the great general *Hamilcar Barca, father of Hannibal; after a succession of adverse campaigns they

raised a new fleet under C. Lutatius Catulus and defeated the Carthaginians off the Aegātēs Insulae (242). They were able to sue for peace on favourable terms: the Carthaginians were to evacuate Sicily (except for the dominion of Hieron II), which then became the first Roman province, and to pay an indemnity of 3,200 talents.

2. When the First Punic War ended, Carthage had to face a serious revolt of her mercenaries, who appealed to Rome, and in consequence Rome annexed Sardinia and Corsica. Carthage turned to Spain to recoup wealth and manpower, and between 237 and 219 Hamilcar, *Hasdrubal, and *Hannibal gradually conquered that country. Hannibal's attack on Rome's Spanish ally Saguntum in 219 deliberately precipitated the Second Punic War (218–202), the great ordeal in which the stubborn courage of Rome was seen at its highest. Hannibal had been vowed by his father Hamilcar to undying hatred of Rome, and his capture of Saguntum was carried out in spite of Rome's protests. Hannibal anticipated the dispatch of Roman expeditions to Spain and Africa and struck first by invading north Italy. Rome had sent an army under P. Scipio; when it failed to intercept Hannibal at the Rhône Scipio turned back but wisely sent a force on to Spain under his brother Cn. Scipio to cut off Carthaginian reinforcements. Hannibal reached Italy after an arduous passage over the Alps in 218, was joined by the Cisalpine Gauls of northern Italy, and defeated one great army after another, that of P. Scipio at the river Ticinus in 218, that of Scipio and Tib. Sempronius Longus at the river Trebia in the same year (both rivers tributaries of the Po), and that of C. Flaminius at Lake Trasimene in 217, when Flaminius was himself killed. Hannibal then moved to the south to detach the allies from Rome.

At this crisis Rome appointed a dictator, Quintus *Fabius Maximus, who acquired the *cognomen* Cunctator, 'delayer', from following the invader and harassing him, while refusing a general engagement. Meanwhile P. Scipio joined his brother in Spain, and they continued to harry the Carthaginians at intervals until 211, when both were killed in battle. In 216 the new consuls C. Terentius Varro and L. Aemilius Paullus were authorized to risk a decisive battle to protect the territory of Rome's allies, with the result that at Cannae Rome suffered the bloodiest of all her defeats, losing perhaps 30,000 men, half of them Roman. The allies wavered; Syracuse went over to Carthage after the death of Hieron II, the friend of Rome, and, most seriously, Capua, the second city of Italy, defected to Hannibal. Rome responded by lowering the property qualification for admission to the army so that even the landless were enrolled (see PROLETARII). Steps had already been taken to prevent reinforcements reaching Hannibal from Spain, and Rome's command of the sea prevented Hannibal's new ally Philip V of Macedon from sending him aid.

Slowly the tide turned for Rome. M. Claudius Marcellus captured Syracuse in 211, despite the weapons of war devised by *Archimedēs, and so weakened the power of Carthage in Sicily. Syracuse was looted, and became subject and tributary to Rome. Campania was recovered. The young P. Cornelius (see SCIPIO 1), son and namesake of that Scipio who was killed in Spain in 211, likewise showed his military genius in Spain and was highly successful. When Hannibal summoned his brother Hasdrubal thence to his aid the latter was intercepted and his army destroyed by C. Claudius Nero and M. Livius Salinator at the river Metaurus (in Umbria, 207). In the following two years Scipio completed the conquest of Punic Spain; the conquered portions were subsequently formed into the two Roman provinces of Hither and Further Spain. The scene of war was now transferred to Africa. Scipio had gained the consulship in 205, and then went to Sicily to plan the invasion of Africa, which he carried out in 204. After defeating the Carthaginians in 203 he permitted an armistice, and Hannibal and the Punic army were recalled from Italy (where they had campaigned for fifteen years). The Carthaginians, with Hannibal's army back in Africa, broke the armistice and tried their luck in a last pitched battle at Zama in 202, but were defeated. Carthage was forced to renounce all her territory except the city of Carthage and the surrounding country in Africa, pay an indemnity of 10,000 talents (in fifty annual instalments), and limit the size of her army. It was the end of her position as a great Mediterranean power. Scipio returned to Rome in triumph and was given the *cognomen* Africanus.

3. Carthage retained, however, her commercial importance; she continued to compete successfully with Rome in trade, and was a source of uneasiness there. She had undertaken to wage no wars in Africa without the consent of Rome, but in 151 the depredations of Masinissa, the ruler of the adjoining Numidian kingdom and the friend of Rome, goaded her into retaliation (150). In 149 Rome declared war on Carthage, initiating the Third Punic War. *Cato (the Censor), from motives of revenge and fear, urged its destruction, and an army under Manilius landed in Africa. Carthage surrendered, handed over hostages and arms, and then heard the terms that the city must be destroyed. Unexpectedly she refused to comply and withstood a siege until 146, when *Scipio Aemilianus captured the city and demolished it. With Carthage destroyed her territory was made into the Roman province of Africa.

purple (Gk. *porphyra*, Lat. *purpura*), dye discovered by the Phoenicians and perhaps known in Homeric times, derived from certain organs of the *mūrex*, a shell-fish found in the Mediterranean. The best kinds of this dye were made in the Phoenician city of Tyre and fetched a high price. It was used for dyeing garments of a distinctive nature such as the mantles of the archons at Athens and the purple stripes on the togas of Roman magistrates (see DRESS).

Pyane'psia or **Pyanopsia**, at Athens, a popular festival held in honour of Apollo, which celebrated the harvest and gave its name to the month Pyanopsion, roughly October. It took its name from the cooked beans (*pyana*) which were offered to the god as first-fruits and partaken of by all the members of the household. An olive-branch (known as *eiresiōnē*) wreathed with wool and hung with various fruits and models of wine cups and bottles of oil was carried about and set before each house and before the temple of the god.

Pydna, in Macedonia on the Thermaic Gulf, the scene of the battle in 168 BC in which the Romans under L. Aemilius Paullus decisively defeated Perseus, king of *Macedonia (see 3), and ended the Third Macedonian War.

Pygmā'lion. 1. Legendary king of Tyre, brother of Elissa (*Dido), whose husband Sychaeus he killed in the hope of obtaining his fortune.

2. Legendary king of Cyprus, who fell in love with a beautiful statue (according to Ovid made by himself). He prayed to Aphroditē to give him a wife resembling the statue; and she did more than this, for she gave the statue life, and Pygmalion married the woman so created. Their child was Paphos, the mother of *Cinyras.

pygmies (pygmaioi, from *pygmē*, a measure of length equivalent to 18 *daktyloi*; see WEIGHTS AND MEASURES 1 (ii)), in Greek myth, a race of dwarves thought to inhabit Africa (usually, but also India or Scythia), with whom the cranes were supposed to carry on war. This belief is frequently referred to by ancient writers, Homer, Aristotle, Ovid, and the Elder Pliny. The fact that tribes of very small stature exist in equatorial Africa may be the origin of the belief.

Pȳ'ladēs. 1. In Greek myth, the constant friend of *Orestes. He was the son of Strophius, king of Phocis, and his wife Anaxibia, sister of Orestes' father Agamemnon. He accompanied Orestes to the land of the Tauri (see IPHIGENEIA), and later to Mycenae when Orestes took vengeance on Clytemnestra and Aegisthus (see ELECTRA, Sophocles' tragedy). He also killed Neoptolemus at Delphi and married Electra.

2. An actor at Rome; see PANTOMIME.

Pylae, see THERMOPYLAE.

Pȳlos. 1. Legendary kingdom of *Neleus and *Nestor in the Peloponnese.

2. Town on the west coast of the Peloponnese, in Messenia. This and the adjoining bay of Pylos, and the island of Sphacteria which almost closes the mouth of the bay, were the scene of an important defeat of the Spartans by the Athenians in 425 BC (see PELOPONNESIAN WAR). The Athenians held it with a garrison until 409 BC.

Py'ramus and Thisbē, hero and heroine of a love story almost unknown in classical literature except through Ovid. The two lovers, who were next-door neighbours in Babylon, were forbidden by their parents to marry, but they spoke to each other through a chink in the party-wall. Finally they arranged to meet at the tomb of Nisus outside the city walls, under a white mulberry tree. Thisbe arrived first, but being frightened by a lion coming from its kill, fled into a cave, dropping her cloak which the lion mauled. On his arrival Pyramus found the tattered and blood-stained cloak and the animal's prints and, concluding that Thisbe was dead, stabbed himself with his sword. Thisbe, emerging from the cave, distraught at the sight of the dying Pyramus, fell upon his sword. Their blood flowed to the roots of the mulberry tree, which thereafter bore dark red fruit. Their parents buried their ashes in a single urn. The story is acted by Bottom and his fellow tradesmen to entertain the wedding-party in Shakespeare's *A Midsummer Night's Dream*.

Pyriphle'gethon, see HADES.

Pyrgopolynī'cēs, the boastful captain of the title in the *Miles gloriosus* of Plautus.

pyrrhic dance (*pyrrhichē*), Spartan mimic war-dance, perhaps a form of the *hyporchema*. It is said to have originated with the Dorians in Crete. It was danced at the Spartan festival of the Gymnopaediae and also at the Athenian festival of the *Panathenaea. The origin of the name is uncertain.

Pyrrhic victory, see PYRRHUS (1).

Pyrrhon, see SCEPTICS.

Pyrrhus. 1. (319–272 BC), king of Epirus in Greece from 307, second cousin of Alexander the Great; his father and Olympias, mother of Alexander, were first cousins. Pyrrhus was ousted from his throne in 302, served under *Demetrius Poliorcetēs of Macedonia (son of Antigonus I) at the battle of Ipsus in 301 (see MACEDONIA 2), and with the help of Ptolemy I of Egypt was restored in 297. He was a skilful commander, a good organizer, and an ambitious military adventurer. He hoped to revive the empire of Alexander the Great and was at one time (286), after a successful war against Demetrius, the most powerful ruler in the

European part of it, having secured Thessaly and a portion of Macedonia. But he was soon driven back to Epirus (283) by Lysimachus (one of the *diadochoi*, Alexander's 'successors'). He then turned to the West and accepted the invitation of the Greek city of Tarentum in Italy to lead the Italian Greeks of *Magna Graecia against Rome. He won battles in 280 and 279 with a large army and twenty elephants but was unable to establish himself in Italy. The expression 'Pyrrhic victory' to describe a victory gained at too great a cost alludes to an exclamation attributed to him after the battle of Asculum in 279 where he routed the Romans but lost the flower of his army: 'One more such victory and we are undone.'

Pyrrhus then transferred his forces to Sicily, and by 277 had almost succeeded in expelling the Carthaginians from that island (they were at that time the allies of Rome, soon to become its enemies with the outbreak of the First Punic War). He broke off the war there and returned to Italy. After an indecisive battle against the Romans at Beneventum (275), he withdrew to Epirus. Once again in 274 he attempted to conquer Macedonia, with some success, but was diverted to an attack on Sparta (272). He was killed in the same year in an attempt to seize Argos. A brilliant tactician, Pyrrhus was quick to take advantage of an opportunity but made no lasting gains. See also FABRICIUS.

2. Alternative name of the Greek hero *Neoptolemus.

Pȳtha'goras, Greek polymath, philosopher, and mystic of the sixth century BC. He wrote no books, but so impressive were his doctrines, his learning, and his way of life that by the end of the fifth century he had become a figure of mystery and legend with a reputation as a great sage and a possessor of miraculous powers (as well as of a golden thigh). The traditions concerning his life are contradictory and confused, but it is believed that he was born at Samos *c*.580 BC and emigrated (perhaps through hostility to the tyranny of Polycratēs) to Croton in *Magna Graecia. There he attracted followers, both men and women, who formed a community and lived according to his rule of life. Even after his death, *c*.500 BC, Pythagorean societies continued to flourish in Croton and elsewhere in Magna Graecia. The members seem to have been active in the politics of the time and, presenting a united front, were no doubt a powerful force; they became unpopular and eventually (*c*.450 BC) the societies were broken up and the members killed or exiled.

Part of Pythagoras' teaching was religious and mystical, and it was presumably this aspect which led his contemporary *Heracleitus to regard him as a fraud. Another contemporary, *Xenophanēs, mocked the most celebrated aspect of his teaching, his doctrine of reincarnation or the transmigration of souls (*metempsychōsis*), with the story that Pythagoras once claimed to recognize a friend's voice in the howling of a puppy which was being beaten. Pythagoras also declared that he remembered his own previous incarnations, including that as the Trojan Euphorbus, killed in the siege. Pythagoras taught that the soul (a combination of life-principle, self, and mind) is immortal, a fallen divinity imprisoned in the body as in a tomb. Since the soul is rational and responsible for its actions, the choices it makes determine the kind of body into which it is reincarnated, human or animal (perhaps even plant; *Empedoclēs, who was greatly influenced by Pythagorean ideas, declares that in one of his incarnations he was a bush). By keeping itself pure from the pollutions of the body the soul may eventually win release from it (see also ORPHEUS and compare Orphic beliefs, with which Pythagoras obviously had much in common). Pythagoras and his followers adhered to a rule of life by which release for the soul might be attained; this was an austere regimen the details of which are not clear but which perhaps entailed silence, self-examination, and abstention from eating flesh and beans (no reason is known for this latter prohibition). The idea of metempsychosis is foreign to Greek tradition and its source uncertain; it may have reached Greece from central Asia or even India. Many precepts of Pythagoras were collected at some time under the name of *acusmata* (Gk. *akousmata*, '(oral) instructions'). Some sound like taboo-prohibitions, e.g. 'Do not poke the fire with a sword' (which *Porphyry interpreted as meaning, 'Do not vex with sharp words a man swollen with anger'). Others sound like traditional wisdom: 'What is the wisest of the things in our power? Medicine. What is the fairest thing? Harmony. What is the most powerful? Knowledge. What is the best? Happiness.'

Pythagoras' name is also linked to the study of numbers and proportions as well as astronomy. It is impossible to ascertain what discoveries should be attributed to him personally, but he is credited with the discovery that the relation between the chief musical intervals produced on a vibrating string can be expressed as ratios between the first four whole numbers: octave, 2 : 1; fifth, 3 : 2; fourth, 4 : 3. From this evolved the idea that the explanation of the universe is to be sought in numbers and their relations, of which the objects of sense are representations. According to Aristotle, even abstracts like 'opinion' or 'opportunity' or 'injustice' were numbers in the Pythagorean system, and had their place in the cosmos. Since the first four whole numbers are important in expressing musical harmonies and since their sum can be represented as an equilateral triangular array of ten dots in rows of one, two, three, and four, it was thought that this pattern, the *tetraktys*, 'foursome', of the dead, was of mystical significance, embracing the whole nature of number: the number one could be identified with the point, two with the line, three with the surface, and four with the solid. Pythagoras is also credited with the theorem that still goes under his name, namely that the square on the hypotenuse of a right-angled triangle is equal to the sum of the squares on the other two sides; on discovering it he is said to have made the important sacrifice of a hecatomb. The Pythagoreans believed that the earth is a sphere; later Pythagoreans had an astronomical system in which the heavenly bodies (the sphere of the fixed stars, the five planets, the sun, moon, earth, and counter-earth, the last included to bring the number of bodies up to ten) revolve around a central fire, a system to which an earlier belief in a '*harmony of the spheres' was accommodated.

Pythagoreanism influenced not only Empedocles but also Plato, whose science and metaphysics are infused with Pythagorean ideas. Later the doctrines were revived at Rome under the early empire, and became confused with Orphic beliefs with which they had affinities.

Py'theas. In the second half of the fourth century BC, a Greek explorer from Massilia (modern Marseilles), who, according to Strabo, Diodorus Siculus, and the Elder Pliny, made a courageous voyage up the west coast of Europe to Britain, Jutland, and the Orkneys and Shetlands. See THULE.

Py'thia, priestess of Apollo at *Delphi. See DELPHIC ORACLE.

Py'thian festival, see GAMES, PUBLIC (1) 3.

Py'thias, see DAMON.

Pÿthon, see DELPHI.

Q

Quadriga'rius, Claudius, see HISTORIOGRA-
PHY 2.

quadri'vium ('meeting place of four roads'), the
four mathematical disciplines of astronomy,
geometry, arithmetic, and music which during
the Middle Ages constituted the advanced part
of the educational curriculum, known as the
*seven liberal arts. The *trivium*, the more
elementary part, consisted of grammar, rhetoric, and logic. The term *quadrivium* seems to
have been invented by *Boethius. For its origin
in fifth-century Greece see EDUCATION 3.

quae'stio, at Rome, a standing criminal court;
see LAW, AT ROME 1.

Quaestiō'nēs, see PAPINIAN.

Quaestiō'nēs convīviā'lēs, etc., see PLUTARCH 3.

quaestors, magistrates at Rome; in the early
republic they were two officers chosen by the
consuls and acting as their deputies in administering criminal justice. Soon after 451 BC the
quaestors became properly constituted magistrates elected annually by the people (see
DECEMVIRI); in 421 their number was increased
to four, of whom two administered the state
treasury, *aerarium*, and were called in consequence *quaestores aerarii* or *urbani* ('of the city').
Four more were instituted in 267 and others
added later as the number of Roman provinces
increased and financial officers were required.
Sulla fixed the total at twenty; Julius Caesar
doubled it, but the emperor Augustus returned
to the former figure. Sulla also made the office
compulsory in the *cursus honorum*, entailing
automatic entry to the senate for the holders,
and declared that 30 was the minimum age for
holding it.

quantity, in metric, see METRE, GREEK 1 and
PROSODY.

quattuo'rviri viis purga'ndis, see VIGINTISEX-
VIRATE.

Quinqua'trus, in Roman religion, a festival
celebrated on 19–23 March, starting five (*quinque*) days after the Ides, whence perhaps its
name. The first day commemorated the birthday of the goddess Minerva; the last day was the
*Tubilustrium. The festival was celebrated
especially by those whose activities were under
the care of the goddess, such as spinners,
weavers, and dyers.

quinque'nnium Nerō'nis ('Nero's five years'),
phrase applied to the early years of the reign of
the emperor Nero (AD 54–68), viewed, in
retrospect, and in contrast with the horrors of
his later years, as a Golden Age.

Quinti'lian (Marcus Fabius Quintiliānus) (b. *c.*
AD 35; the date of his death is not known, but his
Institutio oratoria was published about AD 95).
Born at Calagurris in Spain, Quintilian was a
famous teacher of rhetoric at Rome. He may
have received all his education at Rome; at some
period he returned to Spain, whence he was
brought back by the emperor Galba. He was the
first rhetorician to receive an official salary from
the state treasury (under the emperor Vespasian), and he acquired great wealth; the Younger
Pliny was among his pupils. He also practised
advocacy in the courts. The emperor Domitian
made him consul and tutor to his great-
nephews. He retired, probably in 88, in order to
write. Before he retired he married, but his wife
died before her nineteenth birthday, and his
two sons later, at the ages of 5 and 9; the
introduction to the sixth book of his *Institutio*
makes clear his grief. His earlier work 'The
Decline of Oratory' (*De causis corruptae eloquen-
tiae*) is lost. Two collections of *Declamationēs*
('declamations') are attributed to him, probably
falsely, although some may reproduce themes
used in his school. These are rhetorical themes
on imaginary problems of conduct in various
circumstances or on problems arising out of the
conflict of laws, etc. The *Institutio oratoria*
('education of an orator'), in twelve books, is his
most famous work. It covers the training of an
orator from babyhood to the grown man. The
poet Martial called Quintilian 'the supreme
guide of wayward youth'.

Petrarch (1304–74) had only an imperfect
copy of the *Institutio*, but the Florentine
humanist Poggio Bracciolini (1380–1459) discovered a complete manuscript at the Abbey of
St Gallen (St Gall) in Switzerland in 1416. It was
first printed in 1470 and acquired a great
reputation in the Renaissance, when Quintilian's conception of the purpose of (rhetorical)
education, namely, to produce a man of good
character and cultivation and not merely a
pedant, was in harmony with that of the
humanists. See TEXTS, TRANSMISSION OF
ANCIENT 8 and EDUCATION 5.

Quinti'lius Vārus, see VARUS.

Quintus Cu'rtius, see CURTIUS.

Quintus Smyrnae'us (Quintus of Smyrna). He lived probably in the fourth century AD and was author of an extant epic poem in Greek in fourteen books known by its Latin title, the *Posthomerica* (Gk. *Ta meth' Homēron*), which filled the gap in events between Homer's *Iliad* and *Odyssey*. The work is mainly of antiquarian interest; its sources probably date from the Hellenistic age.

Quirī'nal, most northerly of the seven hills of Rome, traditionally occupied by Sabines, and one of the four regions (see REGIONES) of republican Rome. On it were many famous temples and houses, including at various periods the temple of Quirinus (see below), the residence of the king Numa and his ancient citadel, the temple of Flora, the temple of Salus, goddess of health (adorned with paintings by Fabius Pictor), the shrine of Dius Fidius, a temple of Venus Erycina, and the houses of the poet Martial and of Cicero's friend Atticus.

Quirī'nus, in Roman religion, originally the local deity (perhaps the war god) of the Sabine community settled on the Quirinal hill before the foundation of Rome. When this community came to be incorporated into *Rome (see 2), Quirinus was included among the state gods of the city with Jupiter and Mars. His festival, the Quirinalia, was celebrated on 17 February, but nothing is known of his ritual. Quirinus was identified with the deified Romulus by the Romans of the late republic (but not by Livy). He had his own *flamen, the flamen Quirinalis*.

Quirī'tēs, name given to the earliest inhabitants of Rome, Latin and Sabine (see ROME 2), which survived later in official phraseology to be applied to the Roman people in their civil capacity. It was superseded by the name *Romani* (Romans) or **populus Romanus* (Roman people). The term was not applicable to Romans when serving in the army: Caesar is said to have quelled a mutiny of his soldiers by addressing them as 'Quirites'. The origin of the name is uncertain. The Romans generally believed that it originally signified the inhabitants of the Sabine town of Curēs.

R

Rabi'rius, Gaius, subject of a speech for the defence by *Cicero (see (1) 4).

Ramnēs, one of the three *tribes of which the primitive Roman people is said to have consisted. The other two are Titiēs and Lucerēs. The origin of the names is obscure. See ROME 2.

Rānae, Latin title of the *Frogs of Aristophanes.

Rape of the Sabines, see ROME 2.

Rave'nna, ancient city of north-east Italy, to the south of the river Po, built in the manner of Venice on the lagoons which existed there at that time. After the *Visigothic invasions of AD 401 and 403 its strong and secluded location caused the emperor in the West, Honorius, son of Theodosius the Great, to move his court there from Rome. His successors for the most part followed his example, and not only the Roman emperors ruled from there until the *fall of the Roman empire in 476, but also the Gothic kings who followed them.

recension, critical examination of all the surviving manuscripts (or other evidence) for the constitution of a text, or the text based on such an examination. See TEXTUAL CRITICISM.

recurrent line, palindrome, see SIDONIUS APOLLINARIS.

Rē'gia, at Rome, the royal palace said to have been built by king *Numa at the foot of the Palatine on the edge of the Forum. The earliest foundations have been dated to the sixth and fifth centuries BC. It adjoined the temple of Vesta and the house of the Vestals. In republican times the Regia was the official headquarters of the *pontifex maximus. The building was several times burnt and restored. In 36 BC it was rebuilt of marble and on its walls were inscribed the *fasti consularēs and fasti triumphalēs (records of consuls and of triumphs at Rome).

rēgifu'gium ('flight of the king'), ceremony held at Rome on 24 February, of which all that is known is that the *rex sacrorum, after the sacrifice, concluded the ritual by running away from the *Comitium. It was thought in ancient times that this symbolized the flight of the last Tarquin king from *Rome (see 2).

Rēgi'llus, Lake, in Latium, on the shores of which the Romans in the early days of the republic, c.496 BC, defeated the Latins, who were attempting to re-establish the Tarquins at *Rome (see 4). For the intervention of the gods

Castor and Pollux see DIOSCURI. See also LATIN LEAGUE.

rēgio'nēs (sing. regio), 'regions', at Rome, the four wards into which the city was divided during the republic; these were the Suburana (see SUBURA), which included the Caelian hill, the Esquilina (the *Esquiline hill), the Collina, including the *Quirinal and Viminal hills, and the Palatina (the *Palatine hill). The emperor Augustus divided the city into fourteen new regiones.

Re'gulus, Marcus Atī'lius, Roman consul in 265 and 256 BC. In the latter year he was one of the commanders of the Roman expedition to Africa in the First *Punic War. His colleague was recalled and he was left in sole command with only 15,000 men. After defeating the Carthaginians he proposed exorbitant terms when they attempted to negotiate peace. In despair they then placed the Spartan Xanthippus in command of their army and defeated and captured Regulus (255). Later it is said that he was sent on an embassy to Rome to negotiate peace, the Carthaginians making him swear to return if the negotiations failed. He advised the Romans to continue the war, returned to Carthage, and died in captivity. The story of his death by torture (as related by Horace in Odes III. 5) made him a national hero.

religion. 1. Greek
1. *Minoan and Mycenaean religion.* Virtually nothing is known about the religion of mainland Greece until some time after the arrival of the (*Indo-European) Mycenaean Greeks c.2000 BC, but the religion of Minoan *Crete may possibly be representative of pre-Mycenaean (i.e. non-Indo-European) practice, since Mycenaean Greek influence did not reach there until after about 1450 BC; indeed, in the preceding century and a half the influence was quite the other way.

(i) It is possible to gain some knowledge of Minoan Cretan religion from the archaeological remains, votive gifts, and the scenes and figures, human or divine, depicted on them. The places of worship were at first either caves or mountain-top sanctuaries; in the latter an impressive feature was the lighting of great fires at night, apparently in honour of a goddess. Small shrines are found in the palaces, and recently temples have been discovered, a feature which was hitherto known only through iconography. Iconography has also indicated the existence of tree sanctuaries. The omnipresent cult symbols are the bull horns and the double-axe (see LABYRINTH), which seem to derive from the religious traditions of ancient Anatolia. They perhaps symbolize power, in particular the power to kill in sacrifice, which probably lay in the hands of the king. These objects, as well as the myths of *Pasiphaē and the Minotaur, suggest some sort of bull cult and sacrifice, but nothing has been found to point to a bull-god. Dancing played an important part in cult, but what exactly it is impossible to say. There are representations of numerous goddesses, possibly variants on one Mother- or *Cybelē-type goddess (but see (ii) below), e.g. the Dove Goddess, the Snake Goddess, the Mistress of the Animals. Occasionally a smaller male partner appears with the goddess.

(ii) Mycenaean Greece had an underlying indigenous, non–Indo-European tradition which resulted in different emphases being laid on what appears to have been fundamentally the Minoan religion with its female deities. But the *Linear B tablets have also revealed the names of many gods familiar from later times, thus showing that the Mycenaean religion, if not the Minoan, had a rich polytheistic system. Names appearing on the tablets include *Zeus, *Poseidon, Enyalios, Paian (see PAEAN), *Eileithyia, *Hera, either *Arēs or *Hermēs (the script is ambiguous), and Dionysus. The appearance of numerous goddesses bearing the title *Potnia*, 'mistress', confirms the importance of female deities that Minoan and Mycenaean iconography indicates, and suggests that the Minoan religion may have been more polytheistic than it appears at first sight. The mistresses are differentiated from each other by some individual designation: Mistress of Athana (perhaps indicating a connection with the city of Athens), of the Labyrinth, of the Horses, of the Grain, for example. Offerings to all the gods are generous. The economic importance of some shrines, with their priests and slaves of the god (according to the tablets) must have been considerable. A list from a Pylos tablet enumerates as gifts to Poseidon wheat, wine, one bull, ten cheeses, a ram's fleece, and honey. The order is notably the same as that of the offerings in Greek cult: first grain, then a libation of wine, then the animal sacrifice, then additional bloodless offerings, and the fleece perhaps for purification. The religious organization seems to have been integrated with the palace organization. Correspondences with later Greek religion exist side by side with deities and practices otherwise unknown; clearly the religion of the classical period was rooted in that of the Minoan–Mycenaean age, but with important differences.

2. *The Dark Age.* Despite the upheavals which followed the collapse of the Mycenaean civilization *c.*1125 BC and the great poverty of life during the subsequent Dark Age until *c.*900 BC, there was a certain amount of religious continuity, of which the clearest indication is the fact that half at least of the Mycenaean gods appearing on the Linear B tablets survived. (Two important gods who have not so far been found on these tablets are *Apollo and *Aphroditē.) Some of the festivals of the gods (and the months named after them) seem to date from Mycenaean times, as indicated by the existence of corresponding names in Athens and Ionia, which shows that they were fixed at least before the *migrations. But when life in Greece began to flourish and expand again at the beginning of the eighth century, the sacred sites in existence then very rarely, if ever, show continuity of cult from Mycenaean times, not even at such holy places as Delphi, Delos, Eleusis, or Olympia. Mycenaean votive offerings found at these places seem to have been gifts specially prized for their antiquity and deposited when the sanctuaries were founded during the Dark Age or in the eighth century. Moreover, Mycenaean remains were often subject to reinterpretation (the Mycenaean tombs on Delos regarded as the tombs of the *Hyperborean maidens, for example; see also HEROES). The type of Greek sanctuary that emerged from the Dark Age differed from what went before by the three-fold institution of the open-air altar for burnt sacrifices, the temple, and the cult-image in the temple. (In Greek religion, temples were the houses of their gods, not places where a congregation met for worship.) The oldest Greek sanctuary of this type is the Heraeum on Samos. It may be the case that many changes in Greek religious practice from Mycenaean times should be ascribed to influences from the Near East.

3. *The classical period.* The Greeks would have agreed with the historian Herodotus that it was the poets Homer and Hesiod who gave the gods their names and settled their ritual. The gods in Homer are the twelve Olympians (see GODS), who constitute a divine family of which the individual members are strongly characterized; they are essentially human in their behaviour and motivated by human desires, but differ from men in their power and in their immortality. Hesiod in the *Theogony* related them to one another in a genealogy and systematized all the many other deities of Greek polytheism. Zeus and the Olympian gods are described as the third generation to hold power; the earlier gods were of no real significance except perhaps for *Gaia (Earth). But the Greeks had many other deities apart from the twelve Olympians and there were many other aspects of the divine which Homer excluded but which were of significance in Greek religious life. *Demeter and Dionysus for example, with their emphases on fertility and on ecstasy, were important in cult in ways scarcely hinted at by Homer (see also MYSTERIES and *BACCHAE*).

In popular belief gods were to be found in every locality; every spring and river had its god or *nymph, the object of purely local cult and myth; hero-cult and the cult of the dead generally were important (see HEROES), as were the cults of phratries and demes. Worship was an open-air affair; formal processions, perhaps with musical accompaniment (see LYRIC POETRY), made their way to the altar of the god where *sacrifices were carried out. There was no separate priesthood; *priests were not always a necessary part of the proceedings, and a man might perform his own sacrifices. There was no organization remotely comparable with the Christian church, no dogma, and no firmly asserted connection between religion and morality, linked to an afterlife (except for the mystery religions). But certainly divine attitudes shown in Homer's *Odyssey* and Hesiod's *Works and Days* provided a basis for morality; by the fifth century Zeus was regarded as the upholder of justice, and for the philosophers it was self-evident that god must be good. The Apollo of the poet Pindar and of the Delphic Oracle and the Zeus of Attic tragedy had an intellectual and spiritual dimension which greatly influenced Greek moral thinking. The religious awe with which the gods were regarded is apparent in Greek art as well as literature.

The Greeks did not have a word for 'religion'; *eusebeia*, 'piety', is the word that comes nearest to the idea. Piety lay in the performance of traditional rituals and in the observance of traditional modes of restrained behaviour and thought expressed in the Delphic maxims (see DELPHI). Performance of cult had little to do with men's ideas about god. The philosopher *Socrates seems to have been a scrupulous observer of traditional rites, but accusations of impiety were made against him because his new thoughts on the nature of the divine, particularly when spoken publicly and influentially, were taken by the unsophisticated to be an attempt to substitute new kinds of gods for the old. State gods were important for the safety of the city and were not to be interfered with. A city had its own deities for its own needs, and its particular tutelary deity, Poseidon at Corinth, Hera at Argos, Athena at Athens. The public celebration and worship of Athena at the *Panathenaic festival were tantamount to proud celebration of the city itself. As a city expanded and admitted foreigners so it admitted foreign gods also, as Athens took in the Thracian *Bendis and, influenced by special circumstances, *Pan and *Asclepius. There was no prejudice against foreign cults at home or abroad; Greeks in foreign countries naturally paid homage to the local gods, many of whom were regarded as the familiar Greek deities under different names. However, it was the bond of a common and all-pervasive religion more than any other factor that held the Greeks

together (see HELLAS and OLYMPIA), a religion which had some part to play in virtually every activity of Greek life.

4. *The post-classical period.* The old gods and the old myths finally lost their vitality among the educated classes in the *Hellenistic age, with the disappearance of the *city-state, though the simple cults of the peasantry survived. Among the educated the old religion was replaced, in so far as it was replaced at all, by philosophical systems, notably the Stoic and Epicurean. Ruler-cult became widespread in the Greek world at this time. Alexander the Great and his successors (see DIADOCHOI) were worshipped in various cities; Demetrius I Poliorcetēs of Macedon, for example, was worshipped in Athens and elsewhere. This was a political religion without true religious spirit, the worship of a king as benefactor and protector, more powerful than the discredited gods of Olympus. (For the introduction of a new god in Egypt in the fourth century BC see SERAPIS.) Later the worship of Rome and of Roman governors grew up with the growth of Roman influence in eastern politics.

As well as the references given above see also AFTERLIFE, DAIMONES, FESTIVALS, HERMAE, MAGIC, ORACLES, POLLUTION, SACRIFICES, and TYCHE.

2. Roman

1. The Latin word *religio* is of uncertain derivation, and it is a word of wide application. It may denote people's recognition of an external power that exerts a 'binding' (*ligans*) force upon them, the sense of awe or anxiety felt in a place, such as a grove or a spring, believed to be the abode of a *numen (pl. *numina*, 'will', 'spirit'), and therefore holy. King Evander in Virgil's *Aeneid* (8. 351) says of the primeval forest which clothed the Roman Capitol: 'some god (we do not know what god) has this grove for his dwelling'. People are intruders into this realm of the spirits, and they must therefore propitiate them by suitable offerings and ritual. This sense of spiritual presences permeated daily life, especially the life of the home and the fields. For instances of its influence see LARES, PENATES, JANUS, TERMINUS, VESTA. When families came together to form the first Roman community, state cult was based on the cult and ritual of the family. At first the priest was the king, and after the expulsion of the kings the title survived in the office of 'king of the sacred things', *rex sacrorum*. The festivals of the agricultural year, the harvest, the safeguarding of the boundaries, the hunting of wolves, became the concern of the state, and some of the *numina* took on a new character: *Jupiter, the spirit of the open sky (see INDO-EUROPEAN), became the deity of actions done under the heavens, the god of justice; *Mars, from an agricultural spirit, became, through the farmer-soldiers organized for battle, the god of war. New gods appeared,

especially from Etruria and Magna Graecia, as Roman horizons widened. A triad of divinities, Jupiter, Mars, and *Quirinus, was formed with their temple on the Capitoline hill; later, under Etruscan influence, the triad comprised Jupiter, *Juno, and *Minerva.

There were three ways in which mortals might approach a god: through prayer, by which a request was brought to a god's attention; through *sacrifice, by which the god might be induced to grant a request; and through *divination, by which the god's will could be made known. Religion at Rome came to govern all political activities and consequently to be manipulated for partisan purposes because of the necessity, before all state undertakings, of consulting the will of the gods by taking the *auspices. All religious ceremonial was highly ritualistic, and the most scrupulous attention was paid to the minutiae of procedure. A ceremony might be invalidated by the squeaking of a rat or the falling off of a priest's hat. When trying to get his house back Cicero declared that its consecration had been invalid because the youth performing it had stammered (see CICERO (1) 3 and 4). The formulae of invocation and prayer, and the forms of ritual, were handed down unchanged and recorded by the *colleges, so that in later times the ancient words and actions were barely understood. More attention was paid to the ritual than to the personality and attributes of the deity: it not infrequently happened that the ritual survived when the deity itself was forgotten (see FUR-RINA). The businesslike, contractual nature of the Roman religion is seen in the very frequent use of vows (vota), public and private. The public vota were undertakings given in the name of the state to offer to the gods special sacrifices, games, a share of booty, or a temple, if some peril were averted, success achieved, or prosperity assured for a certain period. Such vows were put down in writing and the record retained by the *pontifices. Similar vows might be made by private individuals, often accompanied by a votive tablet in a temple. Cloanthus vows a white bull if he is successful in the boat-race (Virgil, Aeneid 5. 235); Horace refers to the tablets of sailors escaped from shipwreck (Odes 1. 5). The person under the obligation of a vow was known as voti reus ('one bound to fulfil a vow').

The Roman attitude to the dead remains obscure. It appears to have been thought that the spirits of the dead survived, capable of influencing in some vague way the fortunes of the living. These spirits were at first regarded as hostile (see LEMURES); later the fear of them gave place to a more friendly feeling, and a sense of a bond between the living and the dead members of the family developed (see MANES and PARENT-ALIA). The idea of deities of the underworld arose, perhaps through Greek influence, the di

inferi (see DIS, PROSERPINA, and HECATE) and the di *manes, and other shadowy gods of that region, Vejovis, *Acca Larentia, and *Tarpeia.

For the cult and festivals (fēriae, English 'fair') of the various numina and deities of Roman religion, see under the names of the gods and of the festivals. See also LUSTRATIO, 'lustration'.

2. Greek influences. The primitive Roman religion, coming into contact with Greek thought largely through *Magna Graecia, was deeply modified by the Greek anthropomorphic theology, and the early Roman numina and gods were in many cases identified with the Greek gods and endowed with their attributes and the myths relating to them. Thus Jupiter was identified with Zeus, Minerva with Athena, Vulcan with Hephaestus, and so on. Greek myths supplied the element of story and of the picturesque which the Roman religion lacked. But the primitive faith in the spirits of the home and the countryside survived, especially in rural districts. The third century BC witnessed a change of attitude. Ennius translated the sceptical work of *Euhemerus, and not long after the influence of Greek philosophy was felt. The embassy of the three Greek philosophers in 155 BC (see PHILOSOPHY 2) led to study of the doctrines of the various Greek schools, of which the most important at the time were the Stoic and Epicurean. The Romans were more interested in the ethical than in the speculative side of philosophy; they also picked and chose among the doctrines of the Greeks those which suited them; and in the main it was a modified Stoicism as taught by *Panaetius and *Posidonius which appealed to them as being in accord with the qualities of pietas and gravitas which they so much admired, that is, the punctilious discharge of duties towards gods, family, and state, and self-restraint in all circumstances. The Epicurean ideal, though so ardently promoted by Lucretius, was not widely pursued. Stoicism was in close harmony with religion; it sought to reconcile polytheism with its own monotheism by representing the various gods of popular belief as diverse forms which the single deity assumes.

3. Eastern influences; emperor worship. During the second and first centuries BC new religious influences came from the East. The cult of the Magna Mater, 'great mother' (see CYBELE), was brought from Phrygia to Rome as early as 204 BC in the stress of the Second Punic War. A little later the orgiastic worship of Dionysus spread over Italy, and was suppressed with difficulty in 186 BC (see BACCHANALIA). The wars against Mithridates, king of Pontus, at the beginning of the first century BC brought to Rome the worship of Ma, the goddess of war, from Comana in Cappadocia, to be assimilated to the Italian goddess *Bellona. Contact with Egypt brought *Isis and *Osiris. But evidence of the persistence of early Italian religious beliefs

at the beginning of the empire is seen in Virgil's *Georgics*, in Ovid's *Fasti*, and in the poems of Tibullus; also in the shrines of the ancient gods (*sacrāria* and *larāria*) found in the houses of Pompeii (destroyed AD 79). Nevertheless the new foreign cults found a welcome at Rome. The worship of Isis was soon popular with the masses, and despite initial imperial disapproval, spread from Egypt throughout the empire during the first three centuries AD. The 'shaven, linen-clad' priests of Isis are mentioned by Juvenal, and there is much about the cult in the closing scenes of the *Golden Ass* of *Apuleius, who represents his hero as initiated into the rites of Isis, the supreme deity 'of the thousand names' 'whose godhead under many forms the whole world worships'. In imperial times, in spite of the government's opposition, such deities as the Phrygian *Sabazios and the Syrian *Atargatis were received at Rome, their worship extending to the provinces. In particular the cult of the Persian god of light, *Mithras, spread throughout the Roman empire from the first century AD onwards through the agency of soldiers and merchants. It was confined exclusively to men. Caesar-worship was probably suggested by contact with the East and harmonized with the tendency of the Romans to glorify the heroes of the past. The practice of regarding as a god, or at least god-like, a person who had conferred great benefits was common to both Greeks and Romans (for the Greek ruler-cult and worship of Rome in the Hellenistic age see RELIGION, GREEK 4). Julius Caesar after his death was deified in 42 BC; the emperor Augustus, realizing the value of fostering such devotion, encouraged the spread of this idea in the West in a way that would not clash with Roman religious tradition. The popular attitude is reflected in Virgil, Horace, and Ovid. As *pontifex maximus* in 13/12 BC Augustus organized the imperial cult as part of the state religion, but saw to it that it was devoted not to the living emperor but to his *genius* (tutelary spirit). Augustus and subsequent emperors were deified after their death. This cult of the emperors was the one general test of loyalty to the empire. Subjects might worship any divinity they pleased, but they also had to worship the emperor as a sign of loyalty. Fragments of ancient calendars from the Augustan period indicate an average of two celebrations a month devoted to the emperor or his family.

The oriental cults mentioned above had some influence on Stoicism by introducing a more spiritual and personal relation between god and humanity. The need to reconcile the various beliefs and philosophies led to a revival of a modified Platonism, the core of which was a form of monotheism (see NEOPLATONISM). Into this medley of religions and philosophies *Christianity came, demanding renunciation of the old and a new start, admitting no compro-

mise with alien faiths, refusing worship to the deified emperor, and demanding an exclusive allegiance. This uncompromising spirit caused the persecutions of the Christians but ensured the ultimate triumph of their faith.

The early Roman religion had hardly any obvious connection with morality. It represented merely a businesslike arrangement with the unseen powers, whose favour might be obtained on certain terms. Nevertheless, a strong morality was fostered by this seemingly cold religion, its growth unhampered by mythology. The Romans had no sacred writings except for the formulae of prayer. They were free to think what they liked about the gods: what mattered was the religious acts they performed. It was the necessity for exact fulfilment of their religious duties which promoted discipline and obedience to the state. With the development of Rome, the Romans attached to the gods their own developing sense of morality; a feeling that the gods were just served to sanction human law. In the private sphere the religion of the home, the sense of divine presence in the daily round of domestic events, calling for the maintenance of right relations (*pietas*, see 2 above) both with the gods and with the other members of the family, strengthened the family tie which was the basis of Roman society. The emphasis placed on particular virtues such as patriotism and duty led to a warmth of religious feeling being attached to these virtues, the more so as they were often seen embodied in a line of 'noble Romans', and frequent appeal to them was made by orators and historians. Thus the Roman religion is at the root of the sense of duty that marked so many Romans, duty to home, gods, and state. A national solidarity ensued, maintained by the annual state festivals of the various gods, so that religion became the sanctification of patriotism. For this reason Cicero and above all the emperor Augustus insisted on its value.

See also AUGURS, FATE, FATES, and FLAMENS.

Reme'dia amo'ris ('cures of love'), Latin poem in elegiacs by *Ovid, of some 800 lines. It professes to give instructions for overcoming unfortunate or misplaced love, by hunting, travel, agricultural occupations, avoidance of wine and of the love poets, and other less innocuous precepts.

Rēmus, see ROME 2.

repetu'ndae ('restitution'; in full, *res repetundae*, 'restitution of property'). When a Roman provincial governor returned to Rome, he was examined by the senate upon his administration of the province. Complaints against him by provincials, typically of extortion, were brought before special *ad hoc* tribunals until by a Calpurnian law of 149 BC there was established the first of Rome's standing criminal courts to try cases for the recovery of damages, *quaestio de* *rebus repetundis.* The penalty was simple restitution. See LAW, AT ROME 1 (ii).

republic, Roman. The Latin words *res publica* mean 'affairs affecting the state', 'the state' itself, or 'the constitution' of the state. The Roman constitution was a republic in the modern sense of the word, in that the supreme power rested with the people; arbitrary rule by an individual (monarchy or tyranny) or by a small group (oligarchy) was renounced, and the right to take part in political life was given to all adult male citizens (but not the right to take an equal part; compare DEMOCRACY). For the beginnings of the republic at Rome see ROME 3. Under the republic a man's political role was determined by his wealth (see CENSUS and ROME 2). The republic, in the constitutional sense, lasted from the expulsion of the kings in 510 BC to the death of Mark Antony in 30 BC (see ROME 3–7).

Nominally a democracy in that all laws had to be approved by an assembly of citizens, the republic was in fact organized as an aristocracy or broad-based oligarchy, governed by a fairly small group of about fifty noble families (see NOBILES) who regularly held all the *magistracies. A man could become noble himself and ennoble his descendants by holding the highest magistracy, the *consulship, but to maintain the status it was also necessary for his descendants to continue to be elected to high (*curule) magistracies. Throughout the republic the highest political, military, and religious offices were monopolized by the nobles. Below this rank there was a class of aristocrats drawn from a wider circle who were not noble but who had become members of the *senate (i.e. were now of senatorial rank) through holding important magistracies, and who were ambitious, talented, and above all rich; senators were expected to have substantial means, but were not permitted to enrich themselves by taking a direct part in business activites. Below the rank of senator, but sometimes the wealthiest men in the state, were the *equites* (see EQUESTRIAN ORDER); their wealth was usually acquired through business activities. This was the class whose members had the funds to stand for high magistracies and if successful gain admittance to the senate (see above and see also NOVUS HOMO). Standing for a magistracy was a very expensive business; the candidate's dignity (and sometimes his safety) required that he should be accompanied by a large retinue, which had to be paid, and money gifts were expected by members of his own *tribe or *century in return for their support. These gifts did not constitute bribery, which also might be resorted to (and was illegal). Magistracies had to be held in a fixed order (see CURSUS HONORUM) before a candidate could hold the highest office of all, the consulship. The two consuls, who had exactly equal authority, were in charge of the state for their year of office, their powers limited by the laws and by each other's potential veto and that of the ten *tribunes.

Citizens exercised their political rights in assemblies and were divided into (35) tribes or (193) centuries according to the nature of the assembly (see COMITIA). In elections and all other matters put to the assemblies, decision was reached by the votes of a majority of these groups; an individual's vote merely helped determine that of his group. The groups of the rich and powerful voted first; those to which the poorest people were alloted voted last. Since the result was declared as soon as a simple majority was reached, the last groups rarely voted at all. Voting took place only at Rome, with the consequence that those living in rural areas were usually unable to vote. The assemblies were not deliberative or debating bodies; they could only approve or reject policy that had been decided elsewhere. The sole deliberating body was the senate, which decided upon all policy, relating to both home and foreign affairs. Membership of the senate, once obtained, was for life (although expulsion was possible; see CENSORS). A citizen was not free to address an assembly without the consent of the magistrates and tribunes, who alone had the right to summon a public meeting and to debate. The members of the assembly could only express an unofficial opinion, by shouting for example.

This organization was reflected in the towns (*municipia*) throughout Italy; their citizens were also (in the later republic) citizens of Rome (see ROME 6) but the towns retained local autonomy, with their own senate and senators (known as *decuriones*).

See also DICTATOR.

Republic (Gk. *Politeia*), dialogue in ten books by *Plato. The traditional English title is derived from the Latin translation, *Respublica*, of the Greek title, and is perhaps misleading. The original meaning is closer to 'society' or 'the state'. The *Republic* was written in the early years of the *Academy, the school which Plato founded to give a philosophical education to those embarking on a political career. It is an exposition of the principles on which an ideal society, in Plato's view, should be based. The rulers ('guardians') are to be philosopher-kings who alone have knowledge of the ideas of Justice and the Good (see PLATO 4 and 5); they will rule in the interests of the majority, who have only limited perception. Book 1 has the conversational form of an early Socratic dialogue (see PLATO 2), but the rest of the work is a more or less continuous exposition by *Socrates of what one must suppose to be Plato's own views on society at the time of writing (about 375 BC). The interlocutors are Socrates, an old man Cephalus (father of the orator *Lysias) and his son Polemarchus, Thrasymachus a sophist, and Plato's brothers Glaucon and Adeimantus.

The discussion takes place at the house of Cephalus.

The dialogue starts with the question 'What is justice?', which at its simplest means 'Why should we be good?' The conventional definition offered by the poet Simonidēs, that it means giving a person his due, is shown to be inadequate. Thrasymachus rejects conventional morality and maintains that human behaviour is, and should be, guided by self-interest. Socrates reduces Thrasymachus to silence, but Glaucon and Adeimantus remain unsatisfied and restate his case for him. Glaucon argues that justice is a matter of expediency, and that we would all be unjust to our own advantage if we could. Adeimantus argues that justice is pursued only for mercenary reasons. Socrates must show that justice is preferable to injustice for its own sake and not for the rewards it brings. Socrates suggests that justice will best be seen in the macrocosm of a perfect city-state, and if discovered there, can be found by analogy in individuals. Accordingly Socrates proceeds to construct the ideal state. This is seen to consist of three classes, guardians or magistrates (in whose education Plato is particularly interested), auxiliaries or soldiers, and producers. In the first resides the wisdom of the state, in the second its courage. Temperance or restraint must be present in all three classes, while political justice is that which keeps each class to its proper functions. Similarly, individuals have the qualities of the three classes present in their souls, but in varying proportions. They are wise in respect of the rational element in them, courageous and moved by generous impulses in respect of the spiritual element, and they are moved to satisfy their appetites. In a disciplined individual, spirit and appetite are subordinated to reason; justice consists in the harmony of all these elements. The discussion of the ideal state is continued; Socrates' proposal for the community of women and children is explained, and it is shown that for the efficient working of the constitution the supreme power must be in the hands of philosophers. Socrates expounds the proper education of the guardians (from which the misleading tales of the poets must be excluded) and the nature of true knowledge, which is not of the objects and images of the world of the senses, but of the realities of the intellectual world, apprehended by pure intelligence. The theory of Ideas or Forms (see PLATO 4 and 5) is developed; and the liberating nature of right education is illustrated by the simile of men chained in a subterranean cave representing, in Plato's view, the general human condition, who see only the shadows of objects behind them thrown by firelight on the wall in front of them, so that they take these shadows for the only realities: the guardians will struggle out of the cave into the world of knowledge and wisdom. Socrates resumes (book 8) the subject of the various types of political organization and personal character, and traces the process of degeneration from the perfect type and the perfect man, namely aristocracy and the aristocratic man, through four stages to the worst, namely tyranny and the tyrannical man. Finally the rewards of virtue are considered, chief among these being the reward that the soul receives in the life after death, the soul being immortal, but rewards are merely a secondary consideration. The nature of this afterlife is indicated in the tale of Er the son of Armenius, who twelve days after his death returned to life and described what he had seen in the other world.

Respo'nsa, see PAPINIAN.

Return of the Heracleidae, see HERACLEIDAE.

Revenues (Gk. *Poroi ē peri prosodōn*, Lat. *De vectigalibus*), one of the minor works of *Xenophon, written not before 355 BC and probably his last work. The ascription to him has been doubted.

Xenophon discusses various means of increasing the revenue of Athens, notably by encouraging the resident aliens (metics), who were engaged in manufacturing and trade generally, and by making ingenious suggestions such as for investment in accommodation that could be rented to visitors, and in slaves to be hired out to operators of the Laurium silver-mines (a transaction from which the author expected a return of 33 per cent on the capital expended). See also ISOCRATES 5.

rex sacrō'rum ('king of the sacred things'), at Rome after the expulsion of the kings (510 BC), a priest whose duty it was to perform some of the king's religious functions. He was a patrician, appointed for life, and unlike the *pontifex maximus* (to whom he was superior in rank and precedence though inferior in religious authority) disqualified from holding any other office. He and his wife (*rēgīna*, 'queen', who had some religious duties) performed certain state sacrifices; before the publication of the calendar it fell to him to announce to the people the festivals of each month.

Rhadama'nthys (Lat. Rhadamanthus), in myth, son of Zeus and *Europa; he did not die but went to *Elysium, where he became a ruler; in some accounts he was made judge of the dead in the Underworld, with *Minos and *Aeacus.

Rhampsinī'tus, Rameses (III?), pharaoh of Egypt, of whom the Greek historian Herodotus (2. 121) tells the following folk-tale. He had a treasury built, in the wall of which the builder secretly left a movable stone. After his death the builder's sons, by means of this, were able to creep in and steal the treasure. The king, finding the seals of the door unbroken but the treasure diminished, set a man-trap, in which one of the brothers was caught. He immediately called to his brother and bade him cut off his head and take it away to avoid detection, which was done. (Compare TROPHONIUS.)

rhapsode (or rhapsodist; *rhapsōdos*, 'one who stitches songs together'), in Greece, a professional reciter of poetry, usually of Homer (i.e. epic), but also of other poems. Rhapsodes were a familiar sight at public festivals and games, where they competed for prizes. Plato's dialogue *Ion* is a satire on their pretensions.

Rhēa, in Greek myth, one of the *Titans, daughter of Uranus and Gaia, wife (and sister) of *Cronus, mother of Zeus and other Olympian gods. She was often identified with *Cybelē. The Romans identified her with *Ops.

Rhēa Si'lvia, see ILIA.

Rhēsus, tragedy doubtfully attributed to *Euripides; if it is his work, it would appear to be earlier than any other of his extant plays.

Rhesus is a dramatization of the tenth book of Homer's *Iliad*. The Greeks have been driven back to their ships, and Hector sends the Trojan Dolon by night to spy out their intentions. Rhesus, king of Thrace, arrives with his army to support the Trojans. Hector reproaches him for his delay; Rhesus replies proudly and confidently, and then retires to rest. Odysseus and Diomedēs enter the Trojan camp; they have killed Dolon after learning the password from him. Directed by the goddess Athena they fall upon the sleeping Thracians, kill Rhesus, and lead away his horses. His charioteer relates his death by an unknown hand and accuses Hector of his murder. Hector is exculpated by the Muse Terpsichorē, mother of Rhesus, who descends from heaven to carry off her son's body.

rhētor (Gk. and Lat. *rhētor*), at Athens originally, a public speaker in the *ecclesia*, a politician; later at Athens, and at Rome, a teacher of public speaking, a rhetorician.

rhetoric, the theoretical art of speaking so as to persuade; it is *oratory reduced to a system which can be taught. In the Greek world rhetoric was reputedly first developed in Sicily in the mid-fifth century BC and further refined by the *sophists, most of whom regarded a knowledge and command of it essential for men embarking on a political career. During the first century BC (as a consequence of the spread of Greek culture) the study of rhetoric became an important part of Roman education and exercised an increasing influence on Roman literature during the empire (see EDUCATION). The elements of rhetoric were treated under five headings: invention, arrangement, diction, memory, delivery. 'Invention' was the discovery (*inventio*) of the relevant material; 'arrangement' entailed putting the materials together in

a structured way; 'diction' concerned finding the appropriate style of speech for the occasion, grand, middle, or plain (sometimes known as low). 'Memory' gave guidance on how to memorize speeches; 'delivery' gave guidance on the techniques of public speaking. The following deal with rhetoric: *Aristotle (see 4 (v)); Cicero, *Brutus*, *De inventione*, *De optimo genere oratorum*, *De oratore*; *Demetrius (3); *Dionysius of Halicarnassus, *On the Arrangement of Words*; *Longinus on the Sublime*; Quintilian, *Institutio oratoria*; Tacitus, *Dialogus de oratoribus*; and the *Rhetorica ad Herennium* below.

Rhēto'rica ad Here'nnium, Latin treatise on oratory in four books, written between 86 and 82 BC and addressed to C. Herennius by an unknown author; some attribute it to a certain Cornificius, on slight evidence in Quintilian. It is ascribed in the manuscripts to Cicero, and it seems connected in some way with Cicero's early *De inventione*. *Rhetoric is treated under its five headings; the section on style is the oldest surviving treatment in Latin. The work is modelled on Greek writers, and is interesting as a relatively early example of Latin prose.

Rhodes (Rhŏdos), most easterly of the Aegean islands, close to the mainland of Caria (in Asia Minor), colonized by Dorian Greeks who founded three city-states, Iālysus, Lindus, and Camīrus. Lindus was itself the founder of Gela in Sicily, Phasēlis in Lycia, and Soli in Cilicia. The three Rhodian cities amalgamated in 408 BC into one state with a new federal capital which took its name from the island. The new city was built upon a grid system designed by the town-planner *Hippodamus. During the fifth century BC Rhodes had been a member of the *Delian League, paying tribute to Athens, and Rhodians had been forced to serve against Syracuse and Gela, but in 412 BC Rhodes defected to the Peloponnesians. It joined the Second Athenian League but again revolted in 357 BC (see ATHENS 2 (iv)). During the third century it was a considerable naval power, standing for freedom of trade and suppressing piracy. In the struggles which followed the death of Alexander the Great in 323 BC it tried to follow a policy of neutrality. But Antigonus I, alarmed at the friendly relations between Rhodes and Ptolemy (ruler of Egypt), sent his son Demetrius Poliorcētēs ('besieger') against the island. The capital endured a long and famous siege in 304 at his hands, and Demetrius (having earned his sobriquet) was finally obliged to come to terms with the Rhodians. It was after this that the celebrated *Colossus of Rhodes, a huge statue of the Sun-god, was erected at the entrance to the harbour. Rhodes was associated with Pergamum in a policy of friendship to Rome at the time of the Second Macedonian War and the war with Antiochus III (the *Seleucid king of Asia Minor) in the early second century BC.

After the latter's defeat Rhodes was rewarded with a portion of the opposite coasts of Caria and Lycia, but it soon roused the jealousy of Rome by its independent attitude, especially in the Third Macedonian War (172–168 BC), and was deprived of these new possessions. Its trade was also severely damaged by the Roman free port of *Delos, and sank into relative insignificance. The capital was captured and pillaged by Cassius in 43 BC.

Rhodes was a considerable literary centre; it was the birthplace of *Panaetius and the seat of the school founded by his pupil *Posidonius. *Hipparchus the mathematician probably spent part of his life there. The city was destroyed by an earthquake in 225 BC and again c. AD 155; as rebuilt, it was described by Aelius *Aristeides as the most beautiful of Greek cities. Rhodian maritime law was famous, and portions of it may have passed in later times into that of Venice. Pindar's seventh Olympian ode was written for the victory of the Rhodian boxer Diagoras.

Rhodō'pē or **Rhodō'pis,** Greek courtesan, said to have been a Thracian and a fellow-slave of Aesop, and to have been taken to Naucratis in Egypt. *Aelian relates that one day while Rhodope was bathing, an eagle flew away with one of her slippers and dropped it into the lap of the pharaoh of the day, Psammetichus. The king was struck with the beauty of the slipper, had a search made for the owner, and married her. There was a story (rejected by Herodotus) that she built the third pyramid; Herodotus confuses her with the courtesan Doricha (see SAPPHO).

rhopa'lic verse, verse of which each word in a line contains one more syllable than that before it; e.g. *lux verbo inducta, peccantibus auxiliatrix* ('Light | revealed | by the Word, | a comforter | of all those in sin'). The name is derived from Greek *rhopalon,* 'club', suggesting the gradual increase. See AUSONIUS.

roads

1. *Greek.* The Greeks had a network of roads, levelled but mostly unpaved, many of them connecting cities with the great religious centres, but most serving also the normal purposes of trade and communication. Some stretches of paved road have survived near important sanctuaries such as Delphi. Several roads centred on Olympia. The important roads in Attica led from Athens to Piraeus, Eleusis, Laurium, and Marathon, and from Eleusis to Megara and Plataea. The main road from the Peloponnese to central Greece is still clearly visible, 3 m. (10 ft.) wide, designed for carts. For the *diolkos* at the Isthmus see CORINTH, ISTHMUS OF.

2. *Roman.* The great network of Roman roads was created for military and political, rather than economic, purposes. It was intended for the maintenance of Roman authority in conquered territories and for the defence of Roman frontiers, but it also fostered trade and friendly communication. According to tradition it was initiated by Appius *Claudius the Censor who in 312 BC (during the Second Samnite War; see ROME 4) began the construction of the road which bore his name, the Via Appia (Appian Way), Rome's principal route to south Italy and beyond, running in a straight line south-east from Rome to Tarracina on the Bay of Naples and thence to Capua. (By 244 it had been extended to Beneventum and Brundisium.) An alternative line of communication with Capua was provided by the Via Latina which took an inland route over Mount Algidus and the valleys of the Trerus and Līris, probably having its origin in the Roman conquests of the fifth and early fourth centuries. Pyrrhus and Hannibal both used it.

The other principal roads of the republican period, bearing the names of the censors or consuls who had them constructed, were as follows. The Via Flaminia (in north Italy) was built by the censor C. Flaminius in 220 BC (see PUNIC WARS 2) across the Apennines to Arīminum (Rimini); it was restored several times, notably by the emperor Augustus, whose triumphal arch may still be seen in the main street of Rimini. It was extended to Placentia under the name of Via Aemilia, and helped in the swift Romanization of Cisalpine Gaul; the district through which it passed is still named Emilia. The Via Aurelia, of uncertain date but presumably of the second century BC, ran north-west along the coast from Rome to Genoa. The road running north from Rome through Etruria to Arretium was the Via Cassia, built in the late third or the second century BC, and extended to Bononia in 187 BC by the Via Flaminia Minor. Often confused with it is the Via Clodia which probably followed the same line to near Veii, whence it turned north-west to Saturnia (in central Etruria). The Via Annia (perhaps 153 BC) ran from Aquileia to Bononia, and the Via Popillia linked Ariminum, Atria, and Altinum with Aquileia. The Popillius who built this last is often accredited, probably wrongly, with the extension to the Via Appia from Capua to Rhegium in south Italy. The Via Caecilia connected Rome with the Adriatic by a direct route across the Apennines, but its course is not known. The Via Domitia was a very ancient route from the Rhône to Spain, but owed its name to Cn. Domitius, consul in 121 BC. After the conquest of Macedonia the Via Egnātia, c.130 BC, was the main route from Rome to the East. It began on the eastern Adriatic coast starting from two points, one at Dyrrhachium (Epidamnus), the other at Apollonia; the two branches soon joined, crossed the Balkan range (following the line of an ancient trade route), descended to Thessalonika, and eventually reached Byzantium. (See also VIA SACRA.)

The road system was greatly extended under the empire, spreading through Byzantium far into Asia, to the Euphrates and the Red Sea. It was particularly developed in Gaul; several roads crossed the Alps. In Britain, Roman roads radiated principally from London (Londinium) but also from the tribal capitals such as Canterbury (Durovernum) and Chichester (Regnum). Their Roman names, if they existed, are not known; such apparently Latin names as the Via Devana (running through Cambridge) are of modern origin. The names by which the main roads are known today—Watling Street, Foss(e) Way, Ermine Street, Dere Street, Akeman Street, and Stane Street—were current in Saxon times (and were sometimes applied, as in some cases they still are, confusingly, to other roads in different parts of the country). Watling Street, the main highway from the Channel ports of east Kent through the Midlands to the Welsh border, runs from Dover (Dubris) through Canterbury to London and thence through St Albans (Verulamium) and Towcester (Lactodorum) to Wroxeter (Viroconium, also known as Uriconium, crossing Foss Way at High Cross (Venonae). The same name is given to the north–south road running from Chester (Deva) through Wroxeter to the river Severn and the fort at Caerleon (Isca Silurum). Foss Way runs from the mouth of the river Axe in Devon through Bath (Aquae Sulis), Cirencester (Corinium) and Leicester (Ratae) to Lincoln (Lindum). Ermine Street runs from London to York (Eburacum), continuing as Dere Street to Corbridge (Corstopitum) and into Scotland, by Newstead (the fort Trimontium) to Inveresk and the Antonine Wall. Akeman Street runs from St Albans to Cirencester, and Stane Street from London to Chichester. In many parts modern roads follow the lines of these roads, and in some places there is still visible evidence of the actual Roman construction.

The most important Roman roads were generally 2.5–5 m. (8–16 ft.) wide, running with remarkable straightness in open country, and in broken country keeping to the high ground and avoiding river valleys. Their alignments often demonstrate the accuracy of long-distance surveying by the Romans. Beacons may have been used to obtain a preliminary orientation. Methods of construction vary with the material available, but usually roads were built on a foundation of large stones overlaid with small stones and gravel, the surface being often cobbled or even paved with large blocks. Main roads were often carried on a high causeway (*agger*). Minor roads were less carefully designed and constructed, but all roads were built with a camber for drainage into side ditches. Milestones gave the distance from some centre, and sometimes the name of the constructor of the road and the emperor under whom it was built, thus furnishing historically valuable information (see MILIARIUM AUREUM). On the principal roads there were posting-houses (*mansionēs*) at short intervals, with relays of horses, where travellers might stay (see POSTAL SERVICE). In 20 BC Augustus established highway commissioners, *curatorēs viarum*; the cost of the roads was probably divided between the public treasury, local authorities, and the owners of the land, but the emperors often made large personal contributions. Roads of only minor importance were funded locally.

Rōbī'gus (or Robigo, the female equivalent), in Roman religion, the god of 'blight' who averted red mildew or rust from crops. He was propitiated and the pest averted by the annual sacrifice of a rust-coloured dog at the festival of the Robigalia on 25 April.

Roman age of Greek literature, term used to describe Greek literature written from the time when Rome subjugated the Mediterranean world, i.e. from the second half of the second century BC, to AD 529, when the emperor Justinian closed the schools of philosophy at Athens and ended the long history of that city as the focus of Greek intellectual life and culture. See also SOPHISTIC, SECOND.

romance, see NOVEL.

Roman empire, Roman emperors, see ROME 9–11.

Roman law, see LAW, ROMAN.

Rome (Rōma)

1. *General topography.* Ancient Rome stood on the left bank of the river Tiber, about 22 km. (14 miles) from the sea, in the territory of *Latium near its northern boundary, south of Etruria. The site was already inhabited in the second half of the second millennium BC. According to tradition the original settlement in this area was on the Palatine hill, one of a group of hills some 30–50 m. (100–160 ft.) high near the river. This settlement was on a site later referred to as Roma Quadrāta ('square Rome'), the fortified city supposed to have been built by Romulus (see 2 below). Archaeology shows that this settlement expanded in the mid-eighth century BC and that soon afterwards the Quirinal hill was settled by a different, possibly Sabine, community. Tradition states that the Palatine settlement was extended first to include the region known as the Septimontium ('seven peaks'), the seven *montēs* or peaks apparently being the three spurs of the Palatine, the three of the Esquiline hill, and the Caelian hill, enclosed within a sacred boundary, *pomerium. (The exact meaning and location of the Septimontium remains obscure.) This region was united in its turn with a kindred settlement on the

opposite hills, the Quirinal and Viminal. Within the boundaries of the combined city was included the site of the later Forum ('market-place'); archaeological evidence shows that this area was drained and a market-place built c.625–575. Reputedly under the kingship of Servius Tullius (see below) but more likely in the fourth century BC, the city was enclosed within a wall (the Servian wall, so called) and now comprised the seven hills of Rome (including but to be distinguished from the Septimontium mentioned above), namely the Palatine, Aventine, Capitoline, Caelian, Esquiline, Viminal, and Quirinal. (In Latin, the first five are termed montēs, 'peaks', 'mountains', the last two collēs, 'hills', but the distinction bears no apparent relation to their heights.) The four regions were also created at this time (see REGIONES). Under the kings Rome was a great hill-top fortress, with the Capitoline hill (see CAPITOLIUM) equivalent to the Acropolis at Athens, and with the Aventine as a religious centre.

Under the republic the *Campus Martius ('field of Mars') near the river became a military and athletic training ground, and civic activities became gradually concentrated in the Forum. The Palatine became a desirable residential area; markets were gradually ousted from the Forum by state buildings and spread to an area behind it, and to the bank of the Tiber. The city became crowded, especially in the valleys which served as its main routes, and as early as the third century BC tenement houses were being built, of which later writers bitterly complain (see HOUSES AND FURNITURE 2). Very many temples were built in the early years. *Aqueducts came later, the earliest in 312, 272, and 144 BC, and the second century BC saw intense building activity of every kind. Sulla, Pompey, and Julius Caesar all had their grandiose schemes. Of Caesar's, only the Forum Julium remains; the emperor Augustus built the Forum Augustum, a modest palace on the Palatine, and three new aqueducts, and divided the city into fourteen new regions. His successors Tiberius and Caligula both made their mark, the latter more especially by his *Circus, the site of the many Christian martyrdoms. Nero's contributions, the Domus Aurea (see GOLDEN HOUSE), Colossus, and Via Sacra, attest his Hellenistic taste. Trajan marked his reign with the monumental Forum Trajanum, and his successor Hadrian added other notable buildings to the architecture of Rome. During this time the city had been increasing in size; it was ultimately enclosed by Aurelian (emperor AD 270–5) with a wall which included not only an enlarged area on the left bank but a portion of the Janiculum hill on the right bank of the Tiber.

2. *Legendary origins and regal period.* The surviving traditions about the foundation and early history of Rome depend upon historians and others, most of whom are writing more than 500 years after the event (see HISTORIOGRAPHY 2), by which time it was not easy to distinguish between fact and legend. Moreover, a desire that Rome should share in some way in Greek achievements had led the Romans to connect their history with that of Greece: for the legend that gave the first Romans, through him, a Trojan ancestry, see AENEAS. To reconcile this Trojan origin with the tradition that Rome was a colony of Alba Longa (the chief city of the *Latin League) and to fill the gap between the supposed date of the fall of Troy (1184 BC) and the foundation of Rome in the eighth century by Romulus and Remus, these two were represented as Aeneas' decendants through their mother, and a series of Alban kings was invented, of whom Ascanius, son of Aeneas, was the first. This story was well established by the beginning of the third century BC. The last of the series was Amulius, who ousted his brother Numitor, the rightful king, and made Numitor's only child, Rhea Silvia or Ilia, a Vestal Virgin, so as to ensure that she did not marry and produce an heir. But she became by the god Mars the mother of twin sons, Romulus and Remus. Amulius imprisoned the mother and threw the children into the Tiber. They were washed ashore and suckled by a she-wolf until discovered by the royal herdsman Faustulus, who with his wife Acca Larentia brought them up. They were eventually recognized, overthrew Amulius, and restored Numitor to Alba Longa. They then decided to found a new settlement where they had been washed ashore.

An omen in the form of a flight of birds settled the kingship in favour of Romulus. He proceeded to build the city named after him on the Palatine hill, an event for which various dates in the ninth and eighth centuries have been given: 753 BC has proved the most generally accepted date for the foundation of Rome. Remus showed his contempt for it by jumping over the beginnings of the city wall, and was thereupon killed by Romulus or one of his companions. Romulus expanded his new city by encouraging runaway slaves and even criminals to settle there. To secure wives for his people he invited the neighbouring *Sabines to witness games (the Consualia) which he was celebrating, and while these were proceeding the Romans carried off the Sabine women ('the Rape of the Sabines'). War followed, and the Sabines under Titus Tatius besieged the Capitol, then an outpost of the city. Here *Tarpeia, the daughter of the officer in command, undertook to betray the citadel on the Capitol if, she said, the Sabines would give her 'what they had on their left arms', meaning their gold bracelets. But when the Sabines broke in they rewarded her treachery by crushing her under their shields, also worn on the left arm. (In an alternative version Tarpeia was a heroine, her intention being to gain possession of the Sabine shields in order to help the Romans.) The Romans, who still held the Palatine, were after further fighting reconciled with the Sabines by the captured women, and the two peoples settled down together. Romulus subsequently disappeared from the earth, enveloped in a cloud during a thunderstorm. His divinity was at once proclaimed by those who witnessed the miracle (see QUIRINUS).

According to tradition Rome was ruled after Romulus by a succession of six kings, Numa Pompilius, Tullus Hostilius, Ancus Marcius, Tarquinius Priscus, Servius Tullius, and Tarquinius Superbus ('Tarquin the Proud'), some at least of whom have a historical basis. There is no doubt, for example, that there were kings in early Rome, and that the dynasty of the Tarquins was *Etruscan and not native. From inscriptions and graffiti it is clear that the inhabitants of early Rome spoke Latin, but that there was a brief period when Etruscans dominated the city. The story of Rome's Trojan origins is false, but the tradition that it was a colony founded by the Latins of Alba may have some truth. Some religious festivals (the Lupercalia, Septimontium, the feast of the Argei), which survived into much later times, seem also to reflect different stages of the unification of separate communities into one city. The king (*rex*) was elected by the people and advised by a council (*senatus*, 'senate') of elders (*patrēs*) who comprised the heads of the clans (*gentēs*), into which families with a common ancestor and their dependants were grouped; the people (*populus*) were divided into three tribes, Ramnēs, Titiēs, and Lucerēs (the names are probably Etruscan) and into thirty *curiae* or territorial divisions, 'wards'. The original assembly of the people was known as the *comitia curiata*.

There appear to have been many wars during the early regal period as a result of which Roman territory was enlarged. Rome destroyed Alba, according to legend, when Tullus Hostilius was king (see HORATII AND CURIATII), and under Ancus Marcius founded a colony at Ostia near the mouth of the Tiber. Under Tarquinius Priscus (Tarquin, said to be an adventurer, half Greek and half Etruscan, who came to try his fortune at Rome and won the throne) and his two successors, Etruscan influence became strong at Rome. The Etruscans, a powerful commercial and industrial people, may have conquered Rome; or the Etruscan cities may have accepted Tarquin as their king. *Servius Tullius, a man of humble origin, enlarged the city, enclosing it, it is said, by the wall that bears his name. Other important works, the Cloaca Maxima and the temple of Jupiter on the Capitol for example, are said to have been executed by one or other of the Tarquins.

To Servius Tullius are attributed certain administrative reforms, important features which endured throughout the republican period. He created four urban (and perhaps sixteen rural) tribes (see TRIBES 2; by 241 BC the number was increased to thirty-five in total) based on locality rather than kinship; the census or registration of the citizens and their property, and the *tributum* or wartime tax on property, were dependent upon this organization. Servius Tullius further divided the people into five classes according to their wealth, and the classes into *centuriae*, 'centuries', which for most purposes replaced the older *curiae*; the important assembly of the people was now the *comitia centuriata*, in which the preponderant power was in the hands of the richest class (see REPUBLIC, ROMAN). These reforms had a later political effect in substituting residence and wealth as qualifications for civic rights, instead of birth. Tarquinius Superbus, the last of the kings, is said to have consulted the oracle of Apollo at Delphi about a proposed colony, an illustration of the close relations in early times between Italy and Greece.

The Tarquins were expelled, and with their departure in 510 BC the probable domination by Etruscans was ended; despite the efforts at restoration by Lars Porsen(n)a, monarchy was abolished at Rome. The struggle is reflected in the famous legend of the outrage on *Lucretia.

3. *The republican period: internal struggles.* The constitution which followed the expulsion of the kings in 510 BC was an aristocratic republic. The king was replaced by two magistrates elected annually (*praetors, later called *consuls), invested with *imperium, who had to be patricians (see below). Later, in times of national crisis, their powers might be temporarily superseded by the appointment of a *dictator. The senate retained its former position as council, but was now the real governing force in the state. The history of the republic during the next 250 years consists in the main of two struggles: an internal class struggle (often known as the conflict of the *orders), during which the republican constitution was hammered out and which ended finally in 287 BC with a compromise; and an external struggle with the surrounding peoples, at first mainly defensive but subsequently aggressive, at the end of which Rome emerged supreme as the head of a confederacy embracing all Italy.

The Roman citizens were juridically divided into two 'orders' or 'estates', *patricians and *plebeians (*plebs*), the rich and the poor, the politically powerful and the politically weak. This division almost certainly antedated the end of the monarchy, but was more marked after that event. The plebeians sought to redress their grievances by threats (and acts) of secession (i.e. withdrawal to form a separate community, a state within a state). The grievances of the plebeians were not the same for all. Those of the poorer members arose from their desire for personal security against the arbitrary oppression of the patrician magistrates (see CLAUDIUS, APPIUS), for land, and for relief from debt. The wealthier plebeians desired full social and political equality with the patricians, especially admission to the consulship. During the struggle the plebeians established their own magistrates (tribunes and aediles) and assembly (*concilium plebis*), and eventually forced the patricians to recognize these. The power of the tribunes was gradually enlarged until they had gained the right of veto (*intercessio*) over all acts of the magistrates.

An early turning-point occurred in 451 BC when, after a long struggle, the plebeians obtained the appointment of a commission of ten (*decemviri*) who drew up and published the *Twelve Tables of the law, knowledge of which had hitherto been confined to the magistrates who administered it, the patrician *pontificēs*. These Twelve Tables, the basis of the future Roman law, were of immense value, not only by their definition of rights and of offences, but also as an instrument of education (see PROSE 2). However, the plebeians were not satisfied with the contents, which revealed the full extent of the disabilities under which they lay. A secession of the plebeians to the Aventine hill brought about substantial improvements to their rights. The *concilium plebis* in course of time obtained recognition as a legislative organ of the state. It elected annually the ten tribunes of the *plebs* and two aediles (supervisors of streets and markets, with a general disciplinary role). In 445, according to Livy, a law enacted by the tribune Gaius Canuleius sanctioned inter-marriage between patricians and plebeians, which had been expressly forbidden by the Twelve Tables. For many years during the period 445–376 BC military tribunes, *tribūni militares consulari potestate*, officers who could be plebeians and who were instituted to exercise high military command, replaced the consuls, some of whose powers were transferred to the newly established censors (443 BC).

There followed (the dates are traditional) the admission of plebeians to the quaestorship (421; but the first plebeian was actually elected in 409) and to the consulship (366); the tribunes Licinius and Sextius had made the proposal in about 376 in the 'Licinian rogations' (see LICINIAN–SEXTIAN LAWS), that the plebeians should become eligible for one of the two consulships, but had been vigorously opposed by the patricians, who were finally, after a ten-year struggle, forced to yield. Two *curule aediles had been created in 367 by the patricians, with functions similar to those of the plebeian aediles. After 366 this curule magistracy was held by patricians and plebeians in alternate years. In 356 a distinguished plebeian soldier (C. Marcius Rutilus) was appointed to

the dictatorship; in 351 he was elected to the censorship. The first plebeian praetor was elected in 337. In 304 the aedile Cn. Flavius exhibited in the Forum the calendar of *dies fasti* and *nefasti* (the days on which legal proceedings might and might not take place) and the *formulae* or rules for pleading, so that this knowledge was available to all. Four years later the plebeians gained access to the higher priesthoods, thus preventing the patricians from using religious law to thwart the political activities of the *plebs*. The end to the conflict came in 287 with the Hortensian law, prompted by an economic crisis which left the poorer classes in heavy debt. A secession was threatened, but avoided by the appointment of the plebeian Q. Hortensius as dictator. He took steps to alleviate debt and passed a law which decreed that the resolutions of the *concilium plebis*, *plebiscita*, should be as binding as the laws passed by the *comitia centuriata*.

In theory the sovereignty of the people was established and the conflict of the orders ended. The outcome of the struggle was the formation of a mixed patrician and plebeian oligarchy of *nobilēs*, who monopolized office as exclusively as the patricians alone had done hitherto, and the dominance of the senate (now composed of ex-magistrates). Although the effect of even a small group of plebeian families becoming rich and influential was to lessen hardship generally, the economic situation of the poorer people was still serious. Shortage of food and land was met to a certain extent by land distributions and the establishment of colonies, made possible by the Roman conquest of Italy (see below). Legislators also attacked the harsh laws of debt, which could reduce free men to being virtually serfs.

4. *Republican period: the conquest of Italy*. In its external relations, after the expulsion of the kings, Rome had to face assaults from every side (the legends of Lars *Porsen(n)a, Horatius *Coclēs, *Cloelia, and Mucius *Scaevola all refer to Rome's struggles with Etruria). An attack by the Latins appears to have been defeated in a great battle at Lake *Regillus (496), but a treaty with Latium for common defence was necessitated by external dangers and an alliance was negotiated with the *Latin League through Sp. Cassius in 493. The Roman territory was ravaged from the east by the hill tribes of the Apennines (Volsci and Aedui) and threatened from the north and north-east by Etruscans and Sabines. In the first half of the fifth century Romans, Latins, and Hernici survived the onslaughts of Aequi and Volsci (including events connected with the names of *Coriolanus and *Cincinnatus); in the second half Rome passed from defence to aggression and attacked the Etruscan town of Veii (some 20 km. or 12 miles from Rome), with which it had been intermittently at war for a century, probably with a view to acquiring its valuable

land (see FABIA, GENS). Veii fell after a long siege, captured by the dictator M. Furius Camillus (396). The Etruscans' defence had been indirectly weakened by invasions of Gauls (Celts) in northern and central Italy. In about 390 a body of Gauls pushed south towards Latium and utterly defeated the Roman army at the river Allia (a tributary of the Tiber). The mass of the population fled from Rome, but old men of noble birth remained behind seated in the courtyards of their houses; at first the Gauls were overawed by their silent dignity, but finally massacred them. They then sacked the city, except for the Capitol (according to the usual legend), which was bravely held by a small force under M. Manlius Capitolinus (see MAN-LIUS for the story of the geese saving the Capitol). Finally the Gauls were induced to withdraw by a payment of gold (see BRENNUS), but during their retreat they were annihilated by *Camillus and the gold was recovered. A great part of the ancient Roman records was reputed to have been lost in the destruction.

Thereafter the city was rebuilt and refortified, and Rome entered on a long and arduous period of expansion. A new treaty was imposed upon the Latins in 358 which in effect made them dependants rather than allies, and gave Rome military control of the Latin League, which fought an unsuccessful war of independence in 340–338. The League was dissolved; some of their cities were incorporated in the Roman state; others were forced to make separate agreements with Rome by which they were required to furnish troops when called upon and were subjected to certain restrictions in the matter of trade and intermarriage (see LATIN RIGHTS). Roman interests were now spreading south into Campania, and in 326 Rome made an alliance with Neapolis (Naples). This act brought her into conflict with the *Samnites, the warlike mountain-people of the Abruzzi, east of Rome. After the First Samnite War (343–341, sometimes described as a figment of legend) Rome took control of northern Campania; the Second lasted intermittently from 327 until the Roman victory in 304, and was marked by the notorious disaster of the *Caudine Forks (321) when the consuls, misled by false information, tried to march through the narrow defile of Caudium, were encircled, and obliged to surrender. The repudiation by the senate, quite soon after this, of the terms of the capitulation was the source of increased bitterness on both sides. It is significant that the first important Roman *road, the Via Appia, was constructed for military purposes in 312. The Samnites were finally conquered in the Third Samnite War in the early third century, being defeated at Sentinum in 295 and finally subdued by 290 (see DECIUS MUS and CURIUS DENTATUS). The struggle with them had lasted for seventy years and had been exceedingly destructive.

Southern Italy was devastated by it and never recovered. The Samnites themselves, though subdued, were never reconciled. They supported Pyrrhus in 280, after which Latin colonies were planted at Aesernia and Beneventum; they rose in support of Hannibal and lost territory and population; they revolted in the Social War and fought implacably against Sulla; they supported Marius in his march to Rome. In the end the survivors were Romanized by gradual absorption.

Rome was now drawn into southern Italy, where the Greek cities of Magna Graecia were being hard pressed by Lucanian tribes. When in 282 Rome sent a defensive garrison to Thurii at that city's request, Tarentum, the richest and most powerful of the Greek cities, resented the interference in her sphere of influence, quarrelled with Rome, and when war broke out invited *Pyrrhus, king of Epirus in Greece, to her assistance. Pyrrhus landed in Italy in 280 with his troops and his elephants, as the champion of Hellenism, bringing the knowledge he had acquired of Macedonian military tactics. He won two difficult and inconclusive ('Pyrrhic') victories over the Romans, and saw that he was not strong enough to crush them. He thereupon accepted an invitation to help the Sicilians against the Carthaginians (278), and sought to make peace with Rome. But the war party there, led by the aged Appius *Claudius Caecus, prevailed, and hostilities continued. The double task Pyrrhus had undertaken was too heavy for his forces. He was defeated by M'. Curius Dentatus at Beneventum (east of Capua), abandoned his Italian and Sicilian enterprises, and left Italy in 275 to pursue a new scheme for the conquest of Greece. In the following five years (275–270) Rome captured Tarentum and completed the subjugation of south Italy. By successful wars against the Umbrians, Picentēs, and Sallentīni in 270–266 she became supreme in the whole peninsula from the Arnus and the Rubicon to the southern extremity.

Rome followed a policy of securing strategic points by means of colonies (see COLONIZATION, ROMAN 6) either of Roman citizens (colōniae Romanae), or of Roman and Latin citizens jointly (coloniae Latinae). As she extended her conquests, she dealt with each community she absorbed as appeared advisable. Those nearer were generally given Roman citizenship, in whole or in part; some were given the full franchise, others the civitas sine suffragio ('citizenship without the right to vote'). See MUNICI-PIUM. The more distant communities, known as *socii ('allies'), did not receive citizenship but were bound to Rome by treaties which defined their rights and obligations, the most privileged having ius Latii ('Latin rights'). All, citizens and allies alike, were required to render military service to Rome, but only the citizens paid direct taxes. The allies were subjected to restrictions on their political and commercial relations; otherwise they were left substantially free, and they might look forward to possible promotion to a higher status in their association with Rome.

By about 270 BC Rome had completed the subjugation of the Italian peninsula south of the river Rubicon. Peace was at last substituted for war as the normal condition of life in Italy. Rome did not force her civilization on others, but gradually local languages, cults, and customs gave way to a common culture based on the Latin language and Roman law. When Ptolemaic Egypt entered into a treaty of friendship (amicitia) with Rome in 273 it signalized the fact that Rome was now a Mediterranean power. This was the era to which Romans looked back nostalgically as to an ideal time, the formative period of the Roman character when life was simple and austere, and morality uncorrupted. Many anecdotes exemplifying ancient Roman virtue refer to this period: the stories of the Roman ambassadors who, on their return from Egypt (see above) in 273, delivered to the public treasury the gifts they had received from Ptolemy II Philadelphus; C. Fabricius, who warned Pyrrhus when the latter's physician offered to poison him; and L. Papīrius, who reserved for himself only a wooden cup from the rich booty of Tarentum. It was at the end of this period that Rome first came under the influence of Hellenistic Greek culture, though commerce had already brought some acquaintance with the Greeks, and the Romans had adopted the Greek alphabet in very early times. It was a Greek slave, *Livius Andronicus, taken at the fall of Tarentum, who first introduced Greek drama and epic to the Romans. Greek influence is also seen in the development of the Roman religion (see RELIGION, ROMAN 2).

5. *Republican period: expansion beyond Italy, c.270–c.120 BC.* Rome was now a Mediterranean power, and as such came into contact with Carthaginian interests in Sicily and the western Mediterranean, and with the Hellenistic Greek world in the east. For the conflicts with Carthage and Rome's triumph see PUNIC WARS. Meanwhile Rome had to face another invasion of Italy by the Gauls, who were defeated at the battle of Telamon (in Etruria) in 225; this victory was followed by the pacification of Cisalpine Gaul, and the eventual reduction of the Ligurians and Istrians and of the Dalmatian coast (finally in 129). The depredations of Illyrian pirates in the Adriatic interfered with Rome's growing trade. In two campaigns (229 and 219) Rome subdued the Illyrians and obtained a foothold on the Balkan peninsula by establishing a small protectorate in Illyricum, thus coming into closer contact with the Greeks. The contact became still closer after the Second Punic War. Although in that war the Carthaginians had received little help from their Greek ally

Philip V of Macedon, and Rome had successfully defeated him in the First Macedonian War (214–205), he had shown himself ambitious for a career of conquest in the eastern Mediterranean, and Rome was drawn into war with him again. The Second Macedonian War was terminated by the victory of T. Quinctius Flamininus at Cynoscephalae in 197. Macedon was obliged to surrender her conquests, but was allowed to survive (for a time) as an independent state, while Rome proclaimed freedom (from Macedonian rule) for the rest of Greece; by 194 all Roman troops had left Greece (see MACEDONIA 3).

Rome wished for no further conquests, but she desired security and that meant crushing any rival power. She picked a quarrel with Antiochus III of Syria (see SELEUCIDS) with whom the defeated Carthaginian general Hannibal, expelled from Carthage, had taken refuge, when the Romans thought they were plotting together. When Antiochus, encouraged by Hannibal, invaded Thessaly in 192, the Romans soon drove him out and finally routed him near Magnesia in Lydia (189). Antiochus was forced back into Syria, and most of the Seleucid territory in Asia Minor was given to Pergamum and Rhodes; a few cities were declared free. Rome annexed no territory but received a large war indemnity. Macedon remained quiet until the accession of Perseus, who challenged Rome in the Third Macedonian War (172–168/7) but was defeated by Aemilius Paullus at Pydna in 168. After this a thousand of the citizens of the Achaean League, which had supported Perseus, were transported to Italy, among them the historian Polybius. (For the Greek embassy of 155 BC see PHILOSOPHY 2 and CRATES.) Macedonia was then divided into four republics, but after further disorders was annexed as a province in 146. A revolt of the Achaean League in the same year was rapidly subdued, and L. Mummius captured and destroyed Corinth. Central Greece and the Peloponnese were left independent but were compelled for a time to pay tribute. In 146 also, Carthage was destroyed. It had recovered its economic importance, so much so that in Rome Cato the Censor became alarmed at its renewed wealth and power. It was captured by *Scipio Aemilianus and its territory became a Roman province. A long series of Spanish campaigns, terminated in 133 by the capture of Numantia, resulted in the subjugation of the greater part of Spain.

Meanwhile Rome had subdued in various ways the Hellenistic kingdoms of Bithynia, Galatia, Pergamum, and Rhodes, and had interfered in the politics of Egypt and Syria. In 133 Attalus of Pergamum bequeathed his dominions to Rome (see ATTALIDS). They were formed into the Roman province of Asia. In the West the southern part of Gaul, Gallia

Narbonensis, was made a province in 120. There was thus an enormous expansion of Roman territory in the second century BC. At the same time economic and social life in Rome and Italy underwent profound changes. In many parts peasant husbandry had given place to capitalist farming of huge estates. Industry and commerce had expanded generally and, although the aristocracy did not take part in these enterprises, the *equitēs* (see EQUESTRIAN ORDER) were considerably enriched. Slavery increased, both on the land and in households. Rome quite suddenly acquired immense wealth from booty and tribute, there was a great increase in luxury of all kinds, and great public building works were undertaken. In all spheres, art and architecture, literature and religion, Greek influence was strong. Many nobles, such as the Scipios and their circle, were ardent philhellenes, and the earliest Roman historians actually wrote in Greek. The work of the poet Naevius was strongly Roman in character, but Plautus, Ennius, and Pacuvius show Greek influence, as would Terence not long after. There was for a time a reactionary movement in favour of the old Roman simplicity, led by *Cato the Censor, but it proved ineffectual against the tide of events. Cato himself spent much of his last years learning Greek.

6. *Republican period: the Gracchi, Marius, and Sulla.* The last century of the Roman republic was a period of acute social and political struggle. There was discontent in the provinces. Provincial administration lacked system and a permanent executive and was largely under the control of individual governors who were often unscrupulous and ambitious, seeking to enrich themselves and to acquire power. Army commanders were also personally ambitious, and the army increasingly looked to them rather than to the senate to provide bounties and distributions of land, thus introducing a dangerous element into political life. The senate itself had become more oligarchic and less democratic in its attitudes, leading to the sharper definition of the parties and the struggles of *optimatēs* and *popularēs*. The senate also showed a selfish attitude towards the Italian allies, denying them citizenship and many of the spoils of war which they had helped to win. Other important factors were the rise in influence of a wealthy class outside the senate (see EQUESTRIAN ORDER), the growth of large estates (*latifundia*) devoted to pasturage rather than cereal production, and the diminution of the smallholder class.

The first attempt to deal with some of these problems was made by the *Gracchi. Their eventual failure was followed by a conservative reaction, and by the war with Jugurtha (112–105). This war was conducted so ineffectually by the senate that the people and *equitēs* acting together had the command given to *Marius. In the more serious invasions by the

German tribes of the Cimbri and Teutonēs two consular armies were destroyed before Marius, having instituted military reforms and held repeated consulships, won two notable victories in 102 and 101. Despite the support of his army he was not prepared to use force against the senate, from which instead he sought recognition. Struggles between *optimates* and *populares* were revived; Marius' alliance with the popular leaders Saturninus and Glaucia was short-lived, and Marius supported the senate in its armed conflict with the popular party. More serious were the consequences of the conservative reaction. The proposal of M. Livius Drusus, tribune of the plebs in 91, to extend the Roman franchise to all the Italians, failed amid bitter conservative opposition to it. His assassination precipitated a widespread revolt among Rome's Italian allies, and led to the Social or Marsian War, 90–88 (the former name derived from the Latin *socii*, 'allies', the latter from the Marsi, who began the revolt). Some of the allies were fighting to win Roman citizenship, others, such as the Samnites (see 4 above), to destroy Roman predominance in Italy. From a military point of view the fighting was inconclusive, but the Romans gained victory by conceding the main issue: full citizenship was granted to all Italians south of the Po.

In a literary connection the period is interesting for the development which the stress of politics gave to Roman oratory. Cato the Censor had been a notable orator; the fragments of his speeches which survive show him as a vigorous patriot and an earnest speaker. Scipio Aemilianus and his friend Laelius were famous orators shortly before the time of the Gracchi. Of these two brothers Gaius was the more impassioned and effective speaker, according to Cicero (see ORATORY 2), who names a number of other orators of this period. This was also the age of Lucilius the satirist.

A dispute between (the popular) Marius and (the optimate) *Sulla for the command against Mithridates of Pontus led to Sulla's march on Rome in 88 at the head of his legions, and ushered in a period of civil war and bloodshed. Sulla subdued the East and returned in 83 to overthrow the government set up by Cinna. By 82, after numerous *proscriptions, Sulla was established as dictator and sought to re-establish the power of the senate over the tribunate and over army commanders in a series of measures which did not long survive his retirement in 79.

7. *The last period of the republic, 79–30 BC.* (For the starting-point of the late republic see SALLUST.) This second stage of Rome's civil wars, begun under Marius and Sulla, is associated with the names of *Pompey, Julius *Caesar, *Crassus, and *Cicero. In this struggle all thoughts about the good of the republic gave way to the ambitions of individuals who sought power for themselves alone. Their fortune was

built on their conquests as military commanders and they enjoyed what amounted to private control over loyal and effective troops, who realized that their own profit depended upon the success of their leaders. The consuls in 70 were Pompey, the conqueror of Sertorius in Spain, and Crassus, who had suppressed the revolt of Spartacus in Italy, and they joined forces against the senate to repeal much of Sulla's legislation. While Pompey was subduing the East, Caesar and Crassus became leaders of the popular party, and plotted together in Rome against Pompey's return. However, these intrigues and the attempt at revolution by Catiline (foiled by Cicero in 63) failed to give the *populares* control of Rome. Cicero began to hope for a *concordia ordinum*, a reconciliation of all the moderate elements in the state, but the senate refused to ratify Pompey's settlement for the East or to accede to the demands of Caesar, who in 60 returned from a command in Spain.

In 60 was formed the compact between Caesar, Pompey, and Crassus known (in modern times only) as 'the first triumvirate', by which they secured for themselves a commanding position in the state. It endured, while Caesar was conquering Gaul and Britain, until Crassus was killed after a Roman defeat by the Parthians at Carrhae in 53, after which rivalry between Caesar and Pompey developed into open conflict. For the increasing anarchy of this period see CICERO (1), CLODIUS, and MILO. The senate, fearing the military prestige acquired by Caesar in Gaul, was forced into alliance with Pompey, both sides showing reluctance. When Caesar returned from Gaul in 49 and crossed the river Rubicon into Italy with his army, civil war broke out again, this time between Caesar and Pompey, the latter now representing constitutional republican government. Pompey was utterly defeated at Pharsālus (in Thessaly) and was murdered in Egypt in 48. The republicans continued the war, but their cause collapsed after Cato's suicide in 46 and their defeat by Caesar at Munda (in Spain) in 45. Whether or not Caesar intended to end the republic, his dictatorship introduced the principle of personal autocracy into the constitution. His programme of beneficial legislation was cut short by his assassination at the hands of senatorial conspirators in 44.

Instead of the restoration of the republic which the conspirators had hoped for, a third round of civil war followed. Mark *Antony, Caesar's colleague in the consulship of 44 and at first the natural leader of the Caesarian party, found his position threatened by *Octavian, Caesar's heir; he was also widely thought to be planning to take over Caesar's autocratic powers. Octavian began to co-operate with the republicans in the senate and received their backing, including that of Cicero. The Caesarians were now divided into two parties,

Antony's and Octavian's. The two sides fought each other at Mutina in 43 (see BRUTUS (3)), where Octavian was present with a force of Caesar's veterans on the senatorial side; Antony was defeated and had to withdraw to Narbonese Gaul. When, after Mutina, Octavian's demands were rejected by the senate, he marched on Rome, occupied the city, and had himself elected consul, being then nineteen. A reconciliation took place between him, Antony, and the Caesarian Lepidus so that they could crush their common enemies Brutus and Cassius, the republican murderers of Caesar. The three had themselves appointed triumvirs for five years 'for the settlement of the state' (*triumviri reipublicae constituendae*). They proscribed their political and personal enemies, following the proscriptions with confiscations of land in order to settle 50,000 of their veterans. (Many farmers were made homeless and destitute as a result; see VIRGIL.) They continued the war against the republican party; Brutus and Cassius were defeated at Philippi in 42. Antony and Octavian restored their alliance with the treaty of Brundisium in 40.

Gradually Octavian strengthened his hold on Italy and the West; in 38 the triumvirate was renewed, but Lepidus was forced out in 36. Antony went to the East, became entangled with Cleopatra, and was finally suspected of sacrificing Rome's interests to her. There was a final rupture between Antony and Octavian, ending in Antony's defeat at the battle of Actium in 31 and his death at Alexandria in 30; this left Octavian sole master of Rome and all her territories, and closed the era of republican government.

8. *The Ciceronian age.* The last years of the republic from about 70 BC, the period sometimes described in its intellectual aspect as the Ciceronian age, saw a remarkable flowering of literary activity. It was the age not only of Cicero and Caesar but also of Lucretius, Catullus, and Varro. Virgil is generally associated with the succeeding Augustan age, but by 30 BC he had already written the *Eclogues* and *Georgics*. The most significant fact of the period is that the long process of the unification of Italy was now complete; there came into existence a single Italian nation joined in a common civilization and to some extent in an identity of political and commercial interests. The practical consequences of this union are exemplified by the number of individuals important in literature who came from different regions of Italy (a number which was exceeded in the following period): Catullus from Verona, Varro and Sallust both Sabines, Cicero from Volscian Arpinum, Virgil from Mantua, and Cornelius Nepos from Cisalpine Gaul. A feature of the Ciceronian age is the variety and vigour of the literary activity, stimulated perhaps by the political stress, and certainly by the popularist

tendency of the times, and also by the increasing influence of Greek culture, especially Hellenistic literature. This vigour shows itself in the great diversity of poetic forms evolved, epic, lyric, didactic, pastoral; in the various styles of oratory, ranging from austere Attic to florid Asian; in the conflict of schools of philosophical thought; in the greater independence, freedom of expression, and more personal character of literary works; in the practice of completing a liberal education in the schools of Athens; and in the interest taken in all kinds of learning, including Roman antiquities (see especially VARRO).

9. *The early empire: the Augustan age.* The republic collapsed through lack of a large bureaucracy capable of managing the very complicated empire Rome now governed, and through the rise of military dictators. Using the framework of the old republic *Augustus (a title conferred on Octavian by the senate in 27 BC) created a new system which was to some extent a compromise: he retained sole control of the military forces and foreign policy as well as general supervision over the machinery of government, but he left a share in administration to the senators and, especially, to the *equites* (the membership of these orders was revised by him at intervals throughout his reign, by virtue of his censorial powers). By his first settlement of the constitution in 27 BC, he retained (until 23 BC) the consulship which he had held since 31; he entrusted to the senate the government of Rome and Italy, and of certain provinces (the more peaceful of them, where no legions were required; see PROVINCES). The senate was also given judicial as well as legislative functions (see 12 below and LAW, AT ROME 1); and, most importantly, Augustus consulted it on questions of policy. Augustus himself adopted the outward appearance and mode of life of a republican magistrate. He assumed the title of *princeps* ('chief' or 'leader'). But his real position far exceeded that of a magistrate. He took to himself many of the functions of the senate, which gradually became reconciled to one-man rule as an increasing number of senators attained their rank through his favour.

Up to 23 BC Augustus' authority rested on his annual tenure of the consulship and his provincial command. By his second settlement, in that year, Augustus resigned the consulship, but instead received from the senate and people tribunician power for life, thus placing himself in the tradition of popular leaders. He had proconsular power over all imperial provinces, but his *imperium* was made *maius*, 'superior', to that of other proconsuls so that he had supreme authority in the senatorial provinces as well. By the control which he exercised, in virtue of these and other powers, over legislation, criminal jurisdiction, and a large part of the revenues of the state, as well as by the wide patronage in his

hands, and above all by his command of the army, Augustus was in effect raised to a monarchical position. For the general administration and development of the imperial civil service under the early emperors, see 12 below; for the reorganization of the finances by Augustus, see FINANCE 2; for the provincial administration see PROVINCES.

Augustus made a great effort to restore by legislation the traditional religion and morality of the Roman people (see 4 above), and to encourage desirable marriages as well as restrain luxury. The effect of his laws for this purpose was at best only temporary. As regards foreign policy, ambitious plans in the East were abandoned, a policy of peaceful settlement with Parthia adopted, and the efforts of the empire concentrated on the Romanization of Gaul and the acquisition of a strong frontier in the West. During the subsequent 300 years the centre of gravity of the empire was to shift to the East, the constitution of Augustus was to be radically modified, and in the end the West was to be overrun by barbarians. But none of this was to happen until Augustus' aims of Romanizing western Europe had been achieved in a form that would survive these upheavals.

The change in the political situation which came about with the establishment of the principate is reflected in the literature of the Augustan age. The political tranquillity of the time has its counterpart in the sense of calm after storm which is found in much Augustan poetry, notably in the *Aeneid* and the later poems of Horace. New themes and ideals (Rome's imperial mission, the return of the Golden Age) provide inspiration for poets. On the other hand, the daring and the sense of freedom and vitality which characterized Lucretius and Catullus are gone; Ovid incurs banishment for reasons of morality. Oratory, whether in the senate or before the people, finds itself cramped by the new conditions and degenerates into empty rhetoric. Jurisprudence comes under imperial control. The writing of history labours under similar disadvantages. Nevertheless, the age had in Livy a very great historian who, in spite of his obvious admiration for republican heroes, retained the esteem of Augustus.

10. *The Julio–Claudian emperors: Tiberius, Caligula, Claudius, Nero, AD 14–68.* At Augustus' death in AD 14, *Tiberius, who already had tribunician power and the proconsular *imperium*, was able to carry on the administration during the month that elapsed before the senate proclaimed him emperor. During his reign (14–37) the senate increased its political powers at the expense of the people. Provincial administration was good although there were legionary revolts in Germany; Tiberius followed Augustus' precept not to extend the empire, except that Cappadocia was made a province. In financial matters Tiberius

was considered parsimonious, and at his death left a large fortune. Within his own family there was jealousy and continual intrigue. Embittered and increasingly misanthropic, Tiberius retired to Capri and ruled through *Sejanus, whose career demonstrated the potential power inherent in the office of prefect of praetorians (*praefectus praetorio*) and also in the praetorian guard itself. Informers were rife, and at the end Tiberius' reign was one of terror, with spying, prosecutions, vengeance, and suicides. His life has been painted in the darkest colours by Tacitus and Suetonius, although enthusiastically praised by Velleius Paterculus.

The extravagant reign of *Gaius (Caligula) from 37 to 41 emphasized the autocratic nature of the principate which Tiberius' reign had begun to make evident, and the powerlessness of the senate to check the excesses of a ruler who might well have been insane. When Caligula was assassinated in 41 there was no heir to the principate, but the praetorian guard discovered *Claudius, Caligula's uncle, in the palace, the last member of the Julio–Claudian family, and out of dynastic loyalty proclaimed him emperor. His reign (41–54) was notable for its vigorous foreign policy (Britain was subdued and made a province in 43 and other new provinces were annexed), for the liberal extension of Roman franchise, for great public works, and for the development of the imperial civil service, in which freedmen were given a dominant position. He attempted unsuccessfully to make the senate more effective in government and to restrain professional informers; nevertheless there were conspiracies against him, and his freedmen and his last two wives, *Messalina and *Agrippina, fostered intrigues. It was alleged that Agrippina poisoned Claudius to ensure the succession of *Nero, her son by a previous marriage.

Nero was only 16 when he succeeded in 54, and the first five years of his reign ran smoothly under his mother's guidance and the able administration of Burrus, prefect of praetorians, and Seneca the Younger, his old tutor. In 59 his reign began to degenerate when he had his mother Agrippina and his wife Octavia put to death to facilitate his marriage with his mistress Poppaea Sabina. Seneca was driven into retirement and Burrus, who died in 62, was replaced as prefect by Tigellinus. Nero's passion for chariot-racing and for acting and music, together with his public appearances on the stage, may have scandalized Roman society, but his philhellenism was genuine, and his long-remembered tour of Greece in 67, as well as his generous exemption of the ancient centres of culture from taxation, made him popular at least in the East. The burning, probably accidental, of a great part of Rome in 64 was attributed to the Christians and was followed by the first persecution. The regulations for the rebuilding

of the city were wisely conceived, and in the construction of the new palace, the Golden House, Nero was able to indulge his artistic tastes to great effect. A serious rebellion in Britain in 60 led by Boudicca (see BRITAIN 4), after initial successes, was put down by the Romans in 61, but was caused in part by the abuses of Roman government in the provinces. The discovery of the wide-ranging conspiracy of C. Calpurnius Piso against the emperor in 65 (a result of the unpopularity arising from his excesses) led to the enforced deaths of Lucan, Seneca, and Petronius Arbiter, but failed to bring home to him the danger of his actions. Rebellion spread through Judaea (see 11 below), and finally Vindex (a legate in Gaul of royal Gallic descent) revolted as did Galba, the provincial governor of Spain. The emperor, deserted, fled from Rome and took his own life on 9 June 68.

During the reigns of the Julio–Claudians there was an abrupt decline in literary activity at Rome. The best-known authors of the period are Lucan, Seneca the Younger, Persius, Phaedrus, Petronius, and Columella. Literature, which had been won over to the imperial cause by Augustus, now showed an anti-imperial bias.

11. *Galba, Otho, Vitellius, the Flavians, and the Antonines, AD 69–192.* The 'year of the four emperors' (69) was a time when internal strife and bloodshed accompanied the brief reigns of Galba, Otho, and Vitellius. It was chiefly important for its revelation that emperors might be made elsewhere than at Rome, by the will of the legions. The legions recognized, however, that their nominees had to be accepted by the senate. *Galba was proclaimed by the Spanish army, but the praetorian guard in turn proclaimed *Otho, who was expelled by *Vitellius, the candidate of the legions in Lower Germany, whose legate he was. Although Vitellius was recognized by the senate, the army in the East set up as emperor its own commander, Titus Flavius *Vespasianus, legate of Judaea, with the support of the legions around the Danube. When Vitellius offered to abdicate, his troops would not let him. Rome was stormed and sacked by the Danubian legions and Vitellius killed. In December 69 the senate recognized Vespasian as emperor and he entered Rome early in 70.

The period of strife was followed by a phase of recuperation under the wise and efficient rule of the Flavian emperors Vespasian, Titus, and Domitian. This dynasty, in contrast with the patrician Julio–Claudian line, had relatively humble origins; Vespasian's father was an equestrian tax-collector from the Italian town of Reātē. Vespasian dated his reign from his acclamation by the army in 69 rather than his confirmation by the senate. He restored by prudent economy the finances which had been utterly disorganized by the prodigality of Nero and by the civil war, strengthened the existing frontiers, and admitted more provincials into the senate so that it became more representative of the empire. But he neglected the senate, relying more upon advisers, and there was a marked advance towards absolute monarchy, evidenced by his repeated consulships and his reviving and holding the censorship, which gave control over the composition of the senate. Under the Flavians increasing use was made of *equites* in the bureaucracy in place of freedmen. Vespasian undertook great public works, of which the Colosseum, completed by his successors, is the most striking example. The Jewish Revolt which broke out in 66 was brought to an end under the generalship of his son *Titus. The siege of Jerusalem began in 70 and ended with the storming and destruction of the city; Judaea became a province under an imperial legate. Titus commemorated his victory by the arch which still stands near the *Forum.

At the death of Vespasian in 79 Titus was prefect of praetorians and already shared his father's *imperium*. This made his succession a matter of course. His brief rule was uneventful, except for the eruption of Vesuvius in 79 (see POMPEII) and a fire at Rome in 80 which destroyed Vespasian's new temple to Jupiter Capitolinus.

Titus died in 81 and was succeeded by his younger brother *Domitian, who was saluted as emperor by the praetorian guard and had his succession ratified by the senate. He was an energetic administrator and builder, and a patron of the fine arts, rebuilding the temple to Jupiter Capitolinus and restoring the damaged public libraries. He tried to improve public morality, restricting the performance of *mimes and legislating to suppress vice. His administration of justice was largely free from bribery. Always popular with the army, he made vigorous efforts to secure the provinces, and expanded the area of Britain controlled by Rome, under the generalship of Julius Agricola (see BRITAIN 4). His holding of numerous consulships and a perpetual censorship and his autocratic attitude, as well as his philhellenic leanings, provoked hostility among the senatorial class. After a revolt by the legate of Upper Germany in 88–9 Domitian began to suspect senators and others of conspiracy, and listened to the accusations of informers; his last seven years were a reign of terror with widespread executions. These final years profoundly influenced the attitude of the historian Tacitus towards the principate in general. In 96 Domitian was killed by an assassin and his name erased from public monuments.

Under the terror of Domitian literature declined. The important names of the period are the Elder Pliny, Statius, Martial, and Quintilian. The mild and conciliatory reign of *Nerva (96–8), a leading senator, who had been chosen by the assassins of Domitian as widely acceptable, was followed by the simple, orderly rule of *Trajan (98–117), Nerva's adopted son, who won the unanimous support of the legions. This period, from 96 to 117, brought intense relief at Rome, indicated in the great historical works of Tacitus, the satires of Juvenal, and the letters of the Younger Pliny. The Roman empire was at its peak, and it was a time of peace and stability. With the beneficent governments of *Hadrian (117–38) and the *Antonines (138–92), classical Roman literature (in the widest sense) came practically to an end. Suetonius, Aulus Gellius, and Apuleius are the principal authors of the period.

For later events see BRITAIN 5 ff., BYZANTINE AGE, and FALL OF ROME.

12. *Roman administration.*

(i) *In the republican period.* For the working of the republican constitution see REPUBLIC, ROMAN. The principal regular magistrates (i.e. officers of state) were the consuls, praetors, censors, quaestors, tribunes of the *plebs*, and aediles; dictators (and their assistants, *magistri equitum*) were appointed only in serious emergencies. Their functions are described under the individual entries. For certain minor functionaries see VIGINTISEXVIRATE. For the order in which the various offices might be held and the obligatory intervals between them see CURSUS HONORUM. For the legislative assemblies see SENATE, COMITIA, CONCILIUM PLEBIS. For the administration of justice see LAW, AT ROME. For the administration of conquered territory see 4 above and PROVINCES.

(ii) *Under the early emperors.* The legislative and administrative powers of the state were in fact, if not in theory, gradually gathered up in the hands of the *princeps*, although various emperors made a practice of consulting the senate to a greater or lesser degree. *Senatus consulta* ('resolutions of the *senate*') had the force of law without being ratified by the *comitia* (popular assemblies), and the emperor in addition issued edicts. Legislation by the *comitia* became rare. The *comitia* met to elect magistrates until AD 14 (death of Augustus), after which the senate made the elections. The emperor had a limited (legal) right of nominating the candidates for these. The *quaestiōnēs* (standing criminal courts, see LAW, AT ROME I) continued, but judicial powers were given to the senate, which became the high court of the empire. Moreover the emperor, aided by a council (*consilium*) of assessors, took power to deal with any case. For the provincial administration see PROVINCES.

In effect, a civil service developed, its members appointed by and under the control of the emperor. The latter depended largely on his own household as a source of administrators, and a large staff of secretaries and accountants under his immediate authority was instituted.

From the beginning, freedmen were widely employed and soon given important posts. Some of these freedmen were extremely able and exercised great authority. Their power reached its climax under Claudius. Under the latter even the treasury was supervised by a freedman, known as *procurator a rationibus*, 'controller of the treasury', the equivalent of a magistrate in charge of finance. The principal private secretary of the emperor, a freedman known as *procurator ab epistulis*, answered official letters, dealing for example with the reports from governors of provinces and the grant of personal privileges. Another, in charge of petitions, *a libellis*, had important functions as interpreter of the law. All these were in effect high magistrates of state, so that the household civil service of the emperor encroached on the ancient magistracies. Under Hadrian these posts were entrusted to men of the equestrian order. Other important posts under the empire were *praefectus urbi*, *praefectus praetorio*, *praefectus annonae*, and *praefectus vigilum*. Also to be mentioned are the *curatōrēs viarum* ('keepers of roads') in charge of the upkeep of the Italian roads, the *curatores operum publicorum* ('keepers of public works'), who looked after the public buildings, and the *curator aquarum* ('keeper of the water-supply'; see AQUEDUCTS).

For the financial administration of Rome see FINANCE 2.

13. *The Roman economy*. The Roman state in its first phase was essentially a stock-raising and agricultural community (see AGRICULTURE 2), producing mainly corn; the city itself owed its early importance partly to its position on the chief navigable river on the west coast of Italy, and its possession of a bridge facilitating communication between industrial Etruria and the south of Italy. The only large-scale commercial enterprise was exporting salt from pans at the mouth of the Tiber. With Rome's conquest of Italy (completed by *c*.270 BC), the final reduction of Carthage (146 BC), and the acquisition of Sicily, Sardinia, Corsica, and Spain, the character of the Roman economy changed sharply. Italy itself was not a poor country. Campania and Etruria possessed, besides a prosperous agriculture, metalware and pottery industries. Vineyards, olive farms, and orchards were numerous in suitable regions. Southern Italy (at first), Sardinia, and Sicily produced much corn. (For the Roman corn-supply see ANNONA.) There were, moreover, vast areas of pasture land, including mountain grazing for the summer months; Apulia in particular yielded very fine wool.

From being almost entirely a community of peasant proprietors, including also certain aristocratic families, Rome, during the third to second centuries BC, developed a class of large landowners who were not farmers but who worked large tracts of public land leased from the state with tenant farmers and slaves (see LATIFUNDIA); a factor in the growth of these large estates was the influx of slaves as a result of the continuous warfare of the second century BC. Men like Pompey and Domitius Ahenobarbus owned such large areas that they could raise armies from their tenants. Contact with other countries, especially Greece, brought improvements in agriculture; the cultivation of the vine and olive was intensified. The best *wine of Campania came to rival the choicest wines of Greece. Farming was taken up by Romans in Africa and Gaul. The Spanish *mines were a source of great profit not only to the state but to individual speculators. (For the increase in the numbers of the *equites* at this time see EQUESTRIAN ORDER.) Rome's maritime trade was considerable from early times; it naturally increased with the expansion of the Roman dominions and the development of new needs among the wealthy Romans. The destruction of Corinth in 146 BC and the acquisition of territory in Asia further expanded Italy's trade with the East. *Delos became an important Italian emporium. But although commerce increased, the Roman senatorial class took little interest in it in early republican times, and rather despised it (after 218 BC senators were forbidden to engage in commercial activity outside Italy); and the general carrying trade of the Mediterranean was left to the Greeks and Phoenicians. The rise at Rome of a business and commercial class helped to raise the general standard of living among the well-to-do, but the decline of a free Italian peasantry meant an influx of the impoverished into the city and the growth of an urban proletariat. By 133 BC the city of Rome had a population of perhaps a third of a million people, many of whom lived on the verge of starvation. When in about 138 the staple grain prices rose because a slave war in Sicily interrupted the production of the grain crop, a serious economic crisis ensued, the basic cause of which the Gracchan agrarian reforms of 133 and later aimed to remedy (see GRACCHI).

There is a little evidence of industrial development at Rome before the empire; the only industries in the city appear to have been such as supplied the simple needs of the agricultural and military community, and to have been carried on largely by slaves or the newly enfranchised, with few exceptions on a small scale. However, a small industrial class made an adequate living. Campania was a considerable industrial centre from the second century BC: Capua produced bronze ware, Pompeii textiles, and Puteoli had important iron works, using the ore of Elba and ousting the Etrurian cities from their lead in this industry. Arrētium in Etruria was famous for its pottery, which was widely exported. Both commerce and manufacture increased during the early empire, the former being encouraged by the improved system of roads and the general security. There was a greater use of metals, e.g. lead for water-pipes. The brick-making industry developed at Rome and elsewhere (it was especially stimulated at Rome by the fire of AD 64, in Nero's reign, which destroyed a large part of the city). The glass industry also became of some importance, especially after the discovery of the art of glass-blowing.

If Italian industry was comparatively limited in republican times, banking and finance in general reached a high state of development. The Roman Forum in the first century BC was a great stock-exchange, where men transacted commercial and financial business extending throughout the whole ancient world. Capital was invested in lands, loans, and trading ventures rather than in industry. The rate of interest at Rome in classical times was normally 6 to 10 per cent for safe investments, but capital found more profitable employment in the outlying parts of the empire, where property was less secure. There 12 per cent was regarded as a low rate, and even the virtuous Brutus did not shrink from asking for the not unusual rate of 48 per cent. Apart from the *equites*, who undertook banking and large contracts, the trading class consisted to a great extent of freedmen, many of them men of intelligence and enterprise, who acquired wealth and social status.

At the end of the republican period and under the early empire the principal imports, which exceeded exports by a large amount, were (besides slaves) foodstuffs, raw materials, and manufactured articles, especially luxuries: grain, various metals, marble, linen, papyrus, furs, ivory, amber, silk from China, sometimes woven and dyed in Syria, and Arabian and Indian goods which came to Italy by way of Alexandria. So far as these imports came from provinces of the empire—and the internal trade of the empire was more important than foreign trade—they did not require exports of the same value to pay for them, for the provinces as a whole were tributary to Rome. Imports from the East were paid for in part with gold and silver coins. The chief articles of export from Rome were wine, olive-oil, and manufactured goods, which found active markets in Spain, Gaul, Africa, and even Germany. Trade and industry were not interfered with by the state. Within the empire trade was facilitated by the excellent *roads and by the moderate level of harbour dues. The principal commercial port was now Puteoli on the Bay of Naples, which eclipsed Ostia at the mouth of the Tiber. Pirates ceased to operate in the Mediterranean for nearly a century after Pompey dispersed them in 66 BC; and although there was some revival of piracy in the latter part of the reign of Augustus, the wide distribution of Roman fleets under the succeeding emperors kept it in check.

Thus Rome, from being originally an agricultural community with a frugal way of life, became by the end of the republican period the chief centre of wealth and luxury in the ancient world. Under the empire its temples, basilicas, forums, baths, theatres, circuses, and libraries were built on a magnificent scale. But the task of feeding and entertaining the city proletariat was a costly one. There were 200,000 recipients of free grain at Rome under Augustus and his successors. On the other hand, some few individuals were very rich indeed, such as Lucullus, Crassus, Atticus, and Maecenas. The civil troubles, the conquests in Spain and the East, the opportunities for extortion in the provinces, made many fortunes. Cicero, though a man of integrity, was able to amass 2,000,000 sesterces in his one year's governorship of Cilicia. Among those in the professions, the actors Roscius and Aesopus were extremely rich. Pallas, Callistus, and Narcissus, the famous freedmen of Claudius, became immensely wealthy from the sale of offices and favours. The highest civil officials in the second century AD received salaries of 200,000 sesterces (see MONEY). The traces of fine villas in many parts of the empire are evidence of the wide geographical distribution of wealth. In most of the Roman provinces there was a great development of city life under the early emperors; many splendid cities grew up, well paved, drained, abundantly supplied with water, and beautified with public buildings provided by wealthy donors.

It is difficult to determine the relative value of such prices as are known. Rome and many parts of the empire were dependent on imported corn, the staple food of the people. There were great fluctuations in its market price, owing to variations in the harvest and the difficulties of transport. Prices reported for a *modius* of corn (about a peck, or two imperial gallons, enough for one person for eight days) vary from $1\frac{1}{3}$ asses in a glut to 20 sesterces in a famine. C. Gracchus fixed as a moderate price $6\frac{1}{3}$ asses a *modius* (1 sestertius being worth 4 asses at this time). The price of common Italian wine was very low, but variable. Charges at an Italian inn in the early empire (known from an inscription) were 1 as for bread and wine, 2 asses for 'relish' (*pulmentarium*), and 2 asses for a mule's forage. The bare cost of subsistence for a single man, with corn at a moderate price, may be calculated at about 400 sesterces a year (Cicero reckoned that a life of luxury cost 600,000). The price of a slave varied from roughly 2,000 to 8,000 sesterces according to his age and skills and according to period (see SLAVERY 2). The price of a book of Martial's poetry is referred to as between 4 and 20 sesterces.

Precise information about rates of pay is lacking, but from such evidence as there is it seems probable that at the end of the republican period ordinary unskilled labour was remunerated at about 4 sesterces a day. The pay of a legionary soldier was almost doubled by Julius Caesar in the first century BC to 900 sesterces (225 denarii) a year, with deductions for food, arms, and clothing, and this rate remained unchanged until the time of Domitian at the end of the first century AD. The praetorian guard, from the latter part of Augustus' reign, were paid about 1,500 sesterces a year. A schoolmaster in Horace's native Venusia received 2 sesterces a month for each pupil; for fifty pupils this would amount to 1,200 sesterces a year.

For the finances of Rome see FINANCE 2, AERARIUM, and FISCUS. For the coinage see MONEY AND COINS.

Ro'mulus and Rēmus, see ROME 2.

Ro'mulus Augu'stulus, last emperor of Rome, AD 475–6; see FALL OF ROME.

Ro'scius Gallus, Quintus (d. 62 BC), the most famous comic actor of his day at Rome, although he also played tragic roles. He amassed great wealth. He was on intimate terms with Catullus and Sulla; Cicero defended him in a private suit (see PRO ROSCIO COMOEDO). Though handsome he had a squint, and to conceal it is reported to have introduced into Rome the wearing of masks when acting, wigs having been worn previously. The name of Roscius is occasionally used in English literature to denote a great actor.

Rosetta Stone, slab of black basalt now in the British Museum on which is inscribed an Egyptian decree of 197 BC honouring the king Ptolemy V Epiphanēs. The inscription is given in three versions, Greek and two forms of Egyptian: hieroglyphics ('picture-writing') and demotic, the simplified form of hieroglyphic in common use. The discovery of the stone in Egypt in 1799 made possible the eventual decipherment of hieroglyphics by the French scholar Champollion, in the years following 1820.

Rostra, at Rome, the platform in the *Forum from which speakers addressed the people. It took its name from the bronze prows (*rostra*) of the Latin ships captured at Antium in 338 BC during Rome's Latin War (see ROME 4), with which it was decorated. On it were placed statues of famous men. Here too was erected Rome's first sundial (see CLOCKS).

Royal Road, highway of Persia linking the capital, Susa, with Sardis and other parts of the Persian empire. It carried the royal messenger-service.

Roxa'na (Rōxănē), wife of *Alexander the Great.

Ru'bicon, small Italian river, reddish in colour (hence the name), falling into the Adriatic and marking the boundary in republican times between Italy and the province of Cisalpine Gaul. Julius Caesar, by crossing the river into Italy in 49 BC without disbanding his army as the senate had ordered, effectively declared war on Pompey and the senate. Suetonius gives Caesar the words, *iacta alea est*, 'the die is cast'. 'Crossing the Rubicon' is proverbial for taking an irrevocable decision.

Rudens ('rope'), romantic comedy by *Plautus adapted from a Greek comedy by Diphilus (see COMEDY, GREEK 6). This is one of Plautus' best plays, with a well-integrated plot, interesting characterization, and lively dialogue.

The prologue is spoken by the star Arcturus. The scene is the rocky coast of Cyrēnē near a temple of Venus and the country house of an elderly Athenian, Daemonēs, whose daughter Palaestra was stolen from him in her childhood. She has fallen into the hands of a young pimp, Labrax of Cyrene; a young Athenian, Plesidippus, has fallen in love with her, and made part-payment for her purchase. But Labrax has thought to improve his fortunes by secretly carrying the girl off to Sicily. Thereupon Arcturus has raised a storm and wrecked the ship near the scene of the play. Palaestra and another girl reach land in a boat and are kindly tended by the priestess of Venus. Labrax is also washed ashore; he discovers the girls and tries to carry them off from the temple. They are defended by Daemones and presently rescued by Plesidippus, who marches Labrax off to justice. A box belonging to Labrax is pulled from the sea in the net of a fisherman, who quarrels over it with a slave of Plesidippus while hauling on the rope (*rudens*) of the net; the quarrel leads to the discovery in the box not only of the gold of Labrax but also of trinkets belonging to Palaestra, which show her to be the lost daughter of Daemones. There is joyful recognition, followed by the betrothal of Palaestra to Plesidippus.

Rufus, Quintus Cu'rtius, see CURTIUS.

Rumī'na, in Roman religion, goddess who protected mothers suckling their children. She had a sanctuary at the foot of the Palatine hill, where the *ficus Ruminalis* stood, the fig-tree under which Romulus and Remus were supposed to have been suckled by the wolf (see ROME 2).

running–races, see ATHLETICS (i).

S

Sabā'zios, Phrygian god introduced to Athens in the fifth century BC. He was sometimes identified with the Greek god Dionysus. Aristophanes refers to him, and is said to have written a comedy (now lost) in which Sabazios and other foreign gods are brought to trial and expelled from the state. His worship seems to have had connections with that of the Magna Mater ('great mother'; see CYBELE), and private mysteries were celebrated in his honour. Practically nothing is known of his rites until the time of the Roman empire, when his worship was widely spread in Italy. His chief attribute was the snake.

Sabe'lli, collective name given by the Romans to the tribes of central Italy who spoke the *Oscan-type Italic languages. They include Samnites and Apulians. The Sabelli moved outwards from their original Sabine homeland, imposing their language upon the populations they settled among; these migrations continued into the fourth century BC.

Sabines (Lat. Sabini), an Italian people living north-east of Rome in early times, famous for their bravery, simple morality, and strong religious feelings. Many traditional stories, particularly relating to Roman religious institutions, indicate a Sabine element in the early development of Rome, probably arising rather from amalgamation than from conquest. According to family tradition the Claudian *gens* originated from a Sabine family which settled peacefully at Rome in earliest times. However, Livy records numerous Roman wars against the Sabines, ending in 449 BC with a resounding Roman victory. In 290 BC M'. Curius Dentatus conquered them, and they were absorbed into the Roman state, receiving full citizenship in 268. For the Rape of the Sabines see ROME 2. See also TITUS TATIUS.

Sacred Band (*hieros lochos*), at *Thebes, an élite corps of 300 hoplites chosen from noble families and professionally trained, formed in 378 BC by the general Gorgidas to defend Thebes against Sparta's highly trained army (see SPARTA 2). The special character of the Sacred Band derived from its being composed of 150 pairs of lovers, each member bound to the other by strong emotional ties of love and loyalty. The corps had a notable leader in *Pelopidas. It was partly responsible for the Theban victories over Sparta at Leuctra in 371 and Mantinea in 362, but it was too small to carry a battle by itself, as was shown at the battle of Chaeronea in 338 when Athens and Thebes were beaten by Philip II of Macedon. The Band did not share in the general flight but fought to the death.

Sacred Wars, name given to wars waged by the *Amphictyony (i.e. league of neighbouring states) of Delphi for the protection of Apollo's shrine there and for the punishment of sacrilege. The First Sacred War in the early sixth century BC arose from a quarrel between Delphi and *Crisa (or Cirrha), the latter a neighbouring town, a few kilometres to the south-west, which controlled the route to Delphi. The quarrel concerned Crisa's right to exact tolls from pilgrims. Crisa was destroyed and its fertile plain dedicated to Apollo, with an undertaking that it would never be cultivated.

The Second Sacred War occurred in 448 BC when the Phocians seized control of Delphi, the Spartans intervened to restore the sanctuary to the Delphians, and Athens under Pericles reinstated Phocis. It is not known when Delphi was once again liberated, but under the terms of the Peace of Nicias between Athens and Sparta its independence was guaranteed (421 BC; see PELOPONNESIAN WAR).

The Third Sacred War (355–352 BC) proved to be an event of considerable importance involving most of Greece. Thebes, then in control of the Amphictyony, persuaded it to impose a heavy fine on the Phocians for cultivating the Crisaean plain (see above). The Phocians refused to pay and under Philomēlus seized Delphi (356); in 355 the Amphictyony declared war on Phocis. At first the Phocians, using the treasure of Delphi, were successful. Under Onomarchus, the successor of Philomelus, the power of Phocis was greatly extended until it reached from the Corinthian Gulf to parts of Thessaly. But the intervention of Philip II of Macedon at the request of the Thessalian League and Thebes (see PHILIP (1) 2) turned the scales against Phocis, though the support given to the latter by Athens delayed the end. After defeating Philip in 353 Onomarchus and his army were overcome and he himself killed by Philip in 352 at the battle of the Crocus Field, south of Pherae in Thessaly, before Athenian help could arrive. In 346, after the Peace of Philocratēs between Athens and Macedon, Phocis was isolated and surrendered to Philip, who took her place on the Amphictyonic Council.

In 339 an Amphictyonic war was once more a pretext for the invasion of Greece by Philip, this time with momentous results. The Locrian city of Amphissa had been persuaded by the Thebans to make an accusation against Athens (Thebes' old enemy) at a meeting of the Amphictyonic Council in the autumn of 340, concerning an inscription the Athenians had set up, ostensibly on the grounds that an offence against religion had been committed but in reality because the inscription perpetuated the memory of Thebes' siding with Persia in the *Persian Wars. The Athenian envoy *Aeschinēs turned the tables on the Amphissans by pointing to the Crisaean plain which lay below and which they were cultivating in defiance of the oath that it should be uncultivated for ever (see above). In an impressive speech he persuaded the Amphictyony to punish Amphissa. They marched out intending to lay waste the unlawfully cultivated crops but were driven off, and when Athens and Thebes stood aloof the Amphictyony was not strong enough to enforce the penalties it had decreed. In 338 it therefore called on Philip to assist. He invaded at once, captured Amphissa, and then turned on Thebes, now allied with Athens, and won the victory at Chaeronea which gave him the hegemony of Greece.

Sacred Way, at Rome, see VIA SACRA; at Athens, the road to Eleusis, leaving the Ceramicus by the Sacred Gate (see MYSTERIES).

sacrifice (from the Latin *sacrificium*, 'making sacred').
1. According to the ancient view, sacrifice was a gift to the gods, the latter including for this purpose the heroes and the dead, who were also the recipients of offerings. Sacrifices differed in kind, animals or vegetables, for example, and in the manner in which they were offered, perhaps shared between gods and men in a communal feast, or burnt entirely. Both public and private sacrifices were made.
2. *Bloodless offerings.* Fruit and vegetables were offered in many Greek cults, especially to the gods of the Underworld; they were either laid on the altar or burnt. Cakes were also a common offering, as were cheese, honey, wine, and oil; see LIBATIONS.
3. *Blood offerings.* The slaughter and consumption of a domestic animal for the sake of a god was the most popular form of ancient sacrifice, and could be either a public or a private occasion. The most splendid sacrifice was that of a bull, but more usual was that of a sheep, goat, or pig (see also HECATOMB). Poultry were also commonly sacrificed, other birds and fish rarely. The animal was carefully chosen to be without blemish, and often had to be of a colour considered appropriate, e.g. light-coloured victims for celestial deities, black for the gods of the Underworld and the dead (compare the red dog sacrificed to *Robigus at Rome). In a public

sacrifice of some importance an animal, perhaps an ox, its horns gilded and entwined with ribbons, was escorted to the altar by a procession, preceded by a maiden carrying a basket containing the sacrificial knife concealed in grains of barley or cakes. Someone also carried a vessel of water and perhaps incense.

When all stood around the altar, water was poured over the hands of the participants as well as sprinkled on the animal, causing it to jerk its head 'in consent'. An ox was given water to drink, so that he bowed his head and thus appeared a willing victim. The participants took handfuls of barley, and after a prayer to the god, threw them on the altar and on the animal. The sacrificer took the knife from the basket, cut some hairs from the victim and threw them on the fire. Small animals were held over the altar and their throats cut; an ox was struck with an axe and its neck artery opened to the accompaniment of shrill cries from the women. In Roman sacrifice the head of the animal was sprinkled with wine and sacred cake (*mola salsa*). The blood was caught in a bowl and poured over the altar. The animal was then skinned and cut up, and the entrails roasted on the altar fire. The important participants, perhaps the priests, ate the entrails first. The bones and fat were then burnt on the altar fire for the gods (see PROMETHEUS), together with other offerings such as cakes, and wine poured over so that the flames blazed. After this began the cooking of the meat to make a feast for those taking part. It was often prescribed for a particular sacrifice that all the meat must be consumed within the sanctuary; the priest was often permitted to keep the skin.

In Roman sacrifices the sacrificer kept his head covered with his toga throughout; in Greece the head was kept uncovered. In both Greece and Rome the sacrifice was accompanied by music (usually on the flute, sometimes on the lyre).

4. There were also blood offerings which were not the prelude to a meal and in which the victim was completely burned; these were known as holocausts. They took place at purifications, at burial of the dead, to the gods of the Underworld and heroes, and before battle or at other times of crisis.

5. At some sacrifices animals were offered which were not considered human food, dogs to Hecatē and Eileithyia, horses to Poseidon and Helios, and (at Rome) asses to Priapus, for example. A pregnant sow was offered to Demeter and Dionysus (to promote fertility).

6. Traces of human sacrifice remain in stories. It was reported that at the sacrifice before the battle of Salamis in 480 BC captured Persians were substituted for animals. There were several myths of the—usually willing—sacrifice of maidens before battle, to which class the slaying of *Iphigeneia at Aulis belongs. It seems to be

true that after the defeat at Cannae in 216 BC the Romans buried alive two Greeks and two Gauls in the Forum Boarium at Rome. See also SUOVETAURILIA and RELIGION.

saga, see MYTHOLOGY.

Sagu'ntum (Sagunto), city in Spain about 30 km. (19 miles) north of Valencia. Its alliance with Rome, and its later capture by Hannibal, in 219 BC after a siege, were the immediate cause of the Second *Punic War (218–201). It was recaptured by Rome in 212.

Salami'nia, at Athens, the name of one of the two state warships; see PARALOS.

Sa'lamis. 1. Island separated by a narrow channel from the south-west coast of Attica, near Piraeus. In Greek myth it was the home of Telamon, father of Ajax. It originally belonged to Aegina, was occupied by Megara c.600 BC but was soon after conquered by Athens as a result of a stirring appeal by *Solon, thereafter sharing her fortunes. It was the scene in September 480 BC of the great naval defeat of Persia by the Greeks (see PERSIAN WARS), and it was the birthplace of Euripides.
2. In Greek times the principal city of Cyprus, on the east coast, said to have been founded by Telamon's son *Teucer.

Sale of Lives, see LUCIAN.

Sa'lii, the Salian priests at Rome, so called from the verb *salire,* 'to dance'. They were an ancient college (see COLLEGIUM) of twelve, later twenty-four, priests of Mars; they were required to be of *patrician birth and have both parents living. They wore a striking costume consisting of the old (perhaps Bronze Age) Italian war-dress, with sword, bronze breast-plate, short military cloak, and the distinctive spiked head-dress, the *apex.* They carried in their right hands a spear or staff, and on their left arms the sacred figure-of-eight shields, *ancilia.* They were prominent during March and October (the months that marked the beginning and end of the campaigning season), on certain days going in procession through the city, halting at certain places and performing elaborate ritual dances, beating their shields with their staves and singing the *carmen saliare* ('salian song') in the saturnian metre (see METRE, LATIN 1), a song so ancient that according to Quintilian in the first century AD it had become almost unintelligible even to the priests themselves. A few fragments of it survive. It appears from Virgil's *Aeneid* that *Hercules also had his own Salii. Compare ARVAL PRIESTS.

Sallust (Gaius Sallustius Crispus) (86–35 BC), Roman historian. He was born at Amiternum in the Sabine country, of a plebeian family. He was tribune of the *plebs* in 52 BC, when he acted against *Cicero ((1) 4) and *Milo. It is said that the hostility he showed to Milo after the murder of Clodius in that year was the result of his being horse-whipped by Milo when caught in the act of adultery with the latter's wife. He was expelled from the senate in 50 BC, perhaps for playing a part in fomenting the riots of 52. He then joined Julius Caesar, commanding a legion in 49. Elected praetor in 47 he became governor of the province of Numidia in 46, where he enriched himself considerably at the provincials' expense and was (unsuccessfully) charged with extortion upon his return to Rome. He became the owner of fine gardens, *horti Sallustiāni,* withdrew from public life, and devoted the rest of his life to writing historical monographs, the *Bellum Catilīnae, Bellum Iugurthīnum* (see CATILINE and JUGURTHA), and the *Historiae* of the period 78–67 BC (the years following the abdication of Sulla). The first two works and fragments of the third have survived.

Sallust's work shows an advance on his annalistic predecessors (see HISTORIOGRAPHY 2) both in narrative powers and in its more scientific method: he endeavours to explain the causes of political events and the motives for men's actions. His weaknesses lie in his vagueness and inaccuracy in chronological and geographical matters, and in his biased attitude to the *popularēs* and his hostility to the *nobilēs,* natural perhaps for a *novus homo.* Nevertheless he can recognize merit in political adversaries and faults in his own side. His characters, notably those of Jugurtha and Catiline, Marius, and Sulla, are vividly drawn. For his history of Catiline he must have relied heavily on Cicero ((1) 2) as well as his own recollections of events; for Jugurtha he used a variety of sources, including the autobiography of Sulla and the *History* of Sisenna; he had gathered information while in Africa and had had Punic documents translated. In selecting Catiline and Jugurtha as subjects he was influenced, as he says himself, by the striking and potentially dangerous nature of their actions. All his monographs have a common theme, namely the struggle of the *populares,* at successive stages, against the entrenched nobles. His principal models were Thucydides and the Elder Cato, his narrative enlivened by speeches (in the manner of Thucydides), letters, digressions, and character studies. His political thought is not profound but reflects an essentially Roman moralistic outlook, with emphasis on traditional *virtus* ('virtue'), and a pessimistic attitude towards contemporary corruption. He furnishes us with the starting-point of the late republic, dating Rome's moral collapse from the return of Sulla's booty-laden troops from the East and their bloody seizure of Rome.

The ancient critics noted the characteristics of his style: the use of archaisms, brevity to the point of obscurity, innovative vocabulary, Graecisms, epigrams, rapidity. In these respects he influenced the style of later historical writers, notably Tacitus.

Sa'lmacis, see HERMAPHRODITUS.

Salmō'neus, in Greek myth, son of *Aeolus (2) and father of *Tyro, and consequently the ancestor of Pelias and Jason (see ARGONAUTS). He is placed by Virgil in the lowest depths of Tartarus because of his impious arrogance in claiming to be the equal or even the superior of Zeus, driving about in a chariot of bronze to imitate thunder and throwing firebrands to imitate lightning. Zeus destroyed him and his city with a thunderbolt.

Sā'mia, Greek comedy by *Menander, produced probably between 317 and 307 BC; a considerable part of it has been recovered in modern times from a papyrus.

While two neighbours, Dēmeas and Nicēratus, are abroad, the latter's daughter Plangon gives birth to a baby by Demeas' son Moschion. A marriage is arranged, and Demeas' mistress Chrȳsis, who has suffered a miscarriage, agrees to keep the baby and pass it off as her own by Demeas. The neighbours return; Demeas overhears an old woman speak of the baby as Moschion's and concludes that since Moschion wants to marry Plangon he was unwillingly seduced by Chrysis. Demeas drives Chrysis and the baby out of the house whereupon they are taken in by Niceratus; both fathers are bewildered by conflicting evidence as to the identity of the baby's parents. Moschion, in despair, prepares to go abroad as a soldier, but eventually all is sorted out and the marriage takes place. (The happy resolution of the plot is lost.)

Samian ware. Roman writers of republican and imperial times describe as 'Samian ware' a common type of *pottery (see 2 (i)), probably a variety of table-ware with decoration in relief (*terra sigillata*) brought from the East, originally from Samos. In modern times the name is applied to the red-coated pottery decorated in relief, found in Roman Britain and made in imperial times in Gaul.

Samnite Wars, see ROME 4. Samnium was an *Oscan-speaking region in the southern Apennines, whose inhabitants were particularly warlike. See also SABELLI.

Sāmos, Ionian island off the south-west coast of Asia Minor, between Ephesus and Milētus. During the *migrations from Greece it was settled by Ionians. Its most flourishing period was in the second half of the sixth century BC under the tyranny of Polycratēs. It was famous for its navy, metal-work, and woollen products, and also produced notable architects (who built the island's famous temple of Hera), sculptors, and gem-engravers. A Samian engineer bridged the Bosporus for the Persian king *Darius. Samos joined the *Delian League, revolted

from Athens in 441 BC, and was reduced by Pericles himself. During the oligarchic revolution of the *Four Hundred in 411, the Athenian fleet was stationed at Samos, and the island was the centre of the democratic movement that overthrew the oligarchy. Alone among the subject allies of Athens Samos did not revolt at the end of the *Peloponnesian War, after the defeat at Aegospotami in 405 BC, for which the Samians were rewarded with Athenian citizenship; but the city was reduced by the Spartan general *Lysander in 404. Subsequently it fell into the power of Persia; it was captured for Athens in 365 by *Timotheus (2), and *cleruchs were settled on the land of exiled Samians. These were ousted by Alexander the Great and the exiles restored. Samos was the birthplace of Pythagoras and the astronomer Conon.

Samo'sata, city on the right bank of the Euphrates, the birthplace of *Lucian, and the capital of the kings of Commagēnē, a territory in north Syria.

sapphic, see METRE, GREEK 8 (i).

Sappho, Greek lyric poetess, born in the late seventh century BC at Eresus in *Lesbos, a contemporary of the Lesbian poet Alcaeus. Her father was Scamandronymus, her mother Clēis. While still young she went into exile in Sicily, presumably because of political troubles in Lesbos. (A statue of her erected in Sicily in the fourth century BC was stolen by the notorious Roman governor Verres.) She returned to spend the rest of her life at Mytilene. She had three brothers, one of whom, Charaxus, a merchant, sailed with a cargo of wine to Naucratis in Egypt and there became expensively entangled with an Egyptian courtesan named Doricha (Herodotus, who refers to the story at 2. 135, confuses Doricha with *Rhodopis). Sappho is said to have expressed strong disapproval of the affair. She married Cercylas and had a daughter Cleis. A famous story, perhaps originating in Greek comedy, related that she fell in love with a certain *Phaon who rejected her and in consequence she threw herself off the cliff of Leucas (an island off the west coast of Greece). The date of her death is unknown.

Sappho's poetry, which was almost entirely monody (see LYRIC POETRY), was divided into nine books according to metre; book 1 consisted of poems in the sapphic metre (see METRE, GREEK 8 (i)), book 2 of poems in dactylic pentameters, and so on. The ninth book contained those *Epithalamia which did not fit into the other books for metrical and other reasons. Her dialect was the Lesbian vernacular, a branch of Aeolic Greek (see DIALECTS). Of her poems only the address to Aphroditē is certainly complete; some passages have been preserved in quotations, but for the most part the poems are known from papyrus fragments discovered in the twentieth century (see PAPYROLOGY). Her subject matter seems to be almost entirely confined to her personal world of family and female friends.

Sappho was apparently the leading personality among a circle of women and girls who must have comprised her audience. Whether she was in some formal sense their teacher or mentor remains unclear, but it seems unlikely that they were bound by a common cult of Aphrodite and the Muses, as has been suggested. She was on intimate terms with them and wrote with great simplicity but passionate intensity about her love (and occasionally her hate) for individuals. Her two most famous poems are, first, the address to Aphrodite mentioned above in which she summons the goddess in a style reminiscent of a cult-song and asks to be delivered from unrequited love for a girl; and secondly a declaration of love for a girl, the mere sight of whom moves Sappho intensely while a young man sitting beside her seems godlike in his indifference (Catullus translated this in his poem 51). There are no explicit references to physical relations in the surviving fragments, although the poet *Anacreon a generation later seems to be indicating maliciously that the name of the island connotes female homosexuality. The Epithalamia are different in tone, in some ways more formal and less personal, and contain elements from Lesbian folk song; but they too have a deceptive simplicity. Sappho created a form of subjective personal lyric never equalled in the ancient world in its immediacy and intensity.

Sarā'pis, see SERAPIS.

Sarpē'don, in Homer's *Iliad*, son of Zeus and *Laodameia, leader (with *Glaucus (3), his friend and comrade in battle) of the Lycians, and the best warrior among the allies of the Trojans. His death by the spear of Patroclus (*Iliad* 16) is movingly recounted. His father Zeus had wanted to avert his death, but allowed it after being rebuked by Hera. He ordered Apollo to carry Sarpedon's body off the battle field, and Sleep and Death bore it to Lycia for burial. According to another version Sarpedon was the son of Zeus and Europa, and brother of *Minos and Rhadamanthys.

satire (Lat. *satura*, 'medley', 'farrago', from *satur*, 'full'). Quintilian claimed satire as 'entirely our own', i.e. a Roman creation: *satura quidem tota nostra est* (*Institutio oratoria* X. 1. 93). Although there were satirical elements to be found in Greek literature, notably in Attic Old Comedy (see COMEDY, GREEK 3) with Aristophanes' attacks on personalities of the day, e.g. Cleon, and in the Cynic-Stoic *diatribes of *Bion the Borysthenite and *Menippus, it was the Roman achievement to develop satire as a

separate literary genre characterized by variety of subject matter and occasionally of form (dialogue, fable, anecdote, precept, verse of various metres, combination of verse and prose). Livy (7. 2) describes as *saturae* early dramatic performances (originally put on to placate the gods at a time of plague) combining song, music, and mimetic dancing. On the one hand these contributed to the evolution of Latin comedy, on the other there developed from them the semi-dramatic, mixed literary form of 'satire', a commentary from a personal viewpoint, good-humoured, biting, or moralizing, on current topics, social life, literature, and the faults of individuals. Roman sources say *Ennius (239–169 BC) was the first to write satires in verse (among much else) but apparently without including invective or personalities. *Lucīlius (*c*.180–*c*.102 BC) was the first to confine himself entirely to this genre, and it was he who gave it its character as well as establishing the hexameter as the appropriate metre for it. All later Roman satirists regarded him as their founding father. He was followed by M. Terentius *Varro (116–27 BC), who took as a model the satires of Menippus in which prose and verse in a variety of metres were rather oddly intermingled, but who wrote in a less bitter, mildly didactic vein.

The *Satires* of Horace (see below), written in the 30s BC, show the strong influence of Lucilius but are more genial in tone, containing no dangerous invective against powerful individuals or serious vices, and the personal slant is charmingly autobiographical. *Persius (AD 34–62) also felt Lucilius' influence, but his satires, characterized by earnest Stoic moralizing, contain no direct attacks on individuals. His editor Cornutus toned down a line of verse which the emperor Nero might have resented. Roman satire reached its peak in the *Satires* of Juvenal (published in the first part of the second century AD), whose bitter denunciations of the vice and folly of his own times (safely attached to names of people of the previous generation) embrace most men and all women.

The genre took a different direction in two brilliant Menippean satires which appeared in the reign of the emperor Nero (AD 54–68), Seneca's *Apocolocyntosis*, a caricature of the deification of the late emperor Claudius, and the *Satyricon* of *Petronius. In the fourth century AD the emperor *Julian wrote (in Greek but in the Roman tradition) the *Caesars*. The form of Menippean satire, but not the tone or purpose, was followed by *Martianus Capella in the *Marriage of Mercury and Philology* and by *Boethius in the *Consolation of Philosophy*.

Satires (*Sermōnes*), of *Horace, two books of 'discourses' (in hexameters) written in the 30s BC (the first refers to an event of 37, the second to the events of 31). See also SATIRE. In the first book Horace presents his own personality through his views on a variety of topics, moral and literary criticism, and simple autobiography (including a touching tribute to the author's father). In the second book all the satires except one are written in dialogue form. Painful invective against individuals is almost entirely absent. In this respect Horace differs markedly from his model Lucilius, as he does also in the deliberately casual and easy style of his language and metre, the hexameters conveying an impression of colloquial but urbane Latin.

Among the satires the following are notable: I. 5, 'A Journey to Brundisium' (corresponding to Lucilius' 'Journey to Sicily') describes his travels in the suite of Maecenas with the poet Virgil and the tragedian Varius Rufus; I. 6 is interesting for its autobiographical details, an account of Horace's father and of his own introduction to Maecenas; I. 9, *ibam forte via Sacra* ('I was going by chance along the Sacred Way') is an entertaining description of an encounter with a bore and the author's efforts to get rid of him; I. 8 is the least personal, a story of witches put to flight in the midst of their incantations by the sudden cracking of a wooden statue of Priapus. In the second book, the adoption of dramatic form gives life and humorous variety to the illustrations of Roman life. II. 5 is a parody of epic in which Odysseus, in a continuation of the Underworld episode in *Odyssey* 11, consults Teiresias as to the recovery of his lost fortune and receives advice in the (Roman) art (or vice) of legacy-hunting. II. 6 is the famous satire on town and country life illustrated by the fable of the town mouse and the country mouse. Alexander Pope's imitation (1738) of the last part of this satire is the best known of his *Imitations of Horace*.

Satires (*Saturae*), of *Juvenal.

Satire 1 is an introductory poem in which Juvenal explains that his subject matter is not taken from outworn mythology but is concerned with *quidquid agunt homines* (85), 'all the activities of people'. The vices of the age provide the stimulus: *facit indignatio versum* (79), 'indignation prompts my verse'. But it is safe to write only of the dead; at the present time *probitas laudatur et alget* (74), 'honesty is praised but left out in the cold'. Satire 2 is an attack on those who give the appearance of being stern moralists but are immoral in their private lives: *nemo repente fuit turpissimus* (83), 'no one becomes vicious all at once'. Satire 3 is a picture of life at Rome and is perhaps Juvenal's best satire, imitated by Samuel Johnson in his *London* (1738). Juvenal approves of his honest friend Umbricius for fleeing to the country from the vices and perils of the city, which include 'poets reciting in the month of August'. Umbricius cannot stand the invasion of Greeks and pillories the versatile 'Greek in search of a meal',

Graeculus esuriens (78). The honest and poor Roman has no chance in Rome: *nil habet infelix paupertas durius in se / quam quod ridiculos homines facit* (152), 'luckless poverty has no misery harder to endure than this, that it exposes men to ridicule'. Poverty stands in the way of merit: *haut facile emergunt quorum virtutibus opstat / res angusta domi* (164), 'it is not easy for men to rise when straitened circumstances at home stand in the way of merit'. The city is described: the tall houses with pigeons nesting on the roofs, ready to fall about the ears of the inhabitants; the frequent fires, the impossibility of sleep because of the noise of waggons in the narrow, winding streets and the abuse of drovers, the danger of being crushed by a heavy load or hit by rubbish thrown down from open windows. Then the city at night: a great man passing in his scarlet cloak, with torches and a retinue of clients and slaves, the affray with a bully 'if affray it can be called, when you do all the beating and I get all the blows', *si rixa est, ubi tu pulsas, ego vapulo tantum* (289). When one is finally behind locked doors at home, there is still the danger of being murdered by a burglar.

Satire 4 is a skit on the administration of the emperor Domitian, who had to call a council meeting to consider how to dispose of a mullet too large for any dish. Satire 5 is about the humiliation of poor *clients at the tables of their rich patrons. Satire 6, the longest and most virulent of Juvenal's satires, is a denunciation of women. The poet professes astonishment that a friend should contemplate marriage when there is so much rope to be had, and then depicts, at great length, the vices of women, their insatiable and reckless sexual appetite, their extravagance, tyranny, and quarrelsomeness in the home. The jealous woman, the gossip, the virago, the athlete are among the offenders, worse are the ostentatious pedant and the superstitiously religious. If you chance on a good woman, who is a 'rare bird on earth, as common as a black swan', *rara avis in terris nigroque simillima cygno* (165), she will be haughty. It is useless to set a guard on one's wife, for 'who will guard the guards themselves?', *quis custodiet ipsos custodes?* (O 31).

Satire 7 is on the unprofitability of the literary professions and especially that of teacher (*Quintilian has been lucky). Moreover, the teacher has to endure much monotonous repetition, *crambe repetita* (154), 'cabbage served up again and again'. Satire 8 attacks pride of ancestry. 'Virtue is the only true nobility', *nobilitas sola est atque unica virtus* (20). It is the greatest sin to prefer life to honour 'and to lose for the sake of living all that makes life worth having', *et propter vitam vivendi perdere causas* (84). Satire 9 is an attack on sexual vice, put in the mouth of a repentant sinner. In Satire 10 (the model for Samuel Johnson's poem *The Vanity of Human Wishes*, 1749) Juvenal writes on the folly of human prayers; wealth exposes a man to dangers, whereas 'the empty-handed traveller will cheerfully sing when confronted by a robber', *cantabit vacuus coram latrone viator* (22); power (consider *Sejanus), long life, and beauty are all sources of trouble. Better leave your fate to the gods, or pray for at most 'a healthy mind in a healthy body', *mens sana in corpore sano* (356), and for courage and endurance. The only things the public cares for are 'bread and circuses', *panem et circenses* (80). Satire 11 contrasts extravagance and simplicity of living; in Satire 12 Juvenal celebrates a friend's escape from shipwreck, and attacks legacy-hunters.

Satire 13 is an eloquent plea to a friend not to seek vengeance against one who has defrauded him; the guilty man will be punished by his own conscience: 'it is always the little, weak, and petty mind that delights in vengeance', *quippe minuti | semper et infirmi est animi exiguique voluptas | ultio* (189). The poet refers approvingly to the *Delphic Oracle's condemnation of a man who had merely thought of committing an offence: 'for he who secretly meditates a crime has all the guilt of having done the deed', *nam scelus intra se tacitum qui cogitat ullum, | facti crimen habet* (209). Satire 14 is about the influence of parental example in education. The parents' faults will be copied by the children: 'if you have any shameful deed in mind, the greatest reverence is owed to the young', *maxime debetur puero reverentia, siquid turpe paras* (47). In Satire 15, after describing a conflict in Egypt, resulting in an act of cannibalism, Juvenal praises tenderness of heart as the quality which distinguishes humans from beasts. Satire 16, on the abusive privileges of the military, is unfinished.

satrap, title given to a Persian provincial governor; the territory he governed was known as a satrapy. A satrap had very wide powers over his province and was in effect a vassal king, owing allegiance to the Great King. *Darius divided the Persian empire into twenty satrapies which remained the basis for later territorial administration.

sa'tura, see SATIRE.

Sa'turae Meni'ppeae, see VARRO I.

Saturn (Sāturnus), ancient Italian god whose original function remains obscure. He may have been a blight-god. His name has also been connected with *satus*, 'sowing', and he has been thought of as a seed-god, a supposition supported by the date of his festival (the *Saturnalia) which occurs in the calendar of *Numa on 17 December, between the Consualia for the god of the granary and the Opalia for the god of plenty. Sacrifices to him were made in the Greek manner, with head uncovered (see SACRIFICE 3); the Romans themselves thought that he had been introduced from Greece, and identified him at an early stage with

the Greek god *Cronus, the father of Zeus. Thus he came to symbolize the good old days, the *Golden Age. His temple stood at the foot of the Capitoline hill and served as the treasury (*aerarium*) of the Roman people; there too were kept the Tables of the law and the records of decrees of the senate. He was regarded as the husband of *Ops and father of *Picus.

Saturnā'lia, in Roman religion, festival celebrated from 17 to 19 December, the most cheerful of the year, a time of enjoyment, goodwill, and licence, of present-giving and lighting candles, the prototype of some aspects of the modern Christmas festivities. The holiday began with a sacrifice at the temple of Saturn followed by a public feast open to everyone. All business ceased; everyone dressed in holiday clothes and wore the soft cap, *pilleus* (see DRESS 2). On this one occasion in the year people were allowed to play gambling games in public. Slaves were freed from their duties and might even be waited on by their masters. Each household chose a mock king to preside over the festivities. Not everyone enjoyed it: the Younger Pliny built himself a sound-proof room to which he retired throughout the holiday. By about the fourth century AD many of these customs were transferred to New Year's Day, and hence were added to the traditional Christmas celebrations.

Saturna'lia, dialogue by *Macrobius.

saturnian, see METRE, LATIN I.

Saturnī'nus, Lucius Appule'ius, tribune of the *plebs* in 103 and 100 BC. Of praetorian family, he was quaestor in charge of the corn supply at Ostia in 104 at a time of shortage; when he failed to get adequate supplies to Rome he was superseded in his duties by the leader of the senate; perhaps in consequence of the humiliation he became violently anti-senatorial. As tribune in 103 and 100 he co-operated with the consul *Marius to enable the latter to get land-allotments for his landless veterans, and he was able to pass other popular measures against optimate opposition, often by violence, and with the help of the praetor Glaucia (see ROME 6). His personal influence and his ability to act independently of Marius grew considerably. When in 99 he stood again for the tribunate and Glaucia for the consulship, a rival of Glaucia was assassinated. At this Marius dissociated himself from both of them and with the backing of the senate took action to suppress them; Saturninus and Glaucia were both killed.

satyric drama (satyr-plays). At Athens, at the dramatic festivals, each trilogy (consisting of three tragedies) was followed by a semi-comic satyr-play, written by the same author, in which the chorus was always composed of *satyrs, led by Silenus, wearing horses' tails and ears.

Aristotle at one point in the *Poetics* expresses the belief that tragedy originated from this type of performance. Others believed that satyr-plays were a later development. Euripides' **Cyclops* is the only complete specimen still surviving, but substantial fragments of the *Dictyulci* ('drawers of nets') of Aeschylus and the *Ichneutae* ('trackers') of Sophocles have been found in recent times on papyrus (see PAPYROLOGY). The subject matter of satyr-plays was a burlesque of some mythical episode appropriate to the preceding trilogy, with a certain amount of coarse language and gesturing. *Pratinas of Phlius, writing at the beginning of the fifth century in Athens, is said to have turned the satyr-play into a literary form; he is also said to have written thirty-two satyr-plays himself. Satyric drama continued to be written even in Roman times; rules for its composition are given by Horace in the *Ars poetica*.

Saty'ricōn, see PETRONIUS ARBITER.

satyrs (*satyroi*), in Greek mythology, attendants of the god *Dionysus, boisterous creatures of the woods and hills, represented as mainly of human form but with some bestial aspect, e.g. a horse's tail or the legs of a goat (but they are not usually represented as goats until the fourth century BC). They are lustful and fond of revelry. The Romans identified them with the Fauni (see FAUNUS). The chorus in Attic satyr-plays was dressed to represent satyrs (see SATYRIC DRAMA). See also SILENUS.

Scaean Gate, see TROY.

Scae'vola. 1. Gaius Mu'cius Scaevola, legendary Roman who, when Lars *Porsen(n)a, king of Clusium, was besieging Rome at the end of the sixth century BC, made his way to the enemy camp and attempted to kill Porsena. He was taken prisoner, and to show his indifference to the death with which he was threatened, thrust his right hand into the fire. The king was so impressed that he released Mucius, who thus acquired the *cognomen* Scaevola, 'left-handed'.

2. Publius Mucius Scaevola, see ANNALS, ANNALISTS.

3. Quintus Mucius Scaevola (*c.*170–87 BC), known as 'the augur', consul in 117 BC, son-in-law of *Laelius and father-in-law of L. Licinius Crassus the orator. He was a distinguished jurist and taught (among others) his son-in-law and Cicero, who greatly admired him. He is one of the interlocutors in Cicero's **De oratore*, **De amicitia*, and **De republica*.

4. Quintus Mucius Scaevola (*c.*140–82 BC), *pontifex maximus* in 115, consul with L. Licinius Crassus the orator in 95 BC. He was himself an orator of distinction, noted according to Cicero for the concise accuracy of his language. He published the first systematic treatise on civil law. Cicero in his youth received instruction in the law from him after the death of his relative

and namesake, the augur (see 3 above). In his consulship he and Crassus passed the Licinian–Mucian law, instituting proceedings against aliens who had been illegally enrolled as citizens. This brought about the expulsion of many Italians from Rome and was in consequence a contributory cause of the Social War. Cicero remarked on the fact that such an unfortunate measure was due to such excellent men. Scaevola was assassinated by the Marian party (see ROME 6) in 82 BC in the temple of Vesta.

Scālae Gemō'niae ('stair of sighs'), at Rome, a flight of steps leading to the summit of the Capitoline hill from the Forum, between the Temple of Concord and the Carcer or prison. Criminals were executed in the latter, and their dead bodies thrown out on these steps, down which they were dragged to the Tiber.

scansion, metrical analysis of poetry into long and short (or stressed and unstressed) syllables, and metra or feet. See METRE, GREEK 1.

scāzon, see METRE, GREEK 5.

Sceptics (from Gk. *skepsis*, 'speculation'), Greek philosophers who asserted the impossibility of knowledge. As the name of a particular school of philosophy Scepticism began with Pyrrhon of Elis (*c.*365–*c.*270 BC), but sceptical attitudes were expressed by philosophers, notably the *sophists, long before that. Pyrrhon travelled to India in the train of Alexander the Great and there, tradition relates, met some 'magi' who influenced the development of his philosophical views. He returned and lived the rest of his life quietly at Elis. He left no writings, and only fragments survive of the writings of his pupils. Pyrrhon inferred from the deceptions inherent in sense-perceptions and the contradictions in the teachings of 'dogmatic' philosophers that knowledge of the true nature of things is unattainable. Hence the proper attitude is to follow the appearance of things (*phainomena*), to suspend judgement (*epochē*), and to avoid commitment, with the aim of achieving mental quietude (*ataraxia*). His most influential pupils were *Timon (2) of Phlius, Philo of Larisa (head of the *Academy at Athens in the first century BC), and Nausiphanēs of Teos; our chief source of information on the Sceptics is the lengthy account by *Sextus Empiricus (late second century AD). It remains unclear what the relationship was between Pyrrhon's Scepticism and that of the Academy at Athens, introduced by Arcesilaus (head of the Academy *c.*265 BC) and developed a century later by *Carneades. It seems probable that Arcesilaus was influenced by Pyrrhon.

Sche'ria (Scheriē), name of the island of the Phaeacians (see *Odyssey*, book 5), on the coast of which Odysseus was cast ashore. Some have identified it with Corcyra (modern Corfu).

Schliemann, Heinrich (1822–90), son of a German pastor, who acquired sufficient wealth by means of an indigo business at St Petersburg to devote himself from the age of 36 to archaeology. He excavated the site of *Troy in 1870–3, 1878–9, and 1881. He also excavated *Mycenae in 1876, where he discovered the shaft-graves with their treasures, and *Tiryns in 1884.

schoenus, land-measure used in Egypt, equivalent to 60 stades according to Herodotus (but considerably less in other sources).

scholasticism, see TEXTS, TRANSMISSION OF ANCIENT 7.

schō'lium, in Greek, name given in antiquity to a short explanatory note written to elucidate a difficulty in a text. The plural, scholia, is often used to describe the commentaries on classical texts written in the margins of manuscripts by ancient scholars, and copied along with the text from manuscript to manuscript. In this form they are a compilation, greatly abbreviated and sometimes garbled, made from earlier, fuller commentaries or excerpted from monographs of various dates. Thus they sometimes contain valuable information about antiquity from reliable sources which has not otherwise come down to us. The scholia to Homer, Hesiod, Pindar, Aristophanes, and the tragedians are particularly useful, and although the manuscripts in which they are found are of the later *Byzantine age, the notes sometimes go back to the great scholars of the *Hellenistic age, Zenodotus, Aristophanes (of Byzantium), and Aristarchus. There are also scholia on Latin authors, e.g. Horace.

school, see EDUCATION.

Sci'pio. 1. Publius Corne'lius Scipio Africā'nus Maior (236–183 BC), conqueror of Spain and victor of the Second *Punic War. He was the son of P. Cornelius Scipio who was consul in 218 BC, the first year of the Second Punic War. He is said to have saved his father's life at the battle of Tīcīnus in the same year, and as military tribune to have rallied the survivors of the disaster at Cannae in 216. In 210 when only about 25 his exceptional military ability brought about his appointment by the people to the command in Spain, the first privatus, 'private citizen', to be granted the *imperium of a proconsul. By 206 he had driven the Carthaginians out of Spain and had brought it under Roman control. He was elected consul for 205, and, managing to get the better of senatorial opposition, especially that of Fabius who thought Hannibal should be defeated in Italy, crossed over to Africa with his army, a large number of whom were volunteers. He finally defeated Hannibal at the battle of Zama in 202, and earned the *cognomen* Africanus.

In 199 he was elected censor and became *princeps senatus*, 'leader of the senate'; in 194 he was consul for a second time. In 190, although nominally merely the legate of his brother Lucius in the command against Antiochus of Syria, he led the first Roman army into Asia. When the brothers returned to Rome, political attacks, directed by *Cato the Censor, were launched against them both, accusing them of misconduct in public affairs. A series of trials resulted, and although at the last the charges were not pressed home (Scipio is said at one point to have reminded the people that the day of the trial was the anniversary of Zama) the influence of the Scipios was broken, and Africanus retired to his estate at Līternum in Campania, where he died. The Younger Seneca in Epistle 86 vividly evokes the simplicity of his life there. Like many members of his family he was an ardent philhellene; that and his military brilliance and magnetic personality prompted comparisons with Alexander the Great. He married Aemilia, sister of L. Aemilius *Paullus; one of his daughters was *Cornelia, mother of the Gracchi.

2. Publius Cornelius Scipio Aemiliā'nus, known as Africanus Minor (c.185–129 BC), an important military and political leader at Rome. He was the second son of L. Aemilius *Paullus, the conqueror of Macedonia, and was adopted by P. Scipio, the son of Scipio Africanus Major (see (1) above). He fought under his father at the battle of Pydna in 168 BC, to end the Third Macedonian War (see MACEDONIA 3). When the Greek historian *Polybius was sent to Rome with the other Achaean hostages in 167 BC he became tutor in the family of P. Scipio, and a close and lasting friendship developed between Polybius and Scipio Aemilianus. In 149 and 148 the latter achieved great distinction as military tribune in the Third *Punic War. In 147 when he stood for the aedileship at a critical juncture in the war, he was elected consul instead although he was under the minimum age of 42 and had not been praetor (see CURSUS HONORUM). He brought the siege of Carthage to a successful conclusion (see LAELIUS) and destroyed the city, celebrating a magnificent triumph at Rome. He was elected censor in 142, and in 140 (probably) he led an important embassy to the East. He was made consul for a second time (again unconstitutionally) in 133 BC for the purpose of ending the long and costly war in Spain against the Numantines, and ended it by starving Numantia into surrender.

At his return to Rome (and a second triumph) in 132 he took the lead amongst those opposed to the radical reforms of the *Gracchi but died suddenly in 129 at the height of the political unrest. It was suspected that he had been murdered, perhaps by his wife Sempronia, sister of the Gracchi. There were no children of the marriage. He was a great orator, the leading figure in the philhellenic circle at Rome, and a patron of Greek and Latin literature and learning; his friends included Polybius, Panaetius, Lucilius, Terence, and Laelius. His combination of intellectual and active virtues, of high culture with outstanding military and political success, moved Cicero to unbounded admiration of him as the ideal statesman. Cicero made him the central character in *De republica and *De senectute. His *De amicitia dwells on the friendship of Scipio and Laelius.

3. **Publius Cornelius Scipio Nasi'ca Sera'pio,** consul in 138 BC, a man of strongly conservative and aristocratic views. In 133 he vigorously opposed his cousin Ti. *Gracchus, and was leader of the group of senators and clients who attacked and killed him. In later times the deed sharply divided the *optimatēs* who approved and the *populares* who condemned it.

Scipio's Dream, see SOMNIUM SCIPIONIS.

Scīron, in Greek legend, a brigand who preyed on travellers along the cliff road from Athens to Megara. He made them wash his feet, and as they did so he kicked them over the cliff, where, according to some, they were eaten by a giant tortoise. *Theseus on his way to Athens threw Sciron over the edge, and his bones were turned into the cliffs which bear his name.

Sciropho'ria, Athenian festival, also called Scira, celebrated on the twelfth Scirophorion (midsummer). Many aspects of it were even in late antiquity a matter of dispute, including the meaning of the name, and remain so in modern times. It seems to have been a women's festival, dedicated to Demeter, or perhaps to Athena, in the course of which various offerings, including piglets, were thrown into a pit and recovered three months later at the *Thesmophoria.

sco'lia (from *skolios*, 'crooked'), at a Greek banquet or drinking-party, short songs sung by guests in succession but in random order, 'crookedly'. These songs were accompanied by the lyre. *Athenaeus (book 15) preserves a collection of anonymous Attic scolia of the late sixth and early fifth centuries BC. They either comment on some historical incident (such as the assassination attempt of *Harmodius and Aristogeiton) or contain some personal sentiment or comment on life. The singer held a myrtle branch while he sang, and when he had finished passed the branch to another. Tradition makes *Terpander the originator of the scolion.

Scōpads, Scōpas, see CRANNON and SIMONIDES.

Scopas, of Paros, eminent sculptor of the Attic school in the early fourth century BC (see SCULPTURE I). He was notable for his power of expressing violent emotion. His 'Raging Maenad' survives in a reduced and fragmentary Roman copy; a tritoness from Ostia seems also to be a copy of a figure in one of his

masterpieces, a large, many-figured group of Poseidon and other lesser sea-deities and monsters. Fragments remain of a battle-scene and hunting-scene from the pediment of the temple of Athena at Tegea.

Scribo'nia, wife of *Octavian (later the emperor Augustus). She was married at least three times; by one of her first two husbands she became the mother of that Cornelia whose premature death occasioned an elegy of consolation from Propertius (IV. 11). Octavian married her for political reasons in 40 BC, but divorced her in 39 after the birth of their daughter Julia. She accompanied Julia into exile in 2 BC and remained with her until the latter's death in AD 14. She herself was still alive in 16.

scripts, see BOOKS AND WRITING.

sculpture
1. *Greek.* During the ninth to the early seventh centuries BC statuettes in various materials had been made, but not until the mid-seventh century did the idea of making stone statues life-size or larger come to Greece from Egypt. It seems to have developed simultaneously in mainland Greece, the Peloponnese, southern Italy, the Greek islands, and Asia Minor. Free-standing sculpture was at first confined to a few simple types: the upright male figure, usually naked, standing with the left leg advanced, the so-called *kouros* ('youth'); the draped female figure, with legs close together or the left leg slightly advanced (the *korē*, 'maiden'); or the draped seated figure. The attitude of the figure is rigid and retains the rectilinear appearance of the block from which it was carved. *Kouros* and *kore* remain the principal types of the archaic period (650–480 BC); by the end of it Greek sculptors had come to understand the relation of the parts to the whole in human anatomy. The chief literary authorities for the sculpture of this early period are the Elder Pliny and Pausanias. Two Cretan sculptors, Dipoinos and Scyllis, are said by Pliny to have been working in Argos and Sicyon about 550 BC. An Argive artist at the beginning of the sixth century BC carved the statues of the Argive brothers *Cleobis and Biton, still at Delphi where they were dedicated. The most important sixth-century Peloponnesian statue is the *kouros* from Tenea near Corinth (now in Munich), proud and elegant in comparison with the cruder Argive pair. Peloponnesian sculpture shows a hardness and angularity of line and feature seen typically in the head of Hera (c.600 BC) from the Heraeum at *Olympia. In the second half of the sixth century sculpture from Ionia and the islands, exposed to oriental influences, is marked by greater elegance, softness, and attention to detail.

Attica and, particularly, the Acropolis at Athens have yielded more archaic sculpture than the rest of Greece. A series of pedimental limestone groups from the mid-sixth century has survived more or less entire. One of the most touching statues found is the 'Calf-bearer', a dedication from the late sixth century. Since the protecting deity of Athens was Athena large numbers of *korai* were dedicated to her, mostly from the late sixth and early fifth centuries; these show increasing naturalism in the representation of drapery. Excavations at Aegina in the nineteenth century uncovered the beautiful and dramatic early-fifth-century pediments of the temple of Aphaia, telling the story of how the sons of Aeacus had taken Troy before the Trojan War (see LAOMEDON). From the second half of the sixth century improvements in the process of hollow casting enabled large figures to be cast in bronze, and from the late sixth century onwards bronze was the favourite material for free-standing statuary. Few bronzes survive, but superb examples recovered from a shipwreck off Italy (the Riace bronzes) have been thought to be dedications at Delphi made *c.*450 BC by the Athenians to celebrate the victory of Marathon.

The style of the early classical period in the fifth century is represented by the pediments and metopes of the temple of Zeus at Olympia (*c.*465–457) and the pediments, metopes, and friezes of the *Parthenon (447–431). The principal sculptors of this period were *Myron, *Pheidias, and *Polycleitus of Argos. In the fourth century important buildings with sculptural decoration were erected not only in Greece but in Asia Minor also. Of some of these the sculptures have partly survived, e.g. of the temples of Asclepius at Epidaurus and Athena at Tegea, and of the *Mausoleum at Halicarnassus. The leading sculptors at this time were *Praxiteles of Athens, *Scopas of Paros, and *Lysippus of Sicyon.

At the end of the fourth century, after the time of Alexander the Great, Greek sculpture changed its character. The simplicity of the earlier periods gave place to a striving for theatrical effect, a lack of restraint, and a loss of repose. On the other hand there was increased realism. The most productive schools of this Hellenistic period were those of Pergamum and Rhodes. From the former came the 'Dying Gaul' (popularly known as the 'Dying Gladiator' after Byron, *Childe Harold* 4. 140), a copy of which is now in the Capitol at Rome, and the group of a Gaul with his wife whom he has just killed, turning his sword on himself. Rhodes produced the bronze of the 'Praying Boy' (a Roman copy is now in Berlin), and, more theatrically, the *Laocoon and the Farnese Bull, now in Rome. Among the greatest surviving works of the period are the *Venus de Milo and the Victory of Samothrace (a winged figure of Victory alighting on the prow of a ship), now in the Louvre; see NIKE.

After the Roman conquest of the Greek world in the second century BC the Romans developed a taste for Greek works of the past, which resulted in an age of copying. Greek sculptors retained their mastery of technique but lost their creative impulse. Thousands of Greek works of art were imported into Italy; according to Livy, at the triumph of M. Fulvius Nobilior in 187 BC, 785 bronze statues and 230 marble statues from the spoils of Ambracia were carried in procession before the victor. So great was the desire to possess Greek sculpture that a Roman firm set up branches in Greek cities to deal with the demand. Thus it is that we owe much of our knowledge of Greek sculpture to Roman copies. The recovery of cargoes of sculpture from Roman vessels wrecked in the Mediterranean may yet add to the number of Greek originals.

2. *Roman.* Sculptors working in Rome under the kings and in early republican times seem to have been Etruscan. Etruscan sculpture, strongly influenced by Greek art, is known from the seventh to the first centuries BC; Greek statuary was imported to Rome from the fourth century BC onwards, reaching a flood in the second and early first centuries BC (see 1 above) when Greek sculptors also came to Rome to work. Roman sculpture reached its highest excellence in the first and second centuries AD; it is seen at its best in portrait busts, where it showed great power of expressing character (see PORTRAITURE), and in great bas-reliefs erected on public buildings from the late republic onwards to commemorate historical events. The *Ara Pacis ('altar of peace') illustrates the idealizing Greek style that was favoured under Augustus, and, at a later stage of development, the Arch of Titus shows greater feeling for picture-making qualities. The columns of Trajan and Marcus Aurelius depict a continuous narrative of Rome's wars against the barbarians, unrolled in sequence around the shafts. Inevitably the effect is of a picture overcrowded with detail. There are also many examples of decoration of altars and columns with convolutions and festoons of foliage and flowers.

Scȳlax, of Caryanda in Caria, sent by the Persian king Darius (521–486 BC) on a voyage of exploration from the Indus round the coast of Arabia. The voyage has been doubted, but the book Scylax wrote afterwards (*Periplus*, 'voyage') is apparently quoted by *Hecataeus as well as later authors. The surviving *Periplus* attributed to him dates from the fourth century BC.

Scylla. 1. In Greek myth, daughter of *Phorcys and *Hecatē. She was sometimes described as originally human but turned into a monster by a rival in love. She is represented as having six heads, each with a triple row of teeth, and twelve feet; she lived in a cave (traditionally situated in the Straits of Messina between Sicily and Italy) with the whirlpool of Charybdis opposite. Her diet was fish but she devoured sailors if a ship came near. Homer describes the passage of Odysseus' ship past the cave in *Odyssey* 12. To be 'between Scylla and Charybdis' is to be in a situation where the two possible courses of action are equally dangerous.

2. Daughter of Nīsus, king of Megara, which was besieged by *Minos of Crete. Nisus was inviolable and the city safe as long as a red or purple lock among his white hair remained intact. Scylla cut it off and thus killed him in order to deliver the city to the besiegers, either out of love for Minos or because she had been bribed. Minos was horrified at the deed and drowned her (or she drowned herself). Nisus was turned into an osprey and Scylla into a sea-bird (*ciris*), ever pursued with hatred by her father.

The Latin poets Virgil, Ovid, and Propertius sometimes confuse the two Scyllas.

Seasons (Horai), in Greek myth, daughters of Zeus and *Themis, attendants on the gods and generally three in number (spring, summer, winter). The first two are more often invoked since they are thought of as the goddesses of life and growth, and they are often associated with Aphroditē and the Graces.

Second Sophistic, see SOPHISTIC, SECOND.

secular games (lūdi saeculārēs), see LUDI 2.

seisachthei'a, see SOLON.

Sējā'nus, Lucius Ae'lius, appointed prefect of *praetorians in AD 14, at first jointly with his father L. Seius Strabo, but later on his own. He concentrated the strength of the praetorian guard by quartering them all together in a barracks on the north side of Rome. He exercised a steadily increasing influence over the emperor Tiberius (see ROME 10), and after the latter's son Drusus died suddenly in 23, Sejanus was suspected of poisoning him and of hoping to bring about a dynastic marriage with his widow, Livilla. His background, however, was too humble for the emperor to accede to this request. When at his persuasion Tiberius withdrew to Capri in 27 Sejanus became all-powerful. In 29 he had Agrippina the Younger arrested and deported, together with her son Nero, perhaps as a preparatory move to winning the throne for himself, but Tiberius was alerted by Antonia, the widow of his brother Drusus, and denounced Sejanus in a letter to the senate (the poet Juvenal's *verbosa et grandis epistula*, 'long-winded and lengthy letter'). Sejanus was brought before the senate, condemned of plotting to overthrow the emperor, and executed. It is said that after his execution his body was torn to pieces by the people whose hatred he had incurred, and thrown into the Tiber. Ben Jonson's *Sejanus his Fall* was produced in 1603 with Shakespeare in the cast.

Selē'nē, in Greek myth, the moon-goddess (Roman Luna), according to Hesiod the daughter of the *Titans Hyperion and Theia and sister of Helios and Eos (Sun and Dawn); but some authorities give different genealogies. She has little cult and few myths (but see ENDYMION). She is sometimes identified with the goddess Artemis, perhaps because both had been identified with *Hecatē.

Seleu'cids, dynasty which eventually obtained Syria and much of Asia as its share in the empire of Alexander the Great (see DIADOCHOI). The founder of the dynasty was Seleucus I (*c*.358–281 BC), an officer of Alexander, who, after the latter's death, received the governorship of Babylonia (321). After a shaky beginning, by the end of the fourth century he had extended his rule eastwards over all Alexander's provinces to the banks of the Oxus and Indus. In 301 the issue between him and his chief rival Antigonus I of *Macedonia (see 2) was settled by the defeat and death of Antigonus at the battle of Ipsus, which left Seleucus supreme in Asia and with access through Syria and Cilicia to the Mediterranean; Lysimachus of Thrace, another 'successor' to Alexander's empire and Seleucus' ally at Ipsus, received northern and central Asia Minor as reward. In 281 Seleucus finally acquired this territory too by defeating and killing Lysimachus at the battle of Corupedium. Now entertaining the hope of winning Macedonia, the possession of which was still undecided, he invaded Europe, but was assassinated by Ptolemy Ceraunus, a son of Ptolemy I of Egypt.

His successors, first his son Antiochus I (ruled 281–261), followed by the latter's son Antiochus II (261–246), father of Seleucus II (246–225), his eldest son, whose own eldest son became Seleucus III (225–223), were largely occupied with a succession of wars against the Ptolemies for the possession of Coelē-Syria (roughly Palestine). This was finally annexed in 200 BC by Antiochus III (the Great, 223–187), second son of Seleucus II and a ruler of remarkable energy and enterprise. Succeeding to the throne when little more than 18 he put down the dangerous revolt of several of his eastern governors, and then set about the recovery of the various territories lost by his predecessors. By his eastern expedition (212–206) he acquired Armenia and regained Parthia and Bactria as vassal kingdoms, and finally crossed the Hindu-Kush to the Indus, earning himself, like Alexander, the title 'Great'. But this arduous undertaking had no lasting results: unfortunately for him he underestimated the new power of Rome. When he invaded Europe in 196 to recover Thrace, the Roman senate was alarmed by what they took to be his expansionist policy in the West. There was a protracted diplomatic exchange, and finally, at the invitation of the Aetolian league, Antiochus invaded Greece (192). He then lost three battles to the Romans, including that of Magnesia near Sipylus in 189 at the hands of Lucius, brother of *Scipio Africanus Major (see 1), and was forced to evacuate all Asia Minor west of Mount Taurus. Thereafter, despite its Mediterranean seaboard, the Seleucid empire ceased to be a Mediterranean power.

Antiochus died in 187 and was succeeded first by his second son Seleucus IV (187–175) and then by his third son Antiochus IV Epiphanēs (175–163). This Antiochus was an ardent philhellene, and encouraged the growth of urbanization, particularly in the East. He was eccentric and munificent. It was he who began the rebuilding of the *Olympieum at Athens. He invaded Egypt (169–168) but Rome intervened and he was forced by the Roman envoy, Popilius Laenas, in the most humiliating manner, to withdraw. In his desire to unify his people in religion and culture (perhaps as a means of resisting Rome) he attempted to Hellenize the Jews and abolish the Jewish religion. He thus provoked the rising of the Maccabees; in the Bible the book of Daniel, which dates from this time, reflects his persecution of the Jews. After his death on an expedition in the East against the nascent Parthians, the Seleucid power gradually declined.

Antiochus IV was succeeded first by his son Antiochus V (d. 162) and then by Demetrius I (ruled 162–150), second son of Seleucus IV. The reign of his son Demetrius II (145–139 and 129–125) illustrates the difficulties faced by the later Seleucids faced with attacks by the Parthians and with the break-up of their kingdom through dynastic wars into a multitude of free cities and small kingdoms. A final attempt by Antiochus VII (brother of Demetrius II and king while his brother was in Parthian hands 139–129) to recover the territory lost to the Parthians was defeated in 129 BC, with the final loss of the Seleucid territories in the East. These two brothers were the last true members of the Seleucid line. Syria and Cilicia were finally annexed to Rome by Pompey in 65–63 BC. The importance of the Seleucids lies in their Hellenization of Asia, particularly in founding scores of cities, more or less Greek in character, chiefly by Seleucus I and Antiochus I: the former founded Antioch on the Orontēs as his Syrian capital and Seleucia on the Tigris as the capital of his empire.

sella curū'lis, see CURULE MAGISTRACIES.

Se'melē, see DIONYSUS.

Semnai, see FURIES.

Sēmō'nidēs (mid-seventh century BC), Greek iambic and elegiac poet originally of Samos but always connected with Amorgos (an island of the Sporades in the Aegean Sea), in the colonization of which he is said to have joined.

Very few fragments of his poetry survive. The longest piece, in iambics (see METRE, GREEK 5), describes various types of women by comparing them with animals. There is also a piece of elegiac verse on the shortness of life. Semonides writes with satirical humour in the Ionic *dialect.

sēnā'rius, see METRE, GREEK 5 and LATIN 2.

senate (*senātus*), at Rome, the council of the kings which survived the abolition of the monarchy (see ROME 1). The number of members first attested is 300, increased by Sulla to 600, by Julius Caesar to 900, and reduced by Augustus again to 600. It was at first a purely *patrician body. The origin (and significance) of the distinction between patrician and plebeian senators is not clear, but the latter must have existed by the second half of the fifth century BC. The ancient explanation for the description of senators as *patres conscripti*, 'conscript fathers', was that the original patrician senators were the *patres*, 'fathers', and the plebeian the *conscripti*, 'enrolled members' introduced into the senate by Romulus or at some later time; hence senators in a body were addressed as *patres ⟨et⟩ conscripti*. Membership was permanent (but see CENSORS). In early republican times senators were chosen by the consuls, later by the censors. In the late third century former *curule magistrates were the first to be chosen; Sulla made *quaestors members of the senate. Thus it became in practice an assembly of ex-magistrates. Senators received no payment. Although a property qualification was not stipulated until the time of Augustus (one million sesterces), senators were usually rich men from important families (see OPTIMATES, NOBILES, NOVUS HOMO), and membership of the senate tended to be hereditary.

Owing to its functions and permanence the senate was the real head of the state. It prepared legislative proposals to be brought before the people, and its resolutions, called *decreta* or, more commonly, *senatus consulta*, had some measure of effective if not legal authority (they could be vetoed by the tribunes). It exercised judicial powers through its right of appointing special courts of inquiry (see LAW, AT ROME 1 (ii)). It administered the finances, assigned magistrates to provinces, and dealt with foreign relations. It also supervised the practice of the state religion. Since it was a body of ex-magistrates, serious clashes were avoided between the *imperium* of the magistrates and the authority of the senate, and in general it exercised strong control over holders of office, tending to use them as its tools. The collapse of the republic came about when the authority of the senate was powerless against military leaders backed by their armies. Under the empire, although the senate lost its sovereign power, it was not without important functions, and *Augustus endeavoured to share with it the administration of the state. The senate retained control of certain *provinces and of the *aerarium* or public treasury; *senatus consulta* had force of law without requiring to be ratified by the people; and the judicial functions of the senate were increased. But in fact, partly owing to its own inefficiency, its power gradually diminished.

The senate met for business either in the Curia (senate house), which stood in the Forum, or within a mile of the city in a consecrated place. The first sitting of the year was in the temple of Jupiter Capitolinus. When a decision had to be reached each senator was asked his opinion according to his rank, censors followed by consuls, praetors, aediles, etc., patricians taking precedence over plebeians in each category. The senator heading the list, after Sulla any ex-consul of standing, plebeian as well as patrician, was known as the *princeps senatus, 'leader of the senate'. For senators' special clothing see DRESS 2.

sena'tūs consu'ltum u'ltimum ('the final resolution of the senate'), issued to the magistrates in a grave emergency, authorizing the consuls to use force for the protection of the state and suspending the right of appeal to the people. It took the form, *dent operam consules ne quid respublica detrimenti capiat* ('let the consuls see to it that the state suffer no harm'). It was first used in 122 BC against C. *Gracchus, and, among other occasions, against *Saturninus in 100 and *Catiline in 63. It was last employed (against Salvidienus Rufus) in 40 BC. The senate's legal right to enforce such a measure was always contested by the *populares*, e.g. in connection with C. Rabirius (see PRO RABIRIO).

Se'neca, Lucius Annae'us. 1. 'The Elder' or the 'Rhetorician', born at Corduba (Cordoba) in Spain *c.*55 BC of Italian stock and educated at Rome. He died between AD 37 and 41, before the exile of his son and namesake (see (2) below). By his marriage with Helvia, a fellow countrywoman, he had three sons: Annaeus Novātus, who took the name Gallio Annaeanus after his adoption by L. Junius Gallio (the proconsul of Achaea who dismissed the charges brought against the apostle Paul by the Corinthian Jews; see Acts 18: 12); Seneca (2) the philosopher; and M. Annaeus Mela, father of the poet Lucan. The Elder Seneca devoted himself to the study of rhetoric, and in his old age assembled for his sons a collection of *Controversiae* ('debates') and *Suasoriae* ('speeches of advice'). These were model exercises on rhetorical themes used in the schools of rhetoric: the former covered the oratory of the law courts and took the form of debates about imaginary problems in criminal or civil cases, e.g. whether a soldier has committed sacrilege by fighting bravely with weapons taken from a hero's tomb after losing his own; the latter were exercises in

deliberative (political) oratory and were speeches on such themes as whether 300 Spartans at Thermopylae (see PERSIAN WARS) should fight the Persians or run away. All the examples, dating from the time of Cicero to Seneca's old age, are extracts from rhetoricians whom Seneca had heard during his long life, a testimony to his astonishing memory (which he himself tells us was unrivalled) and an invaluable source for literary history. Of particular interest are the prefaces to the *Controversiae* where he discusses various orators, their analyses (*divisiones*) and lines of approach (*colorēs*) to the debates that follow, with many digressions and anecdotes. Only five of the original ten books of *Controversiae* and one book of *Suasoriae* are extant.

2. 'The Younger' or 'the Philosopher' (*c.*4 BC–AD 65).

1. He was the second son of Seneca the Elder (see above) and was born at Corduba (Cordoba) in Spain. He was brought as a child to Rome and educated there in rhetoric and philosophy. Embarking on a senatorial career he became an advocate, quaestor, and senator, and achieved a considerable reputation as an orator and writer, so much so that he provoked the jealousy of the emperor Caligula and in 39 narrowly escaped being put to death. Under Claudius Seneca occupied a position at court. In 41 he was banished to Corsica for alleged adultery with Julia (sometimes called Livilla), the youngest daughter of Germanicus and Agrippina the Elder, and sister of Caligula. Julia's sister, also called Agrippina (the Younger), mother of *Nero, had him recalled in 49 and he was made tutor to the young Nero. In 51 Burrus, who was to become Seneca's friend and colleague, was made prefect of praetorians. On the accession of Nero in 54 Seneca became the emperor's political adviser, and for the next eight years Rome and the empire enjoyed good government, largely under the direction of Seneca and Burrus. But Nero's behaviour became increasingly wilful, and after the death of Burrus in 62 the willingness of others to condone the emperor's excesses reduced Seneca's influence and he asked permission to retire. He left Rome and devoted the next three years to philosophy and his friends. In 65 he was implicated in the unsuccessful conspiracy of Piso and forced to commit suicide. His courageous death is described by Tacitus (*Annals* 15. 64).

The inconsistencies between Seneca's moral principles, his political life, and the behaviour of his pupil emperor have provoked much speculation, and he has been severely judged. He would appear to have condoned the murders of Claudius, Britannicus, and Agrippina, and he certainly acquired enormous wealth at a court where his professed moral principles were utterly ignored. He conformed to his principles too late to save his reputation. However, he was a humane and tolerant man, for many years a successful politician and an influence for good, and a writer of considerable and varied talent.

2. Seneca wrote voluminously. Besides the works that survive we have titles or fragments of treatises on geography, natural history, and ethics, among many others. His extant prose works comprise, first, the ten ethical treatises given the name *Dialogi* ('dialogues'): *De providentia, De constantia sapientis, *De ira (in three books), De consolatione ad Marciam, *De vita beata, De otio, De tranquillitate animi, *De brevitate vitae, De consolatione ad Polybium, De consolatione ad Helviam matrem. These seem to have been written between 37 and 43. The 'Consolation to Marcia' is an attempt to console the daughter of Cremutius Cordus (a historian, victim of Sejanus) for the death of her sons. The 'Consolation to Helvia' written to his mother to console her for his own exile in 41, shows fortitude and dignity. The 'Consolation to Polybius' is addressed to a freedman of the emperor Claudius, an unattractive piece written c.43 to obtain recall from exile. (This Polybius appears to have translated Homer into Latin prose and Virgil into Greek.) The treatises 'On the constancy of the wise man', 'On tranquillity of the soul', and 'On leisure' (De otio) were addressed to Annaeus Serēnus, *praefectus vigilum under Nero. The theme of the first is that a wise man can suffer neither wrong nor insult. The second is concerned with the pursuit of peace of mind; the third is a defence of leisure and relaxation, and of the value of philosophical speculation and meditation.

Outside this collection of treatises there are further moral essays, *De clementia and *De beneficiis, and the *Epistulae morales*, a collection of 124 letters addressed to his friend Lucilius, divided into twenty books. The letters are also in effect moral essays (the fiction of a genuine correspondence is only sporadically aimed at), and are written in the tradition of the philosophical letter (compare PLATO 6) or the *diatribe. The nature of the subject matter—on happiness, the supreme good, riches, the terrors of death, and so forth—and the charm and informality of style, have made them the most popular of Seneca's works. They are persuasive, not dogmatic, in tone, and furnish interesting personal details about the author himself, as well as being illuminating about contemporary life. They were approved and made use of by early Christian writers. Seneca was thought in the Middle Ages to have been a Christian, and was believed by St Jerome and others to have corresponded with the apostle Paul. His treatises were studied by Petrarch (1304–74) and known to Chaucer (c.1343–1400).

3. Of a different order are the seven books of Seneca's *Naturales quaestiones*, dedicated to Lucilius and written during Seneca's retirement towards the end of his life. This work is an examination of natural phenomena, not from a scientific but from a *Stoic standpoint. It is not a systematic work but a collection of facts about nature. The phenomena are grouped according to their connection with one or other of the four elements, earth, air, fire, and water, with moral observations scattered throughout. The purpose of the work seems to be to find in nature a foundation for Stoic ethic. Though of little scientific value the work was used in the Middle Ages as a text-book of natural science.

The *Apocolocyntosis* is a clever and original piece of satirical burlesque on the death of the emperor Claudius, written in the form of a Menippean satire in a medley of prose and verse.

Most of Seneca's prose work is philosophical, and an important source for the history of Stoicism. His own brand of that philosophy was undogmatic and tempered by experience and common sense, and is often used as the basis for moral exhortation rather than expounded as a system of thought in its own right. The style is lively and rhetorical; it catches the attention immediately, but its unremitting brilliance, lacking depth of thought, is tiring: 'sand without lime' (i.e. cement that crumbles) is how the emperor Caligula described it.

4. Seneca's most important poetical works are nine tragedies adapted from the Greek: *Hercules furens, Medea, Troades (*Trojan Women), Phaedra* (all based at least in part on Euripides), *Agamemnon* (presumably owing a debt to Aeschylus but one not easily traced), *Oedipus, Hercules Oetaeus* (the former very Sophoclean, the latter, which may not be genuinely by Seneca, not very like its presumed source, Sophocles' *Trachiniae), Phoenissae* (owing a little to Sophocles' *Oedipus Coloneus), and Thyestes* (a gruesome story with no extant source). A tenth tragedy attributed to Seneca, *Octavia*, is obviously not by him. (See individual entries for each of these.) The plays are written on Greek lines, that is, with dramatic episodes (written in iambic senarii; see METRE, LATIN 2) separated by choral odes (in lyric metres, most often anapaestic); it is likely that Seneca intended his tragedies for private recitation rather than for acting. They are exaggerations of the Euripidean style, showing psychological insight but markedly rhetorical and pointed in manner, and Seneca loves to dwell on the horrific and macabre elements of the plot. But the *stichomythia is often more effective than that of the Greek original, and the ending of Seneca's *Medea* is more dramatic than that of Euripides. There are fine passages of description, much moralizing, and some striking epigrams. The plays also convey the Euripidean sense of the individual as victim. They exerted a great influence in the Italian Renaissance and in Tudor and Jacobean times in England; stock characters in the romantic plays of Shakespeare, such as the ghost, the nurse, and the barbarous

villain, were transmitted from the Greek through the medium of Seneca.

The *Anthologia Latina* (see ANTHOLOGY 2) includes a number of short poems by Seneca, some containing references to his own life and family.

septenā'rius, see METRE, LATIN 2.

Se'ptuagint (in abbreviation LXX), Greek version of the Hebrew Old Testament which derives its name from a story, now known to be false, contained in an Alexandrian work of the second century BC, the *Letter to Philocratēs*, supposedly by a Greek called Aristeas. The story states that the translation from the Hebrew was made at the request of Ptolemy II Philadelphus (king of Egypt 283–246 BC), who wanted it for the royal library, and that the translators were seventy-two (or seventy, Lat. *septuaginta*) learned Jews, kept in seclusion on the island of Pharos off Alexandria until their task was finished. The translation must in fact have been made by Egyptian Jews working independently of one another and living at different periods in the Hellenistic age. The Septuagint differs from the Old Testament both in the order of the books and in the inclusion of those books which are usually known as the Apocrypha. There are also textual differences. The Christian Fathers down to the late fourth century AD regarded the Septuagint as the standard form of the Old Testament and seldom referred to the Hebrew. *Origen, however, was much interested in its relation to the Hebrew and to other Greek versions. See also VULGATE.

Serā'pis (or Sarapis), new god introduced to Egypt by Ptolemy I Soter (367–283 BC) and apparently derived from a combined Osiris–Apis deity who was the object of cult at Memphis (see EGYPT). Soter's object may have been to give the people of Alexandria a patron deity which they otherwise lacked. No doubt the Egyptian aspects of the new god were important in uniting Greek and Egyptian elements in the population. Before long the cult had spread to other Greek cities. Serapis had retained many of the chthonic aspects of the Egyptian *Osiris, and the two gods were often connected in cult; thus Serapis was sometimes identified with Dionysus in his chthonic role, as well as with Hades (Pluto). He also acquired the role of a god of healing and was identified with Asclepius, an aspect which spread to other cult-centres. Demetrius of Phalērum (a close adviser of Soter) was cured of his blindness, reputedly by the god, in Alexandria, and in consequence wrote a paean to him. Other identifications of Serapis arose, e.g. with Zeus and Helios. The goddess *Isis came to be thought of as his spouse, Harpocratēs or Horus as their child, and Anubis as their faithful companion who conveyed to Osiris the souls of the dead. Ptolemy III Euergetēs (reigned 246–221) built the Serapeum, a vast temple to Serapis, at Alexandria.

As an object of worship he seems to have appealed mostly to Greeks of the official or upper class, that is, to those closely connected with the royal house whose deity he was.

serf, one who is bound, usually on a hereditary basis, to work land belonging to another, keeping a small portion of his produce to maintain himself and his family. Since a serf is not free to leave the land, serfdom may be accounted a form of slavery.

Sermō'nes, see SATIRES of Horace.

Sertō'rius, Quintus, distinguished Roman soldier, supporter of *Marius. He joined Cinna in his march on Rome in 87 BC but opposed Marius' indiscriminate slaughter. He became praetor in 83 and was given Spain as his province. In 80 BC he accepted an invitation by the Lusitanians (in western Spain) to lead them in a revolt against Rome. With the support of some exiles from Rome he was successful against many Roman commanders (including Pompey) and at one time held most of Roman Spain. Gradually losing ground to Metellus and Pompey, and his popularity having waned, he was murdered in 73 or 72 by his lieutenant Perperna.

Se'rvius (Marius Servius Honorātus), Latin grammarian and commentator of the early fifth century AD, whose greatest work was a commentary on Virgil. Since it was intended for school use it dwells mostly upon grammatical, rhetorical, and stylistic points, but some notes on the subject matter are included which contain very valuable information. The commentary is found in the manuscripts in a shorter (the original Servian) and a longer version, the latter known as *Servius auctus* ('augmented Servius') or *Servius Danielis* (named after its discoverer, P. Daniel, and published in 1600), incorporating much earlier material.

Se'rvius Tu'llius, semi-legendary king of Rome, sixth in succession from Romulus; according to tradition he reigned from 578 to 535 BC. He was the successor of Tarquinius Priscus, in whose house he was brought up as a slave. There was a legend of his miraculous birth to a slave-woman and the fire-god Vulcan. His rule is said to have been mild, and a number of public works and constitutional reforms were attributed to him (see ROME 2). He is said to have established a Latin cult of the goddess Diana on the Aventine. Archaeological finds confirm that the temples of Fortuna and Mater *Matuta ascribed to him were founded in the sixth century BC. He was murdered by the order of Lucius Tarquinius, son of Priscus, at the instigation of his own daughter, Tullia, who was Lucius' wife. Lucius succeeded him and was known as Tarquinius Superbus.

seste'rtius (pl. *sestertii*, Eng. sesterces), in Roman currency, a small silver coin; there were 4 sesterces to the denarius. See MONEY AND COINS.

Sestus, in its day the principal Greek town of the Thracian Chersonese, on the Hellespont (Dardanelles) opposite Abydus (see LEANDER). Until eclipsed by *Byzantium it was the usual port of departure for those crossing from Europe to Asia. It was the site of the western end of the bridge of boats constructed by Xerxēs for the passage of the Persian army into Greece. From 478, after the Persian defeat at Mycalē, it remained in Athenian hands until it fell to Sparta at the end of the *Peloponnesian War (see 6). It regained its independence in the early fourth century and retained it against Athenian attack, but in 353 it fell to the Athenian general Charēs, who killed or enslaved the inhabitants.

Seven against Thebes, The (Gk. *Hepta epi Thēbas*, Lat. *Septem contra Thēbas*), tragedy by *Aeschylus, produced in 467 BC, the third play in a trilogy dealing with related events, the first two plays being *Laius* and *Oedipus*; the *satyr-play which followed it was also related in subject matter, being entitled *Sphinx*; all these plays except the *Seven* are lost.

Polyneicēs, son of Oedipus, has come, aided by the Argive army, to claim the kingdom of Thebes, unjustly retained by his brother Eteoclēs (see OEDIPUS). The scene is the city of Thebes, and the chorus is composed of Theban women. A messenger announces the disposition of the Argive army and describes the seven champions preparing to lead the attack, one at each of the seven gates of Thebes. Eteocles appoints a Theban opponent to withstand each one, finding himself left to oppose Polyneices; Eteocles rushes out to face his brother in spite of the dissuasions of the chorus. Their deaths at each other's hands are announced, and their bodies are borne in, mourned by the chorus. In a scene probably added by an imitator their sisters Ismenē and Antigonē join in the lamentation. A herald announces the decree that the body of Polyneices, who has waged war on his own city, shall lie unburied. Antigone at once declares that she will defy the edict: she will bury him herself.

For the Argive background see ADRASTUS. The seven champions in Aeschylus' play are Adrastus, Tydeus (an exile at Argos from Calydon), Parthenopaeus (an Arcadian, son of Atalanta), Capaneus, Hippomedon, Amphiaraus, and Polyneices. In other versions of the story two alternative champions were sometimes included, Eteocles, son of Iphis, instead of Adrastus, and Mecisteus, Adrastus' brother, instead of Polyneices. The story was told in the *Thebais*, a poem of the *Epic Cycle.

seven hills of Rome, the Capitoline, Palatine, Aventine, Quirinal, Viminal, Esquiline, and Caelian hills.

seven liberal arts, a loose classification of the subjects comprising the educational curriculum in the West during the Middle Ages, from the late fifth century AD onwards. The name 'liberal arts' seems to originate with Aristotle who in the *Politics* talks of *eleutherai epistēmai*, 'branches of knowledge worthy of free men', the basic knowledge needed for a properly educated citizen. See EDUCATION 4 and 6. They were divided into the *trivium, namely grammar (i.e. literature), rhetoric, and dialectic, and the more advanced *quadrivium, namely arithmetic, geometry, music, and astronomy. For the original nine see VARRO; see also CASSIODORUS and MARTIANUS CAPELLA.

seven kings of Rome. In its earliest days Rome was ruled by a succession of seven kings. According to tradition these were Romulus (founder of the city), Numa Pompilius, Tullus Hostilius, Ancus Martius, Tarquinius Priscus, Servius Tullius, and Tarquinius Superbus (see ROME 2).

Seven Sages, name given by Greek tradition to seven men of practical wisdom—statesmen, law-givers, and philosophers—of the seventh and sixth centuries BC. The list of sages is variously given in different authorities, but generally it comprises *Solon of Athens, *Thalēs of Miletus, *Pittacus of Mitylēnē, Cleobulus of Rhodes, *Chilon of Sparta, Bias of Priēnē, and *Periander of Corinth. Many pieces of proverbial wisdom were attributed to them, such as those inscribed at *Delphi, 'Know yourself' and 'Nothing in excess'.

Seven Wonders of the Ancient World. Listed in Hellenistic times, these were the Pyramids of Egypt, the Hanging Gardens of Babylon, the Mausoleum at Halicarnassus (see MAUSOLOS), the Temple of Artemis at *Ephesus, the statue of Zeus at Olympia (by *Pheidias), the *Colossus of Rhodes, and the *Pharos of Alexandria.

Seve'rus, Lucius Septi'mius, Roman emperor AD 193–211. See BRITAIN 5.

Sextus Empi'ricus (flourished *c*. AD 200), Greek physician whose writings are the chief source of information on the *Sceptical school of philosophy. In his 'Outlines of Pyrrhonism' (*Pyrrhō-neioi hypotypōseis*) in three books, he states the case for the Sceptics and attacks dogmatic philosophies. In his other work 'Against the Professors' (*Pros tous mathēmatikous*, Lat. *Adversus mathematicos*) he refutes the teachers of the various branches of learning in succession.

shaft-graves, see MYCENAE.

Shield of Heracles (*Aspis Herakleous*), Greek narrative poem in 480 hexameters attributed to *Hesiod but written too late to be by him. The first 56 lines tell the story of Alcmena, mother of Heracles, and come from the *Catalogue of Women* or *Eoeae*, also erroneously attributed to Hesiod. The poem goes on to relate briefly the killing by Heracles of Cycnus, son of Arēs. For the encounter Heracles has put on armour given him by Hephaestus, including a shield, the disproportionately long description of which (in imitation of Homer's description of the shield of Achilles in the *Iliad*) gives the poem its title.

ships, Greek and Roman. The shipping of the Mediterranean in ancient times may be broadly divided into two classes, the slim, light-draught warship and the heavy, slow merchantman. The former was propelled by oars and had a mast (which could be dismantled) and a sail to be used if needed; the latter had a permanent mast and was mainly propelled by sail, with the assistance of a few oars for e.g. changing tack.

The earliest Greek warship was the long penteconter (*pentekonteros*, 'fifty-oarer'), with twenty-five rowers single-banked on each side. The later trireme, having three banks of oars, remained the standard Greek warship until Hellenistic times; the Athenian historian Thucydides says that triremes were first built at Corinth, and that Ameinoclēs of Corinth built four of them for the Samians *c.*700 BC. To judge from the excavated remains of ship-sheds at Piraeus, the Athenian trireme of classical times was up to 37 m. (120 ft.) long and 5 m. (16 ft.) in beam, partially decked to provide a platform for fighting men (see below), and with a hooked prow strengthened with bronze for ramming. It carried a trierarch or commander (see LITURGY) and a complement of 200 comprising 170 oarsmen (*nautai*), ten soldiers (*epibatai*), four archers (*toxotai*), and some sixteen extra men who included the helmsman (*kybernētēs*), the chief technical officer on board, who sat on a raised platform at the stern to steer the ship. There was no spare room on board, nor was the ship very seaworthy, and therefore it was beached at night to let the crew cook and sleep.

The arrangement of oars in a trireme has long been a matter of argument. It now seems that there were on each side of the trireme a top row of 31 oars and below it two rows of 27. The rowers sat in three more or less superimposed rows, called *thranitai*, *zygioi*, and *thalamioi* (at the bottom), the individual positions staggered fore and aft so that none was immediately above or below the other; to the outside view this gave a pattern of oblique lines. Each rower thus had his own oar, and the rowers were not seated three to a bench as has sometimes been suggested. The design was intended to achieve greater oar-power and thus to be most efficient in ramming, with as little increase as possible in the weight and length of the ship. Even so a good speed for a trireme, in favourable conditions but not under pressure, is unlikely to have exceeded 7 or 8 knots.

Between 483 and 480 BC Themistocles had 200 triremes built at Athens for defence against Persia (see PERSIAN WARS). By the beginning of the Peloponnesian War (431 BC) the city had 300 triremes, whose crews were intensively trained. Only in exceptional circumstances were they used to fight on land. They were recruited from the property class of Athenian citizens known as *thētēs* (see SOLON), supplemented as the empire developed by the poorer *metics and by slaves and mercenaries. They were each paid 3 obols a day, with perhaps an equal amount payable upon return at the end of a voyage. At first the main aim of a commander in battle was to sink the enemy ship by ramming it, but in the fifth century BC the Athenians developed a manœuvre for disabling an enemy ship by breaking its oars (*diekplous*).

In the fourth century BC there appeared quadriremes and quinqueremes, the latter becoming the standard warship of the Roman republic. The crew on a Roman quinquereme numbered 300, but the arrangement of oars and rowers is even more obscure than in the case of the trireme. The Roman navy was of little importance until the time of the Punic Wars. For the efficient prosecution of the First Punic War (264–241 BC) the Romans set about building a large fleet, copying a captured Carthaginian quinquereme. They adapted the new ships to the tactics of land warfare, fitting them with grappling-irons and bridges for boarding (*corvi*) and placing a number of soldiers in the bows. With these ships and tactics they won the war, though they were evidently less experienced seamen than the Carthaginians. After the Second Punic War (ended 201 BC) the fleet fell into neglect; in the first century BC Pompey was forced to collect ships from the Rhodians and others for his operations against the pirates, and Julius Caesar had to improvise a fleet in the civil war. Sextus Pompeius, Antony, and Octavian raised large fleets for their struggles with one another, among which figured *liburnae*, so named from the Liburnians who lived on the coast of Illyria. These were fast ships mostly with one or two banks of oars and a very large lateen (i.e. triangular) sail. The Romans had used them in the Second Macedonian War (in 171 BC) and gradually they came to supplant the quinqueremes. Roman ships had a figure-head on the prow appropriate to the name of the ship; a bronze Minerva, now in the British Museum, was found near Actium. (Greek ships had an eye painted on each side of the prow.) Virgil, in *Aeneid* 5, gives names from myth to a number of Aeneas' ships (not all of them female, as was the case with Greek ships).

There was a great extension of Roman naval power under the empire. A fleet stationed on the river Rhine played a very important part in the operations of Drusus, Tiberius, and Germanicus in Germany. From the time perhaps of the emperor Claudius' invasion of Britain in AD 43 there was also a Roman fleet in the Channel, based on Gesoriacum (Boulogne). It circumnavigated Britain and discovered the Orkneys, and its marines helped to build Hadrian's Wall.

Merchant ships were normally propelled by sails and were much wider in proportion to their length (1 : 4) than warships (1 : 7). Greek merchant ships represented on vases have one mast, a yard, and a square sail. Later a second and even a third mast were introduced, also a triangular topsail with its base attached to the main yard and its apex to the masthead. With the spread of commerce vessels increased in size; under the Roman empire a merchantman could carry about 400 tons. Exceptionally large ships were built under Augustus and Caligula to bring to Italy the Flaminian (as it is now called) and Vatican obelisks respectively. (The former was erected in the Circus Maximus, the latter on the Vatican hill, where it stands at present in front of St Peter's.) The Vatican obelisk with its pedestal weighed about 500 tons, and the ship carried in addition some 800 tons (according to Pliny) of lentils as packing. (For Caligula's intention to convey to Rome the statue of Zeus at Olympia see OLYMPIA.)

Sibyl (Sibylla), general name given by the Greeks and Romans to various prophetesses in the Greek and Roman world, who sometimes had individual names as well. Thus the most ancient Sibyl known in legend was Hērophilē, who prophesied to Hecuba, queen of Troy, before the Trojan War. She was also known as the Erythraean Sibyl from her birthplace Erythrae (perhaps the city of that name on the coast of Asia Minor opposite Chios). The Sibyls prophesied in an ecstatic state, and were believed to be possessed by a god, usually Apollo, who spoke through them (compare the Pythia at Delphi). Their utterances were written down, and cities made official collections of what were believed to be their prophecies; at Athens similar collections of oracles were kept on the Acropolis (see ONOMACRITUS and ORACLES).

The most famous Sibyl in antiquity was that of Cumae in Campania (sometimes identified with the Erythraean) whom Virgil represents as being visited by Aeneas (see AENEID 6). The cave in which she lived still exists. Her prophecies were said to have been inscribed on palm-leaves. According to legend she offered nine volumes of oracles to the last king of Rome, Tarquinius Superbus, at a high price. When he refused to buy she burned three volumes and offered the remainder at the same price. When he again refused she burned three more, and finally sold the last three to him at the original price. The king is said to have entrusted these Sibylline books (libri Sibyllini) to the care of two patricians.

However acquired, books of oracles certainly existed in Rome at an early date, and were consulted not only for guidance about the future but in order to find out how to placate divine anger in times of great calamity, such as earthquake and plague. They were kept in a chest in a stone vault under the temple of the Capitoline *Jupiter. In 496 BC they were consulted during a famine and recommended the institution of the cult of the gods Liber, Libera, and Ceres. In 461, after many omens had been seen, they recommended certain rituals and warned of disturbances. During a plague in 433 they were interpreted as recommending the foundation of a temple to Apollo. In 367 the number of custodians was increased to ten (half of them plebeians) and in the first half of the first century BC to fifteen, the quindecimviri sacris faciundis whose business it was to consult the oracles when required to do so by the senate. When the oracles were destroyed in the temple fire of 83 BC, envoys were sent to various places to make a fresh collection of similar oracular sayings, which was subsequently placed by Augustus in the temple of Apollo on the Palatine hill. The last known consultation was in AD 363. The collection was still in existence in the temple when the latter was destroyed by Stilicho, the general of the emperors Theodosius I and Honorius early in the fifth century. Fourteen miscellaneous books of oracles, of Judaeo-Hellenistic and Christian origin, still survive. Because of Christian interpolations in the Sibylline oracles, the Sibyls came to be thought of as on an equality with Old Testament prophets, and frequently figure with them in Christian literature and art.

A famous story told of the Cumaean Sibyl relates that the god Apollo once offered her anything she wished if she would take him as her lover. She asked to live as many years as there were grains of sand in a pile of sweepings, and these numbered a thousand, but she failed to ask for continued youth. Trimalchio, a character in *Petronius' Satyricon, had seen her with his own eyes, he said, hanging from the ceiling of her cave in a bottle, and when children asked her what she wanted, she used to reply, 'I want to die'. In the days of the Greek traveller Pausanias (second century AD) a jar was shown at Cumae said to contain her bones.

Sicilian Expedition, see PELOPONNESIAN WAR 5.

Sicily (Gk. Sikelia, Lat. Sicilia), large island separated from Italy by the Straits of Messina. The Thrīnacia mentioned in Homer's Odyssey (from Greek thrīnax, 'trident') is perhaps to be identified with it. Trīnacria was a Latin poetical name for the island. Its position in the centre of the Mediterranean made it a meeting-place for settlers from east and west, and from Italy and Africa, and gave it great importance in the history of the Mediterranean world. Remains of the Mycenaean period have been found on the island. Ancient writers speak of there being three native peoples: Elymi in the west, Sicani in the west-central, and Siceli in the east. Thucydides says that the Sicanians and Sicels were Iberian and Italian respectively; the Elymi he describes as fleeing from the sack of Troy. He goes on to say that the Phoenicians settled in Sicily before the Greeks, but that may not in fact be the case; and Phoenician colonization may have been limited to Panormus, Solŏeis (Soluntum), and Motya.

In the eighth and seventh centuries BC the Greeks founded many colonies on the coast of Sicily (see COLONIZATION, GREEK 2); the original inhabitants were ejected and driven inland or (at Syracuse) reduced to dependent status (although at Leontini there was peaceful coexistence). Once established, the Greeks soon spread their civilization, the Phoenicians acquiescing but defending their territories against Greek encroachments in the sixth century. In the early fifth century Carthage (a Phoenician colony in North Africa) chose the moment when the Persians under Xerxes were invading Greece to extend Phoenician power in Sicily, acting perhaps in concert with the Persians; but they were defeated by Gelon, tyrant of Syracuse (see SYRACUSE 1), who won a great victory over them at Himera in 480 BC. From this time onwards the history of Sicily is in its main features bound up with that of Syracuse, its principal city.

During the first part of the fifth century BC the courts of the Sicilian tyrants were centres of culture and great wealth, as may be seen from odes written for them by *Pindar in celebration of their victories at the Panhellenic games, as well as from the surviving ruins. After the death of Hieron, tyrant of Syracuse, in 467, democracy was restored in the Sicilian cities, but not effectively enough to deter interference from outside the island. The Athenians twice intervened, in 427–424, without succeeding in their aim of ultimately controlling the island, and disastrously for themselves in 415–413 (see PELOPONNESIAN WAR). Carthage, attempting to profit by the exhaustion of Syracuse, captured Selinus and Himera in 409, Acragas and Gela in 406–5. During this critical time Dionysius I, a Syracusan general, succeeded in establishing himself as tyrant of Syracuse and was able to drive back the invaders in 392 and make peace with them. Syracuse came to control all Sicily except for the Carthaginian territories in the far west. Dionysius' death in 367 was followed by civil war and the establishment of separate tyrannies in the various cities. Carthage again took her chance but her expedition against Sicily in 339 was defeated by Timoleon (see SYRACUSE 3) at the battle of the Crīmīsus, and the Carthaginians were once more confined to the western part of the island. Timoleon's

arrangements collapsed after his death (c.336). Agathoclēs of Syracuse seized the tyranny of that city in 317 and before his death in 289 had gained power over most of the island. A more lasting consequence of his rule was that his ex-mercenaries, the *Mamertini, found a home for themselves in Messana, thereby bringing about the initial clash between Rome and Carthage.

The history of Sicily now becomes merged with that of Rome. In 278 *Pyrrhus was called in by Syracuse, then beset by a Carthaginian fleet and army. But although he drove the Carthaginians out of all Sicily except Lilybaeum, his scheme of empire failed and the venture ended in 275. Carthage recovered the north and west of the island, and this was the occasion for Roman interference. The First *Punic War (264–241) ensued, after which the island, with the temporary exception of the dominions of Hieron II of Syracuse, became a Roman province. After Hieron's death in 215 Syracuse went over to Carthage, but with the Roman capture of Syracuse in 211 (see ARCHIMEDES) all Sicily was included in the province. Large *latifundia grew up there, worked by slaves whose harsh conditions provoked two serious slave revolts in the last years of the second century BC (see SLAVERY 2).

Sicily produced many Greeks famous in literary history, among them the poet Stesichorus, the sophist Gorgias, the scientists Empedoclēs and Archimēdēs, the historian Timaeus, the pastoral poet Theocritus, and Herodas the writer of mimes. It became one of the principal points of contact between Rome and Greek culture. It also earned fame of a sort as the scene of the depredations of the Roman governor Verrēs (see CICERO (1) 1).

Sicyŏ'nius ('the Sicyonian man'), Greek comedy by *Menander, of which some 470 fragmentary lines from the second half have been recovered from a papyrus used by Egyptian mummifiers when making a papier mâché mummy case (see PAPYROLOGY). The play concerns Stratophanēs (the Sicyonian of the title), a successful captain of mercenaries who on returning to Athens after service in Caria has taken a house at Eleusis, and his discovery of his real father and of the identity and Athenian citizenship of a girl whom he has purchased as a slave in Caria and now wishes to marry.

Sīdō'nius (Gaius Sollius Apollināris Sidonius, canonized as St Sidonius Apollinaris, c. AD 430–c.480), a notable Gallo-Roman poet and bishop of Augustonemetum (Clermont-Ferrand), chief town of the Arverni region of Gaul (now the Auvergne). He was born at Lugdunum (Lyons) of a prominent Christian family, and his father and grandfather both held important civic offices. When his wife's father Avītus was proclaimed Roman emperor in the West in 455, Sidonius pronounced a panegyric in verse, for which he was rewarded by a statue in the Ulpian Library of Trajan at Rome. When Avitus was dethroned in 456, Sidonius was reconciled to the new emperor Majorian for whom also he wrote a panegyric (458). When Majorian was overthrown in 461, Sidonius withdrew to Gaul but wrote a third panegyric for a later emperor Anthemius. He became bishop in 469, and resisted an invasion of Visigoths with courage and devotion, giving up the struggle only when the whole Auvergne was ceded to them in 475. Released from imprisonment in 476 he devoted himself to his diocese and to literature until his death. Sidonius was one of the last major figures of classical culture. His poems (twenty-four survive), addressed to friends, are replete with mythological allusions and show great technical skill if limited originality. He also published nine books of letters, many written with an eye to publication and the rest carefully revised. One of the letters records the classic if rather meaningless example of a palindrome (a phrase which reads the same forwards and backwards): *Roma tibi subito motibus ibit amor*, which may be translated, 'Rome, your love, will suddenly collapse in disturbances'. Both letters and poems are often interesting for the light they throw on life and conditions in Gaul in the fifth century.

Si'geum (Gk. Sigeion), see COLONIZATION, GREEK 3.

siki'nnis, in Greece, violent dance associated with the performance of satyr-plays (see SATYRIC DRAMA), the name sometimes said to have been derived from its Cretan inventor. It may have originated with dances performed by votaries of Bacchus or Dionysus.

Silē'nus (Seilēnos). In Greek myth Silenus represented the spirit of wild life in a creature half-man, half-animal in form (compare SATYRS). He is shown on Attic vases of the early sixth century BC having horse-ears and sometimes horse-legs and a tail. Sometimes a collection of sileni are found, and classical authors frequently confuse them with satyrs, but in general, whereas satyrs are young, sileni are thought of as old men, and being old are thought to be wise. A famous story relates how *Midas made Silenus drunk in order to learn his secrets. In Virgil, Eclogue 6, Silenus is caught by two shepherds and sings them songs of ancient myths. He is sometimes represented as Dionysus' tutor, or depicted in the train of Dionysus, making music or getting drunk. (See also the *Cyclops* of Euripides.) *Socrates was often compared with Silenus, and likenesses of the former are remarkably similar to ancient portrait heads of the latter. But the comparison was meant to include not only physical appearance but a common incongruity between outward appearance and inner wisdom.

Sī'lius Ita'licus (Tiberius Catius Ascōnius Silius Italicus; *c.* AD 26–*c.*101), Latin poet. His life is chiefly known to us from a letter of the Younger Pliny (3.7), and from references in Martial's epigrams. He was probably born at Patavium (Padua) and having won fame as an advocate was consul in 68, the last year of the emperor Nero's reign. Later, *c.*77, he won praise as proconsul for his administration of Asia. Thereafter he lived in retirement on his estates near Naples. He was a wealthy man, bought country houses (including a villa once belonging to Cicero, whom he revered), and was a collector of books and works of art. He had a profound admiration for Virgil, whose tomb near Naples, on one of his properties, he restored. Finding that he was suffering from an incurable disease he starved himself to death at the age of 75. He was the author of the longest surviving Latin poem, *Punica*, an epic in seventeen books of hexameters on the Second *Punic War (218–201 BC). It begins with *Hannibal's oath, his appointment to the command, and, except for digressions on the captured Roman general Regulus and Dido's sister Anna, it proceeds in order through the principal episodes of the war, the crossing of the Alps, the battles of the Ticinus, the Trebia, Lake Trasimene, and Cannae, the capture of Syracuse, the battle of the Metaurus, Scipio in Spain and Africa, and the final battle of Zama.

Silius was highly praised as Virgil's poetic heir by Martial, but the Younger Pliny's remark that his epic was written with more diligence than inspiration (*maiore cura quam ingenio*) has been found more apt. The subject matter came from Livy, the form from study of Virgil and Lucan. Following Virgil's practice (and in contrast with Lucan) Silius retained the intervention of the gods in the conflict, traditional in epic since Homer. However, to mythicize the real world of Hannibal and Scipio so as to mingle gods and men without incongruity required more tact and delicacy than Silius shows; it is, for example, bizarre to find the Carthaginian general Hannibal saved from death by the goddess Juno, just as the legendary Turnus is saved in the *Aeneid*. Almost equally incongruous are the traditional epic ingredients of catalogues (of Hannibal's allies, of the Roman forces at Cannae, for example), funeral games, description of a hero's shield (Hannibal's), Nereids (sea-nymphs) disturbed by a vast fleet (Carthaginian), and altercations of antagonists on the battle-field. The greatness of the theme—Rome's heroic rise from defeat to victory—is lost through lack of proportion and good sense, and some aspects repel the reader, notably the excessively realistic descriptions of slaughter (perhaps due to Lucan's influence). The work as a whole is dull and lifeless and lacks the power of Lucan. But the writing is generally lucid and straightforward, the composition runs easily and pleasantly, and the shorter episodes are well told. There are some memorable phrases: *rarae fumant felicibus arae*, 'rarely do the altars of the fortunate smoke [with sacrifices]', and *explorant adversa viros*, 'adversity is the test of men'.

silloi ('squint-eyed' poems, 'lampoons'), see TIMON (2). The name was applied generally to Greek satirical poems, and appears to have been given to certain poems of *Xenophanēs satirizing the myths of Homer and Hesiod.

silvae. The Latin word *silva* in its sense of 'raw material' (compare Greek *hylē*) was extended in a literary sense to the raw material of a literary work; Quintilian explains it as a quickly produced first draft of a poem. It was used in the plural, *silvae*, of collections of occasional poems, and thus it came to be the title given by the poet *Statius to his collection of (mostly) short poems published in five books. The first four books appeared between AD 91 and 95; the fifth was probably put together after Statius' death in 96. The survival of these poems depended on a manuscript discovered in 1417. Most are written in hexameters, but six are in lyric metres, alcaics, sapphics, and hendecasyllables (see METRE, GREEK 3 and 8). Statius wrote them for his patrons, who included the emperor Domitian, on a variety of subjects suggested by incidents in the patrons' lives as well as in the poet's own; his poem on the death of a friend's parrot is well known (2. 4). He has been accused of servility, and it is true that he wrote what his patrons wanted to hear. But some of the poems are sincere and moving: an invocation to sleep (5. 4), an affectionate address to his wife Claudia (3. 5), and an epithalamium on the marriage of his friend Assuntius Stella (1. 2).

Silva'nus, 'of the wood', in Roman religion, the god of the wild land beyond the boundaries of the cultivated fields. He thus resembled the Greek *satyrs or *Silenus, and was sometimes identified with them, but more often with the god *Pan. His cult was regarded as very ancient, and it was important to propitiate him before violating his territory, e.g. cutting down trees.

Silver Age, of Latin literature, term sometimes applied to the post-Augustan period; see LATIN LANGUAGE 2 and ROME 10 and 11.

Sīmo'nidēs. 1. Of Ceos (a small Ionian Greek island off the coast of Attica), 556–468 BC, Greek lyric and elegiac poet and famous writer of sepulchral *epigrams. He was uncle of the poet Bacchylides. As a professional poet he travelled widely in the Greek world. He was the guest of *Hipparchus at Athens during the Peisistratid tyranny, and subsequently went to Thessaly, where he was the guest of the Scopads and later wrote a dirge lamenting their deaths (see below). He seems to have been in Athens in 490, when his epitaph on the Athenian dead at the battle of Marathon (see PERSIAN WARS) was preferred to that of Aeschylus who had fought in it. After the Persian Wars he became the ally of *Themistocles, on whose behalf he attacked in his poetry the Rhodian poet Timocreon. When he was 80 he won the dithyrambic competition at Athens 'in the archonship of Adeimantus' (477). In about 476 he was invited to the court of Hieron, tyrant of *Syracuse (see 1), with whom he stayed until his death; while there he is said to have settled a quarrel between Hieron and Theron (tyrant of Acragas). He died in Sicily and was buried at Acragas.

Very many stories circulated about him, some concerning his fondness for money, which became proverbial (he is said to have been the first Greek poet to write eulogies for pay). The most famous story concerns his visit to the Scopads of Thessaly where at a banquet he sang a lyric glorifying his patron, but including a lengthy digression in praise of Castor and Polydeuces (see DIOSCURI). Scopas said that he would pay the poet only half the fee, and he might apply for the rest to the two heroes to whom he had devoted an equal share of the praise. A little later a message came to say that two young men were asking for Simonides at the door of the hall. Simonides rose to speak to them but found no one there; while he was outside, the roof of the hall collapsed, killing all the other guests. Although the dead were crushed out of recognition Simonides was able to remember where each guest sat and so identify each body for burial (he is also said to have invented a technique for remembering). Aristotle tells of him that, when he was unwilling to compose a victory ode for the not highly esteemed mule-car race (see GAMES, PUBLIC), he did so when he was paid more money. Xenophon in his dialogue *Hieron* on the virtues and vices of tyranny has Simonides and Hieron as his interlocutors.

Despite his great reputation in antiquity, most of Simonides' poetry is lost. Comparatively little survives in quotation, and papyrus finds have been very fragmentary. He wrote *hymns, *scolia, *encomia (including the poem to Scopas from which a long passage survives in Plato's *Protagoras*, quoted there as the basis for discussion), *epinicians (the few surviving lines suggest that these were more playful than Pindar's), and elegies. He was most famed for *dirges and for *epigrams to be inscribed on dedications and tombstones, particularly for those referring to the dead of the Persian Wars, although it is difficult to be sure which ones were genuinely written by him. Probably genuine is that on the Spartan dead at Thermopylae:

> Tell them in Lacedaemon, passer-by,
> That here obedient to their words we lie.

2. Alternative spelling of *Semonides.

Sinis, brigand killed by *Theseus.

Sinon, see TROJAN HORSE.

Sirens (Seirēnēs), in Greek myth, female creatures who had the power of drawing men to destruction by their song. In Homer's *Odyssey* there are two of them who live on an island near *Scylla and Charybdis (in the Straits of Messina). Odysseus, when his ship was about to pass their island, in order to escape them filled the ears of his men with wax but left his own unblocked and had himself lashed to the mast as a precautionary measure. According to later legend the Sirens drowned themselves from vexation at his escape. The body of one of them, Parthenopē, was washed ashore in the bay of Naples, which originally bore her name. The *Argonauts, on their return voyage, passed near the Sirens; Orpheus, by playing on his lyre more beautifully than the Sirens sang, saved the other Argonauts from listening to their song (except for one man, who sprang overboard but was rescued by Aphrodite). In Homer the Sirens are not described, but in art they are represented as half women and half birds; in time they came increasingly to be shown as beautiful women, and also as creators of music; in the Myth of Er at the end of Plato's *Republic* they make the music of the spheres (see HARMONY OF THE SPHERES); thus in Hellenistic art and literature they came to symbolize music. 'What song the Sirens sang' is said by Suetonius to be one of the impossible questions with which the emperor Tiberius used to tease the scholars at his court.

Si'rius (Gk. Seirios), the Dog Star, the brightest of the fixed stars; its appearance marked the season of greatest heat in Greece. In Homer it was already known as *Orion's dog.

Sir'mio, in Italy, promontory on the southern shore of Lacus Bēnācus (Lago di Garda), on which the poet Catullus had a villa.

Sīro (Siron), see VIRGIL.

Sīse'nna, Lucius Corne'lius, Roman historian, praetor in 78 BC, one of the defenders of Verrēs (see CICERO (1) 1) in 70, and legate to Pompey in 67. He was the author of a history of his own times, which has not survived. He also translated into Latin the *Milesian Tales*.

Si'syphus, in Greek myth, son of Aeolus and Enaretē, founder of the city of Corinth (which is called Ephyrē in the *Iliad*), reputedly the most cunning of men. For that reason he was sometimes associated with the master-thief *Autolycus and was perhaps the father of Odysseus. (When Autolycus stole his cattle Sisyphus was able to recognize his own, having marked their hoofs. His revenge was to seduce Autolycus' daughter Anticlea, so that it was suspected that he rather than her husband Laertes was Odysseus' father.) Sisyphus established the Isthmian *games in honour of his

kinsman Melicertēs and fortified the citadel of Corinth (known as Acrocorinth). Having observed the seduction of the nymph Aegina by Zeus he revealed the truth to her father, the river-god Asopus, in return for a spring of fresh water on the citadel. Zeus punished Sisyphus by sending Death for him, but Sisyphus chained Death up in a dungeon, so that mortals ceased to die; the gods in alarm sent Arēs to release Death, who came after Sisyphus once again. Sisyphus instructed his wife Meropē to leave his body unburied and make no offerings, with the result that the Underworld gods Hadēs and Persephonē allowed the supposedly indignant Sisyphus to return from the Underworld to earth to punish his wife and make her bury the body. Once in the world again Sisyphus resumed his life and lived to a great age. However, when he eventually died the gods of the Underworld devised for him a famous punishment: to roll up to the top of a hill a rock which always rolled down again just as it was about to reach the summit. Sisyphus was the father of four sons, one of whom was Glaucus, father of *Bellerophon.

Skirophoria, see SCIROPHORIA.

sky'talē, stick used by the Spartans for sending secret messages. The correspondents had sticks of equal diameter. A strip of leather was wound around the stick of the sender, who wrote his message upon it, across the joins, and then sent the strip of disjointed writing to his correspondent. The latter wound the leather round his own stick and so was able to reconstruct the message.

slavery. A slave is the legal property of another, who has total control over all his activities. He is virtually without rights, and his status as a possession ('living tool' in Aristotle's phrase) is often expressed by the term 'chattel slave'.

1. *In Greece.* It is clear from the vocabulary of the *Linear B tablets that slaves existed in Bronze Age Greece, and they are present in Homer's *Iliad* and *Odyssey*. From Homer onwards the institution of slavery was taken for granted as a fact of life throughout all ancient Greek history. It was not opposed even by those philosophers who believed in the brotherhood of man (Cynics and Stoics) nor by early Christians, largely because they were all indifferent to material concerns. The slaves themselves, except in special cases (see below), did not rebel against their lot.

Slaves were mainly supplied from two sources: through war and conquest, including piracy, by the Greeks and (especially) the Romans themselves; and through full-time slave traders, the slaves being either the victims of wars between *barbarian nations or acquired by purchase: the Greek historian Herodotus says that the Thracians, for example, sold their children into slavery, and this practice was not uncommon. Slave-traders seem to have had a steady and plentiful supply. All slaves were to some degree foreigners in the eyes of their owners; Athenians did not enslave Athenians, nor Romans Romans. Indeed, most slaves in Greece and Rome were not Greek or Italian at all.

There were no specifically servile occupations; slaves could and did perform tasks and have occupations that were upon occasion performed by free men. Although slaves did not have any political rights they were employed at Athens as *police and as secretaries and clerks in the state bureaucracy (in small numbers at Athens compared with those employed at Rome under the empire). They did not fight for their (adopted) country except in times of national emergency, when they were first freed and then conscripted into the army or navy. The slaves who fought for Athens at the battle of Arginusae in 406 (see PELOPONNESIAN WAR) were rewarded with citizenship. Slaves rarely entered the professions, although there were slave doctors (who perhaps treated mostly other slaves). A very large number were employed in domestic service, where virtually no free men or women were employed, and in numbers which seem in modern times unbelievably lavish. Everyone who was not very poor employed at least one slave. In a well-known passage Libanius, a Greek rhetorician of the fourth century AD, describes the impoverished state of his teachers, with heavy mortgages, or living in lodgings 'like cobblers', hardly able to afford to marry let alone have children, in debt to the baker, selling their wives' jewellery to make ends meet, and able to afford at most three slaves, perhaps only two or not even that. Reliable slaves in a managerial position could do well for themselves: in Athens in the fourth century BC the slave *Pasion, who was manager of his master's bank, gained his freedom and even citizenship and inherited the bank, becoming one of the richest men in Athens; when he retired he leased the bank to his own freed slave Phormio. The extent to which slaves were employed on the land in Greece is disputed, since we hear little of agricultural slavery. In the case of Attica it is likely that slaves were employed in sizeable numbers on the farms of large and small land-owners alike. Slaves were commonly employed in industry. All craftsmen and tradesmen who could possibly afford it bought at least one slave and trained him to do his master's work so that the latter could retire in his old age and live on the proceeds of the slave's work. Some citizens possessed quite large industrial concerns manned by slaves: the father of Demosthenes (the orator) owned thirty-two slave cutlers and twenty bed-makers; the brothers Lysias (the orator) and Polemarchus owned a shield factory employing nearly 120 slaves (the largest industrial establishment we know of in Greece).

Hiring out slaves to industrial establishments was an important source of investment income for the rich: the owner kept the slaves' wages, and his profit consisted in the difference between each slave's wage (1 or 1½ drachmas a day) and his keep (notionally 3 obols, i.e. half a drachma, a day). Since the average price of a not-highly-skilled slave was only about 160 drachmas this gave the owner a good return on his capital. It also seems to have been common for owners of industrial slaves to let them work independently and keep the balance of their earnings themselves after they had paid a rent to their owners of 2 or 3 obols a day. 'Living apart' (chōris oikountes) became the technical term to describe slaves working on these conditions. Slave labour was used very extensively in the silver *mines at Laurium, and owning the slaves who did this work was very lucrative. The general *Nicias is said to have hired out a thousand slaves as miners for a return of one obol a day each.

Although reliable figures for population sizes in the ancient world are hard to come by, the most conservative calculation indicates that at the end of the fourth century BC the slave population at Athens numbered about 20,000, or one slave to every three adult free persons. Others have calculated a far higher figure. The Athenian historian Thucydides tells us that in the final ten years of the Peloponnesian War, after the Spartans had set up a fortified post at Decelea, only 22 km. (14 miles) from Athens, more than 20,000 slaves, mostly skilled workers, deserted to the enemy. Clearly there were very large numbers of slaves in Athens who were prepared to flee even for an uncertain future.

It is sometimes stated that the easy availability of slave labour depressed the wages of free men; although it is impossible to disprove this statement, the evidence suggests that except in the case of the mines, which employed very large numbers of slaves from relatively few slave-owners, owners in general, anxious for profits, expected to receive as much for a slave's work as a free labourer received for his; accounts from temple building show that the same wages were paid for hired slaves as for free workers. Thus except in the mines, where the cruel exploitation usually associated with slave labour was evident, slaves and free men worked side by side.

Another category of slaves was comprised by the *helots of Sparta and the penestae of *Thessaly, indigenous populations reduced to *serfdom by conquering invaders. This category of slaves always posed a threat to the rulers, who perpetually feared revolt. Whereas the large slave population of Attica, for example, was ethnically mixed and had no common cause, the helots shared a common language and a national consciousness. (For the helot revolt of

462 see SPARTA 3.) The Athenian *Critias, towards the end of the Peloponnesian War, was said to have tried to mobilize the *penestae* against their Thessalian masters. Another, much smaller, category is that of debt-bondsmen, partially enslaved by debt and under some conditions eligible to be sold into slavery abroad. This last category ceased to exist at Athens after *Solon's legislation in the early sixth century, but continued to be found elsewhere in Greece.

Although a slave belonged to his owner absolutely, and could be treated like any other item of property, sold, bequeathed, or given away, it was not, it seems, permissible for an owner to kill a slave, although he could beat him or otherwise ill-treat him. At Athens one of a slave's few safeguards was to seek asylum in the Theseum (see THESEUS) and ask to be sold to someone else; temples and altars also offered asylum to slaves as they did to free men. Anyone injuring a slave had to pay compensation to the owner. A slave's evidence was admissible in a law-court only if obtained under torture; the assumption was that the slave would only then tell the truth, when fear of further torture outweighed fear of his master.

Like women, slaves were sometimes excluded from religious cults, but during the *Anthesteria at Athens and at the festival of Cronus (in the month Hecatombaion) they were at least given a holiday and allowed to dine with their masters.

It may be wondered why slaves such as Pasion (see above) were preferred to free men in such obviously responsible positions as managers of banks. All Greeks, however, or at least all Athenians, put a very high value on independence, and considered it demeaning to accept employment that involved personal service to a master; this they thought was tantamount to slavery. Employers for their part no doubt preferred to use their own slaves or *freedmen whom they knew well and could rely upon to obey orders. The employment of slaves in responsible positions became particularly marked under the Roman empire.

Very little information can be gleaned about the breeding (or the marriage) of slaves at Athens, to what extent it happened and whether it was considered economic. A person whose parents were slaves was himself a slave from birth.

A master could if he wished give a slave his freedom, a simple declaration before witnesses being all that was required at Athens. Those slaves 'living apart' would hope to earn enough to buy their freedom. The former slave, on becoming a freedman, would be registered not as a citizen, as at Rome, but as a *metic (a resident alien). Conditions were sometimes attached to his freedom, such as that he should continue to perform certain services to his former master (compare MANUMISSION).

2. *At Rome.* The institution of slavery existed at Rome from early times, but the number of slaves in Roman possession rose to large numbers only from the second century BC, when constant wars as well as unchecked piracy brought hundreds of thousands of captives on to the market. We hear of Aemilius *Paullus selling 150,000 slaves after his victory in 168 BC at *Pydna, and of Julius Caesar selling on one occasion 53,000. *Delos became a great slave market, capable of admitting and dispatching 10,000 slaves in a day, according to Strabo (XIV. 5. 2). As in Athens slaves were used on a large scale in the mines; Polybius records that 40,000 worked in the silver mines near Cartagena in Spain in his day (mid-second century BC). The notable use of slaves in the second century BC was in agriculture. Territorial expansion had resulted in the Roman upper classes, both senatorial and equestrian, acquiring vast wealth which they invested in land (see LATIFUNDIA, AGER PUBLICUS, and AGRICULTURE). Great estates grew up and peasant farmers were forced to sell their small properties; the new owners preferred in general to use cheap slave labour, which was suitable for working these estates, rather than free labourers, whom they hired only at harvest and vintage time.

When the great wars of conquest ended in the period following the death of the emperor Augustus (AD 14), and the establishment of law and order suppressed piracy, the main sources of slaves no longer existed. There is evidence that very many slaves were bred during this time, despite the fact that several years must elapse before a slave child is an economic asset. (In the early second century BC Cato the Censor would have allowed on his ideal farm only the slave-bailiff to have a wife.) Slaves thus became very expensive. Horace in the time of Augustus speaks of 500 drachmas as a typical price for an ordinary slave (compare, above, the 160 paid at Athens), and of the equivalent of 2,000 drachmas being the price for a handsome boy who knew some Greek. On the whole, under the empire slaves were too expensive to be employed in unskilled labour, but it was still profitable to employ them in skilled jobs. By the fourth century AD free men instead of slaves were employed in the mines, and although slaves were still found in agriculture and in state employment, in private industry they were rare: factories were manned by free craftsmen. It is clear that slaves were still bred, so much so that on some estates a hereditary slave establishment existed. This, however, was an inheritance of the past, rapidly becoming anomalous. Under the late empire, slaves came to resemble free men in their social and economic position; in industry too, trained slaves, because of their high capital value, were given economic incentives which brought their position close to that of free craftsmen.

The general condition of Roman slaves was much the same as in Greece. They were allowed to attend only a small number of religious cults, such as that of the goddess *Fortuna. Their holidays were few; see COMPITALIA and SATURNALIA. A slave might be granted his freedom for good service or might purchase it by accumulating savings, *peculium* (see MANUMISSION), but if he ran away and was recaptured he might be branded or put to death. When freed in one of the ways legally prescribed he became a Roman citizen. The freedman (*libertus*) continued to belong to the family of his former master (*patronus*; see PATRON) and the two were bound by mutual obligations. The freedman assumed the *nomen* ('name') and *praenomen* ('forename') of his liberator, generally adding his own as *cognomen* (see NAMES 2). Manumissions were very frequent.

Three great slave revolts occurred in Roman history (and were suppressed at great cost), the first two in Sicily (*c.*139–132 and 104–100 BC) at a time when a large number of slaves of the same nationality were put together. The third occurred in Italy, 73–71 BC, and was led by *Spartacus. Again, a large number of slaves with common language and nationality had been brought together. The slaves involved were aiming to seize possession of a territory and live their own lives in freedom, not to destroy the institution of slavery.

There is little reliable information on the number of slaves in Rome, still less in Italy, at various times; as at Athens they may have numbered about one in three of the adult free population.

Sleep (Gk. Hypnos, Lat. Somnus), personified in Greek myth as the brother of Death (Thanatos), son of Night (*Nyx). Homer, in the episode of Hera beguiling Zeus with the aid of Sleep (*Iliad* 14. 225), describes his home as a cave on the island of Lemnos; Ovid places it in the dark mists of the far North.

Smyrna (or Myrrha), see ADONIS and ZMYRNA.

soccus, the low-heeled, loose-fitting shoe worn by Roman actors of comedy, of Greek origin. The word is often used to symbolize comedy; the poet Milton speaks of 'Jonson's learned sock'. Compare COTHURNUS.

Social War. 1. In Greek history, name given to the war (357–355 BC) between Athens on the one hand and Chios, Cos, Rhodes, and Byzantium on the other, all of which had revolted from Athens' second confederacy (see ATHENS 2, iv).

2. In Roman history, the Italian war of 90–88 BC (see ROME 6 and SOCII below).

socii ('allies'), of Rome. Although Rome had allies outside Italy, the term commonly denoted her Italian allies, *socii Italici*, those people, Italian,

Greek, and Etruscan (but excluding the Latins, who had a special relationship with Rome; see LATIN RIGHTS), living in some 150 communities, who were allied to Rome by formal treaties. They differed from the Romans and Latins in language, laws, and customs. All were obliged to provide military aid when required and to surrender to Rome control of foreign affairs. Sometimes they were granted certain privileges that the Latins shared with Rome, chiefly the rights of *commercium* and *conubium*, but in general they did not enjoy the same advantages as the Latins. Their feelings of injustice led to the outbreak of war in 90 BC, when they fought for their liberty against the abuses they suffered from the unrestricted *imperium* of Roman magistrates; their grievances were met by the grant of Roman citizenship under the Julian and Plautian laws of 90–89 BC. See ROME 6.

So'crates (469–399 BC), Greek philosopher, born in the Attic deme of Alōpekē near Athens. His father was Sophroniscus, a sculptor or stonemason, and his mother Phaenaretē, a midwife. He himself was a stonemason. Rather late in life he married the reputedly shrewish Xanthippē, by whom he had three sons who were still young at the time of his death. In the Peloponnesian War he served as a *hoplite during the siege of Potidaea (432–30) and was at Amphipolis and at the retreat from Delium (424); as a soldier he was distinguished by his courage and physical resilience. Although he generally avoided public affairs, when he did take part his behaviour accorded with his principles. He was one of the *prytaneis in 406 when the eight Athenian generals were tried by the assembly after the battle of *Arginusae, and alone objected to the illegality of the accused being sentenced collectively, thereby incurring great popular hostility. A little later, under the *Thirty Tyrants, he refused to assist in the arrest of an innocent man whom the Thirty had condemned to death, thus risking his own life. He preferred to follow his own conviction, irrespective of the will of either the people or the oligarchs. His manner of life won him many enemies, and in 399 he was brought to trial by Anytus (a democratic politician), Meletus, and Lycon on the charge of not believing in the gods whom Athens believed in but of introducing new gods, and of corrupting the youth of the city; the death penalty was asked for.

Two versions of Socrates' speech in his own defence exist in the *Apology (Gk. *apologia*, 'defence') by Plato and (in a less authentic form) in that by Xenophon, but neither makes exactly clear the precise significance of the charges. They were connected, however, with Socrates' well-known association with many of the Thirty Tyrants who overthrew the democracy, notably *Alcibiades and *Critias. The attack on him was not merely because of the political views of his protégés; it was also felt that he had undermined the traditional morality and religion of the city, the practice of which had in former times, it was felt, made Athens great; Alcibiades was suspected of sacrilege and Critias was an atheist. It is unlikely that Socrates' accusers wished or expected the death penalty to be inflicted; it would have been possible for him to follow the usual course of going into voluntary exile before the verdict, or of proposing banishment as an alternative to the death penalty, when it would probably have been accepted. However, his unconditional belief that he had done no harm to the city led to his obviously unacceptable counter-proposal that he should be dined for life at public expense (a privilege afforded to great benefactors of the state) or alternatively that his friends should pay a fine on his behalf; perhaps not surprisingly a greater number of the jury voted for the death-penalty than had condemned him in the first place. Execution was postponed, Xenophon says for a month, during the absence of the state ship on a sacred embassy (see DELOS); during this period Socrates was in prison and visited by his friends, their conversations recorded in Plato's dialogues *Crito and *Phaedo. The latter dialogue movingly describes Socrates' unflinching acceptance of the cup of hemlock (by which the death penalty was carried out at Athens).

Socrates himself wrote no books, and we are dependent mainly upon the widely diverging descriptions of Aristophanes, Xenophon, and above all Plato for our knowledge of his beliefs and also for our understanding of his uncompromising adherence to the philosophic life. This had such a profound effect upon his contemporaries and, through Plato, on subsequent philosophy, that all earlier Greek philosophers are referred to as the Presocratics. Xenophon conveys the deep reverence he felt for the man, but was unable to understand his philosophical concerns. Aristophanes' malicious and satirical portrayal in the *Clouds reflected the anti-intellectual prejudices of his audience, depicting Socrates as no different from the other intellectuals of the day, the *sophists. (In Plato's Apology Socrates refers to the influence of 'the comic poets' as a factor in his unpopularity; Plato in the *Symposium is at pains to show that a friendly relationship existed between Socrates and Aristophanes in real life.) Plato's picture of Socrates is also in some measure his own creation, but it is possible to identify from it some features genuinely those of Socrates: his concern with the difference between true knowledge and opinion which may merely happen to be correct; his search for definitions (What is courage? What is justice?) without which true knowledge is unattainable, in the belief that there are such things as courage and virtue; his particular method of inquiry by question and answer (see ELENCHUS) in order to reach these definitions; the question of whether 'goodness' (aretē, 'virtue', 'excellence of character') can be taught, as the sophists said it could; the feeling that goodness is connected with knowledge of the good, and that once one has that knowledge one cannot deliberately act badly ('no one errs deliberately'). And all this intellectual examination was aimed, as Socrates insisted, at the practical end of achieving happiness in this life by right living: 'the unexamined life is not worth living.'

There is no doubt that this kind of questioning made Socrates highly unpopular with his fellow citizens, if not with the young who enjoyed seeing their elders ridiculed. He compared himself with the gadfly, stinging people out of their complacency. (Alcibiades compared him with a sting-ray, inducing a state of numb helplessness.) Unlike the people he questioned, he himself professed complete ignorance, asking his questions purely for information. When his friend Chaerephon visited the Delphic Oracle to enquire if any man was wiser than Socrates, and returned with the answer that there was none, Socrates concluded that his wisdom consisted of knowing his own ignorance, as others did not know theirs. Some thought his assumption of ignorance was merely a pose and described it as an example of 'Socratic irony'. In a famous passage of Plato's *Theaetetus Socrates is represented as comparing himself with a midwife; he is not a teacher and cannot himself give birth to wisdom, but he can help others to discover and bring to birth the truth within themselves.

Both Plato and Xenophon refer to a less rational aspect of Socrates, his daimonion or 'divine sign', which he often called simply 'the customary sign'. Plato has Socrates describe it in the Apology (where Socrates supposes it to be the reason behind his indictment for introducing new gods into the city) as a kind of inner voice which since childhood has turned him back from action but never urged him towards it; it was this divine sign that prevented him from taking part in politics. He believed that the sign was sent by the gods, in whom, unlike most of the sophists, he believed unquestioningly. He differed from his sophist contemporaries in many other respects: for example, he did not teach, in the sense that he did not impart formal knowledge, nor did he ever take fees from the young men who associated with him; far from being sceptical or a moral relativist, he believed that there was such a thing as virtue, that it was knowable, and that the good life had little to do with material success. But the effect on others of his questioning unexamined assumptions had its destructive and demoralizing aspect.

Socrates' appearance was famous for its ugliness: broad, flat, turned-up nose, prominent bulging eyes, thick lips, and a paunch; he had a characteristic way of looking at people, glancing upwards or sideways with lowered head. Yet his appearance in no way detracted from his magnetic personality. Alcibiades in Plato's *Symposium* contrasted his outward appearance with his inner worth. (See also SILENUS.)

Much of Socrates' later influence was due not so much to his doctrines as to the integrity and consistency of his life and death, and to the memory he left behind of an inspired talker and an outstanding intellect. The scantiness of and uncertainty about his positive doctrines led to schools of the most diverse opinions being founded by his disciples, by *Plato, Antisthenēs the *Cynic, *Eucleidēs of Megara, and *Aristippus, the predecessor of Epicurus.

See also *MEMORABILIA* and *SYMPOSIUM* of Xenophon.

so'leae, see DRESS 2.

Sōlī'nus, Julius, Latin author, probably soon after AD 200, of *Collectanea rerum memorābilium* ('collection of memorable things'), substantially an epitome of the Elder Pliny's *Natural History* and the geography of Pomponius Mela. The title *Polyhistor* is sometimes given to this work. Solinus introduced the name 'Mediterranean Sea'.

Sōlon (*c*.640–after 561 BC), born of a *Eupatrid family at Athens, statesman and poet. He wrote elegiac and iambic poetry to publicize and justify his political policies. For later Greek historians his poetry was the main source of information on the economic and social crisis that he attempted to deal with.

Having won a reputation for giving good advice to Athens in her war with Megara over the possession of Salamis, he was elected *archon for 594/3. This was at a time when Athens was on the brink of revolution, largely owing to an agrarian system in which the rich landowners grew richer and the poor were reduced in some cases to slavery and altogether to despair. Solon's humane and moderate reforms, although they did not entirely avert a tyranny (see PEISISTRATUS), at least delayed it and perhaps produced the constitutional framework that made the eventual transition to democratic rule easier. Selling a debtor as a chattel slave (see SLAVERY) if his possessions failed to cover the debt was an accepted practice in many early societies including Athens. Many Athenians had found themselves unable to meet their obligations and had either been sold over the border of Attica as slaves or had fled into exile to avoid that fate, or still remained in Attica in bondage to their creditors, the latter being perhaps the obscurely named *hektēmoroi*, 'sixth partners', those who, it is thought, paid to someone else a sixth part of their produce. Solon's two relief measures were first of all the cancellation of all debts for which land or freedom was the security (a reform known as the *seisachtheia*, 'shaking-off' of burdens') and secondly the prohibition of all future borrowing on the security of the person himself. He did not institute a redistribution of land, as some of the poorer citizens had hoped, and for this he received some criticism. Other economic reforms were credited to him (perhaps not reliably): the introduction of a native Attic coinage and system of weights and measures (but see MONEY), the prohibition of the export of any crops except the olive (thus keeping for home consumption the surplus grain of the rich landowners who had been selling it outside Attica), and the granting of citizenship to immigrant craftsmen, to strengthen home industry. He also introduced a more humane legal code, repealing all the laws of *Draco except those concerned with homicide.

His great reform of the constitution was to grade eligibility to political office in terms of wealth, not birth, and thus to break the Eupatrid hereditary monopoly of power (and perhaps double the number eligible for high office). In future the nine archons were to be elected from the richest citizens, whether or not nobly born; lesser offices were to be held by the lower property classes; the lowest class was restricted to voting in the assembly (see ECCLESIA), which also became a court of appeal from the decisions of magistrates. His four classes were known (in descending order) as *pentakosiomedimnoi*, those whose annual income, in terms of grain, was not less than 500 *medimnoi* (see WEIGHTS AND MEASURES); *hippeis*, 'knights', 'cavalry' (see HORSES); *zeugitae*, 'yoke-men', i.e. able to keep a team of oxen, the hoplite class; and *thētēs*, freeborn men but without property, 'day-labourers'. After their year of office the archons were to join the council of the *Areopagus so that the composition of that hitherto exclusively Eupatrid body slowly changed. He instituted a second council, the *boulē* of 400 members, 100 members from each *tribe, all elected annually. According to Plutarch it was a deliberative body which considered matters before they came to the assembly for decision (compare CLEISTHENES). In some way that is not clear Solon also redefined the functions of the assembly.

It was said by later writers that after his reforms Solon spent ten years in overseas travel, visiting Egypt and Cyprus among other places (but on chronological evidence almost certainly not meeting Croesus of Lydia, despite . the legends). He returned to find Athens distracted by regional strife and lived long enough to see Peisistratus voted a bodyguard, the first step towards his tyranny.

Solon used verse to express his ideas and explain the motives, indeed the moral philosophy, that lay behind his reforms. His poetic eulogy of 'good order', *Eunomia*, has as much to do with the idea of justice as with its practical application. In a famous reply to the poet Mimnermus, who had said that he wanted to die when he reached 60, Solon declared that the poet should rather say 80. This should probably be taken with another famous line by Solon to the effect that even as he grows old he still continues to learn, *gēraskō d'aiei polla didaskomenos*.

So'mnium, see LUCIAN.

So'mnium Scipiō'nis ('dream of Scipio'), surviving portion of the otherwise lost sixth book of Cicero's *De republica*, preserved in the commentary of *Macrobius. It takes the form of a narrative placed in the mouth of *Scipio Aemilianus. He relates a visit to the court of Masinissa (see SOPHONISBA), a Numidian ally of Rome during the Second Punic War (218–201 BC), during which there was much talk of the first great Scipio, the hero of that war, who was given the *cognomen* Africanus. When the younger Scipio retired to bed, the ghost of the elder appeared to him in a dream, foretold his future, and exhorted him to virtue, patriotism, and disregard of human fame; for those who have served their country well there will be the reward of a heavenly habitation in the afterlife (see also POSIDONIUS for the Stoic origin of this idea). The narrative incidentally indicates Cicero's concept of the universe, borrowed from Greek philosophers. The 'Dream' is largely modelled on the myth of Er in the tenth book of Plato's *Republic*. A poetical summary of it occurs in Geoffrey Chaucer's *Parliament of Fowls* (perhaps 1382).

sophist (*sophistēs*), originally meaning in Greek a man who had a particular skill and therefore a claim to wisdom. In the fifth century BC it came to be specially, though not exclusively, applied to itinerant teachers who went from city to city giving lectures and private instruction for a fee. The subjects they taught were wide ranging, such as geography, mathematics, science, linguistics, but their overriding purpose was to train rich young men to be successful in public life; in their own words they 'taught virtue' (*aretē*). To this end all of them to some extent included in their curriculum the teaching of rhetoric, the art of public speaking; some, notably *Gorgias, concentrated on this subject exclusively and gave public performances to advertise their rhetorical skill; the ability to argue persuasively was essential for political advancement, and politics was the career above all other in the ancient world that offered power, fame, and fortune. The sophists satisfied a need among the ambitious for a kind of advanced education which was not obtainable elsewhere, attuned to the times, inclusive of new knowledge, practical and sophisticated. It is not surprising that sophists enjoyed great popularity among those for whom they catered, and amassed large fortunes. Their emphasis upon worldly success as well as their advocacy of the

idea, which much impressed the Athenians, that the ability to plead a case and win depends on a skill that can be taught rather than on having a just cause (see the *Clouds* of Aristophanes), were factors in promoting the scepticism and moral relativism that were associated with their name. Famous sophists were Gorgias of Leontini, *Protagoras of Abdera, Prodicus of Ceos, *Hippias of Elis, and *Thrasymachus of Chalcedon (see also ANTIPHON). Most Athenians of the day would have included *Socrates, not aware of the radical differences in his outlook, but seeing that he too was an intellectual who questioned people's unexamined beliefs about the gods, the laws, and traditional values.

The dangerous effect of the sophists was evident in the late fifth-century phenomenon of able, cynical, and recklessly self-seeking politicians, but, on the other side, the intellectual stimulus they provided is manifested in the arguments and educational theories of Plato. See EDUCATION 3.

Sophist, The (*Sophistēs*), dialogue by *Plato, a sequel to *Theaetetus*; Plato once more applies himself to problems raised by the *Eleatics. The main speaker is an Eleatic philosopher, left unnamed; Socrates and Theodorus have scarcely anything to say. The dialogue starts with the definition of a *sophist, at the end of which the question arises whether what the sophist produces is false, and whether there can be a 'false' or 'unreal' thing, since the Eleatics believe that 'what is not', and therefore falsehood, cannot exist (see PARMENIDES). The dialogue finds a solution in the doctrine that all things partake of 'difference'; in making a denial we are not making an antithesis between something and nothing, but an opposition between something and something else different from it: 'what is not' is in fact 'what is different'. Plato is thus able to demonstrate the existence of falsehood and error.

Sophistic, Second, in Greek parts of the world under the Roman empire during the second century AD, a revival of the teaching and practice of Greek rhetoric of the late fifth and fourth centuries BC, associated with a general cultural flowering made possible by the peace and security of the times. The term Second Sophistic was coined by Flavius *Philostratus (second to third century AD) who wrote in his 'Lives of the Sophists' the biographies of his predecessors and contemporaries. He used the term to distinguish the later from the the the first sophistic age, the time of the fifth-century *sophist Gorgias; according to him the Second Sophistic, with its interest in historical themes, originated with the orator *Aeschines, but did not emerge as a recognizable movement until the second century AD. The name 'sophist' has a wide meaning in the later context; it includes professional rhetors and teachers, and may include others whose profession was primarily concerned with the written or spoken word, such as lawyers. On the whole the sophists distinguished themselves from philosophers; in the twofold division of higher *education (see 3) philosophy and rhetoric were thought of as separate disciplines.

Despite freedom of speech, the rhetoric of this period was of an artificial kind, consisting of declamations (see DECLAMATIONES) delivered as public entertainment, and subsequently published as literature. These sophists continued the tradition and imitated the virtuoso performances of the fifth-century sophists, as well as carefully imitating the language and style of the best Attic writers, Xenophon, Plato, and Demosthenes. Most of them moved to and settled in the great cultural centres of the time, Athens, Smyrna, Ephesus, and to a lesser extent Pergamum, but their lecture tours took them far afield. The audiences were educated and sophisticated, familiar with the themes (i.e. the subjects for declamation), appreciative of variation, allusion, and subtle effect. Often the audience selected the theme, which the rhetor would meditate on for a few minutes before delivering his declamation extempore. Others preferred to speak on a prepared subject. Although the practice, which concentrated so much on form at the expense of content, could be seen as stultifying, study of the Attic models infused the rhetoric with something of the philosophy of the originals and helped create for some a new Platonism (see PLATO), for others a philosophical Hellenism which amalgamated the central beliefs from different philosophical systems.

Many of the sophists of this period are described by Philostratus (see above). For individuals who were sophists or moved in sophistic circles see ARISTEIDES (3), APULEIUS, DION CHRYSOSTOM, FAVORINUS, FRONTO, GALEN, HERODES ATTICUS, and LUCIAN; see also PLUTARCH.

The unsettled conditions of the mid-third century brought about a decline in literature, but there was a revival in the late third and fourth centuries, the last great peaceful and prosperous classical period, when sophists once again flourished; see HIMERIUS, LIBANIUS, and THEMISTIUS; see also the emperor JULIAN.

Sophists, Against the, see ISOCRATES.

So'phoclēs (*c*.496–406/5 BC), one of the great Athenian tragedians, born at Colōnus near Athens, the son of Sophilus, a wealthy manufacturer of armour. The ancient Life of the poet gives a great deal of information about him, no doubt much of it unreliable. His beauty and his skill in music and dancing early attracted attention; as a boy he led the chorus which sang the paean in honour of the Greek victory over the Persian invaders at Salamis in 480 BC. His

music teacher was Lamprus. His first victory in the tragic competitions was at the Great *Dionysia in 468 BC, at his first attempt it is said, when he defeated Aeschylus. His early life coincided with the expansion of the Athenian empire, and though he took no active part in politics as far as is known, he was twice elected *strategos* ('general'), first as a colleague of Pericles in 440, when he helped to suppress the Samian revolt, and later with Nicias. It was said that he owed his appointment in 440 to the success of *Antigone*. His interesting conversation with the Greek poet *Ion of Chios during the Samian expedition is recorded by Athenaeus (13. 603). After the failure of the Sicilian Expedition in 413 he was made one of the *probouloi* ('commissioners') to deal with the crisis. Sophocles wrote a poem (which has not survived) to the historian Herodotus, who was one of his friends. When the cult of *Asclepius was introduced to Athens, he received the sacred snake representing the god in his house until the temple was ready, and composed a *paean in his honour. He is said to have refused invitations to visit the courts of kings (unlike Aeschylus and Euripides). As well as writing tragedies he was the author of a prose treatise, 'On the Chorus'. Aristophanes in the *Frogs*, writing a year after Sophocles' death, summed up his character in the line (82), 'contented among the living, contented among the dead'; only a few months before his death Sophocles presented his chorus and actors at the *proagon in mourning garb for the death of Euripides. He left two sons: by Nicostratē, Iophon the tragedian; and by Theōris of Sicyon, Agathon, father of the younger Sophocles, also a tragedian. In recognition of his piety in receiving Asclepius he was honoured as a hero after his death.

He is said to have composed 130 plays, of which seven were later judged to be spurious, and to have won twenty-four dramatic competitions with his tetralogies (i.e. ninety-six plays were successful); with the rest he came second, never third. Seven tragedies are extant; the suggested dates seem likely but (except for *Philoctētēs* and *Oedipus Coloneus*) by no means certain: *Antigonē* 441 (see above); *Trachiniae* and *Ajax* probably earlier; *Oedipus Tyrannus* soon after 430; *Electra* between 418 and 410; *Philoctetes* 409; *Oedipus Coloneus* probably written 406/5, produced posthumously in 401 by the younger Sophocles. For the plots of these plays see their individual titles. A large fragment of his satyr-play *Ichneutae* ('trackers'; see SATYRIC DRAMA) has been recovered from a papyrus found in modern times. Its plot concerned the theft of Apollo's cattle by Hermes soon after the latter's birth.

According to Aristotle in the *Poetics*, Sophocles was an innovator in tragedy: he added a third to the previously accepted two actors, introduced 'scene painting', and increased the chorus from twelve to fifteen; he also abandoned the Aeschylean practice of writing trilogies on related events (see TRAGEDY 1), instead giving each play a self-contained plot. Since the actors in Greek tragedy might play more than one part, the introduction of the third actor enabled Sophocles to make plot, dialogue, and the relationship of characters much more complex. His characters were admired by Aristotle for being 'like ourselves only nobler'; Sophocles is said to have remarked that he depicted people as they ought to be, Euripides as they are; nevertheless his characters are not wholly idealized but remain manifestly human. His heroes and heroines are placed in circumstances in which they must act, and by their actions, which often have tragic consequences, they show their heroic stature. More than those of the other tragedians, Sophocles' heroes and heroines give the impression that it is their innate characters that initiate the action, and that they could not have behaved otherwise. When, as in *Ajax*, *Antigone*, and *Trachiniae*, the main character dies well before the end of the play and the plot takes a turn in another direction, some slackening of the tension is inevitably felt; but even so, the concluding part still seems to follow necessarily from what has preceded. In the other plays the unity is complete; in particular, the tight-knit plot of *Oedipus Tyrannus* (which for Aristotle represented Greek tragedy at its greatest) is handled with amazing dexterity and at a rapid pace.

Sophocles rarely introduces into the self-contained world of the play ideas that relate more to contemporary affairs, a factor that makes dating the plays on internal evidence difficult. He was a master of dialogue, both in speeches and in *stichomythia. One feature for which he became famous is dramatic irony, of the kind where the speaker's words have an underlying significance for the audience, already familiar with the outlines of a story drawn from a well-known body of myth (see TRAGEDY 1). The language of Sophocles is dignified, avoiding the grandiose and over-naturalistic, and often dense, rather in aid of economy than at the expense of clarity. Some of the lyric odes are outstanding, moving the action on to a different plane. According to Plutarch, Sophocles distinguished three periods in his own style: the first, when he imitated the 'high-flown' style of Aeschylus; the second, when his style was 'harsh and artificial'; and the third, when it was 'most suitable for expressing characters and best for drama'. All his extant plays seem to belong to the third period.

The plays show a conventional but deeply felt piety: that the gods enforce their justice upon human life, and the wise act as best they may in accordance with divine will. In this connection Matthew Arnold's judgement of Sophocles (in his sonnet, *To a Friend*) as one 'who saw life steadily and saw it whole' is often quoted. The poet Shelley had a volume of Sophocles in his pocket when he was drowned in 1822.

Sophoni'sba, daughter of a Carthaginian general Hasdrubal, son of Gisgo; she married Syphax, king of Numidia, at the time of the Second Punic War (218–202 BC) and drew him away from his alliance with Rome on to the Carthaginian side. When he was defeated in 203 by a Roman army led by Masinissa, a Numidian prince in alliance with Rome, Masinissa fell in love with the captive Sophonisba, and according to the romantic story in Livy sent her poison as the only means of saving her from the disgrace of being sent as a captive to Rome by Scipio, who was afraid of her influence on Masinissa's loyalty. Sophonisba calmly drank the poison. James Thomson's tragedy of 1730 (one among many on the subject) contained the notorious line, 'O! Sophonisba! Sophonisba! O!'.

Sō'phron, see MIME.

sortēs, see ORACLES and VIRGIL.

sortition, election by lot, a method of appointing *magistrates in Greek democracies, best known from its use at Athens. Its introduction there was sometimes ascribed to *Solon in the early sixth century BC. Certainly by the end of the sixth century *Cleisthenes had his council (*boulē*) appointed by lot (from among eligible male citizens). In general, candidates for office had first to present themselves for selection. From 487/6 even archons were appointed by lot, first from a number of nominated candidates, later by a double lottery. Jurors too were selected by lottery, by means of a complicated procedure. This method of appointment, combined with the prohibition of, or severe restriction on, re-election, allowed considerable rotation in office and reinforced the sovereignty of the assembly. The *strategoi and some financial officers, however, in whom technical skill was required, were appointed by vote. See DEMOCRACY.

So'sii, famous booksellers at Rome, referred to by Horace (*Epistles* 1. 20. 2).

Sō'tadēs (third century BC), of Marōnea in Thrace, Greek iambic poet, said to have been put to death for writing lampoons against the marriage in 276/5 of Ptolemy II Philadelphus and his sister Arsinoe II (a marriage of a kind traditional in pharaonic Egypt but scandalous to Greeks). He invented a flexible form of metre named after him (sotadean), which was used for several centuries after his time for coarse satires and mythological burlesques. Only a dozen or so lines and a few titles of his works remain.

South Italy, see MAGNA GRAECIA.

Spain (Gk. Ibēria, from the name of the river Ibērus, Ebro; Lat. Hispania). From earliest times the races of Spain have been mixed; peoples arriving from Africa in Neolithic times (to exploit the mineral resources) spread throughout the south and east, mixing in the centre and west with Celts invading from the north in the late Bronze and early Iron Ages. According to tradition, Phoenicians from Tyre discovered *Tartessus and colonized *Gades c.1100 BC. In the seventh and sixth centuries BC Phocaeans penetrated west to Tartessus (see COLONIZATION, GREEK 2), and their colony Massilia founded other colonies on the eastern coast of Spain. In the third century when Phoenicians from Carthage took control in Spain, the Phocaeans were driven out. After Rome's First Punic War (264–241 BC), the Carthaginians under Hamilcar, Hasdrubal, and Hannibal greatly extended their dominions in Spain, reaching the Ebro and founding Carthāgo Nova (Cartagena) on the Mediterranean coast as their principal centre. They exploited their new territory for mineral wealth and manpower with which to renew the struggle with Rome. In 219 the siege and capture by Hannibal of Rome's ally Saguntum precipitated the Second *Punic War (218–202). Rome sent a force to try to hold Hannibal in Spain, but failed to do so, and operations there ended in disaster with the death of the two Scipios in 211. However they had served a useful purpose by detaining in Spain Carthaginian troops who would otherwise have been sent to Italy. A new Roman army dispatched to Spain in 210 under the young P. Scipio (later given the cognomen Africanus) restored Roman fortunes there, captured Carthago Nova, and by 206 finally expelled the Carthaginians.

Two Roman provinces were established in Spain in 197. They comprised at first only a relatively small portion of the peninsula, and were known as Hispania Citerior, 'Hither Spain', the eastern seaboard, and Hispania Ulterior, 'Further Spain', roughly modern Andalusia. The number of praetors at Rome was increased from four to six to provide governors. But the native population had not then been effectively subdued, and unrest continued for many years. An important pacification was brought about in 179 by Ti. Sempronius Gracchus (father of the Gracchi), who by his personal character won the confidence of the Spaniards. But native risings were renewed in 154, and Numantia resisted the Romans for nine years. Its capture by Scipio Aemilianus in 133 brought the Spanish wars to a close, the Romans then occupying about two thirds of the peninsula, failing to hold only the mountainous region in the north and north-west. No further conquest in Spain was attempted during the republic, nor was systematic Roman colonization attempted at this stage, but two colonies may have existed before the arrival of Julius Caesar (see below), as well as many Roman and Latin townships which in the south and east served as centres of Roman civilization. The valuable *mines were public property at first, but when they were later sold to private ownership they attracted large numbers of Roman and Italian business men to the south and east, which were also very fertile areas. Veterans were settled here also, as well as native townships established.

In the civil wars of the first century BC Spain was held by the Marian leader *Sertorius against the party of Sulla, and later against Pompey, until Sertorius was murdered in 72. The military talent of Julius Caesar was first revealed when he was propraetor in Spain in 61. He subsequently waged war there in 49 against the Pompeian generals Afranius and Petreius, and in 45 against the sons of Pompey, finally making himself master of the Roman empire by his victory at *Munda. Notable among the colonies that he founded were Hispalis (Seville) and Tarraco (Tarragona). A final pacification of the whole peninsula, including the north and north-west, was achieved by the emperor Augustus.

In literature, Spanish colonies produced the two Senecas and Lucan; Columella, Quintilian, and Martial came from native stock. The emperor Trajan was born in Spain, and Hadrian and Marcus Aurelius belonged to Spanish families. The Frankish invasions of the early third century AD severely disrupted northern Spain, but a strong Christian church emerged in the fourth century, inspiring the works of *Prudentius and *Orosius; it survived the barbarian invasions of the fifth century, and converted the Visigothic kings to Christianity. The seventh-century bishop of Seville, *Isidore, was an important link in continuity between classical culture and the Middle Ages.

Of Roman remains in Spain the most striking are perhaps the great bridges at Alcantara and Merida, the latter place-name commemorating its Roman origin (as Augusta Emerita), as does Saragossa (Caesaraugusta).

Sparta (Spartē, or *Lacedaemon), the capital in historical times of Laconia, a state in the southeast of the Peloponnese founded by Dorians (see DORIAN INVASION and HERACLEIDAE). Lacedaemon was the usual name in historical times for both the city and the state; the name Sparta was applied only to the city, and then in poetic or patriotic contexts. The city was situated on high ground on the west bank of the river Eurotas, and consisted of little more than a group of villages, without fine buildings, and unfortified until the end of the fourth century BC.

1. *Early history to the sixth century BC.* During perhaps the tenth century BC a cluster of Dorian villages around the acropolis became united into one political entity; the existence in historical

times of two royal families claiming descent from *Heracles, the Agiads and Eurypontids, from each of which came one of the two hereditary kings who jointly ruled the state, suggests a compromise in the matter of the ruling power. By 700 BC all the territory of the eastern coastal strip of Laconia had been incorporated into the Spartan state, and the population there, both pre-Dorian and Dorian, was either reduced to a condition of limited independence in which they were known as *perioikoi, 'dwellers round about', or had become serfs, known as *helots, bound to the land which they cultivated for their Spartan masters. The creation of this class was the first stage in a way of life that was to distinguish Sparta from every other Greek state.

In the eighth century Sparta fought the First Messenian War (perhaps between c.735 and 715 BC; see ARISTODEMUS) and annexed much of the neighbouring state of Messenia as a result, reducing the population to the same status as the helots of Laconia. The revolt of Messenia in the seventh century, perhaps after rather than before Sparta's serious defeat by Argos at Hysiae in 669 (see PHEIDON), resulted in the Second Messenian War, during which, according to tradition, the Messenians held out for several years against the Spartans, under their hero Aristomenēs. It seems likely that the tensions of this period were related to the reforms associated with the name of *Lycurgus. The political system which resulted was a rigid oligarchy in which considerable power was given to the kings, magistrates (*ephors), and council of elders (*gerousia). The kings were the religious representatives of the state and the leaders of the army in war, but even so they were accompanied and supervised by two ephors, and their power gradually declined. The gerousia was composed of the two kings and twenty-eight members each over 60 years old, elected for life; it was the supreme court of law. The assembly or apella was composed of all Spartan male citizens aged 30 and over, the homoioi ('equals'; they are often referred to in English as the Spartiates, from Gk. Spartiatēs, a Spartan); it was a consultative body, without real authority, but it had to ratify declarations of war (voting was by acclamation). Before the fifth century it numbered 8–9,000, large for an oligarchy but small compared with the citizen body of a democracy such as Athens, and small too for the very large tracts of territory the Spartans possessed, containing a servile population which outnumbered them by about seven to one. The helot system relieved the Spartans of tending the land themselves and allowed the men to spend an abnormally large amount of time training as soldiers, but the helots themselves were a source of permanent anxiety and danger. As a result, along with the constitutional reforms, socio-military institutions were established which,

owing to the inherent stability of the Spartan way of life despite the permanent threat of revolution within its boundaries, lasted unchanged for centuries.

2. In the early part of the seventh century, Sparta was not the closed and self-centred state that she later became, but took a normal part in the life of Greece; her art and industry were highly developed, and she was famous for choral *lyric poetry (see ALCMAN, TERPANDER, and THALETAS); but the only poetry she produced during the Second Messenian War was the martial elegy of *Tyrtaeus, and after that the art of poetry seems to have died.

Each male child appears to have been given at birth an inalienable portion of land to be held for life, if he survived scrutiny and was not rejected and exposed by the elders of his *phratry. An adult Spartan lived in his village, not on his land; as well as his public 'lot' he seems to have been able to own private land; certainly some were richer than others. Spartans were forbidden to take part in any business or trade, which was the province of the perioikoi, as the cultivation of the soil was that of the helots. After the age of 7 the Spartan boy was devoted to a military regime which produced the finest army in Greece (see ARMY, GREEK I) and, gradually, a proverbially famous austerity of life. He was taken from home and enrolled in a group of his contemporaries under the leadership of an older boy, and with this group he lived for the next fourteen years, educated for toughness, endurance, and military discipline. Spartan girls also underwent physical training. Music and *dancing were part of the curriculum because they had military uses, but only the essentials of reading and writing were taught. Other details are obscure. At the end of his education the Spartan joined the eirĕnĕs or young men who had completed their twentieth year, and remained with them living in barracks until he was 30. During this time he might join the *krypteia or secret police. At the age of 30 he became a full citizen with the right to vote in the assembly and to be admitted to a syssition (if this right had not come earlier), a 'mess' where he dined with his fellows until he was 60 (perhaps on the notorious Spartan fare of black broth and much diluted wine). He was now free to marry. It is evident that a society so organized offered virtually no encouragement to the arts.

There was a steady decline in the number of Spartan citizens; the reasons have been much debated, but it seems to have been due not so much to losses in war as, first, to the concentration of property (apart from the inalienable lots) in a few hands, secondly to the fact that there was no source of new blood, and thirdly to a decline in the birth rate attributable to the inadequacy of the basic allotment of land to support a family. Aristotle says that at some time before he was writing (he may mean about the time of the battle of Leuctra, 371 BC) the Spartiates numbered fewer than a thousand; Plutarch says, of c.250 BC, that there were 700 Spartiate families.

3. *Foreign relations in the sixth and fifth centuries.* In foreign relations, Sparta at first followed a policy of conquest and expansion, establishing her predominance in the Peloponnese, and defeating and weakening her principal rival Argos. Towards the middle of the sixth century, perhaps under the influence of the ephor Chīlon, she abandoned this policy and set about consolidating her position. She formed a league of the Peloponnesian states (including Corinth and Megara but neither Argos or Achaea) under her own leadership, with meetings held at Sparta. These states remained autonomous, paid no tribute, but supplied a military contingent in war, of which Sparta retained the direction. Declaration of war by the league required the consent of a majority of member states and the Spartan *apella*. Sparta was now at the height of her power. Her narrow and inward-looking policy was made evident when in 499 she refused assistance to the Ionian Greeks in their revolt against Persia (see PERSIAN WARS I). But when Xerxes prepared for war against Greece itself, Sparta combined with Athens in measures of defiance and showed the bravery of her soldiers at the battles of Thermopylae and Plataea. This co-operation ceased after the final defeat of the Persians at Mycalē, and Sparta no longer took the lead in Greek affairs. This was partly as a result of the disgrace of *Pausanias, the anti-Spartan activities of the Athenian Themistocles, and the consequent rise in importance of Athens (see DELIAN LEAGUE). Sparta also had to face an attempted coalition of Peloponnesian states against her, a devastating earthquake in 464, and a Third Messenian War (464–460) caused by a revolt of the helots. She also survived the first conflict with the imperialism of Athens (460–446). In 431 jealousy and fear of Athenian expansion and the urgings of her allies prompted her to begin another war against Athens for the leadership of Greece (see PELOPONNESIAN WAR).

4. *Foreign relations in the fourth century.* Her defeat of Athens in 404 left Sparta supreme in Greece, but her falling citizen population, rigid institutions, and the individualist ambitions of her leaders (see LYSANDER and AGESILAUS) did not fit her for an imperial role. She entered on a period of arrogant aggrandisement which aroused the hostility of her neighbours and led to the rise of Thebes and her own downfall.

In the last part of the Peloponnesian War Sparta had entered into alliance with the Persian satrap Tissaphernēs and later with the satrap Pharnabazus. But after the war this policy changed. When the Persian king Darius II died in 404, Sparta interfered in the struggles for the succession, assisting Cyrus in his revolt against the new king Artaxerxēs II, Cyrus' brother (see ANABASIS). An appeal from the Ionian cities for help against Tissaphernes, coupled with the hope of easy plunder, induced Sparta to undertake a war against Persia (400–390). The war was successfully conducted by Agesilaus in 396 and 395; then Lysander was killed in Boeotia in 395 and Agesilaus was recalled to deal with trouble nearer home. A league of Thebes, Corinth, Argos, and Athens had been formed against Sparta, and in spite of their defeat by Agesilaus at Coronea in Boeotia in 394, this Corinthian War dragged on until 386 when the Persian king Artaxerxes enforced the pacification known as the King's Peace (or Peace of Antalcidas). This was a triumph for Sparta. It decreed that the Ionian Greek cities including Clazomenae, and Cyprus, were to be restored to Persian rule, and the other cities were to be autonomous, thus breaking up the hegemony which Athens had begun to create but leaving Sparta free not only to dismantle anti-Spartan alliances in the Peloponnese, but also to keep her own Peloponnesian League, which was considered a voluntary association and not subject to the autonomy clause. In 382 she intervened to check the expansion of the *Chalcidic League (composed of Olynthus and other cities of the Chalcidic promontory), forcing it to make peace in 379. Meanwhile the commander of the Spartan army marching through Boeotia accepted the invitation of the pro-Spartan faction to seize Thebes, and occupied the Cadmea, the city's fortress (382). For this act of unprovoked aggression the Spartans fined their general but did not remove the garrison.

In the winter of 379/8 a group of Theban exiles, including the young *Pelopidas, entered Thebes and assassinated the pro-Spartan leaders. As Athens had sent help for this attack and feared retaliations (at some point Sparta made a raid on Piraeus) she set about making alliances, thus creating the beginnings of the Second Athenian League (379/8). Successive Spartan invasions of Boeotia were defeated between 378 and 375. In the latter year the Peace of 386 was renewed, but broken by Sparta in 373. In 371 it seemed that peace between Athens, Sparta, and Thebes could again be renewed, but when Sparta insisted on the independence of the other Boeotian cities from Thebes, the latter refused to sign (see EPAMINONDAS). The Spartans invaded Boeotia to secure this independence and were destroyed at the battle of Leuctra (371). Thereafter Thebes took the role of the aggressor. Sparta was repeatedly invaded by the Theban commander Epaminondas, who dealt her a fatal blow by freeing Messenia (370/69) and refounding it as an independent state after 300 years of servitude to Sparta. The formation of a league of Arcadian cities (see MEGALOPOLIS) after Leuctra also weakened Sparta's influence;

this too was the work of Thebes. A Theban invasion of 362 ended in the battle of Mantinea where Thebes, though nominally victorious, suffered in effect a defeat through the death of Epaminondas. Peace was made in the same year. The success of Thebes during this period was due not only to the military genius of Epaminondas but also to the declining number of Spartan citizens (see above).

5. *Sparta after the rise of Macedon.* Sparta was not actually captured by Philip II of Macedon when he invaded the Peloponnese after the battle of Chaeronea in 338, but her territory and power were further diminished, and her important role in Greek history now came to an end. The most interesting incident in her later history (apart from the brave defence of the city in 272 against an attack by *Pyrrhus, a defence in which the Spartan women took a prominent part) was the social revolution attempted by her king Agis IV (242 BC) and put into effect by king *Cleomenes III (227). At this time the concentration of wealth in a few hands and the reduction in the number of citizens had impaired the stability and power of the state. There was much debt, the institution of *syssitia* was neglected, and the old system of land-allotments was completely disorganized. Agis proposed the cancellation of debts and the redistribution of the Spartan land among 4,500 citizens, *perioikoi*, and selected aliens, who were to constitute the new citizen roll. The scheme was defeated by a conservative ephor (who was also Agis' uncle) and Agis was summarily tried and executed in 241. The scheme was resumed and carried through, with some modification, by Cleomenes who, after defeating the *Achaean League in 227, left his force of citizens in the field, hurried back to Sparta, and staged a sudden coup, deposing the ephors and making himself master of the state. He then carried out his reforms, restoring what he conceived to be the institutions of Lycurgus. After other military successes in 222 Cleomenes was defeated and driven into exile by the Macedonian Antigonus in alliance with the Achaean League, Sparta was captured and enrolled in a Hellenic League, and a Macedonian governor was installed. The debilitating quarrels of Sparta with the Achaean League (the city was captured by *Philopoemen, the Achaean general, in 188) played an important part in the final reduction of Greece by the Romans in 146 BC.

6. *Characteristics of Sparta.* Sparta differed from other Greek states not only in her peculiar constitution and in the supreme importance she attached to military efficiency, but in certain other respects: she did not use coined money until the third century BC, the currency taking the form of iron 'spits', *oboloi* (see MONEY); and women enjoyed a position in some respects approaching equality with men, with greater independence and authority than at Athens, and were expected to interest themselves in the welfare of their country. Their reputation for terseness has given 'laconic' (from Laconia) to the English language—when Philip of Macedon wrote to them, 'If I invade Laconia I shall turn you out,' they wrote back, 'If'.

Spa'rtacus, Thracian slave-gladiator who escaped from a school of gladiators and led a revolt at Capua in 73 BC, joined by large numbers of other slaves and desperate men. Within the year Spartacus had defeated two Roman armies and devastated southern Italy. In 72 he defeated another three armies, and reached Cisalpine Gaul, but marched south again to plunder Italy; he was finally defeated and killed in 71 by M. Licinius *Crassus, who subsequently crucified any rebels he captured. Pompey returned from Spain in time to annihilate the rest, thereby taking credit for ending the war. Spartacus quickly became a legend not only for his daring successes but for personal qualities of bravery, strength, and humanity.

Sparti (Spartoi), see CADMUS.

Spartiā'nus, Ae'lius, see HISTORIA AUGUSTA.

Spa'rtiates (Spartiā'tai), see SPARTA I.

Speusi'ppus (*c.*407–339 BC), nephew of Plato and his successor as head of the *Academy from 347 to 339. Of his voluminous writings only fragments survive, together with accounts of his work by later writers. He seems to have continued along the lines of Platonic dogmatism; Aristotle speaks of him with respect.

Sphactē'ria, see PELOPONNESIAN WAR 4.

spheres, harmony or **music of the,** see HARMONY OF THE SPHERES.

sphinx (from *sphingein*, 'to bind fast'), in Greek myth, a monster usually depicted with the head of a woman on the (winged) body of a lion; bearded male sphinxes are sometimes found in early Greek art. Hesiod made her the child of *Chimaera and *Orthrus; according to others she was the child of *Echidna and *Typhon. In the story of *Oedipus and the Sphinx, the riddle she posed was 'What is it that walks on four legs in the morning, on two at noon, and on three in the evening?' The answer was 'A man', who as an infant crawls on all fours and in old age walks with a stick.

spo'lia opī'ma ('spoils of honour'), the arms taken by a Roman general, in full command of his army, from the body of an enemy leader whom he has killed in single combat. They were reckoned by the Romans to have been won three times: by Romulus from Acron, king of the Caeninenses, in the hostilities that followed the Rape of the Sabines; by Aulus Cornelius Cossus, according to Livy in 437 BC, when he killed Tolumnius the Etruscan king; and by M. Claudius Marcellus who killed the Gaul

Viridomarus in 222 BC. The spoils were dedicated to Jupiter Feretrius; lesser spoils, *spolia secunda* and *tertia*, were dedicated to Mars and Janus Quirinus. A claim was made for the *spolia opima* in 29 BC by M. Licinius Crassus, proconsul of Macedonia, who had defeated the Bastarnae in battle and killed their chieftain Deldo. His claim was disallowed by Octavian on the grounds that he was not the holder of full *imperium*.

spondee, see METRE, GREEK I (ii) and 3.

SPQR, in Roman documents, inscriptions, etc., abbreviation for *senatus populusque Romanus*, 'the senate and people of Rome'; see POPULUS.

stade, stā'dium (*stădion*), Greek unit of length, the 'stade' (see WEIGHTS AND MEASURES), 600 (Greek) feet long, and so in the range 175–200 metres or somewhat less than an English furlong. Because the most famous running-track, that of Olympia, was exactly a stade long, the word came to denote any running-track, 'stadium'. A stadium was generally a piece of level ground a little over 200 m. long and up to about 40 m. wide, with a starting line at each end. In the middle of each line was a turning post round which runners had to make a turn for any race longer than a single length. Since level ground of such a size was not easy to find in mountainous Greece, one end of the stadium was often left curving naturally into the hillside. In this way the stadium came to have what is now considered its characteristic U-shape. The best-preserved ancient stadia may be seen at Olympia, Delphi, Athens, and Epidaurus. The stadium at Athens was rebuilt by *Herodes Atticus in marble, with seats to hold 50,000 spectators. Compare CIRCUS.

Stagei'ra (or Stageiros), Greek town near the east coast of Chalcidicē, famous as the birthplace of Aristotle, who in consequence is sometimes referred to as 'the Stagīrite'. It was destroyed by Philip II of Macedon in 348 BC, but rebuilt by him in honour of Aristotle, whom he appointed as tutor to his son Alexander.

Stane Street, see ROADS 2.

Statei'ra, see ALEXANDER (2) 6.

stater, see MONEY.

Stā'tius. 1. Caeci'lius Statius, see CAECILIUS.
2. **Publius Papi'nius Statius** (*c.* AD 45–*c*.96), Roman poet, born at Naples, the son of a *grammaticus* or schoolmaster and teacher of literature, who was himself a poet and encouraged the literary aptitude of his son. The young man won a prize for poetry at the Neapolitan competition of the Augustalia festival (see LUDI 2). He then appears to have gone to Rome, where he recited his poems to large audiences and won a contest held by the emperor Domitian at Alba. He wrote an (extant) epic in twelve books, the *Thebaid, published in 90 or 91 after twelve years' toil; it tells the story of the quarrel between Oedipus' sons Eteoclēs and Polyneicēs. Soon afterwards Statius began to issue the *Silvae. In (probably) 94 he failed to win the Capitoline poetry competition (see LUDI 2 (iv)), and was deeply disappointed. About this time he retired to Naples, where he began the composition of an epic, the *Achilleid, broken off in book 2 by the poet's death, apparently before the murder of Domitian in September 96.

Statius married Claudia, a widow with one daughter, and was deeply attached to her. He had no children of his own; his sorrow at the death of an adopted son is expressed in the last poem of the *Silvae*. He associated with prominent men, including Domitian himself, whom he flattered obsequiously. His lost works include the libretto for a *pantomime *Agavē*, on the story of Pentheus, and an epic *De bello Germanico* ('on the German war') on Domitian's campaigns. His poetry strikes many as generally over-worked; it is full of literary and rhetorical devices, allusive, and in a highly artificial language; the *Silvae*, being simpler, more spontaneous, and less polished, have for many readers a greater appeal, but the *Thebaid* has attractions for those with a taste for hyperbole and the macabre, and there are episodes of drama and pathos.

Statius was much admired in the Middle Ages; regarded by Dante as a Christian, he appears in Cantos 21 and 22 of the *Purgatorio* where his spirit meets that of Virgil, appropriately enough in view of Statius' reverence for the earlier poet. Statius is made to explain how he was led to Christianity by certain passages in Virgil. The English poets Alexander Pope and Thomas Gray both translated portions of the *Thebaid*.

Stentor, Greek at the siege of Troy who could shout as loudly as fifty men (*Iliad* 5. 785).

Ste'ropēs, name of one of the three *Cyclopēs.

Stēsi'chorus ('choir-setter'), Greek lyric poet writing in the first half of the sixth century BC whose real name was Teisias. He was said to have been born at Matauros (Metaurum) in the toe of Italy and to have lived at Himera in Sicily. He wrote narrative *lyric poetry (of what type is not certain) classified by the ancients as choral lyric because its structure was *triadic, and is even said to have been the inventor of this particular form. It has seemed to some that the great length of his poems precludes their being sung and danced by a chorus, and that it is more likely that the poet performed them himself, to the accompaniment of a lyre, in the manner of a Homeric bard (see HOMER). Certainly the poems were long: the *Geryonēis* exceeded 1,800 lines (by comparison, not many of Pindar's choral odes are much over a hundred lines long), and the *Oresteia* occupied two books. The Alexandrian scholars collected the poems into twenty-six books. Only fragments survive, and most of these have been recovered from papyrus in the twentieth century.

Existing titles indicate that the subjects were taken from a wide range of epic sources, from the *Epic Cycle as well as Homer. His *Oresteia* differed from the story in Homer in placing the death of Agamemnon at Sparta (not Mycenae or Argos); as Aeschylus did in the *Choephoroe*, Stesichorus included Clytemnestra's dream and gave some part to Orestes' nurse. The *Geryoneis*, which told of Heracles' search for the cattle of Geryon (see HERACLES, LABOURS OF 10), is remarkable for an early mention of the silver mines of Tartessus (see SPAIN); it also has a memorable description of the cup of the Sun (see HELIOS). The *Funeral Games of Pelias* is connected with the legends of the Argonauts, the *Boar-hunters* with the Calydonian boar-hunt, the *Eriphylē* with Theban legend. The *Iliupersis*, 'Sack of Troy', drew on the Epic Cycle and included an account of Epeus, who made the Wooden Horse; some believe that it may have been the source for the stories of Aeneas' wanderings to Italy (see TABULA ILIACA). Stesichorus told the story of Helen of Troy twice, first in the usual version as the cause of the Trojan War, and secondly in the form familiar from Euripides' play *Helen*, according to which Helen's phantom went to Troy while she herself remained behind in Egypt. Legend relates that he was struck with blindness for 'slandering' Helen in the first poem, and that his sight was restored after he recanted and wrote his famous *Palinode*, blaming Homer for the earlier story. His language and style show the strong influence of epic, but have many features of later choral lyric, e.g. the rich use of epithets. The metre he used was a form of dactylo-epitrite (see METRE, GREEK 8). His influence on contemporary art was considerable, many of his subjects appearing on the vases of the day.

Stheneboe'a, see BELLEROPHON.

Sthenno, see GORGONS.

stichomy'thia, 'talking by the line', in Greek drama, dialogue that is conducted by two characters speaking in alternate lines (though strict regularity is not always maintained). Stichomythia can be very effective in a confrontation, but the difficulty of maintaining such a form can lead to artificiality of expression, nicely illustrated in A. E. Housman's famous parody, 'Fragment of a Greek Tragedy':

Chorus: Might I then hear at what your presence shoots?
Alcmaeon: A shepherd's questioned mouth informed me that—

Chorus: What? For I know not yet what you will say.
Alcmaeon: Nor will you ever if you interrupt.
Chorus: Proceed, and I will hold my speechless tongue.
Alcmaeon:—This house was Eriphyla's, no one's else.

Stichus, Roman comedy by *Plautus. The title is taken from the name of one of the characters, a slave. The comedy has little plot. The two daughters of Antipho are married to two brothers. These have gone abroad on a trading venture to retrieve their fortunes, and at the opening of the play they have been absent for three years and no news has been received. Antipho urges his daughters to marry again, but they insist on remaining faithful to their husbands. The husbands have prospered and now return, and their home-coming is a matter of celebration. Much comedy is derived from the behaviour of a hungry *parasite and from the portrayal of slaves enjoying themselves.

Stī'licho, Flavius (*c.* AD 365–408), general of the Roman armies and, when the young emperor Honorius (b. 384) succeeded Theodosius I in 395, the effective ruler of the western Roman empire. He successfully repelled the first invasions into Italy of Alaric and the Visigoths in 401 and 403, but was put to death by order of Honorius in 408 (before the sack of Rome by Alaric in 410). See CLAUDIAN and BRITAIN 8.

sto'a, Greek word for a roofed *colonnade or portico (English 'porch') with a wall on one side, erected as a separate building near temples or gymnasia or in market-places as a sheltered place in which to walk and talk or hold meetings. The wall was often decorated with paintings or inscriptions. Thus the Stoa Poikilē ('painted colonnade') in the agora at Athens, built *c.*460 BC, was adorned with frescos by famous artists, including one by *Polygnotus representing the destruction of Troy. It was from this stoa, frequented by the philosopher Zeno and his disciples, that the Stoic school of philosophy derived its name. Later in the fifth century the stoa of Zeus Eleutherios ('Zeus the god of freedom') was built, also in the agora. At Athens too was the Stoa Basileios, where the *archon basileus ('king archon') sat as judge in certain religious matters. In the Hellenistic age, stoas of great magnificence were built; a notable two-storied stoa was erected at Pergamum, and of the same type was the stoa given to Athens by king Attalus II of Pergamum (220–138 BC), now rebuilt to serve as the agora museum. His brother Eumenēs II also gave a stoa to Athens.

Stobae'us, Johannes (i.e. John of Stobi, in Macedonia), compiler in the early fifth century AD of an anthology of excerpts from (pagan) Greek poets and prose-writers, in the first instance for the instruction of his son Septimius. These excerpts were originally arranged in four books whose subjects included philosophy, physics, rhetoric, poetry, ethics, morals, and politics. They were later grouped under the titles *Eklogai* and *Anthologion*. The latter has survived, and preserves quotations from works which have not otherwise come down to modern times.

stoichē'don, see EPIGRAPHY I.

Stoics. The Stoic school of philosophy was founded in Athens *c*.300 BC by *Zeno of Citium (in Cyprus), taking its name from the *Stoa Poikilē at Athens where Zeno did his teaching. He came to Athens *c*.311 BC and first attended lectures at the *Academy (the Platonic school) but was converted to Cynicism by Crates (see CYNIC PHILOSOPHERS). Study of the works of *Antisthenēs, a devoted follower of Socrates (and regarded by some as the founder of Cynicism), turned him to Socratic philosophy, out of which he developed his own 'Stoic' system, embracing logic, theory of knowledge, physics, and above all ethics. At his death Athens honoured him with a public funeral, as a man who 'had made his life an example to all, for he followed his own teaching'. Although the school seems to have been less strictly organized than the Academy and the Lyceum (the school of Aristotelian philosophy), it nevertheless had a succession of heads to at least AD 260, and probably for some years after. It gradually faded out, however, and was no longer in existence when the emperor Justinian closed the philosophical schools at Athens in AD 529.

The main Stoic doctrines were the following. Nature (the whole universe, that is) is controlled by reason, *logos*, which is identified with God and shows itself as fate (also called necessity or providence); whatever happens is in accordance with divine reason. It is thus the aim of the wise man who knows this truth to accept what happens and to live in harmony with nature (or divine reason); this is virtue and the only good. Whatever happens to us cannot be otherwise; the wise man aims to achieve willing acquiescence. Not to do this is to show moral weakness instead of virtue, and this is the only evil. Everything else—pain, poverty, death (even a cold in the head, as the poet Horace ironically observes at the end of his first Epistle)—is indifferent. It is beyond the power of anyone to deprive the wise man of virtue; always knowing the only true good, he is therefore happy. He is also absolutely brave, since he knows that pain and death are not evils, and self-controlled, since he knows that pleasure is not the good.

Matter breaks down into the four elements, earth, air, fire, and water. Fire, the element most closely related to divine reason, periodically consumes the universe, and out of it in time a new universe arises, and so on for ever. Every man possesses a spark of that divine fire. This belief led, importantly, to the Stoic concept of the universal brotherhood of man, without distinction between Greek and barbarian, freeman and slave, and of the consequent duty of universal benevolence and justice. In spite of this, Stoicism was in the main a doctrine of detachment from and independence of the outer world.

The immediate successor of Zeno was *Cleanthēs, followed in 232 BC by *Chrysippus of Soli (in Cilicia), converted to Stoicism by Cleanthēs, who completed and systematized the Stoic doctrine. Among Zeno's pupils was Sphaerus, who inspired the revolution of Cleomenes III at Sparta (see CLEOMENES (2) and SPARTA 5). Antigonus Gonatas, king of Macedon from 277 to 239 (see MACEDON 3), was also influenced by Stoicism. All these philosophers belonged to the Early Stoa. The famous names of the subsequent period, the second and first centuries BC, the so-called Middle Stoa, are those of *Panaetius and Posidonius. The former, who spent much time in Rome, was the first to reject the doctrine of periodic universal conflagrations, and also rejected the belief that only the absolutely wise man can be virtuous, teaching that those who merely aspired to virtue were making progress. While at Rome he joined the circle of P. *Scipio Aemilianus, and his practical version of Stoic ethics, seemingly adapted for the needs of active statesmen and soldiers, had very great influence on the Scipionic circle, including men such as C. *Laelius, Q. Mucius *Scaevola the augur, and his namesake the *pontifex maximus*. Through his writings Panaetius influenced the Younger *Cato, *Brutus, *Cicero (1), and many others. Posidonius submitted the doctrines of the early Stoics to an even more thoroughgoing revision, and his influence was wide and far-reaching.

During the Roman empire the Late Stoics were almost exclusively concerned with ethical questions. The most important Stoics of the first century AD were *Seneca the Younger, *Cornutus, *Musonius Rufus, and, towards the end of the century, *Epictetus. Stoicism provided the philosophical basis for opposition to the one-man rule of the emperors: Paetus *Thrasea and his son-in-law *Helvidius Priscus, resolute opponents of Nero, were Stoics; the emperors Vespasian and Domitian both banished the philosophers from Italy. But after Epictetus the emperor M. *Aurelius was the most famous Stoic in the second century. During the third century the school gradually died out, but it had an important and long-lasting effect on the life and thought of many, influencing *Neoplatonism and permeating the Christianity of some of the early Fathers of the Church.

stola, see DRESS 2.

Strābo (Strabōn, 64 BC–after AD 24), Greek geographer from Amasia in Pontus, a member of a distinguished local family. He came to Rome in 44 BC to complete his education and subsequently visited the city several times. He travelled 'from Armenia to Etruria, from the Black Sea to the borders of Ethiopia', returning to his home in about 7 BC where he remained until his death. At some time he became a *Stoic; he also developed a profound admiration for the Romans: like *Posidonius, he regarded them as the creators of an earthly world-state comparable with the heavenly one.

He was the author of *Historical Sketches* in forty-seven books, now lost, which comprised an outline of historical events up to the opening of Polybius' history, followed by a complete history from 146 BC (where Polybius ended) up to at least the death of Julius Caesar. His surviving great work, the *Geography* in seventeen books, seems to have been completed by 7 BC. It has been suggested that it was originally published at Amasia, where it was perhaps revised and republished in about AD 18, in order to account for the surprising fact that it was not known to the Romans, not even to the Elder Pliny, although it seems to have been known in the East. Strabo insists that his geography is intended for political leaders and its aim is to impart practical wisdom; but it remains unclear whether it was intended for Romans or for the Greeks of his native Pontus. He describes the physical geography of the chief countries in the Roman world, giving the broad features of their historical and economic development and an account of anything remarkable in the customs of their inhabitants or in their animal and plant life. The first two books serve as a general introduction; after a remarkable preface in which he discusses geography as a branch of scientific inquiry, Strabo deals with the dimensions of the inhabited world and the position of various places with reference to a simple grid. Books 3–17 embrace Spain, the Isles of Scilly, Gaul, Britain (of which he knows little), Italy, Sicily, north and east Europe (he knows nothing of northernmost Europe and Asia), central Europe, north Balkans, Greece, Asia around the Black and Caspian Seas, Asia Minor, India, Persia, Mesopotamia, Palestine, Arabia, Egypt, Ethiopia, and North Africa (Strabo takes Africa to be a triangle north of the equator).

Strabo based his geography on *Eratosthenēs, whom he brought up to date. He regarded the world as a sphere, having one land mass, in the northern hemisphere, entirely surrounded by ocean. His whole work is invaluable in informing us about the state of geographical knowledge in his day, as well as containing incidentally many entertaining descriptions: how the Indians capture elephants and long-tailed apes, how the Arabians get fresh water out of the sea, how the Egyptians feed their sacred crocodiles; the Hanging Gardens of Babylon, the whales of the Persian Gulf, the aromatics of the Sabaeans. The work, in an epitomized form, was used as a school-book in the Middle Ages.

Stratēgē'mata, see FRONTINUS and POLYAENUS.

stratē'gos, in Greece, a military commander; at Athens in the fifth century BC *strategoi* were of political as well as military importance. From 501 BC the people as a whole elected annually ten *strategoi,* one from each *tribe with no limits on re-election; each *strategos* commanded the regiment of hoplites from his own tribe, under the supreme command of the *polemarch (see ATHENS 3). In 487 BC all archons including the polemarch came to be selected by lot; since good military leaders could not be guaranteed by this method, the polemarch ceased to command the army and his powers were transferred to the *strategoi,* who continued to be elected and who in some cases became political leaders as well; Themistocles and Cimon were notable early examples. Pericles was *strategos* almost continuously from 443 until his death in 429; Cleon, Nicias, and Alcibiades all held this office. At some time in the fifth century the rule that one *strategos* was elected from each tribe was modified to permit two from a tribe, leaving one tribe unrepresented. Now that the *strategoi* could hold supreme command, taxiarchs (see ARMY, GREEK) took over command of the regiments. When the people decided on a military campaign, they named the *strategos* who was to have supreme command of it, and he seems to have exercised considerable individual authority, although at the end of his term of office he was held accountable (see EUTHYNAE) like any other magistrate. In the fifth century the board of *strategoi* formed an important administrative council, responsible for all duties relating to war, the enlistment of soldiers and sailors and the organization of trierarchies for example (see LITURGY).

strēnae, at Rome, luck-bringing twigs brought at New Year from the grove of Strēnia, goddess of health and physical vigour, and exchanged as presents (French *étrennes*). This ancient custom was preserved at Rome in cult: on New Year's Day by the old reckoning (1 March; see CALENDARS), the previous year's laurel branches at the doors of the oldest shrines were replaced by new. In later times the presents took forms other than twigs, but twigs were still thought to be lucky.

Strife, see ERIS.

strigil, see BATHS.

strophē ('turn'), in Greek *lyric poetry (and Latin written in imitation) a stanza. It was said to have derived its name from the performance of choral lyric, in which a stanza or strophe was sung as the chorus proceeded in its dance in one direction, followed by a second stanza, the antistrophe, corresponding exactly in metre with the strophe, sung when the chorus turned and reversed its dance in the opposite direction. See also TRIAD. 'Astrophic' composition describes extended lyric passages not written in stanza form.

Stymphā'lian Birds, see HERACLES, LABOURS OF 5.

Stymphā'lus, name of a lake in a narrow upland valley under Mount Cyllēnē in northern Arcadia; the emperor Hadrian built an aqueduct to take water to Corinth from one of its springs.

Styx ('the abhorrent'), in Greek myth, the principal river of the Underworld (see HADES) over which the souls of the dead were traditionally said to be ferried by Charon. According to Hesiod, Styx was one of the river-spirits who were daughters of Oceanus and Tethys. Styx and her children, Zēlos (Glory), Nikē (Victory), Kratos (Strength), and Bia (Force), aided Zeus in his quarrel with the *Titans, in consequence of which she was greatly honoured, and an oath by Styx was held inviolable by the gods. According to the Greek historian Herodotus, people swore solemn oaths by a small river of this name in Arcadia which still falls from a tall cliff (the Mavroneri falls), leaving a black stain on the rocks; its water was reputed to be poisonous. Plutarch and Arrian report that Alexander the Great was poisoned by this water, sent to him in a mule's hoof (which withstood its reputedly corrosive nature).

Suāsō'riae, see SENECA (1).

Subli'cian Bridge, see PONS SUBLICIUS.

Sublime, Longinus on the, see LONGINUS.

Subū'ra (or Suburra), at Rome, a densely populated valley between the Viminal and Esquiline hills, occupied largely by traders and workshops, notorious for its noise and dirt. Distinguished residents included Julius Caesar.

Successors, the, see DIADOCHOI.

Suda, The (*hē Souda,* 'fortress', formerly referred to as *Suidas,* as if the name of a person), name of a Greek lexicon or literary encyclopaedia compiled at the end of the tenth century AD and containing many valuable articles on Greek literature and history. It is based partly on earlier lexica (see HESYCHIUS), partly on texts, with *scholia, of Homer, Sophocles, Aristophanes, and the Palatine Anthology which the compiler consulted himself, and partly on excerpts made in earlier times from the works of historians, grammarians, and biographers.

Suetō'nius. 1. Gaius Suetonius Pauli'nus, see BRITAIN 4.

2. Gaius Suetonius Tranqui'llus (b. *c.* AD 70), Roman biographer. He was the son of the equestrian Suetonius Laetus who as a tribune in the thirteenth legion fought at *Bedriacum in AD 69. The son practised in the law-courts at Rome and was a friend of the Younger Pliny, who successfully petitioned the emperor Trajan in 112 for the grant to (the childless) Suetonius of the privileges granted to the parents of three children (see IUS TRIUM LIBERORUM). Shortly afterwards he became a secretary at the imperial palace, where he would have been able to consult the imperial archives. In 121/2 he was dismissed by Hadrian, together with the praetorian prefect, allegedly for some indiscretion involving the emperor's wife. Nothing more is known of his life.

Of his writings, which include works on Roman antiquities, natural sciences, and grammar, much is lost. The surviving works consist of the 'Lives of the Caesars' (*De vita Caesarum*) and part of his 'On Famous Men' (*De viris illustribus*) comprising over half of the sections on the grammarians (*De grammaticis*) and rhetoricians (*De rhetoribus*); in addition his Lives of Terence, Virgil, Horace, and Lucan have been transmitted in manuscripts of these authors' own works; perhaps the Lives of Tibullus and Persius are also by Suetonius. *De grammaticis* sets out what Roman education understands as 'grammar', i.e. broadly the study of literature, and relates its introduction at Rome by *Cratēs (4), as well as giving some account of twenty of the principal grammarians. *De rhetoribus* relates the growth at Rome of the study of rhetoric, which at first was disapproved of by influential Romans, explains the method of teaching it, and illustrates the themes used in the schools. An account of five of the principal teachers of rhetoric follows. The Lives of the poets contain fact, anecdote, and misinformation inextricably confused; passages about the personal appearance of the poets have their own fascination: for instance, that Horace was short and fat.

The 'Lives of the Caesars' include the biographies of Julius Caesar and the eleven subsequent emperors: Augustus, Tiberius, Gaius Caligula, Claudius, Nero, Galba, Otho, Vitellius, Vespasian, Titus, and Domitian. It is clear that Suetonius followed whatever source attracted him, without caring much whether it was reliable or not. It has been thought that he had completed only the Lives of Julius Caesar and Augustus when he was dismissed from the palace, since he makes no direct quotation from correspondence of any emperor later than Augustus. His biographies give an account of the ancestry and career of each emperor, but show little historical grasp or penetration; they consist chiefly of anecdotes, gossipy and salacious, but lively and with interesting detail. There is an account of Caesar's crossing of the Rubicon, and a detailed narrative of his assassination; mention of his dark piercing eyes and his attempts to conceal his baldness.

Augustus is said to have been short but well-proportioned, with an aquiline nose and eyebrows that met, careless in dress, frugal, and sparing in diet. Suetonius gives an interesting account of Tiberius' retirement at Rhodes from 6 BC to AD 2, and reproduces the scandalous and perhaps ill-founded stories of a vicious old age at Capri. There is a vivid picture of the grotesque appearance of Caligula, of his waywardness and insane cruelties; of the awkward walk, loud guffaw, and stammer of Claudius, and his blend of culture and good sense with silliness and excessive timidity. The Life of Nero reveals much about his stage displays and his passion for horses (even after he became emperor he used to play with ivory horses and chariots on a table); about his elaborate organization of a claque to applaud his own productions; about his wanderings incognito at night in the streets of Rome; about his *Golden House, and his conduct while Rome burned. The Life of Titus mentions his notable saying at the end of a day when he had done no good to anyone: 'I have lost a day', and his mastery of shorthand and aptitude for imitating the handwriting of others; and that of Domitian records his restoration of the libraries which had been burnt down and his efforts to collect manuscripts.

The pattern Suetonius followed is always the same: the subject's family and early life, public career, physical appearance, private life. The work became a model for biography in the Middle Ages.

suffect consul, see CONSUL.

Sū'idas, see *SUDA*.

Sulla, Lucius Corne'lius (*c*.138–78 BC), Roman general and leader of the *optimatēs* in the civil war against the *popularis* *Marius. His vindictive cruelty was long remembered. Born of a patrician but not distinguished family, Sulla first came to prominence when as quaestor to Marius in Africa he secured by his courage and diplomacy the surrender of *Jugurtha from Bocchus (107 BC). He also showed his military ability in the campaign against the German tribes which was led by Marius and Catulus. As legate in the Social War (90–88; see ROME 6) he was the most successful Roman commander in south Italy. He gained the consulship in 88 and was designated by the senate for the command against *Mithridates, who had invaded the Roman province of Asia. But the tribune of 88, P. Sulpicius Rufus, a supporter of Marius, transferred the command to the latter, and Sulla was forced to leave Rome. The six legions which Sulla had assembled at Capua, loyal to their leader after two years' fighting under him in the Social War and no doubt attracted by the prospect of Asian booty, were easily prevailed upon to march with him against the (legitimate) government at Rome. Only one officer, however, joined Sulla, the quaestor *Lucullus. For the first time a consul entered the city at the head of his army. Marius escaped with difficulty (arriving in Africa after many adventures), and Sulla took control of the city by force, killing Sulpicius and shocking even his friends by his violent measures.

After devising a temporary political settlement he proceeded to the East, and by 86 had captured Athens and driven Mithridates from Greece; he crossed to Asia Minor and soon came to terms with Mithridates. Meanwhile his command had been transferred, but Sulla refused to relinquish power, behaved tyrannically in Greece and Asia, and in 84, with a devoted army loaded with booty, prepared to invade Italy, Rome being in the hands of the *populares*. Landing at Brundisium in 83 he was joined by *Pompey, Metellus Pius (an influential senator whose presence gave Sulla the optimate seal of approval), and *Crassus. A ruthless civil war ensued and Sulla finally seized Rome in 82 after a victory at the *Colline Gate. He was elected dictator and granted complete immunity, taking the *cognomen* Felix ('fortunate'). He now adopted in his turn Marius' policy of exterminating his enemies, adding the device of proscription, the posting-up of the names of victims who might be killed without trial and their property confiscated, while the murderers and informers were rewarded (see *PRO ROSCIO AMERINO*). The cities that had fought against Sulla were included in his vengeance and in some cases their confiscated lands were distributed among his soldiers. These events marked the advent of a new era, the late republic (see SALLUST), a time when individuals with great personal ambition, made powerful by their leadership of large armies, brought about the ruin of Italy and the collapse of republican government.

After having his eastern settlement ratified, Sulla set about a complete constitutional reform at Rome which aimed to improve administrative efficiency, increase the power of the senate, and restrict that of the people and their tribunes. He raised the numbers of the senate (traditionally 300) to 600 by elevating many of the *equites*, but he removed from the latter the judicial powers they had acquired in the time of the *Gracchi and restored them to the senate. The powers and careers of the magistrates (see CURSUS HONORUM) were strictly defined. Sulla's most important measure was the full organization of a system of criminal procedure, the *quaestiōnēs perpetuae* (see LAW, AT ROME I (ii)). This was one of the few parts of his work which survived the reaction that followed his death. After completing his reforms he abdicated his power, restored constitutional government, becoming consul in 80, and retired to private life in 79. He died in 78, having devoted his last year to the composition of his memoirs in twenty-two books; these have not survived.

Sulmo, birthplace of the Roman poet Ovid, in a valley of the Apennines, east of Rome.

Sulpi'cia, see TIBULLUS.

Sulpi'cius. 1. Publius Sulpicius Rufus, tribune of the *plebs* 88 BC and a supporter of *Marius. He proposed that the newly enfranchised Italians should vote in all the tribes and not be confined to a few (see COMITIA); also that the command against Mithridates should be transferred from *Sulla to Marius. These proposals were carried by force, but when Sulla reacted by marching on Rome Sulpicius had to flee. He was captured and put to death, and his laws annulled.

2. Servius Sulpicius Rufus (*c.*106–43 BC), great Roman jurist and orator, contemporary of Cicero, known to us by the latter's praise of him in his *Brutus* and in the *Ninth Philippic* and by his correspondence with Cicero. He was consul in 51. He wrote to Cicero two celebrated letters, one describing the murder of M. Marcellus in May 45, the other a consolation on the death of Cicero's daughter Tullia, which was admired and copied by St Ambrose as worthy of a Christian. He died in 43 while on an embassy from the senate to Mark Antony.

Sū'nium (Sounion), cape forming the southernmost point of Attica. It is mentioned by Homer (*Odyssey* 3. 278) as the point off which Apollo killed the pilot who guided Menelaus on his way to Troy. A temple to Poseidon was built on the promontory in the 440s BC; eleven of its Doric columns still stand.

Suovetaurī'lia, at Rome, the combined sacrifice of a pig, a sheep, and an ox, the principal animals of the farmer. It was made at certain agricultural festivals such as the *Ambarvalia.

Suppliants, The (Gk. *Hiketidĕs*, Lat. *Supplicēs*, 'suppliants' or 'suppliant women').

1. Greek tragedy by *Aeschylus, of uncertain date, but in a year, possibly 463, in which Sophocles was also a competitor (the latter's first dramatic production was in 468). It was the first play of its trilogy; the others were *Aegyptii* ('sons of Aegyptus') and *Danaidĕs* ('daughters of Danaus'); the satyr-play was the *Amymōnē*.

The suppliants are the fifty daughters of *Danaus who have fled from Egypt to avoid marriage with their cousins, the fifty sons of the usurping king Aegyptus. They have come with their father Danaus to Argos, with which they claim connection through their descent from *Io, to ask for protection from their pursuers. The king of Argos hesitates and consults his people. These vote in favour of the suppliants, and the demand of the enemy herald for their surrender is rejected.

The role of the suppliants themselves is taken by the chorus, which thus becomes virtually the protagonist; it is not therefore inappropriate that choral lyrics occupy more than half the play. The reason for the suppliants' flight from marriage, not made unambiguously clear by Aeschylus, has been much debated, but inconclusively; it does not seem to be of importance to the poet or essential to the plot. The trilogy probably ended with the confirmation of marriage as a natural institution, exemplified by *Hypermnestra's sparing of her husband.

2. Greek tragedy by *Euripides produced probably *c.*422 BC; the goddess Athena's words at the end relate to an Argive alliance, actual or in view at the time of writing.

The Thebans have refused to allow the burial of the bodies of the Argive chieftains (the '*Seven against Thebes') who have unsuccessfully attacked the city, thus violating the sacred custom of the Greeks. The mothers of the chieftains (who form the chorus of suppliants from whom the play is named) have come with Adrastus, king of Argos, surviving leader of the expedition, to Eleusis in Attica and made supplication at the shrine of Demeter to Aethra, mother of Theseus, king of Athens. Theseus rejects the arrogant demand of the Theban herald for their surrender; he yields to the prayer of the suppliants and recovers the bodies for burial by force. Evadnē, widow of Capaneus, one of the chieftains, throws herself on his funeral pyre.

supplicā'tio ('supplication'), at Rome and elsewhere in Italy, on the occasion of some great national misfortune or rejoicing, such as a military defeat or victory; it was a solemn adoration of the gods, when public access was granted to their statues or other emblems, often by placing them on platforms.

Su'pplicēs, see SUPPLIANTS.

Sy'baris, Achaean Greek colony founded *c.*720 BC near a similarly named river on the Gulf of Tarentum in Italy (see COLONIZATION, GREEK 2). In the sixth century it was an important trading centre, and its wealth and luxury became proverbial (hence English 'sybaritic'). It was destroyed *c.*510 BC by its rival *Croton, and the neighbouring river Crathis was diverted from its course to flow over the site. It was never rebuilt. See also THURII.

sy'cophant (sykophantēs, 'fig-denouncer'), at Athens, a man who prosecuted another maliciously, on a trumped-up charge, for the sake of private gain. For most offences at Athens there was no public prosecutor; that role was left to a public-spirited private individual, but the system was open to abuse. Since there could be financial rewards for bringing successful prosecutions (a share of the fines), or a rich victim could be blackmailed into paying off a would-be prosecutor, those individuals who made a habit of such prosecutions earned this abusive name, the origin of which is obscure. Today 'sycophantic' means 'obsequious'.

syllē'psis ('taking together'), figure of speech in which one word is applied to two others in different senses, e.g. 'he bolted the door and his dinner'; thus in Tacitus *Annals* 2. 29: *manus ac supplices voces . . . tendens*, 'raising hands and voices in supplication'. It was sometimes called zeugma.

Sy'mmachus, Quintus Aure'lius (*c.* AD 340–*c.*402), prefect of Rome in 384, a Roman noble, regarded by his contemporaries as an outstanding orator and prose stylist. His eloquence was referred to by *Macrobius as *pingue et floridum*, 'rich and florid'. He was pagan, but of moderate views. His best known work is the *Relatio*, 'report', which, as prefect of Rome, he addressed to the young emperor Valentinian II in 384, defending the ancient religious institutions against Christian inroads (see CHRISTIANITY). In it he urged the restoration to the senate-house of that symbol of the historic greatness of Rome, the Altar of Victory (probably erected by Augustus in 29 BC), which the emperor Gratian under the influence of St *Ambrose had had removed in 382. Symmachus' Report was preserved as a model of eloquence, but was successfully opposed by St Ambrose. His correspondence (over 900 letters) was published by his son in ten books. The first nine consist of carefully composed letters to his friends, trivial and uninteresting to later readers since mostly they ignore external events; the tenth book contains official correspondence.

symmo'riae, see LITURGY and DEMOSTHENES (2) 3.

Symplē'gadĕs ('the clashing ones'), in Greek myth, the 'clashing rocks' at the north end of the Bosporus through which the *Argonauts had to pass to enter the Black Sea. The rocks were believed to clash together, crushing ships that passed between them. The Planctae ('wandering ones') were similar rocks mentioned in the *Odyssey* (12. 61), in an unspecified place.

Sympo'siaca, see PLUTARCH 3.

sympo'sium ('drinking-party', 'banquet'), the male drinking-party, an important social institution in the life of aristocratic Greek men. It was held in the *andrōn*, 'men's apartment' (see HOUSES AND FURNITURE I); the (male) guests, their heads garlanded with flowers, reclined on couches (an Eastern practice introduced into Greece before the sixth century BC), usually two, sometimes more, to a couch (*klinē*), propped on their left arm; low tables to hold food and wine cups were placed in front of the couches. Wine was served from a large mixing-bowl (*kratēr*) where it was blended with water to make it fairly mild (see WINE), and poured by young slaves of both sexes, often chosen for their good looks. At least as important as the drinking was the entertainment, sometimes provided by slaves specially hired to sing and dance (see DANCE and HETAERAE), but often by the guests themselves and of a rather regularized kind; there were riddles and games (*cottabus* being a highly developed example), and lyric poems and *scolia were sung. Much of the lyric of Alcaeus, Anacreon, and Archilochus, and some of the short elegiac poems of Theognis, for example, were written for this kind of setting. Sometimes guests delivered short speeches on agreed topics (see Plato's *SYMPOSIUM* below). *Homosexuality derived much of its vitality as an institution from the circumstances of the symposium, where freeborn respectable women were absent and male beauty, charm, and wit were highly regarded. In a comic scene in Aristophanes' *Wasps*, an 'aristocratic' son tries to teach acceptable symposiastic behaviour to his embarrassingly boorish father. See also *SYMPOSIUM* (2) below. Today, a symposium means no more than a discussion-group.

Sympo'sium ('drinking-party', 'banquet'). I. Dialogue by *Plato written perhaps *c.*384 BC. The dialogue is supposed to have taken place at a banquet held in Athens at the house of the tragic poet *Agathon who is celebrating his first victory in the competitions for tragedy at the Lenaea of 416 BC. The dialogue is narrated by a friend of Socrates, Apollodorus of Phalerum, who was not present (being too young) but had the story from an eye-witness and admirer of Socrates, Aristodemus. Each of the guests delivers a short speech in honour of love, Phaedrus from a mythical standpoint, Pausanias from that of a sophist, Agathon from that of a poet, and so on; Aristophanes turns the dialogue towards comedy. Each speech is a clever parody by Plato of the style of the purported speaker. Socrates takes the discussion on to a higher plane. He has learnt from Diotīma, the priestess of Mantinea, that love may have a nobler aspect. The need in a human being which is manifested on a lower plane by sexual love can also take an intellectual form, the desire of the soul to create conceptions of wisdom and beauty such as poets and legislators produce. One should proceed from the love of a beautiful form to the perception and love of universal divine beauty, which has no physical aspect. *Alcibiades now joins the party, slightly drunk. He confesses the fascination which Socrates exercises on him and his hope of receiving lessons in wisdom from him. He tells of various incidents in the life of Socrates, including his own failure to seduce him. Socrates is like the statuettes of *Silenus that conceal images of gods inside them, and like *Marsyas the satyr who with his pipe could charm the souls of men.

The term 'Platonic love' refers to the argument for the superiority of non-sexual love.

2. A narrative by *Xenophon of an imaginary banquet supposed to have taken place on the occasion of the Great *Panathenaea of 421 BC at the house of *Callias, Socrates being among the guests. Those present at the banquet are all well-known historical characters except for a comedian called Philippus and a Syracusan in charge of the dancers. The narrative gives a vivid picture of the conversation and amusements at an Athenian symposium. The conversation is a mixture of humour and seriousness, and Socrates is presented in a relaxed mood. There are a good many jokes about his personal appearance; he is the central figure, and, amid all the jokes, delivers a serious speeech on the superiority of spiritual to carnal love.

syne'cdoche ('taking up together'), figure of speech in which a part is used to signify the whole, or the singular where the plural is meant, as in Livy's phrase *Romanus proelio victor*, 'The Roman won the battle'.

Syne'sius, see NEOPLATONISM.

synizē'sis ('melting into one'), coalescence of two vowels into one sound without alteration of letters.

Syphax, see SOPHONISBA.

Sȳ'racuse (Gk. Syrakousai, Lat. Syracusae), on the south-east coast of Sicily, a colony founded by Corinth in 733 BC under the leadership of a certain Archias (see COLONIZATION, GREEK 2).

1. *From earliest times to 467 BC.* The city was originally confined to the small island of Ortygia closely adjoining the mainland, but was subsequently extended to include the neighbouring regions of Achradīna and Epipolae. Its early government was in the hands of aristocrats, the *gamoroi* ('land-owners'), who formed an élite, having their lands worked by native labour. It was a flourishing place by the end of the sixth century, founding its own colonies, including Camarīna, but was raised to the position of first city in Sicily by *Gelon. He was originally cavalry-commander to the tyrant of *Gela, Hippocratēs, and when the latter died in battle *c.*490 BC, he seized the tyranny for himself. Under the pretext of restoring to their city the Syracusan aristocrats exiled in a democratic revolution, he seized Syracuse also, and transferred his seat of government there, leaving Gela in the control of his brother *Hieron. He destroyed Camarina and brought its inhabitants, and many of the inhabitants of Gela, to Syracuse. He won great glory by defeating the Carthaginians at the battle of Himera in 480. The inscribed base of Gelon's thank-offering for this victory has been discovered at Delphi.

Gelon was succeeded by his brother Hieron I (478–67), who added to the cultural splendour of Syracuse and was made famous by the Epinician Odes of Pindar and Bacchylides, and by the fact that Aeschylus and Simonides spent some time at his court. Xenophon wrote an imaginary dialogue between the latter and Hieron. The tyrant founded a new city, Aetna, at the foot of the volcano. A bronze helmet dedicated in celebration of his victory over the Etruscans in the naval battle off Cumae (474) has been found at Olympia.

2. *467–353 BC.* Soon after Hieron's death a democracy was set up at Syracuse, and internal dissensions were followed by external aggression against other Sicilian cities (see SICILY), a situation which Athens was led to believe she could turn to her own advantage; her hope of controlling some part of the island led to the disastrous Sicilian Expedition of 415 (see PELOPONNESIAN WAR 5). Its failure was followed by the rise of Dionysius (later Dionysius I), a man of demagogic power, who induced the Syracusan assembly to elect him as the leading *strategos* and grant him a bodyguard, thus enabling him to maintain himself as sole ruler from 405 to 367. He made himself master of half Sicily and extended his conquests to the mainland of Italy, winning effective control over most of Magna Graecia. He was in the midst of a war against Carthage when he died in 367. His rule brought prosperity to Syracuse, but was generally considered oppressive. Plato visited his court (see PLATO I) but there is a legend that when Plato was leaving Syracuse Dionysius contrived to have him sold into slavery, from which Plato's friends rescued him. Dionysius had a taste for literature and bought for himself the writing tablets of Aeschylus. Thus inspired he actually won the prize at the *Lenaea in 367 with a tragedy, the *Ransoming of Hector*; his death is said to have been caused by a drinking-bout in celebration of this victory. A surviving line from a play of his, 'Alas, I've lost a useful wife', rather confirms the ancients' poor view of his talent. It was Dionysius I who built the great wall enclosing Syracuse and the heights of Epipolae.

Dionysius II succeeded his father. According to Plutarch he had been denied an education by his father, and was kept at home making wooden toys. He was at first much under the influence of his uncle and brother-in-law Dion, who induced Plato to visit Sicily again but apparently without good results, for Dion was banished from Sicily. Dionysius II then enjoyed ten years' peaceful reign before Dion challenged his rule (356), conquered Syracuse, and expelled him. Dion was himself assassinated in 353, though he had tried to provide Syracuse with a liberal constitution. The relations of Plato with these tyrants form the subject of several of his Epistles (see PLATO 6).

3. *353 BC to the Roman conquest in 211 BC.* After Dion's death Syracuse became increasingly anarchic and decline began, though Dionysius II

recovered his throne in 346. The Syracusans appealed for assistance against him to their mother-city Corinth, who in 344 sent them *Timoleon; the latter showed himself to be not only an outstanding general (he quickly expelled Dionysius and defeated the Carthaginians in 339 against great odds at the battle of the Crīmīsus) but also a wise and moderate statesman. Dionysius was eventually dispatched to Corinth, where he died. Timoleon restored peace to Sicily, introducing at Syracuse a moderately oligarchic government on the Corinthian model, and then retired into private life, remaining at Syracuse until his death (336) as the adviser of the people.

But party rivalry in Syracuse had not been permanently quelled: after twenty years the government at Syracuse was overthrown by Agathoclēs, a demagogue, who made himself first tyrant (317) and then king (305). While tyrant he attacked other Sicilian cities, who called in the assistance of Carthage. In 311 Syracuse was besieged; thereupon Agathocles took the bold course of slipping out of the harbour with a small force, landing in Africa, and attacking Carthage itself. Though he failed to capture the city the diversion served its purpose by relieving the pressure on Syracuse, and in 306 the Carthaginians agreed to a peace, by which they returned within their former boundaries in the west of the island.

After Agathocles' death (289), there followed a further period of disorder. *Pyrrhus remedied the situation but could not restore the Syracusan empire. Conflict with the *Mamertines produced a new ruler, Hieron II (269–216), mild and just, celebrated by Theocritus in Idyll 16. His reign was the last golden age of Syracuse. He had allied himself with Rome against Carthage in the First Punic War and contributed to her final victory. After his death Syracuse forsook Rome for Carthage, an act which signalled its final downfall. The city was besieged (213–211) and finally sacked by M. Claudius Marcellus; in their defence the Syracusans were substantially aided by *Archimedes, who perished when the city was taken. Under Roman rule Syracuse retained its beauty and to some extent its importance, but it suffered at the hands of the governor *Verrēs.

Sy'ria. The region known as Syria in the ancient world is roughly that of modern Syria, but its boundaries varied and are ill-defined. At its greatest extent it was bounded by the river Euphrates in the east and the Mediterranean in the west, the range of Mt. Taurus ir the north and the Arabian desert in the south. It included *Phoenicia, the coastal strip on the west, and the southern part known as Coelē-Syria. See SELEUCIDS.

sȳrinx, see PAN and MUSIC.

Syrtēs, two wide gulfs on the north coast of Africa, where in antiquity the navigation was considered dangerous. The Greater Syrtis (now the Gulf of Sirte) is east of Tripoli, the Lesser (now the Gulf of Gabes) off the coast of Tunisia.

T

Ta'bula Ï'liaca, marble relief of *c.*15 BC, found by the Via Appia near Bovillae, about 20 km. (12 miles) south-east of Rome. It represents scenes from the Trojan War, and indicates the sources from which they are taken. An inscription states that the central panel represents the (lost) *Iliupersis* of *Stesichorus (Greek lyric poet of the early sixth century BC), and its details have been believed to be Stesichorean. Among other things the panel shows Aeneas bearing his father Anchisēs on his shoulders from Troy, accompanied by his son Ascanius, with an inscription saying that he is sailing to '*Hesperia' (i.e. Italy). If Stesichorus did indeed include this episode, then he is the first authority for the legend of Aeneas' migration to Italy. Many scholars doubt the authenticity of the attribution to Stesichorus.

Ta'bula Peutingeriā'na, see MAPS.

Ta'citus, Publius (or Gaius; sources vary) **Corne'lius** (b. AD 56 or 57, d. after 117), Roman historian. He was possibly a native of Narbonese Gaul. Comparatively little is known about his life, but he had a normal senatorial career, begun under the emperor Vespasian (AD 69–79); he married *Agricola's daughter in 77, was praetor in 88, *consul suffectus* in 97, and governor of Asia in 112–13. His experience of the tyranny of Domitian's reign (81–96), to which he owed advancement, as he admits, led him to write in the introduction to his *Life of Agricola* and *Histories* of the pains and the difficulties of surviving in public life under such an emperor. But he won fame during his lifetime: the Younger *Pliny, who was his friend, was proud to be considered his equal in popular estimation.

His *Agricola* was published in 98, early in Trajan's reign. It is essentially a panegyric of the dead man and especially of his great achievements in *Britain (see 4) on which Tacitus has valuable information; but it is also a defence of the integrity and service of those administrators who, like Agricola and Tacitus himself, as well as Trajan, had managed to survive Domitian's reign. His *Germania* or 'On the Origin and Country of the Germans' was published in the same year. It is an account of the various tribes north of the Rhine and the Danube, heavily dependent on earlier writers such as Livy and the Elder Pliny. The Germans' love of freedom and their vigour and bravery are implicitly compared with the corruption at Rome. His *Dialogus de oratoribus* ('dialogue on orators'), is set in the seventies; four distinguished men of the day discuss the decline of Roman oratory and the reason for it, namely the dependence of oratory on a free political life. It used to be thought an early work but now is agreed to belong to the period 100–5. The fact that its style is very different from that of Tacitus' other works is explained by reference to the requirements of a different literary genre. Tacitus had studied rhetoric as a young man and he became famous as a speaker. In 97 he delivered a funeral oration over the consul Verginius Rufus (a distinguished general whom his soldiers had wanted to become emperor, and whose consulship Tacitus completed), and in 100 he spoke as advocate for the province of Asia against the ex-governor Marius Priscus; the Younger Pliny notes the eloquence and dignity of the latter speech.

His major works were the *Histories* and the *Annals*. A projected work on the happier reigns of Nerva and Trajan 'which I am saving for my old age' did not materialize. The *Histories*, on which Tacitus was working in 106–7, covered the period AD 69–96, the reigns of the emperors Galba, Otho, Vitellius, Vespasian, Titus, and Domitian, and were perhaps written in fourteen books. Only the first four and part of the fifth survive, dealing with the events of 69 and 70, but even those two years justify his description of the period as one 'full of catastrophe, fearful in its fighting, torn by mutinies, bloody even in peace'. He gives a vivid picture of the civil wars of 69 (the 'Year of the Four Emperors') and their contenders, ending with the one emperor who 'changed for the better', Vespasian. The *Annals*, on which Tacitus was working *c.*116, may have consisted of sixteen books covering AD 14–68, i.e. the reigns of Tiberius, Caligula, Claudius, and Nero. Parts of 5 and 6 and the whole of 7–10 are missing; 16 breaks off in AD 66 before Nero's death. His sources overall were the works of other historians, public records, and, where possible, his own experiences.

The *Annals* in particular show Tacitus to have been one of the greatest of historians, with a penetrating insight into character and a sober grasp of the significant issues of the time. He knew that the empire was to be a permanent institution; but he shared the ancient Roman view that it is individuals who create history, and he was deeply pessimistic about Rome's ability to find a good emperor. The impartiality he claimed in writing the histories of the emperors was affected by his preference for the republic at its worst to the imperial system at its best, and he was driven to dwell on the evils of the latter. He saw it as the historian's function to record virtue and ensure that vice was denounced by posterity (*Annals* 3. 65), and to this end he created a style as memorable as the events he records, condensed, rapid, and incisive, with a flavour all of its own and impossible to render in translation. The ironical and pessimistic attitude of mind that informs it is, however, easily appreciated. The works of Tacitus seem to have aroused little admiration in the times that immediately followed, and those we now possess scarcely survived the Middle Ages (see TEXTS, TRANSMISSION OF ANCIENT 6 and 8). Boccaccio possessed a partial manuscript of the *Annals* and *Histories*, but the first political commentary did not appear until 1581. Edward Gibbon (1737–94) admired Tacitus more than any other ancient historian, and his own biting, epigrammatic style comes closest in English to the Latin of his exemplar.

Tagēs, the legendary founder of Etruscan *augury. He is represented as a grandson of Jupiter, who sprang from the ploughed earth in the form of a boy, and taught the Etruscans the interpretation of lightning and other signs.

Tala'ss(i)us, Roman marriage god, the personification of the ritual cry *Talassio* (compare *Hymenaeus* in Greek) when the bride is escorted to the groom's house.

talent, a standard weight in the ancient world, representing a man's load; see WEIGHTS AND MEASURES and MONEY AND COINS.

Tālos. 1. In Greek myth, the bronze man of Crete, made by the god Hephaestus and given by him to king Minos (or by Zeus to *Europa). He guarded the island by walking round it three times a day; if he saw strangers approaching he made himself red-hot and then embraced them when they landed. His one vulnerable spot was a vein of blood which ran through his body and was closed in his head by a nail. When he tried to drive the Argonauts away from Crete, *Medea used her magic powers on him; according to one story she removed the nail, causing him to bleed to death.

2. The nephew of *Daedalus.

Tana'gra. For the battle of Tanagra in 457 BC see ATHENS 2 (ii); for Tanagra figures see POTTERY 3.

Ta'naquil, of noble Etruscan family, in Roman legendary history, the wife of Tarquinius Priscus (see ROME 2 and TARQUIN) who became the fifth king of Rome. She is said to have persuaded him to move from Etruria to Rome, where he gained the throne, and, when he was murdered, to have played an important part in securing the succession of Servius Tullius, thus defeating the designs of the sons of the previous king, Ancus Marcius.

Ta'ntalus, in Greek myth, son of Zeus and the Titaness Pluto ('wealth'), king of the region around Mount Sipylus in Lydia. He married Dionē, daughter of Atlas, by whom he became the father of Niobē and *Pelops, and thus the ancestor of the Pelopidae. Tantalus offended the gods and was punished in *Tartarus by being set, thirsty and hungry, in a pool of water which always receded when he tried to drink from it, and under fruit trees whose branches the wind tossed aside when he tried to pick the fruit. Another account of his punishment was that a great stone was suspended over his head, threatening to crush him, so that he was in too much terror to enjoy a banquet which was set before him. The reason for these punishments is variously described: either he invited the gods to dinner and served them his son's flesh (see PELOPS), or he stole nectar and ambrosia from the gods' table, where he had been invited, and gave them to his friends, or he told his friends the gods' secrets. From his name we have the word 'tantalize'.

Tare'ntum (Taranto), important city and harbour on the 'instep' of south Italy, on the gulf named after it. It was founded (traditionally in 706 BC) by Sparta, soon after she had annexed Messenia, apparently for political reasons since the colonists were known as the Partheniai (perhaps meaning 'children of unmarried mothers') and seem to have been Spartans born in circumstances which denied them full citizenship. Originally an aristocracy, Tarentum became a democracy *c.*475 BC, and flourished especially in the fourth century BC during the lifetime of the philosopher *Archytas. The Tarentines quarrelled with the encroaching Romans in 282, relying on help from *Pyrrhus, and thus provoked Rome's Pyrrhic wars. The Romans conquered Tarentum in 272, but imposed generous terms. *Livius Andronicus, probably a Tarentine captive taken to Rome, was an important figure in early Roman literature. Tarentum played an important part in the Second Punic War: in 213 it was captured by Hannibal, and in 209 recaptured by Fabius Cunctator (and thoroughly plundered). Thereafter it suffered a decline. It lay in very fertile country; its honey, olives, scallops, wool, and purple dye were praised by Horace, its pinewoods by Propertius.

Tarpē'ia, woman in early Roman history whose legend (see ROME 2) explained the name of the Tarpeian Rock at the south-west corner of the Capitoline hill, from which criminals sentenced to death were hurled. The name Tarpeia is Etruscan.

Tarquin (Tarquinius), name of two of the

(semi-legendary) kings of Rome (see ROME 2). They were thought to have been Etruscans, and archaeological discoveries have confirmed a strong Etruscan presence at Rome in the supposed era of the Tarquins. Tarquinius Priscus, the elder Tarquin, was the fifth king of Rome (616–579 BC). Originally named Lucumo, he was the elder son of a certain Demaratus of Corinth who, forced for political reasons to leave his city, had settled in Tarquinii, the chief of the twelve cities of Etruria. Lucumo, born in Etruria of an Etruscan mother, himself married an Etruscan wife Tanaquil and moved to Rome, where he took the name Tarquinius, 'from Tarquinii'. There he won great popularity and when the king Ancus Marcius died he was elected to succeed him. After a reign of thirty-eight years he was murdered at the instigation of his predecessors' sons who felt they had been cheated of their inheritance. However, for the second time these failed to gain the throne, Tanaquil contriving that the succession should pass to *Servius Tullius, who had been brought up in the Tarquin household. Tarquinius and Tanaquil had two sons and two daughters. Of the latter, one married Servius Tullius, the other M. Brutus, becoming the mother of L. *Brutus who expelled the Tarquins from Rome. The sons Lucius and Aruns each married a daughter of Servius Tullius. *Tullia, the wife of Aruns, persuaded Lucius to murder his wife (her own sister) and his brother (her husband Aruns), and then to murder her father, the king Servius Tullius, in order that he, Lucius, might succeed to the throne and she might marry him and become his queen. All this he did, becoming Lucius Tarquinius Superbus, 'the Proud', and reigning from 534 to 510. The achievements and institutions of the two Tarquins are thoroughly confused in the sources, but the younger Tarquin was depicted in later tradition as having all the objectionable characteristics of a Greek tyrant, thereby justifying his expulsion by Brutus. See also LUCRETIA and SIBYL.

Ta'rtarus, in Greek myth, an elemental deity, son of Aither (Sky) and Gaia (Earth), and by his mother the father of Typhon. The name also describes a part of the Underworld where the wicked suffer punishment for their misdeeds on earth, especially (in the early poets) those such as Ixion and Tantalus who have committed some outrage against the gods. See HADES.

Tarte'ssus, vaguely defined region of southern Spain, 'Tarshish' of the Old Testament; the name was also given to the river Baetis (Guadalquivir), which flows to the south of the Sierra Morena, mountains rich in silver, and to a town at its mouth. It was proverbially rich as a result of trading in tin and silver between Brittany and south-west England on the one hand, and the Phoenicians and Carthaginians on

the other. The Phocaean Greeks visited the region in the late seventh century. (For an early reference to Tartessus see STESICHORUS.)

Tauri, the Taurians, the inhabitants of the Tauric Chersonese ('peninsula') in the Black Sea, i.e. the Crimea.

taxation, see FINANCE.

taxiarch, see ARMY, GREEK.

Tay'getē, one of the *Pleiads, the nymph of the high range of mountains named after her in the Peloponnese, west of Sparta. The goddess Artemis turned her into a doe to escape the attentions of Zeus, but by him she became the mother of *Lacedaemon, eponymous ancestor of the Lacedaemonians.

Tecme'ssa, see AJAX.

Te'gea, ancient city in the south-east of Arcadia, mentioned in the *Iliad*; there seems to have been a Mycenaean settlement on the site. In very early times Tegea fought successfully against Sparta; in the first half of the sixth century the Spartans, reputedly trusting an ambiguous oracle from Delphi, advanced into Tegea to seize the land but were defeated, and Spartan prisoners were made to till the land wearing the chains which they had brought with them for use on the Tegeans. In the mid-sixth century, again on advice from Delphi, the Spartans were told to find and bring back to Sparta the bones of the hero Orestes (son of Agamemnon). Having brought the bones from Tegea the Spartans were then victorious over the Tegeans who, after agreeing not to harbour Messenians (see MESSENIA), were taken into alliance with Sparta.

Teire'sias, in Greek myth, the blind Theban seer. Several reasons are given for his blindness: one story is that he saw the goddess Athena bathing and she blinded him, but gave him as compensation, since his mother was her friend, the gift of prophecy and a life seven generations long. In another version, he saw snakes coupling and killed one of them with a stick, whereupon he changed into a woman; later the same thing happened again and he changed back into a man. Since he was now uniquely qualified to answer, Zeus and Hera consulted him as to whether a man or a woman derived more pleasure from the act of love. When Teiresias replied that women received nine times as much pleasure as men, Hera struck him blind, but Zeus gave him the gift of unerring prophecy. Teiresias plays a part in many myths: in Homer's *Odyssey* Odysseus is sent to the Underworld to consult him about his return to Ithaca; he also figures in Sophocles' *Antigonē* and *Oedipus Tyrannus*, in Euripides' *Bacchae* and *Phoenissae*, and in Statius' *Thebaid*.

Teisa'menus, see OMENS.

Tei'sias. 1. Of Syracuse, flourished in the first half of the fifth century BC, an early teacher of *rhetoric, pupil of Corax, with whom he is linked as the founder of forensic oratory.

2. The real name of *Stesichorus.

Te'lamon, in Greek myth, king of the island of Salamis, son of Aeacus (king of Aegina) and Endēis, brother of *Peleus, and father of (the greater) *Ajax and *Teucer. He and Peleus killed their half-brother Phocus (whose mother was the Nereid Psamathē), perhaps at the instigation of Endeis. As a consequence Aeacus exiled them, Telamon going to Salamis. There he married Glaucē, daughter of the king, and inherited the throne. After Glauce's death Telamon married Eriboea (or Periboea) by whom he became the father of (the greater) Ajax. He was one of the Argonauts, and joined in the Calydonian boar-hunt (see MELEAGER). He helped Heracles in an early sack of Troy (see LAOMEDON), and Heracles gave him Laomedon's daughter Hesionē as concubine. Heracles' prayer that Telamon and Eriboea would have a brave son was shown to have been answered by the appearance of an eagle (Gk. *aietos*) sent by Zeus, after which the baby was named Ajax (Gk. Aias). Hesione also bore Telamon a son, Teucer. Telamon's death is variously narrated. He is usually said to have died at Salamis after banishing Teucer for failing to prevent Ajax' death.

Telchī'nēs, in Greek myth, magical and malevolent beings living in Rhodes, perhaps the original inhabitants, who were particularly skilled at metal-work. They were finally destroyed by a god, usually said to be Zeus, by means of a great flood. The poet Callimachus applied the name to his literary critics.

Tele'gonus, according to post-Homeric legend, the son of *Odysseus by Circē, and the unwitting killer of his father. According to Italian legend Telegonus founded the town of *Tusculum in the Alban hills outside Rome.

Tele'machus, in Greek myth, the son of Odysseus and Penelope; for his history see *ODYSSEY*. Post-Homeric legend made Telemachus marry *Circē. Homer in the *Odyssey* represents him as at first diffident, lacking his father's energy and resource, but at the end of the story astonishing his mother by taking command of the house and fighting resolutely against the suitors.

Tē'lephus, in Greek myth, son of Heracles and Augē (daughter of a king of Arcadia), who gave birth to him secretly in a shrine of Athena; as a consequence the land was struck by plague, and when the king discovered the reason he had the child exposed and Auge sold overseas. She came into the possession of Teuthras, king of Teuthrania in Mysia, who adopted her. The child

was rescued by shepherds, and when he grew up went to Mysia. Here he was about to marry Auge when their relationship was revealed. He became king of Mysia; the Greeks on their way to Troy landed in his kingdom, mistaking it for their destination, and in the fighting that ensued Telephus was wounded by Achilles. After the Greeks returned home Telephus' wound was still not healed. To find a cure he went to the Greek camp at Aulis to seek Achilles, having been told by the Delphic Oracle that the wounder would also heal. 'The wounder' was found to mean the spear, rust from which cured the wound. Euripides wrote a (lost) tragedy on the subject containing a scene, twice parodied by Aristophanes, in which Telephus appears disguised as a beggar, dressed in rags, and saves his own life in a melodramatic fashion by seizing Agamemnon's infant son Orestes as hostage. The tetralogy of which it was a part (and which included the still extant *Alcestis*) won second prize in the dramatic competitions of 438 BC.

Telesi'lla, Argive Greek poetess of the fifth century BC, famous for arming the women of Argos after Cleomenēs of Sparta had defeated the Argive men. Only a few fragments of her work survive. The telesillean metre is named after her (see METRE, GREEK 8).

Tellus, in Roman religion, the earth-goddess, associated with agricultural festivals such as the *Fordicidia.

te'menos, 'precinct', in ancient Greece, a piece of land marked off and consecrated to a god, excluded from secular uses. Many small shrines consisted merely of a *temenos* with an *altar, and no temple. In most cases a person had to be purified before entering.

Te'menus, among others of this name, one of the *Heracleidae, descendants of Heracles. After these had conquered the Peloponnese, Temenus received Argos as his share.

temples
1. *Greek*. The Minoans (see CRETE) and the Mycenaean Greeks had no temples; their cults were practised in rooms which were part of palaces and houses, or were associated with caves or mountain-peaks (see RELIGION, GREEK). After the collapse of the Mycenaean civilization and during the subsequent *Dark Age it seems that the fundamental requirement for the worship of a Greek god was an *altar in an open precinct, *temenos. A temple as an independent building, to be the dwelling-place of the god to whom it was dedicated and a shelter for his image, was a construction of the ninth and eighth centuries BC, one of the signs of the return of prosperity to the Greek world after the Dark Age. The first temples were long, narrow buildings made of wood and brick. It was not

until the Greeks had acquired greater building skills, and were also sculpting representations of their gods in statues of considerable size (see SCULPTURE), that the first stone temples were built *c.*700 BC. A temple stood in a walled *temenos*, its front usually facing east like the statues of the gods 'who face the rising sun . . . with gleaming eyes' (*Agamemnon*). The altar was normally erected (or already existed) outside and in front of it. In some cases two or more gods were worshipped in one temple.

In its simplest form the temple was a single room (Gk. *nāos*, Lat. *cella*) containing the cult statue on a pedestal at the end opposite the door. In a few cases it was open to the sky and is known as hypaethral, but more usually it was roofed and received light only through its open doors. Since it was the house of a god and not a place of assembly for a congregation of worshippers there were no seats or other furniture (but compare the Telesterion at Eleusis; see MYSTERIES). In many temples the side walls were continued forwards to form a porch (*pronāos*), with two columns between the walls supporting the front of the roof. Behind the *naos* was often a specially sacred inner chamber (*adyton*, 'not to be entered'), the oracle chamber if the resident god was oracular, or a room in which the temple treasures were kept; sometimes there was also a rear porch (*opisthodomos*). The 'treasuries', small temples at Delphi and Olympia erected by individual cities as demonstrations of piety and to house dedicated objects, were mostly in this form, and the more elaborate temples of later times were still based on this pattern. Since the *pronaos* and the *opisthodomos* frequently housed valuable offerings as well, they were enclosed by metal railings and gates. As the temples were not intended to hold congregations, it is possible that most of the time only privileged people were admitted, others merely catching a glimpse of the god from the open doorway at the east end. For the construction of more elaborate temples see ARCHITECTURE I.

2. *Roman.* The word 'temple' is derived from the Latin *templum*, the area of sky or land designated by the augur as that within which he was taking the auspices (see AUGURY); it was also the space on which to erect the shrine to a god (compare Greek *temenos*), or on which to carry on public business (e.g. the *Rostra* and places where the senate and assemblies of the people met). A building consecrated to a deity was a *templum* only if consecrated by the augurs (who had ascertained the will of the gods) as well as by the pontiffs. If consecration was by the pontiffs only (i.e. by the will of men), the place was not a *templum* but a *sacrum* or *aedēs*. The various *curiae* ('places of assembly') were required to be made *templa* by the augurs before decrees of the senate (*senatus consulta*) could be issued from them. In their earliest temples the Romans followed the Etruscan model (which was itself based on the Greek), having a room (*cella*) containing the statue of the god, and perhaps a small altar for burning incense, fronted by columns. Such was the early temple on the Capitol, according to tradition dedicated in 509 BC, which contained three *cellae* side by side for Jupiter, Juno, and Minerva. Etruscan and Roman temples were raised on a high platform approached by steps from the front only. They were often non-peripteral (see ARCHITECTURE), having a colonnade, if at all, only at the front. Later the Romans imitated the various forms of Greek temple, using mainly the Corinthian order. They also introduced developments of their own, including the circular temple (such as the temple of Vesta) and the use of the arch, vault, and dome.

Ten Thousand, the, see ANABASIS.

Terence (Publius Terentius Āfer) (b. 193 or 183 BC, d. 159), Roman writer of comedy. The main source for his life is the biography written by Suetonius *c.* AD 100 and preserved in Donatus' commentary to Terence, but that itself is uncertain about many events. The manuscripts are divided between those who say he died at the age of 24 and those who say 34. He was said to have been born at Carthage and to have been a slave at Rome. In composing his plays he was alleged to have been aided by *Scipio Aemilianus, C. *Laelius, and others of that circle, allegations to which he himself refers with some pride (at being thought to have such distinguished friends). He is said to have died at sea while returning from a visit to Greece.

Terence wrote six plays (for details see individual titles): *Andria* ('girl from Andros'), *Hecyra* ('mother-in-law'), *Heauton timorumenos* ('self-tormentor'), *Eunuchus* ('eunuch'), *Phormio*, and *Adelphoe* ('brothers').

His plays are *fabulae *palliatae*, and with two exceptions are adapted from *Menander; he follows his Greek originals more closely than *Plautus did, although sometimes combining portions of two plays. He thus represents scenes of the same Greek life as Plautus depicted, but by keeping the settings and conventions of his Greek sources, and excluding specifically Roman elements, he avoided obvious incongruity. Although the characters and subjects (young men's complicated love affairs) are much the same in both playwrights, the spirit is different. In Terence portraiture takes the place of caricature; conversation is much more natural than in Plautus, lacking the boisterous, farcical element of the latter. In all respects Terence is more refined and sophisticated than Plautus, but less robust. He abandoned the expository kind of prologue, and instead inserted necessary background information into the action; he also avoided the somewhat unnatural monologues of his models, rescripting them as dialogues. He introduces a more prosaic note by almost entirely avoiding lyric passages (*cantica*) and opera-like scenes; but only half of his lines are in the spoken metre of iambic senarii (see METRE, LATIN 2); the rest are iambic and trochaic septenarii, which were certainly 'sung' in the form of recitative. In general Terence aims at greater realism.

The plays of Terence did not have popular appeal but were greatly admired by discriminating critics like Cicero and Horace. They were widely known and studied in the Middle Ages, and were adapted into Christian form by Hroswitha (tenth century), the abbess of the Benedictine convent of Gandersheim in Saxony, for her nuns to read. Terence was much read in England in the sixteenth century and even acted (*Phormio* was performed by the boys of St Paul's School before Cardinal Wolsey). His influence can be traced in early English comedy and again in the comedy of manners of the Restoration. Several of his lines have become proverbial: *quot homines, tot sententiae* ('as many opinions as there are men'), and *fortis fortuna adiuvat* ('fortune favours the brave'), both from *Phormio*; see also *HEAUTON TIMORUMENOS*.

Tēreus, see PHILOMELA.

te'rminus, boundary-stone; in Roman religion the *numen* of such stones was the object of an annual ritual (the Terminalia) on 23 February, which included a sacrifice and a feast by the neighbouring land-holders. These rural *termini* had their state counterpart in the god Terminus, whose boundary-stone was located in the temple of Jupiter Optimus Maximus on the Capitol, and according to tradition was there before the temple was built. It was left inside the temple, which had an opening in the roof to ensure that the stone remained under the open sky.

Terpa'nder (Terpandros) (mid-seventh century BC), Greek lyric poet and musician of Lesbos, famous in legend, but of whose life nothing is known for sure. He was said to have won a musical competition during the period 676–673, at the games in honour of Apollo Carneius at Sparta, where he was believed to have founded a music school. The invention of the seven-stringed lyre (*cithara*; see MUSIC 1) was ascribed to him. He composed *nomes* (settings of epic poetry), preludes or introductions to the singing of epic poetry, and *scolia* (drinking songs); it is very doubtful whether the few surviving fragments ascribed to him are authentic; it seems probable that none of his work was known by the Alexandrian scholars of the Hellenistic age.

Terpsichore, the Muse of (choral) dancing; see MUSES.

Tertu'llian (Florens Quintus Septimius Tertulliānus) (*c.* AD 160–*c.*225), the Father of Latin theology. Born at Carthage the son of a centurion and brought up as a pagan, receiving a

good literary and rhetorical education, he was converted to Christianity before 197. He was learned in philosophy and science, and especially in law, and was the author of many apologetic, theological, controversial, and ascetic works. He appeals for the toleration of Christians, who are no danger to the state. It seems to him that natural instinct bears witness to the existence of God: *o testimonium animae naturaliter Christianae* ('O witness of the soul naturally Christian!'). He believed that Christians needed to separate themselves from pagan society to avoid contamination from the latter's immorality and idolatry, and since separation might involve disobeying the law of the state, it could prove necessary to accept martyrdom: Tertullian's actual words are traditionally known in the form, 'The blood of the martyrs is the seed of the Church.'

Both of the above quotations come from the *Apologēticum*, written *c.*197 in the form of a speech by an advocate, addressed to the governors of Roman provinces, in which, with a blend of passion and irony, he seeks to secure for Christians protection from attacks by the populace and, when they are brought up for trial, from illegal procedures. Other treatises are directed to regulating in minute detail the life of Christians in a pagan society, and show Tertullian's strong ascetic slant. At some period of his life he was won over to the ascetic and enthusiastic Montanist movement, which brought about a rupture between him and the Catholic church. Tertullian wrote with much rhetorical skill, and with a rich and varied vocabulary; he created many new words and helped to develop the form and terminology of theological Latin.

Tethys, according to Hesiod, a *Titan, daughter of Gaia (Earth) and Uranus (Heaven), consort of *Oceanus. Homer in the *Iliad* (14. 201) speaks of Tethys and Oceanus as the parents of the gods, but this was a myth that seems to have been forgotten in classical times.

tetra'logy, in Greek, originally a term used in oratory to describe a group of four speeches (*logoi*) delivered in the same law-suit; see LAW, AT ATHENS 3 and ANTIPHON. For its application to Greek drama see TRAGEDY 2.

tetra'meter, see METRE, GREEK 1.

tetrarchy, see AUGUSTUS, THE.

Teucer (Teukros). **1.** In Greek myth, legendary king ruling in the neighbourhood of *Troy who became the ancestor of the Trojan kings through his daughter who married *Dardanus. From him the Trojans are sometimes called Teucri.

2. In Greek myth, son of *Telamon and Hēsionē, and half-brother of *Ajax. He was called Teucer (i.e. Trojan) because his mother was a daugher of *Laomedon, king of Troy. He was the greatest archer among the Greeks at the siege of Troy. On his return to Salamis from the siege he was banished by his father as responsible for his brother's death, and went to Cyprus where he founded a town also called Salamis. See *AJAX*.

texts, transmission of ancient
1. In Greece the first literature, Homeric epic, was composed and handed down orally, without the aid of writing (see HOMER); even when the Phoenician *alphabet had been adopted for writing Greek in the eighth century BC, literature continued to be essentially oral. According to tradition it was the Athenian tyrant *Peisistratus in the middle of the sixth century BC who first ordered an official text of Homer to be written down, and one may guess that the lyric poetry of Archilochus, Alcaeus, and Sappho circulated in written form also. Certainly from the late seventh century onwards the new prose works, which could not have been as easily memorized as poetry, could hardly have survived by oral transmission and must have been written down. The philosopher Heracleitus (who flourished *c.*500 BC) is said to have deposited his treatise *On Nature* in a temple (where, presumably, it could be consulted). Books were not common until well into the fifth century BC, when it is likely that the works chiefly in circulation were those of the early philosophers and historians, the poets studied in schools (for the benefit of teachers), and perhaps the tragedians; later in the fifth century there must have been a demand for the works of the *sophists. Soon after the middle of that century some sort of book-trade developed, which made it possible for individuals to collect books and form libraries (for books at this time see BOOKS AND WRITING 3).

Aristotle's arrangement of the library at the Lyceum served as a model for the library at Alexandria set up in the third century BC (see ALEXANDRIAN LIBRARY); to the editorial labours of the Alexandrian librarians and scholars, in particular to Callimachus, Zenodotus, Eratosthenēs, Aristophanes of Byzantium, and Aristarchus, we owe the texts of classical Greek literature that we still possess today, and some of the ancient notes (*scholia) which have come down with them. The manuscripts which reached Alexandria had been copied with varying degrees of care, and most contained numerous mistakes and deviations ('corruptions') from what the authors had written. The scholars' task was to restore the original texts, as far as was possible, to classify them according to type (in *lyric poetry, for example, there were many different kinds), and also to write commentaries explaining their linguistic, literary, and antiquarian aspects. Restoring the original posed problems of convention; spelling in early texts differed according to the version of the

Greek alphabet used in the author's own city, and these texts had to be transliterated into the Ionic alphabet which was in general use in Greece after 403 BC (see ALPHABET). Some obviously wrong readings found in manuscripts of the Middle Ages go back to errors in transliteration made in the third century BC.

Another problem presented by the manuscripts was that of simple interpretation. Texts were written without word division and continued to be so written long after the Hellenistic age; it was not until the Middle Ages that there was consistent separation of words. *Accents, a Hellenistic invention, were likewise not used consistently until the Middle Ages. *Punctuation was rudimentary and used sporadically; in the texts of plays a change of speaker was indicated by a horizontal stroke at the beginning of a line or by a colon, with inevitable inaccuracy. Lyric poetry was written in continuous lines as if it was prose; *Aristophanes of Byzantium was credited with establishing the colometry of lyric (i.e. of distinguishing the individual metrical units or cola), a discovery which enabled it to be written in lines like modern poetry. The likelihood of making errors of interpretation, and so of wrongly dividing words or lines of poetry, was considerable.

The scholars at Alexandria aimed to collect copies of all the known literature of ancient Greece. It seems probable that the works of some early poets at least had already perished; it is unlikely that the Alexandrians knew any of the poems of Arion or Terpander for example, and they perhaps knew only one or two famous poems or parts of poems by, for example, Eumelus of Corinth or Lasus of Hermionē. Out of all known literature they drew up lists of the best authors in each genre (see CANONS), thus facilitating the survival of their works at the expense, it would appear, of the works of lesser authors.

The critical signs written in the margins by Alexandrian scholars are in some cases still in use today. Lines thought to be spurious were 'obelized', that is, a horizontal stroke, *obelos*, was placed beside the line in the left-hand margin; the *diplē* > indicated that something in the line was notable; the *asteriskos* ※ marked a line incorrectly repeated in another place; the sigma and antisigma (C and Ɔ) marking two consecutive lines showed that they might be interchanged. Thus there gradually developed the business of scholarship and in particular of textual criticism and the standardization of texts. For the scholars the priority in textual criticism had been to detect and remove interpolations, i.e. inauthentic additions; and then to a lesser degree, and with increasing caution as knowledge increased, to replace what they thought to be errors with what they conjectured to be the right readings. But in all their work they respected the manuscript tradition and did not alter without good reason what they read in the manuscripts. Their practice was continued by their successors (see DIDYMUS).

2. In the ensuing *Roman age, Greek was a foreign language to many readers of Greek texts and in consequence the demand was not so much for textual and literary criticism as for popular annotated editions, grammars, and commentaries published separately from the text. These preserved the best of Alexandrian scholarship, and a small fraction of their contents is to be found nowadays, condensed and distorted, in the marginal notes (scholia) written on the manuscripts of the Middle Ages. The notes often contain quotations (*lemmata*) which preserve true readings from Alexandrian editions in places where these were subsequently corrupted. From the second century AD scholarship declined with the disappearance of readers interested in or capable of understanding the classical Greek authors, although there still were scholars engaged in preserving and continuing the tradition of Alexandrian research: in grammar, *Apollonius Dyscolus and *Herodian, in metric *Hephaestion, in the compilation of lexicons Harpocration and *Hesychius. But interest in the old authors was limited to a few names and within these to a few works. Selections and anthologies, e.g. that of *Stobaeus, came to be preferred to the complete work of a poet.

The revival of interest in classical Attic Greek in the second century AD (see SOPHISTIC, SECOND), combined with the emphasis on rhetoric in education, ensured the survival of the admired models, Plato, Xenophon, and Demosthenes, and in verse the popular plays of the tragedians and of Aristophanes; not, however, those of Menander who, though a favourite with anthologists, may have been deemed not to write a pure enough Attic to earn inclusion in the school curriculum. A factor which led to losses at this time was the change in the form of books from the papyrus roll to the parchment codex with leaves as in the modern book (see BOOKS AND WRITING 4). It must always have been the case that works were lost simply by the disintegration of papyrus rolls before they had been recopied, but the general change from roll to codex entailed the complete recopying of ancient literature from one form to another during the second to fourth centuries AD. Inevitably, some works did not seem worth the effort. Also, the absence of a roll or two at the time of copying might mean that a work was thereafter transmitted with part missing.

There is no reason to believe that the early Christians in the Greek (or eastern) half of the Roman empire set about the systematic destruction of classical pagan literature. Classical literature was the basis of the whole educational system for Christian and pagan alike, and there was no possibility of change in that respect since there were no alternative Christian texts. However, most Christians had no further interest in reading pagan literature once their education was over, and hence there was less incentive in a Christian society to copy texts apart from those which appeared on the school curriculum, and not enough, it would appear, to ensure their survival through the wars and destructions of the fourth and subsequent centuries. Thus in one way the spread of Christianity hastened the disappearance of ancient literature. But although the Roman and early *Byzantine periods were a time of loss, it is clear from a comparison of later manuscripts with early papyri, some of the latter not much later than the Alexandrian scholars themselves, that there was no appreciable corruption during this time and that the quality of surviving texts was hardly impaired.

3. By the end of the sixth century a serious decline in learning and literacy had begun in the eastern empire, and for three centuries there is little recorded about classical studies. After the eighth century, the darkest time of this Dark Age of Greek literature, came a period of peace and a revival in the ninth century associated with the names of *Photius and Arethas, who sought out surviving classical books. At the same time there were two important changes in manuscripts, one of material and one of handwriting. Papyrus was no longer plentiful: the plantations seem not to have been cultivated as abundantly as hitherto, and Egyptian supplies not to have been available after the Arab conquest of Egypt in 641. Parchment was greatly in demand but expensive and in limited supply. (It is calculated that the oldest extant manuscript of the Latin *Vulgate required the skins of about 1,550 calves.) However, in 751 the Arabs took prisoner at Samarkand some Chinese who knew the art of paper-making, and soon the Arabs in the East and in Spain were producing enough paper to export to Byzantium.

The second change, that of handwriting, seems to have come about partly as an economy measure (though it also resulted in greater speed and ease of writing). The old hand, uncial, was replaced by minuscule, which could be written rapidly in half the space (see BOOKS AND WRITING 5). The translation of the uncial manuscripts into minuscule was now (in the ninth century) begun and it is obvious that many texts in which there was little interest were not recopied at this time. Photius, for example, whose life spanned most of the ninth century, knew of and read considerably more ancient historians than we now possess. However, it is also the case that recopying ensured the preservation of many works for posterity: most of the surviving manuscripts of ancient authors descend from one or two minuscule manuscripts written at this period.

After the losses of the ninth and tenth centuries, the survival of most of what was left of the Greek classics was virtually certain. The literary texts were copied regularly and so too were those of the medical and mathematical writers. Nevertheless, losses still occurred. An important scholar of the late twelfth century, *Eustathius, archbishop of Thessalonika, seems to have known a little more of Pindar's Epinician Odes than we possess today, and his contemporary John Tzetzes knew more of Callimachus and Hipponax than we now possess. By the twelfth century these seem to have been rare texts indeed, and further losses must have been sustained in 1204 through the destruction of Constantinople by the Franks during the Fourth Crusade. However, serious though this was it did not for long disrupt the progress of learning. It was followed by a flowering of Greek scholarship from the late thirteenth to the fifteenth centuries, when much consolidation of learning took place and resulted in careful editions of the surviving texts.

This period of scholarship is associated particularly with the names of Planudes and Triclinius. The latter sought out manuscripts and was often rewarded by the discovery of different readings, which we now have only in his marginal notes; thus his own manuscripts of an author (or copies of them), although relatively late (fourteenth century), are often no less valuable witnesses to a text than the earliest surviving manuscript perhaps 500 years older. The phrase 'merely late, not worse' (recentiores non deteriores), has been used by a modern scholar to describe manuscripts of this kind. Triclinius' searches had a particularly fortunate outcome in the discovery of a hitherto virtually unknown text of nine plays by Euripides, not selected for reading in schools like the other surviving plays but preserved by chance. When Byzantium fell to the Turks in 1453 the only ancient Greek text known to have been lost as a result was a complete copy of the World History by *Diodorus Siculus. Even before the flight of Byzantine scholars to the West, the Italian humanists had been collecting Greek manuscripts from the Byzantine empire in large numbers. By the time Byzantium fell the survival of Greek literature in the West was assured.

4. Latin literature began in the third century BC and by the middle of the following century a considerable body of texts was in existence, of poetry, plays, and prose. However, although books must have circulated by that time, between the Scipios and their friends for example, very little is known about the way in which texts, presumably written on papyrus rolls as in Greece, were copied and published. The epics of Naevius and Ennius were in a sense a national possession and received some scholarly attention; but dramatic texts, for example, being distributed as acting copies, suffered many alterations and recastings (Plautus' Poenulus and Terence's Andria both have two different endings preserved in the manuscripts). The influence of *Crates (4), a Pergamene grammarian who visited Rome c.168 BC, and scholarship of the Alexandrian school (see HELLENISTIC AGE), gave rise to a desire for authentic texts, and a succession of scholars using the methods of the Alexandrians worked to this end down to the time of the emperor Augustus. (See, for example, the research on Plautus done by *Varro.) On the other hand a revival of interest in the old authors such as Plautus during the early first century BC had a contrary effect. There was a demand for more easily intelligible texts than the original versions with their archaic, obscure, and often recherché vocabulary. Thus popular texts of these authors with considerable variety of readings circulated by the side of the authentic texts. This process was extended to later writers who were more widely read, such as Virgil, and systematic revision of the texts in circulation became necessary; this was carried out with sound scholarship on the basis of the best manuscripts available, at least during the first three centuries AD. *Asconius did important work on Cicero, Virgil, and Sallust, but the outstanding scholar of the later part of the first century AD was M. Valerius *Probus.

In the second century AD there was again a revival of interest in early Roman writers, Ennius, Plautus, and Cato for example, and it is to this revival that we owe most of our knowledge of Ennius and Cato who, though not surviving in manuscript, are quoted and referred to by compilers of excerpts (such as Aulus *Gellius). During the third and fourth centuries many Latin texts were epitomized, continuing and increasing a tendency that had been apparent in the first century AD when Livy was so treated. This was the great age of commentators, among whom were *Donatus and *Servius. The last pagan revival came at the end of the fourth century, in the face of the triumph of *Christianity during the reign of the pious Theodosius (378–95), attested by, among other things, the 'subscriptions' or notes written at the end of a text by whoever originally checked and corrected it, which gave details about when the manuscript was copied and by whom. This subscription was often copied verbatim from manuscript to manuscript, and is valuable as evidence of pedigree. In general, Latin-speaking Christians like their Greek counterparts accepted that the pagan Latin texts were still essential for education and could be used, but with caution. (*Jerome, who suffered crises of conscience over his addiction to pagan literature, uses the analogy of the captive woman in Deuteronomy 21: 10–13 whom her captor may take as wife after she has shaved her head and pared her nails.) The old Roman educational system prevailed until it came to be replaced much later by that of monastic and episcopal schools.

5. The destructions of the fourth and fifth centuries were exceeded by those of the sixth century and by the final collapse of the western Roman empire under the waves of barbarian invaders (see FALL OF ROME). The cultivated world narrowed with the fall of North Africa to the Vandals; Spain, which survived the Frankish invasions of the third century and the Visigothic in the fifth (even transmitting a residuum of Roman culture through *Isidore, bishop of Seville), succumbed early in the eighth century to the Arabs; and Gaul under the Franks was not in a position to preserve classical learning. Nevertheless, books continued to be produced in the fourth and fifth centuries, including luxury copies of Virgil. Although the Latin Church was predominantly hostile to pagan literature, yet pagan Latin texts were included by this time in the important collections of books being made at the ecclesiastical centres of Rome, Ravenna, and Verona. At the beginning of the sixth century it was still possible to obtain copies of most of the important Latin classical and post-classical authors except for the very early literature which had disappeared in the course of the previous centuries. (For the copying of books in a sixth-century monastic library see CASSIODORUS.)

The period from the mid-sixth to the mid-eighth centuries, a dark age in the Latin West as in the Greek East, brought about a steep decline of interest in classical literature, texts of which seem scarcely to have been copied at all, while a large number of biblical and patristic works was produced. Many Latin works perished when old parchments had their original text removed by washing and were then reused for religious texts (reused manuscripts are called *palimpsests), less from hostility than from complete lack of interest in the classics. The surviving part of Cicero's De republica is known only from what has been recovered from underneath the commentary of St Augustine on the Psalms.

But at the same time, from the late sixth century onwards, classical literature was being saved and propagated by missionaries from Ireland; impelled by a zeal for books and learning they spread across Europe founding monasteries to which they passed on their own enthusiasm, e.g. at Luxeuil in Burgundy, Bobbio in northern Italy, and St Gall in Switzerland, and creating a need for books of all kinds. It was the importation of books into England in great quantity which enabled the biblical scholar and historian Bede (673–735), who had never left Northumbria, to acquire his vast learning. Anglo-Saxons in turn became missionaries and scholars. A special variety of Latin handwriting, known as 'insular', is associated with the early scholarship of the British Isles.

At the end of the eighth century came the new interest in learning that was crucial for the preservation of Latin literature, the Carolingian revival, brought about in Charlemagne's reconstituted Roman empire of western Europe, and centred on the monasteries. Of this revival, Alcuin, the perfect exemplar of Anglo-Latin culture, was the chief promoter. Alcuin (735–804), who had been born and educated at York, made the acquaintance of Charlemagne at Parma in 781 and was placed by him at the head of a school attached to his court, where he followed the programme of Cassiodorus in teaching the *seven liberal arts. Later he became Abbot of St Martin's at Tours, where he remained until his death. Among much else he taught his monks to copy manuscripts, and as a result France contributed greatly to the transmission of texts in the ninth and tenth centuries (see BOOKS AND WRITING 6). German monasteries also played an important part, as did the monasteries of Bobbio and Monte Cassino in Italy, particularly notable for the careful copying of manuscripts, and of Cluny and Corbie in Burgundy; the scribes' work was revised by the best scholar in each monastery, and special attention was paid to spelling, punctuation, and comparison with other available manuscripts. A legible script was developed in France, Caroline minuscule, from which evolved eventually a minuscule that became the normal script of western Europe. Our soundest Latin texts, apart from the little that is preserved by manuscripts of greater age, date from this time.

6. By the end of the ninth century the survival of a large number of Latin works was secured by their being part of the educational curriculum or established as works of literature; but there were others which were rarely studied, and some which were represented, as far as can be seen, by one copy only: Cicero's Letters, Tacitus' minor works, Columella, Petronius, Apicius, Valerius Flaccus, Ammianus Marcellinus, were all copied at this time, but by only one or two scribes. Hardly anyone knew of Tibullus, Catullus, the Younger Seneca's tragedies, or Statius' Silvae, and there is no evidence that anyone at the time was reading Propertius' poems, Seneca's Dialogues, Apuleius' Golden Ass, more than a small part of the Histories and Annals of Tacitus, Manilius, Cornelius Nepos, and Velleius Paterculus, texts of which were still nevertheless in existence. Books 40–45 of Livy were preserved on a fifth-century manuscript which was not copied until the sixteenth century. The continued existence of all these works was precarious in the extreme, but they escaped destruction. A great contribution to this survival was made in the eleventh century by the monastery of Monte Cassino, the foundation of St Benedict, at a time when Benedictinism was declining as a cultural force in Europe.

In the late eleventh and early twelfth centuries

there was suddenly a renewed interest in the classics, and books on the verge of extinction began to be copied. Because of this we still possess the texts of Seneca, Apuleius, and Tacitus mentioned above, as well as Varro's *De lingua Latina*, Frontinus' *De aquis*, and the thirty or so lines of Juvenal's sixth satire which are preserved in only one manuscript. During the twelfth century generally the more active intellectual life was no longer being pursued in the monasteries but in the cathedral schools. Although education continued to be based on Latin literature it was becoming more secular, catering for the needs of those who wanted to study law, medicine, and logic, while at the same time there was now a leisured class who wanted from literature a reflection of its own life and desires. It is therefore a matter of regret that when for the first time for many centuries love poetry and satire were in demand for their own sakes, the age was without the poetry of Catullus, Tibullus, and Propertius, who had not yet been rediscovered. As far as classical literature is concerned it was an age of consolidation; its two outstanding scholars were the historian William (librarian) of Malmesbury (d. 1143), and John of Salisbury (*c.*1110–80).

7. The teaching of the seven liberal arts, under the influence of Alcuin, did much to prepare the way in the eleventh century for the application of philosophical method to the study of theology, an educational pattern which became known as scholasticism. To the scholastics, classical literature was no longer important for its form or style or for other literary reasons, but for its material content, information, or moral anecdote. These aspects could be more readily absorbed in excerpts than by reading complete texts. Ovid and Seneca, who can be easily appreciated in selections, became very popular; Virgil, who could not, languished. But perhaps the most significant aspect of scholasticism for classical literature in the long run was the importance acquired by Aristotle, even if only for his works on logic, and the resulting revival of interest in Greek. Until the end of the twelfth century Aristotle was known in the West only in the Latin translations of, and commentaries on, a few of his logical works, by *Boethius and others (see ARISTOTLE 5). Plato similarly was known only from a Latin version of the *Timaeus*, made in the fourth century, and from Latin quotations. From the mid-eighth century onwards, translations into Arabic and Syriac of Greek philosophical works in which Islamic thinkers were particularly interested, initiated by a desire for the medical works but including Plato, Aristotle, Theophrastus, and the mathematical writers, circulated in the Arab world. Towards the end of the twelfth century, Arabic translations and commentaries on these Greek authors by Avicenna (980–1037) and Averroes (1126–98), Aristotle's greatest Muslim disciple,

were themselves translated into Latin at Toledo in Spain and diffused rapidly through Europe. But the great step forward came in the thirteenth century when these Latin translations from the Arabic were superseded by other Latin translations made direct from the original Greek. Robert Grosseteste (*c.*1168–1253) translated Aristotle's *Ethics* and some of the works of Pseudo-Dionysius the Areopagite (see NEOPLATONISM), and William of Moerbeke (*c.*1215–86) a number of Greek commentaries on Aristotle, many at the request of Thomas Aquinas (1225–74). Roger Bacon (*c.*1214–94), a pupil of Grosseteste, lamenting the general ignorance of Greek, tried to remedy matters by compiling a Greek grammar.

8. The Renaissance, the general awakening of enthusiasm for all things intellectual and artistic, covered the period from 1300 to the mid-sixteenth century and was stimulated in the first place by the cultural movement known as humanism (from the Italian *umanista*, a teacher of the 'humanities'). From being at first the study, teaching, and propagation of classical literature the term humanism came to describe the attempt to recapture the *humanitas* (the word coined by Cicero to translate the Greek *paideia*), 'human culture', of Greece and Rome, and to infuse the life of the present with the ideals of the classical past. The movement, which eventually influenced all areas of intellectual and artistic life, started in Italy. There education had not been confined to the monasteries and priesthood, as in the more northern countries, and an educated laity had continued to exist which maintained an interest in ancient literature, in spite of the indifference of the Church to the classics and the invasions and wars of the sixth and following centuries. Stimulated by the general revival of intellectual interests in Europe, Italians of the fourteenth century began to demand more and better texts. But manuscripts were scarce and copyists not very efficient; there was a need for scholarship to match enthusiasm. The combination was found above all in Petrarch (1304–74) and (with more enthusiasm than scholarship) Boccaccio (1313–75). Petrarch's greatest reverence was for Cicero, for whose works he searched throughout Europe; by the end of his life he had collected almost all Cicero's philosophical and rhetorical works and a wide range of speeches, but was most moved by his discovery (which others had made before) of Cicero's Letters to Atticus, to his brother Quintus, and to Brutus. His attempts to learn Greek (from the monk Barlaam) were not successful, but his earnest desire to understand the Greek background to Roman literature moved others to achieve this end. Boccaccio's enthusiasm for collecting classical books stopped short of trying to improve or restore the text, but to his searches we probably owe the rediscovery of, among others,

Martial, Ausonius, Ovid's *Ibis*, parts of the *Appendix Virgiliana* and the *Priapea*. He played some part in propagating the texts of Tacitus, Apuleius, and Varro, which only the library at Monte Cassino possessed. Petrarch and Boccaccio both persuaded Barlaam's pupil Leonzio Pilato to translate Homer into Latin and to teach Greek at Florence. Petrarch's copy of the Latin Homer survives, with his own annotations broken off in book 2 of the *Odyssey* by his death. Discoveries continued until well into the fifteenth century and beyond: the unique source of the Younger Pliny's letters to Trajan (book 10) was found in Paris in 1500, and the only manuscript of Tacitus *Annals* i–vi at Corvey in 1508.

The declining fortunes of the Byzantine empire in the East led to many Greek-speakers moving into Italy even before the exodus which followed the fall of Byzantium in 1453. Spurred on by their new knowledge of Greek, the Italians were keen to collect Greek manuscripts, which included, of course, as well as classical literature the Greek New Testament. Access to the Greek text of this led Bessarion at least to anticipate the attitude of Erasmus, that the proper basis for the interpretation of the New Testament was the Greek text and not the Latin Vulgate of Jerome, and so there were new beginnings in theology also. The latter part of the fifteenth century saw the arrival of the printing press, and a new step was taken in the preservation of the classics (see ALDUS MANUTIUS). See also PAPYROLOGY and TEXTUAL CRITICISM below.

textual criticism. The manuscripts in which the works of Greek and Latin literature are preserved for the most part date from the ninth to the fifteenth centuries AD (see TEXTS, TRANSMISSION OF ANCIENT, and PAPYROLOGY); they are thus at many removes from the authors' autographs. The aim of textual criticism is to restore the original text as far as possible, from manuscripts which, in the course of being copied by hand through many centuries, have been altered ('corrupted') by accidental miscopying and by deliberate insertions ('interpolations'), and have deteriorated by natural wear and tear. The first stage is to compare the manuscript copies of a text with each other so as to understand their relationships (for example, which manuscripts are copied from others still surviving) and to gain an idea of the state of the text of the nearest common ancestor of them all, the archetype. (The archetype, which is very rarely still in existence, is as far back as the manuscript evidence goes, but is itself usually many centuries later than the author's autograph.) This stage is known as recension (*recensio*, 'review'), and the results are if possible set out in a 'family tree of manuscripts' (*stemma codicum*), in which manuscripts are identified by

letters of the alphabet. (Where a scribe has introduced readings from more than one source, his manuscript is said to be 'contaminated', and may not fit easily into a *stemma*.) At this point manuscripts which are found to be direct copies of others still in existence are eliminated as having no independent value.

The next stage is to examine critically the text of the manuscripts selected as significant in the light of the *stemma*. The editor's task is to identify the authentic readings in those places where the manuscripts differ and to detect places where all of them seem to be in error; these last the editor corrects ('emends') if he can; if he cannot, he isolates the error and indicates that the text is not sound by 'obelizing' the corrupt words, i.e. printing a 'dagger' or obelus before and after them. (The dagger thus † is a modern critical sign: the *obelos* of the Alexandrian scholars was a horizontal line; see TEXTS, TRANSMISSION OF ANCIENT I.) In some places in the texts the manuscripts will offer a variety of readings some or all of which have a claim to be considered as authentic; the editor's task is then to decide between them. Nowadays these variant readings, together with the plausible emendations of previous editors, are printed by the editor at the bottom of each page of text. This part of the text, usually written in Latin and with considerable use of abbreviations, is known as the *apparatus criticus*, 'critical apparatus', and enables readers to assess for themselves the evidence for and reliability of the text they are reading.

A famous name in textual criticism is that of Karl Lachmann (1793–1851), who established the principle of *recensio*, leading to the recognition of an archetype, in his work on the Latin poets, and especially in his edition of Lucretius (1850). His study of the manuscripts of the New Testament enabled him to discredit the 'received text' and put the study of the text on a firmer footing.

Thālēs, of Miletus (flourished *c.*600 BC), by tradition the earliest Greek philosopher-scientist, one of the *Seven Sages. He is credited with offering sound advice in many spheres including politics, but he was chiefly famous as an astronomer and geometer. He is said to have predicted an eclipse of the sun within the year 585 BC which actually took place on the day of the battle of the Halys between the Medes and the Lydians. It is, however, impossible for one of his time to have known a system for predicting a solar eclipse at a given geographical latitude. Slightly more plausible is the belief that after visiting Egypt he originated geometry by generalizing from Egyptian land measurement. Aristotle attributed to him the view that all things are modifications of a single eternal (and therefore divine) substance, which Thales held to be water. With this is connected his saying that 'all things are full of gods'. See PHILOSOPHY.

Thale'tas, poet from Gortyn in Crete who came to Sparta in the first half of the seventh century BC in order, it was said, to rid the Spartans of a plague (by appeasing the god Apollo with his poetry). There he composed *paeans and *hyporchemata for the festivals, using paeonic and cretic metres (see METRE, GREEK 1). Nothing of his work survives.

Thali'a, see MUSES.

Tha'myris or **Thamyras,** legendary Thracian poet and musician. According to Homer (*Iliad* 2. 594) he boasted that he would win a contest even if the Muses opposed him, but they blinded him and made him forget his skill. Later authors attribute various musical inventions to him.

Thanatos (Death), see HYPNOS.

Thapsus, city in North Africa, famous as the site of Julius Caesar's victory over the supporters of Pompey in 46 BC.

Tharge'lia, principal festival of Apollo at Athens and throughout Ionia, celebrated on the 7th Thargelion (May–June), a pre-harvest festival with first-fruit offerings from the still unripe crops of all kinds of corn and vegetables cooked together in a pot (the offering being called *thargelos*). The interesting feature of this festival took place on the day before, namely purification (perhaps for a new beginning) by means of scapegoats. Two men (representing the men and women of the city), chosen for their ugliness, were fed and led around the city (so as to absorb all *pollution), then pelted, flogged with branches of figs, and driven out; in early times they were no doubt killed by being beaten with real rods and stoned.

Thasos, rocky island off the coast of Thrace, colonized from Paros *c*.680 BC (see ARCHILOCHUS). It became wealthy from its own gold mines and from the mines which its inhabitants worked on the neighbouring mainland. It joined the Delian League (see ATHENS 2(ii)) but revolted in 465 (and was subdued in 463). It was a permanent member of Athens' second League (see ATHENS 2 (iv)). In 340 it passed into the control of Philip II of Macedon and remained a Macedonian dependency until freed by the Romans in 196. In the seventh and sixth centuries BC it was the home of a flourishing school of sculpture and of the painter *Polygnotus.

Theaete'tus, dialogue by *Plato, named after an Athenian mathematician (*c*.414–369 BC), friend and pupil of Plato. This dialogue deals with the nature of knowledge. In the introductory scene Theaetetus is reported to have been brought home, mortally wounded in the Corinthian War between Athens and Corinth (in 369) in which he has shown great bravery. A conversation is then recalled that took place between him and Socrates shortly before the latter's death in 399, and since it had been written down (in direct dialogue form), a slave is summoned and reads the manuscript. Various definitions of knowledge are considered, such as 'knowledge is sensible perception', but are all found wanting; the problem is left unresolved and is resumed in the *Sophist*. In the course of the dialogue there occurs Socrates' famous comparison of himself to a midwife who brings to birth the thoughts of others.

Thea'genes and Chariclē'a, alternative title of the *Aethiopica* of Heliodorus; see NOVEL.

theatre

1. *Greek.* The Greek theatre appears to have originated with the open-air circular dancing floor (*orchēstra*), a level space of hard earth constructed for performances of choral *lyric, of which one variety, the dithyramb, is according to one tradition the progenitor of Attic *tragedy (see 1). All large Greek theatres were open to the sky (but see ODEUM). The arrangement described below, which may be regarded as typical, is based on that of the theatre of Dionysus at Athens (see DIONYSUS, THEATRE OF). In the middle of the *orchestra* was a *thymelē* or altar of Dionysus, on the steps of which the flute-player who accompanied the *chorus probably stood. For the spectators at Athens there was a *theatron*, 'watching-place', on the slope of the Acropolis above the *orchestra*. Important spectators sat on seats made of stone at the front of the *theatron*; the rest sat on backless wooden benches placed on rising terraces of earth, crossed at intervals by passageways for access. Beyond these bare facts the details of the construction of the theatre are very obscure. At each side of the *orchestra* was a *parodos* or 'way-in', used by the spectators when they entered the theatre and by the chorus and actors on entering and leaving the *orchestra*. In later times a convention grew up that when the scene was Athens, characters purporting to come on the scene from the agora or Piraeus should enter from the audience's right, since these places were situated in fact in that direction; coming from the country they entered from the left. At the back of the *orchestra* was a low platform or stage, perhaps 8 m. (25 ft.) wide and 3 m. (10 ft.) deep, connected by steps with the *orchestra*. Behind it and extending beyond it on each side was a building, the *skēnē* ('tent', 'hut'), containing the dressing rooms, with a wide double door in the façade giving access to the stage. The *skene* provided the backdrop for the stage, and its roof could serve as a stage for action at a higher level, the setting of the solitary watchman on the palace roof in *Agamemnon*, for example.

There were two pieces of stage equipment,

perhaps used mainly in tragedy (which would account for their being the object of mockery in comedy), the *mēchanē* ('machine') and the *ekkyklēma* ('the roll-out'). The *mechane* was a kind of crane which could swing a character round and into view, particularly when a god is announced as being above the house or coming through the sky. The appearance in this manner of a god who provided a solution in an intractable situation originated the Latin phrase *deus ex machina*, 'a god on a machine', to describe an unexpected outside intervention which resolves a difficulty. Euripides was thought by some to be over-fond of this expedient for concluding a play. The *ekkyklema* was a device by which off-stage events in the drama could be revealed to the actors on stage and to the audience; a tableau was arranged on a platform which was then wheeled out through the central door of the *skene* (e.g. in *Agamemnon*, Clytemnestra standing over the murdered bodies of Agamemnon and Cassandra). Various other stage-properties might be used in the Greek theatre, e.g. statues, altars, or other prominent features of the play, and scenery might be painted on boards. There was, however, no curtain. For the actors and their dress see COMEDY, GREEK 3 and TRAGEDY 2. For the admission charge see THEORIC FUND.

Glimpses of the lighter side of Greek theatre-going may be found in the *Characters* of *Theophrastus which include the loquacious man who talked so much that his neighbours could not follow the play, the mean man who availed himself of a free day to bring his children, the shameless man who took advantage of his foreign guests to get admitted without paying, and the stupid man who fell asleep during the play and was left alone in the theatre when the audience had gone. Philochorus writing in the third century BC describes how the audience fill their cups with wine when the chorus enter and fill them again when the chorus leave. Aristotle comments that the eating of sweets is commonest when the actors are bad.

The theatre was used for many kinds of ceremonies apart from plays (see DIONYSIA).

2. *Roman*. There was no permanent theatre at Rome until 55 BC, when Pompey built one in stone from the spoils of the Mithridatic War. It was erected in the Campus Martius, next to the Curia (where Julius Caesar was later assassinated). There seem to have been seats for about 10,000 spectators. Two other stone theatres were subsequently built in Rome, both in the Campus Martius, that of L. Cornelius Balbus dedicated in 13 BC, and that known as the theatre of Marcellus, built by the emperor Augustus and named after his adopted son.

In the time of Plautus, Terence, Ennius, and Pacuvius (late third and the second centuries BC), plays were performed on wooden stages in front of a temporary wooden building having three doors opening on to the stage. These stages would be erected in the Forum or Circus Maximus, with circles of wooden seats; an attempt to erect a permanent theatre in 155 BC was thwarted by the consul Scipio Nasica who induced the senate to demolish the building as it constituted a danger to public morality. But in the first century BC even the temporary theatres became quite elaborate, with linen awnings to keep the sun off the spectators in the auditorium (*cavea*), and ornately decorated stage buildings. The theatre had a semicircular *orchestra*; at the back of it was a stage wider and deeper than the Greek stage (as it existed later at least; see 1 above).

The *orchestra* was not used for dancing, as in Greece, but for seating, reserved for senators, priests, and officials. After 68 BC the *equitēs* had the right to occupy the first fourteen rows of the auditorium behind the *orchestra*. Behind the stage was the stage building which might rise as high as the sloping auditorium. The auditorium was much more enclosed than in a Greek theatre, and could even have the awnings replaced by a roof, as at Pompeii. The uncomfortable nature of the seating is mentioned by Ovid (*Ars amatoria* 1. 141), who refers to the narrow space allotted to each spectator, and to the knees of those behind pressing into the backs of those in front. From the end of the second century BC Roman theatres had a curtain, kept in a slot in the floor of the stage and raised at the end of the play (a convenient way of indicating that the performance was over). Stage scenery was said to have been first introduced in 99 BC. The chorus in the tragedies of Ennius, Pacuvius, and Accius (unlike the chorus of Greek drama) stood on the stage, not in the *orchestra*, and could enter and exit like any other character (whereas with very rare exceptions the Greek chorus did not leave until the end of the play). This was more realistic; the functions of the chorus had changed and there was no longer that important lyrical element in drama for which it had been the mouthpiece.

The players were slaves or freedmen, trained to the profession, and organized in companies (*grex*, *caterva*) under the direction of a manager (*dominus gregis*) paid for by the magistrate who gave the *ludi* ('games') at which the plays were performed (see also AEDILES). The players' pay gradually increased, and although actors (like musicians) were originally despised, the examples of *Roscius and *Aesopus showed that popular actors might become rich and socially acceptable. Female parts (except in mimes and late comedy) were played by men. It is said that the type of character was indicated at first by wigs (white for old men, red for slaves, etc.) and later by masks (see ROSCIUS), but whether masks were in fact worn in the Roman theatre, and if so, when, is a matter of dispute. Tragic actors wore long flowing robes and high buskins (*cothurni*); comic actors wore ordinary dress and the *soccus* or low-heeled shoe.

Thē'băid (*Thēbăis*), Latin epic poem in twelve books of hexameters by *Statius. The author, who spent twelve years on the work, published it in AD 90 or 91.

The subject is the expedition of the *Seven against Thebes in support of the attempt by Polyneicēs to recover the throne from his brother Eteoclēs (see OEDIPUS). The first three books deal with the preliminaries of the war—the arrival of Polyneices and Tydeus at Argos, the embassy of Tydeus to Thebes and the subsequent attempt by some Thebans to destroy him in an ambush (he fights single-handed against fifty Thebans, 2. 496), and the prophecy of Amphiaraus. Books 4, 5, and 6 include the consultation of the seer Teiresias, the Argive march on Thebes, the episode of *Hypsipylē, her account of the massacre at Lemnos, 5. 85, and the funeral games for the child Opheltēs, including the exciting chariot-race, 6. 296. With book 7 the fighting begins, after a vain attempt by Jocasta at mediation. The pious Amphiaraus is swallowed up by the earth; the fighting continues through books 8, 9, and 10, with many incidents: the death of Ismenē's lover Atys, the episode of Tydeus and Melanippus, the feats of Hippomedon, the self-sacrifice (*devotio*) of Menoeceus, the death of Capaneus by a thunderbolt. Book 11 contains the fatal combat of Eteocles and Polyneices, Creon's refusal of burial to the latter, and Jocasta's suicide. Book 12 completes the story with the meeting between Polyneices' wife Argia and Antigonē, the funeral pyre of the two sons of Oedipus, with its divided flames, the intervention of Theseus, and the death of Creon. At the end, Statius takes leave of his long task, and with a humble reference to Virgil speculates whether his own work will endure.

Statius follows epic tradition in having the gods interfere in men's affairs, writing a catalogue of the forces fighting, describing funeral games, and so on. Many of his incidents and much of his language are imitated from Virgil. The modern reader finds an excess of mythological lore; the occasional lively narrative hardly relieves the tedium of the rest.

Thēbā'is, see EPIC CYCLE and *THEBAID*.

Thebes (Thēbai). 1. The principal city of Boeotia in Greece and the most important in Greek history after Athens and Sparta. Its fame in myth and legend was unequalled; Sophocles (in a surviving fragment) described it as 'the only city where mortal women are the mothers of gods' (i.e. Dionysus and Heracles). For its early legendary history see CADMUS, ANTIOPE, HERACLES, and OEDIPUS. According to the usual legend (but see ANTIOPE) the city was founded by the leader of a Phoenician colony, Cadmus,

whose daughter gave birth to the god Dionysus; it was destroyed by the *Epigonoi in the generation before the Trojan War; hence the absence of the name from the catalogue (in *Iliad* 2) of the Greek cities which fought against Troy.

Thebes was among the palace sites of Mycenaean Greece and was probably the centre of a large kingdom. After its eclipse in the *Dark Age, Thebes recovered by the sixth century BC to take the lead in a loose confederation of Boeotian cities (see BOEOTIA), but was never strong enough to unite them into a single state with itself at the head. The government was oligarchic. In historical times Thebes first came into prominence by supporting the Persian cause in the *Persian Wars, and by supplying a base from which the Persian Mardonius acted in the campaign of Plataea, the main Boeotian city-state south of the river Asopus, near Athens. In 519 BC king Cleomenēs of Sparta told Plataea to attach itself to Athens, thus making Thebes implacably hostile to both Athens and Plataea. As a punishment by the Greeks for supporting Persia in 480–479, Thebes lost its predominant position in the Boeotian confederacy and did not recover it until 446 (see ATHENS 2 (ii)). By seizing Plataea in 431 Thebes precipitated the *Peloponnesian War; in 424, by a victory at Delium, the city defeated the ambitious Athenian effort to regain control of Boeotia; and Thebes was one of the states which, on the fall of Athens in 404, urged the destruction of the city.

After the Peloponnesian War came the period of rivalry between Thebes and Sparta for supremacy in Greece, a struggle in which, under the leadership of *Pelopidas and *Epaminondas, Thebes for a time had the advantage (see SPARTA 4). Not only did the city defeat and humiliate Sparta (in the years following the Spartan defeat at Leuctra in 371), it extended its power in the north, bringing parts of Thessaly under its protection and establishing its authority at the court of Macedon (see PELOPIDAS). It was at about this time (368 BC) that Philip (later king Philip II), the youngest son of Amyntas, king of Macedon, was sent as a hostage to Thebes and brought up under Epaminondas. The death of the latter at the battle of Mantinea in 362 brought the hegemony of Thebes to an end (see SPARTA 4). Thebes promoted the designs of Philip on Greece by inviting his interference in the struggle between the Amphictyonic League and Phocis (see PHILIP (1) 3); but at a later stage, when in 338 Philip was threatening Athens, Thebes, dreading the consequences if its neighbour were to be subjugated, allied itself with the Athenians and suffered with them the defeat of Chaeronea. Philip then dissolved the Boeotian confederacy and established a Macedonian garrison in the citadel of Thebes.

Shortly after the accession of *Alexander the Great (see 1) the Thebans revolted (335), but

Alexander, in Illyria, descended upon them in five days and captured the city. By decision of the Corinthian League (of which Alexander was the head), Thebes was razed. The punishment of this once-hated city shocked Greece, and when it was rebuilt by Cassander in 317 (see MACEDONIA 2) many Greek cities helped with contributions. The new Thebes continued to exist throughout Roman times.

*Teiresias and *Amphion in myth, and, historically, the poet Pindar were born at Thebes, and the poetess Corinna at Thebes or Tanagra. In the last destruction of the city the house of Pindar was spared by Alexander's order (the subject of John Milton's sonnet, 'When the assault was intended to the city'). See also CADMEA.

2. Greek name of a city of Upper Egypt, on the site of which Luxor now stands. It became the capital of Egypt at the time of the twelfth dynasty (c.2000 BC), supplanting Memphis, the earlier capital, and attained great splendour under the kings of the eighteenth to twentieth dynasties (c.1400–1100 BC). Homer calls it 'hundred-gated' and speaks of 200 warriors with horses and chariots issuing from each gate. It is now famous for the remains of its great temples and royal tombs.

Themis ('just order'), Greek goddess, according to Hesiod a Titan, daughter of Gaia (Earth), and by Zeus the mother of the *Seasons and the *Fates; in some accounts she is the mother of *Prometheus. Later she is a personification of justice.

Themi'stius (c. AD 317–c.388), Greek rhetorician from Paphlagonia; he opened a rhetorical school in Constantinople c.345, where he was appointed prefect (383–4) by the emperor Theodosius I and tutor to the latter's son, the future emperor Arcadius. He was entrusted with many official missions, and was given the name Euphradēs, 'the eloquent'. Thirty-four of his orations survive, many of them panegyrics on the emperors, but including an interesting funeral oration on his father. He also wrote paraphrases of Aristotle's works, some of which are extant. He was himself a pagan, and advocated toleration of other religious beliefs.

Themi'stocles (c.524–c.459 BC), celebrated statesman of the Athenian democracy, of the ancient *genos* of the Lycomidae but of a non-Athenian mother. He was elected eponymous *archon in 493 and *strategos of his tribe in 490. As archon he began the development of Piraeus as a port; in 483 he persuaded the Athenians to concentrate on strengthening their fleet from 70 to 200 triremes and to devote the produce of the Laurium silver mines to that purpose. Thus the city was prepared for the second Persian invasion under Xerxes (see PERSIAN WARS). In this war he took a prominent part as a *strategos* and commander of the Athenian fleet, and secured victory for Greece in the sea-battle of Salamis (480) by seeing that it was fought in the narrow channel so as to suit Greek tactics. In 479, when the chief Athenian commands had gone to others, he spun out time at Sparta as Athenian envoy while Athens was refortified without the knowledge of the Spartans, who opposed the refortification. Piraeus was also fortified at his urging. However, in the following years he lost influence to Cimon and the aristocrats, and in about 471 was ostracized and retired to Argos, where he stirred up feeling against Sparta. In about 468 Sparta claimed to have evidence that he and *Pausanias were plotting with Persia; he was condemned to death at Athens and his property confiscated. He escaped to Asia by way of Corcyra, Epirus, and Macedonia. When Artaxerxes became king of Persia (464), Themistocles was given many honours and was made governor of Magnesia on the Maeander, where he died of sickness in 459; it was also related that he committed suicide. His remains were brought home, it is said, and buried outside the walls of the Piraeus. There is a famous sketch of his character by Thucydides (1. 138).

Napoleon, writing to the Prince Regent after his defeat at Waterloo in 1815, compared his situation with that of Themistocles, throwing himself on the mercy of the Molossian king in Epirus.

Theocly'menus. 1. In Greek myth, a seer, descended from *Melampus; see ODYSSEY, book 20.

2. See HELEN.

Theo'critus (first half of the third century BC), Hellenistic Greek poet, the originator of pastoral or bucolic poetry. He was born probably at Syracuse in Sicily and may have lived in south Italy; later he went to the island of Cos and to Alexandria during the reign of Ptolemy II Philadelphus. His extant poems, generically known as *Idylls, and mostly in the hexameter metre, include court poems, mythological poems, and epigrams, but his fame stems from the seven or so poems which were primarily *bucolic. These were to have a strong influence on Virgil (in the *Eclogues) and through him on later European literature. Since there is no complete agreement on the criteria that define a bucolic poem, not all readers agree on which of Theocritus' poems are most characteristically bucolic: poems 1, 3, 4, 5, 6, and 11 are always included; 7 and 10 sometimes, and 27 (which is in any case spurious) occasionally; 8 and 9, known and imitated by Virgil, are not now considered authentic. Though Theocritus writes in an artificial, literary Doric dialect (see DIALECTS) for a sophisticated urban circle, the poems still convey an impression of the timeless pastoral life in the hills of Sicily and south Italy.

The first Idyll contains the beautiful lament for *Daphnis, a dirge imitated in the *Adonis* of *Bion 2 and in the *Bion* atttributed to *Moschus, and the prototype of later pastoral elegies, Milton's *Lycidas*, Shelley's *Adonais*, and Matthew Arnold's *Thyrsis*. Idylls 14 and 15, which are set in towns, recall the mimes of *Herodas; the second of these, entitled *Adōniazūsae* ('women at the festival of Adonis'), is a sketch of two simple and admiring Syracusan women, now housewives in Alexandria, visiting a festival at the palace there, closing with a hymn which they hear sung in honour of Adonis and Aphroditē. Idyll 2, *Pharmaceutria* ('woman preparing a love charm'), similarly recalls mime: it tells the story of the unhappy love of Simaetha and her magical incantations to regain her lover. Other Idylls deal with mythological subjects: the love of the one-eyed Cyclops Polyphemus for the nymph Galatea (11), the abduction of Hylas (13), the fight between Pollux and Amycus (24). Two are flattering addresses (in the hope of patronage) to Hieron II, tyrant of Syracuse (17), and Ptolemy II, king of Egypt (16), and one is a poetic epistle accompanying the present of a distaff to the wife of a friend (28). In Idyll 7, entitled *Thalysia* ('harvest festival'), the setting is Cos; the author, calling himself Sīmichidas, sings of the loves of a certain Aratus, in contest with the enigmatic Lycidas; autobiographical details seem to break through the pastoral convention. The end of the poem evokes the feeling of harvest time in an Aegean island. A number of epigrams purportedly written for tombs or statues is also attributed to Theocritus.

Theodo'ric the Great, see BOETHIUS and GOTHS.

Theodo'sius. 1. Theodosius the Elder, Roman general who between AD 368 and 370 restored security in Britain after invasions by Picts, Scots, and Saxons. See BRITAIN 7.

2. Theodosius I, 'the Great', Roman emperor AD 388–95, son of (1) above. He spent the early years of his reign fighting the invading Visigoths and, failing to drive them out of the empire, had to agree to assign them lands in Thrace. He was a devout Christian, an adherent of the Nicene creed, and dealt harshly with heretics. In 391, perhaps under the influence of St *Ambrose, he put an end to all forms of pagan religion in the empire, and thus founded the orthodox Christian state (see CHRISTIANITY). It is for this that he acquired his title. After Theodosius the Roman empire was divided into two halves, eastern and western. See BYZANTINE AGE.

Theo'gnis, of *Megara, Greek elegiac poet, perhaps of the first half of the sixth century BC though his lifetime is put by many half a century later. Nearly 1,400 lines of poetry ascribed to him survive in manuscript, mostly in short poems one to six couplets long, divided into two books; however, it is a matter of dispute how much is authentic, since some of the lines are also found in poems ascribed to Tyrtaeus, Mimnermus, and Solon, and some of the poems were clearly written at a much later date and against a different background. The collection seems to be in the nature of an anthology, based on the authentic poems of Theognis but augmented by other poems of similar theme drawn from various sources. It is usually accepted that poems addressed to the boy Cyrnus, with whom Theognis was in love, were authentic. Theognis' poems seem typical of those sung or recited at *symposia; they express passionate support for the aristocratic belief in the value of good breeding, and deplore the success of new wealth. There are also many poems of moral exhortation and reflection on life which, with the homosexual love poems, are often expressed with great liveliness.

Theo'gony (*Theogonia*), Greek poem in about a thousand hexameter lines by *Hesiod, and unique in surviving Greek literature in being a systematic account of the gods of Greece and their genealogy. The poet begins with a famous description of how, while pasturing sheep on Mount Helicon, he was inspired by the Muses to compose this poem. It begins at the beginning of the world, with the coming into being of primordial Chaos ('chasm', perhaps conceived of as the dark space between Earth and *Tartarus), followed by Gaia (Earth), Tartarus, and Eros (Love). Gaia produced Uranus (Heaven), and these two were the parents of the Titans, Cyclopēs, and other giants. Last-born of the Titans was Cronus, who at his mother's instigation castrated Uranus. The Titans Rhea and Cronus were the parents of the Olympian gods, whom Cronus ate as soon as they were born, except for Zeus. Zeus later overthrew Cronus and made him restore his other children. One of the Titans, *Prometheus, deceived Zeus in the matter of fair division of sacrificed animals between gods and men, and also stole fire from the gods for men. As his punishment Zeus bound him to a rock where an eagle daily ate his liver, and as a punishment for men Zeus created a woman. War broke out between the older gods, the Titans, and the younger (Olympian) gods, the children of Uranus, led by Zeus. The latter were victorious, and the Titans and *Typhoeus, who helped them, were thrown down to Tartarus by Zeus. The gods then chose Zeus to be their king. He took a series of goddesses to wife, the last of whom was Hera. Their child Hēbē married Zeus' mortal son Heracles, who became after death a god himself. The last part of the poem deals with the offspring of goddesses and mortal men, and ends with two lines added in later times to lead into the *Catalogue of Women*.

Theōn, of Alexandria (fourth century AD), Greek mathematician and astronomer. His reworkings of *Ptolemy's astronomical tables are the only form in which these were known to Arabic astronomers and through them became known to medieval Europe. He was the last known member of the Museum at Alexandria, and father of *Hypatia (see also NEOPLATONISM). Others of the same name include a grammarian and commentator on the Hellenistic Greek poets, of the first century BC.

Theophra'stus (c.370–c.287 BC), of Eresus in Lesbos, the pupil and friend of Aristotle and his successor (in 322) as head of the *Peripatetic School of philosophy at Athens. He was the teacher of *Deinarchus and of *Demetrius of Phalerum, and was also on friendly terms with *Cassander and Ptolemy I Soter of Egypt. He wrote in Greek on a great variety of subjects, of which output only a tiny fraction survives, including the following: *Historia plantarum* ('inquiry into plants'), nine books; *De causis plantarum* ('on the aetiology of plants'), six books; a short treatise on metaphysics; and numerous fragments from other philosophical and scientific works. He is best known for a minor work, 'Characters' (*Charaktērěs*), a collection of thirty descriptive sketches of various types of character. Each exemplifies some deviation from the proper norm of behaviour, exhibiting some failing such as tactlessness, followed by a list of the things that the tactless person will do. There are touches of humour (e.g. the children of the loquacious man asking their father to talk to them at bedtime 'so that we may go to sleep'). The 'Characters' delineate in a concise form types similar to those found in the New Comedy of *Menander (who was said to be a pupil of Theophrastus), an aspect of the work which suggests that it was intended less as moral essays prompted by Aristotle and more as dramatic monologues written to entertain, or even as aids to forensic oratory (in which characterization was important). It was popular in the seventeenth and eighteenth centuries, especially in France, influencing La Fontaine's *Fables* and La Bruyère's *Caractères*, as well as the character-sketches in some *Spectator* essays of Addison and Steele.

Theopo'mpus (c.376–after 323 BC), of Chios, Greek historian, pupil of Isocrates, friend of Philip II and Alexander the Great of Macedon. He was exiled from Chios for having Spartan sympathies, restored by Alexander, and fled to Egypt at the latter's death. In spite of his eventful life he wrote numerous books; little remains except for fragments of his two most important works, the *Hellenica* and *Philippica*. The former was a continuation of Thucydides, a history of Greece from 411 to the battle of Cnidus in 394 BC; the latter, a vast work in fifty-eight books, used the life of Philip as the connecting thread in what was virtually a world history composed of extensive digressions. He was a great admirer of Philip and declared that Europe had produced no one to match him.

theo'ric fund (i.e. 'spectators' fund'), at Athens, a state subsidy of 2 obols (see MONEY 1) a head for the poorer citizens to enable them to pay for admission to the theatre at the Dionysiac festivals, introduced, it was said, by Pericles. It was suppressed when Athens was impoverished by the Peloponnesian War but revived by the demagogue Agyrrhius in 394 BC, when the grant was raised threefold to 1 drachma. In the fourth century BC all surpluses from the various state funds were carried to the theoric fund, the administrators being magistrates who had considerable power over state finances, and who used the fund for many civic purposes other than admission to the theatre. A law had been passed prohibiting the diversion to military purposes of any part of the fund, but Demosthenes secured the abolition of the system in 339 BC, so that the state should have extra resources available to it in time of war.

Theoxe'nia, in Greek religion, a festival in honour of various gods in which they were regarded as taking part in a banquet with men, couches being set for them to recline upon. The best known festival of this nature was at Delphi in the month Theoxenios (March–April); Pindar's sixth *paean was written for one such occasion. His third Olympian ode was also written for a Theoxenia at Acragas in Sicily. Compare LECTISTERNIUM.

Thēra (Santorini), Greek island, one of the Sporadēs, formed of part of the cone of an ancient volcano. The island had been colonized from Minoan Crete before a large part of it disappeared beneath the sea in the Middle Bronze Age following what seems to have been the largest volcanic eruption known. It has been generally thought that the eruption occurred c.1500 BC but there is evidence to suggest a date over a century earlier. The settlements destroyed then are now being excavated. In the 630s BC on the advice of the oracle at Delphi Thera colonized Cyrēnē (in North Africa), under the leadership of *Battus, after many difficulties and several false starts. The islanders took no part in the Persian Wars; although *Dorian and therefore likely to sympathize with Sparta (also Dorian) they were allies of Athens in the Peloponnesian War.

Thēra'menēs (d. 404/3 BC), Athenian politician, one of those responsible for the oligarchic revolution of 411 (see ATHENS 2 (iii)) which resulted in the setting up of the oligarchic council of the *Four Hundred. He was, however, a moderate (although Thucydides' picture is hostile) and instrumental in overthrowing the Four Hundred and setting up a broader based voting assembly of 5,000 citizens of moderate means so as to put the new order on a more constitutional footing. This apparent change of policy gave him an appearance of shiftiness, since it wholly supported neither the extreme oligarchs nor the democrats; his enemy *Critias called him 'Cothurnus' (the loose boot, also worn on stage, that fitted either foot). When full democracy was restored in 410 he was in the Hellespont with the newly constituted fleet. In 406 he commanded a ship in the Athenian naval victory over Sparta at Arginusae; the blame for failure to pick up survivors was disputed between Theramenes and the generals, and the latter were put to death. It seems to have been felt that Theramenes' acquittal was due to his adroitness as a politician. After Athens' final defeat in 404 he was sent to negotiate with the Spartans; the blame for the three months' delay during which Athens starved is often laid at his door. When peace was made he was appointed one of the *Thirty Tyrants, but his moderate position brought him into conflict with the extreme oligarch Critias who had him put to death. Aristotle regarded him as a statesman genuinely seeking a moderate political position.

Thē'riaca, see NICANDER.

Thermo'pylae (or Pylae), narrow pass linking Greece with the north, between Thessaly and Locris, having in classical times the sea close by on one side (it has now receded) and on the other steep cliffs, the spurs of Mount Oeta. As a defensive position its weakness was the easy alternative route along the spine of the mountain above for those who could find the way. It was here that in early times the Phocians built a wall to check the southward advance of the Thessalians. In 480 BC the Persians found the mountain track and outflanked and annihilated the Greek defenders (see PERSIAN WARS). In 279 BC the Aetolians were similarly outflanked by the Gauls, and in 191 BC Antiochus III of Syria by Cato (1) and the Romans. It was successfully held by an Athenian force against Philip of Macedon in 352 BC (see PHILIP (1) 2).

Thēron, tyrant of *Acragas in Sicily 488–472 BC, who married his daughter Demaretē to *Gelon, tyrant of *Syracuse (see 1). In 483 he seized the city of Himera, and after the latter appealed for Carthaginian help, he and Gelon won a crushing victory there over the Carthaginians in 480. He made Acragas one of the most beautiful of Greek cities. Pindar wrote his second and third Olympian odes for him. He claimed descent from Thersander (see below).

Thersa'nder, in Greek myth, son of Polyneicēs (son of Oedipus) and Argeia. He took part in the successful expedition of the *Epigonoi against Thebes, and afterwards became king of Thebes. From there he took part in the Greek expedition to Troy, but was killed by *Telephus in Mysia. Theron (see above) claimed descent from him.

Thersī'tēs, in Homer's *Iliad*, the only low-born character among the Greeks at Troy (though in post-Homeric legend said to be of good family), physically ugly and abusive of the Greek leaders. When he attacked Agamemnon for stealing the girl Briseis from Achilles, and suggested that the army should return to Greece, Odysseus beat him for his insolence. For his death see ACHILLES.

Thēsē'um, see THESEUS.

Thēseus, in Greek myth, the national hero of Athens, son of Aegeus, king of Athens (or the sea-god *Poseidon) and of Aethra, daughter of Pittheus, king of Troezen. He was represented as the friend and contemporary of *Heracles (and thus belonged to the generation before the Trojan War), whose exploits he often emulates. When Aegeus left Aethra at Troezen, he told her that when their son reached manhood he was to lift a certain large rock and bring to Athens the sword and sandals which were hidden underneath it. Theseus, the son, in due course lifted the rock easily and with the tokens set out for Athens by the dangerous land route. On the way he destroyed various bandits and monsters including *Procrustēs, *Sciron, and Sinis, who used to tie his victims to two pine trees which he bent to the ground and then released, tearing the victim in two. (It is obvious that these adventures have been influenced by the similar stories told of Heracles.) On his arrival at Athens, Medea (see ARGONAUTS), who had taken refuge with Aegeus, realized who he was and tried to destroy him by persuading Aegeus to send him against the bull of Marathon, according to some, Pasiphae's bull brought from Crete by Heracles. On the way to Marathon he was hospitably received by an old woman, Hecalē; when he returned after killing the bull he found Hecale dead and ordered that her memory should be honoured (see also CALLIMACHUS). He returned to Athens where Medea then tried to poison him, but Aegeus recognized his son in time; Medea was obliged to return to Colchis, taking with her Medus, her son by Aegeus.

Theseus now heard of the tribute which *Minos of Crete had imposed on Athens, that seven youths and seven girls had to be sent to be eaten by the Minotaur, and volunteered to be one of the youths. On the way to Crete he demonstrated that Poseidon was his father by diving into the sea and recovering a gold ring Minos had contemptuously thrown in to test him. *Ariadnē with her thread enabled him to kill the Minotaur in the Labyrinth and find his way out again. Taking Ariadne with him he sailed away with the other Greeks. He abandoned Ariadne at Naxos and sailed thence to

Delos, where he and his companions danced for the first time the Crane dance, with complicated figures which commemorated the Labyrinth. He had arranged with his father that on returning to Athens his ship would carry a white sail if he was safe, but he forgot to change the black sail, seeing which his father, concluding that Theseus had perished, threw himself from the cliffs to his death. According to some, his death-leap is commemorated in the name of the *Aegean Sea.

Theseus was now king of Athens. He is credited with bringing about the union (synoecism) of the various Attic communities into one state with Athens as the capital city. The event is historical, but its date in Attic history is unknown (see ATHENS 2 (i)). With Heracles he took part in an expedition against the Amazons and took the Amazon Antiopē (or Hippolyta, the Amazon queen) as his wife. To recover her the Amazons invaded Attica and occupied the Acropolis, but were defeated and withdrew. When *Pirithous, king of the Lapiths, raided Marathon he was met by Theseus, and the two became friends. Theseus was present at his wedding-feast and at the subsequent fight between Lapiths and *Centaurs, and later helped Pirithous to invade the Underworld in an attempt to carry off Persephonē. Theseus was ultimately rescued by Heracles and in gratitude gave asylum to Heracles after the latter, in a fit of madness, had killed his own wife and children. He is also said to have carried off *Helen when she was a child, but she was rescued by her brothers Castor and Polydeuces (see DIOSCURI). When Creon refused burial to the bodies of the *Seven against Thebes, Theseus supported Adrastus and the sons of the Argive leaders, marched with an army against Creon, and buried the dead. Later he gave refuge to *Oedipus. After the death of his first wife, by whom he became the father of *Hippolytus, he married Phaedra, sister of Ariadne. Theseus was finally driven from Athens by rebellions, took refuge in Scyros, and died or was murdered there. He continued to protect his city, however, and was seen in gigantic size fighting for the Greeks at the battle of Marathon (490 BC). In 475 BC after the Persian Wars the Athenian *Cimon, in obedience to an oracle, brought home from Scyros the bones of a huge man which were believed to be those of Theseus, and buried them at Athens in a shrine, the Theseum, where they received the worship due to a hero. That Theseum was near the site of the later gymnasium of Ptolemy on the southern side of the agora, and seems to have been originally open to the sky, but made into a building in the fourth century BC. Theseus, though probably purely mythical, was believed by the Athenians to have been one of their early kings. There is a Life of him by Plutarch, who brings together the various stories.

thesis, see ARSIS.

Thesmopho'ria, three-day festival held in Athens and in almost every part of the Greek world in honour of *Demeter; it was attended only by women and apparently excluded virgins. Celebrated at Athens during 11–13 Pyanepsion (October/November), its ceremonies were a 'mystery', known only to the participants. Its purpose was evidently to ensure the fertility of the cereal crops sown at this time of year. A distinctive feature was the retrieval of the remains of piglets and other symbols of fertility thrown into a pit at a festival earlier in the year, probably the *Scirophoria. The remains were placed on altars and subsequently put in the earth with the seed to promote fertility. Perhaps the remains were known as *thesmoi*, the carrying of which may have given the festival its name. The first day was devoted to making ready the place for the celebration, the Thesmophorion, where the women camped, and to erecting shelters to sleep in. The second day was a fast, ending with ritualized abuse exchanged among the women (compare the Eleusinian *mysteries); Aristophanes' comedy *Thesmophoriazusae* (see below) is imagined as taking place on this day. The ceremonies of the third day, which was called Kalligeneia, 'day of fine offspring', are unknown.

Thesmophoriazū'sae ('women celebrating the Thesmophoria'), comedy by Aristophanes produced in 411 BC, probably at the Dionysia.

The women are about to celebrate their private festival, the *Thesmophoria (from which men are excluded). Euripides has learnt that, since his portrayal of legendary wicked women in his tragedies has given all women a bad name, they intend to plot his death. Taking an elderly kinsman with him he tries to persuade the effeminate tragic poet *Agathon to disguise himself as a woman, attend the rites, and plead the cause of Euripides. Agathon refuses. Thereupon the elderly relative offers to go instead. He is shaved and suitably dressed and goes off to the festival, having made Euripides swear to come to his aid if there is any trouble. The women gather and speeches are made against Euripides; the old man defends him by pointing out how much worse were the charges he might truthfully have made against women. The general indignation he causes is interrupted by the arrival of Cleisthenēs (notorious for his effeminacy) with news that a man has got into the festival in disguise. Search is made and the old man is discovered and put under guard. Imitating the hero of Euripides' tragedy *Palamēdēs* (now lost) the old man writes a message on a votive tablet of the temple and throws it out. He then assumes the character of Helen from Euripides' extant tragedy of that name, and Euripides appears as Menelaus; there is a recognition scene, the only sustained parody by

Aristophanes of which we possess the original, but the guard prevents the reunion of the pair. A Scythian policeman now arrives and ties up the old man. Euripides reappears as Perseus and the old man takes on the character of Andromeda, from Euripides' lost tragedy of that name, tied to her rock. But the Scythian stops the attempted rescue. Euripides now comes to terms with the women: he will never again slander them if they release his relative. They agree. But the Scythian has to be dealt with. He is lured away by the promise of a dancing girl, and the old man and Euripides escape.

The old man is nowhere given a name in the text. The only manuscript to preserve this play calls him Mnesilochus (the name of Euripides' father-in-law) in the *scholia, but this may be a guess on the part of a commentator.

Thesmo'thetae, see ARCHONS and LAW, AT ATHENS I.

Thespis, from Icaria in Attica, according to one tradition the inventor of Greek tragedy (see TRAGEDY I). He is said to have won the competition when tragedies were first presented at the *Dionysia at Athens between 536 and 533 BC. Aristotle credits him with taking the vital step of transforming a choral performance into drama by inventing an actor, playing the part of a character, who spoke the prologue and conversed with the chorus-leader. He is also said, less credibly, to have invented the mask. Four play titles, drawn from mythology, are known, but they may not be genuine. Nothing can be said about the nature of his plays. 'Thespian' now refers to drama in general.

The'ssaly (Thessalia), district of north-eastern Greece, consisting of two large plains separated by hilly country. It was bounded on the north by the mountain range which ends on the east, Aegean, side with Mount Olympus, and on the west with Mount Pindus. Its chief river was the Pēnēus, flowing into the Aegean through the beautiful Vale of Tempe, between Olympus and Mount Ossa. Because of the extent of its plains Thessaly was richer in cereals, horses, and cattle than other parts of Greece.

During the *Mycenaean period Mycenaean influence spread from a prosperous settlement at Iolcus over most of the rest of Thessaly. In the twelfth century BC the area was overrun by invaders from the north and north-west (see DORIAN INVASION) who passed on southwards, but the Thessali from Thesprotia (in the west, on the coast of Epirus) remained behind to subdue what became known as Thessaly and reduce the indigenous population to the status of *serfs (known as *penestae*, 'labourers'). A few noble families, e.g. the Aleuadae, became supreme, each in its own region, and their success in organizing themselves into a league headed by a *tagos* ('federal ruler') made Thessaly

a power to be reckoned with in the sixth century BC. In the *Persian Wars the Thessalians submitted to the Persian king Xerxes when the Greeks abandoned the defence of Tempē. See also JASON of Pherae. In the reign of Philip II of Macedon in the fourth century Thessaly came under Macedonian control; liberated by Rome in 196, it was incorporated into the Roman province of Macedonia in 148 BC.

In mythology Thessaly was the home of the *Centaurs and Lapiths; it was from Thessaly that the *Argonauts set out, Pelias and Aeson being rulers of Iolcus. It was regarded as pre-eminently the country of magicians (see MAGIC).

thētĕs, see SOLON.

Thetis, see PELEUS and ACHILLES.

Thirty (Tyrants), the. Many Athenians with *oligarchic leanings thought the end of the Peloponnesian War in Greece (404 BC) to be a propitious time to overturn the democracy and set up again an oligarchic constitution (see FOUR HUNDRED). The most extreme exponent of this view was *Critias; *Theramenēs was more moderate. Aided by the Spartan general Lysander they compelled the assembly to appoint a commission of thirty to draw up a constitution. The Thirty proceeded to set up a new council (*boulē*), to abolish the law-courts, and to exterminate their enemies and confiscate their property. A Spartan garrison was stationed on the Acropolis to lend support. To answer the moderates' objections Critias agreed to draw up a list of 3,000 citizens to constitute a voting body, but without implementing it he had Theramenes put to death. About 1,500 citizens and metics are said to have been put to death also, including the brother of the orator *Lysias, who barely escaped with his life (see his speech *Against Eratosthenēs*). A band of exiles led by *Thrasybūlus captured Piraeus, and Critias was killed. The moderate oligarchs gained control of Athens; a reconciliation was brought about between them and Thrasybulus through the mediation of the Spartan king *Pausanias, and the full democracy restored. Most of the Thirty were eventually put to death.

Thirty Years' Peace, the peace which in 446 BC terminated the state of war which had existed between Athens and the Peloponnesians since 459; it was to be for thirty years but in fact lasted barely fifteen (see ATHENS 2 (ii)).

Thisbē, see PYRAMUS.

tholos, public building of circular shape in the agora at Athens, dating to *c.*465 BC, replacing an older building of the mid-sixth century destroyed in the Persian occupation of 480/79 (see PERSIAN WARS). It was the headquarters of the *prytaneis, where they dined at public expense and made sacrifices and libations. The official standard weights and measures were kept here. (Compare PRYTANEUM.)

tholos-tomb, or beehive tomb; see MYCENAE.

Thrace. The boundaries of Thrace were not clearly defined until Roman times, but it was the most northern area of Greece, bounded by the river Ister in the north, the Black Sea and Bosporus in the east, the Propontis, Hellespont, and north Macedonia in the south, and Illyria in the west. The Romans divided it into two parts separated by Mount Haemus and called the northern part Moesia. The Thracians (of *Indo-European stock) were considered by the Greeks to be a primitive people, and until classical times they lived in villages; urban civilization was developed only under the Romans. The coast was extensively colonized by other Greek states, but their influence did not spread inland. Philip II of Macedon imposed tribute and founded Philippopolis in his own honour, and Thrace became a Macedonian protectorate. The Romans incorporated the part west of the river Hebrus into the province of Macedonia.

Thracian Chersonese, see CHERSONESE.

Thra'sea Paetus, Publius Clo'dius, prominent Roman senator under the emperor Nero, leader of the Stoic and republican opposition. His father-in-law was A. Caecina Paetus, husband of Arria (the elder). He modelled himself on *Cato of Utica, of whom he wrote a Life. Condemned for disloyalty, he committed suicide in AD 66. See also HELVIDIUS PRISCUS.

Thraso, the boastful soldier in Terence's comedy *Eunuchus.

Thrasybū'lus. 1. Tyrant of Miletus; see MILETUS and PERIANDER.

2. Athenian naval commander who with *Thrasyllus led the democratic reaction in the Athenian fleet at Samos in 411 BC, against the oligarchic rule of the *Four Hundred (see also ATHENS 2 (iii)), and recalled Alcibiadēs. With Thrasyllus he defeated the Spartan fleet in the same year at Cynossēma. At *Arginusae he was one of the subordinate officers. Banished by the *Thirty Tyrants, Thrasybulus was once more leader of the democratic party in 404/3, and successfully led the exiles to seize Piraeus and defeat the troops of the Thirty. He then led his men to Athens and the democracy was restored. He was killed in 388.

Thrasy'llus, one of the Athenian naval commanders executed after the victory of *Arginusae in 406 BC.

Thrasy'machus, of Chalcēdōn in Bithynia, a Greek *sophist and rhetorician in the last quarter of the fifth century BC, figuring in Plato's *Republic and defending the proposition that might is right. He played a part in the development of Attic oratorical style, emphasiz-

ing the importance of rhythm and of polished sentence structure.

Thrīna'cia (Thrīnakiē), the island where *Helios kept his cattle; see ODYSSEY (book 12) and SICILY.

Thūcy'didēs (Thoukȳdidēs). 1. Athenian politician, born c.500 BC, son of Melēsias and relation by marriage of *Cimon. He was influential in Athens and Greece generally, Cimon's successor as leader of the wealthy aristocratic and oligarchical faction, and political enemy of Pericles, whose use of tribute money from the *Delian League for building works in Athens he attacked. He was ostracized in perhaps 443 BC. In his old age he was brought to trial in a manner condemned by Aristophanes. He is mentioned by Pindar as a famous trainer of wrestlers.

2. Greek historian, author of the (incomplete) History of the *Peloponnesian War between Athens and Sparta (431–404 BC), in eight books. He was born probably between 460 and 455 BC and died c.399; he caught the plague at some time between 430 and 427 but recovered from it. As *strategos in 424 he was sent to protect the coast of Thrace from the Spartan general *Brasidas but failed to save Athens' valuable colony of Amphipolis from falling into Spartan hands, and was condemned in his absence and exiled. He returned to Athens twenty years later when the war was over, and died within a few years; there was a tradition that he was assassinated. He seems to have been related to *Cimon and Thucydides (1) above; his father's name Olorus was the same as that of Cimon's Thracian grandfather, and he had property in Thrace.

Thucydides had intended to take his history down to the fall of Athens in 404, but the narrative breaks off in mid-sentence with the events of the winter 411/10. Its continuation by Theopompus and Cratippus is lost, together with the rest of their works. Thucydides says that at the beginning of the Peloponnesian War he realized that it would have a greater importance in the history of Greece than any previous wars (including the Persian Wars) and would be for that reason more worth writing about. Since he spent most of the war in exile and removed from the immediate action, he was in a good position to gain first-hand information from both sides and to have a clearer perspective. His object was to provide an accurate record of what happened and to be instructive, because knowledge of the past is a useful guide to the future. His work was to be a 'possession for all time' (ktēma es aiei) not something 'written for display, to make an immediate impression'. A feature of the history is the reporting of speeches, for which he does not claim the same degree of accuracy as for events. With regard to these speeches he says that he kept as closely as possible to the sense of what was actually spoken while setting out the arguments which in his opinion the situation required. The speeches serve to reveal the policies or attitudes which lay behind the decisions of the generals and politicians who made them. Often he presents the speeches of two opponents advocating opposite courses of action. Since all the speeches are reported in Thucydides' own idiosyncratic style, some critics have thought that they must be his original compositions, designed to make clear in dramatic form what Thucydides thought to be the fundamental issues, but this is to disbelieve his statement to the contrary. Some critics have also felt that in his search below the surface for underlying causes he resembles the scientists and physicians of his day (see, for example, HIPPO-CRATES); in his analysis of the causes of the Peloponnesian War he distinguishes between the immediate causes and pretexts—quarrels about the alliances of lesser city states, Corcyra and Potidaea—and the primary cause, Sparta's fear of Athenian expansion. It is possible that this last was added at a later stage of composition, with the benefit of deeper reflection.

Of the eight books, book 1 comprises an introduction, giving a brief summary of early Greek history (the so-called 'Archaeology', chapters 1–23) and the author's aims in writing the work, a description of events at Corcyra and Potidaea, and the political manœuvrings of 433–432, followed by a history of the growth of Athenian power during the years 479 to 435 (chapters 89–118, the Pentekontaetia). Books 2–5. 24 describe the main events of the first ten years of war, 431–421, known as the Archidamian War; they include Pericles' Funeral Oration at the end of the first year of war (2. 34–46), the plague at Athens (2. 47–54), the revolt at Mitylene in 428/7 (3. 1–50), the destruction of Plataea in 427 (3. 51–68), civil war in Corcyra in 427 (3. 69–86), the capture of the Spartan garrison on Sphacteria in 425 (4. 1–42), the loss of Amphipolis to Brasidas (4. 102–116), and the deaths of Cleon and Brasidas and the Peace of Nicias (5. 1–24). The rest of book 5 describes the precarious peace, the Mantinea campaign 418–417 (63–83), and ends with the destruction of Melos in 415. Books 6 and 7 are devoted to the Sicilian Expedition. Book 8, which is incomplete and contains no speeches, covers the beginning of the so-called Decelean War (413–404) and describes the revolt of the Athenian allies and the naval warfare off the coast of Asia Minor, before stopping in 411.

Thucydides displayed a passion for accuracy and exactness that no other ancient historian approached and which was probably a product of his own individuality as much as the result of influence from contemporary scientific writers. Moreover, he saw history as explicable entirely in human terms without recourse to the supernatural; omens and oracles earned his contemptuous dismissal. He reported what could be observed, and did not ponder what part if any the gods played in it. He is generally impartial, although it has been felt that his view of Pericles was too favourable and his portrait of a detestable Cleon somewhat prejudiced. His subject is treated with the utmost seriousness and at a high level; there is no room for anecdote or scandal or hearsay, and certainly no room for the romantic. Apart from Thucydides we have no history of the Peloponnesian War; we cannot, except in rare cases, know what he has chosen to omit or test the accuracy of what he includes. His overall attitude is the only justification for our acceptance of his picture of events, both of the facts he gives and his interpretation of them.

His brilliant but difficult style is well-suited to the narration of great events. It has a poetic flavour apparent in, for example, his occasional use of Ionic dialect forms which sound old-fashioned in the context of his normal Attic usage (see DIALECTS 2), other poeticisms include making abstract nouns like 'war' or 'hope' sound like personifications, and using an unnatural word-order, for emphasis. Thucydides' sentences, though not usually short, show remarkable compression, the meaning telescoped into a few words, his rapidity of thought achieved by a plentiful use of abstract nouns. This impression of concentration is particularly apparent in the speeches; in narrative passages the style, though spare, is usually simple.

Thulē, northern land never certainly identified, first noticed by *Pytheas in the fourth century BC on his circumnavigation of Britain and thought from his route to be Norway or Iceland; it lay six days' sail north of Britain and the sun did not set there at midsummer. *Eratosthenēs drew the Arctic circle through it; *Ptolemy located it at Shetland (midnight sun notwithstanding); it was probably Shetland that was seen by Agricola's fleet when they claimed to have seen Thulē. See BRITAIN 4.

Thu'rii (Thourioi), Greek colony situated in south Italy on the Gulf of Tarentum very near the site of *Sybaris (destroyed by the neighbouring city of Croton c.510 BC). The descendants of the Sybarites who had been driven out asked the assistance of Sparta and Athens to refound their city there. Under the direction of Pericles Athens agreed. Athenian colonists were sent out under Lampon (a celebrated soothsayer, satirized in the comedy of the day) and a certain Xenocritus in 443 BC, and were joined by others from all parts of the Greek world, reputedly including Herodotus and Lysias. *Hippodamus may have laid out the city; *Protagoras wrote its code of laws.

Thye'stēs, see PELOPS.

Thye'stēs, Roman tragedy by *Seneca (2), dealing with the gruesome revenge of Atreus against his brother (see PELOPS). No Greek drama on this subject is extant, but the theme had already been used by three Roman writers in tragedies now lost: Ennius in his *Thyestes*, Accius in *Atreus*, and *Varius in his *Thyestes* (a famous play).

thyrsus, in Greece, carried by the worshippers of *Dionysus, a wand wreathed in ivy and vine-leaves, with a pine-cone at the top.

Tiber (Tiberis, also Tibris and Tybris), the chief river of central Italy, rising in the Apennines and flowing in a generally southerly direction between Etruria on the west, Umbria and the country of the Sabines on the east, and Latium on the south. The silt it carries with it on its journey of 400 km. (250 miles) accounts for the yellowish tinge of its water. The Clitumnus, Anio, and Allia among many others are tributaries. Rome stood on its left bank about 25 km. (16 miles) from its mouth at Ostia. See TIBERINUS below.

Tiberi'nus, eponymous hero who gave his name to the river Tiber in Italy. In Roman tradition he is variously described as the son of the god Janus, or as a descendant of Aeneas and king of *Alba Longa (his father then being Capetus); he was drowned in the river then known as Albula, after which the river was renamed.

Tibērius (Tiberius Claudius Nero Caesar), born in 42 BC, Roman emperor AD 14–37, elder son of Tiberius Claudius Nero and *Livia, who was subsequently married to the emperor Augustus. He married first Vipsānia Agrippīna, the daughter of M. *Agrippa and his first wife Attica; he was forced by Augustus to divorce her in 12 BC in order to marry the latter's daughter *Julia (a marriage which ended in her banishment). He was said to have been subsequently moved to tears at the sight of his first wife. After the deaths of Gaius and Lucius Caesar, the two eldest sons of Julia by a previous marriage to the M. Agrippa mentioned above, Augustus seems to have accepted Tiberius as his heir. For his reign see ROME 10.

tibia ('flute'), see MUSIC 2.

Tibu'llus, A'lbius (c.55–19 BC), Roman elegiac poet of equestrian rank who suffered some loss of property in the confiscations after the civil wars (see ROME 7). He was a friend of Horace and Ovid, and belonged to the circle of poets around M. Valerius *Messala Corvinus, whom he may have followed on campaign in Gaul and the Near East between 31 and 27 BC. He wrote two books of elegies, the first published c.27 BC; the date of the second is unknown. The first book contains mostly love elegies, five about his love for Delia (pseudonym for Plania) and three

for a boy Marathus; the second contains only six poems, three concerning his love for a girl Nemesis; the opening poem, a dramatization of the *Ambarvalia, is a notable work. The rest of the works that have come down in his corpus are by other poets, notably the elegies of one Lygdamus, rather sentimental compositions by a poet who writes like Ovid, and six elegies (IV. 7–12) by Sulpicia, the niece of Messala, recording her love for Cerinthus (a pseudonym). Tibullus' favourite themes are romantic love and the pleasures of country life. He is a minor poet, a little dull perhaps, but *tersus atque elegans*, 'polished and discriminating' (Quintilian).

Tibur (Tivoli), town about 28 km. (17 miles) north-east of Rome. Many rich Romans had villas there, including Catullus and the emperor Augustus, and perhaps Horace also; the most famous was the great villa of Hadrian (emperor AD 117–138).

Tigelli'nus, d. AD 69, the emperor Nero's notorious *praefectus praetorio* (62–8) who was the cause of many executions at Rome. He was a Sicilian exiled from Rome in 39 for adultery with the emperor Caligula's sisters, but was again at court early in Nero's reign, becoming first *praefectus vigilum* and then succeeding Burrus (see SENECA (2)) as *praefectus praetorio*. For his part in discovering the conspiracy of *Piso against the emperor in 65 he was lavishly rewarded. He abandoned Nero at the end and transferred his allegiance to Galba, but when Otho became emperor he was forced to commit suicide.

Timae'us (c.356–260 BC), Greek historian of Tauromenium in Sicily, who migrated to Athens c.317 and spent the next fifty years there, probably returning to Sicily under Hieron II. His most important work was a history of Sicily in thirty-eight books from earliest times to 264 BC (before the Romans attacked the Carthaginians there). He seems to have been the first to establish a chronology based on the *Olympiads (see also CALENDARS), and *Eratosthenes must have taken over the system from him. Polybius praised him for his invention, but also attacked him for deliberate falsification and ignorance.

Timae'us, dialogue by *Plato, usually thought to be a late work, in form a sequel to one of the themes of the *Republic*, in which the author places in the mouth of Timaeus, a Pythagorean philosopher, an exposition of the origin and system of the universe. The creator god or demiurge (see DEMIURGUS), being good, created the material universe from the elements earth, air, fire, and water as a unique copy of the ideal universe which exists only in the realm of (Platonic) Ideas or Forms (see PLATO 4). From these elements in various proportions the demiurge also created the soul of the world, the lower gods, and the stars. The lower gods created men's mortal bodies, though the demiurge created their immortal souls. Men who lived a wicked life would suffer reincarnation first as women, and then if unreformed as animals. The origin of sensations and diseases is then traced; the three-fold division of the soul into reason, emotion, and appetite, and the fate of the individual after death are briefly indicated.

In a preliminary myth *Critias recounts the conquest of the empire of Atlantis (a continent west of the Pillars of Hercules, now sunk beneath the sea) by the ancient Athenians, a legend which is continued in the unfinished dialogue *Critias*.

Cicero translated or adapted *Timaeus* but most of his work is lost. *Timaeus* was an influential dialogue in late antiquity, influencing *Neoplatonism with its anticipation of the latter's elaborate spiritual hierarchy; the demiurge was also easily seen by Christians as the Creator God of Genesis. The idea that the demiurge created the stars and other heavenly bodies with souls gave authority to astrology, which regarded them as divine.

time-reckoning, see CALENDARS and CLOCKS.

Tīmo'crates, Against, speech in a public prosecution by *Demosthenes; see (2) 2.

Tīmo'creon (first half of the fifth century BC), Greek lyric and elegiac poet from Rhodes, who took the Persian side when the Persians occupied that island. Only small fragments of his work survive in quotation. He was a personal enemy of *Themistoclēs and *Simonidēs; the latter pilloried him in a couplet purporting to be his epitaph.

Tīmō'leon, idealistic Corinthian who *c.*365 BC conspired with his friends in killing his brother Timophanēs when the latter attempted to make himself tyrant. Timoleon thereafter lived under a cloud until sent by the Corinthians in 345 with a small force of mercenaries to their daughter-city Syracuse whose aristocrats had appealed for help against their tyrant Dionysius II. For his further history see SYRACUSE 3.

Tīmon. 1. Semi-legendary Athenian who, supposedly owing to the ingratitude of his friends, became a notorious misanthrope, refusing to meet anyone except, according to Plutarch, *Alcibiadēs. Aristophanes is the first to refer to him. Shakespeare's *Timon of Athens* is based on his story as told by Plutarch in his Life of Mark Antony, and by Lucian in his dialogue *Timon*.

2. Of Phlius (flourished *c.*250 BC), a Sceptic philosopher, author of a book of lampoons, of which only fragments survive, entitled *Silloi* (i.e. 'squint-eyed' pieces), in mock-Homeric hexameters, in which he ridiculed the dogmatic philosophers.

Tīmo'theus. 1. Greek poet of Miletus (*c.*450–*c.*360 BC), reputedly a friend of Euripides. He is famous for his *nomes and *dithyrambs. Although most of his eighteen books of poems are lost, some 250 lines of the nome *Persae* have been found on an Egyptian papyrus of the fourth century BC, the oldest surviving Greek literary text. It is an impression of the battle of Salamis written in a bombastic imitation of the elevated style of choral lyric; various metres are used (probably the music was as important as the words), and the composition is astrophic (see STROPHE). Timotheus figures in John Dryden's poem 'Alexander's Feast' (1697).

2. Athenian politician of the fourth century BC, son of *Conon (1) and pupil of Isocrates. Elected *strategos in 378 when the Second Athenian League was formed (see ATHENS 2 (iv)), he won many members for it. After the fall from favour of *Callistratus in 366 he promoted an imperialist policy, capturing Samos from the Persians in 365 and extending the dominion of Athens in the Thracian Chersonese and Chalcidicē, although he failed to capture Amphipolis. In consequence of his failure to support his fellow-general Charēs in an attack on Chios in 356 he was tried and fined the enormous sum of 100 talents. He left Athens and died in 354, his son having paid only one tenth of the fine.

Tīre'sias, see TEIRESIAS.

Tīro, Marcus Tu'llius, slave, confidential secretary, and friend of *Cicero ((1) 7), who freed him in 53 BC. He survived his master and was the author of a Life of Cicero (now lost), and editor of some of his speeches and of his letters *Ad familiares* ('to his friends'), which include letters to Tiro himself. He wrote also on grammar, and developed a system of shorthand; a surviving collection of abbreviations is known as *notae Tironiānae.*

Tiryns, ancient Greek city in the southern part of the plain of Argos, inhabited from the early Bronze Age (before 2200 BC) and taken over by the first Greek invaders (see GREECE). The huge Cyclopean walls, built *c.*1400 BC of roughly hewn blocks of stone, are still standing (see CYCLOPES). The city is associated in myth with *Mycenae, some fifteen kilometres to the north, and with the story of *Heracles.

Tīsa'menus, see OMENS.

Tī'sias, see TEISIAS.

Tissaphe'rnēs, the Persian satrap of the coastal provinces of Asia Minor with whom *Sparta (see 4) entered into alliance against Athens in 412 BC, and with whom *Alcibiades intrigued. When in 401 Cyrus the Younger of Persia challenged the army of the Persian king Artaxerxēs, his brother, at the battle of Cunaxa, Tissaphernes with his cavalry played the decisive part in Artaxerxes' victory. Thereafter he harassed Xenophon and the Ten Thousand who had fought for Cyrus (see ANABASIS). He was once more ruler of the Aegean coast when Sparta began war with Persia in 400, and Xenophon relates in his *Hellenica* and *Agesilaus* how Tissaphernes was outwitted and crushingly defeated by the Spartan king *Agesilaus. After this failure he was assassinated by order of Artaxerxes.

Titans (Tītānĕs, of uncertain meaning, perhaps simply 'gods'), in Greek myth the older gods of the generation before the Olympian gods (see GODS 1), children of Uranus (Heaven) and Gaia (Earth). The story of the marriage of Heaven and Earth and the birth of gods from the marriage is very widespread in myth from all parts of the world. According to Hesiod the Titans were twelve in number, six sons and six daughters: Oceanus, Coeus (Koios), Crīus (Krios), Hyperion, Īapetus, Cronus, and Theia, Rhea, Themis, Mnēmosynē, Phoebē, Tethys. The names are a mixture of Greek, non-Greek (e.g. Oceanus, Iapetus, Cronus) and abstractions (Themis, 'justice', and Mnemosyne, 'memory'). Some of their children were also regarded as Titans, notably Prometheus and Atlas. When Zeus, aided by his mother Rhea, compelled *Cronus to disgorge his other children, battle ensued (the Titanomachy) between the Titans on the one hand and Zeus and his brothers and sisters on the other (Prometheus fighting on the side of Zeus). The battle lasted for ten years, shaking the universe to its foundations, but eventually the *Cyclopĕs and *Hecatoncheirĕs came to the help of Zeus, and the Titans were overcome and imprisoned in Tartarus, guarded by the Hecatoncheires; Atlas was punished by being made to support the sky on his shoulders. It was sometimes thought that eventually Zeus freed the Titans. In literature the Titanomachy is often confused with the Battle of Gods and *Giants (the Gigantomachy).

Tithō'nus, in Greek myth, son of Laomedon, king of Troy, and brother of Priam. Eos (Dawn) fell in love with him, and by her he was the father of Emathion (killed while trying to prevent Heracles from stealing the Golden Apples of the Hesperidĕs) and of *Memnon (killed at Troy). Eos obtained immortality for him from Zeus but forgot to ask also for eternal youth, so that Tithonus became an old shrivelled creature little more than a voice, and according to some was turned into a cicada, which renews its skin every year. The story is the subject of a dramatic monologue, 'Tithonus' (pub. 1860), by the English poet Tennyson.

Ti'tiĕs, see RAMNES.

Titi'nius, writer of comedies at Rome, contemporary of Terence, and the earliest known author of *fabulae* *togatae*, comedies with

Roman plots and characters. Only fifteen titles and some fragments survive.

Tītus (Tĭtus Flavius Vespasianus), Roman emperor AD 79–81, elder son of the emperor Vespasian whose rule he had previously shared (see ROME 11). He is famous for the capture of Jerusalem in AD 70 after a long siege. The Arch of Titus commemorating this, erected in the Forum at Rome by his brother Domitian (when the latter succeeded as emperor), is still standing, in part restored. During his campaign in Judaea Titus fell in love with *Berenīcē, daughter of the Jewish king Herod Agrippa I (grandson of Herod the Great); in Acts 25: 13 she is mentioned as assisting her brother Agrippa II in the business of government. She accompanied Titus when he returned to Rome but the Romans disapproved of a connection between the emperor's son and colleague and a Jewess; Titus had to dismiss her, to the sorrow of them both. This is the subject of Racine's tragedy *Bérénice*. Titus was universally popular, and his short reign was remembered as a happy one, despite the eruption of Vesuvius in 79 and the plague and fire in Rome the following year. He gave generous help to those who had suffered; his building works included the completion of the Colosseum (begun by Vespasian) and the Baths of Titus. See also SUETONIUS (*Lives of the Caesars*).

Titus, Arch of, see above.

Tītus Andro'nicus, Roman tragedy by Shakespeare, whose hero has no counterpart in Roman history or literature. The play is set at the time of the Gothic invasions (see GOTHS).

Tītus Tā'tius, legendary king of the *Sabines who, after the reconciliation between his people and the Romans which followed the Rape of the Sabines (see ROME 2), ruled jointly with Romulus over the combined peoples.

Ti'tyus, in Greek myth, a *Giant, son of Gaia (Earth), who was killed, for assaulting the goddess Leto, by Zeus or by Apollo and Artemis (Leto's children). Odysseus (in the *Odyssey*, book 11) saw him lying in the Underworld covering 9 plethra ('acres') of ground, while two vultures tore at his liver.

tmēsis ('division'), in grammar, the division of a word into two parts with other words interposed; e.g. in Ennius, *saxo cere comminuit brum*, 'he shattered his skull (*cerebrum*) with a rock'; more obvious is Virgil's *talis Hyperboreo septem subjecta trioni*, 'beneath the Hyperborean sky' (*septentrioni*).

tōga, see DRESS 2.

tŏgā'ta, fabula ('a play in a toga'). These *fabulae* were Roman comedies of the second century BC about Italian life and characters, set in some small Italian town. Nothing of them has survived except for a few titles and quotations. *Afranius was the chief author; see also ATTA and TITINIUS.

toilet

1. *Greek.* Greek men paid much attention to their physical condition. They rubbed their bodies with olive-oil and unguents to keep the skin supple and used perfumes and scented powder (*diapasma*) as well. Women applied make-up to their faces, white lead to whiten the skin and a rouge made from the root of anchusa. Vase-paintings show them applying it with brushes as well as with their fingers. Xenophon indicates that some men of his day used make-up; Demetrius of Phalerum is said to have done so. Men in early Greece let their hair grow and wore beards. From the fifth century BC they cut their hair short and from the time of Alexander (late fourth century) they were clean-shaven (a fashion not always followed by philosophers and other intellectuals: hence the proverb, 'a long beard does not make a philosopher'). The Spartans were the exception, wearing their hair long and priding themselves on it; a Persian spy found Leonidas and his men combing their hair before the battle of Thermopylae (see PERSIAN WARS). Greek women usually parted their hair in the middle, braided it, and knotted it behind their heads. Blonde hair was prized; it was not unusual for both men and women to dye their hair, especially when it was turning grey.

2. *Roman.* Roman fashions in toilet and hairdressing were much influenced by Greece. Roman men devoted much more time to bathing than the Greeks, with whom it was not the social institution which it became at Rome (see BATHS). Like Greeks, they were fond of perfumes: Seneca speaks of those who applied scented oils two or three times a day. The importance of make-up for women and the many varieties are apparent from Ovid's fragmentary *Medicamina faciei femineae*. From the red colour extracted from a kind of lichen (orchil) called *fucus* all kinds of cosmetic colouring came to be called by that name. Effeminate men wore make-up, or could be accused of doing so; Cicero refers to the 'rouged jowls' of his enemy the consul Piso. Men of fashion liked to have their body-hair removed, with tweezers and plasters. After the arrival of a Sicilian barber in Italy in 300 BC short hair for men and a clean-shaven appearance became fashionable. The first Roman to be shaved every day was reputedly *Scipio Africanus. With the emperor Hadrian (AD 117–38) the beard began to revive and remained fashionable until the time of Constantine in the fourth century. Blonde hair was popular among women, often achieved with a bleach (*spuma caustica*) or by means of wigs of German hair. In the Augustan age women's hair was very elabo-

rately arranged; often special slaves were kept who were trained hairdressers.

Ancient toilet implements seem to have resembled those in use in modern times. Razors, of the 'cut-throat' variety, were made in bronze; combs were double-edged, with one coarse and one fine row of teeth. Mirrors were made of burnished metal, especially silver, and polished translucent stone, mirror *glass being rarely used even after it was known in the empire how to cover a glass plate with a thin leaf of reflecting metal. Mirrors were usually small and held in the hand, though Quintilian says that Demosthenes used to practise his gestures in a full-length mirror.

Tolō'sa (Toulouse), town in the Roman province of Gallia Narbonensis, which at the time of the Gallic rebellion in 107 BC fell into the hands of the invaders. It was recaptured in 106 by the consul Q. Servilius Caepio, who sacked the temples and removed the gold from the sacred offerings. This was regarded as an act of impiety, bound to bring misfortune. The gold mysteriously disappeared on its way to Rome; the escort was said to have been overwhelmed; hence the expression 'Toulouse gold', *aurum Tolosanum*, for ill-gotten goods.

Tŏmis (Lat. Tŏmis, Tomi), colony of Miletus on the west coast of the Black Sea. It was brought under Roman rule in 72 BC, but continued to suffer raids from outlying tribes until that area of north-eastern Thrace became the Roman province of Moesia in the early first century AD. It is famous as the place of Ovid's banishment. See TRISTIA.

To'pica, see ARISTOTLE 4 (i); for Cicero's abstract of the work see CICERO (1) 5.

torch-race (*lampadēdromia*), form of sacred contest common to many cults throughout Greece. In Athens it formed part of the *Panathenaea and of the festivals of the fire gods Prometheus and Hephaestus. In the case of Prometheus the race was run, according to Pausanias, from the altar of Prometheus in the Academy (outside the city walls) to a point in the city. The competitors had to carry lighted torches to the goal, usually the altar of the god or goddess being celebrated. Anyone whose torch went out was disqualified, and the winner placed his torch on the altar. The race was run by teams from each tribe as a relay race, or by single competitors. At the festival of the Thracian goddess Bendis, referred to at the beginning of Plato's *Republic*, there was the novelty of a torch-race on horseback. The preparations for torch-races were among public services borne by wealthy citizens (see LITURGY).

toreutic art, the art of embossing or chasing metal. Decorative metalwork was regarded as one of the major arts in Greece, but its survival has been a matter of chance. It was practised from early times, and there are many references in Homer to the decoration of armour and objects such as brooches and cups. Many examples of the art have been recovered from *Mycenaean tombs, notably the magnificent *Vaphio gold cups of the late fifteenth century BC from a tholos-tomb near Sparta, on which are vivid scenes, all in repoussé work, depicting men hunting bulls. In the Hellenistic Greek world silver was the metal chiefly employed for work of this kind. Embossed and engraved silver vessels were greatly sought after at Rome in the second and first centuries BC, and were imported in large quantities. The Elder Pliny (33. 154) enumerates the artists who were pre-eminent in chasing silver. *Mentor 2 (of very uncertain date) was the most famous; Crassus paid 100,000 sesterces for two cups chased by him; Martial frequently refers to his work, and Propertius compares it with that of another famous artist Mȳs, who engraved the battle of Lapiths and Centaurs on the shield of Athena Promachos, a bronze statue by Pheidias. It appears that Mys always worked from designs by *Parrhasius. *Cicero in the Verrine orations ((1) 1) mentions a water-jug of outstanding workmanship by another jeweller, Boëthus.

Torquā'tus, see MANLIUS TORQUATUS.

Tower of the Winds, see HOROLOGION OF ANDRONICUS.

tra'běa, see DRESS 2.

Trachi'niae ('women of Trachis'), Greek tragedy by *Sophocles, of uncertain date but with indications that, with *Ajax* and *Antigonē*, it is early among his surviving works, written in the years after Aeschylus' *Oresteia* (458 BC).

Since his murder of Iphitus, son of Eurytus, *Heracles and his family have been exiled from Tiryns to Trachis (in Malis, a little west of Thermopylae). The chorus is composed of Trachinian women. When the play opens, Heracles has been absent for fifteen months. He had told Dēianeira, his wife, that at the end of this period the crisis of his life would come, and he would either die or have a happy life thereafter. Deianeira sends Hyllus, their son, in search of his father. As she reflects on her anxieties a messenger announces the arrival of Heracles in Euboea nearby. This is presently confirmed by the report of a herald, who brings with him a train of captive women taken by Heracles when he sacked Oechalia in Euboea, the city of his enemy Eurytus. Deianeira discovers that these include Iolē, daughter of Eurytus, with whom Heracles has fallen in love. With a love-charm which she had been given by Nessus, the Centaur, when he was dying at the hands of Heracles, she decides to win back her husband's love, and smears the charm on a robe she is sending him. Too late she discovers that it

has shrivelled a piece of wool and is a deadly poison. Hyllus returns, describes the agony of Heracles, his flesh consumed by the robe, and denounces his mother as a murderess. Deianeira goes out in silence, and presently her old nurse enters to say that she has killed herself. The dying Heracles is brought in; he tells Hyllus to carry him to Mount Oeta and there burn him on a pyre before the agony returns, and afterwards to marry Iole. Hyllus reluctantly consents, bitterly reproaching the gods for their pitiless treatment of his father.

trade, see ATHENS 4 and ROME 13.

tragedy (i.e. tragic drama), from Greek *tragōi-dia*, 'goat song'. There is no satisfactory explanation of this name. It may have arisen because, it has been suggested, the chorus in tragedy originally wore goat-skins, or in connection with a goat-sacrifice, or even because there was a competition with a goat as prize.

The Monk in Chaucer's *Canterbury Tales* defines the essence of tragedy as he knew it, and as it is in most surviving Greek tragedies:

> Tragedie is to seyn a certeyn storie,
> As olde bookes maken us memorie,
> Of hym that stood in greet prosperitee,
> And is yfallen out of heigh degree
> Into myserie, and endeth wrecchedly.
> And they ben versified communely,
> Of six feet, which men lepen exametron.

> (Tragedy is, as old books inform us, a kind of story concerning someone who has enjoyed great prosperity but has fallen from his high position into misfortune and ends in wretched-ness. Tragedies are commonly written in verse with six feet, called hexameters.)

There are some Greek tragedies which have a happy ending for the good (see e.g. Euripides' *Helen*). Plays of this type Aristotle (in the *Poetics*) considered to be an inferior form of tragedy.

1. *The origin of Greek tragedy.* The only Greek tragedy we possess is Athenian; for that reason it is known as 'Attic' tragedy (from the state of Attica, of which Athens was the chief city). Tragedy was usually regarded as an Attic invention (but not always; see below). It is very difficult to trace its history back beyond the fifth century BC. There were several different ac-counts of its origin current in antiquity. Aristotle (in the *Poetics*) expressed the belief that, it originated 'in the improvisations of those who led the *dithyramb' (choral lyric poetry on a mythical subject sung and danced by a chorus, in honour of Dionysus). Aristotle records that tragedy was said by some to have evolved from choral performances in the (Dorian) Peloponnese. Certainly choral song remained an import-ant constituent of tragedy, and the dialect of the choruses, (literary) Doric, attests the origin of the choral element in a Doric-speaking region (see DIALECTS). Drama, however, requires actors.

A tradition followed by Horace in the *Ars poetica* attributed the invention of the actor to *Thespis, who came to Athens from Icaria in Attica and won the tragedy competition in 533 or a little earlier. Thus Attic tragedy may be thought to have originated no earlier than the mid-sixth century BC.

The tradition which gives tragedy a Peloponnesian origin claims that the decisive step towards drama was taken by *Arion (possibly of the seventh century BC and also credited with the development of the dithyramb into a recognized literary form), who brought on stage '*satyrs speaking verse'. Aristotle also says that tragedy acquired dignity by development from the style of satyr-plays (see SATYRIC DRAMA). The fact that the word *tragoidia* means 'goat-song' suggests that tragic drama may have originated in the performances of a chorus dressed in goat-skins; on the other hand satyrs until the fourth century BC were given the tail and ears of a horse, not a goat. Arion may provide a tenuous link between dithyramb, tragedy, and satyr-plays, but it is still not clear whether (and how) Attic dithyramb and tragedy evolved from the same background as satyr-plays, and to what extent the choral performances in the Peloponnese became dramatic; nothing as specific is said of Arion's supposed innovation as is said of the introduction of an actor by Thespis. The Greek word for actor, *hypokritēs*, probably means 'answerer' (rather than the possible meaning 'interpreter'); the actor's answers to the questions of the chorus provided the occasion for their song, and their exchanges (by this account) brought drama into existence (see CHORUS).

By 472 (the date of the earliest surviving play, Aeschylus' *Persians*) tragedy had acquired the dignity and seriousness of which Aristotle spoke (see above), stemming from its concern with the human condition and the latter's relation to divine ordinance. It is impossible to know how much its development was shaped by Aeschylus, since we know so very little of his predecessors and contemporaries (see 4 below). The plot of a Greek tragedy is nearly always based on an episode from myth (for exceptions see PERSIANS, PHRYNICHUS, and AGATHON), and the influence of Homer is marked.

2. *Performances of Greek tragedies.* Performances of tragedies in Attica were part of religious celebrations and, until the Hellenistic age, appear to have been confined to the festivals of Dionysus. (For the close connection between the god and the performance of drama see DIONYSIA and DIONYSUS, THEATRE OF.) Thus plays were produced on only a few occasions during the year, and for a single performance on each occasion. The most important setting for new tragedies was the Great Dionysia in March, but tragedies were also produced at the *Lenaea in

January, and second productions might be staged at the Rural Dionysia. In the fifth century the only second productions at the Great Dionysia (with one exception; see below) were revised versions of plays which had been unsuccessful in their original form, such as Euripides' *Hippolytus*, but it may be that comedies were more often restaged than tragedies. The one notable exception was in the case of Aeschylus: after his death it was decreed that his plays might be produced at the Great Dionysia by anyone who wished. From 386 BC it was permitted to produce an earlier tragedy and from 339 an earlier comedy.

Tragedy was produced under the auspices of the state. At the Dionysia the magistrate in charge of the dramatic performances was the eponymous *archon; at the Lenaea it was the *archon basileus* (compare COMEDY, GREEK I). Drama at Athens was a matter for competition. Since dramatic competitions at the Dionysia were known to be in existence in the 530s (see I above) it is likely that they were instituted (and the festival itself first organized) by the tyrant *Peisistratus and his sons. Three tragic poets were selected from all those applying and 'granted a chorus' by the archon, i.e. given permission to compete for the prize of best tragic poet. A main actor ('protagonist') was allocated to each poet by lot, from three chosen and paid for by the state. Apart from that the costs of production were borne by the *choregoi. Each poet staged three tragedies (the trilogy) followed by a satyr-play, the set of four being known as the tetralogy. (These terms we owe to the Alexandrian scholars.) The contests were decided by judges, five in number, chosen by lot from lists of names selected by each tribe; no doubt the judges were influenced on occasion by the expressed views of the audience. The successful poet was rewarded with a crown of ivy; from the mid-fifth century the best actor among the protagonists also received a prize. Actors and chorus were all male, and only Athenian citizens were allowed to take part, although *metics were admitted at the Lenaea at a later date.

Greek tragedy contained two elements, choral song in lyric metres, with musical accompaniment, and dramatic spoken exchanges between characters, which were mainly in iambic trimeters (Chaucer's 'hexameters'; see METRE, GREEK 5). Some parts were a blend of the two, spoken or chanted by an actor, solo or with the chorus, to the accompaniment of music (i.e. recitative). These parts were written in tetrameters and iambics interspersed with lyrics. An exchange between an actor and the chorus, each side singing in turn, was known as a *kommos*. The importance of the chorus varied from play to play (in Aeschylus' *Eumenides* it might be considered corporately as one of the main characters); on the whole its role declined in significance towards the end of the fifth century. In general the chorus plays the part of spectators of the action, humble in rank, taking a limited part in but rarely initiating action, sympathizing with one or other of the chief characters, and commenting on or interpreting the dramatic situation. The choral songs were composed in a variety of lyric metres arranged in *strophēs and antistrophēs, occasionally with epodes added (see TRIAD). The chorus comprised twelve performers in the plays of Aeschylus, increased to fifteen by Sophocles. It was drawn up in a rectangular form (in contrast with the circular chorus of the dithyramb) and its movements were based on this arrangement. It was accompanied by the flute. Very little is known about the dances performed by the chorus after the early fifth century when, we are told, Phrynichus and Aeschylus invented many dances. The term *emmeleia* ('gracefulness') was often used to denote the grave and dignified dance of tragedy. At the end of the fifth century BC the dance degenerated. Choruses continued to form a part of tragedies throughout the fifth and for part at least of the fourth century BC, after choruses in comedy had been discontinued; but it is not known precisely how long they survived.

To the single actor of Thespis' invention Aeschylus added a second and Sophocles a third, and three actors seem to have remained the norm. Originally the poet acted in his own plays; this is recorded of Thespis and Aeschylus, and of Sophocles in his earliest plays (not extant). From the time of Sophocles the relative importance of the actors was indicated by the names protagonist ('first actor'), deuteragonist ('second actor'), and tritagonist. To the first was assigned the longest and most difficult part, together with such other parts as could be combined with it. All the actors and the chorus wore masks (according to one tradition introduced by Thespis) appropriate to their parts; this feature was perhaps a relic of Dionysiac cult, for some parts of which the worshippers were masked. Only the flute-player was unmasked. No fifth-century masks have survived, but it is clear from vase-paintings that they covered the whole front half of the head including the ears and had wigs attached. They seem to have been made of linen stiffened with plaster and painted. The wearing of masks facilitated the doubling of parts by a single actor, or even the splitting of a single part between two actors. In Euripides' *Bacchae*, for example, Dionysus and the messenger were probably played by the same actor; in Sophocles' *Oedipus Coloneus* the doubling and splitting of parts has become extremely complicated, with Theseus played by perhaps three actors, and Ismenē by a silent extra (*kōphon prosōpon*, 'dumb mask') unless, exceptionally, a fourth actor was allowed. Non-speaking extras were used, and known, like their modern

equivalents, as 'spear-carriers' (*doryphorēmata*). Aeschylus was said to have given the actors a more dignified costume; by the end of the fifth century they were wearing heavy, long-sleeved, ornamented robes reaching to the ground; Euripides was notorious for clothing his heroes in rags when the plot suggested it. Actors in classical times either went barefooted or wore tall laced boots (*cothurni). Female characters were played by men.

3. *Construction of Greek tragedy.* A Greek tragedy normally contained the following parts.

(i) The prologue (*prologos*), the part preceding the entrance of the chorus, a monologue or dialogue which sets out the subject of the drama and the situation from which it starts. In the earliest tragedies the play begins with the entrance of the chorus, who set the scene without prologue.

(ii) The *parodos*, the song which the chorus sings as it enters. Once on stage, the chorus does not usually leave before the end of the play.

(iii) The episodes (*epeisodia*), scenes in which one or more actors take part, with the chorus. The word *epeisodion* probably meant originally the entrance of an actor to announce something to the chorus. The episodes might also contain lyrical passages, such as lamentations or incidental songs by the chorus, but they were divided from each other by the songs of the chorus known as *stasima* (see below).

(iv) *Stasima*, songs of the chorus 'standing in one place', i.e. in the *orchestra*, in contrast with the *parodos* which was sung during its entrance. In the earlier extant tragedies the *stasima* are usually connected, if only obliquely, with the events of or emotions aroused by the preceding episode. But this connection became more tenuous, until *Agathon became reputedly the first to introduce choral lyrics which had nothing to do with the plot (and could fit any tragedy), called by Aristotle *embolima*, 'interpolations'.

(v) The *exodos* or final scene, after the last *stasimon*.

For Aristotle's analysis of the nature of tragedy and its qualitative elements see POETICS.

4. *Principal Greek tragedians.* Before Aeschylus the principal tragic poets were *Phrynichus, *Pratinas, and *Choerilus. None of their plays survives. Apart from Aeschylus, Sophocles, and Euripides the most famous was Agathon, and after him perhaps *Ion of Chios and *Critias. There were about a dozen others who won the fifth-century tragedy competitions from time to time. The descendants of Aeschylus and Sophocles included some able tragedians. A younger Euripides produced posthumous plays by the elder Euripides and was himself a dramatist. But inspiration was failing by the end of the fourth century, and although tragedy was still being written in the third century at Athens, Alexandria (on a grand scale), and elsewhere, we

know nothing except the (otherwise unknown) names of some of the writers and about forty lines of their work; nothing more was thought worthy of preservation. (See HELLENISTIC AGE 4.)

5. *Roman tragedy*. For the origins of Roman drama see COMEDY, ROMAN 1. A new impulse was given when in 240 BC *Livius Andronicus first staged rough adaptations of a Greek tragedy and a Greek comedy, to be followed by other adaptations from Greek. *Naevius, his contemporary, appears to have been the first to compose, besides tragedies on Greek subjects, *fabulae* *praetextae*, dramas whose themes were drawn from Roman history or legend. His successors *Ennius, *Pacuvius, and *Accius also wrote occasional *praetextae* as well as tragedies modelled on Greek originals. After them Roman tragedy declined, and there was no important tragedian in the later years of the republic. Under the emperor Augustus, Asinius *Pollio wrote tragedies which have perished, as have also the *Medea* of Ovid and the *Thyestes* of Varius Rufus, both of them popular plays praised by Quintilian. To the age of the emperor Nero belong the highly rhetorical tragedies of *Seneca the Younger; like most of his predecessors he borrowed his subjects from Greek sources, and it is improbable that his tragedies were intended for the stage. The ordinary metre of Roman tragedy was the iambic senarius (see METRE, LATIN 2); this was used in dialogue. The sung portions were in simple lyrical metres adapted from the Greek. The chorus, where there was one, appeared on the stage, not, as in Greek tragedy, in the *orchestra*, and could take a greater part in the action.

Horace in his *Ars poetica* gives critical advice on the writing of tragedy, perhaps because the Pisones to whom the poem is addressed were interested in the genre. But conditions at Rome were unfavourable to the development of tragedy. Performances were not, as at Athens, part of a religious festival with cultic associations and social significance. There was no homogeneous audience in sympathy with the poet's view of things, religious, national, ethical, and social. Greek themes did not greatly interest the Roman spectator, and tragedies on Roman themes were perhaps problematical for political reasons; they were certainly few. Tragedy at Rome was moral and didactic, inculcating energy and fortitude, valued for its displays of oratory, and occasionally as appealing to national or political sentiment. But it does not appear to have produced any great original conceptions or the subtlety and character-drawing of its Greek prototype, though Quintilian rated the lost *Thyestes* of Varius as equal to any Greek tragedy. Roman tragedy was further inhibited by the extinction of political life under the empire, which made it difficult for the playwright to choose a subject that was not liable to sinister interpretation by a suspicious emperor.

See also THEATRE.

Trajan (Marcus Ulpius Traiānus), Roman emperor AD 98–117 (see ROME 11). He was born, probably in AD 53, of an Umbrian family which had settled in Spain, his father being of senatorial rank. He had a highly successful military career which earned him his adoption by the emperor Nerva in 97 when he was governor of Upper Germany. After his accession in the following year he did not go immediately to Rome but preferred to organize the Rhine and Danube frontiers. He subsequently conquered the Dacians, whose territory he constituted a Roman province. Later he also conquered a large part of the Parthian empire, capturing its capital Ctesiphon and reaching the Persian Gulf in the course of his expedition. He was a conscientious ruler and competent administrator who earned a high reputation for himself. He strove to be on good terms with the senate, many of whose members he appointed to oversee his schemes such as the system of subsistence allowances (*alimenta*) paid to poor children in Italy, and he showed concern for the well-being of the provinces. He devoted vast sums of money to building projects at Rome, his Forum (Forum Traiani), where the Column of Trajan commemorated his campaigns, new Baths, and the foundation of the library known as the Bibliotheca Ulpia. Pliny the Younger delivered a panegyric on him, and when governor of Bithynia corresponded with him regularly. His decisions and advice on the problems referred to him, notably on the matter of the Christians (Pliny, *Epistles* 10. 97) illustrate his firm humanity and good sense. He died in Cilicia on his way home from the Parthian campaign; his ashes were deposited in the base of his column. Trajan's reign, which saw the Roman empire at its greatest extent, was remembered as a time of peace and prosperity, and set the standard for a good emperor. See ANTONINES.

transmigration of souls, see PYTHAGORAS.

Transpadane Gaul, that part of north-west Italy which is 'beyond the river Padus', i.e. between the Po and the Alps; part of Cisalpine *Gaul.

Trasimene, Lake, battle of; see PUNIC WARS 2.

treasuries, in Greece, see TEMPLES.

Trebe'llius Po'llio, see *HISTORIA AUGUSTA*.

tre'sviri capitā'lēs and **tre'sviri monētā'lēs**, see VIGINTISEXVIRATE.

triad, in a Greek lyric poem, a group of three stanzas, of which the first two, called strophē and antistrophē, are symmetrical, i.e. correspond in metre, but the third, called the epode, has a different though related metrical form. If the poem consists of more than one triad the epodes, at least in Pindar, correspond with one another, as do all the strophes and antistrophes. This form of composition, which broke the monotony of a long series of similar stanzas, was thought to have been introduced by *Stesichorus and followed by Simonides and Pindar. It is generally believed that lyric poetry written in triadic form was sung and danced by a chorus, whereas monodic lyric was usually sung by an individual (see LYRIC POETRY I).

tribes (Gk. *phylai*; Lat. *tribus*)
1. In early times the various Greek peoples were divided into large kinship groups known as tribes, which were further sub-divided into *phratriai*, 'brotherhoods'. Thus the Dorian people were divided into three tribes known as the *Hylleis, Pamphyloi*, and *Dymānĕs* which were found in almost all Dorian cities; the Ionians were divided into four tribes, the *Aigikoreis, Hoplētĕs, Geleontĕs*, and *Argadeis*. Tribes were corporate groups, with hereditary membership and their own priests and officials. In early times they were the basis of state administration for military and governmental purposes. At Athens, *Cleisthenes' reforms of the democracy in the late sixth century BC involved the dismantling of the old tribes and the creation of ten new tribes based on the *demes. These tribes, with new names and cults given divine backing by the Delphic Oracle, were named after one Salaminian and nine Attic heroes, whose statues were erected in the agora. They were called Erechthēis, Aigēis, Pandĭŏnis, Leontis, Akamantis, Oinēis, Kekrŏpis, Hippothontis, Aiantis, and Antiochis (each name being a Greek feminine adjective agreeing with the feminine noun *phylē*, 'tribe'). A similar change was made at Sparta during the Lycurgan reforms, when administration came to be based on the *obai*, the constituent villages, in preference to the tribes.
2. At Rome the people were in the earliest times divided into three tribes based on kinship, Titienses (abbreviated to Tities), Ramnenses (Ramnes), and Luceres. According to tradition, the king *Servius Tullius replaced these with four urban tribes based on locality (compare Cleisthenes' similar reform at Athens), in order to include in the citizen body the large number of aliens who had settled at Rome. These tribes were known as the Sucusana, Esquilina, Collina, and Palatina. To these were gradually added 'rustic' tribes for the country regions, of which the oldest were named after patrician families who presumably owned a large part of the territory in each case. By 387 BC there were twenty-one tribes in all; by 241 BC the number had reached thirty-five, which was never exceeded. The tribes were the administrative units for the census, taxation, and the military

levy, as well as for assemblies of the *plebs* (see COMITIA TRIBUTA).

Tribō'niān (Tribōniānus, d. *c.* AD 545), probably of Sīdē in Pamphylia, a jurist of great learning, particularly in legal history, and 'quaestor of the palace' under the emperor *Justinian; he was the latter's collaborator in the codification of the law.

tribrach, see METRE, GREEK I (vi).

tribunes of the plebs or **people** (*tribūni plēbis*), at Rome, magistrates who were themselves *plebeian and of free birth, first created, according to tradition, in 494 BC, and numbering ten by 450. Their role was to protect the lives and property of the plebeians, and they were inviolable, *sacrosancti*. They had the right of *intercessio*, 'veto' (Lat. *veto*, 'I forbid'), against any act of any magistrate, and thus could thwart elections, laws, and decrees of the senate (*senatus consulta*). They were elected annually by the *concilium plebis* and could summon meetings of the plebeians; *patricians could become tribunes only by getting themselves adopted into a plebeian family (see the case of Clodius under CICERO (I) 3). The tribunate became gradually indistinguishable from the other magistracies (though it lacked *imperium* and the insignia of office), but it never wholly lost its revolutionary flavour. From the time of the Gracchi the power of veto was curtailed. The danger of the tribunate to the senate was evident from the careers of *Saturninus and the younger M. Livius *Drusus. Sulla reduced its attractiveness by forbidding anyone who had held the tribunate to advance to higher office, and curtailed the tribunes' legislative and judicial powers. But these privileges were restored in the 70s BC and tribunes played an important part in the protection of Julius Caesar's interests at Rome during his governorship of Gaul. Under the empire the emperor was invested with tribunician power (*tribunicia potestas*) and the real tribunes lost all importance.

tribū'ni aerā'rii ('tribunes of the treasury'), at Rome, originally officials of the *tribes who collected the *tribūtum* or war-tax on property, and saw to the payment of soldiers (after pay had been introduced, see ARMY, ROMAN I). In the first century BC this name was given to a property class similar to but less wealthy than the *equites* from which certain jurors were drawn (see LAW, AT ROME I (ii)).

tribū'ni mī'litum, at Rome in later republican times, senior army officials, six to a legion; they were elected by the people and ranked as magistrates (which meant that they did not command subsections of the legion as subordinate officers). Under Julius Caesar the tribunes declined in importance with the rise of *legati* as legion commanders.

tribū'ni plēbis, see TRIBUNES OF THE PEOPLE.

tribute lists, Athenian, name given to a series of fragmentary inscriptions on stone of the fifth century BC, recovered from the Athenian Acropolis, relating to the finances of the *Delian League. They record the sum of money paid each year by each allied city in the Delian League to (the treasurers of) the goddess Athena, which amounted to one sixtieth part of the city's total tribute. It is thus possible to calculate how much a city paid in tribute. These inscriptions cover the years following 454 BC (when the Delian treasury was moved from Delos to Athens). The money was brought to Athens in 454–415 (except perhaps in 449) and 410–406. Modern historians have elicited a great deal of political and social information from the lists.

tribū'tum, at Rome, property-tax; see FINANCES, ROMAN and ROME 2.

triclī'nium. The Romans imitated from the Greeks the practice of reclining on a couch to dine; the *triclinium* was originally an arrangement of couches with three places on each around three sides of a square table, and the name was subsequently transferred to the dining-room itself. The diners leaned on their left elbows, their feet pointing away from the table and perhaps supported by foot-stools. The left-hand couch, as seen from the (empty) foot of the table, was the lowest in rank (*lectus īmus*), and here the host and his family reclined, the host being at the upper end of it. The chief guest reclined in the place of honour (*locus consulāris*), at the left-hand end of the middle couch (*lectus medius*), next to his host. The so-called top couch (*lectus summus*) was set along the right-hand side of the table. Reclining on couches at meals was the custom of the rich and leisured class; poor people or slaves reclined on pallets or sat upright.

Tricli'nius, Deme'trius, see TEXTS, TRANSMISSION OF ANCIENT 3.

triēra'rchia ('trierarchy'), see LITURGY.

triglyph, see METOPE.

trilogy, see TRAGEDY 2.

Trima'lchio's Banquet, see PETRONIUS ARBITER.

tri'meter, see METRE, GREEK 1.

Trīna'cria, Trinacia, Thrinacia, see SICILY.

Trinu'mmus ('three pieces of silver'), Roman comedy by *Plautus adapted from a Greek Comedy by Philemon (see COMEDY, GREEK 6). The play takes its name from a coin paid as a day's wages to a hired impostor, whose part in the plot is relatively unimportant. The exact value of the coin is disputed.

While Charmidēs, a wealthy Athenian, is out of the country, his dissolute son Lesbonīcus has spent all his father's money and even put the house up for sale. At his departure Charmides had entrusted his son and daughter to the care of his friend Calliclēs, and confided to the latter that a treasure was concealed in the house. Callicles therefore, anxious about the treasure, has bought the house himself. Lesbonicus' friend, Lysitelēs, wishing to help the financial situation, offers to marry Lesbonicus' sister without a dowry. Lesbonicus, though approving the match, will not accept an arrangement discreditable to his family, and Callicles thinks the sister should have a dowry out of the treasure. The difficulty is how to arrange this without revealing to Lesbonicus the existence of the treasure. Callicles' solution is to hire 'for three pieces of silver' a 'sycophant' (i.e. a man prepared to do anything for money), who is to deliver to Lesbonicus a thousand gold pieces and a letter purporting to come from his father, explaining that the money is to be used for a dowry (while in fact being part of the treasure). Charmides himself now arrives unexpectedly and meets the sycophant knocking at the door. Learning his errand he reveals the imposture, and then discovers that the house is no longer his own but belongs to Callicles. He begins to abuse the latter, but when all is revealed warmly thanks him, gives his daughter, with a dowry, to Lysitelēs, and pardons the now penitent Lesbonicus.

tripod, any utensil or article of furniture supported on three feet but, in Greece, especially the cauldron used for boiling meat, which either rested on a three-legged stand or was made with three legs all in one piece. This was a utensil of great value; tripods are included among the prizes offered at the Funeral Games of Patroclus in Homer, *Iliad* 23. In a religious context the tripod was put to practical use as a cooking vessel for the meat from a sacrifice, and thus it came to be thought of as a suitable object for dedication to a god. One peculiar use was at Delphi, where the god Apollo was represented as seated on a tripod as if it were a throne; as his mouthpiece the Pythia too sat on the tripod when making prophecies (see DELPHIC ORACLE). It is not known why it should have been used in this way.

Tripto'lemus, in Greek myth, the young man chosen by the goddess *Demeter to go about the world and teach men the skills of agriculture, in some accounts identified with the child whom Demeter tried to make immortal. His parentage is variously described: he is said to be the son of the hero Eleusis (after whom the town was named), or, in Orphic literature, of Oceanus and Gaia (Earth). He was the recipient of sacrifice at Eleusis, where the Greek traveller Pausanias reports having seen his temple. Probably because of his Orphic connections Plato made him, with Minos and Rhadamanthys, judge of the dead in the Underworld.

trireme, see SHIPS.

Tri'stia ('sorrows'), Latin elegiac poems by *Ovid in five books, written in AD 8–12, the early years of the poet's exile to Tomis. The metre must have seemed appropriate, since elegiac was commonly thought in ancient times to have been originally the metre of lament (see ELEGY). Most of the poems are in the form of letters to his wife and friends, written to ensure that he was not forgotten at Rome, in which he laments his fate and prays for some mitigation of his severe punishment. The poems appear to have been sent individually to Rome and then collected in groups for publication.

Book I consists of poems composed on the long journey to Tomis and sent back to Rome on Ovid's arrival. They include descriptions of storms and hardships encountered. The real destination of these poems is Augustus, on whom Ovid brings moral pressure to rescind his banishment; he reminds the emperor of his status as a poet and of his achievement. The third poem of the book is the moving account of the poet's last night at Rome.

Book II is a single poem, written at times in a satirical manner, but still a serious defence of the autonomy of poetry, in the face of which the emperor's attitude to the poet is made to seem beside the point. (The fact that Ovid's first loyalty has always been to poetry is made clear in his autobiographical poem IV. 10, written to show that poetry was not for him a matter of choice but a true vocation; like Alexander Pope he 'lisped in numbers for the numbers came': *et quod temptabam scribere versus erat*, 'all I attempted to write turned out as verse' (IV. 10. 26).)

Books III, IV, and V include glimpses of life at Tomis, a precariously held outpost of civilization: the flat, treeless landscape, the rigorous climate, the attacks of barbarians on the town (when even Ovid is constrained to take up arms for its defence), the poet's loneliness among his Getic hosts. The casual reader may become bored by a certain monotony in Ovid's complaints, but these are by no means abject, and often run the risk of making too clear for safety the poet's view that he was a victim of tyrannical injustice.

Trīton, in Greek myth, a merman, son of *Poseidon and Amphitritē, with human head and shoulders and a fish tail from the waist down. The origin of his name (as also of Amphitrite) is obscure and may not be Greek. He is commonly shown blowing on a conchshell, and Virgil describes how the trumpeter Misenus challenged him to a contest on this instrument and was drowned by him. In some stories there are several Tritons (as in the case of Eros). *Pausanias on his travels saw what he was told was a Triton preserved in brine.

Trītō'nia (or Tritogeneia), epithet sometimes used of the goddess Athena; the origin is unknown, but it was explained that she was born beside a river Triton or a Lake Tritonis, variously found in Boeotia, Libya, and Crete.

trittys, at Athens, 'a third', i.e. of a *tribe. *Cleisthenes (2) in his constitutional reforms created thirty *trittyěs*, territorial divisions, each containing a number of demes. Each of his (new) ten tribes was composed of three *trittyes*, one each from the city, interior, and coastal regions. See DEME.

triumph, at Rome, the celebratory procession of a victorious Roman general to the temple of Jupiter Capitolinus. It was Etruscan in origin, and was regulated by strict rules of a religious nature. To be granted a triumph it was at first necessary for the general to hold a magistracy with *imperium* (even Scipio Africanus had been denied a triumph after his victories in Spain through not holding a regular magistracy), to have won a great victory over a foreign enemy, with at least 5,000 of the enemy killed, and to have brought home at least a token army to show that the war was won. Later, holding a regular magistracy was not a prerequisite (see POMPEY), but the other requirements meant that a triumph was a relatively rare event.

Because *imperium* did not include the city itself, the *triumphator* had to wait outside until the senate had suspended the law and allowed him to retain his *imperium* within the city for one day only. Preceded by his lictors he stood, richly dressed and wreathed in bay, on a fourhorse chariot, a slave murmuring to him words to avert the possible ill consequences of outstanding success such as 'remember you are mortal'. The army shouted '*io triumphe*' and also sang rude songs (see FESCENNINE VERSES). The procession was joined by the magistrates and senators, captives, spoils, and sacrificial animals. It proceeded from the Campus Martius outside the city through the Triumphal Gate, the Circus Flaminius and Circus Maximus, around the Palatine hill, along the Via Sacra to the Capitol. At the temple of Jupiter Capitolinus the general made sacrifice and surrendered his bays to the god.

When a triumph was disallowed an *ovatio* was usually granted. This was a less spectacular form of triumph, the general entering Rome on foot or on horseback rather than in a chariot, wearing the *toga praetexta* (see DRESS 2) and wreathed in myrtle. The last recorded *ovatio* was in AD 47.

triumvirate. The unofficial coalition of Julius Caesar, Pompey, and Crassus in 60 BC is often referred to for convenience, but strictly

speaking incorrectly, as the first triumvirate (see
CAESAR). For the (second) officially constituted
triumvirate in 43 BC of Antony, Lepidus, and
Octavian see ROME 7.

Tri'via, see DIANA.

tri'vium, see EDUCATION 6.

Trō'adĕs, see *TROJAN WOMEN.*

Troas, the Troad, the territory around *Troy,
forming the north-west extremity of Asia
Minor, between the Hellespont and the island of
Lesbos, including Mount Ida.

trŏchee, trocha'ic, see METRE, GREEK I (v).

Troezen, in Greece, a city of the Peloponnese
in the north-east corner of the promontory of
Argolis, opposite and to the south of Athens
across the Saronic Gulf. Many of its legends are
connected with Athens. It was the home of
Aithra, mother of Theseus, and the location of
the death of Theseus' son *Hippolytus, who had
an important cult there. Many Athenian women
and children fled to Troezen at the time of the
Persian invasion in 480 BC.

Trogus, Pompē'ius, Roman historian in the
time of Augustus (emperor 27 BC–AD 14), a
native of Narbonese Gaul, whose father had
been a lieutenant of Julius Caesar. He wrote a
universal history in forty-four books entitled
Historiae Philippicae ('Philippic histories'),
centred as the name indicates on the history of
Macedon, especially under Philip II, and probably based on Greek sources (e.g. the important
*Theopompus). We have only an epitome of it
by *Justin which is nevertheless very valuable
for the history of Macedon and the Hellenistic
kingdoms.

Trŏilus, in Greek myth, a younger son of
Priam king of Troy and Hecuba, mentioned
briefly in Homer's *Iliad* as already killed by
Achilles. For the post-classical story of Troilus
and Cressida (which Chaucer and Shakespeare
get from Boccaccio) see PANDARUS. Cressida is
the Greek maiden called *Chryseis in the *Iliad.*

Trojan Horse, also known as the Wooden
Horse, a device resorted to by the Greeks, after
the death of Achilles, to capture Troy. The story
is known to Homer and is referred to in the
Odyssey as well as being part of the cycle of
stories about Troy (see EPIC CYCLE; ILIAD, LITTLE;
and ILIUPERSIS), but the *Iliad* ends well before this
event. Epēius, a skilful craftsman, constructed a
very large wooden horse inside which picked
Greek warriors, including Odysseus, were concealed. Then the Greek army sailed out of sight,
leaving Sinon, one of their number, behind. He
pretended to the Trojans that he was a deserter
and that the horse was an offering to Athena; if
brought within the city it would render it
impregnable. In spite of the warning given to

the Trojans by Lāocŏon (a priest of Apollo) not
to trust 'Greek gifts', the Trojans dragged the
horse into the city, convinced that the destruction of Laocoon and his sons by two serpents
after he had given his warning was a punishment for impiety. Cassandra too prophesied
disaster but was disbelieved. At night the Greeks
came out of the horse and the city was taken. In
Homer's *Odyssey* (book 4) Menelaus reminds
Helen how, when the horse was inside the walls
of Troy, she had walked round it calling out the
names of the men she suspected might be inside,
and Odysseus had prevented anyone from
answering. In book 8 Odysseus at the court of
Alcinous asks the bard to sing the story of the
Wooden Horse. Virgil in *Aeneid* 2 tells the story
of the entry of the horse and of the following
sack of Troy.

Trojan War, the subject of the most important
and most pervasive of Greek legends; an episode
in the war is the subject of Homer's *Iliad,* the
war's aftermath that of his *Odyssey.* The ancient
city of *Troy stood on the Asian side of
the Hellespont; its destruction by violence
*c.*1250 BC, revealed by archaeologists at the level
known as VIIa, is possibly the historical basis of
the Homeric Trojan War, representing the last
concerted effort of Mycenaean Greece against a
foreign power, and preceding the widespread
destructions in the Greek world by a few
decades (see MYCENAE). The archaeological date
is not far removed from Erastosthenes' calculation of 1184 for the fall of Troy. In the Homeric
account the war was waged by the *Achaeans
(i.e. the Greeks) led by Agamemnon to recover
*Helen, the wife of Agamemnon's brother
Menelaus and the most beautiful woman in the
world, who had been abducted by *Paris, a
prince of Troy. The Achaeans laid siege to the
city but at the end of nine years had still failed to
take it. Then followed the events recounted in
the *Iliad.* After this, according to post-Homeric
legend, occurred the arrival of the Amazons
under Penthesilēa (see ACHILLES) and of the
Ethiopians under *Memnon to reinforce the
Trojans, the death of Achilles, the summoning
of *Neoptolemus and *Philoctētes, the incident
of the Trojan Horse, and the fall of the city.

Medieval legend relating to the Trojan War is
mainly based on Latin works which purported
to be translations of the narratives of *Darēs
Phrygius and *Dictys Cretensis. Dares, supposed to have been on the Trojan side, appears
to have influenced more than Dictys the western
European countries, some of which claimed a
Trojan ancestry. Thus the Trojan hero Hector
rather than the Greek hero Achilles became the
ideal of chivalry. In England the most prominent form of the medieval legend was the story
which Geoffrey of Monmouth (d.1155) made
popular: that Brutus ('Brut'), great-grandson of
Aeneas, collected a remnant of Trojans, settled

in Britain, which was uninhabited at the time ('except for a few giants'), and became the progenitor of a line of British kings which included King Arthur; and that he founded 'New Troy', Troynovant, later known as London. (The name was based on that of the British tribe the Trinovantes whose territory was north and east of London.) This legend was taken seriously even beyond medieval times.

Trojan Women (*Trōadĕs*). 1. Greek tragedy by *Euripides. It was produced in 415 BC, shortly after the capture of *Melos by the Athenians, who slaughtered its male inhabitants and enslaved its women and children. One of the most poignant of Euripidean dramas, it presents not so much a narrative as a tragic situation: the condition of the Trojan women when their men-folk have been killed and they are at the mercy of their captors. Grieving and anxious they await their fate. Talthybius, the herald, announces that they are to be distributed among the victors. The Trojan queen Hecuba is to become the possession of the hated Odysseus; her daughter Cassandra has been allotted to Agamemnon, and it is revealed that her other daughter Polyxena has been slaughtered on the tomb of Achilles. The tragic figure of Cassandra appears; being a prophetess she foretells some of the disasters which will come upon the conquerors. Andromachē enters with her small son Astyanax; she is to be the prize of Neoptolemus. Talthybius returns to carry off Astyanax whose death has been ordered by the Greeks. The meeting of Menelaus and Helen follows; he is determined to destroy her, and Hecuba encourages his anger. But Helen pleads her cause, and when Helen and Menelaus depart their reconciliation has been foreshadowed. Talthybius appears once more with the broken body of Astyanax, and Hecuba prepares the burial. Finally Troy is set on fire and its towers collapse as the women turn to captivity.
2. Roman tragedy by *Seneca (2), based on (1) above and combining with it the sacrifice of Polyxena from Euripides' *Hecuba. This is one of the best (to modern taste) of the Senecan tragedies, containing passages of great passion and pathos.

Trophō'nius ('nourisher') **and Agamē'dēs**, in Greek myth, sons of Ergīnus of Orchomenus (in Boeotia) who lived in the time of Heracles. Trophonius is sometimes said to be the son of Apollo. They were architects and reputedly built the temple of Apollo at Delphi and a treasury for the Boeotian king Hyrieus (or for Augēas, king of Elis). The story told about them is similar to that told of *Rhampsinitus. The two brothers robbed the treasury by means of a movable stone in the wall; the king set a trap, and when Agamedes was caught Trophonius cut off his head to avoid identification. Trophonius was subsequently swallowed up by the

earth at Lebadeia in Boeotia. When the Boeotians were suffering from a drought the oracle at Delphi told them to consult Trophonius' oracle. They did not know how to find it, but one of the envoys, following a swarm of bees into a cave, saw a vision of Trophonius who told him he was now the oracle of the cave.

The oracle was consulted by Croesus, king of Lydia, in the sixth century BC, Epaminondas, and Philip II of Macedon, and was still in existence in Roman times. According to Plutarch it was the only Boeotian oracle that remained active in his day (early second century AD). The method of consulting the oracle was highly unusual, as we know from Pausanias (IX. 39. 4) who consulted it himself. After elaborate preparations, which included drinking from the springs of Forgetfulness and Memory, the enquirer descended into a chasm, at the bottom of which was a small opening. Into this he inserted his legs and was immediately snatched away to another place 'as if a deep fast river was catching a man in a current and sucking him down'. Here the enquirer learned the future from things he saw or heard, before being returned feet first the same way. The priests then took him to the Throne of Memory and asked him what he had learnt; this was written down and the tablet dedicated to the god. The enquirer emerged pale and terrified, so that it became proverbial to say of people looking gloomy that they had consulted the oracle of Trophonius. See also ORACLES.

Trōs, see TROY below.

Troy (Troia), otherwise known as Ilium, an ancient city famous in legend; its siege by the Greeks is the subject of Homer's *Iliad* (see TROJAN WAR and TROJAN HORSE above). Its site in north-west Asia Minor some 6 km. (4 miles) from the Aegean Sea, a little south of the Hellespont, was identified at the modern Hissarlik by Heinrich *Schliemann, who between 1870 and 1890 excavated the occupation mound, composed of the accumulated debris of centuries. There is no evidence for occupation in the Neolithic Age; the earliest habitation levels, layers I–IV, extend through the Early Bronze Age which lasted for most of the third millennium. From the beginning Troy was a fortified stronghold, occupied during this period by a single people with their own unbroken culture. Layer VI shows the arrival *c*.1900 BC of a new people who introduced a new culture, that of the Middle Bronze Age. They brought with them the horse and a different kind of pottery known as Minyan ware (see POTTERY), and seem thus to have been akin to the Greek-speaking invaders of mainland *Greece *c*.2000–1900 BC. Their city, Troy VI (*c*.1900–1300), was built on a completely different plan, which took no account of the houses and streets that had gone before. It prospered, was fortified, and eventually resembled a Mycenaean stronghold inside a massive wall, over 3 m. (10 ft.) thick and still in parts 6 m. (20 ft.) high, with gates and square towers for its defence, and a central citadel.

By 1300 Troy had enjoyed settled prosperity for six centuries. The source of its wealth has been much disputed. It is clear that by its position it could control a large part of east-west trade, and was itself the possessor of rich agricultural lands; it was famous for its horses, according to Homer, and, to judge from the large number of spinning whorls discovered there, was a flourishing producer of textiles. The city was destroyed by a massive earthquake *c.*1300; the population seems to have survived and to have set about the rebuilding at once (Troy VIIa). There is evidence that a larger number of people than hitherto began to live within the fortification walls. This phase of Troy's life lasted not much more than a generation. The archaeological evidence shows that by 1250 BC Troy VIIa was once more destroyed, this time by human agency; it was consumed by fire, and traces of human bones in houses and streets suggest violence. If there is any fact at all behind the story of the Trojan War, 1250 or thereabout seems to be the latest reasonable date for mainland Greece to be making a concerted attack on the city, since after that time Greece herself was involved in the general upheavals of the Mediterranean world which began in the middle of the century. Greek authors gave different dates for the Trojan War, from *c.*1280 to 1184 and even later. The second date was that arrived at by *Eratosthenes, and subsequently favoured. He worked backwards from the established date of the first Olympic games, 776 BC, using the genealogies of the Spartan kings, which gave him 1104 for the *Dorian Invasion. According to tradition this happened two generations, i.e. 80 years, after the Trojan War.

The legendary family tree of the kings of Troy is as follows. *Dardanus son of Zeus 'established Dardania' (as Homer says), a district north-east of Troy, and married the daughter of the local king Teucer (Teukros). He had as descendants Trōs (from whom the Troad and the Trojans were named) and Ilus, who founded the city of Troy, sometimes called after him Ilium (Ilion). Ilus had two sons, *Laomedon father of *Priam, and *Tithonus, and a daughter Hesionē, mother by *Telamon of another Teucer, half-brother of Ajax.

Trucule'ntus ('the boor'), Roman comedy by *Plautus.

The play, which has little plot, is mainly concerned with the doings of a covetous prostitute who shamelessly exploits her three lovers, a dissolute young Athenian, a boastful soldier, and a young man from the country (whose sour and aggressive slave gives the play its title). She palms off on the soldier a child she has acquired, by pretending that it is his. The child turns out to be that of the dissolute Athenian and a free-born girl, whom the penitent seducer agrees to marry. The slave tries to prevent his master wasting his money on the prostitute, but then falls in love himself with her maid.

Tryphiodō'rus (third or fourth century AD), Greek epic poet, a native of Egypt. Only his *Capture of Troy* survives. A short epic of 691 lines, it resembles in style the epic of *Nonnus.

Tubilu'stria, in Roman religion, a festival of the god *Mars on 23 March, when the sacred trumpets (*tubae*), originally used in war and later on ceremonial occasions, were purified. See QUINQUATRUS.

Tucca, Plō'tius, see AENEID (at the end of the preamble).

Tu'llia. 1. In Roman legendary history, daughter of king Servius Tullius and wife of Tarquinius Superbus; see ROME 2 and TARQUIN. She incited her husband to overthrow her father, and when the latter had been murdered, drove her chariot over his dead body.

2. The much-loved daughter of Cicero (1) and Terentia, born *c.*79 BC. She was three times married, to Calpurnius Piso Frugi, of whom Cicero was fond, but who died during the latter's exile; to Furius Crassipēs, who divorced her; and thirdly to the dissolute P. Cornelius Dolabella who supported alternately Julius Caesar and Brutus in the civil war. Her death in 45 BC threw her father into despair; see CICERO (1) 4 and SULPICIUS RUFUS.

Tulliā'num, at Rome, the underground execution cell of the prison, at the foot of the Capitoline hill, where most state prisoners were executed, including Jugurtha, the Catilinarian conspirators, and the Gaul Vercingetorix.

Tullus Hosti'lius, in Roman legendary history the third king of Rome (673–642 BC; see ROME 2). His reign was said to have been occupied by constant warfare (hence his name), which included the capture and destruction of Alba Longa (see HORATII AND CURIATII).

Tully, name by which Marcus Tullius *Cicero (1) was known to English readers down to the early nineteenth century.

tu'nica, see DRESS 2.

Tū'riae laudā'tio, see WOMEN, POSITION OF 2.

Turnus, in Virgil's *Aeneid*, Italian hero, son of Daunus and the nymph Venilia, brother of the nymph Juturna. He was the king of the Rutulians and suitor of Lavinia, daughter of king *Latinus. The Latins joined with the Rutulians to fight the Trojans; Turnus killed

Pallas, son of Evander, was twice saved by Juno, but was finally killed by Aeneas (see AENEID, books 7–12).

Tu'sculan Disputations (*Tusculānae disputatiōnēs*, 'discussions at Tusculum'), philosophical treatise in five books by Cicero on the conditions for happiness. The work was completed in 44 BC (see CICERO (I) 5) and is addressed to Marcus *Brutus. It takes the form of conversations between two characters indicated as M and A.

After an introduction defending the adoption of philosophy as a subject for treatment in Latin literature, Cicero in book I deals with the proposition that death is an evil and an impediment to happiness. His answer is that death is either a change of place for the soul or annihilation; in neither case is it an evil; 'How can what is necessary for all be an evil for one?' In a famous sentence Cicero says that he would rather be wrong with Plato than right with some other philosophers: *errare, mehercule, malo cum Platone* . . .

Book 2 deals with physical suffering and shows that it is of trifling importance by the side of virtue, that it can be borne with fortitude, and that death is a refuge from it.

Book 3 discusses mental suffering and grief, whether due to mourning, envy, compassion, vexation, or despondency, and shows that it originates in a mistaken judgement, is an act of will, and can be overcome by reflection, fortitude, and self-restraint.

Book 4 asserts that other mental disorders, excessive delight, lust, and fear, are similarly due to errors of judgement and can be overcome by philosophy.

Book 5 discusses whether virtue alone is sufficient for happiness, whether e.g. the virtuous man can be happy under torture. Cicero here adopts the *Stoic view that the wise and virtuous man is happy always.

Tu'sculum, ancient Italian town in the mountains near Frascati about 24 km. (15 miles) south-east of Rome. Under the late republic and early empire it was a fashionable resort. Lucullus, Maecenas, and Cicero all had villas there. For the legendary founder see TELEGONUS.

Twelve gods, see GODS.

Twelve Tables, the earliest Roman code of laws drawn up by a special commission of ten, *decemviri legibus scribundis* ('ten men for writing out the laws'), in 451/0 BC, on the demand of the plebeians; see ROME 3. No complete text of the code survives, and it is known only from quotations and references. Most of the quotations are a series of succinct and laconic commands, generally in a revised and classical-sounding Latin, but a few survive in a very archaic and obscure form. According to tradi-

tion envoys were sent to Athens to study Greek laws before the decemvirs started work. The Twelve Tables embraced all spheres of law, private, criminal, public, and sacred; they were never abolished, but later enactments made them obsolete. As late as Cicero's day, although not for much longer, schoolboys still learned them by heart.

Tȳchē, 'chance', 'fortune', good or bad, in Greek religious thought the incalculable element in life. In popular belief each person and city had its own *tyche*, much like a *daimon*. Belief in this abstraction strengthened after the fifth century BC as worship of the old gods declined. Pindar calls Tyche one of the Fates, stronger than her sisters, but she never became fully personified or a subject of myth. Compare Latin FORTUNA.

Tȳdeus, in Greek myth, son of Oineus, king of Calydon. Exiled for homicide (his victim is variously given), at Argos he married Dēïpylē, daughter of Adrastus, while Polyneicēs married her sister Argeia. He was one of the leaders in the expedition of the *Seven against Thebes and was father of *Diomedēs.

Tynda'ridae ('the Tyndarids'), name sometimes given to Castor and Polydeucēs (Pollux; see DIOSCURI), whose mother *Leda was wife of Tyndareus, king of Sparta.

Typhō'eus or **Tȳphon,** according to Hesiod, son of *Tartarus and Gaia (Earth), born after Zeus' defeat of the *Titans. He was a monster with a hundred serpent heads, fiery eyes, and a tremendous voice; Zeus at once attacked him with thunderbolts and cast him into Tartarus, setting Aetna on fire on the way. In Pindar and Aeschylus he is the force under that volcano, and he is the source of storm winds which cause shipwreck and devastation. For the identification of Typhon with the Egyptian god Set, see OSIRIS.

tyrant (*tyrannos*, 'king', perhaps a Lydian word), in Greece, name given to an absolute monarch who seized power illegally. There were many such in Greek cities of the seventh and sixth centuries BC, who were often originally members of a ruling oligarchy but who led a popular revolt against oppressive government. In such cases they sometimes paved the way for democratic government. Under the later democracies of classical Greece, when the idea of tyranny became repugnant, the word 'tyrant' acquired its pejorative overtone. Most of the early tyrants made important contributions to the adornment and general cultural standing of their cities. A tyranny rarely lasted for more than two generations. Among the best-known tyrants were Pheidon, Polycrates, Cypselus, Periander, Cleisthenes of Sicyon, Peisistratus,

Hippias, and the Sicilian tyrants Gelon, Theron, and Hieron. A second period of tyranny arose at Syracuse in the third century BC under Dionysius I.

Tȳro, in Greek myth, daughter of *Salmoneus, a king of Elis, brought up by a cruel stepmother. Tyro was loved by the god Poseidon, who took the form of the Thessalian river Enipeus and made a great wave curl over them. She bore two sons, Pelias (see ARGONAUTS) and Nēleus (father of Nestor), whom she abandoned. She was married to Salmoneus' brother Crētheus and became the mother of Aeson and grand-mother of Jason. See also MELAMPUS.

Tyrrhē'nians, see ETRUSCANS.

Tyrtae'us (seventh century BC), Greek elegiac poet who lived at Sparta at the time of the Second Messenian War (see SPARTA 1) and was probably of Spartan birth. The story that he was an Athenian schoolmaster who was sent to Sparta as the result of an oracle must be a fabrication. He encouraged the Spartans to capture Messēnē by his war-songs and exhortations in verse. The Alexandrian scholars collected his works in five books, but only fragments survive.

Tzetzēs, see TEXTS, TRANSMISSION OF ANCIENT 3.

U

Uli'xēs or **Ulyssēs,** see ODYSSEUS.

U'lpian (Domitius Ulpiānus), famous Roman jurist, born of a family long established at Tyre (in Syria). His writings, which numbered nearly 280 books, date mostly from the reign of the emperor Caracalla (AD 212–17). With *Paulus he assisted *Papinian when the latter was praetorian prefect in 203 (see PRAEFECTUS PRAE-TORIO). He was banished by the emperor Elagabalus (218–22) but became praetorian prefect at the beginning of the reign of the next emperor, Alexander Severus. In 223 he was murdered by the praetorian guard ostensibly over his plans for its reform.

Ulpian's summing-up of earlier legal writings was so thorough and effective that the codifiers of Justinian's reign used him far more than any other writer. Nearly a third of the *Digesta* is taken from his works (see JUSTINIAN).

U'lpian Library, at Rome, built by Trajan, emperor AD 98–117, and so called from his own name, Ulpius. See LIBRARIES.

Uly'ssēs, see ODYSSEUS.

U'mbria, region of central Italy, north-east of Rome. The Umbrian language, an Italic dialect, survives in inscriptions from *c.*400–90 BC. It was written partly in the Latin alphabet and partly in Greek (through the influence of Etruria). See LATIN LANGUAGE.

uncials, in Greek and Latin handwriting, one of the two forms of majuscules or large letters used in papyri and early manuscripts, the other being capitals. Uncials are a curvilinear form of the latter, being easier to write with a pen on soft material than the angular capitals, which are more readily cut on metal or stone. The name first appears in Jerome's preface to the Old Testament book of Job, and is generally taken to mean 'letters an inch long' (Lat. *uncia*, 'inch'), but the derivation is uncertain.

Underworld, see HADES and AFTERLIFE.

Ūra'nia. 1. One of the *Muses.

2. Title of the goddess *Aphroditē, describing her as 'heavenly', i.e. spiritual, to distinguish her from Aphrodite Pandemos, 'vulgar' love, as in Plato's *Symposium*.

Ū'ranus (Heaven), in Greek myth, the personification of the heavens. Uranus and *Gaia (Earth), who herself gave birth to Uranus, are the primeval parents in Greek cosmogony. Uranus fathered numerous children but prevented them from being born. Gaia called upon her son *Cronus to help, and he castrated his father with a sickle (an act which seems to represent the separation of Heaven and Earth, a frequent motif of myth all over the world). Uranus' children could then be born (see TITANS, CYCLOPES, and HECATONCHEIRES), after which he himself loses importance and disappears from view. Various divine monsters were born from the drops of his blood which fell on the earth, Erinyes (see FURIES), *Giants, and Meliae (tree-nymphs); his genital organs were flung into the sea by Cronus, and from the foam that bubbled around them Aphrodite was born.

V

Vacū'na, a Sabine goddess whose functions were already forgotten by the time Horace in his *Epistles* (1. 10. 49) puns on her name to make her a goddess of vacation.

Valē'rius Flaccus, Gaius, Latin poet of whose life little is known except that dateable references in his only known work, the *Argonautica*, suggest that he began it in the early 70s AD, that he died prematurely in 92 or 93 before completing it, and that he was one of the *quindecimviri sacris faciundis* (see SIBYL). The *Argonautica*, an epic poem written in hexameters, ends abruptly in the eighth book. Valerius' main source was the similarly entitled Hellenistic Greek epic of *Apollonius Rhodius, but other poets including *Varro Atacinus had treated the same subject and he may have consulted their works; the Underworld scene in book 1 is indebted to similar scenes in Homer's *Odyssey* and, especially, to Virgil's *Aeneid*, but Valerius also introduces scenes of his own invention. Book 7, and the incomplete book 8, the episode of Jason and Medea, are the best part of the poem, where with some subtlety and in a graver, less playful manner than Apollonius, he develops the character of Medea, torn between her passion for Jason and loyalty to her father, and enlists the reader's sympathy for her. He leaves Jason contemplating the betrayal of the bride on whom his success depends.

Valē'rius Maximus, Latin compiler of an extant collection of anecdotes in the early first century AD. Very little is known of his life; he followed his patron Sextus Pompeius (consul AD 14) to Asia in AD 27, and dedicated his work to the emperor Tiberius after the fall of Sejanus in AD 31. His nine books of *Facta et dicta memorabilia* ('memorable deeds and sayings'), anecdotes and examples for the use of orators, are arranged roughly as follows: book 1, religion, omens, prophecies; book 2, social customs; books 3–6, virtuous conduct (fortitude, moderation, humanity, etc.); books 7–8, a miscellaneous group including good fortune, military stratagems, famous law-suits, eloquence, and many other items; book 9, evil conduct. The examples on each topic are divided into 'Roman' and 'foreign'. The work shows little originality and the style is highly rhetorical, but it proved useful and was very popular in the Middle Ages; two epitomes were made of it, perhaps in the fourth or fifth centuries.

Vandals, a Germanic people who left their original homes in Scandinavia and settled on the south coast of the Baltic Sea, then gradually moved further south until they became the western neighbours of the *Visigoths. They attacked the Roman provinces in the third and fourth centuries AD. On 31 December 406 they crossed the Rhine near Mogontiacum (Mainz), moved on to devastate Gaul, and in 409 invaded Spain. Here too they caused great destruction, but subsequently made apparently permanent settlements. However, in 429 most of them crossed over into Africa under Gaiseric (see AUGUSTINE and CARTHAGE), who built a fleet and controlled the western Mediterranean; in 455 he captured Rome and carried off many works of art. The last Vandal king Gelimer was defeated by a Roman army under *Belisarius in 533 and subsequently captured and taken to Constantinople.

Vaphī'o cups, two very fine gold cups found in a *Mycenaean tholos-tomb at Vaphio southeast of Sparta. The style and craftsmanship strongly suggest that they were made in Minoan Crete, although the tomb is of a period (LH II, 1500–1400 BC) when the Mycenaeans, under Minoan influence, were producing comparable work themselves, and it is conceivable that the cups were made in Greece. They show in repoussé work scenes connected with bull-hunting and bull-leaping (one scene shows a bull charging two athletes). See also TOREUTIC ART.

Va'rius Rufus, Lucius, Roman poet, friend of Virgil and Horace, who both admired his poetry, and regarded as a leading epic poet in his day. He was the author of a tragedy on the story of *Thyestes, performed in 29 BC at the games in celebration of Octavian's victory at Actium, which earned him a million sesterces from the victor, and which Quintilian thought the equal of any Greek tragedy. He also wrote epics on Julius Caesar and the wars of Augustus. None of his works has survived. After Virgil's death Varius and Plotius Tucca edited the *Aeneid*, upon instructions from Augustus.

Varro. 1. Marcus Tere'ntius Varro (116–27 BC), called 'Reātīnus' because he was born at Reātē in Sabine territory, 'the most learned of Romans' according to Quintilian. He was opposed to Julius Caesar in politics and was a Pompeian officer in Spain at the time of the civil war, but was reconciled to Caesar and was to have been the head of the public library whose creation Caesar was contemplating in 47. In 43 he was proscribed by Mark Antony, but escaped with the loss of some property and books. He was a poet, satirist, antiquarian, jurist, geographer, grammarian, and scientist, and wrote on education and philosophy also. His enormous literary output ran to more than 600 volumes. Of these only his *De re rustica ('on farming') survives complete; we also have six books out of the twenty-five of his De lingua Latina ('on the Latin language'), and some 600 fragments of his Saturae Menippeae ('Menippean satires'). He died pen in hand.

De lingua Latina is a systematic treatise on Latin grammar, dealing successively with etymology, inflexion, and syntax, a pioneer work showing occasional penetration, amid many absurd derivations. Books 5–10, which we possess, are dedicated to Cicero.

The Saturae Menippeae were satires on the model of *Menippus, in a mixture of prose and verse, some of them in dialogue or semi-dramatic form. They were critical sketches of Roman life with a wide range of characters and scenes including some from myth; the language is vigorous, earthy, and inventive. Many of the sketches were directed, with humour and nostalgia for the decencies of the previous century, against the greed, luxury, and sophisticated pretensions of Varro's day, as exemplified by the contemporary Greek schools of philosophy, for example.

His Hebdomadĕs ('sevens'), or Imaginēs ('portraits'), in fifteen books, now lost, was a collection of character sketches in prose of celebrated Greeks and Romans, accompanied by coloured portraits of the subjects, to each of which an epigram was appended. Much of our knowledge about the lives of eminent Romans derives ultimately from Varro.

Among his other more important works were (i) the antiquarian treatise Antiquitatēs rerum humanarum et divinarum ('human and divine antiquities'), a historical encyclopaedia, of which roughly speaking the first part dealt with the history of Rome and the second part with Roman religion (the arrangement of facts followed a simple pattern of people, places, dates, and events); (ii) De gente populi Romani ('on the Roman nation'), concerning the prehistory and early chronology of Rome; (iii) De vita populi Romani ('on the way of life of the Roman people'), concerning the history and style of Roman society; (iv) Disciplinae ('studies'), on the liberal arts (grammar, dialectic, rhetoric, geometry, arithmetic, astronomy, music, medicine, and architecture), all except the last two forming the medieval trivium and quadrivium, and subsequently utilized by *Martianus Capella; and (v) a treatise on philosophy, De philosophia. Many fragments survive of the Res divinae ('on religion') preserved by St

Augustine when he attacked it in the City of God. Varro was highly praised by Cicero (who dedicated to him the second edition of his Academica) and by Quintilian. He was influenced by the Platonism of Antiochus of Ascalon (see ACADEMY), as well as by Stoic and Pythagorean ideas, yet he insisted that an ancient city should adhere to its traditional religion, and accepted that the greatness of Rome had depended in part on its religious observances: at the least, religion, even if untrue, was useful.

2. Publius Terentius Varro, 'Atacīnus' (i.e. from the valley of the river Atax in Narbonese Gaul), Latin poet, b. 82 BC. Nothing is known of his life, and his work survives only in fragments. He wrote an epic poem on Julius Caesar's exploits in Gaul in 58 BC called Bellum Sequanicum ('war against the Sequani'). He also wrote a geographical poem called Chōrographia and a free translation of the Argonautica of the Greek poet *Apollonius Rhodius.

Vārus. 1. The cognomen of a friend of Horace, given the name Quintilius in some manuscripts. He may be P. Alfenus Varus, a jurist and patron of literature, to whom Catullus may also have written a poem.

2. Quinti'lius Varus, Roman general who in AD 9 was entrusted with the settlement of Germany. He and his three legions were lured by the German chief Arminius (whence 'Hermann'), whom he had trusted, into the Teutoburgian forest and ambushed. The legions were annihilated and Varus committed suicide. The scene of the disaster was afterwards visited by *Germanicus with a Roman army. The numbers of the lost legions were never used again, and Roman expansion in north Germany was ended for ever.

vase-painting, Greek. The art of decorative *pottery was highly developed in *Crete under the ancient civilization of that island in the second millennium BC. It reached its summit there in the Middle Minoan period (very roughly, the second millennium down to c.1600), with designs drawn in a graceful and natural style from flowers, shells, and fish (especially cuttlefish), usually in white, red, orange, and black, the pottery often being of extreme thinness. The industry declined in the Late Minoan period after the destructions of the early fifteenth century and, although artistic work continued to be produced, inspiration had somehow failed.

By this time *Mycenaean craftsmen in mainland Greece under Minoan influence were producing very similar vases themselves and exporting them to Crete. In the period 1600 to c.1450 Mycenaean design was strongly influenced by the naturalistic painting on Minoan vases; it was the period of the 'palace style' vases, so called in modern times from large but elegant storage-jars, decorated in a florid style, which imitated those found in excavations at the palace at Cnossus. Another style of Mycenaean vase at this time is the Ephyrean (first found in the region of 'Ephyra', i.e. Corinth), which has a stylized flower painted on both sides of the vase, a familiar Minoan motif. After this, vase-painting in mainland Greece became increasingly formal and abstract, although fine pieces continued to be produced until the end of the Mycenaean age (compare the *Vaphio cups).

The Proto-geometric style of mainland Greece was a continuation in style and technique of the pottery of the Late Bronze Age, though standards at first declined after the collapse of the Mycenaean civilization. Proto-geometric emerged as a revival at the beginning of the Iron Age, c.1050 BC, at Athens, and lasted there until c.900. (In the rest of Greece it began and ended later.) In this pottery the exposed surfaces of the clay are light to medium brown, sometimes covered in a yellowish wash; the decoration, consisting of simple geometric shapes or concentric circles, is painted on in dark brown or black.

The Geometric style appeared at Athens c.900 BC and lasted for roughly two centuries. The amount of ornamentation increased and, among new ornaments, the rectilinear meander ('key-pattern') was introduced, becoming the characteristic motif. By the mid-eighth century at Athens the bands of geometric pattern were interspersed with silhouette figures of men and horses, later other animals, deer and goats, in stylized poses. Figures first appear to great effect on the vases of the Dipylon painter, who was working c.750 BC at Athens and is so called from his best-known vase, found at the Dipylon Gate. In the cemetery nearby from the tenth century onwards graves were marked by a stone pillar and a libation vessel; during the eighth century very tall vases were made for the purpose.

The Orientalizing period, which derived its name from the adoption of motifs from eastern art, began soon after 725 BC at Corinth. Geometric did not die out at once, but retained vitality in various parts of Greece for some years. The new patterns were imitations of decorative motifs from north Syria and Phoenicia and designs created under their influence. New curving shapes appear, reminiscent of plant forms, rosettes, palmettes, lotus flowers, and of animals, lions, bulls, boars, goats, deer. Fabulous beasts appear too, sphinxes, griffins, chimaeras. A new 'black-figure' technique of drawing was also used: the larger figures hitherto depicted in partial outline came to be painted in black silhouette with incised linear details, the pale clay showing through the black. Touches of red or white paint were added as required, and all paint was applied before the vase was fired. Orientalizing motifs were most popular in the seventh century; by the mid-sixth century animals were less common, and by the classical period rare. Plant motifs, on the other hand, debased, revived, and transmuted, became a regular feature.

The Orientalizing style flourished for about a century until a new style began to make itself felt in about 625 BC, the start of the Archaic age. At Corinth, where the Orientalizing vases are known as proto-Corinthian, from about 700 BC the black-figure technique (see above) had been employed; while at Athens the figures were painted both in outline and in silhouette, but for most of the seventh century are very rarely found with incised detail. By c.625, when the proto-Corinthian style evolved into 'Ripe Corinthian', Athenian artists also were beginning to use the Corinthian technique for all their figures, and by the end of the century for the surrounding ornament as well. Corinth felt the effect of growing Athenian competition, based on the excellence of Athenian clay, and soon after 550 Corinthian vase-painting suffered a sharp decline while vase-painting at Athens showed rapid development. A notable Athenian vase of the early sixth century is the François vase (c.570 BC), named after its finder; it is a large wine bowl of a new shape, signed by its potter Ergotīmus and its painter Cleitias, whose masterpiece it is. It has five zones containing in all 270 human and animal figures, most delicately painted (and labelled). All but one of the zones are devoted to scenes from myth. No other surviving vase of this period is as rich or as fully lettered. Notable black-figure painting was produced on the Panathenaic vases from the late 560s onwards and retained, for reasons of tradition, long after black-figure painting was abandoned elsewhere. These vases were large amphoras (see below) full of olive oil, presented to victors in the games at the Greater Panathenaic festival at Athens. They had a painting of an armed Athena on one side, and on the other a representation of the event for which the prize was won. They were still being given as prizes in the third and second centuries BC. Among the famous black-figure vase-painters were the Nessus Painter, Amasis Painter, Cleitias, Exekias, Lydus, Sophilus, Antimerēs Painter, and the Leagrus Group. (Many Greek vase-painters, identifiable from their style, remain anonymous. They are often referred to by the subject or location of their most famous vase.)

During the sixth century depiction of the anatomy and poses of the human figure was improved, but c.530 BC the technique of red-figure vase painting was invented and made possible great advances in figure drawing. Black-figure painting was still flourishing, however, and remained popular until c.500, after which it declined in quality (except on the Panathenaic vases). Red-figure painting was an Athenian invention and virtually all figure-decorated vases of the fifth and fourth centuries BC are Athenian (except for the Athens-inspired

South Italian schools which started in the mid-fifth century). It is the reverse of the black-figure technique: figures and patterns are left unglazed on the clay (hence 'red'), with linear detail painted on them in black and brown, and the background painted in black. Later there were vases of great beauty painted with a white ground, specially intended for religious and funeral ceremonies. Mythical scenes were still represented, but the most interesting vases are those depicting scenes of everyday life. Iconographic conventions that had grown up in the black-figure period were now broken or expanded, and scenes of life were diversified with much realistic detail, especially of dress. Architecture, on the other hand, receives very summary treatment, a token column usually sufficing for most buildings. The great artists of this period include Euphronius, Euthymidēs, the Cleophradēs Painter, the Berlin Painter, Dūris, the Brygos Painter, and the Pan Painter. In the middle of the fourth century BC red-figure vase-painting enjoyed a last flowering, but thereafter the industry declined and finally ceased in about 100 BC. Interest in vases was not revived in the Renaissance, and it was not until the eighteenth century and as a result of the keen interest of Sir William Hamilton, the British envoy at Naples, that the art form came to be studied. See also PORTLAND VASE.

vases, Greek. The word 'vase' covers a great variety of shapes and sizes of pottery vessels designed, since all Greek vases are functional, for many purposes. The commonest kinds include the amphora (Gk. *amphoreus*, 'carried on both sides'), a jar for storing oil or wine, having a narrow neck and two upright handles, and sometimes a pointed base so that it had to be supported in a stand; the *hydria* or water-jar, having globular body and cylindrical neck, with two horizontal handles for lifting and one upright for pouring; and the *crater* or open mixing-bowl for wine (see François vase above) with a pair of high handles at the rim. The *cylix* is a cup, of any form, but usually in a shallow bowl shape on a foot, with a pair of horizontal handles; the *pyxis* is a lidded box, rather like a modern powder-box; the *lecythos* is a small, elongated oil-flask having a narrow chimney neck with an upright handle; the *aryballos* was also intended for oil, and is spherical, with a flat base but no foot, narrow neck, and disc lip; the *oenochŏē* is a pouring vase, with a fairly bulbous body, narrower neck and high handle, like a modern jug, but with a wide rim rather than a spout. See also VASE-PAINTING, GREEK.

Vatican, at Rome in classical times, an outlying district on the west bank of the river Tiber on the Vatican hill, north-west of the ancient city. (The hill was not one of the seven hills of Rome.) The region was noted for its unhealthy air, unproductive soil, and bad wine.

Its only claim to fame in republican times was that here *Cincinnatus was cultivating his four acres when he was summoned to be dictator. Its only building of note was the Mausoleum of the emperor Hadrian, now the Castello di S. Angelo. Here was the infamous Circus of Nero, where Christians were enveloped in pitch and burnt to serve as torches for the midnight games, and where the martyrdom of St Peter took place.

Vati'nius, Publius, tribune 59 BC. In 56 Cicero, defending Sestius, delivered an invective against Vatinius, but successfully defended him in 54 (see CICERO (1) 4). He was consul in 46. One of his letters to Cicero (*Ad familiares* 5. 10) survives. He is mentioned by Catullus as the enemy of his friend *Calvus.

vau, see DIGAMMA.

Vē'diovis (Vēiovis, Vendius), in Roman religion, an ancient deity about whom little is known; he was taken by the Romans to be 'the opposite of Jupiter', i.e. harmful. His festival was on 21 May.

Vē'dius Po'llio, see SLAVERY 2.

Vege'tius (Flāvius Vegetius Renātus), military writer under the emperor Theodosius (AD 379–95). His *Epitoma rei militaris* ('military epitome') is a compilation of material from many periods but aims to describe and advocate the training and organization of the classic Roman legion.

Veii, see ROME 4.

Vēlā'brum, at Rome, the low ground between the Palatine and the Capitoline hills, a densely populated and squalid part of the city. Through it ran the Vīcus Tuscus, connecting the Forum Romanum with the Forum Boarium.

Vellē'ius Pate'rculus, Gaius (*c.*19 BC–after AD 30), Roman historian. He served for several years with the army in Germany, was quaestor in AD 7 and praetor in AD 15. He was the author of a compendium of Roman history from earliest times to AD 29 in two books, the first of which (down to 146 BC) is incomplete. The history shows partiality for the imperial house of the Caesars and enthusiasm reaching adulation for Tiberius. The work is not profound (he admits that he wrote hurriedly), but his interest is in individuals and the work is especially valuable for its biographical sketches, e.g. that of Tiberius (which is in strong contrast with the picture given by Tacitus) and on a small scale those of Caesar, Pompey, and Maecenas. The history is notable also for its chapters on the evolution of Latin literature. He discusses the reasons for its decline and suggests that the perfection reached in the Augustan age had driven later writers in despair to seek minor fields. The style of the history is artificial and rhetorical, but some of his epigrams are acute.

vellum, a fine kind of parchment made from the skins of calves. See TEXTS, TRANSMISSION OF ANCIENT 3.

venatiō'nēs ('huntings'), at Rome, fights of men against animals or animals against animals, introduced in 186 BC as entertainment, and frequently occurring in the first century BC as part of the various public games (see LUDI I). *Elephants are said to have first fought in the Circus in 99 BC. Sulla in 93 BC exhibited a hundred lions. The *venationes* displayed by Pompey in 55 BC lasted for five days and there was an immense slaughter of animals, which not only Cicero but even the general public regarded with distaste, moved to pity by the elephants. 'There was even an impulse of compassion, a feeling that the beasts had something human about them' (Cicero, *Ad familiares* 7. 1). Roman spectators seem to have become more bloodthirsty under the empire. 3,500 elephants were killed in the Circus in the reign of Augustus, and at the opening of the Colosseum under Titus, 5,000 wild and 4,000 tame animals. The men who fought with the animals, *bestiarii*, were condemned criminals or prisoners of war, or trained individuals who did it for money. How long these spectacles continued is uncertain, but they were taking place after the abolition of gladiatorial shows, and still existed at Constantinople as late as the sixth century AD.

Ve'neti, see ITALY.

Vēnus, originally an Italian goddess of whom virtually nothing is known; her name means 'charm', 'beauty', and she seems to have presided over the fertility of vegetable gardens. In Rome at an early date she became identified with and acquired the mythology of the Greek goddess *Aphroditē, the goddess of love, through the cult of Aphrodite on Mount Eryx in Sicily which, according to tradition, had been founded by Aeneas after the death of his father Anchisēs. Venus of Eryx (Venus Erycina) had a temple on the Capitoline hill in Rome dedicated in 217 BC at a dire moment in the Second Punic War, and another outside the Colline Gate. Aeneas was the son of Aphrodite/Venus; the story of his wanderings and final settlement in Italy was particularly important to the Julian family (of which Julius Caesar and the emperors down to and including Nero were members) because it was claimed that they were descended from Aeneas' son Iulus (Ascanius) and so from Venus. Julius Caesar, in gratitude to her for his success at the battle of Pharsalus, dedicated a temple to Venus Genetrix, 'universal mother', in 46 BC in the Forum Iulium. It is this aspect of Venus that *Lucretius extols at the beginning of his poem, *De rerum natura*, and that is celebrated

in the *Pervigilium Veneris written for the spring festival. Venus was also thought of as concerned in the origin of the Roman people as the consort of *Mars. 'Venus' was the name given to the highest throw at dice.

Venus de Milo, statue of the Greek goddess Aphroditē from the Aegean island of Melos, now in the Louvre in Paris. It was found in 1820 with other marbles intended for a lime-kiln. The sculptor's name is half obliterated; the ending ...andros suggests Agesandros or Alexandros, son of Menidēs, of Antioch on the river Meander, of the mid-second century BC. It is a modification of an earlier type of statue which is also exemplified in a Roman version, known as the Venus of Capua, now in the museum at Naples. Aphrodite is naked to the waist; it has been thought that, like the Capua Venus, she is looking at her reflection in the shield of Arēs which she holds.

Venu'sia (Venosa), town on the river Aufidus in Apulia, south Italy, near the border of Lucania, famed as the birthplace of Horace.

Vēra histo'ria, see LUCIAN.

Vercinge'torix, king of the Gallic tribe of the Arverni who in 52 BC raised a revolt in Gaul against Rome and was eventually defeated by Julius Caesar. See *COMMENTARIES* I (book 7). He surrendered and was brought to Rome for Caesar's triumph in 46 BC before being put to death (see TULLIANUM).

Vergil, see VIRGIL.

Verginia, see VIRGINIA.

Verrēs, Gaius, Roman propraetor in Sicily 73–71 BC. He plundered the province for his personal enrichment, in a way that was typical of many Roman governors of the time but perhaps more thoroughgoing than most (see PROVINCES, ROMAN). He must have expected to survive a prosecution in the *repetundae (extortion) courts, with the help of bribery, powerful allies, and Q. *Hortensius to defend him, but he was defeated by the oratorical and legal genius of *Cicero (see (1) 1) whose *Verrine Orations* have made Verres' crimes notorious. He retired to Massilia and kept much of his plundered treasures. These later attracted the greed of Mark Antony, and Verres was proscribed and murdered in 43.

Ve'rrius Flaccus, a freedman of the time of the emperor Augustus (d. AD 14), the most learned scholar of his age and tutor to the grandsons of Augustus. We hear that he gave fine ancient books as prizes to his pupils. He wrote various works on antiquities but is best known for his (lost) *De significatu verborum* ('on the meaning of words'), in which he quoted from early republican authors. We have a portion of an abridgement surviving in the lexicon compiled by Sextus Pompeius Festus in the second century AD, and the gaps in Festus' text may be supplemented from an epitome of the latter by Paulus Diaconus in the eighth century. Verrius was also interested in the calendar and erected in Praenestē, his native town, an annotated stone calendar, of which a copy survives in a damaged condition.

ver sacrum ('sacred spring'), in ancient Italy (and apparently in some parts of Greece also), at a time of great emergency, the dedication to a god, often Jupiter, of all that was born in the spring. The animals were sacrificed, and the children born then (*sacrani*), when aged 20, were expelled from the country to go where they pleased and found a new community. The ceremony (without the expulsions) was revived at Rome during the Second Punic War in 217 BC, together with many other religious acts in that desperate year (see e.g. VENUS, LECTISTER-NIUM, PUNIC WARS). The progeny of the pigs, sheep, goats, and oxen in the ensuing spring was dedicated to Jupiter (Livy 22. 10).

verse. As well as having the obvious meaning of poetry in general, 'verse' in the context of Latin and Greek poetry usually means 'metrical line', rarely 'stanza'.

Vertu'mnus, see VORTUMNUS.

Vespae, see WASPS.

Vespā'sian (Titus Flavius Sabinus Vespasianus) (AD 9–79), Roman emperor 69–79, the first of the Flavians. For the events leading to his accession in 69, the 'year of the four emperors', see ROME 11. He was a successful soldier, responsible for the pacification of southern Britain in the invasion of AD 43. He was also a sound and just ruler, though firm (see HELVIDIUS PRISCUS), remarkable for the simplicity of his life and the economy and efficiency of his administration. Among his public works at Rome were the *Colosseum (completed by his son and heir Titus), the reconstruction of the temple of Jupiter Capitolinus, and a temple to Peace (after his victory over Jerusalem), thought by the Elder Pliny to be one of the most beautiful buildings in the world. It was adorned with works of art from the emperor Nero's palace as well as with spoils from the temple at Jerusalem, including the great golden candlestick.

Vespi'llo, Lucrē'tius, see WOMEN, POSITION OF 2.

Vesta, in Roman religion, the ancient Roman goddess of the hearth, the etymological and religious equivalent of the Greek goddess Hestia (but unaffected by Greek influence). She was worshipped at the hearth in every Roman household, and since the state cult was based on family cult (see RELIGION, ROMAN 1) the sacred fire on the symbolic hearth of the state was kept

burning, in a small round temple in the Forum. This fire was rekindled every year on 1 March (the ancient New Year's Day; see CALENDARS), by rubbing two sticks together, and was looked after for the rest of the year by the *Vestal Virgins. The round temple of Vesta was thought to have represented the original round house and hearth of the king of Rome in ancient times, and the Vestals his daughters. In the temple was the storehouse, *penus,* of the state (see PENATES), where sacred objects were kept including the *Palladium, and generally only the Vestals and the *pontifex maximus* were allowed to enter. On 9 June each year for the festival of Vesta, the Vestālia, it was opened to married women, who walked barefoot to it in procession, bringing simple food-offerings. This festival was also regarded as the bakers' holiday; asses were freed from the treadmill and decked with garlands and little cakes. From 9 to 15 June the temple stood open, a time of ill-omen while the building was cleaned. 15 June was marked in the calendar Q(uando) St(ercus) D(elatum) F(as), which meant that it was a normal working day 'when the dirt has been lawfully cleaned away'.

Vestal Virgins, in Roman religion, virgins who were considered to represent the daughters of the early Roman kings and whose duty it was to watch in turn, by day and night, the fire in the temple of *Vesta on the state hearth. They also made the salt cake (*mola salsa*) for various festivals and had custody of a number of sacred objects including the *Palladium and the ashes for the Parilia (see PALES). The Vestals, said to have been instituted by the king Numa, and originally drawn from patrician families, were four (later six) in number, chosen by the *pontifex maximus* from suitable girls aged between 6 and 10. Their period of service was for thirty years, but generally the Vestals continued to serve the goddess for the rest of their lives. They lived in a house near the Forum known as the Atrium Vestae ('hall of Vesta') and were maintained at public expense. They were under the control of the *pontifex maximus* and could be scourged for offences such as letting the fire out. Their purity was all-important: any Vestal found guilty of unchastity was entombed alive. A letter of the Younger Pliny (4. 11) describes such an event under the emperor Domitian. Vestals were held in high repute, and great weight was attached to their intervention on behalf of those in trouble. They wore a linen dress of old-fashioned style.

veto, see TRIBUNES OF THE PLEBS.

Via A'ppia, the Appian Way; see ROADS.

Via Sacra, the Sacred Way, the street connecting the Forum with Velia (a narrow ridge joining the Palatine and Oppian hills). Its name is derived from the sacred buildings, including the temple of Vesta and the Regia, which it passed. There Horace famously encountered his Bore (*Satires* 1. 9).

Vidula'ria ('wallet'), title of a play by *Plautus surviving in a *palimpsest of which only fragments are legible. The plot appears to have resembled that of the *Rudens*.

vi'gilēs, at Rome, the fire-brigade, instituted by the emperor Augustus after the fire of 23 BC. After another fire in AD 6 he created a corps of 7,000 freedmen under the command of a *praefectus vigilum* appointed by the emperor.

vigintise'xvirate ('the office of the twenty-six'), at Rome, a company of lesser magistrates who manned boards known by the number of magistrates involved (*duoviri, tresviri*, 'board of two', 'board of three', etc.) for the performance of various duties. They included the *decemviri stlitibus iudicandis*; *tresviri capitales*, assistants to the magistrates in criminal cases; *tresviri monē-tāles*, in charge of the mint (see MONEY AND COINS); *quattuorviri* ('board of four') *viis purgandis*, in charge of street-cleaning in Rome; likewise *duoviri* for the care of roads outside the city; and the four *praefecti Capuam Cumas* who administered justice on behalf of the *praetor urbanus* in Capua, Cumae, and other Campanian towns. These last two boards, comprising six officers, were suppressed by the emperor Augustus, leaving twenty officers, the vigintivirate. As the *quaestors under the empire were also twenty in number it was usual for men elected to this board to pass on to the quaestorship.

villa, Latin term covering (i) the *villa rustica* or farmstead of courtyard style attached to an estate, containing, besides the actual farm buildings, quarters for the use of the owner of the estate when he visited it; (ii) a later development of the second century BC, the large country house of a wealthy Roman which served as a retreat from city life. We hear of Scipio Africanus occupying a modest villa of this kind at the end of his life; Cicero and his brother each owned several, and villas became very numerous and luxurious under the empire. A particularly magnificent specimen was the villa of the emperor Hadrian at Tībur, the vast ruins of which may still be seen. For Roman villas in Britain see BRITAIN 8.

Villano'vans, see ITALY.

Vīnā'lia, two festivals held at Rome in connection with wine-production, the *Vinalia priora* ('first V.') on 23 April and the *Vinalia rustica* ('country V.') on 19–20 August. At the first the wine casks which had been filled the preceding autumn were opened, the first draught being offered as a libation, called *calpar*, to Jupiter. It supposedly had its origins in Aeneas' vowing the vintage to Jupiter if he won the war against Turnus. The second festival inaugurated the grape harvest. Lambs were sacrificed to Jupiter, and the *flamen dialis* broke off the first grapes.

Vi'rbius, see DIANA.

Virgil (Publius Vergilius Maro) (70–19 BC), Roman poet, born at Andēs near Mantua (Mantova) in Cisalpine Gaul on 15 October in the year of Pompey's first consulship. He was thus of Gallic origin, and a little older than the poet Horace and the emperor Augustus. According to ancient sources which may not be altogether reliable his father was quite rich but of humble origins, his mother perhaps well-connected. He was educated at Cremona and Mediolānum (Milan), and later studied philosophy and rhetoric at Rome; at some time he was a pupil of the Epicurean philosopher Sīro at Naples. His family estate suffered loss, it was said, in the confiscations of land for the army veterans of Antony and *Octavian which followed the battle of Philippi in 42 BC, but he was on friendly terms with the commissioners for the redistribution of the confiscated lands (*Gallus, *Varus, and *Pollio), and may have been given a property near Naples in recompense. It was around 42 BC when he began the composition of the *Eclogues*. Pollio was the first to recognize Virgil's talents, but with the publication of the *Eclogues* (perhaps finally in 37) Virgil moved from the circle of Pollio to the patronage of *Maecenas (to whom he introduced Horace) and Octavian. At this time he lived chiefly in Campania, at Naples and Nola. In 37 Horace records their journey together to Brundisium (*Satires* 1. 5). He spent the following seven years in the composition of the *Georgics*, published in 29 BC, and immediately afterwards began on the *Aeneid*, which was to occupy him for the remaining ten years of his life. In his last year he undertook a voyage to the East to visit some of the places he had described; he fell ill at Megara in Greece and returned to Italy, but died on 20 September 19 BC at Brundisium. His body was brought to Naples and buried outside the city, where his tomb was soon honoured as a shrine. He is said to have dictated the inscription for it on his death-bed:

> *Mantua me genuit, Calabri rapuere, tenet nunc Parthenope: cecini pascua, rura, duces.*

> 'Mantua brought me life, Calabria death; now Naples holds me: I sang of flocks and farms and heroes.' (For the name Parthenopē see SIRENS.)

The *Aeneid* was incomplete at the author's death, and Virgil is said to have made Varius promise to burn it if he died before his return, but on the orders of Augustus it was published after the literary executors Varius and Tucca had 'lightly corrected' it.

The *Eclogues, Georgics*, and *Aeneid* are described under those titles. A number of minor poems attributed to the poet are collected in the *Appendix Virgiliana*.

Virgil is described by *Donatus as tall and

dark, with the appearance of a countryman. His health was weak, he was shy and led a retired life, rarely appearing in Rome. Although he became famous during his lifetime, he was diffident of his own poetic powers. His fame was based primarily on his position as the epic poet who revealed the greatness of the Roman empire, but his poetic eminence rests also on the technical perfection of his verse and its sustained beauty and melodiousness, and on the poet's tenderness and melancholy, and his love of nature. He is the poet not only of the destiny of Rome but of the beauty and fertility of Italy, its morality and its religion.

Virgil's fame grew after his death into superstitious reverence. In the first century AD his birthday was celebrated and his works and tomb were almost the object of cult by *Silius Italicus. He came to be regarded as a magician and miraculous powers were attributed to him. The *sortes Virgilianae*, 'Virgilian lots', attempts to foretell the future by opening his books and picking a line at random, were widely practised from an early date (reputedly as early as the emperor Hadrian). Memoirs of King Charles I relate that when the king was in the Bodleian Library at Oxford during the Civil War he sought his future by this method and hit upon Dido's curse against Aeneas (*Aeneid* 4. 615), *At bello audacis populi vexatus et armis . . .*, 'harassed by war and the hostility of a bold nation . . .' Virgil's works soon became one of the most widely used of school books and the subject of commentaries and learned discussion by Donatus, *Servius, *Macrobius, and others. Early Christian writers often reveal a conflict in their minds between admiration for his poetry and distrust of his paganism (see JEROME). The number and high quality of the manuscripts surviving from the third to the fifth centuries AD attest the high estimation in which he was then held. His ideas were made acceptable to Christians by allegory (book 2 signifying the trauma of birth, book 6 the acquisition of enlightenment, for example), this kind of interpretation persisting even in the thirteenth century in Dante (although not in the *Divine Comedy*). The widespread feeling that only mischance prevented Virgil from dying a Christian is expressed in the legend that the apostle Paul wept over his tomb at Naples, described by an anonymous poet at Paris in the twelfth or thirteenth century:

> '*quem te', inquit, 'reddidissem*
> *si te vivum invenissem*
> *poetarum maxime.'*

'What would I have made of you, greatest of poets,' he said, 'had I found you alive!'

Dante regarded Virgil not only as *il nostro maggior poeta* ('our greatest poet'), but as a prophet of Christianity, who guided him to the Gates of Paradise but had himself to be excluded. Several translations preceded John Dryden's famous version of the whole of Virgil in 1697. Alfred Lord Tennyson in his lines 'To Virgil' (1882), for the nineteenth centenary of his death, paid a tribute to him as 'Wielder of the stateliest measure / Ever moulded by the lips of man'. In the twentieth century he is perhaps not so much thought of as the composer of melodious lines as the poet who understood that 'at the heart of things there are tears', *sunt lacrimae rerum (Aeneid* 1. 462).

Virgi'nia (Verginia), according to Roman tradition, daughter of L. Verginius, a centurion, around 450 BC when the *decemvirs had been appointed at Rome to publish a code of laws (see TWELVE TABLES). Appius Claudius, one of the decemvirs, intended to seduce her and in order to get her into his possession had one of his dependants claim her as a slave belonging to his own household; Appius Claudius himself pronounced judgement in the case, in favour of his dependant. Before Virginia could be taken away her father stabbed her to death, declaring that her death was better than her dishonour, and made his escape to the army camp. A rising followed in which the decemvirs were overthrown and more democratic procedures instituted (see ROME 3). The story is told by Livy (3. 44) and retold by Petrarch and by Chaucer in *The Physician's Tale*.

Visigoths, i.e. west *Goths, a Germanic tribe which in the late third century AD occupied Dacia, north of the Danube. They were driven across that river by the Huns in 376, and in 378 they killed the Roman emperor Valens at the great battle of Adrianople. After devastating Greece they invaded Italy in 401 under their leader *Alaric and again in 403, but were driven back. In 410, however, they sacked Rome itself; it was the first occasion the city had been entered by an enemy since the Gallic invasion of 390 BC. Later they moved to Gaul and Spain. In the sixth century most of those in Gaul were driven out and retreated to Spain. There the Visigothic kingdom survived until it was overrun by the Arabs in 711. In the fourth century the Visigoths were converted to Arian Christianity, and became Catholics in the late sixth century. See FALL OF ROME.

Vision, The, see LUCIAN.

Vita'rum au'ctio, see LUCIAN.

Vite'llius, Aulus, Roman emperor. Proclaimed by his troops in Germany, he became emperor after the defeat and death of Otho in April 69, the 'year of the four emperors' (see ROME 11). He was notorious for his gluttony. In December his forces were defeated by those of Vespasian, who captured Rome and killed Vitellius.

Vitru'vius Po'llio, Roman engineer and architect of the first century BC, who saw military service under Julius Caesar and Octavian. He wrote a treatise in ten books, *De architectura* ('on architecture'), compiled partly from his own experience and partly from similar works by earlier architects, mostly Greek. He was interested in preserving what he regarded as the classical tradition of design, but his work was based largely on Hellenistic Greek practice. It is the only treatise of its kind to have survived, and was an important influence on the principles of building adopted during the Italian Renaissance, when architects regarded Vitruvius as the supreme architectural authority. Bramante, Michelangelo, and Palladio all studied him in order to put his precepts into practice. The term 'Vitruvian man' refers to his theory of human proportion, in which the human figure is shown to fit into a square circumscribed by a circle (illustrated by Leonardo da Vinci).

In his treatise book 1 deals with town planning, architecture in general, and the qualifications necessary for an architect; 2, building materials; 3 and 4, temples and the 'orders' of *architecture (see 1); 5, theatres (and their acoustics), baths, and other public buildings; 6, domestic architecture; 7, interior decoration, *mosaic pavements, decorative plaster-work, and the use of colouring; 8, water supplies; 9 includes geometry, astronomy, mensuration, etc., with interesting remarks about water-clocks; 10, machines, civil and military. The work is illustrated with diagrams.

Volcā'tius Gallicā'nus, see HISTORIA AUGUSTA.

Volsci, tribe of central Italy, who spoke an Italic dialect resembling Umbrian. By 500 BC they had moved to an area south-east of Rome; three important Volscian towns were Arpinum (birthplace of Cicero), Antium, and Tarracina (Volscian name, Anxur). They were a threat to the independence of Rome, which Rome met by making alliances with the Latins. The exploits of *Coriolanus relate to this time. By the end of the fourth century BC the Volscians were subject to Rome and they rapidly became Romanized.

Voltu'rnus, see TIBERINUS.

Volu'mnia, wife of *Coriolanus.

Vopi'scus, Flavius, see HISTORIA AUGUSTA.

Vortu'mnus (or Vertumnus), Roman god of orchards and fruit, who presided over the changes of the year. He was regarded as the husband of *Pomona, whom he wooed in a succession of various forms, reaper, ploughman, pruner, etc. His name, connected with *vertere*, 'to turn', was explained variously, as of the god who changes his shape, or who presides over the 'turn' of the year (autumn), or who once turned back a flood of the Tiber.

Voyage to the Lower World, see LUCIAN.

Vulcan (Volcānus), early Roman deity, the god of fire, perhaps a god of the smithy, later identified with the Greek god *Hephaestus. His festival of 23 May coincided with the *Tubilustria, and there was another festival in his honour on 23 August. He was the patron deity of Ostia, where he had an important cult.

Vulgate (Lat. *editio* or *lectio vulgāta*, 'the common text').

1. In textual criticism, the version of an author's text in general circulation (not necessarily the most accurate or authentic; see TEXTS, TRANSMISSION OF ANCIENT 4).

2. The Latin version of the Bible most widely used in the West, largely the work of St *Jerome. Its various books came to be collected into a single Bible (probably in the sixth century), with the following constituent parts: Jerome's translation from the Hebrew of the Old Testament, except for the Psalms (see SEPTUAGINT); the Psalms, translated by Jerome earlier from the text of *Origen (the 'Gallican Psalter'); Jerome's translation of Tobit and Judith, and the rest of the Apocrypha in the Old Latin (unrevised) version; Jerome's revision of the Gospels, for which he used a Greek text; and a revised text of Acts, Epistles, and Revelation, not by Jerome. *Cassiodorus writing in the sixth century is the first to refer unambiguously to a collection of biblical books within one cover. The oldest extant manuscript of the Vulgate is the Codex Amiatinus written at Wearmouth or Jarrow between c.690 and 700.

W

Wall of A'ntonine (Antoninus Pius), **Wall of Hadrian**, see BRITAIN 5.

Wasps (*Sphēkĕs*, Lat. *Vespae*), comedy by *Aristophanes, produced in 422 BC at the *Lenaea, where it won second prize.

The play is a satire on the system of the jury courts at Athens (see LAW, AT ATHENS 2) which at that time provided, through payment of 3 obols for a day's jury service, an important means of support for a sizeable number of poor and elderly men who were Athenian citizens. Philocleon ('love-*Cleon') is consumed by a passion for serving on juries. His son Bdelycleon ('loathe-Cleon') has tried to cure him and has finally imprisoned him in his house. Philocleon's friends, the chorus of old jurymen, dressed as wasps to show their readiness to inflict punishment, come along before dawn to take him with them to the courts, and try to effect his escape. There is a scuffle, and Bdelycleon eventually persuades the chorus to listen while he urges his father to change his ways. A debate follows between father and son, the father dwelling upon the pleasures and benefits of exercising power irresponsibly, the son demonstrating that the jurors' power is an illusion; they are really manipulated by the politicians, who divert the city's revenues for their own ends. The chorus are converted, but Philocleon is reluctant, and as consolation Bdelycleon arranges for him to play the juror at home, the first to be tried being Labēs, the house dog, who has stolen a cheese. Tricked by his son, Philocleon unintentionally acquits the prisoner, the first that he has ever let off. Bdelycleon now takes in hand his father's social life, polishing his manners for the more relaxed pleasures of a dinner party (see SYMPOSIUM). Philocleon takes to this with gusto and returns drunk and in high spirits with a kidnapped slave-girl, and followed by threatening tradespeople whom he has assaulted on the way home. Bdelycleon is dismayed, but the play ends in a riotous dance, *cordax*, led by Philocleon. Racine imitated the *Wasps* in *Les Plaideurs*.

Watling Street, see ROADS 2.

weeks, see CALENDARS and NUNDINAE.

weights and measures
1. *In Greece*
(i) *Units of weight.* In Greece, units of weight had the same names as units of *money (since these latter denote weights of metal) and were based on natural products and physical capacity; thus a talent represented the load carried by a man, and the silver obol was thought of as the weight of 12 barley corns. As in the case of money, the standards of weight varied from place to place and from time to time, but the internal relations remained the same, thus

6 obols	= 1 drachma
100 drachmas	= 1 mina
60 minas	= 1 talent

At Athens, which used the so-called Attic-Euboic standard, the mina weighed 431 g., almost a pound avoirdupois (1 lb. = 454 g.). Thus the talent weighed 25.86 kg. (about 57 lb. or half a hundredweight), the drachma 4.31 g. (about $\frac{1}{7}$ of an ounce), and the obol 0.72 g. Another common standard of weight was the stater (see MONEY), equal to 2 drachmas.

(ii) *Units of length.* These were based primarily on parts of the human body, with the foot as the fundamental unit. As with weights, the standards varied from place to place but the internal relations were always the same. Fractions of a foot and a few longer measures were reckoned in fingers (*daktyloi*) as follows:

2 fingers	= 1 *kondylos* (middle joint of finger)
4 "	= 1 *palastē* (palm)
12 "	= 1 *spithamē* (span)
16 "	= 1 *pous* (foot)
18 "	= 1 *pygmē* (short cubit, from elbow to knuckles)
20 "	= 1 *pygon* (short cubit, from elbow to first joint)
24 "	= 1 *pēchys* (cubit, elbow to fingertips)
27 "	= 1 'royal' cubit

Multiples of feet were:

$2\frac{1}{2}$ feet	= 1 *bēma* (pace)
6 "	= 1 *orguia* (a stretch of both arms, a fathom)
100 "	= 1 *plethron*

(An area 100 feet square, the Greek 'acre', representing the amount of land which could be ploughed in one day in Greece, was also known as a *plethron*.) The later Greek unit the *stadion* (*stade) is equivalent to 600 Greek feet; the parasang (*parasangēs*), consisting of 30 stades, was adopted from Persia. An Egyptian land measure, the *schoinos*, was equivalent to sixty stades, according to Herodotus.

The Greek foot as used in building measured 294–6 mm. and the Olympic foot (as used in the running track at Olympia) 320 mm. (the modern foot is 305 mm.). The stade may therefore be taken to be 192 m. (210 yards).

(iii) *Units of capacity or volume.* The principal dry measures, used chiefly for corn, were these:

4 *kotylai*	= 1 *choinix* (a day's ration)
48 *choinikĕs*	= 1 *medimnus*

but for liquids

12 *kotylai*	= 1 *chous* (pl. *choĕs*; compare CHOEPHOROE)

The *kotylē*, used for both dry and liquid measures, was typically about ¼ litre (rather less than a half-pint) and the *medimnus* would then be 48 litres (about 10½ imperial gallons, or 1⅓ bushels).

2. *At Rome*

(i) *Units of weight.* The Roman units of weight were based on the pound, *libra* (or *as*), their highest weight, equivalent to 327 g. (about ¾ lb). It was subdivided into 12 ounces (*unciae*, 'twelfth parts', each roughly equivalent to the ounce avoirdupois), and the ounce was subdivided down to the *scrīpulum* ('scruple'), its 24th part.

(ii) *Units of length.* The Roman foot, *pes* (pl. *pedēs*), was sometimes divided into 16 fingers (*digiti*), as in the Greek system but more usually into 12 inches (*unciae*, 'twelfth parts'). The other units were:

5 feet	= 1 *passus* (pace)
125 paces	= 1 *stadium* (stade)
1,000 paces	= *mille passus*, 1 (Roman) mile

The Roman foot measured 296 mm. (about ⅓ inch less than the modern) and the mile 1480 m. (about 140 yards less than the modern mile).

(iii) *Units of capacity or volume.* The principal dry measure, used for corn, was the *sextarius*, a little over half a litre; 16 *sextarii* were equal to one *modius*, roughly two imperial gallons (one peck or quarter of a bushel). Liquid capacity was based on the *amphora*, the volume of a cubic Roman foot, subdivided thus:

12 *heminae*	= 1 *congius*
8 *congii*	= 1 *amphora*

The *amphora* was equivalent to about 26 litres (almost 6 gallons) and the *hemina* to rather more than ⅓ litre, or almost a half-pint.

winds, wind gods. The winds were thought of as gods by both Greeks and Romans. In Homer the winds are sometimes under the control of *Aeolus, sometimes independent, invoked by men with prayer and sacrifice, or acting under the orders of Zeus. They had well-defined personalities, particularly (in Greece) Boreas, the North Wind, and Zephyrus, the West Wind. Hesiod speaks of three winds, Boreas, Zephyrus, and Notus (the South Wind), the children of Astraeus and Eos. Four, including the East Wind, Eurus, are found in Homer. The 'Tower of the Winds' at Athens (see HOROLOGION OF ANDRONICUS) depicts eight winds in human form; in compass order they are (in their Greek

forms) Boreas, Kaikias, Apēliōtēs, Euros, Notos, Lips, Zephyros, Skīrōn.

In Italy the West Wind, Favonius, was the favourite. The name of the North Wind, Aquilo ('eagle'), suggests the idea of the wind as a mighty bird. Sacrifices were made to the winds where necessary (compare IPHIGENEIA). At Rome there was a temple to the Tempestatēs or weather-goddesses where sacrifices were offered. White animals were sacrificed to the beneficent winds, black animals to the stormy winds. See TYPHOEUS.

wine. Both in Greece and Rome in classical times wine formed part of the staple diet but was nearly always drunk diluted with water (see SYMPOSIUM). After the grapes were pressed the juice was stored in large jars (Gk. *pithoi*, Lat. *dolia*) to ferment. In Italy in the early period native wine was scarce. A famous year for wine was 121 BC, the year in which C. Gracchus was killed and L. Opimius was consul. According to the Elder Pliny some *vinum Opimianum* still survived in his day, nearly 200 years later. Four kinds of wine were first served at a banquet given by Julius Caesar in 46 BC. By this time Italian wines were felt to be the equal of Greek. Greek wines, in which fermentation was never completely arrested, were drunk when between 3 and 4 years old; most Roman wines were drunk at the same age, though some required ten to fifteen years to mature, and there are references to older vintages. Scores of different wines, named by locality, are known. Homer mentions only Thracian and the most mysteriously named 'Pramnian' wine, but the wines most highly regarded by later Greeks were those of Chios, Thasos, Lesbos, and Cos. Lesbian wine tasted naturally of sea-water, which the Greeks occasionally added to wine as a flavouring. The most favoured among Italian wines were those of Alba, Setia, and the Caecuban territory (all in Latium), and of the Falernian territory (in Campania). Also popular was the Mamertine wine from Messana and the Mareotic from the area near Alexandria in Egypt.

Winged Victory of Samothrace, see NIKE.

women, position of

1. *In Greece.* Homer and the Greek tragedians depict their female characters—Penelopē, Nausicăa, Andromachē, Helen, Clytemnestra, Electra, and others—as enjoying a moderately free social life, but naturally the heroines' behaviour is governed by literary convention, and need not be taken to be completely realistic. Yet it is clear that in Lesbos in the seventh century BC the poet *Sappho enjoyed considerable social freedom within her circle of female acquaintance, however restricted she might have been in other aspects of her life, and there are indications that in the families of tyrants and aristocrats women were allowed a measure of independence

(Plutarch in his Life of *Cimon gives an interesting glimpse of this when he mentions Cimon's sister Elpinicē). This probably reflects these women's social value when the family and marriage alliances were important.

In democratic Athens women had severely limited rights (in some other states their position was somewhat better). They had no political rights whatsoever and could take no part in the running of the city, an activity which took up so large a part of the lives of their menfolk. A woman was allowed very little room by law for independent action. Her marriage was arranged by her father or nearest male relation. She could not inherit or hold property or enter into any transaction that involved more than the value of a bushel of grain. Any business that concerned her had to be dealt with on her behalf by husband, father, or guardian. If she had no brothers to inherit her father's property, she as heiress (*epiklēros*) 'went with the property' (the literal meaning of the Greek word), i.e. the male next-of-kin who took the property had to marry her, divorcing his previous wife if he had one, unless he renounced his inheritance. The heiress herself might have to divorce her husband in order to comply (in fact we know of no instance of such a drastic recourse). Women were kept in seclusion in the home, though the comedies of Aristophanes (see especially LYSISTRATA and THESMOPHORIAZUSAE) provide a counterbalance to the declaration of Pericles in his Funeral Oration (Thucydides, book 2), that the best reputation a woman can achieve is not to have her name mentioned at all for praise or blame. The women at Athens had their separate quarters in the house (see HOUSES AND FURNITURE) in which the girls would remain under their mothers' close supervision so that, according to Xenophon, 'they might see, hear, and enquire as little as possible'.

But in matters of religion women had a very important role to play, in family rites (weddings, funerals) and in public festivals (see PANATHENAEA). Virtually all women of citizen status were married, and at an early age (about 15), to men much older than themselves (probably about 30); they were regarded as responsible for organizing the household including the slaves, raising the children, and with the help of the female slaves doing all the spinning, weaving, and clothes-making that the household required (see MARRIAGE I). They seldom left the house, and if they did were always accompanied by a slave. Poor women, especially poor widows, went out to work, often selling goods in the market (it was a too-often repeated joke in comedy that Euripides' mother had been a vegetable seller). Foundlings, foreign women, and slaves (but not citizens) were often taken as concubines (a class that was legally defined and had specific rights) or became *hetaerae; these last were sometimes educated

and talented women (like *Aspasia), and became more so by having the freedom to join men's society, at symposia for example (see SYMPOSIUM), and may have had some control of their property.

Plato in the *Republic* proposed a radically different society in which the family was displaced from its central position, but reverted to a more traditional view in the *Laws*. Both he and Aristotle, who accepted the family as the basic unit of society, believed that men and women should have the same education and training. *Cynic philosophers such as Crates rejected marriage and family life altogether.

During the Hellenistic age several powerful Macedonian women exercised great authority in their own kingdoms (see MACEDONIA 4). Stoicism also played a part in encouraging the independence of women by providing a philosophical basis for the idea of equality between the sexes. Women in Alexandria seem to have enjoyed some measure of freedom (see THEOCRITUS, Idyll 15). Finds of papyri include many private letters written by women attesting widespread literacy: education was by that time clearly within their reach.

2. *At Rome.* In early Rome the *paterfamilias had complete control over his wife and family, but in general Roman law allowed more rights to women than Greek. In quite early times it became possible, and by the end of the republic usual, for a woman to marry without passing wholly into her husband's control. However, it was necessary in this case for a woman to have a guardian through whom to conduct business, and until the time of Augustus only *Vestal Virgins were the exceptions to this rule. Later, women with three children became independent. Married women at Rome always had a position of greater dignity and a more public role to play than in Greece. They did not live in seclusion, and they took their meals with their husbands; the all-male *symposium* was not the social centre of the life of upper-class Roman men as it was of Greek. Roman women were free to leave the house (wearing the *stola mātronālis*; see DRESS 2) and visit not only shops but public places such as theatres or law-courts. Many upper-class Roman women were influential, taking an active part in the business discussed in their houses. They were educated, clever, and good company; some (see FULVIA and CLODIA) wielded power conspicuously; others stayed in the background (see CORNELIA, mother of the Gracchi).

Marriage under the empire became unpopular, and measures had to be taken to encourage it by penalizing the unmarried (see IUS TRIUM LIBERORUM). In this connection Suetonius records in his Life of Augustus (AD 89) that the emperor recommended that Romans should read a famous speech which had been delivered in the senate in 131 BC by the censor Q.

Caecilius Metellus Macedonicus, urging compulsory marriage to stimulate the birthrate: 'If we could get on without a wife, Romans, we would all avoid the annoyance, but since nature has ordained that we can neither live very comfortably with them nor at all without them, we must take thought for our lasting well-being rather than for the pleasure of the moment'. If one takes Juvenal's *Satires* as serious social comment on the early empire they point to demoralization at this time of a section at least of Roman women. On the other hand there is evidence in literature that there were happy marriages in which both partners were equal in their informed concern for each other, even if the wife's responsibilities were confined to the home (see e.g. Statius and the Younger Pliny). The most striking instance is the loving encomium preserved in an inscription (the so-called *Laudatio Turiae*), supposed to be that of a certain Lucretius Vespillo (who served under Pompey in 48 BC and was consul under Augustus in 19 BC) on his wife Turia. It records how courageously she concealed her husband during the proscriptions of 43–42 BC until his pardon was obtained, and how loyal she was both when they were betrothed and during the romantic and dangerous adventures of their forty-one years of married life.

Works and Days (*Erga kai hēmerai*), Greek poem in 828 hexameters by *Hesiod; the 'works' are the activities of the farming year, the 'days' (from line 765 onward) are an almanac of days in the month that are favourable or unfavourable for different activities. No reason is given for the category of a particular day except for the implication that Zeus has ordained it so. Lucky or unlucky days are scarcely mentioned again until Hellenistic times.

The chief themes of the poem are justice and the need for hard work. After an invocation to the Muses the poet addresses his brother Persēs, urging him to a reconciliation of their quarrel (see HESIOD). To explain why men have to work hard and act justly he uses myth: *Prometheus and the story of Pandora, the five ages or generations (*Golden, Silver, Bronze, Heroic, and Iron), and the fable of the hawk and the nightingale, illustrating the unjust use of power; the whole is blended with proverbs, moral maxims, and threats of divine anger. In the remaining two thirds of the poem Hesiod gives Perses instructions on how to work as a farmer, which are mostly an enumeration of the tasks of the various seasons with some practical advice, for example on how to construct a plough; there is a fine descriptive passage on the rigours of winter (504–35), balanced by a picture of the farmer enjoying the languorous heat of summer (582–96). There follow some brief advice on sea trading, a collection of proverbial maxims about religious and social conduct, and the almanac of lucky and unlucky days. The poem is a work of exhortation and instruction, for which parallels exist, but in Near Eastern literature rather than in Greek; the poems of *Phocylidēs and *Theognis are comparable in tone, but much more limited in scope. *Works and Days* is given unity chiefly by the personality of the author. Whether the circumstances of its composition are real or imaginary, the poem represents the life-experience of a cautious and conservative farmer, inured to hardship and adversity, suspicious of pleasure, and no lover of women, but one who by reflection had come to believe that the conditions of life were divinely and justly ordained.

wrestling, see ATHLETICS (ii).

writing, writing materials, see ALPHABET and BOOKS AND WRITING 5.

X

Xanthi'ppē, wife of *Socrates.

Xanthi'ppus. I. Father of *Pericles. In the *Persian Wars he commanded the Athenian fleet after the battle of Salamis and in 479 BC at the battle of Mycalē, where he had a large share in the victory. He had earlier married Agaristē, niece of Cleisthenēs (2) and a member of the *Alcmaeonidae whose political ally he was. He had been ostracized in 484, but recalled at the time of the invasion by Xerxes.

2. A Spartan who, in the course of the First Punic War, reorganized and commanded the Carthaginian defence force in Africa and in 255 BC inflicted a crushing defeat on the Romans under *Regulus.

Xanthus, of Lydia, see LOGOGRAPHERS (1).

Xanthus and Ba'lius ('bay' and 'dapple'), in Greek myth, the immortal horses of Achilles, offspring of Zephyrus the West Wind and the *Harpy Podargē ('swift-foot') and given by the gods to Achilles' father Peleus as a wedding-present. After the death of Patroclus, their charioteer and Achilles' friend, the two horses wept bitterly, and Zeus regretted having allowed immortal creatures to become involved in the sufferings of mortal men. Xanthus had the gift of speech but the Furies struck him dumb after he had prophesied Achilles' death to him.

xe'nia ('guest-friendship'), see HOMERIC AGE.

Xeno'cratēs, head of the *Academy 339–314 BC.

Xeno'phanēs, of Colophon, in Ionia, an early Greek philosopher who spent most of his long life wandering in Greek lands, chiefly perhaps in Sicily. His own words, written when he was 92, indicate that he was born c.570, and he is said to have lived on to the time of Hieron (tyrant of Syracuse 478–467 BC). According to tradition he was the teacher of *Parmenidēs, and thus in some sense connected with the origins of *Eleatic philosophy. He is said to have written a poem in hexameters on the foundation of Colophon and the colonization of Elea (in *Magna Graecia), but the surviving fragments of his writings are either from his satirical *Silloi or from occasional elegiac poems. He was not an original philosopher, but the fragments, dealing with theological or physical matters, indicate that he thought deeply about religion and the gods. He was well known for his revolutionary attack on the polytheism and anthropomor-

phism of the traditional Greek religion, and on the immoral stories about the gods found in Homer and Hesiod. His god is single and eternal, in no way resembling men, effecting things by mind alone. This radical monotheism was new in Greek thought. From the presence of sea shells in the mountains and the impression of a fossil fish and of seaweed in the Syracusan quarries, Xenophanes deduced that the land was once covered with water, and infers that it may be so again. In other fragments he shows the same radical approach to accepted opinions, denouncing athletic success in the games as of less value than his own intellectual achievement.

Xe'nophon. I. (c.428–c.354 BC), Greek historian and disciple of Socrates. He was an Athenian, son of Gryllus, and had two sons Gryllus and Diodorus. As a knight (see HIPPEIS) and an associate of the aristocratic circle of young men around Socrates, he may have found life difficult in Athens during the oligarchic revolution and the democratic restoration (see ATHENS 2 (iii)), and he left in 401. At the invitation of his Boeotian friend Proxenus he joined the expedition of *Cyrus the Younger, described in his *Anabasis*. After having extricated the Ten Thousand from this failed adventure by his own determination and military skill, he accepted service in 396 with the Spartan king *Agesilaus to whom he became strongly attached, against the Persian Pharnabazus. When Agesilaus was recalled by events in Greece Xenophon accompanied him and was present (perhaps as a non-combatant) on the Spartan side at the battle of Coronea, against Athens and Boeotia, in 394. Already it seems he had been banished from Athens and his property confiscated. The Spartans provided him with an estate at Scillus near Olympia, and elected him the Spartan *proxenos* for the entertainment of Spartans visiting Olympia. Here he spent the next twenty years, enjoying the country life and writing his books. In 371 Elis claimed Scillus and Xenophon retired to Corinth. The decree of his banishment from Athens was revoked, probably c.368. When the Athenians were expelled from Corinth in 366 he returned to Athens; his two sons fought in the Athenian contingent on the Spartan side at the battle of Mantinea in 362 and the elder, Gryllus, was killed.

Xenophon wrote on numerous subjects suggested by his varied experience (see individual titles). Socrates' personality made a profound impression on him and he wrote three books of recollections, *Memorabilia*, *Apology*, and *Symposium*. However, he has no real grasp of philosophy and seems to have misunderstood Socrates as profoundly as he admired him. (It is related that Socrates first met Xenophon, then a boy, in the street, and stopping him asked where various articles could be got. Xenophon told him. Socrates then asked, 'Where can you get brave and virtuous men?' and when Xenophon was puzzled told him to come with him.) *Oeconomicus* was inspired by his home life; *Anabasis* and *Cyropaedia* by his experiences in Persia; his treatises *The Cavalry Commander*, *Horsemanship*, and *Cynegeticus* by his military career and devotion to sport; *Hellenica*, *Agesilaus*, *Constitution of the Lacedaemonians*, *Hieron*, and *Revenues*, by his acquaintance with political affairs in various countries. The **Constitution of the Athenians*, preserved among his works, is certainly not by him. As a historian Xenophon sometimes omits matters of importance and is guilty of taking sides. On military and sporting matters he is an expert and an enthusiast and writes engagingly. He was a pious man, possessed of great common sense, an easy, lucid, and agreeable writer. Quintilian speaks warmly of his unaffected charm.

2. Of Ephesus, see NOVEL.

Xerxēs, see PERSIAN WARS.

Xūthus (Xouthos). In Greek myth, the ancestor of the Ionians and Achaeans. He is presented either as the son of Hellen and brother of Dorus and Aeolus (see HELLEN and DEUCALION), or as the son of Aeolus (see ION).

Y

'year of the four emperors', AD 69; see ROME 11.

Z

Za'greus, see DIONYSUS ZAGREUS.

Zama, Battle of, in Numidia in 202 BC, the final defeat of Hannibal by Scipio Africanus to end the Second Punic War. See PUNIC WARS.

Zēno (Zēnōn). **1.** Of Elea (c.490–after 445 BC), Greek philosopher. Little is known of his life except that he was a disciple of *Parmenidēs and thus belonged to the so-called *Eleatic school of Greek philosophy which believed that the basic matter of the universe is single, indivisible, and unchanging. He seems to have written, in support of this belief and against those who made fun of it, a book of philosophical paradoxes which reduce to absurdity the supposition that plurality and motion exist. (Because of his method he was called by Aristotle the inventor of *dialectic.) Only two of his forty arguments against plurality have survived, and the essence of these can be summarized as follows. If there are many things, they must be both limited and unlimited in number (which is absurd): limited, because they are as many as they are; unlimited, because things are only two in number when they can be distinguished from one another, i.e. when they are separated; but things are only separated where there is something in between; that in turn must be separated by two intervening things from those it originally separated, and so on *ad infinitum*.

Of his four arguments (according to Aristotle) against the possibility of motion, the most famous is the paradox of Achilles and the tortoise. If a tortoise is given a start in a race against Achilles, Achilles will never be able to overtake it because when he arrives at the tortoise's starting point it will have moved ahead to a new position, and when he reaches that position the tortoise will again have moved ahead, and so on indefinitely. On this basis the tortoise must always be ahead, by however small a margin. The simplest and usual explanation of fallacy in the argument is that while it takes Achilles an infinite number of these increments of distance to catch the tortoise, their sum, i.e. the total distance required, is in fact finite. Nevertheless, the argument raises questions about the ideas of infinity and divisibility which are philosophically important, and formal refutation is not a trivial matter. One of Zeno's other arguments against motion similarly divides the distance to be covered by an athlete in the stadium into the geometrical series $\frac{1}{2} + \frac{1}{4} + \frac{1}{8} + \ldots$ and asserts that the distance, having an infinite number of divisions, can never be covered, and therefore motion is impossible. It is an argument of the same nature as that of Achilles and the tortoise.

Zeno appears in the dialogue *Parmenides* of Plato.

2. Greek philosopher of Citium in Cyprus (c.333–262 BC), and founder of the *Stoic school, regarded by his contemporaries as of Phoenician stock.

Zēno'bia, widow, successor, and perhaps murderer in AD 266 or 267 of Odaenathus, ruler of *Palmyra, a city state in Syria which from the second century AD had enjoyed the protection of successive Roman emperors. She embarked on wars of expansion; in 269 she conquered Egypt and in 270 overran Asia Minor except Bithynia. When in 271 she proclaimed her son Augustus (for the title see AUGUSTUS, THE) the emperor Aurelian reoccupied Asia Minor and after a series of battles captured Palmyra, the queen herself, and her sons. Palmyra was utterly destroyed, but the queen, having been exhibited in Aurelian's *triumph, was granted a pension and a villa at Tibur. See also LONGINUS, CASSIUS.

Zēno'dotus, of Ephesus, scholar at Alexandria, pupil of Philetas of Cos, who became the first head of the *Alexandrian Library c.285–c.270 BC. He is reputed to have divided Homer's *Iliad* and *Odyssey* into twenty-four books each, and to have worked on the text, perhaps even produced an edition. He seems also to have worked on the lyric poets. Traces of his critical work and views survive in the Homeric *scholia.

Ze'phyrus, in Greek myth, the personification of the west wind, sometimes said to be the husband of Iris, goddess of the rainbow. By the *Harpy Podargē he became the father of Achilles' horses *Xanthus and Balius. See WINDS, FLORA, and HYACINTHUS.

Zētēs, see CALAIS.

Zēthus, see ANTIOPE.

zeugī'tae, see SOLON.

zeugma, see SYLLEPSIS.

Zeus, in Greek myth and religion, the supreme god, the youngest (according to Homer the eldest) son of *Cronus whom he overthrew and succeeded. His name indicates an *Indo-

European origin, being found in the Indic sky-god Dyaus pita, the Roman Jupiter, the Germanic Tues-day, Latin *deus*, 'god', *dies*, 'day', and Greek *eudia*, 'fine weather'. For the Greeks he is the god of weather rather than of the 'bright sky' of day. According to his Homeric epithets he is the cloud-gatherer, the thunderer on high, hurler of thunderbolts. He was born in Crete, according to what is probably the oldest myth, or was born in Arcadia and brought to Crete, where he was hidden in a cave on Mount *Dictē or Mount *Ida and fed by the goat *Amalthea. The *Curētĕs, in order to conceal him, drowned his cries by their noisy ritual. (The Cretans also had a peculiar myth of Zeus dead and buried.) After the overthrow of Cronus, Zeus and his brothers divided the universe by casting lots, Zeus obtaining the heavens, Poseidon the sea, and Hadēs the underworld. Zeus dwells on the tops of mountains where the storm clouds gather, on Mount *Lycaeus in Arcadia, or Mount Ida near Troy, or on Mount Olympus, the highest mountain in northern Thessaly. The thunderbolt, which only he commands, signifies his irresistible power, over other gods as well as men, and it enabled him to defeat the *Titans, the *Giants, and *Typhoeus. Thus it is Zeus who must be supplicated to grant victory in war. He is the protector of political freedom, Zeus Eleutherios ('liberator'), or Sōtēr ('saviour'), and festivals were instituted in his honour. After the Greek victory at Plataea in 479 BC (see PERSIAN WARS) a sanctuary for Zeus Eleutherios and the festival of the *Eleutheria were instituted.

Zeus is the only Greek god to have as children other powerful gods, Apollo, Artemis, Hermēs, Dionysus, Athena, and Persephonē. By his wife Hera he was the father only of Arēs, Hebē, and Eileithyia. The mother of *Athena, Mētis (Wisdom), was fated to have a second child more powerful than its father, and so Zeus swallowed her, thereafter combining supreme power and wisdom within himself. His mortal children included Heracles, Helen, Perseus, Epaphos, Minos, and the brothers Amphion and Zethus (see DIOSCURI). Zeus is called 'the father of gods and men' and had perhaps been so addressed since Indo-European times, although he is not the father of all the gods and did not create men (for stories about the creation of men see DEUCALION and PROMETHEUS). Epithets added to his name indicate his particular roles: he is father in the sense of ruler and protector, defender of the house (Herkeios), of the hearth (Ephestios), of the rights of hospitality (Xenios and Hikēsios), of oaths (Horkios), and the guardian of property (Ktēsios), his image set up in the store room. He is also the protector of law and morals; in that capacity the poet Hesiod invokes him in *Works and Days, and represents the goddess of justice, Dikē, as enthroned beside

him. The impartiality of his judgements is represented by Homer in the *Iliad* in the image of Zeus holding golden scales in his hand; as Achilles and Hector fight, the fall of a pan indicates that Hector is doomed. Zeus has the power, if he wishes, to save Hector whom he loves, as he might have saved his own son *Sarpedon, but it is men's 'fate' (*moira*) or 'portion' (*aisa*) to die, and Zeus does not overrule the apportionment (see FATE).

Zeus is also called Chthonios, 'of the Earth'. Sometimes the phrase simply stands for Hades or Pluto, the god of the Underworld; the sky god is not meant. More often the phrase signifies Zeus whose all-embracing power extends into the earth as well, from whom the growth of crops is expected. Apart, however, from general overseership given by his position of supremacy, Zeus had little to do with the day to day concerns of men, war, agriculture, crafts, etc.; but the wide scope of his functions made him unique in his importance to all Greece. His festival at *Olympia asserted his supreme position and the essential unity of all who worshipped him. To participate in his festival was to be a Hellene; the admission of the Macedonians and later of the Romans were events of great political significance. His universality, of which the beginnings are apparent in Aeschylus, paved the way for the later philosophical pantheism of the *Stoics. He corresponds to, and was identified with, the Roman *Jupiter.

Zeus confūtā'tus, see LUCIAN.

Zeuxis, of Heraclea in *Magna Graecia, one of the most famous painters of ancient Greece, working in the late fifth century BC. He was famous for his skill in depicting the female form. His success in producing illusion is attested by the story that birds flew down to peck at a bunch of grapes he had painted (see also PARRHASIUS). One of his most celebrated paintings was a picture of Helen (of Troy) for the temple of Hera on the Lacinian promontory in Magna Graecia. Another, a picture of a female Centaur with her young, is described by Lucian. Zeuxis is said to have given a painting of Pan to the artistically inclined Archelaus, king of Macedonia, at the end of the fifth century. See also PAINTING.

Zmyrna, short Latin epic poem in hexameters on the myth of Myrrha and *Adonis by C. Helvius *Cinna (*c*.70–44 BC). Only three lines survive. It was worked on by its author for nine years, and seems to have typified the influence of *Alexandrianism on Roman poetry. Catullus predicted immortality for it.

Zō'ilus, of Amphipolis, *Cynic philosopher, rhetorician, and critic of the fourth century BC, also perhaps a sophist, who earned notoriety for the bitterness of his attacks on Isocrates, Plato, and especially Homer, earning himself the name of Homēromastix, 'scourge of Homer', by his nine books of criticism. He found fault with Homer mainly on points of invention (such as the description of the companions of Odysseus 'weeping' when turned into swine), but also on points of grammar. His name became proverbial for a carping critic.

Zo'simus (late fifth century AD), Greek historian, author of an extant history, in Greek in four books, of the Roman empire from Augustus to AD 410 (the sack of Rome by the Visigoths). Book 1 summarizes the events of the first three centuries, books 2–4 give a fuller account of the fourth century, and particularly of the years 395–410, for which he is the most important source. Being a pagan he attributes the decline of the empire to the rejection of the pagan gods.

CHRONOLOGICAL TABLE

Many of the dates given are approximate, especially before *c*.600 BC. The abbreviation *fl*. (*floruit, floruerunt*: flourished) after writers' names is meant only to give an impression of relative dates.

EVENTS		LITERATURE	
	BC		
2800–1050	Greek Bronze Age		
2200	Coming of the Greeks		
1800–1000	Italian Bronze Age		
1600–1125	Mycenaean period		
1300–1200	Linear B tablets		
1200–1125	Destruction of Mycenaean cities in Greece		
1184	Destruction of Troy		
1100	Beginning of Dark Age; Dorian Invasion		
1050	Beginning of Iron Age in Greece		
1050–875	Proto-geometric pottery; migration of mainland Greeks to Asia Minor		
1000	Beginning of Iron Age in Italy		
875–750	Geometric pottery		
814	Phoenicians found Carthage		
776	First Olympian (Olympic) games		
753	Foundation of Rome		
750–720	Sub-geometric pottery; early Greek writing		
735–715	First Messenian War		
734	Greek colonization of Sicily begins		
733	Foundation of Syracuse		
720	Greek colonization of S. Italy begins		
720–620	Orientalizing period in pottery		
700–680	Colonization of Hellespont and Bosporus	*c*.700	Homer and Hesiod *fl*.
664	Psammetichus I begins Saite dynasty of Egypt	675	Terpander and Callinus *fl*.
660	Foundation of Byzantium		
650–620	Second Messenian War	650	Archilochus and Semonides *fl*.
		640	Tyrtaeus *fl*.
625–600	Thrasybulus tyrant of Miletus	630	Alcman and Mimnermus *fl*.
625–585	Periander tyrant of Corinth		

Events		Literature	
621	Laws of Draco		
620–480	Archaic period		
610	Black-figure pottery begins	610–575	Alcaeus and Sappho *fl.*
		610–545	Anaximander
600	Foundation of Massilia	600	Thales *fl.*
594	Reforms of Solon	594	Solon's poetry
582	Pythian games established		
581	Isthmian games established		
573	Nemean games established		
		570–478	Xenophanes
560–556	Peisistratus tyrant at Athens	570	Stesichorus *fl.*
560–546	Croesus king of Lydia		
		556–468	Simonides
		550	Anaximenes and Phocylides *fl.*
546–527	Peisistratus again tyrant		
545	Persians conquer Ionia		
		540	Hipponax, Ibycus, and Theognis *fl.*
533	Thespis wins first tragedy competition at the Dionysia		
530	Red-figure pottery begins	530	Anacreon and Pythagoras *fl.*
		518	Pindar born
514	Hipparchus murdered by Harmodius and Aristogeiton		
510	Hippias expelled from Athens		
509	Foundation of Roman republic		
508	Reforms of Cleisthenes		
		500	Hecataeus, Heracleitus, and Phrynichus *fl.*
499	Ionian Revolt		
496	Battle of Lake Regillus, Italy		
494	Battle of Lade: Persians sack Miletus		
490	Persians invade Greece and are defeated at Marathon	490–425	Herodotus
486	First comedy produced at the Dionysia	484	Aeschylus: first victory in tragedy competitions
480	Persian invasion of Greece: battles of Artemisium, Thermopylae, and Salamis; Carthaginian invasion of Sicily: battle of Himera; beginning of Classical period	480	Parmenides *fl.*
479	Battles of Plataea and Mycale		
478	Delian League formed	470	Bacchylides *fl.*
		468	Sophocles: first victory in tragedy competitions

Events		*Literature*	
467	Battle of Eurymedon		
464	Helot revolt		
462	Reforms of Ephialtes	462	Anaxagoras in Athens
461–429	Ascendancy of Pericles		
461–456	Long Walls built		
460–446	First Peloponnesian War		
		458	Aeschylus: *Oresteia*
		458–380	Lysias
		456	Death of Aeschylus
		455	Euripides: first production
450	Twelve Tables published at Rome; Peace of Callias	450	Empedocles and Zeno the Eleatic *fl.*
447	Battle of Coronea; Parthenon begun		
446	Thirty Years' Peace		
		440–390	Andocides
		436	Isocrates born
		435	Leucippus *fl.*
431	Start of (Second) Peloponnesian War	431	Thucydides begins his history
430	Plague at Athens	430	Democritus, Hippocrates, Meton, Protagoras, and Socrates *fl.*
429	Death of Pericles		
		427	Plato born; Gorgias arrives at Athens
425	Capture of Sphacteria; Cleon influential at Athens	425	Aristophanes: *Acharnians*; Hellanicus *fl.*
424	Battle of Delium		
422	Deaths of Brasidas and Cleon		
421	Peace of Nicias		
		420	Hippias and Prodicus *fl.*
419	Peloponnesian War resumed		
415–413	Sicilian Expedition		
411	Oligarchic revolution at Athens	411	Execution of Antiphon
407	Battle of Notium		
406	Battle of Arginusae	406	Deaths of Euripides and Sophocles
405	Battle of Aegospotami	405	Aristophanes: *Frogs*.
404	Capitulation of Athens: the Thirty Tyrants		
404–371	Sparta supreme in Greece		
403	Restoration of democracy at Athens		
401	Expedition of the Ten Thousand: battle of Cunaxa		

Events		*Literature*	
400–386	Sparta at war with Persia	400	Antisthenes and Eucleides *fl.*
		400–325	Diogenes
		399	Trial and death of Socrates
395–386	Corinthian War		
		390	Aeschines born; Isocrates, Plato, and Xenophon (428–354) *fl.*
387	Gauls sack Rome		
386	Peace of Antalcidas; Academy founded at Athens	384	Aristotle and Demosthenes born
377	Second Athenian League		
371	Battle of Leuctra		
		370–287	Theophrastus
369	Epaminondas founds Megalopolis		
		365–285	Crates the Cynic
		365–270	Pyrrhon
362	Battle of Mantinea: death of Epaminondas		
		360	Aeschines, Aristotle, and Demosthenes *fl.*
359–336	Philip II king of Macedon		
357–355	Social War		
356	Alexander the Great born		
355–352	Sacred War		
		347	Death of Plato
346	Peace of Philocrates		
343–341	First Samnite War in Italy		
		342–292	Menander
		340	Ephorus and Theopompus *fl.*
339	Timoleon defeats Carthaginians at the battle of the Crimisus		
338	Battle of Chaeronea	338	Death of Isocrates; Lycurgus in control of Athenian finance
336–323	Alexander the Great king of Macedon	335	Aristotle founds Lyceum
334	Battle of the Granicus		
333	Battle of Issus		
331	Alexandria founded; battle of Gaugamela		
330	Persepolis destroyed		
327–304	Second Samnite War in Italy		
326	Battle of Hydaspes		
323	Death of Alexander		
323–322	Lamian War		
		322	Deaths of Aristotle and Demosthenes
321	Battle of the Caudine Forks		

Events		Literature	
317–307	Demetrius of Phalerum governor of Athens		
311–306	War of Agathocles of Syracuse against Carthage		
		307	Epicurus founds his school at Athens
301	Battle of Ipsus		
		300	Zeno of Citium founds Stoic school at Athens
298–290	Third Samnite War in Italy		
297–272	Campaigns of Pyrrhus		
		285	Zenodotus head of the Alexandrian Library; Philetas and Euclid *fl.*
283	Accession of Ptolemy II Philadelphus		
		280	Bion the Borysthenite *fl.*
		271	Death of Epicurus
		270	Aratus, Aristarchus of Samos, Callimachus, Herodas, and Theocritus *fl.*
266–262	Chremonidean War		
264–241	First Punic War		
		260	Death of Timaeus
		250	Apollonius Rhodius *fl.*
		240	Archimedes, Eratosthenes, and Livius Andronicus *fl.*
		235	Naevius *fl.*
221–179	Philip V king of Macedon		
219	Hannibal captures Saguntum		
218–202	Second Punic War		
217	Battle of Lake Trasimene		
216	Battle of Cannae		
214–205	First Macedonian War		
		212	Archimedes killed; Fabius Pictor *fl.*
202	Battle of Zama: subjugation of Carthage		
200–197	Second Macedonian War	200	Aristophanes of Byzantium head of Alexandrian Library; Ennius and Plautus *fl.*
		180	Aristarchus of Samothrace head of Alexandrian Library; Pacuvius *fl.*
172–168	Third Macedonian War		
168	Battle of Pydna		
167	Polybius taken to Rome		
		166–159	Terence's plays produced
		155	Carneades at Rome
149–146	Third Punic War	149	Cato the Censor: *Origines*
146	Sack of Corinth: Greece becomes a Roman protectorate		
		145	Lucilius *fl.*
		144	Panaetius at Rome

Events		Literature	
		140	Accius *fl.*
		135	Nicander *fl.*
133, 123	Tribunates of the Gracchi		
		116	Varro born
112–105	War against Jugurtha		
107–100	Reforms of Marius		
		106	Cicero born
100	Julius Caesar born	100	Meleager *fl.*
		98	Lucretius born
90–88	Social War		
89–85	First Mithridatic War		
		87–51	Posidonius *fl.*
86	Sulla sacks Athens		
		84	Catullus born
83–82	Second Mithridatic War		
82–80	Reforms of Sulla		
		75–35	Philodemus in Italy
74–63	Third Mithridatic War		
73–71	Slave revolt under Spartacus		
70	Consulate of Crassus and Pompey; trial of Verres		
66–62	Pompey in the East		
		65	Horace born
63	Catilinarian conspiracy; birth of Augustus (Octavian)		
60	First triumvirate	60	Cornelius Nepos *fl.*
		60–30	Diodorus Siculus compiles his history
		59	Livy born
58–57	Cicero in exile	58–52	Caesar: *Commentaries* on the Gallic War
58–49	Caesar in Gaul		
		57–56	Catullus visits Asia Minor
55–54	Caesar in Britain	55	Death of Lucretius
		54	Death of Catullus
53	Battle of Carrhae		
49	Caesar crosses the Rubicon		
48	Battle of Pharsalus; murder of Pompey		
47–44	Caesar dictator		
		45	Sallust begins his histories
44	Murder of Caesar	44	Strabo arrives at Rome
43	Second triumvirate; murder of Cicero	43	Ovid born
42	Battle of Philippi		
		37	Virgil: *Eclogues*

Events		Literature	
31	Battle of Actium		
30	Deaths of Mark Antony and Cleopatra	30	Didymus *fl.*
		29	Virgil: *Georgics*; Propertius: *Elegies* I
		28–23	Vitruvius: *de Architectura*
27	Principate of Augustus begins	27	Death of Varro
		23	Horace: *Odes* I–III
		20	Ovid: *Amores*, first edition
		19	Deaths of Tibullus and Virgil
		8	Deaths of Horace and Maecenas
4	Death of Herod the Great		

AD

Events		Literature	
14	Death of Augustus	8	Ovid exiled
14–37	Tiberius emperor	17	Deaths of Livy and Ovid
31	Execution of Sejanus	30	Manilius, Valerius Maximus, and Velleius Paterculus *fl.*
37	Caligula emperor	37	Death of Seneca the Elder
		39–40	Philo the Jew in Rome
41	Claudius emperor		
43	Invasion of Britain		
54–68	Nero emperor		
60	British revolt under Boudicca	60	Persius (34–62) and Lucan (39–65) *fl.*
64	Fire of Rome		
65	Pisonian conspiracy	65	Suicides of Lucan, Petronius, and Seneca the Younger
66–70	Jewish revolt		
69	Year of the four emperors: Galba, Otho, Vitellius, and Vespasian		
70	Destruction of the Temple at Jerusalem	70	Valerius Flaccus begins *Argonautica*
		74	Frontinus consul
78–85	Agricola governor of Britain		
79–81	Titus emperor		
79	Eruption of Vesuvius: destruction of Herculaneum and Pompeii	79	Death of Pliny the Elder
80	Colosseum inaugurated		
81–96	Domitian emperor	81	Dio Chrysostom, Josephus, Martial, and Quintilian *fl.*
		89	Epictetus banished

Events		Literature	
		92–3	Plutarch in Rome
96–8	Nerva emperor		
		97	Tacitus consul
98–117	Trajan emperor		
		100	Pliny the Younger consul
		100–27	Juvenal: *Satires* written
117–38	Hadrian emperor		
		119–22	Suetonius: *Lives* published
135	Final dispersal of the Jews		
138–61	Antoninus Pius emperor		
		140	Ptolemy (mathematician) *fl.*
		143	Fronto consul
		150	Lucian *fl.*
		155	Apuleius *fl.*
		160	Appian begins his history; Aristeides, Aulus Gellius, and Pausanias *fl.*
161–80	Marcus Aurelius emperor; first Germanic invasions into Italy	161	Herodian (grammarian) *fl.*
		162–6	Galen in Rome
		174–80	M. Aurelius: *Meditations*
180–92	Commodus emperor	185	Clement of Alexandria *fl.*
193–211	Lucius Septimius Severus emperor	200	Alexander of Aphrodisias, Athenaeus, Papinian, Sextus Empiricus, and Tertullian *fl.*
211	Death of Severus at York		
211–17	Caracalla emperor		
218–22	Elagabalus emperor		
		223	Murder of Ulpian
		224	Philostratus: *Lives of the Sophists*
		229	Second consulate of Cassius Dio
		230	Herodian (historian) and Origen *fl.*
		240	Plotinus *fl.*
247	Millenary celebrations at Rome	248	Cyprian bishop of Carthage
267	Herulians (Germanic tribe) sack Athens		
272	Emperor Aurelian captures Palmyra	280	Porphyry *fl.*
284–305	Diocletian emperor		
293	Tetrarchy established		
		300	Eusebius, Iamblichus, and Lactantius *fl.*
303–5	Great Persecution of Christians		

Events   *Literature*

306–37	Constantine (the Great) emperor		
312	Battle of the Milvian bridge: toleration and imperial favour given to Christianity		
325	Council of Nicaea		
330	Constantinople capital of the Roman empire	330	Tryphiodorus *fl.*
		350	Ausonius and Donatus *fl.*
360–3	Julian the Apostate emperor	360	Libanius and Themistius *fl.*
		370	Ambrose, Ammianus Marcellinus, and Jerome *fl.*
378–95	Theodosius (the Great) emperor	380	Quintus of Smyrna *fl.* *Historia Augusta*
		384	Symmachus *praefectus urbi*
395	Division of the empire into East and West	400	Claudian *fl.*
410	Sack of Rome by Alaric the Visigoth	420	Martianus Capella and Servius *fl.*
		430	Death of Augustine Macrobius *fl.*
439	Vandals conquer Roman Africa		
452	Attila invades Italy	450	Nonnus *fl.*
455	Vandals plunder Rome		
476	Fall of Rome		
527	Justinian emperor in the East	524	Boethius executed
529	Philosophical schools at Athens closed		

MAPS

The place-names on the following maps include the majority of those which appear in the text. Sites of battles are not distinguished from those of cities, nor are distinctions made on grounds of relative importance or of period. Mountains are shown as peaks except in a few cases where the names describe a range. Classical names are given in commonly accepted spellings, with the Latinized form generally preferred (thus: Abydus, not Abydos). Modern place-names are shown in italic.

1. Asia Minor and the Middle East
2. Greece and the Aegean
3. Greece
4. Italy
5. The Western Roman Empire
6. Roman Britain

Map 1

Tanais (Don)

Hypanis
(Kuban)

COLCHIS   C A U C A S U S

Caspian Sea

Phasis • Phasis
(Rioni)

△ Trapezus (Trebizond)
THECHES

Araxes
(Araks or Aras)

ARMENIA

M E D I A

MAGENE
• Samosata

Nineveh•   • Arbela
Gaugamela•

ASSYRIA

Royal Road

• Ecbatana
(Hamadan)
• Bisotun

• Hierapolis
or Bambyce

RIA
• Palmyra

MESOPOTAMIA

Euphrates

Tigris

Opis
Cunaxa• • Ctesiphon
Babylon • Seleucia

BABYLONIA

SUSIANA   PERSIS

• Susa

Pasargadae
•

Persepolis
•

Persian Gulf

Map 2

E u x i n e
(Black Sea)

Hebrus (Maritsa)

Hadrianopolis
(Adrianople)

A C E

Bosporus

Byzantium or
Constantinople
(Istanbul)

Chalcedon

Nicomedia
(Izmit)

B I T H Y N I A

Perinthus

P r o p o n t i s
(Sea of Marmora)

Abdera   Maronea

Proconnesus

Cios

Lysimacheia

Cardia

Parium

THRACIAN
CHERSONESE

Granicus

Cyzicus

Samothrace

Imbros

Aegospotami

Lampsacus

Sestus

Abydus

M Y S I A

Lemnos

Cynossema

Hellespont

Sigeum

Cape Rhoeteum

Troy

Tenedos

TROAS
(THE TROAD)

△IDA

P H R Y G I A

Colonae

Assos

Methymna

Antissa

Pyrrha

Atarneus

Pergamum

Eresus

Mitylene

Pitane

Lesbos

Arginusae

Elaea

Cyme

Magnesia
(Manisa)

Phocaea

Hermus

L Y D I A

△SIPYLUS

Sardis

Pactolus

Smyrna

Chios

Clazomenae

Erythrae

Teos

Colophon

Notium

Ephesus

Maeander

Hierapolis

Andros

Magnesia

Tenos

Samos

Icaria

Priene

Rheneia

MYCALE△

Lade

Miletus

C A R I A

Myconos

Sea

Syros

Delos

Paros

Leros

Caryanda

Naxos

Halicarnassus

Amorgos

Cos

L Y C I A

Ios

Cnidus

Xanthus

Telos

Ialysus

Rhodes

Camirus

Thera
(Santorini)

Rhodes

Lindus

A E O L I S

I O N I A

S p o r a d e s

Map 3

Cape Artemisium

Scyros

E U B O E A

Aegean Sea

Elatea
Halae
Chaeronea
Tegyra
Orchomenus
Anthedon
Lebadeia
L. Copais
BOEOTIA
Chalcis
Eretria
Coronea
Haliartus
Aulis
Delium
Ascra
Thebes
Tanagra
Oropus
HELICON
Thespiae
Oenophyta
Rhamnus
Leuctra
Plataea
CITHAERON
Decelea
PARNES
Cephissia
Eleutherae
Marathon
Eleusis
PENTELICUS
Carystus
Megara
Piraeus
Pallene
Nisaea
Salamis
Athens
Psyttaleia
Phalerum
HYMETTUS
Brauron
Tenea
ATTICA
Andros
ARGOLIS
Epidaurus
Aegina
Ceos
Tiryns
Saronic Gulf
Sunium
LAURIUM
Nauplia
Cyclades
Troezen
Calaureia
Rheneia
Hermione

Seriphos

N I A
(EMON)
Myrtoan Sea

Melos

Cythera

PANNONIA

Savus

ILLYRICUM

DALMATIA

Is. of
Diomedes (*Tremiti*)

Adriatic   Sea

APULIA

Aufidus •Cannae

•Venusia

CALABRIA

Brundisium
(*Brindisi*)

LUCANIA• Tarentum
•Metapontum   •Rudiae
•Heraclea

•Sybaris

Thurii

BRUTTIUM

•Croton

•Locri
Rhegium

Map 4

BRITANNIA

GERMANIA

Gesoriacum
(*Boulogne*) **BELGICA**
Colonia
Agrippina (*Cologne*)
Aduatuca

Corbie
Samarobriva
(*Amiens*)

Mogontiacum (*Mainz*)

Augusta Treverorum (*Trier*)

Cenabum
(*Orleans*)
Tours **CÉLTICA** Alesia
Avaricum
(*Bourges*) Luxovium (*Luxeuil*)
Augustodunum (*Autun*)
Bibracte Vesontio
(*Besançon*) St' Gall **NORICUM**

Augustonemetum
(*Clermont*) Cluny **RAETIA** **PANNONIA**
Burdigala
(*Bordeaux*) Gergovia Geneva
Lugdunum (*Lyons*) **ILLYRICUM**

AQUITANIA **DALMATIA**

GAUL
Tolosa Arelate
(*Arles*) Aquae
Sextiae
(*Aix*) **CISALPINE
GAUL**
Nicaea
Antipolis Adriatic Sea
**HISPANIA ULTERIOR
(FURTHER SPAIN)** Iberus **NARBONESE**
Calagurris Narbo Agathe Forum
Julii
Durius Numantia Caesaraugusta
(*Saragossa*) Martius Nemausus
(*Nimes*)
Bilbilis Massilia
Ilerda **Corsica** Rome

LUSITANIA
Norba Toletum
Caesariana Tarraco **Sardinia** Tyrrhenian
Sea
(*Alcantara*)
Augusta Emerita
(*Merida*) Saguntum
SIERRA MORENA **HISPANIA CITERIOR
(HITHER SPAIN)**
Hispalis *Cordoba*
(*Seville*) Munda
Tartessus
Gades (*Cadiz*) Carthago Nova
(*Cartagena*)
Tingentera Malaca
Caesarea *M e d i t e r r a n e a n*
Hippo
Pillars of Hercules Regius Utica *Ionian
Sea*
S e a
MAURETANIA Cirta Carthage
or Constantina Thagaste
Madaura
ATLAS MTS. **NUMIDIA** Zama Thapsus

GAETULIA **BYZACIUM** *Lesser
Syrtis*

Map 5

CALEDONIA

PICTI

Tay • Inchtuthil

Bodotria
(Forth)
ANTONINE
WALL

DUMNONII

VOTADINI

Clota
(Clyde) • Trimontium
(Newstead) *Tweed*

SELGOVAE

Corstopitum
(Corbridge) • Wallsend

NOVANTAE HADRIAN'S
WALL • Tyne
• Bowness

Solway Firth

North Sea

PARISI

DERE STREET

Mona
(I. of Man)

BRIGANTES

Wharfe • Eburacum
(York)

Humber

Mona
(Anglesey)

ERMINE

• Deva *(Chester)* *Trent* Lindum
(Lincoln)

CORNOVII CORITANI STREET *Ouse* ICENI

ORDOVICES

• Viriconium
(Wroxeter) WAY • Venonae *(High Cross)*

WALES *Sabrina* *Avon* CATUVELLAUNI

(Severn) FOSSE WATLING • Lactodorum TRINOVANTES
(Towcester) STREET • Camulodunum
(Colchester)

Wye • Glevum *(Gloucester)* AKEMAN STREET • Verulamium *(St Albans)*

SILURES *Tamesis* *(Thames)*
Isca Silurum • Corinium Londinium *(London)* Rutupiae
(Caerleon) • *(Cirencester)* *(Richborough)*

ATREBATES Durovernum
(Canterbury)

MENDIP
HILLS • Aquae Sulis STANE STREET
(Bath) BELGAE • Venta Belgarum CANTIACI Dubris
(Winchester) *(Dover)*

Exe DUROTRIGES

DUMNONII Noviomagus Regensium or Regnum
Tamarus • Durnovaria *(Chichester)*
(Tamar) Isca Dumnoniorum *(Dorchester)* Portus Adurni *(Portchester)*

CORNWALL *(Exeter)* Vectis
(I. of Wight)

• St. Michael's Mount

English Channel Map 6